The Little Oxford Thesaurus

Second Edition

Edited by
Martin Nixon

With
Lucinda Coventry

OXFORD
UNIVERSITY PRESS

Great Clarendon Street, Oxford OX2 6DP

Oxford University Press is a department of the University of Oxford.
It furthers the University's objective of excellence in research, scholarship,
and education by publishing worldwide in

Oxford New York

Athens Auckland Bangkok Bogotá Buenos Aires Cape Town
Chennai Dar es Salaam Delhi Florence Hong Kong Istanbul Karachi
Kolkata Kuala Lumpur Madrid Melbourne Mexico City Mumbai Nairobi
Paris São Paulo Shanghai Taipei Tokyo Toronto Warsaw

with associated companies in Berlin Ibadan

Published in the United States
by Oxford University Press Inc., New York

First published 1992

British Library Cataloguing in Publication Data

Data available

Library of Congress Cataloging in Publication Data

Data available

ISBN 0–19–860461–0

ISBN 0–19–860450–5

10 9 8 7 6 5 4 3 2 1

Typeset in Swift and Arial
by Kolam Information Services, India
Printed in Great Britain
by Clays Ltd, Bungay, Suffolk

Guide to the thesaurus

part of speech of the entry word

core synonym—the closest synonym to the entry word

assistance noun HELP, aid, support, cooperation, collaboration, succour, a (helping) hand, encouragement, patronage, sponsorship, subsidy, contribution.
–OPPOSITES hindrance, impedance.

combined synonym group standing for *a hand* and *a helping hand*

numbered sense of the entry word

approve verb ❶ approve of his behaviour: BE PLEASED WITH, think well of, like, look on with favour, give one's blessing to, hold in regard/esteem, admire, respect, praise. ❷ approve the application: AGREE TO, accept, consent to, permit, pass, allow, sanction, authorize, bless, support, back, uphold, endorse, ratify, validate, accede to, countenance; *informal* go along with, rubber-stamp.
–OPPOSITES disapprove, condemn, refuse, veto.

combined synonym group standing for *hold in regard* and *hold in esteem*

example of use, to help distinguish different senses

label indicating the style of English in which the following synonym(s) are used (see over for complete list)

often adverb FREQUENTLY, a lot, many a time, repeatedly, again and again, time and again, time after time, over and over, over and over again, {day in, day out}; *poetic/literary* oft, oft-times.
–OPPOSITES seldom, never.

word(s) meaning the opposite of the entry word; most have entries of their own, where a wider choice will be found

brackets showing that the phrase they contain is one complete synonym

child noun ❶ BOY, GIRL, youngster, young person, infant, baby, toddler, tot, tiny tot, youth, adolescent, juvenile, minor; *Scottish* bairn; *informal* kid, nipper, shaver, brat, guttersnipe; *Brit. informal* sprog. ❷ SON, DAUGHTER, offspring, progeny, descendant, scion; *Law* issue.

label indicating the region of the world in which the following synonym(s) are used (see over for abbreviations)

label indicating the specialist field in which the following synonym(s) are used

Most of the synonyms given are part of standard English, but some have restricted use. These are placed at the end of each group and have the following labels in front of them:

informal, e.g. *swig*: normally only used in speech or informal writing.

formal, e.g. *thereupon*: normally only used in writing, such as official documents.

technical, e.g. *admixture*. Words used in specific fields are labelled *Medicine*, *Nautical*, etc.

poetic/literary, e.g. *plenteous*.

dated, e.g. *rotter*.

historical, e.g. *serfdom*: only used today to refer to things that are no longer part of modern life.

humorous, e.g. *posterior*.

archaic, e.g. *aliment*: not in use today except for old-fashioned effect.

Synonyms are also labelled if they are exclusively or mainly British (abbreviated to *Brit.*), Scottish, North American (*N. Amer.*), Australian (*Austral.*), or New Zealand (*NZ*).

After the main thesaurus section are handy lists of foods, animals, collective names, countries, currencies, and words that are useful in games and puzzles. See the Contents at the very end of the book.

Note on trademarks and proprietary status

Aa

abandon verb ❶ DESERT, leave, forsake, depart from, leave behind, cast aside, jilt; *informal* run out on. ❷ abandon hope: GIVE UP, renounce, relinquish, dispense with, forgo, desist from; *formal* forswear. ❸ abandon his right: YIELD, surrender, give up, cede, relinquish, abdicate, deliver up, resign.
– OPPOSITES keep.
► noun LACK OF RESTRAINT/INHIBITION, wildness, impulse, impetuosity, immoderation, wantonness.
– OPPOSITES self-control.

abandoned adjective ❶ an abandoned wife: DESERTED, forsaken, cast aside. ❷ abandoned behaviour: RECKLESS, unrestrained, uninhibited, impetuous, wild, careless, wanton.

abashed adjective EMBARRASSED, ashamed, shamefaced, mortified, humiliated, taken aback, disconcerted, nonplussed, discomfited, discomposed, perturbed, confounded, dismayed, dumbfounded, confused, put out of countenance, discountenanced.

abbreviate verb SHORTEN, reduce, cut, cut short/down, contract, condense, compress, abridge, truncate, crop, shrink, constrict, summarize, abstract, precis, synopsize, digest.
– OPPOSITES expand.

abdicate verb ❶ RESIGN, stand down, retire; *informal* quit. ❷ abdicate responsibility: GIVE UP, renounce, relinquish, abjure, repudiate, reject, disown, waive, yield, forgo, refuse, abandon, surrender, cast aside.

abduct verb KIDNAP, carry off, run away/off with, make off with, seize, hold as hostage, hold to ransom; *informal* snatch.

aberrant adjective DEVIANT, anomalous, abnormal, irregular, atypical, freakish.
– OPPOSITES normal, typical.

aberration noun DEVIATION, anomaly, abnormality, irregularity, variation, freak.

abhorrent adjective DETESTABLE, loathsome, hateful, hated, abominable, repellent, repugnant, repulsive, revolting, disgusting, distasteful, vile, horrible, horrid, heinous, obnoxious, odious, offensive, execrable; *informal* yucky.
– OPPOSITES delightful, admirable.

abide verb STAND, tolerate, bear, put up with, endure, accept, stomach; *formal* brook; *archaic* suffer.
■ **abide by** KEEP TO, comply with, observe, follow, obey, agree to, hold to, conform to, adhere to, stick to, stand by.

ability noun ❶ TALENT, competence, competency, proficiency, skill, expertise, expertness, adeptness, aptitude, dexterity, adroitness, qualification, cleverness, flair, gift, knack, savoir faire; *informal*

know-how. ❷ CAPACITY, capability, potential, potentiality, power, facility, faculty, propensity.
– OPPOSITES inability.

abjure verb GIVE UP, renounce, relinquish, retract, abandon, deny, abdicate, disclaim, disavow; *formal* forswear.

ablaze adjective ❶ ON FIRE, burning, blazing, alight, flaming, aflame; *poetic/literary* afire. ❷ LIT UP, gleaming, glowing, aglow, illuminated, brilliant, radiant, shimmering, sparkling, flashing, incandescent.

able adjective COMPETENT, capable, talented, skilful, skilled, clever, intelligent, accomplished, gifted, proficient, fit, expert, adept, efficient, effective, qualified, adroit.
– OPPOSITES incompetent.

abnormal adjective UNUSUAL, strange, odd, peculiar, uncommon, curious, queer, eccentric, extraordinary, unexpected, exceptional, irregular, weird, unnatural, erratic, singular, atypical, anomalous, deviant, deviating, divergent, aberrant; *informal* oddball, off the wall, wacko.
– OPPOSITES normal.

abolish verb DO AWAY WITH, put an end to, end, stop, terminate, axe, eliminate, eradicate, exterminate, destroy, annihilate, stamp out, obliterate, wipe out, extinguish, quash, expunge, extirpate, annul, cancel, invalidate, nullify, void, rescind, repeal, revoke, abrogate.
– OPPOSITES retain.

abominable adjective HATEFUL, loathsome, detestable, odious, obnoxious, base, despicable, contemptible, damnable, cursed, disgusting, revolting, repellent, repulsive, offensive, repugnant, abhorrent, foul, vile, wretched, horrible, nasty, disagreeable, unpleasant, execrable; *informal* yucky, god-awful.
– OPPOSITES good, admirable.

abominate verb DETEST, loathe, hate, abhor, dislike, feel aversion/revulsion to, shudder at, recoil from.

aboriginal adjective INDIGENOUS, native, original, earliest, first, ancient, primitive, primeval, primordial, autochthonous.
– OPPOSITES immigrant.

abortive adjective FAILED, unsuccessful, non-successful, vain, futile, useless, worthless, ineffective, ineffectual, fruitless, unproductive, unavailing.
– OPPOSITES successful.

abound verb BE PLENTIFUL, proliferate, teem, overflow, swarm, thrive, flourish; *informal* be two/ten a penny.

abrasive adjective ❶ an abrasive substance: EROSIVE, eroding, corrosive, chafing, rubbing, coarse, harsh. ❷ an abrasive manner: CAUSTIC, cutting, grating, biting, rough, harsh, irritating, sharp, nasty.
– OPPOSITES smooth, kind, gentle.

abridge verb SHORTEN, cut down, summarize, condense, precis, abstract, epitomize, synopsize, digest, contract, compress, abbreviate, reduce, decrease, diminish, curtail, truncate, lessen, trim.
– OPPOSITES expand.

abridgement noun ❶ SUMMARY, synopsis, precis, abstract, outline, résumé, digest, cut-down version. ❷ SHORTENING, cutting,

condensation, contraction, reduction, summarization.
– OPPOSITES expansion.

abrupt adjective ❶ an abrupt ending: SUDDEN, quick, hurried, hasty, swift, rapid, precipitate, headlong, instantaneous, surprising, unexpected, unanticipated, unforeseen. ❷ an abrupt manner: CURT, blunt, brusque, short, terse, brisk, crisp, gruff, unceremonious, rough, rude; *informal* snappish.
– OPPOSITES gradual, gentle.

abscond verb RUN AWAY, bolt, clear out, flee, make off, escape, take flight, fly, decamp, slip/steal/sneak away, take to one's heels, run for it, make a quick getaway, beat a hasty retreat; *informal* show a clean pair of heels, skedaddle, skip; *Brit. informal* do a bunk, do a runner.

absent adjective ❶ AWAY, off, out, gone, missing, truant. ❷ an absent expression: ABSENT-MINDED, distracted, preoccupied, daydreaming, dreaming, dreamy, faraway, blank, empty, vacant, inattentive, vague, absorbed, abstracted, musing, unheeding.
– OPPOSITES present, attentive.

absent-minded adjective DISTRACTED, preoccupied, absorbed, abstracted, vague, inattentive, forgetful, oblivious, in a brown study, distrait; *informal* scatterbrained.
– OPPOSITES alert.

absolute adjective ❶ absolute trust: COMPLETE, total, utter, out-and-out, outright, perfect, entire, undivided, unqualified, unadulterated, unalloyed, downright, undiluted, solid, consummate, unmitigated. ❷ an absolute standard: FIXED, independent, non-relative, non-variable, rigid, established, set, definite. ❸ absolute power: UNLIMITED, unrestricted, unrestrained, unbounded, boundless, infinite, ultimate, total, supreme, unconditional, full, utter, sovereign, omnipotent.
– OPPOSITES qualified.

absolve verb FORGIVE, pardon, excuse, reprieve, give amnesty to, give dispensation/indulgence to, clear, set free, vindicate.

absorb verb ❶ SOAK UP, suck up, draw up/in, take up/in, blot up, mop, sponge up, sop up. ❷ absorb the extra workers: TAKE IN, incorporate, assimilate, appropriate, co-opt. ❸ absorb her attention: OCCUPY, engage, preoccupy, captivate, engross, spellbind, rivet.

absorbent adjective SPONGY, sponge-like, porous, permeable, pervious, penetrable, absorptive, assimilative, receptive.
– OPPOSITES impervious.

absorbing adjective FASCINATING, gripping, interesting, captivating, engrossing, riveting, spellbinding, intriguing.
– OPPOSITES boring.

abstain verb REFRAIN, decline, forbear, desist, hold back, keep from, refuse, renounce, avoid, shun, eschew.

abstemious adjective MODERATE, temperate, abstinent, self-denying, austere, sober, self-restrained, ascetic, puritanical.
– OPPOSITES self-indulgent.

abstract adjective ❶ THEORETICAL, conceptual, notional, intellectual, metaphysical, philosophical.

❷ NON-REPRESENTATIONAL, non-realistic, unrealistic.
– OPPOSITES actual, concrete
▶ **verb** EXTRACT, remove, take out/away, separate, detach, draw away, isolate.
▶ **noun** SUMMARY, synopsis, precis, résumé, outline, abridgement, condensation, digest.

abstruse adjective OBSCURE, deep, profound, complex, hidden, esoteric, mysterious, incomprehensible, unfathomable, inscrutable, enigmatic, perplexing, puzzling, recondite, arcane, nebulous.
– OPPOSITES comprehensible.

absurd adjective RIDICULOUS, foolish, silly, idiotic, stupid, nonsensical, senseless, inane, crazy, ludicrous, funny, laughable, comical, preposterous, farcical, hare-brained, asinine; *Brit. informal* daft.
– OPPOSITES sensible.

abundance noun PLENTY, plentifulness, profusion, copiousness, amplitude, affluence, lavishness, bountifulness; *informal* heaps, bags, stacks, loads, tons, oodles.
– OPPOSITES scarcity.

abundant adjective PLENTIFUL, large, great, huge, ample, well supplied, well provided, profuse, copious, lavish, bountiful, teeming, overflowing, galore.
– OPPOSITES scarce.

abuse verb ❶ abuse power/alcohol: MISUSE, misapply, misemploy, mishandle, exploit. ❷ abuse children: MISTREAT, maltreat, ill-use, ill-treat, manhandle, injure, hurt, harm, beat, damage, wrong, oppress, torture. ❸ INSULT, swear at, curse, scold, rebuke, upbraid, reprove, inveigh against, revile, vilify, slander; *formal* castigate; *archaic* vituperate against.
▶ **noun** ❶ MISUSE, misapplication, misemployment, mishandling, exploitation. ❷ MISTREATMENT, maltreatment, ill-use, ill-treatment, manhandling, injury, hurt, harm, beating, damage, wronging, oppression, torture. ❸ SWEARING, cursing, scolding, rebuke, upbraiding, reproval, invective, revilement, vilification, vituperation, defamation, slander, insults, curses, expletives, swear words; *formal* castigation.

abusive adjective INSULTING, rude, offensive, disparaging, denigratory, derogatory, defamatory, derisive, scornful, vituperative, opprobrious, slanderous, libellous; *formal* castigating, calumniating.

abut verb ADJOIN, border, verge on, join, touch, meet, impinge on.

abysmal adjective VERY BAD, dreadful, awful, terrible, frightful, atrocious, deplorable, lamentable; *informal* rotten, appalling, pathetic, pitiful, woeful, lousy, dire; *Brit. informal* chronic.
– OPPOSITES excellent.

abyss noun CHASM, gorge, ravine, canyon, crevasse, cavity, void, pit, bottomless pit, hole, gulf, depth.

academic adjective
❶ EDUCATIONAL, scholastic, instructional, pedagogical.
❷ SCHOLARLY, studious, literary, well read, intellectual, erudite, highbrow, learned, cultured, bookish, pedantic, donnish, cerebral; *informal* brainy.
❸ THEORETICAL, hypothetical, abstract, conjectural, notional,

impractical, unrealistic, speculative.
▶ **noun** SCHOLAR, lecturer, don, teacher, tutor, professor, fellow.

accede
■ **accede to** AGREE TO, consent to, accept, assent to, acquiesce in, endorse, comply with, go along with, concur, grant, yield to.

accelerate **verb** SPEED UP, go faster, pick up speed, hasten, hurry, quicken.
– OPPOSITES decelerate.

accent **noun** ❶ PRONUNCIATION, intonation, enunciation, articulation, inflection, tone, modulation, utterance. ❷ STRESS, emphasis, accentuation, force, beat, prominence. ❸ EMPHASIS, stress, prominence, importance, accentuation, priority, underlining, underscoring.

accentuate **verb** EMPHASIZE, stress, highlight, underline, draw attention to, give prominence to, heighten, point up, underscore, accent.

accept **verb** ❶ RECEIVE, take, get, gain, obtain, acquire. ❷ **accept the decision:** ACCEDE TO, agree to, consent to, acquiesce in, concur with, endorse, comply with, go along with, defer to, put up with, recognize, acknowledge, cooperate with, adopt, admit. ❸ **accept their story:** BELIEVE, trust, credit, be convinced of, have faith in, count/rely on.
– OPPOSITES reject.

acceptable **adjective** ❶ WELCOME, agreeable, delightful, pleasing, desirable, satisfying, gratifying. ❷ SATISFACTORY, good enough, adequate, passable, admissible, tolerable.
– OPPOSITES unacceptable.

accepted **adjective** ❶ **an accepted opinion:** APPROVED, recognized, sanctioned, authorized, received, allowable, acceptable. ❷ **the accepted way:** USUAL, customary, normal, expected, standard, conventional, recognized, acknowledged, established, traditional.

access **noun** ENTRY, entrance, way in, means of entry/entrance, admittance, admission, approachability, accessibility, approach, means of approach.

accessible **adjective** ❶ ATTAINABLE, reachable, available, approachable, obtainable, achievable; *informal* get-at-able. ❷ APPROACHABLE, available, easy-going, informal, friendly, pleasant, agreeable, obliging, congenial, affable, cordial.
– OPPOSITES inaccessible.

accessory **noun** ❶ ATTACHMENT, fitment, extra, addition, adjunct, appendage, supplement. ❷ ACCOMPLICE, associate, confederate, abetter, helper, assistant, partner.
▶ **adjective** **an accessory part/factor:** ADDITIONAL, extra, supplementary, contributory, subsidiary, ancillary, auxiliary, secondary.

accident **noun** ❶ MISHAP, misfortune, misadventure, injury, disaster, tragedy, blow, catastrophe, calamity. ❷ CRASH, smash, collision; *informal* pile-up; *Brit. informal* shunt. ❸ **met by accident:** CHANCE, mere chance, fluke, fate, twist of fate, fortune, good fortune, luck, good luck, fortuity, hazard.

accidental **adjective** CHANCE, unintentional, unintended,

inadvertent, unexpected, unforeseen, unlooked for, fortuitous, unanticipated, unplanned, uncalculated, unpremeditated, unwitting, adventitious.
– OPPOSITES intentional.

acclaim verb APPLAUD, cheer, celebrate, salute, welcome, approve, honour, praise, commend, hail, extol, eulogize, exalt; *formal* laud.
▶ noun APPLAUSE, ovation, praise, commendation, approval, approbation, homage, tribute, extolment, cheers, congratulations, plaudits, bouquets, salutes, eulogies; *formal* laudation.

acclimatize verb ADJUST, adapt, accustom, get used, accommodate, become seasoned, familiarize oneself, become inured.

accommodate verb
❶ accommodated in a hotel: PUT UP, house, cater for, board, lodge, shelter, give someone a roof over their head, harbour, billet. ❷ try to accommodate everyone: HELP, assist, aid, oblige, meet the needs/wants of, cater for, fit in with, satisfy.

accommodating adjective
OBLIGING, cooperative, helpful, considerate, amenable, unselfish, willing, polite, kindly, hospitable, kind, friendly, agreeable.

accommodation noun
HOUSING, lodging, board, shelter, place of residence, house, billet, lodgings, quarters; *informal* digs, pad.

accompany verb ❶ ESCORT, go with, go along with, keep someone company, attend, usher, show, see, conduct, squire, chaperone, convoy. ❷ OCCUR WITH, go with, go together with, go hand in hand with, coexist with, supplement.

accomplice noun PARTNER IN CRIME, associate, accessory, CONFEDERATE, collaborator, abetter, henchman, fellow conspirator; *informal* sidekick.

accomplish verb ACHIEVE, carry out, fulfil, perform, attain, realize, succeed in, bring off, bring about, effect, execute; *formal* effectuate.
– OPPOSITES fail in.

accomplished adjective
SKILLED, skilful, expert, gifted, talented, proficient, adept, masterly, polished, practised, capable, able, competent, experienced, professional, deft, consummate.
– OPPOSITES incompetent.

accomplishment noun
TALENT, ability, skill, gift, attainment, achievement, capability, proficiency.

accord verb AGREE, concur, fit, correspond, tally, match, conform, harmonize, suit, be in tune.
– OPPOSITES disagree, differ.
▶ noun AGREEMENT, consensus, unanimity, harmony, rapport, unison, amity; *formal* concord.
– OPPOSITES disagreement.

account noun ❶ DESCRIPTION, report, statement, record, narration, narrative, story, recital, explanation, tale, chronicle, history, relation, version.
❷ FINANCIAL RECORD, ledger, balance sheet, financial statement, books. ❸ BILL, invoice, reckoning, tally, charges, debts.
❹ a person of little account:

IMPORTANCE, consequence, significance.

accumulate verb ❶ the dust accumulated: GATHER, pile up, build up, collect, amass, increase, augment, cumulate, accrue. ❷ accumulate money: AMASS, gather, collect, stockpile, pile up, heap up, store, hoard.

accumulation noun PILE, heap, build-up, mass, collection, store, supply, stockpile, hoard, stock, conglomeration, gathering, growth.

accurate adjective CORRECT, right, true, exact, precise, authentic, factual, truthful, faultless, reliable, scrupulous, faithful, meticulous, careful, sound, sure, certain, strict; *Brit. informal* spot on, bang on; *formal* veracious.
– OPPOSITES inaccurate.

accusation noun CHARGE, allegation, indictment, complaint, summons, arraignment, citation, denunciation, imputation; *N. Amer.* impeachment.

accuse verb ❶ CHARGE, indict, bring/prefer charges against, make allegations against, arraign, prosecute, summons, cite; *N. Amer.* impeach. ❷ blame, hold responsible, denounce, censure, condemn, incriminate, tax; *informal* point the finger at.
– OPPOSITES defend.

accustomed adjective ❶ his accustomed style: USUAL, customary, habitual, regular, established, normal, conventional, expected, routine, familiar, common, fixed, traditional, ordinary, set, prevailing; *poetic/literary* wonted. ❷ accustomed to doing: USED TO, familiar with, habituated, adapted.
■ **become/get accustomed** *see* ADAPT.

ache noun PAIN, soreness, discomfort, hurt, distress, throbbing, twinge, pang, suffering, anguish, smart.
▶ verb HURT, be sore, be painful, smart, sting, pound, throb, suffer.
■ **ache for** *see* DESIRE.

achieve verb ❶ SUCCEED IN, accomplish, manage, do successfully, carry out, complete, attain, bring off, effect, perform, conclude, finish, discharge, fulfil, execute, engineer, consummate. ❷ achieve success: GAIN, obtain, get, acquire, earn, reach, win, score, procure.

acid adjective ❶ acid taste: SHARP, tart, sour, vinegary, tangy, stinging. ❷ acid wit: CAUSTIC, acerbic, sharp, sardonic, scathing, trenchant, vitriolic.
– OPPOSITES sweet, pleasant.

acknowledge verb ❶ acknowledge the truth: ADMIT, concede, accept, agree, confirm, allow, confess, grant, own, affirm, profess. ❷ acknowledge someone: GREET, salute, address, hail, say hello to. ❸ acknowledge a letter: ANSWER, reply to, respond to, react to, return.
– OPPOSITES deny, ignore.

acme noun PEAK, top, highest point, pinnacle, summit, height, culmination, zenith, apex, climax, optimum.
– OPPOSITES nadir.

acquaint verb FAMILIARIZE, make familiar, make aware of, inform of, advise of, notify of, apprise of, let know, get up to date, brief, prime; *informal* fill in on.

acquaintance noun ❶ a business acquaintance: CONTACT, associate, colleague. ❷ acquaintance with someone: ASSOCIATION, relationship, contact. ❸ acquaintance with something: FAMILIARITY, awareness, knowledge, experience, understanding, grasp.

acquire verb GET, obtain, buy, purchase, procure, come by, pick up, receive, earn, secure, appropriate; *informal* get hold of, get one's hands on.
– OPPOSITES lose.

acquisition noun POSSESSION, gain, purchase, property, prize, addition, accession; *informal* buy.
– OPPOSITES loss.

acquit verb CLEAR, find innocent, declare innocent, absolve, set free, free, release, liberate, discharge, reprieve, vindicate, exonerate; *informal* let off; *formal* exculpate.
– OPPOSITES condemn.
■ **acquit oneself** *see* BEHAVE (1).

acrid adjective PUNGENT, sharp, bitter, harsh, acid, caustic.

acrimonious adjective BITTER, angry, rancorous, caustic, acerbic, scathing, sarcastic, acid, harsh, sharp, cutting, virulent, spiteful, vicious, vitriolic, hostile, venomous, bad-tempered, ill-natured, malicious, waspish.
– OPPOSITES good-natured.

act verb ❶ you must act: DO SOMETHING, take action, move, react, take steps. ❷ acting strangely: BEHAVE, carry on, conduct oneself; *formal* comport oneself. ❸ act a part: PERFORM, play, appear as, enact, portray, represent, assume the character of, overact; *informal* tread the boards. *See also* PRETEND (1). ❹ act as a preservative: FUNCTION, work, operate, have an effect, take effect, serve.
▶ noun ❶ an act of courage: DEED, action, feat, exploit, undertaking, effort, enterprise, achievement, step, move, operation, proceeding. ❷ an act of parliament: LAW, statute, bill, decree, order, enactment, edict. ❸ a comedy act: PERFORMANCE, routine, number, turn, item, sketch.

acting adjective TEMPORARY, provisional, interim, stopgap, substitute, stand-in, fill-in, surrogate, deputy, pro tem.
– OPPOSITES permanent.

action noun ❶ DEED, act, feat, exploit, undertaking, process, enterprise, measure, step, effort, endeavour, proceeding, performance, work. ❷ ACTIVITY, movement, motion, exertion, drama, liveliness, excitement, vigour, energy, vitality, initiative, exercise, enterprise. ❸ STORY, events, incidents, happenings. ❹ the action of a clock: MECHANISM, works, operation, functioning, working.

activate verb SET OFF, set in motion, operate, start, trigger, initiate, actuate, energize, trip.

active adjective ❶ ENERGETIC, lively, sprightly, spry, mobile, vigorous, vital, dynamic, sporty, busy, occupied; *informal* on the go, full of beans. ❷ HARD-WORKING, busy, industrious, diligent, tireless, effective, enterprising, involved, enthusiastic, keen, committed, devoted, zealous. ❸ OPERATIVE, working, functioning, functional,

operating, operational, in action, in operation, live; *informal* up and running.
– OPPOSITES inactive.

activity noun ❶ MOVEMENT, action, bustle, motion, excitement, liveliness, commotion, energy, industry, hurly-burly, animation, life, hustle, stir. ❷ HOBBY, pastime, interest, task, job, venture, project, occupation, undertaking, scheme, pursuit. *See also* WORK noun.

actual adjective REAL, authentic, genuine, true, factual, verified, realistic, bona fide, definite, existing, current, legitimate, indisputable, unquestionable, tangible, certain, truthful, in existence, living, confirmed, corporeal.
– OPPOSITES imaginary.

acute adjective ❶ acute shortage: SERIOUS, urgent, pressing, grave, critical, crucial, precarious. ❷ acute illness: SEVERE, critical, intense. ❸ acute pains: SHARP, piercing, intense, severe, extreme, fierce, excruciating, cutting, sudden, violent, shooting, keen, exquisite, racking. ❹ acute analysis: INTELLIGENT, shrewd, sharp, quick, penetrating. *See also* CLEVER (1).
– OPPOSITES mild, chronic, dull.

adapt verb ❶ adapt to a new environment: GET USED, adjust, get accustomed, habituate oneself, acclimatize, reconcile oneself, attune, accommodate, become hardened, become inured. ❷ a specially adapted machine: ALTER, change, modify, adjust, convert, remodel, transform, rebuild, remake, refashion, reshape, reconstruct, tailor.

add verb ATTACH, append, put on, affix, tack on, include, combine.
– OPPOSITES subtract.
■ **add up** TOTAL, count, reckon, tot up. **add to** *see* INCREASE verb (2).

addict noun ABUSER, user; *informal* junkie, druggy, — freak, —head.

addiction noun DEPENDENCY, craving, habit, compulsion, obsession, enslavement, dedication, devotion.

addition noun ❶ INCREASE, enlargement, expansion, supplement, extension, increment, augmentation, gain, adjunct, accessory, addendum, appendage, development, additive, appendix, postscript, afterthought, attachment, annex, amplification, accession; *technical* admixture. ❷ the addition of figures: ADDING UP, counting, totalling, calculation, reckoning, computation; *informal* totting up.
– OPPOSITES reduction, subtraction.

additional adjective EXTRA, more, further, added, supplementary, other, new, fresh, increased, spare, supplemental.

address noun ❶ move to a new address: LOCATION, whereabouts, place, home, house, residence, situation; *formal* dwelling, abode, domicile. ❷ an address to the crowd: SPEECH, talk, lecture, oration, disquisition, sermon, homily, diatribe, discourse, disquisition, harangue; *poetic/literary* philippic.
▶ verb ❶ address the crowd: SPEAK TO, talk to, lecture, give a speech to, declaim to, harangue, preach to. ❷ address a person: GREET, speak to, talk to, engage in conversation, approach, accost, hail, salute; *informal* buttonhole.

3 address an envelope: DIRECT, label, inscribe, superscribe.
■ **address oneself to** *see* TACKLE verb (1).

adduce verb MENTION, put forward, cite, point out, quote, name, propose, advance, instance.

adept adjective EXPERT, proficient, clever, accomplished, talented, gifted, practised, masterly. *See also* SKILFUL.
– OPPOSITES inept.

adequate adjective **1** adequate work: TOLERABLE, passable, all right, average, satisfactory, competent, unexceptional, acceptable, unexceptionable, mediocre, good enough; *informal* OK, so-so. **2** adequate to the task: COMPETENT, up to, capable, able, qualified.
– OPPOSITES inadequate.

adhere verb STICK, cling, bond, attach, bind, fuse.

adherent noun SUPPORTER, follower, devotee, disciple, advocate, fan, upholder, defender, stalwart, partisan.

adjacent adjective NEIGHBOURING, adjoining, bordering, next, close, next door, touching, attached, abutting, contiguous.

adjourn verb BREAK OFF, interrupt, discontinue, postpone, put off, delay, defer, shelve, suspend, prorogue.

adjournment noun INTERRUPTION, break, breaking off, postponement, pause, delay, deferral, deferment, recess, suspension, prorogation.

adjust adjective **1** adjust to a new situation: ADAPT, become accustomed to, get used to, reconcile oneself, accommodate, acclimatize, habituate oneself, conform. **2** adjust the brakes: ADAPT, alter, fix, repair, regulate, modify, put right, put in working order, rectify, change, arrange, amend, set to rights, tune, rearrange, tailor, balance, vary, position, set, refashion, remake, remodel, reorganize.

administer verb **1** administer a business: MANAGE, direct, run, administrate, control, organize, supervise, oversee, preside over, superintend, regulate, govern, conduct, rule, command. **2** administer the medicine: GIVE, dispense, issue, provide, supply, treat with, hand out, deal out, distribute, measure out, dole out. **3** administer justice: DISPENSE, provide, implement, carry out, mete out, distribute, disburse, bestow, execute.

admirable adjective COMMENDABLE, worthy, praiseworthy, laudable, good, excellent, fine, exemplary, wonderful, great, marvellous, enjoyable, respectable, creditable, pleasing, meritorious, first-rate, first-class, masterly, awe-inspiring, deserving, estimable.
– OPPOSITES deplorable.

admiration noun APPROVAL, regard, respect, praise, appreciation, commendation, approbation, esteem, awe, veneration, honour.
– OPPOSITES contempt.

admire verb APPROVE OF, like, respect, appreciate, praise, have a high opinion of, look up to, think highly of, applaud, wonder at, esteem, value, commend, sing someone's praises, love, honour, idolize, revere, venerate,

hero-worship, marvel at, be delighted by; *formal* laud. *See also* LOVE verb (1).
– OPPOSITES hate.

admissible adjective ALLOWABLE, allowed, accepted, permitted, permissible, tolerable, justifiable.

admission noun ❶ ADMITTANCE, entry, entrance, access, entrée, ingress. ❷ an admission of guilt: ACKNOWLEDGEMENT, acceptance, confession, declaration, disclosure, profession, divulgence, utterance, avowal, revelation, affirmation.
– OPPOSITES denial.

admit verb ❶ the ticket admits two people: ALLOW IN, let in, permit entry to, grant access to. ❷ admit one's guilt: ACKNOWLEDGE, confess, reveal, concede, own up to, declare, make known, accept, disclose, agree, profess, recognize, allow.
– OPPOSITES exclude, deny.

admonish verb *see* REPRIMAND verb.

adolescent adjective TEENAGE, youthful, pubescent, immature, childish, juvenile, puerile, girlish, boyish.
▶ noun TEENAGER, youth, youngster, young person, juvenile.

adopt verb ❶ adopt a child: TAKE IN, foster, take care of, take under one's wing. ❷ adopt the new measures: ACCEPT, endorse, approve, support, back, sanction, ratify. ❸ adopt eastern customs: EMBRACE, assume, take on, espouse, appropriate, affect.

adore verb LOVE, worship, dote on, cherish, idolize, adulate, revere, venerate, honour, glorify. *See also* ADMIRE.
– OPPOSITES hate.

adorn verb DECORATE, embellish, ornament, enhance, beautify, grace, emblazon, bedeck, trim.

adrift adjective ❶ a boat adrift: DRIFTING, unmoored, unanchored, floating. ❷ come adrift: UNFASTENED, untied, loose, detached. ❸ plans went adrift: WRONG, amiss, astray, awry, off course.

adult adjective FULLY GROWN, grown up, mature, fully developed, of age, nubile.
– OPPOSITES immature.

adulterate verb CONTAMINATE, make impure, taint, pollute, debase, degrade, doctor, corrupt, alloy, defile, dilute, thin, water down, weaken.

advance verb ❶ the army advanced: MOVE FORWARD, move ahead, go forward, proceed, forge ahead, gain ground, make headway, approach, push forward, press on, press ahead, push on, bear down, make strides. ❷ her career advanced: PROGRESS, move forward, go ahead, improve, flourish, thrive, prosper. ❸ advance the schedule: SPEED UP, bring forward, accelerate, step up, expedite, forward, hurry, hasten. ❹ advance a suggestion: PUT FORWARD, suggest, present, submit, propose, introduce, offer, proffer, adduce, furnish. ❺ advance money: LEND, pay in advance, loan, provide, supply, proffer.
– OPPOSITES retreat.
▶ noun medical advances: DEVELOPMENT, breakthrough, discovery, finding, progress, improvement, invention.

advanced adjective ❶ advanced technology: SOPHISTICATED, modern, latest, up to date.

❷ advanced thinking: PROGRESSIVE, innovative, original, new, forward-looking, inventive, contemporary, revolutionary, experimental, novel, avant-garde, pioneering, trendsetting, ahead of the times; *informal* way-out. ❸ advanced studies: HIGHER-LEVEL, complex, complicated, difficult, hard. ❹ MATURE, grown up, precocious, sophisticated, well developed.
– OPPOSITES backward.

advantage noun ❶ BENEFIT, good point, asset, gain, convenience, profit, use, boon, blessing. ❷ an advantage over him: SUPERIORITY, dominance, edge, upper hand, whip hand, trump card.
– OPPOSITES disadvantage.
■ **take advantage of** *see* EXPLOIT verb (2).

advantageous adjective ❶ BENEFICIAL, helpful, useful, of benefit, profitable, valuable, worthwhile. ❷ an advantageous position: FAVOURABLE, dominant, superior, powerful.

adventure noun ❶ the soldier's adventures: EXPLOIT, deed, feat, experience, incident, escapade, venture, undertaking, operation. ❷ a spirit of adventure: EXCITEMENT, danger, hazard, risk, peril, precariousness.

adventurous adjective ❶ an adventurous man: DARING, brave, bold, courageous, heroic, enterprising, intrepid, daredevil, valiant, venturesome, reckless, rash. ❷ adventurous activities: RISKY, dangerous, exciting, hazardous, challenging, perilous, precarious.
– OPPOSITES cautious, boring, uneventful.

adverse adjective ❶ adverse circumstances: UNFAVOURABLE, unfortunate, harmful, disadvantageous, inauspicious, unlucky, detrimental, untoward, prejudicial, unpropitious, uncongenial, deleterious, contrary. ❷ adverse criticism: HOSTILE, unfriendly, antagonistic, negative, disapproving, derogatory, attacking, uncomplimentary, opposing, unkind, unsympathetic, hurtful, unfavourable, censorious, inimical.
– OPPOSITES favourable.

adversity noun MISFORTUNE, bad luck, trouble, disaster, sorrow, misery, hard times, tribulation, woe, affliction.

advertise verb PUBLICIZE, promote, market, display, tout, make known, call attention to, merchandise, flaunt, show off, announce, promulgate, proclaim; *informal* push, puff, plug, hype.

advertisement noun COMMERCIAL, promotion, display, publicity, announcement, notice, circular, handout, small ad, leaflet, placard; *informal* ad, plug, puff, blurb; *Brit. informal* advert.

advice noun GUIDANCE, help, counsel, suggestions, recommendations, hints, pointers, tips, ideas, views, warnings, caution, admonition.

advisable adjective PRUDENT, recommended, sensible, appropriate, expedient, judicious, politic. *See also* WISE (2).
– OPPOSITES inadvisable.

advise verb GIVE GUIDANCE, guide, counsel, enjoin, offer suggestions, caution, instruct, urge, exhort,

advocate, warn, encourage, commend, admonish.
■ **advise someone of** *see* INFORM (1).

advocacy noun SUPPORT, backing, promotion, argument for, advising, recommendation.

advocate noun SUPPORTER, proponent, backer, spokesman, exponent, apologist.
▶ verb ADVISE, recommend, support, back, argue for, urge, favour, endorse, champion.

aesthetic adjective ARTISTIC, tasteful, beautiful, sensitive, in good taste, cultivated.

affable adjective FRIENDLY, agreeable, pleasant, amiable, good-natured, civil, courteous.
– OPPOSITES unfriendly.

affair noun ❶ a sad affair: EVENT, occurrence, episode, incident, happening, circumstance, case, proceeding, occasion, matter, issue, subject, topic. ❷ that's my affair: BUSINESS, concern, activity, responsibility, province, preserve, problem, worry; *Brit. informal* lookout. ❸ an affair with a married man: RELATIONSHIP, love affair, romance, involvement, liaison, intrigue, amour, attachment; *Brit. informal* carry-on.

affect[1] verb ❶ HAVE AN EFFECT ON, influence, act on, change, have an impact on, modify, shape, transform. ❷ the experience affected him deeply: MOVE, touch, upset, trouble, disturb, concern, perturb, stir, agitate, hit, grieve.

affect[2] verb affect an accent: ADOPT, assume, feign, sham, simulate; *informal* put on. *See also* PRETEND (1).

affectation noun PRETENCE, affectedness, pretentiousness, pretension, posturing, artificiality. *See also* PRETENCE (3).

affected adjective UNNATURAL, contrived, put on, artificial, mannered, insincere, studied. *See also* PRETENTIOUS.
– OPPOSITES natural.

affecting adjective MOVING, touching, heart-rending, poignant, upsetting, pathetic.

affection noun FONDNESS, liking, love, warmth, devotion, attachment, tenderness, friendship, partiality, amity, warm feelings; *informal* soft spot. *See also* LOVE noun (1).
– OPPOSITES dislike, hatred.

affectionate adjective FOND, loving, caring, devoted, tender, doting, warm, friendly. *See also* LOVING.
– OPPOSITES cold.

affinity noun ❶ LIKING, fondness, closeness, relationship, kinship, like-mindedness, rapport, empathy, understanding; *informal* chemistry. ❷ LIKENESS, closeness, similarity, resemblance, correspondence, similitude.

affirm verb STATE, assert, declare, maintain, attest, avow, swear, pronounce, proclaim; *formal* aver.
– OPPOSITES deny.

affirmation noun STATEMENT, assertion, declaration, confirmation, proclamation, pronouncement, oath, attestation; *formal* averment.
– OPPOSITES denial.

affirmative adjective ASSENTING, agreeing, concurring, consenting, positive, approving.
– OPPOSITES negative.

afflict verb TROUBLE, burden, distress, affect, try, worry, bother, harm, oppress, pain, hurt, torture, plague, rack, torment, beset, harass, wound, bedevil, grieve, pester, annoy, vex.

affluence noun WEALTH, prosperity, riches, fortune, substance, resources.
– OPPOSITES poverty.

affluent adjective RICH, wealthy, prosperous, well off, well-to-do, moneyed, opulent, comfortable; *informal* well heeled, loaded.
– OPPOSITES poor.

afford verb ❶ PAY FOR, find enough for, have the means for, spare the price of, meet the expense of, run to, stretch to, spare. ❷ *See* PROVIDE (2).

affray noun FIGHT, brawl, fracas, scuffle, tussle; *informal* scrap, punch-up, set-to.

afraid adjective ❶ FRIGHTENED, scared, terrified, fearful, apprehensive, terror-stricken, timid, intimidated, nervous, alarmed, anxious, trembling, cowardly, panicky, panic-stricken, uneasy, agitated, pusillanimous, faint-hearted, reluctant, craven, diffident, daunted, cowed, timorous; *informal* chicken, yellow, jittery; *Brit. informal* windy. ❷ I'm afraid I can't help: SORRY, apologetic, regretful, unhappy.
– OPPOSITES brave, confident.

aftermath noun AFTER-EFFECTS, consequences, repercussions, results, outcome, end result, upshot.

afterwards adverb LATER, subsequently, then, next, after; *formal* thereupon.
– OPPOSITES beforehand.

age noun ❶ wisdom comes with age: MATURITY, old age, advancing years, seniority, elderliness; *Biology* senescence. ❷ the nuclear age: ERA, epoch, period, time, generation. ❸ it took ages: A LONG TIME, an eternity, aeons, hours, days, months, years; *Brit. informal* yonks.
▶ verb GROW OLD, mature, grow up, ripen, develop, mellow, wither, fade.

aged adjective OLD, elderly, ancient, long in the tooth, superannuated; *Biology* senescent; *informal* getting on, over the hill.
– OPPOSITES young, youthful.

agent noun REPRESENTATIVE, middleman, go-between, broker, negotiator, intermediary, mediator, emissary, envoy, proxy, factor, trustee, delegate, spokesperson, spokesman, spokeswoman, executor.

aggravate verb ❶ MAKE WORSE, worsen, exacerbate, intensify, inflame, exaggerate, make more serious, compound, increase, heighten, magnify, add to. ❷ *See* ANNOY.
– OPPOSITES alleviate, improve.

aggressive adjective ❶ an aggressive act: HOSTILE, violent, belligerent, combative, attacking, destructive, quarrelsome, warlike, antagonistic, provocative, pugnacious, bellicose, bullying, contentious, jingoistic, militant. ❷ an aggressive salesman: ASSERTIVE, forceful, pushy, insistent, vigorous, dynamic, bold, enterprising, energetic, zealous, pushing; *informal* go-ahead.
– OPPOSITES peaceable, retiring.

aggrieved adjective RESENTFUL, affronted, indignant, angry, distressed, piqued, disturbed; *informal* peeved.

agile adjective NIMBLE, lithe, fit, supple, sprightly, graceful, acrobatic, lively, spry, adroit, deft, quick-moving, limber, in good condition; *informal* nippy.
– OPPOSITES clumsy, stiff.

agitate verb ❶ UPSET, worry, fluster, perturb, disturb, disconcert, trouble, alarm, work up, ruffle, disquiet, unsettle, unnerve, rouse, excite, discomfit, confuse, shake up; *informal* rattle. ❷ agitate the mixture: STIR, whisk, beat, shake, toss, work, churn, froth up, ruffle, ferment.
– OPPOSITES calm.

agitator noun TROUBLEMAKER, rabble-rouser, agent provocateur, instigator, firebrand, fomenter, revolutionary, demagogue.

agonizing adjective EXCRUCIATING, painful, acute, harrowing, searing, unendurable, torturous.

agony noun SUFFERING, anguish, hurt, torment, torture, distress. *See also* PAIN.

agree verb ❶ I agree with you: CONCUR, be of the same mind, comply, see eye to eye. ❷ the statements agree: MATCH, correspond, accord, conform, coincide, fit, tally. ❸ agree to the proposal: CONSENT TO, accept, assent to, approve, allow, admit, acquiesce in.
– OPPOSITES disagree.

agreeable adjective PLEASING, enjoyable, nice, delightful, acceptable, likable, to one's liking, pleasurable. *See also* PLEASANT.
– OPPOSITES disagreeable.

agreement noun ❶ be in agreement: ACCORD, concurrence, harmony, accordance, unity, assent; *formal* concord. ❷ a business agreement: CONTRACT, deal, compact, settlement, pact, bargain, treaty, covenant, concordat. ❸ agreement between our views: CORRESPONDENCE, similarity, conformity, match, harmony, accordance, coincidence.
– OPPOSITES disagreement.

agricultural adjective ❶ FARMING, farm, agrarian, pastoral, rural. ❷ FARMED, cultivated, planted, productive, tilled.
– OPPOSITES urban.

agriculture noun FARMING, cultivation, tillage, husbandry, agronomy, agronomics, agribusiness; *Brit.* crofting.

aground adverb & adjective GROUNDED, beached, ashore, shipwrecked, on the bottom, stranded, stuck, high and dry.
– OPPOSITES afloat.

aid noun ❶ HELP, assistance, support, succour, encouragement, a helping hand, cooperation. ❷ foreign aid: CONTRIBUTION, gift, donation, subsidy, loan, debt remission, relief, sponsorship, backing, grant; *historical* alms.
– OPPOSITES hindrance.
▶ verb ❶ HELP, assist, support, succour, lend a hand, sustain, second. ❷ aid recovery: FACILITATE, speed up, hasten, help, encourage, expedite, promote, contribute to, sustain.
– OPPOSITES hinder.

ailing adjective UNWELL, sick, poorly, sickly, indisposed, infirm; *informal* under the weather. *See also* ILL adjective (1).
– OPPOSITES healthy.

ailment noun ILLNESS, disease, sickness, disorder, complaint, malady, infirmity, affliction. *See also* ILLNESS.

aim verb ❶ aim a gun: POINT, direct, take aim, train, sight, focus, address, zero in on. ❷ aim to increase profits: INTEND, mean, resolve, wish, aspire, want, plan, propose, seek, try, strive, endeavour.
▶ noun AMBITION, objective, object, end, goal, purpose, intention, intent, plan, target, hope, aspiration, desire, wish, design, direction, focus, dream, destination.

aimless adjective ❶ an aimless life: POINTLESS, purposeless, futile, undirected, goalless, objectless. ❷ aimless people: PURPOSELESS, drifting, wandering, undirected, unambitious, undisciplined, wayward.
– OPPOSITES purposeful.

air noun ❶ SKY, atmosphere, airspace; *poetic/literary* heavens, ether. ❷ let's get some air: OXYGEN, breath of air, breeze, draught, puff of wind; *poetic/literary* zephyr. ❸ an air of peace: APPEARANCE, impression, look, mood, atmosphere, quality, feeling, ambience, character, flavour, demeanour, effect, manner, bearing, tone, aspect, mien. ❹ put on airs: AFFECTATIONS, pretension, pretentiousness, affectedness, airs and graces, posing, posturing. ❺ play an old air: MELODY, tune, song, theme, strain.
▶ verb ❶ air one's views: EXPRESS, make known, voice, publicize, broadcast, give vent to, publish, communicate, reveal, proclaim, divulge, circulate, disseminate, vent, disclose. ❷ air the room: VENTILATE, aerate, freshen, refresh.

airless adjective STUFFY, close, stifling, suffocating, muggy, unventilated, oppressive, sultry.
– OPPOSITES airy.

airtight adjective ❶ airtight tin: SEALED, closed, impermeable, shut tight. ❷ airtight alibi: INDISPUTABLE, incontrovertible, irrefutable, incontestable, unassailable.

airy adjective ❶ an airy room: WELL VENTILATED, fresh, spacious, uncluttered, light, bright. ❷ an airy reply: NONCHALANT, casual, light-hearted, breezy, cheerful, jaunty, flippant, blithe, insouciant; *dated* gay.
– OPPOSITES stuffy, studied.

aisle noun PASSAGE, passageway, gangway, walkway, corridor, lane, alley.

akin adjective RELATED TO, allied with, connected with, corresponding to, similar to.
– OPPOSITES unrelated, different.

alacrity noun READINESS, promptness, eagerness, enthusiasm, willingness, haste, swiftness.
– OPPOSITES reluctance, sluggishness.

alarm noun ❶ feel alarm: FEAR, apprehension, anxiety, uneasiness, distress, consternation, panic, fright, trepidation, disquiet. *See also* FEAR noun (1). ❷ WARNING SOUND, siren, alert, alarm bell/signal, danger/distress signal; *archaic* tocsin.
▶ verb FRIGHTEN, scare, panic, terrify, unnerve, agitate, distress, disturb, startle, shock, upset, worry; *Brit. informal* put the wind up.
– OPPOSITES reassure.

alcohol noun DRINK, liquor, spirits; *informal* booze, hard stuff, the demon drink, the bottle, grog, tipple; *Brit. informal* bevvy.

alcoholic adjective INTOXICATING, strong, inebriating, hard; *formal* spirituous.
– OPPOSITES soft.
▶ noun DRUNKARD, drunk, hard/heavy drinker, dipsomaniac, problem drinker, inebriate, tippler, sot, imbiber; *informal* boozer, lush, dipso, wino, alky.
– OPPOSITES teetotaller.

alert adjective ❶ alert to danger: AWARE, alive to, watchful, vigilant, observant, wary, wide awake, on one's guard, attentive, on the alert, sharp-eyed, heedful, circumspect, on the lookout, on one's toes. ❷ an alert mind: SHARP, quick, bright, perceptive, keen, lively, wide awake; *informal* on the ball, quick off the mark.
– OPPOSITES inattentive, slow, absent-minded.
▶ verb WARN, make aware, caution, advise, forewarn, inform, apprise, notify; *informal* tip off.

alibi noun EXCUSE, defence, justification, explanation, pretext, plea, vindication.

alien adjective FOREIGN, strange, unfamiliar, outlandish, remote, exotic, extraterrestrial.
– OPPOSITES familiar.
▶ noun FOREIGNER, stranger, outsider, newcomer, extraterrestrial.
– OPPOSITES native.

alight[1] verb GET OFF, come down, get down, dismount, disembark, come to rest, land, descend, touch down, settle, perch.

alight[2] adjective ❶ set alight: ON FIRE, burning, ablaze, blazing, lighted, lit, aflame. ❷ alight with joy: LIT UP, shining, bright, illuminated, brilliant.

align verb ❶ align the books: LINE UP, arrange in line, put in order, straighten, rank, range. ❷ aligned with a political party: ALLY, associate, affiliate, cooperate, side, join, unite, combine, join forces.

alike adjective SIMILAR, like, resembling, indistinguishable, identical, interchangeable, corresponding, matching, the same, twin, uniform.
– OPPOSITES different.
▶ adverb think alike: SIMILARLY, just the same, identically, in a like manner, in the same way.
– OPPOSITES differently.

alive adjective ❶ LIVING, breathing, live, animate; *informal* alive and kicking, in the land of the living; *archaic* quick. ❷ alive to the possibilities: *see* ALERT.
– OPPOSITES dead.

allay verb LESSEN, diminish, reduce, alleviate, calm, assuage, ease, quell, relieve, appease, moderate, mitigate, check, lull, subdue, soothe.
– OPPOSITES increase, stimulate.

allegation noun CHARGE, accusation, claim, assertion, statement, declaration, testimony, deposition, avowal.

allege verb CLAIM, declare, state, profess, assert, maintain, affirm, avow, attest, contend, lay a charge; *formal* aver.

alleged adjective SUPPOSED, claimed, declared, so-called, professed, stated.

allegiance noun LOYALTY, faithfulness, adherence, fidelity, devotion, duty, obedience; *historical* fealty.

allergic adjective ❶ HYPERSENSITIVE, sensitive, sensitized, susceptible. ❷ AVERSE, opposed, antagonistic, disinclined, hostile, antipathetic, loath.

alleviate verb REDUCE, lessen, diminish, relieve, ease, allay, mitigate, assuage, abate, palliate, lighten, soothe, subdue, temper, ameliorate, check, quell, soften, make lighter.
– OPPOSITES aggravate.

alliance noun ASSOCIATION, union, coalition, partnership, affiliation, agreement, league, confederation, federation, relationship, connection, pact, bond, understanding, treaty, marriage, compact, concordat, syndicate, cartel, consortium, bloc, combination, covenant, entente.

allot verb ALLOCATE, assign, apportion, distribute, give out, share out, award, dispense, deal out, ration, divide up, mete out, dole out, dish out.

allow verb ❶ **allow to enter:** PERMIT, let, give permission to, authorize, consent to, sanction, approve, license, enable; *informal* give the go-ahead to, give the green light to. ❷ **allow that you're right:** ADMIT, acknowledge, concede, recognize, grant, confess.
– OPPOSITES forbid, deny.

allowance noun ❶ **a baggage allowance:** QUOTA, allocation, ration, portion, share. ❷ **a monthly allowance:** PAYMENT, subsidy, remittance, grant, contribution. ❸ **a tax allowance:** REBATE, discount, deduction, concession, reduction.
■ **make allowances** ❶ TAKE INTO ACCOUNT, bear in mind, have regard to. ❷ EXCUSE, make excuses, forgive, pardon.

alloy noun MIXTURE, blend, amalgam, combination, compound, composite; *technical* admixture.

allude
■ **allude to** REFER TO, mention, speak of, touch on, make an allusion to, cite, suggest, hint at; *formal* advert to.

allure verb ATTRACT, fascinate, charm, seduce, captivate, enchant, bewitch, beguile, tempt, magnetize, lure, entice, cajole, draw, inveigle.

allusion noun REFERENCE, mention, suggestion, citation, hint, intimation.

ally noun ASSOCIATE, colleague, partner, friend, supporter, collaborator, confederate, accomplice, abetter, accessory.
– OPPOSITES enemy, opponent.
▶ verb JOIN, unite, join forces, combine, merge, go into partnership, band together, form an alliance, team up, link up, affiliate, be in league, cooperate, collaborate, side.

almighty adjective
❶ ALL-POWERFUL, supreme, most high, omnipotent. ❷ **almighty explosion:** *See* HUGE, LOUD (1).

almost adverb NEARLY, just about, close to, not quite, practically, virtually, as good as, approaching, not far from, verging on, well-nigh.

alone adjective & adverb BY ONESELF, on one's own, solitary, apart, unaccompanied, isolated, single, separate, unassisted, solo, lonely, friendless, forlorn, deserted, desolate, lonesome.
– OPPOSITES accompanied.

aloof adjective DISTANT, unapproachable, remote,

stand-offish, unfriendly, unsociable, reserved, unresponsive, reticent, supercilious, cold, chilly, haughty, formal, inaccessible, detached, undemonstrative, unsympathetic, unforthcoming.
- OPPOSITES familiar, friendly.

aloud adverb OUT LOUD, clearly, audibly, distinctly, plainly, intelligibly.
- OPPOSITES silently.

already adverb ❶ BY NOW, by this time, previously, before, before now. ❷ AS SOON AS THIS, as early as this, so soon, so early.

also adverb IN ADDITION, additionally, moreover, besides, too, to boot, on top of that.

alter verb CHANGE, make different, adjust, adapt, modify, convert, reshape, remodel, remake, vary, amend, revise, transform, emend, edit.

alteration noun CHANGE, adjustment, modification, adaptation, revision, amendment, transformation, conversion, metamorphosis, reorganization, transfiguration.

alternate verb TAKE TURNS, follow each other, rotate, interchange, substitute for each other, replace each other, oscillate, see-saw.

alternative noun ❶ CHOICE, option, preference. ❷ SUBSTITUTE, back-up, replacement.

alternatively adverb ON THE OTHER HAND, as an alternative, instead, otherwise, if not, or.

although conjunction THOUGH, even though, even if, despite the fact that, whilst, albeit.

altogether adverb COMPLETELY, totally, entirely, thoroughly, fully, utterly, absolutely, perfectly, quite, wholly.

always adverb ❶ EVERY TIME, on every occasion, invariably, consistently, repeatedly, unfailingly. ❷ CONTINUALLY, constantly, repeatedly, forever, perpetually, incessantly, eternally. ❸ FOREVER, forever and ever, evermore, endlessly, everlastingly, eternally.
- OPPOSITES never.

amalgamate verb COMBINE, merge, unite, join, blend, integrate, mingle, intermingle, mix, intermix, incorporate, fuse, come together, join forces, coalesce, associate, compound, link up.
- OPPOSITES split.

amass verb COLLECT, gather, accumulate, pile up, assemble, store up, hoard.

amateur noun NON-PROFESSIONAL, layman, dabbler, dilettante, enthusiast.
▶ adjective UNPAID, inexperienced, lay, unqualified.
- OPPOSITES professional, expert.

amateurish adjective UNPROFESSIONAL, unskilful, untrained, unskilled, incompetent, inexpert, clumsy, crude, bungling, shoddy, unpolished, inept, second-rate, rough and ready.
- OPPOSITES skilled.

amaze verb ASTONISH, surprise, astound, startle, dumbfound, rock, shock, stagger, stun, bewilder, stupefy, daze, disconcert, confound, awe; *informal* flabbergast, bowl over.

amazement noun ASTONISHMENT, surprise, bewilderment, shock, wonder, stupefaction.

amazing adjective ASTONISHING, astounding, stunning, staggering, surprising, breathtaking, extraordinary, incredible, remarkable, sensational, phenomenal, prodigious, stupendous, exceptional; *informal* mind-boggling.

ambassador noun ENVOY, consul, diplomat, emissary, representative, plenipotentiary; *archaic* legate.

ambiguous adjective ❶ AMBIVALENT, equivocal, double-edged. ❷ OBSCURE, cryptic, vague, unclear, uncertain, indefinite, woolly, indeterminate, confusing, puzzling, perplexing, enigmatic.

ambition noun ❶ **full of ambition**: DRIVE, enterprise, desire, initiative, eagerness, thrust, push, zeal, pushiness, striving, yearning, hankering; *informal* get-up-and-go, oomph. ❷ GOAL, aim, objective, desire, object, intent, purpose, design, target, wish, aspiration, dream, hope, ideal.

ambitious adjective ❶ FORCEFUL, enterprising, purposeful, assertive, pushy, aspiring, zealous, enthusiastic, committed, eager, energetic; *informal* go-ahead, on the make. ❷ **an ambitious task**: CHALLENGING, formidable, demanding, difficult, exacting, bold, unrealistic.
– OPPOSITES aimless, apathetic, easy.

ambivalent adjective EQUIVOCAL, ambiguous, uncertain, doubtful, inconclusive, unclear, unresolved, unsettled, confusing, mixed, conflicting, clashing, opposing, vacillating, two-faced.
– OPPOSITES unequivocal.

ambush noun TRAP, snare, surprise attack, pitfall, lure; *archaic* ambuscade.
▶ **verb** LIE IN WAIT FOR, lay a trap for, pounce on, entrap, ensnare, intercept, surprise, waylay, swoop on, decoy; *archaic* ambuscade.

amenable adjective AGREEABLE, accommodating, persuadable, cooperative, tractable, compliant, responsive, willing, acquiescent, adaptable, open-minded, biddable, complaisant, submissive, deferential.
– OPPOSITES uncooperative.

amend verb ❶ ALTER, change, revise, correct, modify, adjust, emend, reorganize, reshape, transform. ❷ IMPROVE, remedy, fix, set right, repair, enhance, better, ameliorate, mend.

amenity noun FACILITY, service, convenience, resource, advantage.

amiable adjective FRIENDLY, agreeable, pleasant, charming, likeable, sociable, genial, amicable, congenial, good-natured, well disposed.
– OPPOSITES unfriendly, disagreeable.

amnesty noun PARDON, general pardon, reprieve, forgiveness, absolution, dispensation, indulgence.

amorous adjective LOVING, passionate, sexual, sexy, erotic, carnal, lustful, affectionate, ardent, fond, enamoured, impassioned; *Brit. informal* randy.
– OPPOSITES unloving, cold.

amorphous adjective FORMLESS, shapeless, structureless, unstructured, unformed, nebulous, vague, ill-organized, indeterminate.
– OPPOSITES shaped, definite.

amount noun QUANTITY, number, total, aggregate, sum, volume, mass, weight, measure, bulk, extent, expanse.
■ **amount to** ADD UP TO, total, come to, equal, make, correspond to, approximate to.

ample adjective ENOUGH, sufficient, plenty, more than enough, enough and to spare, abundant, considerable, copious, lavish, substantial, bountiful, profuse, liberal, generous, munificent, unstinting; *poetic/literary* plenteous.
– OPPOSITES insufficient.

amplify verb ❶ **amplify a signal:** BOOST, increase, intensify, augment, heighten, magnify, supplement. ❷ **amplify a statement:** EXPAND, enlarge on, add to, expound on, go into detail about, elaborate on, fill out, make longer, flesh out, develop, extend, lengthen, broaden, explicate, expatiate on, dilate on, supplement.

amputate verb CUT OFF, sever, chop off, saw off, remove, lop off, excise, dismember, truncate, dock, poll.

amuse verb ❶ ENTERTAIN, delight, enliven, gladden, cheer, make laugh, please, divert, beguile, regale with, raise a smile in. ❷ **amuse yourselves when I'm out:** OCCUPY, entertain, divert, interest, absorb, engross.

amusement noun ❶ LAUGHTER, mirth, hilarity, fun, gaiety, pleasure, delight, enjoyment, merriment. ❷ **a range of amusements:** ENTERTAINMENT, interest, diversion, recreation, pastime, hobby, sport, game, pleasure.

amusing adjective *see* FUNNY (1), ENJOYABLE.

anaemic adjective PALE, colourless, pallid, ashen, sickly, unhealthy, wan, bloodless, weak, feeble, powerless, ineffective, ineffectual, impotent, vigourless.
– OPPOSITES healthy, rosy, vigorous.

analogous adjective SIMILAR, comparable, parallel, corresponding, related, matching, equivalent, like, kindred, homologous.

analyse verb ❶ BREAK DOWN, dissect, separate out, anatomize, fractionate, test, assay. ❷ STUDY, examine, investigate, review, evaluate, interpret, scrutinize, enquire into, dissect.

analysis noun ❶ BREAKDOWN, dissection, anatomization, fractionation, assay. ❷ STUDY, examination, investigation, enquiry, review, evaluation, interpretation.

analytical, analytic adjective INVESTIGATIVE, inquisitive, critical, diagnostic, interpretative, enquiring, searching, systematic, questioning, rational, methodical, in depth.

anarchy noun ❶ ABSENCE OF GOVERNMENT, lawlessness, nihilism, misrule, misgovernment, mobocracy, revolution. ❷ **anarchy in the classroom:** DISORDER, riot, chaos, pandemonium, tumult, mayhem, rebellion, insurrection, mutiny.
– OPPOSITES order, law.

ancestor noun FOREBEAR, forerunner, forefather, progenitor, predecessor, precursor, antecedent.
– OPPOSITES descendant, successor.

ancestry noun ❶ LINEAGE, descent, parentage, extraction, origin, genealogy, stock, blood, pedigree, derivation. ❷ ANTECEDENTS, forebears, forefathers, progenitors, family tree.

anchor noun MAINSTAY, cornerstone, linchpin, bulwark, support.
▶ verb ❶ MOOR, berth, make fast, tie up. ❷ SECURE, fasten, attach, connect, bind.

ancient adjective ❶ ancient times: EARLY, earliest, prehistoric, primeval, primordial, immemorial, bygone. ❷ an ancient custom: VERY OLD, time-worn, age-old, antique, long-lived, venerable, elderly. ❸ positively ancient ideas: OLD-FASHIONED, antiquated, out of date, outmoded, obsolete, archaic, superannuated, antediluvian, atavistic.

ancillary adjective SECONDARY, auxiliary, subsidiary, supplementary, additional, subordinate, extra.

anew adverb AGAIN, afresh, once again, once more, over again.

angelic adjective ❶ HEAVENLY, seraphic, cherubic, ethereal, beatific, holy, divine, blessed. ❷ an angelic child: INNOCENT, pure, virtuous, saintly, beautiful, adorable. *See also* GOOD adjective (1).

anger noun RAGE, fury, wrath, rancour, temper, annoyance, irritability, antagonism, vexation, exasperation, outrage, indignation, spleen, pique, passion, hostility, tantrum; *poetic/literary* ire, choler.
▶ verb MAKE ANGRY, infuriate, enrage, madden, incense, outrage, irritate, annoy, exasperate, provoke, antagonize, rile, vex, inflame, aggravate; *informal* make someone's blood boil, needle, bug, drive crazy.
– OPPOSITES pacify, placate.

angle noun ❶ BEND, corner, fork, nook, niche, recess, elbow. ❷ what's his angle? POINT OF VIEW, approach, viewpoint, standpoint, opinion, position, slant.
▶ verb ❶ TILT, slant, slope, turn, bend. ❷ SLANT, distort, skew.

angry adjective FURIOUS, irate, enraged, incensed, maddened, outraged, wrathful, seething, raging, annoyed, irritated, exasperated, fuming, indignant, bitter, irascible, vexed, heated, provoked, raving, wild, fiery, apoplectic, hot-tempered, ill-humoured; *informal* hot under the collar, mad, up in arms; *Brit. informal* aerated.
– OPPOSITES calm, pleased.

angst noun ANXIETY, apprehension, fear, disquiet, foreboding.

anguish noun AGONY, suffering, pain, distress, torment, torture, misery, sorrow, grief, woe, heartache, tribulation.
– OPPOSITES pleasure, happiness.

angular adjective ❶ BENT, crooked, jagged, zigzag, pointed, V-shaped, Y-shaped, forked, bifurcate. ❷ an angular woman: BONY, gaunt, spare, scrawny, skinny, lean.
– OPPOSITES rounded.

animal noun ❶ CREATURE, beast, brute, organism, being. ❷ the man is an animal: BRUTE, beast, savage,

fiend, barbarian, monster; *informal* swine.
▶ **adjective** animal passions: SENSUAL, carnal, physical, bodily, fleshly, brutish, bestial.

animate verb ENLIVEN, give life to, liven up, cheer up, gladden, brighten up, make lively, revitalize, perk up, inspire, excite, exhilarate, rouse, stir, stimulate, invigorate, fire, move, energize, rejuvenate, revive, encourage, galvanize, urge, arouse, activate, spark, kindle, incite; *informal* buck up, pep up.
▶ **adjective** LIVING, alive, live, breathing, conscious, sentient.
– OPPOSITES inanimate.

animated adjective LIVELY, energetic, excited, enthusiastic, spirited, exuberant, vivacious, bubbling, vibrant, cheerful, bright, ebullient, dynamic, eager, zestful, busy, brisk, active, alive, sprightly, passionate, vigorous, quick.
– OPPOSITES lethargic, lifeless.

animation noun LIVELINESS, energy, excitement, enthusiasm, passion, dynamism, vitality, vivacity, eagerness, ebullience, exhilaration, zest, exuberance, life, spirit, high spirits, verve, buoyancy, forcefulness, sparkle, briskness, activity, vigour, sprightliness; *informal* pep, zing.
– OPPOSITES apathy, lethargy.

animosity noun DISLIKE, enmity, unfriendliness, hostility, resentment, antagonism, hate, hatred, loathing, antipathy, bitterness, spite, bad blood, rancour, venom, ill will, acrimony, vindictiveness, malice, animus, asperity, sourness, malignancy, malignity, odium, acerbity, virulence, sharpness.
– OPPOSITES goodwill, friendliness.

annals plural noun RECORDS, archives, history, chronicles, accounts, registers.

annex verb SEIZE, take over, conquer, appropriate, acquire, occupy, usurp.

annihilate verb DESTROY, wipe out, exterminate, obliterate, eliminate, eradicate, extirpate, erase, liquidate, raze, extinguish, slaughter, kill off, finish off.

annotate verb COMMENT ON, gloss, add notes to, explain, interpret, elucidate, explicate.

annotation noun NOTE, comment, gloss, footnote, commentary, explanation, interpretation, elucidation, observation.

announce verb ❶ announce the result: MAKE KNOWN, make public, publish, put out, report, state, give out, reveal, declare, disclose, divulge, broadcast, proclaim, advertise, notify of, promulgate, propound, blazon, intimate. ❷ announce a guest: INTRODUCE, present, give someone's name, name, usher in, herald.
– OPPOSITES suppress.

announcement noun ❶ the announcement of the results: DECLARATION, reporting, proclamation, disclosure, publication, statement, promulgation, notification, advertisement, intimation, revelation. ❷ make an announcement: STATEMENT, report, bulletin, message, communiqué.

announcer noun PRESENTER, newsreader, broadcaster, newscaster, reporter, commentator, anchorman, anchor, herald, master of ceremonies, compère, MC.

annoy verb ❶ IRRITATE, exasperate, displease, infuriate, anger, madden, vex, provoke, upset, put out, try someone's patience, drive mad, antagonize, irk, gall, nettle, make cross, pique, jar; *Brit.* rub up the wrong way; *informal* get on someone's nerves, aggravate, bug, peeve, get to. ❷ BOTHER, disturb, pester, harass, trouble, fret, worry, plague, harry, badger, molest; *informal* bug.

annoyance noun ❶ IRRITATION, exasperation, anger, displeasure, vexation, chagrin, pique; *poetic/literary* ire. ❷ NUISANCE, pest, bother, irritant, trial, offence, provocation; *informal* pain, hassle, pain in the neck, bind, bore.

annoyed adjective IRRITATED, exasperated, cross, displeased, upset, vexed, riled, put out; *informal* miffed, peeved, huffy, in a huff; *Brit. informal* shirty; *N. Amer. informal* sore.
– OPPOSITES pleased.

annoying adjective IRRITATING, infuriating, exasperating, maddening, upsetting, trying, galling, tiresome, grating, troublesome, worrying, vexing, irksome, bothersome, vexatious, wearisome; *informal* aggravating, pestilential.

annul verb NULLIFY, cancel, declare null and void, invalidate, rescind, revoke, repeal, quash, void, negate, abrogate.

anoint verb ❶ anoint the body: OIL, apply ointment to, spread over, rub, smear, lubricate, grease. ❷ anoint a new king: CONSECRATE, bless, sanctify, ordain, hallow.

anomalous adjective ABNORMAL, irregular, atypical, aberrant, deviant, exceptional, unusual, odd, eccentric, bizarre, peculiar.

anonymous adjective ❶ an anonymous donor/donation: UNNAMED, unidentified, nameless, unknown, unspecified, incognito, uncredited, unattributed, unsigned. ❷ an anonymous place: CHARACTERLESS, unremarkable, impersonal, nondescript, boring, dull, uninteresting.
– OPPOSITES named, known.

answer noun ❶ REPLY, response, acknowledgement, rejoinder, retort, riposte; *informal* comeback. ❷ SOLUTION, explanation, resolution. ❸ an answer to the accusation: DEFENCE, plea, refutation, rebuttal, vindication.
▶ verb ❶ REPLY TO, respond to, acknowledge, react to, come back, retort, riposte, make a rejoinder, rejoin. ❷ SOLVE, explain, resolve. ❸ answer our requirements: MEET, satisfy, fulfil, suit, measure up to, serve. ❹ answer a description: FIT, match, correspond to, be similar to, conform to, correlate to.
■ **answer back** TALK BACK, argue with, be cheeky, contradict, be impertinent. **answer for** ❶ PAY FOR, suffer for, be punished for, make amends for, atone for. ❷ VOUCH FOR, be accountable for, be responsible for, be liable for.

answerable adjective RESPONSIBLE, accountable, liable.

antagonism noun ANIMOSITY, hostility, enmity, antipathy, rancour, opposition, rivalry, friction, conflict, dissension.
– OPPOSITES friendship.

antagonize verb ANNOY, anger, irritate, alienate, offend, provoke, put out, upset, make an enemy of, arouse hostility in.
– OPPOSITES pacify.

antediluvian adjective OLD-FASHIONED, antiquated, out of date, outmoded, archaic, obsolete.

anthem noun HYMN, psalm, song of praise, chorale, chant, canticle, paean.

anthology noun COLLECTION, compilation, miscellany, selection, treasury, compendium, digest.

anticipate verb ❶ EXPECT, predict, forecast, foresee, await, prepare for, reckon on, look for, look forward to. ❷ anticipate his move: PREVENT, intercept, forestall, pre-empt; *informal* beat to it, beat to the draw.

anticipation noun ❶ anticipation of success: EXPECTATION, prediction, preparation, contemplation. ❷ full of anticipation: EXPECTANCY, hopefulness, hope.

anticlimax noun DISAPPOINTMENT, let-down, disillusionment, comedown, bathos; *Brit.* damp squib.

antics plural noun PRANKS, capers, escapades, tricks, romps, frolics, clowning, horseplay, skylarking; *informal* larking about.

antidote noun COUNTERMEASURE, antitoxin, neutralizing agent, cure, remedy, corrective.

antipathy noun DISLIKE, hostility, enmity, opposition, hatred, animosity, antagonism, loathing, repugnance, animus.
– OPPOSITES liking, affinity.

antiquated adjective OLD-FASHIONED, out of date, outmoded, old, dated, outdated, ancient, aged, archaic, antique, obsolete, antediluvian, outworn, passé, medieval, primitive, primeval, quaint; *informal* prehistoric, past it, superannuated.

antique adjective ❶ ANTIQUARIAN, collectable, vintage, historic, traditional, veteran. ❷ *See* ANTIQUATED.
▶ noun COLLECTOR'S ITEM, heirloom, collectable, curiosity, curio, objet d'art, rarity, relic.

antiquity noun CLASSICAL TIMES, former times, bygone age, the past, days gone by, olden days.

antiseptic adjective ❶ DISINFECTED, disinfectant, sterile, sterilized, sterilizing, hygienic, sanitized, germ-free, medicated, germicidal, bactericidal. ❷ antiseptic surroundings: CLINICAL, characterless, anonymous, unexciting, undistinguished.

antisocial adjective ❶ feel antisocial: UNSOCIABLE, unfriendly, uncommunicative, reserved, withdrawn, retiring, misanthropic, alienated. ❷ antisocial behaviour: DISRUPTIVE, disorderly, rude, unruly, nasty, undisciplined, offensive, obnoxious, rebellious, lawless, asocial.
– OPPOSITES sociable.

antithesis noun OPPOSITE, reverse, converse, inverse, other extreme.

anxiety noun ❶ anxiety about the future: WORRY, concern, apprehension, disquiet, uneasiness, nervousness, dread, stress, tension, tenseness, strain,

misgiving, foreboding, fear, uncertainty, fretfulness, distress, angst. ❷ **anxiety to win:** DESIRE, eagerness, longing, keenness, enthusiasm, avidity.
– OPPOSITES serenity.

anxious adjective ❶ WORRIED, concerned, apprehensive, fearful, nervous, nervy, uneasy, disturbed, afraid, perturbed, agitated, alarmed, edgy, troubled, upset, tense, distraught, fraught, overwrought, fretful; *informal* jittery, on edge. ❷ **anxious to win:** EAGER, keen, longing, desperate, yearning, impatient, intent, avid, desirous; *informal* dying, itching.
– OPPOSITES unconcerned, nonchalant.

anyhow adverb ❶ **anyhow, you must go:** IN ANY CASE, in any event, no matter what, at all events. ❷ **clothes strewn anyhow:** HAPHAZARDLY, carelessly, heedlessly, negligently; *informal* all over the place.

apathetic adjective UNINTERESTED, indifferent, unenthusiastic, unconcerned, unmotivated, impassive, half-hearted, uncommitted, uninvolved, unresponsive, casual, cool, dispassionate, unfeeling, unemotional, emotionless, phlegmatic, unambitious.
– OPPOSITES enthusiastic.

apathy noun INDIFFERENCE, lack of interest, lack of enthusiasm, unconcern, impassivity, unresponsiveness.
– OPPOSITES enthusiasm, passion.

aperture noun OPENING, gap, hole, crack, slit, window, orifice, fissure, breach, eye.

apex noun ❶ TOP, peak, summit, tip, head, crest, crown, pinnacle, vertex. ❷ HIGH POINT, height, zenith, climax, culmination, apogee, acme.
– OPPOSITES nadir.

aphrodisiac adjective STIMULATING, erotic, arousing, sexy.

apocryphal adjective UNVERIFIED, unsubstantiated, debatable, questionable, dubious, spurious, mythical, fictitious, untrue, false; *informal* phoney.
– OPPOSITES authentic.

apologetic adjective REGRETFUL, sorry, remorseful, contrite, repentant, penitent, conscience-stricken, ashamed, rueful.
– OPPOSITES unrepentant, impenitent.

apologize verb SAY SORRY, make an apology, express regret, ask forgiveness, ask for pardon, beg pardon, eat humble pie.

apology noun ❶ REGRETS, expression of regret. ❷ **an apology for a man:** MOCKERY, travesty, caricature, substitute, poor excuse.

apostle noun EVANGELIST, missionary, spreader of the word, preacher, crusader, teacher, supporter, advocate, propagandist.

appal verb SHOCK, dismay, horrify, sicken, disgust, outrage, astound, alarm, nauseate, revolt.

appalling adjective SHOCKING, horrifying, disgusting, dreadful, awful, frightful, ghastly, dire, hideous, harrowing. *See also* BAD.

apparatus noun DEVICE, equipment, instrument, contraption, mechanism, appliance, machine, machinery, tackle, gadget, tool, plant; *informal* gear.

apparel noun CLOTHING, clothes, dress, garments, garb, attire, costume; *informal* gear.

apparent adjective ❶ the problem is apparent: OBVIOUS, clear, plain, evident, recognizable, noticeable, perceptible, manifest, discernible, visible, unmistakable, patent, perceivable. ❷ apparent calm: SEEMING, ostensible, superficial, outward.
– OPPOSITES hidden.

apparition noun GHOST, phantom, spirit, presence, spectre, manifestation, vision, wraith, shade, chimera; *informal* spook; *poetic/literary* phantasm.

appeal noun ❶ REQUEST, plea, call, application, entreaty, petition, prayer, solicitation, cri de cœur, supplication. ❷ hold little appeal: ATTRACTION, interest, allure, charm, temptation, fascination, seductiveness.
▶ verb ❶ ASK, request, beg, plead, implore, entreat, solicit, call, petition; *poetic/literary* beseech. ❷ the idea appeals to her: INTEREST, tempt, fascinate, charm, engage, entice, enchant, beguile.

appear verb ❶ a woman appeared: TURN UP, come into view, come out, emerge, materialize, loom up, arrive, enter, surface, bob up; *informal* show up. ❷ a solution appeared: OCCUR, materialize, be revealed, be seen, arise, develop, originate, crop up, spring up. ❸ appear sad: SEEM, look, give the impression of, have the appearance of. ❹ appear on stage: PERFORM, act, take part, play, come on.
– OPPOSITES disappear.

appearance noun ❶ COMING INTO VIEW, emergence, arrival, advent, materialization, surfacing. ❷ a handsome appearance: LOOK, impression, air, manner, bearing, demeanour, aspect, expression, mien. ❸ give the appearance of: IMAGE, impression, semblance, guise, pretence.
– OPPOSITES disappearance.

appease verb ❶ appease the enemy: PLACATE, pacify, conciliate, mollify, soothe, propitiate. ❷ appease someone's curiosity: SATISFY, assuage, relieve, blunt, diminish, take the edge off.
– OPPOSITES provoke.

appendage noun ❶ ADDITION, attachment, addendum, adjunct, appurtenance, affix. ❷ LIMB, extremity, projection, protuberance.

appendix noun SUPPLEMENT, addition, addendum, postscript, adjunct, codicil, rider, epilogue, extension.

appetite noun ❶ an appetite for food: HUNGER, taste, relish, desire, palate, stomach. ❷ an appetite for life: KEENNESS, eagerness, passion, desire, lust, hunger, thirst, yearning, longing, craving, zest, gusto, relish, zeal, hankering, yen, predilection.

appetizing adjective ❶ DELICIOUS, mouth-watering, tasty, succulent, palatable. ❷ INVITING, tempting, appealing, enticing, alluring.
– OPPOSITES unappetizing.

applaud verb ❶ CLAP, cheer, give a standing ovation to; *informal* put one's hands together for, give someone a big hand, bring the house down. ❷ PRAISE, admire, express approval of, commend,

compliment on, congratulate, salute, acclaim, hail, extol.
– OPPOSITES condemn, criticize.

applause noun ❶ CLAPPING, ovation, cheering, bravos, encores, curtain calls. ❷ PRAISE, acclaim, admiration, approval, commendation, approbation, accolades, plaudits.

appliance noun DEVICE, gadget, instrument, apparatus, machine, mechanism, tool, implement, contraption.

applicable adjective RELEVANT, appropriate, pertinent, apposite, apropos.
– OPPOSITES inapplicable.

applicant noun CANDIDATE, interviewee, competitor, claimant, enquirer, petitioner, supplicant, suitor, postulant.

apply verb ❶ apply force: USE, employ, exercise, bring to bear, utilize, put into practice, bring into effect. ❷ apply ointment: PUT ON, rub on/in, cover with, spread, smear, administer. ❸ regulations which apply: BE RELEVANT, relate, have a bearing on, be germane, appertain. ❹ apply for a job: ENQUIRE AFTER, put in for, request, try for, seek, appeal.
■ **apply oneself** MAKE AN EFFORT, be industrious, commit oneself, devote oneself, persevere, persist.

appoint verb ❶ appoint a time: SET, fix, arrange, decide on, establish, settle on, determine, ordain, designate. ❷ appoint him manager: SELECT, name, choose, designate, settle on, plump for, elect, assign, delegate, install as, vote for, co-opt.

appointment noun ❶ cancel an appointment: MEETING, engagement, date, arrangement, interview, rendezvous, assignation, fixture; *poetic/literary* tryst. ❷ his appointment as manager: SELECTION, choice, naming, nomination, commissioning, election. ❸ her new appointment: JOB, post, position, office, situation, place.

appreciable adjective CONSIDERABLE, substantial, sizeable, significant, goodly.

appreciate verb ❶ appreciate your help: BE GRATEFUL FOR, be thankful for, be appreciative of, be indebted for. ❷ appreciate good wine: RATE HIGHLY, prize, value, enjoy, admire, approve of, respect, treasure, hold in high regard, think much of, esteem. ❸ appreciate its importance: RECOGNIZE, realize, acknowledge, see, know, be aware of, understand, comprehend, perceive. ❹ appreciate in value: INCREASE, rise, grow, go up, gain, mount, soar, escalate.
– OPPOSITES disparage, ignore, depreciate.

appreciative adjective GRATEFUL, thankful, obliged, indebted, beholden.
– OPPOSITES ungrateful.

apprehensive adjective WORRIED, uneasy, nervous, frightened, afraid, alarmed, fearful, mistrustful, concerned, troubled; *informal* on edge, jittery.
– OPPOSITES fearless, unconcerned.

apprentice noun TRAINEE, learner, pupil, student, beginner, novice, probationer, neophyte, cub, tyro; *informal* rookie; *N. Amer. informal* greenhorn.

apprise verb TELL, inform, notify, let know; *informal* fill in, clue in.

approach verb ❶ approach the house: REACH, come/draw near, come/draw close, near, move/advance towards, bear down on. ❷ approach someone for a contribution: APPEAL TO, make overtures to, proposition, solicit, sound out. ❸ approach the problem: SET ABOUT, tackle, begin, start, make a start on, embark on, commence, undertake. ❹ a price approaching £500: COME NEAR/CLOSE TO, compare with, be comparable with, approximate to.
– OPPOSITES leave.
▶ noun ❶ a new approach: METHOD, procedure, way, style, attitude, manner, technique, means, mode, modus operandi. ❷ made an approach to his employer: APPEAL, application, proposal, overture, proposition. ❸ COMING NEAR, advance, arrival, advent. ❹ the approach to the manor: DRIVE, driveway, avenue, access road.

approachable adjective FRIENDLY, open, affable, relaxed, accessible, sympathetic, well disposed.
– OPPOSITES aloof.

appropriate adjective SUITABLE, fitting, right, apt, timely, applicable, seemly, proper, becoming, correct, well judged, relevant, germane, well suited, pertinent, apposite, opportune, apropos.
– OPPOSITES inappropriate.
▶ verb ❶ appropriate a house: TAKE OVER, take possession of, seize, confiscate, requisition, commandeer, annex, expropriate, arrogate. ❷ appropriate money: STEAL, embezzle, misappropriate, pilfer, purloin, pocket; *informal* filch, swipe; *Brit. informal* nick, pinch.

approval noun ❶ ADMIRATION, acceptance, praise, liking, support, favour, appreciation, respect, esteem, commendation, approbation. ❷ approval of the minutes: ACCEPTANCE, agreement, endorsement, authorization, confirmation, assent, consent, ratification, sanction, blessing, permission, mandate, concurrence, acquiescence, licence, seal, validation, imprimatur; *informal* OK, thumbs up, go-ahead, green light.
– OPPOSITES disapproval, rejection, refusal.

approve verb ❶ approve of his behaviour: BE PLEASED WITH, think well of, like, look on with favour, give one's blessing to, hold in regard/esteem, admire, respect, praise. ❷ approve the application: AGREE TO, accept, consent to, permit, pass, allow, sanction, authorize, bless, support, back, uphold, endorse, ratify, validate, accede to, countenance; *informal* go along with, rubber-stamp.
– OPPOSITES disapprove, condemn, refuse, veto.

approximate adjective ROUGH, estimated, near, close, inexact, imprecise, loose.
– OPPOSITES exact.
■ **approximate to** BE CLOSE/NEAR TO, come near to, approach, border on, verge on, resemble, be similar to, roughly equal.

approximately adverb ROUGHLY, about, round about, around, just about, circa, more or less, nearly, close to, near to, in the region/neighbourhood of, approaching, almost, not far off.
– OPPOSITES precisely.

apt adjective ❶ an apt remark: SUITABLE, appropriate, fitting, applicable, apposite, felicitous. ❷ apt to get angry: LIKELY, inclined, prone, liable, given, disposed.
– OPPOSITES inappropriate, unlikely.

aptitude noun TALENT, ability, gift, skill, flair, knack, bent, capability, capacity, faculty.

arbiter noun JUDGE, authority, determiner, controller, director, governor, expert, master, pundit.

arbitrary adjective ❶ an arbitrary decision: CAPRICIOUS, unreasonable, whimsical, irrational, illogical, personal, subjective, random, chance, erratic, wilful, unreasoned, inconsistent, unpredictable, unplanned, unjustified. ❷ an arbitrary ruler: DICTATORIAL, despotic, autocratic, absolute, tyrannical, imperious, domineering, high-handed.
– OPPOSITES rational, reasoned.

arbitrate verb ADJUDICATE, judge, referee, sit in judgement, mediate, umpire, settle, decide, determine, decide the outcome of.

arbitration noun ADJUDICATION, judgement, settlement, decision, determination, mediation, negotiation, good offices.

arbitrator noun ADJUDICATOR, judge, referee, umpire, arbiter, ombudsman, mediator, negotiator, intermediary, go-between, peacemaker.

arc noun CURVE, bend, bow, crescent, semicircle, half-moon, arch, curvature.

arcane adjective SECRET, mysterious, concealed, hidden, recondite, enigmatic, abstruse, esoteric, cryptic.

arch[1] noun ARCHWAY, vault, span, bridge.
▶ verb CURVE, bend, bow, arc.

arch[2] adjective PLAYFUL, mischievous, roguish, artful, sly, knowing.

archetype noun PROTOTYPE, example, pattern, model, original, standard, ideal, paradigm, precursor.

architect noun ❶ DESIGNER, planner, building consultant, draughtsman. ❷ CREATOR, author, engineer, originator, planner, deviser, instigator, founder, prime mover.

ardent adjective PASSIONATE, fervent, impassioned, eager, enthusiastic, intense, keen, zealous, vehement, fierce.
– OPPOSITES apathetic.

arduous adjective HARD, difficult, demanding, exhausting, laborious, strenuous, tiring, gruelling, punishing, tough, onerous, heavy, rigorous, back-breaking, taxing, Herculean.
– OPPOSITES easy, effortless.

area noun ❶ the area around the town: REGION, district, environment, vicinity, locality, zone, territory, neighbourhood, environs, terrain, sector, quarter, province, precinct, realm, domain. ❷ specialize in an area: FIELD, subject, sphere, discipline, sector, realm. ❸ the area of the room: SIZE, extent, expanse, measurement, space, compass, range, square footage, acreage, dimensions.

argue verb ❶ argued that he was right: CLAIM, maintain, hold, reason, insist, contend, declare, assert, demonstrate, make a case, plead, suggest. ❷ QUARREL, differ, disagree, fall out, have an argument, bicker, have words, bandy words, fight, squabble, debate, dispute, answer back, object, take exception, wrangle, feud, remonstrate; *informal* row. ❸ argue the point: DISPUTE, debate, discuss.

argument noun ❶ DISAGREEMENT, quarrel, fight, squabble, dispute, difference of opinion, falling-out, altercation, wrangle, conflict, clash, feud, controversy, remonstration; *informal* row, tiff, set-to, dust-up. ❷ the argument against capital punishment: CASE, reasoning, reasons, line of reasoning, grounds, logic, evidence, polemic, argumentation. ❸ the argument of the book: SUBJECT MATTER, theme, topic, gist, outline, storyline, summary, synopsis, abstract, precis.

argumentative adjective QUARRELSOME, contentious, combative, belligerent, disputatious, litigious.

arid adjective ❶ arid areas: DRY, dried up, waterless, parched, moistureless, scorched, desiccated, barren, infertile, desert, lifeless, sterile. ❷ an arid discussion: DULL, tedious, dreary, dry, boring, uninteresting, monotonous, flat, vapid, lifeless.
– OPPOSITES wet, fertile, interesting.

arise verb ❶ COME TO LIGHT, turn/crop up, emerge, occur, begin, come into being. *See also* APPEAR. ❷ accidents arising from carelessness: RESULT, be caused, originate, follow, proceed, emanate, ensue.

aristocracy noun NOBILITY, peerage, upper class, gentry, high society, elite, ruling class, patriciate; *informal* upper crust.

aristocratic adjective ❶ NOBLE, titled, high-born, blue-blooded, upper-class, patrician. ❷ WELL BRED, dignified, refined, courtly, elegant, gracious, haughty, proud.

arm[1] noun ❶ an arm of the sea: INLET, creek, cove, fjord, bay, estuary, firth, sound. ❷ an arm of the civil service: BRANCH, department, section, wing, division, sector, offshoot, extension.

arm[2] verb EQUIP, supply, provide, issue, furnish.

armaments plural noun WEAPONS, guns, arms, firearms, weaponry, munitions, ordnance.

armistice noun CEASEFIRE, truce, peace, treaty, agreement, suspension of hostilities.

armoury noun ARSENAL, arms depot, ammunition dump, magazine, ordnance depot.

army noun ❶ ARMED FORCE, troops, soldiers, infantry, land force, soldiery. ❷ an army of tourists: CROWD, horde, throng, swarm, pack, host, multitude, mob.

aroma noun SMELL, scent, odour, fragrance, perfume, bouquet, savour; *poetic/literary* redolence.

arouse verb ❶ arouse suspicion: INDUCE, prompt, trigger, kindle, provoke, engender, stir up, spark off. ❷ WAKE, wake up, awaken, rouse.
– OPPOSITES allay.

arrange verb ❶ arrange the books: PUT IN ORDER, set out, sort, lay out, organize, position, group, sift, align, tidy, file, rank, classify, categorize, array, systematize.

❷ arrange a meeting: FIX, settle on, set up, agree, determine, plan, organize, schedule, bring about, coordinate, make preparations for. ❸ music arranged for piano: SCORE, adapt, set, orchestrate, harmonize.
– OPPOSITES disturb, cancel.

arrangement noun ❶ ORDER, ordering, organization, positioning, grouping, distribution, disposition, system, alignment, filing, marshalling, ranging, spacing, tabulation. ❷ make an arrangement: AGREEMENT, plan, deal, contract, compact, bargain, pact, understanding, settlement, terms, preparations, provisions. ❸ a musical arrangement: SCORE, orchestration, adaptation, instrumentation, setting, harmonization.

array noun ❶ ARRANGEMENT, collection, line-up, formation, presentation, display, exhibition, show, parade, assemblage, muster. ❷ DRESS, attire, clothing, garments, garb, finery; *formal* apparel.
▶ verb ❶ *See* ARRANGE (1). ❷ CLOTHE, dress, fit out, adorn, garb, rig out, deck, robe, accoutre.

arrest verb ❶ TAKE INTO CUSTODY, apprehend, take prisoner, capture, detain, seize, catch, lay hold of; *informal* pick up, pinch, collar, haul in, nab, bust, run in; *Brit. informal* nick. ❷ arrest the spread of disease: STOP, halt, block, end, prevent, obstruct, hinder, impede, interrupt, delay, slow down, bring to a standstill, check, restrain, stem, retard, nip in the bud.
– OPPOSITES release, start.
▶ noun APPREHENSION, capture, detention, seizure, taking into custody.
– OPPOSITES release.

arresting adjective STRIKING, remarkable, extraordinary, impressive, outstanding, unusual, stunning, conspicuous, noticeable.
– OPPOSITES inconspicuous.

arrival noun ❶ COMING, appearance, approach, advent, entrance, entry, occurrence. ❷ recent arrivals: VISITOR, incomer, guest, immigrant, newcomer, caller.
– OPPOSITES departure, leaver.

arrive verb ❶ COME, appear, enter, get here/there, turn up, get in, put in/make an appearance, drop by/in; *informal* show up, roll in/up, blow in. ❷ *See* SUCCEED (1).
– OPPOSITES leave, depart.

arrogant adjective HAUGHTY, proud, conceited, self-important, pompous, overbearing, patronizing, superior, high-handed, egotistical, condescending, snobbish, disdainful, imperious, lordly, swaggering, presumptuous, cocky, boastful, supercilious, overweening, blustering, insolent; *informal* stuck up, high and mighty, snooty, uppity.
– OPPOSITES modest, diffident.

arrogate verb APPROPRIATE, assume, seize, expropriate, commandeer, avail oneself of.

art noun ❶ PAINTING, drawing, fine art, design, visual art. ❷ the art of conversation: SKILL, craft, talent, flair, aptitude, gift, knack, facility, technique, proficiency, expertise, ingenuity, skilfulness, mastery, dexterity, virtuosity, adroitness.

artful adjective CUNNING, sly, wily,

clever, shrewd, canny, crafty, devious, tricky, subtle, ingenious, astute, scheming, designing; *informal* smart, foxy; *Brit. informal* fly.
– OPPOSITES ingenuous.

article noun ❶ THING, object, item, commodity. ❷ a magazine article: STORY, piece, item, account, report, feature, column.

articulate adjective FLUENT, eloquent, lucid, expressive, clear, comprehensible, coherent, intelligible, understandable, glib, silver-tongued.
– OPPOSITES inarticulate.
▶ verb ENUNCIATE, say, utter, express, pronounce, vocalize, voice.

articulated adjective HINGED, jointed, segmented, flexible, bendy.

artifice noun TRICKERY, cunning, deceit, deception, craftiness, artfulness, slyness, duplicity, guile, chicanery.

artificial adjective ❶ MANUFACTURED, man-made, fabricated, synthetic, imitation, simulated, ersatz. ❷ an artificial smile: FALSE, affected, fake, unnatural, insincere, forced, sham, contrived, pretended, assumed, put on, mock, unreal, feigned, bogus, pseudo, laboured, hollow, spurious, meretricious; *informal* phoney.
– OPPOSITES natural, genuine.

artist noun ❶ PAINTER, drawer, sculptor, old master. ❷ CRAFTSMAN, craftswoman, expert, master, past master, genius, adept. ❸ *See* PERFORMER.

artistic adjective ❶ an artistic person: CREATIVE, imaginative, talented, gifted, accomplished, sensitive, cultured, cultivated. ❷ an artistic flower arrangement: ATTRACTIVE, tasteful, decorative, beautiful, stylish, elegant, graceful, aesthetic, ornamental, exquisite.
– OPPOSITES ugly.

artistry noun SKILL, art, talent, ability, flair, gift, expertise, creativity, proficiency, craftsmanship, workmanship, brilliance.

artless adjective INNOCENT, naive, simple, childlike, ingenuous, guileless, sincere, frank, unpretentious.
– OPPOSITES scheming.

ascend verb CLIMB, go/move up, rise, mount, soar, take off, lift off, fly up, levitate, scale.
– OPPOSITES descend.

ascendancy noun DOMINATION, dominance, control, authority, power, rule, command, supremacy, sway, mastery, sovereignty, the upper hand.

ascent noun CLIMB, rise, hill, slope, ascension, gradient, ramp.
– OPPOSITES descent.

ascertain verb FIND OUT, establish, discover, learn, determine, decide, identify, confirm, make certain, get to know, verify, make sure/certain, settle, pin down.

ascetic adjective ABSTEMIOUS, abstinent, moderate, temperate, spartan, puritanical, self-denying, self-disciplined, self-controlled, strict, restrained, austere, frugal, rigorous, harsh, celibate, chaste.
– OPPOSITES self-indulgent.
▶ noun HERMIT, recluse, abstainer, anchorite.

ascribe verb ATTRIBUTE, put down, assign, impute, credit, accredit, chalk up, lay on, blame, charge with.

ashamed adjective
❶ EMBARRASSED, shamefaced, sorry, apologetic, sheepish, red-faced, blushing, humiliated, conscience-stricken, remorseful, mortified, crestfallen, discomfited, bashful, contrite, penitent, repentant, rueful, chagrined; *informal* with one's tail between one's legs.
❷ **ashamed to say:** RELUCTANT, loath, unwilling, indisposed.
– OPPOSITES proud, shameless.

ashen adjective PALE, white, pallid, wan, colourless, grey, grey-faced, washed out, bleached, ghostly, leaden.

asinine adjective IDIOTIC, stupid, foolish, nonsensical, ridiculous, half-witted, imbecilic, fatuous, moronic; *informal* batty, nutty, dumb, gormless; *Brit. informal* daft.
– OPPOSITES intelligent, sensible.

ask verb ❶ QUESTION, inquire, query, quiz, put a question to, interrogate, cross-examine, give the third degree to; *informal* grill, pump. ❷ **ask someone a favour:** REQUEST, demand, appeal to, apply to, beg, solicit, implore, plead, seek, supplicate; *poetic/literary* beseech. ❸ **ask them to dinner:** INVITE, summon, bid.
– OPPOSITES answer.

asleep adjective ❶ SLEEPING, fast/sound asleep, in a deep sleep, dozing, resting, slumbering, snoozing, napping, catnapping, reposing, comatose, unconscious, sedated, dormant; *informal* out like a light, dead to the world; *Brit. informal* kipping; *humorous* in the land of Nod. ❷ **my leg's asleep:** NUMB, without feeling, deadened.
– OPPOSITES awake.

aspect noun ❶ **every aspect of the problem:** FEATURE, viewpoint, facet, side, circumstance, angle, characteristic, element, light, standpoint, slant, attribute. ❷ **a fierce aspect:** APPEARANCE, look, expression, features, air, manner, demeanour, bearing, countenance, mien, visage. ❸ **a northern aspect:** DIRECTION, outlook, prospect, orientation, view, exposure, situation, location, position.

asperity noun BITTERNESS, harshness, hostility, sharpness, acrimony, sourness, severity, virulence, acerbity, rancour, venom, abrasiveness, crossness, irascibility, astringency.

asphyxiate verb SUFFOCATE, choke, smother, stifle, strangle, throttle, strangulate.

aspiration noun AIM, desire, objective, ambition, goal, wish, hope, dream, longing, yearning, craving, eagerness, enthusiasm.

aspire verb DESIRE, hope to/for, long for/to, wish to/for, dream of, yearn for/to, seek, pursue, crave, hunger for.

aspiring adjective WOULD-BE, potential, hopeful, expectant, ambitious, optimistic, wishful, striving.

assail verb ATTACK, assault, set on/upon, fall on, rush, storm; *informal* lay into, tear into, pitch into.

assassin noun MURDERER, killer, executioner, contract killer, liquidator; *informal* hit man; *poetic/literary* slayer.

assassinate verb MURDER, kill, execute, eliminate, liquidate; *informal* hit; *poetic/literary* slay.

assault verb ❶ ATTACK, charge, storm, rush at, set about/on, strike at. ❷ STRIKE, hit, attack, beat up, aim blows at; *informal* lay into, pitch into, wade into, do over. ❸ MOLEST, rape, sexually assault, interfere with.

assay verb TEST, check, analyse, examine, assess, evaluate, appraise, investigate, scrutinize.

assemble verb ❶ **the crowd assembled**: GATHER, collect, come together, congregate, meet, convene, join up, flock together, converge, rally round, throng around. ❷ **assemble the children/evidence**: GATHER, collect, bring/put together, round up, summon, muster, mobilize, accumulate, marshal, rally, amass; *formal* convoke. ❸ **assemble the device**: CONSTRUCT, build, erect, put together, set up, piece together, fit together, fabricate, manufacture, connect, join.
– OPPOSITES disperse, dismantle.

assembly noun GATHERING, meeting, crowd, group, congregation, throng, rally, convention, conference, congress, conclave, synod; *informal* get-together. *See also* CROWD.

assent noun AGREEMENT, consent, acceptance, approval, permission, sanction, acquiescence, compliance, accord, accordance, approbation.
– OPPOSITES dissent.
▶ **verb** AGREE, accept, consent, be willing, comply, approve, acquiesce, concede, concur, give one's permission, submit, yield, accede.
– OPPOSITES refuse.

assert verb ❶ DECLARE, state, maintain, proclaim, pronounce, emphasize, insist on, profess, claim, swear to, stress, affirm, avow; *formal* aver. ❷ **assert one's rights**: UPHOLD, insist on, stand up for, defend, press/push for, vindicate.
■ **assert oneself** BEHAVE CONFIDENTLY, make one's presence felt, stand up for oneself, exert one's influence.

assertive adjective CONFIDENT, self-assured, assured, forceful, pushy, strong-willed, positive, authoritative, dominant, domineering, strong, aggressive, decisive, firm, definite, emphatic, uncompromising, stubborn, opinionated; *informal* bossy.

assess verb JUDGE, evaluate, estimate, gauge, appraise, weigh up, rate, determine, reckon, work out, assay, compute, calculate, fix; *informal* size up.

asset noun ADVANTAGE, benefit, strength, strong point, help, aid, resource, support, blessing, boon, godsend.
■ **assets** WEALTH, money, resources, capital, means, property, possessions, belongings, holdings, goods, valuables, reserves, securities, estate, effects, chattels.

assiduous adjective DILIGENT, industrious, hard-working, persistent, indefatigable, zealous, persevering, sedulous.

assign verb ❶ **assign duties**: ALLOCATE, allot, distribute, share out, give out, dispense, apportion, consign. ❷ **assign him to a post**: APPOINT, select for, nominate, designate, name, install, delegate, commission. ❸ **assign her behaviour to jealousy**: ASCRIBE, put down, attribute, accredit, credit, chalk up. ❹ **assign the property**: TRANSFER, make over, convey.

assignation noun RENDEZVOUS, date, meeting, appointment; *poetic/literary* tryst.

assignment noun ❶ a tough assignment: TASK, job, duty, mission, responsibility, obligation, charge, commission. ❷ the assignment of tasks: ALLOCATION, distribution, allotment, apportionment, dispensation, consignment. ❸ the assignment of property: TRANSFER, making over, handing down, consignment.

assimilate verb ❶ ABSORB, take in, incorporate, ingest, digest. ❷ ADAPT, adjust, accustom, become like, acclimatize, blend in, homogenize.

assist verb ❶ HELP, help out, aid, support, lend a hand, rally round, cooperate with, collaborate with, work with, play a part, abet, succour. ❷ FACILITATE, make easier, boost, further, promote, expedite.
– OPPOSITES impede, hinder.

assistance noun HELP, aid, support, cooperation, collaboration, succour, a (helping) hand, encouragement, patronage, sponsorship, subsidy, contribution.
– OPPOSITES hindrance, impedance.

assistant noun ❶ DEPUTY, subordinate, second-in-command, auxiliary, right-hand man/woman, man/girl Friday, henchman, minion. ❷ HELPER, collaborator, associate, partner, colleague, mainstay, accessory, abetter. ❸ SHOP/SALES ASSISTANT, salesperson, salesman, saleswoman, checkout operator, server; *N. Amer.* clerk.

associate verb ❶ associate wine with France: LINK, connect, identify, equate, bracket, relate. ❷ associate with criminals: MIX, socialize, keep company, mingle, fraternize; *informal* hobnob, run/go around, hang out. ❸ the clubs are associated: AFFILIATE, connect, combine, join, attach, band together, team up, ally, incorporate, syndicate.
– OPPOSITES dissociate.

association noun FEDERATION, affiliation, alliance, partnership, union, confederation, syndicate, coalition, combination, league, fellowship, merger, cartel, consortium, club.

assorted adjective MIXED, varied, various, diverse, miscellaneous, sundry, multifarious, manifold, motley, heterogeneous, variegated; *poetic/literary* divers.

assortment noun MIXTURE, selection, variety, collection, range, jumble, miscellany, medley, diversity, melange, farrago, pot-pourri, mishmash, hotchpotch.

assuage verb EASE, relieve, soothe, alleviate, lessen, moderate, temper, mitigate, diminish, mollify, abate, palliate.
– OPPOSITES aggravate, intensify.

assume verb ❶ SUPPOSE, presume, think, presuppose, take for granted, believe, suspect, understand, expect, imagine, guess, gather, surmise, fancy. ❷ assume an air of authority: TAKE ON, adopt, take up, acquire, put on, affect, come to have, don. ❸ assume responsibility: UNDERTAKE, accept, take upon oneself, shoulder, embark on, enter upon. ❹ assume power:

SEIZE, take over, appropriate, commandeer, usurp, pre-empt.

assumption noun SUPPOSITION, presumption, belief, hypothesis, presupposition, theory, suspicion, guess, expectation, conjecture, surmise, premise.

assurance noun ❶ shows remarkable assurance: SELF-CONFIDENCE, confidence, self-assurance, poise, nerve. ❷ you have my assurance: GUARANTEE, commitment, word, promise, undertaking, oath, pledge, affirmation.

assure verb ❶ DECLARE, give one's word, affirm, guarantee, promise, swear, pledge, certify, vow, attest. ❷ success is assured: ENSURE, make sure/certain, guarantee, confirm, secure, clinch, seal.

assured adjective CONFIDENT, self-confident, self-assured, self-reliant, poised, positive.

astonish verb AMAZE, astound, stagger, stun, surprise, dumbfound, leave speechless, take someone's breath away, take aback, startle, stupefy, daze, bewilder, dazzle; *informal* flabbergast, floor, wow.

astonishing adjective AMAZING, astounding, staggering, surprising, breathtaking, striking, stunning, bewildering, impressive.
– OPPOSITES unremarkable.

astound verb *see* ASTONISH.

astray adverb & adjective ❶ OFF COURSE, lost, off the right track, adrift. ❷ WRONG, into sin, into wrongdoing, into error; *informal* off the rails.

astringent adjective SEVERE, stern, harsh, rough, acerbic, stringent, caustic, trenchant, mordant.

astute adjective SHREWD, clever, quick, quick-witted, acute, cunning, intelligent, sly, artful, knowing, canny, ingenious, perceptive, observant, crafty, wily, calculating, perspicacious, sagacious; *informal* foxy; *Brit. informal* fly.
– OPPOSITES stupid, dull.

asylum noun ❶ REFUGE, sanctuary, shelter, safety, protection, safe keeping, haven, retreat, harbour, port in a storm. ❷ MENTAL HOSPITAL, psychiatric hospital, institution; *informal* loony bin, madhouse, funny farm.

asymmetrical adjective UNEVEN, irregular, crooked, distorted, lopsided, unbalanced, misshapen, malformed.
– OPPOSITES symmetrical.

atheist noun UNBELIEVER, disbeliever, non-believer, sceptic, freethinker, heretic, heathen, pagan, infidel.
– OPPOSITES believer.

athletic adjective ❶ athletic build/person: MUSCULAR, strong, well built, powerful, fit, active, energetic, sturdy, robust, strapping, wiry, hardy, vigorous, brawny. ❷ athletic event: SPORTING, sports, gymnastics.
– OPPOSITES puny.

atmosphere noun ❶ AIR, sky, aerospace, stratosphere; *poetic/literary* heavens, ether. ❷ ENVIRONMENT, climate, mood, feeling, spirit, ambience, surroundings, setting, milieu, character, tone, quality, flavour, vibrations, aura, tenor; *informal* vibes.

atom noun BIT, particle, scrap,

shred, speck, spot, fragment, jot, trace, iota, dot, crumb, grain, morsel; *informal* smidgen.

atone verb MAKE AMENDS, compensate, pay for, be punished, do penance, answer, pay the penalty/price, make reparations, redeem oneself, redress, expiate.

atrocious adjective ❶ **atrocious crimes:** WICKED, vicious, brutal, barbaric, evil, dreadful, horrific, horrifying, sickening, abominable, savage, cruel, murderous, frightful, revolting, villainous, heinous, ruthless, monstrous, inhuman, gruesome, hideous, fiendish, diabolical, outrageous, vile. ❷ **atrocious weather:** VERY BAD, terrible, appalling, dreadful.
– OPPOSITES commendable, excellent.

atrocity noun OUTRAGE, crime, offence, horror, abomination, monstrosity, violation, evil.

atrophy verb WASTE AWAY, wither, shrivel, decay, wilt, deteriorate, decline, degenerate.

attach verb ❶ FASTEN, stick, affix, join, connect, link, tie, couple, pin, hitch, bond, add, append, annex. ❷ **attach no significance to it:** PLACE, put, ascribe, assign, attribute, lay, impute, invest with. ❸ **attached to a unit:** ASSIGN, appoint, second, allocate, detail.
– OPPOSITES detach.

attached adjective ❶ MARRIED, engaged, spoken for, having a partner. ❷ FOND OF, devoted to, having a regard for.

attack verb ❶ ASSAULT, set on/upon, beat up, strike, strike at, rush, storm, charge, pounce upon, beset, besiege, beleaguer; *informal* lay/wade into, let someone have it, do over. ❷ CRITICIZE, berate, reprove, censure, rebuke, find fault with, denounce, revile, blame, harangue, vilify, snipe at, fulminate against, impugn, malign, inveigh against, traduce. ❸ **attack a pile of work:** BEGIN, set about, get/go to work on, get started on, embark on, undertake.
– OPPOSITES defend, praise.
▶ noun ❶ ASSAULT, offensive, raid, ambush, sortie, onslaught, charge, strike, invasion, rush, foray, incursion, battery, bombardment. ❷ CRITICISM, abuse, censure, outburst, tirade, rebuke, reproval, vilification, diatribe, impugnment, invective. ❸ **an asthmatic attack:** FIT, seizure, bout, spasm, convulsion, paroxysm, stroke.

attacker noun ASSAILANT, aggressor, assaulter, mugger, opponent, raider, critic, detractor, persecutor, slanderer.

attain verb ACHIEVE, accomplish, gain, obtain, get, win, earn, acquire, reach, realize, arrive at, fulfil, succeed in, bring off, grasp, secure, procure.

attempt verb TRY, strive, endeavour, tackle, seek, set out to, venture, aim, undertake, make an effort, bid; *informal* have a go/shot at, give something a whirl, have a crack at.
▶ noun TRY, effort, endeavour, venture, undertaking; *informal* go, shot, crack.

attend verb ❶ BE PRESENT, be at, be there/here, appear, put in an appearance, turn up, visit, show, frequent, haunt; *informal* show up. ❷ PAY ATTENTION, listen, concentrate, follow, heed, pay heed, take note, notice, mark, watch. ❸ **attend the sick:** LOOK AFTER, take care of, care for, nurse, tend, see to, mind, minister to. ❹ **attended by her bodyguard:** ESCORT, accompany, guard, follow, chaperone, squire, usher, convoy.

attendant noun ❶ **a sleeping car attendant:** STEWARD, waiter, waitress, porter, servant. ❷ **a royal attendant:** ESCORT, companion, retainer, aide, lady in waiting, equerry, chaperone.
▶ adjective RELATED, accompanying, consequent, resulting, concomitant, accessory.

attention noun
❶ CONCENTRATION, attentiveness, notice, observation, scrutiny, heed, regard, diligence, thought, thinking, studying. ❷ **attract their attention:** NOTICE, awareness, observation, recognition, regard, consciousness. ❸ **medical attention:** CARE, treatment, therapy, ministration. ❹ **effusive in his attentions:** OVERTURES, approaches, suit, wooing, compliments, flattery; *dated* courting.

attentive adjective ❶ ALERT, aware, watchful, awake, observant, wide awake, vigilant, intent, mindful, on guard, heedful. ❷ **an attentive host:** CONSIDERATE, thoughtful, conscientious, polite, kind, obliging, accommodating, gallant.
– OPPOSITES inattentive.

attenuated adjective ❶ THIN, slender, stretched out, drawn out. ❷ WEAKENED, reduced, lessened, decreased, diminished, impaired.
– OPPOSITES broad, strengthened.

attire noun CLOTHING, dress, clothes, garments, garb, costume, outfit, wear, ensemble, accoutrements; *informal* gear, togs, glad rags, rig; *formal* apparel; *archaic* habit.
▶ **verb** *see* DRESS verb (1).

attitude noun ❶ VIEW, point of view, opinion, viewpoint, outlook, belief, standpoint, frame of mind, position, approach, perspective, reaction, stance, thoughts, ideas. ❷ POSITION, pose, stance, bearing, carriage; *Brit.* deportment.

attract verb ❶ APPEAL TO, interest, fascinate, charm, entice, captivate, tempt, engage, bewitch, seduce, beguile, lure, allure, inveigle; *informal* turn on. ❷ **attract controversy:** CAUSE, generate, encourage, provoke, incite, stir up. ❸ **magnets attract iron filings:** DRAW, pull, magnetize.
– OPPOSITES repel.

attractive adjective ❶ **an attractive woman/man:** GOOD-LOOKING, beautiful, handsome, pretty, lovely, stunning, striking, gorgeous, irresistible, glamorous, desirable, appealing, captivating, fascinating, charming, adorable, enchanting, alluring, enticing, seductive, bewitching, fetching, prepossessing, winsome; *informal* tasty; *N. Amer. informal* cute; *archaic* comely. ❷ **an attractive proposal:** APPEALING, agreeable, interesting, tempting, pleasing, inviting.
– OPPOSITES ugly, uninviting.

attribute noun QUALITY, feature, characteristic, property, mark, sign, trait, indicator, distinction, idiosyncrasy.
▶ **verb** ASCRIBE, assign, put down,

accredit, credit, impute, chalk up, lay at the door of.

attrition noun ❶ WEAKENING, wearing down, debilitation, sapping, enfeebling. ❷ ABRASION, friction, rubbing, corrosion, corroding, erosion, wearing/eating away, grinding, scraping, excoriation.

attune verb ACCUSTOM, adjust, familiarize, adapt, acclimatize.

audacious adjective BOLD, daring, fearless, brave, courageous, adventurous, intrepid, valiant, plucky, reckless, brazen, daredevil; *informal* gutsy.
– OPPOSITES timid.

audacity noun ❶ BOLDNESS, daring, fearlessness, bravery, courage, valour, pluck; *Brit. informal* guts. *See also* COURAGE.
❷ EFFRONTERY, cheek, impudence, brazenness, impertinence, shamelessness, presumption; *informal* sauce.
– OPPOSITES timidity.

audible adjective DISCERNIBLE, perceptible, clear, distinct, recognizable, hearable, detectable.
– OPPOSITES inaudible, faint.

audience noun ❶ SPECTATORS, LISTENERS, viewers, onlookers, crowd, gathering, assembly, house, turnout, congregation, gallery. ❷ INTERVIEW, meeting, hearing, consultation, discussion, reception.

audit noun INSPECTION, examination, investigation, scrutiny, review, check.
▶ verb INSPECT, examine, review, check, scrutinize, investigate, go over/through.

augment verb INCREASE, enlarge, make larger/greater, add to, expand, multiply, grow, extend, boost, enhance, raise, inflate, heighten, strengthen, intensify, amplify, swell, supplement, magnify.
– OPPOSITES decrease, diminish.

augur verb BE A SIGN OF, bode, foretell, predict, herald, prophesy, foreshadow, harbinger, portend, forecast, presage.

august adjective DIGNIFIED, solemn, stately, majestic, noble, imposing, impressive, exalted, grand, illustrious.
– OPPOSITES obscure, insignificant.

auspicious adjective FAVOURABLE, promising, hopeful, encouraging, bright, fortunate, propitious, timely, felicitous.
– OPPOSITES inauspicious.

austere adjective ❶ an austere style: PLAIN, severe, simple, unadorned, unornamented, stark, subdued, sombre, unembellished. ❷ an austere manner: STERN, formal, serious, solemn, severe, cold, distant, aloof, stiff, forbidding, unsmiling, unbending, unyielding, harsh, rigorous, stringent, unrelenting. ❸ an austere life: STRICT, abstemious, disciplined, puritanical, spartan, frugal, ascetic, self-denying, restrained, chaste, celibate, abstinent.
– OPPOSITES elaborate, genial, immoderate.

authentic adjective ❶ an authentic document: GENUINE, real, true, bona fide, actual, legitimate, valid, undisputed; *informal* the real McCoy. ❷ an authentic account: TRUE, accurate, honest, credible, reliable, dependable; *informal* straight from the horse's mouth.
– OPPOSITES fake, unreliable.

authenticate verb VERIFY, validate, confirm, substantiate, certify, guarantee, endorse, ratify.

author noun ❶ WRITER, composer, novelist, dramatist, playwright, poet, screenwriter, essayist, journalist, reporter, columnist. ❷ CREATOR, originator, producer, designer, architect, planner, cause, prime mover, maker, initiator, inventor; *poetic/literary* begetter.

authoritarian adjective DICTATORIAL, tyrannical, strict, domineering, despotic, autocratic, imperious, harsh, Draconian, disciplinarian, dogmatic; *informal* bossy.
– OPPOSITES democratic, liberal.

authoritative adjective ❶ authoritative information: RELIABLE, accurate, authentic, sound, dependable, factual, definitive, valid, certified. ❷ an authoritative manner: CONFIDENT, self-assured, assertive, commanding, masterful, imposing, arrogant, overbearing, imperious.
– OPPOSITES unreliable, timid.

authority noun ❶ the authority to decide | a person in authority: RIGHT, power, jurisdiction, authorization, influence, might, prerogative, rule, command, charge, dominion, sovereignty, supremacy, ascendancy; *informal* say-so. ❷ you have authority to act: PERMISSION, authorization, consent, sanction, licence, mandate, warrant. ❸ the authorities: GOVERNMENT, administration, officialdom, management, establishment, bureaucracy; *informal* powers that be. ❹ an authority on linguistics: EXPERT, specialist, master, scholar, pundit, adept.

authorize verb PERMIT, allow, agree to, give permission, consent to, approve, sanction, endorse, back, license, ratify, legalize, certify, countenance, give leave for, warrant, commission; *informal* give the go-ahead for, give the green light to.

authorized adjective *see* OFFICIAL.

automatic adjective ❶ AUTOMATED, mechanical, mechanized, electronic, self-regulating, self-activating, push-button, programmable, robotic. ❷ an automatic reaction: INSTINCTIVE, spontaneous, involuntary, unconscious, reflex, habitual, natural, unintentional, unthinking, mechanical, conditioned. ❸ promotion is automatic: INEVITABLE, routine, certain, assured.
– OPPOSITES manual, deliberate.

autonomous adjective INDEPENDENT, free, self-governing, sovereign.

autonomy noun INDEPENDENCE, self-determination, self-sufficiency, individualism, autarchy.

auxiliary adjective SECONDARY, subsidiary, subordinate, ancillary, supporting, additional, extra, reserve, back-up, spare, supplementary, substitute.

available adjective FREE, untaken, obtainable, to hand, handy, procurable, unoccupied, vacant, usable, ready, convenient, accessible, employable.
– OPPOSITES unavailable, inaccessible.

avarice noun GREED, acquisitiveness, covetousness,

materialism, meanness, miserliness.
– OPPOSITES generosity.

avaricious adjective GREEDY, grasping, covetous, acquisitive, miserly, parsimonious; *informal* tight-fisted, stingy.
– OPPOSITES generous.

average adjective ❶ average size: NORMAL, typical, ordinary, common, regular, usual, commonplace, everyday, widespread, unexceptional, medium, middling, moderate; *informal* run-of-the-mill. ❷ no better than average: MEDIOCRE, unexceptional, moderate, second-rate, pedestrian, banal.
– OPPOSITES exceptional, outstanding.
▶ noun MEAN, midpoint, median, centre, norm, standard, rule, yardstick.
▶ verb EVEN OUT, equalize, normalize, standardize.

averse adjective OPPOSED, hostile, antagonistic, unwilling, disinclined, reluctant, resistant, loath, ill-disposed.

aversion noun DISLIKE, distaste, hatred, repugnance, antipathy, reluctance, unwillingness, evasion, avoidance, shunning.
– OPPOSITES liking, inclination.

avert verb DEFLECT, ward off, fend off, turn aside/away, parry, stave off, prevent.

avid adjective KEEN, eager, enthusiastic, fervent, dedicated, ardent, fanatical, zealous, passionate.
– OPPOSITES apathetic, indifferent.

avoid verb ❶ EVADE, elude, hide from, keep away from, keep clear of, shun, ignore, dodge, steer clear of, give a wide berth to, shirk, eschew; *informal* duck. ❷ ABSTAIN FROM, circumvent, refrain from, bypass; *Brit. informal* skive off.
– OPPOSITES face, seek.

await verb ❶ WAIT FOR, expect, anticipate, hope for, look out for. ❷ BE IN STORE FOR, WAIT FOR, be ready for, lie ahead for, lie in wait for, be round the corner.

awake adjective ❶ WAKEFUL, sleepless, wide awake, insomniac, open-eyed, restless, tossing and turning. ❷ AWARE, alert, conscious, attentive, vigilant.
– OPPOSITES asleep, unaware.

awaken verb ❶ WAKE, wake up, awake, waken, rouse, call, alert. ❷ awaken a response: KINDLE, arouse, stimulate, call forth, stir up, excite, revive.

award noun ❶ PRIZE, reward, trophy, honour, decoration, medal, badge, cup, grant, scholarship. ❷ GIFT, grant, conferment, bestowal, presentation.
▶ verb CONFER, present, give, grant, accord, allot, assign, bestow, endow.

aware adjective CONSCIOUS, alive to, informed, knowledgeable, familiar, acquainted, mindful, heedful, sensitive, responsive, observant, attentive, sensible, conversant, cognizant, versed in.
– OPPOSITES ignorant, insensitive.

awareness noun CONSCIOUSNESS, perception, realization, knowledge, sense, feeling, understanding, sensitivity, perceptiveness.
– OPPOSITES ignorance, insensitivity.

awe noun WONDER, amazement, admiration, reverence, veneration, respect, dread, fear.

awesome adjective BREATHTAKING, awe-inspiring, magnificent, stupendous, overwhelming, sublime, majestic, solemn, imposing, dramatic, grand, formidable, marvellous, amazing, staggering, stunning, fearful, impressive; *informal* mind-blowing; *poetic/literary* wondrous. *See also* WONDERFUL.
– OPPOSITES unimpressive.

awful adjective ❶ an awful day | awful work: *see* BAD. ❷ *See* AWESOME.

awfully adverb ❶ awfully sorry: VERY, extremely, intensely, deeply, exceedingly; *informal* terribly, dreadfully; *Brit. informal* ever so; *informal, dated* frightfully. ❷ we played awfully: TERRIBLY, badly, dreadfully, appallingly, atrociously, disgracefully, frightfully.

awkward adjective ❶ awkward to carry: UNWIELDY, cumbersome, unmanageable, inconvenient, bulky. ❷ an awkward time: INCONVENIENT, difficult, troublesome, problematic, unhelpful, unsuitable. ❸ an awkward question: TRICKY, difficult, perplexing, taxing, puzzling, thorny, troublesome, trying, vexed. ❹ awkward characters: UNCOOPERATIVE, unhelpful, disobliging, contrary, obstructive, perverse, troublesome, trying, exasperating, obstinate, stubborn, refractory, intractable; *Brit. informal* bloody-minded, bolshie; *N. Amer.* ornery. ❺ CLUMSY, blundering, bungling, ungainly, uncoordinated, inelegant, inexpert, clownish, inept, unskilled, maladroit, gawky, gauche, wooden; *informal* ham-fisted. ❻ an awkward pause: UNCOMFORTABLE, uneasy, strained, embarrassing, unnatural; *informal* edgy.
– OPPOSITES convenient, handy, cooperative, graceful, skilful, relaxed.

axe verb GET RID OF, discontinue, terminate, cancel, withdraw, remove, make redundant, dismiss, discharge; *informal* sack.

Bb

babble verb CHATTER, prattle, burble, gabble, jabber, gibber, murmur, mutter; *informal* waffle; *Brit. informal* rabbit.
▶ noun CHATTER, chat, gabble, prattling, murmur, clamour.

baby noun INFANT, newborn, child; *poetic/literary* babe; *technical* neonate.
▶ adjective TINY, miniature, mini, little, dwarf, diminutive, minute.
▶ verb COSSET, pamper, spoil, indulge, coddle, mollycoddle, pet.

babyish adjective CHILDISH, infantile, immature, juvenile, puerile, silly, inane.
– OPPOSITES mature.

back noun ❶ REAR, rear end, stern, tail end, hindquarters,

posterior, end. ❷ REVERSE, reverse side, other side.
– OPPOSITES front.
▶ **adjective** ❶ REAR, hind, end, hindmost, last. ❷ DORSAL, spinal.
– OPPOSITES front.
▶ **verb** ❶ *See* SUPPORT verb (5), UPHOLD. ❷ REVERSE, go backwards, move back, back away, back off, retreat, retire, recede, recoil, withdraw, backtrack.
■ **back down** *see* WITHDRAW (4).

backer noun SUPPORTER, sponsor, promoter, patron, advocate, benefactor, champion, seconder; *informal* angel.

background noun ❶ BACKDROP, setting, surroundings, context, circumstances, conditions, framework, environment. ❷ **a person's background:** FAMILY, origins, ancestry, upbringing, education, milieu, culture, training, tradition, experience, qualifications, credentials, history.
– OPPOSITES foreground.

backing noun ❶ SUPPORT, encouragement, approval, endorsement, promotion, recommendation, assent, agreement, assistance, help, aid, sponsorship, funding, patronage, subsidy, funds, grant, loan. ❷ **musical backing:** ACCOMPANIMENT, obbligato.

backlash noun REACTION, recoil, rebound, response, retaliation, counterblast, repercussion, reversal.

backslide verb RELAPSE, lapse, go astray, weaken, slip, regress, deteriorate, degenerate, fall away.

backward adjective ❶ REVERSE, retreating, rearward, retrograde, regressive, retrogressive. ❷ SLOW, late-starting, behind, behindhand, retarded, undeveloped, unprogressive, underdeveloped, disadvantaged, handicapped; *dated* subnormal. ❸ SHY, bashful, timid, diffident, hesitant, self-effacing, reticent, unforthcoming, reserved, unassertive, modest, coy, inhibited.
– OPPOSITES forward, advanced, precocious, confident.

bad adjective ❶ **bad workmanship:** POOR, inadequate, unsatisfactory, substandard, inferior, imperfect, defective, deficient, faulty, incompetent, inefficient, incorrect, unsound, useless, worthless, shoddy, abysmal, awful, appalling, disgraceful, atrocious, dreadful, frightful, hopeless, abominable; *informal* lousy, rotten, diabolical; *Brit. informal* grotty, ropy. ❷ **a bad moment; bad for you:** UNSUITABLE, unpropitious, unfavourable, inappropriate, adverse, unhelpful, inconvenient, unlucky, dangerous, harmful, deleterious, detrimental, damaging, unhealthy, risky, injurious, hurtful, destructive. ❸ **bad weather; a bad day:** UNPLEASANT, disagreeable, nasty, horrid, horrible, harsh, unwelcome, gloomy, distressing, dreadful, awful, frightful, terrible, foul, appalling, atrocious. ❹ **a bad accident/mistake:** SERIOUS, severe, grave, dangerous, disastrous, calamitous, terrible, awful, dreadful, frightful, critical, acute, dire, hideous. ❺ **a bad character:** IMMORAL, wicked, evil, wrong, corrupt, sinful, vicious, criminal, depraved, villainous, vile, rotten, delinquent, guilty, blameworthy, reprehensible, dishonest, dishonourable, ignoble, base,

reprobate. ❻ bad behaviour: NAUGHTY, mischievous, unruly, wayward, disobedient, disorderly. ❼ go bad: ROTTEN, decayed, mouldy, off, rancid, tainted, spoiled, sour, decomposing, putrid, contaminated, foul, polluted, mildewed, diseased. ❽ feel bad after eating too much: *see* ILL adjective (1). ❾ I felt bad about leaving: REMORSEFUL, regretful, ashamed, guilty, sorry, unhappy, contrite, apologetic, penitent.
– OPPOSITES good, favourable, fine, fresh.

badge noun EMBLEM, pin, crest, insignia, medal, token, sign, mark, symbol, logo, device, characteristic, trademark; *N. Amer.* button.

badger verb PESTER, bother, plague, nag, harass, chivvy, torment, persecute; *informal* hassle, bug.

bad-tempered adjective IRRITABLE, short-tempered, quick-tempered, peevish, touchy, prickly, crotchety, irascible, cross, angry, ill-humoured, testy, quarrelsome, truculent, grumpy, acrimonious, querulous, petulant, gruff, sullen, moody, sulky, disgruntled, grumbling, scowling, churlish, cantankerous, dyspeptic, bilious, crabbed, shrewish; *informal* snappy; *Brit. informal* shirty.
– OPPOSITES good-humoured, affable.

baffle verb ❶ BEWILDER, bemuse, mystify, perplex, puzzle, confuse, confound, nonplus, floor; *informal* flummox, bamboozle, stump. ❷ THWART, foil, frustrate, defeat, prevent, check, hinder, block, obstruct.

bag noun HANDBAG, carrier bag, shoulder bag, case, grip, satchel, sack, holdall, rucksack, haversack, reticule.
▶ verb ❶ CATCH, capture, shoot, kill, trap, snare, land. ❷ bag a seat: GET, gain, acquire, obtain, reserve, secure, get hold of.

baggage noun LUGGAGE, bags, cases, belongings, things, equipment, accoutrements, paraphernalia, impedimenta; *informal* gear.

bait noun LURE, attraction, enticement, temptation, incentive, inducement, bribe, decoy, carrot.
▶ verb TEASE, provoke, goad, pester, annoy, harass, plague, torment, persecute, taunt; *informal* needle; *Brit. informal* wind up.

balance noun ❶ STABILITY, poise, steadiness, equilibrium. ❷ CORRESPONDENCE, equivalence, symmetry, equality, parity, equipoise, evenness, proportion. ❸ pay the balance: REMAINDER, rest, difference, surplus, excess, residue. ❹ SCALES, weighing machine.
– OPPOSITES imbalance, instability.
▶ verb ❶ KEEP BALANCED, poise, steady, stabilize, support. ❷ OFFSET, cancel out, counterbalance, match, compensate for, even up, level, equalize, parallel, counterpoise, counteract, neutralize.

bald adjective ❶ HAIRLESS, bare, smooth, bald-headed; *informal* thin on top. ❷ a bald statement: BLUNT, frank, plain, straightforward, forthright, direct, not beating about the bush, stark, uncompromising, downright,

simple, unadorned, unembellished.
– OPPOSITES hairy.

ball noun SPHERE, globe, orb, globule, spheroid.

ballot noun VOTE, poll, election, referendum, plebiscite.

ban verb PROHIBIT, forbid, veto, outlaw, put a ban on, proscribe, suppress, disallow, interdict, bar, debar, prevent, suppress, restrict, exclude, banish, ostracize.
– OPPOSITES authorize, permit, sanction.
▶ **noun** PROHIBITION, veto, embargo, boycott, bar, interdict, interdiction, proscription, restriction, taboo, suppression.

banal adjective TRITE, clichéd, hackneyed, commonplace, unoriginal, cliché-ridden, unimaginative, uninspired, stale, boring, dull, everyday, stock, stereotyped, platitudinous, obvious, predictable, tired, pedestrian, humdrum, prosaic, vapid, fatuous; *informal* corny, old hat.
– OPPOSITES interesting, original.

band[1] noun ❶ **a band of colour:** STRIPE, strip, line, belt, bar, streak, border, swathe. ❷ **a band for the hair:** BRAID, belt, fillet, sash, tie, ribbon, cord, loop, girdle.

band[2] noun ❶ GROUP, troop, crowd, crew, gang, company, body, pack, mob, horde, flock, bunch, gathering, party, throng, society, club, clique, set, association. ❷ **a brass band:** GROUP, orchestra, ensemble; *informal* combo.

bandit noun BRIGAND, outlaw, robber, highwayman, footpad, marauder, desperado, gangster, gunman, pirate, buccaneer, hijacker, plunderer, thief.

bandy[1] adjective **bandy legs:** BOWED, crooked, curved, bent, bow-legged, misshapen.

bandy[2] verb ❶ **bandy words:** EXCHANGE, swap, trade, pass, reciprocate. *See also* ARGUE. ❷ **bandy rumours about:** SPREAD, circulate, pass on, disseminate.

bang noun ❶ BOOM, crash, thud, slam, knock, clash, clap, report, explosion. ❷ **a bang on the head:** BLOW, bump, hit, knock, slap, punch, stroke, cuff, smack, rap; *informal* whack.
▶ **adverb** ❶ WITH A BANG, crash, thump, thud, noisily, violently. ❷ EXACTLY, precisely, absolutely, right; *informal* slap bang.

banish verb ❶ EXILE, expel, exclude, deport, expatriate, ostracize, transport, eject, evict, outlaw, oust, throw out, proscribe. ❷ DISMISS, drive away, dispel, shut out, eliminate, get rid of, dislodge, remove, bar, ban, suppress.

bank[1] noun ❶ **a grassy bank:** SLOPE, mound, embankment, hillock, incline, ridge, rise, rampart, ramp, dyke, pile, mass. ❷ **a river bank:** EDGE, shore, brink, side, margin, embankment. ❸ **a bank of switches:** ROW, array, collection, display, panel, rank, tier.
▶ **verb** **the plane banked:** TILT, lean, slope, slant, list, tip, incline.

bank[2] noun **a blood bank:** STORE, reserve, supply, fund, stock, hoard, repository, pool, reservoir.
▶ **verb** **bank your savings:** DEPOSIT, save, put by, save up, keep, store, hoard.
– OPPOSITES withdraw.
■ **bank on** *see* RELY ON.

bankrupt adjective ❶ INSOLVENT, ruined, failed, in liquidation, destitute, penniless; *informal* broke, bust. ❷ MORALLY BANKRUPT, deficient, lacking, poor, impoverished, worthless.
–OPPOSITES solvent.

banner noun FLAG, standard, pennant, pennon, colours, ensign, banderole, streamer.

banquet noun FEAST, repast, dinner, meal, party; *informal* binge, blowout, spread.

banter noun TEASING, joking, repartee, chaff, badinage, persiflage, pleasantry, raillery, jesting, wordplay; *informal* ribbing.

bar noun ❶ BEAM, rod, pole, shaft, stake, stick, spar, rail, batten, girder, crosspiece. ❷ BARRIER, obstacle, obstruction, impediment, hindrance, check, deterrent, drawback, prohibition, prevention, problem, difficulty. ❸ BAND, stripe, belt, strip, streak, line. ❹ **a bar of chocolate/soap**: CAKE, slab, chunk, block, piece, wedge, lump, hunk, nugget, ingot. ❺ HOSTELRY, inn, tavern; *Brit.* pub, public house; *Brit. informal* local, boozer.
▶ **verb** ❶ EXCLUDE, ban, banish, keep out, prohibit, forbid, preclude, outlaw, ostracize, proscribe. ❷ **bar someone's passage**: BLOCK, check, impede, obstruct, prevent, hinder, stop, halt, deter, restrain, arrest, thwart.

barbarian noun SAVAGE, vandal, boor, yahoo, churl, brute, ruffian, hooligan, heathen, pagan, philistine, ignoramus; *Brit. informal* yob, yobbo.
▶ **adjective** *See* BARBARIC.

barbaric adjective ❶ UNCIVILIZED, primitive, wild, savage, barbarian, uneducated, unsophisticated, crude, brutish. ❷ CRUEL, brutal, savage, bestial, barbarous, vicious, ferocious, inhuman. *See also* CRUEL.
–OPPOSITES civilized.

bare adjective ❶ NAKED, nude, undressed, unclad, uncovered, stripped, unclothed, exposed, denuded; *informal* in the buff; *Brit. informal* starkers; *N. Amer. informal* buck naked. ❷ **a bare room**: EMPTY, unfurnished, undecorated, plain, austere, unadorned, vacant. ❸ **a bare landscape**: BLEAK, barren, featureless, treeless, unsheltered, desolate, open. ❹ **the bare facts**: PLAIN, simple, unadorned, unvarnished, unembellished, uncompromising, basic, essential, literal, straightforward, bald, stark, direct, uninterpreted, unelaborated. ❺ **the bare minimum**: MERE, basic, essential, minimum, minimal, least, smallest, meagre, scanty, inadequate.
▶ **verb** REVEAL, uncover, expose, lay bare, undress, unmask, unveil, show, disclose, make known, publish, betray.
–OPPOSITES conceal.
■ **bare of** LACKING, without, devoid of, deprived of, wanting, destitute of, deficient in.

barely adverb HARDLY, scarcely, just, only just, by the skin of one's teeth, with difficulty.

bargain noun ❶ **make a bargain**: AGREEMENT, deal, pact, contract, arrangement, settlement, treaty, transaction, understanding, promise, pledge, compact, covenant, concordat, engagement, negotiation. ❷ GOOD BUY, good deal, special offer,

discount, reduction; *informal* snip, giveaway.
▶ verb NEGOTIATE, haggle, barter, argue, discuss, deal, trade, traffic, compromise, agree, settle, promise, pledge, engage.
■ **bargain for** EXPECT, allow for, anticipate, be prepared for, take into account. **into the bargain** *see* MOREOVER.

barmy adjective MAD, foolish, insane, idiotic, silly, odd, eccentric, weird, peculiar; *informal* crazy, batty, zany, nutty, loony, off one's rocker, round the bend, out to lunch; *Brit. informal* daft.
– OPPOSITES sane.

barrage noun ❶ BROADSIDE, gunfire, bombardment, fusillade, salvo, volley, battery, shelling, cannonade. ❷ **a barrage of criticism:** ONSLAUGHT, deluge, torrent, stream, hail, storm, flood, mass, avalanche, abundance, plethora. ❸ *See* BARRIER (1).

barrel noun CASK, keg, vat, butt, tub, tank, firkin, hogshead.

barren adjective ❶ **barren land:** INFERTILE, unproductive, unfruitful, waste, desert, arid, bare, bleak, desolate, lifeless, empty. ❷ STERILE, infertile, childless; *technical* infecund. ❸ **a barren life:** POINTLESS, worthless, fruitless, useless, purposeless, empty, arid, valueless, futile, unrewarding, unfulfilling, uninspiring, dull, boring, prosaic.
– OPPOSITES fertile.

barricade noun *see* BARRIER (1).
▶ verb BLOCK OFF, blockade, bar, obstruct, close up, fortify, defend.

barrier noun ❶ BAR, fence, railing, barricade, obstruction, blockade, barrage, roadblock, rampart, palisade, bulwark, dam, stockade. ❷ OBSTACLE, hindrance, impediment, handicap, difficulty, problem, restriction, check, bar, limitation, drawback, stumbling block.

barter verb BARGAIN, trade, traffic, exchange, swap, deal, haggle.

base[1] noun ❶ FOUNDATION, bed, foot, bottom, basis, support, stand, rest, pedestal, prop, plinth, substructure. ❷ BASIS, core, fundamentals, essence, essentials, root, heart, source, origin, mainspring. ❸ HEADQUARTERS, centre, camp, station, post, starting point, settlement, site.
▶ verb ❶ FOUND, build, settle, support, ground, rest, derive from, construct, establish.
❷ **based in London:** LOCATE, station, centre, post, situate, place, install.

base[2] adjective IGNOBLE, mean, low, sordid, contemptible, shameful, vulgar, shabby, despicable, unworthy, inferior, corrupt, depraved, vile, dishonourable, disreputable, unprincipled, immoral, evil, wicked, sinful, detestable, degrading.
– OPPOSITES noble.

bashful adjective SHY, diffident, timid, shrinking, backward, modest, self-effacing, retiring, nervous, self-conscious, reserved, inhibited, reticent, unforthcoming, hesitant, coy, demure, shamefaced, abashed, sheepish, embarrassed, blushing, uneasy.
– OPPOSITES confident.

basic adjective ❶ FUNDAMENTAL, essential, intrinsic, underlying, primary, elementary, central, key, indispensable, vital, main, principal, chief, crucial,

rudimentary. ❷ basic accommodation: PLAIN, simple, austere, spartan, unadorned, stark, minimal.
– OPPOSITES luxurious.

basin noun BOWL, dish, pan, vessel, container, receptacle.

basis noun ❶ FOUNDATION, base, grounding, support, rest, stand, stay, infrastructure, bottom. ❷ STARTING POINT, source, origin, core, essence, beginning, impetus, impulse, material, ingredients, stimulus. ❸ a regular basis: FOOTING, position, arrangement, condition, status, procedure, way, manner, fashion.

bask verb ❶ LIE, laze, relax, sunbathe, lounge, loll. ❷ REVEL, wallow, exult, delight, take pleasure, luxuriate, glory, rejoice, enjoy, relish, savour.

bastard noun ❶ ILLEGITIMATE CHILD; *dated* love child; *archaic* natural child. ❷ SCOUNDREL, villain, brute, rogue; *informal* beast; *dated* cad, blackguard.
▶ adjective DEBASED, corrupt, adulterated, impure, imperfect, hybrid, inferior, alloyed, counterfeit, spurious.

batch noun SET, group, lot, cluster, bunch, quantity, collection, accumulation, assemblage, pack, crowd, aggregate, conglomeration.

bathe verb ❶ WASH, clean, cleanse, rinse, soak, steep, moisten, wet, immerse. ❷ SWIM, go swimming, take a dip. ❸ SUFFUSE, envelop, cover, soak.

bathos noun ANTICLIMAX, let-down, comedown, sentimentality, mawkishness, banality, inanity, fatuousness, stupidity.
– OPPOSITES climax.

baton noun STICK, wand, rod, bar, cane, staff, club, truncheon, mace.

batter verb ❶ BEAT, hit, strike, bludgeon, assault, belabour; *informal* bash. *See also* HIT (1). ❷ DAMAGE, injure, hurt, harm, crush, shatter, exhaust, ruin, destroy, buffet, wear down, wear out, impair, squash, mar, spoil, demolish.

battle noun CONFLICT, fight, fighting, clash, engagement, skirmish, struggle, confrontation, combat, encounter, collision, campaign, war, tussle, scuffle, melee, action, strife, hostilities, fray, crusade; *informal* scrap.
▶ verb STRUGGLE, fight, contend, compete, contest, combat, feud, quarrel, wrangle, argue, war, cross swords.

battlefield noun BATTLEGROUND, front, battle lines, combat zone, theatre of war, arena.

bawdy adjective RIBALD, lewd, indecent, salacious, earthy, broad, suggestive, indelicate, naughty, racy, risqué, off colour, obscene, dirty, filthy, smutty, erotic, prurient, pornographic, gross, coarse, titillating, licentious, lascivious, unseemly, vulgar, Rabelaisian; *informal* blue, raunchy.
– OPPOSITES decent, proper.

bawl verb ❶ SHOUT, cry, yell, roar, bellow, thunder, clamour, vociferate; *informal* holler. ❷ SOB, wail, cry, roar, howl, weep, blubber, squall, snivel, grizzle.

bay[1] noun COVE, inlet, gulf, basin, harbour, indentation, sound, arm, bight, creek, firth, fjord, estuary.

bay[2] noun ALCOVE, recess, niche, opening, nook, booth.

bay[3] verb BARK, howl, yelp, roar, growl, clamour, ululate.

bazaar noun ❶ MARKET, mart, souk, exchange. ❷ FÊTE, fair, sale; *Brit.* jumble sale, bring-and-buy (sale); *N. Amer.* rummage sale.

be verb ❶ EXIST, live, be alive, breathe. ❷ BE SITUATED, be located, be positioned, stay, remain, continue, dwell, live, inhabit, be present, attend, persist, survive, endure, last. ❸ **the party is tomorrow**: TAKE PLACE, occur, be due, be planned for, happen, come about, arise, transpire; *poetic/literary* come to pass, befall.

beach noun SHORE, seashore, sands, sand, seaside, coast, coastline, littoral, margin, foreshore, water's edge, waterfront; *poetic/literary* strand.

beached adjective STRANDED, aground, grounded, ashore, high and dry, stuck, cast up, marooned, wrecked, abandoned.

bead noun ❶ BALL, pellet, pill, drop, globule. ❷ **beads of sweat**: DROP, droplet, globule, drip, blob, dot, dewdrop, teardrop.

beaker noun CUP, mug, glass, goblet, tumbler, tankard.

beam noun ❶ BAR, spar, rafter, girder, support, boom, plank, board, joist, timber, stanchion, scantling. ❷ **a beam of sunlight**: RAY, shaft, bar, stream, streak, pencil, gleam, glimmer, glow, glint.

▶ verb ❶ EMIT, radiate, shine, broadcast, transmit, direct, aim. ❷ SMILE, grin, laugh, be radiant.

– OPPOSITES frown.

bear verb ❶ HOLD, support, carry, uphold, sustain, prop up, shoulder, take. ❷ BRING, carry, transport, convey, fetch, deliver, move, take, transfer; *informal* tote. ❸ **bear a signature**: BE MARKED WITH, display, exhibit, show, present. ❹ ENDURE, tolerate, abide, accept, stand, put up with, submit to, suffer, sustain, cope with, live with, stomach, admit, allow, resign oneself to; *formal* brook. ❺ **bear fruit**: PRODUCE, yield, give, give forth, supply, provide. ❻ **bear children**: GIVE BIRTH TO, produce, breed, generate; *archaic* bring forth. ❼ **bear a grudge**: HARBOUR, hold, maintain, feel, nurture, cherish, entertain, possess.

■ **bear out** *see* CONFIRM (1), SUPPORT verb (4). **bear up** COPE, survive, endure, manage, keep on, hold out, keep going. **bear with** BE PATIENT WITH, be tolerant towards, make allowances for, tolerate, suffer, indulge.

bearable adjective ENDURABLE, tolerable, supportable, sustainable, sufferable, acceptable, admissible, manageable.

– OPPOSITES intolerable, unbearable.

bearing noun ❶ CARRIAGE, posture, gait, demeanour, air, aspect, behaviour, manner, attitude, mien, composure, stance, style; *Brit.* deportment; *formal* comportment. ❷ COURSE, direction. ❸ **this has no bearing on the issue**: RELEVANCE, pertinence, connection, implication, significance, relation, relationship, application, effect, consequence.

bearings plural noun ORIENTATION, location, position, sense of direction, whereabouts, situation, track, way.

beast noun ❶ ANIMAL, creature, brute. ❷ BRUTE, savage, monster, fiend, devil, sadist, barbarian, wretch; *archaic* blackguard.

beastly adjective HORRID, nasty, loathsome, vile, foul, awful, horrible, frightful, ghastly, atrocious, unpleasant, disagreeable; *informal* rotten.
– OPPOSITES pleasant, kind.

beat verb ❶ HIT, strike, batter, thrash, slap, whip, lash, cuff, cudgel, buffet, cane, scourge, smack, thwack, thump, pound, drub, hammer, flog, chastise; *informal* bash, whack, clout, wallop, lay into, rough up, knock about, tan, biff. ❷ **a beating heart**: PULSATE, throb, pound, pulse, palpitate, thump, vibrate. ❸ DEFEAT, outdo, conquer, surpass, trounce, vanquish, overcome, excel, subdue, master, best, outclass, outdistance, outpace, outwit, quash, worst; *informal* thrash, lick. ❹ **beat eggs**: WHISK, whip, stir, agitate, blend, mix. ❺ **beating wings**: FLAP, flutter, quiver, vibrate, tremble.
▶ **noun** ❶ PULSE, vibration, throb, throbbing, pounding, palpitation. ❷ RHYTHM, stress, accent, pulse, tempo, metre, measure, time. ❸ **a policeman's beat**: ROUND, rounds, route, circuit, path, track, course, way, itinerary.

beautiful adjective LOVELY, attractive, pretty, gorgeous, ravishing, stunning, handsome, good-looking, elegant, exquisite, charming, delightful, pleasing, picturesque, decorative, scenic, spectacular, superb, fine, glamorous, graceful; *poetic/literary* beauteous, pulchritudinous; *archaic* fair, comely; *Scottish & N. English* bonny.
– OPPOSITES ugly.

beautify verb ADORN, embellish, decorate, ornament, bedeck, enhance, improve, prettify, glamorize, smarten, gild; *informal* do up, doll up, titivate.
– OPPOSITES spoil.

beauty noun ATTRACTIVENESS, loveliness, prettiness, handsomeness, good looks, allure, appeal, charm, picturesqueness, glamour, elegance, grace, magnificence, radiance, splendour, artistry; *poetic/literary* pulchritude.
– OPPOSITES ugliness.

because conjunction SINCE, as, for the reason that, in that, seeing that.
■ **because of** ON ACCOUNT OF, owing to, due to, as a result of, in view of, by reason of, by virtue of, thanks to.

beckon verb ❶ GESTURE, signal, motion, gesticulate, call, summon, bid, invite, encourage. ❷ ATTRACT, tempt, pull, draw, allure, entice.

become verb ❶ TURN INTO, turn out to be, change into, grow into, develop into, be transformed into, evolve into, metamorphose into. ❷ **your dress becomes you**: SUIT, flatter, look good on, sit well on, set off, enhance, go well with, grace. ❸ BE APPROPRIATE TO, be suited to, be fitting for, be worthy of; *formal* behove.
■ **become of** HAPPEN TO; *poetic/literary* befall.

becoming adjective ❶ FLATTERING, pretty, attractive, elegant, stylish, chic. ❷ SUITABLE, seemly, proper, right, fitting, decent, decorous, dignified, graceful, comme il faut.
– OPPOSITES unflattering, improper.

bed noun ❶ COUCH, cot, berth;

informal the sack, the hay; *Brit. informal* one's pit. ❷ BASE, foundation, bottom, basis, support, substratum, substructure, layer.

bedraggled adjective DISHEVELLED, untidy, unkempt, disordered, muddy, wet, soiled, drenched, soaked, stained, soaking, sodden, soggy, messy, dirty, muddied.
– OPPOSITES neat, clean.

beef noun ❶ BRAWN, muscle, strength, sinew, physique, bulk, burliness, robustness, muscularity. ❷ COMPLAINT, grumble, grumbling, grievance, criticism, protest, objection; *informal* whine, moan, gripe, grouse, nit-picking.

befall verb HAPPEN, occur, happen to, take place, come about, chance, arise, ensue, follow, transpire; *poetic/literary* come to pass, betide.

before preposition ❶ IN FRONT OF, ahead of, earlier than, sooner than, prior to. ❷ IN FRONT OF, in the presence of, in the sight of. ❸ RATHER THAN, in preference to, sooner than.
– OPPOSITES after.
▶ adverb EARLIER, previously, beforehand, in advance, formerly, ahead.

befriend verb ❶ MAKE FRIENDS WITH, get to know, make the acquaintance of, become acquainted with. ❷ TAKE UNDER ONE'S PROTECTION, protect, look after, take under one's wing, support, assist, succour.

befuddled adjective CONFUSED, bemused, dazed, bewildered, muddled, numbed, stupefied, muzzy, groggy; *informal* woozy.
– OPPOSITES clear.

beg verb ❶ ASK FOR MONEY, solicit; *informal* scrounge, cadge. ❷ PLEAD, entreat, ask, request, seek, crave, importune, implore, pray, supplicate, petition, cajole, wheedle; *poetic/literary* beseech.

beget verb ❶ FATHER, sire, engender, generate, procreate, propagate, spawn. ❷ PRODUCE, give rise to, bring about, cause, result in, lead to, occasion, effect.

beggar noun VAGRANT, tramp, down-and-out, derelict, vagabond, mendicant; *informal* scrounger, sponger, cadger.
▶ verb RUIN, impoverish, reduce to poverty, bankrupt, pauperize.

begin verb ❶ START, commence, set about, start on, set in motion, set going, activate, spark off, embark on, initiate, establish, institute, inaugurate, originate, found, pioneer, open, launch, give rise to, cause, instigate, be the source of. ❷ COME INTO BEING, start, commence, arise, emerge, appear, occur, happen, originate, materialize, dawn, spring up.
– OPPOSITES finish, disappear.

beginner noun ❶ NOVICE, learner, trainee, apprentice, student, recruit, tyro, fledgling, neophyte, novitiate; *N. Amer.* tenderfoot; *informal* rookie; *N. Amer. informal* greenhorn. ❷ ORIGINATOR, starter, founder, creator, pioneer, initiator.
– OPPOSITES expert, veteran.

beginning noun ❶ START, origin, opening, commencement, outset, dawn, birth, inception, starting point, source, emergence, onset, genesis, conception, germ, root, spring. ❷ ESTABLISHMENT, foundation, institution, inauguration, opening, creation,

introduction. ❸ PRELUDE, introduction, preface, opening.
– OPPOSITES end, conclusion.

begrudge verb GRUDGE, resent, give unwillingly, be jealous of, object to, envy, mind, be dissatisfied with.

beguile verb ❶ CHARM, attract, delight, enchant, allure, bewitch, please, entice, seduce, tempt. ❷ AMUSE, absorb, engross, engage, divert, entertain, distract, occupy. ❸ WHILE AWAY, pass, spend.

behalf
■ **on behalf of** ❶ IN THE INTERESTS OF, for the sake of, in support of, for the good of, on account of. ❷ REPRESENTING, in the name of, in place of.

behave verb ❶ ACT, conduct oneself, perform, operate, function, acquit oneself; *formal* comport oneself. ❷ BE GOOD, be polite, mind one's manners, be obedient; *informal* mind one's Ps and Qs.

behaviour noun CONDUCT, actions, demeanour, manners, ways, activity, functioning, performance, operation; *N. Amer.* deportment; *formal* comportment.

behold verb SEE, look at, gaze at, stare at, contemplate, scan, survey, observe, notice, take note of, pay heed to, mark, consider.

being noun ❶ CREATURE, living thing, entity, animal, person, individual, human, mortal. ❷ EXISTENCE, life, living, animation, actuality, reality. ❸ ESSENCE, spirit, soul, nature, substance; *Philosophy* quiddity.

belated adjective LATE, overdue, delayed, unpunctual, tardy, behind time, behindhand.
– OPPOSITES early.

belief noun ❶ OPINION, judgement, view, thought, feeling, conviction, way of thinking, theory, notion, impression. ❷ TRUST, faith, credence, reliance, assurance, certainty, confidence, security, sureness. ❸ FAITH, creed, credo, doctrine, dogma, persuasion, conviction, tenet, teaching, ideology.
– OPPOSITES doubt.

believe verb ❶ ACCEPT, be convinced by, trust, subscribe to, rely on, swear to; *informal* swallow, buy, fall for, take as gospel. ❷ THINK, hold, suppose, reckon, be of the opinion, assume, presume, imagine, consider, conjecture, guess, hypothesize, theorize, maintain, understand, surmise, postulate.
– OPPOSITES disbelieve.

believer noun ADHERENT, devotee, follower, supporter, disciple.
– OPPOSITES sceptic.

belittle noun DISPARAGE, decry, slight, depreciate, deprecate, make light of, underestimate, underrate, undervalue, detract from, denigrate, downgrade, minimize, criticize, scoff at, sneer at.
– OPPOSITES praise.

belligerent adjective ❶ AGGRESSIVE, argumentative, pugnacious, combative, antagonistic, confrontational, disputatious, bellicose, provocative, militant, quarrelsome, hot-tempered, quick-tempered, irascible, captious. ❷ **belligerent nations:** WARRING, at war, hostile, battling, combatant, contending, militant, warmongering, warlike, martial.
– OPPOSITES peaceable.

belong verb ❶ **belong to someone:** BE OWNED BY, be the property of, be held by. ❷ **belong to a society:** BE A MEMBER OF, be part of, be one of, be connected with, be associated with, be affiliated to, be allied to, be included in, be an adherent of. ❸ **the book belongs on the shelf:** HAVE A PLACE, be supposed to be. ❹ BE AT HOME, be suited, be welcome, fit in, be accepted.

belongings plural noun PROPERTY, possessions, things, effects, goods, chattels, paraphernalia, appurtenances, accoutrements, impedimenta; *informal* stuff, gear, junk.

beloved adjective LOVED, adored, dear, dearest, cherished, worshipped, treasured, prized, precious, sweet, idolized, darling.
– OPPOSITES hated.
▶ **noun** SWEETHEART, lover, love, girlfriend, boyfriend, inamorata, inamorato; *archaic* paramour.
■ **beloved of** POPULAR WITH, liked by, valued by, esteemed by.

belt noun ❶ GIRDLE, sash, waistband, band, cummerbund, girth; *poetic/literary* cincture. ❷ STRIP, stretch, band, stripe, streak, bar, region, zone, area, district, tract, extent.
▶ **verb** HIT, strike, beat, thump, cuff; *informal* whack, wallop. *See also* HIT (1).

bemused adjective BEWILDERED, dazed, confused, stunned, muddled, puzzled, perplexed, baffled, befuddled, stupefied, amazed, astounded, astonished, overwhelmed, disconcerted.

bend verb ❶ CURVE, crook, make crooked, arch, bow, twist, flex, warp, fold, contort, mould, shape. ❷ **the road bends:** TURN, curve, twist, curl, veer, swerve, loop, diverge, deviate, wind, coil, spiral, incurvate. ❸ **bend over:** STOOP, lean, crouch, bow, hunch, duck. ❹ **bend someone to one's will:** CONTROL, influence, subdue, sway, compel, force, mould, direct, persuade, subjugate.
– OPPOSITES straighten.
▶ **noun** CURVE, corner, turn, twist, arc, angle, loop, coil, spiral, crook, swerve, deflection, deviation, zigzag, dog-leg.
– OPPOSITES straight.

beneath preposition ❶ BELOW, under, underneath, lower than. ❷ INFERIOR TO, lower than, subservient to, subordinate to, secondary to. ❸ UNWORTHY OF, not proper for, degrading to, undignified for, unsuitable for, inappropriate for, unbecoming for.
– OPPOSITES above.

benefactor noun HELPER, supporter, sponsor, patron, backer, donor, promoter, subsidizer, subscriber, well-wisher, sympathizer, philanthropist, fairy godmother; *informal* angel.

beneficial adjective ADVANTAGEOUS, profitable, helpful, useful, worthwhile, valuable, gainful, healthy, rewarding, fruitful, productive, salutary, salubrious, wholesome, improving, serviceable, propitious, promising, favourable, obliging, accommodating, nutritious, nourishing, nurturing.
– OPPOSITES disadvantageous.

beneficiary noun HEIR, heiress, inheritor, recipient, legatee, payee, assignee, receiver, successor.

benefit noun ❶ ADVANTAGE, asset, blessing, boon, plus, plus point; *informal* perk; *formal* perquisite. ❷ **for the benefit of all:** GOOD, well-being, advantage, interest, profit, gain, welfare, convenience, prosperity, good fortune, aid, assistance, help, service, privilege, betterment. ❸ AID, allowance, subsidy, grant, payment, assistance; *Brit. informal* dole.
– OPPOSITES disadvantage, detriment.
▶ **verb** ❶ HELP, profit, be advantageous to, be good for, serve, aid, assist, advance, further, promote, advantage, forward, boost, avail, enhance, improve, better. ❷ GAIN, profit, do well, reap benefits/reward, prosper, put to good use, do well out of; *informal* cash in.
– OPPOSITES damage, suffer.

benevolent adjective KIND, kind-hearted, kindly, generous, warm-hearted, caring, benign, amiable, friendly, beneficent, liberal, magnanimous, bountiful, humane, humanitarian, altruistic, philanthropic, compassionate, sympathetic, considerate, thoughtful, obliging, well meaning, helpful.
– OPPOSITES malicious, unkind.

benign adjective ❶ KINDLY, benevolent, kind-hearted, kind, generous, cordial, genial, amiable, warm, gentle, tolerant, gracious, friendly, accommodating. ❷ **benign circumstances/climate:** FAVOURABLE, auspicious, propitious, opportune, lucky, advantageous, helpful, providential, suitable, appropriate, healthy, wholesome, health-giving, salubrious, pleasant, refreshing, agreeable, mild, temperate, balmy. ❸ **benign tumour:** NON-MALIGNANT, curable, treatable, remediable, innocent, harmless.
– OPPOSITES unfriendly, unfavourable, malignant.

bent adjective ❶ CURVED, crooked, twisted, angled, bowed, arched, warped, distorted, contorted, folded, coiled, buckled, hunched. ❷ CORRUPT, dishonest, fraudulent, criminal, untrustworthy, unprincipled, immoral; *informal* crooked.
– OPPOSITES straight, honest.
▶ **noun** TENDENCY, inclination, predisposition, leaning, talent, gift, flair, ability, aptitude, penchant, predilection, propensity, proclivity.
■ **bent on** DETERMINED, resolved, set, fixated, insistent, resolute, undeterred, obsessed, obsessive.

bequeath verb LEAVE (IN ONE'S WILL), will, make over, pass on, hand on/down, transfer, donate, give, endow on, bestow on, confer on.

bequest noun LEGACY, inheritance, endowment, settlement, estate, heritage.

bereavement noun DEATH IN THE FAMILY, loss, passing (away), demise; *formal* decease.

berserk adjective MAD, crazy, insane, out of one's mind, hysterical, frenzied, crazed, demented, maniacal, manic, frantic, raving, wild, amok, on the rampage; *informal* off the deep end, ape, bananas, bonkers; *Brit. informal* spare.

berth noun ❶ BUNK, bed, cot,

hammock. ❷ **the vessel left its berth**: MOORING, dock, quay, pier.
▶ **verb** DOCK, moor, land, tie up, make fast.
■ **give someone/something a wide berth** AVOID, shun, keep/stay away from, steer clear of, keep at arm's length, dodge, sidestep, skirt.

beseech **verb** IMPLORE, beg, entreat, plead with, appeal to, call on, supplicate, importune, pray to, ask, petition.

besiege **verb** ❶ LAY SIEGE TO, beleaguer, blockade. ❷ **fans besieged his hotel**: SURROUND, mob, crowd round, swarm round, ring, encircle.

best **adjective** FINEST, greatest, top, foremost, leading, pre-eminent, premier, prime, first, supreme, of the highest quality, superlative, par excellence, unrivalled, second to none, without equal, nonpareil, unsurpassed, peerless, matchless, unparalleled, unbeatable, optimum, optimal, ultimate, ideal, perfect; *informal* star, number-one.
– OPPOSITES worst.
▶ **noun** FINEST, top, cream, choice, prime, elite, crème de la crème, flower, jewel in the crown; *informal* pick of the bunch.

bestial **adjective** SAVAGE, animal, brutish, brutal, barbaric, cruel, vicious, violent, inhuman, depraved, degenerate.
– OPPOSITES civilized, humane.

bestow **verb** CONFER, grant, accord, afford, endow with, vest in, present, award.

bet **verb** WAGER, gamble, stake, risk, venture, hazard, chance, put/lay money, speculate; *Brit. informal* have a flutter, have a punt.
▶ **noun** WAGER, gamble, stake, ante; *Brit. informal* flutter, punt.

betray **verb** ❶ **he betrayed his brother**: BREAK ONE'S PROMISE TO, be disloyal to, be unfaithful to, break faith with, play someone false, inform on/against, give away, denounce, sell out, stab in the back; *informal* split on, rat on, peach on, stitch up, do the dirty on, sell down the river, squeal on; *Brit. informal* grass on, shop, sneak on; *N. Amer. informal* finger. ❷ **he betrayed a secret**: REVEAL, disclose, divulge, tell, give away, leak, let slip, let out, blurt out; *informal* blab, spill.

better **adjective** ❶ SUPERIOR, finer, of higher quality; *informal* a cut above, streets ahead, head and shoulders above. ❷ **are you better?** WELL, healthy, cured, healed, recovered, recovering, on the road to recovery; *informal* on the mend.
– OPPOSITES worse, inferior.
▶ **verb** *See* IMPROVE (1, 4).

beware **verb** BE ON YOUR GUARD, watch out, look out, mind out, be alert, be on the lookout, keep your eyes open/peeled, keep an eye out, take care, be careful, be cautious, have a care, watch your step.

bewilder **verb** BAFFLE, mystify, bemuse, perplex, puzzle, confuse, nonplus; *informal* flummox, stump, beat, fox, discombobulate.

bewitch **verb** CAPTIVATE, enchant, entrance, cast/put a spell on, enrapture, charm, beguile, fascinate, enthral.

bias **noun** PREJUDICE, partiality, partisanship, favouritism, unfairness, one-sidedness, tendency, inclination, predilection, bigotry, intolerance, discrimination.
– OPPOSITES impartiality.

▶ verb PREJUDICE, influence, colour, sway, predispose, distort, skew.

biased adjective PREJUDICED, partial, partisan, one-sided, blinkered, jaundiced, distorted, warped, twisted, skewed, bigoted, intolerant, discriminatory.
– OPPOSITES impartial.

bid verb ❶ they bid £1m: OFFER, put up, tender, proffer, propose. ❷ she is bidding for a place: TRY TO GET, go for, make a pitch for, make a bid for.
▶ noun ❶ a bid of £30: OFFER, tender, proposal. ❷ a bid to cut crime: ATTEMPT, effort, endeavour, try; *informal* crack, go, shot, stab.

big adjective ❶ LARGE, great, of considerable size, sizeable, substantial, goodly, tall, high, huge, immense, enormous, colossal, massive, mammoth, broad, vast, prodigious, gigantic, giant, monumental, stupendous, gargantuan, man-size, king-size, outsize, considerable; *informal* whopping, mega, astronomical, humongous; *Brit. informal* ginormous. ❷ a big decision: IMPORTANT, significant, major, momentous, weighty, consequential, far-reaching, key, vital, critical, crucial.
– OPPOSITES small, trivial.

bigot noun DOGMATIST, partisan, sectarian, racist, sexist, chauvinist.

bigoted adjective PREJUDICED, biased, one-sided, sectarian, discriminatory, opinionated, dogmatic, intolerant, narrow-minded, blinkered, racist, sexist, chauvinistic, jingoistic.
– OPPOSITES open-minded.

bill noun ❶ INVOICE, account, statement; *N. Amer.* check; *informal* tab. ❷ a parliamentary bill: DRAFT LAW, proposed legislation, measure.
▶ verb INVOICE, charge, debit, send a statement to.

billow verb ❶ her dress billowed around her: PUFF UP/OUT, balloon (out), swell, fill (out), belly out. ❷ smoke billowed from the chimney: SWIRL, spiral, roll, undulate, eddy, pour, flow.

bind verb ❶ they bound her feet: TIE (UP), fasten (together), hold together, secure, make fast, attach, rope, strap, lash, truss, tether. ❷ he bound up the wound: BANDAGE, dress, cover, wrap, strap up, tape up. ❸ misfortune bound them: UNITE, join, bond, knit.
– OPPOSITES untie, separate.

binding adjective IRREVOCABLE, unalterable, inescapable, unbreakable, contractual, compulsory, obligatory, mandatory.

birth noun ❶ CHILDBIRTH, delivery, nativity, birthing; *dated* confinement. ❷ the birth of science: BEGINNING(S), emergence, genesis, dawn, rise, start. ❸ noble birth: ANCESTRY, lineage, blood, descent, parentage, family, extraction, origin, genealogy, stock.
– OPPOSITES death, demise, end.
■ **give birth to** HAVE, bear, produce, be delivered of, bring into the world; *N. Amer.* birth; *informal* drop.

bisect verb CUT IN HALF, halve, divide/cut/split in two, cross, intersect.

bit noun ❶ PIECE, portion, segment, section, part, fragment, scrap, shred, crumb, grain, speck, snippet, snatch, spot, drop, pinch, dash, soupçon, morsel, iota, jot,

whit, atom, particle, trace, touch, suggestion, hint; *informal* smidgen, tad. ❷ **wait a bit:** MOMENT, minute, second, (little) while; *informal* sec, jiffy; *Brit. informal* mo, tick.
– OPPOSITES lot.
■ **bit by bit** GRADUALLY, little by little, in stages, step by step, piecemeal, slowly.

bite verb ❶ SINK ONE'S TEETH INTO, chew, munch, nibble at, gnaw, crunch, champ, tear at. ❷ **my boots failed to bite:** GRIP, hold, get a purchase. ❸ **the measures begin to bite:** TAKE EFFECT, be effective, work, act, have results.
▶ noun ❶ CHEW, munch, nibble, gnaw, nip. ❷ **a bite to eat:** SNACK, mouthful, refreshments; *informal* a little something. ❸ **a fresh, lemony bite:** PIQUANCY, pungency, spiciness, tang, zest, sharpness, tartness; *informal* kick, punch.

biting adjective *See* COLD (1), SCATHING.

bitter adjective ❶ ACRID, tart, sour, sharp, acid, unsweetened, harsh, biting, acerbic, astringent, pungent, vinegary, acetous, unpleasant. ❷ RESENTFUL, angry, sullen, embittered, sour, sore, rancorous, acerbic, acrimonious, peevish, petulant, spiteful, malicious, vicious, sharp, waspish, piqued, jaundiced, jealous, envious, indignant, morose, begrudging, crabbed. ❸ **bitter experience:** PAINFUL, unhappy, hard, distressing, upsetting, difficult, grievous, sad, tragic, harrowing, heartbreaking, heart-rending, agonizing, sorrowful, distressful, poignant, distasteful, galling, vexatious, troublesome, unpleasant. ❹ **a bitter wind:** COLD, icy, freezing, biting, piercing, penetrating, harsh.
– OPPOSITES sweet, happy, pleasant.

bizarre adjective EXTRAORDINARY, outlandish, eccentric, fantastic, surreal, freakish, grotesque, peculiar, odd, strange, curious, abnormal, weird, unusual, uncommon, outré, unconventional, queer, aberrant, deviant, ludicrous, droll; *informal* offbeat, oddball, way-out, wacky; *Brit. informal, dated* rum.
– OPPOSITES ordinary.

black adjective ❶ JET, ebony, sable, inky, sooty, pitch-black, pitch-dark, dark, dusky, coal-black, funereal, raven; *poetic/literary* Stygian. ❷ **a black heart:** EVIL, wicked, sinful, bad, cruel, devilish, diabolic, depraved, vile, villainous, criminal, corrupt. ❸ **a black day:** DISASTROUS, bad, unfortunate, calamitous, melancholy, depressing, distressing, doleful, dismal, inauspicious, ominous, foreboding, menacing.

blacken verb ❶ DARKEN, make dark, dirty, smudge, stain, soil, begrime, befoul. ❷ DEFAME, slander, libel, sully, malign, impugn, run down, decry, traduce, denigrate, disparage, dishonour, tarnish, taint, stain, besmirch, drag through the mud; *formal* calumniate.

blame verb ❶ ACCUSE, hold responsible, condemn, find guilty, find fault with, criticize, censure, reprimand, reproach, admonish, reprove, reprehend, scold, upbraid, chide, berate, take to task. ❷ **blame it on me:** ATTRIBUTE, ascribe, impute, pin on.

▶ noun ❶ the blame for the accident: RESPONSIBILITY, accountability, guilt, fault, culpability, liability, onus. ❷ CRITICISM, condemnation, censure, accusation, incrimination, stricture, reproach, reproof, recrimination, reprimand, indictment, complaint, berating; *informal* stick, rap; *formal* castigation.

blameless adjective INNOCENT, faultless, guiltless, in the clear, irreproachable, unimpeachable, above reproach, upright, moral, virtuous, unoffending, impeccable, stainless, unblemished.
– OPPOSITES guilty.

bland adjective ❶ TASTELESS, insipid, flavourless, mild. ❷ DULL, boring, uninspired, uninspiring, unoriginal, unexciting, tedious, nondescript, trite, vapid, mediocre, humdrum, weak. ❸ a bland manner: SUAVE, smooth, urbane, genial, cordial, gracious, courteous, affable, amiable, congenial, agreeable, soothing.
– OPPOSITES tangy, interesting, emotional.

blank adjective ❶ BARE, plain, clean, unmarked, empty, vacant, clear, void, unfilled, spotless. ❷ a blank face: EXPRESSIONLESS, inscrutable, impassive, unresponsive, deadpan, poker-faced, indifferent, vacant, empty, uncomprehending, vacuous, glazed, emotionless, uninterested. ❸ my mind went blank: EMPTY, vacant, at a loss, nonplussed, confused, baffled, bewildered, lost, dumbfounded, uncomprehending, puzzled, perplexed.
– OPPOSITES full, expressive.

▶ noun GAP, void, space, vacancy, emptiness, vacuum, nothingness, vacuity.

blasphemous adjective PROFANE, sacrilegious, irreligious, impious, irreverent, ungodly, godless, sinful, disrespectful, unholy.
– OPPOSITES reverent.

blasphemy noun ❶ SACRILEGE, profanity, impiety, impiousness, irreverence, irreligiousness, profaneness, ungodliness, desecration, unholiness, execration. ❷ OATH, curse, swear word, profanity.

blast noun ❶ GUST, draught, rush, gale, storm, squall, blow. ❷ EXPLOSION, detonation, blowing up, discharge, burst, bang, eruption. ❸ a blast of noise: BURST, roar, blare, din, clamour, boom, clang, uproar.
▶ verb ❶ BLOW UP, blow to pieces, explode, shatter, demolish, burst, ruin. ❷ BOOM, roar, blare, screech, trumpet. ❸ BLIGHT, kill, wither, shrivel, destroy, ruin, wreck, spoil, crush, dash, put an end to, mar, annihilate, frustrate. ❹ CRITICIZE, rebuke, attack, shout at, rail at, reprimand, upbraid, berate; *formal* castigate.

blatant adjective FLAGRANT, glaring, obvious, unconcealed, undisguised, overt, manifest, brazen, shameless, unembarrassed, barefaced, naked, sheer, conspicuous, prominent, obtrusive, apparent, stark, unmistakable, unmitigated, outright, out-and-out.
– OPPOSITES discreet, inconspicuous.

blaze noun ❶ FIRE, conflagration, burning, flame, inferno. ❷ a blaze of light: BEAM, gleam, glitter, shine,

radiance, dazzle, brightness, brilliance, flash, flare.
▶ **verb** ❶ BURN, be on fire, be ablaze, flame, catch fire, flare up, burst into flame. ❷ SHINE, gleam, glimmer, dazzle, beam, flare, flash, glitter.

bleach **verb** FADE, blanch, discolour, turn white/pale, etiolate, decolorize, lighten, whiten, peroxide.

bleak **adjective** ❶ DESOLATE, bare, barren, forbidding, exposed, cold, unwelcoming, unsheltered, waste, desert, windswept, windy, arid, uncultivated, wild, dreary, lonely, grim. ❷ DISMAL, dreary, gloomy, depressing, melancholy, wretched, hopeless, sombre, discouraging, disheartening, unpromising, comfortless, miserable, cheerless, joyless.
– OPPOSITES lush, promising.

bleary **adjective** BLURRED, blurry, dim, unclear, indistinct, fuzzy, cloudy, clouded, foggy, misty, hazy, filmy, smeary, obscured, fogged, murky, watery, rheumy.
– OPPOSITES clear.

blemish **noun** DEFECT, stain, flaw, fault, disfigurement, imperfection, deformity, ugliness, blot, mark, smear, blotch, crack, chip, taint.
▶ **verb** SPOIL, mar, damage, injure, flaw, mark, stain, taint, impair, disfigure, discolour, tarnish, blot, deface, sully, besmirch.

blend **verb** ❶ MIX, combine, intermix, mingle, amalgamate, unite, commix, commingle, merge, compound, fuse, coalesce, integrate, homogenize, synthesize, meld, alloy; *technical* admix. ❷ HARMONIZE, complement, fit, suit, go with.
▶ **noun** MIXTURE, mix, combination, amalgam, compound, fusion, union, amalgamation, synthesis, composite, alloy, melange, concoction.

bless **verb** ❶ SANCTIFY, consecrate, hallow, dedicate, anoint, make sacred. ❷ **bless God's name:** GLORIFY, extol, praise, exalt, adore; *formal* laud.
– OPPOSITES curse.
■ **blessed with** ENDOWED WITH, favoured with, having, lucky to have.

blessed **adjective** ❶ SACRED, holy, divine, venerated, consecrated, hallowed, sanctified, beatified, revered. ❷ HAPPY, fortunate, blissful, lucky, favoured, joyful, joyous, glad, cheerful, contented; *poetic/literary* blithe. ❸ WONDERFUL, marvellous, welcome, longed for.
– OPPOSITES cursed, wretched.

blessing **noun** ❶ BENEDICTION, consecration, dedication, prayer, grace, thanksgiving, commendation, invocation. ❷ **he gave the project his blessing:** APPROVAL, permission, consent, sanction, backing, endorsement, assent, support, concurrence, agreement, encouragement, approbation; *informal* go-ahead, the green light. ❸ GODSEND, boon, gift, favour, benefit, advantage, asset, comfort, convenience, help, bit of luck.
– OPPOSITES veto.

blight **noun** ❶ DISEASE, plague, pestilence, fungus, infestation, canker, mildew. ❷ AFFLICTION, misfortune, plague, disaster, calamity, trouble, ruin, catastrophe, curse, bane, scourge, tribulation, woe.
▶ **verb** RUIN, destroy, spoil, shrivel, wither, crush, blast, mar.

blind **adjective** ❶ SIGHTLESS,

unseeing, visually impaired, visionless, partially sighted, purblind. ❷ OBTUSE, blinkered, imperceptive, unaware, insensible, insensitive, unseeing, heedless, careless, unobservant, oblivious, indifferent, neglectful, slow, slow-witted, dense, stupid. ❸ **love is blind**: UNCRITICAL, unthinking, unreasoning, undiscerning, unreasoned, irrational, indiscriminate, injudicious, partial, prejudiced, biased.

▶ **verb** ❶ MAKE BLIND, deprive of sight, blinker, blindfold. ❷ DAZZLE, deceive, delude, beguile, infatuate, confuse, bewilder, hoodwink; *informal* pull the wool over someone's eyes.

▶ **noun** ❶ SHUTTER, shade, curtain, screen. ❷ COVER, pretext, camouflage, screen, smokescreen, front, facade, disguise, cloak, mask, masquerade, feint, pretence.

bliss **noun** JOY, ecstasy, delight, rapture, euphoria, elation, happiness, pleasure, gladness, blessedness, beatitude, heaven, paradise, seventh heaven.
– OPPOSITES misery.

bloated **adjective** SWOLLEN, distended, puffy, puffed up, inflated, enlarged, expanded, dilated.

blob **noun** DROP, droplet, globule, dollop, gobbet, bubble, ball, bead, daub, blotch, dab, spot, splash, blot, smudge, smear; *informal* glob.

block **verb** ❶ CLOG, choke, jam, close, obstruct, constrict, stop up, plug, dam, bung up, barricade, bar. ❷ HINDER, prevent, obstruct, hamper, impede, bar, frustrate, thwart, check, resist, deter, oppose, arrest, stop, halt, scotch, stonewall.

▶ **noun** ❶ BLOCKADE, barrier, barricade, obstacle, bar, hindrance, impediment, obstruction, deterrent, check, stumbling block, difficulty, drawback, hitch. ❷ **a block of soap**: BAR, piece, chunk, hunk, cake, lump, mass, slab, ingot, brick. ❸ **a block of seats**: GROUP, set, batch, section, quantity.

blockage **noun** OBSTRUCTION, congestion, constriction, stoppage, occlusion, block, impediment, jam, bottleneck.

blood **noun** ❶ GORE, vital fluid; *poetic/literary* lifeblood, ichor. ❷ ANCESTRY, lineage, family, descent, birth, extraction, pedigree, origin, genealogy, inheritance, stock, race, kinship. ❸ **his blood was up**: TEMPER, spirit, feeling, temperament, nature, disposition, humour.

blood-curdling **adjective** TERRIFYING, horrifying, spine-chilling, chilling, frightening, fearful, dreadful, terrible, horrendous, horrific, appalling, frightful.

bloodshed **noun** KILLING, carnage, slaughter, murder, massacre, butchery, bloodletting, bloodbath; *poetic/literary* slaying.

bloodthirsty **adjective** SAVAGE, cruel, murderous, ferocious, homicidal, vicious, brutal, ruthless, barbaric, barbarous, inhuman, sadistic, bloody, slaughterous, violent, warlike, bellicose; *archaic* sanguinary.

bloody **adjective** ❶ BLEEDING, bloodstained, blood-soaked, blood-spattered, unstaunched, raw. ❷ **a bloody battle**: SAVAGE, fierce, gory, cruel, slaughterous; *archaic* sanguinary.

bloom noun ❶ BLOSSOM, flower, floret. ❷ FRESHNESS, radiance, lustre, glow, sheen, flush, perfection, blush, beauty. ❸ PERFECTION, prime, heyday, vigour, strength, flourishing.
▶ verb ❶ FLOWER, blossom, burgeon, bud. ❷ FLOURISH, prosper, thrive, be healthy, be happy, do well.

blot noun ❶ SPOT, smudge, speck, blotch, stain, mark, dot, patch, blob, smear; *Brit. informal* splodge. ❷ BLEMISH, imperfection, eyesore, defect, stain, fault, flaw, taint, ugliness.
▶ verb MARK, stain, dot, speckle, smudge, spoil, blotch, spot, spatter, bespatter, disfigure; *poetic/literary* besmirch.
■ **blot out** OBLITERATE, erase, efface, wipe out, delete, expunge, destroy, obscure, conceal, darken, dim, shadow.

blotchy adjective SPOTTED, speckled, blotted, discoloured, patchy, smudged, uneven, streaked, stained, blotched, spattered.

blow[1] noun WIND, gale, breeze, blast, gust, storm, tempest.
▶ verb ❶ PUFF, blast, gust, flurry, bluster. ❷ WAFT, flutter, buffet, whirl, whisk, sweep, drive, carry, transport, convey. ❸ BREATHE, breathe out, exhale, puff, pant, gasp, whistle. ❹ **blow a trumpet**: SOUND, play, blare, toot, blast.
■ **blow over** SUBSIDE, die down, pass, cease, settle, end, vanish. **blow up** ❶ EXPLODE, shatter, burst, detonate, go off, blast, erupt. ❷ INFLATE, pump up, expand, swell, distend, puff up. ❸ ENLARGE, magnify, heighten, exaggerate, overstate, embroider, colour, improve on. ❹ LOSE ONE'S TEMPER, rage, fume, erupt, go wild; *informal* blow one's top, hit the roof, fly off the handle.

blow[2] noun ❶ HIT, bang, knock, stroke, slap, smack, punch, buffet, rap, impact, jolt; *informal* whack, wallop, clout, bash, belt, biff, thwack. ❷ AFFLICTION, misfortune, shock, upset, disaster, calamity, catastrophe, grief, disappointment, setback, reversal, bombshell.

blueprint noun DESIGN, plan, draft, prototype, model, pattern, scheme, sketch, diagram, outline, layout, representation.

blues plural noun DEPRESSION, despondency, gloom, gloominess, dejection, sadness, melancholy, moroseness, downheartedness, glumness, low spirits, discouragement, despair; *informal* the dumps.

bluff[1] verb TRICK, deceive, mislead, hoodwink, hoax, take in, dupe, delude, fool, sham, feign, fake, lie; *poetic/literary* cozen.
▶ noun BLUSTER, deceit, deception, trickery, fraud, fake, front, facade, pretence, sham, subterfuge, humbug.

bluff[2] adjective BLUNT, straightforward, frank, candid, outspoken, direct, hearty, rough.

blunder verb ❶ MAKE A MISTAKE, slip, err, be in error, miscalculate, misjudge, mismanage, bungle; *informal* slip up, screw up, botch, blow it, put one's foot in it. ❷ STUMBLE, stagger, lurch, flounder, be clumsy.
▶ noun ERROR, fault, mistake, slip, miscalculation, misjudgement, false/wrong move, faux pas,

oversight, inaccuracy, gaffe; *informal* slip-up, boo-boo, howler, clanger; *Brit. informal* boob, cock-up.

blunt adjective ❶ DULL, edgeless, unsharpened, unpointed, rounded. ❷ DIRECT, frank, straightforward, candid, forthright, bluff, outspoken, plain-spoken, unceremonious, undiplomatic, tactless, rude, brusque, curt, abrupt, insensitive; *informal* upfront.
– OPPOSITES sharp.
▶ verb DULL, take the edge off, deaden, weaken, dampen, allay, abate, lessen, appease, impair.

blur verb SMEAR, besmear, smudge, mist, cloud, fog, befog, bedim, blear, becloud, obscure, mask.

blurred adjective INDISTINCT, blurry, hazy, misty, cloudy, foggy, fuzzy, vague, unfocussed, unclear, obscure, ill-defined, nebulous, dim, faint, smeary, smudged.
– OPPOSITES clear.

blurt
■ **blurt out** SAY, utter, let slip, blab, disclose, reveal, let out, divulge, tell, babble, exclaim; *informal* spill the beans, let the cat out of the bag, give the game away.

blush verb REDDEN, go red/pink, flush, colour, crimson, glow, be ashamed, be embarrassed.

bluster verb ❶ BLOW, storm, rage, blast, gust, roar. ❷ BOAST, bluff, brag, swagger, show off, vaunt, lord it, hector, bully, domineer, threaten, rant, harangue, be overbearing; *informal* throw one's weight about.
▶ noun BOASTING, bravado, bluff, bombast, bragging, braggadocio, hectoring, domineering, swagger.

blustery adjective STORMY, windy, gusty, squally, wild, tempestuous, violent.
– OPPOSITES calm.

board noun ❶ PLANK, beam, panel, slat, timber, sheet, block. ❷ FOOD, meals, sustenance, provisions, keep. ❸ PANEL, committee, council, directorate.
▶ verb ❶ GET ON, get aboard/on board, enter, embark, mount. ❷ LODGE, stay, live, room, billet.

boast verb ❶ BRAG, swank, crow, swagger, vaunt, show off, exaggerate, bluster, blow one's own trumpet, pat oneself on the back; *informal* talk big. ❷ POSSESS, have, own, pride oneself on, take pride in, enjoy, benefit from, exhibit, display.
▶ noun ❶ BRAG, self-praise, vaunt, overstatement; *informal* swank. ❷ PRIDE, treasure, joy, gem; *informal* pride and joy, apple of someone's eye.

boastful adjective CONCEITED, bragging, vain, arrogant, cocky, egotistical, proud, swaggering, swollen-headed, blustering, vaunting, braggart, overbearing; *informal* swanky, big-headed; *poetic/literary* vainglorious.
– OPPOSITES modest.

bob verb BOUNCE, dip, jump, nod, leap, hop, jerk, jolt, quiver, wobble, toss, shake, oscillate.

bodily adjective CORPOREAL, physical, carnal, corporal, fleshly, material, substantial, tangible, incarnate.

body noun ❶ FIGURE, frame, form, physique, shape, build, anatomy, skeleton, trunk, torso. ❷ CORPSE, carcass, remains, relics, mummy; *Medicine* cadaver; *informal* stiff. ❸ MAIN PART, hub, core, bulk, majority, preponderance. ❹ SET, group, band, party, company, crowd, number, assembly, association. ❺ ACCUMULATION, collection, quantity, mass, corpus.

bog noun MARSH, swamp, marshland, fen, quagmire, morass, mire, slough, mud.
■ **bog down** MIRE, stick, hamper, hinder, obstruct, impede, delay, stall, detain, entangle, ensnare, embroil, swamp, overwhelm.

bogus adjective COUNTERFEIT, fake, sham, false, spurious, forged, fraudulent, artificial, pretended, pretend, pseudo, imitation, mock, inauthentic, suppositious, soi-disant; *informal* phoney.
– OPPOSITES genuine.

bohemian adjective UNCONVENTIONAL, eccentric, unorthodox, nonconformist, original, avant-garde, artistic, alternative, exotic, bizarre; *informal* offbeat, way-out, oddball, arty.

boil verb ❶ BUBBLE, seethe, simmer, stew, heat, cook, effervesce, foam, fizz, steam. ❷ RAGE, fume, seethe, storm, rant, rave, fulminate, flare up.

boisterous adjective ❶ LIVELY, bouncy, playful, exuberant, frisky, romping, unruly, disorderly, rough, wild, irrepressible, undisciplined, spirited, animated, obstreperous, riotous, rollicking, uproarious, rowdy, noisy; *Brit. informal* rumbustious. ❷ ROUGH, choppy, stormy, wild, squally, breezy, turbulent, tempestuous, raging, gusty, blustery.
– OPPOSITES restrained, calm.

bold adjective ❶ DARING, brave, adventurous, dauntless, unafraid, courageous, plucky, intrepid, audacious, fearless, valiant, gallant, hardy, heroic, valorous, undaunted, confident, venturesome, enterprising, daredevil, reckless, resolute. ❷ FORWARD, audacious, presumptuous, impudent, pert, impertinent, brazen, shameless, immodest, insolent, brash, cheeky, rude, barefaced, blatant, unashamed; *informal* saucy. ❸ STRIKING, eye-catching, prominent, pronounced, conspicuous, noticeable, emphatic, obvious, vivid, bright, showy, flashy, strong, distinct, marked.
– OPPOSITES timid, modest, faint, subdued.

bolster noun CUSHION, pillow, support, prop, stay, rest.
▶ **verb** SUPPORT, prop up, shore up, hold up, reinforce, buttress, strengthen, boost, maintain, build up, aid, assist, augment.

bolt noun ❶ BAR, latch, lock, catch, fastening, pin, peg, rivet, rod. ❷ **a bolt of lightning:** FLASH, streak, flare, shaft, burst. ❸ ARROW, dart, missile, projectile, shaft. ❹ RUN, dash, sprint, dart, rush, bound, escape.
▶ **verb** ❶ BAR, lock, fasten, secure, rivet, pin, nail, clamp. ❷ RUN, dash, sprint, dart, rush, hurtle, hurry, fly, flee, run for it, escape, abscond; *Brit. informal* scarper, do a bunk. ❸ **bolt one's food:** GOBBLE, guzzle, wolf, stuff, gulp, cram, devour.

bombard verb ❶ SHELL, bomb, blitz, strafe, blast, pound, fire at, attack, assault, assail, batter. ❷ BADGER, pester, harass, bother, hound, plague, besiege, beset, assail, importune, belabour.

bombardment noun ASSAULT, attack, bombing, shelling, strafing, blitz, air raid, cannonade, fusillade, barrage, broadside.

bombastic adjective POMPOUS, pretentious, grandiose, grandiloquent, turgid, verbose, ranting, extravagant, magniloquent, blustering, ostentatious, affected, inflated, periphrastic.

bonanza noun WINDFALL, godsend, bonus, boom, plenty, cornucopia, surplus, amplitude, sufficiency.

bond noun ❶ CHAIN, fetter, rope, cord, shackle, manacle, tie, restraint, restriction, limitation, harness, straitjacket. ❷ LINK, connection, tie, attachment, affinity, union, relation, relationship, closeness, intimacy, nexus, ligature. ❸ CONTRACT, compact, agreement, deal, bargain, covenant, treaty, pledge, promise, guarantee, word, transaction, obligation.
▶ **verb** UNITE, join, bind, connect, link, attach, fasten, secure, stick, glue, fuse, weld, blend, merge.

bondage noun SLAVERY, servitude, enslavement, subjection, captivity, oppression; *historical* serfdom, vassalage, thraldom.
– OPPOSITES freedom.

bonus noun ❶ GAIN, advantage, extra, plus, benefit, boon. ❷ GIFT, gratuity, tip, present, bounty, reward, commission, honorarium; *informal* perk.

bony adjective THIN, skinny, scrawny, angular, lean, skeletal, emaciated, cadaverous, gaunt, raw-boned.
– OPPOSITES plump.

book noun VOLUME, tome, work, title, publication, paperback, hardback, folio, edition, copy.
▶ **verb** RESERVE, engage, charter, secure, bag, order, sign up, arrange, organize, schedule, programme.

bookish adjective STUDIOUS, scholarly, scholastic, learned, erudite, highbrow, bluestocking, intellectual, academic, literary, pedantic, impractical; *informal* brainy, egghead.

booklet noun LEAFLET, pamphlet, brochure, notebook.

boom noun ❶ CRASH, bang, report, explosion, blast, rumble, roar, thunder, reverberation. ❷ BOOST, surge, increase, upturn, improvement, growth, expansion, spurt, upsurge, success, bonanza, prosperity, advance, popularity, development.
– OPPOSITES decline.
▶ **verb** RESOUND, reverberate, rumble, roar, thunder, bang, blast.

boorish adjective RUDE, crude, loutish, churlish, unrefined, coarse, ill-mannered, impolite, uncouth, gross, oafish, uncultured, philistine, unsophisticated, vulgar, ignorant, indelicate, insensitive; *Brit. informal* yobbish.
– OPPOSITES refined.

boost verb ❶ LIFT, raise, push, thrust, elevate, support, hoist, heave, shove. ❷ ENCOURAGE, support, uplift, increase, raise, heighten, promote, further, advance, improve, foster, assist, expand, enlarge, develop, facilitate, sustain; *informal* hike up, jack up.
▶ **noun** ❶ PUSH, shove, lift, thrust, helping hand. ❷ IMPETUS, impulse, encouragement, support, increase, expansion, rise,

improvement, advance, stimulus; *informal* shot in the arm.

boot verb KICK, knock, punt.
■ **boot out** THROW OUT, kick out, dismiss, eject, expel, oust; *informal* sack.

booth noun ❶ STALL, stand, kiosk, counter. ❷ CUBICLE, compartment, enclosure, hut, carrel.

booty noun LOOT, plunder, haul, spoils, gains, prizes, profits, takings, pickings, winnings; *informal* swag, boodle, the goods.

bordello noun BROTHEL, whorehouse; *Brit. informal* knocking shop; *archaic* house of ill repute, bawdy house.

border noun ❶ EDGE, perimeter, verge, boundary, limit, margin, periphery, brink, fringe, hem, brim, rim, skirt, surround. ❷ FRONTIER, boundary, borderline, limit.
▶ verb ❶ BE NEXT/ADJACENT TO, be close to, neighbour, adjoin, abut, touch, join, connect, edge, skirt, bound. ❷ EDGE, fringe, hem, trim, bind, decorate, rim.
■ **border on** VERGE ON, approach, come close to, approximate, be near/similar to, resemble.

bore[1] verb PIERCE, penetrate, drill, puncture, perforate, burrow, tap, tunnel, mine, dig out, sink.

bore[2] verb BE TEDIOUS TO, weary, tire, fatigue, exhaust, depress, jade, pall on, send to sleep, leave cold, bore to tears, bore to death; *informal* turn off.
– OPPOSITES interest, amuse.

boring adjective TEDIOUS, dull, uninteresting, uninspiring, unexciting, unstimulating, monotonous, unvaried, repetitive, dreary, humdrum, commonplace, flat, lacklustre, dry, dry as dust, stale, soporific, dead, soul-destroying, tiring, tiresome, wearisome; *informal* deadly.
– OPPOSITES interesting, amusing.

borrow verb ❶ BE LENT, ask for the loan of, beg, take as a loan, have temporarily, lease, hire; *informal* cadge, scrounge, bum; *N. Amer. informal* mooch. ❷ COPY, plagiarize, take, imitate, adopt, appropriate, commandeer, steal, pirate, purloin, help oneself to; *informal* filch, grab; *Brit. informal* nick, pinch.
– OPPOSITES lend.

boss noun HEAD, chief, leader, supervisor, manager, director, employer, superintendent, foreman, overseer, controller, master; *informal* numero uno; *Brit. informal* gaffer, governor; *N. Amer. informal* head honcho.
▶ verb ORDER ABOUT/AROUND, give orders/commands to, control, bully, push around, domineer, dominate; *informal* throw one's weight about.

bossy adjective DOMINEERING, overbearing, dictatorial, high-handed, authoritarian, autocratic, tyrannical, despotic, assertive, pushy, imperious, oppressive, bullying, lordly, officious, hectoring.
– OPPOSITES submissive.

botch verb BUNGLE, make a mess of, do badly, spoil, muff, mismanage, fumble; *informal* mess/screw up, make a hash of; *Brit. informal* cock up.

bother verb ❶ **don't bother him:** DISTURB, trouble, worry, pester, harass, annoy, upset, irritate, vex, inconvenience, plague, torment, nag, molest; *informal* hassle, get in

someone's hair. ❷ **bother oneself with:** CONCERN/TROUBLE ONESELF, take the time, make the effort, take the trouble, go to the trouble, inconvenience oneself. ❸ **it bothers me:** TROUBLE, worry, concern, distress, perturb, disconcert.
▶ **noun** ❶ NUISANCE, annoyance, irritation, pest, trouble, worry, vexation. ❷ TROUBLE, disturbance, commotion, disorder, uproar, fighting, violence, furore, brouhaha.

bottle **noun** FLASK, container, carafe, pitcher, decanter, flagon, phial, magnum, jeroboam, carboy, demijohn.
■ **bottle up** *see* SUPPRESS (2).

bottleneck **noun** NARROWING, constriction, obstruction, congestion, blockage, jam, hold-up.

bottom **noun** ❶ BASE, foundation, basis, support, substructure, pedestal, substratum, underpinning. ❷ LOWEST POINT, foot, base, nadir. ❸ UNDERNEATH, underside, lower side, belly. ❹ BUTTOCKS, rear end, rear, seat, rump; *informal* backside, behind; *Brit. informal* bum, arse, jacksie; *N. Amer. informal* butt, fanny; *humorous* posterior.
– OPPOSITES top, surface.
▶ **adjective** LOWEST, deepest, least, last, minimum.

bottomless **adjective** ❶ DEEP, immeasurable, fathomless, unfathomable, unplumbable. ❷ UNLIMITED, inexhaustible, infinite, boundless.

bounce **verb** JUMP, leap, spring, bob, rebound, skip, recoil, ricochet, jounce.
▶ **noun** SPRINGINESS, spring, elasticity, give, resilience.

bound[1] **adjective** ❶ **she's bound to win:** CERTAIN, sure, definite, very likely, fated, predestined. ❷ **bound by the rules:** OBLIGATED, obliged, required, forced, compelled, constrained, duty-bound. ❸ **the bound prisoners:** TIED, tied up, roped, tethered, fettered, secured.
■ **bound for** GOING/TRAVELLING TOWARDS, going to, heading for, making for, off to.

bound[2] **verb** LEAP, jump, spring, skip, hop, vault, bounce, hurdle, bob, gambol, romp, prance, caper.

boundary **noun** ❶ FRONTIER, border, limit, edge, dividing line, perimeter, verge, margin, threshold, bounds, periphery, fringe, borderline, brink, extremity. ❷ **the boundaries of knowledge:** BOUNDS, borders, limits, outer limits, extremities.

boundless **adjective** LIMITLESS, unlimited, infinite, endless, unbounded, unending, never-ending, without end, unrestricted, inexhaustible, immeasurable, incalculable, vast, great, immense.
– OPPOSITES limited, restricted.

bountiful **adjective** ABUNDANT, plentiful, ample, superabundant, copious, lavish, profuse, princely; *poetic/literary* plenteous, bounteous.
– OPPOSITES mean, meagre.

bounty **noun** ❶ REWARD, recompense, remuneration, gratuity, tip, premium, bonus. ❷ GENEROSITY, munificence, altruism, largesse, benevolence, kindness, philanthropy.

bouquet **noun** ❶ BUNCH OF FLOWERS, spray, posy, wreath, garland, nosegay, corsage, buttonhole. ❷ SMELL, aroma, odour, fragrance, scent, perfume; *poetic/literary* redolence.

bout noun ❶ MATCH, contest, fight, engagement, round, competition, encounter, struggle; *informal* set-to. ❷ a bout of flu: ATTACK, spell, fit, period, paroxysm.

bow verb ❶ CURTSY, incline the head/body, bob, stoop, make obeisance, genuflect, bend the knee, prostrate oneself, kowtow, salaam. ❷ bow to the inevitable: SUBMIT, yield, give in, surrender, accept, capitulate, comply with, acquiesce in.
■ **bow out** LEAVE, resign, retire, withdraw, step down, give up, pull out, back out; *informal* quit.

bowels plural noun ❶ INTESTINES, entrails, viscera, vitals; *informal* insides, innards, guts. ❷ the bowels of the earth: INTERIOR, depths, inside, core, heart, belly.

bowl[1]
■ **bowl over** ❶ KNOCK DOWN, bring, down, floor, fell. ❷ ASTOUND, amaze, astonish, stagger, dumbfound, stun, surprise; *informal* flabbergast.

bowl[2] noun BASIN, dish, pan, container, vessel.

box[1] noun CONTAINER, receptacle, crate, case, carton, pack, package, chest, trunk, bin, coffer, casket.

box[2] verb FIGHT, spar, punch, thump, cuff, batter, pummel; *informal* belt, sock, clout, whack, slug, slam.

boxer noun FIGHTER, pugilist, sparring partner, prizefighter.

boy noun YOUTH, lad, youngster, stripling, schoolboy; *informal* kid, whippersnapper.

boycott verb ❶ SHUN, ostracize, stay away from, avoid, spurn, reject, eschew, send to Coventry, blacklist, blackball. ❷ BAN, bar, prohibit, embargo, proscribe, blacklist, debar.

brace verb ❶ STRENGTHEN, support, reinforce, shore up, prop up, buttress. ❷ braced his foot against the wall: STEADY, secure, stabilize, make fast. ❸ brace oneself: PREPARE, ready, fortify, tense.

bracing adjective INVIGORATING, refreshing, stimulating, energizing, reviving, restorative, vitalizing, fresh, brisk, crisp.

brag verb BOAST, show off, blow one's own trumpet, crow, sing one's own praises.

brain noun ❶ CEREBRUM, cerebral matter, encephalon; *informal* grey matter. ❷ INTELLIGENCE, intellect, mind, sense, cleverness, wit, understanding, acumen; *informal* nous, savvy.

brainy adjective CLEVER, intelligent, bright, brilliant, gifted; *informal* smart.
– OPPOSITES stupid.

branch noun ❶ BOUGH, limb, stem, twig, shoot, sprig, arm. ❷ DEPARTMENT, division, subdivision, section, subsection, part, wing, office.
▶ verb FORK, divide, diverge, separate, bifurcate, split, subdivide.
■ **branch out** EXTEND, spread out, diversify, expand, proliferate, multiply.

brand noun ❶ MAKE, variety, line, trade name, trademark. ❷ KIND, type, sort, variety, style, stamp, cast.
▶ verb ❶ STAMP, mark, burn,

scorch, sear, tag, identify. ❷ **branded as a thief:** STIGMATIZE, characterize, mark, taint, vilify, disgrace, discredit, denounce.

brandish verb FLOURISH, wave, wield, raise, swing, display, shake, wag, flaunt, show off.

brash adjective BOLD, self-confident, cocky, audacious, assertive, brazen, aggressive, forward, insolent, impudent, bumptious.
– OPPOSITES meek.

bravado noun BLUSTER, swaggering, arrogance, boldness, audacity, bombast, braggadocio.

brave adjective COURAGEOUS, valiant, fearless, intrepid, plucky, unafraid, heroic, bold, daring, resolute, indomitable, audacious, unshrinking, determined, undaunted, lion-hearted, spirited, dauntless, gallant, valorous, stalwart, doughty, stout-hearted, venturesome, game; *informal* gutsy, spunky.
– OPPOSITES cowardly, fearful.

bravery noun COURAGE, courageousness, fearlessness, pluck, pluckiness, intrepidity, boldness, heroism, audacity, daring, nerve, fortitude, resolution, grit, spirit, dauntlessness, mettle, valour, tenacity, doughtiness, hardihood; *informal* guts, spunk; *Brit. informal* bottle.
– OPPOSITES cowardice.

brawl noun FIGHT, scuffle, fracas, rumpus, altercation, clash, free-for-all, tussle, brouhaha, quarrel, wrangle, commotion, uproar, ruckus; *informal* punch-up, scrap; *Law, dated* affray.
▶ verb *see* FIGHT verb (1).

brawny adjective MUSCULAR, powerful, burly, strong, powerfully built, robust, sturdy, strapping, sinewy.
– OPPOSITES scrawny, puny.

brazen adjective BOLD, shameless, unashamed, unabashed, audacious, defiant, brash, forward, pushy, presumptuous, brassy, impudent, insolent, cheeky, immodest, pert; *informal* saucy.
– OPPOSITES reserved, modest.

breach noun ❶ BREAK, rupture, split, opening, crack, gap, hole, fissure, rent, fracture, rift, cleft, aperture, gulf, chasm. ❷ **a breach of confidence:** BREAKING, violation, infringement, contravention, transgression, infraction. ❸ **a breach in diplomatic relations:** BREAKING OFF, severance, estrangement, parting, parting of the ways, rift, split, falling-out, schism, alienation, disaffection, quarrel, discord.
▶ verb ❶ BREAK THROUGH, split, rupture, open up, burst through, make a gap in. ❷ **breach the contract:** BREAK, contravene, violate, infringe, transgress against, defy, disobey, flout.

break verb ❶ SMASH, crack, shatter, split, burst, fracture, fragment, splinter, crash, snap, rend, tear, divide, sever, separate, part, demolish, disintegrate. ❷ **break a law:** VIOLATE, contravene, infringe, breach, disobey, defy, flout, transgress against. ❸ **break for tea:** STOP, take a break, pause, rest, discontinue, give up; *informal* knock off, take five. ❹ **break the record:** BEAT, surpass, outdo, better, exceed, outstrip, top, cap. ❺ **break the news:** TELL, announce, reveal,

impart, disclose, divulge, make public, proclaim.
– OPPOSITES repair, mend, obey.
▶ **noun** ❶ CRACK, hole, gap, opening, chink, split, fissure, tear, rent, gash, rupture, rift, chasm, cleft. ❷ **a break for tea:** INTERVAL, pause, stop, halt, intermission, rest, respite, breathing space, interlude; *informal* breather, let-up, time out. ❸ **a break in diplomatic relations:** BREACH, split, rupture, rift, discontinuation, schism, disaffection, alienation.
■ **break away** LEAVE, break with, separate from, part company with, detach oneself from, secede from. **break down** ❶ **his van broke down** STOP WORKING, give out, go wrong, malfunction; *informal* conk out; *Brit. informal* pack up ❷ *See* ANALYSE. ❸ *See* COLLAPSE verb (3). **break in** *see* INTERRUPT (1). **break off** END, bring to an end, finish, cease, discontinue, call a halt to, suspend. **break out** *see* ESCAPE verb (1). **break up** ❶ *See* DISPERSE. ❷ *See* SEPARATE verb (4).

breakdown noun ❶ STOPPAGE, failure, malfunctioning, seizing up; *informal* conking out. ❷ **the breakdown of the talks:** COLLAPSE, failure, disintegration, foundering, falling through. ❸ **a breakdown of the figures:** ANALYSIS, classification, itemization, categorization, explanation, examination, dissection.

breakthrough noun ADVANCE, step/leap forward, leap, quantum leap, discovery, find, invention, innovation, development, improvement, revolution.

breast noun BUST, bosom, chest, front, thorax; *informal* boob, knocker.

breath noun ❶ INHALATION, pant, gasp, gulp of air, inspiration, exhalation, expiration. ❷ **a breath of air:** PUFF, waft, gust, breeze.

breathe verb ❶ INHALE, EXHALE, respire, puff, pant, gasp, wheeze, gulp. ❷ **breathe his name:** WHISPER, murmur, purr, sigh, say.

breathless adjective OUT OF BREATH, panting, wheezing, wheezy, puffing, gasping, winded, choking.

breathtaking adjective SPECTACULAR, magnificent, impressive, awesome, awe-inspiring, astounding, exciting, astonishing, amazing, thrilling, stunning; *informal* out of this world.

breed verb ❶ REPRODUCE, procreate, multiply, give birth, bring forth young, propagate; *poetic/literary* beget. ❷ **breed resentment:** PRODUCE, bring about, give rise to, create, generate, stir up, engender, make for, foster, arouse, induce, originate, occasion.
▶ **noun** ❶ FAMILY, variety, type, kind, class, strain, stock, line. ❷ STOCK, species, race, lineage, extraction, pedigree.

breeze noun BREATH OF WIND, gentle wind, draught, puff of air, gust, flurry, current of air; *poetic/literary* zephyr.

breezy adjective ❶ WINDY, blowy, blustery, gusty, squally, fresh. ❷ **a breezy manner:** CHEERFUL, jaunty, cheery, light-hearted, carefree, easy-going, casual, airy, blithe.

brevity noun SHORTNESS, briefness, conciseness, concision, terseness, compactness, pithiness, succinctness, economy, curtness, condensation, pointedness.

brew verb ❶ MAKE, prepare, infuse, ferment, mash. ❷ **trouble is brewing**: BE IMMINENT, loom, gather, form, be threatening, be impending, impend. ❸ **they brewed a plot**: PLAN, scheme, hatch, concoct, devise, invent, foment; *informal* cook up.
▶ noun DRINK, beverage, liquor, ale, beer, tea, infusion, mixture, potion.

bribe verb CORRUPT, entice, suborn, get at, buy off, pay off; *informal* grease someone's palm, sweeten, fix, square.
▶ noun INDUCEMENT, enticement, incentive; *informal* backhander, sweetener, graft, kickback.

bridge noun ❶ ARCH, span, overpass, flyover, viaduct. ❷ BOND, link, tie, connection, cord, binding.
▶ verb SPAN, cross, go over, pass over, traverse, extend across, reach across, arch over.

bridle verb ❶ **bridle your anger**: RESTRAIN, curb, check, keep control of, govern, master, subdue. ❷ **she bridled at his insults**: BRISTLE, become/get angry, draw oneself up, feel one's hackles rise, rear up.

brief adjective ❶ **a brief speech**: SHORT, concise, succinct, to the point, terse, economic, abbreviated, pithy, pointed, curt, crisp, condensed, compressed, sparing, thumbnail, epigrammatic. ❷ **a brief life**: SHORT, short-lived, fleeting, momentary, temporary, impermanent, passing, fading, transitory, ephemeral, transient.
– OPPOSITES long.
▶ verb INSTRUCT, inform, direct, guide, advise, enlighten, prepare, prime; *informal* fill in, put in the picture, give someone the low-down.
▶ noun ❶ INFORMATION, advice, instructions, directions, guidance, briefing, preparation, priming, intelligence; *informal* low-down, rundown. ❷ **the barrister's brief**: ARGUMENT, case, proof, defence, evidence, contention, demonstration.

briefly adverb ❶ **speak briefly**: CONCISELY, succinctly, to the point, tersely, sparingly, economically. ❷ **survived briefly**: FLEETINGLY, temporarily, momentarily, ephemerally. ❸ **briefly, the plot is as follows**: IN SHORT, in brief, to cut a long story short, in a word, in a nutshell, in essence.

briefs plural noun UNDERPANTS, pants, Y-fronts, knickers; *Brit.* camiknickers; *N. Amer.* shorts; *informal* panties.

brigand noun BANDIT, outlaw, robber, criminal, thief, marauder, desperado, gangster, pirate, buccaneer, freebooter.

bright adjective ❶ **bright light**: SHINING, brilliant, vivid, intense, blazing, dazzling, beaming, sparkling, glittering, gleaming, radiant, glowing, glistening, shimmering, luminous, lustrous, incandescent. ❷ **bright colours**: VIVID, intense, rich, brilliant, bold, glowing. ❸ **a bright day**: CLEAR, cloudless, unclouded, sunny, pleasant, clement. ❹ **a bright child**: INTELLIGENT, clever, sharp, quick-witted, astute, acute, ingenious, resourceful, accomplished; *informal* brainy, smart. ❺ **a bright future**: PROMISING, optimistic, favourable, hopeful,

auspicious, propitious, encouraging, lucky, golden.
– OPPOSITES dark, dull, stupid.

brighten verb ❶ MAKE BRIGHT/BRIGHTER, light up, lighten, illuminate, irradiate; *poetic/literary* illumine. ❷ CHEER UP, gladden, liven up, enliven, perk up, animate; *informal* buck up, pep up.

brilliant adjective ❶ brilliant light: BRIGHT, shining, intense, radiant, beaming, gleaming, sparkling, dazzling, lustrous. ❷ a brilliant decision: CLEVER, intelligent, astute, masterly, inventive, resourceful, discerning; *informal* smart. ❸ a brilliant film: EXCELLENT, superb, very good, outstanding, exceptional; *Brit. informal* brill, smashing.
– OPPOSITES dull, bad.

brim noun RIM, lip, edge, brink, margin, circumference, perimeter, verge.
▶ verb BE FULL, be filled up, be full to capacity, overflow, run over, well over.

bring verb ❶ FETCH, carry, bear, take, convey, transport, deliver, lead, guide, conduct, usher, escort. ❷ the war brought hardship: CAUSE, create, produce, result in, engender, contribute to, occasion, wreak, effect.
■ **bring about** *see* CAUSE verb (1), CREATE. **bring in** *see* EARN (1). **bring off** *see* ACHIEVE. **bring up** *see* RAISE (6, 8).

brink noun ❶ EDGE, verge, margin, limit, rim, extremity, boundary, fringe. ❷ the brink of disaster: VERGE, edge, threshold, point.

brisk adjective ❶ a brisk pace: QUICK, rapid, fast, swift, speedy, energetic, lively, vigorous, sprightly, spirited. ❷ a brisk manner: ABRUPT, brusque, no-nonsense, sharp, curt, crisp; *informal* snappy. ❸ brisk weather: FRESH, bracing, biting, keen, crisp, invigorating, refreshing, energizing; *informal* nippy.
– OPPOSITES slow, leisurely.

bristle noun HAIR, stubble, whisker, prickle, spine, quill, thorn, barb.
▶ verb GROW ANGRY/INDIGNANT, be irritated, bridle, flare up, draw oneself up, rear up.

brittle adjective ❶ BREAKABLE, hard, crisp, fragile, frail, delicate; *formal* frangible. ❷ a brittle laugh: EDGY, nervous, on edge, tense, stiff; *informal* uptight.
– OPPOSITES flexible, relaxed.

broach verb ❶ PIERCE, puncture, tap, draw off. ❷ INTRODUCE, raise, bring up, mention, suggest, open, put forward, propound.

broad adjective ❶ WIDE, large, extensive, vast, spacious, expansive, sweeping, boundless, ample, capacious, open. ❷ a broad range of subjects: WIDE, wide-ranging, general, comprehensive, inclusive, encyclopedic, all-embracing, universal, unlimited. ❸ a broad outline: GENERAL, non-specific, unspecific, imprecise, vague, loose, sweeping. ❹ broad daylight: FULL, complete, total, clear, open. ❺ a broad hint: CLEAR, obvious, direct, plain, explicit, straightforward, undisguised, unmistakable, unconcealed. ❻ broad humour: COARSE, vulgar, gross, indecent, indelicate, near the bone, improper, ribald, racy; *informal* blue.
– OPPOSITES narrow.

broadcast verb ❶ TRANSMIT, relay, send out, put on the air, beam, televise, telecast. ❷ ANNOUNCE, make public, report, publicize, publish, advertise, proclaim, air, spread, circulate, disseminate, promulgate.
▶ noun PROGRAMME, show, transmission, telecast.

broaden verb ❶ WIDEN, make broader, extend, spread, enlarge. ❷ broaden his knowledge: WIDEN, expand, enlarge, extend, increase, augment, add to, develop, amplify, swell.

broad-minded adjective OPEN-MINDED, liberal, tolerant, unprejudiced, flexible, unbiased, undogmatic, catholic, fair, progressive, freethinking, enlightened, permissive.
– OPPOSITES narrow-minded.

brochure noun BOOKLET, catalogue, prospectus, leaflet, pamphlet, handbill, handout, advertisement.

broke adjective PENNILESS, insolvent, bankrupt, poverty-stricken, impoverished, impecunious, destitute, indigent, ruined; *informal* flat broke, strapped for cash, cleaned out, on one's uppers; *Brit. informal* skint, stony broke.

broken-hearted adjective GRIEF-STRICKEN, desolate, despairing, devastated, inconsolable, miserable, overwhelmed, wretched, forlorn, woeful, crestfallen.

brood noun OFFSPRING, young, family, clutch, nest, litter, children, youngsters.
▶ verb ❶ WORRY, agonize, fret, dwell on, meditate, mull over. ❷ SIT ON, hatch, incubate.

brook[1] noun STREAM, streamlet, channel, rivulet, runnel; *N. English* beck; *Scottish & N. English* burn; *N. Amer. & Austral./NZ* creek.

brook[2] verb TOLERATE, stand, bear, allow.

browbeat verb BULLY, force, coerce, intimidate, compel, badger, hector, harangue, terrorize, tyrannize.

brown adjective ❶ HAZEL, chestnut, nut-brown, brunette, chocolate, coffee, walnut, ochre, sepia, mahogany, russet, umber, burnt sienna, dun, khaki, beige, tan. ❷ TANNED, sunburnt, browned, bronze, bronzed, swarthy.
▶ verb GRILL, toast, sear, seal.

browse verb ❶ LOOK THROUGH, skim, scan, glance at, thumb through, leaf through, peruse. ❷ GRAZE, feed, eat, crop, nibble.

bruise noun CONTUSION, swelling, bump, mark, blemish, welt.
▶ verb CONTUSE, injure, blacken, mark, discolour, make black and blue.

brunt noun IMPACT, full force, burden, shock, thrust, violence, pressure, strain, stress, repercussions, consequences.

brush noun ❶ BROOM, sweeper, besom, whisk. ❷ a brush with the law: ENCOUNTER, clash, confrontation, conflict, skirmish, tussle, fight, engagement.
▶ verb ❶ SWEEP, clean, groom, buff. ❷ his lips brushed her cheek: TOUCH, graze, kiss, glance, contact.
■ **brush aside** *see* DISMISS (1).
brush off *see* REBUFF verb.

brusque adjective ABRUPT, curt,

blunt, short, terse, caustic, gruff, rude, discourteous, impolite.
– OPPOSITES polite.

brutal adjective SAVAGE, cruel, vicious, sadistic, violent, bloodthirsty, ruthless, callous, murderous, heartless, merciless, pitiless, remorseless, inhuman, barbarous, barbaric, ferocious, wild, brutish, bestial.
– OPPOSITES gentle.

brute noun ❶ ANIMAL, beast, creature. ❷ SAVAGE, monster, animal, sadist, barbarian, fiend, devil, lout, oaf, boor; *informal* swine.
▶ adjective CRUDE, rough, mindless, physical, unfeeling.

brutish adjective SAVAGE, brutal, cruel, barbaric, barbarous, crude, loutish, animal, coarse, boorish, mindless, insensitive, beastly, cold-blooded.
– OPPOSITES gentle.

bubble noun GLOBULE, bead, drop, air pocket.
▶ verb FIZZ, foam, froth, gurgle, effervesce, sparkle, boil, simmer, seethe, percolate.

bubbly adjective ❶ FIZZY, foamy, frothy, effervescent, sparkling, sudsy. ❷ VIVACIOUS, lively, animated, sparkling, excited, effervescent, bouncy, ebullient, elated.

bucket noun PAIL, pitcher, can, scuttle.

buckle noun ❶ CLASP, fastener, clip, catch, fastening, hasp. ❷ KINK, warp, distortion, wrinkle, bulge.
▶ verb ❶ FASTEN, hook, secure, do up, strap, tie, clasp, clip. ❷ BEND, twist, contort, warp, crumple, distort.

bud noun SHOOT, sprout.
▶ verb SPROUT, germinate, shoot, burgeon.

budge verb ❶ MOVE, shift, stir, yield, go, proceed. ❷ you won't budge her: PERSUADE, convince, influence, sway, bend.

budget noun FINANCIAL PLAN, estimate, statement, account, allowance, means, resources.
▶ verb ❶ PLAN, allow, set aside, allocate, save. ❷ PLAN, schedule, allocate, ration, apportion.

buff[1] verb POLISH, shine, rub, smooth, burnish.

buff[2] noun FAN, enthusiast, aficionado, devotee, admirer, expert; *informal* freak, nut.

buffer noun BULWARK, fender, bumper, cushion, guard, safeguard, shield, screen, intermediary.

buffet[1] noun CAFE, cafeteria, snack bar, refreshment counter/stall.

buffet[2] verb BATTER, strike, knock against, hit, bang, beat against.

buffoon noun FOOL, idiot, dot, nincompoop; *informal* dope, chump, numbskull, halfwit; *Brit. informal* nitwit.

bug noun ❶ INSECT, flea, mite; *informal* creepy-crawly; *Brit. informal* minibeast. ❷ GERM, virus, bacterium, microbe, micro-organism. ❸ ILLNESS, sickness, disease, infection, disorder, upset, complaint; *Brit. informal* lurgy. ❹ FAULT, flaw, defect, error, imperfection, failing, obstruction; *informal* gremlin.
▶ verb ❶ TAP, wiretap, listen in on, intercept, spy on. ❷ it really bugs me: *see* ANNOY.

build verb CONSTRUCT, make, erect,

put up/together, assemble, set up, manufacture, fabricate, raise, form.
▶ noun PHYSIQUE, body, frame, shape.
■ **build up** *see* INTENSIFY.

building noun STRUCTURE, construction, edifice, pile, erection.

build-up noun GROWTH, increase, expansion, enlargement, accumulation, escalation, development.

bulbous adjective DISTENDED, bulging, swollen, rotund, convex, bloated, spherical, rounded.

bulge verb SWELL, swell out, project, protrude, stick out, balloon, jut out, enlarge, billow, distend, bloat.
▶ noun SWELLING, bump, protuberance, protrusion, lump, knob, projection, prominence, distension.

bulk noun ❶ SIZE, volume, quantity, weight, extent, mass, substance, magnitude, dimensions, amplitude. ❷ MAJORITY, preponderance, greater part, mass, body, generality.

bulky adjective UNWIELDY, awkward, large, big, substantial, massive, immense, voluminous, weighty, ponderous; *informal* hulking.

bulldoze verb ❶ DEMOLISH, flatten, level, raze. ❷ bulldoze his way: FORCE, push, shove, drive, propel.

bulletin noun REPORT, announcement, statement, newsflash, account, message, communiqué, communication, dispatch, notification.

bullish adjective OPTIMISTIC, hopeful, confident, positive, assured, cheerful, sanguine.

bully noun INTIMIDATOR, persecutor, oppressor, browbeater, tyrant, tormentor, bully boy, thug; *informal* tough.
▶ verb INTIMIDATE, coerce, browbeat, oppress, domineer, persecute, torment, pressurize, pressure, terrorize, tyrannize, cow; *informal* push around.

bulwark noun ❶ RAMPART, embankment, fortification, bastion, redoubt, outwork, breastwork. ❷ SUPPORT, defence, guard, protection, safeguard.

bumbling adjective CLUMSY, awkward, blundering, incompetent, bungling, inept, inefficient, stumbling, lumbering, foolish.

bump verb ❶ HIT, bang, strike, knock, jar, crash into, collide with, smash into. *See also* HIT (1). ❷ BOUNCE, jolt, shake, jerk, rattle, jounce.
▶ noun ❶ BANG, crash, thud, thump, knock, smash, collision. ❷ a bump on his head: LUMP, swelling, contusion, injury, protrusion, bulge, projection, protuberance, hump, knob, distension.
■ **bump into** *see* MEET (1). **bump off** *see* KILL (1).

bumpkin noun YOKEL, clodhopper, peasant, rustic, country cousin; *N. Amer. informal* hillbilly, hick, hayseed, rube.

bumptious adjective SELF-IMPORTANT, conceited, arrogant, cocky, full of oneself, overconfident, brash, overbearing, puffed up, self-opinionated, egotistical,

immodest, boastful, presumptuous, pompous, officious, swaggering, forward, pushy; *informal* big-headed.
– OPPOSITES modest.

bumpy adjective ❶ a bumpy road: ROUGH, uneven, rutted, potholed, pitted, lumpy, knobby. ❷ a bumpy flight: JOLTING, jarring, bouncy, jerky, rough.
– OPPOSITES smooth.

bunch noun ❶ COLLECTION, cluster, batch, set, quantity, bundle, heap, sheaf, clump. ❷ BOUQUET, spray, posy, sheaf, corsage, nosegay. ❸ a bunch of people: GROUP, crowd, party, band, gathering, swarm, gang, party, flock, mob, knot, cluster, multitude.
▶ verb ❶ GATHER, cluster, huddle, group, flock, mass, cram, pack, herd, bundle. ❷ cloth bunching up: GATHER, fold, pleat.
– OPPOSITES disperse.

bundle noun BATCH, pile, collection, heap, stack, bunch, parcel, bale, sheaf, mass, quantity, accumulation.
▶ verb ❶ TIE, tie up, wrap, bind, fasten together, pack, parcel, roll, truss. ❷ bundled him outside: PUSH, shove, hurry, hustle, rush, thrust, throw.

bungle verb MAKE A MESS OF, mismanage, spoil, ruin, blunder, muff, mar; *informal* screw up, foul up, mess up, louse up, botch, make a hash of, muck up; *Brit. informal* cock up.

bungling adjective CLUMSY, incompetent, inept, unskilful, blundering, maladroit; *informal* ham-fisted, cack-handed.

buoy noun FLOAT, marker, beacon.

buoyant adjective ❶ FLOATING, afloat, floatable, light. ❷ *See* CHEERFUL (1).

burden noun ❶ LOAD, weight, cargo, freight. ❷ RESPONSIBILITY, duty, obligation, onus, charge, care, worry, anxiety, problem, trouble, difficulty, strain, stress, affliction, weight, trial, tribulation, encumbrance, millstone, cross, albatross.
▶ verb ❶ LOAD, overload, weigh down, encumber, hamper. ❷ TROUBLE, worry, oppress, bother, distress, afflict, torment, strain, tax, overwhelm, saddle, encumber; *informal* land.

burdensome adjective HARD, difficult, onerous, trying, worrying, oppressive, heavy, exacting, weighty, taxing, troublesome.

bureau noun ❶ AGENCY, office, department, service. ❷ DESK, writing desk, writing table.

bureaucracy noun OFFICIALDOM, officials, administration, civil servants, civil service, government, directorate, regulations, paperwork, red tape.

burglar noun HOUSEBREAKER, thief, robber, raider, looter, cat burglar, intruder; *N. Amer. informal* second-story man.

burglary noun HOUSEBREAKING, breaking and entering, breaking in, break-in, forced/forcible entry, theft, robbery.

burial noun INTERMENT, burying, entombment, funeral, obsequies; *formal* exequies.
– OPPOSITES exhumation.

burlesque noun PARODY, caricature, mockery, travesty, imitation, pastiche, satire, lampoon, farce; *informal* send-up, take-off, spoof.

burly adjective WELL BUILT, muscular, brawny, stout, thickset,

stocky, sturdy, big, powerful, strong, strapping, hefty, athletic, tough, husky; *informal* beefy, hulking.
– OPPOSITES puny.

burn verb ❶ BE ON FIRE, be alight, be ablaze, go up, blaze, be aflame, smoulder, flare, flash, glow, smoke, flicker. ❷ SET ON FIRE, set fire to, set alight, ignite, light, kindle, put a match to, incinerate, reduce to ashes, cremate, consume, sear, char, scorch. ❸ **burning to succeed**: LONG, yearn, desire, hunger for/after, lust, pant, wish, want, be consumed with desire; *informal* itch.

burning adjective ❶ ON FIRE, blazing, ablaze, aflame, alight, flaring, glowing, smouldering, ignited, flickering, scorching, incandescent; *poetic/literary* afire. ❷ **a burning sensation**: STINGING, smarting, biting, prickling, irritating, searing, caustic, corrosive, painful. ❸ **a burning desire**: INTENSE, eager, passionate, fervent, ardent, fervid. ❹ **burning issues**: IMPORTANT, crucial, significant, urgent, pressing, critical, compelling, vital, essential, acute, pivotal.

burnish verb POLISH, shine, brighten, rub, buff, buff up, smooth.

burrow noun TUNNEL, hole, hollow, excavation, lair, den, earth, warren, set.
► verb DIG, tunnel, excavate, mine, hollow out, gouge out, scoop out.

burst verb ❶ SPLIT, break open, rupture, crack, shatter, explode, give way, fracture, disintegrate, fragment, fly open. ❷ **burst into the room**: RUSH, thrust, shove, push, dash, run, erupt, surge.

bury verb ❶ INTER, lay to rest, entomb, consign to the grave; *informal* plant. ❷ **buried his head in his hands**: CONCEAL, hide, cover with, submerge, tuck, sink, cup.
– OPPOSITES exhume.

bush noun ❶ SHRUB, thicket, undergrowth, shrubbery. ❷ SCRUB, brush, wilds, backwoods; *Austral./NZ* outback.

bushy adjective THICK, shaggy, dense, tangled, hairy, bristly, fuzzy, luxuriant, unruly, untidy, spreading.

business noun ❶ OCCUPATION, profession, line, career, job, trade, vocation, work, employment, pursuit, métier. ❷ TRADE, commerce, industry, buying and selling, trading, merchandising, trafficking, bargaining, dealing, transactions. ❸ COMPANY, firm, enterprise, corporation, concern, organization, venture, shop, establishment, partnership. ❹ **none of your business**: CONCERN, affair, responsibility, duty, function, task, assignment, obligation, problem. ❺ **a strange business**: AFFAIR, matter, thing, case, set of circumstances, issue.

businesslike adjective ❶ PROFESSIONAL, efficient, organized, methodical, systematic, well ordered, practical, thorough, painstaking, meticulous, correct. ❷ ROUTINE, conventional, unimaginative, prosaic, down-to-earth, workaday.
– OPPOSITES unprofessional, disorganized.

bust[1] noun BREASTS, bosom, chest, torso; *informal* boobs, knockers.

bust[2] verb ❶ BREAK, destroy, wreck, rupture, fracture, crack. ❷ ARREST, capture, catch, seize; *informal* pinch, nab, collar; *Brit. informal* nick.

bustle noun ACTIVITY, flurry, stir, restlessness, movement, hustle, hurly-burly, busyness, commotion, tumult, excitement, agitation, fuss; *informal* to-do.
▶ verb HURRY, rush, dash, scurry, dart, hasten, scramble, fuss, scamper, flutter; *informal* tear.

busy adjective ❶ ACTIVE, industrious, tireless, energetic, hectic, strenuous, full, bustling, exacting; *informal* on the go. ❷ **the doctor's busy:** OCCUPIED, working, engaged, at work, on duty, otherwise engaged; *informal* tied up. ❸ **busy doing something:** ENGAGED IN, occupied in, absorbed in, engrossed in, working at, preoccupied with, toiling at, labouring at, slaving at. ❹ **a busy pattern:** ORNATE, over-elaborate, over-decorated, fussy, cluttered.
– OPPOSITES idle.

busybody noun MEDDLER, interferer, troublemaker, mischief-maker, gossip, scandalmonger, muckraker; *informal* snooper, nosy parker.

butt[1] verb ❶ KNOCK, strike, shove, ram, bump, push, thrust, prod, poke, jab, thump, buffet. ❷ **butt into the conversation:** INTERRUPT, intrude, interfere in; *informal* stick one's nose/oar in.

butt[2] noun **the butt of his jokes:** TARGET, victim, object, subject, scapegoat, dupe.

butt[3] noun ❶ HANDLE, shaft, hilt, haft. ❷ STUB, end, remnant, tail end; *Brit. informal* fag end.

buttocks noun CHEEKS, rump, behind, hindquarters, seat; *Brit.* bottom; *informal* BTM, backside, derrière; *Brit. informal* bum, arse; *N. Amer. informal* butt, fanny; *humorous* posterior, fundament.

buttonhole verb ACCOST, waylay, importune, detain, grab, catch, take aside.

buttress noun SUPPORT, prop, reinforcement, strut, stanchion, pier.
▶ verb STRENGTHEN, support, reinforce, prop up, shore up, brace, underpin, uphold, defend, back up.

buxom adjective BIG-BREASTED, big-bosomed, full-figured, voluptuous, well rounded, Rubenesque, plump, robust, shapely, ample; *informal* busty, well endowed.

buy verb PURCHASE, pay for, get, acquire, obtain, come by, procure, invest in.
– OPPOSITES sell.
▶ noun PURCHASE, acquisition, bargain, deal.
– OPPOSITES sale.

buzz verb HUM, murmur, drone, whirr, whisper; *poetic/literary* susurrate.

bygone adjective PAST, departed, dead, gone, former, previous, one-time, forgotten, lost, old, antiquated, ancient, obsolete, outmoded.

bypass verb ❶ GO ROUND, make a detour round, pass round. ❷ CIRCUMVENT, avoid, evade, get round, pass over, ignore, skirt, sidestep, miss out, go over the head of, short-circuit.

bystander noun ONLOOKER, spectator, eyewitness, witness, watcher, viewer, passer-by.

Cc

cabal noun CLIQUE, faction, coterie, league, confederacy, gang, band, party, ring, set.

cabin noun ❶ HUT, shack, shed, chalet, lodge, shelter, bothy. ❷ BERTH, compartment, stateroom, sleeping quarters, saloon, deckhouse.

cable noun ROPE, cord, wire, line, lead, hawser, mooring line, chain, guy.

cache noun HOARD, store, supply, collection, fund; *informal* stash.

cacophonous adjective DISCORDANT, atonal, dissonant, noisy, harsh, unmusical.
– OPPOSITES harmonious.

cacophony noun DISCORDANCE, dissonance, atonality, noise, racket, row, caterwauling, jangle, tumult, stridency, rasping.

cadaverous adjective CORPSE-LIKE, death-like, gaunt, haggard, drawn, emaciated, skeletal, hollow-eyed, ashen, pale, wan, ghostly.

cadence noun RHYTHM, beat, pulse, tempo, measure, metre, swing, lilt, intonation, inflection, accent, modulation.

cafe noun CAFETERIA, snack bar, buffet, coffee bar/shop/house, tea room/shop, diner, bistro, restaurant, brasserie.

cage noun PEN, enclosure, pound, coop, lock-up, hutch, aviary.
▸ verb *see* CONFINE (1).

cagey adjective GUARDED, secretive, cautious, non-committal, wary, careful, chary, wily.

cajole verb COAX, wheedle, beguile, seduce, persuade, flatter, humour, lure, entice, tempt, inveigle; *informal* sweet-talk, soft-soap, butter up.

cake noun ❶ BUN, gateau, pastry. ❷ BLOCK, bar, slab, piece, lump, cube, mass, loaf, chunk.
▸ verb ❶ HARDEN, solidify, thicken, dry, bake, congeal, coagulate, consolidate. ❷ COVER, coat, plaster, encrust, clog.

calamitous adjective DISASTROUS, catastrophic, devastating, cataclysmic, ruinous, dire, dreadful, terrible, tragic, fatal, wretched, woeful, ghastly, unfortunate.

calamity noun DISASTER, catastrophe, tragedy, misfortune, cataclysm, accident, devastation, misadventure, mischance, mishap, ruin, tribulation, woe.

calculate verb ❶ WORK OUT, estimate, determine, compute, count up, figure out, reckon up, evaluate, total. ❷ ESTIMATE, gauge, judge, measure, weigh up, reckon, rate. ❸ calculated to appeal to children: DESIGN, plan, aim, intend.

calculated adjective *see* DELIBERATE adjective (1).

calculating adjective *see* CRAFTY.

calibre noun ❶ a man of his calibre: QUALITY, worth, stature, distinction, ability, merit, talent, capability, excellence, competence, capacity, endowments, gifts, strengths, scope. ❷ BORE, gauge, diameter, size.

call verb ❶ CRY, cry out, shout, bellow, exclaim, yell, scream, roar, shriek. ❷ **call her tomorrow**: TELEPHONE, phone, call up; *Brit.* ring; *informal* buzz, give someone a buzz/tinkle; *Brit. informal* give someone a ring. ❸ **call at the house**: VISIT, pay a visit/call, call on, stop by; *informal* drop in/by, pop in. ❹ **call a meeting**: convene, summon, assemble, ANNOUNCE, order; *formal* convoke. ❺ **called her Sara**: NAME, christen, baptize, entitle, dub, designate, describe as, label, term. ❻ **call a doctor/taxi**: SEND FOR, summon, ask for, contact, order, fetch, bid. ❼ **call him in the morning**: AWAKEN, wake, arouse, rouse.

▶ **noun** ❶ CRY, shout, exclamation, yell, scream, shriek, roar, bellow. ❷ **a call for unity**: PLEA, request, appeal, order, command, summons. ❸ **there's no call to be rude**: NEED, occasion, reason, cause, justification, grounds, excuse. ❹ **no call for it here**: DEMAND, requirement, request, need, want, requisition.

■ **call for** NEED, require, be grounds for, justify, necessitate, demand, entail. **call off** *see* CANCEL.

call girl noun *see* PROSTITUTE.

calling noun VOCATION, occupation, job, line, line of work, career, profession, métier, business, work, employment, trade, craft, pursuit, province, field.

callous adjective INSENSITIVE, unfeeling, hard, hardened, heartless, hard-hearted, hard-bitten, tough, cold, cool, stony-hearted, cruel, uncaring, unsympathetic, indifferent, unresponsive, dispassionate, unconcerned, unsusceptible, merciless, pitiless, soulless; *informal* hard-nosed, hard-boiled.

–OPPOSITES compassionate.

callow adjective IMMATURE, inexperienced, naive, unsophisticated, innocent, uninitiated, raw, green, young, adolescent; *informal* wet behind the ears.

–OPPOSITES mature, experienced.

calm adjective ❶ COMPOSED, relaxed, collected, cool, controlled, restrained, self-controlled, self-possessed, quiet, tranquil, unruffled, serene, unexcited, unflappable, undisturbed, imperturbable, unemotional, unmoved, impassive, undemonstrative, poised, level-headed, patient, equable, stoical, pacific; *informal* laid-back, together. ❷ **a calm day**: STILL, windless, mild, tranquil, balmy, quiet, peaceful, restful, undisturbed, halcyon.

–OPPOSITES excitable, stormy.

▶ **verb** ❶ SOOTHE, quieten, pacify, hush, tranquillize, mollify, appease, allay, alleviate, assuage. ❷ QUIETEN, settle, settle down, die down, still.

–OPPOSITES agitate.

▶ **noun** ❶ COMPOSURE, coolness, self-control, tranquillity, serenity, quietness, peace, peacefulness, harmony, restfulness, repose. ❷ STILLNESS, tranquillity, serenity, quietness, quietude.

calumny noun SLANDER, libel, defamation, misrepresentation, false accusation, insult, abuse, denigration, vilification, vituperation, aspersions, backbiting, detraction, disparagement, deprecation, revilement, obloquy, smear campaign; *informal* mud-slinging.

camouflage **noun** DISGUISE, mask, screen, cover, protective colouring, cloak, cover-up, front, false front, guise, facade, blind, concealment, masquerade, subterfuge.
▶ **verb** DISGUISE, hide, conceal, mask, screen, cloak, veil, cover, cover up, obscure.

camp[1] **noun** ENCAMPMENT, settlement, campsite, camping ground, tents, bivouac, cantonment.

camp[2] **adjective** EFFEMINATE, effete, mincing, affected, artificial, mannered, posturing, studied.
– OPPOSITES macho.

campaign **noun** ❶ BATTLE, war, offensive, expedition, attack, crusade. ❷ DRIVE, push, operation, plan, promotion, strategy, movement, manoeuvre.
▶ **verb** FIGHT, battle, work, crusade, push, strive, struggle.

cancel **verb** ❶ **cancel a holiday:** CALL OFF, scrap, drop, axe, abandon, stop, discontinue. ❷ **cancel an order:** ANNUL, declare void, invalidate, quash, nullify, set aside, retract, negate, countermand, rescind, revoke, repudiate, abrogate, abolish.
– OPPOSITES confirm.
■ **cancel out** COUNTERBALANCE, offset, counteract, neutralize, redeem.

cancer **noun** MALIGNANT GROWTH, cancerous growth, tumour, malignancy; *technical* carcinoma, sarcoma.

candid **adjective** FRANK, open, honest, truthful, direct, plain-spoken, blunt, straightforward, straight from the shoulder, outspoken, sincere, forthright, no-nonsense, unequivocal, undisguised, bluff, brusque.
– OPPOSITES guarded.

candidate **noun** APPLICANT, contender, nominee, contestant, competitor, runner, entrant, aspirant, possibility.

candour **noun** FRANKNESS, honesty, truthfulness, openness, directness, bluntness, outspokenness, sincerity, forthrightness.

canny **adjective** SHREWD, sharp, astute, discerning, penetrating, clever, perspicacious, judicious, wise, sagacious, circumspect.
– OPPOSITES foolish.

canopy **noun** AWNING, shade, sunshade, cover, tarpaulin.

canvass **verb** ❶ SEEK VOTES, solicit votes, campaign, electioneer, drum up support, persuade, convince. ❷ **canvass people's views:** INVESTIGATE, survey, find out, enquire into, look into, examine, scrutinize, explore, study, analyse, evaluate.
▶ **noun** SURVEY, poll, opinion poll, census, investigation, market research.

canyon **noun** RAVINE, valley, gorge, gully, defile, chasm, gulf, abyss.

capability **noun** ABILITY, capacity, potential, aptitude, faculty, facility, power, skill, skilfulness, competence, efficiency, effectiveness, proficiency, adeptness.

capable adjective ABLE, competent, effective, efficient, proficient, accomplished, talented, gifted, adept, skilful, experienced, practised, expert, masterly, qualified, adequate, clever, intelligent; *informal* smart.
– OPPOSITES incapable, incompetent.
■ **capable of** UP TO, equal to, inclined to, disposed to, liable to, prone to, likely to.

capacity noun ❶ SPACE, room, size, scope, extent, volume, largeness, dimensions, proportions, magnitude, ampleness, amplitude. ❷ ABILITY, capability, aptitude, facility, competence, competency, potential, proficiency, skill, talent, accomplishment, cleverness, intelligence. ❸ in his capacity as teacher: POSITION, role, job, post, office, function, responsibility, appointment, province.

cape[1] noun CLOAK, shawl, wrap, coat, robe, cope.

cape[2] noun HEADLAND, point, promontory, peninsula, neck, tongue.

caper verb FROLIC, romp, skip, gambol, cavort, prance, dance, jig, leap, hop, jump, bound, spring, bounce.

capital noun ❶ FIRST CITY, seat of government, metropolis. ❷ MONEY, funds, finance, cash, wealth, principal, savings, resources, means, assets, reserves, property, wherewithal.
▶ adjective capital letters: UPPER-CASE, block.

capitulate verb SURRENDER, yield, give in/up, back down, submit, concede, throw in the towel/sponge, succumb, cave in, relent, accede, acquiesce.
– OPPOSITES resist.

caprice noun WHIM, impulse, fancy, vagary, notion, fad, quirk.

capricious adjective FICKLE, unpredictable, impulsive, changeable, inconstant, mercurial, whimsical, volatile, erratic, variable, wayward, fitful, quirky, fanciful, uncertain, irregular, unreliable.
– OPPOSITES stable, consistent.

capsize verb OVERTURN, turn over, upset, upend, tip over, knock over, keel over, turn turtle, invert.

capsule noun PILL, tablet, caplet, lozenge; *informal* tab.

captain noun ❶ COMMANDER, master, officer in charge; *informal* skipper. ❷ CHIEF, head, leader, principal; *informal* boss.

caption noun HEADING, title, wording, head, legend, inscription, description.

captious adjective CRITICAL, criticizing, carping, fault-finding, quibbling, cavilling; *informal* nit-picking.
– OPPOSITES forgiving.

captivate verb CHARM, delight, enchant, bewitch, fascinate, dazzle, beguile, entrance, enrapture, attract, hypnotize, mesmerize, enthral, allure, win, infatuate, seduce, ravish, ensnare, steal someone's heart.
– OPPOSITES repel, bore.

captive adjective IMPRISONED, locked up, caged, incarcerated, jailed, confined, detained, taken prisoner, interned, penned up, captured, ensnared, restrained, in captivity, in bondage; *informal* under lock and key.
– OPPOSITES free.

▶ noun PRISONER, detainee, prisoner-of-war, convict, internee, slave; *informal* jailbird, con.

captivity noun IMPRISONMENT, custody, detention, confinement, internment, incarceration, restraint, constraint, committal, bondage, slavery, servitude, enslavement, subjugation, subjection; *historical* thraldom.
– OPPOSITES freedom.

capture verb CATCH, arrest, apprehend, take prisoner, take into custody, seize, trap, take, lay hold of, take captive; *informal* nab, pinch, collar, lift, bag; *Brit. informal* nick.
– OPPOSITES free, liberate.
▶ noun ARREST, apprehension, detention, imprisonment, seizure, trapping.

car noun MOTOR CAR, motor, automobile; *informal* wheels; *N. Amer. informal* auto.

carafe noun FLASK, decanter, jug, pitcher, flagon.

carcass noun ❶ BODY, corpse, remains; *Medicine* cadaver; *informal* stiff. ❷ FRAME, framework, skeleton, remains, structure, shell, hulk.

cardinal adjective FUNDAMENTAL, basic, main, chief, primary, prime, principal, paramount, key, essential.
– OPPOSITES unimportant.

care noun ❶ WORRY, anxiety, sadness, trouble, stress, unease, distress, disquiet, sorrow, anguish, grief, woe, hardship, tribulation, affliction, responsibility, pressure, strain, burdens. ❷ CAREFULNESS, attention, thought, regard, thoroughness, conscientiousness, pains, vigilance, accuracy, precision, meticulousness, fastidiousness, punctiliousness, mindfulness, solicitude, forethought, heed. ❸ in the care of her uncle: CHARGE, supervision, custody, protection, safe keeping, guardianship, control, management, ministration, wardship.
– OPPOSITES happiness, inattention, carelessness.
▶ verb MIND, be concerned, be interested, worry oneself, bother, trouble, have regard.
■ **care for** *see* LOVE verb (1), LOOK AFTER.

career noun PROFESSION, occupation, job, vocation, calling, livelihood, employment, work, métier.

carefree adjective CHEERFUL, light-hearted, happy, nonchalant, unworried, untroubled, cheery, happy-go-lucky, jolly, merry, buoyant, easy-going, relaxed, unconcerned, breezy, jaunty, insouciant, blithe; *informal* upbeat, laid-back.
– OPPOSITES worried, miserable.

careful adjective ❶ be careful: CAUTIOUS, alert, attentive, watchful, aware, vigilant, wary, on one's guard, prudent, heedful, circumspect, mindful, observant, chary. ❷ a careful worker: CONSCIENTIOUS, painstaking, meticulous, diligent, attentive, accurate, precise, scrupulous, fastidious, punctilious, methodical, organized, systematic, thorough, well organized.
– OPPOSITES careless.

careless adjective ❶ a careless driver: INATTENTIVE, thoughtless, negligent, unthinking, irresponsible, lax, slipshod,

sloppy, forgetful, absent-minded, remiss. ❷ a careless piece of work: CURSORY, perfunctory, hasty, inaccurate, disorganized, slapdash, slipshod, sloppy, messy. ❸ a careless remark: THOUGHTLESS, unthinking, insensitive, indiscreet, unguarded, ill-considered, reckless, rash, imprudent.
– OPPOSITES careful.

caress verb FONDLE, stroke, smooth, touch, pet, cuddle, pat, nuzzle, kiss, embrace, hug.

caretaker noun JANITOR, superintendent, porter, warden, watchman, keeper, steward, curator, concierge.

careworn adjective *see* WEARY adjective (1).

cargo noun FREIGHT, payload, load, consignment, contents, goods, merchandise, baggage, shipment, boatload, lorryload, truckload, lading.

caricature noun PARODY, mimicry, lampoon, distortion, burlesque, travesty, cartoon, satire, farce; *informal* take-off, send-up.
▶ verb PARODY, mimic, lampoon, mock, ridicule, distort, satirize, burlesque; *informal* take off, send up.

carnage noun SLAUGHTER, massacre, mass murder, butchery, bloodbath, bloodshed, holocaust, pogrom.

carnal adjective SEXUAL, sensual, erotic, fleshly, lustful, lewd, lecherous, lascivious, libidinous, coarse, gross, prurient, salacious, lubricious.

carnival noun FESTIVAL, celebration, fair, fiesta, fête, gala, jamboree, festivity, revelry.

carouse verb MAKE MERRY, party, go on a spree, binge, roister, overindulge; *informal* live it up, paint the town red, go on a bender.

carp verb COMPLAIN, find fault, criticize, quibble, grumble, object, reproach, censure, cavil, nag; *informal* nit-pick, gripe, go on.

carpenter noun WOODWORKER, cabinetmaker, joiner; *Brit. informal* chippy.

carriage noun ❶ COACH, vehicle. ❷ BEARING, posture, stance, gait, manner, presence, air, demeanour, mien, behaviour, conduct; *Brit.* deportment; *formal* comportment. ❸ TRANSPORT, transportation, freight, conveyance, delivery, carrying.

carry verb ❶ CONVEY, transport, move, transfer, take, bring, fetch, bear, haul, shift, transmit, relay, manhandle; *informal* lug, cart. ❷ SUPPORT, bear, sustain, maintain, hold up, shoulder. ❸ carry the audience: AFFECT, influence, have an effect on, stimulate, motivate, spur on, drive, impel, urge. ❹ carry a heavy fine: INVOLVE, lead to, result in, require, entail, demand.
■ **carry on** *see* CONTINUE. **carry out** *see* DO (1).

cart noun BARROW, wheelbarrow, handcart, pushcart.
▶ verb *see* CARRY (1).

carton noun BOX, container, package, case, packet, pack.

cartoon noun ❶ CARICATURE, parody, lampoon, burlesque, satire; *informal* send-up, take-off. ❷ ANIMATED FILM, animation, comic strip, photostory.

cartridge noun ❶ CASE, container, cylinder, capsule,

cassette, magazine. ❷ ROUND, shell.

carve verb ❶ SCULPT, sculpture, chisel, cut, hew, whittle, form, shape, fashion, mould. ❷ ENGRAVE, etch, incise, notch, cut in. ❸ SLICE, cut up.
■ **carve up** *see* DIVIDE (3).

cascade noun WATERFALL, falls, shower, fountain, torrent, flood, deluge, outpouring, avalanche, cataract.
▶ verb GUSH, pour, surge, spill, overflow, tumble, descend.

case[1] noun ❶ in this case: SITUATION, occasion, context, circumstances, instance, position, conditions, event, occurrence, predicament, contingency, plight. ❷ a case of cheating: INSTANCE, example, occurrence, occasion, illustration, specimen. ❸ the case comes up next week: TRIAL, proceedings, lawsuit, action, suit. ❹ a terminal case: PATIENT, victim, sufferer, invalid.

case[2] noun a packing case: CONTAINER, box, receptacle, canister, crate, carton, pack, suitcase, trunk, luggage, baggage.

cash noun MONEY, funds, finance, capital, resources, currency, change, notes, coins, legal tender; *informal* dough, bread, moolah; *Brit. informal* readies, the ready.
▶ verb EXCHANGE, change, turn into money/cash, realize; *Brit.* encash.

cashier[1] noun TELLER, clerk, banker, treasurer, purser, bursar, controller.

cashier[2] verb DISMISS, discharge, drum out, expel; *informal* throw out, boot out.

cask noun BARREL, keg, vat, butt, tub, vessel, tun, hogshead, firkin, pipe.

cast verb ❶ THROW, toss, fling, pitch, hurl, sling, lob, launch, let fly; *informal* chuck, heave. ❷ cast a soft light: EMIT, give off, send out, shed, radiate, diffuse, spread. ❸ cast figures in bronze: MOULD, form, fashion, sculpt, model.
▶ noun ❶ FIGURE, shape, mould, form, sculpture. ❷ a cast of mind: SORT, kind, type, style, stamp.
■ **cast about** *see* SEARCH verb (2).

castaway adjective MAROONED, shipwrecked, stranded, abandoned, exiled, deserted.

caste noun CLASS, order, rank, level, grade, position, station, place, status, standing, grading.

castigate verb REBUKE, reprimand, scold, censure, upbraid, berate, admonish, chide, take to task, criticize; *informal* tell off, dress down, haul over the coals.

castle noun FORTRESS, fort, citadel, stronghold, fortification, keep, palace, chateau, tower.

castrate verb NEUTER, geld, desex, sterilize; *Brit. informal* doctor.

casual adjective ❶ a casual attitude: INDIFFERENT, careless, lax, unconcerned, uninterested, unenthusiastic, easy-going, nonchalant, offhand, throwaway, relaxed, apathetic, lackadaisical, blasé, insouciant, unprofessional; *informal* laid-back. ❷ a casual acquaintance: SLIGHT, superficial, shallow. ❸ casual work: TEMPORARY, part-time, freelance, irregular. ❹ a casual meeting: ACCIDENTAL, chance, unintentional, unplanned, unexpected, unforeseen, unanticipated, fortuitous, serendipitous, incidental. ❺ casual clothes: INFORMAL,

relaxed, leisure, unceremonious; *informal* sporty.
– OPPOSITES diligent, permanent, deliberate, formal.

casualty noun FATALITY, victim, sufferer, dead/wounded/injured person.

cat noun FELINE, tomcat, tom, kitten; *informal* pussy, pussy cat, puss, kitty; *Brit. informal* moggie, mog.

catacombs plural noun CRYPT, tomb, vault, sepulchre.

catalogue noun LIST, record, register, inventory, index, directory, roll, table, guide, classification, calendar, schedule.
▶ verb LIST, file, classify, categorize, register, record, make an inventory of, alphabetize.

catapult verb LAUNCH, hurl, propel, shoot, fling, fire. *See also* THROW (1).

cataract noun WATERFALL, falls, cascade, rapids, torrent, downpour.

catastrophe noun DISASTER, calamity, cataclysm, tragedy, misfortune, blow, mishap, misadventure, reverse, debacle, fiasco, trouble, trial, adversity, affliction.

catch verb ❶ GRASP, seize, grab, clutch, grip, hold, pluck, clench, intercept, snare, trap, receive, acquire. ❷ catch a criminal: CAPTURE, apprehend, arrest, seize, take prisoner, lay hold of, trap, snare; *informal* collar, nab, pinch; *Brit. informal* nick. ❸ catch what he said: HEAR, understand, follow, grasp, comprehend, make out, take in, discern, perceive, fathom. ❹ catch him unawares: SURPRISE, startle, come across, discover, detect, find. ❺ catch pneumonia: CONTRACT, get, develop, become infected by, suffer from, succumb to; *Brit.* go down with.
▶ noun ❶ BOLT, lock, fastening, fastener, clasp, hasp, hook, clip, latch, snib. ❷ what's the catch? SNAG, disadvantage, drawback, difficulty, hitch, fly in the ointment, stumbling block, trick, snare. ❸ YIELD, take, haul, bag, net, prize.
■ **catch on** ❶ BECOME POPULAR, come into fashion, succeed, become all the rage; *informal* become trendy. ❷ *See* UNDERSTAND (1).

catching adjective CONTAGIOUS, infectious, communicable, transmissible, transmittable.

catchy adjective MEMORABLE, popular, haunting, appealing, captivating, melodious, singable.

categorical adjective UNQUALIFIED, unconditional, unequivocal, unambiguous, unreserved, definite, absolute, explicit, emphatic, positive, express, firm, direct, conclusive, decided, forceful, downright, utter, out-and-out.
– OPPOSITES equivocal, tentative.

category noun CLASS, group, classification, grouping, type, sort, kind, variety, grade, order, rank, division, heading, section, department.

cater
■ **cater for** ❶ cater for vegetarians: FEED, provide food for, provision, serve, cook for; *dated* victual. ❷ cater for all tastes: TAKE INTO ACCOUNT/CONSIDERATION, allow for, bear in mind, make provision for, have regard for.

cathartic adjective PURGATIVE,

purifying, cleansing, releasing, lustral.

catholic adjective WIDE, broad, wide-ranging, all-embracing, general, comprehensive, varied, all-inclusive, eclectic, universal.
– OPPOSITES narrow.

cattle noun COWS, bovines, livestock, stock, bulls, heifers, calves, bullocks, steers.

catty adjective SPITEFUL, malicious, nasty, mean, ill-natured, venomous, malevolent, vicious; *informal* bitchy.

cause noun ❶ ORIGIN, source, root, beginning, genesis, occasion, mainspring, author, originator, creator, produce, agent, prime mover, maker. ❷ **no cause for alarm**: REASON, basis, grounds, justification, call, motive, motivation. ❸ **devoted to the cause**: PRINCIPLE, ideal, belief, conviction, object, end, aim, objective, purpose, charity.
▶ verb ❶ BRING ABOUT, produce, create, make happen, give rise to, lead to, result in, provoke, originate, generate, engender, arouse, effect, occasion, precipitate. ❷ **cause him to worry**: FORCE, make, compel, induce.

caustic adjective ❶ CORROSIVE, acid, corroding, burning, destructive, mordant, acrid. ❷ **caustic wit**: CUTTING, biting, sarcastic, stinging, scathing, virulent, waspish, trenchant, pungent, astringent, acidulous, acrimonious, mordant.
– OPPOSITES gentle, mild.

caution noun ❶ CARE, carefulness, attention, alertness, wariness, prudence, watchfulness, vigilance, heed, heedfulness, guardedness, circumspection, discretion, forethought, mindfulness. ❷ **receive a caution**: WARNING, reprimand, admonition, injunction; *informal* dressing-down; *Brit. informal* ticking-off.
▶ verb ❶ WARN, advise, urge, counsel, inform, alert, forewarn, admonish. ❷ REPRIMAND, admonish, warn, give a warning to, censure; *informal* tell off; *Brit. informal* tick off.

cautious adjective ❶ CAREFUL, wary, prudent, discreet, guarded, alert, circumspect, watchful, vigilant, mindful, shrewd, chary. ❷ **a cautious statement**: GUARDED, tactful, non-committal, restrained, tentative, suspicious; *informal* cagey.
– OPPOSITES incautious, reckless.

cavalcade noun PARADE, march, procession, caravan, cortège, column, file, train.

cavalier adjective OFFHAND, arrogant, haughty, disdainful, supercilious, insolent, condescending, lofty, patronizing.

cave noun CAVERN, hollow, grotto, pothole, cavity, dugout, underground chamber.
■ **cave in** *see* COLLAPSE.

cavil verb CARP, quibble, find fault, complain, object, criticize; *informal* nit-pick.

cavity noun HOLE, hollow, crater, pit, orifice, gap, dent, aperture.

cease verb STOP, finish, end, bring to a halt, halt, break off, discontinue, conclude, suspend, terminate, desist, leave off, refrain from; *informal* quit, knock off, lay off.
– OPPOSITES start, begin.

ceaseless adjective UNENDING, endless, constant, continual,

continuous, non-stop, perpetual, never-ending, incessant, persistent, relentless, unremitting, interminable, everlasting, untiring, chronic.
– OPPOSITES intermittent.

celebrate verb ❶ ENJOY ONESELF, rejoice, make merry, revel, party; *informal* go out on the town, paint the town red, whoop it up.
❷ celebrate his birthday: COMMEMORATE, remember, honour, observe, make, keep, toast, drink to. ❸ celebrate a religious ceremony: PERFORM, officiate at, observe.

celebrated adjective *see* FAMOUS.

celebration noun ❶ PARTY, festival, carnival, gala, fête, festivity, revelry, merrymaking, jollification, spree; *informal* bash, shindig; *Brit. informal* beanfeast, rave-up. ❷ COMMEMORATION, remembrance, observance, honouring, keeping.

celebrity noun ❶ *See* FAME.
❷ FAMOUS PERSON, star, dignitary, luminary, notable, personage; *informal* bigwig, big shot, big noise.

celestial adjective
❶ ASTRONOMICAL, cosmic, heavenly, stellar, interstellar, extraterrestrial. ❷ DIVINE, heavenly, supernatural, transcendental, godlike, ethereal, sublime, spiritual, immortal, angelic, seraphic, cherubic.

celibacy noun CHASTITY, purity, abstinence, self-denial, asceticism, virginity, bachelorhood, spinsterhood, monasticism, monkhood, nunhood, continence, abnegation.

celibate adjective CHASTE, pure, abstinent, virgin, immaculate, continent.

cell noun ❶ ENCLOSURE, dungeon, lock-up, cubicle, room, apartment, chamber, stall.
❷ CAVITY, compartment, hole, unit.

cement noun ADHESIVE, glue, paste, bonding, binder.

cemetery noun GRAVEYARD, burial ground, churchyard, necropolis.

censor verb EXPURGATE, bowdlerize, cut, delete, edit, remove, make cuts/changes to, amend, prohibit, forbid, ban.

censorious adjective CRITICAL, hypercritical, disapproving, condemnatory, judgemental, moralistic, fault-finding, captious, carping, cavilling.

censure verb CRITICIZE, blame, disapprove of, denounce, reprove, rebuke, reproach, reprimand, upbraid, berate, scold, chide, reprehend; *informal* tell off; *Brit. informal* tick off, carpet; *formal* castigate.
▶ noun CRITICISM, blame, condemnation, denunciation, disapproval, reproval, reproof, reproach, rebuke, reprimand, scolding, berating, upbraiding, obloquy, reprehension, vituperation; *informal* talking-to, dressing-down; *formal* castigation.

central adjective ❶ MIDDLE, mid, median, mean, mesial. ❷ MAIN, chief, principal, foremost, basic, fundamental, key, essential, primary, pivotal, core, focal, cardinal.
– OPPOSITES side, outer, subordinate.

centralize verb CONCENTRATE, centre, consolidate, condense, amalgamate, unify, incorporate, streamline, focus, rationalize.

centre noun MIDDLE, middle point, heart, core, nucleus, midpoint, hub, kernel, focus, focal point, pivot, inside, interior.
– OPPOSITES periphery.
▶ verb CONCENTRATE, focus, converge, close in, pivot.

ceremonial adjective FORMAL, official, ritual, ritualistic, celebratory, liturgical, stately, dignified, solemn.

ceremonious adjective DIGNIFIED, majestic, imposing, impressive, solemn, stately, formal, courtly, scrupulous, precise, punctilious, deferential, stiff, rigid.
– OPPOSITES casual.

ceremony noun ❶ RITE, service, ritual, sacrament, formality, observance, celebration, commemoration, function, event, parade. ❷ conducted with ceremony: FORMALITY, pomp, decorum, formalities, niceties, etiquette, propriety, ritual, attention to detail, protocol, punctiliousness, pageantry, grandeur, ceremonial.

certain adjective ❶ I'm certain: SURE, confident, convinced, satisfied, persuaded, assured, unwavering, secure, unshaken. ❷ her success is certain: ASSURED, inevitable, definite, destined, inescapable, bound to happen, inexorable, unarguable, ineluctable. ❸ it's certain he'll go: DEFINITE, sure, unquestionable, beyond question, evident, plain, clear, indubitable, undeniable, obvious, incontrovertible, incontestable, conclusive. ❹ a certain cure: DEFINITE, sure, unquestionable, undisputed, reliable, dependable, sound, infallible, trustworthy, foolproof; *informal* sure-fire. ❺ a certain place: PARTICULAR, specific, precise, special, individual.
– OPPOSITES doubtful, possible, unlikely.

certainly adverb DEFINITELY, surely, assuredly, undoubtedly, undeniably, obviously, plainly, clearly.

certainty noun ❶ say with certainty: SURENESS, authority, positiveness, confidence, assurance, assuredness, conviction, reliability, conclusiveness, authoritativeness, validity. ❷ FACT, inevitability, foregone conclusion, indubitability; *informal* sure thing; *Brit. informal* dead cert.
– OPPOSITES uncertainty.

certificate noun CERTIFICATION, authorization, document, licence, warrant, credentials, pass, permit, guarantee, voucher, diploma, qualification, testimonial.

certify verb ❶ AUTHENTICATE, document, verify, validate, confirm, bear witness to, attest to, testify to, substantiate, corroborate, endorse, vouch for, ratify, warrant. ❷ certified as a teacher: ACCREDIT, license, recognize, authorize, qualify, give a certificate/diploma to.

cessation noun END, finish, termination, conclusion, halt, pause, break, respite, let-up.

chagrin noun ANNOYANCE, irritation, dissatisfaction, resentment, anger, vexation, displeasure, disquiet, discomposure.

chain noun ❶ SHACKLE, fetter, manacle, bonds, coupling, link.

❷ a chain of events: SERIES, succession, progression, sequence, string, set, cycle, line, row, concatenation.
▶ verb FASTEN, secure, tie, bind, tether, shackle, fetter, manacle, handcuff, hitch.

chair verb PRESIDE OVER, lead, direct, manage, control, oversee, supervise.

chalky adjective WHITE, pale, wan, pallid, ashen, pasty, waxen, blanched, bleached, colourless.

challenge verb ❶ DARE, summon, invite, throw down the gauntlet to, defy. ❷ challenge his authority: QUESTION, dispute, call into question, protest against, object to, take exception to, disagree with, argue against, contest, oppose, query, demur against, impugn. ❸ the job really challenges him: STIMULATE, test, tax, inspire, excite, arouse, spur on.

challenging adjective STIMULATING, exciting, inspiring, testing, thought-provoking.
– OPPOSITES easy.

chamber noun ❶ ROOM, cubicle, bedroom, bedchamber, boudoir. ❷ CAVITY, compartment, hollow, cell.

champion noun ❶ WINNER, prizewinner, medallist, record-breaker, victor, title-holder, conqueror, hero. ❷ a champion of the cause: SUPPORTER, defender, upholder, advocate, backer, patron, protector, vindicator. ❸ KNIGHT, hero, warrior, contender, fighter, man-at-arms, paladin.
▶ adjective WINNING, victorious, unrivalled, leading, great, supreme, record-breaking.
▶ verb DEFEND, support, uphold, stand up for, back, advocate, promote, espouse.

chance noun ❶ meet by chance: ACCIDENT, coincidence, luck, fate, destiny, fluke, providence, fortune, serendipity, fortuity. ❷ a good chance he'll win: POSSIBILITY, likelihood, prospect, probability, likeliness, odds, conceivability. ❸ a second chance: OPPORTUNITY, time, occasion, turn, opening; *informal* shot.
▶ adjective ACCIDENTAL, unforeseen, unexpected, coincidental, lucky, unplanned, unintended, unintentional, unpremeditated, casual, inadvertent, unanticipated, unforeseeable, random, haphazard, unlooked for, fortuitous, serendipitous, adventitious, fluky.
– OPPOSITES intentional, deliberate.
▶ verb ❶ *See* HAPPEN. ❷ *See* RISK verb (2, 3).
■ **chance on/upon** MEET, encounter, come across, stumble on; *informal* bump into, run into.

chancy adjective RISKY, dangerous, hazardous, unsafe, uncertain, precarious, perilous, insecure, speculative, unpredictable; *informal* dicey; *Brit. informal* dodgy.
– OPPOSITES safe.

change verb ❶ ALTER, adjust, transform, modify, convert, vary, amend, rearrange, reorganize, remodel, reorder, reform, reconstruct, restyle, recast, tailor, transmute, accustom, metamorphose, transmogrify, permutate, permute. ❷ the world's changed: ALTER, be transformed, evolve, develop, move on, mutate, shift, do an

about-face, do a U-turn; *Brit. informal* chop and change. ❸ **change jobs/sides:** EXCHANGE, swap, switch, substitute, replace, trade, interchange, barter, transpose.
▶ **noun** ❶ ALTERATION, modification, adaptation, difference, transformation, conversion, variation, development, remodelling, reorganization, rearrangement, reconstruction, shift, transition, metamorphosis, mutation, transmutation, transmogrification, innovation, vicissitude, permutation. ❷ **a change of jobs:** EXCHANGE, switch, swap, trade, substitution, interchange, bartering. ❸ **have no change:** COINS, silver, small change, cash, petty cash.

changeable **adjective** VARIABLE, changing, varying, shifting, vacillating, fluctuating, volatile, capricious, wavering, unstable, unsteady, irregular, erratic, unreliable, inconsistent, unpredictable, fickle, inconstant, mercurial, fluid, fitful, kaleidoscopic, protean, mutable, chequered, vicissitudinous.
– OPPOSITES constant.

channel **noun** ❶ PASSAGE, sea passage, strait, narrow, neck, waterway, watercourse, fiord. ❷ GUTTER, furrow, groove, conduit, duct, culvert, ditch, gully. ❸ PATH, route, direction, way, approach, course. ❹ **channels of communication:** MEDIUM, means, agency, vehicle, route.
▶ **verb** CONVEY, conduct, transmit, transport, guide, direct.

chant **noun** SONG, hymn, chorus, carol, psalm.
▶ **verb** INTONE, recite, sing, cantillate.

chaos **noun** DISORDER, anarchy, mayhem, bedlam, pandemonium, turmoil, tumult, uproar, disruption, upheaval, confusion, disarray, lawlessness, riot, disorganization.
– OPPOSITES order.

chaotic **adjective** ANARCHIC, in chaos, disordered, disorganized, confused, disorderly, unruly, uncontrolled, tumultuous, jumbled, upset, askew, disrupted, in disarray, awry, lawless, riotous, ungovernable, rebellious, orderless; *informal* topsy-turvy, haywire, higgledy-piggledy; *Brit. informal* shambolic.
– OPPOSITES disorderly.

chap **noun** MAN, boy, male; *informal* guy, fellow, sort, customer; *Brit. informal* bloke; *Brit. informal, dated* cove.

character **noun** ❶ PERSONALITY, nature, disposition, temperament, temper, make-up, constitution, cast, attributes, bent, complexion. ❷ **a person of character:** STRENGTH, honour, integrity, moral fibre, uprightness, rectitude, fortitude, backbone. ❸ **he's a character:** ECCENTRIC, original, individual, oddity; *informal* oddball, odd fellow, queer fish; *informal, dated* card. ❹ **they're friendly characters:** PERSON, individual, human being; *informal* fellow, guy, type, sort, customer; *Brit. informal* bloke, chap. ❺ **damage his character:** REPUTATION, name, standing, position, status. ❻ **in bold characters:** TYPE, sign, symbol, mark, figure, hieroglyph, cipher, ideogram.

characteristic **noun** QUALITY, attribute, feature, trait, property, peculiarity, quirk, mannerism,

idiosyncrasy, hallmark, trademark.
▶ **adjective** TYPICAL, distinctive, distinguishing, particular, special, individual, peculiar, specific, representative, symbolic, idiosyncratic, symptomatic.

characterize **verb** PORTRAY, depict, describe, present, identify, draw, brand, typify, delineate, denote, indicate, specify, designate.

charade **noun** PRETENCE, travesty, mockery, fake, sham, deception, pose, farce, absurdity, parody, pantomime, play-acting, masquerade.

charge **verb** ❶ ASK IN PAYMENT, ask, ask for, expect, make someone pay, impose, levy, require. ❷ ACCUSE OF, arraign, indict, prosecute, impute, blame, incriminate. ❸ **charge the fort**: ATTACK, storm, assault, rush, open fire on, assail, fall on; *informal* lay into, wade into. ❹ **charge with the responsibility**: ENTRUST, burden, impose on, give, load, encumber, saddle. ❺ **charge with emotion**: FILL, load, imbue, instil, suffuse, permeate, pervade.
– OPPOSITES absolve.
▶ **noun** ❶ COST, rate, price, amount, fee, payment, expense, outlay, expenditure, levy, toll, terms, dues. ❷ **a charge of murder**: ACCUSATION, allegation, indictment, arraignment, impeachment, citation, imputation, blame, incrimination. ❸ **lead a charge**: ATTACK, assault, offensive, storming, raid, strike, onrush, onslaught, sally, incursion, sortie. ❹ **in their charge**: CARE, custody, responsibility, protection, supervision, safe keeping, keeping, trust, guardianship, surveillance.

charitable **adjective** ❶ GENEROUS, kind, giving, philanthropic, magnanimous, liberal, munificent, bountiful, open-handed, benevolent. ❷ **a charitable interpretation**: GENEROUS, liberal, tolerant, understanding, broad-minded, sympathetic.
– OPPOSITES uncharitable.

charity **noun** ❶ DONATIONS, contributions, handouts, financial assistance, funding, endowments, almsgiving, philanthropy, benefaction. ❷ **show some charity**: COMPASSION, humanity, goodwill, kindliness, sympathy, love, tolerance, thoughtfulness, generosity, altruism, humanitarianism, benevolence.

charm **noun** ❶ ATTRACTIVENESS, attraction, appeal, allure, fascination, desirability, charisma, lure, delightfulness, captivation, allurement. ❷ SPELL, magic words, incantation, sorcery, witchcraft, wizardry. ❸ **a lucky charm**: AMULET, trinket, talisman, mascot.
▶ **verb** DELIGHT, please, attract, captivate, fascinate, win over, bewitch, beguile, enchant, seduce, hypnotize, mesmerize, enthral, intrigue, disarm, enamour, allure, draw.
– OPPOSITES repel.

chart **noun** GRAPH, table, diagram, map, plan, blueprint, guide, scheme, tabulation.
▶ **verb** MAP, map out, plot, graph, delineate, sketch, draft.

chase **verb** PURSUE, run/go after, follow, hunt, hound, track, trail, tail.

chasm **noun** ABYSS, ravine, pit,

canyon, opening, void, crater, crevasse, gap, fissure, rift.

chaste adjective ❶ CELIBATE, virginal, abstinent, pure, innocent, virtuous, undefiled, moral, immaculate, unmarried. ❷ chaste conduct: VIRTUOUS, good, pure, innocent, decent, moral, modest, wholesome, upright, righteous, becoming, restrained, unsullied.
– OPPOSITES promiscuous.

chasten verb ❶ SUBDUE, restrain, tame, curb, check, humble, cow. ❷ PUNISH, discipline, penalize, scold, reprimand, upbraid, chide, take to task; *informal* haul over the coals; *formal* castigate.

chastise verb *see* CHASTEN (2).

chastity noun CHASTENESS, celibacy, abstinence, virginity, self-restraint, self-denial, virtue, purity, innocence, continence, sinlessness.

chat verb TALK, gossip, chatter, have a conversation with, converse, prattle, jabber.
▶ noun TALK, gossip, conversation, heart-to-heart; *informal* confab, chinwag; *Brit. informal* natter.

chatty adjective TALKATIVE, garrulous, loquacious, voluble, effusive, gushing, gossipy.
– OPPOSITES taciturn.

chauvinism noun JINGOISM, prejudice, bigotry, bias, machismo.

cheap adjective ❶ INEXPENSIVE, low-cost, low-priced, economical, reasonable, bargain, economy, reduced, marked down, discounted, sale; *informal* bargain-basement, knock-down. ❷ POOR-QUALITY, inferior, shoddy, common, tawdry, tatty, paltry, worthless, second-rate, gimcrack; *informal* tacky, trashy. ❸ a cheap joke: DESPICABLE, contemptible, tasteless, unpleasant, unworthy, mean, low, base, sordid, vulgar.
– OPPOSITES expensive.

cheapen verb DEGRADE, debase, belittle, demean, devalue, denigrate, discredit, prostitute, lower the tone of.

cheat verb ❶ DECEIVE, trick, swindle, take in, defraud, dupe, hoodwink, double-cross, take advantage of, exploit, gull; *informal* rip off, take for a ride, con, diddle, bamboozle, finagle, bilk, fleece. ❷ cheat death: AVOID, elude, evade, dodge, escape, shun, eschew.
▶ noun ❶ CHEATER, swindler, fraud, confidence trickster, deceiver, trickster, double-crosser, impostor, crook, hoaxer, rogue, charlatan, mountebank, shark; *informal* con man, phoney; *Brit. informal* twister. ❷ SWINDLE, fraud, deception, deceit, trick, trickery, ruse, misrepresentation, chicanery, imposture, artifice; *informal* con, rip-off, fiddle, racket; *Brit. informal* swizz.

check verb ❶ EXAMINE, inspect, look over/at, scrutinize, test, monitor, investigate, probe, enquire into, study; *informal* give the once-over to. ❷ check the vehicle's movement: STOP, halt, arrest, bring to a standstill, slow down, brake, obstruct, inhibit, bar, impede, block, retard, curb, delay, thwart.
▶ noun ❶ EXAMINATION, inspection, scrutiny, test, monitoring, investigation, enquiry, probe, study; *informal* once-over, going-over. ❷ STOP, stoppage, halt, obstruction, break, slowing down, slowdown, delay,

interruption, suspension, hiatus, retardation.

cheek noun IMPUDENCE, impertinence, insolence, effrontery, boldness, audacity, temerity, brazenness; *informal* brass, neck, gall, lip; *Brit. informal* sauce.

cheeky adjective IMPUDENT, impertinent, insolent, disrespectful, insulting, impolite, presumptuous, mocking, irreverent, forward, pert; *informal* saucy; *N. Amer. informal* sassy.
– OPPOSITES respectful.

cheep verb CHIRP, chirrup, tweet, twitter, warble, trill.

cheer verb ❶ ACCLAIM, applaud, hail, hurrah, encourage, clap, shout/yell at. ❷ MAKE CHEERFUL, please, hearten, gladden, brighten, perk up, comfort, console, buoy up, solace, uplift; *informal* buck up.
▶ noun ❶ the cheers of the crowd: ACCLAIM, acclamation, applause, hurray, hurrah, ovation, plaudit, shout, shouting, hailing, clapping, encouragement, approval. ❷ a time of cheer: CHEERFULNESS, happiness, gladness, merriment, glee, mirth, gaiety, joy, pleasure, jubilation, rejoicing, festivity, revelry.
■ **cheer up** BRIGHTEN, liven up, perk up, rally, take heart.

cheerful adjective ❶ HAPPY, bright, glad, merry, sunny, joyful, delighted, good-humoured, jolly, animated, buoyant, light-hearted, carefree, gleeful, breezy, cheery, jaunty, perky, smiling, laughing, optimistic, hopeful, positive, in good spirits, sparkling, happy-go-lucky, sprightly, rapturous; *informal* chirpy; *poetic/literary* blithe. ❷ BRIGHT, sunny, cheering, pleasant, agreeable, friendly, happy.
– OPPOSITES sad, cheerless, dull.

cheerless adjective GLOOMY, miserable, dreary, dull, dismal, depressing, bleak, drab, grim, austere, dark, dingy, desolate, sombre, uninviting, forbidding, melancholy, comfortless, forlorn, joyless, disconsolate, funereal, woeful.
– OPPOSITES cheerful, bright.

cheery adjective CHEERFUL, happy, bright, merry, glad, in good spirits. *See also* CHEERFUL (1).
– OPPOSITES sad.

chemist noun PHARMACIST, pharmacy; *N. Amer.* drugstore; *archaic* apothecary.

chequered adjective a chequered career: MIXED, varied, diverse, diversified, eventful.

cherish verb ❶ TREASURE, prize, hold dear, love, adore, dote on, idolize, cosset, nurture, look after, protect, value. ❷ cherish hopes: HAVE, entertain, harbour, cling to, nurture, foster.
– OPPOSITES neglect.

chest noun ❶ BREAST, thorax, sternum, ribcage. ❷ BOX, crate, case, trunk, container, coffer, casket.

chew verb BITE, crunch, gnaw, masticate, champ, grind.
■ **chew over** *see* CONSIDER (1).

chic adjective STYLISH, fashionable, smart, elegant, modish, voguish.

chide verb SCOLD, upbraid, rebuke, reprimand, reproach, admonish, lecture, take to task, berate; *formal* castigate.

chief noun ❶ CHIEFTAIN, head, headman, ruler, leader, overlord, suzerain. ❷ HEAD, ruler, principal, leader, director, manager,

supervisor, superintendent, chairman, chairperson, chief executive, proprietor, master, mistress, overseer, foreman, controller, captain, commander; *informal* boss, kingpin, top dog, big cheese, bigwig, number one, supremo; *Brit. informal* gaffer, governor.
▶ **adjective** ❶ SUPREME, foremost, principal, highest, leading, senior, superior, premier, head, directing, grand, top. ❷ **the chief point**: MAIN, principal, most important, cardinal, key, primary, prime, central, fundamental, predominant, pre-eminent, foremost, vital, paramount, uppermost.
– OPPOSITES minor, subordinate.

chiefly **adverb** MAINLY, principally, primarily, in the main, predominantly, especially, particularly, mostly, essentially, on the whole, for the most part, above all.

child **noun** ❶ BOY, GIRL, youngster, young person, infant, baby, toddler, tot, tiny tot, youth, adolescent, juvenile, minor; *Scottish* bairn; *informal* kid, nipper, shaver, brat, guttersnipe; *Brit. informal* sprog. ❷ SON, DAUGHTER, offspring, progeny, descendant, scion; *Law* issue.

childbirth **noun** LABOUR, delivery, confinement, parturition, accouchement.

childhood **noun** YOUTH, infancy, babyhood, boyhood, girlhood, adolescence, minority; *informal* teens, pre-teens.

childish **adjective** IMMATURE, infantile, juvenile, puerile, irresponsible, foolish, jejune. *See also* SILLY (1).
– OPPOSITES mature.

childlike **adjective** INNOCENT, simple, unsophisticated, trusting, gullible, naive, ingenuous, guileless, artless, unaffected, credulous.

chill **verb** COOL, freeze, refrigerate, make cold/cool.
– OPPOSITES heat.
▶ **noun** ❶ COOLNESS, chilliness, coldness, iciness, rawness, frigidity, nip, bite. ❷ COLDNESS, coolness, aloofness, unfriendliness, hostility, distance, unresponsiveness.
– OPPOSITES warmth.

chilly **adjective** ❶ COLD, cool, icy, freezing, chill, fresh, sharp, biting, raw, brisk, penetrating, wintry, frigid. ❷ **a chilly manner**: COLD, cool, unfriendly, aloof, distant, unresponsive, reserved, unsympathetic, unwelcoming, hostile, remote, frigid.
– OPPOSITES warm, friendly.

chime **verb** RING, peal, toll, strike, sound, clang, tinkle, resound.
▶ **noun** PEAL, striking, tolling.

china **noun** ❶ DISHES, tableware, dinner/tea service. ❷ PORCELAIN.

chink **noun** CRACK, gap, cleft, rift, slit, fissure, crevice, split, opening, aperture, cranny, cavity.

chip **noun** ❶ SHARD, flake, fragment, splinter, paring, sliver, bit, fleck, shred, scrap, snippet. ❷ NICK, crack, notch, snick, scratch, splinter, gash, fault, flaw, dent.
▶ **verb** ❶ NICK, crack, notch, scratch, splinter, gash, damage, snick. ❷ CHISEL, whittle, hew.
■ **chip in** *see* INTERRUPT (1), CONTRIBUTE (1).

chirpy **adjective** CHEERFUL, cheery, happy, light-hearted, carefree, merry, in good spirits; *informal* upbeat.

chivalrous adjective ❶ COURTEOUS, polite, gallant, gentlemanly, gracious, well mannered, thoughtful, protective. ❷ COURTLY, knightly, courageous, brave, valiant, heroic, daring, intrepid, honourable, just, fair, constant, true, magnanimous.
– OPPOSITES rude, boorish.

choice noun ❶ open to choice: SELECTION, option, choosing, preference, picking, election, adoption. ❷ I had no choice: ALTERNATIVE, option, possibility, solution, answer, way out. ❸ a wide choice of: SELECTION, range, variety, assortment, mixture, store, supply, display, array, miscellany.
▶ adjective BEST, excellent, superior, first-rate, first-class, prize, prime, select, special, exclusive, rare, hand-picked.
– OPPOSITES inferior.

choke verb ❶ STRANGLE, asphyxiate, throttle, suffocate, smother, stifle. ❷ choked on a fish bone: GAG, gasp, retch, struggle for air, asphyxiate, suffocate. ❸ roads were choked: CLOG, congest, jam, block, obstruct, fill up, constrict, plug, stop up.
■ **choke back** *see* SUPPRESS (2).

choose verb SELECT, pick, pick on/out, decide on, opt for, settle on, agree on, fix on, plump for, prefer, designate, elect, single out, adopt, espouse, hand-pick, name, nominate, vote for, show a preference for.

choosy adjective FUSSY, particular, discriminating, exacting, finicky, pernickety, fastidious, hard to please, selective, discerning; *informal* picky.

chop verb ❶ CUT DOWN, fell, hack down, hew, bring down, saw down, lop, split. ❷ CUT UP, dice, cube, fragment, crumble. ❸ *See* CUT (2).

choppy adjective ROUGH, turbulent, stormy, squally, blustery, tempestuous.
– OPPOSITES calm.

chorus noun ❶ CHOIR, ensemble, choral group, choristers, singers, vocalists. ❷ REFRAIN, response.

christen verb BAPTIZE, anoint, name, dub, call, designate, style, term.

chronic adjective ❶ chronic illness: PERSISTENT, long-lasting, long-standing, lingering, continual, constant, incessant, deep-rooted, deep-seated, ingrained. ❷ chronic liar: HABITUAL, inveterate, confirmed, hardened. ❸ a chronic book: BAD, dreadful, appalling, awful, atrocious.
– OPPOSITES acute.

chronicle noun RECORD, account, history, story, description, calendar, annals, narrative, journal, archive, log.
▶ verb RECORD, report, document, set down, relate, tell about, register.

chronological adjective CONSECUTIVE, in sequence, sequential, ordered, historical, serial, progressive.

chubby adjective PLUMP, tubby, flabby, dumpy, paunchy, fleshy, stout, portly, rotund. *See also* FAT (1).
– OPPOSITES skinny.

chunk noun LUMP, piece, block, hunk, slab, square, portion, mass, wedge; *informal* dollop.

church noun PLACE OF WORSHIP, house of God, cathedral, chapel, abbey, minster, temple, tabernacle, mosque, synagogue.

churlish adjective RUDE, impolite, boorish, oafish, ill-mannered, discourteous, surly, curt, sullen, brusque.
– OPPOSITES polite.

churn verb ❶ BEAT, whip up, agitate, stir up, shape up, disturb. ❷ SEETHE, foam, boil, froth, swirl, toss, convulse.

cinema noun FILMS, movies, pictures, motion pictures; *informal* silver screen, big screen.

circle noun ❶ RING, disc, round, loop, circumference, ball, globe, sphere, orb. ❷ GROUP, circle of friends, set, company, crowd, ring, coterie, clique, assembly, fellowship, class.
▶ verb ❶ MOVE ROUND, revolve, rotate, orbit, circumnavigate, wheel, gyrate, whirl, pivot, swivel. ❷ SURROUND, ring, encircle, enclose, envelop, hedge in, hem in, gird, belt, circumscribe.

circuit noun LAP, round, cycle, loop, circumference, turn, ambit.

circuitous adjective WINDING, indirect, meandering, roundabout, twisting, tortuous, rambling, zigzag, labyrinthine, maze-like, serpentine.
– OPPOSITES direct.

circular adjective ROUND, spherical, spheroid, ring-shaped, globular, annular.
▶ noun PAMPHLET, leaflet, notice, advertisement.

circulate verb ❶ circulate the news: SPREAD, spread round, make known, broadcast, publish, distribute, give out, disseminate, propagate, issue, pronounce, advertise; *informal* put about. ❷ blood circulating: MOVE/GO ROUND, flow, revolve, rotate, whirl, gyrate.

circumference noun PERIMETER, border, boundary, periphery, bounds, limits, confines, edge, rim, verge, margin, fringe, outline, skirt, circuit, compass, extremity.

circumspect adjective CAUTIOUS, wary, careful, guarded, vigilant, watchful, prudent, suspicious, apprehensive, observant, leery, chary, judicious, politic.
– OPPOSITES unguarded.

circumstances plural noun ❶ SITUATION, set of affairs, conditions, facts, position, context, occurrence, event, background, particulars, surroundings. ❷ poor circumstances: STATE, situation, conditions, financial position, plight, predicament, means, resources, station.

circumstantial adjective INDIRECT, incidental, presumed, conjectural, inferential.

citadel noun FORTRESS, fort, fortification, stronghold, bastion, castle, tower, keep, fastness.

citation noun QUOTATION, quote, reference, extract, excerpt, allusion, passage, source.

cite verb QUOTE, mention, refer to, allude to, name, adduce, specify, excerpt, extract.

citizen noun SUBJECT, national, native, passport-holder, resident, inhabitant, denizen, dweller, householder, taxpayer, voter, freeman, freewoman, burgher, burgess.

city noun TOWN, conurbation, metropolis, urban area,

municipality; *informal* concrete jungle, urban sprawl.

civil adjective ❶ a civil young man: POLITE, courteous, well mannered, well bred, gentlemanly, ladylike, refined, urbane, polished, cultured, cultivated, cordial, civilized, genial, pleasant. ❷ civil responsibilities: CIVIC, public, municipal, community, local.
– OPPOSITES rude.

civility noun COURTESY, politeness, courteousness, good manners, graciousness, cordiality, pleasantness, geniality, affability, amiability, urbanity, gallantry.
– OPPOSITES rudeness.

civilization noun ❶ modern civilization: DEVELOPMENT, advancement, progress, enlightenment, culture, cultivation, refinement, sophistication. ❷ ancient civilizations: SOCIETY, culture, community, nation, country, people, way of life.

civilize verb ENLIGHTEN, educate, cultivate, instruct, improve, refine, polish, domesticate, socialize, humanize, edify.

civilized adjective ENLIGHTENED, advanced, developed, cultured, cultivated, educated, sophisticated, refined, sociable, urbane, well behaved.
– OPPOSITES uncivilized, barbarous.

claim verb ❶ DEMAND, request, ask for, lay claim to, require, insist on, command, exact, requisition. ❷ PROFESS, maintain, state, declare, assert, allege, protest, insist, contend, hold, avow, affirm, postulate; *formal* aver.

clairvoyance noun PSYCHIC POWERS, second sight, ESP, extrasensory perception, telepathy, sixth sense.

clamber verb SCRAMBLE, climb, scrabble, scale, ascend, mount, shin, shinny, claw one's way.

clammy adjective MOIST, damp, humid, sweaty, sticky, close, muggy, dank.

clamour noun NOISE, uproar, outcry, racket, row, din, shouts, shouting, yelling, babel, commotion, hubbub, hullabaloo, brouhaha, vociferation.
▶ verb SHOUT, yell, call/cry out, exclaim.

clamp noun VICE, press, brace, clasp, fastener, hasp.
▶ verb GRIP, hold, press, squeeze, clench, fix, secure, make fast.

clandestine adjective SECRET, undercover, surreptitious, furtive, concealed, hidden, underhand, cloak-and-dagger.

clarify verb ❶ MAKE CLEAR, explain, clear up, make plain, illuminate, resolve, throw light on, make simple, simplify. ❷ clarify butter: PURIFY, refine.
– OPPOSITES confuse.

clash verb ❶ BANG, strike, crash, clang, clatter, rattle, jangle. ❷ FIGHT, contend, quarrel, wrangle, do battle, feud, grapple, cross swords. ❸ *See* COINCIDE (1).

clasp noun ❶ CATCH, fastener, fastening, clip, hook, buckle, pin, hasp. ❷ EMBRACE, hug, cuddle, hold, grip, grasp.
▶ verb EMBRACE, hug, squeeze, clutch, grip, grasp, hold.

class noun ❶ CATEGORY, group, sort, type, kind, set, division, order, rank, classification, grade, section, denomination, species, genus, genre, domain. ❷ SOCIAL ORDER/DIVISION, rank,

stratum, level, status, standing, station, group, grouping, caste, lineage, pedigree, descent. ❸ a player of class: QUALITY, excellence, distinction, ability, stylishness, elegance, chic.
▶ verb *see* CLASSIFY.

classic adjective ❶ EXCELLENT, memorable, notable, lasting, brilliant, finest, first-rate, first-class, outstanding, exemplary, consummate, masterly, legendary, immortal. ❷ a classic example: TYPICAL, archetypal, definitive, standard, model, stock, prototypical, paradigmatic, copybook. ❸ classic styles: TRADITIONAL, simple, timeless, ageless, enduring, abiding, long-lasting, time-honoured, long-established.
▶ noun MASTERPIECE, master work, great work, standard work.

classical adjective ❶ ANCIENT, Greek, Grecian, Hellenic, Attic, Roman, Latin. ❷ classical music: SERIOUS, symphonic, traditional, concert, highbrow. ❸ classical styles: ELEGANT, balanced, well proportioned, symmetrical, austere, pure, simple, plain, harmonious, restrained.

classification noun CATEGORIZATION, ordering, organization, grouping, arrangement, grading, systemization, codification, tabulation, taxonomy.

classify verb CATEGORIZE, class, arrange, order, sort, organize, group, catalogue, systematize, type, rank, index, file, bracket.

clause noun SECTION, subsection, paragraph, article, item, point, passage, part, heading, provision, proviso, stipulation, note.

claw noun NAIL, talon, pincer, nipper, chela.
▶ verb SCRATCH, tear, scrape, lacerate, rip, maul.

clean adjective ❶ UNSTAINED, spotless, unsoiled, unblemished, unsullied, immaculate, speckless, hygienic, sanitary, disinfected, sterile, sterilized, washed, cleansed, laundered, scrubbed. ❷ clean air: PURE, clear, unpolluted, natural, unadulterated, uncontaminated, untainted. ❸ living clean lives: GOOD, upright, virtuous, pure, decent, respectable, moral, upstanding, exemplary, chaste, undefiled. ❹ a clean piece of paper: UNUSED, unmarked, blank, untouched, new, vacant, void. ❺ clean lines: WELL DEFINED, clean-cut, smooth, streamlined, regular, symmetrical, elegant, simple, graceful, trim, shapely. ❻ a clean break: COMPLETE, thorough, total, conclusive, decisive, final, entire. ❼ a clean fight: FAIR, honest, sporting, sportsmanlike, honourable.
– OPPOSITES dirty.
▶ verb WASH, cleanse, wipe, sponge, scour, swab, dry-clean, launder, tidy, vacuum, hoover, dust, mop, sweep.
– OPPOSITES dirty, soil.

cleanse verb WASH, clean, bathe, rinse, disinfect.

clear adjective ❶ a clear day: BRIGHT, cloudless, fine, fair, light, sunny, sunshiny. ❷ clear water: TRANSPARENT, translucent, limpid, pellucid, crystalline, diaphanous. ❸ it was clear he was guilty: OBVIOUS, plain, evident, apparent, sure, definite, unmistakable, beyond question, indisputable, patent, manifest,

incontrovertible, irrefutable, palpable. ❹ a clear account: COMPREHENSIBLE, plain, intelligible, understandable, lucid, coherent, distinct. ❺ a clear road/view: OPEN, empty, unobstructed, unimpeded, free, unhindered, unlimited. ❻ a clear conscience: UNTROUBLED, undisturbed, innocent, guilt-free, guiltless, clean, peaceful, tranquil, serene, sinless, stainless. ❼ four clear days: WHOLE, full, entire, complete, total.
– OPPOSITES cloudy, opaque, vague, incoherent.
▶ adverb ❶ stand clear: AWAY FROM, at a distance from, apart from, out of contact with. ❷ got clear away: COMPLETELY, entirely, fully, wholly, thoroughly.
▶ verb ❶ the weather cleared: BRIGHTEN, clear up, lighten, break. ❷ clear the drains: UNBLOCK, unclog, unstop, clean out, free. ❸ clear a room: EMPTY, vacate, evacuate. ❹ cleared of all charges: ACQUIT, absolve, discharge, let go, exonerate, vindicate, excuse, pardon. ❺ clear the fence: JUMP, vault, leap, hop, pass over. ❻ clear 500 pounds: MAKE/REALIZE A PROFIT OF, net, earn, gain, make, acquire, secure, bring, reap. ❼ cleared to enter: AUTHORIZE, sanction, give consent to, approve, permit, allow, pass; *informal* give the go-ahead to.
■ **clear up** *see* EXPLAIN (1).

clearance noun ❶ CLEARING, removal, emptying, evacuation, eviction, depopulation, withdrawal. ❷ clearance under the bridge: GAP, space, headroom, allowance, margin, leeway, room to spare. ❸ AUTHORIZATION, permission, consent, sanction, leave, endorsement; *informal* go-ahead, green light.

clear-cut adjective DEFINITE, specific, precise, explicit, unequivocal.

clearly adverb OBVIOUSLY, plainly, undoubtedly, undeniably, surely, certainly, incontestably, patently, incontrovertibly.

cleave verb SPLIT, crack, lay open, divide, hew, hack, chop/slice up, sever, sunder, rend.

cleft noun SPLIT, crack, fissure, gap, crevice, rift, break, fracture.

clemency noun MERCY, leniency, compassion, kindness, humanity, pity, sympathy, fairness, magnanimity, moderation, indulgence.
– OPPOSITES ruthlessness.

clench verb GRIP, grasp, clutch, hold, seize, clamp, squeeze.

clergyman noun MINISTER, priest, pastor, preacher, vicar, rabbi, imam, cleric, churchman, churchwoman, man of the cloth, bishop, archbishop, cardinal, prelate, ecclesiastic, divine.

clerical adjective ❶ clerical duties: OFFICE, secretarial. ❷ ECCLESIASTICAL, spiritual, priestly, episcopal, churchly, pastoral, canonical, rabbinical, sacerdotal, apostolic, prelatic.

clever adjective ❶ INTELLIGENT, bright, sharp, quick-witted, quick, gifted, talented, brilliant, able, capable, knowledgeable, educated, sagacious; *informal* brainy, smart. ❷ a clever move: SHREWD, cunning, ingenious, astute, skilful, skilled, resourceful, wily, inventive, subtle, canny, artful, adroit, guileful; *informal* foxy; *N. Amer. informal* cute. ❸ clever with his

hands: DEXTEROUS, skilful, deft, nimble, handy.
– OPPOSITES stupid, awkward.

cliché noun HACKNEYED/WELL-WORN PHRASE, platitude, commonplace, banality, truism, saw, maxim; *informal* old chestnut.

click verb ❶ CLINK, clack, snap, tick. ❷ BECOME CLEAR, make sense, fall into place, come home to one. ❸ TAKE TO EACH OTHER, get on, feel a rapport, be compatible, be on the same wavelength; *informal* hit it off. ❹ BE SUCCESSFUL, prove popular, succeed, be a success, go down well.

client noun CUSTOMER, patron, regular, buyer, purchaser, shopper, consumer, user, patient.

cliff noun PRECIPICE, rock face, crag, bluff, escarpment, scar, scarp, promontory, tor.

climate noun **the political climate**: ATMOSPHERE, mood, environment, temper, spirit, feeling, ambience, aura, ethos.

climax noun CULMINATION, high point, crowning point, height, peak, pinnacle, summit, top, highlight, acme, zenith, apex, apogee, ne plus ultra.
– OPPOSITES anticlimax, nadir.

climb verb ❶ GO UP, ascend, mount, scale, clamber up, shin up. ❷ RISE, increase, shoot up, soar. ❸ SLOPE UPWARD, incline, bank.
– OPPOSITES descend, fall.
■ **climb down** ❶ DESCEND, go down, shin down. ❷ BACK DOWN, retreat, retract, eat one's words, eat humble pie.

clinch verb COMPLETE, settle, secure, seal, set the seal on, confirm, conclude, assure, cap, close, wind up.

cling verb STICK, adhere, hold, grip, clasp, clutch.
■ **cling to** EMBRACE, clutch, hold on to, grasp, grip, cleave to.

clinic noun MEDICAL CENTRE, health centre, infirmary, surgery, sickbay.

clip[1] verb PIN, staple, fasten, fix, attach, hold.
▶ noun FASTENER, clasp, pin.

clip[2] verb CUT, crop, trim, snip, shear, prune.
▶ noun EXCERPT, cutting, snippet, fragment, portion, bit, passage, section, trailer.

clique noun COTERIE, in-crowd, set, group, gang, faction, band, ring, fraternity.

cloak noun ❶ CAPE, robe, wrap, poncho, mantle. ❷ COVER, screen, mask, veil, shroud, cloud, shield, camouflage, disguise.
▶ verb HIDE, conceal, cover, screen, mask, veil, shroud, shield, camouflage, obscure, disguise.

clog verb OBSTRUCT, block, jam, congest, stop up, plug, dam, bung up, impede, hinder, hamper.

cloistered adjective SECLUDED, sheltered, insulated, confined, sequestered, withdrawn, restricted, reclusive, hermitic.

close[1] adjective ❶ NEAR, adjacent, neighbouring, in close proximity, adjoining, abutting, hard by. ❷ **a close resemblance**: NEAR, similar, like, alike, comparable, corresponding, akin, parallel. ❸ **a close description**: ACCURATE, precise, near, true, faithful, literal, conscientious. ❹ **a close friend**: INTIMATE, devoted, loving, inseparable, bosom, close-knit, confidential. ❺ **close print**: DENSE, condensed, crowded, compact,

packed, solid, tight, cramped, congested, squeezed. ❻ **a close game**: HARD-FOUGHT, well matched, evenly matched, sharply contested; *informal* neck-and-neck, nose-to-nose, fifty-fifty. ❼ **close attention**: CAREFUL, keen, rigorous, thorough, vigilant, alert, concentrated, minute, detailed, intent, assiduous, painstaking, searching. ❽ **close weather**: HUMID, muggy, airless, stuffy, suffocating, oppressive, stifling, musty, unventilated; *Brit. informal* fuggy. ❾ **close with his money**: MEAN, miserly, parsimonious, niggardly, penny-pinching, near; *informal* tight-fisted, tight, stingy.
– OPPOSITES distant, remote.

close[2] **verb** ❶ SHUT, slam, fasten, secure, lock, bolt, bar, latch. ❷ **close an opening**: SEAL OFF, stop up, obstruct, block, clog, choke. ❸ **close the meeting**: END, bring to an end, conclude, finish, terminate, wind up, adjourn, discontinue. ❹ **the gap closed**: NARROW, lessen, grow smaller, dwindle, reduce.
– OPPOSITES open.

closet **noun** CUPBOARD, wardrobe, cabinet, locker, storage room.
▶ **verb** SHUT AWAY, sequester, cloister, seclude, confine, isolate.
▶ **adjective** SECRET, undisclosed, hidden, concealed, furtive.

clot **noun** LUMP, clump, mass, obstruction, thrombus; *informal* glob.
▶ **verb** COAGULATE, set, congeal, solidify, thicken, jell, cake, curdle.

cloth **noun** FABRIC, material, textile, stuff.

clothe **verb** DRESS, attire, garb, robe, outfit, fit out, turn out, deck out, rig out, drape, accoutre; *informal* doll up, kit out; *archaic* apparel.
– OPPOSITES undress.

clothes **plural noun** GARMENTS, clothing, dress, attire, costume, garb, wardrobe, outfit, finery, ensemble, vestments; *informal* get-up, gear, togs, weeds; *Brit. informal* clobber; *formal* apparel; *dated* raiment.

cloud **noun** ❶ **a cloud of smoke**: HAZE, pall, shroud, cloak, screen, cover. ❷ SHADOW, threat, gloom, darkness.

cloudless **adjective** CLEAR, sunny, bright, unclouded.
– OPPOSITES cloudy.

cloudy **adjective** ❶ **a cloudy sky**: OVERCAST, dark, grey, hazy, sombre, leaden, heavy, gloomy, dim, sunless, starless. ❷ **cloudy liquids**: OPAQUE, murky, muddy, milky, turbid. ❸ **cloudy recollections**: BLURRED, vague, indistinct, hazy, obscure, confused, muddled, nebulous.
– OPPOSITES cloudless, clear.

clown **noun** ❶ JESTER, fool, buffoon, harlequin, pierrot. ❷ JOKER, comedian, comic, humorist, funny man, wag, wit, prankster.

cloying **adjective** SICKLY SWEET, sugary, saccharine, sickening, nauseating.

club[1] **noun** SOCIETY, group, association, organization, circle, set, league, union, federation, fellowship, fraternity, brotherhood, sisterhood, sorority.
■ **club together** COMBINE, join forces, pool resources, divide costs; *informal* have a whip-round.

club[2] noun CUDGEL, baton, truncheon, bludgeon, staff; *Brit. informal* cosh.
▶ verb *see* HIT (1).

clue noun SIGN, lead, hint, indication, indicator, suggestion, pointer, evidence, information, guide, tip, tip-off, suspicion, trace, inkling.

clump noun CLUSTER, bunch, bundle, collection, mass, assembly, assemblage. *See also* GROUP noun (2).

clumsy adjective ❶ AWKWARD, uncoordinated, ungainly, blundering, inept, bungling, bumbling, maladroit, fumbling, lumbering, heavy-handed, unhandy, unskilful, inexpert, graceless, ungraceful; *informal* cack-handed, ham-fisted, butterfingered, like a bull in a china shop. ❷ UNWIELDY, awkward, cumbersome, bulky, heavy, solid, inconvenient, inelegant, ponderous; *informal* hulking. ❸ a clumsy apology: CRUDE, boorish, crass, inappropriate, ill-judged, tactless, graceless, insensitive, uncouth, inept, gauche, unpolished.
– OPPOSITES graceful, adroit.

cluster noun BUNCH, clump, group, collection, gathering, crowd, assembly, assemblage, knot.
▶ verb GATHER, collect, assemble, congregate, group, come together, flock together.

clutch verb GRIP, grasp, clasp, cling to, hang on to, clench, grab, seize, catch at, claw at.

clutches plural noun fall into his clutches: HANDS, power, control, hold, grip, grasp, claws, possession, keeping, custody.

clutter noun MESS, jumble, litter, disorder, junk, untidiness, chaos, confusion, heap, odds and ends, hotchpotch, tangle.
▶ verb LITTER, make untidy, make a mess of, be strewn about, be scattered about; *informal* mess up.

coach[1] noun BUS, carriage; *dated* omnibus; *historical* charabanc.

coach[2] noun INSTRUCTOR, trainer, teacher, tutor, mentor.
▶ verb INSTRUCT, train, teach, tutor, guide, prepare, direct, drill, cram, prime, put someone through their paces.

coagulate verb CONGEAL, clot, thicken, set, gel, solidify, stiffen, curdle.

coalesce verb COMBINE, unite, join together, blend, fuse, amalgamate, integrate, affiliate, commingle.

coalition noun UNION, alliance, league, affiliation, association, federation, bloc, confederacy, amalgamation, merger, conjunction, fusion.

coarse adjective ❶ ROUGH, uneven, harsh, lumpy, bristly, prickly, gritty, hairy, shaggy, scratchy. ❷ coarse manners: RUDE, ill-mannered, uncivil, boorish, loutish, uncouth, crass, churlish. ❸ coarse humour: VULGAR, indecent, obscene, crude, smutty, offensive, indelicate, bawdy, immodest, unrefined, earthy, ribald, lewd, improper, foul, prurient, pornographic; *informal* blue, raunchy.
– OPPOSITES fine, refined.

coarsen verb ROUGHEN, toughen, thicken, harden, harshen.
– OPPOSITES soften, refine.

coast noun SHORE, seashore,

coastline, shoreline, beach, foreshore, seaboard, water's edge; *poetic/literary* strand.
▶ **verb** GLIDE, cruise, freewheel, drift, taxi, sail, skim, slide.

coat **noun** ❶ JACKET, overcoat. ❷ FUR, hair, wool, fleece, hide, pelt. ❸ **a coat of paint:** LAYER, covering, coating, overlay, film, patina, veneer, wash, glaze, finish, membrane.
▶ **verb** *see* COVER verb (1).

coax **verb** CAJOLE, persuade, wheedle, beguile, inveigle, talk into, induce, entice, win over, prevail upon; *informal* sweet-talk, soft-soap.

cocky **adjective** ARROGANT, conceited, egotistical, vain, swollen-headed, cocksure, swaggering, brash.
– OPPOSITES modest.

coddle **verb** PAMPER, spoil, indulge, cosset, humour, mollycoddle, baby, pet, feather-bed.

code **noun** ❶ CIPHER, secret writing, cryptograph. ❷ SYSTEM, laws, rules, regulations, rule book.

coerce **verb** FORCE, compel, pressure, pressurize, drive, bully, intimidate, frighten, terrorize, browbeat, impel, constrain, oblige; *informal* lean on, twist someone's arm, strong-arm, put the screws on.

coffer **noun** BOX, chest, case, casket, strongbox, safe, trunk, cabinet.

cogent **adjective** CONVINCING, persuasive, compelling, forceful, effective, conclusive, indisputable, sound, unanswerable, powerful, strong, weighty, potent, influential, telling, authoritative, well argued.
– OPPOSITES unconvincing.

cohere **verb** COMBINE, coalesce, join, unite, stick together, fuse, bind, hold together, consolidate.

coherent **adjective** LOGICAL, rational, reasoned, consistent, lucid, articulate, systematic, orderly, structured, well structured, well ordered, cohesive, organized, comprehensible, intelligible, unified, integrated.
– OPPOSITES incoherent, muddled.

cohort **noun** TROOP, brigade, squad, squadron, group, company, body, band, legion, column.

coil **verb** LOOP, wind, spiral, curl, twist, snake, turn, wreathe, entwine, twine, convolute.

coin **noun** ❶ PIECE, bit. ❷ CHANGE, small/loose change, silver, copper, coppers, coinage, specie.
▶ **verb** ❶ MINT, stamp, mould, die, forge. ❷ **coin a word:** INVENT, create, make up, devise, conceive, originate, introduce, think/dream up, formulate, concoct, produce, fabricate.

coincide **verb** ❶ **the dates coincided:** OCCUR SIMULTANEOUSLY, fall together, be concurrent, concur, coexist, synchronize, happen together, clash. ❷ **stories coincided:** AGREE, accord, match, correspond, concur, square, tally, harmonize.

coincidence **noun** CHANCE, accident, luck, fluke, fortuity, serendipity.

coincidental **adjective** ACCIDENTAL, chance, unintentional, unplanned, lucky, casual, fortuitous, serendipitous.

cold adjective ❶ CHILLY, cool, freezing, bitter, icy, chill, wintry, frosty, raw, perishing, biting, glacial, numbing, piercing, frigid, inclement, windy, Siberian, crisp, sunless, polar; *informal* nippy; *Brit. informal* parky. ❷ **feeling cold:** CHILLY, chilled, freezing, frozen, frozen stiff, frostbitten, cool, shivering, shivery. ❸ **a cold response/person:** DISTANT, reserved, aloof, remote, unfriendly, unresponsive, unfeeling, unemotional, indifferent, dispassionate, stand-offish, frigid, glacial, passionless, unmoved, unexcitable, phlegmatic, lukewarm, apathetic, spiritless, unsympathetic, uncaring, heartless, callous, cold-hearted, stony-hearted, inhospitable.
– OPPOSITES hot, warm.

cold-blooded adjective RUTHLESS, callous, savage, inhuman, barbaric, heartless, pitiless, merciless, hard-hearted.
– OPPOSITES kind, humane.

collaborate verb ❶ COOPERATE, work together, join forces, join, unite, combine; *informal* team up, pull together. ❷ COLLUDE, connive, turn traitor, conspire, fraternize; *informal* rat.

collaborator noun ❶ CO-WORKER, colleague, associate, fellow worker, partner, helper, confederate, accomplice, team mate, co-author; *humorous* partner in crime. ❷ TRAITOR, turncoat, quisling, colluder, fraternizer, conspirator; *informal* Judas, blackleg.

collapse verb ❶ FALL IN/DOWN, cave in, give way, crumple, disintegrate, subside, buckle, tumble down, fall to pieces, come apart, break up, fold up, sink, give in. ❷ **the man collapsed:** FAINT, pass out, black out, fall down, lose consciousness, fall unconscious, swoon; *informal* keel over. ❸ **the business/talks collapsed:** BREAK DOWN, fail, fold, fall through, founder, come to nothing, disintegrate, fall flat, miscarry, crash; *informal* flop.
▶ noun ❶ CAVE-IN, fall-in, subsidence, disintegration, break-up. ❷ FAINTING, loss of consciousness, swoon. ❸ **the collapse of the talks:** BREAKDOWN, failure, disintegration, foundering.

collate verb ARRANGE, put in order, order, sort, categorize.

colleague noun CO-WORKER, fellow worker, associate, workmate, partner, collaborator, confederate.

collect verb ❶ GATHER, accumulate, pile up, assemble, stockpile, amass, store, hoard, put by, save, reserve, heap up, aggregate. ❷ **a crowd collected:** GATHER, assemble, congregate, converge, mass, flock together, convene, rally. ❸ **collect money:** RAISE, gather, solicit, obtain, acquire, secure. ❹ **collect the dry-cleaning:** FETCH, call for, go and get, pick up, bring.
– OPPOSITES disperse.

collected adjective COMPOSED, cool, poised, unperturbed, serene, unruffled, unshaken. *See also* CALM adjective (1).

collection noun ❶ ACCUMULATION, pile, stockpile, store, stock, supply, heap, hoard, mass, conglomeration, array, aggregation. ❷ DONATIONS, contributions, gifts, offerings, alms.

collective adjective JOINT, united, combined, shared, common, cooperative, concerted, collaborative, corporate, aggregate.
– OPPOSITES individual.

college noun UNIVERSITY, polytechnic, institute, college of further education, school, conservatory.

collide verb CRASH, come into collision, bang into, smash into, knock into, run into, slam into, cannon into.

collision noun CRASH, impact, accident, smash, pile-up, bump, scrape, knock, clash, wreck.

colloquial adjective CONVERSATIONAL, informal, casual, familiar, chatty, everyday, idiomatic, demotic, vernacular.
– OPPOSITES formal.

collusion noun COMPLICITY, connivance, collaboration, secret understanding, plotting, intrigue; *informal* cahoots.

colonize verb OCCUPY, settle, populate, people, subjugate, pioneer, open up, found.

colony noun ❶ DEPENDENCY, possession, settlement, territory, province, dominion, protectorate, satellite state. ❷ COMMUNITY, group, ghetto, quarter.

colossal adjective ENORMOUS, huge, immense, gigantic, vast, massive, mammoth, gargantuan, monumental, prodigious, monstrous, titanic, mountainous, towering, elephantine, Brobdingnagian.
– OPPOSITES small.

colour noun ❶ HUE, tint, shade, tone, tinge, coloration, colouring, pigmentation, pigment. ❷ add colour to her cheeks: PINKNESS, rosiness, redness, ruddiness, blush, flush, glow, bloom.
▶ verb ❶ TINT, dye, paint, colour-wash, tinge, stain, shade, pigment. ❷ attitudes coloured by his experiences: INFLUENCE, affect, prejudice, distort, bias, slant, taint, sway, pervert, warp.

colourful adjective ❶ BRIGHT, vivid, intense, brilliant, vibrant, multi-coloured, deep-coloured, iridescent, psychedelic, gaudy, variegated. ❷ colourful descriptions: VIVID, graphic, lively, interesting, animated, rich, striking, picturesque, stimulating, telling. ❸ a colourful character: INTERESTING, eccentric, unusual, flamboyant, dynamic, flashy.
– OPPOSITES colourless, dull.

colourless adjective ❶ UNCOLOURED, achromatic, white, bleached, faded. ❷ DULL, boring, uninteresting, tame, lifeless, dreary, insipid, lacklustre, characterless, vapid, vacuous.
– OPPOSITES colourful.

colours plural noun ❶ FLAG, standard, banner, ensign. ❷ BADGE, insignia, uniform.

column noun ❶ PILLAR, post, support, upright, shaft, pilaster, obelisk, caryatid. ❷ a column of people: LINE, row, file, queue, procession, train, rank, string, progression, cavalcade. ❸ a newspaper column: ARTICLE, piece, item, feature, editorial, leader, leading article.

comb verb ❶ GROOM, arrange, tidy, smarten up, spruce up, untangle, curry, dress. ❷ comb the area: SEARCH, hunt through, scour, ransack, rummage, rake, sift, go over with a fine-tooth comb.

combat noun BATTLE, fighting, conflict, hostilities, fight, clash, skirmish, duel, contest, engagement, encounter.
▶ **verb** FIGHT, battle against, oppose, resist, contest, make a stand against, stand up to, grapple with, struggle against, tackle, withstand, defy, strive against. *See also* FIGHT verb.

combative adjective AGGRESSIVE, belligerent, pugnacious, bellicose, quarrelsome, argumentative, antagonistic, contentious, truculent.
– OPPOSITES conciliatory.

combination noun ❶ BLEND, mixture, compound, amalgamation, amalgam, mix, alloy, composite, aggregate, fusion, marriage, synthesis, concoction. ❷ UNION, association, alliance, federation, merger, grouping, confederation, confederacy, cooperation, coalition, partnership, league, consortium, syndication.

combine verb ❶ JOIN, join forces, unite, form an alliance, get together, cooperate, ally, pool resources, associate, unify, integrate; *informal* team up, gang together, club together. ❷ MIX, blend, add together, fuse, compound, mingle, merge, amalgamate, bind, alloy, bond, incorporate, synthesize, interweave.
– OPPOSITES separate, part.

combustible adjective FLAMMABLE, inflammable, incendiary, explosive.
– OPPOSITES incombustible.

come verb ❶ MOVE TOWARDS, approach, advance, draw near, near, reach, bear down on, close in on. ❷ ARRIVE, appear, turn up, put in an appearance, materialize; *informal* show up, fetch up, blow in. ❸ it comes in all colours: BE AVAILABLE, be made, be produced, be on offer.
– OPPOSITES go, leave.
■ **come about** *see* HAPPEN. **come across** *see* MEET (1), FIND (1). **come clean** *see* CONFESS. **come off** *see* SUCCEED (2). **come out with** *see* SAY (2).

comedian noun ❶ COMIC, stand-up comedian, humorist. ❷ WIT, wag, joker, clown, jester; *informal* laugh; *informal, dated* card.

comedy noun HUMOUR, joking, funniness, wit, wittiness, fun, farce, hilarity, levity, slapstick, clowning, buffoonery, facetiousness, drollery.

comfort noun ❶ EASE, well-being, affluence, contentment, tranquillity, luxury, opulence, serenity, repose, cosiness, plenty, sufficiency. ❷ bring comfort to the bereaved: SOLACE, help, support, sympathy, consolation, succour, cheer, condolence, relief, easement, alleviation, gladdening.
– OPPOSITES discomfort, grief, pain.
▶ **verb** HELP, support, bring comfort to, console, sympathize with, solace, reassure, succour, cheer, soothe, hearten, gladden, assuage.
– OPPOSITES distress.

comfortable adjective ❶ comfortable shoes: WELL FITTING, snug, loose-fitting, roomy. ❷ a comfortable room: COSY, homely, snug, relaxing, tranquil. ❸ a comfortable lifestyle: PLEASANT, well off, affluent, prosperous, well-to-do, luxurious, opulent,

free from hardship, untroubled, happy, contented.
– OPPOSITES uncomfortable.

comic adjective FUNNY, humorous, amusing, entertaining, comical, witty, hilarious, farcical, jocular, hysterical, diverting, joking, droll, zany, side-splitting, ridiculous, facetious, whimsical, uproarious, waggish; *informal* rich, priceless.
– OPPOSITES serious.
▶ noun *see* COMEDIAN.

command verb ❶ ORDER, give orders to, direct, instruct, charge, require, prescribe, ordain, demand, compel, bid, summon, enjoin; *formal* adjure. ❷ **he commands the unit:** BE IN CHARGE OF, have charge of, control, have control of, lead, head, rule, direct, supervise, manage, govern, preside over, superintend.
▶ noun ❶ ORDER, instruction, decree, directive, edict, direction, dictate, injunction, requirement, prescription, bidding, mandate, fiat, commandment, precept. ❷ **under his command:** CHARGE, control, authority, power, direction, mastery, government, management, supervision, administration, dominion, sway, domination, ascendancy. ❸ **her command of English:** KNOWLEDGE, grasp, mastery.

commander noun LEADER, head, chief, director, officer-in-charge; *informal* boss, top dog, kingpin, big cheese. *See also* CHIEF.

commemorate verb CELEBRATE, remember, honour, salute, mark, memorialize, pay tribute to, pay homage to, immortalize, solemnize.

commence verb BEGIN, start, initiate, originate, embark on, go ahead, inaugurate, launch; *informal* set the ball rolling, get the show on the road.
– OPPOSITES finish, end, conclude.

commend verb PRAISE, applaud, speak highly of, acclaim, extol, compliment, approve of, eulogize; *formal* laud.
– OPPOSITES criticize.

commendable adjective ADMIRABLE, praiseworthy, laudable, creditable, worthy, estimable, meritorious, reputable, deserving.
– OPPOSITES reprehensible.

comment verb ❶ SAY, observe, state, remark, speak, express an opinion on, interpose, interject, opine. ❷ EXPLAIN, annotate, write notes, interpret, elucidate, clarify, shed light on.
▶ noun ❶ REMARK, opinion, observation, view, statement, reaction, criticism, animadversion. ❷ NOTE, annotation, explanation, interpretation, footnote, gloss, exposition, interpolation, marginalia.

commentary noun ❶ NARRATION, description, account, review, analysis. ❷ **a textual commentary:** ANNOTATION, notes, interpretation, analysis, critique, elucidation, exegesis.

commerce noun BUSINESS, trade, trading, dealing, dealings, financial transactions, buying and selling, merchandising, trafficking.

commercial adjective ❶ BUSINESS, trade, profit-making, marketing, mercantile, merchandising, sales. ❷ PROFIT-ORIENTATED,

materialistic, mercenary, mercantile.
▶ **noun** ADVERTISEMENT, advertising break; *informal* ad, plug; *Brit. informal* advert.

commission **noun** ❶ **a commission to paint his portrait:** TASK, employment, piece of work, work, duty, charge, mission, responsibility. ❷ **a commission on the sale:** PERCENTAGE, brokerage, share, fee, compensation; *informal* cut, rake-off. ❸ **the commission of a crime:** PERFORMANCE, perpetration, execution, committal.
▶ **verb** ❶ **commission an artist:** ENGAGE, employ, appoint, contract, book, authorize. ❷ **commission a portrait:** ORDER, place an order for, contract for, pay for, authorize.

commit **verb** ❶ **commit a crime:** PERFORM, carry out, perpetrate, execute, enact, effect, do. ❷ **commit to her care:** ENTRUST, trust, deliver, hand over, give, consign, assign, transfer.
■ **commit oneself** PROMISE, pledge, engage, bind oneself, obligate oneself, covenant.

commitment **noun** ❶ DEDICATION, involvement in, devotion, zeal, loyalty, allegiance, adherence. ❷ **make a commitment:** PROMISE, pledge, undertaking, vow, assurance, guarantee, covenant. ❸ **have too many commitments:** OBLIGATION, duty, responsibility, undertaking, appointment, arrangement, liability, task, engagement, tie.

committed **adjective** DEDICATED, enthusiastic, devoted, keen, passionate, resolute, earnest, single-minded, whole-hearted, unwavering, ardent, zealous; *informal* card-carrying.
– OPPOSITES apathetic.

commodious **adjective** SPACIOUS, roomy, large, capacious, extensive, ample.
– OPPOSITES cramped.

common **adjective** ❶ ORDINARY, average, normal, conventional, typical, unexceptional, plain, commonplace, run-of-the-mill, simple, habitual, undistinguished, unsurprising, pedestrian, humdrum, everyday, workaday, customary, stock; *Brit. informal* common or garden. ❷ **a common belief:** WIDESPREAD, general, universal, popular, accepted, prevalent, prevailing, shared, public, communal, collective. ❸ **she's very common:** VULGAR, coarse, rude, uncouth, unrefined, boorish, churlish, inferior, disreputable, lower-class, plebeian, lowly, proletarian; *Brit. informal* yobbish.
– OPPOSITES uncommon, unusual, rare.
▶ **noun** PARK, heath, parkland.

commonplace **adjective** ORDINARY, unexceptional, undistinguished, routine, pedestrian, mediocre, dull, uninteresting, humdrum, trite, hackneyed.
– OPPOSITES remarkable.

commotion **noun** DISTURBANCE, racket, uproar, disorder, chaos, tumult, clamour, pandemonium, rumpus, hubbub, riot, fracas, hullabaloo, row, furore, brouhaha, confusion, upheaval, disruption, bother, turmoil, agitation, contretemps, excitement, fuss, disquiet, ferment, bustle, hustle and bustle; *informal* to-do, bedlam, stir, palaver.

communal adjective COMMON, collective, shared, joint, general, public, community, cooperative.
– OPPOSITES individual, private.

communicable adjective INFECTIOUS, contagious, catching, transmittable, transmissible, transferable.

communicate verb ❶ **communicate ideas:** MAKE KNOWN, pass on, convey, spread, impart, get across, publish, transmit, broadcast, announce, report, relay, disseminate, proclaim, promulgate, divulge, disclose, express, mention, reveal, intimate, transfer.
❷ **communicate with someone:** GET ONE'S IDEAS/MESSAGE ACROSS, talk, get in touch, converse, confer, correspond, commune, have dealings, interface.
❸ **communicate diseases:** TRANSMIT, pass on, spread, give, infect with, transfer. ❹ **her room communicates with his:** CONNECT, be connected to, lead to, adjoin, abut on.

communication noun ❶ CONTACT, interaction, getting in touch, link, dissemination, communion. ❷ **received a communication:** MESSAGE, dispatch, letter, report, statement, news, information, data, intelligence, word.

communicative adjective TALKATIVE, chatty, open, frank, candid, expansive, forthcoming, voluble, loquacious, informative, conversational.
– OPPOSITES uncommunicative, reserved.

communion noun EMPATHY, rapport, sympathy, affinity, closeness, togetherness, unity, accord, fellowship, harmony, fusion; *formal* concord.

commute verb ❶ TRAVEL TO AND FROM, travel back and forth, shuttle. ❷ **commute a sentence:** LESSEN, reduce, shorten, curtail, mitigate, modify.

compact[1] adjective ❶ DENSE, compressed, condensed, packed close, tight-packed, solid, firm, close, consolidated. ❷ **a compact style:** CONCISE, succinct, terse, brief, condensed, pithy, to the point, epigrammatic, abridged, abbreviated, compendious.
❸ SMALL, neat, portable, handy.
– OPPOSITES loose, rambling, large.

compact[2] noun AGREEMENT, contract, pact, covenant, treaty, alliance, bargain, deal, settlement, entente.

companion noun ❶ ESCORT, friend, partner, consort, chaperone, confederate, colleague, associate, ally, crony, comrade. ❷ **a companion to this volume:** COUNTERPART, fellow, match, twin, complement, mate.

companionship noun FRIENDSHIP, company, fellowship, togetherness, society, camaraderie, intimacy, rapport, comradeship.

company noun ❶ BUSINESS, firm, organization, corporation, conglomerate, consortium, concern, enterprise, house, establishment, partnership, syndicate. ❷ *See* COMPANIONSHIP.
❸ **expecting company:** VISITORS, callers, guests. ❹ **a company of actors:** GROUP, band, party, body,

association, society, troupe, fellowship, circle, collection, league, crew, guild. ❺ **address the company:** ASSEMBLY, gathering, audience, crowd, group, throng.

comparable adjective SIMILAR, like, parallel, analogous, related, equivalent, matching, compatible, commensurable, corresponding, proportionate, proportional, cognate.
– OPPOSITES dissimilar.

compare verb ❶ CONTRAST, make a comparison between, measure against, juxtapose, differentiate, collate. ❷ **his work does not compare:** BEAR COMPARISON, be comparable, be the equal, be on a par, be in the same class, compete, approach, match, come up to; *informal* hold a candle to.

comparison noun ❶ CONTRAST, juxtaposition, correlation, distinction, collation, differentiation. ❷ **there is no comparison:** RESEMBLANCE, likeness, similarity, correlation, analogy, comparability.

compass noun SCOPE, range, extent, area, reach, span, limits, bounds, field, sphere, zone, circumference, stretch.

compassionate adjective TENDER, gentle, kindly, soft-hearted, understanding, sympathetic, humane, pitying, lenient, charitable, benevolent.

compatible adjective ❶ WELL SUITED, suited, like-minded, in agreement, in tune, of the same mind, in harmony. ❷ CONSISTENT, in keeping, reconcilable, consonant, congruent, congruous.
– OPPOSITES incompatible.

compel verb FORCE, make, coerce, drive, pressure, pressurize, order, constrain, impel, oblige, press, necessitate, urge; *informal* put the screws on, strong-arm, railroad, bulldoze.

compelling adjective ❶ FASCINATING, gripping, enthralling, hypnotic, mesmerizing. ❷ **compelling reasons:** CONVINCING, telling, forceful, powerful, weighty, conclusive, irrefutable, cogent.
– OPPOSITES boring, weak.

compensate verb ❶ RECOMPENSE, repay, reimburse, make amends, make up for, atone, redress, make restitution, make reparation, make good, expiate, requite. ❷ OFFSET, counterbalance, counteract, balance, cancel out, neutralize, counterpoise, nullify.

compensation noun ❶ RECOMPENSE, damages, repayment, reimbursement, indemnification, requital. ❷ AMENDS, restitution, redress, atonement, expiation.

compete verb ❶ TAKE PART, be a contestant, participate, enter, go in for; *informal* throw one's hat in the ring. ❷ CONTEND, struggle, fight, oppose, rival, be in competition, vie, strive.
– OPPOSITES cooperate.

competent adjective CAPABLE, able, proficient, skilful, skilled, adept, accomplished, qualified, expert, efficient, effective, trained, workmanlike.
– OPPOSITES incompetent, inept.

competition noun ❶ CONTEST, match, game, heat, tournament, championship, event, meet, quiz, race, rally, trial, challenge. ❷ CONTENTION, opposition, rivalry, contest, struggle, vying, strife.

competitive adjective
❶ AMBITIOUS, aggressive, combative, antagonistic, hard-fought, keen, cut-throat, lively, contentious. ❷ **prices were not competitive:** REASONABLE, moderate, fair, comparable, similar, average.
– OPPOSITES uncompetitive.

competitor noun ❶ CONTESTANT, contender, challenger, participant, candidate. ❷ RIVAL, opponent, adversary, antagonist, opposition.

compile verb COLLECT, gather, accumulate, amass, assemble, put together, marshal, organize, arrange, collate, anthologize.

complain verb ❶ CRITICIZE, make/lodge a complaint, find fault, carp, make a fuss; *informal* kick up a fuss. ❷ **she's always complaining:** GRUMBLE, whine, lament, bewail; *informal* moan, gripe, grouch, grouse, bellyache, bitch.

complaint noun ❶ GRIEVANCE, criticism, protest, accusation, charge, remonstrance, objection, grumble; *informal* gripe, grouse, moan, beef, whine, whinge. ❷ ILLNESS, disease, sickness, ailment, disorder, affliction, malady, infection, malaise. *See also* ILLNESS.

complaisant adjective
AMENABLE, obliging, tractable, compliant, obedient, biddable, pliant, cooperative, willing, accommodating, deferential, submissive, docile, acquiescent.

complement noun ❶ **the perfect complement:** COMPANION, addition, supplement, accessory, finishing/final touch. ❷ **the full complement:** AMOUNT, total, allowance, aggregate, load, capacity, quota.
▶ verb COMPLETE, round/set off, go well with, add the finishing/final touch to, supplement.

complementary adjective
MATCHING, finishing, perfecting, interdependent, reciprocal.

complete adjective ❶ ENTIRE, whole, full, total, intact, comprehensive, undivided, uncut, unshortened, unabridged, unexpurgated. ❷ **the task is complete:** FINISHED, completed, accomplished, achieved, done, concluded, ended, finalized. ❸ **a complete idiot:** ABSOLUTE, utter, total, out-and-out, downright, thorough, thoroughgoing, unmitigated, unqualified, sheer, rank, dyed-in-the-wool.
– OPPOSITES incomplete, partial, unfinished, .
▶ verb ❶ **complete the task:** FINISH, conclude, end, accomplish, achieve, do, perform, execute, fulfil, effect, discharge, realize, settle, clinch; *informal* wrap up, polish off. ❷ **complete the outfit:** ROUND OFF, finish off, make perfect, crown, cap, add the final/finishing touch.

completely adverb TOTALLY, utterly, absolutely, thoroughly, quite, wholly, altogether.

complex adjective
❶ COMPLICATED, difficult, intricate, convoluted, involved, knotty, puzzling, perplexing, cryptic, problematic, enigmatic, tortuous, labyrinthine; *informal* tricky. ❷ **a complex structure:** COMPOSITE, compound, elaborate, multiple, manifold, heterogeneous, multiplex.
– OPPOSITES simple, elementary.

complicate verb MAKE DIFFICULT, confuse, make involved/intricate, muddle, jumble, entangle, compound; *informal* snarl up, screw up.
– OPPOSITES simplify.

complicated adjective *see* COMPLEX (1).

complication noun
❶ DIFFICULTY, problem, obstacle, snag, drawback, setback.
❷ DIFFICULTY, confusion, complexity, muddle, intricacy.

compliment noun PRAISE, tribute, admiration, flattery, commendation, congratulations, accolade, honour, plaudits, bouquet, testimonial, eulogy, panegyric; *formal* encomium.
▶ verb CONGRATULATE, praise, speak highly of, commend, flatter, acclaim, honour, pay tribute to, salute, admire, sing someone's praises, extol, felicitate, eulogize; *formal* laud.
– OPPOSITES insult, criticize.

complimentary adjective CONGRATULATORY, admiring, approving, appreciative, flattering, commendatory, eulogistic, panegyrical; *formal* encomiastic, laudatory.
– OPPOSITES insulting, abusive.

comply verb OBEY, conform to, observe, abide by, keep to, adhere to, assent to, consent to, agree with, accord with, acquiesce in, follow, respect, yield, submit, defer to.
– OPPOSITES disobey, ignore.

component noun PART, piece, element, bit, section, constituent, ingredient, unit, item, module.

compose verb ❶ WRITE, make up, create, think up, produce, devise, invent, concoct, compile, fashion, formulate. ❷ COMPRISE, form, make up, constitute.
❸ **compose oneself**: CALM, quiet, collect, control, soothe, pacify, assuage, still.

composed adjective *see* CALM adjective (1).

composition noun ❶ **the composition of the soil**: STRUCTURE, make-up, organization, layout, configuration, constitution, character, formulation. ❷ STORY, article, essay, poem, novel, work of art, piece, work, opus. ❸ **the painting's composition**: ARRANGEMENT, proportions, balance, harmony, symmetry.

compound noun BLEND, mixture, amalgam, combination, fusion, alloy, conglomerate, synthesis, medley, hybrid; *technical* admixture.
▶ adjective COMPOSITE, blended, complex, fused, conglomerate.
▶ verb ❶ *See* COMBINE. ❷ **compound the problem**: WORSEN, make worse, add to, exacerbate, aggravate, magnify, intensify, heighten.

comprehend verb UNDERSTAND, grasp, take in, follow, appreciate, see, realize, assimilate, fathom, perceive, discern, apprehend; *Brit. informal* twig.

comprehensible adjective UNDERSTANDABLE, clear, straightforward, intelligible, self-explanatory, lucid, explicit, discernible, graspable, fathomable.
– OPPOSITES incomprehensible.

comprehensive adjective COMPLETE, all-inclusive, full, all-embracing, total, encyclopedic, wholesale, universal, exhaustive, detailed,

thorough, extensive, widespread, broad, wide-ranging, far-reaching, blanket, umbrella, catholic.
– OPPOSITES selective.

compress verb ❶ COMPACT, squeeze, press down/together, crush, squash, flatten, cram, condense, constrict, tamp; *informal* jam together. ❷ SHORTEN, abbreviate, abridge, reduce, contract, summarize, truncate.
– OPPOSITES expand.

compressed adjective *see* COMPACT[1] (1).

comprise verb ❶ CONSIST OF, include, contain, be composed of, take in, embrace, encompass. ❷ MAKE UP, form, constitute, compose.

compromise verb ❶ COME TO AN UNDERSTANDING, make concessions, strike a balance, meet halfway, come to terms, make a deal, give and take, find the middle ground, find a happy medium, reach a formula, negotiate a settlement. ❷ **compromised his reputation:** DAMAGE, injure, undermine, discredit, dishonour, bring into disrepute, shame, embarrass, endanger, jeopardize, imperil, weaken.
▶ noun UNDERSTANDING, deal, balance, concession, happy medium, trade-off, middle course, give and take, adjustment.

compulsion noun ❶ OBLIGATION, force, constraint, duress, coercion, pressure, oppression. ❷ URGE, need, desire, drive, necessity, addiction, preoccupation, obsession.

compulsive adjective ❶ **a compulsive desire:** OBSESSIVE, uncontrollable, irresistible, compelling, overwhelming, driving, urgent, besetting. ❷ **a compulsive gambler:** OBSESSIVE, obsessional, addicted, habitual, incorrigible, incurable, dependent, out of control; *informal* hooked.

compulsory adjective OBLIGATORY, mandatory, required, binding, forced, necessary, essential, unavoidable, inescapable, requisite, prescribed, set, statutory, de rigueur, stipulated.
– OPPOSITES optional.

compunction noun REMORSE, regret, guilt, scruples, qualms, contrition, pangs of conscience, penitence, repentance, contriteness.

compute verb CALCULATE, count, add up, work out, reckon, determine, total, figure out, estimate, tally, measure, evaluate, rate, enumerate, sum.

comrade noun FRIEND, companion, colleague, partner, associate, confederate, co-worker, fellow worker, teammate, ally; *informal* pal; *Brit. informal* mate.

con verb DECEIVE, swindle, trick, cheat, mislead, hoodwink, delude; *informal* bamboozle.

conceal verb ❶ **conceal her face:** HIDE, cover, keep hidden, keep out of sight, obscure, screen, mask, disguise, camouflage, shelter, bury, tuck away. ❷ **conceal his identity:** HIDE, keep secret, keep dark, cover up, hush up, dissemble; *informal* keep the lid on.
– OPPOSITES reveal, expose.

concealed adjective *see* HIDDEN.

concede verb ❶ **concede defeat:** ADMIT, acknowledge, accept, allow, grant, accede, confess, recognize, own. ❷ **concede territory:** GIVE UP,

yield, surrender, hand over, relinquish, cede.
– OPPOSITES deny, retain.

conceit noun PRIDE, arrogance, vanity, egotism, self-importance, self-satisfaction, self-admiration, boasting, swagger, narcissism; *poetic/literary* vainglory.
– OPPOSITES humility.

conceited adjective PROUD, arrogant, vain, self-important, swollen-headed, haughty, immodest, egotistical, egocentric, self-satisfied, smug, cocky, boastful, swaggering, narcissistic, supercilious, overweening, complacent, bumptious; *informal* big-headed, stuck up, toffee-nosed, snooty; *poetic/literary* vainglorious.
– OPPOSITES modest, humble.

conceivable adjective CREDIBLE, believable, thinkable, imaginable, possible, understandable, comprehensible.
– OPPOSITES inconceivable.

conceive verb ❶ BECOME PREGNANT, be impregnated. ❷ conceive a strategy: THINK UP, formulate, create, work out, form, devise, originate, produce, frame, draw up, develop, imagine, dream up, contrive, envisage; *informal* cook up.

concentrate verb ❶ concentrate on his studies: GIVE ONE'S ATTENTION TO, be absorbed in, focus on, be engrossed in, put one's mind to, consider closely. ❷ troops concentrated on the border: COLLECT, gather, crowd, mass, accumulate, congregate, amass, cluster, converge, rally. ❸ concentrated liquid: CONDENSE, reduce, compress, boil down, distil.
– OPPOSITES disperse, dilute.

concentrated adjective a concentrated effort: INTENSIVE, intense, rigorous, vigorous, all-out.
– OPPOSITES half-hearted.

concern noun ❶ full of concern: WORRY, anxiety, disquiet, distress, apprehension, disturbance, perturbation. ❷ of concern to us all: INTEREST, importance, relevance, bearing, applicability. ❸ not your concern: BUSINESS, matter of interest, affair, department, involvement, responsibility, duty, job, task, occupation. ❹ a going concern: BUSINESS, company, firm, enterprise, organization, corporation, establishment.
– OPPOSITES indifference.
▶ verb ❶ AFFECT, be the business of, be relevant to, involve, apply to, be of interest to, touch. ❷ WORRY, disturb, trouble, bother, make anxious, perturb, distress.

concerned adjective ❶ the men concerned: INVOLVED, implicated, relevant, party to, connected, interested. ❷ concerned parents: WORRIED, disturbed, anxious, upset, bothered, apprehensive, uneasy, distressed, perturbed, exercised.

concerning preposition ABOUT, relating to, regarding, as regards, involving, with reference to, with respect to, in the matter of, re, apropos.

concerted adjective JOINT, combined, united, collective, coordinated, collaborative, cooperative, synchronized.

conciliate verb PLACATE, calm down, appease, pacify, mollify, assuage, soothe.
– OPPOSITES provoke.

concise adjective SUCCINCT, brief, short, compact, condensed, terse, compressed, to the point, pithy, laconic, epigrammatic, synoptic, compendious.
– OPPOSITES lengthy, wordy.

conclude verb ❶ END, finish, come/bring to an end, halt, cease, terminate, discontinue; *informal* wind up. ❷ COME TO A CONCLUSION, deduce, infer, gather, judge, assume, presume, suppose, conjecture, surmise.
– OPPOSITES start.

conclusion noun ❶ END, finish, close, completion, termination, cessation, culmination, halting, discontinuance. ❷ DEDUCTION, inference, decision, opinion, judgement, verdict, conviction, assumption, presumption, interpretation, resolution, solution.
– OPPOSITES beginning.

conclusive adjective DECISIVE, definitive, certain, incontestable, unquestionable, unequivocal, final, clinching, ultimate, categorical, irrefutable, convincing, cogent.
– OPPOSITES inconclusive.

concoct verb INVENT, devise, think up, dream up, put together, plan, fabricate, formulate, form, hatch, plot, forge, design, fashion, brew; *informal* cook up.

concomitant adjective ATTENDANT, accompanying, associated, linked, affiliated.

concrete adjective ACTUAL, real, definite, genuine, factual, substantial, solid, physical, visible, material, tangible, palpable, specific, objective, firm, existing.
– OPPOSITES abstract, unreal.

concur verb AGREE, assent, acquiesce, accord, be of the same mind.
– OPPOSITES disagree.

concurrent adjective SIMULTANEOUS, parallel, coexisting, overlapping, coexistent, coincident, contemporaneous, synchronous, side by side.

condemn verb ❶ DENOUNCE, criticize, censure, damn, deplore, berate, reprove, upbraid, reproach, blame, reprehend, deprecate, disapprove of, disparage, revile, execrate, decry, reprobate; *informal* slam; *Brit. informal* slate; *formal* castigate. ❷ **condemn to death**: SENTENCE, pass sentence on, convict. ❸ **condemned to poverty**: DAMN, doom, compel, coerce, impel.
– OPPOSITES praise, acquit.

condense verb ❶ SHORTEN, abridge, abbreviate, cut, reduce, compress, curtail, summarize, contract, compact, synopsize, encapsulate. ❷ THICKEN, concentrate, reduce, distil, solidify, coagulate.
– OPPOSITES lengthen.

condescend verb DEIGN, lower oneself, stoop, descend, unbend, humble/demean oneself.

condescending adjective PATRONIZING, supercilious, disdainful, superior, snobbish, lofty, lordly; *informal* snooty, snotty, toffee-nosed.

condition noun ❶ STATE, state of affairs, situation, circumstance, position, predicament, plight, quandary. ❷ **athletes in good condition**: SHAPE, fitness, health, state of health, order, trim; *informal* nick, fettle, kilter. ❸ **on one condition**: RESTRICTION, proviso,

provision, stipulation, prerequisite, rule, limitation, terms, limit. ❹ **a heart condition:** DISEASE, illness, disorder, complaint, problem, ailment, malady.
▶ **verb** TRAIN, accustom, habituate, adapt, influence, mould, determine, govern, educate, inure.

conditional **adjective** PROVISIONAL, dependent, contingent, qualified, limited, restricted, provisory; *informal* with strings attached.
– OPPOSITES unconditional.

condone **verb** ALLOW, tolerate, excuse, pardon, make allowances for, forgive, overlook, disregard, turn a blind eye to, let pass; *informal* wink at.
– OPPOSITES condemn.

conducive **adjective** CONTRIBUTORY, helpful, favourable, useful, instrumental, advantageous, supportive, beneficial.

conduct **noun** ❶ BEHAVIOUR, actions, habits, practices, bearing, manners; *N. Amer.* deportment; *formal* comportment. ❷ **the conduct of the war:** RUNNING, handling, operation, direction, management, organization, administration, control, regulation, guidance, supervision, leadership.
▶ **verb** ❶ **conduct oneself:** BEHAVE, act, acquit, deport; *formal* comport. ❷ **conduct the proceedings:** DIRECT, run, manage, administer, be in charge of, lead, organize, handle, control, supervise, regulate, preside over. ❸ **conduct them to their seats:** SHOW, guide, lead, escort, accompany, take.

confer **verb** ❶ BESTOW, present, award, grant, give, hand out, invest, accord. ❷ **confer with colleagues:** TALK, have discussions, exchange views, consult, debate, deliberate, compare notes, converse, seek advice; *informal* put their/your/our heads together.

conference **noun** MEETING, seminar, discussion, deliberation, convention, council, congress, forum, symposium, colloquium, convocation.

confess **verb** ADMIT, acknowledge, own up to, make known, disclose, reveal, divulge, accept responsibility, make a clean breast of, unburden oneself, come clean; *informal* spill the beans, get something off one's chest, blurt out.

confidant **noun** FRIEND, crony, intimate, familiar, alter ego; *informal* pal, chum; *Brit. informal* mate.

confide **verb** CONFESS, reveal, disclose, tell, divulge, admit, unburden oneself, unbosom oneself, open one's heart.

confidence **noun** ❶ **no confidence in them:** BELIEF, reliance, faith, certainty, trust, credence, dependence. ❷ **full of confidence:** SELF-ASSURANCE, self-confidence, self-reliance, self-possession, nerve, poise, courage, boldness, conviction, panache, composure, mettle, fortitude, verve.
– OPPOSITES distrust, uncertainty, doubt.

confident **adjective** ❶ CERTAIN, sure, convinced, positive, sanguine. ❷ SELF-ASSURED, self-possessed, self-confident, unafraid, fearless, secure, bold, assertive, cocksure.
– OPPOSITES uncertain.

confidential adjective ❶ SECRET, top secret, private, classified, restricted, off the record, suppressed, personal, intimate. ❷ a confidential friend: CLOSE, trusted, intimate, faithful, reliable, trustworthy.

confine verb ❶ ENCLOSE, cage, lock up, imprison, detain, jail, shut up, intern, hold captive, incarcerate, restrain, impound, keep, pen, coop up, box up, immure, wall up. ❷ confine your remarks to: RESTRICT, limit, keep within the limits of, circumscribe, curb.
– OPPOSITES free.

confirm verb ❶ VERIFY, prove, bear out, corroborate, validate, endorse, authenticate, establish, substantiate, give credence to, evidence. ❷ confirm the appointment: RATIFY, endorse, approve, sanction, authorize, underwrite, warrant, accredit. ❸ confirm that he would appear: GUARANTEE, assure, affirm, promise, pledge, assert, reassert.
– OPPOSITES contradict, deny.

confiscate verb SEIZE, impound, take possession of, remove, take away, appropriate, commandeer, expropriate, sequester, sequestrate, arrogate.

conflict noun ❶ DISPUTE, quarrel, squabble, wrangle, feud, hostility, disagreement, dissension, discord, friction, antagonism, strife, contention; *informal* row. ❷ WAR, battle, fight, warfare, clash, engagement, encounter, hostilities, combat, struggle. ❸ CLASH, incompatibility, incongruity, mismatch, variance, divergence, inconsistency.
– OPPOSITES agreement, peace, harmony.
▶ verb CLASH, differ, disagree, be at odds, be in opposition, be at variance, be incompatible, contrast, oppose each other, collide.
– OPPOSITES agree.

conform verb ❶ COMPLY, obey the rules, adapt, adjust, be conventional; *informal* run with the pack, swim with the stream. ❷ conform with his ideas: FIT, match, agree with, correspond to, tally with, square with, accord with.
– OPPOSITES rebel, differ.

conformity noun ❶ CONVENTIONALITY, traditionalism, orthodoxy. ❷ COMPLIANCE, obedience, observance, adaptation, adjustment, accommodation.

confront verb FACE, face up to, tackle, stand up to, defy, challenge, take on, resist, attack, assault, accost, waylay, meet head on.
– OPPOSITES avoid.

confuse verb ❶ BEWILDER, puzzle, perplex, bemuse, baffle, mystify, befuddle, disorientate, disorient, agitate, nonplus; *informal* rattle, throw, flummox. ❷ confuse the issue: MUDDLE, mix up, jumble, tangle up, disorder; *informal* snarl up. ❸ confuse with each other: MISTAKE, mix/muddle up.
– OPPOSITES enlighten, simplify.

confused adjective ❶ a confused recollection: UNCLEAR, hazy, indistinct, foggy, obscure, garbled, incoherent, woolly. ❷ a confused mess: MUDDLED, jumbled, untidy, disordered, disorderly, out of order, chaotic, disorganized, upset, disarranged; *informal* topsy-turvy, at sixes and sevens,

higgledy-piggledy. ❸ a confused old man: BEWILDERED, disorientated, disoriented, flustered, befuddled, addled, unbalanced, unhinged, demented, at sea, nonplussed; *informal* in a tizzy, discombobulated.
– OPPOSITES clear, orderly.

confusion noun
❶ BEWILDERMENT, perplexity, bafflement, puzzlement, mystification, bemusement, muddle, disorientation, befuddlement, distraction. ❷ the room in a state of confusion: MUDDLE, jumble, untidiness, disorder, chaos, shambles, disorderliness, disorganization, disarrangement. ❸ the confusion at the airport: MUDDLE, disorganization, upheaval, commotion, bustle, uproar, turmoil, riot, tumult, pandemonium, hubbub, fuss, disturbance, bother, mess, anarchy, bedlam, mayhem, hullabaloo, maelstrom.
– OPPOSITES clarity, order.

congeal verb SOLIDIFY, coagulate, thicken, clot, set, harden, cake, jell, condense, coalesce, curdle.

congenial adjective AGREEABLE, friendly, pleasant, amiable, amicable, nice, kindly, good-natured, companionable, sympathetic, like-minded, pleasing, understanding, well suited, kindred.
– OPPOSITES unfriendly, unpleasant.

congenital adjective ❶ a congenital disease: HEREDITARY, inherited, innate, constitutional, inborn, inbred. ❷ a congenital liar: INVETERATE, utter, complete, thoroughgoing, dyed-in-the-wool.

congested adjective
❶ congested lungs: BLOCKED, clogged, choked, plugged, stopped up, gorged. ❷ congested roads: PACKED, jammed, overcrowded, crowded, blocked, obstructed, overflowing, teeming.
– OPPOSITES clear.

congratulate verb COMPLIMENT, offer good wishes to, wish joy to, praise, felicitate.
– OPPOSITES criticize.

congregate verb GATHER, assemble, come together, collect, mass, group, convene, flock together, converge, meet, crowd, cluster, throng, swarm, rendezvous, muster, rally, foregather.
– OPPOSITES disperse.

conjecture noun GUESS, suspicion, theory, hypothesis, presumption, presupposition, notion, fancy, surmise, inference; *informal* guesstimate.

conjugal adjective CONNUBIAL, matrimonial, nuptial, marital, married, wedded, spousal, bridal, hymeneal, epithalamic.

connect verb ❶ ATTACH, link, fix, couple, affix, clamp, secure, tie, rivet, fuse, solder, weld.
❷ ASSOCIATE, link, relate to, equate, identify, bracket, draw a parallel with.
– OPPOSITES separate.

connection noun
❶ ATTACHMENT, fastening, coupling, clamp, joint, clasp.
❷ LINK, relationship, association, relation, correspondence, parallel, analogy.

connive verb CONSPIRE, collude, be in collusion with, collaborate, plot, scheme, abet, be a party to, intrigue.

connotation noun NUANCE, undertone, intimation, hint, suggestion, implication, allusion, insinuation, reference.

conquer verb ❶ DEFEAT, beat, vanquish, overpower, overthrow, subdue, rout, trounce, subjugate, triumph over, overwhelm, crush, overrun, prevail over, quell, worst; *informal* thrash, lick. ❷ **conquer territory:** SEIZE, occupy, invade, annex, overrun, win, appropriate. ❸ **conquer his fears:** OVERCOME, master, get the better of, surmount, quell, vanquish.

conquest noun ❶ VICTORY, beating, defeat, overthrow, overpowering, subjugation, trouncing, rout, triumph, mastery, crushing. ❷ OCCUPATION, seizure, possession, annexation, invasion, overrunning, appropriation. ❸ **her conquests:** ADMIRER, worshipper, fan, adherent, follower, supporter.

conscience noun MORAL SENSE, morals, principles, ethics, scruples, standards, qualms, reservations, misgivings.

conscientious adjective DILIGENT, careful, meticulous, thorough, attentive, precise, accurate, exact, punctilious, dedicated, hard-working, painstaking, scrupulous, rigorous, detailed.
– OPPOSITES casual.

conscious adjective ❶ **a conscious state:** AWAKE, aware, alert, sentient, responsive. ❷ **a conscious attempt:** DELIBERATE, premeditated, intentional, intended, on purpose, calculated, voluntary, studied, knowing, volitional.
– OPPOSITES unconscious.

consecrate verb SANCTIFY, bless, make holy/sacred, devote, hallow.

consecutive adjective SUCCESSIVE, succeeding, following, in sequence, sequential, serial, in turn, progressive, continuous, uninterrupted, unbroken, chronological.

consensus noun AGREEMENT, common consent, consent, unanimity, harmony, unity, concurrence; *formal* concord.
– OPPOSITES disagreement.

consent noun AGREEMENT, assent, acceptance, approval, permission, acquiescence, sanction, compliance, concurrence; *informal* go-ahead, green light.
▶ verb AGREE TO, accept, approve, go along with, acquiesce in, accede to, concede to, yield to, give in to, submit to, comply with, abide by, concur with.
– OPPOSITES dissent, refuse.

consequence noun ❶ **the consequences of the decision:** RESULT, effect, outcome, aftermath, repercussion, upshot, reverberation, by-product, event, issue, end. ❷ **a matter of consequence:** IMPORTANCE, significance, note, value, concern, substance, weight, import, moment, portent.
– OPPOSITES cause.

consequent adjective RESULTING, subsequent, following, ensuing, resultant, consequential, successive, sequential.

conservation noun PRESERVATION, protection, safe keeping, safeguarding, saving, guarding, care, charge, custody, husbandry, upkeep, maintenance.
– OPPOSITES destruction.

conservative adjective ❶ RIGHT-WING, reactionary, Tory; *N. Amer.* Republican. ❷ CONVENTIONAL, traditional, reactionary, orthodox, cautious, prudent, careful, moderate, middle-of-the-road, unadventurous, temperate, stable, unchanging, old-fashioned, hidebound, sober. ❸ a conservative estimate: MODERATE, reasonable, cautious.
– OPPOSITES radical.

conserve verb PRESERVE, save, keep, protect, take care of, use sparingly, husband, hoard, store up, nurse.
– OPPOSITES squander, waste.

consider verb ❶ consider the matter: THINK ABOUT, weigh up, give thought to, examine, study, ponder, contemplate, deliberate over, mull over, meditate on, ruminate over, chew over, turn over in one's mind. ❷ consider him suitable: THINK, believe, regard as, deem, hold to be, judge, rate.

considerable adjective ❶ a considerable amount: SUBSTANTIAL, sizeable, appreciable, tolerable, goodly, fair, reasonable, ample, plentiful, abundant, marked, noticeable, comfortable, decent, great, lavish. ❷ a considerable artist: DISTINGUISHED, noteworthy, noted, important, significant, influential, illustrious, renowned.
– OPPOSITES negligible.

considerate adjective THOUGHTFUL, kind, helpful, concerned, attentive, solicitous, kindly, unselfish, compassionate, sympathetic, charitable, patient, generous, obliging, accommodating, neighbourly, altruistic.
– OPPOSITES thoughtless.

consign verb HAND OVER, give over, deliver, send, pass on, transfer, assign, entrust, commend, remit, bequeath.

consignment noun LOAD, batch, delivery, shipment, cargo, container load.

consist verb BE COMPOSED OF, be made up of, comprise, contain, include, incorporate, add up to, involve, embody.

consistent adjective ❶ consistent attitudes: CONSTANT, unchanging, unvarying, undeviating, steady, dependable, steadfast, stable, reliable, faithful, uniform, true to type. ❷ injuries consistent with stabbing: COMPATIBLE, conforming to, consonant, agreeing, congruous, accordant.
– OPPOSITES inconsistent.

consolation noun COMFORT, sympathy, solace, compassion, pity, commiseration, relief, help, support, cheer, encouragement, soothing, assuagement, alleviation.

consolidate verb MAKE STRONGER, strengthen, make secure, secure, make stable, stabilize, reinforce, fortify, cement.
– OPPOSITES weaken.

consort
■ **consort with** ASSOCIATE WITH, keep company with, mix with, spend time with, fraternize with, have dealings with; *informal* hang around with.

conspicuous adjective CLEAR, visible, obvious, evident, apparent, prominent, notable, noticeable, marked, plain, unmistakable, observable,

recognizable, discernible, perceptible, distinguishable, manifest, patent, vivid, striking, glaring, blatant, flagrant, obtrusive, showy, bold ostentatious, eminent.
– OPPOSITES inconspicuous, unobtrusive.

conspiracy noun PLOT, scheme, plan, stratagem, machinations, cabal, intrigue, collusion, connivance, machination, treason.

conspirator noun PLOTTER, conspirer, schemer, intriguer, colluder, collaborator, confederate, traitor; *informal* wheeler-dealer.

conspire verb PLOT, scheme, form conspiracy, hatch a plot, intrigue, collude, collaborate, connive, combine, be in league; *informal* be in cahoots.

constant adjective ❶ a constant temperature: EVEN, regular, uniform, stable, steady, unchanging, fixed, consistent, invariable, unvarying, sustained, immutable. ❷ constant chattering: CONTINUAL, unending, non-stop, sustained, incessant, endless, unceasing, perpetual, persistent, interminable, unflagging, unremitting, relentless, unrelenting. ❸ a constant friend: LOYAL, faithful, devoted, dependable, staunch, true, trustworthy, trusty, resolute, steadfast, unwavering, unswerving.
– OPPOSITES variable, fickle.

consternation noun DISMAY, anxiety, bewilderment, distress, alarm, surprise, astonishment, amazement, confusion, mystification, panic, fear, fright, dread, horror, trepidation, shock, terror, awe.

construct verb BUILD, make, assemble, erect, put up, set up, manufacture, produce, put together, fabricate, fashion, forge, establish, raise, elevate, engineer, form.
– OPPOSITES demolish.

construction noun ❶ BUILDING, assembly, erection, manufacture, fabrication, elevation. ❷ BUILDING, structure, edifice, framework. ❸ put a different construction on: INTERPRETATION, meaning, reading, explanation, inference.

constructive adjective USEFUL, helpful, productive, practical, positive, valuable, worthwhile, beneficial, creative.
– OPPOSITES destructive, negative.

consult verb ❶ consult with colleagues: CONFER, discuss, talk, talk over, speak to, exchange views, deliberate; *informal* put heads together, talk turkey. ❷ consult an expert: ASK, seek advice from, call in, turn to, take counsel from.

consume verb ❶ EAT, drink, swallow, ingest, devour, guzzle; *informal* gobble, tuck into; *Brit. informal* scoff. ❷ consume electricity: USE, utilize, expend, deplete, absorb, exhaust, waste, squander, drain, dissipate.

contact verb COMMUNICATE WITH, get/be in touch with, be in communication with, approach, write to, phone, call, ring up, speak to, reach, get hold of, notify, sound out.
▶ noun TOUCH, proximity, exposure, joining, junction, contiguity, tangency.

contagious adjective CATCHING, communicable, transmittable, transmissible, infectious, spreadable, pandemic.

contain verb ❶ HOLD, carry, have capacity for, accommodate, seat. ❷ INCLUDE, comprise, take in, embrace, incorporate, involve. ❸ contained his mirth: RESTRAIN, hold in/back, control, keep in check, keep under control, suppress, repress, curb, stifle.

container noun RECEPTACLE, vessel, holder, repository.

contaminate verb ADULTERATE, pollute, debase, defile, corrupt, taint, dirty, infect, foul, spoil, tarnish, sully, soil, stain, befoul.

contemplate verb ❶ contemplate the future: THINK ABOUT, meditate over/on, consider, ponder, reflect over/on, muse on, dwell on, deliberate over, ruminate over, cogitate on. ❷ contemplate doing something: THINK ABOUT, envisage, consider, intend, plan, propose, foresee, expect to. ❸ contemplate the picture: LOOK AT, view, regard, examine, inspect, observe, scrutinize, survey, eye.

contemplative adjective THOUGHTFUL, pensive, reflective, meditative, ruminative, musing, intent, rapt, lost in thought.

contemporary adjective ❶ contemporary fashion: CURRENT, modern, present-day, up to date, latest, fashionable, recent, newest; *informal* trendy, with it. ❷ contemporary with Shakespeare: CONTEMPORANEOUS, concurrent, coexistent, coeval, synchronous.
– OPPOSITES old-fashioned.

contempt noun SCORN, disdain, disgust, loathing, abhorrence, detestation, disrespect, derision, mockery, condescension. *See also* HATRED.
– OPPOSITES admiration.

contemptible adjective DESPICABLE, detestable, beneath contempt, disgraceful, loathsome, odious, ignominious, lamentable, pitiful, discreditable, low, mean, shameful, abject, unworthy, worthless, base, vile, shabby, cheap, sordid, wretched, degenerate.
– OPPOSITES admirable.

contemptuous adjective SCORNFUL, disdainful, insulting, disrespectful, derisive, derisory, insolent, mocking, sneering, jeering, belittling, dismissive, condescending, patronizing, haughty, lofty, supercilious, arrogant, superior, snide, imperious; *informal* snooty, high and mighty, snotty; *formal* contumelious.
– OPPOSITES respectful, admiring.

contend verb ❶ COMPETE, oppose, challenge, contest, vie, clash, strive, struggle, grapple, tussle, wrestle. ❷ contend with a problem: COPE WITH, face, grapple with, take on. ❸ contend that he is right: STATE, declare, assert, maintain, hold, claim, profess, allege, affirm; *formal* aver.

content[1] noun *see* CONTENTMENT.
▶ adjective *see* CONTENTED.
▶ verb *see* SATISFY (2).

content[2] noun CONSTITUENT, part, ingredient, element.

contented adjective SATISFIED, content, pleased, happy,

cheerful, glad, gratified, fulfilled, at ease, at peace, comfortable, relaxed, serene, tranquil, unworried, untroubled, uncomplaining, complacent.
– OPPOSITES discontented, dissatisfied.

contentment noun SATISFACTION, content, contentedness, happiness, pleasure, cheerfulness, gladness, gratification, fulfilment, relaxation, ease, comfort, peace, serenity, equanimity, tranquillity, complacency.
– OPPOSITES dissatisfaction.

contest noun ❶ *See* COMPETITION (1). ❷ STRUGGLE, conflict, battle, fight, combat, tussle, skirmish.
▶ verb ❶ **contest the seat:** COMPETE FOR, contend for, fight for/over, vie for, battle for, struggle for, tussle over; *informal* make a bid for. ❷ **contest the verdict:** CHALLENGE, question, call into question, oppose, doubt, dispute, object to, query, resist.

contestant noun COMPETITOR, entrant, candidate, contender, participant, rival, opponent, adversary, player.

context noun CIRCUMSTANCES, situation, conditions, state of affairs, background, environment, setting, frame of reference, framework, surroundings, milieu.

contingency noun EVENT, eventuality, incident, happening, occurrence, juncture, accident, chance, possibility, emergency, uncertainty, fortuity.

continual adjective ❶ **continual noise:** CONSTANT, perpetual, endless, interminable. *See also* CONTINUOUS. ❷ **continual complaints:** FREQUENT, regular, constant, habitual, persistent, recurrent, repeated.
– OPPOSITES occasional, temporary.

continue verb ❶ CARRY ON, go on, keep on, persist, persevere, stay, endure, remain, survive, last, sustain, linger; *informal* stick at. ❷ **continue the session:** PROLONG, extend, sustain, maintain, protract, perpetuate. ❸ **continue after a break:** RESUME, carry on with, recommence, restart, start again, return to, take up.
– OPPOSITES stop.

continuous adjective CONSTANT, uninterrupted, non-stop, perpetual, sustained, ceaseless, incessant, relentless, unceasing, unremitting, endless, never-ending, interminable, lasting, everlasting, unbroken.
– OPPOSITES sporadic, intermittent.

contour noun OUTLINE, silhouette, profile, figure, shape, form, line, curve.

contract noun AGREEMENT, pact, arrangement, settlement, covenant, compact, understanding, treaty, bargain, deal, convention, concordat, entente.
▶ verb ❶ GET/BECOME/MAKE SMALLER, shrink, reduce, shrivel, narrow, tighten, draw in, constrict, tense, diminish, decrease, shorten, compress, curtail, concentrate, abbreviate, abridge. ❷ **contract with him to do the work:** AGREE, arrange, come to terms, reach an agreement, negotiate, bargain, strike a

bargain, engage, settle, covenant. ❸ **contracted a disease:** CATCH, develop, get, become infected with; *Brit.* go down with.
– OPPOSITES expand.

contradict verb SAY THE OPPOSITE OF, oppose, challenge, counter, be at variance with, clash with, dissent from, rebut, refute, controvert, impugn, confute.
– OPPOSITES agree.

contradictory adjective OPPOSING, opposite, opposed, conflicting, clashing, contrasting, incompatible, inconsistent, irreconcilable, dissenting, contrary, dissident, antithetical.

contraption noun DEVICE, machine, mechanism, gadget, contrivance, apparatus, appliance; *informal* whatsit, thingamajig, thingamabob, thingummy, whatchamacallit, gizmo, doodah.

contrary adjective ❶ **contrary views:** OPPOSING, opposite, contradictory, conflicting, contrasting, clashing, incompatible, irreconcilable, inconsistent, incongruous, antithetical. ❷ **a contrary woman:** AWKWARD, wilful, perverse, obstinate, stubborn, headstrong, wayward, intractable, unaccommodating, recalcitrant, intransigent, refractory, cantankerous; *informal* pig-headed, cussed; *Brit. informal* stroppy.
– OPPOSITES compatible, accommodating.

contrast noun DIFFERENCE, dissimilarity, disparity, distinction, differentiation, divergence, opposition, dissimilitude.
▶ verb ❶ COMPARE, set side by side, juxtapose, distinguish, differentiate, discriminate. ❷ FORM A CONTRAST, differ, contradict, clash, conflict, be at variance, be contrary, diverge.

contribute verb ❶ GIVE, donate, provide, subscribe, present, hand out, supply, grant, endow, bestow, confer, furnish; *informal* chip in. ❷ **diet contributes to good health:** LEAD TO, be conducive to, be instrumental in, help, add to, promote, advance; *informal* have a hand in.

contribution noun ❶ DONATION, gift, subscription, offering, present, grant, allowance, subsidy, endowment; *informal* handout. ❷ PARTICIPATION, input; *informal* one's pennyworth.

contrite adjective PENITENT, repentant, remorseful, regretful, sorry, conscience-stricken, guilt-stricken, chastened, in sackcloth and ashes.
– OPPOSITES unrepentant.

control noun ❶ AUTHORITY, power, charge, management, command, direction, rule, government, supervision, oversight, regulation, jurisdiction, dominance, mastery, leadership, reign, supremacy, sway, superintendence, guidance. ❷ **import controls:** LIMITATION, restriction, regulation, check, restraint, curb, brake. ❸ **the machine's controls:** INSTRUMENT, switch, dial, knob, lever.
▶ verb ❶ BE IN CHARGE OF, be in control of, manage, head, direct, command, rule, govern, oversee, dominate, preside over, conduct, reign over; *informal* be the boss of, be in the driver's seat, be in the saddle. ❷ **control prices:** REGULATE, restrain, keep in check, restrict,

curb, hold back, contain, limit, subdue, bridle.

controversial adjective DISPUTED, contentious, at issue, open to question/discussion, disputable, debatable, under discussion, problematical, doubtful, questionable, contended, controvertible.

controversy noun DISPUTE, argument, debate, disagreement, dissension, contention, altercation, wrangle, wrangling, quarrelling, squabbling, bickering, war of words, polemic.

conundrum noun RIDDLE, puzzle, problem, enigma, mystery; *informal* brain-teaser.

convalesce verb GET BETTER, recover, recuperate, improve, return to health, be on the mend, regain strength.

convene verb ❶ convene a meeting: CALL, call together, summon, round up, rally; *formal* convoke. ❷ the meeting convened: ASSEMBLE, gather, meet, collect, congregate, muster.

convenient adjective ❶ a convenient time: SUITABLE, suited, appropriate, fitting, fit, favourable, advantageous, opportune, timely, well timed, expedient, useful, serviceable. ❷ shops convenient for the houses: ACCESSIBLE, nearby, close at hand, handy, at hand, within reach, just round the corner.
– OPPOSITES inconvenient.

convention noun ❶ *See* ASSEMBLY. ❷ PROTOCOL, formality, code, custom, tradition, practice, usage, etiquette, propriety.

conventional adjective ❶ ACCEPTED, expected, customary, usual, normal, standard, regular, correct, proper, orthodox, traditional, prevailing, prevalent, conformist, decorous, conservative, formal, ritual. ❷ COMMONPLACE, common, run-of-the-mill, everyday, prosaic, routine, stereotyped, pedestrian, hackneyed, unoriginal, clichéd, trite, platitudinous, bourgeois; *Brit. informal* common or garden.
– OPPOSITES unconventional.

converge verb MEET, intersect, join, merge, unite, come together, become one, coincide, concur.
– OPPOSITES diverge, separate.

conversant adjective ACQUAINTED WITH, familiar with, knowledgeable about, well versed in, informed about, apprised of, au fait with, experienced in, proficient in, practised in, skilled in; *informal* well up on.

conversation noun TALK, discussion, chat, dialogue, communication, gossip, exchange of views, conference, tête-a-tête, discourse, colloquy, intercourse, heart to heart, palaver; *informal* powwow, confab, chinwag; *Brit. informal* natter.

convert verb ❶ CHANGE, transform, alter, modify, reshape, refashion, remodel, remake, rebuild, reorganize, metamorphose, transfigure, transmogrify, transmute. ❷ convert to Islam: CONVINCE, persuade, reform, re-educate, baptize, save, proselytize.

convey verb ❶ TRANSPORT, carry, bring, fetch, take, move, deliver, bear, shift, transfer, ship, conduct, channel, transmit; *informal* cart, lug. ❷ convey information: TRANSMIT, communicate, pass on, send, make known, tell, announce, relate, impart, hand on, dispatch, reveal, disclose.

convict noun PRISONER, criminal, offender, felon, law-breaker, malefactor; *informal* jailbird, con, old lag.
▶ verb DECLARE/FIND GUILTY, sentence, condemn.
– OPPOSITES acquit.

conviction noun ❶ speak with conviction: CONFIDENCE, assurance, belief, certainty, persuasion, firmness, earnestness, certitude. ❷ his religious convictions: BELIEF, view, principle, opinion, thought, idea, creed, tenet, persuasion.
– OPPOSITES uncertainty.

convince verb PERSUADE, prove to, satisfy, assure, talk round, bring round, win over, sway.

convincing adjective ❶ a convincing argument: PERSUASIVE, powerful, plausible, conclusive, cogent, incontrovertible. ❷ a convincing person: PERSUASIVE, plausible, credible.
– OPPOSITES unconvincing.

convivial adjective FRIENDLY, genial, cordial, sociable, affable, amiable, congenial, agreeable, jolly, cheerful.

convoy noun GROUP, company, line, fleet, cortège, caravan, assemblage.
▶ verb ESCORT, accompany, attend, protect, guard, defend, guide, shepherd, flank.

cook verb PREPARE, make, put together, concoct, improvise.
■ **cook up** MAKE UP, concoct, devise, invent, create, contrive, fabricate, plot, plan, scheme.

cool adjective ❶ CHILLED, chilly, fresh, refreshing, unheated, breezy, draughty; *informal* nippy. *See also* COLD (1). ❷ cool in an emergency: CALM, relaxed, composed, collected, self-possessed, level-headed, self-controlled, unexcited, unmoved, unperturbed, unruffled, unemotional, placid, serene. ❸ a cool young woman: ALOOF, distant, reserved, stand-offish, unfriendly, offhand, indifferent, uninterested, undemonstrative, unwelcoming, uncommunicative, chilly, frigid, impassive, dispassionate. ❹ SOPHISTICATED, urbane, cosmopolitan, elegant.
– OPPOSITES warm.
▶ verb ❶ CHILL, refrigerate, freeze. ❷ cool his ardour: LESSEN, diminish, reduce, dampen, abate, moderate, temper, soothe, assuage, allay, mollify.
– OPPOSITES heat, inflame.

cooperate verb WORK TOGETHER, join forces, unite, help each other, act jointly, combine, collaborate, pool resources, conspire, connive, coordinate; *informal* pull together, pitch in, play ball.

cooperative adjective ❶ a cooperative venture: JOINT, united, shared, unified, combined, concerted, collective, collaborative, coordinated. ❷ be cooperative: HELPFUL, of assistance, obliging, accommodating, supportive, responsive, willing.
– OPPOSITES uncooperative.

coordinate verb ARRANGE, organize, order, integrate, correlate, systematize, synchronize, harmonize.

cope verb MANAGE, succeed, survive, carry on, get through, get on, get by, subsist, come through; *informal* make out.

■ **cope with** HANDLE, deal with, take care of, contend with, grapple with, struggle with.

copious adjective ABUNDANT, plentiful, ample, profuse, full, extensive, generous, lavish, superabundant, rich, liberal, bountiful, exuberant, luxuriant, overflowing, abounding; *poetic/literary* plenteous, bounteous.
– OPPOSITES scarce.

copy noun ❶ REPRODUCTION, imitation, replica, likeness, representation, twin, counterfeit, forgery, fake, sham. ❷ a copy of a document: DUPLICATE, facsimile, carbon, carbon copy, photocopy, Xerox, photostat, transcript.
▶ verb ❶ IMITATE, mimic, emulate, mirror, echo, follow, simulate, ape, parrot. ❷ copy a document: DUPLICATE, photocopy, Xerox, photostat. ❸ copy the painting: REPRODUCE, replicate, forge, counterfeit.

cord noun STRING, rope, twine, cable, line, ligature.

cordon noun BARRIER, line, chain, ring, picket line.
■ **cordon off** CLOSE OFF, fence off, shut off, separate off, isolate, enclose, encircle, surround, picket.

core noun CENTRE, heart, nucleus, nub, kernel, crux, essence, heart of the matter, substance, gist, pith; *informal* nitty-gritty.

corner noun ❶ BEND, angle, curve, turn, crook. ❷ JUNCTION, turn, intersection, crossroads, fork, convergence. ❸ hidden in odd corners: NOOK, cranny, recess, crevice, hideaway, niche, cavity, hole; *informal* hidey-hole.
▶ verb TRAP, capture, run to earth, bring to bay.

corny adjective BANAL, inane, trite, hackneyed, stale, commonplace, platitudinous, fatuous, mawkish, feeble; *informal* old hat.

corpse noun BODY, remains, cadaver, carcass; *informal* stiff.

correct adjective ❶ the correct answer: RIGHT, accurate, true, actual, exact, precise, unerring, faithful, strict, faultless, flawless, confirmed, verified; *informal* on the mark; *Brit. informal* spot on, bang on. ❷ correct behaviour: PROPER, suitable, appropriate, accepted, fit, fitting, seemly, apt, approved, conventional, usual, customary.
– OPPOSITES wrong, incorrect, improper.
▶ verb ❶ RECTIFY, amend, set right, remedy, repair, emend, redress, cure, improve, better. ❷ ADJUST, regulate, fix, set, standardize, normalize. ❸ *See* REPRIMAND verb.

correspond verb ❶ AGREE, be in agreement, accord, concur, coincide, conform, match, fit together, square, tally, dovetail, correlate. ❷ correspond with a friend: EXCHANGE LETTERS, write to, communicate, keep in touch/contact.

correspondence noun LETTERS, mail, post, notes, messages.

corroborate verb CONFIRM, verify, bear out, authenticate, validate, certify, endorse, ratify, substantiate, uphold, attest to; *informal* back up.

corrode verb ❶ EAT AWAY, wear away, erode, abrade, destroy, consume, rust, oxidize. ❷ WEAR AWAY, rust, deteriorate, disintegrate, crumble, fragment.

corrugated adjective FURROWED, ridged, wrinkled, creased, grooved, crinkled, ribbed, channelled, puckered, fluted.

corrupt adjective ❶ DISHONEST, fraudulent, unscrupulous, dishonourable, untrustworthy, venal; *informal* crooked, bent, shady. ❷ IMMORAL, depraved, wicked, evil, sinful, degenerate, perverted, dissolute, debauched, decadent, abandoned, lascivious, lecherous.
–OPPOSITES honest, pure.
▶ verb ❶ BRIBE, buy, buy off, pay off, suborn, induce, lure, entice; *informal* grease someone's palm. ❷ DEPRAVE, pervert, warp, debauch, lead astray.

cosmic adjective ❶ UNIVERSAL, worldwide. ❷ VAST, huge, enormous, immense, immeasurable, infinite, limitless.

cosmopolitan adjective ❶ INTERNATIONAL, global, universal. ❷ SOPHISTICATED, liberal, urbane, worldly, wordly-wise, well travelled.
–OPPOSITES parochial.

cost noun PRICE, charge, amount, rate, value, quotation, payment, expense, outlay; *informal* damage.
▶ verb BE PRICED AT, be worth, come to, fetch, amount to, realize; *informal* set someone back.

costly adjective ❶ EXPENSIVE, dear, exorbitant, extortionate, extravagant; *informal* steep. ❷ **a costly victory:** DISASTROUS, harmful, ruinous, catastrophic, pyrrhic.
–OPPOSITES cheap, inexpensive.

cosy adjective COMFORTABLE, snug, restful, warm, relaxed, homely, sheltered, secure, safe; *informal* comfy, snug as a bug.
–OPPOSITES uncomfortable.

coterie noun CLIQUE, set, crowd, circle, gang, club, league, alliance, faction, cabal.

counsel noun ❶ *See* ADVICE. ❷ *See* LAWYER.
▶ verb ADVISE, guide, direct, recommend, warn, admonish, caution.

count verb ❶ ADD UP, keep a count of, calculate, work out, total, estimate, reckon up, enumerate, check, tally, compute, tell; *informal* tot up. ❷ **count himself lucky:** REGARD, consider, think, look upon, hold, judge, deem. ❸ **that doesn't count:** MATTER, be of account, signify, enter into consideration, mean anything, amount to anything, rate.
■ **count on** *see* RELY ON.

countenance noun FACE, features, expression, look, mien, appearance, visage, air.
▶ verb *see* PERMIT verb, STAND verb (4).

counter[1] noun ❶ TOP, surface, worktop, table, checkout, stand. ❷ TOKEN, disc, piece, marker, wafer, man.

counter[2] verb OPPOSE, resist, combat, dispute, argue against, rebut, contradict, retaliate, ward off, parry; *informal* hit back at, come back at.

counteract verb OFFSET, balance, counterbalance, neutralize, act counter to, be an antidote to, oppose, work against, thwart, negate, annul, impede, hinder, invalidate, countervail.

counterbalance verb BALANCE, compensate for, make up for, offset, neutralize, equalize, set off, undo, counterpoise.

counterfeit adjective FAKE, faked, forged, copied, imitation,

pseudo, fraudulent, sham, bogus, spurious, feigned, ersatz; *informal* phoney.
– OPPOSITES genuine.
▶ **noun** FAKE, copy, forgery, imitation, reproduction, fraud, sham.
▶ **verb** FAKE, copy, imitate, reproduce, simulate, feign, falsify, pretend.

counterpart **noun** EQUIVALENT, equal, opposite number, parallel, complement, match, twin, mate, fellow, analogue, correlative, copy, duplicate.

countless **adjective** INNUMERABLE, incalculable, infinite, immeasurable, endless, limitless, without limit/end, untold, inexhaustible, boundless, myriad, legion, no end of.

country **noun** ❶ STATE, nation, realm, kingdom, land, territory, power, commonwealth, domain, people, principality. ❷ LAND, terrain, landscape, territory, scenery, region, area, district, neighbourhood.

coupon **noun** VOUCHER, token, ticket, slip, stub, certificate.

courage **noun** BRAVERY, fearlessness, valour, heroism, intrepidity, pluck, nerve, grit, boldness, daring, audacity, mettle, spirit, fortitude, firmness, resolution, tenacity, determination, lion-heartedness, gallantry, stout-heartedness, dauntlessness, indomitability, hardihood, fibre; *informal* guts, spunk; *Brit. informal* bottle.
– OPPOSITES cowardice, fear.

courageous **adjective** BRAVE, fearless, heroic, bold, daring, plucky, audacious, unshrinking, dauntless, lion-hearted, intrepid, valiant, valorous, gallant, tenacious, indomitable, resolute, determined, game, spirited, stout-hearted, undaunted, stalwart.
– OPPOSITES cowardly.

course **noun** ❶ ROUTE, way, track, direction, path, trail, line, road, passage, lane, tack, trajectory, circuit, ambit, orbit. ❷ **a course of action:** WAY, method, line of action, procedure, process, system, policy, programme, regimen. ❸ **in the course of the day:** DURATION, passing, passage, period, lapse, term, span. ❹ **an English course:** CLASSES, lectures, curriculum, schedule, syllabus, programme.

court **noun** ❶ LAW COURT, court of law, tribunal, forum, bench, chancery, assizes. ❷ ATTENDANTS, household, retinue, entourage, train, suite. ❸ **paying court:** HOMAGE, suit, wooing, courtship, respects, blandishments.
▶ **verb** ❶ WOO, pursue, run after, go out (with); *informal* date, go steady (with). ❷ **court disaster:** INVITE, risk, provoke, lead to, cause, bring on, elicit.

courteous **adjective** POLITE, well mannered, civil, gentlemanly, gracious, mannerly, well bred, civilized, urbane.
– OPPOSITES discourteous, rude.

courtier **noun** ATTENDANT, follower, steward, page, squire, cup-bearer, train-bearer, liegeman.

cove **noun** BAY, inlet, sound, creek, bight, anchorage; *Scottish* firth.

cover **verb** ❶ PLACE OVER, spread over, protect, shield, shelter, conceal, coat, extend over, cloak, overlay, blanket, carpet, drape,

overlie, overspread, shroud, surface, veil, enclose, mask, screen, obscure, enshroud, house, secrete, bury, hide, submerge, layer, film, mantle, pave, clothe, wrap, swaddle, attire, garb, robe, encase, sheathe. ❷ **cover several matters:** DEAL WITH, involve, take in, contain, encompass, embrace, incorporate, treat, examine, survey. ❸ **reporters covering the trial:** REPORT, write up, describe, tell of, give an account of, give details of, investigate.
▶ **noun** ❶ COVERING, surface, top, lid, cap, screen, layer, coat, coating, carpet, canopy, crust, mantle, blanket, overlay, mask, cloak, veil, film, sheath, shield, veneer, wrapping, housing, cocoon, casing, cladding, skin, tarpaulin, encrustation, rind. ❷ **a cover for spying:** DISGUISE, front, camouflage, pretence, facade, false front, smokescreen, window-dressing, pretext, cloak, veil, mask. ❸ **cover against fire:** INSURANCE, protection, compensation, indemnity, indemnification.

covert **adjective** SECRET, concealed, hidden, surreptitious, furtive, stealthy, private, underground.
– OPPOSITES overt.

covet **verb** DESIRE, want, wish for, long/yearn for, crave, hanker after, lust after, thirst for, hunger for, set one's heart on, aspire to, aim for, envy, begrudge.

cowardly **adjective** FEARFUL, timid, timorous, faint-hearted, spineless, lily-livered, chicken-hearted, craven, base, shrinking, pusillanimous, afraid of one's shadow, submissive, unheroic, unchivalrous, ungallant; *informal* chicken, yellow, yellow-bellied, gutless, wimpish.
– OPPOSITES brave, courageous.

cower **verb** CRINGE, shrink, flinch, draw back, recoil, crouch, wince, slink, blench, quail, quake, tremble, quiver, grovel, skulk.

coy **adjective** COQUETTISH, arch, kittenish, evasive, shy, modest, unforthcoming, demure, bashful, reticent, diffident, retiring, self-effacing, hesitant, shrinking, withdrawn, timid, prudish, lacking confidence, unsure.
– OPPOSITES brazen.

crack **noun** ❶ FRACTURE, break, chip, split, fissure, crevice, breach, rupture, rift, chink, gap, cavity, slit, cleft, cranny. ❷ ATTEMPT, try, shot, opportunity; *informal* go, stab. ❸ *See* JOKE noun (1).
▶ **verb** ❶ FRACTURE, break, fragment, chip, split, splinter, snap. ❷ **crack under questioning:** BREAK DOWN, give way, collapse, yield, succumb; *informal* go to pieces, come apart at the seams.

cradle **noun** ❶ CRIB, cot, carry-cot, bassinet. ❷ BIRTHPLACE, source, fount, wellspring, beginnings, nursery.
▶ **verb** HOLD, rock, nestle, shelter, support.

craft **noun** ❶ SKILL, skilfulness, expertise, ability, mastery, artistry, art, technique, aptitude, dexterity, talent, flair, knack, genius. ❷ TRADE, occupation, vocation, calling, pursuit, business, line, work, employment. ❸ VESSEL, ship, boat, aircraft, plane, spacecraft.

crafty **adjective** CUNNING, artful, calculating, designing, scheming, wily, sly, devious, tricky, foxy, shrewd, astute, canny, sharp,

Machiavellian, shifty, guileful, deceitful, duplicitous, insidious, treacherous, fraudulent, underhand; *informal* crooked.
– OPPOSITES honest.

crag noun CLIFF, bluff, escarpment, scarp, ridge, peak, pinnacle, tor.

cram verb ❶ STUFF, push into, force into, pack in, ram down, press into, squeeze into, compress, compact, condense. ❷ *See* STUDY (1).

cramped adjective CONFINED, crowded, packed, narrow, small, restricted, limited, uncomfortable, closed in, hemmed in, tight, overfull, squeezed, jammed in, congested.
– OPPOSITES spacious.

crash verb ❶ COLLIDE WITH, bump into, smash into, plough into, pitch into, jolt, jar. ❷ FALL, topple, tumble, overbalance, pitch, plunge, hurtle, lurch.
▶ noun ❶ COLLISION, accident, smash, pile-up, bump; *Brit. informal* prang. ❷ CLASH, clang, clank, bang, smash, clangour, racket, din, boom, explosion. ❸ a stock-market crash: COLLAPSE, failure, fall, plummet, ruin, downfall, depression, debacle.

crate noun BOX, case, chest, carton, basket, hamper, receptacle.

crater noun HOLE, hollow, pit, cavity, depression, dip, chasm, abyss.

crawl verb ❶ CREEP, move on hands and knees, go on all fours, slither, squirm, wriggle, writhe, worm one's way, sneak. ❷ FAWN, flatter, grovel, cringe, toady; *informal* suck up.

craze noun TREND, fashion, fad, vogue, enthusiasm, passion, obsession, mania, fixation, whim, fascination, preoccupation, rage, infatuation.

crazy adjective ❶ MAD, insane, unbalanced, demented, lunatic, crazed, of unsound mind, deranged, unhinged, touched, berserk; *informal* batty, loony, nuts, nutty, cuckoo, bonkers, mental, round the bend/twist; *Brit. informal* potty. ❷ a crazy idea: ABSURD, idiotic, stupid, ridiculous, silly, foolish, peculiar, odd, strange, queer, eccentric, bizarre, weird, fantastic, inane, fatuous, unwise, preposterous; *informal* half-baked; *Brit. informal* potty. ❸ crazy about football: ENTHUSIASTIC, mad, keen, passionate, smitten, fanatical, devoted, fervent, excited.
– OPPOSITES sensible, uninterested.

cream noun LOTION, paste, ointment, salve, unguent, liniment, emulsion.

crease noun WRINKLE, furrow, line, fold, crinkle, ridge, corrugation, pucker, ruck, pleat, tuck.
▶ verb CRUMPLE, wrinkle, rumple, crinkle, ruck up, pucker, ridge, furrow, corrugate, pleat, tuck.

create verb ❶ create a new system: PRODUCE, originate, generate, design, establish, set up, invent, make, build, construct, develop, initiate, engender, frame, fabricate, erect, found, institute, constitute, inaugurate, shape, form, mould, forge, concoct, hatch. ❷ create new life: BRING INTO BEING, give birth/life to, father, sire, spawn, procreate; *poetic/literary* beget. ❸ create a good impression: PRODUCE, make, result in, bring about, give rise to, lead to.
– OPPOSITES destroy.

creative adjective INVENTIVE, imaginative, original, artistic, inspired, visionary, talented, gifted, resourceful, ingenious, clever, productive, fertile, fecund.

creator noun ❶ INVENTOR, originator, author, maker, designer, initiator, deviser, producer, manufacturer, architect, builder, prime mover, parent, generator; *poetic/literary* begetter. ❷ GOD, the Almighty.

creature noun ❶ ANIMAL, beast, being, living thing, organism; *N. Amer. informal* critter. ❷ **beautiful creatures:** PERSON, human being, individual, character, soul, mortal; *informal* fellow. ❸ **the King's creatures:** LACKEY, minion, puppet, toady, sycophant, hireling, retainer, dependant, hanger-on, vassal.

credentials plural noun DOCUMENTS, references, documentation, qualifications, certificate, diploma, testimonial, warrant, licence, permit, card, voucher, passport, letter of introduction.

credible adjective ❶ BELIEVABLE, plausible, convincing, likely, conceivable, imaginable, persuasive, tenable. ❷ ACCEPTABLE, reliable, trustworthy, dependable.
– OPPOSITES incredible, untrustworthy.

credit noun ❶ **credit for his performance:** PRAISE, acclaim, approval, commendation, acknowledgement, tribute, kudos, glory, recognition, esteem, regard, respect, merit, veneration; *formal* laudation. ❷ FINANCIAL STANDING/STATUS, solvency.
▶ verb ❶ **he couldn't credit it:** BELIEVE, accept, trust, have faith in, rely on, depend on, put confidence in; *informal* fall for, swallow, buy. ❷ **credit him with the discovery:** ASCRIBE TO, attribute to, assign to, give credit to, accredit to, impute to, chalk up to, put down to.

creditable adjective PRAISEWORTHY, admirable, commendable, laudable, meritorious, exemplary, worthy, respectable, reputable, estimable, honourable, deserving.
– OPPOSITES discreditable.

credulous adjective GULLIBLE, easily taken in, over-trusting, naive, unsuspicious, uncritical; *informal* green, wet behind the ears.
– OPPOSITES suspicious.

creed noun BELIEF, principle, teaching, doctrine, dogma, tenet, catechism, article of faith.

creek noun INLET, bay, cove, estuary, bight; *Scottish* firth.

creep verb CRAWL, move on hands and knees, go on all fours, slither, squirm, wriggle, writhe, move stealthily, sneak, tiptoe, slink, skulk, worm one's way.
▶ noun SYCOPHANT, toady, fawner, sneak; *informal* bootlicker.

creepy adjective HORRIFYING, horrific, horrible, frightening, scary, terrifying, hair-raising, awful, disturbing, eerie, sinister, weird, nightmarish, macabre, ominous, menacing, threatening, disgusting, repellent, repulsive, revolting.

crest noun ❶ COMB, tuft, cockscomb, plume. ❷ **the crest of the hill:** SUMMIT, top, peak, crown, brow, apex, ridge, heights. ❸ BADGE, emblem, regalia, insignia, device, coat of arms, seal, shield, sign, symbol.

crestfallen adjective DOWNCAST, dejected, depressed, glum, downhearted, disheartened, discouraged, dispirited, despondent, disconsolate; *informal* down in the dumps, in the doldrums.
– OPPOSITES cheerful.

crevice noun FISSURE, cleft, crack, cranny, split, rift, slit, gash, rent, fracture, opening, gap, hole, interstice.

crick noun PAIN, cramp, twinge, spasm, pang, stiffness.

crime noun ❶ OFFENCE, violation, felony, misdemeanour, misdeed, wrong, transgression, fault, injury; *archaic* trespass. ❷ LAWBREAKING, illegality, misconduct, wrongdoing, delinquency, villainy, wickedness, evil; *Law* malfeasance.

criminal adjective ❶ UNLAWFUL, illegal, illicit, lawless, felonious, delinquent, indictable, culpable, wrong, villainous, corrupt, evil, wicked, iniquitous, nefarious; *informal* crooked, bent. ❷ **a criminal waste:** DEPLORABLE, scandalous, shameful, reprehensible, senseless, foolish, ridiculous, sinful, immoral.
– OPPOSITES lawful, commendable.
▶ noun OFFENDER, lawbreaker, wrongdoer, malefactor, felon, delinquent, miscreant, culprit, villain, gangster, racketeer, hoodlum, bandit, transgressor, sinner; *informal* crook, con, baddy; *archaic* trespasser.

cringe verb COWER, shrink, draw back, quail, flinch, recoil, start, shy, dodge, duck, crouch, wince, tremble, quiver, shake.

cripple verb ❶ DISABLE, incapacitate, lame, debilitate, impair, damage, maim, weaken, enfeeble, paralyse. ❷ **business crippled by the recession:** DAMAGE, injure, ruin, destroy, weaken, hamstring, enfeeble, paralyse, bring to a standstill.

crisis noun EMERGENCY, disaster, catastrophe, calamity, predicament, plight, mess, trouble, difficulty, extremity, dilemma, quandary, exigency; *informal* fix, pickle, scrape.

crisp adjective ❶ BRITTLE, breakable, crunchy, crispy, friable. ❷ **a crisp manner:** BRISK, decisive, vigorous, brusque, curt, abrupt.
– OPPOSITES flaccid.

criterion noun MEASURE, standard, benchmark, norm, yardstick, scale, touchstone, barometer, exemplar, canon.

critic noun ❶ REVIEWER, commentator, pundit, arbiter, judge, evaluator. ❷ ATTACKER, fault-finder, detractor, reviler, vilifier, carper, backbiter; *informal* knocker, nit-picker.

critical adjective ❶ CENSORIOUS, disapproving, disparaging, derogatory, fault-finding, carping, depreciatory, niggling, cavilling, judgemental, uncomplimentary, scathing, unfavourable, captious; *informal* nit-picking. ❷ **a critical essay:** EVALUATIVE, analytic, interpretative, expository, explanatory, explicative, elucidative, annotative. ❸ **a critical point in history:** CRUCIAL, decisive, pivotal, key, important, vital, urgent, pressing. ❹ **in a critical condition:** DANGEROUS, grave, serious, risky, perilous, hazardous, precarious.
– OPPOSITES complimentary, unimportant.

criticism noun ❶ CONDEMNATION, censure, disapproval, disparagement, fault-finding, reproof, carping, cavilling, captiousness, animadversion; *informal* nit-picking, brickbats, flak, knocking, slamming. ❷ literary criticism: EVALUATION, comment, commentary, assessment, appreciation, appraisal, analysis, interpretation, judgement, elucidation, explication, annotation.

criticize verb FIND FAULT WITH, censure, denounce, condemn, disapprove of, disparage, cast aspersions on, snipe at, impugn, scold, decry, carp at, cavil at, excoriate, animadvert on; *informal* nit-pick, pick holes in, knock, slam, pan, lash, get at, pitch into, rap, flay, hand out brickbats; *Brit. informal* slate.
– OPPOSITES praise.

crockery noun DISHES, tableware, pottery, porcelain, china, earthenware.

crook noun ❶ *See* CRIMINAL. ❷ the crook of one's arm: BEND, curve, curvature, angle, bow, hook.

crooked adjective ❶ *See* CRIMINAL adjective (1). ❷ BENT, curved, twisted, warped, contorted, angled, bowed, irregular, hooked, flexed, winding, twisting, zigzag, misshapen, out of shape, lopsided, off-centre, meandering, sinuous, tortuous, serpentine.
– OPPOSITES straight.

crop noun HARVEST, growth, yield, produce, vintage, fruits, gathering, reaping.
▶ verb CUT, trim, clip, shear, lop, snip, prune, mow, graze, nibble, browse.
■ **crop up** HAPPEN, arise, occur, turn up, emerge, appear; *poetic/literary* come to pass.

cross noun ❶ a cross to bear: AFFLICTION, trouble, worry, burden, trial, disaster, tribulation, misfortune, misery, adversity, woe, pain, suffering, catastrophe, calamity. ❷ a cross between two breeds: HYBRID, mixture, cross-breed, amalgam, blend, combination, mongrel.
▶ verb ❶ crossing the river: GO ACROSS, span, stretch/extend across, pass over, bridge, ford, traverse. ❷ the lines crossed: INTERSECT, meet, join, converge, criss-cross, interweave, intertwine. ❸ he hates being crossed: OPPOSE, resist, thwart, frustrate, obstruct, foil, impede, hinder, hamper, check, contradict.
▶ adjective ANNOYED, irritated, vexed, bad-tempered, short-tempered, irascible, touchy, fractious, peevish, crotchety, grouchy, querulous, cantankerous, testy, waspish; *informal* snappy.
– OPPOSITES pleased, good-humoured.
■ **cross out** *see* DELETE.

crossing noun ❶ JUNCTION, crossroads, intersection. ❷ PEDESTRIAN/PELICAN CROSSING, underpass, subway, level crossing, bridge, ford, causeway, flyover.

crotchety adjective *see* CROSS.

crouch verb SQUAT, bend, duck, stoop, hunch over, hunker, cower, cringe.

crowd noun ❶ crowds of people: HORDE, throng, mob, mass, multitude, host, rabble, army, herd, flock, drove, swarm, troupe, pack, press, crush, flood, assembly, gathering, collection, congregation, convention. ❷ a capacity crowd: AUDIENCE, house,

turnout, gate, attendance, spectators, viewers, listeners.
▶ **verb** ❶ GATHER, cluster, flock, swarm, throng, huddle, concentrate, foregather. ❷ PRESS, push, shove, thrust, jostle, elbow, squeeze, pile, pack, cram, jam, bundle, stuff.

crowded **adjective** FULL, busy, packed, congested, overflowing, teeming, swarming, crammed, thronged, populous; *informal* jam-packed, full to bursting.
– OPPOSITES empty.

crown **noun** ❶ the power of the Crown: ROYALTY, monarchy, monarch, king, queen, emperor, empress. ❷ the crown of the hill: TOP, crest, summit, apex, tip, head, pinnacle.
▶ **verb** ❶ the crowned king: INVEST, enthrone, inaugurate, install, induct, anoint. ❷ crown his career: CAP, be the culmination/climax of, round off, complete, perfect, conclude, top off.

crucial **adjective** IMPORTANT, vital, critical, decisive, pivotal, central, urgent, pressing, high-priority, essential.
– OPPOSITES unimportant.

crude **adjective** ❶ RAW, unrefined, natural, coarse, unprocessed, unpolished. ❷ a crude drawing: ROUGH, primitive, rudimentary, rough and ready, unpolished, makeshift, rough-hewn, unskilful, amateurish, clumsy, inartistic, awkward, inept. ❸ crude jokes: *see* VULGAR (1).
– OPPOSITES refined.

cruel **adjective** BRUTAL, savage, barbaric, inhuman, barbarous, vicious, ferocious, fierce, evil, callous, pitiless, fiendish, sadistic, venomous, cold-blooded, ruthless, merciless, unrelenting, implacable, remorseless, unfeeling, heartless, malevolent, inhumane, severe, harsh, stern, stony-hearted, hard-hearted, flinty, bestial, tyrannical.
– OPPOSITES kind, merciful.

cruelty **noun** BRUTALITY, savagery, savageness, inhumanity, barbarism, barbarousness, viciousness, ferocity, fierceness, callousness, heartlessness, evil, fiendishness, sadism, ruthlessness, pitilessness, relentlessness, severity, harshness, inclemency.
– OPPOSITES kindness, compassion.

cruise **noun** TRIP, voyage, sail.
▶ **verb** SAIL, voyage, journey, drift, coast.

crumb **noun** BIT, fragment, morsel, particle, grain, speck, scrap, snippet, atom, sliver.

crumble **verb** ❶ CRUSH, break up, pulverize, pound, grind, powder, fragment. ❷ DISINTEGRATE, fall apart, break down/up, collapse, deteriorate, decompose, rot, rot away, perish.

crumple **verb** CRUSH, crease, rumple, wrinkle, crinkle, fold, pucker, dent, mangle.

crunch **verb** BITE, chew, gnaw, masticate, champ, chomp, munch, crush, grind, pulverize.

crusade **noun** CAMPAIGN, drive, movement, push, struggle, cause, war.
▶ **verb** FIGHT, campaign, work, take up arms, take up a cause.

crush **verb** ❶ SQUASH, squeeze, press, mash, compress, mangle, pound, pulverize, smash, crunch, grind, pulp, shiver. ❷ crush the rebellion: PUT DOWN, defeat, suppress, subdue, overpower,

overwhelm, quash, stamp out, conquer, extinguish. ❸ **felt crushed:** HUMILIATE, mortify, shame, abash, chagrin.
▶ **noun** CROWD, jam, congestion.

crust **noun** CASING, outer layer, rind, shell, husk, covering, skin, encrustation, scab, concretion.

crusty **adjective** CRISP, crispy, brittle, hard, well done, friable.

cry **verb** ❶ WEEP, sob, wail, snivel, blubber, whimper, whine, bawl, howl. ❷ CALL OUT, yell, exclaim, screech, bellow, howl.
▶ **noun** ❶ SOB, wail, blubbering, keening. ❷ CALL, exclamation, scream, screech, yell, shout, bellow, howl.
■ **cry off** BACK OUT, pull out, cancel, withdraw, change one's mind; *informal* get cold feet, cop out.

crypt **noun** TOMB, vault, burial chamber, sepulchre, catacomb, undercroft.

cryptic **adjective** MYSTERIOUS, obscure, enigmatic, arcane, esoteric, puzzling, perplexing, secret, concealed, coded, unintelligible, hidden, unclear, veiled.
– OPPOSITES clear.

cuddle **verb** HUG, embrace, clasp, fondle, pet, snuggle, nestle, curl up, enfold, nurse, dandle; *informal* canoodle, neck, smooch.

cudgel **noun** CLUB, bludgeon, stick, truncheon, blackjack, baton, bat, bastinado; *Brit. informal* cosh.
▶ **verb** BLUDGEON, club, beat, strike, pound, pummel, thrash, thump; *informal* clobber, thwack; *Brit. informal* cosh.

cue **noun** SIGNAL, sign, hint, indication, suggestion, reminder, intimation.

culminate **verb** PEAK, come to/reach a climax, come to an end, come to a head, end, finish, close, conclude, terminate; *informal* wind up.

culpable **adjective** GUILTY, in the wrong, at fault, blameworthy, to blame, answerable, wrong, reprehensible, reproachable, sinful.
– OPPOSITES blameless, innocent.

culprit **noun** GUILTY PARTY, person responsible, sinner, evil-doer, miscreant, lawbreaker, criminal, delinquent, reprobate, transgressor, malefactor.

cult **noun** ❶ SECT, church, religion, body, denomination, faith, belief, persuasion. ❷ CRAZE, fashion, fad, vogue, trend, obsession.

cultivate **verb** ❶ TILL, farm, work, plough, dig, prepare, fertilize. ❷ **cultivate the mind:** EDUCATE, improve, better, develop, train, civilize, enlighten, refine, elevate, enrich. ❸ **cultivate people:** WOO, court, pursue, ingratiate oneself with, curry favour with; *informal* butter up, suck up to. ❹ **cultivate a friendship:** FOSTER, develop, pursue, devote oneself to, encourage, support, further, aid.

cultivated **adjective** *see* CULTURED.

cultural **adjective** ARTISTIC, aesthetic, educational, improving, educative, enlightening, intellectual, civilizing, elevating, broadening, developmental.

culture **noun** ❶ CULTIVATION, enlightenment, education, accomplishment, edification, erudition, refinement, polish, sophistication, urbanity, discernment, discrimination, good taste, breeding, politeness, savoir faire. ❷ CIVILIZATION, way of life, lifestyle, customs, habits, ways, mores.

cultured adjective ARTISTIC, cultivated, educated, learned, enlightened, intellectual, knowledgeable, highbrow, scholarly, well informed, well read, erudite, accomplished, well versed, refined, genteel, polished, sophisticated, urbane.

cunning adjective ❶ CRAFTY, devious, wily, sly, artful, shrewd, astute, knowing, sharp, Machiavellian, deceitful, shifty, guileful; *informal* tricky, foxy. ❷ CLEVER, ingenious, resourceful, inventive, imaginative, skilful, deft, subtle, adroit.
– OPPOSITES ingenuous.
▶ noun ❶ CRAFTINESS, artfulness, wiliness, slyness, shrewdness, guile, astuteness, sharpness. ❷ CLEVERNESS, ingenuity, resourcefulness, inventiveness, skill, deftness, adroitness, finesse, capability.

cup noun ❶ MUG, teacup, beaker, tumbler, tankard, wine glass, chalice, goblet. ❷ TROPHY, prize, award.

cupidity noun GREED, avarice, acquisitiveness, covetousness, rapacity, rapaciousness, voracity, voraciousness, avidity.

curator noun KEEPER, caretaker, custodian, guardian, conservator, steward.

curb verb RESTRAIN, check, keep in check, control, contain, hold back, repress, suppress, moderate, dampen, put a brake on, impede, retard, subdue, bridle, muzzle.
– OPPOSITES encourage.

curdle verb CONGEAL, turn, coagulate, clot, solidify, thicken, condense.

cure noun REMEDY, antidote, treatment, therapy, alleviation, medicine, restorative, panacea, corrective.
▶ verb ❶ HEAL, make better, rehabilitate, remedy, put right, repair, fix, restore, palliate, rectify, relieve. ❷ **cure meat:** PRESERVE, smoke, salt, dry, kipper, pickle.
– OPPOSITES aggravate.

curiosity noun INQUISITIVENESS, interest, questioning, prying, meddling; *informal* snooping, nosiness.

curious adjective ❶ INQUISITIVE, inquiring, interested, searching, querying, questioning, interrogative, puzzled, intrusive, prying, interfering; *informal* snooping. ❷ *See* STRANGE (1).
– OPPOSITES incurious.

curl verb ❶ SPIRAL, coil, bend, twist, wind, loop, twirl, wreathe, meander, snake, corkscrew. ❷ **curl the hair:** CRIMP, perm, crinkle, frizz, wave.
▶ noun ❶ SPIRAL, twist, coil, whorl, helix. ❷ **curls in one's hair:** RINGLET, coil, kink,wave, curlicue, corkscrew.

curly adjective CURLED, crimped, kinked, crinkly, wavy, frizzy, permed, fuzzy.
– OPPOSITES straight.

current adjective PRESENT, present-day, contemporary, up to date, up to the minute, existing, modern, fashionable, popular, prevailing, prevalent, accepted, common, general, widespread, rife; *informal* trendy, now, in.
– OPPOSITES obsolete.
▶ noun FLOW, stream, tide, river, channel, drift, jet, draught, undercurrent, undertow.

curse noun ❶ DAMNATION, execration, imprecation, evil eye, malediction, anathema; *informal* jinx. ❷ SWEAR WORD, obscenity, oath, profanity, expletive, blasphemy, bad language.
▶ verb ❶ PUT A CURSE ON, damn, execrate, put the evil eye on, anathematize. ❷ SWEAR, use bad/foul language, utter oaths, blaspheme, be foul-mouthed.

cursory adjective HASTY, rapid, hurried, quick, perfunctory, slapdash, casual, superficial, desultory, fleeting, passing, ephemeral, transient.
– OPPOSITES thorough.

curt adjective TERSE, abrupt, brusque, blunt, short, sharp, crisp, tart, gruff, uncommunicative, laconic, offhand, rude, summary, impolite, unceremonious, ungracious, uncivil, brief, concise, succinct, pithy, compact; *informal* snappy, snappish.
– OPPOSITES expansive.

curtail verb REDUCE, shorten, cut, cut back/down, decrease, lessen, diminish, slim down, tighten up, pare down, trim, dock, lop, truncate, abridge, abbreviate, contract, compress, shrink.
– OPPOSITES lengthen, expand.

curtain noun DRAPE, hanging, blind, screen.
■ **curtain off** SCREEN OFF, separate off, mask, shield, conceal, hide, isolate.

curtsy verb BOW, genuflect, bend the knee, bob, salaam.

curve noun BEND, arch, arc, bow, turn, loop, hook, crescent, spiral, twist, swirl, whorl, corkscrew, curvature, undulation, camber, meander.
▶ verb BEND, arc, arch, bow, turn, swerve, twist, wind, hook, loop, spiral, coil, meander, snake, swirl, bulge, camber, inflect, incurve.

curved adjective BENT, arched, rounded, bowed, twisted, crooked, humped, concave, serpentine, whorled, undulating, tortuous, sinuous.
– OPPOSITES straight.

cushion noun PILLOW, bolster, pad, headrest, hassock, mat, squab, pillion, scatter cushion, beanbag.
▶ verb ❶ PILLOW, bolster, cradle, support, prop up. ❷ **cushion the blow:** SOFTEN, lessen, diminish, mitigate, allay, deaden, muffle, stifle.

custody noun ❶ CARE, charge, guardianship, keeping, safe keeping, protection, supervision, superintendence, control, tutelage. ❷ DETENTION, imprisonment, incarceration, confinement, restraint, constraint, duress.

custom noun ❶ HABIT, practice, routine, way, policy, rule, convention, procedure, ritual, ceremony, form, usage, observance, fashion, mode, style. ❷ **thank them for their custom:** TRADE, business, patronage, support, customers, buyers.

customary adjective USUAL, accustomed, regular, typical, common, habitual, traditional, routine, fixed, set, established, familiar, everyday, prevailing, confirmed, normal, ordinary, expected, favourite, popular, stock, well worn; *poetic/literary* wonted.
– OPPOSITES unusual, exceptional.

customer noun BUYER, purchaser, shopper, consumer, patron, client.

cut verb ❶ **cut his finger:** GASH, slash, lacerate, slit, nick, pierce, notch, penetrate, wound, lance, incise, score. ❷ **cut the meat:** CARVE, slice, chop, sever, divide, cleave. ❸ **cut a key:** SHAPE, fashion, form, mould, chisel, carve, sculpt, chip away, whittle. ❹ **cut his hair/the grass:** TRIM, clip, crop, snip, shear, dock, shave, pare, mow. ❺ **cut expenditure:** REDUCE, decrease, lessen, lower, diminish, contract, prune, curb, curtail, slash, rationalize, economize on. ❻ **cut the text:** SHORTEN, abridge, condense, abbreviate, contract, compact, precis, summarize.
▶ noun ❶ GASH, laceration, slash, incision, slit. ❷ **cut in spending:** CUTBACK, decrease, reduction, curtailment, contraction. ❸ **I want my cut:** SHARE, portion, proportion.
■ **cut in** *see* INTERRUPT (1).

cutting adjective WOUNDING, hurtful, caustic, acid, barbed, acrimonious, sarcastic, spiteful, sardonic, vicious, malicious, sharp, trenchant, mordant.

cycle noun ❶ SERIES, sequence, succession, round, run, rotation. ❷ BICYCLE, bike, tandem, tricycle, monocycle.

cyclic adjective RECURRING, repetitive, circular, rotating.

cynical adjective SCEPTICAL, pessimistic, doubting, unbelieving, disbelieving, distrustful, suspicious, misanthropic, critical, sardonic, scoffing.
– OPPOSITES optimistic.

Dd

dab verb PAT, blot, press, touch, smudge, besmear, bedaub.
▶ noun ❶ PAT, blot, press, touch, smudge. ❷ **a dab of butter:** BIT, speck, touch, trace, dash, drop, tinge, suggestion, hint, modicum.

dabble verb ❶ PADDLE, dip, splash, slosh. ❷ **dabble in politics:** FLIRT WITH, toy with, dally with, dip into.

dabbler noun DILETTANTE, amateur, trifler.

daily adjective ❶ EVERYDAY, quotidian, diurnal. ❷ COMMON, regular, commonplace, usual, habitual, customary.
▶ adverb EVERY DAY, once a day, day after day, day by day, per diem.

dainty adjective ❶ **a dainty figure:** PETITE, delicate, neat, exquisite, graceful, elegant, trim, pretty, fine, refined. ❷ **a dainty eater:** PARTICULAR, discriminating, fastidious, fussy, choosy, finicky, refined, scrupulous, meticulous, squeamish, nice. ❸ **a dainty morsel:** TASTY, delicious, appetizing, palatable, choice, savoury, flavoursome, luscious, juicy, succulent.
– OPPOSITES unwieldy, undiscriminating, unpalatable.

▶ noun TITBIT, delicacy, confection, sweetmeat, bonne bouche.

dally verb DAWDLE, loiter, delay, linger, take one's time, loaf, saunter, procrastinate, waste time; *informal* dilly-dally, hang about; *archaic* tarry.
– OPPOSITES hurry.

dam noun BARRIER, wall, obstruction, barricade, embankment, barrage, bank, weir.
▶ verb BLOCK, obstruct, hold back, check, stop, staunch, stem.

damage noun ❶ HARM, injury, destruction, hurt, impairment, defacement, abuse, defilement, vandalism, ruin, devastation, havoc, detriment, mischief, outrage, accident, loss, suffering. ❷ what's the damage? COST, charge, expense, bill, total.
▶ verb HARM, injure, do damage to, spoil, vandalize, destroy, wreck, ruin, mar, deface, devastate, defile, play havoc with, do mischief to, mutilate, impair, disable, sabotage, warp.

damages plural noun COMPENSATION, reparation, reimbursement, restitution, satisfaction, indemnity.

damaging adjective *see* HARMFUL.

damn verb ❶ CURSE, execrate, anathematize, imprecate. ❷ damned by the critics: CRITICIZE, attack, flay; *informal* pan, slam, knock, blast, take apart; *Brit. informal* slate.
– OPPOSITES bless, praise.

damning adjective damning evidence: INCRIMINATING, condemnatory, condemning, implicating, accusatorial.

damp adjective ❶ damp clothes: MOIST, soggy, wettish, dank. ❷ a damp day: RAINY, wettish, drizzly, humid, clammy, muggy, misty, foggy, vaporous.
– OPPOSITES dry.
▶ verb ❶ MOISTEN, dampen, sprinkle, humidify. ❷ damp their enthusiasm: DISCOURAGE, dampen, check, curb, restrain, stifle, inhibit; *informal* put a damper on, pour cold water on. ❸ damp down the vibrations: REDUCE, lessen, diminish, decrease, moderate.

dance verb CAPER, trip, jig, skip, prance, cavort, hop, frolic, gambol, jump, leap, romp, bounce, whirl, spin.

dandy noun FOP, man about town, boulevardier; *informal* sharp dresser; *dated* beau, popinjay, blade; *archaic* coxcomb.

danger noun ❶ RISK, peril, hazard, jeopardy, endangerment, precariousness, insecurity, instability. ❷ a danger of rain: CHANCE, possibility, threat, risk.
– OPPOSITES safety.

dangerous adjective ❶ RISKY, perilous, unsafe, hazardous, precarious, insecure, exposed, defenceless, uncertain, unsound, critical, alarming; *informal* hairy, chancy. ❷ a dangerous criminal: MENACING, threatening, ruthless, nasty, violent, desperate, treacherous, unmanageable, wild, volatile.
– OPPOSITES safe, harmless.

dangle verb ❶ HANG, swing, sway, trail, droop, flap, wave. ❷ dangling an offer: TEMPT WITH, entice with, lure with, hold out.

dank adjective DAMP, wet, moist, humid, clammy, chilly.
– OPPOSITES dry.

dappled adjective SPOTTED, marked, mottled, flecked, stippled, freckled, dotted, streaked, patchy, marbled, blotchy, blotched, piebald, motley, brindled, pinto, variegated, particoloured.

dare verb ❶ RISK, hazard, venture, have the courage, take the risk, be brave enough, make bold. ❷ **dare him to go**: CHALLENGE, provoke, goad, taunt.

daring adjective BOLD, adventurous, brave, courageous, audacious, intrepid, fearless, undaunted, unshrinking, rash, reckless, foolhardy.

dark adjective ❶ BLACK, pitch-black, pitch-dark, jet-black, inky, unlit, shadowy, shady, murky, dim, indistinct, dingy, foggy, misty, cloudy, overcast, sunless, gloomy, funereal. ❷ **dark skin**: SALLOW, swarthy, black, olive-skinned, ebony, tanned. ❸ **a dark mood**: MOODY, brooding, angry, sullen, dour, glum, morose, sulky, frowning, glowering, forbidding, ominous. ❹ **dark deeds**: EVIL, wicked, villainous, sinful, iniquitous, vile, base, foul, horrible, atrocious, nefarious, fiendish, satanic, damnable. ❺ *See* MYSTERIOUS.
– OPPOSITES light, pale, cheerful.

darken verb ❶ GROW DARK/DARKER, blacken, cloud over, dim, grow dim. ❷ MAKE DARK/DARKER, blacken, black, dim, shade, overshadow, eclipse.
– OPPOSITES lighten, brighten.

darling noun ❶ **goodbye, darling**: DEAR, dearest, sweetheart, love, beloved, honey. ❷ **a little darling**: CHARMER, pet, sweetheart; *informal* sweetie, poppet.

dart noun ARROW, bolt, missile.
► verb RUSH, dash, bolt, sprint, run, tear, hurtle, fly, bound, flash, shoot, leap, spring, scuttle, flit; *informal* scoot, zip, whizz.

dash verb ❶ RUSH, run, hurry, race, sprint, tear, speed, fly, dart, bolt, hasten. ❷ **dash her hopes**: SHATTER, destroy, ruin, spoil, frustrate, thwart, blight, baulk, check.
► noun ❶ RUSH, bolt, run, race, flight, dart, sprint, sortie, spurt. ❷ **a dash of salt**: BIT, pinch, drop, sprinkling, touch, trace, tinge.

dashing adjective DEBONAIR, stylish, lively, spirited, dynamic, energetic, animated, gallant, bold, daring, swashbuckling, dazzling.

data plural noun INFORMATION, facts, figures, details, statistics, material, input.

date noun ❶ DAY, point in time. ❷ MEETING, appointment, engagement, rendezvous, assignation; *poetic/literary* tryst. ❸ PARTNER, escort, girlfriend, boyfriend; *dated* beau.

dated adjective OUT OF DATE, outdated, old-fashioned, outmoded, antiquated; *informal* old hat.
– OPPOSITES up to date, modern.

daunt verb INTIMIDATE, frighten, overawe, scare, alarm, dismay, unnerve, abash, cow, dishearten, dispirit.

dawdle verb LOITER, delay, move slowly, linger, take one's time, waste time, idle, dally, straggle, trail behind, potter about, move at a snail's pace.
– OPPOSITES hurry, hasten.

dawn noun ❶ DAYBREAK, break of day, sunrise, first light, cockcrow. ❷ BEGINNING, start, birth, rise,

commencement, onset, advent, arrival, appearance, emergence, origin, inception, genesis, unfolding, development.
– OPPOSITES dusk.

day noun ❶ DAYTIME, daylight, daylight hours, broad daylight. ❷ in those days: PERIOD, time, epoch, age, era, generation.

daze verb STUN, stupefy, confuse, bewilder, befuddle, addle, numb, benumb, paralyse.

dazzle verb ❶ BLIND, bedazzle, daze. ❷ OVERPOWER, overwhelm, overawe, awe, stagger, fascinate, dumbfound, amaze, astonish.

dead adjective ❶ DECEASED, lifeless, gone, passed on/away, departed, no more, late, inanimate, defunct; *informal* done for. ❷ a dead language/issue: OBSOLETE, extinct, outmoded, outdated, lapsed, inactive. ❸ dead to his pleas: UNRESPONSIVE, indifferent, unsympathetic, unfeeling, insensitive, cold, lukewarm, apathetic, emotionless, wooden. ❹ the place was dead: DULL, boring, uninteresting, tedious, uneventful, flat, wearisome, humdrum, stale, moribund, vapid. ❺ a dead stop: ABRUPT, sudden, quick, rapid, swift, hurried, instantaneous.
– OPPOSITES alive, lively.
▶ adverb dead serious/tired: COMPLETELY, totally, absolutely, entirely, utterly, thoroughly, categorically.

deaden verb ❶ emotions deadened: DESENSITIZE, numb, anaesthetize, paralyse, dull. ❷ deaden the pain: REDUCE, suppress, moderate, blunt, dull, muffle, diminish, mitigate, alleviate, smother, stifle.

deadlock noun STALEMATE, impasse, stand-off, standstill, halt, stop.

deadly adjective FATAL, lethal, dangerous, destructive, toxic, poisonous, venomous, virulent, noxious. *See also* HARMFUL (1).
– OPPOSITES harmless.

deafening adjective LOUD, ear-splitting, thunderous, resounding, ringing, reverberating.

deal noun ❶ AGREEMENT, transaction, arrangement, contract, bargain, understanding, settlement, compact, pact. ❷ a great deal of money: AMOUNT, quantity, volume.
▶ verb ❶ TRADE, do business, buy and sell, traffic. ❷ deal cards: DISTRIBUTE, share out, allocate, divide out, hand out, dole out, apportion, mete out. ❸ deal him a blow: ADMINISTER, deliver, give, direct, aim.
■ **deal with** ATTEND TO, see to, take care of, cope with, handle, manage, tackle.

dealer noun TRADER, broker, retailer, wholesaler, supplier, distributor, vendor, tradesman, merchant, trafficker, chandler, pedlar.

dear adjective ❶ BELOVED, loved, adored, cherished, intimate, close, esteemed, respected. ❷ EXPENSIVE, costly, overpriced, exorbitant, high-priced; *informal* pricey, steep.
– OPPOSITES cheap.

dearth noun LACK, scarcity, scarceness, shortage, deficiency, insufficiency, paucity.
– OPPOSITES abundance.

death noun ❶ DYING, demise, end, final exit, passing on/away.

❷ KILLING, murder, massacre, slaughter; *poetic/literary* slaying.
– OPPOSITES life.

debacle noun FIASCO, disaster, catastrophe, failure, collapse, ruin, defeat, rout, havoc.

debase verb DEGRADE, devalue, demean, disgrace, dishonour, shame, discredit, cheapen, humble, humiliate, diminish, ruin, soil, sully, vulgarize.
– OPPOSITES enhance.

debatable adjective ARGUABLE, questionable, open to question, disputable, controversial, contentious, doubtful, open to doubt, dubious, uncertain, unsure, undecided, borderline, moot.
– OPPOSITES certain.

debate noun ARGUMENT, dispute, discussion, difference of opinion, altercation, disputation, wrangle, controversy, war of words, polemic.
▶ verb ARGUE, dispute, argue the pros and cons of, discuss, bandy words, wrangle, contend, moot; *informal* kick around.

debauched adjective DEGENERATE, dissipated, dissolute, immoral, abandoned, promiscuous, wanton.
– OPPOSITES wholesome.

debris noun RUBBLE, wreckage, detritus, rubbish, litter, waste, flotsam, remains, ruin, fragments.

debt noun ❶ pay his debts: BILL, account, money owing, score, tally, dues, arrears. ❷ his debt to his family: OBLIGATION, liability, indebtedness.

decamp verb RUN OFF/AWAY, make off, flee, take off, abscond, escape; *informal* cut and run, skedaddle, vamoose, skip, hightail it; *Brit. informal* do a moonlight flit.

decay verb ❶ ROT, decompose, go bad, putrefy, spoil, perish, corrode. ❷ DEGENERATE, decline, deteriorate, fail, wane, ebb, dwindle, crumble, disintegrate, wither, die, atrophy.

deceit noun DECEPTION, cheating, dishonesty, duplicity, double-dealing, fraud, fraudulence, trickery, subterfuge, untruthfulness, duping, chicanery, underhandedness, cunning, wiliness, dissimulation, pretence, artifice, treachery.
– OPPOSITES honesty.

deceitful adjective DECEPTIVE, misleading, fraudulent, double-dealing, sneaky, treacherous, untruthful, dishonest, underhand, false, untrustworthy, lying, unfaithful, two-faced, duplicitous, mendacious, insincere, disingenuous, sham, bogus, spurious, perfidious; *informal* crooked, tricky.
– OPPOSITES honest.

deceive verb MISLEAD, take in, fool, delude, misguide, lead on, trick, hoodwink, dupe, hoax, swindle, outwit, ensnare, entrap, double-cross, gull; *informal* con, take for a ride, pull someone's leg, pull the wool over someone's eyes, pull a fast one on, bamboozle, diddle.

decelerate verb SLOW DOWN, go slower, reduce speed, brake, put the brakes on, ease up.
– OPPOSITES accelerate.

decent adjective ❶ PROPER, acceptable, respectable, correct, appropriate, seemly, fitting, fit, suitable, modest, becoming,

tasteful, decorous, pure. ❷ **a decent fellow**: HONEST, trustworthy, dependable, respectable, worthy, upright, kind, thoughtful, obliging, helpful, generous, courteous, civil. ❸ **a decent salary**: SUFFICIENT, acceptable, reasonable, adequate, ample.
– OPPOSITES indecent.

deception noun ❶ TRICK, ruse, dodge, subterfuge, fraud, cheat, swindle, sham, pretence, bluff, stratagem, confidence trick, imposture; *informal* con. ❷ *See* DECEIT.

deceptive adjective
❶ **appearances can be deceptive**: MISLEADING, false, illusory, ambiguous, unreliable, wrong, distorted, deceiving, delusive, spurious, treacherous. ❷ *See* DECEITFUL.
– OPPOSITES genuine.

decide verb ❶ COME TO A DECISION, reach/make a decision, make up one's mind, resolve, choose, come to a conclusion, conclude, commit oneself, opt for, select. ❷ JUDGE, adjudicate, arbitrate, make a judgement on, make a ruling, give a verdict.

decided adjective CLEAR, distinct, definite, obvious, certain, marked, pronounced, emphatic, categorical, unequivocal.

decision noun CONCLUSION, resolution, judgement, verdict, pronouncement, determination, outcome, findings.

decisive adjective ❶ **a decisive person**: DETERMINED, resolute, firm, sure, purposeful, unhesitating, unswerving, unwavering, unfaltering, incisive, emphatic. ❷ **the decisive factor**: DECIDING, determining, conclusive, final, critical, crucial, significant, influential.
– OPPOSITES irresolute, inconclusive.

declaration noun ❶ STATEMENT, announcement, proclamation, pronouncement, broadcast, promulgation, edict, notification, manifesto. ❷ ASSERTION, protestation, insistence, profession, claim, allegation, avowal, contention, affirmation, swearing; *formal* averment.

declare verb STATE, announce, proclaim, make known, assert, pronounce, broadcast, report, trumpet, profess, claim, allege, affirm, maintain, swear, emphasize, insist, avow, attest.

decline verb ❶ **decline an invitation**: REFUSE, turn down, reject, say no, rebuff, forgo, send one's regrets; *informal* give the thumbs down to. ❷ **his influence declined**: LESSEN, decrease, dwindle, wane, fade, ebb, fall/taper off, tail off, flag, abate. ❸ **her strength is declining**: DETERIORATE, diminish, weaken, fail, degenerate, wither, fade away, sink.
– OPPOSITES accept, flourish, increase.
▶ **noun** DECREASE, reduction, lessening, downturn, downswing, slump, plunge, diminution, ebb, waning, falling-off, deterioration, degeneration; *informal* nosedive.

decode verb DECIPHER, unravel, make out, unscramble, solve, explain, interpret, read; *informal* crack, figure out.
– OPPOSITES encode.

decompose verb ROT, decay, putrefy, go bad, go off, break down, disintegrate, fester.

decor noun DECORATION, furnishings, furbishing, colour scheme, ornamentation.

decorate verb ❶ ADORN, ornament, festoon, beautify, prettify, embellish, garnish, trim, enhance, garland. ❷ PAINT, wallpaper, paper, renovate, refurbish, furbish; *informal* do up. ❸ decorated for bravery: HONOUR, give a medal to, pin a medal on, confer an award on.

decoration noun ❶ ADORNMENT, ornamentation, embellishment, beautification, prettification, enhancement. ❷ ORNAMENT, trinket, bauble, frill, flourish, frippery, knick-knack, tinsel, trimming. ❸ MEDAL, award, order, badge, star, ribbon, laurel, colours, insignia.

decorative adjective ORNAMENTAL, ornate, fancy, elaborate.

decorous adjective PROPER, seemly, decent, becoming, fitting, tasteful, in good taste, correct, appropriate, suitable, presentable, apt, apposite, polite, well mannered, well behaved, refined, genteel, well bred, respectable, dignified.
– OPPOSITES indecorous, unseemly.

decorum noun PROPRIETY, decency, correctness, appropriateness, seemliness, respectability, good taste, politeness, courtesy, refinement, breeding, etiquette, protocol, conformity, good form; *informal* the thing to do.

decoy noun LURE, bait, temptation, diversion, distraction, snare, trap, inducement, attraction, enticement.
▶ verb LURE, attract, tempt, seduce, inveigle, draw, lead, ensnare, entrap, snare, trap, trick.

decrease verb ❶ LESSEN, reduce, grow less, diminish, drop, fall off, decline, contract, dwindle, shrink, lower, cut down/back, curtail. ❷ DIE DOWN, abate, subside, let up, slacken, ebb, wane, taper off, peter out, tail off.
– OPPOSITES increase.
▶ noun REDUCTION, drop, lessening, decline, falling-off, downturn, cutback, diminution, curtailment, contraction, shrinkage.
– OPPOSITES increase.

decree noun ❶ EDICT, order, law, statute, act, ordinance, regulation, injunction, rule, enactment, command, mandate, proclamation, precept, dictum. ❷ RULING, verdict, judgement, decision, finding.
▶ verb ORDAIN, rule, order, command, dictate, lay down, prescribe, pronounce, declare, proclaim, direct, determine, decide, promulgate, enact, adjudge, enjoin.

decrepit adjective DILAPIDATED, battered, ramshackle, derelict, broken-down, run down, worn out, rickety, antiquated; *informal* the worse for wear, on its last legs.
– OPPOSITES sound.

dedicate verb ❶ DEVOTE, commit, give, give over, pledge, surrender. ❷ INSCRIBE, address, assign, name.

dedicated adjective COMMITTED, devoted, wholehearted, enthusiastic, keen, zealous, single-minded, sworn.

deduce verb CONCLUDE, come to the conclusion that, infer, gather, work out, reason, understand, come to understand, surmise, divine, assume, presume, glean; *informal* put two and two together; *Brit. informal* suss out.

deduct verb SUBTRACT, take away, take off, withdraw, remove, discount, abstract.
– OPPOSITES add.

deduction noun ❶ CONCLUSION, inference, reasoning, assumption, presumption, findings, result. ❷ SUBTRACTION, reduction, decrease, taking off, removal, withdrawal, discount.

deed noun ❶ ACT, action, feat, exploit, performance, undertaking, effort, accomplishment, enterprise, achievement, endeavour, stunt. ❷ DOCUMENT, title, contract, instrument, indenture.

deep adjective ❶ FATHOMLESS, bottomless, yawning, cavernous, profound, unplumbed, abyssal. ❷ **deep distrust**: PROFOUND, extreme, intense, great, deep-seated, deep-rooted, grave. ❸ **deep affection**: INTENSE, heartfelt, fervent, ardent, impassioned. ❹ **a deep voice**: LOW, low-pitched, bass, rich, powerful, resonant, sonorous, rumbling, booming, resounding. ❺ **a deep secret**: OBSCURE, unclear, mysterious, abstruse, hidden, secret, recondite, esoteric, arcane. ❻ **deep in thought**: ENGROSSED, absorbed, preoccupied, rapt, immersed, engaged, lost. ❼ **a deep thinker**: CLEVER, intellectual, wise, learned, sagacious, penetrating, discerning, perspicacious. ❽ **deep sleep**: HEAVY, sound.
– OPPOSITES shallow, light.

deface verb SPOIL, disfigure, blemish, mar, deform, ruin, sully, tarnish, damage, mutilate, vandalize, injure, uglify.

defame verb SLANDER, libel, blacken someone's name, cast aspersions on, smear, malign, insult, speak evil of, vilify, traduce, besmirch, drag through the mud, defile, stigmatize, disparage, denigrate.

defeat verb ❶ BEAT, conquer, get the better of, win a victory over, vanquish, rout, trounce, overcome, overpower, overwhelm, crush, quash, subjugate, subdue, quell; *informal* thrash, wipe the floor with, lick, smash, clobber, zap. ❷ **the problem defeats me**: BAFFLE, puzzle, perplex, confound, frustrate. ❸ **the motion was defeated**: REJECT, throw out, outvote.
– OPPOSITES lose.
▶ noun CONQUEST, beating, vanquishing, thrashing, rout, overpowering, overthrow, reverse, setback, subjugation, humiliation, failure, repulse; *informal* drubbing, licking.

defect[1] noun FAULT, flaw, imperfection, deficiency, shortcoming, weak spot/point, weakness, mistake, error, failing, inadequacy, omission, absence, snag, kink, deformity, blemish, crack, break, tear, scratch; *informal* bug.

defect[2] verb DESERT, change sides, go over, apostatize.

defective adjective FAULTY, flawed, imperfect, malfunctioning, broken, in disrepair, inadequate, deficient, incomplete, weak, unsatisfactory,

cracked, torn, scratched, insufficient, wanting.
– OPPOSITES intact.

defence noun ❶ PROTECTION, guard, shield, security, safeguard, cover, shelter, fortification, screen, resistance, deterrent. ❷ JUSTIFICATION, argument, apology, apologia, vindication, plea, explanation, excuse, extenuation, exoneration.

defenceless adjective VULNERABLE, helpless, exposed, weak, powerless, unguarded, unprotected, unarmed, open to attack, wide open.

defend verb ❶ PROTECT, guard, watch over, safeguard, keep from harm, preserve, secure, shelter, screen, shield, cover, fight for. ❷ JUSTIFY, argue for, speak on behalf of, make a case for, give reasons for, plead for, champion, stand up for, explain, exonerate.
– OPPOSITES attack.

defendant noun ACCUSED, prisoner at the bar, respondent, appellant, litigant.

defensive adjective ❶ PROTECTIVE, watchful, shielding, opposing. ❷ a defensive attitude: OVERSENSITIVE, prickly, apologetic, thin-skinned.
– OPPOSITES offensive.

defer verb POSTPONE, put off, delay, adjourn, hold over, suspend, stay, hold in abeyance, prorogue; *informal* put on ice, shelve.

deference noun RESPECT, reverence, homage, veneration, dutifulness, consideration, regard, attentiveness, attention, thoughtfulness.

defiant adjective CHALLENGING, aggressive, provocative, rebellious, disobedient, uncooperative, insolent, resistant, insubordinate, mutinous, obstinate, headstrong, antagonistic, refractory, contemptuous, scornful, bold, brazen, daring, audacious, truculent, unruly, self-willed.

deficiency noun ❶ LACK, shortage, scarcity, scantiness, want, dearth, insufficiency, inadequacy, deficit, absence, paucity. ❷ *See* DEFECT[1].

defile verb CORRUPT, contaminate, taint, tarnish, pollute, foul, dirty, soil, sully, pervert, infect, besmirch, desecrate, dishonour.

define verb ❶ define one's terms: EXPLAIN, give the meaning of, spell out, elucidate, describe, interpret, expound, clarify. ❷ define the boundary: MARK OUT/OFF, fix, establish, determine, settle, bound, demarcate, delineate, delimit, circumscribe, describe.

definite adjective ❶ definite plans: SPECIFIC, precise, particular, exact, well defined, clear, clear-cut, explicit, fixed, established, confirmed, determined, express. ❷ it's definite that: CERTAIN, sure, decided, positive, settled, guaranteed, assured, conclusive, final. ❸ definite boundaries: FIXED, marked, delimited, demarcated, circumscribed.
– OPPOSITES indefinite, uncertain, indeterminate.

definitely adverb CERTAINLY, surely, for sure, without doubt/question, beyond any doubt, undoubtedly, indubitably, positively, absolutely, undeniably, unmistakably, plainly, clearly, obviously, decidedly.

definition noun ❶ MEANING,

description, elucidation, exposition, interpretation, clarification. ❷ definition of the image: SHARPNESS, clearness, clarity, distinctness, focus, precision.

definitive adjective CONCLUSIVE, authoritative, final, decisive, unconditional, unqualified, absolute, categorical, settled, official, ultimate, decided, agreed, standard, complete, correct.

deflect verb TURN ASIDE, turn, divert, parry, fend off, ward off, intercept, glance off, veer, swerve, deviate, switch, avert, sidetrack.

deformed adjective MISSHAPEN, malformed, distorted, contorted, twisted, crooked, crippled, maimed, disfigured, damaged, mutilated, marred, warped, gnarled, mangled, perverted, corrupted, depraved.

defraud verb CHEAT, swindle, rob, trick, fool; *informal* rip off, fleece, con, gyp.

deft adjective DEXTEROUS, nimble, adroit, agile, skilful, skilled, adept, proficient, able, clever, expert, quick.
– OPPOSITES clumsy, maladroit.

defy verb ❶ DISOBEY, disregard, rebel, ignore, flout, deride, slight, scorn; *informal* thumb one's nose at, scoff at, snap one's fingers at. ❷ defy the enemy: RESIST, stand up to, confront, face, repel, repulse, thwart, frustrate, foil, withstand, brave; *informal* meet head-on.
– OPPOSITES obey.

degenerate adjective *see* DEBAUCHED.
► verb DETERIORATE, decline, worsen, decay, rot, regress, fail, fall off, sink, slide, slip; *informal* go to the dogs, go to pot, hit the skids.
– OPPOSITES improve.

degrade verb ❶ DEBASE, discredit, cheapen, belittle, demean, lower, devalue, reduce, shame, disgrace, dishonour, humble, humiliate, abase, mortify; *formal* vitiate. ❷ DEMOTE, downgrade, strip of rank, cashier, unseat, dethrone.
– OPPOSITES dignify.

degree noun ❶ a high degree of talent: LEVEL, stage, grade, step, rung, point, mark, measure, gradation, limit. ❷ to a marked degree: EXTENT, measure, magnitude, level, amount, intensity, quality, proportion, ratio.

dehydrate verb DRY, dry up, lose water, parch, sear, desiccate.

deign verb CONDESCEND, lower oneself, stoop, think/see fit, deem worthy, consent.

deity noun GOD, goddess, supreme being, divinity, godhead, divine being, demiurge.

dejected adjective DEPRESSED, dispirited, discouraged, disheartened, downhearted, crestfallen, downcast, disappointed, unhappy, sad, miserable, despondent, forlorn, woebegone, disconsolate, morose; *informal* down in the dumps, blue, long-faced.
– OPPOSITES cheerful.

delay verb ❶ POSTPONE, put off, hold over, adjourn, defer, stay, hold in abeyance; *informal* shelve, put on ice, put on the back burner. ❷ delayed by traffic: HOLD UP/BACK, detain, hinder, obstruct, hamper, impede, check, restrain, arrest; *informal* bog down. ❸ don't delay!

LINGER, loiter, dawdle, dally, lag/fall behind, procrastinate; *informal* dilly-dally; *archaic* tarry.
– OPPOSITES advance, hurry.
▶ **noun** ❶ POSTPONEMENT, adjournment, deferment, suspension, stay. ❷ HOLD-UP, wait, setback, check, stoppage, halt, interruption, detention, hindrance, obstruction, impediment.

delectable **adjective** *see* DELICIOUS (1).

delegate **verb** ❶ APPOINT, designate, nominate, name, depute, commission, mandate, choose, select, elect, ordain. ❷ **delegate tasks:** PASS ON, hand over, transfer, give, entrust, assign, commit.
▶ **noun** REPRESENTATIVE, agent, envoy, legate, emissary.

delegation **noun** DEPUTATION, legation, mission, commission, embassy.

delete **verb** ERASE, cross out, rub out, cut out, cancel, edit out, remove, take out, expunge, obliterate, blue-pencil, efface.

deliberate **adjective** ❶ INTENTIONAL, planned, intended, calculated, considered, designed, studied, conscious, purposeful, wilful, premeditated, pre-arranged, preconceived, aforethought. ❷ **slow deliberate steps:** CAREFUL, unhurried, cautious, thoughtful, steady, regular, measured, unwavering, unhesitating, unfaltering, determined, resolute, ponderous, laborious.
– OPPOSITES unintentional, hasty.
▶ **verb** *see* THINK (3).

deliberately **adverb** INTENTIONALLY, on purpose, purposefully, by design, knowingly, wittingly, consciously, premeditatedly, calculatingly; *informal* in cold blood.

delicate **adjective** ❶ **delicate material:** FINE, fragile, dainty, exquisite, slender, slight, elegant, graceful, flimsy, wispy, gossamer. ❷ **delicate health:** FRAIL, sickly, weak, unwell, in poor health, infirm, ailing, debilitated. ❸ **requires delicate handling:** CAREFUL, sensitive, tactful, discreet, considerate, diplomatic, politic. ❹ **delicate colours:** SUBTLE, subdued, muted, pastel, pale, understated. ❺ **a delicate matter:** DIFFICULT, awkward, tricky, sensitive, critical, precarious; *informal* ticklish, touchy. ❻ **a delicate touch:** DEFT, skilled, skilful, expert.
– OPPOSITES coarse, robust.

delicious **adjective** ❶ APPETIZING, tasty, delectable, mouth-watering, savoury, palatable, luscious, flavoursome, toothsome, ambrosial; *informal* yummy, scrumptious. ❷ DELIGHTFUL, enchanting, enjoyable, pleasant, agreeable, charming, pleasurable, entertaining, amusing, diverting.
– OPPOSITES revolting, disgusting.

delight **noun** JOY, pleasure, happiness, gladness, bliss, ecstasy, rapture, elation, jubilation, satisfaction, excitement, entertainment, amusement, transports.
– OPPOSITES dismay.
▶ **verb** PLEASE, gladden, thrill, cheer, gratify, enchant, excite, transport, captivate, charm, entertain, amuse, divert.
– OPPOSITES dismay, displease.

delighted adjective *see* HAPPY (1, 2).

delightful adjective PLEASING, agreeable, enjoyable, pleasant, pleasurable, amusing, entertaining, diverting, gratifying, delectable, enchanting, captivating, entrancing, ravishing, attractive, beautiful, engaging, winning, joyful, exciting, thrilling.

delinquent noun OFFENDER, wrongdoer, lawbreaker, criminal, hooligan, culprit, ruffian, hoodlum, miscreant, transgressor, malefactor; *Brit.* tearaway.

delirious adjective ❶ RAVING, incoherent, babbling, light-headed, irrational, deranged, demented, unhinged, insane; *informal* off one's head. ❷ ECSTATIC, euphoric, carried away, wild with excitement, frantic, transported.

deliver verb ❶ DISTRIBUTE, carry, bring, take, transport, convey, send, dispatch, remit. ❷ **deliver a speech:** GIVE, give voice to, pronounce, enunciate, announce, proclaim, declare, read, recite, broadcast, promulgate. ❸ **delivered from their enemies:** SET FREE, save, liberate, free, release, rescue, set loose, emancipate, redeem. ❹ **deliver a blow:** DIRECT, aim, give, deal, administer, inflict, throw, pitch.

delivery noun ❶ DISTRIBUTION, transport, carriage, conveyance, dispatch. ❷ CONSIGNMENT, batch, load. ❸ **his clear delivery:** ENUNCIATION, articulation, intonation, elocution, utterance, presentation. ❹ CHILDBIRTH, labour, confinement, parturition.

deluge noun FLOOD, downpour, inundation, spate, rush.
▶ **verb** FLOOD, inundate, swamp, engulf, drown, submerge, soak, drench, douse, overwhelm.

delusion noun MISCONCEPTION, illusion, fallacy, misapprehension, mistake, misunderstanding, hallucination, fantasy, fancy.

delve verb SEARCH, rummage, dig into, hunt through, investigate, probe, examine.

demand verb ❶ ASK FOR, request, insist on, press for, urge, clamour for, claim, lay claim to. ❷ EXPECT, impose, insist on, order, requisition. ❸ **work demanding care:** REQUIRE, need, necessitate, involve, want, call for, cry out for. ❹ ASK, inquire, question, interrogate.
▶ **noun** ❶ REQUEST, entreaty, claim, requisition. ❷ REQUIREMENT, need, necessity, claim, imposition, exigency. ❸ INQUIRY, question, interrogation, challenge.

demanding adjective *see* DIFFICULT (1).

demean verb DEGRADE, lower, debase, devalue, humble, abase, humiliate, disgrace, shame, belittle.

demeanour noun AIR, appearance, bearing, conduct, behaviour, mien, deportment, carriage; *formal* comportment.

demolish verb KNOCK DOWN, pull/tear down, flatten, bring down, raze, level, bulldoze, wreck, topple, dismantle, break up, pulverize.
– OPPOSITES build.

demonic adjective HELLISH, diabolical, satanic, infernal, evil, wicked, fiendish.
– OPPOSITES angelic.

demonstrable adjective PROVABLE, verifiable, indisputable, incontrovertible, irrefutable, conclusive, undeniable, unquestionable, confirmable, attestable, evincible.

demonstrate verb ❶ SHOW, indicate, display, exhibit, manifest, evince, evidence. ❷ SHOW, indicate, determine, prove, confirm, validate, verify, establish. ❸ PROTEST, march, parade, rally, picket.

demonstration noun ❶ EXPLANATION, exposition, illustration, description. ❷ INDICATION, confirmation, substantiation, verification, validation, affirmation. ❸ PROTEST, march, parade, rally, vigil, lobby, picket; *informal* demo, sit-in.

demonstrative adjective EMOTIONAL, unrestrained, expressive, open, effusive, expansive, gushing, affectionate, loving, warm.
– OPPOSITES undemonstrative, reserved.

demoralize verb DISCOURAGE, dishearten, dispirit, depress, crush, shake, undermine.
– OPPOSITES hearten.

demur verb OBJECT, raise objections, take exception, express doubts, be unwilling, protest, refuse, dissent, balk at, cavil.

demure adjective MODEST, unassuming, bashful, retiring, shy, meek, diffident, reticent, timid, shrinking, timorous, sober.
– OPPOSITES brazen.

denial noun ❶ CONTRADICTION, repudiation, disaffirmation, negation, dissent, abjuration. ❷ REFUSAL, rejection, dismissal, veto, repulse; *informal* thumbs down.
– OPPOSITES confession.

denigrate verb DISPARAGE, belittle, diminish, deprecate, detract from, decry, defame, slander, libel, cast aspersions on, malign, vilify, besmirch, abuse, revile; *informal* bad-mouth, put down.
– OPPOSITES praise.

denomination noun ❶ CREED, faith, church, sect, persuasion, communion, order, school. ❷ CATEGORY, type, classification, group, grouping.

denote verb BE A SIGN OF, indicate, mean, stand for, signify, represent, symbolize, express, betoken.

denouement noun FINALE, resolution, solution, outcome, result, upshot, culmination, climax, last act.

denounce verb ❶ CONDEMN, attack, criticize, censure, decry, fulminate against, inveigh against, revile; *formal* castigate. ❷ ACCUSE, inform against, incriminate, implicate, charge, inculpate, indict, impeach.

dense adjective ❶ TIGHTLY PACKED, close-packed, crowded, jammed together, crammed, compressed, compacted, closely set. ❷ CONCENTRATED, heavy, condensed, thick, viscous, impenetrable, opaque. ❸ STUPID, slow-witted, slow, dull-witted, obtuse, blockheaded; *informal* thick, dim.
– OPPOSITES sparse, light, clever.

deny verb ❶ deny the charge: REPUDIATE, dispute, reject,

contradict, disagree with, disclaim, dissent from, negate, disaffirm, abjure, controvert. ❷ **deny the request**: REFUSE, reject, turn down, decline, dismiss, repulse, veto; *informal* give the thumbs down to, give the red light to.
– OPPOSITES admit, allow, grant.

depart verb ❶ LEAVE, go, take one's leave/departure, withdraw, absent oneself, set off, start out, get under way, quit, make an exit, decamp, retire, retreat; *informal* make tracks, shove off, split, vamoose, hightail it. ❷ *See* DEVIATE.

departed adjective DEAD, deceased, late, gone, passed away/on.

department noun ❶ SECTION, division, unit, branch, office, bureau, agency, compartment. ❷ AREA OF RESPONSIBILITY, area, concern, sphere, line, province, domain, field, realm, jurisdiction.

departure noun LEAVING, going, starting out, embarkation, escape, exit, withdrawal, retreat, retirement.
– OPPOSITES arrival.

depend verb ❶ BE DEPENDENT ON, turn/hinge on, be subject to, rest on, be contingent on, revolve around, be influenced by. ❷ RELY ON, count/bank on, trust in, put one's faith in, swear by, be sure of, be supported by.

dependable adjective RELIABLE, trustworthy, trusty, faithful, steady, responsible, sure, stable, unfailing, sound.
– OPPOSITES unreliable.

dependent adjective ❶ DEPENDING ON, conditional on, contingent on, subject to, determined by, connected with, relative to. ❷ RELYING ON, reliant on, supported by, sustained by. ❸ **dependent children**: RELIANT, helpless, weak, defenceless, vulnerable.
– OPPOSITES independent.

depict verb PORTRAY, represent, draw, paint, sketch, illustrate, delineate, outline, reproduce, render, describe, set out, relate, detail, narrate, recount, chronicle.

deplete verb EXHAUST, use up, consume, expend, spend, drain, empty, milk.
– OPPOSITES augment, increase.

deplorable adjective DISGRACEFUL, shameful, reprehensible, scandalous, shocking, dishonourable, discreditable, despicable, contemptible, blameworthy, abominable, lamentable, dire, pitiable, calamitous, base, sordid, vile, execrable, opprobrious.
– OPPOSITES admirable.

deplore verb ❶ *See* CONDEMN (1). ❷ BE SCANDALIZED BY, be shocked by, be offended by, disapprove of, abhor.
– OPPOSITES applaud.

deploy verb ❶ ARRANGE, position, dispose, distribute, station. ❷ USE, utilize, set out/up, bring into play, have recourse to.

deport verb EXPEL, banish, evict, transport, oust, expatriate, extradite.

depose verb UNSEAT, oust, remove, dismiss, dethrone, discharge, cashier; *informal* sack, fire, give someone the boot; *Brit. informal* give someone the push.

deposit noun ❶ DOWN PAYMENT, instalment, retainer, security,

pledge, stake. ❷ SEDIMENT, accumulation, layer, precipitation, deposition, sublimate, dregs, silt, alluvium.
▶ verb ❶ BANK, lodge, consign, entrust, store, hoard, stow, put away, lay in; *informal* squirrel away. ❷ PUT, place, lay, drop, let fall; *informal* dump, park.

depot noun ❶ STATION, garage, terminus, terminal. ❷ STORE, storehouse, warehouse, repository, depository, magazine, arsenal, cache.

deprave verb CORRUPT, debauch, lead astray, pervert, debase, degrade, defile, pollute, contaminate.

depraved adjective *see* CORRUPT adjective (2).

depreciate verb ❶ DECREASE IN VALUE, lose value, decline in price. ❷ *See* DISPARAGE.

depress verb ❶ SADDEN, make gloomy/despondent, dispirit, dishearten, discourage, weigh down, grieve, oppress, dampen someone's spirits, burden. ❷ **depress the economy**: SLOW DOWN/UP, weaken, lower, reduce, impair, enfeeble, drain, sap, debilitate, devitalize.
– OPPOSITES cheer.

depressed adjective *see* SAD (1).

depression noun ❶ SADNESS, unhappiness, despair, gloom, dejection, downheartedness, despondency, melancholy, desolation, moodiness, moroseness, pessimism; *informal* the dumps, the blues. ❷ HOLLOW, indentation, cavity, dip, valley, pit, hole, bowl, excavation, concavity. ❸ **an economic depression**: RECESSION, slump, slowdown, stagnation, decline.
– OPPOSITES happiness, boom.

deprive verb DISPOSSESS, take away from, strip, deny, expropriate, divest, wrest, rob.

deprived adjective *see* POOR (1).

deputize verb TAKE THE PLACE OF, stand in for, act for, do someone's job, substitute for, take over from, replace, cover for, understudy.

deputy noun SUBSTITUTE, representative, stand-in, delegate, envoy, proxy, agent, ambassador, commissioner, legate.

derelict adjective ❶ ABANDONED, deserted, neglected, rejected, discarded, forsaken, relinquished, cast off. ❷ DILAPIDATED, ramshackle, tumbledown, run down, broken-down, in disrepair, crumbling, rickety.
▶ noun VAGRANT, beggar, down and out, tramp, outcast; *N. Amer.* hobo; *Brit. informal* dosser.

deride verb MOCK, ridicule, jeer at, scoff at, sneer at, make fun of, poke fun at, laugh at, scorn, lampoon, satirize, taunt, insult, rag, tease, chaff, disparage, slight, vilify; *informal* pooh-pooh.

derogatory adjective DISPARAGING, deprecatory, depreciatory, detracting, disapproving, unflattering, insulting, defamatory.
– OPPOSITES complimentary.

descend verb ❶ GO/COME DOWN, climb down, fall, drop, sink, subside, plunge, plummet, tumble, slump. ❷ **descend from the train**: GET DOWN, get off, alight, disembark, dismount, detrain, deplane.
– OPPOSITES ascend.

descent noun ❶ SLOPE, incline, dip, drop, gradient, declivity, slant. ❷ ANCESTRY, parentage, origins, lineage, extraction, heredity, genealogy, succession, stock, line, pedigree, blood, strain.
– OPPOSITES ascent.

describe verb ❶ GIVE DETAILS OF, detail, tell, narrate, put into words, express, recount, relate, report, set out, chronicle, illustrate, characterize, portray, depict. ❷ **describe a circle**: DRAW, mark out, delineate, outline, trace, sketch.

description noun ACCOUNT, statement, report, chronicle, narration, recounting, commentary, explanation, illustration, designation, characterization, portrayal, depiction, elucidation, relation.

descriptive adjective DETAILED, graphic, vivid, striking, expressive, illustrative, depictive, pictorial.

desecrate verb DEFILE, profane, blaspheme, pollute, treat sacrilegiously, contaminate, befoul, infect, debase, degrade, dishonour.
– OPPOSITES honour.

desert[1] verb ❶ ABANDON, forsake, give up, leave, turn one's back on, betray, jilt, strand, leave stranded, maroon, neglect, shun, relinquish; *informal* walk out on, leave in the lurch, leave high and dry. ❷ ABSCOND, defect, run away, flee, decamp, bolt, depart, quit; *informal* go AWOL, turn tail, take French leave.

desert[2] adjective ARID, dry, parched, scorched, torrid.
▶ noun WASTELAND, wilderness, barrenness, wilds.

deserted adjective ABANDONED, empty, neglected, vacant, uninhabited, unoccupied, untenanted, desolate, lonely, solitary, godforsaken.
– OPPOSITES crowded.

deserter noun ❶ ABSCONDER, runaway, defector, fugitive, truant, escapee. ❷ RENEGADE, turncoat, traitor, betrayer, apostate; *informal* rat.

deserve verb MERIT, warrant, be worthy of, rate, justify, earn, be entitled to, have a right to, have a claim on.

deserving adjective *see* WORTHY.

design noun ❶ PLAN, blueprint, drawing, sketch, outline, map, plot, diagram, draft, scheme, model. ❷ PATTERN, style, arrangement, composition, configuration, shape. ❸ INTENTION, aim, purpose, plan, objective, goal, end, target, point, hope, desire, wish, aspiration.
▶ verb ❶ PLAN, draw, sketch, outline, map out, block out, delineate, draft, depict. ❷ CREATE, invent, think up, originate, conceive, fashion. ❸ INTEND, aim, contrive, plan, tailor, mean, destine.

designer noun CREATOR, inventor, deviser, originator, architect, author.

designing adjective *see* CRAFTY.

desire verb ❶ WISH FOR, want, long for, yearn for, thirst for, hunger after, crave, ache for, set one's heart on, hanker after, fancy, have a fancy for, covet, aspire to; *informal* have a yen for. ❷ LUST AFTER, burn for; *informal* have the hots for.

▶ **noun** ❶ WISH, want, fancy, inclination, preference, longing, yearning, craving, eagerness, enthusiasm, hankering, predilection, aspiration. ❷ LUST, lustfulness, passion, lechery, sexual appetite, libido, sensuality, sexuality, lasciviousness, salaciousness, libidinousness; *informal* the hots.

desolate **adjective** ❶ ABANDONED, deserted, barren, uninhabited, unoccupied, lonely, isolated, bare, desert, bleak, depopulated, forsaken, unfrequented, remote, cheerless, dismal, godforsaken. ❷ SAD, unhappy, miserable, broken-hearted, wretched, downcast, dejected, downhearted, melancholy, gloomy, depressed, forlorn, disconsolate, despondent, distressed, grieving, bereft.
– OPPOSITES populous, joyful.

despair **noun** HOPELESSNESS, depression, dejection, despondency, pessimism, melancholy, gloom, misery, wretchedness, distress, anguish.
▶ **verb** LOSE HOPE, give up hope, give up, lose heart, be discouraged, resign oneself.

desperate **adjective** ❶ **a desperate act:** RECKLESS, rash, foolhardy, risky, hazardous, daring, wild, imprudent, incautious, injudicious, ill-conceived, precipitate. ❷ **in desperate need:** URGENT, pressing, acute, critical, crucial, drastic, serious, grave, dire, extreme, great. ❸ **a desperate state:** BAD, appalling, grave, intolerable, deplorable, lamentable.

despise **verb** DISDAIN, scorn, hate, detest, loathe, be contemptuous of, abhor, abominate, look down on, deride, spurn, shun, scoff at, jeer at, mock, revile, execrate, undervalue.
– OPPOSITES admire.

despondent **adjective** DOWNCAST, miserable, sad, sorrowful, disheartened, discouraged, disconsolate, low-spirited, dispirited, downhearted, in despair, despairing, melancholy, gloomy, glum, morose, woebegone.
– OPPOSITES cheerful, happy.

despotic **adjective** AUTOCRATIC, dictatorial, tyrannical, authoritarian, absolute, oppressive, totalitarian, domineering, imperious, arrogant, high-handed, arbitrary.

destination **noun** JOURNEY'S END, stop, terminus, port of call, goal.

destined **adjective** ❶ BOUND FOR, en route for, heading for/towards, directed towards, scheduled for. ❷ **destined to die young:** FATED, ordained, preordained, predestined, predetermined, doomed, certain, sure, bound; *informal* written in the cards.

destiny **noun** ❶ FATE, lot, portion, due, future, doom. ❷ FATE, fortune, predestination, luck, chance, karma, kismet.

destitute **adjective** PENNILESS, impoverished, poverty-stricken, poor, impecunious, penurious, indigent, insolvent, deprived, down-and-out, beggarly; *informal* on one's uppers; *Brit. informal* skint.
– OPPOSITES rich, wealthy.

destroy **verb** ❶ DEMOLISH, wreck, smash, annihilate, knock down, pull down, tear down, level, raze, shatter, dismantle, blow up, wipe out, bomb, torpedo, ruin, spoil, devastate, lay waste to, ravage, wreak havoc on, extinguish,

vaporize, extirpate. ❷ KILL, slaughter, put to sleep, exterminate, wipe out, massacre, liquidate, decimate.
– OPPOSITES build, construct.

destruction noun ❶ DEMOLITION, annihilation, devastation, levelling, razing, blowing up, wiping out, tearing down, ruination, desolation, ruin, havoc, termination, extinction. ❷ KILLING, slaughter, massacre; *poetic/literary* slaying.

destructive adjective ❶ RUINOUS, devastating, disastrous, catastrophic, calamitous, cataclysmic, fatal, deadly, dangerous, lethal, damaging, noxious, pernicious, injurious, harmful, detrimental, deleterious. ❷ **destructive comments**: NEGATIVE, adverse, unfavourable, contrary, antagonistic, hostile, unfriendly, derogatory, disparaging, disapproving, undermining.
– OPPOSITES constructive.

desultory adjective HALF-HEARTED, rambling, aimless, irregular, fitful, haphazard, erratic, inconsistent.
– OPPOSITES keen.

detach verb DISCONNECT, unfasten, remove, undo, take off, release, unhitch, separate, uncouple, loosen, free, sever, tear off, disengage, part.
– OPPOSITES attach.

detached adjective DISPASSIONATE, impersonal, indifferent, aloof, unconcerned, reserved, remote, cool.
– OPPOSITES passionate, involved.

detail noun ❶ ITEM, point, particular, factor, nicety, fact, element, aspect, circumstance, intricacy, feature, respect, attribute, component, part, unit. ❷ **a detail of soldiers**: UNIT, detachment, task force, patrol.

detailed adjective FULL, comprehensive, exhaustive, thorough, all-inclusive, itemized, precise, exact, specific, meticulous, particularized.
– OPPOSITES general.

detain verb ❶ DELAY, hold up/back, keep, slow down/up, hinder, impede, check, retard, inhibit, stay. ❷ PUT/KEEP IN CUSTODY, imprison, confine, lock up, jail, incarcerate, intern, restrain, hold, arrest, impound; *informal* collar; *Brit. informal* nick.

detect verb ❶ **detected the theft**: FIND OUT, discover, turn up, uncover, bring to light, expose, unearth, reveal, unmask, unveil; *informal* track down, ferret out. ❷ **detect hostility**: NOTICE, note, perceive, discern, make out, observe, spot, become aware of, recognize, distinguish, identify, catch, sense, see, smell.

detective noun INVESTIGATOR, police officer; *informal* private eye, sleuth, tec, dick; *N. Amer. informal* gumshoe.

detention noun CUSTODY, confinement, imprisonment, incarceration, internment, detainment, arrest, quarantine.

deter verb PREVENT, put off, stop, discourage, talk out of, dissuade, check, restrain, caution, frighten, intimidate, daunt, scare off, warn against, prohibit, hinder, impede, obstruct.
– OPPOSITES encourage.

deteriorate verb ❶ GET WORSE, worsen, decline, degenerate, go

downhill, sink, slip, lapse, fall, drop; *informal* go to the dogs, go to pot. ❷ DISINTEGRATE, crumble, fall apart, fall to pieces, break up, decay, decompose.
– OPPOSITES improve.

determination noun FIRMNESS, persistence, resoluteness, tenacity, perseverance, steadfastness, single-mindedness, resolve, drive, fortitude, dedication, backbone, stamina, mettle, conviction, doggedness, stubbornness, intransigence, obduracy, push, thrust, pertinacity; *informal* grit, guts.

determine verb ❶ DECIDE, agree on, fix, settle, establish, judge, arbitrate, decree, ordain. ❷ FIND OUT, discover, learn, establish, calculate, work out, check, ascertain, verify. ❸ AFFECT, influence, act/work on, regulate, decide, condition, direct, control, rule, dictate, govern, form, shape.

determined adjective FIRM, resolute, purposeful, single-minded, steadfast, tenacious, strong-willed, dedicated, persistent, persevering, dogged, unflinching, tough, assertive, mettlesome, plucky, unwavering, stubborn, obdurate, intransigent, indomitable, inflexible.
– OPPOSITES irresolute, hesitant.

deterrent noun DISINCENTIVE, inhibition, restraint, discouragement, curb, check, impediment, hindrance, obstacle, block, obstruction, barrier, warning, threat.
– OPPOSITES incentive.

detest verb LOATHE, hate, abhor, despise, abominate, execrate. *See also* HATE verb (1).
– OPPOSITES love.

detestable adjective LOATHSOME, abhorrent, hateful, odious, despicable, contemptible, disgusting, repugnant, distasteful, abominable.

detract verb TAKE AWAY FROM, diminish, reduce, lessen, lower, devalue.

detrimental adjective HARMFUL, damaging, injurious, hurtful, destructive, pernicious, deleterious, inimical, prejudicial, unfavourable.
– OPPOSITES benign.

devastate verb ❶ DESTROY, ruin, lay waste to, demolish, wreck, flatten, obliterate, level, raze, annihilate, ravage, despoil, sack. ❷ *See* DISMAY verb (1).

develop verb ❶ GROW, evolve, mature, improve, expand, spread, enlarge, advance, progress, flourish, prosper, make headway. ❷ develop a theme: ELABORATE, unfold, work out, enlarge on, expand, broaden, add to, augment, amplify, dilate on, magnify, supplement, reinforce. ❸ develop a cough: ACQUIRE, begin to have, contract, pick up, get. ❹ a row developed: BEGIN, start, come about, follow, happen, result, ensue, break out. ❺ develop into adults: GROW, mature, turn.

development noun ❶ GROWTH, evolution, advance, improvement, expansion, spread, progress, maturing, furtherance, extension, headway. ❷ new developments: EVENT, turn of events, occurrence, happening, incident, circumstance, situation, issue, outcome, upshot. ❸ a housing development: ESTATE, complex, building, structure, conglomeration.

deviate verb DIVERGE, branch off, turn aside, depart from, make a detour, digress, deflect, differ, vary, change, veer, swerve, wander, bend, drift, stray, tack, slew.

device noun ❶ APPLIANCE, gadget, implement, tool, utensil, piece of equipment, apparatus, instrument, machine, contraption, contrivance, invention; *informal* gizmo. ❷ SCHEME, ploy, plan, plot, stratagem, trick, deception, artifice, ruse, dodge, stunt, gambit, subterfuge, manoeuvre, expedient, fraud, imposture. ❸ EMBLEM, symbol, insignia, crest, coat of arms, seal, badge, token, motif, design, figure, motto, slogan, legend.

devil noun ❶ DEMON, fiend, evil spirit, imp. ❷ **the Devil**: SATAN, Lucifer, the Prince of Darkness, the Evil One; *informal* Old Nick.

devilish adjective DEMONIC, diabolical, fiendish, satanic, infernal, hellish, demoniacal.

devious adjective ❶ CUNNING, underhand, sly, crafty, wily, artful, scheming, designing, calculating, deceitful, dishonest, double-dealing, guileful, treacherous, furtive, secretive; *informal* slippery, crooked. ❷ INDIRECT, roundabout, circuitous, rambling, winding, tortuous, wandering, erratic, digressive.
– OPPOSITES honest, direct.

devise verb CREATE, invent, originate, concoct, work out, contrive, plan, form, formulate, plot, scheme, compose, frame, construct, think up, imagine, fabricate, hatch, put together, prepare.

devoted adjective COMMITTED, faithful, loyal, true, dedicated, staunch, devout, steadfast, constant, unswerving, zealous.

devotee noun FAN, enthusiast, admirer, follower, adherent, disciple, supporter, champion, advocate, fanatic, zealot; *informal* buff, freak.

devotion noun FAITHFULNESS, loyalty, steadfastness, commitment, staunchness, allegiance, dedication, devoutness, fervour, zeal.
– OPPOSITES disloyalty, indifference.

devour verb EAT GREEDILY, consume, swallow, gorge oneself on, guzzle down, feast on; *informal* tuck into, pig out on.

devout adjective PIOUS, religious, godly, churchgoing, reverent, holy, righteous, orthodox, saintly.
– OPPOSITES impious.

dexterity noun DEFTNESS, adroitness, nimbleness, agility, skilfulness, adeptness, expertise, talent, craft, mastery, finesse.

diabolical adjective ❶ *See* DEVILISH. ❷ VERY BAD, horrible, dreadful, appalling, shocking, outrageous, atrocious.

diagnose verb IDENTIFY, detect, find, determine, recognize, distinguish, isolate, pinpoint.

diagonal adjective CROSSWAYS, crosswise, slanting, slanted, sloping, oblique, angled, cornerways, cornerwise.

diagram noun PLAN, picture, representation, blueprint, sketch, illustration, outline, draft, table, chart, figure.

dialect noun REGIONAL LANGUAGE, vernacular, patois, regionalism, localism, provincialism; *informal* lingo.

dialectic noun DEBATE, argument, discussion, dialogue, reasoning, polemic; *informal* war of words.

dialogue noun CONVERSATION, talk, chat, communication, debate, argument, exchange of views, discussion, conference, discourse, parley, colloquy, interlocution, palaver; *informal* powwow, chinwag, rap session.

diary noun JOURNAL, chronicle, account, record, log, history, annals, calendar.

dictate verb ❶ **dictate a letter:** READ ALOUD, read out, speak, say, utter, recite. ❷ ORDER, command, decree, ordain, direct, enjoin, give orders, order about, impose one's will, domineer, lay down the law; *informal* boss about, throw one's weight about.

dictator noun ABSOLUTE RULER, despot, autocrat, tyrant, oppressor.

dictatorial adjective TYRANNICAL, oppressive, despotic, overbearing, domineering, repressive, imperious, high-handed, authoritarian, totalitarian, peremptory, dogmatic, arbitrary, fascistic; *informal* bossy.

diction noun ENUNCIATION, articulation, elocution, pronunciation, intonation, inflection, delivery.

dictum noun UTTERANCE, pronouncement, direction, injunction, statement, dictate, command, order, decree, edict.

die verb ❶ EXPIRE, perish, pass on/away, lose one's life, meet one's end, lay down one's life, breathe one's last, be no more, go to one's last resting place; *informal* give up the ghost, kick the bucket, bite the dust, be pushing up daisies, croak, turn up one's toes, cash in one's chips, pop off; *Brit. informal* snuff it, pop one's clogs. ❷ **hope died:** COME TO AN END, end, pass, disappear, vanish, fade, decline, ebb, dwindle, melt away, wane, wither, subside. ❸ **the engine died:** FAIL, break down, halt, stop, lose power.
– OPPOSITES live.

diehard adjective INTRANSIGENT, inflexible, uncompromising, indomitable, unyielding, rigid, immovable, adamant, dyed-in-the-wool, conservative, reactionary.

differ verb ❶ BE DIFFERENT, vary, contrast, diverge, be dissimilar, be distinguishable. ❷ DISAGREE, be in dispute, dissent, be at variance, oppose, take issue, contradict, dispute, conflict, clash, quarrel, argue, wrangle, squabble, quibble, altercate.
– OPPOSITES agree.

difference noun ❶ DISSIMILARITY, contrast, distinction, variance, variation, divergence, deviation, contradiction, disparity, imbalance, incongruity, dissimilitude, differentiation, antithesis, nonconformity, contrariety. ❷ DIFFERENCE OF OPINION, dispute, disagreement, argument, debate, misunderstanding, quarrel, altercation, wrangle, clash, contretemps, feud, vendetta; *informal* row, tiff, set-to. ❸ **pay the difference:** BALANCE, remainder, rest, residue, excess.
– OPPOSITES similarity.

different adjective ❶ DISSIMILAR, contrasting, diverse, disparate,

divergent, incompatible, opposed, inconsistent, at variance, at odds, clashing, conflicting, discrepant, unlike. ❷ **appearing different:** CHANGED, altered, modified, transformed, metamorphosed. ❸ **different people:** VARIOUS, several, many, numerous, sundry, assorted, diverse. ❹ **looking for something different:** UNUSUAL, uncommon, out of the ordinary, distinctive, rare, unique, novel, special, remarkable, singular, noteworthy, unconventional, atypical, strange, odd, bizarre.
– OPPOSITES similar, ordinary.

difficult adjective ❶ HARD, demanding, laborious, onerous, burdensome, tough, strenuous, arduous, exhausting, exacting, tiring, wearisome, back-breaking, painful, oppressive; *informal* no picnic. ❷ **a difficult problem:** COMPLEX, complicated, hard, problematic, intricate, involved, puzzling, baffling, perplexing, knotty, thorny, delicate, obscure, abstruse, enigmatic, abstract, recondite, profound, deep. ❸ **a difficult child:** TROUBLESOME, demanding, tiresome, unmanageable, intractable, perverse, recalcitrant, obstreperous, refractory, fractious, uncooperative, unamenable. ❹ **a difficult time:** INCONVENIENT, ill-timed, unfavourable.
– OPPOSITES easy, simple.

difficulty noun ❶ **encounter a difficulty:** PROBLEM, complication, snag, hitch, obstacle, hindrance, hurdle, pitfall, impediment, obstruction, barrier. ❷ **raise difficulties:** PROTEST, objection, complaint, gripe, demur, cavil. ❸ **financial difficulties:** PREDICAMENT, quandary, dilemma, plight, distress, embarrassment, trouble, straits; *informal* fix, jam, spot, scrape. ❹ **in difficulty:** HARDSHIP, trial, tribulation, ordeal, exigency.

diffident adjective SHY, modest, bashful, sheepish, unconfident, timid, unassertive, fearful, timorous, shrinking, apprehensive, reserved, withdrawn, hesitant, tentative, reluctant, doubtful, unsure, insecure, unobtrusive, self-effacing, unassuming, humble, meek, distrustful, suspicious.
– OPPOSITES bold, assertive.

diffuse adjective ❶ SPREAD OUT, scattered, dispersed, diffused. ❷ WORDY, verbose, long-winded, prolix, discursive, rambling, wandering, meandering, digressive, circumlocutory; *informal* waffly.
– OPPOSITES concentrated, concise.

dig verb ❶ CULTIVATE, turn over, work, spade, till, harrow, fork over. ❷ EXCAVATE, dig out, burrow, mine, quarry, hollow out, scoop out, tunnel, gouge. ❸ **dig him in the ribs:** POKE, nudge, prod, jab, thrust, punch.
■ **dig up** EXHUME, unearth, disinter.

digest verb ❶ ABSORB, assimilate, break down, dissolve, process, macerate. ❷ ABSORB, take in, understand, comprehend, grasp, master, consider, think about, mull over, weigh up.
▶ **noun** SUMMARY, abstract, precis, outline, review, compendium, abridgement, epitome.

dignified adjective FORMAL, grave, solemn, stately, noble, decorous,

reserved, ceremonious, courtly, majestic, august, lofty, exalted, regal, lordly, imposing, grand, impressive.
– OPPOSITES undignified.

dignitary noun LUMINARY, worthy, notable, VIP, big name, leading light, celebrity, star, lion, pillar of society; *informal* somebody, bigwig, big shot, big noise, celeb, top brass, lord/lady muck; *N. Amer. informal* big wheel.

dignity noun STATELINESS, nobleness, nobility, formality, solemnity, gravity, gravitas, decorum, propriety, respectability, reserve, courtliness, ceremoniousness, majesty, augustness, loftiness, exaltedness, regality, grandeur, lordliness, impressiveness.

digress verb STRAY FROM THE POINT, get off the subject, go off at a tangent, ramble, wander, deviate, turn aside, depart, drift, meander, maunder; *informal* lose the thread.

dilapidated adjective RUN-DOWN, ramshackle, broken-down, in ruins, ruined, tumbledown, falling to pieces, falling apart, in disrepair, shabby, battered, rickety, shaky, crumbling, decayed, decrepit, worn out, neglected, uncared for.

dilate verb ENLARGE, widen, expand.
– OPPOSITES contract.

dilemma noun DIFFICULTY, problem, quandary, predicament, puzzle, plight, trouble, perplexity, confusion, embarrassment; *informal* catch-22, tight spot, devil and the deep blue sea.

diligent adjective ASSIDUOUS, industrious, conscientious, hard-working, painstaking, meticulous, thorough, careful, attentive, heedful, earnest, studious, persevering, persistent, tenacious, zealous, active, busy, untiring, tireless, indefatigable, dogged, plodding, laborious.
– OPPOSITES lazy.

dilute verb WATER DOWN, weaken, thin out, cut, adulterate, mix.
– OPPOSITES concentrate.

dim adjective ❶ a dim light: DULL, muted, faint, weak, feeble, pale, dingy, lustreless. ❷ dim corridors: DARK, gloomy, badly lit, poorly lit, dingy, dismal. ❸ a dim shape: VAGUE, ill-defined, indistinct, unclear, shadowy, blurred, blurry, fuzzy, imperceptible, obscured, nebulous, bleary, obfuscated. ❹ a dim recollection: VAGUE, indistinct, hazy, confused, blurred, imperfect, obscure, remote. ❺ *See* STUPID (1).
– OPPOSITES bright, clear.
▶ verb ❶ dim the lights: DIP, turn down, lower. ❷ the light/sky dimmed: GROW DARKER, darken, cloud over.
– OPPOSITES brighten.

dimension noun ❶ SIZE, extent, length, width, area, volume, capacity, proportions. ❷ add another dimension: ASPECT, facet, side, feature, element.

diminish verb ❶ LESSEN, grow less, decrease, reduce, shrink, contract, abate, grow weaker, lower, curtail, cut, narrow, constrict, truncate. ❷ SUBSIDE, wane, recede, dwindle, slacken, fade, decline, peter out.
❸ diminish his reputation: DISPARAGE, denigrate, belittle, deprecate, devalue, detract from, cheapen, defame, vilify.
– OPPOSITES increase, boost.

diminutive adjective SMALL, tiny,

little, petite, minute, miniature, microscopic, undersized, dwarfish.
– OPPOSITES enormous.

din noun NOISE, uproar, row, racket, commotion, hullabaloo, tumult, hubbub, clamour, outcry, shouting, yelling, pandemonium, bedlam, rumpus, brouhaha, babel.

dingy adjective DARK, dull, dim, gloomy, drab, dismal, dreary, cheerless, dusky, sombre, murky, smoggy, dirty, sooty, grimy, discoloured, faded, shabby, worn, seedy, run-down, tacky.
– OPPOSITES bright.

dinky adjective SMALL, petite, dainty, neat, trim, cute, diminutive, miniature.

dip verb ❶ GO DOWN, descend, sink, subside, fall, drop, decline, sag, droop. ❷ dip it in water: IMMERSE, plunge, submerge, duck, dunk, lower, sink, soak, drench, steep, bathe.
– OPPOSITES rise.
▶ noun ❶ take a dip: SWIM, bathe, plunge, dive, paddle. ❷ a dip in the ground: HOLLOW, hole, basin, concavity, depression, declivity, slope, incline, slant.

diplomacy noun TACTFULNESS, tact, discretion, subtlety, sensitivity, delicacy, politeness, finesse, prudence, judiciousness, cleverness, artfulness, cunning, care, skill.

diplomatic adjective TACTFUL, subtle, discreet, careful, delicate, sensitive, thoughtful, considerate, prudent, judicious, polite, politic, clever, skilful, artful.
– OPPOSITES tactless.

dire adjective TERRIBLE, dreadful, awful, appalling, frightful, horrible, atrocious, grim, cruel, disastrous, ruinous, wretched, miserable, woeful, calamitous, catastrophic.

direct adjective ❶ a direct road: STRAIGHT, uncircuitous, unswerving, undeviating. ❷ a direct journey/train: NON-STOP, straight through, through, uninterrupted, unbroken. ❸ a direct approach: PERSONAL, face-to-face, immediate, head-on, interventionist. ❹ a direct manner/statement: FRANK, blunt, straightforward, straight to the point, straight, clear, plain, explicit, candid, open, honest, sincere, outspoken, unambiguous, unequivocal, outspoken, plain-spoken, forthright, matter-of-fact. ❺ the direct opposite: EXACT, absolute, complete, diametrical, downright.
– OPPOSITES indirect.
▶ verb ❶ direct them to the station: SHOW THE WAY, give directions, guide, steer, lead, conduct, usher, navigate, pilot. ❷ direct the operation: BE IN CHARGE OF, lead, run, command, control, supervise, oversee, superintend, regulate, govern, conduct, handle, preside over, mastermind, orchestrate; *informal* call the shots. ❸ remarks directed at her: AIM AT, address to, intend/mean for, destine for, point at, train on, fix on. ❹ direct him to go: COMMAND, order, instruct, charge, bid, enjoin; *formal* adjure.

directive noun COMMAND, direction, order, instruction, charge, bidding, injunction, ruling, regulation, dictate, decree, edict, notice, ordinance, prescription, mandate, fiat.

director noun MANAGER, administrator, executive, head, chief, chairperson, leader, governor, president, superintendent, supervisor, overseer; *informal* boss; *Brit. informal* gaffer.

dirge noun LAMENT, elegy, requiem, keen, funeral song, threnody.

dirt noun ❶ GRIME, dust, soot, muck, mud, filth, sludge, slime, ooze, waste, dross, pollution, smudge, stain, tarnish; *informal* crud; *Brit. informal* gunge. ❷ EARTH, soil, clay, silt, loam. ❸ *See* OBSCENITY (1).

dirty adjective ❶ UNCLEAN, filthy, stained, grimy, soiled, grubby, messy, dusty, mucky, sooty, muddy, bedraggled, slimy, polluted, sullied, foul, smudged, tarnished, defiled, spotted; *informal* cruddy, yucky; *Brit. informal* grotty, gungy. ❷ **dirty jokes**: OBSCENE, indecent, vulgar, ribald, salacious, smutty, coarse, bawdy, suggestive, prurient, lewd, lascivious, licentious. ❸ **a dirty trick**: UNFAIR, unsporting, dishonourable, dishonest, unscrupulous, illegal, deceitful, double-dealing, treacherous; *informal* crooked. ❹ **a dirty look**: MALEVOLENT, bitter, angry, annoyed, resentful, indignant, offended, smouldering. ❺ **dirty weather**: UNPLEASANT, foul, stormy, squally, rainy, gusty, misty, gloomy, murky, overcast.
– OPPOSITES clean.
▶ verb SOIL, stain, muddy, begrime, blacken, mess up, spatter, smudge, smear, spot, splash, sully, pollute, foul, defile; *poetic/literary* besmirch.
– OPPOSITES clean.

disability noun HANDICAP, infirmity, impairment, affliction, disorder, complaint, ailment, illness, malady, disablement.

disable verb INCAPACITATE, impair, damage, injure, cripple, lame, handicap, debilitate, indispose, weaken, enfeeble, render infirm, immobilize, paralyse, hamstring, maim, prostrate, mutilate.

disadvantage noun ❶ DRAWBACK, snag, weak point, downside, fly in the ointment, weakness, flaw, defect, fault, handicap, liability, trouble, hindrance, obstacle; *informal* minus. ❷ **to their disadvantage**: DETRIMENT, prejudice, harm, damage, loss, injury, hurt.
– OPPOSITES advantage.

disaffected adjective ALIENATED, estranged, unfriendly, disunited, dissatisfied, disgruntled, discontented, disloyal, rebellious, mutinous, seditious, hostile, antagonistic; *informal* up in arms.
– OPPOSITES contented.

disagree verb ❶ DIFFER, fail to agree, be in dispute, dissent, be at variance/odds, quarrel, argue, bicker, wrangle, squabble, dispute, debate, take issue; *informal* have words, fall out. ❷ BE DIFFERENT, be dissimilar, vary, conflict, clash, contrast, diverge.
– OPPOSITES agree.

disagreeable adjective UNPLEASANT, objectionable, disgusting, horrible, nasty, dreadful, hateful, detestable, offensive, repulsive, obnoxious, odious, repellent, revolting, sickening.
– OPPOSITES pleasant.

disallow verb REJECT, say no to, refuse, dismiss, forbid, prohibit, veto, embargo, proscribe, rebuff, repel, repudiate, repulse, ban, bar, cancel, disclaim, disown, abjure, disavow.

disappear verb ❶ VANISH, pass from sight, be lost to view, fade, recede, dematerialize, evaporate. ❷ *See* LEAVE[1] verb (1). ❸ DIE OUT, come to an end, end, pass away, vanish, expire, perish, fade away, leave no trace, pass into oblivion.
– OPPOSITES appear.

disappoint verb LET DOWN, fail, dishearten, depress, dispirit, upset, sadden, dash someone's hopes, dismay, chagrin, disgruntle, disenchant, disillusion, dissatisfy, vex.
– OPPOSITES delight.

disappointed adjective SADDENED, let down, disheartened, downhearted, downcast, depressed, despondent, dispirited, disenchanted, disillusioned.
– OPPOSITES pleased.

disapproval noun DISAPPROBATION, displeasure, criticism, blame, censure, condemnation, dislike, disfavour, discontent, dissatisfaction, reproach, reproof, remonstration, deprecation, animadversion.
– OPPOSITES approval.

disapprove verb FIND UNACCEPTABLE, dislike, deplore, have a poor opinion of, be displeased with, frown on, criticize, look askance at, censure, condemn, denounce, object to, take exception to, reprove, remonstrate, disparage, deprecate; *informal* take a dim view of, look down one's nose at.
– OPPOSITES approve.

disarray noun DISORDER, confusion, untidiness, chaos, mess, muddle, clutter, jumble, mix-up, tangle, shambles, dishevelment; *Scottish* guddle.
– OPPOSITES tidiness.

disaster noun CATASTROPHE, calamity, cataclysm, tragedy, act of God, accident, mishap, misadventure, mischance, stroke of bad luck, heavy blow, shock, adversity, trouble, misfortune, ruin, ruination.
– OPPOSITES success.

disastrous adjective CATASTROPHIC, cataclysmic, calamitous, devastating, tragic, dire, terrible, shocking, appalling, dreadful, harmful, black, ruinous, unfortunate, unlucky, ill-fated, ill-starred, injurious, detrimental, hapless.
– OPPOSITES successful.

disbelieve verb REJECT, discount, give no credence to, be incredulous, question, suspect, challenge, scoff at, mistrust, distrust.
– OPPOSITES believe.

disburse verb PAY OUT, spend, expend, lay out, dish out; *informal* fork out, shell out.

discard verb THROW OUT/AWAY, dispose of, get rid of, jettison, toss out, dispense with, scrap, cast aside, reject, repudiate, abandon, relinquish, forsake, shed; *informal* have done with, dump, ditch.
– OPPOSITES keep.

discern verb SEE, notice, observe, perceive, make out, distinguish, detect, recognize, determine.

discernible adjective VISIBLE, noticeable, observable, perceptible, perceivable, detectable, recognizable, apparent, obvious, clear, manifest, conspicuous, patent.

discerning adjective DISCRIMINATING, astute, shrewd, ingenious, clever, perceptive, penetrating, perspicacious, percipient, judicious, sensitive, knowing.

discharge verb ❶ EMIT, exude, release, give off, eject, send out, leak, dispense, void, gush, excrete, ooze, belch, secrete, spew, spit out. ❷ **discharge from employment:** DISMISS, expel, get rid of, oust, cashier; *informal* fire, sack, axe, send packing, give someone the boot, boot out. ❸ **discharge a weapon:** FIRE, shoot, let off, set off, detonate. ❹ **discharge the prisoner:** SET FREE, free, release, liberate, acquit, clear, absolve, exonerate, pardon, emancipate, exculpate. ❺ **discharge a duty:** CARRY OUT, perform, do, accomplish, achieve, fulfil, execute.

disciple noun APOSTLE, follower, supporter, adherent, devotee, advocate, student, pupil, believer, proponent, partisan, votary.

disciplinarian noun MARTINET, authoritarian, hard taskmaster, tyrant, despot, stickler for order, autocrat, dictator, hardliner; *informal* slave-driver.

discipline noun ❶ CONTROL, self-control, self-restraint, strictness, restraint, orderliness, regulation, direction, restriction, limitation, check, curb. ❷ PUNISHMENT, correction, chastisement, penalty, reprimand, rebuke, reproof. ❸ FIELD OF STUDY, subject, area, course, speciality, specialty.
▶ verb ❶ CONTROL, restrain, regulate, restrict, govern, limit, check, curb. ❷ PUNISH, chastise, correct, penalize, reprimand, rebuke, reprove; *formal* castigate.

disclaim verb DENY, renounce, repudiate, reject, refuse, decline, disown, abandon, abjure; *informal* wash one's hands of.

disclose verb REVEAL, divulge, tell, impart, communicate, broadcast, unveil, leak, let slip, blurt out.

discolour verb STAIN, soil, mark, streak, spot, tarnish, tinge, fade, bleach.

discomfort noun ❶ PAIN, ache, soreness, irritation, pang, throb, smart. ❷ HARDSHIP, unpleasantness, trouble, distress.

disconcert verb UNSETTLE, shake, disturb, take aback, perturb, ruffle, upset, agitate, worry, discomfit, discompose, confound, throw off balance, distract, confuse, nonplus; *informal* throw, put someone off their stroke, faze, rattle.

disconnect verb UNDO, detach, disengage, uncouple, unfasten, unhook, unhitch, unplug, cut off, break off, sever, part, turn off, switch off.
– OPPOSITES connect.

disconnected adjective DISJOINTED, confused, garbled, jumbled, mixed up, incoherent, unintelligible, rambling, disordered, wandering.

discontented adjective DISSATISFIED, displeased, disgruntled, unhappy, miserable, disaffected; *informal* fed up, browned off, hacked off; *Brit. informal* cheesed off.

discord noun ❶ DISAGREEMENT, dispute, argument, conflict, friction, strife, opposition,

hostility, disharmony, incompatibility, disunity. *See also* QUARREL noun. ❷ DISHARMONY, dissonance, cacophony.
– OPPOSITES harmony.

discordant adjective
❶ CONFLICTING, differing, contrary, opposed, opposing, opposite, contradictory, contentious, hostile, divergent, incompatible, incongruous. ❷ DISSONANT, atonal, tuneless, cacophonous, inharmonious, jangling, grating, jarring, harsh, strident, shrill.
– OPPOSITES harmonious.

discount noun REDUCTION, price cut, rebate, concession; *informal* mark-down.
▶ verb DISREGARD, ignore, dismiss, overlook, pass over, pay no attention to, take no notice of, gloss over, brush off.

discourage verb ❶ **discouraged by failure**: DISHEARTEN, dispirit, depress, demoralize, deject, disappoint, disenchant, dismay, cast down, frighten, put off, scare, daunt, intimidate, cow, unnerve, unman; *informal* pour cold water on. ❷ **discourage him from going**: DISSUADE, put off, deter, talk out of, advise against, urge against, caution against, restrain, inhibit, divert from. ❸ **discourage the idea**: OPPOSE, disapprove of, repress, deprecate; *informal* put a damper on.
– OPPOSITES encourage.

discouragement noun
❶ OPPOSITION, disapproval, repression, deprecation.
❷ DETERRENT, disincentive, impediment, hindrance, obstacle, barrier, curb, damper, check, restraint, constraint.
– OPPOSITES encouragement.

discourse noun ❶ ADDRESS, speech, lecture, oration, sermon, homily, essay, treatise, dissertation, paper, study, disquisition. ❷ *See* CONVERSATION.
▶ verb *see* SPEAK (1), TALK verb (1).

discover verb ❶ FIND, come across/upon, locate, stumble upon, chance upon, light upon, bring to light, unearth, uncover, turn up; *informal* dig up. ❷ FIND OUT, come to know, learn, realize, detect, ascertain, determine, recognize, see, spot, notice, perceive; *informal* get wise to; *Brit. informal* twig. ❸ INVENT, devise, originate, pioneer, conceive of, contrive.

discoverer noun ❶ INVENTOR, originator, pioneer, deviser, designer, initiator. ❷ FOUNDER, explorer, pioneer.

discovery noun ❶ DETECTION, recognition, disclosure, finding, determination, revelation.
❷ INNOVATION, invention, breakthrough, finding, find.

discredit verb ❶ ATTACK, denigrate, disparage, defame, slur, slander, libel, detract from, cast aspersions on, vilify, bring into disrepute, deprecate, decry, dishonour, devalue, degrade, belittle, disgrace, censure. ❷ DISPROVE, invalidate, refute, dispute, challenge, reject, deny.

discreet adjective CAREFUL, circumspect, cautious, wary, guarded, sensitive, prudent, judicious, chary, tactful, reserved, diplomatic, muted, understated, delicate, considerate, politic, wise, sensible, sagacious.
– OPPOSITES indiscreet, tactless.

discrepancy noun INCONSISTENCY, disparity, deviation, variance, variation, divergence, incongruity, difference, disagreement, dissimilarity, conflict, discordance, gap, lacuna.
– OPPOSITES similarity.

discretionary adjective OPTIONAL, voluntary, open, open to choice, elective, non-mandatory, unrestricted, volitional.
– OPPOSITES compulsory.

discriminate verb ❶ DISTINGUISH, differentiate, tell the difference, tell apart, separate, discern. ❷ BE BIASED AGAINST, show prejudice against/towards, treat differently, favour.

discriminating adjective *see* PERCEPTIVE.

discrimination noun ❶ DISCERNMENT, good taste, taste, perception, penetration, perspicacity, shrewdness, astuteness, acumen, judgement, refinement, sensitivity, insight, subtlety, cultivation, artistry. ❷ PREJUDICE, bias, intolerance, bigotry, narrow-mindedness, favouritism, chauvinism, racism, sexism, unfairness.

discuss verb TALK OVER, talk/chat about, debate, argue about/over, exchange views about, converse about, deliberate, consider, go into, examine, review, analyse, weigh up, consult about, ventilate; *informal* kick about, thrash out.

discussion noun CONVERSATION, talk, dialogue, chat, argument, dispute, conference, debate, discourse, exchange of views, seminar, consultation, symposium, deliberation, review, analysis; *informal* confab. *See also* TALK noun (1).

disdainful adjective SCORNFUL, contemptuous, derisive, sneering, disparaging, arrogant, proud, supercilious, haughty, superior, lordly, pompous, snobbish, aloof, indifferent.
– OPPOSITES respectful.

disease noun *see* ILLNESS.

diseased adjective UNHEALTHY, unwell, sick, sickly, infected, abnormal, blighted, unsound, cankerous. *See also* ILL adjective (1).

disembark verb LAND, arrive, get off, step off, alight, go ashore, deplane, detrain.
– OPPOSITES embark.

disfigure verb MUTILATE, deface, deform, blemish, scar, spoil, mar, damage, injure, maim, vandalize, ruin, make ugly, uglify.

disgrace noun ❶ SHAME, humiliation, dishonour, scandal, ignominy, degradation, discredit, infamy, debasement. ❷ such behaviour is a disgrace: SCANDAL, black mark, stain, blemish, stigma, blot, smear.
– OPPOSITES honour.

disgraceful adjective SCANDALOUS, outrageous, shocking, shameful, dishonourable, disreputable, contemptible, despicable, ignominious, reprehensible, improper, unseemly.
– OPPOSITES admirable.

disgruntled adjective DISSATISFIED, displeased, unhappy, discontented, annoyed, exasperated, irritated, vexed, grumpy, testy, petulant; *informal* fed up; *Brit. informal* cheesed off.

disguise noun CAMOUFLAGE, costume, pretence, mask, cover, cloak; *informal* get-up, smokescreen.

▶ **verb** ❶ DRESS UP, camouflage, cover up, conceal, hide, mask, veil, cloak, shroud. ❷ **disguise the truth:** COVER UP, falsify, misrepresent, fake, feign, dissemble, dissimulate, varnish.

disgust **noun** REVULSION, repugnance, repulsion, aversion, abhorrence, loathing, detestation, distaste, nausea.
▶ **verb** SICKEN, nauseate, revolt, repel, put off, offend, outrage, shock, appal, scandalize, displease, dissatisfy, annoy, anger; *informal* turn someone's stomach.

dish **noun** ❶ PLATE, platter, bowl, basin, container, receptacle, salver. ❷ FOOD, recipe, fare, concoction, item on the menu.
■ **dish out** *see* DISTRIBUTE (1). **dish up** SERVE, serve up, spoon, ladle, scoop.

dishearten **verb** DISCOURAGE, dispirit, depress, crush, sadden, disappoint, deter, weigh down; *informal* put a damper on.
– OPPOSITES encourage.

dishevelled **adjective** UNTIDY, rumpled, messy, scruffy, bedraggled, disordered, disarranged, tousled, unkempt, slovenly, uncombed, slatternly, blowsy, frowzy.
– OPPOSITES tidy, neat.

dishonest **adjective** UNTRUTHFUL, deceitful, lying, underhand, cheating, fraudulent, false, misleading, dishonourable, unscrupulous, unprincipled, corrupt, deceptive, crafty, cunning, designing, mendacious, double-dealing, two-faced, treacherous, perfidious, unfair, unjust, unethical, disreputable, rascally, knavish, roguish; *informal* crooked, shady, bent, slippery.
– OPPOSITES honest.

dishonour **noun** DISGRACE, shame, humiliation, discredit, blot, blemish, stigma, scandal, infamy, ignominy, disrepute, disfavour, abasement, odium, opprobrium, obloquy.
▶ **verb** DISGRACE, bring shame to, shame, discredit, degrade, humiliate, sully, stain, stigmatize, insult, abuse, affront, slight, offend.

dishonourable **adjective** ❶ **a dishonourable man:** UNPRINCIPLED, unscrupulous, untrustworthy, corrupt, treacherous, perfidious, traitorous, disreputable, discreditable; *informal* shady; *archaic* blackguardly. ❷ **a dishonourable act:** DISGRACEFUL, shameful, ignoble, shameless, ignominious, contemptible, blameworthy, despicable, reprehensible, base.
– OPPOSITES honourable.

disillusion **verb** DISABUSE, disenchant, shatter someone's illusions, open someone's eyes, set straight, enlighten, disappoint; *informal* make sadder and wiser.

disinclined **adjective** RELUCTANT, unenthusiastic, unwilling, hesitant, loath, averse, resistant, antipathetic, opposed, recalcitrant, not in the mood.

disinfect **verb** STERILIZE, sanitize, clean, cleanse, purify, fumigate, decontaminate.

disingenuous **adjective** INSINCERE, deceitful, feigned, underhand, duplicitous, two-faced, false, untruthful, artful, cunning, wily, scheming, calculating.

disintegrate **verb** FALL APART, fall to pieces, break up, break apart, shatter, crumble, come apart, crack up, smash, splinter, decompose, decay, rot, dissolve, degenerate, erode, moulder.

disinterested adjective UNBIASED, unprejudiced, impartial, detached, objective, dispassionate, impersonal, open-minded, neutral, fair, just, even-handed.
– OPPOSITES biased, partial.

disjointed adjective INCOHERENT, rambling, unconnected, disconnected, wandering, disorganized, confused, muddled, jumbled, disordered, aimless, directionless, uncoordinated, fitful, spasmodic, dislocated, discontinuous.
– OPPOSITES coherent.

dislike verb HAVE NO LIKING FOR, have an aversion to, regard with distaste, feel hostility towards, be unable to stomach, have no taste for, object to, hate, detest, loathe, abominate, abhor, despise, scorn, execrate, shun, have a grudge against.
– OPPOSITES like.
▶ noun AVERSION, distaste, disapproval, animosity, hostility, antipathy, hate, antagonism, detestation, loathing, disgust, repugnance, enmity, abhorrence, animus.

dislocate verb DISPLACE, put out, disjoint, disengage, disconnect, put out of joint; *Medicine* luxate.

disloyal adjective UNFAITHFUL, faithless, false, untrue, inconstant, untrustworthy, treacherous, traitorous, perfidious, disaffected, seditious, subversive, unpatriotic, renegade, apostate, dissident, double-dealing, two-faced, deceitful.
– OPPOSITES loyal.

disloyalty noun UNFAITHFULNESS, faithlessness, infidelity, breaking of faith, breach of trust, falseness, falsity, inconstancy, untrustworthiness, treachery, treason, perfidiousness, disaffection, sedition, subversion, apostasy, dissidence, double-dealing.
– OPPOSITES loyalty.

dismal adjective GLOOMY, sad, bleak, miserable, wretched, drab, dreary, dingy, cheerless, desolate, depressing, grim, funereal, uninviting.
– OPPOSITES cheerful, bright.

dismantle verb TAKE APART, take to pieces, disassemble, pull apart, strip down, tear down, demolish.
– OPPOSITES assemble.

dismay noun DISAPPOINTMENT, distress, consternation, discouragement, anxiety, apprehension, gloom, horror, agitation.
– OPPOSITES pleasure, relief.
▶ verb ❶ DISCOURAGE, dishearten, dispirit, put off, depress, disappoint, daunt, abash, cast down, devastate. ❷ SHOCK, horrify, take aback, startle, alarm, frighten, scare, surprise, disturb, perturb, upset, unsettle, unnerve.
– OPPOSITES encourage.

dismiss verb ❶ **dismiss the thought:** BANISH, put away, lay/set aside, reject, drop, put out of one's mind, brush aside, think no more of, spurn, repudiate; *informal* pooh-pooh. ❷ **dismissed from the firm:** EXPEL, discharge, give notice to, lay off, make redundant, remove, oust, cashier; *informal* sack, fire, boot out, give the boot/push to, give someone their marching orders, send packing. ❸ **dismiss the men:** DISPERSE, send away, disband, let go, release, free, discharge.

disobedient adjective INSUBORDINATE, rebellious, defiant, unruly, wayward, undisciplined, mutinous, recalcitrant, intractable, wilful, refractory, fractious, obdurate, stubborn, obstreperous, disorderly, delinquent, uncontrollable, disruptive, wild, non-compliant, perverse, naughty, mischievous, contrary; *formal* contumacious.
– OPPOSITES obedient.

disobey verb DEFY, not comply with, disregard, ignore, oppose, contravene, flout, infringe, resist, overstep, rebel against, transgress, violate; *informal* fly in the face of.

disobliging adjective UNHELPFUL, uncooperative, unaccommodating, unfriendly, unsympathetic, discourteous, uncivil.
– OPPOSITES helpful.

disorder noun ❶ MESS, untidiness, chaos, muddle, clutter, jumble, confusion, disorderliness, disarray, disorganization, shambles. ❷ **disorder on the streets:** DISTURBANCE, disruption, riot, tumult, fracas, rumpus, unrest. ❸ DISEASE, complaint, affliction, illness, sickness, malady.
– OPPOSITES tidiness, peace.

disorderly adjective ❶ *See* UNTIDY. ❷ *See* UNDISCIPLINED (1).

disorganized adjective CONFUSED, disorderly, untidy, chaotic, jumbled, muddled, in disarray, unsystematic, haphazard, random, unorganized, scatterbrained, unmethodical, careless, sloppy, slipshod, slapdash, messy, hit-or-miss, aimless, unplanned, unstructured; *Brit. informal* shambolic.
– OPPOSITES organized, systematic.

disown verb RENOUNCE, repudiate, reject, abandon, forsake, disclaim, disavow, deny, disallow, abnegate, disinherit; *informal* turn one's back on.

disparage verb BELITTLE, slight, deprecate, denigrate, depreciate, dismiss, ridicule, malign, scorn, insult, impugn, vilify, traduce; *informal* put down, bad-mouth; *Brit. informal* rubbish.
– OPPOSITES praise.

disparity noun DISCREPANCY, difference, dissimilarity, contrast, gap, inequality, unevenness, inconsistency, imbalance, incongruity.

dispassionate adjective CALM, level-headed, cool, unflappable, unruffled, collected, nonchalant, sober, equable, serene, unperturbed, detached, objective, disinterested, indifferent.
– OPPOSITES emotional.

dispatch verb ❶ SEND, post, mail, forward, transmit, consign, remit, convey. ❷ *See* KILL (1).
▶ **noun** LETTER, message, bulletin, communication, report, account, missive, document.

dispense verb ❶ DISTRIBUTE, hand out, share out, measure out, divide out, dole out, allocate, assign, apportion, allot, supply, disburse, bestow, mete out, confer. ❷ **dispense medicines:** MAKE UP, prepare, mix, supply.
■ **dispense with** OMIT, do without, waive, forgo, give up, relinquish, renounce.

disperse verb ❶ **the crowd dispersed:** BREAK UP, disband, separate, scatter, dissolve, go separate ways, leave, vanish, melt away. ❷ **wind dispersed the clouds:** BREAK UP, scatter, dissipate, dispel, drive away, banish.
– OPPOSITES gather.

displace verb ❶ **displace from office:** REMOVE, dismiss, discharge, depose, dislodge, eject, expel, force out; *informal* sack, fire. ❷ **displaced the old manager:** REPLACE, take the place of, take over from, succeed, oust, supersede, supplant.

display verb ❶ **display the goods:** SHOW, exhibit, put on show/view, present, unveil, set forth, demonstrate, advertise, publicize. ❷ **display emotion:** SHOW, manifest, evince, betray, show evidence of, reveal, disclose.
– OPPOSITES conceal, hide.
▶ noun ❶ SHOW, exhibition, exhibit, presentation, demonstration, array. ❷ SHOW, spectacle, parade, pageant.

displease verb ANNOY, irritate, anger, put out, dissatisfy, irk, vex, offend, pique, gall, nettle, incense, exasperate, disgust, perturb; *informal* aggravate.

dispose verb ❶ ARRANGE, order, position, place, range, line up, array, marshal, organize, group, rank, regulate. ❷ **not disposed to believe him:** INCLINE, make willing, predispose, make, prompt, lead, induce, motivate.
■ **dispose of** *see* DISCARD.

disposed adjective INCLINED, willing, predisposed, minded, of a mind to, in the mood to, prepared, ready, prone, liable, given, apt.

disprove verb PROVE FALSE, invalidate, refute, negate, confute, rebut, give the lie to, deny, contradict, discredit, controvert, expose, demolish.
– OPPOSITES prove.

dispute noun ARGUMENT, quarrel, altercation, clash, wrangle, squabble, feud, disturbance, fracas, brawl; *informal* row.
▶ verb ❶ DEBATE, discuss, argue, disagree, clash, quarrel, bicker, wrangle, squabble. ❷ **dispute his right:** QUESTION, call into question, challenge, contest, doubt, deny, object to, oppose, controvert, impugn, gainsay.
– OPPOSITES agree.

disqualify verb RULE OUT, bar, exclude, reject, turn down, prohibit, debar, preclude.

disquiet noun UNEASINESS, anxiety, nervousness, agitation, upset, worry, concern, distress, alarm, fear, fretfulness, dread, foreboding.
– OPPOSITES calm.

disregard verb IGNORE, pay no attention to, take no notice of, neglect, discount, set aside, brush aside, overlook, turn a blind eye to, pass over, forget, gloss over, make light of, play down, laugh off, skip, snub, cold-shoulder; *informal* pooh-pooh.
– OPPOSITES attention.

disrepair noun DILAPIDATION, decay, collapse, shabbiness, ruin, deterioration, decrepitude.

disreputable adjective INFAMOUS, notorious, dishonourable, dishonest, unprincipled, villainous, corrupt, unworthy, questionable, unsavoury, contemptible, unscrupulous, despicable, disgraceful, reprehensible,

discreditable, shocking, outrageous, scandalous.
– OPPOSITES reputable.

disrespectful adjective IMPOLITE, discourteous, ill-mannered, rude, uncivil, irreverent, insolent, inconsiderate, impertinent, impudent, cheeky, scornful, contemptuous, insulting, churlish, derisive, uncomplimentary.
– OPPOSITES respectful.

disrupt verb UPSET, interrupt, break up, throw into disorder, cause turmoil in, disturb, interfere with, obstruct, impede, hamper, unsettle; *Brit.* throw a spanner in the works.

dissatisfaction noun DISCONTENT, displeasure, disappointment, disapproval, frustration, unhappiness, dismay, disquiet, annoyance, irritation, anger, exasperation, resentment, malaise, restlessness, disapprobation.
– OPPOSITES satisfaction.

dissatisfied adjective DISCONTENTED, displeased, disgruntled, unsatisfied, disapproving, disappointed, frustrated, unhappy, angry, vexed, irritated, annoyed, resentful, restless, unfulfilled.
– OPPOSITES satisfied.

disseminate verb SPREAD, circulate, broadcast, publish, publicize, proclaim, promulgate, propagate, dissipate, scatter, distribute, disperse, diffuse, bruit abroad.

dissident noun DISSENTER, rebel, objector, protestor, nonconformist, recusant, apostate.
– OPPOSITES conformist.

dissimilar adjective DIFFERENT, distinct, unlike, varying, disparate, unrelated, divergent, deviating, diverse, various, contrasting, mismatched.
– OPPOSITES similar.

dissipate verb ❶ DISPERSE, scatter, drive away, dispel, dissolve. ❷ SQUANDER, waste, fritter away, misspend, deplete, use up, consume, run through.

dissipated adjective *see* DEBAUCHED.

dissociate verb SEPARATE, set apart, segregate, isolate, detach, disconnect, sever, divorce.
– OPPOSITES associate.

dissolve verb ❶ LIQUEFY, become liquid, melt, deliquesce. ❷ **dissolve the partnership:** END, bring to an end, break up, terminate, discontinue, wind up, disband, suspend. ❸ **dissolve in tears:** BE OVERCOME WITH, break into, collapse into.

dissuade verb PERSUADE AGAINST, advise against, warn against, put off, stop, talk out of, argue out of, discourage from, deter from, divert, turn aside from.
– OPPOSITES persuade.

distance noun ❶ SPACE, extent, interval, gap, separation, span, stretch, measurement, length, width, breadth, depth, range, mileage. ❷ ALOOFNESS, reserve, coolness, remoteness, reticence, coldness, stiffness, frigidity, restraint, formality, unresponsiveness, unfriendliness; *informal* stand-offishness.
■ **distance oneself** SEPARATE ONESELF, dissociate oneself, keep one's distance, set oneself apart, remove oneself, stay away, keep

away, detach oneself, be unfriendly.

distant adjective ❶ a distant place: FAR, faraway, far-off, remote, out of the way, outlying, far-flung, inaccessible. ❷ three miles distant: AWAY, off, apart, separated, dispersed, scattered. ❸ a distant smile: RESERVED, aloof, uncommunicative, remote, withdrawn, unapproachable, restrained, reticent, cool, cold, stiff, formal, unfriendly, unresponsive, haughty, condescending.
– OPPOSITES close, friendly.

distasteful adjective DISAGREEABLE, unpleasant, displeasing, undesirable, off-putting, objectionable, offensive, obnoxious, repugnant, disgusting, unsavoury, revolting, nauseating, sickening, loathsome, abhorrent, detestable.
– OPPOSITES pleasant.

distinct adjective ❶ a distinct resemblance: CLEAR, clear-cut, well defined, marked, sharp, decided, visible, perceptible, definite, unmistakable, obvious, recognizable, plain, plain as day, evident, apparent, manifest, patent, unambiguous, palpable, unequivocal. ❷ two distinct things: SEPARATE, individual, different, unconnected, contrasting, discrete, disparate, dissimilar, detached, unassociated.
– OPPOSITES indistinct, vague.

distinction noun ❶ CONTRAST, difference, dissimilarity, division, dividing line, separation, differentiation, contradistinction, peculiarity. ❷ a man of distinction: NOTE, consequence, importance, account, significance, greatness, prestige, eminence, prominence, renown, fame, celebrity, mark, honour, merit, worth, excellence, name, rank, quality, superiority.
– OPPOSITES similarity, mediocrity.

distinctive adjective DISTINGUISHING, characteristic, typical, individual, particular, special, peculiar, different, uncommon, unusual, remarkable, singular, extraordinary, noteworthy, original, idiosyncratic.
– OPPOSITES ordinary.

distinguish verb ❶ TELL APART, differentiate, discriminate, tell the difference between, decide between, determine. ❷ SET APART, single out, separate, characterize, individualize. ❸ MAKE OUT, see, perceive, discern, observe, notice, recognize, pick out, espy.

distinguished adjective FAMOUS, renowned, well known, prominent, famed, noted, notable, illustrious, celebrated, respected, acclaimed, esteemed, legendary.
– OPPOSITES obscure.

distort verb ❶ TWIST, bend, warp, contort, buckle, deform, misshape, mangle, wrench. ❷ distort the facts: MISREPRESENT, pervert, twist, falsify, slant, bias, colour, tamper with, alter, change, garble.

distract verb ❶ DIVERT, deflect, sidetrack, interrupt, interfere, draw away, turn aside. ❷ AMUSE, entertain, divert, beguile, engage, occupy. ❸ CONFUSE, bewilder, disturb, fluster, agitate, disconcert, discompose, harass, annoy, trouble; *informal* hassle.

distracted adjective *see* DISTRAUGHT.

distraction noun ❶ DIVERSION, interruption, disturbance, interference, obstruction. ❷ CONFUSION, bewilderment, agitation, befuddlement, harassment. ❸ DIVERSION, amusement, entertainment, recreation, pastime, divertissement.

distraught adjective DISTRESSED, disturbed, excited, overcome, overwrought, frantic, distracted, beside oneself, wild, hysterical, grief-stricken, mad, maddened, insane, crazed, deranged; *informal* out of one's mind, worked up.
– OPPOSITES calm.

distress noun ❶ ANGUISH, suffering, pain, agony, affliction, torment, misery, wretchedness, torture, sorrow, grief, sadness, discomfort, heartache, desolation, trouble, worry, anxiety, uneasiness, perturbation, angst. ❷ HARDSHIP, adversity, trouble, misfortune, poverty, need, destitution, privation, impoverishment, indigence, penury, beggary, dire straits.
– OPPOSITES happiness, prosperity.
▶ verb UPSET, pain, trouble, worry, bother, disturb, perturb, torment, grieve, sadden, make miserable, vex, shock, scare, alarm.
– OPPOSITES calm.

distribute verb ❶ GIVE OUT, hand out, share out, divide out, dole out, measure out, parcel out, mete out, allocate, allot, issue, dispense, apportion, administer, deal out, dish out, assign, dispose. ❷ distribute leaflets: CIRCULATE, pass around, hand out, deliver, convey, transmit. ❸ distribute seeds: DISSEMINATE, disperse, scatter, strew, spread, sow, diffuse.

district noun AREA, region, place, locality, neighbourhood, sector, vicinity, quarter, territory, domain, precinct, province, zone, ward, department, parish, community.

distrust verb MISTRUST, be suspicious of, have doubts about, doubt, be wary/chary of, have misgivings about, question, wonder about, suspect, disbelieve; *informal* be leery of.
– OPPOSITES trust.

disturb verb ❶ disturb him at work: INTERRUPT, distract, bother, trouble, intrude on, butt in on, interfere with, harass, plague, pester, hinder; *informal* hassle. ❷ disturb the papers: MUDDLE, disorder, disarrange, confuse, throw into confusion; *informal* jumble up, mess about with. ❸ disturbed by the news: CONCERN, trouble, worry, perturb, upset, fluster, agitate, discomfit, alarm, frighten, dismay, distress, unsettle, ruffle.

disturbed adjective ❶ UPSET, troubled, worried, concerned, agitated, alarmed, dismayed, unsettled, ruffled. ❷ UNBALANCED, disordered, maladjusted, neurotic, psychotic; *informal* screwed up.

disused adjective UNUSED, neglected, abandoned, discontinued, obsolete, superannuated, withdrawn, discarded, idle, closed.

ditch noun TRENCH, channel, dyke, canal, drain, gutter, gully, moat, furrow, rut.
▶ verb THROW OUT, abandon, discard, drop, jettison, scrap, get rid of, dispose of; *informal* dump.

dive verb PLUNGE, plummet, jump, leap, bound, spring, nosedive, fall, descend, submerge, drop, swoop, dip, pitch, bellyflop.

diverge verb SEPARATE, fork, branch off, radiate, spread out, bifurcate, divide, split, part, go off at a tangent, divaricate, ramify.
– OPPOSITES converge.

diverse adjective ASSORTED, various, miscellaneous, mixed, varied, diversified, variegated, heterogeneous, different, differing, distinct, unlike, dissimilar, distinctive, contrasting, conflicting.

diversify verb BRANCH OUT, expand, bring variety to, develop, extend, enlarge, spread out, vary, mix, change, transform.

diversion noun ❶ DETOUR, deviation, alternative route. ❷ AMUSEMENT, entertainment, distraction, fun, relaxation, recreation, pleasure, enjoyment, delight, divertissement.

divert verb ❶ DEFLECT, turn aside, change the course of, redirect, draw away, switch, sidetrack. ❷ AMUSE, entertain, distract, delight, beguile, give pleasure to, enchant, interest, occupy, absorb, engross.

diverting adjective AMUSING, entertaining, distracting, fun, enjoyable, pleasurable, interesting, absorbing, engrossing.
– OPPOSITES boring.

divide verb ❶ divide it in two: SPLIT, cut up, separate, sever, halve, bisect, sunder, rend, part, segregate, partition, detach, disconnect, disjoin. ❷ the road divides: BRANCH, fork, diverge, split in two. ❸ divide the food: SHARE OUT, allocate, allot, apportion, distribute, dispense, hand out, dole out, measure out, parcel out, carve up. ❹ politics divided them: BREAK UP, separate, alienate, split up, disunite, set/pit against one another, set at odds, come between, sow dissension. ❺ divide into types: SORT, classify, arrange, order, group, rank, grade, categorize, segregate.
– OPPOSITES unite.

divine[1] adjective ❶ HEAVENLY, celestial, holy, angelic, spiritual, saintly, seraphic, sacred, consecrated, godlike, godly, supernatural. ❷ looking divine: LOVELY, beautiful, wonderful, glorious, marvellous, admirable; *informal* super, stunning.
– OPPOSITES mortal.

divine[2] verb FORETELL, predict, foresee, forecast, presage, augur, portend, prognosticate.

divinity noun ❶ DIVINE NATURE, divineness, deity, godliness, holiness, sanctity. ❷ THEOLOGY, religious studies, religion, scripture.

division noun ❶ ALLOCATION, distribution, apportionment, allotment. ❷ DIVIDING LINE, boundary, limit, border, partition, demarcation, frontier, margin. ❸ SECTION, part, portion, slice, fragment, chunk, component, share, compartment, category, class, group, family, grade. ❹ BRANCH, department, section, arm, sector, unit. ❺ a bitter division: DISAGREEMENT, conflict, dissension, discord, difference of opinion, feud, breach, rupture, split, variance, disunion, estrangement, alienation, schism.

divorce noun BREAK-UP, split,

dissolution, annulment, separation, breach, rupture.
▶ **verb** BREAK UP, split up, separate, part, annul/end the marriage.

dizzy **adjective** ❶ LIGHT-HEADED, giddy, faint, shaky, off balance, reeling, staggering; *informal* weak at the knees, wobbly, woozy. ❷ **dizzy young girls:** FOOLISH, silly, scatterbrained, giddy, fickle, capricious.

do **verb** ❶ **do the job:** PERFORM, carry out, undertake, execute, accomplish, discharge, achieve, implement, complete, finish, bring about, effect, produce, engineer. ❷ **do as you like:** ACT, behave, conduct oneself; *formal* comport oneself. ❸ **this will do:** BE ENOUGH, be adequate, suffice, be sufficient, be satisfactory, serve the purpose, fit the bill, pass muster, measure up. ❹ **do the sum:** WORK OUT, solve, resolve, figure out, decipher, puzzle out. ❺ **do him a favour:** GRANT, bestow, render, pay, give, afford. ❻ **how are you doing?** GET ON/ALONG, progress, fare, make out, manage, continue.
■ **do away with** *see* ABOLISH. **do in** *see* KILL (1).

docile **adjective** AMENABLE, compliant, tractable, manageable, accommodating, obedient, pliant, biddable, submissive, dutiful, malleable.
– OPPOSITES disobedient.

dock[1] **noun** PIER, quay, wharf, jetty, berth, harbour, port, slipway, marina, waterfront.

dock[2] **verb** ❶ CUT, shorten, crop, lop, truncate. ❷ DEDUCT, subtract, remove, take off.

doctor **noun** PHYSICIAN, medical practitioner, GP, general practitioner, consultant, registrar; *informal* medic, doc; *Brit. informal* quack.

doctrine **noun** CREED, belief, teaching, credo, dogma, conviction, tenet, principle, maxim, axiom, precept, article of faith, canon, theory, thesis, orthodoxy, postulate.

document **noun** PAPER, form, certificate, record, report, deed, voucher, charter, instrument, licence, parchment, visa, warrant.
▶ **verb** RECORD, detail, report, register, chart, cite, instance.

documentary **adjective** ❶ **documentary evidence:** DOCUMENTED, recorded, written, registered. ❷ **documentary film:** FACTUAL, non-fiction, true-to-life, real-life, realistic.

dodge **verb** ❶ DART, duck, dive, swerve, veer, jump, move aside. ❷ **dodge the police:** EVADE, avoid, elude, fend off, escape, steer clear of, deceive, trick. ❸ **dodge questions:** EVADE, parry, fend off, fudge. ❹ **dodge hard work:** AVOID, evade, shun, shirk.
▶ **noun** RUSE, ploy, stratagem, trick, subterfuge, wile, deception, manoeuvre, contrivance, expedient; *Brit. informal* wheeze.

dog **noun** HOUND, bitch, cur, mongrel, tyke, pup, puppy, whelp; *informal* doggy, pooch, mutt, bow-wow.
▶ **verb** FOLLOW, pursue, track, shadow, trail, hound, plague, trouble, haunt.

dogged **adjective** DETERMINED, obstinate, stubborn, tenacious, relentless, single-minded, unflagging, unwavering, persistent, obdurate, firm, steadfast, staunch.

dogmatic adjective OPINIONATED, peremptory, assertive, insistent, pushy, emphatic, categorical, authoritarian, domineering, imperious, arrogant, overbearing, dictatorial, intolerant, biased, prejudiced.

dole noun BENEFIT, welfare, social security, income support.
■ **dole out** *see* DISTRIBUTE (1).

doleful adjective MOURNFUL, sad, sorrowful, dejected, depressed, miserable, disconsolate, wretched; *informal* blue, down in the dumps.

domestic adjective ❶ HOME, family, household, private. ❷ **a domestic animal:** DOMESTICATED, tame, pet, trained; *Brit.* house-trained; *N. Amer.* housebroken.

domesticate verb ❶ TAME, train, break in; *Brit.* house-train; *N. Amer.* housebreak. ❷ **domesticate a plant:** NATURALIZE, acclimatize, habituate, accustom, familiarize, assimilate.

dominant adjective ❶ **dominant person:** COMMANDING, ruling, controlling, presiding, governing, supreme, ascendant, domineering, most influential, most assertive, authoritative. ❷ **the dominant issue:** CHIEF, most important, predominant, main, leading, principal, paramount, pre-eminent, primary, outstanding, prevailing.
– OPPOSITES submissive.

dominate verb ❶ RULE, govern, control, exercise control over, have the whip hand, command, direct, preside over, have mastery over, domineer, tyrannize, intimidate; *informal* call the shots, have under one's thumb, be in the driver's seat, wear the trousers. ❷ **the hill dominates the town:** OVERLOOK, tower above, stand over, project over, hang over, loom over, bestride.

domineering adjective OVERBEARING, authoritarian, autocratic, imperious, high-handed, peremptory, arrogant, dictatorial, haughty, masterful, forceful, pushy, tyrannical, despotic, oppressive, iron-fisted; *informal* bossy.
– OPPOSITES meek, servile.

donate verb GIVE, contribute, present, make a gift of, hand over, grant, subscribe; *informal* chip in, kick in.

donation noun CONTRIBUTION, gift, subscription, present, grant, offering, gratuity, charity, benefaction, largesse.

donor noun CONTRIBUTOR, giver, benefactor, benefactress, supporter, backer, philanthropist; *informal* angel.

doom noun ❶ RUIN, ruination, downfall, destruction, disaster, catastrophe, annihilation, extinction, death, termination, quietus. ❷ FATE, destiny, fortune, lot, portion.
▶ verb DESTINE, condemn, ordain, preordain, consign, predestine.

doomed adjective DAMNED, cursed, hopeless, accursed, ill-fated, ill-starred, ruined, bedevilled.

door noun ❶ DOORWAY, opening, portal, entrance, exit, way out, barrier. ❷ **the door to success:** ENTRY, entrance, opening, access, gateway, way, path, road, ingress.

dope noun ❶ DRUGS, narcotics. ❷ *See* IDIOT. ❸ INFORMATION, story,

news, facts, details; *informal* info, gen, low-down.
▶ **verb** DRUG, administer drugs, knock out, sedate, narcotize.

dormant **adjective** ❶ SLEEPING, asleep, hibernating, resting, slumbering, inactive, inert, comatose, quiescent. ❷ HIDDEN, latent, potential, untapped, unused.
– OPPOSITES awake, active.

dose **noun** ❶ AMOUNT, quantity, measure, portion, draught. ❷ **a dose of flu:** BOUT, attack, spell.

dot **noun** SPOT, speck, fleck, point, mark, dab, particle, atom, iota, jot, mote, mite.

dote
■ **dote on** ADORE, idolize, love, treasure, prize, make much of, lavish affection on, indulge, spoil, pamper.

double **adjective** ❶ DUPLICATE, twinned, twin, paired, in pairs, dual, coupled, twofold. ❷ **a double meaning:** AMBIGUOUS, dual, ambivalent, equivocal, double-edged.
▶ **noun** TWIN, clone, lookalike, Doppelgänger, duplicate, replica, copy, facsimile, counterpart, match, mate, fellow; *informal* spitting image, dead ringer.

double-cross **verb** BETRAY, cheat, defraud, trick, mislead, deceive, swindle, hoodwink; *informal* two-time, take for a ride.

doubt **verb** ❶ **I doubt his motives:** BE SUSPICIOUS OF, suspect, distrust, mistrust, have misgivings about, feel uneasy about, call into question, question, query. ❷ **I doubt if it's true:** HAVE DOUBTS, be dubious, be undecided, lack conviction, have scruples.
– OPPOSITES trust.
▶ **noun** ❶ **have doubts about:** DISTRUST, mistrust, suspicion, scepticism, lack of confidence, uneasiness, reservations, misgivings, qualms. ❷ **full of doubt:** UNCERTAINTY, indecision, hesitancy, hesitation, vacillation, wavering, irresolution, lack of conviction.

doubtful **adjective** ❶ IN DOUBT, uncertain, unsure, improbable, unlikely. ❷ **doubtful about his motives:** SUSPICIOUS, distrustful, mistrustful, sceptical, having reservations, apprehensive, uneasy, questioning, unsure, incredulous. ❸ **its genuineness is doubtful:** DUBIOUS, uncertain, open to question, questionable, debatable, inconclusive, unresolved, unconfirmed. ❹ **the meaning is doubtful:** UNCLEAR, dubious, ambiguous, equivocal, obscure, vague, nebulous. ❺ **doubtful people:** DUBIOUS, suspicious, questionable, suspect, under suspicion, unreliable, disreputable.
– OPPOSITES certain.

dour **adjective** MOROSE, unsmiling, gloomy, sullen, sour, gruff, churlish, uncommunicative, unfriendly, forbidding, grim, stern, austere, severe, harsh, dismal, dreary.
– OPPOSITES cheerful.

dowdy **adjective** FRUMPISH, drab, dull, unfashionable, inelegant, unstylish, slovenly, shabby, dingy, untidy, frowzy.
– OPPOSITES smart.

downcast **adjective** DISHEARTENED, downhearted, dispirited, depressed, dejected,

dismayed, disconsolate, crestfallen, despondent, sad, unhappy, miserable, wretched, gloomy, glum, melancholy; *informal* down, low, blue.
– OPPOSITES elated.

downright adverb COMPLETELY, totally, absolutely, utterly, thoroughly, profoundly, categorically, positively.

downward adjective DECLINING, descending, falling, downhill, going down, earthbound.
– OPPOSITES upward.

drab adjective ❶ DULL, colourless, grey, mousy, dingy, dreary, cheerless, gloomy, sombre, depressing.
❷ UNINTERESTING, boring, tedious, dry, dreary, lifeless, lacklustre, uninspired.
– OPPOSITES bright, interesting.

draft noun ❶ OUTLINE, plan, rough version, skeleton, abstract, notes.
❷ MONEY ORDER, cheque, bill of exchange, postal order.

drag verb ❶ PULL, haul, draw, tug, yank, trail, tow, lug. ❷ the film dragged: GO ON TOO LONG, go on and on, become tedious, pass slowly, be boring, crawl, creep.
■ **drag out** PROTRACT, prolong, draw out, spin out, stretch out, lengthen, extend.

dragoon verb FORCE, compel, coerce, drive, impel, constrain, browbeat, bully, tyrannize; *informal* strong-arm, put the screws on.

drain verb ❶ drain the water: DRAW OFF, extract, remove, pump out, bleed, milk, tap, filter. ❷ the water drained away: FLOW OUT, seep out, leak, trickle, ooze, well out, discharge, exude, effuse.
❸ draining resources: USE UP, exhaust, deplete, consume, sap, bleed, tax, strain.
▶ noun TRENCH, channel, duct, sewer, gutter, ditch, culvert, pipe, outlet, conduit.

dramatic adjective ❶ THEATRICAL, stage, thespian, dramaturgical.
❷ EXCITING, sensational, startling, spectacular, thrilling, tense, suspenseful, electrifying, stirring, affecting. ❸ a dramatic view: STRIKING, impressive, vivid, breathtaking, moving, affecting, graphic.

dramatist noun PLAYWRIGHT, scriptwriter, screenwriter, dramaturge.

dramatize verb ❶ ADAPT, put into dramatic form.
❷ EXAGGERATE, make a drama of, overstate, overdo; *informal* ham it up, lay it on thick.

drape verb COVER, envelope, swathe, blanket, cloak, veil, shroud, decorate, adorn, deck, festoon, array, overlay.
▶ noun CURTAIN, drapery, screen, hanging, tapestry, valance.

drastic adjective SEVERE, extreme, strong, vigorous, draconian, desperate, radical, dire, harsh, forceful, rigorous, sharp.

draw verb ❶ draw up a chair: PULL, haul, drag, tug, yank, tow, trail, lug. ❷ draw attention: ATTRACT, lure, entice, invite, engage, interest, win, capture, captivate, tempt, seduce, fascinate, allure.
❸ draw liquid: DRAIN, siphon off, pump out, tap, milk, bleed, filtrate. ❹ draw a house/picture: SKETCH, portray, depict, delineate, make a drawing of, represent, paint, design, trace, map out,

chart, mark out. ❺ **draw lots:** CHOOSE, pick, select, opt for, decide on, make a choice of, single out. ❻ **draw a salary:** TAKE, receive, be in receipt of, get, procure, obtain, earn. ❼ **draw a conclusion:** DEDUCE, infer, conclude, derive, gather, glean. ❽ **draw a breath:** BREATHE IN, inhale, suck in, inspire, respire. ❾ **draw a gun:** PULL OUT, take out, bring out, extract, withdraw, unsheathe.

▶ **noun** ❶ LURE, attraction, pull, enticement, allure, magnetism. ❷ LOTTERY, raffle, sweepstake. ❸ TIE, dead heat, stalemate.

■ **draw on** MAKE USE OF, have recourse to, exploit, employ, rely on. **draw out** EXTEND, protract, prolong, lengthen, drag out, spin out.

drawback noun DISADVANTAGE, catch, problem, snag, difficulty, trouble, flaw, hitch, fly in the ointment, stumbling block, handicap, obstacle, impediment, hindrance, barrier, hurdle, deterrent, nuisance, defect.

– OPPOSITES benefit.

drawing noun PICTURE, sketch, illustration, portrayal, representation, depiction, composition, study, outline, diagram.

dread noun FEAR, fearfulness, terror, alarm, nervousness, uneasiness, anxiety, apprehension, trepidation, horror, concern, foreboding, dismay, perturbation; *informal* blue funk, the heebie-jeebies.

▶ **verb** FEAR, be afraid of, be terrified by, worry about, have forebodings about, shrink from, flinch from; *informal* have cold feet about.

dreadful adjective ❶ **a dreadful sight:** TERRIBLE, horrible, frightful, awful, dire, frightening, terrifying, distressing, alarming, shocking, appalling, harrowing, ghastly, fearful, hideous, gruesome, horrendous, calamitous, grievous. ❷ **a dreadful man:** NASTY, unpleasant, disagreeable, repugnant, distasteful, odious.

– OPPOSITES pleasant, agreeable.

dream noun ❶ VISION, nightmare, hallucination, fantasy, daydream, reverie, illusion, delusion. ❷ AMBITION, aspiration, goal, design, plan, aim, hope, desire, wish, daydream, fantasy.

▶ **verb** ❶ DAYDREAM, be in a reverie, be in a trance, be lost in thought, muse, be preoccupied. ❷ **wouldn't dream of it:** THINK, consider, conceive, suppose, visualize.

■ **dream up** THINK UP, invent, concoct, devise, create, hatch; *informal* cook up.

dreamy adjective ❶ **a dreamy recollection:** DREAMLIKE, vague, dim, hazy, shadowy, misty, faint, indistinct, unclear. ❷ **a dreamy young man:** WONDERFUL, marvellous, heavenly; *informal* fabulous, terrific.

dreary adjective DULL, drab, uninteresting, colourless, lifeless, dry, flat, tedious, boring, humdrum, monotonous, wearisome, routine, unvaried.

– OPPOSITES interesting.

drench verb SOAK, drown, saturate, flood, inundate, steep, permeate, douse, souse, wet, slosh.

dress noun ❶ FROCK, gown, garment, robe. ❷ CLOTHES, garments, attire, costume, outfit,

ensemble, garb; *informal* get-up, togs, duds.
▶ **verb** ❶ CLOTHE, attire, garb, fit out, turn out, robe, accoutre; *archaic* apparel. ❷ **dressed his wound:** BANDAGE, bind up, cover.
– OPPOSITES undress.
■ **dress down** REPRIMAND, scold, rebuke, upbraid, reprove, berate; *informal* tell off; *formal* castigate.

dressmaker **noun** TAILOR, tailoress, couturier, seamstress, needlewoman.

dribble **verb** ❶ DROOL, slaver, slobber; *Scottish* slabber. ❷ DRIP, trickle, leak, run, ooze, seep, exude.

drift **verb** ❶ BE CARRIED ALONG, float, coast, be borne, be wafted. ❷ **people drifting:** WANDER, roam, rove, meander, stray. ❸ **snow drifting:** PILE UP, accumulate, gather, form heaps, bank up, amass.
▶ **noun** ❶ **the drift of his argument:** GIST, essence, substance, meaning, significance, import, purport, tenor. ❷ **a snow drift:** PILE, heap, bank, mound, mass, accumulation.

drill **verb** ❶ TRAIN, instruct, coach, teach, exercise, rehearse, ground, inculcate, discipline; *informal* put someone through their paces. ❷ BORE A HOLE IN, pierce, penetrate, puncture, perforate.
▶ **noun** ❶ TRAINING, instruction, coaching, teaching, indoctrination. ❷ **know the drill:** PROCEDURE, routine, practice.

drink **verb** ❶ SWALLOW, sip, gulp down, drain, guzzle, imbibe, quaff, partake of; *informal* swig, swill, toss off. ❷ **he drinks a lot:** TAKE ALCOHOL, indulge, imbibe, tipple; *informal* booze, take a drop, hit the bottle, knock back a few.
▶ **noun** ❶ SWALLOW, gulp, sip, draught; *informal* swill, swig. ❷ ALCOHOL, liquor, spirits; *informal* booze, the hard stuff, hooch.

drip **verb** DRIBBLE, trickle, drizzle, leak, ooze, splash, sprinkle, leak; *informal* plop.
▶ **noun** DROP, dribble, splash, trickle, leak, bead.

drive **verb** ❶ **drive a bus:** OPERATE, steer, handle, guide, direct, manage. ❷ **drive cattle:** MOVE, herd, get going, urge, press, impel, push, round up. ❸ **driven to steal:** FORCE, make, compel, coerce, oblige, impel, pressure, goad, spur, prod. ❹ **drive in the stake:** HAMMER, thrust, ram, strike, bang, sink, plunge.
▶ **noun** ❶ **go for a drive:** TRIP, run, outing, journey, jaunt, tour, excursion; *informal* spin, joyride. ❷ **drive and ambition:** ENERGY, determination, enthusiasm, industry, vigour, push, motivation, persistence, keenness, enterprise, initiative, aggressiveness, zeal, verve; *informal* get-up-and-go, pizzazz, zip. ❸ **a sales drive:** CAMPAIGN, effort, push, crusade.
■ **drive at** MEAN, suggest, imply, indicate, intimate, have in mind; *informal* get at.

drivel **noun** NONSENSE, rubbish, garbage, gibberish, balderdash; *informal* rot, poppycock, twaddle, waffle, tripe, hogwash, mumbo-jumbo; *Brit. informal* stuff and nonsense; *informal, dated* bunkum, tommyrot.
▶ **verb** TALK NONSENSE/RUBBISH, babble, gibber, blather, prate, maunder; *informal* waffle, talk

through one's hat; *Brit. informal* witter on.

drop verb ❶ FALL, descend, plunge, dive, plummet, tumble, dip, sink, subside, swoop. ❷ **prices dropped:** FALL, decrease, lessen, diminish, dwindle, sink, plunge, plummet. ❸ **dropped his girlfriend:** LEAVE, finish with, desert, abandon, jilt, reject, discard, renounce, disown; *informal* ditch, chuck, run out on. ❹ **drop from exhaustion:** FALL DOWN, collapse, faint, swoon, drop/fall dead.
– OPPOSITES rise, increase.
▶ noun ❶ DROPLET, globule, bead, bubble, blob, spheroid, oval. ❷ **add a drop:** BIT, dash, trace, pinch, dap, speck, modicum, dribble, splash, trickle, sprinkle. ❸ **a drop in prices:** DECREASE, fall, decline, reduction, cut, lowering, depreciation, slump. ❹ **the path ends in a drop:** INCLINE, slope, descent, declivity, plunge, abyss, chasm, precipice, cliff.
■ **drop off** ❶ DELIVER, deposit, set down, unload, leave. ❷ FALL ASLEEP, doze off, have a nap, catnap, drowse; *informal* nod off, get some shut-eye.

drown verb ❶ FLOOD, submerge, inundate, deluge, swamp, engulf, drench. ❷ **the sound drowned her speech:** BE LOUDER THAN, muffle, overpower, overwhelm, stifle.

drowsy adjective SLEEPY, tired, lethargic, weary, dozy, dozing, sluggish, somnolent, heavy-eyed; *informal* dopey.
– OPPOSITES alert.

drudge noun SERVANT, slave, menial, labourer, toiler, factotum; *Brit. informal* skivvy, dogsbody; *Brit. dated* charwoman, char.

drug noun ❶ MEDICINE, medication, medicament, remedy, cure, panacea; *informal* magic bullet; *dated* physic. ❷ NARCOTIC, opiate; *informal* dope, junk.
▶ **verb** ANAESTHETIZE, tranquillize, sedate, knock out, render unconscious, stupefy, poison, narcotize, befuddle; *informal* dope.

drum verb TAP, beat, rap, knock, tattoo, strike, thrum.
■ **drum out** EXPEL, dismiss, discharge, throw out, oust. **drum up** GATHER, collect, round up, summon, obtain, get, attract, canvass, solicit, petition.

drunk adjective INTOXICATED, inebriated, blind drunk, the worse for drink, under the influence, befuddled, merry, tipsy, incapable, tight; *informal* tiddly, squiffy, plastered, smashed, paralytic, sloshed, blotto, sozzled, drunk as a lord, pie-eyed, three sheets to the wind, well oiled, stewed, pickled, tanked up, steaming, out of it, one over the eight, canned, tired and emotional; *Brit. informal* legless, bevvied.
– OPPOSITES sober.
▶ **noun** DRUNKARD, heavy drinker, alcoholic, dipsomaniac, inebriate; *informal* soak, boozer, alky, lush, wino.

dry adjective ❶ ARID, parched, dehydrated, scorched, waterless, moistureless, desiccated, withered, shrivelled, wizened, rainless, torrid, barren, unproductive, sterile. ❷ **a dry talk:** DULL, uninteresting, boring, tedious, dreary, monotonous, tiresome, wearisome, flat, unimaginative, prosaic, humdrum. ❸ **a dry response:**

COOL, cold, indifferent, aloof, unemotional, remote, impersonal.
– OPPOSITES wet.
▶ **verb** ❶ DRY UP, mop, blot, towel, drain. ❷ MAKE DRY, dry up, parch, scorch, dehydrate, sear, desiccate, wither, wilt, shrivel, mummify.

dub **verb** CALL, name, christen, designate, term, entitle, style, label, tag, nickname, denominate, nominate.

dubious **adjective** ❶ DOUBTFUL, uncertain, unsure, hesitant, undecided, wavering, vacillating, irresolute, suspicious, sceptical; *informal* iffy. ❷ SUSPICIOUS, questionable, suspect, untrustworthy, unreliable, undependable; *informal* shady, fishy.
– OPPOSITES certain, trustworthy.

duck **verb** ❶ **duck behind the wall:** BEND, bob down, crouch, stoop, squat, hunch down, hunker down. ❷ **duck her in the pond:** IMMERSE, submerge, dip, plunge, douse, souse, dunk.

duct **noun** PIPE, tube, conduit, channel, passage, canal, culvert.

due **adjective** ❶ **money due:** OWING, owed, payable, outstanding, receivable. ❷ **recognition due:** DESERVED, merited, earned, justified, appropriate, fitting, suitable, right. ❸ **due respect:** PROPER, correct, rightful, fitting, appropriate, apt, adequate, ample, satisfactory, requisite, apposite.

dulcet **adjective** SWEET, melodious, musical, lyrical, silver-toned, euphonious, pleasant, agreeable, soothing, mellow.

dull **adjective** ❶ **dull colours:** DRAB, dreary, sombre, dark, subdued, muted, toned down, lacklustre, lustreless, faded, washed out. ❷ **dull weather:** OVERCAST, cloudy, gloomy, dismal, dreary, dark, leaden, murky, sunless, lowering. ❸ **dull reactions:** INSENSITIVE, unfeeling, indifferent, unemotional, unresponsive, apathetic, blank, uncaring, passionless. ❹ **a dull speech:** UNINTERESTING, boring, tedious, tiresome, wearisome, dry, monotonous, flat, bland, unimaginative, humdrum, prosaic, vapid. ❺ **a dull sound:** MUTED, muffled, indistinct, feeble, deadened. ❻ **trade is dull:** SLOW, depressed, sluggish, stagnant.
– OPPOSITES bright, interesting.

dumbfound **verb** ASTOUND, amaze, astonish, startle, surprise, stun, stagger, take aback, bewilder, overwhelm, confound, baffle, confuse, disconcert; *informal* throw, knock sideways; *Brit. informal* knock for six.

dummy **noun** ❶ MODEL, mannequin, figure, doll. ❷ COPY, reproduction, imitation, representation, sample, substitute, counterfeit, sham. ❸ *See* IDIOT.

dump **verb** ❶ DISPOSE OF, get rid of, discard, throw away/out, scrap, jettison. ❷ **dumped her boyfriend:** LEAVE, abandon, desert, walk out on, forsake; *informal* leave in the lurch.
▶ **noun** ❶ TIP, rubbish dump, scrapyard, junkyard. ❷ **what a dump!** PIGSTY, hovel, slum, shack; *informal* hole.

dunce noun FOOL, dolt, idiot, ass, ignoramus, imbecile, simpleton; *informal* chump, booby, nincompoop, ninny, dunderhead, blockhead, fathead, halfwit, cretin, moron, dummy, numbskull, dimwit; *Brit. informal* twerp, clot, twit, nitwit.

duplicate noun ❶ COPY, replica, reproduction, likeness, twin, double, clone, match; *informal* lookalike, spitting image, dead ringer. ❷ COPY, carbon copy, photocopy, photostat, Xerox.
▶ adjective MATCHING, twin, identical, corresponding, second, paired.
▶ verb ❶ COPY, photocopy, reproduce, replicate, clone, photostat. ❷ REPEAT, do again, replicate, perform again.

duplicity noun DECEITFULNESS, double-dealing, dishonesty, two-facedness, trickery, guile, chicanery, artifice.

durable adjective ❶ *durable clothes*: LONG-LASTING, hard-wearing, strong, sturdy, tough, resistant, imperishable. ❷ *a durable affection*: LASTING, long-lasting, enduring, persistent, abiding, continuing, stable, constant, firm, permanent, unchanging, dependable, reliable.
– OPPOSITES flimsy, ephemeral.

dusk noun TWILIGHT, sunset, sundown, nightfall, evening, dark.

dust noun ❶ DIRT, grime, powder, soot. ❷ EARTH, soil, clay, ground, dirt.

dusty adjective ❶ DUST-COVERED, dirty, grimy, grubby, unclean, sooty, undusted. ❷ POWDERY, chalky, crumbly, sandy, fine, friable.

dutiful adjective CONSCIENTIOUS, obedient, submissive, compliant, deferential, respectful, filial, reverent, reverential, devoted, considerate, thoughtful, pliant, docile.
– OPPOSITES disrespectful, remiss.

duty noun ❶ *a sense of duty*: RESPONSIBILITY, obligation, service, loyalty, allegiance, obedience, faithfulness, respect, deference, fidelity, homage. ❷ *perform his duties*: TASK, job, assignment, requirement, responsibility, obligation, mission, commission, function, office, charge, role, burden, onus. ❸ *pay duty*: TAX, levy, tariff, excise, toll, fee, impost.

dwarf verb TOWER OVER, overshadow, dominate, stand head and shoulders above, diminish, minimize.

dwell verb LIVE, reside, stay, lodge; *informal* hang out; *formal* abide.

dwindle verb BECOME/GROW LESS, diminish, decrease, lessen, shrink, contract, fade, wane.
– OPPOSITES increase, grow.

dye noun COLOUR, shade, tint, hue.
▶ verb COLOUR, tint, stain, pigment, shade.

dynamic adjective ENERGETIC, active, lively, spirited, aggressive, pushy, enthusiastic, driving, eager, motivated, zealous, alive, vigorous, strong, forceful, powerful, high-powered, potent, vital, effective; *informal* go-ahead, go-getting, zippy, peppy.

Ee

each adjective EVERY, every single. ▶ **pronoun** EACH ONE, every one, each and every one, one and all. ▶ **adverb** APIECE, per person, per capita, to each, for each, from each, individually.

eager adjective ❶ KEEN, enthusiastic, avid, fervent, impatient, zealous, passionate, wholehearted, earnest, diligent, ambitious, enterprising; *informal* bright-eyed and bushy-tailed, raring to go. ❷ **eager for news:** LONGING, yearning, anxious, intent, agog, wishing, desirous, hopeful, thirsty, hungry, greedy; *informal* dying, itching, hot.
– OPPOSITES indifferent, apathetic.

early adverb ❶ AHEAD OF TIME, too soon, beforehand, before the appointed time, prematurely. ❷ IN GOOD TIME, ahead of schedule, before the appointed time.
– OPPOSITES late.
▶ **adjective** ❶ **an early birth:** ADVANCED, forward, premature, untimely, precocious. ❷ **early man:** PRIMITIVE, primeval, prehistoric, primordial.
– OPPOSITES overdue.

earn verb ❶ GET, make, receive, obtain, draw, clear, collect, bring in, take home, gross, net; *informal* pull in, pocket. ❷ **earn their respect:** GAIN, win, attain, merit, achieve, rate, secure, obtain, deserve, be entitled to, be worthy of, warrant.

earnest adjective ❶ SERIOUS, solemn, grave, intense, thoughtful, studious, staid, diligent, steady, hard-working, committed, dedicated, assiduous, keen, zealous. ❷ **an earnest request:** SINCERE, fervent, intense, ardent, passionate, heartfelt, wholehearted, enthusiastic, urgent, zealous, fervid, warm.
– OPPOSITES flippant.

earnings plural noun INCOME, salary, wage, pay, remuneration, fee, stipend, emolument, honorarium.

earth noun SOIL, clay, loam, turf, clod, dirt, sod, ground.

earthly adjective ❶ WORLDLY, temporal, secular, mortal, human, material, materialistic, non-spiritual, mundane, carnal, fleshly, physical, corporeal, gross, sensual, base, sordid, vile, profane. ❷ **not an earthly chance:** POSSIBLE, feasible, conceivable, imaginable, likely.
– OPPOSITES spiritual.

earthy adjective ❶ UNSOPHISTICATED, down-to-earth, unrefined, homely, simple, plain, unpretentious, natural, uninhibited, rough, robust. ❷ **earthy humour:** CRUDE, bawdy, coarse, ribald, indecent, obscene, indecorous; *informal* blue.

ease noun ❶ **succeed with ease:** EFFORTLESSNESS, no difficulty, simplicity, deftness, proficiency, facility, adroitness, dexterity, mastery. ❷ **a life of ease:** COMFORT,

contentment, enjoyment, content, affluence, wealth, prosperity, luxury, opulence. ❸ ease of mind: PEACE, peacefulness, calmness, tranquillity, composure, serenity, restfulness, quiet, security.
– OPPOSITES difficulty.
▶ verb ❶ ease the pain: LESSEN, mitigate, reduce, lighten, diminish, moderate, ameliorate, relieve, assuage, allay, soothe, palliate, appease. ❷ ease it into position: GUIDE, manoeuvre, edge, inch, steer, glide, slip. ❸ ease her mind: COMFORT, console, soothe, solace, calm, quieten, pacify.
– OPPOSITES aggravate.

easy adjective ❶ SIMPLE, uncomplicated, straightforward, undemanding, effortless, painless, trouble-free, facile; *informal* idiot-proof. ❷ an easy manner: NATURAL, casual, informal, unceremonious, easy-going, amiable, unconcerned, affable, carefree, nonchalant, composed, urbane, insouciant, suave; *informal* laid-back. ❸ an easy mind: UNTROUBLED, unworried, relaxed, at ease, calm, tranquil, composed, serene, comfortable, contented, secure. ❹ an easy pace: MODERATE, steady, regular, undemanding, leisurely, unhurried.
– OPPOSITES difficult, formal, uneasy.

easy-going adjective EVEN-TEMPERED, relaxed, carefree, happy-go-lucky, placid, serene, nonchalant, insouciant, tolerant, undemanding, amiable, patient, understanding, imperturbable; *informal* laid-back, together.
– OPPOSITES intolerant.

eat verb CONSUME, devour, swallow, chew, munch, gulp down, bolt, wolf, ingest; *informal* tuck into, put away; *Brit. informal* scoff.
■ **eat away** ERODE, wear away, corrode, gnaw away, dissolve, waste away, rot, decay, destroy.

eavesdrop verb LISTEN IN, spy, monitor, tap, wire-tap, overhear; *informal* bug, snoop.

ebb verb ❶ GO OUT, flow back, retreat, fall back, draw back, recede, abate, subside. ❷ *See* DECLINE verb (2, 3).

ebullience noun EXUBERANCE, buoyancy, high spirits, exhilaration, elation, euphoria, high-spiritedness, jubilation, animation, sparkle, vivacity, zest, irrepressibility.

eccentric adjective ODD, strange, queer, peculiar, unconventional, idiosyncratic, quirky, bizarre, weird, outlandish, irregular, uncommon, abnormal, freakish, aberrant, anomalous, capricious, whimsical; *informal* offbeat, way-out, dotty, nutty, screwy.
– OPPOSITES ordinary, conventional.
▶ noun CHARACTER, oddity, crank; *informal* queer fish, weirdo, oddball, nut; *Brit. informal* nutter; *N. Amer. informal* screwball.

echo verb ❶ REVERBERATE, resound, ring, repeat, reflect. ❷ COPY, imitate, repeat, reproduce, reiterate, mirror, parrot, reflect, parallel, parody, ape.

eclectic adjective WIDE-RANGING, broad, broad-based, comprehensive, varied, diverse, catholic, liberal, all-embracing, many-sided, multifaceted, multifarious.

eclipse verb ❶ BLOCK, cover, blot out, obscure, conceal, cast a shadow over, darken, shade, veil, shroud. ❷ OUTSHINE, overshadow, dwarf, put in the shade, surpass, exceed, outstrip, transcend.

economical adjective ❶ THRIFTY, sparing, careful, prudent, frugal, scrimping, mean, niggardly, penny-pinching, parsimonious; *informal* stingy. ❷ CHEAP, inexpensive, reasonable, low-price, low-cost, budget.
– OPPOSITES extravagant.

economize verb BUDGET, cut back, scrimp, save, be economical, be sparing, retrench; *informal* cut corners, tighten one's belt, draw in one's horns.

economy noun ❶ WEALTH, resources, financial state. ❷ THRIFTINESS, carefulness, prudence, frugality, thrift, care, restraint, meanness, stinginess, miserliness, niggardliness, parsimony, penny-pinching, husbandry, conservation.

ecstasy noun BLISS, delight, rapture, joy, joyousness, happiness, elation, euphoria, jubilation, exultation, transports of delight, rhapsodies; *informal* seventh heaven, cloud nine.
– OPPOSITES misery.

ecstatic adjective BLISSFUL, enraptured, rapturous, joyful, joyous, overjoyed, jubilant, gleeful, exultant, elated, in transports of delight, delirious, in a frenzy of delight, rhapsodic, orgasmic, transported; *informal* on cloud nine, in seventh heaven, over the moon.
– OPPOSITES miserable.

eddy noun WHIRL, whirlpool, vortex, maelstrom, swirl, countercurrent, counterflow.
▶ verb SWIRL, whirl, spin, turn.

edge noun ❶ BORDER, boundary, side, rim, margin, fringe, outer limit, extremity, verge, brink, lip, contour, perimeter, periphery, parameter, ambit. ❷ **an edge in her voice**: STING, bite, sharpness, severity, pointedness, acerbity, acidity, acrimony, virulence, trenchancy, pungency. ❸ **have an edge**: ADVANTAGE, lead, superiority, upper hand, whip hand, dominance, ascendancy; *informal* head start.
▶ verb ❶ **edge with lace**: TRIM, hem, border, fringe, rim, bind, verge. ❷ **edge forward**: INCH, creep, sidle, steal. ❸ **edge one's way**: INCH, ease, sidle, elbow, worm, work, sidestep.

edgy adjective NERVOUS, nervy, tense, anxious, apprehensive, on tenterhooks, uneasy, irritable, touchy, irascible, tetchy; *informal* twitchy, uptight.
– OPPOSITES calm.

edit verb REVISE, correct, emend, polish, check, modify, rewrite, rephrase, prepare, adapt, amend, alter.

edition noun ❶ ISSUE, number, version, printing. ❷ PRINTING, impression, publication, issue.

educate verb TEACH, instruct, tutor, coach, school, train, drill, inform, enlighten, inculcate, prime, indoctrinate, edify, cultivate, develop, improve, prepare, rear, nurture, foster.

educated adjective LITERATE, well read, informed, knowledgeable, learned, enlightened, erudite, cultivated, refined, cultured, schooled.
– OPPOSITES illiterate, ignorant.

education noun ❶ TEACHING, schooling, instruction, tuition, training, tutelage, enlightenment, edification, cultivation, development, improvement, preparation, indoctrination, drilling. ❷ a man of education: LITERACY, knowledge, scholarship, letters, cultivation, refinement, culture.

eerie adjective UNCANNY, unearthly, ghostly, mysterious, strange, weird, unnatural, frightening, chilling, fearful, spine-chilling, blood-curdling, spectral; *informal* spooky, scary, creepy.

effect noun ❶ RESULT, outcome, consequence, upshot, repercussion, impact, aftermath, conclusion, issue, fruit. ❷ to great effect: EFFECTIVENESS, success, influence, efficacy, weight, power. ❸ words to that effect: SENSE, meaning, drift, essence, tenor, significance, import, purport.
▶ verb BRING ABOUT, carry out, execute, initiate, cause, make, create, produce, perform, achieve, accomplish, complete, fulfil, implement, actuate.

effective adjective ❶ SUCCESSFUL, competent, productive, capable, able, efficient, useful, efficacious, adequate, active. ❷ effective from today: VALID, in force, in operation, operative, active, effectual. ❸ effective arguments: FORCEFUL, powerful, telling, cogent, compelling, persuasive, convincing, moving.
– OPPOSITES ineffective.

effeminate adjective WOMANISH, unmanly, girlish, effete, weak, camp; *informal* wimpish, sissy, pansy-like.
– OPPOSITES manly, virile.

effervesce verb FIZZ, bubble, foam, froth, sparkle, ferment.

effervescent adjective ❶ BUBBLY, fizzy, frothy, foamy, sparkling, carbonated. ❷ VIVACIOUS, lively, animated, exuberant, buoyant, ebullient, sparkling, merry, irrepressible.
– OPPOSITES flat.

efficient adjective WELL ORGANIZED, organized, capable, competent, effective, productive, proficient, adept, skilful, businesslike, workmanlike.
– OPPOSITES inefficient.

effigy noun IMAGE, likeness, statue, bust, model, dummy, representation, carving.

effort noun ❶ EXERTION, force, power, energy, work, application, muscle, labour, striving, endeavour, toil, struggle, strain, stress; *informal* elbow grease. ❷ his last effort: ATTEMPT, try, endeavour; *informal* go, shot, crack, stab. ❸ his artistic efforts: ACHIEVEMENT, accomplishment, attainment, creation, result, production, feat, deed, opus.

effrontery noun IMPERTINENCE, insolence, impudence, cheek, audacity, temerity, presumption, gall, rashness, bumptiousness; *informal* nerve, neck, brass neck.

effusive adjective GUSHING, unrestrained, extravagant, fulsome, lavish, enthusiastic, expansive, profuse, demonstrative, exuberant, verbose, wordy, long-winded; *informal* over the top, OTT.

egg
■ **egg on** ENCOURAGE, urge, push, drive, goad, spur on, prod, exhort, prompt.

egotistic, egotistical adjective EGOCENTRIC, self-absorbed, egoistic, narcissistic, conceited, vain, proud, arrogant, self-important, boastful, superior, bragging, self-admiring.

egregious adjective GLARING, flagrant, blatant, gross, outrageous, monstrous, rank, shocking, scandalous, appalling, heinous, intolerable, infamous, notorious, arrant.

eject verb ❶ EMIT, discharge, expel, cast out, exude, excrete, spew out, disgorge, spout, vomit, ejaculate. ❷ EVICT, expel, turn out, put out, remove, oust, banish, deport, exile; *informal* kick out, chuck out, turf out, boot out.

elaborate adjective ❶ elaborate plans: COMPLICATED, detailed, complex, involved, intricate, studied, painstaking, careful. ❷ elaborate patterns: COMPLEX, detailed, ornate, fancy, showy, fussy, ostentatious, extravagant, baroque, rococo.
– OPPOSITES simple.
■ **elaborate on** EXPAND ON, enlarge on, flesh out, amplify, add detail to, expatiate on.

elastic adjective STRETCHY, stretchable, flexible, springy, pliant, pliable, supple, yielding, rubbery, plastic, resilient.
– OPPOSITES rigid.

elderly adjective OLD, aging, aged, ancient, superannuated, long in the tooth, past one's prime; *Biology* senescent; *informal* getting on, over the hill.
– OPPOSITES young, youthful.

elect verb VOTE FOR, cast one's vote for, choose by ballot, choose, pick, select, appoint, opt for, plump for, decide on, designate.

election noun BALLOT, poll, vote, referendum, plebiscite, general election.

electric adjective ❶ ELECTRICALLY OPERATED, battery-operated; *Brit.* mains-powered. ❷ an electric moment: EXCITING, charged, tense, thrilling, stirring, galvanizing, stimulating, jolting.

electrify verb THRILL, excite, startle, arouse, rouse, stimulate, move, stir, animate, fire, charge, invigorate, galvanize.

elegant adjective STYLISH, graceful, tasteful, artistic, fashionable, cultured, beautiful, lovely, charming, exquisite, polished, cultivated, refined, suave, debonair, modish, dignified, luxurious, sumptuous, opulent.
– OPPOSITES inelegant.

elegiac adjective FUNEREAL, doleful, mournful, dirge-like, melancholic, plaintive, keening, sad, valedictory.

element noun ❶ PART, piece, ingredient, factor, feature, component, constituent, segment, unit, member, subdivision, trace, detail, module. ❷ in his natural element: ENVIRONMENT, habitat, medium, milieu, sphere, field, domain, realm, circle, resort, haunt.

elementary adjective ❶ BASIC, introductory, preparatory, fundamental, rudimentary, primary. ❷ EASY, simple, straightforward, uncomplicated, facile, simplistic.
– OPPOSITES advanced, difficult.

elevate verb ❶ RAISE, lift, hoist, hike. ❷ PROMOTE, upgrade, advance, prefer, exalt, aggrandize.
– OPPOSITES lower, demote.

elevated adjective ❶ RAISED, upraised, lifted up, aloft, high up. ❷ *his elevated position*: HIGH, great, grand, lofty, dignified, noble, exalted, magnificent, inflated. ❸ *elevated style*: LOFTY, exalted, inflated, pompous, bombastic, orotund, fustian.

elf noun FAIRY, pixie, sprite, goblin, hobgoblin, imp, puck, troll.

elicit verb BRING OUT, draw out, obtain, extract, extort, exact, wrest, evoke, derive, educe, call forth.

eligible adjective SUITABLE, fitting, fit, appropriate, proper, acceptable, qualified, worthy, authorized, competent, allowed.
– OPPOSITES ineligible.

elite noun ❶ THE BEST, the pick, the cream, the elect. ❷ ARISTOCRACY, nobility, gentry, high society, beau monde; *informal* beautiful people, jet set.

eloquent adjective ARTICULATE, expressive, well spoken, fluent, silver-tongued, smooth-tongued, well expressed, vivid, graphic, pithy, persuasive, glib, forceful, effective, plausible.
– OPPOSITES inarticulate, tongue-tied.

elude verb AVOID, dodge, evade, lose, escape, duck, flee, circumvent; *informal* shake off, give the slip to, throw off the scent, slip away from.

elusive adjective ❶ *an elusive person*: DIFFICULT TO FIND/CATCH, slippery, evasive; *informal* shifty, cagey. ❷ *an elusive answer*: EVASIVE, ambiguous, misleading, equivocal, deceptive, baffling, puzzling, fraudulent.

emaciated adjective THIN, skinny, wasted, skeletal, gaunt, anorexic, starved, scrawny, cadaverous, shrunken, haggard, withered, shrivelled, drawn, pinched, wizened, attenuated, atrophied.
– OPPOSITES fat.

emancipate verb FREE, set free, liberate, release, let loose, deliver, unchain, discharge, unfetter, unshackle, unyoke; *historical* manumit.

emasculate verb WEAKEN, enfeeble, debilitate, erode, undermine, cripple, pull the teeth of; *informal* water down.

embargo noun BAN, bar, prohibition, stoppage, proscription, restriction, restraint, blockage, check, barrier, obstruction, impediment, hindrance.

embarrass verb MAKE UNCOMFORTABLE/AWKWARD, make self-conscious, upset, disconcert, discomfit, discompose, confuse, fluster, agitate, distress, chagrin, shame, humiliate, abash, mortify, discountenance, nonplus; *informal* show up, put one on the spot.

embed verb INSERT, drive in, hammer in, ram in, sink, implant, plant, set/fix in, root.

embellish verb DECORATE, adorn, ornament, dress up, beautify, festoon, enhance, garnish, trim, gild, varnish, embroider, deck, bedeck, emblazon, bespangle; *informal* tart up.

embezzle verb STEAL, rob, thieve, pilfer, misappropriate, pocket, appropriate, purloin, abstract; *informal* filch, put one's hand in the till, rip off; *formal* peculate.

embitter verb MAKE RESENTFUL, make bitter, sour, anger,

disillusion, disaffect, poison, envenom.

emblazon verb DECORATE, adorn, ornament, embellish, illuminate, colour, paint.

emblem noun CREST, insignia, badge, symbol, sign, device, representation, token, image, figure, mark.

embody verb ❶ PERSONIFY, represent, symbolize, stand for, typify, exemplify, incarnate, manifest, incorporate, realize, reify. ❷ INCORPORATE, combine, bring together, comprise, include, collect, contain, integrate, constitute, consolidate, encompass, assimilate, systematize.

embrace verb ❶ TAKE/HOLD IN ONE'S ARMS, hold, hug, cuddle, clasp, squeeze, clutch, seize, grab, enfold, enclasp, encircle; *informal* canoodle with, neck with. ❷ **embrace the suggestion:** WELCOME, accept, take up, adopt, espouse.

emend verb ALTER, change, edit, correct, revise, rewrite, improve, polish, refine, expurgate, censor, bowdlerize, redact.

emerge verb ❶ COME OUT, come into view, appear, become visible, surface, crop up, spring up, materialize, arise, proceed, issue, come forth, emanate. ❷ BECOME KNOWN, come out, come to light, become apparent, transpire, come to the fore.

emergency noun CRISIS, difficulty, predicament, danger, accident, quandary, plight, dilemma, crunch, extremity, exigency; *informal* pickle.

eminence noun IMPORTANCE, greatness, prestige, reputation, fame, distinction, renown, pre-eminence, prominence, illustriousness, rank, standing, note, station, celebrity.

eminent adjective IMPORTANT, great, distinguished, well known, celebrated, famous, renowned, noted, prominent, esteemed, noteworthy, pre-eminent, outstanding, superior, high-ranking, exalted, revered, elevated, august, paramount.
– OPPOSITES unimportant.

emit verb DISCHARGE, give out/off, throw out, issue, disgorge, vent, vomit, send forth, eject, spew out, emanate, radiate, ejaculate, exude, ooze, leak, excrete.

emolument noun PAY, wages, salary, earnings, income, fee, reward, stipend, revenue, compensation, recompense, honorarium, profits, proceeds, gain.

emotional adjective ❶ PASSIONATE, demonstrative, feeling, hot-blooded, warm, responsive, tender, loving, sentimental, ardent, fervent, sensitive, excitable, temperamental, melodramatic. ❷ **an emotional farewell:** MOVING, touching, affecting, poignant, emotive, tear-jerking, pathetic, heart-rending, soul-stirring, impassioned.
– OPPOSITES unfeeling.

emotive adjective SENSITIVE, delicate, controversial, touchy, awkward.

emphasis noun ❶ STRESS, attention, importance, priority, weight, significance, prominence, urgency, force, insistence, accentuation, pre-eminence, import, mark. ❷ STRESS, accent, accentuation, weight.

emphasize verb LAY/PUT STRESS ON, stress, accent, dwell on, focus on, underline, accentuate, call attention to, highlight, give prominence to, point up, spotlight, insist on, play up, feature, intensify, strengthen, heighten, deepen, underscore.
– OPPOSITES understate, minimize.

emphatic adjective ❶ an emphatic denial: FORCEFUL, forcible, categorical, unequivocal, definite, decided, certain, determined, absolute, direct, earnest, energetic, vigorous. ❷ emphatic change: MARKED, pronounced, decided, positive, definite, distinctive, unmistakable, important, significant, striking, strong, powerful, resounding, telling, momentous.
– OPPOSITES hesitant.

empirical adjective PRACTICAL, observed, seen, pragmatic, experimental, experiential, heuristic.

employ verb ❶ HIRE, engage, take on, sign up, put on the payroll, enrol, apprentice, commission, enlist, retain, indenture. ❷ USE, make use of, utilize, apply, exercise, bring to bear, ply.

employed adjective ❶ WORKING, in work, in employment, in a job. ❷ OCCUPIED, busy, engaged, preoccupied.
– OPPOSITES unemployed, unoccupied.

employee noun WORKER, member of staff, hand, hired hand, hireling, labourer, assistant.

employer noun MANAGER, owner, proprietor, patron, contractor, director; *Brit. informal* gaffer, governor.

empower verb ❶ AUTHORIZE, license, certify, accredit, qualify, sanction, warrant, commission, delegate. ❷ ALLOW, enable, give strength to, equip.

empty adjective ❶ UNFILLED, vacant, unoccupied, hollow, void, uninhabited, bare, desolate, unadorned, barren, blank, clear. ❷ empty gestures: MEANINGLESS, futile, ineffective, ineffectual, useless, worthless, insubstantial, fruitless, idle. ❸ an empty life: PURPOSELESS, aimless, hollow, barren, senseless, unsatisfactory, banal, inane, frivolous, trivial, worthless, valueless, profitless. ❸ an empty expression: BLANK, expressionless, vacant, deadpan, vacuous, absent.
– OPPOSITES full.
► verb VACATE, clear, evacuate, unload, unburden, void, deplete, sap.

enable verb ALLOW, permit, make possible, give the means to, equip, empower, facilitate, prepare, entitle, authorize, sanction, fit, license, warrant, validate, accredit, delegate, legalize.
– OPPOSITES prevent.

enchant verb BEWITCH, hold spellbound, fascinate, charm, captivate, entrance, beguile, enthral, hypnotize, mesmerize, enrapture, delight, enamour.

enchanting adjective BEWITCHING, charming, delightful, attractive, appealing, captivating, irresistible, fascinating, engaging, endearing, entrancing, alluring, winsome, ravishing.

enclose verb ❶ SURROUND, circle, hem in, ring, shut in, hedge in, wall in, confine, encompass, encircle, circumscribe, encase, gird. ❷ enclose a cheque: INCLUDE, send with, put in, insert, enfold.

enclosure noun COMPOUND, yard, pen, pound, ring, fold, paddock, stockade, corral, run, sty, cloister, close, kraal.

encompass verb INCLUDE, cover, embrace, contain, comprise, take in, incorporate, envelop, embody.

encounter verb ❶ MEET, run into/across, come upon, stumble across, chance upon, happen upon; *informal* bump into. ❷ encounter problems: BE FACED WITH, contend with, confront, tussle with.
▶ noun an encounter with the enemy: FIGHT, battle, clash, conflict, confrontation, engagement, skirmish, scuffle, tussle, brawl; *informal* run-in, set-to, brush.

encourage verb ❶ encourage the losers: CHEER, rally, stimulate, motivate, inspire, stir, incite, hearten, animate, invigorate, embolden; *informal* buck up. ❷ encourage him to go: URGE, persuade, prompt, influence, exhort, spur, goad, egg on. ❸ encourage exports: PROMOTE, advance, foster, help, assist, support, aid, advocate, back, boost, abet, forward, strengthen.
– OPPOSITES discourage.

encroach verb TRESPASS, intrude, invade, infringe, infiltrate, overrun, impinge, usurp, appropriate; *informal* tread on someone's toes, muscle in on, invade someone's space.

encumber verb INCONVENIENCE, constrain, handicap, hinder, impede, obstruct, retard, check, restrain.

encyclopedic adjective COMPREHENSIVE, complete, wide-ranging, all-inclusive, exhaustive, all-embracing, thorough, universal, all-encompassing, compendious, vast.

end noun ❶ the end of the affair: ENDING, finish, close, conclusion, cessation, termination, completion, resolution, climax, finale, culmination, denouement, epilogue, expiry; *informal* wind-up, pay-off. ❷ the north end: EDGE, border, boundary, limit, extremity, margin, point, tip, extent. ❸ a cigarette end: REMAINDER, remnant, fragment, vestige, leftover. ❹ achieve her end: AIM, goal, purpose, intention, objective, design, motive, aspiration, intent, object. ❺ the marketing end of the business: SIDE, section, area, field, part, share, portion, segment, province, responsibility, burden, load. ❻ a peaceful end: DEATH, demise, extinction, doom, annihilation, extermination, ruin, ruination, destruction, dissolution.
– OPPOSITES beginning, start.
▶ verb ❶ the show ended: COME TO AN END, finish, stop, close, cease, conclude, terminate, discontinue, break off, fade away, peter out; *informal* wind up. ❷ end the relationship: BRING TO AN END, finish, stop, cease, conclude, close, terminate, break off, complete, dissolve, resolve. ❸ ended his life: PUT AN END TO, destroy, extinguish, annihilate.
– OPPOSITES begin, start.

endanger verb THREATEN, put at risk, put in danger, jeopardize,

imperil, risk, expose, hazard, compromise.
– OPPOSITES protect.

endearing adjective CHARMING, adorable, lovable, attractive, engaging, disarming, appealing, winning, sweet, captivating, enchanting, winsome.

endearment noun ❶ SWEET TALK, sweet nothings, soft words, blandishments. ❷ AFFECTION, love, fondness, liking, attachment.

endeavour verb TRY, attempt, strive, venture, aspire, undertake, struggle, labour, essay; *informal* work at, have a go/stab at.

endless adjective ❶ endless patience: UNENDING, unlimited, infinite, limitless, boundless, continual, perpetual, constant, everlasting, unceasing, unfading, interminable, incessant, measureless, untold, incalculable. ❷ an endless chain: CONTINUOUS, unbroken, uninterrupted, never-ending, whole, entire. ❸ endless talk: NON-STOP, interminable, overlong, unremitting, monotonous, boring.
– OPPOSITES finite, limited.

endorse verb ❶ endorse the cheque: SIGN, countersign, validate, autograph, superscribe, underwrite. ❷ endorse his choice: APPROVE, support, back, favour, recommend, advocate, champion, subscribe to, uphold, authorize, sanction, ratify, affirm, warrant, confirm, vouch for, corroborate.

endow verb PROVIDE, give, present, confer, bestow, gift, enrich, supply, furnish, award, invest; *poetic/literary* endue.

endurance noun ❶ STAMINA, staying power, perseverance, tenacity, fortitude, durability, continuance, longevity. ❷ beyond endurance: TOLERATION, sufferance, forbearance, acceptance, patience, resignation.

endure verb ❶ LAST, continue, persist, remain, live on, hold on, survive, abide; *archaic* bide, tarry. ❷ STAND, bear, put up with, tolerate, suffer, abide, submit to, countenance, stomach, swallow; *Brit. informal* stick; *formal* brook.
– OPPOSITES fade.

enemy noun ADVERSARY, opponent, foe, rival, antagonist, competitor.
– OPPOSITES friend.

energetic adjective ❶ energetic exercises/person: ACTIVE, lively, vigorous, strenuous, dynamic, brisk, spirited, animated, vibrant, sprightly, vital, tireless, indefatigable; *informal* zippy, peppy, bright-eyed and bushy-tailed. ❷ an energetic approach: FORCEFUL, forcible, determined, aggressive, emphatic, driving, powerful, effective, potent.
– OPPOSITES lethargic.

energy noun VIGOUR, strength, stamina, power, forcefulness, drive, push, exertion, enthusiasm, life, animation, liveliness, vivacity, vitality, spirit, spiritedness, fire, zest, exuberance, buoyancy, verve, dash, sparkle, effervescence, brio, ardour, zeal, passion, might, potency, effectiveness, efficiency, efficacy, cogency; *informal* vim, zip, zing.

enfold verb ENCLOSE, fold, envelop, encircle, swathe, shroud, swaddle.

enforce verb ❶ enforce the law: APPLY, carry out, administer, implement, bring to bear, impose, prosecute, execute, discharge, fulfil. ❷ enforce silence: FORCE, compel, insist on, require, coerce, necessitate, urge, exact.

engage verb ❶ engage a servant: EMPLOY, hire, take on, appoint, enlist, enrol, commission. ❷ engage someone's interest: OCCUPY, absorb, hold, engross, grip, secure, preoccupy, fill. ❸ engage in a project: TAKE PART, enter into, become involved in, undertake, embark on, set about, join in, participate in, tackle, launch into. ❹ engage gear: FIT TOGETHER, join together, mesh, intermesh, interconnect.
– OPPOSITES dismiss.

engender verb CAUSE, produce, create, bring about, give rise to, lead to, arouse, rouse, provoke, excite, incite, induce, generate, instigate, effect, hatch, occasion, foment; *formal* effectuate.

engine noun MOTOR, mechanism, machine, power source, generator.

engineer verb BRING ABOUT, cause, plan, plot, contrive, devise, orchestrate, mastermind, originate, manage, control, superintend, direct, conduct, handle, concoct.

engrave verb INSCRIBE, etch, carve, cut, chisel, imprint, impress, mark.

enhance verb ADD TO, increase, heighten, stress, emphasize, strengthen, improve, augment, boost, intensify, reinforce, magnify, amplify, enrich, complement.

enjoy verb ❶ TAKE PLEASURE IN, delight in, appreciate, like, love, rejoice in, relish, revel in, savour, lap up, luxuriate in; *informal* fancy. ❷ enjoy good health: HAVE, possess, benefit from, own, have the advantage of, be blessed with.
– OPPOSITES dislike.
■ **enjoy oneself** HAVE FUN, have a good time, make merry, celebrate, party, have the time of one's life; *informal* have a ball, let one's hair down.

enjoyable adjective ENTERTAINING, amusing, delightful, diverting, satisfying, gratifying, pleasant, lovely, agreeable, pleasurable, fine, good, great, nice.
– OPPOSITES boring, disagreeable.

enlarge verb MAKE BIGGER/LARGER, expand, extend, add to, augment, amplify, supplement, magnify, multiply, widen, broaden, lengthen, elongate, deepen, thicken, distend, dilate, swell, inflate.

enlighten verb INFORM, make aware, advise, instruct, teach, educate, tutor, illuminate, apprise, counsel, edify, civilize, cultivate.

enlist verb ❶ enlist soldiers/help: ENROL, sign up, conscript, recruit, hire, employ, take on, engage, muster, obtain, secure. ❷ enlist in the army: JOIN, join up, enrol in, sign up for, enter into, volunteer for.

enliven verb BRIGHTEN UP, cheer up, perk up, hearten, gladden, excite, stimulate, exhilarate, invigorate, revitalize, buoy up, give a boost to, wake up, rouse, refresh; *informal* jazz up, ginger up, light a fire under.

enormous adjective HUGE, immense, massive, vast, gigantic, colossal, mammoth, astronomic, gargantuan, mountainous, prodigious, tremendous, stupendous, titanic, excessive, Herculean, Brobdingnagian; *informal* jumbo.
– OPPOSITES tiny.

enough adjective SUFFICIENT, adequate, ample, abundant.
– OPPOSITES insufficient, inadequate.

enquire verb *see* INQUIRE.

enrage verb MADDEN, infuriate, incense, exasperate, provoke, annoy, irritate, inflame, incite, irk, agitate; *informal* make someone's hackles rise, make someone's blood boil, get someone's back up; *Brit. informal* wind up.
– OPPOSITES placate.

enrapture verb DELIGHT, thrill, captivate, charm, fascinate, enchant, beguile, bewitch, entrance, enthral, transport, ravish; *informal* blow someone's mind, turn on.

ensue verb FOLLOW, come next/after, result, occur, happen, turn up, arise, transpire, proceed, succeed, issue, derive, stem, supervene; *poetic/literary* come to pass, befall.

ensure verb MAKE CERTAIN, make sure, guarantee, confirm, certify, secure, effect, warrant.

entail verb INVOLVE, require, call for, necessitate, demand, impose, cause, bring about, produce, result in, lead to, give rise to, occasion.

enter verb ❶ COME/GO INTO, pass/move into, invade, infiltrate, penetrate, pierce, puncture. ❷ **enter into negotiations**: BEGIN, start, commence, embark on, engage in, undertake, venture on. ❸ **entered the competition**: TAKE PART IN, participate in, go in for, gain entrance/admittance to. ❹ **enter a protest**: SUBMIT, put forward, present, proffer, register, tender. ❺ **enter your date of birth**: RECORD, register, put down, note, mark down, document, list, file, log.

enterprise noun ❶ VENTURE, undertaking, project, operation, endeavour, task, effort, plan, scheme, campaign. ❷ RESOURCEFULNESS, initiative, drive, push, enthusiasm, zest, energy, vitality, boldness, audacity, courage, imagination, spirit, spiritedness, vigour; *informal* get-up-and-go, vim, oomph. ❸ BUSINESS, firm, industry, concern, operation, corporation, establishment, house.

enterprising adjective RESOURCEFUL, entrepreneurial, energetic, determined, ambitious, purposeful, pushy, adventurous, audacious, bold, daring, active, vigorous, imaginative, spirited, enthusiastic, eager, keen, zealous, vital, courageous, intrepid; *informal* go-ahead, up-and-coming, peppy.

entertain verb ❶ AMUSE, divert, delight, please, charm, cheer, interest, beguile, engage, occupy. ❷ **entertain at home**: PLAY HOST/HOSTESS, receive guests, provide hospitality, have people round, have company, keep open house, hold/throw a party. ❸ **entertain the proposal**: CONSIDER, give consideration to, take into consideration, give some thought to, think about/over, contemplate, weigh up, ponder, muse over, bear in mind.

entertainment noun ❶ AMUSEMENT, fun, enjoyment, recreation, diversion, distraction, pastime, hobby, sport. ❷ SHOW, performance, concert, play, presentation, spectacle, pageant.

enthralling adjective CAPTIVATING, enchanting, spellbinding, fascinating, bewitching, gripping, riveting, charming, delightful, intriguing, mesmerizing, hypnotic.

enthusiasm noun ❶ EAGERNESS, keenness, fervour, ardour, passion, zeal, warmth, vehemence, zest, fire, excitement, exuberance, ebullience, avidity, wholeheartedness, commitment, devotion, fanaticism, earnestness. ❷ HOBBY, pastime, interest, recreation, passion, fad, craze, mania.
– OPPOSITES apathy.

enthusiast noun SUPPORTER, follower, fan, devotee, lover, admirer, fanatic, zealot, aficionado; *informal* buff, freak.

enthusiastic adjective EAGER, keen, fervent, ardent, passionate, warm, zealous, vehement, excited, spirited, exuberant, ebullient, avid, wholehearted, hearty, committed, devoted, fanatical, earnest; *informal* mad about.
– OPPOSITES apathetic, indifferent.

entice verb TEMPT, lure, seduce, inveigle, lead on/astray, beguile, coax, wheedle, cajole, decoy, bait.

entire adjective ❶ his entire life: WHOLE, complete, total, full, continuous, unbroken. ❷ remain entire: INTACT, undamaged, unbroken, sound, unmarked, perfect, unimpaired, unblemished, unspoiled.
– OPPOSITES partial.

entirely adverb COMPLETELY, absolutely, totally, fully, wholly, altogether, utterly, in every respect, without exception, thoroughly, perfectly.

entitle verb ❶ GIVE THE RIGHT TO, make eligible, qualify, authorize, allow, sanction, permit, enable, empower, warrant, enfranchise, accredit. ❷ CALL, name, term, style, dub, designate.

entity noun BEING, body, person, creature, individual, organism, object, thing, article, substance, quantity, existence.

entourage noun RETINUE, escort, cortège, train, suite, bodyguard, attendants, companions, followers, associates; *informal* groupies.

entrails plural noun INTESTINES, internal organs, bowels, vital organs, viscera; *informal* guts, insides, innards.

entrance noun ❶ WAY IN, entry, means of entry/access, access, door, doorway, gate, gateway, drive, driveway, foyer, lobby, porch, threshold, portal. ❷ ENTRY, coming in, appearance, arrival, introduction, ingress. ❸ ENTRY, admission, permission to enter, right of entry, access, ingress.
– OPPOSITES exit, departure.

entrant noun ❶ NEWCOMER, beginner, new arrival, probationer, trainee, novice, tyro, initiate, neophyte; *informal* cub, rookie; *N. Amer. informal* greenhorn. ❷ CONTESTANT, competitor, participant, player, candidate, applicant, rival, opponent.

entreat verb BEG, implore, plead with, appeal to, petition, solicit, pray, crave, exhort, enjoin, importune, supplicate; *poetic/literary* beseech.

entrenched adjective DEEP-SEATED, deep-rooted, rooted, well established, fixed, set, firm, ingrained, unshakeable, immovable, indelible, dyed in the wool.

envelop verb ENFOLD, cover, wrap, swathe, swaddle, cloak, blanket, surround, engulf, encircle, encompass, conceal, hide, obscure.

envelope noun WRAPPER, wrapping, cover, covering, case, casing, jacket, shell, sheath, skin, capsule, holder, container.

enviable adjective EXCITING ENVY, desirable, covetable, worth having, tempting, excellent, fortunate, lucky, favourable.

envious adjective JEALOUS, covetous, desirous, green-eyed, green, grudging, begrudging, resentful, bitter, jaundiced; *informal* green with envy.

environment noun SURROUNDINGS, habitat, territory, domain, medium, element, milieu, situation, location, scene, locale, background, conditions, circumstances, setting, context, atmosphere, ambience, mood.

envisage verb PREDICT, foresee, imagine, visualize, picture, anticipate, envision, contemplate, conceive of, think of, dream of.

envy noun ENVIOUSNESS, jealousy, covetousness, desire, cupidity, longing, resentment, bitterness, resentfulness, discontent, spite, dissatisfaction.
▶ verb BE ENVIOUS OF, be jealous of, covet, be covetous of, begrudge, grudge, resent.

ephemeral adjective FLEETING, short-lived, transitory, transient, momentary, brief, short, temporary, passing, impermanent, evanescent, fugitive.
– OPPOSITES permanent.

epidemic noun OUTBREAK, pandemic, plague, scourge, upsurge, wave, upswing, upturn, increase, growth, rise, mushrooming.
▶ adjective RIFE, rampant, widespread, extensive, wide-ranging, prevalent, sweeping, predominant.

episode noun ❶ PART, instalment, chapter, section, passage, scene. ❷ INCIDENT, occurrence, event, happening, experience, adventure, matter, occasion, affair, business, circumstance, interlude.

epitome noun PERSONIFICATION, embodiment, essence, quintessence, archetype, representation, model, typification, example, exemplar, prototype.

epoch noun ERA, age, period, time, date.

equal adjective ❶ equal height: IDENTICAL, alike, like, comparable, commensurate, equivalent, the same as, on a par with. ❷ an equal contest: EVEN, evenly matched, balanced, level, evenly proportioned; *Brit.* level pegging; *informal* fifty-fifty, neck and neck. ❸ equal to the task: CAPABLE OF, up to, fit for, good enough for,

adequate for, sufficient for, suited, ready for.
▶ noun EQUIVALENT, match, parallel, peer, twin, alter ego, counterpart.
▶ verb ❶ *equal him in strength*: BE EQUAL/LEVEL WITH, be equivalent to, match, measure up to, equate with, vie with, rival, emulate.
❷ *equal the record*: MATCH, reach, achieve, parallel, come up to, measure up to.

equality noun ❶ SAMENESS, identity, parity, likeness, similarity, uniformity, evenness, levelness, balance, correspondence, comparability.
❷ FAIRNESS, justice, justness, impartiality, egalitarianism, even-handedness.
– OPPOSITES inequality.

equanimity noun COMPOSURE, presence of mind, self-control, self-possession, level-headedness, equilibrium, poise, aplomb, sangfroid, calmness, calm, coolness, serenity, placidity, tranquillity, phlegm, imperturbability, unflappability.
– OPPOSITES anxiety.

equilibrium noun ❶ BALANCE, stability, steadiness, evenness, symmetry, equipoise, counterpoise. ❷ *See* EQUANIMITY.

equip verb FIT OUT, rig out, provide, supply, furnish, prepare, stock, arm, attire, array, dress, outfit, accoutre, endow; *informal* kit out.

equitable adjective FAIR, fair-minded, just, even-handed, right, rightful, proper, reasonable, honest, impartial, unbiased, unprejudiced, open-minded, non-discriminatory, disinterested, dispassionate.
– OPPOSITES inequitable, unfair.

equivalent adjective EQUAL, identical, similar, the same, alike, like, comparable, corresponding, commensurate, matching, interchangeable, on a par, tantamount, synonymous, homologous.
– OPPOSITES different, dissimilar.

equivocal adjective AMBIGUOUS, ambivalent, vague, unclear, obscure, roundabout, non-committal, hazy, oblique, evasive, misleading, duplicitous, indeterminate, uncertain.
– OPPOSITES unequivocal.

equivocate verb EVADE THE QUESTION, parry questions, vacillate, quibble, fence, hedge, prevaricate, pussyfoot around, beat about the bush; *Brit.* hum and haw; *N. Amer. informal* waffle.

era noun AGE, epoch, period, time, eon, generation, stage, cycle, season.

eradicate verb REMOVE, get rid of, wipe out, eliminate, do away with, extirpate, abolish, annihilate, stamp out, obliterate, extinguish, excise, expunge, destroy, kill.

erase verb DELETE, rub out, wipe out, remove, cross out, strike out, blot out, efface, expunge, obliterate, cancel.

erect adjective ❶ UPRIGHT, straight, vertical. ❷ RIGID, stiff, hard, firm.
▶ verb BUILD, construct, put up, assemble, put together, raise, elevate, mount.

erode verb WEAR AWAY, wear, eat away at, corrode, abrade, gnaw away at, grind down, consume, devour, spoil, disintegrate, destroy, excoriate.

erotic adjective AROUSING, stimulating, aphrodisiac,

exciting, titillating, seductive, sensual, sexy, carnal, salacious, suggestive, pornographic; *informal* steamy.

err verb BE WRONG, be incorrect, make a mistake, be mistaken, blunder, misjudge, miscalculate, misunderstand, misconstrue, get it wrong, be wide of the mark; *informal* be barking up the wrong tree, slip up; *Brit. informal* boob.

errand noun TASK, job, commission, chore, assignment, undertaking, message, charge, mission.

erratic adjective ❶ **erratic behaviour**: INCONSISTENT, variable, irregular, unstable, unpredictable, unreliable, capricious, whimsical, fitful, wayward, abnormal, eccentric, aberrant, deviant. ❷ **an erratic course**: WANDERING, meandering, wavering, directionless, haphazard.
– OPPOSITES consistent.

error noun ❶ MISTAKE, inaccuracy, miscalculation, blunder, fault, flaw, oversight, misprint, erratum, misinterpretation, misreading, fallacy, misconception, delusion; *Brit.* literal; *informal* slip-up, boo-boo, howler, typo; *Brit. informal* boob; *Brit. informal, dated* bloomer. ❷ **the error of his ways**: WRONGNESS, misconduct, misbehaviour, lawlessness, criminality, delinquency, sinfulness, evil.

erupt verb ❶ EJECT, gush, pour forth, spew, vent, boil over, vomit. ❷ **violence erupted**: BREAK OUT, flare up, blow up, explode.

escalate verb GROW, increase, be stepped up, mushroom, intensify, heighten, accelerate, be extended, be magnified, be amplified.

escapade noun STUNT, prank, adventure, caper, romp, frolic, fling, spree, antics; *informal* lark, scrape, shenanigans.

escape verb ❶ GET AWAY, break out, run away, break free, flee, bolt, abscond, decamp, fly, steal away, slip away; *informal* skedaddle, vamoose, fly the coop; *Brit. informal* do a bunk, do a runner. ❷ **escape punishment**: AVOID, evade, dodge, elude, circumvent, sidestep, steer clear of, shirk; *informal* duck, bilk; *Brit. informal* skive (off). ❸ **gas escaping**: LEAK, seep, pour out, gush, spurt, issue, flow, discharge, emanate, drain.
▶ **noun** ❶ BREAKOUT, getaway, flight. ❷ AVOIDANCE, evasion, dodging, eluding, elusion, circumvention. ❸ LEAK, leakage, seepage, gush, spurt, issue, flow, discharge, outflow, emanation, efflux.

eschew verb AVOID, abstain from, give up, refrain from, forgo, shun, renounce, abjure, swear off.

escort noun ❶ ENTOURAGE, retinue, attendants, train, cortège, bodyguard, protector, convoy, defender, contingent. ❷ PARTNER, companion, gigolo, hostess, geisha; *informal* date; *dated* beau.
▶ **verb** ❶ ACCOMPANY, guide, conduct, lead, usher, shepherd, guard, protect, safeguard, defend. ❷ PARTNER, accompany, take out, go out with, attend on.

esoteric adjective ABSTRUSE, obscure, cryptic, arcane, recondite, abstract, mysterious, hidden, secret, mystic, magical, occult, cabbalistic.

essence noun ❶ FUNDAMENTAL NATURE, substance, crux, quintessence, heart, lifeblood, kernel, marrow, pith, reality, actuality; *Philosophy* quiddity. ❷ EXTRACT, concentrate, distillate, tincture, elixir, abstraction.

essential adjective ❶ NECESSARY, important, indispensable, vital, crucial, needed, requisite. ❷ the essential theme: BASIC, fundamental, chief, intrinsic, inherent, innate, elemental, characteristic, principal, cardinal. – OPPOSITES unimportant.

establish verb ❶ SET UP, found, institute, form, start, begin, bring about, create, inaugurate, organize, build, construct, install, plant. ❷ establish his guilt: PROVE, show to be true, show, demonstrate, confirm, attest to, certify, verify, evidence, substantiate, corroborate, validate, authenticate, ratify. – OPPOSITES disprove.

established adjective ACCEPTED, official, proven, settled, conventional, traditional, fixed, entrenched, inveterate, dyed in the wool.

establishment noun ❶ FORMATION, foundation, founding, setting up, creation, inception, inauguration, building, construction, organization, installation. ❷ RESIDENCE, house, household, home, estate; *formal* dwelling, abode, domicile. ❸ FIRM, business, company, shop, store, concern, office, factory, organization, enterprise, corporation, conglomerate.

estate noun ❶ PROPERTY, landholding, lands, manor, domain. ❷ AREA, piece of land, region, tract, development. ❸ ASSETS, resources, effects, possessions, belongings, wealth, fortune, property.

esteem verb RESPECT, admire, value, honour, look up to, think highly of, revere, venerate, appreciate, favour, approve of, like, love, cherish, prize, treasure.

estimate verb WORK OUT, calculate, assess, gauge, reckon, weigh up, evaluate, judge, appraise, guess, compute. ▶ noun ❶ ESTIMATION, valuation, costing, assessment, appraisal, evaluation. ❷ in my estimate: OPINION, estimation, judgement, consideration, thinking, mind, point of view, viewpoint, feeling, conviction, deduction, conclusion, guess, conjecture, surmise.

estimation noun *see* ESTIMATE noun (2).

estrangement noun ALIENATION, parting, separation, divorce, break-up, split, breach, severance, division, hostility, antagonism, antipathy, disaffection.

estuary noun INLET, river mouth, bay, cove, creek, arm of the sea; *Scottish* firth.

eternal adjective ENDLESS, everlasting, never-ending, without end, immortal, infinite, enduring, deathless, undying, permanent, indestructible, imperishable, immutable, ceaseless, incessant, constant, continuous, unchanging, unremitting, interminable, relentless, perpetual.

eternity noun IMMORTALITY, afterlife, everlasting life, the hereafter, the next world, heaven, paradise, nirvana.

ethical adjective MORAL, honourable, upright, righteous, good, virtuous, decent, principled, honest, just, fair, right, correct, proper, fitting, seemly, high-minded, decorous. – OPPOSITES unethical, immoral.

euphoric adjective ELATED, joyful, ecstatic, jubilant, enraptured, rapturous, blissful, exhilarated, gleeful, excited, high-spirited, exalted, buoyant, intoxicated, merry; *informal* on cloud nine, in seventh heaven, over the moon, on a high.

evacuate verb ❶ evacuate the town: LEAVE, abandon, vacate, move out of, pull out of, quit, withdraw from, retreat from, flee, depart from, go away from, retire from, decamp from, desert, forsake. ❷ evacuate waste matter: EXPEL, excrete, eject, discharge, eliminate, void, purge, drain.

evade verb ❶ AVOID, dodge, escape from, elude, circumvent, sidestep, shake off, keep out of the way of, keep one's distance from, steer clear of, shun, shirk; *informal* duck, give the slip to, chicken out of. ❷ evade the question: DODGE, avoid, parry, fend off, quibble about, fudge, not give a straight answer to; *informal* duck, cop out of.

evaluate verb ASSESS, put a price on, appraise, weigh up, size up, gauge, judge, rate, estimate, rank, calculate, reckon, measure, determine.

evaporate verb ❶ BECOME VAPOUR, vaporize, volatilize. ❷ DRY, dry up/out, dehydrate, desiccate, sear, parch. ❸ VANISH, fade, disappear, melt away, dissolve, dissipate.

evasive adjective EQUIVOCAL, equivocating, prevaricating, quibbling, indirect, roundabout, circuitous, oblique, cunning, artful, casuistic; *informal* cagey, waffling.

even adjective ❶ an even surface: FLAT, level, smooth, plane, uniform, flush, true. ❷ even breathing: CONSTANT, steady, uniform, consistent, stable, unvarying, unchanging, unwavering, regular, unfluctuating. ❸ even amounts: EQUAL, identical, the same, alike, like, similar, comparable, commensurate, parallel, on a par. ❹ scores are even: TIED, level, all square; *informal* neck and neck, nip and tuck, even-steven.
– OPPOSITES bumpy, uneven.
▶ adverb ❶ even colder: YET, still, more so, all the more, all the greater. ❷ couldn't even stand: AT ALL, so much as, hardly, barely, scarcely.
▶ verb ❶ even out the bumps: SMOOTH, level, flatten, make flush. ❷ even up the differences: EQUALIZE, make equal, make the same, balance up, standardize, regularize.

evening noun NIGHT, close of day, twilight, dusk, nightfall, sunset, sundown.

event noun ❶ OCCASION, affair, business, matter, occurrence, happening, episode, circumstance, fact, eventuality, experience, phenomenon. ❷ track events: COMPETITION, contest, fixture, engagement, game, tournament, round, bout, race. ❸ in the event he won: END, conclusion, outcome, result, upshot, consequence, effect, aftermath.

eventful adjective BUSY, action-packed, lively, full, active, important, noteworthy, memorable, notable, remarkable, outstanding, fateful, momentous, significant, crucial, historic, critical, decisive, consequential. – OPPOSITES uneventful, dull, insignificant.

eventual adjective FINAL, closing, concluding, end, last, ultimate, resulting, resultant, later, ensuing, consequent, subsequent.

eventually adverb IN THE END, ultimately, finally, at the end of the day, in the long run, when all is said and done, one day, some day, sooner or later, sometime.

everlasting adjective NEVER-ENDING, endless, without end, eternal, perpetual, undying, immortal, deathless, indestructible, abiding, enduring, infinite, boundless, timeless.

evermore adverb FOREVER, always, for all time, endlessly, without end, ceaselessly, unceasingly, constantly.

evict verb TURN OUT, throw out, eject, expel, remove, oust, dispossess, dislodge; *informal* throw out on the streets, throw someone out on their ear, chuck out, kick/turf out, give the heave-ho to, give the bum's rush to.

evidence noun ❶ PROOF, verification, confirmation, substantiation, corroboration, authentication, support, grounds. ❷ TESTIMONY, sworn statement, deposition, declaration, allegation, affidavit, attestation.

evident adjective OBVIOUS, clear, apparent, plain, unmistakable, noticeable, conspicuous, perceptible, visible, discernible, transparent, manifest, patent, tangible, palpable, indisputable, undoubted, incontrovertible, incontestable.

evil adjective ❶ evil deeds: WICKED, wrong, bad, immoral, sinful, corrupt, nefarious, vile, base, depraved, iniquitous, heinous, villainous, nefarious, sinister, reprobate, vicious, atrocious, malevolent, demonic, malicious, devilish, diabolic. ❷ evil influence: BAD, harmful, injurious, destructive, deleterious, pernicious, mischievous, malignant, venomous, noxious. ❸ evil times: UNFAVOURABLE, adverse, unfortunate, unhappy, disastrous, catastrophic, ruinous, calamitous, unpropitious, inauspicious, dire, woeful. – OPPOSITES good.

▶ noun ❶ WICKEDNESS, wrong, bad, wrongdoing, sin, sinfulness, immorality, vice, iniquity, vileness, baseness, corruption, depravity, villainy, malevolence, devilishness. ❷ the evils of war: HARM, hurt, pain, misery, sorrow, suffering, disaster, misfortune, catastrophe, ruin, calamity, affliction, woe. – OPPOSITES goodness.

evince verb SHOW, indicate, reveal, display, exhibit, make clear/plain, manifest, demonstrate, signify, evidence.

evoke verb BRING ABOUT, cause, produce, bring forth, induce, arouse, excite, awaken, give rise to, stir up, stimulate, kindle, elicit, educe, summon up, call forth, conjure up, invoke, raise.

evolution noun DEVELOPMENT, progress, growth, progression, unrolling, expansion, natural selection, Darwinism.

evolve verb DEVELOP, grow, progress, emerge, mature,

expand, unfold, unroll, open out, work out.

exacerbate verb AGGRAVATE, make worse, worsen, intensify; *informal* add fuel to the fire, put salt on the wound.

exact adjective ❶ an exact description: PRECISE, accurate, correct, faithful, close, true, unerring, literal, strict; *informal* on the nail; *Brit. informal* spot on, bang on; *formal* veracious. ❷ an exact person: PRECISE, careful, meticulous, painstaking, methodical, conscientious, punctilious, rigorous, scrupulous, exacting.
– OPPOSITES inaccurate, careless.
▶ verb REQUIRE, demand, extract, extort, insist on, request, compel, call for, command, impose, wring, wrest, squeeze.

exacting adjective *see* DIFFICULT (1).

exaggerate verb OVERSTATE, overemphasize, overstress, overestimate, overvalue, magnify, embellish, amplify, embroider, colour, add colour, over-elaborate, aggrandize, overdraw, hyperbolize; *informal* make a mountain out of a molehill, lay it on thick, lay it on with a trowel.
– OPPOSITES understate, minimize.

exalted adjective ❶ his exalted position: HIGH, high-ranking, lofty, grand, eminent, elevated, prestigious, august. ❷ an exalted mood: ELATED, exultant, jubilant, triumphant, joyful, rapturous, ecstatic, blissful, rhapsodic, transported.

examination noun ❶ STUDY, inspection, scrutiny, investigation, review, analysis, research, observation, exploration, consideration, appraisal. ❷ a physical examination: CHECK-UP, inspection, observation, assessment. ❸ the examination of witnesses: QUESTIONING, cross-examination, cross-questioning.

examine verb ❶ examine the facts: LOOK AT/INTO, study, investigate, inquire into, survey, analyse, review, research, explore, sift, probe, check out, consider, appraise, weigh, weigh up, scan, inspect, vet. ❷ examine a patient: INSPECT, look at, check over, assess, observe, give a check-up to, scrutinize. ❸ examine the witness: PUT QUESTIONS TO, question, interrogate, quiz, test, cross-examine, cross-question; *informal* give the third-degree to, grill, pump.

example noun ❶ SAMPLE, specimen, instance, representative, case, case in point, illustration. ❷ follow his example: MODEL, pattern, ideal, standard, paradigm, criterion.

exasperate verb ANGER, infuriate, annoy, irritate, madden, incense, enrage, provoke, irk, vex, gall, pique, try someone's patience; *informal* get on someone's nerves, make someone's blood boil, bug, needle, get to, rile.

excavate verb DIG, dig out, quarry, mine, burrow, hollow out, scoop out, gouge, cut out, unearth.

exceed verb BE GREATER THAN, surpass, beat, outdo, outstrip, outshine, transcend, go beyond, better, pass, top, cap, overshadow, eclipse.

exceedingly adverb EXTREMELY, very, extraordinarily, unusually, tremendously, enormously, vastly, greatly, highly, supremely, hugely, inordinately, superlatively.

excellence noun EMINENCE, merit, pre-eminence, distinction, greatness, fineness, quality, superiority, transcendence, supremacy, value, worth, skill.

excellent adjective VERY GOOD, first-rate, first-class, of a high standard, of high quality, great, fine, distinguished, superior, superb, outstanding, marvellous, eminent, pre-eminent, noted, notable, supreme, admirable, superlative, sterling, worthy, prime, select, model, exemplary, consummate, remarkable; *informal* A1, top-notch, ace, tip-top, super; *Brit. informal* smashing, brilliant, brill.
– OPPOSITES poor, inferior.

except preposition WITH THE EXCEPTION OF, excepting, excluding, besides, leaving out, barring, bar, other than, omitting, saving, save.

exception noun ❶ EXCLUSION, omission. ❷ SPECIAL CASE, anomaly, irregularity, peculiarity, oddity, deviation, departure, quirk, freak.
■ **take exception** OBJECT, be offended, take offence, resent, take umbrage, demur, disagree, cavil.

exceptional adjective ❶ UNUSUAL, uncommon, abnormal, out of the ordinary, atypical, rare, odd, anomalous, singular, peculiar, inconsistent, aberrant, deviant, divergent. ❷ exceptional ability: UNUSUALLY GOOD, excellent, extraordinary, remarkable, outstanding, special, phenomenal, prodigious.
– OPPOSITES normal, usual, average.

excerpt noun EXTRACT, quote, citation, quotation, passage, selection, highlight, part, section, fragment, piece, portion.

excess noun ❶ an excess of fat: SURPLUS, over-abundance, glut, surfeit, superfluity, plethora, superabundance, overkill. ❷ throw out the excess: REMAINDER, residue, leftovers, overflow, overload. ❸ a life of excess: IMMODERATION, lack of restraint, overindulgence, intemperance, debauchery, dissipation, dissolution.
– OPPOSITES shortage, moderation.
▶ adjective EXTRA, additional, too much, surplus, spare, superfluous, redundant.

excessive adjective TOO MUCH, immoderate, extravagant, lavish, superabundant, unreasonable, undue, uncalled for, extreme, inordinate, unjustifiable, unwarranted, unnecessary, needless, disproportionate, exorbitant, outrageous, intemperate, unconscionable.

exchange verb TRADE, swap, barter, interchange, reciprocate, bandy.
▶ noun TRADE, trade-off, barter, swapping, traffic, dealings, interchange, giving and taking, reciprocity.

excise verb ❶ CUT OUT/OFF, remove, eradicate, extirpate; *technical* resect. ❷ DELETE, remove, cut out, cross/strike out, erase, expunge, eliminate, blue-pencil, expurgate, bowdlerize.

excitable adjective TEMPERAMENTAL, emotional, highly strung, nervous, edgy, mercurial, volatile, tempestuous, hot-tempered, quick-tempered, hot-headed, passionate, fiery, irascible, testy, moody, choleric.
– OPPOSITES calm.

excite verb ❶ **excite someone:** STIMULATE, animate, rouse, arouse, move, thrill, inflame, provoke, stir up, electrify, intoxicate, titillate, discompose; *informal* turn on, get going, work up; *Brit. informal* wind up. ❷ **excite feelings:** BRING ABOUT, cause, rouse, arouse, awaken, incite, provoke, stimulate, kindle, evoke, stir up, elicit, engender, foment, instigate.

excited adjective AROUSED, animated, stimulated, thrilled, agitated, impassioned, hysterical, frenzied, delirious, enthusiastic, lively, exuberant, exhilarated, overwrought, feverish, wild; *informal* wound up, high, turned on.
– OPPOSITES calm, indifferent.

excitement noun ❶ ANIMATION, enthusiasm, passion, agitation, emotion, exhilaration, anticipation, elation, feverishness, ferment, tumult, discomposure, perturbation. ❷ THRILL, adventure, stimulation, pleasure; *informal* kick. ❸ **the excitement of feelings:** AROUSAL, stimulation, awakening, evocation, kindling.

exciting adjective THRILLING, exhilarating, stimulating, gripping, dramatic, stirring, intoxicating, rousing, electrifying, invigorating, spine-tingling, riveting, moving, inspiring, provocative, titillating, sensational.
– OPPOSITES boring, uninteresting.

exclaim verb CALL, cry, call/cry out, shout, yell, roar, bellow, shriek, proclaim, utter, vociferate; *dated* ejaculate.

exclamation noun CALL, cry, shout, yell, roar, bellow, shriek, utterance, interjection, expletive; *dated* ejaculation.

exclude verb ❶ BAR, debar, keep out, shut out, prohibit, forbid, prevent, disallow, refuse, ban, veto, blackball, proscribe, interdict, stand in the way of. ❷ **exclude the possibility:** ELIMINATE, rule out, preclude, reject, set aside, omit, pass over, leave out, ignore, repudiate, except. ❸ **the price excludes drinks:** BE EXCLUSIVE OF, not include, not be inclusive of, omit, leave out.
– OPPOSITES include.

exclusive adjective ❶ **an exclusive club:** SELECT, selective, restrictive, restricted, private, closed, limited, discriminating, cliquish, snobbish, fashionable, chic, elegant, upmarket; *informal* ritzy; *Brit. informal* posh, swish. ❷ **exclusive of drinks:** NOT INCLUDING, excluding, with the exception of, except for, not counting, leaving out, omitting.
– OPPOSITES inclusive.

excommunicate verb EXCLUDE, expel, cast out, banish, eject, remove, bar, debar, proscribe, anathematize, interdict, repudiate.

excrement noun WASTE MATTER, excreta, faeces, stools, droppings, ordure, dung, manure.

excrete verb DEFECATE, urinate, pass, void, discharge, eject, evacuate, expel, eliminate, emit.

excruciating adjective AGONIZING, unbearable, insufferable, harrowing, searing, acute, piercing, racking, torturous, severe, intense.

excusable adjective FORGIVABLE, pardonable, defensible, justifiable, understandable, condonable, venial.

excuse noun ❶ EXPLANATION, reason, grounds, justification, defence, apology, vindication, mitigation, mitigating circumstances. ❷ PRETEXT, pretence, cover-up, front, subterfuge, fabrication, evasion. ❸ an excuse for a man: APOLOGY, travesty, mockery, pitiful example.
▶ verb ❶ FORGIVE, pardon, absolve, acquit, exonerate, make allowances for, bear with, tolerate, indulge, exculpate. ❷ excused from work: LET OFF, exempt, spare, release, absolve, relieve, free, liberate.
– OPPOSITES condemn.

execute verb ❶ PUT TO DEATH, kill, carry out a sentence of death. ❷ execute a plan: CARRY OUT, accomplish, perform, implement, effect, bring off, achieve, complete, fulfil, enact, enforce, put into effect, do, engineer, prosecute, discharge, realize, attain, render.

exemplar noun MODEL, ideal, standard of perfection/excellence, epitome, paradigm, benchmark, pattern, criterion, paragon.

exemplary adjective MODEL, ideal, perfect, excellent, admirable, commendable, faultless, praiseworthy, laudable, honourable, meritorious.

exemplify verb TYPIFY, personify, epitomize, represent, embody, illustrate, show, demonstrate, symbolize.

exempt verb FREE FROM, release from, make an exception for, exclude from, excuse from, absolve from, spare, liberate from, relieve of, discharge from, dismiss from; *informal* let off.

exercise noun ❶ physical exercise: ACTIVITY, exertion, effort, action, work, movement, training, gymnastics, sports, aerobics, callisthenics, keep-fit, workout, warm-up, limbering up, drill. ❷ the exercise of patience: EMPLOYMENT, use, application, utilization, implementation, practice, operation, exertion, discharge.
▶ verb ❶ WORK OUT, train, do exercises, exert oneself, drill. ❷ exercise patience: EMPLOY, use, make use of, utilize, apply, implement, exert. ❸ exercise the mind: WORRY, disturb, trouble, perplex, distress, preoccupy, annoy, make uneasy, perturb, vex.

exert verb ❶ exert pressure: EMPLOY, exercise, use, make use of, utilize, apply, wield, bring to bear, set in motion, expend, spend. ❷ exert oneself: APPLY ONESELF, make an effort, spare no effort, try hard, do one's best, give one's all, strive, endeavour, struggle, labour, toil, strain, work, push, drive; *informal* put one's back into it.

exhaust verb ❶ TIRE, wear out, fatigue, drain, weary, sap, debilitate, prostrate, enfeeble, disable; *informal* knock out; *Brit. informal* knacker, fag out; *N. Amer.*

informal poop. ❷ **exhaust the supplies:** USE UP, deplete, consume, finish, expend, run through, waste, squander, dissipate, fritter away; *informal* blow.
– OPPOSITES invigorate, replenish.

exhausting adjective TIRING, fatiguing, wearing, gruelling, punishing, strenuous, arduous, back-breaking, taxing, laborious, enervating, sapping, debilitating.

exhaustion noun TIREDNESS, fatigue, weariness, weakness, collapse, debility, prostration, faintness, lassitude, enervation.

exhaustive adjective ALL-INCLUSIVE, comprehensive, intensive, all-out, in-depth, total, all-embracing, thorough, encyclopedic, complete, full, thoroughgoing, extensive, profound, far-reaching, sweeping.
– OPPOSITES perfunctory.

exhibit verb ❶ PUT ON DISPLAY, show, display, demonstrate, set out/forth, present, model, expose, air, unveil, flaunt, parade. ❷ **exhibit signs of distress:** SHOW, express, indicate, reveal, display, demonstrate, betray, give away, disclose, manifest, evince, evidence.

exhibition noun DISPLAY, show, fair, demonstration, presentation, exposition, spectacle.

exhilarate verb MAKE HAPPY, elate, delight, gladden, brighten, enliven, excite, thrill, animate, invigorate, lift, perk up, stimulate, raise someone's spirits, revitalize, exalt, inspirit; *informal* pep up.

exhilaration noun ELATION, joy, happiness, delight, gladness, high spirits, excitement, gaiety, glee, animation, vivacity, exaltation, mirth, hilarity.

exhort verb URGE, persuade, press, encourage, prompt, sway, advise, counsel, incite, goad, stimulate, push, entreat, bid, enjoin, admonish, warn.

exile verb BANISH, deport, expatriate, expel, drive out, eject, oust, uproot.
▶ **noun** ❶ BANISHMENT, deportation, expatriation, uprooting, separation. ❷ EXPATRIATE, deportee, refugee, displaced person, outcast, pariah.

exist verb ❶ LIVE, be, have existence, have being, have life, breathe, draw breath, subsist, be extant, be viable. ❷ **enough money to exist on:** SURVIVE, live, stay alive, subsist, eke out a living.
– OPPOSITES die.

existing adjective IN EXISTENCE, existent, extant, living, surviving, remaining, enduring, prevailing, abiding, present, current.

exit noun ❶ WAY OUT, door, doorway, gate, gateway, opening, egress, portal. ❷ DEPARTURE, withdrawal, leaving, going, retirement, leave-taking, retreat, flight, exodus, farewell, adieu.
– OPPOSITES entrance, arrival.

exonerate verb ABSOLVE, clear, acquit, discharge, vindicate, exculpate, dismiss, let off, excuse, pardon, justify.
– OPPOSITES incriminate.

exorbitant adjective EXCESSIVE, unreasonable, extortionate, extreme, immoderate, outrageous, inordinate, preposterous, monstrous, unwarranted, undue, unconscionable.
– OPPOSITES moderate.

exotic adjective ❶ FOREIGN, tropical, imported, alien, novel, introduced, external, extraneous. ❷ STRIKING, outrageous, colourful, extraordinary, sensational, extravagant, unusual, remarkable, astonishing, strange, outlandish, bizarre, peculiar, impressive, glamorous, fascinating, mysterious, curious, different, unfamiliar.

expand verb ❶ GROW/BECOME/MAKE LARGER, enlarge, increase in size, swell, inflate, magnify, amplify, add to, distend, lengthen, heighten, broaden, thicken, prolong, stretch, extend, multiply, dilate. ❷ OPEN OUT, spread out, unfold, unfurl, unravel, unroll.
– OPPOSITES contract.

expanse noun AREA, stretch, region, tract, extent, breadth, space, sweep, field, plain, surface, extension.

expansive adjective SOCIABLE, outgoing, friendly, affable, talkative, communicative, uninhibited, open, frank, genial, extrovert, garrulous, loquacious.

expect verb ❶ SUPPOSE, assume, believe, imagine, think, presume, surmise, calculate, reckon, conjecture. ❷ **expect a large crowd**: ANTICIPATE, envisage, predict, forecast, await, look for, look forward to, watch for, hope for, contemplate, bargain for, have in prospect. ❸ **expect cooperation**: DEMAND, insist on, require, count on, rely on, call for, look for, wish, want, hope for.

expectant adjective ❶ HOPEFUL, eager, anticipating, anticipatory, ready, watchful, in suspense, anxious, on tenterhooks; *informal* keyed up. ❷ **expectant mothers**: PREGNANT, expecting, in the family way; *technical* gravid.

expectation noun ❶ ASSUMPTION, belief, supposition, presumption, assurance, conjecture, surmise, reckoning, calculation, confidence. ❷ **great expectations**: PROSPECTS, hopes, outlook, good fortune.

expedient adjective CONVENIENT, useful, pragmatic, advantageous, beneficial, profitable, gainful, practical, desirable, appropriate, suitable, advisable, apt, fit, effective, helpful, politic, judicious, timely, opportune, propitious.
▶ **noun** MEANS, measure, stratagem, plan, scheme, plot, manoeuvre, trick, ploy, ruse, device, artifice, contrivance, invention.

expeditious adjective IMMEDIATE, speedy, quick, instant, prompt, swift, rapid, fast, punctual, ready, brisk, nimble, hasty, summary.
– OPPOSITES slow.

expel verb ❶ EVICT, banish, oust, drive out, exile, throw out, cast out, expatriate, deport, proscribe, outlaw; *informal* chuck out, kick out, boot out, turf out, heave out, send packing, give the bum's rush to. ❷ **expel smells**: DISCHARGE, eject, eliminate, excrete, evacuate, void, belch, spew out.

expend verb SPEND, pay out, lay out, disburse, lavish, squander, waste, fritter away, use up, consume, exhaust, deplete, sap, empty, finish off.

expendable adjective DISPOSABLE, dispensable, replaceable, non-essential, inessential, unimportant.
– OPPOSITES indispensable.

expense noun COST, price,

outlay, payment, expenditure, outgoings, charge, amount, fee, rate, figure, disbursement.

expensive adjective OVERPRICED, exorbitant, steep, costly, dear, high-priced, extortionate, extravagant, lavish. *See also* EXORBITANT.
– OPPOSITES cheap.

experience noun ❶ experience of teaching: FAMILIARITY, knowledge, involvement, practice, participation, contact, acquaintance, exposure, observation, understanding. ❷ a wonderful experience: EVENT, incident, occurrence, happening, affair, episode, adventure, encounter, circumstance, test, trial, case, ordeal. ❸ experience needed: PRACTICAL KNOWLEDGE, skill, training, practice, learning, maturity; *informal* know-how.
▶ verb HAVE EXPERIENCE OF, undergo, encounter, meet, feel, become familiar with, come into contact with, go through, live through, suffer, sustain.

experienced adjective PRACTISED, proficient, accomplished, skilful, seasoned, trained, expert, competent, adept, capable, knowledgeable, qualified, well versed, professional, mature, veteran, master.
– OPPOSITES novice.

experiment noun TEST, investigation, trial, trial run, try-out, examination, observation, enquiry, demonstration, venture.
▶ verb CONDUCT EXPERIMENTS, carry out tests/trials, conduct research, test, examine, investigate, explore, observe.

experimental adjective TRIAL, exploratory, pilot, tentative, speculative, preliminary, under review.

expert noun AUTHORITY, specialist, professional, master, adept, pundit, maestro, virtuoso, connoisseur; *informal* old hand, ace, wizard, buff, pro; *Brit. informal* dab hand.
▶ adjective ACCOMPLISHED, brilliant, competent, adept, master, able, proficient, skilful, experienced, practised, qualified, knowledgeable, capable, specialist, adroit, deft, dexterous, clever; *informal* crack, top-notch, wizard.
– OPPOSITES incompetent.

expiate verb ATONE FOR, make amends for, make up for, do penance for, pay for, redress, make reparations for, make recompense for.

expire verb ❶ RUN OUT, lapse, finish, end, come to an end, terminate, conclude, discontinue, stop, cease. ❷ *See* DIE (1).

explain verb ❶ DESCRIBE, give an explanation of, make clear/plain, teach, illustrate, demonstrate, define, spell out, interpret, clear up, throw light on, clarify, elucidate, explicate, decipher, expound, decode, delineate, expose, resolve, solve, gloss, unravel, unfold; *informal* get across. ❷ explain their actions: ACCOUNT FOR, justify, give a reason for, give a justification for, excuse, defend, vindicate, legitimize, rationalize, mitigate.

explanation noun ❶ DESCRIPTION, interpretation, elucidation, explication, demonstration, definition, clarification, deciphering, decoding, expounding, illustration, exposure, resolution,

solution. ❷ ACCOUNT, justification, reason, excuse, defence, apology, vindication, mitigation, apologia.

explanatory adjective EXPOSITORY, descriptive, interpretative, illustrative, demonstrative, elucidative, elucidatory, explicative, justificatory, exegetic.

expletive noun SWEAR WORD, oath, curse, obscenity, epithet, exclamation, four-letter word, dirty word.

explicit adjective ❶ explicit instructions: CLEAR, understandable, detailed, crystal-clear, direct, plain, obvious, precise, exact, straightforward, definite, categorical, specific, unequivocal, unambiguous. ❷ explicit sex: UNRESTRAINED, unreserved, uninhibited, open, candid, frank, direct, full-frontal, no holds barred.
– OPPOSITES vague, implicit.

explode verb ❶ BLOW UP, detonate, go off, erupt, burst, fly apart, fly into pieces; *informal* go bang. ❷ explode a myth: DISPROVE, invalidate, refute, discredit, debunk, repudiate, belie, give the lie to, ridicule; *informal* blow up, blow sky-high, knock the bottom from.

exploit verb ❶ exploit resources: MAKE USE OF, use, put to use, utilize, turn/put to good use, profit from/by, turn to account, capitalize on, make capital out of; *informal* milk, cash in on. ❷ exploit the workers: TAKE ADVANTAGE OF, abuse, impose on, misuse; *informal* take for a ride, walk all over, put one over on.
▶ noun FEAT, deed, adventure, stunt, achievement, accomplishment, attainment.

explore verb ❶ TRAVEL, tour, range over, traverse, survey, inspect, scout, reconnoitre, prospect. ❷ explore possibilities: INVESTIGATE, look into, enquire into, consider, examine, scrutinize, research, study, review, take stock of.

explosion noun ❶ BLAST, bang, detonation, eruption, discharge, boom, rumble, report, thunder, crash, clap, crack. ❷ an angry explosion: OUTBURST, flare-up, fit, outbreak, eruption, paroxysm.

explosive adjective ❶ VOLATILE, unstable, inflammable, eruptive. ❷ an explosive situation: TENSE, charged, serious, critical, dangerous, hazardous, overwrought, ugly, volcanic.

exponent noun ❶ ADVOCATE, supporter, upholder, backer, defender, champion, spokesperson, promoter, proponent, propagandist. ❷ PRACTITIONER, performer, interpreter, player, presenter, executant.

expose verb ❶ UNCOVER, bare, lay bare, strip, reveal, denude. ❷ expose someone's ignorance: REVEAL, show, display, make obvious, exhibit, disclose, manifest, unveil. ❸ expose a crime: REVEAL, bring to light, disclose, uncover, divulge, let out, denounce, unearth, unmask, detect, betray; *informal* spill the beans on, blow the whistle on.
– OPPOSITES cover, conceal.

expository adjective EXPLANATORY, interpretative, descriptive, illustrative, elucidatory, explicatory, explicative; *formal* exegetic, hermeneutic.

expression noun ❶ a public expression of apology: STATEMENT, utterance, pronouncement, assertion, proclamation, articulation, voicing. ❷ an apt expression: WORD, phrase, term, choice of words, turn of phrase, wording, language, phrasing, speech, diction, idiom, style, delivery, intonation; *formal* locution. ❸ a sad expression on his face: LOOK, countenance, appearance, air, mien, aspect. ❹ play music with expression: FEELING, emotion, passion, intensity, power, force, imagination, artistry, poignancy, depth, spirit, vividness, ardour.

expressionless adjective ❶ an expressionless face: BLANK, deadpan, inscrutable, emotionless, impassive, poker-faced, straight-faced, vacuous. ❷ expressionless reading: DULL, dry, boring, wooden, undemonstrative, apathetic, devoid of feeling.
– OPPOSITES expressive.

expressive adjective ❶ an expressive face/gesture: EMOTIONAL, demonstrative, eloquent, suggestive, telling, vivid. ❷ expressive music: EMOTIONAL, intense, passionate, moving, poignant, striking, eloquent, vivid, evocative, artistic, sympathetic.
– OPPOSITES expressionless, unemotional.

expressly adverb ❶ expressly forbidden: ABSOLUTELY, explicitly, clearly, plainly, distinctly, specifically, unequivocally, precisely. ❷ expressly made: SPECIALLY, especially, particularly, solely, specifically, singularly.

extend verb ❶ EXPAND, increase, enlarge, lengthen, widen, broaden, stretch, draw out, elongate. ❷ extend its scope: INCREASE, widen, add to, expand, augment, enhance, develop, supplement, amplify. ❸ extend the holiday: PROLONG, increase, lengthen, protract, drag out, stretch out, spin out. ❹ extend a welcome: OFFER, give, proffer, present, hold out, confer, advance, impart. ❺ the road extends for miles: CONTINUE, stretch, carry on, run on, last, unroll, range.
– OPPOSITES contract, curtail.

extensive adjective ❶ extensive grounds: LARGE, sizeable, substantial, spacious, considerable, vast, immense. ❷ extensive knowledge: BROAD, wide, wide-ranging, comprehensive, thorough, complete, all-embracing, inclusive.
– OPPOSITES small, limited.

extent noun ❶ LENGTH, area, expanse, stretch, range, scope. ❷ the extent of her knowledge: BREADTH, range, scope, degree, comprehensiveness, completeness, thoroughness.

exterior noun OUTSIDE, surface, front, covering, facade, shell, skin.
▶ adjective OUTER, outside, outermost, outward, external, surface, superficial.
– OPPOSITES interior.

exterminate verb KILL, destroy, annihilate, eradicate, extirpate, abolish, eliminate; *informal* wipe out, bump off.

extinguish verb ❶ PUT OUT, blow out, quench, smother, douse, snuff out, dampen down, stifle, choke off. ❷ **extinguish passion:** DESTROY, kill, end, remove, annihilate, wipe out, eliminate, abolish, eradicate, erase, expunge, suppress, extirpate.
– OPPOSITES light, kindle.

extol verb PRAISE, sing someone's praises, applaud, acclaim, pay tribute to, commend, exalt, congratulate, compliment, celebrate, glorify, eulogize; *formal* laud.
– OPPOSITES condemn.

extra adjective ❶ ADDITIONAL, further, supplementary, supplemental, added, subsidiary, auxiliary, ancillary, other, accessory. ❷ SPARE, surplus, left over, excess, redundant, superfluous, reserve, unused.

extract verb ❶ **extract a tooth:** PULL OUT, draw out, take out, pluck out, wrench out, prise out, tear out, uproot, withdraw. ❷ **extract money:** EXTORT, exact, force, coerce, elicit, wring, wrest, squeeze.
▶ noun ❶ **extract of malt:** CONCENTRATE, essence, distillate, juice, solution, decoction. ❷ **extracts from newspapers:** EXCERPT, passage, cutting, clipping, abstract, citation, selection, quotation, fragment.

extraordinary adjective ❶ **extraordinary talent:** EXCEPTIONAL, unusual, rare, uncommon, unique, singular, outstanding, striking, remarkable, phenomenal, marvellous, wonderful, signal, peculiar, unprecedented. ❷ **how extraordinary!** AMAZING, surprising, unusual, remarkable, strange, astounding, odd. ❸ **an extraordinary colour:** ODD, strange, curious, bizarre, unconventional, weird.
– OPPOSITES ordinary, commonplace.

extravagant adjective ❶ **extravagant way of life:** SPENDTHRIFT, profligate, wasteful, lavish, reckless, imprudent, excessive, improvident, prodigal, thriftless. ❷ **extravagant compliments:** EXAGGERATED, excessive, unrestrained, outrageous, immoderate, preposterous, absurd, irrational, reckless, wild; *informal* over-the-top, OTT. ❸ **extravagant prices:** EXORBITANT, excessive, unreasonable, extortionate, inordinate, immoderate, expensive, steep, dear, costly, overpriced.
– OPPOSITES thrifty, restrained.

extreme adjective ❶ **extreme danger/cold:** GREAT, greatest, acute, intense, severe, highest, utmost, maximum, supreme, high, ultimate, exceptional, extraordinary. ❷ **extreme measures:** SEVERE, harsh, Draconian, stringent, drastic, strict, stern, unrelenting, relentless, unbending, uncompromising, unyielding, radical, overzealous. ❸ **extreme views:** FANATICAL, immoderate, intemperate, militant, radical, intransigent, extremist, exaggerated, excessive, unreasonable, overzealous, outrageous.
– OPPOSITES moderate.
▶ **noun** MAXIMUM, highest point, pinnacle, climax, acme, zenith, apex, ne plus ultra.

extremely adverb VERY, exceedingly, exceptionally, intensely, greatly, acutely, utterly, excessively, inordinately, markedly, extraordinarily, uncommonly, severely, terribly; *informal* awfully.

extroverted adjective OUTGOING, sociable, friendly, social, lively, cheerful, effervescent, exuberant.
– OPPOSITES introverted.

exuberant adjective ❶ ELATED, exhilarated, cheerful, sparkling, full of life, animated, lively, high-spirited, spirited, buoyant, effervescent, vivacious, excited, ebullient, exultant, enthusiastic, irrepressible, energetic, vigorous, zestful; *informal* upbeat, bouncy. ❷ exuberant foliage: PROFUSE, luxuriant, lush, thriving, abundant, superabundant, prolific, teeming, lavish, copious, rich, plentiful, abounding, overflowing, rank.
– OPPOSITES depressed, meagre.

exultant adjective JOYFUL, overjoyed, jubilant, triumphant, delighted, ecstatic, cock-a-hoop, gleeful, enraptured, transported.

eyeful noun ❶ LOOK, good look, view, stare, gaze; *informal* load, gander; *Brit. informal* butcher's, shufti. ❷ VISION, dream, beauty, dazzler; *informal* stunner, knockout, sight for sore eyes, bobby-dazzler.

eyesore noun BLEMISH, blot, scar, blight, disfigurement, defacement, defect, monstrosity, carbuncle, atrocity, disgrace, ugliness.

eyewitness noun WITNESS, observer, onlooker, bystander, passer-by, spectator, watcher, viewer, beholder.

Ff

fabric noun ❶ CLOTH, material, textile, stuff. ❷ the fabric of society/the building: STRUCTURE, make-up, framework, frame, constitution, essence.

fabricate verb ❶ ASSEMBLE, construct, build, make, manufacture, erect, put together, form, produce, fashion, frame, shape. ❷ fabricate an excuse: MAKE UP, invent, concoct, think up, hatch, devise, trump up, coin.

fabulous adjective ❶ *See* MARVELLOUS. ❷ MYTHICAL, legendary, fantastical, imaginary, fictional, fictitious, unreal, made up, fanciful, apocryphal.

face noun ❶ COUNTENANCE, visage, physiognomy, features, lineaments; *informal* mug, clock, dial; *Brit. informal* phizog, phiz. ❷ a furious face: EXPRESSION, look, demeanour, air, aspect.
▸ verb ❶ buildings facing the sea: LOOK ON TO, overlook, look towards, give on to, be opposite to. ❷ face criticism/danger: ENCOUNTER, meet, confront, withstand, cope with, deal with, brazen out, defy, brave, oppose; *informal* get to grips with, meet

head-on. ❸ **face stone:** DRESS, finish, polish, smooth, level, coat, surface, clad, veneer.
– OPPOSITES evade.

facet noun ASPECT, feature, characteristic, factor, element, angle, side, point, part.

facetious adjective FLIPPANT, jocular, frivolous, light-hearted, tongue-in-cheek, waggish, jocose.
– OPPOSITES serious.

facile adjective ❶ **facile speeches:** INSINCERE, superficial, glib, shallow, slick, urbane, suave, bland. ❷ **facile tasks:** EASY, simple, uncomplicated, unchallenging.

facility noun ❶ EASE, effortlessness, skill, adroitness, smoothness, fluency, slickness. ❷ **leisure facilities:** AMENITY, resource, service, benefit, convenience, equipment, aid, opportunity.

fact noun ❶ TRUTH, actuality, reality, certainty, certitude. ❷ **all the facts:** DETAIL, particular, information, point, item, factor, element, feature, circumstance, specific.
– OPPOSITES falsehood.

faction noun GROUP, section, side, party, band, set, ring, division, contingent, lobby, camp, bloc, clique, coalition, confederacy, coterie, caucus, cabal, junta, ginger group, splinter group, pressure group; *informal* gang, crew.

factor noun ELEMENT, part, component, ingredient, constituent, point, detail, item, facet, aspect, feature, characteristic, consideration, influence, circumstance, thing, determinant.

factual adjective REAL, realistic, true, fact-based, true-to-life, truthful, authentic, genuine, accurate, sure, exact, precise, honest, faithful, literal, matter-of-fact, verbatim, word-for-word, objective, unbiased, unprejudiced, unvarnished, unadorned, unadulterated, unexaggerated.
– OPPOSITES untrue, fictitious.

fad noun CRAZE, mania, enthusiasm, vogue, fashion, trend, mode, fancy, whim.

fade verb ❶ GROW PALE, lose colour, become paler, become bleached, become washed out, dull, dim, lose lustre. ❷ **hope fading:** GROW LESS, dwindle, diminish, decline, die away, disappear, vanish, die, peter out, dissolve, melt away, grow faint, wane, fail, evanesce.
– OPPOSITES increase.

fail verb ❶ **the attempt failed:** NOT SUCCEED, be unsuccessful, fall through, be frustrated, break down, be defeated, be in vain, collapse, founder, misfire, meet with disaster, come to grief, come to nothing, run aground, go astray; *informal* come a cropper, bite the dust, fizzle out, miss the mark, not come up to scratch. ❷ **his business failed:** GO BANKRUPT, collapse, crash, go under, become insolvent, go into receivership, cease trading, be closed, close down; *informal* fold, flop, go bust, go broke. ❸ **he failed them:** LET DOWN, desert, neglect, abandon, forsake, disappoint. ❹ **failed to do it:** OMIT, neglect, forget, be unable.
– OPPOSITES succeed.

failing noun FAULT, shortcoming, weakness, imperfection, defect, flaw, blemish, frailty, foible, drawback.
– OPPOSITES strength.

failure noun ❶ **plan was a failure:** FIASCO, vain attempt, defeat, debacle, blunder; *informal* botch, flop, washout. ❷ **he feels a failure:** LOSER, incompetent, non-achiever, disappointment, ne'er-do-well; *informal* no-hoper, dud, flop, washout. ❸ **his failure to attend:** OMISSION, neglect, negligence, dereliction, remissness, delinquency.
– OPPOSITES success.

faint adjective ❶ **a faint mark:** INDISTINCT, unclear, obscure, dim, pale, faded, bleached. ❷ **a faint noise:** SOFT, muted, indistinct, low, weak, feeble, subdued, stifled, whispered. ❸ **a faint chance:** SLIGHT, small, remote, vague, minimal. ❹ **feeling faint:** DIZZY, giddy, light-headed, muzzy, weak, weak-headed, vertiginous; *informal* woozy.
– OPPOSITES clear, loud.
▶ **verb** LOSE CONSCIOUSNESS, black out, pass out, collapse, swoon; *informal* keel over, conk out, flake out.

fair[1] adjective ❶ **a fair trial:** JUST, impartial, unbiased, unprejudiced, objective, even-handed, disinterested, dispassionate, equitable, detached, above board, lawful, legal, legitimate, proper, square; *informal* on the level. ❷ **a fair chance of winning:** REASONABLE, tolerable, passable, satisfactory, respectable, decent, goodish, moderate, average, middling, adequate, sufficient, ample, so-so. ❸ **fair hair:** BLOND/BLONDE, light, yellow, golden, flaxen, light brown, strawberry blonde. ❹ **fair maidens:** BEAUTIFUL, pretty, lovely, attractive, good-looking; *Scottish & N. English* bonny; *poetic/literary* beauteous; *archaic* comely. ❺ **fair weather:** FINE, dry, bright, clear, sunny, cloudless, unclouded.
– OPPOSITES unfair, ugly.

fair[2] noun ❶ EXHIBITION, display, show, exhibit, exposition, expo. ❷ FESTIVAL, carnival, fête, gala.

fairly adverb ❶ JUSTLY, equitably, impartially, even-handedly, without prejudice, objectively. ❷ **fairly good:** REASONABLY, quite, pretty, passably, tolerably, moderately, satisfactorily, rather, somewhat, adequately.

faith noun ❶ TRUST, belief, confidence, conviction, credence, reliance, credit, optimism, hopefulness. ❷ RELIGION, church, denomination, belief, creed, persuasion, teaching, doctrine, sect.
– OPPOSITES mistrust.

faithful adjective ❶ LOYAL, devoted, constant, dependable, true, reliable, trustworthy, staunch, unswerving, unwavering, steadfast, dutiful, dedicated, committed. ❷ **a faithful copy:** ACCURATE, true, exact, precise, close, strict, unerring; *Brit. informal* spot on, bang on.
– OPPOSITES unfaithful, inaccurate.

fake adjective ❶ **fake money/furs:** SHAM, imitation, false, counterfeit, forged, fraudulent, bogus, spurious, pseudo, mock, simulated, artificial, synthetic, reproduction, ersatz; *informal* phoney. ❷ **a fake accent:** ASSUMED, affected, feigned, put on, pseudo, insincere; *informal* phoney.
– OPPOSITES genuine, authentic.
▶ **noun** ❶ SHAM, imitation, forgery, counterfeit, copy, reproduction, hoax. ❷ **he is a fake:** FRAUD,

charlatan, impostor, hoaxer, cheat, humbug, mountebank, quack; *informal* phoney.

fall verb ❶ leaves falling: DROP, descend, come/go down, sink, plummet, cascade, gravitate. ❷ the child fell: FALL DOWN/OVER, collapse, fall in a heap, trip, trip over, stumble, slip, tumble, slide, topple over, keel over, go head over heels, take a spill. ❸ prices fell: DECREASE, dwindle, go down, grow less, diminish, plummet, depreciate, slump, deteriorate. ❹ the town fell to the enemy: SURRENDER, yield, submit, give in/up, give way, capitulate, succumb, be taken by, be defeated by, be conquered by, pass into the hands of. ❺ it so fell that she died: OCCUR, take place, happen, come about; *poetic/literary* come to pass.
▶ noun ❶ the child had a fall: TUMBLE, trip, spill, stumble, slide, collapse. ❷ the fall of the Roman Empire: DOWNFALL, demise, collapse, ruin, failure, decline, deterioration, destruction, overthrow. ❸ a fall in demand: DECREASE, lessening, cut, dip, reduction, depreciation, slump.
■ **fall apart** *see* DISINTEGRATE. **fall back** *see* RETREAT verb (1). **fall back on** RESORT TO, have recourse to, call into play, call upon, make use of, use, employ, rely on. **fall for** FALL IN LOVE WITH, become infatuated with, be smitten by, lose one's heart to. **fall out** QUARREL, argue, fight, differ, squabble, bicker, disagree, clash, wrangle.

fallacious adjective WRONG, false, erroneous, untrue, incorrect, flawed, mistaken, inaccurate, misleading, fictitious, spurious, faulty, inexact, imprecise, fraudulent, delusory, illusory.
– OPPOSITES correct.

fallacy noun MISCONCEPTION, false notion, error, mistake, misapprehension, miscalculation, delusion, misjudgement.

fallow adjective UNCULTIVATED, unploughed, unused, dormant, resting, inactive, undeveloped, neglected.

false adjective ❶ a false account: UNTRUE, untruthful, fictitious, inaccurate, misleading, invented, concocted, fabricated, incorrect, wrong, faulty, erroneous, unfounded, invalid, forged, fraudulent, spurious. ❷ a false friend: TREACHEROUS, disloyal, unfaithful, faithless, traitorous, two-faced, double-dealing, untrustworthy, deceitful, untrue, deceiving, deceptive, duplicitous, dishonourable, perfidious, dishonest, hypocritical, unreliable, unsound, lying, mendacious.
– OPPOSITES true, loyal, faithful.

falsehood noun LIE, untruth, false statement, fib, falsification, fabrication, invention, piece of fiction, fairy story, exaggeration; *informal* whopper.
– OPPOSITES truth.

falsify verb ALTER, doctor, tamper with, forge, counterfeit, distort, pervert, adulterate.

falter verb ❶ HESITATE, waver, delay, drag one's feet, vacillate, shilly-shally, blow hot and cold, be undecided, sit on the fence, oscillate, fluctuate; *Brit.* hum and haw. ❷ STAMMER, stutter, speak haltingly.

fame noun RENOWN, celebrity, eminence, notability, note,

distinction, prominence, mark, esteem, importance, greatness, account, pre-eminence, glory, honour, illustriousness, stardom, reputation, repute, notoriety, infamy.
– OPPOSITES obscurity.

familiar adjective ❶ familiar face/excuse: WELL KNOWN, known, recognized, accustomed, common, customary, everyday, ordinary, commonplace, frequent, habitual, usual, repeated, stock, routine, mundane, run-of-the-mill, conventional, household; *Brit. informal* common or garden. ❷ being familiar with the staff: OVERFAMILIAR, presumptuous, disrespectful, forward, bold, impudent, impertinent, intrusive, pushy.
– OPPOSITES unfamiliar.
■ **familiar with** ACQUAINTED WITH, knowledgeable about, informed about, expert in, conversant with, well up on, au fait with, at home with, no stranger to, au courant with.

family noun ❶ HOUSEHOLD, ménage, clan, tribe. ❷ she wants a family: CHILDREN, offspring, progeny, brood, descendants; *informal* kids; *Law* issue, scions. ❸ ANCESTRY, extraction, parentage, pedigree, birth, background, descent, lineage, genealogy, line, bloodline, stock, dynasty, house, forebears, forefathers.

famine noun ❶ STARVATION, hunger, lack of food. ❷ SCARCITY, shortage, insufficiency, lack, want, dearth, paucity, deficiency.

famished adjective STARVING, starved, ravenous, hungry, undernourished.

famous adjective WELL KNOWN, renowned, celebrated, famed, noted, prominent, notable, eminent, great, pre-eminent, distinguished, esteemed, respected, venerable, illustrious, acclaimed, honourable, exalted, glorious, remarkable, signal, popular, legendary, much publicized.
– OPPOSITES unknown, obscure.

fan noun ADMIRER, follower, devotee, enthusiast, aficionado, disciple, adherent, supporter, backer, champion; *informal* buff, freak, nut, groupie.

fanatic noun EXTREMIST, zealot, militant, activist, partisan, bigot, sectarian, devotee, addict, enthusiast, visionary.

fanatical adjective ❶ EXTREMIST, extreme, zealous, radical, militant, sectarian, bigoted, dogmatic, prejudiced, intolerant, narrow-minded, partisan, rabid. ❷ ENTHUSIASTIC, eager, keen, fervent, passionate, obsessive, immoderate, frenzied, frenetic; *informal* wild, gung-ho.

fanciful adjective ❶ fanciful notions: UNREAL, imaginary, illusory, made up, fantastic, romantic, mythical, legendary, fairy-tale. ❷ a fanciful child: IMAGINATIVE, inventive, whimsical, capricious, visionary, impractical.

fancy noun ❶ have a fancy for something: DESIRE, urge, wish, want, yearning, longing, inclination, bent, hankering, impulse, fondness, liking, love, partiality, preference, taste, predilection, relish, penchant; *informal* yen, itch. ❷ the poet's fancy: IMAGINATION, creativity, conception, images, visualizations.

▶ **verb** ❶ **I fancy it will rain:** HAVE AN IDEA, think, guess, believe, suppose, reckon, suspect, conjecture, surmise. ❷ **he fancies her:** FIND ATTRACTIVE, be attracted to, be infatuated by, take to, desire, lust after; *informal* go for, be wild/mad about, have taken a shine to.
▶ **adjective** ORNATE, elaborate, ornamented, decorative, embellished, intricate, lavish, ostentatious, showy, luxurious, sumptuous; *informal* jazzy, snazzy, ritzy.

fantastic **adjective** ❶ **fantastic notions:** FANCIFUL, imaginary, unreal, illusory, romantic, make-believe, extravagant, irrational, wild, mad, absurd, incredible, strange, eccentric, whimsical. ❷ **fantastic shapes:** STRANGE, weird, queer, peculiar, outlandish, eccentric, bizarre, grotesque, freakish, fanciful, quaint, exotic, elaborate, ornate, intricate, rococo, baroque. ❸ *See* MARVELLOUS.
– OPPOSITES ordinary.

fantasy **noun** ❶ IMAGINATION, fancy, creativity, invention, originality, vision, myth, romance. ❷ SPECULATION, fancy, daydreaming, reverie, flight of fancy, fanciful notion, dream, daydream, pipe dream.

far **adverb** A LONG WAY, a great distance, a good way, afar.
▶ **adjective** FARAWAY, far-flung, distant, remote, out of the way, far removed, outlying, inaccessible.
– OPPOSITES near.

farcical **adjective** RIDICULOUS, ludicrous, absurd, laughable, preposterous, nonsensical, silly, foolish, asinine.

farewell **noun** GOODBYE, adieu, leave-taking, parting, send-off, departure, departing.
▶ **exclamation** GOODBYE, so long, adieu, au revoir, see you, see you later; *Brit. informal* cheerio, cheers.

far-fetched **adjective** IMPROBABLE, unlikely, implausible, remote, incredible, unbelievable, doubtful, dubious, unconvincing, strained, laboured, fanciful, unrealistic; *informal* hard to take/swallow.
– OPPOSITES likely.

fascinate **verb** CAPTIVATE, enchant, beguile, bewitch, infatuate, enthral, enrapture, entrance, hold spellbound, rivet, transfix, mesmerize, hypnotize, lure, allure, tempt, entice, draw, tantalize, charm, attract, intrigue, delight, absorb, engross.
– OPPOSITES bore, repel.

fashion **noun** ❶ STYLE, vogue, trend, latest thing, taste, mode, craze, rage, fad, convention, custom, practice. ❷ CLOTHES, design, couture; *informal* rag trade. ❸ **the usual fashion:** WAY, manner, style, method, system, mode, approach.
▶ **verb** MAKE, build, construct, manufacture, create, devise, shape, form, mould, forge, hew, carve.

fashionable **adjective** STYLISH, in fashion, up to date, up to the minute, contemporary, modern, voguish, in vogue, modish, popular, all the rage, trendsetting, latest, smart, chic, elegant; *informal* trendy, natty, with it, ritzy.
– OPPOSITES unfashionable.

fast **adjective** ❶ **a fast pace:** QUICK, rapid, swift, speedy, brisk, hurried, breakneck, hasty, accelerated, flying, express, fleet;

informal nippy. ❷ **fast friends:** LOYAL, devoted, faithful, steadfast, firm, staunch, constant, lasting, unchanging, unwavering, enduring. ❸ **fast women:** LICENTIOUS, promiscuous, dissolute, loose, wanton. ❹ **lead fast lives:** WILD, dissipated, debauched, dissolute, promiscuous, intemperate, immoderate, unrestrained, reckless, profligate, extravagant.
– OPPOSITES slow.
▶ **adverb** ❶ **run fast:** QUICKLY, rapidly, swiftly, speedily, briskly, hastily, hurriedly, in a hurry, post-haste, expeditiously; *informal* hell for leather, like a shot, like a bat out of hell, lickety-split. ❷ **stuck fast:** FIRMLY, tightly, securely, immovably, fixedly.

fasten **verb** ❷ **fasten the door:** BOLT, lock, secure, chain, seal. ❶ **fasten the hook to the wall:** ATTACH, fix, affix, clip, pin, tack, stick. ❸ **fastened his horse to a tree:** tie, bind, tether, hitch, anchor, lash. ❹ **fastened his gaze on her:** DIRECT, aim, point, focus, fix, concentrate, rivet, zero in.

fastidious **adjective** FUSSY, finicky, over-particular, critical, hard to please, overcritical, hypercritical; *informal* choosy, picky, pernickety.
– OPPOSITES easy-going.

fat **adjective** ❶ PLUMP, stout, overweight, obese, heavy, large, solid, corpulent, tubby, chubby, portly, rotund, pudgy, flabby, pot-bellied, gross, paunchy, bloated, dumpy, bulky, fleshy, stocky, well fed, massive, elephantine; *informal* beefy, roly-poly. ❷ **a fat book/cheque:** SUBSTANTIAL, large, major, sizeable, significant, considerable.
– OPPOSITES thin, lean.

fatal **adjective** ❶ **fatal illness:** MORTAL, deadly, lethal, terminal, final, incurable. ❷ **fatal to the plan:** RUINOUS, disastrous, destructive, catastrophic, calamitous, cataclysmic. ❸ **the fatal moment:** CRITICAL, fateful, decisive, crucial, pivotal, determining, momentous, important.

fatalism **noun** STOICISM, resignation, acceptance.

fatality **noun** DEATH, casualty, mortality, loss.

fate **noun** ❶ DESTINY, providence, predestination, predetermination, kismet, chance, one's lot in life, the stars. ❷ FUTURE, outcome, issue, upshot, end.

fated **adjective** PREDESTINED, preordained, destined, inevitable, inescapable, sure, ineluctable, doomed, foreordained.

father **noun** PARENT, paterfamilias, patriarch; *informal* dad, daddy, pop, poppa, pa, old boy, old man; *Brit. informal, dated* pater; *poetic/literary* begetter.

fathom **verb** UNDERSTAND, comprehend, grasp, perceive, divine, penetrate, search out, get to the bottom of, ferret out.

fatigue **noun** TIREDNESS, weariness, exhaustion, lethargy, prostration, lassitude, debility, listlessness, enervation.
– OPPOSITES vigour.
▶ **verb** TIRE, tire out, weary, exhaust, wear out, drain, prostrate, enervate; *informal* take it out of, do in, whack; *Brit. informal* fag out; *N. Amer. informal* poop.

fatuous **adjective** SILLY, foolish, stupid, senseless, nonsensical,

idiotic, puerile, brainless, mindless, asinine, vacuous, moronic, witless.
– OPPOSITES sensible.

fault noun ❶ DEFECT, flaw, imperfection, blemish, failing, weakness, weak point, deficiency, snag, error, mistake, inaccuracy, blunder, oversight. ❷ MISDEED, wrongdoing, offence, misdemeanour, sin, vice, misconduct, lapse, indiscretion, transgression, peccadillo; *archaic* trespass.
▶ **verb** FIND FAULT WITH, criticize, complain about, censure, quibble about, find lacking, impugn; *informal* pick holes in.
■ **at fault** TO BLAME, in the wrong, culpable, responsible, accountable, answerable, blameworthy.

faultless adjective ❶ **faultless work:** PERFECT, flawless, without fault, unblemished, impeccable, accurate, correct, exemplary, model. ❷ **faultless person:** INNOCENT, blameless, guiltless, above reproach, irreproachable, pure, sinless, unsullied.
– OPPOSITES imperfect.

faulty adjective ❶ **a faulty lock:** DEFECTIVE, malfunctioning, broken, out of order, damaged, unsound; *informal* on the blink, kaput. ❷ **faulty reasoning:** DEFECTIVE, flawed, unsound, wrong, inaccurate, incorrect, erroneous, fallacious, impaired, weak, invalid.
– OPPOSITES working, correct.

favour noun ❶ **do him a favour:** SERVICE, good turn, kindness, courtesy, good deed. ❷ **look on him with favour:** APPROVAL, approbation, good will, esteem, kindness, benevolence, friendliness. ❸ **the favour of the king:** BACKING, support, patronage, aid, assistance, championship.
– OPPOSITES disservice, disfavour.
▶ **verb** ❶ APPROVE OF, advocate, recommend, support, back, endorse, sanction. ❷ BE TO THE ADVANTAGE OF, be advantageous to, benefit, help, assist, aid, advance, abet, succour.
– OPPOSITES oppose.

favourable adjective ❶ **a favourable report:** APPROVING, good, enthusiastic, well disposed, commendatory. ❷ **circumstances were favourable:** ADVANTAGEOUS, in one's favour, beneficial, on one's side, helpful, good, hopeful, promising, fair, auspicious, propitious, opportune, timely, encouraging, conducive, convenient, suitable, fitting, appropriate. ❸ **a favourable impression:** GOOD, pleasing, agreeable, successful, positive.
– OPPOSITES unfavourable.

favourite adjective BEST-LOVED, most-liked, favoured, preferred, chosen, ideal, treasured, pet, well liked.
▶ **noun** FIRST CHOICE, pick, beloved, darling, idol, god, goddess, jewel; *informal* teacher's pet; *Brit. informal* blue-eyed boy.

fear noun ❶ FEARFULNESS, fright, terror, alarm, panic, trepidation, apprehensiveness, dread, nervousness, timidity, disquiet, trembling, anxiety, worry, unease, agitation, concern, foreboding, misgiving, doubt, angst, quaking, quivering, consternation, dismay, shivers, tremors; *informal* funk, blue funk, butterflies. ❷ **no fear of that happening:** LIKELIHOOD,

probability, chance, prospect, possibility.
▶ **verb** BE AFRAID OF, be scared of, dread, live in fear of, go in terror of, take fright at, shudder at, shrink from, quail at, tremble at, have cold feet.

fearful **adjective** ❶ AFRAID, frightened, scared, terrified, apprehensive, alarmed, uneasy, nervous, tense, panicky, timid, faint-hearted, timorous, diffident, intimidated, hesitant, trembling, quaking, quivering, cowering, cowardly, pusillanimous; *informal* jumpy, jittery. ❷ **a fearful accident:** TERRIBLE, dreadful, appalling, frightful, ghastly, horrific, horrible, horrendous, shocking, awful, hideous, atrocious, monstrous, dire, grim, unspeakable, gruesome, distressing, harrowing, fearsome, alarming.
– OPPOSITES fearless.

fearless **adjective** UNAFRAID, brave, courageous, intrepid, valiant, gallant, plucky, lion-hearted, stout-hearted, heroic, bold, daring, confident, game, audacious, indomitable, doughty, undaunted, unflinching, unshrinking, unabashed; *informal* gutsy, spunky.
– OPPOSITES fearful, cowardly.

fearsome **adjective** *see* FEARFUL (2).

feasible **adjective** PRACTICABLE, possible, achievable, doable, likely, attainable, workable, accomplishable, realizable, viable, reasonable, realistic, within reason.
– OPPOSITES impractical, impossible.

feast **noun** ❶ BANQUET, dinner, repast, junket, revels; *informal* blowout, spread, bash, thrash; *Brit. informal* beanfeast, beano. ❷ FEAST DAY, festival, saint's day, holy day, holiday, fête, gala, festivity.
▶ **verb** EAT ONE'S FILL OF, gorge on, indulge in, gormandize; *informal* stuff one's face with, stuff oneself with.

feat **noun** DEED, act, action, exploit, achievement, accomplishment, performance, attainment, manoeuvre, move, stunt.

feather **noun** PLUME, quill, pinion, plumule, pinna, plumage, down, hackles.

feature **noun** ❶ ASPECT, characteristic, facet, side, point, attribute, quality, property, trait, mark, hallmark, trademark, peculiarity, idiosyncrasy. ❷ **feature in a magazine:** ARTICLE, piece, item, report, story, column.
▶ **verb** ❶ PRESENT, give prominence to, promote, star, spotlight, highlight, emphasize, accentuate, play up. ❷ PLAY A PART, have a place, have prominence.

features **plural noun** FACE, countenance, visage, physiognomy, lineaments; *informal* mug, kisser.

federation **noun** CONFEDERATION, confederacy, league, alliance, coalition, union, syndicate, association, amalgamation, combination, entente, fraternity.

feeble **adjective** ❶ **a feeble old man:** WEAK, weakly, weakened, frail, infirm, sickly, puny, delicate, slight, failing, ailing, helpless, powerless, debilitated, decrepit, doddering, tottering, enfeebled, enervated, effete, etiolated. ❷ **he's so feeble:** INEFFECTUAL, inadequate, ineffective, weak,

indecisive, wishy-washy. ❸ a **feeble attempt:** INEFFECTUAL, unsuccessful, ineffective, unconvincing, poor, weak, futile, tame, paltry, slight.
– OPPOSITES strong.

feed verb ❶ NOURISH, sustain, cater for, provide for, wine and dine. ❷ EAT, take nourishment, graze, browse. ❸ **feed information to him:** GIVE, supply, provide, furnish.

feel verb ❶ **feel her face:** TOUCH, stroke, caress, fondle, handle, finger, manipulate, paw, maul. ❷ **feel the ship's motion:** BE AWARE OF, notice, be conscious of, perceive, observe, be sensible of. ❸ **feel pain:** EXPERIENCE, undergo, have, know, go through, bear, endure, suffer. ❹ **feel one's way:** GROPE, fumble, explore, poke. ❺ **feels that he should go:** THINK, believe, consider, be of the opinion, hold, judge, deem.
■ **feel for** SYMPATHIZE WITH, be sorry for, pity, empathize with, feel compassion for, be moved by, weep for, grieve for, commiserate with.

feeling noun ❶ **a feeling of pain:** SENSATION, sense, perception, awareness, consciousness. ❷ **I had a feeling you would go:** IDEA, suspicion, funny feeling, impression, notion, inkling, hunch, apprehension, presentiment, premonition, foreboding. ❸ **show feeling:** SYMPATHY, pity, compassion, understanding, concern, sensitivity, tenderness, commiseration, empathy, fellow-feeling. ❹ **a feeling of neglect:** ATMOSPHERE, air, aura, feel, mood, ambience, impression; *informal* vibes.

felicitous adjective ❶ **a felicitous expression:** APT, well chosen, well expressed, well put, fitting, suitable, appropriate, pertinent, apposite, germane. ❷ **a felicitous event:** HAPPY, joyful, fortunate, lucky, successful, prosperous.
– OPPOSITES inappropriate, unfortunate.

fellow noun MAN, male, boy, person, individual; *informal* guy, character, customer, codger; *Brit. informal* bloke, chap.

feminine adjective ❶ WOMANLY, girlish, ladylike, soft, delicate, gentle, tender, graceful, refined, modest. ❷ EFFEMINATE, womanish, effete, unmanly, unmasculine, weak; *informal* sissy, limp-wristed.
– OPPOSITES masculine.

fence noun BARRIER, railing, rail, paling, wall, hedge, barricade, rampart, stockade, palisade.
▶ verb ❶ ENCLOSE, surround, encircle, circumscribe, encompass. ❷ SHUT IN, confine, pen, separate off, secure, imprison.

fend
■ **fend for oneself** PROVIDE FOR ONESELF, take care of oneself, get by, look after oneself, support, oneself, survive. **fend off** WARD OFF, stave off, parry, turn aside, keep off, divert, deflect, avert, defend oneself against, guard against, forestall.

ferment noun ❶ FERMENTATION AGENT, yeast, mould, bacteria, leaven, leavening. ❷ **a ferment of excitement:** FRENZY, furore, fever, tumult, commotion, uproar, agitation, turbulence, stir, confusion, fuss, brouhaha, hubbub, stew, hurly-burly, racket, imbroglio.
▶ verb ❶ UNDERGO FERMENTATION,

foam, froth, bubble, effervesce, seethe, boil, rise, work. ❷ fermenting the crowd: EXCITE, inflame, agitate, incite.

ferocious adjective ❶ FIERCE, savage, brutal, brutish, ruthless, cruel, pitiless, merciless, vicious, barbarous, violent, barbaric, inhuman, inexorable, bloodthirsty, murderous, wild, untamed, predatory, rapacious. ❷ ferocious heat: INTENSE, very great, fierce, extreme, acute.
– OPPOSITES gentle.

ferret verb ❶ RUMMAGE, search about, scrabble around, rifle through, forage around, sift through. ❷ ferret out the facts: SEARCH OUT, unearth, discover, bring to light, elicit, disclose, get at, run to earth, track down, dig out/up, root out, hunt out, nose out, sniff out.

ferry verb CARRY, transport, convey, run, ship, shuttle, chauffeur.

fertile adjective ❶ fertile soil: FRUITFUL, productive, rich, fecund. ❷ fertile imagination: INVENTIVE, creative, original, ingenious, resourceful, productive, visionary, constructive.
– OPPOSITES sterile.

fertilize verb ❶ ADD FERTILIZER TO, feed, enrich, mulch, dress, compost, top-dress. ❷ IMPREGNATE, inseminate, make pregnant, fecundate.

fertilizer noun PLANT FOOD, manure, dung, compost, dressing, top-dressing, bonemeal, guano, marl.

fervent adjective PASSIONATE, ardent, impassioned, intense, vehement, heartfelt, emotional, fervid, emotive, warm, devout, sincere, eager, zealous, earnest, enthusiastic, excited, animated, spirited; *poetic/literary* perfervid.
– OPPOSITES apathetic, unemotional.

fervour noun PASSION, ardour, intensity, vehemence, emotion, warmth, devoutness, sincerity, eagerness, zeal, enthusiasm, earnestness, excitement, animation, spirit, vigour.
– OPPOSITES apathy, indifference.

fester verb ❶ SUPPURATE, run, discharge, ulcerate, rot, decay, go bad, go off, decompose, disintegrate, gather, come to a head. ❷ RANKLE, chafe, cause bitterness/resentment, gnaw.

festival noun ❶ SAINT'S DAY, holy day, feast day, holiday, anniversary, day of observance. ❷ CARNIVAL, gala day, fête, celebrations, festivities.

festive adjective JOYFUL, joyous, happy, jolly, merry, jovial, light-hearted, cheerful, cheery, jubilant, convivial, gleeful, mirthful, uproarious, rollicking, backslapping, celebratory, carnival, sportive, festal.

festoon verb GARLAND, wreathe, hang, drape, decorate, adorn, ornament, array, deck, bedeck, swathe, beribbon.
▸ noun GARLAND, wreath, chaplet, lei, swathe, swag.

fetch verb ❶ GET, go and get, bring, carry, deliver, convey, transport, escort, conduct, lead, usher in. ❷ SELL FOR, realize, go for, bring in, yield, earn, cost, afford.

fetching adjective ATTRACTIVE, charming, enchanting, sweet, winsome, captivating, fascinating, alluring.

feud noun VENDETTA, conflict, quarrel, argument, hostility, enmity, strife, discord, bad blood, animosity, grudge, antagonism, estrangement, schism, unfriendliness.

fever noun FEVERISHNESS, high temperature, delirium; *formal* pyrexia.

feverish adjective ❶ FEVERED, febrile, hot, burning. ❷ **feverish excitement:** FRENZIED, excited, frenetic, agitated, nervous, overwrought, frantic, distracted, worked up, flustered, impatient, passionate.

few adjective ❶ NOT MANY, hardly any, scarcely any, one or two, a handful of, a sprinkling of, a couple of, few and far between, infrequent, sporadic, irregular. ❷ SCARCE, rare, negligible, scant, thin on the ground.
– OPPOSITES many.

fiasco noun FAILURE, disaster, debacle, catastrophe, mess, ruination, abortion; *informal* flop, washout.

fibre noun ❶ THREAD, strand, tendril, filament, fibril. ❷ CHARACTER, nature, make-up, spirit, disposition, temperament.

fickle adjective CAPRICIOUS, unpredictable, mercurial, changeable, variable, volatile, inconstant, unstable, vacillating, unsteady, unfaithful, faithless, undependable, inconsistent, irresolute, flighty, giddy, erratic, fitful, irregular, mutable.
– OPPOSITES constant, stable.

fiction noun ❶ STORY TELLING, narration, romance, fable, fantasy, legend. ❷ **a polite fiction:** FABRICATION, lie, piece of fiction, untruth, falsehood, invention, concoction, fib, improvisation, prevarication; *informal* cock and bull story, whopper.
– OPPOSITES fact.

fictional adjective FICTITIOUS, invented, made up, imaginary, unreal, non-existent, make-believe, fabricated, mythical, fanciful.
– OPPOSITES real, actual.

fictitious adjective ❶ INVENTED, made up, imaginary, imagined, untrue, false, apocryphal. ❷ **a fictitious address:** FALSE, bogus, sham, counterfeit, fake, fabricated, spurious, concocted.
– OPPOSITES true, genuine.

fidelity noun FAITHFULNESS, loyalty, devotedness, devotion, allegiance, commitment, constancy, trustworthiness, dependability, reliability, staunchness, obedience.
– OPPOSITES disloyalty.

fidget verb ❶ MOVE RESTLESSLY, wriggle, squirm, twitch, jiggle; *informal* have ants in one's pants. ❷ FIDDLE WITH, play with, fuss with.

fidgety adjective RESTLESS, restive, on edge, uneasy, nervous, nervy, twitchy; *informal* jittery, jumpy, like a cat on hot bricks.

field noun ❶ PASTURE, meadow, grassland, paddock, sward; *literary* lea, mead, greensward; *archaic* glebe. ❷ AREA, area of activity, sphere, province, department, subject, discipline, line, speciality, domain, territory, regime. ❸ **my field of vision:** RANGE, scope, limits, confines, purview.

fiend noun ❶ DEVIL, demon, evil spirit. ❷ BRUTE, monster, savage, beast, barbarian, sadist, ogre; *archaic* blackguard. ❸ ADDICT, fanatic, maniac, enthusiast, devotee, fan, aficionado; *informal* buff, freak, nut.

fiendish **adjective** WICKED, cruel, savage, brutal, brutish, barbaric, barbarous, inhuman, vicious, bloodthirsty, ferocious, ruthless, heartless, pitiless, merciless, black-hearted, unfeeling, malevolent, villainous, odious, malignant, devilish, diabolical, demonic, satanic.

fierce **adjective** ❶ FEROCIOUS, savage, wild, vicious, bloodthirsty, dangerous, brutal, cruel, murderous, menacing, threatening, slaughterous, terrible, grim, tigerish, wolfish, feral. ❷ **a fierce love:** PASSIONATE, intense, ardent, impassioned, fervent, fiery, uncontrolled, fervid. ❸ **fierce competition:** KEEN, strong, intense, relentless, cut-throat.
– OPPOSITES gentle, mild.

fight **verb** ❶ ATTACK/ASSAULT EACH OTHER, hit each other, come to blows, exchange blows, grapple, scuffle, brawl, box, skirmish, tussle, collide, spar, joust, clash, wrestle, battle, do battle, give battle, war, wage war, go to war, make war, take up arms, combat, engage, meet; *informal* scrap. ❷ QUARREL, argue, feud, bicker, squabble, fall out, wrangle, dispute, be at odds, disagree, battle, altercate. ❸ **fight the decision:** OPPOSE, contest, take a stand against, object to, resist, defy, withstand, struggle against, take issue with.
▶ **noun** ❶ BRAWL, scuffle, tussle, skirmish, struggle, fracas, battle, engagement, clash, conflict, combat, contest, encounter, exchange, brush; *informal* set-to, scrap, punch-up, dust-up; *Law, dated* affray. ❷ QUARREL, disagreement, difference of opinion, dispute, argument, altercation, feud.
■ **fight back** ❶ DEFEND ONESELF, put up a fight, retaliate, counter-attack. ❷ SUPPRESS, repress, check, curb, restrain, contain, bottle up. **fight off** WARD OFF, beat off, stave off, repel, repulse, hold at bay, resist.

figurative **adjective** METAPHORICAL, symbolic, allegorical, non-literal, representative, emblematic, imagistic.
– OPPOSITES literal.

figure **noun** ❶ NUMBER, numeral, digit, integer, sum, value, symbol, cipher. ❷ COST, price, amount, value, total, sum, aggregate. ❸ SHAPE, form, outline, silhouette. ❹ BODY, physique, build, frame, torso, proportions. ❺ DIAGRAM, illustration, picture, drawing, sketch, chart, plan, map.
▶ **verb** ❶ **she figures in the book:** APPEAR, feature, play a part, be featured, be conspicuous. ❷ **that figures:** BE LIKELY, be probable, be understandable, make sense.
■ **figure out** ❶ *See* CALCULATE. ❷ *See* UNDERSTAND (1).

file[1] **noun** ❶ FOLDER, portfolio, box, document case, filing cabinet. ❷ DOSSIER, information, documents, records, data, particulars, case notes.
▶ **verb** RECORD, enter, store, categorize, classify, put in place, put in order, put on record, pigeonhole.

file[2] **noun** **a file of people:** LINE, column, row, string, chain, queue.

▶ verb WALK/MARCH IN A LINE, march, parade, troop, stream.

fill verb ❶ fill the room: OCCUPY ALL OF, crowd, overcrowd, congest, cram, pervade. ❷ fill the shelves: PACK, load, stack, supply, furnish, provide, replenish, restock, refill. ❸ fill the hole: STOP UP, block up, plug, seal, bung up, close, clog. ❹ fill an order: CARRY OUT, execute, perform, complete, fulfil.

fillip noun STIMULUS, incentive, encouragement, inducement, motivation, spur, goad, prod, push.

film noun ❶ MOVIE, picture, motion picture, video; *informal* flick. ❷ LAYER, coat, coating, covering, cover, dusting, sheet, blanket, skin, tissue, membrane, pellicle. ❸ HAZE, mist, cloud, blur, veil, murkiness.

filter noun STRAINER, sieve, riddle, sifter, colander, gauze, netting. ▶ verb STRAIN, sieve, sift, riddle, filtrate, clarify, purify, clear, refine.

filth noun DIRT, muck, grime, mud, sludge, mire, slime, excrement, dung, manure, ordure, sewage, rubbish, refuse, garbage, trash, contamination, pollution; *informal* crud; *Brit. informal* gunge.

filthy adjective DIRTY, unclean, mucky, muddy, slimy, murky, squalid, foul, nasty, polluted, contaminated, unwashed, grubby, dirt-encrusted, black, blackened, begrimed, rotten, decaying, smelly, fetid, putrid, faecal.
– OPPOSITES clean, spotless.

final adjective ❶ LAST, closing, concluding, finishing, terminal, end, ultimate, eventual, endmost. ❷ the decision is final: ABSOLUTE, conclusive, irrevocable, unalterable, incontrovertible, indisputable, decisive, definite, definitive, settled.
– OPPOSITES first.

finale noun END, finish, close, conclusion, climax, culmination, denouement, last act, final scene, final curtain, epilogue; *informal* wind-up.

finalize verb COMPLETE, conclude, settle, decide, agree on, work out, tie up, wrap up, put the finishing touches to, clinch, sew up.

finance noun ❶ MONEY MATTERS, financial affairs, economics, commerce, business, investment, banking, accounting. ❷ finances are low: MONEY, funds, cash, resources, assets, capital, wealth, wherewithal, revenue, stock. ▶ verb PAY FOR, fund, back, support, subsidize, underwrite, capitalize, guarantee, provide capital for.

financial adjective MONETARY, fiscal, pecuniary, economic, budgetary.

find verb ❶ found a gold watch: COME ACROSS, chance upon, stumble on, light on, happen upon. ❷ find a cure/answer: DISCOVER, come up with, hit upon, turn up, bring to light, uncover, unearth, ferret out, locate, lay one's hands on, encounter. ❸ find the missing glove: RECOVER, get back, retrieve, regain, repossess, recoup. ❹ find happiness: GET, obtain, achieve, attain, acquire, gain, earn, procure. ❺ find it pays to be honest: DISCOVER, realize, learn, conclude, detect, observe, notice, note, perceive. ❻ found its mark: REACH, attain, arrive at, gain, achieve.

finding noun DECISION, conclusion, verdict, judgement,

pronouncement, decree, order, recommendation.

fine adjective ❶ a fine performance: EXCELLENT, first-class, first-rate, great, exceptional, outstanding, admirable, superior, magnificent, splendid, quality, beautiful, exquisite, choice, select, prime, supreme, rare; *informal* A1, top-notch; *Brit. informal, dated* top-hole. ❷ a fine day: FAIR, dry, bright, clear, cloudless, sunny, balmy, clement. ❸ fine material: SHEER, light, lightweight, thin, flimsy, diaphanous, filmy, chiffony, gossamer, gauze-like, gauzy, transparent, translucent, airy, ethereal. ❹ fine clothes: ELEGANT, stylish, expensive, smart, chic, fashionable, modish, high-fashion, lavish. ❺ a fine mind: KEEN, acute, sharp, quick, clever, perspicacious, intelligent, brilliant. ❻ that's fine with me: ALL RIGHT, satisfactory, acceptable, agreeable, convenient, suitable; *informal* OK. ❼ fine taste: DISCRIMINATING, discerning, tasteful, fastidious, critical, refined, sensitive, intelligent.

finish verb ❶ finish the task: COMPLETE, conclude, accomplish, carry out, execute, discharge, deal with, do, get done, fulfil, achieve, attain, end, close, bring to a conclusion, finalize, terminate, round off, put the finishing touches to; *informal* wind up, wrap up, sew up, polish off, knock off. ❷ finish working: STOP, cease, give up, suspend, have done with, discontinue. ❸ finish the milk: USE, use up, consume, exhaust, empty, deplete, drain, expend, dispatch, dispose of. ❹ the job finished her: OVERCOME, defeat, overpower, overwhelm, conquer, get the best of, best, worst, rout, bring down, put an end to, dispose of; *informal* wipe out, do in.
– OPPOSITES start, begin.
▶ noun ❶ END, completion, conclusion, close, closing, cessation, final act, finale, accomplishment, fulfilment, achievement, consummation, execution. ❷ a table with a lovely finish: SURFACE, veneer, coating, texture, glaze, lustre, gloss, polish, shine, patina.

finite adjective LIMITED, restricted, bounded, delimited, demarcated, subject to limitations, determinate, measurable, countable.
– OPPOSITES infinite.

fire noun ❶ BLAZE, conflagration, inferno, flames, combustion. ❷ GUNFIRE, sniping, bombardment, flak, shelling, barrage, fusillade, salvo. ❸ the fire in her eyes: PASSION, intensity, ardour, zeal, energy, spirit, vivacity, sparkle, vigour, fervour, enthusiasm.
▶ verb ❶ SET FIRE TO, set on fire, set alight, set ablaze, light, ignite, kindle, put a match to. ❷ fire a gun: SHOOT, let off, discharge, trigger. ❸ fire with enthusiasm: STIMULATE, animate, arouse, rouse, stir up, excite, enliven, inflame, inspire, motivate, incite, galvanize, electrify, impassion. ❹ fire an employee: DISMISS, discharge, get rid of, oust, depose, cashier; *informal* give someone their marching orders, show someone the door, sack, give someone the sack, axe, give someone the bullet.

firebrand noun TROUBLEMAKER, agitator, rabble-rouser, demagogue, tub-thumper.

fireproof adjective NON-FLAMMABLE, non-inflammable, fire-resistant, flame-resistant, flame-retardant, incombustible, unburnable.
– OPPOSITES inflammable.

firm[1] adjective ❶ **a firm surface:** HARD, hardened, stiff, rigid, inflexible, unyielding, inelastic, resistant, solid, solidified, compacted, compressed, condensed, dense, close-grained, congealed, frozen, set, jelled, stony. ❷ **firm plans:** SETTLED, fixed, decided, definite, established, unalterable, unchangeable. ❸ **a firm handshake:** STRONG, vigorous, sturdy, powerful. ❹ **firm friendship:** CONSTANT, unchanging, enduring, abiding, durable, deep-rooted, long-standing, long-lasting, steady, stable, staunch. ❺ **firm about not going:** DETERMINED, resolute, decided, resolved, unfaltering, unwavering, unflinching, unswerving, unyielding, unbending, inflexible, obstinate, stubborn, obdurate, strict, intransigent, unmalleable.
– OPPOSITES soft.

firm[2] noun BUSINESS, company, concern, establishment, organization, corporation, conglomerate, partnership; *informal* outfit.

first adjective ❶ INITIAL, earliest, original, introductory, opening, primitive, premier, primordial, primeval. ❷ **first principles:** BASIC, fundamental, rudimentary, key, cardinal, primary, beginning.
– OPPOSITES last.
▶ **adverb** ❶ AT FIRST, to begin with, at the beginning, at the outset, initially. ❷ FIRSTLY, before anything else, first and foremost, in the first place.

fish verb GO FISHING, angle, cast, trawl.
■ **fish out** PULL OUT, haul out, extricate, extract, retrieve, produce.

fishy adjective SUSPICIOUS, dubious, questionable, doubtful, suspect, odd, queer, peculiar, strange, not quite right; *informal* funny, shady, not kosher.

fit[1] adjective ❶ **feeling fit:** WELL, healthy, in good health, in shape, in good shape, in good trim, in good condition, strong, robust, hale and hearty, sturdy, hardy, vigorous. ❷ **fit to drive:** CAPABLE, able, competent, good enough, adequate, ready, prepared, satisfactory, qualified, trained, equipped, worthy, eligible; *informal* up to scratch. ❸ **a fit occasion/fit behaviour:** FITTING, proper, seemly, decent, right, decorous, correct, apt, appropriate, suitable, apposite, relevant, pertinent.
– OPPOSITES unfit, inappropriate.
▶ **verb** ❶ **the facts fit the theory:** AGREE WITH, be in agreement with, accord with, concur with, correspond with, match, tally with, suit, go with, conform to, dovetail with, be consonant with, be congruent with. ❷ **fit the parts together:** JOIN, connect, put together, put in place, fix, arrange, insert, adjust, shape.

fit[2] noun ❶ CONVULSION, spasm, paroxysm, seizure, attack. ❷ **a fit of giggles:** BOUT, burst, outburst, outbreak.

fix verb ❶ FASTEN, secure, attach, connect, join, couple, stick, glue, cement, pin, nail, screw, bolt, clamp, bind, tie, pinion, anchor, plant, embed, establish, position, station. ❷ **fix a date:** DECIDE ON,

settle, set, agree on, arrange, arrive at, determine, establish, name, specify. ❸ **fix the car**: REPAIR, mend, put right, patch up, put to rights, restore, adjust, rectify, sort out, see to.
▶ **noun** PREDICAMENT, difficulty, quandary, plight, dilemma, trouble, muddle, mess, corner, tricky situation, tight spot; *informal* pickle, jam, hole, scrape; *Brit. informal* spot of bother.

fixation **noun** OBSESSION, preoccupation, compulsion, complex, mania, monomania; *informal* hang-up, thing.

fizz **verb** BUBBLE, effervesce, froth, sparkle, foam, fizzle, sputter.

fizzy **adjective** BUBBLY, bubbling, sparkling, effervescent, gassy, carbonated.

flag[1] **noun** STANDARD, ensign, banner, pennant, streamer, bunting, colours, pennon, gonfalon.

flag[2] **verb** ❶ **I'm flagging**: TIRE, become tired/weary, weaken, grow weak, lose one's strength. ❷ **his interest is flagging**: FADE, decline, fail, wane, diminish, ebb, decrease, taper off.

flagrant **adjective** OBVIOUS, glaring, blatant, outrageous, shameless, disgraceful, shocking, scandalous, terrible, dreadful.

flair **noun** ❶ ABILITY, capability, aptitude, facility, skill, talent, gift, knack, bent, genius. ❷ STYLE, panache, dash, elan, good taste, discrimination, discernment.

flap **verb** FLUTTER, beat, thresh, thrash, wave, wag, agitate, waggle, swing, shake, oscillate.

flash **verb** ❶ GLARE, beam, gleam, shine out, glint, sparkle, flicker, shimmer, twinkle, glimmer, glisten, scintillate, coruscate. ❷ SHOW OFF, flaunt, flourish, display, exhibit.

flat **adjective** ❶ **a flat surface**: LEVEL, horizontal, levelled, even, smooth, unbroken, plane. ❷ **lying flat**: STRETCHED OUT, prone, spreadeagled, prostrate, supine, recumbent. ❸ **a flat tyre**: DEFLATED, punctured, burst, collapsed, ruptured. ❹ **a flat voice**: MONOTONOUS, boring, dull, tedious, uninteresting, lifeless, dead, lacklustre, bland, insipid, vapid, prosaic. ❺ **a flat denial**: OUTRIGHT, direct, out-and-out, definite, positive, downright, firm, conclusive, utter, complete, categorical, unconditional.
■ **flat out** AT FULL SPEED, all out, as fast as possible, at full tilt, full steam ahead, post-haste; *informal* hell for leather.

flatten **verb** ❶ LEVEL, level out/off, even out, smooth, compress, trample, press down, crush, squash, compact. ❷ DEMOLISH, tear down, knock down, raze, raze to the ground. ❸ KNOCK SOMEONE OFF THEIR FEET, knock to the ground, floor, prostrate, fell.

flatter **verb** COMPLIMENT, praise, sing someone's praises, praise to excess, praise to the skies, pay court to, pay blandishments to, fawn upon, cajole, humour, flannel, wheedle; *informal* sweet-talk, soft-soap, butter up, lay it on thick, play up to.
– OPPOSITES insult.

flattering **adjective** ❶ **flattering remarks**: COMPLIMENTARY, adulatory, fulsome, laudatory, honeyed, sugary, ingratiating, cajoling. ❷ **a flattering dress**: ENHANCING, becoming.
– OPPOSITES unflattering.

flattery noun PRAISE, adulation, fulsomeness, unctuousness, fawning, puffery, cajolery, wheedling, compliments, blandishments, honeyed words; *informal* sweet talk, soft soap, flannel.

flaunt verb SHOW OFF, parade, display, exhibit, draw attention to, make a show of, wave, dangle, brandish.

flavour noun ❶ TASTE, savour, tang, relish. ❷ FLAVOURING, seasoning, tastiness, tang, relish, piquancy, spiciness, zest. ❸ the flavour of the place: ATMOSPHERE, spirit, essence, nature, character, soul, quality, feel, feeling, ambience, tone, style.

flaw noun ❶ a character flaw: FAULT, defect, imperfection, failing, shortcoming, blemish, weakness, weak spot, foible. ❷ a flaw in the glass: FAULT, defect, crack, chip, fracture, break, crevice, fissure, rent, spit, tear.
– OPPOSITES strength.

flawless adjective ❶ flawless performance: PERFECT, impeccable, faultless. ❷ flawless complexion: UNBLEMISHED, perfect, blemish-free, unmarred, unimpaired. ❸ flawless piece of china: PERFECT, whole, intact, sound, undamaged, unbroken.
– OPPOSITES imperfect, flawed.

flee verb RUN AWAY, run off, make off, fly, take flight, beat a hasty retreat, bolt, abscond, retreat, depart hastily, make a quick exit, run for it, make a run for it, take off, take to one's heels, decamp, escape, make one's getaway, vanish; *informal* do a disappearing act, cut and run, beat it, skedaddle, split, scram, light out; *Brit. informal* scarper, do a bunk, do a runner.

fleet adjective SWIFT, quick, rapid, speedy, expeditious, nimble, swift-footed.

fleeting adjective BRIEF, short-lived, transient, momentary, rapid, swift, transitory, ephemeral, temporary, impermanent, here today and gone tomorrow, evanescent, fugitive, vanishing, flying, passing, flitting.
– OPPOSITES lasting.

flesh noun MUSCLE, tissue, fat, brawn, body.
■ **flesh out** ❶ PUT ON WEIGHT, fatten up, grow fatter. ❷ FILL OUT, expand, add substance/detail to, make more substantial.

flexible adjective ❶ BENDABLE, pliable, pliant, elastic, plastic, springy, mouldable, rubbery. ❷ flexible bodies: SUPPLE, agile, limber, lithe, lissom, double-jointed. ❸ flexible arrangements: ADAPTABLE, adjustable, changeable, open to change, variable, open, open-ended, provisional, mutable. ❹ he is very flexible: COOPERATIVE, accommodating, tractable, compliant, manageable, amenable, malleable, biddable, docile, submissive, yielding.
– OPPOSITES inflexible, rigid.

flick verb ❶ STRIKE, hit, whip, rap, tap, touch. ❷ CLICK, switch, snap, flip.
■ **flick through** SKIM, glance over/through, browse through, thumb through.

flight noun ❶ AVIATION, flying, air transport, aeronautics. ❷ a flight of geese: FLOCK, group, skein, bevy, covey, migration.

flimsy adjective ❶ a flimsy box: INSUBSTANTIAL, fragile, frail, slight, makeshift, rickety, shaky, jerry-built, ramshackle, gimcrack. ❷ flimsy material: THIN, light, fine, delicate, lightweight, sheer, filmy, diaphanous, transparent, gossamer, gauzy. ❸ a flimsy excuse: FEEBLE, weak, poor, inadequate, thin, unconvincing, transparent, implausible, unsatisfactory, trivial, shallow, paltry.
– OPPOSITES strong.

flinch verb DRAW BACK, shrink back, pull back, start back, recoil, withdraw, shy away, cringe, cower, quail, crouch, wince, blench.
■ **flinch from** SHIRK, evade, avoid, shy away from, dodge, duck, baulk at.

fling verb THROW, hurl, toss, pitch, cast, launch, catapult, propel, send flying, let fly, shy, lob; *informal* chuck, heave.

flippant adjective FRIVOLOUS, glib, offhand, impertinent, insouciant, impudent, irreverent, superficial, carefree, thoughtless, shallow, cheeky, pert; *informal* flip.
– OPPOSITES serious.

flirt verb CHAT UP, make eyes at, toy with, lead on, trifle with, dally with, tease.
▶ noun COQUETTE, tease, vamp, heartbreaker, trifler, philanderer.

flirtatious adjective PROVOCATIVE, teasing, coquettish, playful, amorous, philandering, come-hither.

float verb ❶ STAY AFLOAT, be buoyant, sail, bob, glide, drift, slip. ❷ MOVE AIMLESSLY, drift, wander, meander; *N. Amer. informal* bum around.
– OPPOSITES sink.

flock noun ❶ HERD, drove. ❷ FLIGHT, bevy, gaggle, skein. ❸ CROWD, gathering, assembly, group, company, collection, congregation, throng, mass, host, multitude, troop, convoy.

flog verb WHIP, lash, horsewhip, flay, flagellate, birch, scourge, belt, cane, strap, thrash, beat, whack, wallop, chastise, trounce; *informal* tan someone's hide.

flood noun ❶ DELUGE, torrent, inundation, spate, overflow, flash flood. ❷ ABUNDANCE, superabundance, profusion, glut, surfeit, plethora, superfluity; *informal* tons, heaps, loads.
– OPPOSITES trickle.
▶ verb ❶ INUNDATE, deluge, pour over, immerse, submerge, swamp, drown, engulf, saturate. ❷ flood the market: OVERSUPPLY, saturate, overfill, glut, overwhelm.
– OPPOSITES trickle.

floor noun STOREY, level, tier, deck.
▶ verb KNOCK DOWN, knock out, fell, prostrate.

flop verb ❶ COLLAPSE, slump, drop, fall, tumble, droop, sag, dangle. ❷ FAIL, be unsuccessful, be a disaster, miss the mark, founder, fall flat; *informal* bomb, go down like a lead balloon.
– OPPOSITES succeed.

florid adjective ❶ a florid complexion: RED, ruddy, flushed, high-coloured, rubicund, rubescent, erubescent. ❷ florid prose: FLOWERY, over-elaborate, verbose, purple, grandiloquent.
– OPPOSITES pale, plain.

flounder verb ❶ THRASH, struggle, blunder, stumble, fumble, grope. ❷ STRUGGLE, falter, be in difficulties, be confused, be in the dark, be out of one's depth.

flourish verb ❶ flourish the sword/prize: BRANDISH, wave, wield, swing, hold aloft, display, exhibit, flaunt, show off, parade, vaunt. ❷ plants are flourishing: THRIVE, grow, do well, develop, burgeon, bloom, blossom, bear fruit, flower, succeed, prosper.

flout verb DEFY, disdain, scorn, show contempt for, scoff at, mock, laugh at, deride, ridicule, sneer at.
– OPPOSITES obey, observe.

flow verb ❶ MOVE, course, run, go along, proceed, glide, stream, ripple, swirl, surge, sweep, roll, whirl, rush, drift, slide, trickle, gurgle. ❷ GUSH, stream, well, spurt, spout, squirt, spew, jet, spill, leak, seep, ooze, drip.
▶ noun ❶ CURRENT, course, drift, stream, tide, spate. ❷ GUSH, stream, outflow, outpouring, welling.

flower noun ❶ BLOOM, blossom, floweret, floret, annual, perennial. ❷ the flower of the nation: BEST, finest, pick, cream, elite.

fluctuate verb ❶ RISE AND FALL, go up and down, see-saw, yo-yo, be unstable, vary, change, alter, swing, oscillate, ebb and flow, undulate. ❷ WAVER, vacillate, hesitate, change one's mind, blow hot and cold, shilly-shally, alternate, veer, teeter, totter; *Brit.* hum and haw.

fluent adjective ❶ ARTICULATE, eloquent, silver-tongued, smooth-spoken, voluble. ❷ fluent prose: SMOOTH, flowing, fluid, natural, effortless, graceful, elegant, mellifluous, euphonious.
– OPPOSITES inarticulate.

fluff noun ❶ DOWN, fuzz, lint, nap, pile, dust. ❷ MISTAKE, error, bungle; *informal* foul-up, screw-up; *Brit. informal* cock-up.

fluid adjective ❶ LIQUID, liquefied, gaseous, gassy, melted, molten, running, flowing, uncongealed. ❷ a fluid movement: SMOOTH, fluent, flowing, graceful, elegant, effortless, easy, natural. ❸ our plans are fluid: FLEXIBLE, open to change, adaptable, not fixed, adjustable, variable, mutable. ❹ the situation is fluid: UNSTABLE, likely to change, unsteady, fluctuating, shifting.
– OPPOSITES solid.
▶ noun LIQUID, gas, solution.

flunkey noun LACKEY, toady, minion, yes-man, sycophant, hanger-on, puppet, camp follower, cat's paw; *informal* bootlicker, creep.

flush verb ❶ BLUSH, turn red, redden, colour, colour up, crimson, burn up, flame up, glow, suffuse with colour. ❷ flush the toilet: WASH OUT, rinse out, cleanse, hose down, swab. ❸ flush it away: EXPEL, eject.

fluster verb AGITATE, ruffle, unsettle, upset, bother, put on edge, panic, disconcert, discompose, confuse, throw off balance, confound, nonplus; *informal* hassle, rattle, faze, throw into a tizz.

flutter verb ❶ flutter its wings: BEAT, flap, quiver, agitate, vibrate, ruffle. ❷ flutter one's eyelashes: BAT, flicker, flit. ❸ flags fluttering: FLAP, wave, flop, ripple, quiver, shiver, tremble.

fly verb ❶ SOAR, take wing, take to the air, wing, wing its way, hover, swoop. ❷ fly the flag: DISPLAY, show, exhibit, wave, hoist, raise, hang out. ❸ **he flew past:** DASH, race, rush, tear, bolt, zoom, dart, speed, hurry, career, hasten; *informal* hare off, be off like a shot. ❹ FLEE, run away, bolt, take flight, make off, abscond, beat a retreat, run for it, decamp, make one's escape; *informal* cut and run, skedaddle; *Brit. informal* scarper, do a bunk.

foam **verb** FROTH, froth up, bubble, fizz, cream, lather, spume, effervesce.
▶ **noun** FROTH, bubbles, fizz, head, spume, lather, effervescence, suds.

focus **noun** ❶ **focus of attention:** CENTRE, central point, focal point, centre of attention, core, hub, pivot, magnet, cynosure. ❷ FOCAL POINT, point of conversion.
▶ **verb** AIM, fix, concentrate, bring to bear, zero in on, zoom in on, centre, pinpoint, rivet.

foe **noun** ENEMY, opponent, adversary, rival, antagonist, combatant, contestant.
– OPPOSITES friend.

fog **noun** MIST, smog, haze, murk, murkiness, gloom; *informal* pea-souper.

foggy **adjective** ❶ MISTY, smoggy, dark, grey, dim, overcast, murky, hazy, gloomy. ❷ **foggy recollections:** VAGUE, indistinct, cloudy, hazy, unclear, obscure, befuddled, confused, muddled, dazed.
– OPPOSITES clear.

foible **noun** WEAKNESS, weak point, failing, shortcoming, flaw, blemish, defect, frailty, quirk, idiosyncrasy; *informal* hang-up.

foil **verb** THWART, frustrate, stop, baffle, defeat, check, checkmate, circumvent, counter, baulk, disappoint, impede, obstruct, hamper, hinder.

fold **noun** ❶ LAYER, pleat, overlap, turn, gather, crease, knife-edge. ❷ WRINKLE, pucker, furrow, crinkle, crows feet.
▶ **verb** ❶ DOUBLE UP, turn under, turn up, bend, tuck, crease, gather, pleat, crimp, crumple. ❷ **fold her in his arms:** WRAP, enfold, clasp, embrace, envelop, hug, squeeze. ❸ **the firm folded:** FAIL, collapse, go out of business, go bankrupt, crash, go to the wall; *informal* go bust, go under, flop.

folk **noun** PEOPLE, populace, population, citizenry, general public, public, clan, tribe.

follow **verb** ❶ GO/COME BEHIND, walk behind, go with, escort, accompany, keep pace with, attend, chase, pursue, run after, trail, shadow, hunt, stalk, track, dog, hound; *informal* tread on someone's heels, tail, tag after. ❷ **follow the rules:** OBEY, observe, comply with, heed, conform to, pay attention to, stick to, adhere to, note, have regard to, mind, be guided by, accept, yield to. ❸ **follow logically:** RESULT FROM, arise from, be consequent on, develop from, ensue from, emanate from, issue from, proceed from, spring from, flow from. ❹ **follow the logic of it:** UNDERSTAND, comprehend, take in, see, grasp, fathom, get, catch on to, appreciate. ❺ **she follows tennis:** BE A FOLLOWER OF, be a supporter of, be interested in, be devoted to, support, keep abreast of, keep up to date with.
■ **follow through** CONTINUE, complete, bring to completion, see something through. **follow up** INVESTIGATE, research, find out

about, look into, check out, pursue.

following adjective NEXT, ensuing, succeeding, subsequent, successive.
▶ noun SUPPORTERS, backers, fans, admirers, devotees, public, audience, adherents, patrons.

foment verb INCITE, instigate, stir up, provoke, excite, arouse, encourage, initiate, agitate. *See also* STIMULATE.

fond adjective ❶ ADORING, devoted, loving, affectionate, caring, warm, tender, amorous, doting, indulgent. ❷ fond hopes: FOOLISH, naive, deluded, delusory, absurd, vain, empty.
– OPPOSITES hostile.

fondle verb CARESS, stroke, pat, pet, cuddle, hug, nuzzle.

food noun NOURISHMENT, sustenance, nutriment, subsistence, diet, fare, menu, bread, board, provender, cooking, cuisine, foodstuffs, refreshments, edibles, meals, provisions, rations, stores, commons, comestibles, solids; *informal* nosh, grub, eats, chow; *Brit. informal* scoff; *dated* victuals.

fool noun ❶ IDIOT, dolt, dunce, ass, ignoramus, imbecile, simpleton; *informal* chump, booby, nincompoop, ninny, dunderhead, blockhead, fathead, halfwit, cretin, moron, dummy, numbskull, dimwit; *Brit. informal* twerp, clot, twit, nitwit. ❷ make a fool of him: DUPE, butt, laughing stock, gull, easy mark, cat's paw; *informal* stooge, sucker, pushover, sap, fall guy; *Brit. informal* mug.
▶ verb ❶ TRICK, deceive, hoax, make a fool of, dupe, take in, mislead, hoodwink, bluff, delude, beguile, gull; *informal* con, bamboozle, kid, have on. ❷ he was only fooling: PRETEND, make believe, feign, put on an act, sham, fake.

foolish adjective ❶ a foolish idea: SILLY, absurd, senseless, nonsensical, pointless, ridiculous, laughable, fatuous, risible, derisible, imprudent, incautious, injudicious, irresponsible, indiscreet, unwise, unreasonable, ill-advised, ill-considered; *informal* dotty, nutty. ❷ a foolish person: STUPID, idiotic, silly, half-witted, brainless, doltish, dull-witted, ignorant, dense, moronic, witless, mad, crazy, weak-minded; *informal* dotty, dippy, batty, screwy, wacky; *Brit. informal* daft, potty, barmy.
– OPPOSITES sensible.

foolproof adjective INFALLIBLE, certain, sure, guaranteed, safe, dependable, trustworthy, never-failing.

fop noun DANDY, poseur; *Brit. informal* toff; *informal, dated* swell; *dated* beau, popinjay.

forbid verb PROHIBIT, ban, bar, debar, outlaw, veto, proscribe, disallow, preclude, interdict, exclude, rule out, stop.
– OPPOSITES allow.

forbidden adjective PROHIBITED, out of bounds, banned, outlawed, vetoed, proscribed, taboo, debarred, interdicted.

forbidding adjective ❶ a forbidding manner: STERN, harsh, grim, hard, tough, hostile, unfriendly, disagreeable, nasty, mean, repellent, off-putting. ❷ a forbidding landscape: FRIGHTENING, ominous, threatening, menacing, sinister, daunting, foreboding.
– OPPOSITES friendly.

force noun ❶ POWER, strength, vigour, energy, potency, muscle, might, effort, impact, exertion, pressure, stamina, vitality, stimulus, dynamism. ❷ COERCION, duress, compulsion, pressure, constraint, enforcement, violence; *informal* arm-twisting. ❸ arguments with force: PERSUASIVENESS, validity, weight, effectiveness, influence, power, strength, vehemence, efficacy; *informal* punch, bite. ❹ a task force: DETACHMENT, unit, squad, squadron, battalion, division, regiment, army, patrol.
▶ verb ❶ COMPEL, coerce, make, bring pressure on, use force on, pressure, pressurize, impel, drive, oblige, necessitate, constrain, urge, press-gang; *informal* use strong-arm tactics on, put the squeeze on. ❷ force them back: DRIVE, push, propel, thrust, shove, press. ❸ force a confession from: WREST, extract, extort, wring, drag.

forceful adjective ❶ forceful speakers: POWERFUL, vigorous, strong, potent, dynamic, energetic, assertive. ❷ forceful arguments: PERSUASIVE, telling, convincing, compelling, effective, cogent, impressive, valid.
– OPPOSITES weak, unconvincing.

forecast verb PREDICT, foretell, foresee, prophesy, forewarn, prognosticate, augur, divine, guess, conjecture, speculate, calculate.
▶ noun PREDICTION, prophecy, prognostication, augury, prognosis, guess, conjecture, projection.

foregoing adjective PRECEDING, prior, previous, former, above, aforesaid, antecedent, anterior.

foreign adjective ❶ from foreign parts: OVERSEAS, distant, remote, alien, exotic. ❷ foreign objects: STRANGE, unfamiliar, unknown, exotic, outlandish, odd, peculiar, curious. ❸ foreign to the discussion: IRRELEVANT, unrelated, not pertinent, unconnected, inappropriate, extraneous, outside, extrinsic, inapposite.
– OPPOSITES domestic, native, familiar.

foreigner noun ALIEN, non-native, immigrant, incomer, newcomer, stranger, outsider.
– OPPOSITES native.

foremost adjective LEADING, principal, premier, top, first, primary, front, paramount, chief, main, most important, supreme, highest.

forerunner noun PREDECESSOR, precursor, antecedent, ancestor, forefather, harbinger, herald, usher, advance guard.

foreshadow verb FOREBODE, bode, presage, augur, portend, indicate, show, signify, point to, prefigure, promise.

foresight noun FAR-SIGHTEDNESS, perspicacity, anticipation, forethought, presence of mind, preparedness, readiness, prescience, provision, discernment, care, caution.

forest noun WOODLAND, wood, woods, trees, plantation.

forestall verb PRE-EMPT, anticipate, intercept, thwart, frustrate, stave off, ward off, fend off, prevent, avert, hinder, impede, obstruct; *informal* steal a march on, get ahead of.

foretell verb ❶ PREDICT, forecast, prophesy, foresee, forewarn, prognosticate, augur, divine.

❷ PRESAGE, augur, forebode, portend, foreshadow, prefigure, point to, indicate, betoken.

forethought noun FORESIGHT, far-sightedness, anticipation, provision, circumspection, prudence, judiciousness, care, precaution.

forever adverb ALWAYS, evermore, ever, for all time, until the end of time, eternally, perpetually; *informal* till the cows come home, till hell freezes over, for keeps, for good and all.

forfeit noun FINE, penalty, confiscation, damages, loss, relinquishment.
▶ verb GIVE UP, hand over, relinquish, be stripped of.

forge verb ❶ BEAT INTO SHAPE, hammer out, shape, form, fashion, mould, cast, found, make, manufacture, frame, construct, create. ❷ FAKE, fabricate, falsify, counterfeit, copy, imitate.

forgery noun FAKE, counterfeit, sham, fraud, imitation, reproduction; *informal* phoney.

forget verb ❶ FAIL TO REMEMBER, lose track of, overlook, let slip. ❷ DISREGARD, put out of one's mind, ignore, let bygones be bygones. ❸ I forgot my gloves: LEAVE BEHIND, omit to take, overlook.
– OPPOSITES remember.

forgetful adjective
❶ ABSENT-MINDED, vague, apt to forget, abstracted, amnesiac.
❷ forgetful of his duties: NEGLECTFUL, negligent, careless, heedless, unmindful, inattentive, lax, remiss, oblivious.

forgive verb PARDON, excuse, absolve, exonerate, acquit, let off, let bygones be bygones, bury the hatchet, bear no malice, harbour no grudge; *informal* let someone off the hook.

forgiveness noun PARDON, amnesty, reprieve, absolution, exoneration, acquittal, remission, clemency, tolerance, compassion, exculpation, indulgence, leniency.

forgiving adjective MERCIFUL, lenient, magnanimous, understanding, compassionate, humane, clement, soft-hearted, forbearing, tolerant, mild.
– OPPOSITES unforgiving.

forgo verb DO/GO WITHOUT, waive, renounce, sacrifice, relinquish, abjure, surrender, cede, abandon, yield, abstain from, refrain from, eschew; *formal* forswear.

fork verb BRANCH, branch off, diverge, bifurcate, divide, split, separate, go separate ways, divaricate.

forlorn adjective UNHAPPY, sad, miserable, wretched, pathetic, woebegone, disconsolate, lonely, cheerless, desolate, pitiable, pitiful, uncared for.

form noun ❶ SHAPE, formation, configuration, structure, construction, conformation, arrangement, appearance, exterior. ❷ help in the form of the police: APPEARANCE, shape, character, guise, description, manifestation, semblance. ❸ a form of work: TYPE, kind, sort, variety, species, genre, stamp, kidney, genus. ❹ the book lacks form: STRUCTURE, organization, order, planning, symmetry, proportion, orderliness, framework, format. ❺ the team's form: CONDITION, fitness, health, shape, trim, fettle. ❻ **not good form:** MANNERS, polite behaviour, acceptable conduct, etiquette, convention, protocol; *informal* the done thing. ❼ **fill in a form:** APPLICATION, document, paper, sheet of paper. ❽ **know the form:** MANNER, method, style, mode, system, formula, procedure, usual way, convention, custom, ritual, protocol.

▶ **verb** ❶ **form shapes:** MAKE, fashion, shape, model, mould, forge, construct, build, assemble, put together, set up, erect, produce, concoct, devise. ❷ **form plans:** DEVISE, formulate, think up, plan, draw up, frame, hatch, forge, develop, organize, dream up. ❸ **form an alliance:** BRING ABOUT, set up, establish, found, organize, institute, inaugurate. ❹ **a shape began to form:** TAKE SHAPE, appear, materialize, show, become visible, come into being. ❺ **form bad habits:** ACQUIRE, get into, contract, develop, get, pick up, grow into.

formal adjective ❶ **a formal person:** CORRECT, proper, conventional, reserved, aloof, remote, precise, exact, punctilious, stiff, unbending, inflexible, stand-offish, prim, stuffy, strait-laced. ❷ **formal procedures:** OFFICIAL, set, fixed, conventional, standard, regular, customary, approved, prescribed, pro forma, legal, lawful, ceremonial, ritual. ❸ **formal gardens:** ORDERLY, arranged, symmetrical, regular, methodical.
– OPPOSITES informal.

formation noun ❶ **planes in formation:** ARRANGEMENT, pattern, order, grouping, configuration, structure, format, layout, disposition, design. ❷ **the formation of a government:** ESTABLISHMENT, setting up, institution, founding, creation, inauguration. ❸ **the formation of the committee:** COMPOSITION, make-up, constitution, organization.

former adjective ❶ **the former president:** PREVIOUS, ex-, prior, preceding, earlier, late, sometime, erstwhile, one-time, foregoing, antecedent, anterior, ci-devant; *formal* quondam. ❷ **former times:** EARLIER, past, long past, bygone, long departed, long gone, old, ancient, of yore.

formidable adjective ❶ **formidable appearance:** INTIMIDATING, daunting, alarming, frightening, terrifying, horrifying, dreadful, awesome, fearsome, menacing, threatening, dangerous; *informal* scary. ❷ **a formidable opponent:** STRONG, powerful, impressive, mighty, great, redoubtable, terrific, indomitable, invincible. ❸ **a formidable task:** DIFFICULT, arduous, onerous, tough, mammoth, colossal, challenging, overwhelming, staggering.
– OPPOSITES weak, easy.

formula noun ❶ FORM OF WORDS, set expression, wording, rubric, formulary. ❷ RECIPE, prescription, method, blueprint, procedure, convention, modus operandi, ritual, principles, rules, precepts, rubric.

formulate verb ❶ **formulate plans:** DRAW UP, work out, plan, map out, prepare, compose, devise, think up, conceive, create, invent, coin, design. ❷ **formulate one's thoughts:** DEFINE, state clearly, set down, frame, give form to, specify, itemize, detail, indicate, systematize.

forsake verb ❶ DESERT, abandon, leave, quit, jilt, throw over, cast off, discard, repudiate, reject, disown; *informal* leave in the lurch, leave flat. ❷ GIVE UP, renounce, relinquish, forgo, turn one's back on, repudiate, have done with, discard, set aside.

forthcoming adjective ❶ FUTURE, coming, expected, prospective, imminent, impending. ❷ COMMUNICATIVE, informative, talkative, expansive, voluble, chatty, loquacious, open.

forthright adjective DIRECT, frank, open, candid, blunt, outspoken, plain-speaking, plain-spoken, straightforward, honest.
– OPPOSITES evasive.

fortify verb ❶ BUILD DEFENCES ROUND, protect, secure, garrison, cover, guard, buttress, shore up. ❷ **fortify himself with drink**: STRENGTHEN, invigorate, energize, revive, embolden, give courage to, encourage, cheer, hearten, buoy up, reassure, make confident, brace, sustain.

fortitude noun STRENGTH, firmness, courage, nerve, grit, backbone, bravery, pluck, mettle, fearlessness, valour, intrepidity, stout-heartedness, forbearance, tenacity, perseverance, resolution, resoluteness, determination.
– OPPOSITES cowardice.

fortunate adjective LUCKY, blessed, favoured, in luck, having a charmed life, happy, felicitous, prosperous, well off, successful, flourishing; *informal* sitting pretty, born with a silver spoon in one's mouth; *Brit. informal* jammy.

fortune noun ❶ WEALTH, affluence, treasure, opulence, prosperity, riches, property, assets, means, possessions. ❷ **cost a fortune**: HUGE AMOUNT, mint, king's ransom; *informal* packet, bundle, bomb, pile. ❸ **by good fortune**: CHANCE, accident, luck, coincidence, happy chance, fortuity, serendipity, contingency, providence.
– OPPOSITES pittance.

fortune-teller noun SEER, soothsayer, prophet, prophetess, augur, diviner, sibyl, oracle, clairvoyant, astrologer.

forward adjective ❶ **forward movement**: ONWARD, advancing, progressing, progressive, frontal. ❷ ADVANCED, well advanced, early, premature, precocious. ❸ **the forward unit**: FRONT, at the front/fore, fore, frontal, foremost, head, leading, advance. ❹ **a forward young woman**: BOLD, brash, brazen, audacious, presumptuous, cocky, familiar, assertive, confident, overweening, aggressive, pushy, thrusting, pert, impudent, impertinent, cheeky, insolent; *informal* brass-necked, fresh.
– OPPOSITES backward, shy.
▶ adverb ❶ **move forward**: TOWARDS THE FRONT, onward, onwards, on, ahead, forth. ❷ **step forward**: OUT, into view, into the open, into public view.
▶ verb ❶ **forward the letter**: SEND ON, pass on, dispatch, transmit, post, mail, ship, freight, deliver. ❷ **forward his plans**: ADVANCE, further, hasten, speed up, hurry along, accelerate, expedite, step up, aid, assist, help, encourage, foster, promote, favour, support, back, give backing to.

foster verb ❶ ENCOURAGE, promote, further, stimulate, boost, advance, forward, cultivate, foment, help, aid, assist, support, uphold, back, give backing to, facilitate. ❷ **foster children:** BRING UP, rear, raise, care for, look after, take care of, mother, parent. ❸ **foster hopes:** CHERISH, harbour, hold, entertain, nurse, nourish, nurture, sustain.

foul adjective ❶ **looks foul:** DISGUSTING, revolting, repulsive, nauseating, sickening, loathsome, odious, abominable, offensive, nasty. ❷ **smells foul:** EVIL-SMELLING, stinking, high, rank, fetid; *poetic/literary* mephitic, noisome. ❸ **foul water:** IMPURE, contaminated, polluted, adulterated, infected, tainted, defiled, filthy, dirty, unclean. ❹ **foul language:** BLASPHEMOUS, profane, obscene, vulgar, offensive, coarse, filthy, dirty, indecent, indelicate, smutty, salacious, suggestive, off colour, low, ribald, lewd, scatological; *informal* blue. ❺ **a foul man/crime:** ABHORRENT, detestable, hateful, loathsome, despicable, contemptible, offensive, odious, disgusting, revolting, dishonourable, disgraceful, base, low, mean, sordid, vile, wicked, heinous, execrable, iniquitous, nefarious, infamous. ❻ **foul play:** UNFAIR, dishonourable, dishonest, underhand, unsportsmanlike, unsporting, dirty, unprincipled, unscrupulous, immoral, fraudulent; *informal* crooked.
▶ verb DIRTY, soil, stain, blacken, muddy, begrime, smear, spatter, besmear, defile, pollute, contaminate, taint, sully; *poetic/literary* besmirch.

found verb ESTABLISH, set up, institute, originate, initiate, bring into being, create, start, inaugurate, constitute, endow, organize, develop.

foundation noun ❶ BASE, bottom, substructure, bedrock, substratum, understructure, underpinning. ❷ **the foundations of maths:** BASIS, groundwork, principles, fundamentals, rudiments. ❸ **the foundation of the company:** ESTABLISHMENT, founding, institution, inauguration, initiation, constitution, endowment.

founder noun ESTABLISHER, builder, constructor, maker, initiator, institutor, beginner, inventor, discoverer, framer, designer, architect, creator, author, originator, organizer, developer, generator, prime mover, father, patriarch.

fountain noun ❶ SPRAY, jet, spout, well, fount, stream, fountainhead. ❷ **a fountain of knowledge:** SOURCE, fount, fountainhead, origin, wellspring, commencement, beginning, cause, birth, genesis, root, mainspring, derivation, inception, inspiration.

fracas noun DISTURBANCE, quarrel, fight, brawl, rumpus, scuffle, tussle, skirmish, free-for-all, brouhaha, riot, uproar, commotion, tumult, trouble, pandemonium, turmoil; *informal* scrap, punch-up, dust-up; *Law, dated* affray.

fractious adjective BAD-TEMPERED, cross, irritable, ill-humoured, ill-natured, petulant, testy, querulous, touchy, irascible, sulky, sullen, morose; *informal* snappish.

fracture noun BREAK, breakage, rupture, split, crack, fissure, cleft, rift, rent, chink, crevice, gap, opening, aperture.
▶ verb BREAK, crack, split, rupture, splinter.

fragile adjective ❶ FLIMSY, breakable, frail, delicate, insubstantial, brittle, dainty, fine. ❷ ILL, unwell, sickly, ailing, delicate, weak, infirm.
– OPPOSITES strong.

fragment noun PIECE, part, particle, shred, chip, shard, sliver, splinter, scrap, bit, snip, snippet, wisp, tatter, remnant, remainder, fraction.
▶ verb *see* BREAK verb (1).

fragmentary adjective INCOMPLETE, partial, piecemeal, disconnected, broken, disjointed, discontinuous, uneven, incoherent, scrappy, bitty, sketchy, unsystematic.
– OPPOSITES complete, whole.

fragrance noun SCENT, smell, perfume, aroma, bouquet, balm, balminess; *poetic/literary* redolence.

fragrant adjective SWEET-SMELLING, aromatic, scented, perfumed, balmy, odorous, odoriferous; *poetic/literary* redolent.
– OPPOSITES smelly.

frail adjective ❶ FRAGILE, breakable, delicate, easily broken; *formal* frangible. ❷ frail old lady: WEAK, infirm, ill, unwell, sickly, ailing, delicate, slight, slender, puny, unsound.
– OPPOSITES strong, robust.

frame noun ❶ STRUCTURE, framework, foundation, body, chassis, skeleton, scaffolding, shell, casing, support. ❷ BODY, physique, build, figure, shape, size, carcass. ❸ a picture frame: MOUNT, mounting, setting, border.
▶ verb ❶ frame a policy: FORMULATE, put together, draw up, plan, think up, draft, map out, shape, compose, form, devise, create, establish, conceive. ❷ framed for murder: INCRIMINATE, fabricate charges/evidence against; *Brit. informal* fit up.

framework noun ❶ *See* FRAME noun (1). ❷ the framework of society: ORDER, organization, frame, scheme, fabric.

frank adjective ❶ a frank reply/person: CANDID, direct, straightforward, plain, plain-spoken, straight, outspoken, blunt, open, sincere, honest, truthful, artless, guileless, explicit, downright. ❷ show frank admiration: OPEN, obvious, transparent, patent, undisguised, manifest, unmistakable, evident, noticeable, visible.
– OPPOSITES evasive.

frantic adjective DISTRAUGHT, overwrought, panic-stricken, panicky, beside oneself, at one's wits' end, frenzied, wild, hysterical, frenetic, berserk, worked up, fraught, distracted, agitated, distressed, out of control, uncontrolled, unhinged, mad, crazed, out of one's mind, maniacal.
– OPPOSITES calm.

fraud noun ❶ FRAUDULENCE, sharp practice, cheating, swindling, crookedness, embezzlement, trickery, deceit, double-dealing, duplicity, treachery, chicanery, imposture, skulduggery; *informal* monkey business. ❷ RUSE, trick, deception, swindle, hoax, subterfuge, wile, stratagem, artifice. ❸ he is a fraud: IMPOSTOR, fake, sham, cheat, cheater, swindler, trickster, charlatan, quack, mountebank; *informal* phoney, con man.

fraudulent adjective DISHONEST, cheating, swindling, criminal, deceitful, double-dealing, duplicitous, unscrupulous, dishonourable; *informal* crooked, shady, sharp.
– OPPOSITES honest.

fraught adjective ❶ fraught with danger: FILLED WITH, full of, attended by, teeming with, accompanied by. ❷ feeling fraught: ANXIOUS, distraught, overwrought, agitated, worked up, distracted, distressed.

fray verb ❶ UNRAVEL, wear, wear thin, wear out/away, become threadbare, become tattered/ragged. ❷ tempers fraying: STRAIN, tax, overtax, irritate, put on edge, make edgy/tense.

freak noun ❶ ABERRATION, abnormality, oddity, irregularity, monster, monstrosity, mutant, malformation. ❷ ODDITY, peculiar person; *informal* queer fish, odd bod, oddball, weirdo, nutcase, nut. ❸ film freaks: FAN, enthusiast, fanatic, addict, aficionado, devotee; *informal* buff, fiend, nut.
▶ adjective ABNORMAL, unusual, aberrant, atypical, exceptional, unaccountable, unpredictable, unforeseeable, bizarre, queer, odd, unparalleled, fluky.

free adjective ❶ a free ticket: FREE OF CHARGE, complimentary, for nothing, without charge, gratis, at no cost, for free, on the house. ❷ free from responsibilities: WITHOUT, devoid of, lacking in, exempt from, not liable to, safe from, immune to, unaffected by, clear of, unencumbered by, relieved of, released from, rid of. ❸ she is not free today: AVAILABLE, unoccupied, at leisure, with time on one's hands, with time to spare. ❹ a free seat: UNOCCUPIED, empty, vacant, available, spare, untaken, uninhabited. ❺ a free country: INDEPENDENT, self-governing, autonomous, sovereign, emancipated, democratic, enfranchised. ❻ the animals are free: AT LIBERTY, at large, loose, on the loose, unconfined, unchained, unrestrained, unshackled, unfettered. ❼ a free flow: UNOBSTRUCTED, unimpeded, clear, unblocked, unhampered. ❽ free in his manner: FAMILIAR, overfamiliar, bold, assertive, presumptuous, cocky, forward, cheeky, aggressive, impudent.
▶ verb ❶ SET FREE, release, let go, set at liberty, liberate, turn loose, untie, unchain, unfetter, unshackle, uncage, unleash, deliver. ❷ RESCUE, release, extricate, get loose, disentangle, disengage, disencumber. ❸ EXEMPT, make exempt, excuse, except, relieve.

freedom noun ❶ LIBERTY, emancipation, release, deliverance, independence, autonomy, sovereignty, self-government, enfranchisement; *historical* manumission. ❷ freedom to operate: SCOPE, latitude, flexibility, wide margin, elbow room, licence, facility, free rein. ❸ freedom of manner: NATURALNESS, openness, lack of reserve, informality, lack of ceremony, spontaneity.
– OPPOSITES captivity.

freeze verb ❶ ICE OVER/UP, glaciate, solidify, harden. ❷ CHILL, cool, make cold, deep-freeze. ❸ STAND STILL, stop dead, stop in one's tracks, go rigid, become motionless. ❹ **freeze prices**: FIX, hold, peg, suspend.

freezing adjective BITTERLY COLD, chilling, frosty, glacial, arctic, wintry, raw, biting, piercing, penetrating, cutting, numbing, Siberian.

freight noun CARGO, load, consignment, lading, merchandise, goods.

frenzy noun MADNESS, mania, insanity, wild excitement, wildness, hysteria, agitation, distraction, fit, seizure, paroxysm, outburst, spasm.

frequent adjective ❶ **frequent accidents**: MANY, numerous, several, repeated, recurrent, persistent, continuing, quite a lot/few. ❷ **frequent caller**: REGULAR, habitual, common, customary, usual, familiar, everyday, continual, constant, incessant.
– OPPOSITES infrequent.
▶ verb VISIT, attend, haunt, patronize; *informal* hang out at.

fresh adjective ❶ **fresh fruit**: NATURAL, unprocessed, raw, newly harvested, crisp, unwilted, undried, uncured. ❷ **fresh ideas**: NEW, brand new, recent, latest, up to date, modern, new-fangled, innovative, different, original, novel, unusual, unconventional, unorthodox. ❸ **feeling fresh**: ENERGETIC, vigorous, invigorated, lively, vibrant, spry, sprightly, bright, alert, bouncing, refreshed, rested, restored, revived, fresh as a daisy; *informal* full of beans, bright-eyed and bushy-tailed. ❹ **fresh supplies**: ADDITIONAL, more, further, extra, supplementary. ❺ **a fresh complexion**: HEALTHY, clear, bright, wholesome, blooming, glowing, fair, rosy, pink, ruddy. ❻ **fresh air/a fresh morning**: CLEAR, bright, cool, crisp, sparkling, pure, clean, refreshing. ❼ **a fresh young man**: FAMILIAR, overfamiliar, forward, presumptuous, cocky, bold, audacious, brazen, cheeky, impudent, impertinent, insolent, disrespectful; *informal* brass-necked. ❽ **fresh recruits**: NEW, untrained, newly arrived, raw, untried, callow, green, immature, artless, ingenuous, naive; *informal* wet behind the ears.
– OPPOSITES stale, old, tired.

fret verb ❶ WORRY, be upset, be distressed, be anxious, agonize, pine, brood, mope, fuss, complain, grumble, whine. ❷ *See* ANNOY (2).

friction noun ❶ ABRASION, attrition, rubbing, chafing, scraping, rasping. ❷ **friction in the family**: DISSENSION, dissent, disagreement, discord, strife, conflict, contention, dispute, argument, quarrelling, bickering, squabbling, hostility, rivalry, animosity, antagonism, resentment, bad feeling.
– OPPOSITES harmony.

friend noun COMPANION, crony, bosom friend, comrade, playmate, soul mate, intimate, confidante, alter ego, ally, acquaintance, associate, familiar, shadow; *informal* pal, chum; *Brit. informal* mate; *N. Amer. informal* buddy.
– OPPOSITES enemy.

friendless adjective ALONE, companionless, by oneself, lone, lonely, lonesome, with no one to turn to, solitary, with no ties, unattached, single, forlorn, unpopular, unloved, forsaken, deserted, ostracized, abandoned.

friendliness noun AMIABILITY, affability, geniality, warmth, affection, companionability, cordiality, conviviality, sociability, neighbourliness, approachability, communicativeness, good-naturedness, amenability, benevolence.
– OPPOSITES hostility.

friendly adjective ❶ a friendly person: AMIABLE, affable, warm, genial, agreeable, companionable, cordial, convivial, sociable, hospitable, comradely, neighbourly, outgoing, approachable, accessible, communicative, open, unreserved, easy-going, good-natured, kindly, benign, amenable, well disposed, sympathetic, benevolent; *informal* chummy; *Brit. informal* matey. ❷ on friendly terms: AMICABLE, close, cordial, congenial, intimate, familiar, peaceable, conciliatory.
– OPPOSITES unfriendly.

friendship noun ❶ CLOSE RELATIONSHIP, companionship, intimacy, rapport, affinity, attachment, alliance, harmony, fellowship, mutual understanding, amity, comradeship. ❷ FRIENDLINESS, affability, amiability, warmth, geniality, cordiality, neighbourliness, good-naturedness, kindliness.

fright noun ❶ FEAR, terror, alarm, horror, dread, fearfulness, apprehension, trepidation, consternation, dismay, disquiet, nervousness, panic; *informal* blue funk, jitters, heebie-jeebies, willies. ❷ SCARE, shock, shivers.

frighten verb SCARE, terrify, startle, alarm, terrorize, give a shock to, shock, panic, appal, throw into a panic, unnerve, unman, intimidate, cow, daunt, dismay, make someone's blood run cold, freeze someone's blood; *informal* scare the living daylights out of, scare stiff, scare someone out of their wits, scare witless, make someone's hair stand on end, make someone's hair curl, throw into a blue funk, make someone jump out of their skin, spook; *Brit. informal* put the wind up.

frightful adjective ❶ a frightful sight: DREADFUL, terrible, horrible, horrid, hideous, ghastly, gruesome, grisly, macabre, grim, dire, abhorrent, revolting, repulsive, loathsome, odious, fearful, fearsome, terrifying, alarming, shocking, harrowing, appalling, daunting, unnerving. ❷ a frightful woman: DISAGREEABLE, unpleasant, dreadful, horrible, terrible, awful, ghastly, insufferable, unbearable, annoying, irritating. ❸ a frightful cold: VERY BAD, terrible, dreadful, awful, ghastly, nasty.

frigid adjective ❶ a frigid look/welcome: COLD, icy, distant, austere, aloof, remote, unapproachable, forbidding, stiff, formal, unbending, cool, unfeeling, unemotional, unfriendly, hostile, unenthusiastic. ❷ a frigid woman: PASSIONLESS, cold, unresponsive, passive. ❸ frigid conditions: VERY COLD, bitterly cold, freezing, frozen, icy, frosty, chilly, wintry, arctic, glacial, Siberian, polar, gelid.

frills plural noun ORNAMENTATION, decoration, embellishment, fanciness, ostentation, fuss, trimmings, extras, affectations, additions, superfluities, bits and pieces.

fringe noun ❶ BORDER, frill, ruffle, gathering, trimming, tassels, edging. ❷ OUTER EDGE, edge, border, perimeter, periphery, margin, rim, limits, outskirts, verge.

frisky adjective LIVELY, bouncy, active, playful, spirited, romping, rollicking, sportive, in high spirits, high-spirited, exuberant, joyful, sprightly, perky, jaunty; *informal* full of beans; *poetic/literary* frolicsome.

frivolity noun ❶ LIGHT-HEARTEDNESS, gaiety, levity, fun, silliness, foolishness. ❷ EMPTY-HEADEDNESS, frivolousness, giddiness, flightiness, dizziness, flippancy, silliness, zaniness.

frivolous adjective ❶ SILLY, flighty, foolish, dizzy, facetious, flippant, senseless, giddy, light-hearted, merry, superficial, shallow, empty-headed, feather-brained. ❷ **a frivolous remark**: FLIPPANT, ill-considered, inane, facetious, superficial, shallow; *informal* flip. ❸ **frivolous clothes**: IMPRACTICAL, frothy, flimsy.
– OPPOSITES serious.

frolic verb GAMBOL, cavort, skip, frisk, caper, cut capers, dance, leap, romp, trip, prance, hop, jump, bounce, rollick, sport, curvet.
▶ **noun** ROMP, lark, antics, caper, escapade, prank, revels, spree, high jinks.

front noun ❶ FACE, facade, frontage, fore, forepart, foremost part, forefront, foreground, anterior. ❷ HEAD, top, lead, beginning. ❸ **the front in the battle**: FRONT LINE, vanguard, van, firing line. ❹ **put a brave front on it**: LOOK, appearance, face, exterior, air, manner, demeanour, expression, show, countenance, bearing, mien, aspect. ❺ **a front for drug dealing**: COVER, blind, facade, disguise, pretext, mask.
– OPPOSITES back.
▶ **adjective** LEADING, lead, first, foremost.
■ **front on** FACE TOWARDS, look out on, overlook, lie opposite to.

frontier noun BORDER, boundary, limit, edge, rim, bounds, confines, marches.

frosty adjective ❶ FREEZING, frozen, cold, glacial, frigid, arctic, icy, wintry, bitter. ❷ **a frosty welcome**: UNFRIENDLY, cold, unwelcoming, unenthusiastic, icy, glacial.

froth noun FOAM, fizz, lather, head, scum, effervescence, bubbles, suds, spume.

frown verb ❶ SCOWL, glare, glower, knit one's brows, lower, lour; *informal* look daggers at, give a dirty look to. ❷ **frown on/at something**: DISAPPROVE OF, view with dislike/disfavour, dislike, not take kindly to, not think much of, take a dim view of, look askance at.

frugal adjective THRIFTY, economical, sparing, careful, prudent, abstemious, scrimping, niggardly, cheese-paring, penny-pinching, miserly, parsimonious; *informal* stingy.
– OPPOSITES extravagant, spendthrift.

fruitful adjective ❶ FERTILE, fecund, potent, abundant, flourishing, lush, copious,

bountiful; *poetic/literary* bounteous. ❷ **fruitful discussions:** USEFUL, worthwhile, productive, well spent, profitable, advantageous, beneficial, rewarding, gainful, successful, effective.
– OPPOSITES barren, futile, fruitless.

fruition noun FULFILMENT, realization, materialization, achievement, attainment, success, completion, consummation, actualization, perfection, maturation, maturity, ripening.

fruitless adjective FUTILE, useless, vain, in vain, to no avail, worthless, pointless, abortive, to no effect, idle, ineffectual, ineffective, inefficacious, unproductive, unrewarding, profitless, unsuccessful, unavailing.
– OPPOSITES fruitful, productive.

frustrate verb ❶ DISCOURAGE, dishearten, dispirit, depress, dissatisfy, make, discontented, anger, annoy, vex, irritate, embitter, irk. ❷ **frustrate their attempts:** DEFEAT, thwart, obstruct, impede, hamper, hinder, check, block, counter, foil, baulk, forestall, disappoint, baffle, stymie, stop, cripple, spoil, circumvent.

fudge verb ❶ EVADE, dodge, avoid, shift ground about. ❷ EQUIVOCATE, hedge; *Brit.* hum and haw; *N. Amer. informal* waffle.

fuel verb ❶ SUPPLY WITH FUEL, fire, stoke up, charge, power. ❷ **fuel her anger:** INFLAME, fan, incite, provoke, goad, stimulate, encourage.

fugitive noun ESCAPEE, runaway, deserter, refugee, renegade.
▶ **adjective** TRANSIENT, transitory, fleeting, ephemeral, passing, impermanent, momentary, short-lived, short, brief, evanescent, fugacious.

fulfil verb ❶ ACCOMPLISH, achieve, carry out, execute, perform, discharge, complete, implement, finish, conclude, effect; *formal* effectuate. ❷ **fulfil his desire:** SATISFY, realize, attain, consummate. ❸ **fulfil the requirements:** SATISFY, conform to, fill, answer, meet, comply with, obey.

full adjective ❶ **the cup is full:** FILLED UP, filled, filled to the brim, brimming, overflowing, filled to capacity. ❷ **the shop was full:** CROWDED, packed, crammed, solid with people, chock-a-block, chock-full; *informal* jam-packed. ❸ **feeling full:** SATISFIED, sated, gorged, replete, glutted, cloyed. ❹ **a full list:** COMPLETE, entire, whole, comprehensive, thorough, exhaustive, detailed, all-inclusive, all-encompassing, extensive, unabridged. ❺ **a full programme:** ABUNDANT, plentiful, copious, ample, sufficient, broad-ranging, complete, satisfying. ❻ **a full figure:** WELL ROUNDED, rounded, plump, buxom, shapely, curvaceous, voluptuous; *informal* busty. ❼ **a full skirt:** BAGGY, voluminous, loose-fitting, capacious. ❽ **a full voice:** RICH, deep, resonant, loud, strong; *informal* fruity.
– OPPOSITES empty, incomplete.

fully adverb COMPLETELY, entirely, wholly, totally, thoroughly, in all respects, utterly, amply, satisfactorily.

fumble verb ❶ **fumble a ball:** FAIL TO CATCH, miss, drop, mishandle, misfield. ❷ **fumble for his keys:** GROPE, feel about, search blindly, scrabble about/around.

fume verb BE ENRAGED, seethe, boil, be livid, rage, rant and rave, be furious, be incensed, flare up; *informal* be up in arms, get hot under the collar, fly off the handle, foam at the mouth, get all steamed up, flip one's lid, blow one's top.

fumes plural noun VAPOUR, gas, exhaust, smoke, pollution, smog, fog.

fun noun ❶ AMUSEMENT, entertainment, recreation, relaxation, enjoyment, pleasure, diversion, play, playfulness, tomfoolery, buffoonery, distraction, good time, jollification, merrymaking, junketing; *informal* living it up, skylarking. ❷ **full of fun:** MERRIMENT, gaiety, mirth, laughter, hilarity, glee, cheerfulness, gladness, jollity, joy, high spirits, zest.
– OPPOSITES misery.
■ **make fun of** RIDICULE, deride, mock, scoff at, sneer at, taunt, jeer at, lampoon, parody; *informal* send up, rib, take off.

function noun ❶ ROLE, capacity, responsibility, duty, task, job, post, situation, office, occupation, employment, business, charge, province, concern, activity, operation, mission. ❷ SOCIAL EVENT, gathering, affair, reception, party; *informal* do; *Brit. informal* beanfeast.
▶ **verb** WORK, go, run, be in working order, operate.

functional adjective ❶ PRACTICAL, useful, serviceable, utilitarian, working, workaday, hard-wearing. ❷ WORKING, in working order, going, running, operative, in commission.

fund noun RESERVE, collection, pool, kitty, endowment, foundation, grant, investment, capital, savings.
▶ **verb** FINANCE, pay for, back, subsidize, stake, endow, support.

fundamental adjective BASIC, rudimentary, elemental, underlying, primary, cardinal, initial, original, prime, first, principal, chief, key, central, structural, organic, inherent, intrinsic, vital, essential, important, indispensable, necessary.
– OPPOSITES unimportant.

fundamentally adverb BASICALLY, at heart, at bottom, deep down, essentially, intrinsically.

funds plural noun MONEY, ready money, cash, hard cash, capital, the wherewithal, means, assets, resources, savings; *informal* dough, bread, folding stuff.

funereal adjective DARK, gloomy, dismal, drab, depressing, dreary, sombre, grave, solemn, melancholy, sad, lugubrious.
– OPPOSITES cheerful.

funny adjective ❶ AMUSING, comical, comic, humorous, hilarious, entertaining, diverting, laughable, hysterical, side-splitting, witty, jocular, riotous, droll, absurd, rich, facetious, ludicrous, ridiculous, farcical, risible, silly, slapstick, waggish. ❷ PECULIAR, odd, strange, curious, queer, bizarre, mysterious, suspicious, dubious; *informal* weird.
– OPPOSITES serious.

furious adjective ❶ ENRAGED, very angry, raging, infuriated, livid, fuming, boiling, incensed, inflamed, frenzied, indignant, mad, maddened, wrathful, beside oneself, in high dudgeon; *informal* hot under the collar, up in arms, foaming at the mouth. ❷ a furious storm/struggle: VIOLENT, fierce, wild, intense, vehement, unrestrained, tumultuous, tempestuous, stormy, turbulent, boisterous.
– OPPOSITES calm.

furnish verb ❶ furnish a room: PROVIDE WITH FURNITURE, fit out, outfit, appoint. ❷ furnish with details: SUPPLY, provide, give, present, offer, equip, grant, bestow, endow, provision.

furniture noun FURNISHINGS, house fittings, effects, movables, appointments, chattels.

furore noun COMMOTION, uproar, disturbance, hullabaloo, turmoil, tumult, brouhaha, tempest, stir, excitement, outburst, outcry; *informal* to-do.

furrow noun ❶ GROOVE, trench, channel, rut, trough, ditch, seam, hollow. ❷ CREASE, line, wrinkle, crinkle, corrugation, crow's foot.

further adjective ADDITIONAL, more, extra, supplementary, other, new, fresh.
▶ adverb FURTHERMORE, moreover, what's more, also, besides, additionally, as well, to boot, on top of that, over and above that, by the same token.
▶ verb ADVANCE, forward, facilitate, aid, assist, help, lend a hand to, promote, back, contribute to, encourage, foster, champion.

furthest adjective FARTHEST, furthermost, most distant, most remote, outermost, outmost, extreme, uttermost, ultimate.

furtive adjective SECRETIVE, secret, stealthy, surreptitious, clandestine, sneaky, sneaking, hidden, disguised, shifty, skulking, covert, cloaked, conspiratorial, sly, underhand, under the table, wily.
– OPPOSITES open, above board.

fury noun ❶ ANGER, rage, wrath, madness, passion, frenzy; *poetic/literary* ire. ❷ the fury of the storm: FIERCENESS, violence, ferocity, intensity, force, power, severity, turbulence, tempestuousness.

fuse verb COMBINE, amalgamate, join, put together, unite, blend, intermix, intermingle, merge, coalesce, integrate, meld, compound, agglutinate, weld, solder.
– OPPOSITES separate.

fuss noun FLUSTER, agitation, excitement, bother, commotion, stir, confusion, uproar, tumult, upset, worry; *informal* palaver, storm in a teacup, flap, tizzy, stew.
▶ verb BE WORRIED/AGITATED, worry, rush about, dash about; *informal* get worked up, be in a tizzy, flap, be in a stew, make a big thing out of it.

fussy adjective ❶ PARTICULAR, over-particular, finicky, pernickety, fastidious, hard to please, difficult, exacting, demanding, selective, discriminating, faddish; *informal* choosy, picky, nit-picking; *Brit. informal* faddy. ❷ fussy rooms: CLUTTERED, busy, over-decorated, ornate, overdone, over-elaborate, rococo, over-embellished.

futile adjective ❶ a futile search: USELESS, vain, in vain, to no avail, ineffectual, unsuccessful, unproductive, unprofitable, abortive, unavailing, inefficacious, barren, impotent, hollow. ❷ a futile statement: UNIMPORTANT, trivial, petty, trifling, valueless, worthless, inconsequential.
– OPPOSITES fruitful, significant.

future noun ❶ TIME TO COME, time ahead, hereafter, coming times. ❷ PROSPECTS, expectations, anticipation, outlook, likely success/advancement.
▶ adjective FORTHCOMING, coming, impending, approaching, prospective, expected, planned, destined, awaited.

fuzzy adjective ❶ DOWNY, down-covered, frizzy, woolly, furry, fleecy, fluffy, linty, napped. ❷ fuzzy recollections: CONFUSED, muddled, fuddled, befuddled, foggy, misty, shadowy, blurred. ❸ picture's gone fuzzy: OUT OF FOCUS, unfocused, blurred, blurry, indistinct, unclear, misty, distorted, ill-defined, bleary.

Gg

gadget noun APPLIANCE, apparatus, device, contrivance, mechanism, instrument, tool, implement, invention, contraption; *informal* widget, gismo.

gaffe noun MISTAKE, blunder, slip, indiscretion, faux pas, solecism, gaucherie; *informal* clanger, howler, boo-boo; *Brit. informal* boob; *Brit. informal, dated* bloomer.

gag noun JOKE, witticism, jest, quip, funny remark, hoax, prank; *informal* crack, wisecrack.

gaiety noun ❶ CHEERFULNESS, light-heartedness, merriment, glee, happiness, high spirits, gladness, delight, joy, joyfulness, joyousness, pleasure, exuberance, elation, jollity, hilarity, mirth, joviality, liveliness, animation, vivacity, effervescence, buoyancy, sprightliness, exultation; *poetic/literary* blitheness. ❷ COLOURFULNESS, brightness, sparkle, brilliance, glitter, showiness, gaudiness, garishness.
– OPPOSITES gloom.

gain verb ❶ gain an advantage: OBTAIN, get, acquire, secure, procure, attain, build up, achieve, arrive at, come to have, win, capture, pick up, net, reap, gather. ❷ gain weight: INCREASE IN, add on, get more of. ❸ they were gaining on him: CATCH UP WITH, get nearer to, close in on, narrow the gap between, overtake, come up to, approach. ❹ gain the shore: REACH, arrive at, get to, come to, attain.
– OPPOSITES lose.
▶ noun ❶ INCREASE, addition, rise, augmentation, increment, accumulation, accretion. ❷ PROFIT, earnings, income, advantage, benefit, reward, yield, return, winnings, proceeds, dividend, interest, emolument; *informal* pickings.

gainful adjective PROFITABLE,

rewarding, remunerative, lucrative, productive, beneficial, fruitful, advantageous, worthwhile, useful.

gait noun WALK, step, stride, pace, tread, manner of walking, bearing, carriage.

gale noun STORM, tempest, hurricane, squall, tornado, cyclone, typhoon.

gallant adjective ❶ CHIVALROUS, gentlemanly, courtly, courteous, polite, attentive, gracious, considerate, thoughtful, obliging, deferential. ❷ BRAVE, courageous, valiant, bold, daring, plucky, fearless, intrepid, dashing, heroic, lion-hearted, mettlesome.
– OPPOSITES rude, cowardly.

galvanize verb ELECTRIFY, shock, stir, startle, jolt, arouse, awaken, spur, prod, stimulate, invigorate, fire, animate, vitalize, energize, thrill, inspire.

gamble verb ❶ BET, wager, lay a bet, place a wager, stake, game, try one's luck; *informal* punt; *Brit. informal* have a flutter. ❷ TAKE A CHANCE/RISK, speculate, venture; *informal* stick one's neck out, go out on a limb, take a flier.

game noun ❶ PASTIME, diversion, recreation, entertainment, amusement, sport, play, distraction, frolic, romp, fun, merriment. ❷ MATCH, contest, tournament, meeting, event, round, bout. ❸ **in the oil game:** BUSINESS, line, trade, occupation, profession, industry, activity, calling. ❹ **shooting game:** WILD ANIMALS, quarry, prey, big game.

gang noun GROUP, band, company, crowd, gathering, pack, horde, mob, herd.

gangly adjective LANKY, rangy, skinny, angular, spindly, awkward.

gangster noun RACKETEER, crook, criminal, hoodlum, Mafioso, gang member, mobster, robber, brigand, bandit, desperado, thug; *informal* tough; *N. Amer. informal* hood.

gap noun ❶ OPENING, hole, aperture, cavity, space, breach, break, fracture, rift, fissure, rent, cleft, chink, crack, crevice, divide, cranny, orifice, interstice. ❷ PAUSE, break, intermission, interval, interlude, lull, respite, breathing space, rest, suspension, hiatus, recess. ❸ OMISSION, blank, lacuna, void, vacuity. ❹ DIFFERENCE, disparity, inconsistency, incompatibility, disagreement, divergence, breach, discrepancy, distance, division.

gape verb ❶ STARE, gaze, goggle, ogle; *informal* gawk, rubberneck. ❷ OPEN WIDE, open up, yawn, part, split, crack.

garb noun CLOTHES, garments, clothing, dress, attire, costume, outfit, wear, uniform, vestments, livery, trappings; *informal* gear, get-up, togs, rig-out, duds; *formal* apparel; *archaic* habit.
▶ **verb** CLOTHE, dress, attire, array, robe, cover, outfit, fit; *informal* kit out, rig out; *archaic* apparel.

garbage noun WASTE, rubbish, refuse, litter, debris, junk, filth, detritus, scraps, leftovers, remains, slops.

garble verb DISTORT, twist, warp, slant, doctor, falsify, pervert, corrupt, misstate, misquote, misreport, misrepresent, misinterpret, misunderstand.

garish adjective FLASHY, flash, showy, loud, gaudy, lurid, bold,

glaring, brassy, tinselly, vivid, tawdry, tasteless, in poor taste, vulgar, cheap, meretricious, crude, Brummagem.
– OPPOSITES sober, tasteful.

garner verb GATHER, collect, accumulate, heap, pile up, amass, stack up, assemble, hoard, stockpile, deposit, husband, reserve, save, preserve.

garrison noun ❶ FORCE, detachment, unit, brigade, platoon, squadron. ❷ BARRACKS, base, fort, fortress, fortification, stronghold, camp, encampment, citadel.
▶ verb STATION, post, assign, position, billet, send in.

garrulous adjective TALKATIVE, chatty, verbose, loquacious, long-winded, effusive; *informal* mouthy, gabby.
– OPPOSITES taciturn.

gash verb CUT, slash, tear, lacerate, wound, gouge, incise, slit, rend, split, rent, nick, cleave.

gasp verb PANT, puff, puff and blow, blow, catch one's breath, gulp, choke, fight for breath, wheeze; *informal* huff and puff.

gate noun BARRIER, door, gateway, doorway, access, entrance, exit, opening, turnstile, passage, egress, portal, wicket, postern.

gather verb ❶ crowds gathered: COME TOGETHER, collect, assemble, congregate, meet, group, cluster, mass, crowd, flock together, convene, foregather, muster, converge, accumulate. ❷ gather them together: CALL TOGETHER, summon, assemble, collect, convene, round up, muster, marshal. ❸ gather stocks/facts: COLLECT, accumulate, assemble, amass, store, garner, stockpile, heap up, pile up, stack up, hoard; *informal* stash away. ❹ we gather he's dead: UNDERSTAND, be given to understand, believe, hear, learn, infer, deduce, conclude, come to the conclusion, surmise, assume. ❺ gather in the harvest: COLLECT, pick, harvest, reap, glean, garner, cull, pluck. ❻ gather in strength: INCREASE, grow, rise, build, expand, enlarge, swell, extend, intensify, deepen, heighten, thicken.
– OPPOSITES disperse.

gathering noun ASSEMBLY, congregation, company, collection, group, crowd, band, throng, mass, horde, meeting, convention, conclave, rally, congress, convocation.

gauche adjective AWKWARD, clumsy, ungainly, bumbling, maladroit, lumbering, inept, inelegant, unpolished, graceless, unsophisticated, uncultured, uncultivated.
– OPPOSITES sophisticated, adroit.

gaudy adjective *see* GARISH.

gauge noun ❶ SIZE, measure, extent, degree, capacity, magnitude, height, width, thickness, span, bore. ❷ MEASURE, basis, standard, guide, guideline, touchstone, yardstick, benchmark, criterion, rule, norm, example, model, pattern, exemplar, sample, test, indicator.

gaunt adjective ❶ HAGGARD, drawn, cadaverous, skeletal, emaciated, skinny, skin and bone, spare, bony, angular, lanky, lean, raw-boned, spindly, pinched, hollow-cheeked, scrawny, scraggy, wasted, shrivelled, withered. ❷ BLEAK, barren, desolate, bare, dreary, dismal,

forlorn, grim, stern, harsh, forbidding.
– OPPOSITES fat, lush.

gawky adjective UNGAINLY, clumsy, gauche, maladroit, ungraceful, gangling, inept, lumbering, blundering, lanky, oafish, loutish, doltish, lumpish; *informal* clodhopping.
– OPPOSITES graceful.

gay adjective ❶ LIGHT-HEARTED, jolly, merry, cheerful, jovial, glad, mirthful, happy, bright, joyful, elated, exuberant, animated, cock-a-hoop, lively, sprightly, vivacious, buoyant, effervescent, playful; *poetic/literary* frolicsome. ❷ HOMOSEXUAL, lesbian, homoerotic; *informal* queer; *Brit. informal* bent, poofy.
– OPPOSITES gloomy, heterosexual.

gaze verb STARE, gape, take a good look, look fixedly, goggle, stand agog, watch in wonder, ogle, eye, contemplate; *informal* gawk, rubberneck, give the once-over.

gear noun ❶ EQUIPMENT, tools, kit, apparatus, implements, tackle, appliances, utensils, supplies, accessories, paraphernalia, accoutrements, contrivances, trappings; *informal* stuff. ❷ BELONGINGS, possessions, things, luggage, baggage, kit, effects, goods, paraphernalia, impedimenta, chattels.

genealogy noun FAMILY TREE, ancestry, pedigree, line, lineage, descent, parentage, birth, derivation, extraction, family, strain, stock, bloodline, heritage, roots.

general adjective ❶ general practice: USUAL, customary, common, ordinary, normal, standard, regular, everyday, typical, conventional, habitual, run-of-the-mill. ❷ the general feeling: COMMON, accepted, widespread, shared, broad, wide, prevalent, prevailing, universal, popular, public, generic, extensive. ❸ a general pay rise: UNIVERSAL, blanket, comprehensive, all-inclusive, across-the-board, broad-ranging, broad, sweeping, indiscriminate, catholic, encyclopedic. ❹ general knowledge: MIXED, assorted, miscellaneous, diversified, variegated, composite, heterogeneous. ❺ a general account: BROAD, loose, rough, approximate, non-specific, vague, ill-defined, indefinite, inexact, imprecise.
– OPPOSITES unusual, specific, detailed.

generally adverb ❶ USUALLY, in general, as a rule, normally, ordinarily, almost always, customarily, habitually, typically, regularly, for the most part, mainly, by and large, on average, on the whole, in most cases. ❷ COMMONLY, widely, extensively, universally, comprehensively.

generate verb CAUSE, give rise to, produce, make, bring into being, create, engender, originate, initiate, occasion, arouse, whip up, propagate.

generosity noun LIBERALITY, kindness, magnanimity, benevolence, munificence, open-handedness, bounty, hospitality, charitableness, lavishness.

generous adjective ❶ LIBERAL, kind, magnanimous, benevolent, munificent, beneficent, bountiful, hospitable, open-handed,

charitable, ungrudging, lavish, unstinting, free-handed, princely; *poetic/literary* bounteous. ❷ a generous spirit: NOBLE, magnanimous, high-minded, honourable, good, unselfish, altruistic, unprejudiced, disinterested. ❸ a generous supply: ABUNDANT, liberal, plentiful, lavish, ample, rich, copious, superabundant, overflowing.
– OPPOSITES mean, selfish, meagre.

genial adjective AMIABLE, affable, friendly, sociable, congenial, amicable, convivial, good-humoured, good-natured, agreeable, warm, pleasant, cordial, amenable, well disposed, cheerful, cheery, kind, kindly, benign, happy, sunny, jovial, easy-going, sympathetic.
– OPPOSITES unfriendly.

genius noun ❶ he's a genius: BRILLIANT PERSON, mental giant, prodigy, virtuoso, master, mastermind, maestro, intellectual, intellect, expert, adept; *informal* brain, Einstein. ❷ a person of genius: BRILLIANCE, intelligence, cleverness, capability, flair, talent, aptitude, ability, capacity, endowment.

genteel adjective ❶ RESPECTABLE, refined, patrician, ladylike, gentlemanly, well bred, aristocratic, noble, blue-blooded, well born. ❷ POLITE, well mannered, courteous, mannerly, civil, gracious, decorous, courtly, polished, cultivated, stylish, elegant.
– OPPOSITES uncouth.

gentle adjective ❶ a gentle person: TENDER, kind, kindly, humane, benign, merciful, lenient, compassionate, tender-hearted, placid, sweet-tempered, mild, serene, soft, quiet, tranquil, still, peaceful, pacific, meek, dove-like. ❷ a gentle wind: MILD, moderate, light, temperate, soft, balmy. ❸ a gentle touch: SOFT, tender, light, smooth, soothing. ❹ a gentle animal: PLACID, docile, tame, biddable, tractable, manageable, meek, easily handled, broken, trained, schooled. ❺ a gentle slope: GRADUAL, slight, easy, imperceptible.
– OPPOSITES cruel, fierce, rough.

genuine adjective ❶ REAL, authentic, true, pure, actual, bona fide, veritable, sound, pukka, sterling, legitimate, lawful, legal, valid, original, unadulterated, unalloyed; *informal* kosher, honest-to-goodness. ❷ a very genuine person: SINCERE, truthful, honest, frank, candid, open, natural, unaffected, artless, ingenuous; *informal* upfront.
– OPPOSITES fake, insincere.

germ noun ❶ MICROBE, micro-organism, bacillus, bacterium, virus; *informal* bug. ❷ BEGINNING, start, genesis, seed, embryo, root, bud, origin, source, fount, fountain, rudiment.

germane adjective RELEVANT, pertinent, applicable, material, related, connected, akin, allied, analogous, à propos, apposite, appropriate, fitting, apt, suited, felicitous, proper, to the point.
– OPPOSITES germane.

gesture noun SIGNAL, motion, sign, wave, indication, gesticulation.
▶ verb GESTICULATE, signal, make a sign, motion, wave, indicate.

get verb ❶ ACQUIRE, obtain, come by, come into possession of,

secure, procure, buy, purchase. ❷ get a letter: RECEIVE, be sent, be given. ❸ go and get it: GO FOR, fetch, bring, collect, carry, transport, convey. ❹ get £200 a week: EARN, be paid, make, bring in, clear, gross, net, take home, pocket; *informal* pull in. ❺ they got the thief: CAPTURE, seize, arrest, apprehend, take, trap, lay hold of, grab, bag, take captive, grasp; *informal* collar, nab; *Brit. informal* nick. ❻ get what he means: UNDERSTAND, comprehend, grasp, see, fathom, work out, follow; *informal* make head or tail of, catch on, get the hang of. ❼ get her to go: PERSUADE, induce, coax, talk into, wheedle into, prevail upon, influence, sway, convince, win over. ❽ get cold: BECOME, grow, come to be, turn. ❾ I'll get him for that: GET EVEN WITH, avenge oneself on, take vengeance on, pay back, settle the score with, return like for like; *informal* get back at, get one's own back on. ❿ beginning to get to me: IRRITATE, get on someone's nerves, annoy, vex, anger, provoke, exasperate, infuriate, rile, upset, bother, nettle, pique; *Brit.* rub up the wrong way; *informal* get someone's back up, bug, get someone's goat.
– OPPOSITES lose.
■ **get ahead** SUCCEED, do well, make good, be successful, prosper, flourish, rise in the world. **get at** ❶ FIND FAULT WITH, pick on, criticize, carp, nag, taunt. ❷ SUGGEST, mean, imply, hint, intend, lead up to. **get by** SURVIVE, cope, manage, subsist, exist, get along, fare, make both ends meet; *informal* keep one's head above water, make out. **get out of** AVOID, dodge, evade, shirk, escape.

getaway noun ESCAPE, flight, breakout, break, absconding.

ghastly adjective ❶ a ghastly murder: TERRIBLE, horrible, frightful, dreadful, awful, horrid, horrendous, hideous, shocking, grim, gruesome, terrifying, frightening. ❷ a ghastly man: LOATHSOME, odious, nasty, contemptible, dreadful, appalling, foul. ❸ a ghastly mistake: VERY BAD, serious, grave, critical, unforgivable, awful, terrible.

ghost noun ❶ APPARITION, spectre, spirit, phantom, wraith, shade; *informal* spook; *poetic/literary* phantasm. ❷ ghost of a smile: SUGGESTION, hint, trace, glimmer, shadow, impression, semblance.

ghostly adjective SPECTRAL, phantom, ghost-like, wraithlike, unearthly, supernatural, other-wordly, illusory, insubstantial, shadowy, eerie, creepy, scary, weird, uncanny; *informal* spooky; *poetic/literary* phantasmal.

giant noun COLOSSUS, behemoth, man mountain, titan, Goliath.
▶ adjective GIGANTIC, enormous, huge, colossal, immense, vast, mammoth, gargantuan, titanic, elephantine, prodigious, stupendous, Brobdingnagian; *informal* jumbo.

gibberish noun NONSENSE, drivel, rubbish, balderdash, blather, prattle; *informal* gobbledegook, bosh, piffle, twaddle, poppycock, mumbo-jumbo; *informal, dated* tommyrot.

gibe noun *see* JIBE.

giddy adjective DIZZY, faint, light-headed, unsteady, reeling, vertiginous; *informal* woozy.

gift noun ❶ PRESENT, offering, donation, contribution, grant, bonus, bounty, largesse, boon, gratuity, benefaction, bequest, legacy, inheritance, endowment. ❷ TALENT, aptitude, flair, facility, knack, bent, ability, faculty, capacity, capability, skill, attribute, expertise, genius, mind for.

gifted adjective TALENTED, brilliant, clever, bright, intelligent, ingenious, sharp, able, accomplished, capable, masterly, skilled, adroit, proficient, expert; *informal* smart.
– OPPOSITES inept.

gigantic adjective *see* GIANT adjective.

giggle verb TITTER, snigger, snicker, chuckle, chortle, laugh, cackle; *informal* tee-hee.

gimcrack adjective SHODDY, cheap, tawdry, flimsy, kitsch, badly made, jerry-built, useless, worthless; *informal* tacky, tatty, trashy.

gingerly adverb CAUTIOUSLY, warily, carefully, attentively, heedfully, vigilantly, watchfully, guardedly, prudently, circumspectly, judiciously, suspiciously, hesitantly, reluctantly, timidly, timorously.
– OPPOSITES recklessly.

girdle noun CORSET, sash, band, braid, cummerbund.
▶ verb SURROUND, encircle, circle, ring, enclose, encompass, gird.

girl noun ❶ YOUNG WOMAN, female, young lady, miss; *Scottish & N. English* lass, lassie; *informal* chick, filly; *Brit. informal* bird; *N. Amer. informal* babe, broad; *Austral./NZ informal* sheila. ❷ GIRLFRIEND, lover, sweetheart, mistress, inamorata.

girth noun CIRCUMFERENCE, perimeter, size, bulk, measure.

gist noun ESSENCE, substance, drift, sense, crux, significance, idea, import, core, quintessence, nucleus, kernel, nub, pith, marrow, burden.

give verb ❶ PRESENT, hand, hand over, bestow, donate, contribute, confer, turn over, award, grant, accord, leave, will, bequeath, make over, entrust, consign, vouchsafe. ❷ **give them time:** ALLOW, permit, grant, accord. ❸ **give advice:** PROVIDE, supply, furnish, proffer, offer. ❹ **give news:** COMMUNICATE, impart, announce, transmit, convey, send, purvey. ❺ **give good results:** PRODUCE, yield, afford, result in. ❻ **give no trouble:** CAUSE, be a source of, make, create. ❼ **give a yell:** LET OUT, utter, emit, issue, voice. ❽ **gave him to believe:** LEAD, make, cause. ❾ **the bridge gave:** GIVE WAY, collapse, break, break down, fall apart, come apart, bend, buckle, warp, yield.
■ **give away** REVEAL, disclose, divulge, let slip, leak, let out, expose, uncover. **give in** GIVE UP, surrender, admit defeat, concede, yield, capitulate, submit, comply, succumb, retreat; *informal* quit. **give off** EMIT, send out, throw out, discharge, exude, release, vent, produce. **give up** STOP, cease, leave off, desist from, swear off, renounce, abandon, discontinue; *informal* quit, cut out, chuck; *formal* forswear.

glad adjective ❶ **glad you're here:** HAPPY, pleased, delighted, thrilled, gratified, overjoyed, elated, satisfied, contented; *informal* over the moon, tickled pink; *Brit. informal* chuffed. ❷ **glad to help:** WILLING,

eager, ready, prepared, happy, pleased. ❸ **the glad news:** HAPPY, joyful, welcome, cheering, cheerful, pleasing, gratifying.
– OPPOSITES unhappy, reluctant.

gladden **verb** MAKE HAPPY, delight, cheer, cheer up, hearten, brighten up, raise someone's spirits, please, elate, buoy up, give a lift to; *informal* buck up.
– OPPOSITES sadden.

glamorous **adjective** ❶ ALLURING, dazzling, smart, elegant, beautiful, lovely, attractive, charming, fascinating, exciting, beguiling, bewitching, enchanting, entrancing, irresistible, tantalizing. ❷ **a glamorous life:** EXCITING, fascinating, stimulating, thrilling, glossy, glittering; *informal* ritzy, glitzy.
– OPPOSITES dowdy, boring.

glamour **noun** ❶ BEAUTY, loveliness, attractiveness, allure, attraction, elegance, charm, fascination. ❷ EXCITEMENT, allure, charm, fascination, enchantment, captivation, magic, spell.

glance **verb** LOOK QUICKLY/HURRIEDLY, take a quick look, glimpse, catch a glimpse, peek, peep, sneak a look.

glare **verb** ❶ **glare at him:** SCOWL, glower, frown, look threateningly, look daggers, give someone dirty looks, lour. ❷ **lights glaring:** DAZZLE, beam, flare, blaze, flame.

glaring **adjective** ❶ DAZZLING, blazing, flaring. ❷ **a glaring mistake:** OBVIOUS, conspicuous, manifest, overt, patent, visible, flagrant, blatant, outrageous, egregious, gross.

glass **noun** TUMBLER, wine glass, flute, schooner, balloon, goblet, beaker, chalice.

glasses **plural noun** SPECTACLES, eyeglasses, bifocals, sunglasses, monocle, lorgnette, pince-nez, field glasses, binoculars, opera glasses.

glassy **adjective** ❶ SHINY, glossy, smooth, mirror-like, clear, transparent, translucent, limpid, pellucid. ❷ **a glassy look:** GLAZED, blank, expressionless, empty, vacant, deadpan, vacuous, fixed, unmoving, lifeless, motionless.

glaze **verb** VARNISH, coat, polish, enamel, lacquer, gloss, burnish.
▶ **noun** GLOSS, lustre, finish, lacquer, enamel.

gleam **verb** SHINE, radiate, flash, glow, glint, flare, glisten, glitter, beam, shimmer, glimmer, sparkle, twinkle, scintillate.
▶ **noun** ❶ BEAM, flash, glow, shaft, ray, flare, glint. ❷ LUSTRE, glow, shine, gloss, sheen, brightness, flash, brilliance, coruscation.

glee **noun** MIRTH, merriment, gaiety, delight, joy, joyfulness, joyousness, gladness, happiness, pleasure, jollity, hilarity, jocularity, joviality, exhilaration, high spirits, cheerfulness, exaltation, elation, exuberance, liveliness, verve, triumph; *poetic/literary* blitheness.

glib **adjective** SMOOTH-TALKING, fast-talking, slick, smooth, fluent, smooth-tongued, silver-tongued, plausible, talkative, voluble, loquacious, unctuous, having the gift of the gab; *informal* sweet-talking.
– OPPOSITES tongue-tied, inarticulate.

glimpse **verb** CATCH SIGHT OF, catch a glimpse of, spot, spy, discern, make out, distinguish, notice, observe, sight, espy, descry.

▶ **noun** GLANCE, brief look, peek, peep, look, sight, view.

glint **verb** SHINE, sparkle, flash, twinkle, glitter, glimmer, blink, gleam, wink, shimmer, glisten, dazzle, scintillate.

glisten **verb** SHINE, shimmer, sparkle, twinkle, flicker, glint, blink, wink, gleam, flash, scintillate, coruscate.

glitter **verb** SPARKLE, twinkle, flicker, blink, wink, shimmer, glimmer, glint, flash, gleam.
▶ **noun** ❶ SPARKLE, twinkle, flicker, blink, winking. ❷ SHOWINESS, flashiness, glamour, ostentation, pageantry, splendour, fanfare; *informal* razzle-dazzle, glitz, pizzazz.

gloat **verb** RELISH, revel in, glory in, rejoice in, exult in, triumph over, crow about; *informal* rub it in.

global **adjective** ❶ WORLDWIDE, universal, international, planetary. ❷ GENERAL, comprehensive, all-encompassing, exhaustive, encyclopedic, thorough, total, with no exceptions, across-the-board.

globule **noun** BEAD, drop, ball, droplet, pearl, particle.

gloom **noun** ❶ DIMNESS, darkness, dark, blackness, murkiness, shadowiness, shadiness, dullness, obscurity, dusk, twilight. ❷ SADNESS, melancholy, unhappiness, sorrow, woe, grief, despondency, misery, dejection, glumness, desolation, depression, despair, pessimism, hopelessness.
– OPPOSITES light, cheer.

gloomy **adjective** ❶ DARK, overcast, cloudy, dull, sunless, dim, shadowy, black, unlit, murky, sombre, dismal, dreary, shady, dingy. ❷ SAD, melancholy, unhappy, miserable, sorrowful, despondent, woebegone, disconsolate, dejected, downcast, downhearted, glum, dispirited, desolate, depressed, blue, pessimistic, morose; *informal* down in the mouth.
– OPPOSITES bright, cheerful.

glorious **adjective** ❶ ILLUSTRIOUS, celebrated, noble, famous, famed, renowned, distinguished, honoured, eminent, magnificent, excellent, majestic, splendid, resplendent, supreme, triumphant, sublime, victorious. ❷ **a glorious day:** BEAUTIFUL, bright, sunny, brilliant, perfect. ❸ **a glorious time:** MARVELLOUS, splendid, wonderful, delightful, enjoyable, pleasurable, fine, excellent, great; *informal* fab, terrific.

glory **noun** ❶ **to the glory of God:** EXALTATION, worship, adoration, honour, reverence, extolment, veneration, thanksgiving. ❷ **glory in battle:** DISTINCTION, fame, kudos, renown, honour, prestige, acclaim, illustriousness, credit, accolade, recognition; *formal* laudation. ❸ **the glory of Versailles:** SPLENDOUR, resplendence, magnificence, grandeur, majesty, pomp, pageantry, beauty.
– OPPOSITES disgrace.
■ **glory in** EXULT IN, rejoice in, take pleasure in, be proud of, delight in, revel in, boast about, crow about, gloat about.

gloss **noun** ❶ SHINE, sheen, lustre, gleam, brightness, brilliance, sparkle, polish, shimmer, burnish. ❷ **a gloss of respectability:** FRONT, facade, disguise, mask, semblance,

camouflage, show, veneer, surface.
■ **gloss over** EVADE, avoid, smooth over, conceal, hide, cover up, disguise, mask, veil, whitewash.

glossy **adjective** SHINING, shiny, gleaming, bright, smooth, lustrous, glistening, brilliant, polished, burnished, glazed, silky, silken, sleek, waxed.
– OPPOSITES dull, lustreless.

glow **verb** ❶ GLEAM, shine, glimmer, smoulder, shed a glow, light up. ❷ **glow with pleasure**: BLUSH, flush, redden, grow pink, go scarlet, colour, crimson, radiate, thrill, tingle.
▶ **noun** ❶ GLEAM, glimmer, luminosity, incandescence, phosphorescence, lambency. ❷ BRIGHTNESS, vividness, colourful ness, brilliance, radiance, splendour, richness. ❸ BLUSH, rosiness, flush, pinkness, redness, crimson, reddening, scarlet, bloom.

glower **verb** SCOWL, stare angrily, glare, frown, give someone black/ dirty looks, look daggers, lour.
– OPPOSITES smile.

glowing **adjective** ❶ LUMINOUS, bright, vivid, brilliant, radiant, rich, smouldering, incandescent, phosphorescent, aglow, lambent. ❷ **a glowing report**: FAVOURABLE, enthusiastic, complimentary, laudatory, adulatory, ecstatic, rhapsodic, eulogistic, panegyrical; *informal* rave.

glue **noun** ADHESIVE, gum, fixative, paste, cement, epoxy resin, mucilage.
▶ **verb** STICK, paste, gum, fix, affix, cement, bond, seal.

glum **adjective** GLOOMY, melancholy, sad, despondent, miserable, dejected, downcast, downhearted, dispirited, depressed, in low spirits; *informal* down in the mouth.
– OPPOSITES cheerful.

glut **noun** SURPLUS, excess, surfeit, over-abundance, superabundance, oversupply, overprovision, saturation, superfluity.
– OPPOSITES dearth.

glutinous **adjective** STICKY, viscous, tacky, mucous, gummy, adhesive, viscid, glue-like, mucilaginous.

gluttonous **adjective** GREEDY, voracious, insatiable, ravenous, gormandizing; *informal* piggish, hoggish.

gnarled **adjective** KNOTTY, knotted, lumpy, bumpy, rough, twisted, crooked, distorted, contorted, warped, nodular, knurled.

gnaw **verb** CHEW, munch, bite, nibble, masticate, worry.

go **verb** ❶ **go forward/back**: MOVE, proceed, progress, walk, pass, travel, journey, repair. ❷ **time to go**: LEAVE, go away, depart, withdraw, retire, set off, set out, decamp; *informal* beat it, scram. ❸ **the machine won't go**: WORK, be in working order, function, operate, be operative, run, perform. ❹ **go grey**: BECOME, grow, get, come to be, turn. ❺ **the road goes to the sea**: EXTEND, reach, stretch, lead to, give access to. ❻ **the book goes there**: BELONG, have a place, fit in, be located, be situated, be found, lie, stand. ❼ **her headache has gone**: STOP, cease, disappear, vanish, be no more, fade away, melt away. ❽ **it/ he will have to go**: BE DISCARDED, be

thrown away, be disposed of, be got rid of, be dismissed, be made redundant; *informal* be sacked/fired, get the axe/chop. **9 how did it go?** TURN OUT, work out, fare, progress, develop, result, end, end up, eventuate. **10 the carpet and curtains don't go:** MATCH, go together, be compatible, blend, suit each other, complement each other, harmonize, accord, be in accord.
▶ **noun** TRY, attempt, turn, opportunity, effort, bid, endeavour, essay; *informal* shot, stab, crack, whirl, whack.
■ **go down 1** SINK, submerge, founder, go under. **2** DECREASE, fall, drop, be reduced, decline, plummet. **go far** DO WELL, be successful, succeed, make progress, get on, get ahead, make a name for oneself, advance; *informal* set the world on fire. **go in for** ENGAGE IN, take part in, participate in, practise, pursue, take up, adopt, espouse, embrace. **go off 1** EXPLODE, detonate, blow up, erupt, burst; *informal* go bang. **2** GO BAD, go stale, go sour, be rotten.

goad **noun** STIMULUS, incentive, incitement, inducement, stimulation, impetus, motivation, pressure, spur, jolt, prod, poke.
▶ **verb** PROMPT, stimulate, induce, motivate, spur, urge, chivvy.

go-ahead **noun** PERMISSION, authorization, assent, consent, sanction, leave, confirmation, imprimatur; *informal* green light, OK, okay, thumbs up.
▶ **adjective** ENTERPRISING, ambitious, pioneering, progressive; *informal* up-and-coming, go-getting.

goal **noun** AIM, objective, end, purpose, ambition, target, design, intention, intent, aspiration, ideal.

go-between **noun** INTERMEDIARY, mediator, middleman, liaison, contact, messenger, agent, broker, medium, dealer, factor, pander.

godforsaken **adjective** DESOLATE, dismal, dreary, bleak, wretched, miserable, gloomy, deserted, abandoned, forlorn, neglected, remote, backward, in the back of beyond.

godless **adjective** ATHEISTIC, agnostic, sceptical, faithless, pagan, heathen, ungodly, impious, irreligious, unrighteous, sinful, wicked, evil, depraved.

godsend **noun** PIECE OF GOOD FORTUNE, stroke of luck, blessing, boon, windfall, bonanza, gift, benediction.
– OPPOSITES curse.

goggle **verb** STARE, gape, gaze, ogle; *informal* gawk, rubberneck.

good **adjective** **1 a good person:** VIRTUOUS, moral, ethical, righteous, right-minded, right-thinking, honourable, upright, honest, high-minded, noble, worthy, admirable, estimable, exemplary. **2 that's good:** SATISFACTORY, acceptable, good enough, passable, tolerable, adequate, fine, excellent; *informal* great, hunky-dory, OK. **3 a good child:** WELL BEHAVED, well mannered, obedient, manageable, tractable, malleable. **4 a good thing to do:** CORRECT, right, proper, fitting, suitable, appropriate, decorous, seemly. **5 a good driver:** COMPETENT, capable, able, accomplished, skilful, efficient, adept, proficient, expert, excellent, first-rate, first-class;

informal top-notch, tip-top, A1. ❻ **good friends:** RELIABLE, dependable, trustworthy. ❼ **good condition:** FINE, healthy, sound, robust, strong, vigorous. ❽ **good of you:** KIND, kindly, kind-hearted, good-hearted, friendly, obliging, well disposed, charitable, gracious, sympathetic, benevolent, altruistic, benign. ❾ **milk is good for you:** WHOLESOME, healthy, nutritious, nutritional, beneficial. ❿ **the food is good:** DELICIOUS, tasty, appetizing; *informal* scrumptious, yummy. ⓫ **a good reason:** VALID, legitimate, genuine, authentic, sound, bona fide. ⓬ **a good number:** CONSIDERABLE, substantial, goodly, sizeable, large, sufficient, ample; *informal* tidy. ⓭ **good weather:** FINE, fair, mild, clear, bright, cloudless, sunny, calm, balmy, tranquil, clement, halcyon.
– OPPOSITES bad.
▶ **noun** ❶ **for your own good:** BENEFIT, advantage, gain, profit, interest, well-being, welfare. ❷ **tell good from bad:** VIRTUE, goodness, righteousness, morality, ethics, rectitude, honour, uprightness, honesty, integrity, probity, worth, merit.

goodbye exclamation FAREWELL, adieu, au revoir; *informal* bye, bye-bye, see you later, see you, so long, ciao; *Brit. informal* cheerio, cheers, ta-ta.

good-humoured adjective AMIABLE, affable, easy-going, genial, cheerful, cheery, happy, pleasant, good-tempered.
– OPPOSITES grumpy.

good-looking adjective ATTRACTIVE, handsome, pretty, lovely, beautiful, personable, well favoured; *archaic* comely, fair.

goodly adjective CONSIDERABLE, substantial, sizeable, significant, large, great, ample, sufficient; *informal* tidy.
– OPPOSITES paltry.

good-natured adjective KIND, kindly, kind-hearted, warm-hearted, generous, benevolent, charitable, friendly, helpful, accommodating, amiable, tolerant.

goods plural noun PROPERTY, belongings, possessions, effects, things, paraphernalia, chattels, movables, appurtenances, trappings, accoutrements; *informal* stuff, gear.

gorge noun CHASM, canyon, ravine, abyss, defile, pass, cleft, crevice, rift, fissure.

gorgeous adjective ❶ **a gorgeous woman:** BEAUTIFUL, attractive, lovely, good-looking, sexy; *informal* stunning. ❷ **a gorgeous sight:** SPLENDID, magnificent, superb, grand, impressive, sumptuous, imposing, dazzling, brilliant, glittering, breathtaking.

gory adjective BLOODY, bloodstained, horrific, violent, bloodthirsty, brutal, murderous, savage.

gossamer adjective SILKY, gauzy, chiffony, feathery, light, fine, delicate, frail, flimsy, insubstantial, airy, diaphanous, sheer, transparent, see-through, translucent.

gossip noun ❶ RUMOURS, scandal, tittle-tattle, tattle, hearsay, whispering campaign; *informal* mud-slinging, dirt. ❷ GOSSIPMONGER, rumour-monger, scandalmonger, busybody, babbler, chatterer, prattler.

▶ verb SPREAD RUMOURS, chat, chit-chat, blather, blether, talk, tattle, babble, gabble, prattle, prate; *informal* chinwag, jaw, yack.

gouge verb DIG, incise, chisel, gash, scoop, hollow.

govern verb ❶ RULE, reign over, be in power over, exercise control over, hold sway over, preside over, administer, lead, be in charge of, control, command, direct, order, guide, manage, conduct, oversee, supervise, superintend, pilot, steer. ❷ **govern one's passions:** CONTROL, restrain, keep in check, check, curb, hold back, keep back, rein in, bridle, subdue, constrain, arrest, contain. ❸ **govern our decision:** DETERMINE, decide, sway, rule, influence, have an influence on, be a factor in.

government noun ADMINISTRATION, regime, parliament, ministry, executive, rule, leadership, command, direction, control, guidance, management, conduct, supervision, superintendence.

gown noun DRESS, frock, garment, costume, garb, habit.

grab verb ❶ GRASP, clutch, grip, clasp, lay hold of, catch hold of, take hold of, fasten upon; *informal* collar. ❷ SEIZE, snatch, pluck, snap up, appropriate, capture; *informal* bag, nab.

grace noun ❶ ELEGANCE, refinement, charm, attractiveness, beauty, loveliness, polish, suaveness, culture, cultivation, good taste, taste, tastefulness, smoothness, suppleness, fluidity. ❷ **have the grace to apologize:** MANNERS, courtesy, decency, consideration, tact, breeding, decorum, propriety. ❸ **by grace of the king:** FAVOUR, good will, generosity, kindness, kindliness, indulgence, benefaction, mercy, mercifulness, compassion, clemency. ❹ **say grace:** BLESSING, prayer, thanksgiving, thanks, benediction.

▶ verb ADORN, decorate, ornament, embellish, enhance, beautify, prettify, set off, deck.

graceful adjective ELEGANT, refined, smooth, agile, flowing, nimble, cultured, cultivated, polished, suave, charming, appealing, attractive, beautiful, lovely; *archaic* comely.

– OPPOSITES inelegant.

gracious adjective ❶ **a gracious lady:** COURTEOUS, cordial, kindly, kind-hearted, warm-hearted, benevolent, friendly, amiable, considerate, affable, pleasant, polite, civil, well mannered, chivalrous, charitable, indulgent, obliging, accommodating, beneficent, benign. ❷ **a gracious way of life:** ELEGANT, tasteful, comfortable, luxurious. ❸ **gracious God:** MERCIFUL, compassionate, gentle, mild, humane, clement.

grade noun ❶ LEVEL, degree, stage, echelon, rank, standing, station, position, order, class. ❷ CATEGORY, class, classification, type, brand. ❸ GRADIENT, slope, incline, hill, rise, bank, declivity.

▶ verb CLASSIFY, class, categorize, sort, group, order, brand, size, rank, evaluate, rate, value, range, graduate.

gradient noun SLOPE, incline, hill, rise, bank, acclivity, declivity, grade.

gradual adjective PROGRESSIVE, regular, steady, even, moderate,

slow, measured, unhurried, step-by-step, successive, continuous, systematic.
– OPPOSITES sudden, abrupt.

gradually adverb SLOWLY, steadily, moderately, evenly, bit by bit, little by little, by degrees, step by step, inch by inch, piece by piece, drop by drop.

graduate verb ❶ TAKE A DEGREE, receive one's degree, become a graduate. ❷ graduate a scale: MARK OFF, measure off, divide into degrees, grade, calibrate. ❸ graduate to a better job: MOVE UP, progress, advance, gain promotion, be promoted.

graft noun ❶ SHOOT, bud, scion, new growth, slip, sprout, splice. ❷ a skin graft: TRANSPLANT, implant, implantation.

grain noun ❶ PARTICLE, granule, bit, piece, scrap, crumb, fragment, morsel, speck, trace, scintilla, mite, iota. ❷ the grain of the wood/cloth: TEXTURE, weave, fibre, pattern, nap.

grand adjective ❶ grand houses: IMPRESSIVE, imposing, magnificent, splendid, superb, striking, palatial, stately, large, monumental, majestic. ❷ a grand feast: SPLENDID, sumptuous, luxurious, lavish, magnificent, opulent, princely. ❸ grand people: GREAT, noble, aristocratic, distinguished, august, illustrious, eminent, elevated, esteemed, celebrated, pre-eminent, leading, prominent, notable, renowned, famous.
– OPPOSITES unimpressive, lowly.

grandiloquent adjective POMPOUS, high-flown, pretentious, bombastic, ornate, rhetorical, elaborate, florid, magniloquent, orotund, ostentatious, periphrastic, euphuistic, fustian.
– OPPOSITES understated.

grandiose adjective ❶ grandiose plans: OVERAMBITIOUS, ambitious, extravagant, high-flown, high-sounding, pompous, flamboyant, pretentious; *informal* OTT. ❷ grandiose buildings: GRAND, impressive, magnificent, imposing, striking, splendid, superb, stately, majestic.
– OPPOSITES modest.

grant verb ❶ grant them an interview: AGREE TO, consent to, assent to, accede to, permit, give one's permission for, allow, concede, accord, vouchsafe. ❷ grant that you may be right: ACKNOWLEDGE, concede, accept, cede, yield, go along with.
▶ noun AWARD, endowment, contribution, donation, allowance, subsidy, allocation, allotment, gift, present, subvention, sponsorship, honorarium; *Brit.* bursary.

granule noun GRAIN, particle, fragment, crumb, bit, scrap, molecule, atom, mite, iota, jot.

graphic adjective VIVID, striking, expressive, descriptive, illustrative, lively, forcible, detailed, well defined, well drawn, telling, effective, cogent, clear, lucid, explicit.
– OPPOSITES dull.

grapple verb ❶ grapple with the enemy: FIGHT WITH, wrestle with, struggle with, tussle with, clash with, engage with, close with, battle with, combat with, brawl with. ❷ grapple with the problem: TACKLE, face, cope with, deal with, handle, manage, confront, address oneself to, attack, get down to, come to grips with.

grasp verb ❶ GRIP, clutch, hold, clasp, clench, grab, snatch, get/take hold of, seize. ❷ grasp the point: UNDERSTAND, comprehend, follow, see, take in, realize, apprehend, perceive; *informal* get, get the picture, get the drift, catch on.

grasping adjective GREEDY, acquisitive, avaricious, rapacious, covetous, mean, parsimonious, niggardly, penny-pinching, selfish, possessive; *informal* grabby, tight-fisted, stingy.
– OPPOSITES generous.

grate verb ❶ grate cheese: SHRED, pulverize, mince, grind, granulate, triturate. ❷ grate on the metal: RASP, scrape, jar, scratch, grind, creak, rub, grit. ❸ his voice grates on them: IRRITATE, annoy, jar on, irk, vex, gall, rankle with, anger, rile, exasperate, chafe; *Brit.* rub up the wrong way; *informal* set someone's teeth on edge, get on someone's nerves, aggravate.

grateful adjective THANKFUL, appreciative, obliged, indebted, obligated, beholden, filled with gratitude.
– OPPOSITES ungrateful.

gratify verb PLEASE, make happy, delight, give pleasure to, gladden, satisfy, thrill; *informal* warm the cockles of the heart.

gratis adverb FREE OF CHARGE, free, for free, without charge, for nothing, at no cost, without payment, freely, gratuitously; *informal* on the house.

gratitude noun GRATEFULNESS, thankfulness, thanks, appreciation, thanksgiving, indebtedness, acknowledgement, recognition, sense of obligation.
– OPPOSITES ingratitude.

gratuitous adjective ❶ gratuitous violence: UNPROVOKED, unjustified, groundless, without cause, without reason, unfounded, baseless, uncalled for, unwarranted, unmerited, needless, unnecessary, superfluous. ❷ FREE, complimentary, voluntary, unpaid, unrewarded, unasked for, without charge, at no cost.

gratuity noun TIP, bonus, gift, present, donation, reward, recompense, largesse.

grave adjective ❶ a grave expression/mood: SOLEMN, serious, earnest, sober, sombre, severe, unsmiling, long-faced, stony-faced, grim-faced, grim, gloomy, preoccupied, thoughtful, pensive, subdued, muted, quiet, dignified, sedate, dour, staid. ❷ grave matters: SERIOUS, important, significant, weighty, momentous, urgent, pressing, vital, crucial, life-and-death, acute, pivotal, perilous, hazardous, dangerous, threatening, menacing.
– OPPOSITES carefree, trivial.

graveyard noun CEMETERY, burial ground, churchyard, memorial park, necropolis, charnel house; *informal* boneyard; *N. Amer. informal* potter's field.

gravitate verb ❶ MOVE TOWARDS, head towards, be drawn to, be pulled towards, be attracted to, drift towards, lean towards, incline towards. ❷ SINK, fall, drop, descend, precipitate, be precipitated, settle.

gravity noun ❶ SOLEMNITY, seriousness, earnestness, sobriety, sombreness, severity, grimness, thoughtfulness, pensiveness, sedateness, dignity, dourness, staidness. ❷ **the gravity of the situation:** SERIOUSNESS, importance, significance, momentousness, weightiness, acuteness, criticalness, consequence, perilousness, peril, hazard, danger.

graze verb ❶ **graze the wall:** BRUSH, touch, rub, glance off, shave, skim, kiss. ❷ **grazed his knee:** SCRAPE, abrade, skin, scratch, chafe, bark, bruise, contuse.

greasy adjective ❶ FATTY, fat, oily, buttery, oleaginous, sebaceous, adipose. ❷ **greasy roads:** SLIPPERY, slippy, slimy. ❸ **a greasy fellow:** SLIMY, oily, unctuous, smooth, smooth-tongued, glib, suave, slick, fawning, ingratiating, grovelling, sycophantic, toadying, flattering, gushing; *informal* smarmy.

great adjective ❶ **a great expanse:** LARGE, big, extensive, vast, immense, boundless, unlimited, huge, spacious, enormous, gigantic, colossal, mammoth, monstrous, prodigious, tremendous, stupendous. ❷ **in great detail:** SUBSTANTIAL, considerable, exceptional, pronounced, inordinate, sizeable. ❸ **great cities:** MAJOR, main, most important, leading, chief, principal, capital, paramount, primary. ❹ **a great occasion:** IMPRESSIVE, grand, magnificent, imposing, splendid, majestic, glorious, sumptuous. ❺ **great people:** PROMINENT, eminent, pre-eminent, distinguished, illustrious, august, celebrated, renowned, noted, notable, noteworthy, famous, famed, leading, top, high, high-ranking, noble. ❻ **a great player:** GIFTED, talented, outstanding, remarkable, exceptional, first-rate, incomparable, expert, skilful, skilled, able, masterly, adept, proficient, adroit; *informal* crack, ace. ❼ **a great time:** EXCELLENT, enjoyable, marvellous, wonderful, first-class, first-rate, fine, very good, admirable; *informal* fab, super.

greatly adverb VERY MUCH, considerably, to a great extent, extremely, exceedingly, vastly, enormously, immensely, tremendously, hugely, markedly, mightily, remarkably, abundantly.

greed noun ❶ GLUTTONY, voraciousness, voracity, ravenousness, insatiability; *informal* hoggishness, piggishness, swinishness. ❷ AVARICE, acquisitiveness, rapacity, covetousness, cupidity, miserliness, parsimony; *informal* tight-fistedness. ❸ **greed for knowledge:** DESIRE, eagerness, avidity, hunger, craving, longing, enthusiasm, impatience.

greedy adjective ❶ GLUTTONOUS, voracious, ravenous, ravening, famished, gourmandizing, insatiable, omnivorous; *informal* piggish, hoggish, gutsy; *archaic* esurient. ❷ **a greedy miser:** AVARICIOUS, acquisitive, grasping, rapacious, grabbing, covetous, miserly, hoarding, niggardly, close-fisted, parsimonious; *informal* grabby, money-grubbing, tight-fisted. ❸ **greedy for knowledge:** EAGER, hungry, avid,

desirous, anxious, impatient, enthusiastic, longing, craving.
– OPPOSITES generous.

green adjective ❶ GRASSY, verdant, leafy. ❷ **a green apprentice:** INEXPERIENCED, untrained, new, raw, immature, inexpert, unqualified, unversed, simple, unsophisticated, callow, ingenuous; *informal* wet behind the ears. ❸ **green issues:** ENVIRONMENTALIST, conservationist, ecological.

greenhouse noun HOTHOUSE, glasshouse, conservatory.

greet verb SAY HELLO TO, address, salute, hail, nod to, wave to, raise one's hat to, acknowledge, accost, receive, meet, welcome.

greeting noun HELLO, salute, salutation, address, nod, wave, acknowledgement, welcome.

greetings plural noun GOOD WISHES, best wishes, regards, kind regards, congratulations, compliments, respects.

grey adjective ❶ **a grey day:** CLOUDY, overcast, dull, dark, sunless, gloomy, dim, dreary, dismal, cheerless, depressing, misty, foggy, murky. ❷ **grey people:** DULL, uninteresting, boring, characterless, anonymous, colourless. ❸ **a grey area:** UNCLEAR, doubtful, uncertain, indistinct, mixed.

grief noun SORROW, mourning, mournfulness, bereavement, lamentation, misery, sadness, anguish, pain, distress, agony, suffering, affliction, heartache, heartbreak, broken-heartedness, heaviness of heart, trouble, woe, tribulation, desolation, trial, despondency, dejection, despair, remorse, regret.
– OPPOSITES joy, delight.

grievance noun ❶ COMPLAINT, protest, charge, moan, axe to grind, bone to pick; *informal* grouse, gripe, beef. ❷ INJUSTICE, unfairness, injury, damage, hardship, offence, affront, insult.

grieve verb ❶ MOURN, lament, be sorrowful, sorrow, be sad, weep and wail, cry, sob, suffer, ache, be in anguish, be distressed, bemoan, bewail; *informal* eat one's heart out. ❷ **it grieved her:** HURT, wound, pain, sadden, break someone's heart, upset, distress, cause suffering to, crush.
– OPPOSITES rejoice.

grim adjective ❶ **looking grim:** STERN, forbidding, fierce, formidable, threatening, ferocious, menacing, harsh, sombre, cross, crabbed, churlish, morose, surly, ill-tempered, sour, implacable, cruel, ruthless, merciless. ❷ **grim determination:** RESOLUTE, determined, firm, decided, obstinate, adamant, unyielding, unwavering, unfaltering, unshakeable, obdurate, inflexible, unrelenting, relentless, inexorable, dead set. ❸ **a grim sight:** DREADFUL, horrible, horrendous, terrible, horrid, dire, ghastly, awful, appalling, frightful, shocking, unspeakable, harrowing, grisly, hideous, gruesome, macabre.
– OPPOSITES amiable.

grimy adjective DIRTY, grubby, stained, soiled, dusty, sooty, muddy, filthy, besmeared; *poetic/literary* besmirched.
– OPPOSITES clean.

grind verb ❶ **grind coffee:** CRUSH, pound, pulverize, mill, powder, granulate, crumble, mash, smash, triturate, kibble, levigate. ❷ **grind knives:** SHARPEN, file, whet, smooth, polish, sand. ❸ grind one's teeth: GNASH, grit, grate, scrape, rasp.

■ **grind down** OPPRESS, persecute, ill-treat, torture, torment, harass, harry.

grip verb ❶ GRASP, clutch, hold, clasp, clench, take/lay hold of, grab, seize, catch, latch on to. ❷ grip the audience: ABSORB, engross, rivet, spellbind, hold spellbound, entrance, fascinate, enthral, hold, catch, mesmerize, hypnotize, compel.

▶ noun ❶ GRASP, clutch, clasp, clench, handshake, clinch. ❷ a grip on the problem: UNDERSTANDING, comprehension, awareness, perception.

■ **come to grips with** FACE, face up to, confront, meet head on, deal with, cope with, handle, tackle, take on.

grisly adjective GRUESOME, frightful, horrifying, horrid, grim, horrendous, awful, dreadful, terrible, fearful, disgusting, hideous, repulsive, revolting, repugnant, repellent, macabre, spine-chilling, sickening, appalling, loathsome, abhorrent, odious, abominable.

– OPPOSITES pleasant.

grit noun ❶ GRAVEL, sand, dust, dirt. ❷ PLUCK, courage, bravery, mettle, backbone, spirit, gameness, fortitude, toughness, determination, resolution, tenacity; *informal* guts, spunk; *Brit. informal* bottle.

groan verb ❶ MOAN, cry, call out, sigh, murmur, whine, whimper. ❷ COMPLAIN, grumble, object, lament; *informal* moan, grouse, gripe, beef, bellyache, bitch. ❸ CREAK, grate, squeak, screech.

groove noun ❶ CHANNEL, furrow, trench, trough, canal, gouge, rut, gutter, cutting, cut, score, rabbet, rebate. ❷ RUT, routine, habit, treadmill, daily grind.

grope verb ❶ grope one's way: FEEL, fumble, move blindly, pick. ❷ grope for the keys: FUMBLE FOR, fish for, scrabble for, cast about for, search for, hunt for, look for.

gross adjective ❶ OBESE, massive, huge, immense, colossal, big, large, overweight, fat, corpulent, bloated, bulky, lumpish, cumbersome, unwieldy; *informal* hulking. ❷ gross jokes: COARSE, crude, vulgar, obscene, rude, lewd, ribald, bawdy, dirty, filthy, smutty, earthy, risqué, indecent, indelicate, improper, unseemly, impure, offensive, sexual, sensual, pornographic; *informal* blue. ❸ gross behaviour/person: BOORISH, loutish, oafish, coarse, vulgar, crass, ignorant, unrefined, unsophisticated, uncultured, uncultivated, undiscriminating, tasteless, insensitive, unfeeling, imperceptive, callous; *Brit. informal* yobbish. ❹ a gross error: FLAGRANT, blatant, glaring, outrageous, shocking, serious, egregious, manifest, obvious, plain, apparent. ❺ gross salary: TOTAL, whole, entire, aggregate, before deductions, before tax.

– OPPOSITES slender, refined, net.

▶ **verb** EARN, make, bring in, take home, rake in.

grotesque adjective ❶ a grotesque sight: BIZARRE, weird, outlandish, freakish, strange, odd, peculiar, unnatural, surreal, macabre, queer, fantastic, whimsical, fanciful, ridiculous, ludicrous, absurd, incongruous, preposterous, extravagant.

❷ a grotesque shape: DISTORTED, misshapen, twisted, deformed, malformed, misproportioned.
– OPPOSITES normal.

ground noun ❶ EARTH, floor, terra firma; *informal* deck. ❷ SOIL, earth, dirt, land, terrain, clay, turf, loam, clod, sod, dust. ❸ PITCH, stadium, field, arena, park. *See also* GROUNDS.
▶ verb ❶ grounded on fact: BASE, establish, settle, set, found. ❷ ground him in maths: TEACH, instruct, train, tutor, coach, educate, drill, school, prepare, familiarize with, acquaint with, inform.

groundless adjective WITHOUT BASIS, baseless, without foundation, unfounded, unsupported, imaginary, illusory, false, unsubstantiated, unwarranted, unjustified, unjustifiable, uncalled for, unprovoked, without cause/reason, unreasonable, irrational, illogical, empty, idle, chimerical.

grounds plural noun ❶ grounds of the house: SURROUNDINGS, land, property, estate, acres, lawns, gardens, park, parkland, area, domain, holding, territory. ❷ grounds for concern: REASON, cause, basis, base, foundation, justification, call, rationale, argument, premise, occasion, factor, excuse, pretext, motive, inducement. ❸ coffee grounds: DREGS, deposit, lees, sediment, precipitate, settlings, grouts.

groundwork noun FOUNDATION, basis, base, cornerstone, footing, underpinning, fundamentals, basics, elements, essentials, preliminaries, spadework, preparations.

group noun ❶ SET, lot, category, classification, class, batch, family, species, genus, bracket. ❷ a group of people: COMPANY, band, party, body, gathering, congregation, assembly, collection, bunch, cluster, crowd, flock, pack, troop, gang, batch. ❸ a radical group: FACTION, set, coterie, clique, circle. ❹ a sewing group: SOCIETY, association, league, guild, circle, club, work party. ❺ a group of trees: CLUMP, cluster.
▶ verb ❶ grouped according to ability: CLASSIFY, class, categorize, sort, grade, rank, bracket. ❷ group them together: ASSEMBLE, collect, gather together, arrange, organize, marshal, range, line up, dispose. ❸ they grouped themselves around him: COLLECT, gather, assemble, cluster. ❹ they grouped together: GET TOGETHER, band together, associate, consort.

grouse verb COMPLAIN, grumble, groan, protest; *informal* moan, gripe, bellyache, beef, bitch, grouch, whinge.

grovel verb ❶ ABASE ONESELF, toady, fawn, flatter, curry favour, humble oneself, kowtow, bow and scrape, lick someone's boots; *informal* crawl, butter someone up. ❷ PROSTRATE ONESELF, fall on one's knees, crawl, creep, kneel, slither.

grow verb ❶ GET BIGGER, get larger, get taller, stretch, lengthen, heighten, enlarge, extend, expand, spread, thicken, widen, fill out, swell, increase, multiply. ❷ plants growing: DEVELOP, sprout, shoot up, spring up, germinate, bud, burgeon, flourish, thrive, pullulate. ❸ business is growing: FLOURISH, thrive, prosper, succeed, progress, make progress, make headway, advance, improve, expand. ❹ fear grows from insecurity: ARISE, originate, stem, issue, spring. ❺ grow prettier: BECOME, come to be, get to be, get, turn, wax. ❻ grow corn: PRODUCE, cultivate, farm, propagate, raise. – OPPOSITES shrink.

grown-up noun ADULT, grown man, man, grown woman, woman, mature man/woman.

growth noun ❶ INCREASE, expansion, enlargement, development, augmentation, proliferation, multiplication, extension, evolution, magnification, amplification, growing, deepening, heightening, widening, thickening, broadening, swelling, aggrandizement. ❷ growth of plants: DEVELOPMENT, maturation, germination, burgeoning, sprouting, shooting up, blooming, vegetation, pullulation. ❸ growth of industry: EXPANSION, rise, progress, success, advance, advancement, improvement, headway. ❹ a growth in his lungs: TUMOUR, lump, cancer, swelling, excrescence, intumescence, tumefaction.

grubby adjective DIRTY, filthy, unwashed, grimy, messy, soiled, scruffy, shabby, untidy, unkempt, slovenly, sordid, squalid; *informal* mucky, cruddy; *Brit. informal* gungy. – OPPOSITES clean.

grudge noun RESENTMENT, spite, malice, bitterness, ill will, pique, umbrage, grievance, hard feelings, rancour, malevolence, venom, hatred, dislike, aversion, animosity, animus.
▶ verb ❶ BEGRUDGE, give unwillingly, give reluctantly. ❷ RESENT, mind, take ill, begrudge, envy, be jealous of.

gruelling adjective EXHAUSTING, tiring, fatiguing, wearying, taxing, demanding, trying, arduous, laborious, back-breaking, strenuous, punishing, crushing, draining, hard, difficult, harsh, severe, grinding, stiff, brutal, relentless, unsparing, inexorable.

gruesome adjective GRISLY, ghastly, frightful, horrible, horrifying, horrid, horrendous, awful, dreadful, grim, terrible, fearful, hideous, disgusting, repulsive, revolting, repugnant, repellent, macabre, spine-chilling, sickening, appalling, shocking, abominable, loathsome, abhorrent, odious.

grumble verb COMPLAIN, groan, protest, object, find fault, carp, whine; *informal* moan, grouse, gripe, bellyache, beef, bitch, grouch, whinge.

grumpy adjective BAD-TEMPERED, surly, churlish, crotchety, tetchy, crabby, crusty, ill-natured, bearish; *informal* grouchy. – OPPOSITES good-humoured.

guarantee noun ❶ WARRANTY, warrant, covenant, bond, contract, guaranty. ❷ PLEDGE, promise, assurance, word, word of honour, oath, bond.
▶ verb ❶ guarantee a loan: UNDERWRITE, sponsor, back, support, provide collateral for, vouch for, provide surety for. ❷ PROMISE, pledge, give a pledge, give an assurance, give one's word, swear.

guard verb ❶ DEFEND, shield, safeguard, stand guard over, protect, watch over, cover, patrol, police, preserve, save, conserve, secure, screen, shelter. ❷ guard against thieves: BEWARE, keep

watch, be alert, take care, be on the lookout; *informal* keep an eye out, keep one's eyes peeled/ skinned.
▶ **noun** ❶ DEFENDER, guardian, bodyguard, custodian, sentry, sentinel, watchman, nightwatchman, lookout, scout, watch, picket, garrison, escort, convoy, patrol; *informal* minder. ❷ **prison guards**: WARDER, jailer, keeper; *informal* screw.

guarded **adjective** CAREFUL, cautious, circumspect, wary, chary, reluctant, non-committal, reticent, restrained, reserved, discreet, prudent; *informal* cagey.

guess **noun** CONJECTURE, surmise, estimate, hypothesis, guesswork, theory, reckoning, judgement, supposition, feeling, assumption, inference, prediction, speculation, notion; *informal* guesstimate.
▶ **verb** ❶ CONJECTURE, surmise, estimate, reckon, hypothesize, postulate, predict, speculate. ❷ SUPPOSE, believe, think, imagine, judge, consider, feel, suspect, dare say, fancy, divine, deem, surmise, reckon.

guest **noun** ❶ VISITOR, caller, company. ❷ **a guest at the hotel**: RESIDENT, boarder, lodger, patron, tenant.

guidance **noun** ❶ **the guidance of the headmaster**: DIRECTION, leadership, management, auspices, control, handling, conduct, government, charge, rule, teaching, instruction. ❷ **career guidance**: ADVICE, counselling, counsel, direction, recommendation, suggestion, tip, hint, pointer, intelligence, information, instruction.

guide **verb** ❶ LEAD, lead the way, conduct, show, usher, shepherd, direct, show the way, pilot, steer, escort, accompany, convoy, attend. ❷ **guide the firm**: CONTROL, direct, manage, steer, command, be in charge of, govern, rule, preside over, superintend, supervise, handle, regulate, manipulate, manoeuvre. ❸ **guide schoolchildren**: ADVISE, give advice to, counsel, give counselling to, make suggestions/ recommendations to, give someone pointers/tips, inform, instruct.
▶ **noun** ❶ ESCORT, chaperone, leader, courier, pilot, usher, attendant, director. ❷ ADVISER, counsellor, mentor, tutor, teacher, guru, confidant. ❸ GUIDEBOOK, handbook, manual, ABC, instructions, key, catalogue.

guile **noun** CUNNING, duplicity, craftiness, artfulness, craft, wiliness, artifice, foxiness, slyness, deception, deceit, underhandedness, double-dealing, trickery, trickiness, sharp practice, treachery, chicanery, skulduggery, fraud, gamesmanship, knavery.
– OPPOSITES candour.

guileless **adjective** OPEN, artless, ingenuous, sincere, genuine, naive, simple, innocent, unsophisticated, unworldly, trusting, trustful, honourable, frank, candid.

guilty **adjective** ❶ **found guilty**: TO BLAME, blameworthy, culpable, blameable, at fault, responsible, censurable, convicted, criminal, reproachable, condemnable, erring, errant, wrong, delinquent, offending, sinful, wicked, evil, unlawful, illegal, illicit,

reprehensible, felonious, iniquitous. ❷ feel guilty: REMORSEFUL, ashamed, conscience-stricken, shamefaced, regretful, contrite, repentant, penitent, rueful, sheepish, hangdog, compunctious.
– OPPOSITES innocent, unrepentant.

guise noun ❶ COSTUME, clothes, likeness, outfit, dress, appearance, style. ❷ under the guise of friendship: PRETENCE, disguise, screen, cover, blind, appearance, form.

gulf noun ❶ BAY, cove, inlet, bight. ❷ CHASM, abyss, hollow, pit, hole, opening, rift, cleft, fissure, split, crevice, gully, canyon, gorge, ravine.

gullible adjective CREDULOUS, trustful, over-trustful, easily deceived, easily taken in, unsuspecting, unsuspicious, ingenuous, naive, innocent, simple, inexperienced, green, foolish, silly; *informal* wet behind the ears.
– OPPOSITES cynical, suspicious.

gulp verb ❶ gulp a drink: SWALLOW, quaff, toss off, drain one's glass; *informal* swig, swill. ❷ gulp one's food: BOLT, wolf, gobble, guzzle, devour; *informal* tuck into. ❸ gulp back the tears: FIGHT BACK, suppress, stifle, smother, choke back, strangle.
▶ noun SWALLOW, mouthful, draught; *informal* swig.

gumption noun INITIATIVE, resourcefulness, enterprise, spirit, forcefulness, backbone, pluck, mettle, nerve, courage; *informal* get-up-and-go, grit, spunk; *Brit. informal* bottle.

gunman noun ARMED ROBBER, sniper, gangster, terrorist, assassin, murderer, killer, bandit; *informal* gunslinger, hit man, hired gun, trigger man, gunfighter; *N. Amer. informal* hood.

gurgle verb BUBBLE, murmur, babble, burble, lap, splash, tinkle, plash, purl.

gush verb ❶ water gushing: STREAM, rush, spout, spurt, surge, jet, well, pour, burst, cascade, flood, flow, run, issue, emanate. ❷ she gushed about the new house: BE EFFUSIVE, enthuse, wax lyrical, bubble over, get carried away, fuss, babble, prattle, jabber, gabble, blather, chatter, make too much, overstate the case.
▶ noun STREAM, outpouring, spurt, jet, spout, rush, burst, surge, cascade, flood, torrent, spate, freshet.

gusto noun ZEST, enthusiasm, relish, zeal, fervour, verve, enjoyment, delight, exhilaration, pleasure, appreciation, liking, fondness, appetite, savour, taste.
– OPPOSITES apathy, indifference.

gut noun STOMACH, belly, abdomen, bowels, colon, intestines, entrails, vital organs, viscera; *informal* insides, innards.
▶ verb ❶ gut the fish: EVISCERATE, disembowel, dress, clean, draw. ❷ gut the house: STRIP, ransack, empty, plunder, loot, rob, rifle, ravage, sack, clear out, destroy, devastate, lay waste.

guts plural noun COURAGE, bravery, valour, nerve, fortitude, pluck, mettle, spirit, boldness, audacity, daring, hardiness, toughness, forcefulness, will power, tenacity; *informal* grit, gumption, spunk; *Brit. informal* bottle.

gutter noun DRAIN, sewer, sluice, culvert, conduit, pipe, duct, channel, trench, trough, ditch, furrow.

guttural adjective HUSKY, throaty, gruff, gravelly, harsh, croaking, rasping, deep, low, rough, thick.

gyrate verb ROTATE, revolve, wheel round, turn round, circle, whirl, pirouette, twirl, swirl, spin, swivel.

Hh

habit noun ❶ CUSTOM, practice, wont, procedure, way, routine, matter of course, style, pattern, convention, policy, mode, rule. ❷ TENDENCY, propensity, predisposition, proclivity, penchant, leaning, bent, inclination, custom, practice, quirk. ❸ ADDICTION, dependence, weakness, obsession, fixation. ❹ **a riding habit**: COSTUME, dress, garb, attire, clothes, clothing, garments, livery, uniform; *formal* apparel.

habitable adjective INHABITABLE, liveable in, usable, fit to live in, fit to occupy, tenantable.
– OPPOSITES uninhabitable.

habitual adjective ❶ **his habitual place**: USUAL, customary, accustomed, regular, normal, set, fixed, established, routine, common, ordinary, familiar, traditional; *poetic/literary* wonted. ❷ **habitual grumbling**: PERSISTENT, constant, continual, repeated, recurrent, perpetual, non-stop, continuous, frequent. ❸ **a habitual smoker**: CONFIRMED, addicted, chronic, inveterate, hardened, ingrained.
– OPPOSITES unaccustomed, infrequent, occasional.

habituate verb ACCUSTOM, make used to, adapt, acclimatize, condition, break in, inure, harden, season, train, school, familiarize.

hackneyed adjective BANAL, trite, overused, overworked, tired, worn out, time-worn, stale, clichéd, platitudinous, unoriginal, commonplace, common, unimaginative, pedestrian, prosaic, run-of-the-mill, stock, conventional; *informal* corny, old hat, played out.
– OPPOSITES fresh, original.

hag noun CRONE, witch, harridan, gorgon, ogress, harpy, shrew, virago, vixen, fury, hellcat, termagant; *informal* battleaxe, old bat.

haggard adjective GAUNT, drawn, pinched, hollow-cheeked, scraggy, scrawny, withered, exhausted, ghost-like, death-like, wan, pallid, ghastly, cadaverous, peaked, drained, careworn, emaciated, wasted, thin.
– OPPOSITES plump.

hail verb ❶ GREET, salute, acknowledge, lift one's hat to. ❷ SIGNAL, make a sign, flag, flag down, wave down, call, shout to. ❸ *See* ACCLAIM.

hair noun ❶ LOCKS, tresses, shock

of hair, mop of hair, head of hair. ❷ COAT, fur, pelt, hide, wool, fleece, mane.

hair-raising adjective SPINE-CHILLING, blood-curdling, terrifying, horrifying, petrifying, frightening, alarming, shocking, exciting, thrilling; *informal* scary, creepy.

hairy adjective HIRSUTE, woolly, shaggy, bushy, fuzzy, bristly, fleecy, downy, bearded, unshaven, bewhiskered, stubbly.

half-baked adjective ILL-CONCEIVED, poorly-planned, unplanned, not thought through, premature, undeveloped, unformed, ill-judged, short-sighted, injudicious, impractical; *informal* crackpot.
– OPPOSITES sensible.

half-hearted adjective LUKEWARM, unenthusiastic, apathetic, indifferent, uninterested, unconcerned, cool, listless, unemotional, lacklustre, dispassionate, cursory, perfunctory, superficial, passive, neutral.
– OPPOSITES enthusiastic.

half-witted adjective SIMPLE-MINDED, feeble-minded, simple, stupid, idiotic, foolish, silly, dim-witted, moronic, crazy, doltish, dull-witted; *informal* cracked, crackpot, nutty, batty; *Brit. informal* barmy.

hallmark noun MARK, trademark, stamp, sign, badge, device, symbol, indicator, indication.

hallucinate verb IMAGINE THINGS, see things, have hallucinations, dream, fantasize, be delirious; *informal* be on a trip.

hallucination noun ILLUSION, delusion, figment of the imagination, vision, fantasy, apparition, dream, mirage, chimera, delirium, phantasmagoria.

halt verb ❶ COME TO A HALT, stop, come to a stop/standstill, pull up, draw up, wait. ❷ STOP, finish, cease, break off, call it a day, desist, discontinue; *informal* knock off; *Brit. informal* down tools. ❸ STOP, arrest, terminate, block, curb, put an end/stop to, bring to an end, crush, frustrate, obstruct, baulk, impede, hold back.
– OPPOSITES begin.
▶ **noun** STOP, stoppage, cessation, close, end, standstill, pause, interval, interlude, intermission, break, hiatus, rest, respite.

halve verb CUT IN HALF, divide in two, divide equally, split in two, bisect.

hammer verb ❶ BEAT, batter, pound, pummel, hit, strike, cudgel, slap, bludgeon, club; *informal* wallop, clobber. ❷ **hammer the opposition**: DEFEAT, trounce, thrash, worst, drub, give someone a drubbing; *informal* clobber, beat hollow.

hamper verb HINDER, obstruct, impede, hold back, inhibit, retard, slow down, hold up, restrain, block, check, frustrate, thwart, foil, curb, interfere with, cramp, restrict, bridle, handicap, stymie, hamstring, shackle, fetter, encumber, trammel, cumber; *Brit.* throw a spanner in the works.
– OPPOSITES expedite.

hand noun ❶ FIST, palm; *informal* mitt, paw, duke. ❷ POINTER, indicator, needle. ❸ WORKER, workman, employee, operative, hired hand, labourer, artisan.
▶ **verb** GIVE, pass, pass over, hand over, deliver, present.

■ **hand on/down** PASS ON/DOWN, bequeath, will, give, transfer. **hand out** DISTRIBUTE, give out, pass out, deal out, dole out, mete out, dispense, apportion, disseminate, disburse, dish out.

handicap noun ❶ DISABILITY, impairment, abnormality, disadvantage, defect. ❷ IMPEDIMENT, disadvantage, hindrance, obstruction, obstacle, encumbrance, check, block, curb, barrier, stumbling block, constraint, restriction, limitation, drawback, shortcoming.
– OPPOSITES advantage.
▶ **verb** DISADVANTAGE, put at a disadvantage, impede, hinder, impair, hamper, obstruct, check, block, encumber, curb, trammel, bridle, hold back, constrain, restrict, limit.

handiwork noun ❶ HANDICRAFT, craft, craftsmanship. ❷ ACTION, achievement, work, doing, creation, design, product, production, result.

handle verb ❶ TOUCH, feel, hold, finger, grasp, grip, pick up, lift, pat, caress, stroke, fondle, poke, maul; *informal* paw. ❷ **handle him:** COPE WITH, deal with, treat, manage, control. ❸ **handle the matter:** BE IN CHARGE OF, control, manage, administer, direct, guide, conduct, supervise, take care of. ❹ **handle a car:** DRIVE, steer, operate, manoeuvre. ❺ **handle goods:** DEAL IN, trade in, traffic in, market, sell, stock, carry.
▶ **noun** SHAFT, grip, handgrip, hilt, haft, knob, stock, helve.

handsome adjective ❶ **a handsome man:** GOOD-LOOKING, attractive, personable; *informal* dishy. ❷ **a handsome woman:** ATTRACTIVE, good-looking, lovely, elegant, fine, personable, well formed, well proportioned, stately, dignified. ❸ **a handsome present:** GENEROUS, magnanimous, liberal, lavish, considerable, sizeable, large, ample, abundant, plentiful; *poetic/literary* bounteous.
– OPPOSITES ugly.

handy adjective ❶ TO HAND, at hand, within reach, available, accessible, near, nearby, close, at one's fingertips, convenient; *informal* on tap. ❷ **a handy tool:** USEFUL, helpful, practicable, practical, serviceable, functional, expedient, easy-to-use, neat, convenient. ❸ **a handy person:** DEFT, dexterous, nimble-fingered, adroit, proficient, adept, skilful, skilled, expert, clever/good with one's hands.
– OPPOSITES inaccessible, useless, inept.

hang verb ❶ BE SUSPENDED, dangle, swing, sway, be pendent. ❷ **hang the prisoner:** SEND TO THE GALLOWS, send to the gibbet, execute; *informal* string up. ❸ **hang wallpaper:** STICK UP, attach, fix, fasten on, paste, glue, cement. ❹ **room hung with tapestries:** ADORN, decorate, deck, ornament, drape, cover, furnish.
■ **hang about/around** WAIT, linger, loiter, dally, waste time; *archaic* tarry. **hang back** HOLD BACK, stay back, stay in the background, be reluctant, hesitate, recoil, demur, shrink back. **hang on** WAIT, hold on, stop, stay, remain, persevere.

hang-up noun FIXATION, preoccupation, obsession, phobia, problem; *informal* thing, bee in one's bonnet.

hanker
■ **hanker after/for** LONG FOR, have a longing for, yearn for,

crave, desire, hunger for, thirst for, be bent on, covet, want, wish for, set one's heart on, pine for, lust after; *informal* be itching for, be dying for, have a yen for.

haphazard adjective UNPLANNED, random, indiscriminate, undirected, unforeseen, chaotic, chance, unsystematic, unorganized, unmethodical, orderless, aimless, irregular, slapdash, thrown together, careless, casual, hit-or-miss.
– OPPOSITES methodical, systematic.

hapless adjective UNLUCKY, unfortunate, out of luck, ill-starred, forlorn, wretched, unhappy, woebegone; *informal* down on one's luck.
– OPPOSITES lucky.

happen verb TAKE PLACE, occur, come about, present itself, arise, materialize, appear, come into being, chance, arrive, transpire, crop up, develop, eventuate, supervene; *poetic/literary* come to pass.

happening noun OCCURRENCE, event, incident, occasion, affair, circumstance, action, case, phenomenon, eventuality, episode, experience, adventure, scene, proceedings, chance.

happiness noun CHEERFULNESS, cheeriness, merriness, gaiety, good spirits, high spirits, light-heartedness, joy, joyfulness, glee, joviality, carefreeness, enjoyment, gladness, delight, exuberance, elation, ecstasy, bliss, blissfulness, euphoria, transports; *poetic/literary* blitheness.
– OPPOSITES unhappiness, sadness.

happy adjective ❶ CHEERFUL, cheery, merry, in good/high spirits, joyful, joyous, light-hearted, jovial, gleeful, buoyant, carefree, untroubled, smiling, glad, delighted, elated, ecstatic, blissful, euphoric, overjoyed, exuberant, in seventh heaven, floating/walking on air; *informal* over the moon, on cloud nine, on top of the world; *dated* gay; *poetic/literary* blithe. ❷ **happy to see you:** GLAD, pleased, delighted, contented, satisfied, gratified, thrilled. ❸ **a happy chance:** LUCKY, fortunate, advantageous, favourable, beneficial, opportune, helpful, timely, convenient, welcome, propitious, auspicious, felicitous, fortuitous. ❹ **a happy choice:** APPROPRIATE, fitting, apt, fit, good, right, proper, seemly.
– OPPOSITES unhappy, sad, displeased, unfortunate.

harangue noun LECTURE, tirade, diatribe, speech, talk, sermon, exhortation, declamation, oration, address, homily, peroration; *informal* spiel.

harass verb ❶ BOTHER, pester, annoy, exasperate, worry, fret, disturb, agitate, provoke, badger, hound, torment, plague, persecute, harry, tease, bait, nag, molest, bedevil; *informal* hassle, give someone a hard time, drive someone up the wall. ❷ **harass the enemy:** HARRY, attack repeatedly, raid, beleaguer, press hard, oppress.

harassed adjective STRESSED, under pressure, distraught, under stress, strained, worried, careworn, troubled, vexed, agitated, fretting; *informal* hassled.
– OPPOSITES carefree.

harbinger noun FORERUNNER, herald, precursor, sign, portent, omen, augury.

harbour noun ❶ PORT, anchorage, dock, haven, marina. ❷ REFUGE, shelter, haven, sanctuary, retreat, asylum, sanctum, covert.
▶ verb ❶ **harbour criminals:** SHELTER, give shelter to, house, lodge, put up, take in, billet, provide refuge for, shield, protect, conceal, hide, secrete. ❷ **harbour resentment:** NURSE, maintain, nurture, hold on to, cherish, cling to, retain, entertain.

hard adjective ❶ **hard ground:** FIRM, solid, compact, compacted, compressed, condensed, dense, rigid, stiff, unyielding, resistant, inflexible, unpliable, tough, strong, stony, unmalleable, close-packed, rock-like. ❷ **hard work:** STRENUOUS, arduous, heavy, tiring, fatiguing, exhausting, back-breaking, laborious, rigorous, exacting, formidable, tough, difficult, uphill, toilsome, Herculean. ❸ **a hard problem:** DIFFICULT, complicated, complex, involved, intricate, puzzling, perplexing, baffling, knotty, thorny, bewildering, insoluble, enigmatic, unfathomable, incomprehensible. ❹ **a hard master:** HARSH, severe, stern, hard-hearted, cold, unfeeling, unsympathetic, grim, ruthless, oppressive, tyrannical, pitiless, merciless, unrelenting, unsparing, callous, cruel, vicious, implacable, obdurate, unyielding, unjust, unfair. ❺ **hard conditions:** DIFFICULT, grim, harsh, unpleasant, disagreeable, uncomfortable, intolerable, unendurable, unbearable, insupportable, distressing, painful, disastrous, calamitous. ❻ **a hard blow:** FORCEFUL, violent, heavy, strong, powerful, fierce, harsh, sharp. ❼ **hard words:** ANGRY, bitter, antagonistic, acrimonious, hostile, resentful, rancorous. ❽ **hard drugs:** ADDICTIVE, habit-forming, harmful, noxious, injurious.
– OPPOSITES soft, easy.

hard-boiled adjective CYNICAL, tough, unsentimental, down-to-earth, world-weary.

harden verb ❶ SOLIDIFY, become hard, set, stiffen, cake, congeal, clot, coagulate, bake, anneal. ❷ TOUGHEN, make insensitive/unfeeling, deaden, numb, benumb.

hard-hitting adjective TOUGH, uncompromising, unsparing, strongly worded, vigorous, straight-talking, blunt, frank, critical; *informal* pulling no punches.

hardly adverb SCARCELY, barely, only just, just, almost not, with difficulty, with effort.
– OPPOSITES fully.

hardship noun ADVERSITY, deprivation, privation, want, need, destitution, poverty, austerity, desolation, misfortune, distress, suffering, affliction, pain, misery, wretchedness, tribulation, trials, burdens, calamity, catastrophe, disaster, ruin, ruination, torment, torture; *poetic/literary* travail.
– OPPOSITES ease, comfort.

hardy adjective HEALTHY, fit, strong, robust, sturdy, tough, rugged, vigorous, in good condition, resilient, lusty, stalwart, hale and hearty, fit as a fiddle, sound in

body and limb, in fine fettle, in good kilter.
– OPPOSITES delicate.

harm noun ❶ HURT, injury, pain, suffering, trauma, destruction, loss, ruin, havoc, adversity, disservice, abuse, damage, mischief, detriment, defacement, defilement, impairment. ❷ EVIL, badness, wrongdoing, wrong, wickedness, vice, iniquity, sin, sinfulness, immorality, nefariousness.
▶ verb HURT, injure, wound, inflict pain/suffering on, abuse, maltreat, ill-treat, ill-use, molest, do violence to, destroy, damage, do mischief to, deface, defile, impair, spoil, mar, blemish.

harmful adjective ❶ harmful effects: HURTFUL, injurious, wounding, abusive, detrimental, damaging, deleterious, disadvantageous, destructive, dangerous, pernicious, noxious, baneful, toxic. ❷ a harmful influence: BAD, evil, wicked, malign, corrupting, subversive.
– OPPOSITES harmless.

harmless adjective ❶ a harmless substance: INNOCUOUS, safe, non-toxic, mild, non-irritant. ❷ a harmless old man: INNOCUOUS, inoffensive, unoffending, innocent, blameless, gentle.
– OPPOSITES harmful.

harmonious adjective
❶ MELODIOUS, tuneful, musical, harmonizing, sweet-sounding, mellifluous, dulcet, euphonious, symphonious, consonant. ❷ a harmonious atmosphere: PEACEFUL, peaceable, friendly, amicable, cordial, amiable, agreeable, congenial, united, cooperative, in harmony, in tune, attuned, in accord, compatible, sympathetic.
– OPPOSITES discordant, hostile.

harmonize verb ❶ BE IN ACCORD, coincide, agree, correspond, tally, be in unison, be congruent, be of one mind. ❷ RECONCILE, settle differences, restore harmony to, make peaceful, patch up, negotiate peace between, heal the breach, pour oil on troubled waters.

harmony noun ❶ work in harmony: AGREEMENT, accord, accordance, concordance, concurrence, unanimity, cooperation, unity, unison, oneness, amicability, good will, amity, affinity, rapport, sympathy, like-mindedness, friendship, fellowship, comradeship, peace, peacefulness. ❷ harmony of the colours: COMPATIBILITY, congruity, consonance, coordination, blending, balance, symmetry, suitability; *formal* concord.
❸ musical harmony: TUNE, melody, tunefulness, melodiousness, mellifluousness, euphony.
– OPPOSITES disagreement, incongruity, dissonance.

harrowing adjective DISTRESSING, agonizing, excruciating, traumatic, heart-rending, heartbreaking, painful, racking, afflicting, chilling, disturbing, vexing, alarming, perturbing, unnerving, horrifying, terrifying.

harsh adjective ❶ a harsh reply: ABRUPT, brusque, blunt, curt, gruff, short, surly, concise, clipped, impolite, discourteous, uncivil, ungracious. ❷ a harsh ruler: CRUEL, brutal, savage, barbarous, hard-hearted, despotic, tyrannical, ruthless, unfeeling, merciless, pitiless, relentless,

unrelenting, inhuman. ❸ **harsh measures:** SEVERE, stringent, stern, grim, austere, uncompromising, inflexible, punitive, draconian. ❹ **a harsh noise:** GRATING, jarring, grinding, rasping, strident, jangling, raucous, ear-piercing, discordant, dissonant, unharmonious. ❺ **a harsh voice:** ROUGH, coarse, guttural, hoarse, croaking, raucous, strident, gravelly. ❻ **harsh conditions/countryside:** SEVERE, grim, desolate, stark, austere, barren, rough, bleak, wild, bitter, inhospitable, comfortless, spartan. ❼ **harsh colours:** GARISH, gaudy, glaring, bold, loud, flashy, showy, crass, crude, vulgar.
– OPPOSITES lenient, gentle.

harvest **noun** REAPING, crop, yield, produce, vintage, ingathering.
▶ **verb** GATHER, gather in, reap, glean, pick, pluck, collect, amass, accumulate, garner.

hassle **verb** ANNOY, badger, harass, hound, pester, bother, trouble, worry, torment, plague; *informal* give someone a hard time.
▶ **noun** TROUBLE, bother, inconvenience, annoyance, nuisance, harassment, difficulty, problem, struggle, fight, quarrel, altercation, disagreement, dispute, wrangle, tussle.

haste **noun** SPEED, swiftness, rapidity, rapidness, quickness, fastness, briskness, urgency, alacrity, promptness, dispatch, expeditiousness, promptitude, expedition, celerity, fleetness.

hasty **adjective** ❶ SWIFT, rapid, quick, fast, speedy, hurried, hurrying, running, prompt, expeditious, brisk, urgent, fleet. ❷ **a hasty visit:** QUICK, short, brief, rushed, short-lived, fleeting, transitory, cursory, perfunctory, superficial, slight. ❸ **a hasty decision:** HURRIED, rushed, impetuous, reckless, rash, foolhardy, precipitate, impulsive, headlong, thoughtless, heedless, careless, ill-conceived.
– OPPOSITES slow, cautious.

hatch **verb** ❶ INCUBATE, brood, sit on, cover. ❷ **hatch a plan:** DEVISE, concoct, contrive, plan, scheme, design, invent, formulate, originate, conceive, dream up, think up; *informal* cook up.

hate **verb** ❶ LOATHE, detest, abhor, dislike, despise, abominate, execrate, have an aversion to, feel hostile towards, be unable to stand/bear, view with dislike, be sick of, be tired of, shudder at, be repelled by, recoil from. ❷ **I hate to say it:** BE RELUCTANT, be loath, be unwilling, feel disinclined, be sorry, dislike, not have the heart, shy away from, flinch from.
– OPPOSITES love, relish.
▶ **noun** *see* HATRED.

hateful **adjective** DETESTABLE, loathsome, abhorrent, abominable, despicable, execrable, odious, revolting, repugnant, repellent, disgusting, obnoxious, offensive, insufferable, horrible, unpleasant, nasty, disagreeable, foul, vile, heinous.
– OPPOSITES admirable.

hatred **noun** HATE, loathing, detestation, abhorrence, dislike, aversion, hostility, ill will, enmity, animosity, antagonism, antipathy, animus, revulsion, repugnance, odium, rancour, grudge, execration, abomination.
– OPPOSITES love.

haughty **adjective** ARROGANT,

proud, conceited, self-important, egotistical, vain, swollen-headed, overweening, overbearing, pompous, smug, presumptuous, condescending, supercilious, lofty, patronizing, snobbish, imperious, boastful, scornful, lordly, high-handed; *informal* snooty, on one's high horse, high and mighty, stuck up, hoity-toity, uppity, uppish.
–OPPOSITES modest, humble.

haul verb DRAG, pull, tug, draw, heave, trail, lug, tow, take in tow, cart, carry, convoy, ship.

haunt verb **1** haunt bars: FREQUENT, visit regularly, patronize; *informal* hang out in. **2** haunted by guilt: OBSESS, prey on someone's mind, prey on, torment, plague, disturb, trouble, worry, oppress, burden, beset, harry, weigh on, come back to, stay with.

have verb **1** she has a car: OWN, possess, keep, keep for one's use, use, hold, retain. **2** he had a cup of tea: GET, be given, receive, accept, obtain, acquire, procure, secure, gain. **3** the flat has five rooms: CONTAIN, include, comprise, embrace, take in, incorporate, embody, comprehend. **4** have some trouble: EXPERIENCE, undergo, go through, encounter, meet, find, be subjected to, submit to, suffer from, endure, tolerate, put up with. **5** have doubts: FEEL, entertain, have/keep/bear in mind, harbour, foster, nurse, cherish. **6** had her doing the work: MAKE, cause, oblige, require, force, coerce, induce, prevail upon, talk into, persuade. **7** won't have such behaviour: PERMIT, allow, put up with, tolerate, stand, support, endure, abide; *formal* brook. **8** have a baby: GIVE BIRTH TO, bear, deliver, be delivered of, bring into the world, bring forth.
■ **have had it** BE FINISHED, be out, be defeated, have lost, have no chance, have no hope. **have on** **1** WEAR, be wearing, be dressed/clothed in. **2** HAVE PLANNED, have arranged, be committed to, have on the agenda. **3** TEASE, joke with, play a joke on, trick, play a trick on, pull someone's leg, kid. **have to** MUST, have got to, be bound to, be obliged to, be forced to, be compelled to.

haven noun REFUGE, shelter, sanctuary, asylum, retreat, sanctum, sanctum sanctorum, covert.

havoc noun **1** DEVASTATION, destruction, damage, ruination, ruin, rack and ruin, despoliation, waste, gutting, wreckage, desolation, disaster, catastrophe, cataclysm. **2** CHAOS, disorder, confusion, disruption, disorganization, mayhem; *informal* shambles.

hazard noun **1** DANGER, peril, risk, jeopardy, threat, menace. **2** CHANCE, accident, luck, contingency, fortuity, fortuitousness.
▶ verb **1** RISK, put at risk, endanger, expose to danger, imperil, put in jeopardy, jeopardize. **2** hazard a guess: VENTURE, put forward, proffer, offer, submit, advance, volunteer.

hazardous adjective DANGEROUS, risky, perilous, fraught with danger/risk, chancy, uncertain, unpredictable, precarious, parlous, unsafe, insecure; *informal* dicey, hairy, tricky.
–OPPOSITES safe.

haze noun MIST, mistiness, fog, cloud, cloudiness, smog, vapour.

hazy adjective ❶ MISTY, foggy, cloudy, smoggy, overcast. ❷ *hazy memories:* VAGUE, indefinite, blurred, fuzzy, faint, confused, muddled, unclear, obscure, dim, indistinct, ill-defined.
– OPPOSITES clear.

head noun ❶ SKULL, cranium; *informal* nut, noodle, noddle; *Brit. informal* bonce; *informal, dated* conk. ❷ *use your head:* MIND, intelligence, intellect, brain, brains, mentality, wit, sense, wisdom, reasoning, rationality, understanding. ❸ *the head of the business:* LEADER, chief, commander, director, manager, superintendent, controller, administrator, supervisor, principal, captain. ❹ *the head of the hill:* TOP, summit, peak, crest, crown, tip, brow, apex. ❺ *the head of the queue:* FRONT, fore, forefront, van, vanguard.
▶ verb ❶ *head the expedition:* LEAD, be at the head of, be in charge of, be in command/control of, command, control, run, supervise, rule, govern, guide. ❷ *head for town:* MAKE FOR, go to, go in the direction of, aim for, set out for, start out for, go towards, steer towards, make a beeline for.
■ **head off** DIVERT, intercept, deflect, turn aside, block off, cut off, forestall.

headlong adverb ❶ HEAD FIRST, head on, on one's head. ❷ HASTILY, hurriedly, impatiently, without thinking, rashly, recklessly, wildly, prematurely, carelessly, precipitately, heedlessly.
– OPPOSITES cautiously.

headquarters noun CENTRE OF OPERATIONS, base, command post, main office/branch, head office.

heal verb ❶ CURE, make well, make better, remedy, treat, mend, restore, regenerate. ❷ RECUPERATE, get better/well, mend, be cured, be on the mend, improve, be restored. ❸ *heal the breach:* RECONCILE, patch up, settle, set right, put right, harmonize, conciliate.

health noun ❶ HEALTHINESS, fitness, well-being, good condition, good shape, soundness, robustness, strength, vigour, fine fettle, salubrity. ❷ *his health is not good:* STATE OF HEALTH, constitution, physical state, shape, condition, form, tone.

healthy adjective ❶ IN GOOD HEALTH, fit, in good condition, robust, strong, vigorous, hardy, flourishing, blooming, hale and hearty, hale; *informal* in the pink. ❷ *healthy diet/climate:* HEALTH-GIVING, beneficial, invigorating, bracing, stimulating, refreshing, nutritious, nourishing, wholesome, good for one.
– OPPOSITES unhealthy.

heap noun ❶ PILE, stack, mound, mass, stockpile, accumulation, collection, agglomeration, conglomeration, hoard, store, stock, supply. ❷ *a heap of/heaps of money:* A LOT, lots, a great deal, abundance, plenty, a mint; *informal* oodles, loads, tons, pots, stacks; *Brit. informal* lashings.
▶ verb PILE UP, stack, amass, stockpile, mound, accumulate, collect, assemble, hoard, store, stock up, set aside, lay by.

hear verb ❶ TAKE IN, catch, perceive, overhear; *informal* get, latch on to. ❷ I heard he was dead: BE INFORMED, be told of, be made aware, receive information, find out, discover, learn, gather, pick up, hear tell, get wind of. ❸ the judge heard the case: TRY, judge, pass judgement on, adjudicate, examine, investigate, inquire into, consider.

hearing noun INQUIRY, trial, inquest, investigation, review.

heart noun ❶ with all his heart: PASSION, love, affection, emotions, feelings. ❷ have no heart: TENDERNESS, compassion, sympathy, empathy, humanity, responsiveness, fellow feeling, goodwill, kindness, kindliness. ❸ have the heart to go on: SPIRIT, enthusiasm, keenness, eagerness, liveliness. ❹ the heart of the matter: ESSENCE, crux, substance, core, quintessence.

heartache noun SORROW, grief, sadness, anguish, pain, hurt, agony, suffering, misery, wretchedness, despair, desolation, woe, despondency; *poetic/literary* dolour.
– OPPOSITES happiness.

heartbreaking adjective SAD, pitiful, tragic, poignant, painful, agonizing, distressing, affecting, grievous, bitter, cruel, harsh, tear-jerking, harrowing, excruciating.

hearten verb CHEER, raise someone's spirits, revitalize, energize, invigorate, animate, exhilarate, uplift, elate, comfort, encourage, buoy up; *informal* buck up, give someone a shot in the arm.

heartfelt adjective DEEPLY FELT, deep, profound, wholehearted, sincere, earnest, honest, devout, genuine, unfeigned, ardent, fervent, passionate, warm, enthusiastic, eager.

heartless adjective UNFEELING, unsympathetic, unkind, uncaring, unmoved, untouched, cold, cold-hearted, cold-blooded, hard-hearted, cruel, harsh, stern, hard, brutal, merciless, pitiless, ruthless.
– OPPOSITES compassionate.

heat noun ❶ HOTNESS, warmth, warmness, torridness, torridity, sultriness, calefaction. ❷ the heat in his voice: PASSION, warmth, intensity, vehemence, ardour, fervour, fervency, zeal, eagerness, enthusiasm, animation, earnestness, excitement, agitation.
– OPPOSITES cold, apathy.
▶ verb ❶ heat the milk: WARM, warm up, make hot/warm, reheat, cook. ❷ the day heated up: GROW HOT/WARM, become hotter/warmer.

heated adjective VEHEMENT, passionate, fierce, angry, furious, stormy, tempestuous, frenzied, raging, intense, impassioned, violent, animated, inflamed, enraged.

heathen noun UNBELIEVER, infidel, pagan, disbeliever, atheist, heretic, idolater/idolatress.
▶ adjective PAGAN, godless, infidel, heathenish, irreligious, idolatrous, atheistic, heretical.

heave verb ❶ LIFT, haul, tug, raise, hoist. ❷ THROW, cast, toss, fling, hurl, let fly, pitch; *informal* sling, chuck. ❸ VOMIT, throw up, retch, spew; *Brit.* be sick.

heaven noun ❶ PARADISE, the next life, the hereafter, the life to come, the next world, the

afterlife, nirvana. ❷ ECSTASY, bliss, rapture, joy, happiness, contentment, seventh heaven. ❸ **the heavens opened**: SKY, skies; *poetic/literary* firmament, empyrean, ether.
– OPPOSITES hell.

heavenly adjective ❶ CELESTIAL, divine, angelic, seraphic, cherubic, beatific, blessed, holy, god-like, immortal, paradisiacal. ❷ DELIGHTFUL, pleasurable, enjoyable, marvellous, wonderful, gratifying, blissful, rapturous, sublime, glorious, divine. ❸ **a heavenly dress**: BEAUTIFUL, exquisite, perfect, superb, ravishing, enchanting, alluring.
– OPPOSITES hellish.

heavy adjective ❶ **a heavy load**: WEIGHTY, bulky, hefty, big, large, substantial, massive, enormous, unwieldy, cumbersome, burdensome. ❷ **a heavy responsibility**: ONEROUS, burdensome, oppressive, difficult, unbearable, intolerable. ❸ **a heavy blow**: HARD, forceful, strong, severe, harsh, intense, sharp. ❹ **a heavy man**: OVERWEIGHT, fat, stout, obese, tubby, corpulent, paunchy, lumbering, bulky; *informal* hulking. ❺ **heavy fighting**: SEVERE, intense, serious, grave. ❻ **heavy ground**: MUDDY, sticky, boggy, difficult. ❼ **heavy reading**: DIFFICULT, dull, serious, tedious, boring, uninteresting, dry, wearisome. ❽ **heavy seas**: ROUGH, wild, stormy, tempestuous, turbulent, violent.
– OPPOSITES light.

heavy-handed adjective *see* CLUMSY (1, 3).

hectic adjective BUSY, active, frantic, frenetic, frenzied, bustling, flurried, fast and furious, turbulent, tumultuous, confused, exciting, excited, wild.
– OPPOSITES leisurely.

hedge noun ❶ HEDGEROW, row of bushes, quickset, barrier, screen, protection, windbreak. ❷ **a hedge against inflation**: SAFEGUARD, guard, protection, shield, cover, insurance.
▶ verb ❶ SURROUND, enclose, encircle, circle, border, edge, skirt. ❷ **she hedged when questioned**: EQUIVOCATE, prevaricate, be vague/ambivalent, be non-committal, dodge the question/issue, beat about the bush, sidestep the question/issue, temporize, quibble; *Brit.* hum and haw; *N. Amer. informal* waffle.

heed noun ATTENTION, attentiveness, notice, note, regard, mindfulness, mind, respect, consideration, thought, care, caution, watchfulness, wariness, chariness.
▶ verb PAY HEED/ATTENTION TO, attend to, take notice/note of, notice, note, bear in mind, be mindful of, mind, mark, take into account, follow, obey, adhere to, observe, take to heart, be alert to, be cautious of, watch out for.

heedful adjective ATTENTIVE, careful, mindful, cautious, prudent, circumspect, wary, observant, watchful, vigilant, alert, on guard.
– OPPOSITES heedless.

heedless adjective INATTENTIVE, unheeding, careless, incautious, unmindful, regardless, unthinking, thoughtless, unwary, oblivious, unobservant, negligent, neglectful, rash, reckless, foolhardy, precipitate.
– OPPOSITES heedful.

heft verb LIFT, lift up, raise, hoist, hike up, heave, boost.

hefty adjective ❶ HEAVY, bulky, big, large, stout, massive, huge, muscular, brawny, strapping, sturdy, solidly built, strong; *informal* beefy, hulking. ❷ **a hefty bill:** SUBSTANTIAL, sizeable, huge, colossal, expensive.
– OPPOSITES light.

height noun ❶ HIGHNESS, altitude, loftiness, elevation, tallness, stature. ❷ **a mountain height:** TOP, mountain top, hilltop, summit, peak, crest, crown, pinnacle, apex, vertex, apogee. ❸ **the height of his powers:** PEAK, zenith, apex, culmination, crowning point, climax, consummation, perfection.

heighten verb ❶ RAISE, make higher, lift, elevate. ❷ **heighten the tension:** MAKE GREATER, intensify, raise, increase, add to, build up, augment, boost, strengthen, amplify, magnify, aggravate, enhance.
– OPPOSITES lower.

heinous adjective ABOMINABLE, atrocious, abhorrent, odious, detestable, loathsome, hateful, wicked, monstrous, horrible, ghastly, shocking, flagrant, contemptible, reprehensible, despicable.

hellish adjective ❶ DEMONIC, diabolical, devilish, fiendish, satanic, infernal. ❷ **a hellish day:** UNPLEASANT, nasty, disagreeable, horrible, horrid, awful.

help verb ❶ ASSIST, aid, give someone a (helping) hand, lend a hand, guide, be of service to, be useful to, succour, befriend. ❷ **help the charity:** SUPPORT, back, contribute to, promote, boost. ❸ **help the pain:** SOOTHE, relieve, ameliorate, alleviate, mitigate, assuage, cure, heal, improve, ease. ❹ **can I help you?** SERVE, be of assistance, give help. ❺ **help oneself to:** TAKE, appropriate, commandeer, steal, make free with; *informal* walk off with; *Brit. informal* pinch, nick.
▶ noun ❶ ASSISTANCE, aid, service, helping hand, guidance, benefit, advantage, support, backing, succour. ❷ RELIEF, alleviation, amelioration, mitigation, remedy, cure, improvement, ease, corrective, balm. ❸ SERVANT, maid, worker, hired help; *Brit. informal* daily.

helper noun ASSISTANT, aide, deputy, adjutant, second-in-command, auxiliary, right-hand man/woman, henchman, colleague, associate, co-worker, partner, ally, collaborator.

helpful adjective ❶ **a helpful suggestion:** USEFUL, of use, of service, beneficial, valuable, advantageous, constructive, practical, productive, instrumental. ❷ **helpful people:** SUPPORTIVE, kind, friendly, obliging, accommodating, cooperative, sympathetic, considerate, caring, neighbourly, charitable, benevolent.
– OPPOSITES useless, unhelpful.

helping noun PORTION, serving, ration, piece, plateful, amount, share.

helpless adjective ❶ **a helpless invalid:** WEAK, feeble, disabled, incapable, infirm, debilitated, powerless, dependent, unfit, invalid, bedridden, paralysed; *informal* laid up. ❷ **left him helpless:**

DEFENCELESS, unprotected, vulnerable, exposed, abandoned, destitute, forlorn, desolate.
– OPPOSITES independent.

hem noun BORDER, edge, edging, trim, trimming, fringe, frill, flounce, valance.
▶ verb ❶ hem the dress: BIND, edge, trim, fringe. ❷ trees hemming the lake: BORDER, edge, skirt, surround, encircle, circle, enclose, encompass. ❸ he was hemmed in: SHUT IN, hedge in, close in, pen in, confine, constrain, restrict, limit, trap, keep within bounds.

herd noun FLOCK, pack, mob, crowd, throng, swarm, press, multitude.
▶ verb DRIVE, round up, assemble, collect, muster, shepherd, guide, lead, force, urge, goad.

hereditary adjective
❶ hereditary characteristics: GENETIC, congenital, innate, inborn, inherent, family, inbred, transmissible, transferable.
❷ hereditary property: INHERITED, handed down, bequeathed, willed, transferred, transmitted, family, ancestral.

heresy noun APOSTASY, dissent, nonconformity, unorthodoxy, free thinking, dissidence, scepticism, agnosticism, atheism, heterodoxy, revisionism, paganism.

heretic noun DISSENTER, apostate, unbeliever, sceptic, agnostic, atheist, nonconformist, free thinker, renegade, revisionist, schismatic, pagan, idolater, recusant.

heretical adjective DISSIDENT, sceptical, nonconformist, atheistical, agnostic, freethinking, unorthodox, heterodox, renegade, revisionist, schismatic, idolatrous, pagan, recusant.
– OPPOSITES orthodox.

heritage noun HISTORY, tradition, background, ancestry, lineage, descent, family, extraction, heredity, birth.

hermit noun RECLUSE, solitary, anchorite, anchoress, eremite, stylite.

heroic adjective ❶ BRAVE, courageous, valiant, intrepid, fearless, gallant, valorous, stout-hearted, lion-hearted, bold, daring, undaunted, dauntless, manly, virile, doughty, chivalrous.
❷ heroic characters/myths: LEGENDARY, mythological, classic, classical, fabulous. ❸ heroic language: EPIC, epical, Homeric, grandiloquent, high-flown, high-sounding, extravagant, grandiose, bombastic, rhetorical, pretentious, turgid, magniloquent, orotund, elevated.
– OPPOSITES cowardly.

heroism noun BRAVERY, courage, courageousness, valour, intrepidity, fearlessness, gallantry, stout-heartedness, lion-heartedness, boldness, daring, dauntlessness, doughtiness, manliness, virility, mettle, spirit, fortitude, chivalry.

hesitant adjective ❶ UNCERTAIN, unsure, doubtful, dubious, sceptical, irresolute, indecisive, vacillating, wavering, oscillating, shilly-shallying, stalling, delaying, disinclined, unwilling, half-hearted, lacking confidence, diffident, timid, shy.
❷ RELUCTANT, unwilling,

disinclined, diffident, having qualms about.
– OPPOSITES determined, decisive.

hesitate verb ❶ DELAY, pause, hang back, wait, be uncertain, be unsure, be doubtful, be indecisive, vacillate, waver, dither, shilly-shally, dally, stall, temporize, dilly-dally. ❷ BE RELUCTANT, be unwilling, be disinclined, shrink from, hang back from, think twice about, baulk at, demur from, scruple to, have misgivings about, be diffident about. ❸ STAMMER, stumble, falter, fumble for words; *Brit.* hum and haw.

hew verb ❶ CHOP, hack, axe, cut, saw, fell, lop, sever, trim, prune. ❷ CARVE, sculpt, sculpture, shape, fashion, form, model, whittle, chip, hammer, chisel, rough-hew.

hidden adjective ❶ hidden treasure: CONCEALED, secret, unseen, out of sight, not visible, not on view, covered, masked, shrouded, unrevealed. ❷ hidden motives: CONCEALED, secret, obscure, indistinct, indefinite, unclear, vague, cryptic, mysterious, covert, under wraps, abstruse, arcane, recondite, clandestine, ulterior, unfathomable, inexplicable, occult, mystical.
– OPPOSITES obvious.

hide verb ❶ hide from the police: CONCEAL ONESELF, go into hiding, take cover, find a hiding place, lie low, keep out of sight, secrete oneself, go to ground, go underground, cover one's tracks; *informal* hole up. ❷ hide the jewels: CONCEAL, secrete, store away, stow away, lock up; *informal* stash. ❸ clouds hiding the sun: OBSCURE, block, obstruct, darken, eclipse, cloud. ❹ hide one's motives: CONCEAL, keep secret, keep dark, withhold, suppress, mask, veil, shroud, camouflage, disguise, hush up; *informal* keep mum about, keep under one's hat.
– OPPOSITES reveal.

hideous adjective ❶ a hideous sight: UGLY, unsightly, grotesque, monstrous, repulsive, repellent, revolting, gruesome, disgusting, grim, ghastly, macabre. ❷ a hideous crime: AWFUL, horrible, horrific, horrendous, horrifying, frightful, shocking, dreadful, outrageous, monstrous, appalling, terrible, terrifying, heinous, abominable, foul, vile, odious, loathsome, contemptible, execrable.
– OPPOSITES beautiful.

hiding noun BEATING, thrashing, whipping, caning, spanking, flogging, drubbing, battering; *informal* licking, walloping, tanning, whaling, lathering.

hierarchy noun SOCIAL ORDER, ranking, grading, class system, pecking order.

high adjective ❶ TALL, lofty, elevated, soaring, towering, steep. ❷ a high official: HIGH-RANKING, leading, top, powerful, important, prominent, eminent, principal, chief, influential, distinguished, notable, illustrious, exalted. ❸ high cost: DEAR, expensive, steep, excessive, stiff, inflated, exorbitant, extortionate, high-priced, extravagant, costly. ❹ a high opinion: GOOD, favourable, approving, admiring, flattering. ❺ a high wind: INTENSE, strong, powerful, extreme, forceful, vigorous, potent, violent.

❻ high on drugs: DRUGGED, intoxicated, inebriated, delirious, hallucinating; *informal* stoned, on a trip, turned on.
– OPPOSITES low.
■ **high and dry** STRANDED, marooned, abandoned, helpless, destitute, bereft. **high and mighty** HAUGHTY, arrogant, self-important, proud, conceited, egotistical, overweening, overbearing, snobbish, condescending, supercilious, imperious.

highbrow noun INTELLECTUAL, scholar, genius, mastermind; *informal* egghead, brain; *Brit. informal* brainbox.
▶ adjective INTELLECTUAL, scholarly, bookish, cultured, cultivated, educated, sophisticated; *informal* brainy.
– OPPOSITES lowbrow.

high-handed adjective AUTOCRATIC, tyrannical, despotic, domineering, oppressive, overbearing, imperious, haughty, lordly; *informal* bossy.

hike verb ❶ WALK, march, tramp, trek, trudge, plod, ramble, wander, backpack. ❷ HITCH UP, pull up, jack up, lift up. ❸ RAISE, increase, add to, put up, jack up.
▶ noun WALK, march, tramp, trek, ramble, trudge, wander.

hilarious adjective VERY FUNNY, extremely amusing, comical, uproarious, humorous, entertaining, side-splitting; *informal* priceless.

hill noun ❶ ELEVATION, heights, hillock, hilltop, knoll, hummock, mound, mount, fell, ridge. ❷ SLOPE, incline, rise, gradient, ramp, acclivity, declivity.

hinder verb IMPEDE, hamper, hold back, interfere with, delay, hold up, slow down, retard, obstruct, inhibit, handicap, hamstring, block, interrupt, check, trammel, forestall, curb, baulk, thwart, frustrate, baffle, foil, stymie, stop, bring to a halt, arrest, defer, abort, prevent, debar.
– OPPOSITES facilitate.

hindrance noun IMPEDIMENT, obstacle, obstruction, interference, handicap, block, restraint, interruption, check, bar, barrier, drawback, snag, difficulty, stumbling block, encumbrance, curb, stoppage, trammel, deterrent, prevention, debarment.
– OPPOSITES aid, help.

hinge
■ **hinge on** DEPEND ON, turn on, hang on, be contingent on, pivot on, revolve around, rest on, centre on.

hint noun ❶ CLUE, inkling, suggestion, innuendo, tip-off, insinuation, implication, indication, mention, allusion, intimation, whisper, a word to the wise. ❷ TIP, pointer, advice, help, suggestion. ❸ a hint of garlic: TOUCH, trace, suggestion, dash, soupçon, sprinkling, tinge, whiff, breath, taste, scent.
▶ verb SUGGEST, insinuate, imply, indicate, mention, allude to, intimate, let it be known, signal, refer to, make a reference to.

hire verb ❶ RENT, lease, charter, engage. ❷ hire staff: APPOINT, sign on, take on, engage, employ, secure someone's services, enlist, contract with.

historic adjective FAMED, notable, famous, celebrated, renowned, momentous, significant, important, consequential, memorable, remarkable, outstanding, extraordinary, epoch-making, red-letter.

historical adjective DOCUMENTED, recorded, factual, chronicled, archival, authentic, actual, attested, verified, confirmed.

history noun ❶ ANNAL, records, chronicles, account, study, tale, saga, narrative, recital, reports, memoirs, biography. ❷ LIFE STORY, background, antecedents, experiences, adventures, fortunes. ❸ THE PAST, former times, bygone days, yesterday, the old days, the good old days, time gone by, antiquity.

hit verb ❶ STRIKE, smack, slap, punch, box, cuff, buffet, thump, batter, pound, pummel, thrash, hammer, bang, knock, club, swat; *informal* whack, wallop, bash, belt, clout, clip, clobber, sock, biff, swipe. ❷ **the car hit the lorry**: RUN INTO, collide with, bang into, smash into, crash into, knock into, bump, meet head-on. ❸ **her death hit him hard**: AFFECT, have an effect on, make an impression on, influence, make an impact on, leave a mark on, impinge on, move, touch, overwhelm, devastate, hurt; *informal* knock back; *Brit. informal* knock for six. ❹ **hit the right tone**: ACHIEVE, accomplish, reach, attain, arrive at, gain, secure, touch, strike.
■ **hit it off** GET ON, get on good terms, become friends, take to each other, warm to each other, be on the same wavelength. **hit on/upon** STUMBLE ON, chance on, light on, come upon, discover, uncover, arrive at, think of, come up with.

hoard verb STORE, store up, stock up, stockpile, put by, put away, lay by, lay in, set aside, pile up, stack up, stow away, husband, save, buy up, accumulate, amass, heap up, collect, gather, squirrel away, garner.
▶ **noun** STORE, stockpile, supply, reserve, fund, cache, reservoir, accumulation, heap, pile, mass, aggregation, conglomeration; *informal, dated* stash.

hoarse adjective CROAKY, croaking, gruff, rough, throaty, harsh, husky, gravelly, rasping, guttural, raucous, cracked.
– OPPOSITES smooth.

hoax noun PRACTICAL JOKE, joke, prank, jest, trick, ruse, deception, fraud, imposture, cheat, swindle; *informal* con, fast one, spoof, scam.
▶ **verb** TRICK, fool, deceive, hoodwink, delude, bluff, dupe, take in, cheat, swindle, defraud, gull; *informal* con, pull a fast one on, pull the wool over someone's eyes, take for a ride, spoof.

hobble verb WALK WITH DIFFICULTY, limp, falter, shuffle, totter, stagger, reel; *Scottish* hirple.

hobby noun INTEREST, pursuit, pastime, diversion, recreation, relaxation, sideline, divertissement, entertainment, amusement.

hobnob verb ASSOCIATE, fraternize, socialize, mingle, mix with, keep company, go around, consort; *informal* hang around, hang out.

hold verb ❶ **hold her hand**: CLASP, clutch, grasp, grip, clench, seize, cling to. ❷ **hold his weight**: BEAR, carry, take, support, hold up, buttress, keep up, sustain, prop up, brace, suspend. ❸ **police are holding the suspect**: DETAIN, hold in custody, confine, impound, constrain, lock up, imprison, put behind bars, incarcerate. ❹ **hold his interest:** KEEP, maintain, occupy, engage, involve, absorb, engross, monopolize, catch, arrest, fascinate, rivet. ❺ **hold a job:** OCCUPY, be in, hold down, fill, continue in. ❻ **the bottle holds a litre:** CONTAIN, take, accommodate, have a capacity for. ❼ **hold that he's guilty:** MAINTAIN, think, believe, consider, regard, deem, judge, assume, presume, reckon, suppose. ❽ **the rule still holds:** HOLD GOOD, stand, apply, be in force, be in operation, operate, remain valid, exist, be the case. ❾ **hold a meeting:** CALL, convene, assemble, conduct, run, preside over, officiate at.

▶ **noun** ❶ GRIP, grasp, clutch, clasp. ❷ **his hold on them:** CONTROL, grip, power, dominance, influence, mastery, dominion, authority, ascendancy.

■ **hold forth** SPEAK, talk, declaim, lecture, discourse, harangue, preach, orate, sermonize, perorate. **hold out** STAND FAST, stand firm, resist, withstand, maintain one's position, stay put. **hold up** DELAY, hinder, impede, obstruct, retard, slow down, set back, stop, bring to a halt, prevent.

holder **noun** ❶ OWNER, possessor, bearer, proprietor, keeper, custodian, purchaser, incumbent; *Brit.* occupier. ❷ CONTAINER, case, casing, receptacle, stand, cover, covering, housing, sheath.

hole **noun** ❶ OPENING, aperture, gap, orifice, space, breach, break, fissure, crack, rift, puncture, perforation, cut, incision, split, gash, rent, slit, vent, notch. ❷ **a hole in the ground:** PIT, crater, excavation, mine, shaft, dugout, cave, cavern, pothole, depression, hollow, chamber, pocket, cavity, dip.

holiness **noun** SANCTITY, sanctitude, saintliness, sacredness, divineness, divinity, godliness, blessedness, spirituality, religiousness, piety, righteousness, goodness, virtue, purity, sanctimoniousness.

hollow **adjective** ❶ EMPTY, vacant, not filled, not solid, hollowed out. ❷ **hollow cheeks:** SUNKEN, deep-set, indented, depressed, concave, caved in, cavernous, incurvate. ❸ **a hollow sound:** MUFFLED, muted, low, dull, deep, rumbling, flat, dead, sepulchral. ❹ **hollow victories:** WORTHLESS, valueless, empty, profitless, fruitless, unprofitable, pointless, meaningless, insignificant, specious, pyrrhic. ❺ **hollow words:** INSINCERE, false, dissembling, deceitful, sham, untrue, spurious.

– OPPOSITES solid.

▶ **noun** INDENTATION, depression, concavity, dent, dip, dint, dimple, hole, crater, cavern, pit, cavity, well, trough.

holocaust **noun** ❶ DEVASTATION, destruction, inferno, conflagration, demolition. ❷ GENOCIDE, mass murder, annihilation, massacre, carnage, slaughter, extermination, butchery, ethnic cleansing.

holy **adjective** ❶ **a holy person:** DEVOUT, God-fearing, pious, spiritual, religious, righteous, good, virtuous, moral, saintly, saintlike, sinless, pietistic. ❷ **a holy place:** SACRED, blessed, blest,

sanctified, consecrated, hallowed, sacrosanct, dedicated, venerated, divine, religious.
– OPPOSITES impious.

home noun ❶ HOUSE, residence, habitation; *formal* dwelling, abode, domicile. ❷ HOMELAND, birth place, native land, fatherland, motherland, country of origin. ❸ HABITAT, environment, natural element, territory, ground, haunts, domain; *formal* abode.
■ **home in on** AIM AT, focus on, focus attention on, concentrate on, pinpoint, zero in on, zoom in on.

homeless adjective OF NO FIXED ABODE, destitute, derelict, without a roof over one's head, down-and-out, vagrant, itinerant, nomadic, dispossessed, rootless.

homely adjective ❶ COMFORTABLE, cosy, snug, welcoming, informal, relaxed, modest, unassuming, unpretentious, simple, natural, plain. ❷ PLAIN, unattractive, ugly, plain-featured, ill-favoured; *informal* not much to look at, short on looks.
– OPPOSITES grand, beautiful.

homicide noun MURDER, manslaughter, killing, slaughter, assassination, patricide, matricide, infanticide; *poetic/literary* slaying.

homily noun SERMON, lecture, speech, address, discourse, lesson, talk, oration.

homosexual adjective GAY, lesbian, homoerotic; *informal* queer; *Brit. informal* bent, poofy.
– OPPOSITES heterosexual.

honest adjective ❶ **honest people:** PRINCIPLED, upright, honourable, ethical, moral, righteous, right-minded, virtuous, good, worthy, decent, law-abiding, high-minded, upstanding, just, fair, truthful, incorruptible, true, trustworthy, trusty, reliable, conscientious, scrupulous, reputable, dependable, loyal, faithful; *formal* veracious. ❷ **an honest reply:** TRUTHFUL, frank, candid, direct, forthright, straightforward, open, genuine, plain-speaking, matter-of-fact, outspoken, blunt, undisguised, unfeigned, unequivocal.
– OPPOSITES dishonest.

honestly adverb ❶ **earns his living honestly:** LAWFULLY, legally, legitimately, fairly, by fair means, honourably, decently, ethically, morally, without corruption; *informal* on the level, on the straight and narrow. ❷ **honestly, he's not here:** SPEAKING TRUTHFULLY, truthfully, to be honest, speaking frankly, in all sincerity, candidly, frankly, openly, plainly, in plain language, to someone's face, without dissembling; *informal* straight out, straight up, Scout's honour.

honorary adjective NOMINAL, titular, in name only, unofficial, ex officio, complimentary, unpaid.

honour noun ❶ **a man of honour:** HONESTY, uprightness, integrity, ethics, morals, high principles, righteousness, virtue, rectitude, goodness, decency, probity, worthiness, worth, fairness, justness, justice, truthfulness, trustworthiness, reliability, dependability, faithfulness, fidelity. ❷ **the honour of winning:** GLORY, prestige, renown, fame, illustriousness, notability, esteem, distinction, credit, kudos. ❸ **treat him with honour:** ACCLAIM,

acclamation, applause, accolades, tributes, homage, praise, compliments, eulogy, paeans, adoration, reverence, adulation.
– OPPOSITES dishonour.
▶ **verb** ❶ ESTEEM, respect, hold in esteem, have a high regard for, admire, defer to, revere, venerate, worship, adore, idolize. ❷ ACCLAIM, applaud, pay homage to, pay tribute to, lionize, cheer, praise, eulogize. ❸ **honour the agreement:** FULFIL, discharge, carry out, observe, keep, be true to, live up to.

honourable **adjective** HONEST, upright, ethical, moral, principled, upstanding, righteous, right-minded, virtuous, good, decent, worthy, fair, just, true, truthful, trustworthy, trusty, reliable, dependable, faithful.

hoodwink **verb** DECEIVE, dupe, outwit, fool, delude, get the better of, cheat, take in, hoax, mislead, defraud, swindle, gull; *informal* con, lead up the garden path, pull a fast one on, pull the wool over someone's eyes, take for a ride, make a sucker of.

hook **verb** ❶ FASTEN, secure, fix, close the clasp. ❷ SNARE, trap, ensnare, entrap, enmesh.

hooligan **noun** THUG, vandal, lout, rowdy, delinquent, ruffian, mugger, hoodlum; *Brit.* tearaway; *informal* tough; *Brit. informal* yob, yobbo.

hoop **noun** RING, band, circle, loop, wheel, girdle.

hop **verb** JUMP, leap, bound, spring, vault, bounce, skip, caper, dance, frisk.

hope **noun** EXPECTATION, hopefulness, expectancy, anticipation, desire, longing, wish, wishing, craving, yearning, aspiration, ambition, dream, belief, assurance, confidence, assumption, conviction, faith, trust, optimism.
– OPPOSITES despair, pessimism.
▶ **verb** BE HOPEFUL OF, expect, anticipate, look forward to, await, contemplate, desire, long, wish, crave, yearn, aspire, be ambitious, dream, believe, assume, have confidence, be convinced, rely on, count on, trust in.

hopeful **adjective** ❶ **hopeful candidates:** FULL OF HOPE, expectant, optimistic, confident, positive, assured, buoyant, sanguine. ❷ **hopeful news:** ENCOURAGING, promising, heartening, reassuring, gladdening, optimistic, favourable, auspicious, propitious, cheerful, bright, pleasant, rosy.
– OPPOSITES hopeless.

hopefully **adverb** ❶ **travelling hopefully:** WITH HOPE, full of hope, expectantly, optimistically, confidently, with assurance, buoyantly, sanguinely. ❷ **hopefully, he will win:** IT IS TO BE HOPED THAT, with luck, all being well, if all goes well, probably, conceivably, feasibly.

hopeless **adjective** ❶ WITHOUT HOPE, despairing, in despair, desperate, pessimistic, dejected, downhearted, despondent, demoralized, disconsolate, downcast, wretched, forlorn, suicidal, woebegone. ❷ **a hopeless task:** IMPOSSIBLE, impracticable, futile, useless, vain, pointless, worthless, unattainable, unachievable, no-win. ❸ **she's hopeless at maths:** POOR, incompetent,

inadequate, inferior, ineffective, ineffectual; *informal* no good, useless.
– OPPOSITES hopeful, accomplished.

horde noun CROWD, throng, mob, mass, group, multitude, host, army, pack, gang, troop, drove, crew, band, flock, swarm, gathering, assembly.

horrible adjective ❶ a horrible accident/sight: AWFUL, dreadful, terrible, horrid, horrifying, terrifying, frightful, fearful, horrendous, shocking, gruesome, hideous, grim, ghastly, harrowing, disgusting, revolting, repulsive, loathsome, abhorrent, detestable, hateful, abominable. ❷ a horrible child/picture: DISAGREEABLE, nasty, unpleasant, obnoxious, odious, awful, dreadful, ghastly, frightful, hideous, revolting, appalling.
– OPPOSITES pleasant.

horrify verb SHOCK, appal, outrage, scandalize, disgust, revolt, repel, nauseate, sicken, offend, dismay; *informal* turn off.

horror noun ❶ TERROR, fear, fearfulness, alarm, fright, dread, awe, panic, trepidation, apprehensiveness, uneasiness, nervousness, dismay, consternation. ❷ ABHORRENCE, abomination, loathing, hate, detestation, repulsion, revulsion, disgust, distaste, aversion, hostility, antipathy, animosity.

horse noun PONY, foal, colt, stallion, mare, steed, mount, hack, cob, nag, racehorse, filly, draught horse, carthorse, packhorse, hunter, bay, sorrel, pinto, piebald, grey, jade, palfrey; *Brit. informal* gee-gee.

horseman, horsewoman noun RIDER, equestrian, jockey, horse soldier, cavalryman, dragoon, cavalier, cowboy, cowgirl.

horseplay noun CLOWNING, fooling, tomfoolery, buffoonery, pranks, antics, capers, high jinks, rough and tumble, skylarking; *informal* shenanigans, monkey business.

hospitable adjective WELCOMING, generous, open-handed, sociable, friendly, bountiful, neighbourly, kind, warm, helpful.
– OPPOSITES inhospitable.

hospital noun CLINIC, infirmary, health centre, medical centre, sanatorium, nursing home, hospice, sick bay.

host noun ❶ PROPRIETOR, proprietress, landlord, landlady, innkeeper, hotel-keeper, hotelier. ❷ PRESENTER, compère, master of ceremonies, MC, anchorman, anchorwoman.

hostage noun CAPTIVE, prisoner, pawn, pledge, security.

hostile adjective ❶ hostile to the idea: OPPOSED, antagonistic, averse, ill-disposed, against, inimical; *informal* anti. ❷ a hostile crowd: AGGRESSIVE, angry, belligerent, bellicose, warlike, warring, militant, antagonistic, unfriendly, unkind, unsympathetic, malevolent, malicious, spiteful, wrathful. ❸ hostile weather conditions: ADVERSE, unfavourable, inauspicious, unpropitious, disadvantageous.
– OPPOSITES favourable, friendly.

hostility noun ❶ ANTAGONISM, opposition, ill will, aversion, animosity, enmity. ❷ AGGRESSION,

belligerence, anger, bellicosity, militancy, antagonism, unfriendliness, unkindness, malevolence, spite, malice, wrath.
– OPPOSITES friendship.

hot adjective ❶ HEATED, very warm, boiling, boiling hot, piping hot, scalding, red-hot, sizzling, steaming, scorching, roasting, searing, blazing hot, sweltering, blistering, baking, oven-like, torrid, sultry. ❷ *a hot curry*: SPICY, peppery, piquant, fiery, pungent, sharp, biting, acrid. ❸ *hot on the idea*: EAGER, enthusiastic, keen, fervent, ardent, zealous, vehement, passionate, animated, excited. ❹ *a hot temper/argument*: VIOLENT, furious, heated, fierce, ferocious, stormy, tempestuous, savage.
– OPPOSITES cold, mild.

hot-headed adjective HOT-TEMPERED, quick-tempered, short-tempered, fiery, excitable, volatile, hasty, rash, impetuous, impulsive, reckless, foolhardy, wild, unruly.

house noun ❶ RESIDENCE, home, habitation; *informal* pad; *Brit. informal* gaff; *formal* dwelling, abode, domicile. ❷ FAMILY, clan, line, dynasty, lineage, ancestry.
▶ verb ❶ ACCOMMODATE, lodge, put up, take in, have room for, sleep, shelter, harbour. ❷ COVER, sheathe, protect, shelter, guard, contain, keep.

household noun FAMILY, home, house, ménage, establishment.
▶ adjective DOMESTIC, family, ordinary, everyday, common, usual, run-of-the-mill.

hover verb ❶ FLOAT, fly, be suspended, hang, drift, be wafted, flutter. ❷ LINGER, loiter, hang about, wait, stay. ❸ VACILLATE, fluctuate, oscillate, alternate, see-saw; *Scottish* swither.

however adverb NEVERTHELESS, be that as it may, nonetheless, notwithstanding, anyway, anyhow, regardless, despite that, still, yet, just the same, though.

howl verb BAY, yowl, ululate, yelp, wail, bawl, scream, bellow, caterwaul, cry.

hub noun ❶ PIVOT, axis, nave. ❷ CENTRE, middle, core, heart, focus, focal point.

huddle verb ❶ CROWD, throng, press, pack, cluster, cram, herd, squeeze, gather, congregate. ❷ CURL UP, snuggle, cuddle, nestle, hunch up.
▶ noun GATHERING, crowd, cluster, pack, press.

hue noun ❶ COLOUR, tone, shade, tint, tinge, dye. ❷ COMPLEXION, cast, aspect, light.

hug verb ❶ EMBRACE, cuddle, take in one's arms, hold close, enfold in one's arms, clasp/press to one's bosom, squeeze, snuggle against. ❷ KEEP CLOSE TO, stay near, follow closely.

huge adjective ENORMOUS, immense, great, massive, colossal, vast, prodigious, gigantic, giant, gargantuan, mammoth, monumental, monstrous, elephantine, bulky, extensive, mountainous, titanic, Brobdingnagian, Herculean; *informal* jumbo.
– OPPOSITES tiny.

hulk noun ❶ WRECK, shipwreck, derelict, ruin, shell, skeleton, hull, frame. ❷ OAF, lout, lump, lubber.

hulking adjective ❶ CUMBERSOME, unwieldy, bulky, weighty, massive, ponderous. ❷ CLUMSY, awkward, ungainly, lumbering, loutish, lumpish, overgrown.

hull noun FRAMEWORK, body, frame, skeleton, structure, casing, covering.

hum verb ❶ MURMUR, drone, vibrate, thrum, buzz, whirr, purr. ❷ SING, croon, whisper, mumble.

human adjective ❶ MORTAL, physical, bodily, fleshly, carnal, corporal. ❷ KIND, kindly, considerate, understanding, sympathetic, compassionate, approachable, humane, accessible. ❸ **only human:** FLESH AND BLOOD, fallible, weak, frail, vulnerable, erring.

humane adjective KIND, kindly, kind-hearted, good, good-natured, compassionate, understanding, considerate, sympathetic, forgiving, merciful, lenient, forbearing, gentle, tender, mild, benign, clement, benevolent, charitable, generous, magnanimous, approachable, accessible.
– OPPOSITES cruel, inhumane.

humble adjective ❶ MODEST, unassuming, self-effacing, meek, unassertive, unpretentious, unostentatious, servile, docile, submissive, obsequious, subservient, deferential, over-respectful, slavish, sycophantic. ❷ COMMON, ordinary, simple, poor, low-born, of low birth, low-ranking, low, lowly, inferior, plebeian, proletarian, base, mean, unrefined, vulgar, unimportant, insignificant, inconsequential, undistinguished, ignoble.
– OPPOSITES arrogant, important.

▶ verb ❶ HUMILIATE, mortify, subdue, chasten, shame, put to shame, abash, degrade. ❷ DEFEAT, crush, trounce, rout, break, conquer, vanquish, overwhelm, bring someone to their knees.

humdrum adjective COMMONPLACE, routine, run-of-the-mill, unvaried, unvarying, ordinary, everyday, mundane, monotonous, repetitious, dull, uninteresting, boring, tedious, banal, tiresome, wearisome.
– OPPOSITES remarkable.

humiliate verb MORTIFY, shame, humble, put to shame, make ashamed, disgrace, embarrass, discomfit, chasten, subdue, deflate, abash, debase, abase, degrade, crush, make someone eat humble pie, demean; *informal* take someone down a peg or two, put down, show up; *N. Amer.* make someone eat crow.

humiliation noun MORTIFICATION, loss of pride, humbling, disgrace, loss of face, dishonour, indignity, discredit, embarrassment, discomfiture, affront, abasement, debasement, degradation, submission; *informal* put-down.

humility noun HUMBLENESS, lack of pride, modesty, meekness, self-effacement, unpretentiousness, unobtrusiveness, diffidence, servility, submissiveness, obsequiousness, subservience, deference, sycophancy.
– OPPOSITES arrogance, pride.

humorous adjective ❶ **a humorous story:** FUNNY, comic, comical, witty, jocular, amusing, hilarious, side-splitting, rib-tickling, farcical, facetious, ridiculous, ludicrous, absurd,

droll. ❷ **a humorous person:** FUNNY, amusing, entertaining, witty, facetious, jocular, waggish, whimsical.
– OPPOSITES serious, solemn.

humour noun ❶ FUNNINESS, comic side, funny side, comical aspect, comedy, farce, jocularity, hilarity, ludicrousness, absurdness, absurdity, drollness. ❷ COMEDY, jokes, joking, jests, jesting, wit, wittiness, witticisms, waggishness, pleasantries, buffoonery; *informal* gags, wisecracks. ❸ MOOD, temper, temperament, frame of mind, state of mind, disposition, spirits.

hump noun PROTRUSION, protuberance, projection, bulge, swelling, lump, bump, knob, hunch, mass, nodule, node, intumescence, tumefaction.
▶ verb ❶ HUNCH, arch, curve, curl up, crook. ❷ CARRY, lift, lug, heave, shoulder, hoist.

hunch noun ❶ FEELING, presentiment, premonition, intuition, sixth sense, suspicion, inkling, impression, idea. ❷ *See* HUMP noun.

hunger noun ❶ HUNGRINESS, lack of food, starvation, ravenousness, emptiness, famine, voracity, greediness. ❷ LONGING, craving, yearning, desire, want, need, thirst, appetite, hankering, lust; *informal* itch.

hungry adjective ❶ FAMISHED, famishing, ravenous, starving, starved, half-starved, empty, greedy, voracious; *dated* sharp-set. ❷ **hungry for knowledge:** LONGING, yearning, craving, in need/want of, eager, keen, desirous of, covetous of.
– OPPOSITES full.

hunt verb ❶ CHASE, give chase, pursue, stalk, track, trail, follow, shadow, hound, tail. ❷ **hunt for her keys:** SEARCH FOR, look for, seek, try to find, scour for, forage for, fish for, rummage for, scrabble for.

hurdle noun ❶ FENCE, barrier, railing, rail, wall, hedge, hedgerow, bar, barricade. ❷ OBSTACLE, barrier, hindrance, impediment, obstruction, stumbling block, snag, complication, difficulty, handicap.

hurl verb THROW, fling, pitch, cast, toss, heave, fire, launch, let fly, shy, propel, project, dart, catapult; *informal* sling, chuck.

hurried adjective ❶ QUICK, rapid, fast, swift, speedy, hasty, breakneck. ❷ HASTY, quick, swift, rushed, cursory, superficial, perfunctory, offhand, passing, fleeting, transitory.
– OPPOSITES slow.

hurry verb ❶ MOVE QUICKLY, hurry up, be quick, make haste, hasten, speed, lose no time, press on, push on, run, dash, rush; *informal* go hell for leather, get a move on, put one's foot down, step on it, get cracking, shake a leg, go like a bat out of hell, hightail it, hotfoot it. ❷ SPEED UP, quicken, hasten, accelerate, expedite, urge on, drive on, push on, goad, prod, hustle.
– OPPOSITES dawdle.

hurt verb ❶ **my foot hurts:** BE SORE, be painful, cause pain, ache, smart, sting, nip, throb, tingle, burn. ❷ **he's hurt his leg:** INJURE, wound, bruise, cut, scratch, lacerate, maim, damage, mutilate, disable, incapacitate, impair, debilitate. ❸ **his words hurt her:**

UPSET, sadden, grieve, wound, distress, pain, cut to the quick, sting, offend, give offence to, discompose. ❹ **hurt his reputation:** HARM, damage, spoil, blight, mar, blemish, impair.

hurtful adjective ❶ **hurtful remarks:** UPSETTING, wounding, injurious, distressing, unkind, nasty, mean, spiteful, malicious, cutting, cruel, mischievous, offensive. ❷ **hurtful to his reputation:** HARMFUL, damaging, injurious, detrimental, deleterious, destructive, prejudicial, ruinous, inimical.

husband noun SPOUSE, partner, consort, groom, bridegroom; *informal* hubby, old man; *Brit. informal* other half.

hush verb SILENCE, quieten, quieten down, shush, shut up. ▶ noun QUIET, quietness, silence, stillness, still, peace, calm, tranquillity.

hustle verb ❶ PUSH, shove, thrust, crowd, jostle, elbow, nudge, shoulder. ❷ *See* HURRY. ❸ COERCE, force, impel, pressure, badger, urge, goad, prod, spur, propel.

hut noun SHED, lean-to, shack, cabin, shanty, hovel; *Scottish* bothy.

hygiene noun CLEANLINESS, sanitation, public health, sanitary measures.

hygienic adjective SANITARY, clean, germ-free, disinfected, sterilized, sterile, aseptic, unpolluted, uncontaminated, healthy, pure.
– OPPOSITES dirty, unsanitary.

hypnotic adjective MESMERIC, mesmerizing, sleep-inducing, soporific, somniferous, numbing, sedative, stupefacient.

hypnotize verb ❶ PUT UNDER, put out, send into a trance, mesmerize, put to sleep. ❷ FASCINATE, bewitch, entrance, beguile, spellbind, magnetize.

hypocrisy noun INSINCERITY, falseness, sanctimoniousness, falsity, deceptiveness, deceit, deceitfulness, deception, dishonesty, duplicity, imposture, cant, two-facedness, double-dealing, pretence, Pharisaism, pietism.
– OPPOSITES sincerity.

hypocritical adjective FALSE, insincere, sanctimonious, fraudulent, deceitful, deceptive, dishonest, untruthful, lying, dissembling, duplicitous, two-faced, double-dealing, untrustworthy, perfidious, specious, spurious; *informal* phoney.

hypothesis noun THEORY, thesis, theorem, proposition, axiom, premise, postulate, supposition, assumption, presumption, conjecture, speculation.

hypothetical adjective ASSUMED, presumed, theoretical, putative, speculative, conjectured, imagined, notional, academic.

hysteria noun HYSTERICS, frenzy, loss of control, agitation, madness, delirium; *informal* the screaming habdabs.

hysterical adjective ❶ FRENZIED, in a frenzy, frantic, out of control, berserk, beside oneself, distracted, distraught, overwrought, agitated, in a panic, mad, crazed, delirious, raving. ❷ VERY FUNNY/AMUSING, hilarious, uproarious, side-splitting, comical, farcical, screamingly funny.
– OPPOSITES calm.

Ii

ice noun FROZEN WATER, frost, icicle, iceberg, glacier, rime.

icy adjective ❶ FREEZING, chill, chilly, frigid, frosty, biting, raw, bitter, arctic, glacial, Siberian, polar, gelid. ❷ FROZEN, ice-bound, frosty, rimy, glassy, slippery, slippy. ❸ **an icy welcome:** COLD, cool, frigid, frosty, stiff, aloof, distant, unfriendly, unresponsive, uncommunicative, reserved, reticent, restrained.

idea noun ❶ CONCEPT, thought, conception, conceptualization, image, abstraction, perception, notion. ❷ THOUGHT, theory, view, viewpoint, opinion, feeling, outlook, belief, judgement, conclusion. ❸ IMPRESSION, feeling, notion, suspicion, inkling. ❹ ESTIMATION, approximation, guess, surmise; *informal* guesstimate. ❺ PLAN, design, aim, scheme, intention, objective, object, purpose, end, goal, target.

ideal adjective ❶ PERFECT, consummate, supreme, absolute, complete, flawless, exemplary, classic, archetypal, model, quintessential. ❷ UNATTAINABLE, utopian, unreal, impracticable, imaginary, ivory-towered, romantic, visionary, fanciful.
► **noun** ❶ ARCHETYPE, prototype, model, pattern, exemplar, paradigm, example, criterion, yardstick. ❷ PRINCIPLE, standard, moral value, morals, ethics.

idealistic adjective IMPRACTICAL, utopian, perfectionist, visionary, romantic, quixotic, unrealistic; *informal* starry-eyed.
– OPPOSITES practical, realistic.

ideally adverb IN A PERFECT WORLD, all things being equal, theoretically, hypothetically, in theory.

identical adjective ❶ THE SAME, the very same, one and the same, selfsame. ❷ ALIKE, like, similar, much the same, indistinguishable, corresponding, matching, twin.
– OPPOSITES different.

identify verb ❶ RECOGNIZE, single out, pick out, spot, point out, pinpoint, discern, distinguish, name; *informal* put the finger on. ❷ **identify the problem:** ESTABLISH, find out, ascertain, diagnose, select, choose. ❸ **identify someone with:** ASSOCIATE, connect, think of in connection with. ❹ **identify with:** RELATE TO, empathize with, sympathize with, have a rapport with, respond to, feel for.

identity noun ❶ NAME, specification. ❷ PERSONALITY, self, selfhood, ego, individuality, distinctiveness, singularity, uniqueness. ❸ **mistaken identity:** IDENTIFICATION, recognition, naming. ❹ SAMENESS, interchangeability, likeness, similarity, closeness, accordance.

ideology noun DOCTRINE, creed, credo, teaching, dogma, theory, thesis, tenets, beliefs, opinions, principles, convictions, attitudes.

idiocy noun STUPIDITY, foolishness, absurdity, inanity, fatuity, fatuousness, asininity, lunacy, craziness, insanity, dumbness; *Brit. informal* daftness.
– OPPOSITES sense.

idiom noun ❶ PHRASE, expression, locution, turn of phrase, set phrase, fixed expression. ❷ LANGUAGE, style of speech, speech, talk, usage, parlance, vernacular, jargon, patois; *informal* lingo.

idiomatic adjective COLLOQUIAL, informal, vernacular, natural.

idiosyncrasy noun PECULIARITY, oddity, eccentricity, trait, singularity, mannerism, quirk, habit, characteristic, speciality, quality, feature.

idiot noun FOOL, dolt, dunce, ass, ignoramus, imbecile, simpleton; *informal* chump, booby, nincompoop, ninny, dunderhead, blockhead, fathead, halfwit, cretin, moron, dummy, numbskull, dimwit; *Brit. informal* twerp, clot, twit, nitwit.

idiotic adjective STUPID, foolish, senseless, absurd, fatuous, inane, asinine, unintelligent, half-witted, hare-brained, lunatic, crazy, insane, mad, moronic, dumb, irrational, nonsensical, ridiculous; *Brit. informal* daft.
– OPPOSITES sensible.

idle adjective ❶ an idle fellow: LAZY, indolent, slothful, sluggish, apathetic, torpid, slow, shiftless, loafing, dronish. ❷ machines lying idle: INOPERATIVE, not in operation, inactive, out of action, unused, mothballed. ❸ idle hours: EMPTY, unfilled, unoccupied, vacant. ❹ idle rumours: GROUNDLESS, baseless, worthless, futile, casual. ❺ idle remarks: TRIVIAL, unimportant, insignificant, trifling, superficial, shallow, foolish, inane, fatuous.
– OPPOSITES industrious, busy.
▶ verb ❶ idle away the time: WHILE, loaf, lounge, loiter, dawdle, fritter, dally, potter. ❷ stop idling! DO NOTHING, laze, loaf, be inactive, mark time, shirk, slack, vegetate, take it easy, rest on one's oars.

idol noun ❶ GOD, icon, effigy, image, graven image, fetish, likeness. ❷ HERO, heroine, favourite, darling, pet, beloved, star, superstar, apple of one's eye; *Brit. informal* blue-eyed boy/girl.

idolize verb ❶ WORSHIP, bow down before, glorify, exalt, revere, deify. ❷ HERO-WORSHIP, worship, adulate, adore, love, look up to, admire, dote on, lionize, revere, venerate.

if conjunction ❶ ON CONDITION THAT, provided, providing, supposing, assuming, allowing. ❷ WHETHER, whether or not. ❸ ALTHOUGH, even though.

ignite verb ❶ SET FIRE TO, light, set on fire, set alight, fire, kindle, inflame, touch off, put a match to. ❷ CATCH FIRE, catch, burst into flames, burn up, burn, flame up, kindle.
– OPPOSITES extinguish.

ignominious adjective ❶ an ignominious defeat: SHAMEFUL, dishonourable, disgraceful, humiliating, mortifying, discreditable, disreputable, undignified, infamous, ignoble, inglorious, scandalous, abject, sorry, base. ❷ ignominious behaviour: CONTEMPTIBLE, despicable, offensive, revolting, wicked, vile, base, low.
– OPPOSITES glorious.

ignorance noun UNFAMILIARITY, unconsciousness, lack of knowledge, inexperience, greenness, innocence; *poetic/literary* nescience.
– OPPOSITES knowledge.

ignorant adjective ❶ **ignorant of the law:** UNAWARE OF, unfamiliar with, unconscious of, unacquainted with, uninformed about, unconversant with, unenlightened about, inexperienced in, blind to, unschooled in, naive about, innocent about; *informal* in the dark about. ❷ **ignorant children:** UNEDUCATED, unschooled, illiterate, unlettered, uninformed, unknowledgeable, unintelligent, stupid, benighted. ❸ **ignorant louts:** RUDE, crude, coarse, vulgar, gross, oafish, insensitive.
– OPPOSITES knowledgeable.

ignore verb ❶ **ignore that remark:** DISREGARD, pay no attention to, take no notice of, brush aside, pass over, shrug off, shut one's eyes to, be oblivious to, turn a blind eye to, turn a deaf ear to. ❷ **ignore her friend:** SLIGHT, spurn, cold-shoulder, look right through, look past, turn one's back on, send to Coventry, cut, cut dead.
– OPPOSITES acknowledge.

ill adjective ❶ SICK, unwell, not well, poorly, ailing, sickly, infirm, feeling bad, afflicted, indisposed, out of sorts, diseased, bedridden, invalided, weak, feeble; *Brit.* off colour; *informal* under the weather, laid up, queasy, funny, seedy; *Brit. informal, dated* queer. ❷ **ill feeling:** HOSTILE, unfriendly, antagonistic, acrimonious, belligerent, bellicose, unkind, spiteful, rancorous, malicious, resentful, malevolent, bitter. ❸ **ill repute:** BAD, infamous, notorious, wicked, nefarious, vile, evil, foul, sinful, corrupt, depraved, degenerate.
– OPPOSITES healthy.
▶ **adverb speak ill of them:** BADLY, unfavourably, with disfavour, with disapproval, with hostility, unkindly, maliciously, spitefully.
■ **ill at ease** UNCOMFORTABLE, uneasy, awkward, embarrassed, self-conscious, out of place, strange, unsure, uncertain, unsettled, hesitant, restless, disturbed, troubled, anxious, on edge, edgy, nervous, tense, on tenterhooks, apprehensive.

ill-advised adjective UNWISE, ill-considered, imprudent, incautious, injudicious, ill-judged, impolitic, misguided, foolish, foolhardy, rash, hasty, overhasty, short-sighted, thoughtless, careless, reckless.

illegal adjective UNLAWFUL, illegitimate, illicit, lawless, criminal, felonious, actionable, unlicensed, unauthorized, unsanctioned, unwarranted, unofficial, outlawed, banned, forbidden, barred, prohibited, proscribed, contraband, black-market, under the counter, bootleg.
– OPPOSITES legal.

illegible adjective INDECIPHERABLE, unreadable, unintelligible, scrawled, scribbled, unclear, obscure, squiggly.
– OPPOSITES legible.

illegitimate adjective ❶ ILLEGAL, illicit, unlawful, lawless, criminal, unauthorized, unsanctioned, irregular, invalid. ❷ **an illegitimate child:** BORN OUT OF WEDLOCK; *dated* love, born on the wrong side of the blanket; *archaic* bastard, natural. ❸ **an illegitimate**

deduction: UNSOUND, illogical, invalid, incorrect, spurious.
– OPPOSITES legitimate.

ill-fated adjective UNLUCKY, luckless, unfortunate, hapless, unhappy, doomed, blighted, ill-starred, ill-omened.

ill-judged adjective *see* ILL-ADVISED.

illness noun SICKNESS, ailment, disease, complaint, malady, disorder, affliction, disability, attack, indisposition, infection, contagion, ill health, poor health.

illogical adjective UNSOUND, fallacious, unproved, invalid, specious, unreasonable, unreasoned, fallible, untenable, unscientific, casuistic, sophistic, inconsistent, incorrect, wrong, absurd, preposterous, meaningless, senseless.
– OPPOSITES logical.

ill-treat verb TREAT BADLY, abuse, harm, injure, damage, handle roughly, mishandle, ill-use, maltreat, misuse; *informal* knock about.

illuminating adjective INSTRUCTIVE, informative, enlightening, explanatory, revealing, helpful.

illusion noun ❶ DELUSION, misapprehension, misconception, deception, false/mistaken impression, fallacy, error, misjudgement, fancy. ❷ HALLUCINATION, figment of the imagination, spectre, phantom, mirage, fantasy, will-o'-the-wisp; *poetic/literary* phantasm.

illusory adjective FALSE, mistaken, deceptive, delusory, delusional, delusive, fallacious, erroneous, misleading, untrue, specious, unreal, imagined, imaginary, fancied, non-existent, fanciful, notional, chimerical, dreamlike.
– OPPOSITES genuine.

illustrate verb ❶ ADD PICTURES TO, adorn, decorate, ornament, embellish. ❷ **illustrate the point**: DEMONSTRATE, exemplify, show, point up, instance, make plain/clear, clarify, bring home, emphasize, interpret.

illustration noun ❶ PICTURE, drawing, sketch, figure, plate, artwork. ❷ EXAMPLE, demonstration, typical case, case in point, instance, specimen, sample, exemplar, analogy.

image noun ❶ LIKENESS, representation, painting, picture, portrait, effigy, figure, statue, sculpture, bust. ❷ **he's the image of his father**: DOUBLE, twin, replica, clone, copy, reproduction, counterpart, doppelganger; *informal* spit, spitting image, ringer, dead ringer. ❸ FIGURE OF SPEECH, conceit, trope, expression.

imaginary adjective UNREAL, non-existent, illusory, fanciful, unsubstantial, chimerical, notional, assumed, supposed, suppositious, fictitious, fictional, mythical, mythological, made up, invented, hallucinatory, ghostly, spectral, dreamlike, visionary, shadowy; *poetic/literary* phantasmic.
– OPPOSITES real, actual.

imagination noun ❶ CREATIVITY, vision, inspiration, inventiveness, originality, innovation, ingenuity, insight, fancifulness. ❷ **just my imagination**: ILLUSION, figment of the imagination, fancy, vision, dream, unreality.

imaginative adjective CREATIVE, inventive, original, innovative, visionary, inspired, fanciful, resourceful, ingenious,

enterprising, clever, whimsical.
– OPPOSITES unimaginative.

imagine verb ❶ PICTURE, visualize, see in the mind's eye, envision, envisage, conjure up, dream about, dream up, think up, conceive, fantasize about, conceptualize, plan, scheme, project. ❷ I imagine he'll come: ASSUME, presume, expect, suppose, think, believe, be of the opinion that, take it, gather, fancy, judge, deem, infer, deduce, conjecture, surmise, guess, reckon, suspect, realize.

imbue verb FILL, impregnate, inject, inculcate, instil, ingrain, inspire, permeate, charge.

imitate verb ❶ COPY, emulate, simulate, mirror, follow someone's example, take after, follow, follow suit, take a page from someone's book, follow in someone's footsteps, echo. ❷ MIMIC, ape, impersonate, do an impression of, parody, mock, caricature, burlesque, travesty; *informal* send up, take off, spoof, do.

imitation noun ❶ COPY, reproduction, forgery, fake, counterfeit, resemblance, emulation, duplication, likeness, replica, simulation. ❷ MIMICKING, mimicry, aping, impersonation, impression, parody, mockery, caricature, burlesque, travesty; *informal* send-up, take-off, spoof.
▶ adjective ARTIFICIAL, simulated, synthetic, man-made, mock, sham, fake, reproduction, pseudo, ersatz; *informal* phoney.

immature adjective ❶ UNRIPE, undeveloped, unformed, imperfect, unfinished, incomplete, half-grown, crude, raw, green, unfledged, untimely. ❷ CHILDISH, juvenile, adolescent, infantile, babyish, puerile, callow, jejune, inexperienced, green; *informal* wet behind the ears.
– OPPOSITES mature.

immediate adjective ❶ INSTANT, instantaneous, prompt, swift, speedy, sudden, abrupt. ❷ his immediate neighbour: NEAR, nearest, next, next-door, close, closest, adjacent, adjoining, abutting, contiguous, proximate. ❸ his immediate plans: CURRENT, present, existing, actual, existent, extant, urgent, pressing.
– OPPOSITES delayed, distant.

immediately adverb RIGHT AWAY, right now, straight away, at once, instantly, now, this minute, directly, promptly, without delay; *informal* before you can say Jack Robinson, pronto.

immense adjective HUGE, vast, massive, enormous, gigantic, colossal, giant, great, extensive, infinite, immeasurable, illimitable, monumental, tremendous, prodigious, elephantine, monstrous, titanic, Brobdingnagian; *informal* mega; *Brit. informal* ginormous.
– OPPOSITES tiny, minute.

immerse verb ❶ SUBMERGE, plunge, dip, dunk, duck, sink, souse, soak, drench, imbue, saturate. ❷ immerse oneself in work: ABSORB, engross, occupy, engage, preoccupy, involve, engulf, lose oneself in.

immigrant noun SETTLER, alien, incomer, non-native, new arrival, migrant, naturalized citizen, expatriate.

imminent adjective IMPENDING, approaching, close, fast-approaching, at hand, near, coming, forthcoming, on the way,

about to happen, upon us, in the offing, on the horizon, in the air, brewing, threatening, menacing, looming.
-OPPOSITES distant.

immobile adjective UNMOVING, motionless, immovable, still, static, at rest, stationary, at a standstill, stock-still, dormant, rooted, fixed to the spot, rigid, frozen, stiff, riveted, like a statuej; *technical* immotile, immotive.

immobilize verb STOP, halt, bring to a standstill, paralyse, put out of action, inactivate, disable, cripple, freeze, transfix.

immodest adjective BOLD, brazen, forward, impudent, unblushing, shameless, wanton, improper, indecent, cheeky.

immoral adjective BAD, wicked, evil, unprincipled, dishonest, unethical, sinful, impure, corrupt, iniquitous, depraved, vile, base, degenerate, debauched, abandoned, dissolute, villainous, nefarious, reprobate, indecent, lewd, licentious, pornographic, unchaste, bawdy, of easy virtue.
-OPPOSITES ethical, chaste.

immortal adjective ❶ UNDYING, eternal, deathless, everlasting, never-ending, endless, imperishable, timeless, indestructible, unfading, perennial, evergreen, perpetual, lasting, enduring, constant, abiding, immutable, indissoluble; *poetic/literary* sempiternal, perdurable. ❷ FAMOUS, celebrated, renowned.
-OPPOSITES mortal.

immortalize verb COMMEMORATE, memorialize, eternalize, eternize, perpetuate, exalt, glorify; *formal* laud.

immovable adjective ❶ FIXED, set fast/firm, fast, firm, secure, stable, rooted, riveted, moored, anchored, stuck, jammed, stiff, unbudgeable. ❷ MOTIONLESS, unmoving, stationary, still, stock-still, at a standstill, dead still, statue-like. ❸ FIRM, adamant, steadfast, unwavering, unswerving, resolute, determined, tenacious, stubborn, dogged, obdurate, inflexible, unyielding, unbending, uncompromising, unshakeable, inexorable.

immune adjective NOT SUBJECT TO, not liable to, protected from, safe from, unsusceptible to, secure against, exempt from, clear of, free from, absolved from, released from, excused from, relieved of, spared from, exempted from, unaffected by, resistant to, proof against.
-OPPOSITES liable, susceptible.

immunize verb INOCULATE, vaccinate, protect, shield, safeguard.

impact noun ❶ COLLISION, crash, contact, smash, striking, clash, bump, knock, bang, jolt, thump, whack, thwack, slam, smack, slap. ❷ INFLUENCE, effect, impression, results, consequences, repercussions.

impair verb WEAKEN, lessen, decrease, reduce, blunt, diminish, enfeeble, debilitate, enervate, damage, mar, spoil, injure, harm, hinder, disable, cripple, impede, undermine; *formal* vitiate.
-OPPOSITES improve, enhance.

impart verb PASS ON, convey, communicate, transmit, relate, tell, make known, report, disclose, reveal, divulge, proclaim, broadcast.

impartial adjective UNBIASED, unprejudiced, disinterested, objective, detached, neutral, equitable, even-handed, fair, fair-minded, open-minded, non-partisan, without fear or favour, with no axe to grind.
– OPPOSITES biased, partisan.

impartiality noun DETACHMENT, disinterest, objectivity, neutrality, even-handedness, fairness, justness, open-mindedness.

impassable adjective ❶ CLOSE, blocked, obstructed, unnavigable, untraversable, impenetrable. ❷ INSURMOUNTABLE, insuperable, unconquerable.

impatient adjective ❶ **impatient to see him**: EAGER, keen, anxious, avid, desirous, yearning, longing. ❷ **an impatient crowd**: RESTLESS, restive, excitable, agitated, nervous, edgy, impetuous. ❸ **an impatient answer**: ABRUPT, brusque, terse, short, irritated, angry, testy, short-tempered, quick-tempered, curt, querulous, peevish, intolerant; *informal* snappy.
– OPPOSITES patient.

impede verb HINDER, obstruct, hamper, handicap, block, check, curb, bar, hold back, hold up, delay, interfere with, disrupt, retard, slow, slow down, brake, restrain, thwart, frustrate, baulk, stop; *Brit.* throw a spanner in the works.
– OPPOSITES facilitate.

impediment noun HINDRANCE, obstruction, obstacle, handicap, block, stumbling block, check, encumbrance, bar, barrier, curb, brake, restraint, drawback, difficulty, snag, setback.

impel verb URGE, press, exhort, force, oblige, constrain, necessitate, require, demand, make, apply pressure, pressure, pressurize, spur, goad, incite, prompt, chivvy, persuade, inspire.

impending adjective *see* IMMINENT.

impenetrable adjective ❶ IMPERVIOUS, impermeable, solid, dense, thick, hard, closed, sealed, resistant, waterproof, tight, unpierceable. ❷ **impenetrable forests**: IMPASSABLE, inaccessible, thick, dense, overgrown. ❸ **impenetrable jargon**: INCOMPREHENSIBLE, baffling, puzzling, abstruse, obscure, inexplicable, unfathomable, recondite, inscrutable, enigmatic.

imperceptible adjective UNNOTICEABLE, unobtrusive, unapparent, slight, small, gradual, subtle, faint, fine, inconsequential, tiny, minute, minuscule, microscopic, infinitesimal, undetectable, indistinguishable, indiscernible, invisible, indistinct, unclear, obscure, vague, indefinite, shadowy, inaudible, muffled, impalpable.
– OPPOSITES obvious.

imperceptibly adverb UNNOTICEABLY, unobtrusively, unseen, gradually, slowly, subtly, undetectable, little by little, bit by bit.

imperfect adjective ❶ **imperfect goods**: FAULTY, flawed, defective, blemished, damaged, broken, impaired. ❷ **imperfect knowledge**: DEFICIENT, inadequate, insufficient, rudimentary, limited, patchy, sketchy.
– OPPOSITES flawless.

imperfection noun ❶ FAULT, flaw, defect, blemish, deformity, crack, break, scratch, cut, tear, stain, spot. ❷ FAILING, foible, deficiency, weakness, weak point, shortcoming, fallibility, frailty, infirmity, peccadillo.

imperious adjective OVERBEARING, overweening, domineering, peremptory, high-handed, assertive, commanding, authoritative, lordly, masterful, dictatorial, tyrannical.
– OPPOSITES humble.

impersonal adjective ❶ an impersonal assessment: OBJECTIVE, detached, disinterested, dispassionate, neutral, unbiased, unprejudiced, fair, equitable, even-handed. ❷ an impersonal manner: COLD, cool, aloof, frigid, stiff, rigid, wooden, starchy, stilted, stuffy, businesslike, bureaucratic, matter-of-fact.
– OPPOSITES biased.

impersonate verb IMITATE, mimic, personate, ape, mock, parody, caricature, masquerade as, burlesque, pose as, pass oneself off as; *informal* take off, do.

impertinent adjective INSOLENT, impudent, cheeky, rude, impolite, unmannerly, ill-mannered, uncivil, coarse, uncouth, crude, discourteous, disrespectful, bold, brazen, audacious, presumptuous, forward, pert, brash, shameless; *informal* saucy, brass-necked, fresh, flip.
– OPPOSITES polite.

imperturbable adjective SELF-POSSESSED, composed, collected, calm, cool, tranquil, serene, unexcitable, unflappable, even-tempered, easy-going, at ease, unruffled, untroubled, undismayed, unmoved, nonchalant.
– OPPOSITES nervous, excitable.

impetuous adjective ❶ an impetuous person: IMPULSIVE, hasty, impatient, excitable, headstrong, rash, reckless, foolhardy, wild, uncontrolled, eager, enthusiastic, spontaneous, passionate, ardent, zealous. ❷ an impetuous act: HASTY, precipitate, impulsive, spontaneous, impromptu, spur-of-the-moment, unthinking, unplanned, ill-conceived, ill-considered, unreasoned, heedless, reckless, rash.
– OPPOSITES cautious.

impetus noun ❶ MOMENTUM, energy, force, power, propulsion, motion. ❷ STIMULUS, motivation, incentive, inducement, inspiration, encouragement, influence, push, urging, pressing, spur, goading, goad, instigation, actuation.

impinge
■ **impinge on** ❶ ENCROACH ON, infringe, intrude on, invade, trespass on, violate, usurp, make inroads on, obtrude on. ❷ AFFECT, have an effect on, have a bearing on, impress, touch, exert influence on, bear upon.

impious adjective UNHOLY, godless, ungodly, irreligious, sinful, sacrilegious, unrighteous, profane, blasphemous, irreverent, disrespectful, atheistic, agnostic, pagan, heathen.
– OPPOSITES pious.

implausible adjective UNLIKELY, improbable, hard to believe, incredible, unbelievable, unimaginable, inconceivable, debatable, questionable, doubtful.
– OPPOSITES plausible.

implement noun TOOL, utensil, appliance, instrument, gadget,

device, apparatus, contrivance; *informal* gismo.
▶ verb CARRY OUT, fulfil, execute, perform, discharge, accomplish, achieve, realize, put into effect, bring about, effect, enforce.

implicate verb INCRIMINATE, involve, compromise, accuse, charge, blame, entangle, impeach, inculpate.
– OPPOSITES absolve.

implication noun
❶ INCRIMINATION, involvement, connection, entanglement, embroilment, association.
❷ SUGGESTION, inference, insinuation, innuendo, hint, allusion, reference, assumption, presumption.

implicit adjective ❶ implicit criticism: IMPLIED, indirect, inferred, unspoken, undeclared, unexpressed, unstated, tacit, understood, suggested. ❷ implicit trust: ABSOLUTE, complete, total, wholehearted, utter, unqualified, unconditional, unreserved, unquestioning, firm, steadfast.
– OPPOSITES explicit.

implore verb BEG, appeal to, entreat, plead with, ask, pray, request, solicit, supplicate, importune, press, crave, plead for, appeal for; *poetic/literary* beseech.

imply verb INSINUATE, hint, suggest, intimate, give to understand, signal, indicate.

impolite adjective *see* RUDE (1).

important adjective
❶ SIGNIFICANT, crucial, of great consequence/import, far-reaching, critical, pivotal, momentous, substantial, weighty, valuable, serious, grave, urgent, of great moment, consequential, salient, chief, main, principal, major, of concern, of interest, relevant, of value, necessary, essential. ❷ important people: EMINENT, prominent, pre-eminent, leading, foremost, outstanding, distinguished, esteemed, notable, noteworthy, of note, influential, of influence, powerful, high-ranking, high-level, top-level, prestigious.
– OPPOSITES unimportant.

importunate adjective
PERSISTENT, insistent, dogged, unremitting, relentless, pertinacious, pressing, urgent, demanding, exacting, clamorous, entreating, solicitous, imprecatory.

importune verb BEG, implore, plead with, appeal to, call upon, supplicate, petition, press; *poetic/literary* beseech.

impose verb ❶ impose a tax: ENFORCE, apply, exact, levy, charge, lay on, set, establish, fix, ordain, introduce, promulgate, decree. ❷ impose her views: FORCE, inflict, foist, thrust, obtrude.

imposing adjective IMPRESSIVE, striking, grand, splendid, majestic, august, lofty, stately.

impossible adjective ❶ NOT POSSIBLE, out of the question, inconceivable, unthinkable, unimaginable, impracticable, unattainable, unachievable, unobtainable, beyond one, hopeless. ❷ an impossible story: UNBELIEVABLE, incredible, absurd, ludicrous, ridiculous, preposterous, outlandish. ❸ an impossible child: UNMANAGEABLE, intractable, recalcitrant, wayward, intolerable, unbearable.
– OPPOSITES possible, plausible.

impostor noun DECEIVER, pretender, fake, fraud, sham, charlatan, mountebank, hoodwinker, bluffer, trickster, cheat, cheater, swindler, confidence man/woman, rogue; *informal* con man/woman, con artist.

impracticable adjective IMPOSSIBLE, out of the question, unfeasible, unworkable, unattainable, unrealizable, unsuitable.
– OPPOSITES feasible, possible.

impractical adjective ❶ USELESS, ineffective, ineffectual, unrealistic, impossible, unviable. ❷ UNREALISTIC, idealistic, romantic, quixotic, starry-eyed.
– OPPOSITES practical.

imprecise adjective ❶ INEXACT, approximate, estimated, rough, inaccurate, incorrect. ❷ VAGUE, loose, hazy, blurred, indefinite, woolly, confused, ambiguous, equivocal.
– OPPOSITES precise.

impregnate verb ❶ SUFFUSE, permeate, imbue, penetrate, fill, infuse, pervade, soak, steep, saturate, drench, inundate. ❷ MAKE PREGNANT, inseminate, fertilize; *informal* put in the family way.

impress verb ❶ MAKE AN IMPRESSION/IMPACT ON, move, sway, influence, affect, stir, rouse, excite, inspire, galvanize. ❷ STAMP, imprint, print, mark, engrave, emboss.

impression noun ❶ EFFECT, influence, impact, sway, hold, power, control. ❷ MARK, indentation, dent, hollow, outline, stamp, imprint. ❸ FEELING, sense, sensation, awareness, perception, notion, idea, thought, belief, opinion, conviction, suspicion, inkling, intuition, hunch, funny feeling. ❹ IMPERSONATION, imitation, mimicry, parody, caricature, take-off, send-up, burlesque, travesty. ❺ PRINT RUN, printing, issue, edition.

impressionable adjective SUGGESTIBLE, susceptible, persuadable, receptive, responsive, sensitive, open, gullible, ingenuous, pliable, malleable, mouldable.

impressive adjective IMPOSING, striking, magnificent, splendid, moving, touching, affecting, stirring, rousing, exciting, powerful, inspiring.
– OPPOSITES ordinary, unexciting.

imprison verb PUT IN PRISON, send to prison, jail, lock up, take into custody, put under lock and key, put away, incarcerate, confine, shut in/up, intern, detain, constrain, immure; *informal* send down.

imprisonment noun CUSTODY, incarceration, internment, confinement, detention, restraint; *Brit. informal* porridge.

improbable adjective UNLIKELY, doubtful, questionable, dubious, implausible, far-fetched, unconvincing, unbelievable, incredible, ridiculous, ludicrous, preposterous.
– OPPOSITES probable.

impromptu adjective UNREHEARSED, ad lib, unprepared, extempore, extemporized, extemporaneous, spontaneous, improvised, unscripted,

unpremeditated, unstudied; *informal* off-the-cuff, off the top of one's head, on the spur of the moment.
– OPPOSITES rehearsed.

improper adjective ❶ improper behaviour: UNSEEMLY, unbecoming, indecorous, unfitting, indiscreet, injudicious. ❷ an improper remark: INDECENT, off colour, indelicate, risqué, suggestive, smutty, obscene, lewd, pornographic; *informal* blue. ❸ an improper inference: INCORRECT, inaccurate, wrong, erroneous, false, fallacious.
– OPPOSITES proper.

improve verb ❶ MAKE BETTER, better, ameliorate, mend, amend, reform, rehabilitate, set/put right, correct, rectify, help, advance, upgrade, revamp, modernize; *informal* give something a facelift. ❷ GET/GROW BETTER, advance, come along, make headway, develop, progress, make progress, pick up, perk up, take a turn for the better, take on a new lease of life, rally, look up. ❸ GET BETTER, recuperate, be on the mend, turn the corner, recover, gain strength, convalesce. ❹ improve on the offer: INCREASE, make larger, raise, put up; *informal* jack up.
– OPPOSITES worsen.

improvement noun BETTERMENT, amelioration, advance, reform, reformation, rehabilitation, rectification, upgrade, upgrading, progress, growth, revamp, change for the better, development, rally, recovery, upswing, comeback.

improvident adjective UNTHRIFTY, thriftless, spendthrift, wasteful, prodigal, extravagant, uneconomical, shiftless.
– OPPOSITES thrifty.

improvise verb ❶ EXTEMPORIZE, ad lib; *informal* speak off the cuff, play it by ear, make it up as you go along. ❷ THROW/PUT TOGETHER, contrive, devise, concoct, rig, jury-rig.

impudent adjective IMPERTINENT, insolent, cheeky, bold, audacious, brazen, cocky, pert, presumptuous, forward, bumptious, impolite, rude, disrespectful, ill-mannered, unmannerly, ill-bred, shameless, immodest; *informal* saucy, brass-necked.

impugn verb CHALLENGE, call into question, question, dispute, query, cast aspersions on, look askance at, attack, berate, assail, criticize, denounce, censure.

impulse noun ❶ DRIVE, urge, instinct, appetite, proclivity. ❷ STIMULUS, inspiration, stimulation, incitement, incentive, inducement, motivation.

impulsive adjective ❶ an impulsive act: HASTY, sudden, quick, precipitate, impetuous, impromptu, spontaneous, snap, ill-considered, unplanned, unpremeditated, thoughtless, rash, reckless. ❷ an impulsive person: IMPETUOUS, rash, reckless, spontaneous, instinctive, passionate, intuitive, emotional, foolhardy, madcap, devil-may-care.
– OPPOSITES deliberate, cautious.

impure adjective ❶ ADULTERATED, debased, contaminated, polluted, tainted, infected, dirty, foul, unclean, filthy, sullied, defiled, unwholesome, poisoned, feculent. ❷ LEWD, lustful, obscene,

indecent, lecherous, ribald, smutty, pornographic, improper, crude, vulgar, coarse, gross.
– OPPOSITES pure.

inaccessible adjective UNREACHABLE, out of reach, cut off, beyond reach, unapproachable, impenetrable, unattainable, out of the way, isolated, lonely, remote, godforsaken, off the beaten track.
– OPPOSITES accessible.

inaccurate adjective ❶ INCORRECT, wrong, erroneous, faulty, inexact, imprecise, out. ❷ WRONG, false, not true, erroneous, fallacious, not right, imperfect, flawed, defective, unsound, unreliable, wide of the mark; *informal* full of holes.
– OPPOSITES accurate.

inactive adjective ❶ IMMOBILE, motionless, inert, stationary, idle, sluggish, slow, indolent, lazy, lifeless, slothful, lethargic, stagnant, vegetating, dilatory, torpid. ❷ inactive machines: INOPERATIVE, idle, out of service, unused, out of use, unoccupied, mothballed, unemployed. ❸ an inactive volcano: DORMANT, quiescent, latent, passive.

inadequate adjective ❶ INSUFFICIENT, not enough, too little, too few, lacking, found wanting, deficient, short, in short supply, meagre, scanty, scant, niggardly, scarce, sparse, skimpy, sketchy, incomplete. ❷ INCAPABLE, incompetent, unfit, ineffective, ineffectual, inefficient, unskilful, inexpert, inept; *informal* not up to scratch.
– OPPOSITES adequate.

inadvertent adjective ACCIDENTAL, unintentional, chance, unpremeditated, unplanned, unconscious, uncalculated, unwitting, involuntary.
– OPPOSITES deliberate.

inadvisable adjective UNWISE, ill-advised, ill-judged, misguided, injudicious, imprudent, foolish, impolitic, inexpedient.
– OPPOSITES shrewd.

inanimate adjective ❶ LIFELESS, without life, dead, inert, insentient, insensate, extinct, defunct. ❷ APATHETIC, spiritless, lazy, inactive, listless, lethargic, sluggish, torpid.
– OPPOSITES living.

inappropriate adjective UNSUITABLE, unfitting, out of place, unseemly, unbecoming, improper, indecorous, inapposite, incongruous, out of keeping, inexpedient, inadvisable, injudicious, infelicitous, untimely.
– OPPOSITES appropriate.

inarticulate adjective ❶ inarticulate sounds: UNINTELLIGIBLE, incomprehensible, incoherent, unclear, indistinct, blurred, muffled, mumbled, muttered. ❷ an inarticulate person: POORLY SPOKEN, faltering, hesitating, halting, stumbling, stuttering, stammering. ❸ inarticulate emotion: UNSPOKEN, unuttered, unexpressed, unvoiced, wordless, silent, mute, dumb, speechless, voiceless, soundless, taciturn, tongue-tied.
– OPPOSITES articulate.

inattentive adjective ❶ NEGLECTFUL, negligent, remiss, forgetful, careless, thoughtless, heedless, indifferent, unconcerned, inconsiderate. ❷ DISTRACTED, preoccupied, absent-minded, daydreaming,

wool-gathering, lost in thought; *informal* in a world of one's own, miles away, with one's head in the clouds, in a brown study.
– OPPOSITES attentive.

inauspicious adjective UNPROPITIOUS, unpromising, unlucky, unfortunate, unhappy, infelicitous, unfavourable, ill-omened, ominous, ill-fated, ill-starred, untoward, untimely.
– OPPOSITES auspicious.

incapable adjective ❶ INCOMPETENT, ineffective, ineffectual, inadequate, inefficacious, unfit, unfitted, unqualified, inept, inapt, useless, feeble; *informal* not up to scratch. ❷ UNABLE TO, not capable of, lacking the ability to.
– OPPOSITES capable.

inception noun BEGINNING, commencement, start, starting point, outset, opening, debut, inauguration, initiation, institution, birth, dawn, origin, rise; *informal* kick-off.
– OPPOSITES end.

incessant adjective UNCEASING, ceaseless, non-stop, endless, unending, never-ending, everlasting, eternal, constant, continual, perpetual, continuous, uninterrupted, unbroken, on-going, unremitting, persistent, recurrent.
– OPPOSITES intermittent.

incident noun ❶ EVENT, happening, occurrence, episode, experience, proceeding, adventure, occasion, circumstance, fact, matter. ❷ DISTURBANCE, commotion, scene, row, fracas, contretemps, skirmish, clash, conflict, confrontation, brush.

incidental adjective ❶ ACCIDENTAL, by chance, chance, random, fortuitous. ❷ RELATED, connected, associated, accompanying, attendant, concomitant, contingent. ❸ SECONDARY, subsidiary, subordinate.

incise verb CUT, cut into, make an incision in, slit, slit open, gash, slash, notch, nick, furrow.

incite verb ❶ **incite a rebellion:** INSTIGATE, provoke, foment, whip up, stir up, prompt. ❷ **incite someone:** ENCOURAGE, urge, egg on, goad, spur on, prod, stimulate, drive on, excite, arouse, agitate, inflame, stir up, provoke.
– OPPOSITES discourage.

inclination noun ❶ TENDENCY, leaning, propensity, proclivity, predisposition, weakness, penchant, predilection, partiality, preference, affinity, attraction, fancy, liking, fondness, affection, love. ❷ **an inclination of the head:** BEND, bow, nod, lowing, stooping.

incline verb ❶ TEND, lean, swing, veer, have a preference for, be attracted to, have an affinity for. ❷ BEND, slope, slant, bank, cant, bevel, tilt, lean, tip, list, deviate.
▶ **noun** SLOPE, gradient, hill, drop, declivity, descent, ascent, ramp, rise.
■ **be inclined to** HAVE A TENDENCY TO, be liable to, be likely to, be predisposed to.

include verb ❶ CONTAIN, hold, take in, admit, incorporate, embrace, encompass, comprise, embody, comprehend, subsume. ❷ ADD, insert, allow for, put in, enter, introduce, count in, take account of, build in, number, incorporate.
– OPPOSITES exclude.

incoherent adjective UNCONNECTED, disconnected, disjointed, disordered, confused, mixed up, muddled, jumbled, scrambled, rambling, wandering, discursive, illogical, unintelligible, inarticulate, mumbled, muttered, stuttered, stammered.
– OPPOSITES coherent.

incombustible adjective NON-COMBUSTIBLE, uninflammable, non-flammable, flameproof, fireproof, flame-retardant, flame-resistant.
– OPPOSITES flammable, inflammable.

income noun SALARY, pay, earnings, wages, remuneration, takings, profits, revenue, gains, proceeds, means.

incomparable adjective BEYOND COMPARE, inimitable, unequalled, matchless, nonpareil, unrivalled, peerless, unparalleled, unsurpassed, superlative, supreme, transcendent.

incompatible adjective ❶ UNSUITED, mismatched, ill-assorted, incongruous, antagonistic, conflicting, antipathetic, discordant; *Brit.* like chalk and cheese. ❷ CLASHING, discordant, jarring, inharmonious. ❸ incompatible with his behaviour: CONTRARY TO, differing from, at odds with, inconsistent with, in opposition to, diametrically opposed to.
– OPPOSITES compatible.

incompetent adjective ❶ INCAPABLE, inept, inefficient, ineffectual, unqualified, unable, unfitted, unsuitable, useless, inadequate, deficient. ❷ an incompetent performance: INEXPERT, unskilful, inept, bungling, awkward, maladroit, clumsy, floundering, gauche; *informal* botched.
– OPPOSITES competent.

incomplete adjective ❶ an incomplete job: UNFINISHED, partial, unaccomplished, undone, undeveloped, unexecuted, unperformed. ❷ an incomplete set: IMPERFECT, broken, defective, lacking, wanting, deficient. ❸ an incomplete text: SHORTENED, deficient, curtailed, abridged, expurgated, bowdlerized.
– OPPOSITES complete.

incomprehensible adjective ❶ UNINTELLIGIBLE, too difficult/hard, complicated, complex, involved, intricate; *informal* over one's head. ❷ ILLEGIBLE, indecipherable, unintelligible, unreadable.
– OPPOSITES intelligible, clear.

inconceivable adjective UNIMAGINABLE, unthinkable, incomprehensible, incredible, unbelievable, implausible, impossible, out of the question, preposterous, ridiculous, ludicrous.
– OPPOSITES plausible.

inconclusive adjective INDEFINITE, indeterminate, indecisive, undetermined, open to question, open to doubt, vague, unsettled, unresolved, questionable, ambiguous, equivocal, unestablished; *informal* up in the air.
– OPPOSITES conclusive.

incongruous adjective OUT OF PLACE, inappropriate, incompatible, discordant, jarring, out of keeping, inconsistent, contrary, unsuited, at odds, in opposition, opposed, conflicting,

irreconcilable, strange, odd, absurd, unsuitable.
– OPPOSITES appropriate, suitable.

inconsequential adjective
INSIGNIFICANT, negligible, unimportant, trivial, trifling, petty; *informal* piddling.
– OPPOSITES important.

inconsiderate adjective
THOUGHTLESS, unthinking, uncaring, heedless, unmindful, regardless, undiscerning, insensitive, tactless, uncharitable, unkind, ungracious, selfish, self-centred, egotistical.
– OPPOSITES considerate.

inconsistent adjective
❶ INCOMPATIBLE, out of keeping, out of place, contrary, at odds, at variance, in opposition, conflicting, in conflict, irreconcilable, discordant, discrepant. ❷ an inconsistent character: UNSTABLE, unsteady, changeable, erratic, irregular, unpredictable, capricious, fickle, whimsical, mercurial, volatile.
– OPPOSITES consistent.

inconspicuous adjective
UNOBTRUSIVE, unnoticeable, indistinct, ordinary, plain, run-of-the-mill, unremarkable, undistinguished, unostentatious, unimposing, hidden, insignificant, quiet, retiring, unassuming, in the background; *informal* low-key.
– OPPOSITES conspicuous.

inconvenience noun
❶ TROUBLE, bother, disruption, disturbance, vexation, worry, annoyance, disadvantage, difficulty, embarrassment. ❷ AWKWARDNESS, unwieldiness, cumbersomeness, unhandiness.
▶ verb DISTURB, bother, trouble, worry, disrupt, put out, impose upon, burden, distract, annoy, discommode.

inconvenient adjective
❶ AWKWARD, unsuitable, inappropriate, inopportune, disadvantageous, inexpedient, disturbing, troublesome, bothersome, tiresome, vexatious, annoying, embarrassing, ill-timed, untimely, unseasonable. ❷ UNWIELDY, cumbersome, awkward, unmanageable, unhandy, difficult.
– OPPOSITES convenient.

incorporate verb ❶ INCLUDE, embrace, absorb, embody, assimilate, subsume. ❷ MERGE, coalesce, fuse, blend, mix, amalgamate, combine, unite, integrate, unify, compact.
– OPPOSITES exclude.

incorrect adjective ❶ incorrect answers: WRONG, inaccurate, erroneous, wide of the mark. ❷ an incorrect account: MISTAKEN, inaccurate, faulty, inexact, untrue, false, fallacious, non-factual, flawed; *informal* full of holes. ❸ incorrect behaviour: IMPROPER, unsuitable, indecorous, inappropriate, lacking in propriety, unseemly, ungentlemanly, unladylike.
– OPPOSITES correct.

incorrigible adjective
INVETERATE, irredeemable, hardened, dyed-in-the-wool, incurable, irreformable, hopeless, beyond hope, beyond redemption, impenitent, uncontrite, unrepentant, obdurate, habitual, shameless.

incorruptible adjective
❶ VIRTUOUS, honest, upright, honourable, moral, ethical, trustworthy, straight, unbribable,

high-principled. ❷ IMPERISHABLE, indestructible, indissoluble, everlasting, non-biodegradable. – OPPOSITES corrupt.

increase verb ❶ GROW, become greater/larger/bigger, expand, extend, multiply, intensify, heighten, mount, escalate, mushroom, snowball, swell, wax. ❷ ADD TO, enhance, build up, enlarge, augment, expand, extend, spread, heighten, raise, intensify, strengthen, magnify, proliferate, inflate, step up.
– OPPOSITES decrease.
▶ noun GROWTH, rise, enlargement, expansion, extension, increment, addition, development, intensification, escalation, heightening, boost, augmentation, snowballing, mushrooming, strengthening, magnification, inflation.
– OPPOSITES decrease.

incredible adjective ❶ find his story incredible: UNBELIEVABLE, hard to believe, beyond belief, far-fetched, inconceivable, unimaginable, unthinkable, impossible, implausible, highly unlikely, improbable, absurd, preposterous, questionable, dubious, doubtful, fictitious, mythical. ❷ an incredible performance: EXTRAORDINARY, wonderful, great, supreme, tremendous, marvellous, amazing, astounding, prodigious, awe-inspiring, awesome, superhuman; *informal* fantastic, fab, magic.
– OPPOSITES credible.

incredulous adjective DISBELIEVING, unbelieving, sceptical, cynical, distrusting, distrustful, mistrusting, mistrustful, doubtful, doubting, dubious, unconvinced, suspicious, uncertain.
– OPPOSITES credulous.

incriminate verb IMPLICATE, involve, inculpate, inform against, charge, blame, pin the blame on, accuse, indict, impeach, arraign, stigmatize, blacken someone's name; *informal* point the finger at, finger, rat on; *Brit. informal* grass on.

incumbent adjective ❶ BINDING, obligatory, mandatory, necessary, compulsory. ❷ CURRENT, existing, present, in office, in power.

incur verb BRING UPON ONESELF, expose oneself to, lay oneself open to, provoke, be liable to, contract, meet with, experience.

incurable adjective ❶ UNTREATABLE, inoperable, beyond cure, fatal, terminal, irremediable. ❷ *See* INCORRIGIBLE.

incursion noun RAID, foray, sortie, attack, assault, onslaught, invasion, sally.

indecent adjective ❶ IMPROPER, suggestive, indelicate, impure, risqué, off colour, ribald, bawdy, foul, vulgar, gross, crude, obscene, dirty, smutty, coarse, lewd, lascivious, salacious, licentious, pornographic, scatological; *informal* blue, raunchy. ❷ indecent haste: UNSEEMLY, improper, inappropriate, unsuitable, unfitting, unacceptable, offensive, outrageous.
– OPPOSITES proper, seemly.

indecisive adjective IRRESOLUTE, hesitant, in two minds, wavering, vacillating, ambivalent, undecided, uncertain, unresolved, sitting on the fence, blowing hot and cold.

indefatigable adjective TIRELESS, untiring, unflagging, persistent, tenacious, dogged, assiduous, industrious, indomitable, relentless, unremitting.

indefensible adjective ❶ indefensible behaviour: INEXCUSABLE, unjustifiable, unpardonable, unforgivable, inexpiable. ❷ an indefensible theory: UNTENABLE, insupportable, flawed, faulty, implausible, specious, unarguable.

indefinite adjective ❶ an indefinite answer: VAGUE, unclear, imprecise, inexact, ambiguous, ambivalent, equivocal, confused, evasive. ❷ an indefinite number: INDETERMINATE, unspecified. ❸ an indefinite shape: BLURRED, ill-defined, indistinct, fuzzy, hazy, dim, vague, obscure.
– OPPOSITES definite.

indemnify verb INSURE, underwrite, guarantee, protect, secure, make secure, give security to, endorse.

indenture noun CONTRACT, agreement, compact, covenant, certificate, deed, document, lease, warranty, bond, commitment.

independence noun ❶ SELF-GOVERNMENT, autonomy, self-determination, sovereignty, freedom, home rule, autarchy. ❷ FREEDOM, liberty, self-sufficiency, self-reliance.

independent adjective ❶ SELF-GOVERNING, autonomous, free, sovereign, self-determining, non-aligned, neutral, autarchic. ❷ FREETHINKING, bold, liberated, individualistic, unconventional, unrestrained, untrammelled, unfettered, unconstrained. ❸ SEPARATE, unconnected, unrelated, unattached, distinct, individual.
– OPPOSITES subservient, biased, related.

indescribable adjective INEXPRESSIBLE, undefinable, beyond words/description, incommunicable, ineffable, unutterable, incredible, extraordinary, remarkable, prodigious.

indestructible adjective UNBREAKABLE, imperishable, durable, enduring, infrangible, inextinguishable, perennial, deathless, undying, immortal, endless, everlasting.
– OPPOSITES fragile.

indeterminate adjective UNFIXED, indefinite, undetermined, unspecified, unstipulated, unknown, uncertain, unpredictable, uncounted, uncalculated.

index noun KEY, guide, directory, catalogue, table of contents.

indicate verb ❶ SHOW, demonstrate, exhibit, display, manifest, evince, express, make known, tell, state, reveal, disclose, register, record, signal, denote, betoken, suggest, imply. ❷ POINT TO/AT, designate, specify.

indication noun ❶ SIGN, symptom, mark, manifestation, signal, omen, augury, portent, warning, hint. ❷ SHOW, demonstration, exhibition, display, manifestation, revelation, disclosure.

indicator noun ❶ POINTER, needle, marker, meter, display. ❷ INDEX, guide, mark, sign, signal, symbol, signpost.

indifferent adjective

❶ indifferent to his pain: UNCONCERNED, apathetic, heedless, uncaring, uninterested, unimpressed, aloof, detached, distant, cold, cool, impassive, dispassionate, unresponsive, unemotional, emotionless, unmoved, unexcited, unfeeling, unsympathetic, callous. ❷ an indifferent player: MEDIOCRE, middling, moderate, fair, not bad, passable, adequate, barely adequate, average, ordinary, commonplace, undistinguished, uninspired; *informal* so-so, OK.
– OPPOSITES enthusiastic.

indigenous adjective NATIVE, original, aboriginal, autochthonous.

indignant adjective ANGRY, angered, irate, furious, incensed, infuriated, annoyed, irritated, wrathful, enraged, exasperated, heated, riled, in a temper, in high dudgeon, provoked, piqued, disgruntled, fuming, livid, mad, seeing red; *informal* miffed, in a huff, up in arms, huffy; *Brit. informal* narked.

indirect adjective ❶ CIRCUITOUS, roundabout, wandering, meandering, winding, curving, tortuous, zigzag, divergent, deviant. ❷ DISCURSIVE, oblique, digressive, long-drawn-out, rambling, circumlocutory, periphrastic, allusive. ❸ BACKHANDED, devious, insidious, underhand, sneaky, surreptitious.
– OPPOSITES direct.

indiscreet adjective IMPRUDENT, unwise, incautious, injudicious, ill-advised, ill-judged, ill-thought-out, ill-considered, foolish, impolitic, careless, unwary, hasty, rash, reckless, impulsive, precipitate, foolhardy, tactless, insensitive, undiplomatic.

indiscriminate adjective ❶ indiscriminate choice: UNSELECTIVE, undiscriminating, uncritical, careless, aimless, hit-or-miss, haphazard, random, unsystematic, unmethodical, sweeping, general, broad-based, wholesale. ❷ an indiscriminate collection: JUMBLED, mixed, haphazard, motley, miscellaneous, diverse, varied, confused, mongrel, chaotic, thrown together; *informal* higgledy-piggledy.
– OPPOSITES systematic.

indispensable adjective ESSENTIAL, vital, crucial, imperative, key, necessary, requisite, needed, important, urgent, pressing, high-priority, fundamental.
– OPPOSITES superfluous.

indisputable adjective INCONTESTABLE, incontrovertible, undeniable, irrefutable, unquestionable, indubitable, beyond dispute/question, beyond the shadow of a doubt, unassailable, certain, sure, positive, definite, absolute, final, conclusive.
– OPPOSITES debatable.

indistinct adjective ❶ indistinct shapes: BLURRED, fuzzy, out of focus, bleary, hazy, misty, shadowy, dim, obscure, indefinite, indistinguishable, barely perceptible. ❷ indistinct sounds: MUFFLED, muted, low, muttered, mumbled, slurred.
– OPPOSITES distinct.

indistinguishable adjective IDENTICAL, alike, very similar,

interchangeable, the same; *informal* like two peas in a pod.
– OPPOSITES different.

individual adjective ❶ SINGLE, separate, lone, sole, solitary, distinct, distinctive, particular, specific, peculiar, isolated. ❷ an individual style: CHARACTERISTIC, distinctive, peculiar, personal, personalized, own, private, special, singular, original, unique, idiosyncratic.

indolent adjective LAZY, idle, slothful, lethargic, slow-moving, slack, lackadaisical, apathetic, listless, inert, torpid.
– OPPOSITES active.

induce verb ❶ induce them to go: PERSUADE, talk into, get, prevail upon, move, prompt, inspire, instigate, influence, press, urge, incite, encourage, impel, motivate, inveigle, coax, wheedle. ❷ induce a reaction: BRING ABOUT, bring on, cause, produce, effect, create, give rise to, generate, originate, engender, occasion, set in motion, develop, lead to.

inducement noun INCENTIVE, encouragement, attraction, bait, carrot, lure, reward, incitement, stimulus, spur, goad, impetus, motive, provocation; *informal* come-on.

indulge verb PAMPER, spoil, coddle, mollycoddle, cosset, pander to, humour, go along with, baby, pet.

indulgent adjective PERMISSIVE, easy-going, compliant, fond, doting, forbearing, compassionate, humane, kind, understanding, sympathetic, liberal, forgiving, lenient, merciful, clement.
– OPPOSITES intolerant.

industrious adjective HARD-WORKING, diligent, assiduous, conscientious, sedulous, laborious, steady, busy, active, bustling, energetic, on the go, vigorous, determined, dynamic, indefatigable, tireless, persistent, pertinacious, zealous, productive.
– OPPOSITES idle, lazy.

industry noun ❶ MANUFACTURING, production, fabrication, construction, business, trade, field, line, craft. ❷ INDUSTRIOUSNESS, diligence, assiduity, application, activity, energy, vigour, effort, determination, dynamism, tirelessness, persistence, zeal, pertinacity, productiveness, sedulousness, sedulity, conscientiousness.

ineffable adjective INDESCRIBABLE, inexpressible, unutterable, beyond words, undefinable.

ineffective adjective ❶ ineffective attempts: INEFFECTUAL, useless, to no avail, unavailing, worthless, unsuccessful, futile, fruitless, unproductive, profitless, abortive, inadequate, inefficient, inefficacious, impotent, idle, feeble, weak, incompetent, inept, lame, barren, sterile. ❷ ineffective people: INEFFECTUAL, unproductive, inadequate, incompetent, inept, feeble, weak, impotent.
– OPPOSITES effective.

inelegant adjective ❶ an inelegant position: AWKWARD, clumsy, ungainly, ungraceful, graceless. ❷ inelegant manners: UNREFINED, uncultured, uncultivated, unpolished, unsophisticated, unfinished,

gauche, crude, uncouth, ill-bred, coarse, vulgar.
- OPPOSITES graceful, refined.

ineligible adjective UNSUITABLE, unqualified, unfit, unfitted, inappropriate, unequipped, unacceptable, undesirable, disqualified.
- OPPOSITES eligible.

inept adjective ❶ INCOMPETENT, incapable, unskilled, inexpert, clumsy, awkward, maladroit, heavy-handed; *informal* cack-handed. ❷ an inept remark: INAPPROPRIATE, badly timed, inapt, unsuitable, infelicitous.
- OPPOSITES competent, appropriate.

inequality noun DISPARITY, imbalance, lack of balance, disproportion, variation, variability, difference, discrepancy, contrast, dissimilarity, unevenness, incongruity.
- OPPOSITES equality.

inequitable adjective UNFAIR, unjust, prejudiced, biased, discriminatory, partisan, partial, preferential, one-sided, intolerant, bigoted.
- OPPOSITES fair.

inert adjective ❶ UNMOVING, inactive, motionless, immobile, still, stock-still, stationary, static, lifeless, inanimate, unconscious, passive, out cold, comatose, dormant, dead. ❷ IDLE, inactive, indolent, slack, lazy, slothful, dull, sluggish, lethargic, stagnant, languid, lackadaisical, listless, torpid.
- OPPOSITES active.

inertia noun INERTNESS, inactivity, inaction, motionlessness, immobility, stagnation, passivity, stasis, idleness, indolence, laziness, sloth, slothfulness, dullness, sluggishness, lethargy, languor, listlessness, torpor.
- OPPOSITES activity.

inescapable adjective UNAVOIDABLE, inevitable, unpreventable, inexorable, assured, certain, bound to happen, ineludible, ineluctable.
- OPPOSITES avoidable.

inestimable adjective IMMEASURABLE, measureless, incalculable, priceless, precious, invaluable, unparalleled, supreme, superlative.

inevitable adjective UNAVOIDABLE, unpreventable, inexorable, inescapable, fixed, settled, irrevocable, fated, destined, predestined, ordained, decreed, out of one's hands, assured, certain, bound/sure to happen, for sure, necessary, ineluctable.
- OPPOSITES avoidable.

inexhaustible adjective UNLIMITED, limitless, illimitable, infinite, boundless, endless, never-ending, unrestricted, bottomless, measureless, copious, abundant.
- OPPOSITES limited.

inexpensive adjective *see* CHEAP (1).

inexperienced adjective UNTRAINED, untutored, unqualified, undrilled, unpractised, amateur, unskilled, uninitiated, uninformed, ignorant, unacquainted, unversed, naive, unsophisticated, unfledged, untried, unseasoned, new, callow, immature, fresh, green, raw; *informal* wet behind the ears.

inexplicable adjective UNEXPLAINABLE, unaccountable,

incomprehensible, beyond comprehension, unintelligible, unfathomable, baffling, puzzling, mysterious, strange, weird, abstruse, enigmatic, inscrutable.
– OPPOSITES understandable.

infallible adjective ❶ an infallible remedy: UNFAILING, foolproof, dependable, trustworthy, reliable, sure, certain; *informal* sure-fire. ❷ an infallible memory: UNERRING, unfailing, error-free, faultless, flawless, impeccable, unimpeachable, perfect.
– OPPOSITES fallible.

infamous adjective NOTORIOUS, disreputable, ill-famed, of ill-repute, iniquitous, ignominious, dishonourable, discreditable, villainous, wicked, evil, vile, nefarious.

infant noun BABY, little child, little one, tot, toddler; *Scottish* bairn.

infantile adjective CHILDISH, babyish, puerile, immature, juvenile, adolescent.
– OPPOSITES mature.

infatuated adjective BESOTTED, enamoured, captivated, bewitched, beguiled, spellbound, fascinated, enraptured, carried away, obsessed, swept off one's feet, smitten.

infatuation noun PASSING FANCY, crush, fancy, passion, obsession, fixation, craze, mania.

infect verb ❶ CONTAMINATE, pollute, taint, blight, spoil, mar. ❷ INFLUENCE, affect, imbue, infuse, stimulate, inspire, corrupt, pervert.

infectious adjective ❶ an infectious disease: CONTAGIOUS, infective, communicable, transmittable, transmissible, catching, spreading. ❷ infectious material: GERM-LADEN, pestilential, contaminating, toxic, noxious, virulent, poisonous. ❸ laughter is infectious: CATCHING, spreading, contagious, communicable, irresistible, compelling.

infer verb DEDUCE, conclude, work out, derive, reason, gather, understand, presume, conjecture, surmise, theorize, hypothesize; *informal* figure; *Brit. informal* suss.

inferior adjective ❶ an inferior position: LOWER, lesser, subordinate, junior, secondary, subsidiary, ancillary, minor, subservient, lowly, humble, servile, menial. ❷ inferior goods: FAULTY, imperfect, defective, substandard, low-quality, low-grade, shoddy, cheap, reject, gimcrack; *Brit. informal* grotty. ❸ an inferior performer: SECOND-RATE, indifferent, mediocre, incompetent, poor, bad, awful.
– OPPOSITES superior.

infernal adjective HELLISH, diabolical, devilish, demonic, demoniac, fiendish, satanic.

infest verb SPREAD THROUGH, overrun, take over, pervade, permeate, penetrate, infiltrate, invade, swarm over, beset, plague.

infidelity noun UNFAITHFULNESS, adultery, cheating, cuckoldry, affair, liaison, intrigue, amour.

infinite adjective ❶ infinite space: BOUNDLESS, unbounded, unlimited, limitless, without end, extensive, vast. ❷ infinite numbers: COUNTLESS, without number, numberless, innumerable, immeasurable, incalculable, untold, uncountable, inestimable, indeterminable, vast, enormous, stupendous, prodigious. ❸ infinite

patience: UNLIMITED, boundless, endless, unending, never-ending, inexhaustible, interminable, absolute, total.
–OPPOSITES limited.

infinitesimal adjective TINY, minute, microscopic, minuscule, inappreciable, insignificant, trifling; *informal* piddling, teeny.
–OPPOSITES huge.

infinity noun LIMITLESSNESS, boundlessness, unlimitedness, endlessness, infinitude.

infirm adjective FEEBLE, enfeebled, weak, frail, debilitated, decrepit, disabled, in poor health, failing, ailing, doddery, lame, crippled.
–OPPOSITES fit.

inflame verb INCITE, excite, arouse, rouse, stir up, work up, whip up, agitate, fire, ignite, kindle, foment, impassion, provoke, stimulate, actuate.
–OPPOSITES cool.

inflammable adjective FLAMMABLE, combustible, burnable, ignitable, incendiary.
–OPPOSITES incombustible.

inflate verb ❶ BLOW UP, pump up, puff up/out, dilate, distend, swell, aerate. ❷ EXAGGERATE, increase, extend, amplify, augment, expand, intensify.
–OPPOSITES deflate.

inflexible adjective ❶ RIGID, stiff, non-flexible, unbendable, unyielding, taut, hard, firm, inelastic, unmalleable. ❷ inflexible rules: UNCHANGEABLE, unalterable, immutable, unvarying, firm, fixed, hard and fast, uncompromising, stringent, rigorous, inexorable. ❸ inflexible people/attitudes: ADAMANT, firm, immovable, unaccommodating, dyed-in-the-wool, stubborn, obdurate, obstinate, intractable, unbending, intolerant, relentless, merciless, pitiless, uncompromising, inexorable, steely, iron-willed.
–OPPOSITES flexible.

inflict verb ADMINISTER, deal out, mete out, serve out, deliver, apply, lay on, impose, levy, exact, wreak.

influence noun ❶ EFFECT, impact, control, sway, ascendancy, power, mastery, agency, guidance, domination, rule, supremacy, leadership, direction, pressure. ❷ under the influence of drugs: EFFECT, control, sway, hold, power.
▶ verb ❶ AFFECT, have an effect on, impact on, sway, bias, incline, motivate, determine, guide, control, change, alter, transform. ❷ PERSUADE, induce, impel, incite, manipulate, prompt.

influential adjective ❶ an influential person: POWERFUL, important, leading, authoritative, controlling, dominant, predominant, prestigious. ❷ an influential reason: INSTRUMENTAL, guiding, significant, important, persuasive, telling, meaningful.
–OPPOSITES unimportant.

influx noun RUSH, inflow, inundation, flood, invasion, intrusion, incursion, ingress, convergence.

inform verb ❶ TELL, let know, advise, apprise, notify, announce to, impart to, relate to, communicate to, acquaint, brief, instruct, enlighten, make conversant, send word to; *informal* put in the picture, fill in, clue in, put wise, spill the beans to, tip off, tip the wink to, give the inside story to. ❷ inform on his accomplices: DENOUNCE, betray, incriminate, inculpate; *informal* blab on, rat on, squeal on, tell on, blow the whistle on, put the finger on, finger, sell down the river, snitch on, peach on; *Brit. informal* grass on.

informal adjective ❶ CASUAL, non-formal, unceremonious, unofficial, simple, unpretentious, everyday, relaxed, easy. ❷ **informal language**: COLLOQUIAL, vernacular, non-literary, simple, natural, unofficial, unpretentious; *informal* slangy.
–OPPOSITES formal.

information noun ❶ DATA, facts. ❷ KNOWLEDGE, intelligence, news, notice, word, advice, counsel, instruction, enlightenment, tidings, message, report, communiqué, communication; *informal* info, gen, low-down, dope, inside story, bumf, dirt.

informative adjective INSTRUCTIVE, illuminating, enlightening, edifying, educational, revealing, telling, communicative, newsy, chatty, gossipy.
–OPPOSITES uninformative.

informed adjective KNOWLEDGEABLE, well briefed, posted, abreast of the facts, well versed, primed, up to date, au fait, au courant.

informer noun INFORMANT, betrayer, traitor, Judas, whistle-blower; *informal* rat, squealer, stool pigeon, canary, snitch, peacher; *Brit. informal* grass, nark, snout.

infraction noun BREACH, violation, transgression, contravention, infringement, intrusion, encroachment, invasion.

infrequent adjective RARE, occasional, irregular, sporadic, uncommon, unusual, exceptional, few and far between, intermittent; *informal* once in a blue moon.
–OPPOSITES frequent.

infringe verb BREAK, disobey, violate, contravene, transgress, breach, disregard, take no notice of, defy, flout.

ingenious adjective CLEVER, intelligent, shrewd, astute, sharp, bright, talented, brilliant, masterly, resourceful, inventive, creative, original, subtle, crafty, wily, cunning, skilful, adroit, deft, capable; *informal* smart.
–OPPOSITES stupid, unimaginative.

ingenuous adjective OPEN, sincere, honest, frank, candid, direct, forthcoming, artless, guileless, simple, naive, innocent, genuine, unaffected, trustful, trusting, truthful, unsuspicious.
–OPPOSITES insincere, artful.

ingratiating adjective SYCOPHANTIC, toadying, fawning, unctuous, obsequious, servile, crawling, flattering, wheedling; *informal* bootlicking.

inhabit verb LIVE IN, dwell in, reside in, occupy, lodge in, tenant, make one's home in, settle in, people, populate.

inhabitant noun RESIDENT, dweller, occupant, habitant, settler, native, tenant; *Brit.* occupier.

inherent adjective ❶ **an inherent part**: INTRINSIC, innate, built-in, inseparable, essential, basic, fundamental, ingrained. ❷ **an inherent tendency**: INBORN, inbred, innate, hereditary, inherited, in the family, congenital, familial.

inherit verb BE LEFT, be willed, be bequeathed, come into, fall heir to, succeed to, accede to, assume, take over.

inheritance noun LEGACY, bequest, endowment, birthright, heritage, patrimony.

inhibit verb IMPEDE, hold back, prevent, stop, hamper, hinder, obstruct, interfere with, curb, check, restrict, restrain, constrain, bridle, rein in, baulk, frustrate, arrest.
– OPPOSITES assist, encourage.

inhibited adjective SHY, reticent, self-conscious, reserved, constrained, repressed, embarrassed, tongue-tied, subdued, withdrawn; *informal* uptight.
– OPPOSITES uninhibited.

inhibition noun ❶ OBSTRUCTION, prevention, stopping, hindrance, hampering, impediment, curb, check, restriction, restraint, frustration, arrest. ❷ SHYNESS, reticence, reserve, self-consciousness, repression, constraint, embarrassment.

inhospitable adjective ❶ UNWELCOMING, unfriendly, unsociable, unsocial, antisocial, uncivil, discourteous, ungracious, ungenerous, cool, cold, chilly, aloof, unkind, unsympathetic, ill-disposed, hostile, inimical, xenophobic. ❷ an inhospitable landscape: BLEAK, bare, uninviting, barren, desolate, lonely, empty, forbidding, hostile.
– OPPOSITES hospitable.

inimical adjective ❶ an inimical atmosphere: HOSTILE, unfriendly, inhospitable, unwelcoming, unfavourable, cold, unsociable, antagonistic, antipathetic. ❷ inimical to their survival: HARMFUL, injurious, detrimental, deleterious, damaging, dangerous, destructive, pernicious, noxious.
– OPPOSITES advantageous, friendly.

initial adjective FIRST, beginning, starting, commencing, opening, early, prime, primary, elementary, introductory, inaugural, foundational, inceptive.
– OPPOSITES final.

initiate verb ❶ BEGIN, start, commence, open, institute, inaugurate, get under way, set in motion, lay the foundations of, launch, actuate, instigate, trigger off, originate, pioneer, sow the seeds of; *informal* start the ball rolling. ❷ TEACH, instruct, coach, tutor, school, train, prime, familiarize, indoctrinate.
– OPPOSITES finish.

initiative noun ENTERPRISE, resourcefulness, inventiveness, resource, originality, creativity, drive, push, dynamism, ambition, ambitiousness, verve, dash, leadership; *informal* get-up-and-go, pep, zip.

injunction noun COMMAND, instruction, order, ruling, direction, directive, dictate, dictum, mandate, enjoinment, admonition, precept, ultimatum.

injure verb HURT, harm, damage, wound, maim, cripple, lame, disable, mutilate, deform, mangle, impair, weaken, enfeeble, blight, blemish.

injurious adjective HARMFUL, hurtful, damaging, deleterious,

detrimental, disadvantageous, unfavourable, destructive, pernicious, ruinous, disastrous, calamitous, malignant.
– OPPOSITES innocuous.

injury noun ❶ HARM, hurt, wounding, damage, impairment, affliction. ❷ WOUND, sore, cut, bruise, gash, laceration, abrasion, lesion, contusion, trauma.

injustice noun UNFAIRNESS, unjustness, inequity, bias, prejudice, favouritism, partiality, one-sidedness, discrimination, partisanship.
– OPPOSITES justice.

inkling noun HINT, clue, intimation, suggestion, indication, whisper, suspicion, insinuation, notion, glimmering; *informal* the foggiest idea, the foggiest.

innate adjective INBORN, inbred, congenital, hereditary, inherited, inherent, intrinsic, ingrained, natural, native, indigenous.

inner adjective INTERIOR, inside, central, middle, further in.
– OPPOSITES outer.

innocence noun ❶ GUILTLESSNESS, blamelessness, irreproachability, clean hands. ❷ SIMPLENESS, ingenuousness, naivety, guilelessness, openness, credulity, inexperience, gullibility.
– OPPOSITES guilt.

innocent adjective ❶ NOT GUILTY, guiltless, blameless, clear, in the clear, above suspicion, above reproach, unimpeachable, irreproachable. ❷ innocent fun: HARMLESS, innocuous, safe, unobjectionable, inoffensive, playful. ❸ SIMPLE, naive, ingenuous, unsophisticated, artless, guileless, childlike, frank, open, trustful, trusting, credulous, inexperienced, unworldly, green, gullible; *informal* wet behind the ears.
– OPPOSITES guilty.

innocuous adjective ❶ SAFE, harmless, non-poisonous. ❷ an innocuous person: INOFFENSIVE, harmless, unobjectionable, unexceptionable, mild, peaceful, bland, commonplace, insipid.

innuendo noun INSINUATION, implication, suggestion, hint, overtone, allusion, inkling, imputation, aspersion.

innumerable adjective VERY MANY, numerous, countless, untold, incalculable, numberless, unnumbered, infinite, myriad; *informal* umpteen, masses, oodles.
– OPPOSITES few.

inquire verb ASK, make inquiries about, investigate, question, query, research, look into, examine, explore, probe, scan, scrutinize, study.

inquiry noun ❶ INVESTIGATION, examination, exploration, probe, review, search, scrutiny, scrutinization, inspection, study, interrogation. ❷ QUESTION, query.

inquisitive adjective INQUIRING, questioning, probing, scrutinizing, curious, burning with curiosity, interested, intrusive, meddlesome, prying; *informal* nosy, nosy-parker, snooping.
– OPPOSITES uninterested.

insane adjective MAD, crazy, deranged, demented, unhinged, out of one's mind, non compos mentis; *informal* not all there, bonkers, cracked, batty, bats, cuckoo, loony, loopy, nuts, nutty,

screw, bananas, off one's rocker, round the bend; *Brit. informal* barmy, crackers, off one's trolley.
– OPPOSITES sane.

inscrutable adjective ENIGMATIC, impenetrable, unreadable, cryptic, deadpan, sphinx-like, poker-faced.
– OPPOSITES transparent.

insecure adjective ❶ VULNERABLE, open to attack, defenceless, unprotected, unguarded, exposed, in danger, dangerous, perilous, hazardous. ❷ UNCONFIDENT, lacking confidence, timid, diffident, uncertain, unsure, doubtful, hesitant, anxious, fearful, apprehensive, worried.
– OPPOSITES secure.

insensible adjective UNCONSCIOUS, senseless, insentient, insensate, anaesthetized, comatose, knocked out, stupefied, inert; *informal* out, out cold, out for the count, zonked.
– OPPOSITES conscious.

insensitive adjective ❶ insensitive to the cold: IMPERVIOUS TO, immune to, oblivious to, unmoved by, indifferent to, proof against, insusceptible to, unaffected by, unreactive to. ❷ insensitive people: HEARTLESS, uncaring, unfeeling, callous, tactless, thick-skinned, unconcerned, unsympathetic.
– OPPOSITES sensitive.

insert verb DRIVE IN, push in, put in, press in, stick in, thrust in, work in, slide in, slip in, tuck in, pop in.
– OPPOSITES extract.
▶ noun INSERTION, inset, supplement, circular, advertisement, ad.

inside noun ❶ INTERIOR, inner part, contents. ❷ STOMACH, abdomen, gut, intestines, viscera, entrails, bowels, vital organs.
▶ adjective INTERIOR, inner, internal, innermost, inward, on the inside, intramural.

insidious adjective SURREPTITIOUS, sneaky, cunning, crafty, stealthy, subtle, artful, Machiavellian, sly, wily, slick, deceitful, deceptive, underhand, double-dealing, duplicitous, dishonest, insincere, treacherous, perfidious; *informal* tricky.
– OPPOSITES straightforward.

insignificant adjective UNIMPORTANT, trivial, trifling, negligible, inconsequential, of no consequence, not worth mentioning, nugatory, meagre, paltry, scanty, petty, insubstantial, flimsy, irrelevant, immaterial.
– OPPOSITES significant, important.

insincere adjective UNTRUTHFUL, dishonest, deceptive, not candid, not frank, disingenuous, dissembling, dissimulating, pretended, devious, hypocritical, deceitful, duplicitous, underhand, double-dealing, false, faithless, disloyal, treacherous, two-faced, lying, mendacious, evasive, shifty, slippery.
– OPPOSITES sincere.

insinuate verb IMPLY, hint, whisper, suggest, indicate, give the impression, intimate, mention.

insist verb ❶ BE FIRM, stand one's ground, stand firm, make a stand, be resolute, be determined, be emphatic, not take no for an answer; *formal* brook no refusal. ❷ MAINTAIN, assert, state, declare, contend, pronounce, proclaim, avow, vow, swear, stress, reiterate; *formal* aver.

insistent adjective FIRM, emphatic, determined, resolute, tenacious, persistent, unyielding, obstinate, dogged, unrelenting, unremitting, relentless, inexorable, importunate.

insolence noun IMPERTINENCE, impudence, cheek, cheekiness, rudeness, disrespect, incivility, insubordination, contempt, abuse, offensiveness, audacity, boldness, brazenness, brashness, pertness, forwardness, effrontery, insults; *informal* gall, chutzpah; *Brit. informal* sauce, backchat.

insolent adjective IMPERTINENT, impudent, cheeky, rude, ill-mannered, disrespectful, insubordinate, contemptuous, insulting, abusive, offensive, audacious, bold, brash, brazen, pert, forward; *informal* saucy, fresh.
– OPPOSITES respectful.

insoluble adjective
❶ UNSOLVABLE, baffling, unfathomable, indecipherable, perplexing, complicated, intricate, involved, impenetrable, inscrutable, enigmatic, obscure, mystifying, inexplicable, incomprehensible, mysterious.
❷ INDISSOLUBLE.

insolvent adjective BANKRUPT, ruined, penniless, impoverished, penurious, impecunious; *informal* gone bust, in the red, broke, strapped for cash.

inspect verb EXAMINE, check, go over, look over, survey, scrutinize, vet, audit, study, pore over, view, scan, observe, investigate, assess, appraise; *informal* give the once-over to.

inspection noun EXAMINATION, check, check-up, survey, scrutiny, view, scan, observation, investigation, probe, assessment, appraisal; *informal* once-over, look-see.

inspector noun EXAMINER, checker, scrutinizer, scrutineer, auditor, surveyor, observer, investigator, overseer, supervisor, assessor, appraiser, critic.

inspiration noun ❶ STIMULUS, stimulation, motivation, fillip, encouragement, influence, muse, goad, spur, incitement, arousal. ❷ CREATIVITY, originality, inventiveness, genius, insight, vision, afflatus. ❸ BRIGHT IDEA, revelation, illumination, enlightenment.

inspire verb ❶ STIMULATE, motivate, encourage, influence, rouse, stir, goad, energize, galvanize, animate. ❷ **she inspired affection**: AROUSE, excite, touch off, spark off, ignite, kindle, give rise to, produce, bring about, prompt, instigate.

instability noun ❶ UNSTEADINESS, unsoundness, shakiness, frailty, flimsiness, insubstantiality.
❷ IMPERMANENCE, temporariness, transience, inconstancy.
❸ CAPRICIOUSNESS, volatility, changeableness, flightiness, vacillation, wavering, fitfulness, oscillation.
– OPPOSITES stability.

install verb ❶ PUT IN, insert, put in place, position, place, fix, locate, situate, station, lodge. ❷ INVEST, ordain, establish, initiate, ensconce, induct, institute.
– OPPOSITES remove.

instalment noun PART, portion,

section, segment, chapter, episode, division.

instance noun CASE, case in point, example, illustration, occasion, occurrence.
▶ verb CITE, mention, name, specify, quote, adduce.

instant adjective
❶ INSTANTANEOUS, immediate, prompt, rapid, sudden, abrupt.
❷ PRE-PREPARED, ready-prepared, ready-mixed, pre-cooked.
▶ noun MOMENT, minute, second, split second, trice, twinkling, twinkling of an eye, flash; *informal* jiffy, tick, shake.

instigate verb ❶ BRING ABOUT, start, initiate, generate, actuate, incite, provoke, inspire, foment, kindle, stir up, whip up. ❷ INCITE, encourage, egg on, urge, prompt, goad, prod, induce, impel, constrain, press, persuade, prevail upon, sway, entice.
– OPPOSITES discourage.

instigator noun INCITER, prime mover, motivator, agitator, fomenter, troublemaker, mischief-maker, ringleader, leader.

instil verb IMBUE, infuse, inculcate, introduce, inject, implant, insinuate, ingrain, indoctrinate, teach, drill, arouse.

instinct noun ❶ NATURAL FEELING, tendency, inclination, intuition, sixth sense, inner prompting. ❷ TALENT, gift, ability, capacity, faculty, aptitude, knack, bent, trait, characteristic.

instinctive adjective
❶ AUTOMATIC, reflex, mechanical, spontaneous, involuntary, impulsive, intuitive, unthinking, unpremeditated. ❷ INBORN, inbred, innate, inherent, natural, intuitive, untaught, unlearned.
– OPPOSITES learned.

institute verb ❶ BEGIN, start, commence, set in motion, put into operation, initiate. ❷ FOUND, establish, launch, bring into being, set up, constitute, organize, develop, create, originate, pioneer.
▶ noun INSTITUTION, establishment, organization, foundation, society, association, league, guild, consortium.

institutional adjective
❶ institutional methods: ORGANIZED, established, bureaucratic, accepted, orthodox, conventional, customary, formal, systematic, methodical, orderly.
❷ institutional food: UNIFORM, same, unvarying, unvaried, unchanging, monotonous, bland, dull, insipid. ❸ an institutional atmosphere: COLD, cheerless, clinical, dreary, drab, unwelcoming, uninviting, impersonal, formal, forbidding.

instruct verb ❶ TELL, order, direct, command, bid, charge, enjoin, demand, require. ❷ TEACH, educate, tutor, coach, train, school, drill, ground, prepare, prime, guide, inform, enlighten, discipline, edify.

instruction noun ❶ TEACHING, education, tutoring, tutelage, coaching, training, schooling, drilling, grounding, preparation, priming, guidance, information, enlightenment, edification, lessons, classes, lectures.
❷ DIRECTIVE, direction, briefing, order, command, charge, injunction, requirement, ruling, mandate.

instructive adjective INFORMATIVE, educational, educative, enlightening, illuminating, revealing, useful, helpful, edifying, uplifting, informational, cultural, academic, didactic, doctrinal.

instructor noun TEACHER, schoolmaster, schoolmistress, educator, lecturer, professor, tutor, coach, trainer, adviser, counsellor, guide, mentor, demonstrator.

instrument noun IMPLEMENT, tool, appliance, apparatus, mechanism, utensil, gadget, contrivance, device, aid.

instrumental adjective HELPFUL, of use, of help, of assistance, useful, of service, contributory, active, involved, influential, significant, important, valuable, beneficial.

insubordinate adjective DEFIANT, rebellious, mutinous, disobedient, refractory, recalcitrant, undisciplined, ungovernable, uncontrollable, unmanageable, unruly, disorderly, seditious, riotous, insurgent, contumacious.
– OPPOSITES obedient.

insufferable adjective INTOLERABLE, unbearable, unendurable, insupportable, impossible, dreadful, excruciating, grim, outrageous.
– OPPOSITES bearable.

insufficient adjective INADEQUATE, deficient, in short supply, scarce, meagre, scant, scanty, too small/few/little, not enough, lacking, wanting, at a premium.
– OPPOSITES sufficient.

insular adjective ❶ insular lives: ISOLATED, detached, separate, solitary, insulated, self-sufficient. ❷ insular attitudes: NARROW, narrow-minded, illiberal, prejudiced, biased, bigoted, provincial, blinkered, parochial, limited, restricted.
– OPPOSITES broad-minded.

insulate verb ❶ COVER, wrap, encase, enwrap, envelop, pad, cushion, seal, heatproof, soundproof. ❷ SEPARATE, segregate, isolate, detach, cut off, keep apart, exclude, sequester, protect, shield.

insult noun SLIGHT, affront, gibe, snub, barb, slur, dig, abuse, disparagement, depreciation, impugnment, revilement, insolence, rudeness, aspersions.
▶ verb OFFEND, affront, slight, hurt someone's feelings, hurt, abuse, injure, wound, mortify, humiliate, disparage, discredit, depreciate, impugn, slur, revile.
– OPPOSITES compliment.

insuperable adjective INSURMOUNTABLE, impassable, overwhelming, invincible, unconquerable, unassailable.

insure verb ASSURE, indemnify, cover, underwrite, guarantee, warrant.

insurgent noun REBEL, revolutionary, mutineer, rioter, insurrectionist, insurrectionary, malcontent.

intact adjective WHOLE, complete, entire, perfect, in one piece, sound, unbroken, undamaged, unblemished, faultless, flawless.
– OPPOSITES damaged.

intangible adjective ❶ IMPALPABLE, untouchable, incorporeal, phantom, spectral, ghostly. ❷ INDEFINABLE,

indescribable, vague, subtle, unclear, obscure, mysterious.
– OPPOSITES tangible.

integral adjective ❶ an integral part: ESSENTIAL, necessary, indispensable, requisite, basic, fundamental, inherent, intrinsic, innate. ❷ an integral design: ENTIRE, complete, whole, total, full, intact, unified, integrated, undivided.
– OPPOSITES peripheral, fragmented.

integrate verb JOIN, unite, combine, amalgamate, consolidate, blend, incorporate, coalesce, fuse, merge, intermix, mingle, commingle, assimilate, homogenize, mesh, harmonize, concatenate.
– OPPOSITES separate.

integrity noun ❶ HONESTY, uprightness, rectitude, righteousness, virtue, probity, morality, honour, goodness, decency, truthfulness, fairness, sincerity, candour. ❷ UNITY, wholeness, entirety, completeness, totality, cohesion.
– OPPOSITES dishonesty.

intellect noun INTELLIGENCE, understanding, reason, comprehension, mind, brain, thought, sense, judgement.

intellectual adjective ❶ an intellectual exercise: MENTAL, cerebral, academic, rational, logical. ❷ an intellectual person: INTELLIGENT, academic, well educated, well read, erudite, learned, bookish, donnish, highbrow, scholarly, studious.
▶ noun INTELLECT, genius, thinker, mastermind, academic, don, man/woman of letters, bluestocking, highbrow, pedant; *informal* egghead, bookworm.

intelligence noun ❶ INTELLECT, mind, brain, brainpower, mental capacity, aptitude, reason, understanding, comprehension, acumen, wit, cleverness, brightness, sharpness, brilliance, quickness of mind, discernment, alertness, perception, perspicacity, penetration, sense, brains, sagacity; *informal* grey matter, nous. ❷ INFORMATION, news, notice, notification, knowledge, account, advice, rumour, facts, data, reports, tidings; *informal* gen, low-down, dope. ❸ SPYING, observation, information collection, investigation, surveillance.

intelligent adjective CLEVER, bright, sharp, brilliant, quick, quick-witted, perceptive, penetrating, discerning, sagacious, thinking, well informed, educated, knowledgeable, enlightened; *informal* brainy, smart.

intelligentsia plural noun INTELLECTUALS, academics, literati, cognoscenti, illuminati, highbrows, pedants, the enlightened.

intelligible adjective UNDERSTANDABLE, comprehensible, clear, lucid, plain, explicit, unambiguous, legible, decipherable, straightforward, meaningful.
– OPPOSITES unintelligible, incomprehensible.

intemperate adjective IMMODERATE, self-indulgent, excessive, inordinate, extreme, extravagant, unreasonable, outrageous.
– OPPOSITES moderate.

intend verb ❶ he intends to go: MEAN, plan, have in mind/view, propose, aim, resolve, be resolved, be determined, expect, purpose, contemplate, think of. ❷ intended it for him: MEAN, aim, destine, purpose, plan, scheme, devise.

intense adjective ❶ intense heat/cold: ACUTE, fierce, severe, extreme, harsh, strong, powerful, potent, vigorous, great, profound, deep, concentrated, consuming. ❷ an intense desire: EARNEST, ardent, eager, keen, enthusiastic, zealous, excited, impassioned, passionate, fervent, burning, fervid, consuming, vehement, fanatical. ❸ an intense person: NERVOUS, nervy, tense, overwrought, fraught, highly strung, emotional.
– OPPOSITES mild.

intensify verb STRENGTHEN, increase, deepen, heighten, enhance, add to, fuel, build up, reinforce, magnify, fan, extend, boost, augment, escalate, step up, aggravate, exacerbate, worsen, inflame, raise.
– OPPOSITES reduce, decrease.

intensive adjective CONCENTRATED, in-depth, thorough, exhaustive, all-out, thoroughgoing, total, all-absorbing, high-powered, unremitting, comprehensive.
– OPPOSITES cursory.

intent adjective ❶ an intent expression: CONCENTRATED, concentrating, fixed, steady, steadfast, absorbed, attentive, engrossed, focused, occupied, preoccupied, rapt, enrapt, wrapped up, observant, watchful, alert, earnest, committed, intense. ❷ intent on doing it: SET ON, bent on, committed to, firm about, determined to, resolved to; *informal* hell-bent on.

intention noun ❶ AIM, purpose, objective, goal, intent, end, end in view, target, aspiration, wish, ambition, plan, design, resolve, resolution, determination. ❷ PREMEDITATION, design, plan, calculation, preconception.

intentional adjective INTENDED, deliberate, meant, done on purpose, wilful, purposeful, planned, calculated, designed, premeditated, preconceived, predetermined, pre-arranged, considered, weighed up, studied.
– OPPOSITES accidental, inadvertent.

inter verb BURY, entomb, consign to the grave, lay to rest; *informal* put six feet under.

intercept verb CUT OFF, stop, deflect, head off, catch, check, arrest, block, obstruct, impede, interrupt, thwart.

intercourse noun ❶ DEALINGS, trade, traffic, commerce, association, communication, connection, contact, correspondence, congress, communion. ❷ SEX, sexual intercourse, sexual relations, copulation, coitus, coition, carnal knowledge, lovemaking, sexual congress, congress, intimacy.

interest noun ❶ look with interest: ATTENTIVENESS, attention, absorption, engrossment, heed, regard, notice, scrutiny, curiosity, inquisitiveness. ❷ an object of interest: CURIOSITY, attraction, appeal, fascination, charm, allure. ❸ a matter of interest: CONCERN, importance, consequence, import, moment, significance, note, relevance, seriousness, weight, gravity, priority, urgency. ❹ PASTIME, hobby, activity, diversion, amusement,

pursuit, relaxation; *informal* thing, scene. ❺ an interest in the business: SHARE, stake, portion, claim, investment, involvement, participation, stock, equity.
– OPPOSITES boredom.
▶ **verb** ATTRACT, absorb, hold/engage someone's interest, engross, fascinate, rivet, grip, captivate, amuse, intrigue, arouse curiosity in, concern.
– OPPOSITES bore.

interested adjective ❶ ATTENTIVE, intent, absorbed, engrossed, curious, fascinated, riveted, gripped, captivated, intrigued. ❷ interested parties: CONCERNED, involved, implicated. ❸ PARTIAL, involved, partisan, biased, prejudiced.
– OPPOSITES uninterested, disinterested.

interesting adjective ABSORBING, engrossing, fascinating, riveting, gripping, compelling, compulsive, spellbinding, captivating, appealing, engaging, amusing, entertaining, stimulating, thought-provoking, diverting, exciting, intriguing.
– OPPOSITES boring, uninteresting.

interfere verb ❶ interfering with his work: HINDER, inhibit, impede, obstruct, get in the way of, check, block, hamper, handicap, cramp, frustrate, trammel, thwart, baulk. ❷ interfere in other people's business: MEDDLE WITH, butt into, pry into, intrude into, intervene in, get involved in, tamper with, intercede in; *informal* poke one's nose into, horn in, stick one's oar in.

interim adjective TEMPORARY, provisional, pro tem, stopgap, caretaker, acting, makeshift, improvised.

interior adjective INNER, internal, inside, inward.
– OPPOSITES exterior, outer.
▶ **noun** ❶ INSIDE, inner part, centre, middle, nucleus, core, heart. ❷ HINTERLAND, centre, heartland.
– OPPOSITES exterior.

interject verb INTRODUCE, interpose, interpolate, add, insinuate, intersperse.

interlude noun INTERVAL, intermission, break, pause, recess, rest, respite, halt, stop, stoppage, breathing space, delay, wait, hiatus.

intermediary noun MEDIATOR, go-between, broker, agent, middleman, arbitrator, negotiator.

intermediate adjective HALFWAY, in-between, middle, in the middle, mid, midway, intervening, interposed, transitional, medial, median, intermediary.

interminable adjective ENDLESS, never-ending, everlasting, incessant, ceaseless, unlimited, infinite, boundless, countless, untold, innumerable, incalculable, immeasurable, indeterminable.

intermittent adjective FITFUL, spasmodic, irregular, sporadic, occasional, periodic, cyclic, recurrent, recurring, broken, discontinuous, on and off, erratic.
– OPPOSITES continuous.

internal adjective ❶ INNER, inside, inward, interior. ❷ DOMESTIC, home, civil, interior, in-house.
– OPPOSITES external, foreign.

international adjective

WORLDWIDE, cosmopolitan, global, universal, intercontinental.

interpolate verb INSERT, interject, interpose, introduce, add, inject, insinuate, put in, work in, intercalate.

interpret verb ❶ TRANSLATE, transliterate, transcribe, paraphrase. ❷ EXPLAIN, elucidate, expound, explicate, clarify, make clear, illuminate, shed light on, gloss, simplify, spell out. ❸ DECODE, decipher, solve, crack, unravel, untangle. ❹ UNDERSTAND, take, take to mean, read.

interrogate verb QUESTION, put/pose questions to, examine, cross-examine, give the third degree to, inquire of, quiz, probe; *informal* put the screws on, pump, grill.

interrogation noun QUESTIONING, cross-examination, inquisition, investigation, grilling, probing, inquiry; *informal* the third degree.

interrogative adjective INQUISITIVE, questioning, quizzical, inquiring, curious, investigative, inquisitorial, probing.

interrupt verb ❶ CUT IN ON, break in on, barge in on, intrude on, butt in on, disturb, heckle, interfere with; *informal* chime in on, horn in on, muscle in on; *Brit. informal* chip in on. ❷ SUSPEND, discontinue, break, break off, hold up, delay, lay aside, leave off, postpone, stop, put a stop to, halt, bring to a halt/standstill, cease, end, cancel, sever.

interruption noun ❶ INTERFERENCE, disturbance, intrusion, butting in, obtrusion; *informal* horning in. ❷ SUSPENSION, discontinuance, breaking off, delay, postponement, stopping, halt, cessation. ❸ INTERMISSION, interval, interlude, break, pause, recess, gap, hiatus.

intersect verb ❶ CUT ACROSS/THROUGH, cut in two, divide, bisect. ❷ CROSS, criss-cross, meet, connect.

intersection noun JUNCTION, interchange, crossroads, roundabout, spaghetti junction.

interval noun ❶ INTERLUDE, interim, intervening time, time, period, meantime, meanwhile, wait, space. ❷ INTERMISSION, break, half-time, pause, lull, respite, breather, breathing space, gap, hiatus, delay.

intervene verb ❶ **the years that intervened:** COME/OCCUR BETWEEN, occur, happen, arise, take place, ensue, supervene, succeed; *poetic/literary* come to pass. ❷ **intervene in the dispute:** INTERCEDE, mediate, arbitrate, negotiate, step in, involve oneself, come into, interpose, interfere, intrude.

interview noun ❶ APPRAISAL, evaluation, discussion, meeting, talk, dialogue. ❷ AUDIENCE, question and answer session, exchange, dialogue, colloquy, interlocution.
▶ verb TALK TO, have a discussion/dialogue with, hold a meeting with, confer with, question, put questions to, sound out, examine, interrogate, cross-examine, evaluate.

interweave verb ❶ **interweave strands:** WEAVE, intertwine, twine, twist, interlace, braid, plait. ❷ **their financial affairs are interwoven:** INTERMINGLE, mingle, interlink, intermix, mix, blend, interlock, knit, connect, associate.

intimate[1] adjective ❶ intimate friends: CLOSE, near, dear, nearest and dearest, cherished, bosom, familiar, confidential, warm, friendly, comradely, amicable. ❷ an intimate atmosphere: INFORMAL, warm, cosy, friendly, comfortable, snug. ❸ intimate details: PERSONAL, private, confidential, secret, privy.
–OPPOSITES distant.

intimate[2] verb ❶ ANNOUNCE, make known, state, tell, inform, communicate, impart. ❷ IMPLY, suggest, let it be known, hint, insinuate, give an inkling that, indicate, signal; *informal* tip someone the wink.

intimidate verb FRIGHTEN, terrify, scare, alarm, terrorize, overawe, awe, cow, subdue, daunt, domineer, browbeat, bully, tyrannize, coerce, compel, bulldoze, pressure, pressurize, threaten; *informal* push around, lean on, twist someone's arm.

intolerable adjective UNBEARABLE, unendurable, beyond endurance, insufferable, insupportable, not to be borne, more than one can stand, impossible, painful, excruciating, agonizing.

intolerant adjective BIGOTED, illiberal, narrow-minded, narrow, parochial, provincial, insular, small-minded, prejudiced, biased, partisan, one-sided, warped, twisted, fanatical, chauvinistic, jingoistic, racist, xenophobic, sexist, ageist, homophobic.
–OPPOSITES tolerant.

intonation noun PITCH, tone, timbre, cadence, lilt, inflection, accentuation, emphasis, stress.

intoxicate verb ❶ INEBRIATE, make drunk, befuddle, fuddle, stupefy. ❷ EXHILARATE, elate, thrill, invigorate, animate, enliven, excite, arouse, inflame, enrapture.

intoxicated adjective *see* DRUNK.

intractable adjective UNMANAGEABLE, ungovernable, uncontrollable, stubborn, obstinate, obdurate, perverse, disobedient, indomitable, refractory, recalcitrant, insubordinate, rebellious, wild, unruly, rowdy.
–OPPOSITES manageable.

intricate adjective ❶ intricate patterns: TANGLED, entangled, ravelled, twisted, knotty, convoluted, involute, maze-like, labyrinthine, winding, serpentine, circuitous, sinuous, fancy, elaborate, ornate, Byzantine, rococo. ❷ intricate problems: COMPLEX, complicated, difficult, involved, perplexing, puzzling, thorny, mystifying, enigmatic, obscure.
–OPPOSITES simple.

intrigue verb ❶ INTEREST, absorb, arouse someone's curiosity, attract, draw, pull, rivet someone's attention, rivet, fascinate, charm, captivate, divert, pique, titillate. ❷ PLOT, conspire, scheme, connive, manoeuvre, machinate, devise.
–OPPOSITES bore.
▶ noun PLOT, conspiracy, collusion, cabal, scheme, ruse, stratagem, wile, dodge, artifice, manoeuvre, machination, trickery, sharp practice, double-dealing.

intrinsic adjective INHERENT, inborn, inbred, congenital, natural, native, indigenous, constitutional, built-in, ingrained, implanted, basic, fundamental, elemental, essential, true, genuine, real, authentic.

introduce verb ❶ PRESENT, make known, acquaint, make acquainted. ❷ PRESENT, announce, give an introduction to. ❸ PREFACE, precede, lead into, commence, start off, begin. ❹ BRING IN, bring into being, originate, launch, inaugurate, institute, initiate, establish, found, set in motion, organize, develop, start, begin, commence, usher in, pioneer. ❺ introduce a note of solemnity: INSERT, inject, interject, interpose, interpolate, intercalate, add, bring, infuse, instil.

introduction noun FOREWORD, preface, front matter, preamble, prologue, prelude, exordium, lead-in; *informal* intro, prelims.
– OPPOSITES afterword.

introductory adjective ❶ introductory remarks: PREFATORY, preliminary, precursory, lead-in, initiatory, opening, initial, starting. ❷ an introductory course: PREPARATORY, elementary, basic, basal, rudimentary, fundamental, initiatory.
– OPPOSITES closing.

introspective adjective INWARD-LOOKING, inner-directed, introverted, self-analysing, self-examining, subjective, contemplative, reflective, meditative, musing, pensive, brooding, preoccupied.

intrude verb ❶ INTERRUPT, push/thrust oneself in, gatecrash, barge in, encroach, butt in, interfere, obtrude. ❷ intrude on their grief: ENCROACH ON, invade, impinge on, infringe on, trespass on, obtrude on, violate.

intruder noun ❶ BURGLAR, housebreaker, thief, raider, invader, prowler, trespasser. ❷ UNWELCOME GUEST/VISITOR, gatecrasher, interloper, infiltrator.

intuition noun ❶ INSTINCT, sixth sense, divination, presentiment, clairvoyance, second sight, extrasensory perception, ESP. ❷ FEELING, feeling in one's bones, hunch, inkling, presentiment, foreboding.

inundate verb ❶ FLOOD, deluge, overrun, swamp, submerge, engulf, drown, cover, saturate, soak. ❷ OVERWHELM, overpower, overburden, swamp, bog down, glut.

inure verb HARDEN, toughen, season, temper, habituate, familiarize, accustom, naturalize, acclimatize.

invade verb ❶ ATTACK, assail, assault, overrun, occupy, storm, take over, descend upon, make inroads on, raid, plunder. ❷ invade their privacy: INTRUDE ON, obtrude on, encroach on, infringe on, trespass on, burst in on, violate.
– OPPOSITES withdraw.

invalid adjective ❶ INOPERATIVE, legally void, null, null and void, void, not binding, nullified, revoked, rescinded, abolished. ❷ an invalid argument: UNJUSTIFIED, unsubstantiated, unwarranted, untenable, illogical, irrational, unscientific, false, faulty, fallacious, spurious, unacceptable, inadequate, unconvincing, ineffectual, unsound, weak, useless, worthless.

invaluable adjective PRICELESS, beyond price, inestimable,

precious, costly, worth its weight in gold, worth a king's ransom.
– OPPOSITES worthless.

invariable adjective UNCHANGING, changeless, unchangeable, constant, unvarying, unvaried, invariant, unalterable, immutable, fixed, stable, set, steady, unwavering, static, uniform, regular, consistent.
– OPPOSITES varied.

invariably adverb ALWAYS, every/each time, on every occasion, at all times, without fail/exception, regularly, consistently, repeatedly, habitually, unfailingly, infallibly, inevitably.

invasion noun ❶ OVERRUNNING, occupation, incursion, offensive, attack, assailing, assault, raid, foray, onslaught, plundering. ❷ invasion of privacy: INTRUSION, obtrusion, encroachment, infringement, breach, infraction, trespass, violation.

inveigle verb PERSUADE, talk into, cajole, wheedle, coax, beguile, tempt, decoy, lure, entice, seduce, deceive; *informal* sweet-talk.

invent verb ❶ ORIGINATE, create, innovate, discover, design, devise, contrive, formulate, think up, conceive, come up with, hit upon, compose, frame, coin. ❷ MAKE UP, fabricate, concoct, hatch, trump up, forge; *informal* cook up.

invention noun ❶ ORIGINATION, creation, innovation, discovery, design, contrivance, construction, coinage; *informal* brainchild. ❷ INVENTIVENESS, originality, creativity, creativeness, imagination, artistry, inspiration, ingenuity, resourcefulness, genius.

inventive adjective ORIGINAL, creative, innovational, imaginative, artistic, inspired, ingenious, resourceful, innovative, gifted, talented, skilful, clever.
– OPPOSITES unimaginative.

inventor noun ORIGINATOR, creator, innovator, discoverer, author, architect, designer, deviser, developer, initiator, coiner, father, prime mover, maker, framer, producer.

inventory noun LIST, listing, checklist, catalogue, record, register, tally, account, description, statement.

inverse adjective OPPOSITE, converse, contrary, reverse, counter.

invert verb ❶ TURN UPSIDE DOWN, upturn, turn inside out. ❷ TURN UPSIDE DOWN, overturn, upturn, turn turtle, capsize, upset.

invest verb ❶ invest in the business: PUT/SINK MONEY INTO, lay out money on, provide capital for, fund, subsidize. ❷ invest money/energy in the venture: SPEND, expend, lay out, put in, use up, devote, contribute, donate, give. ❸ invest power in: VEST, endow, confer, bestow, grant, entrust, give, place.

investigate verb INQUIRE INTO, make inquiries about, go/look into, research, probe, explore, search, scrutinize, study, examine, inspect, consider, sift, analyse; *informal* check out; *Brit. informal* suss out.

investigation noun INQUIRY, fact-finding, search, scrutinization, scrutiny, research, probe, exploration, study, survey, review, examination, inspection, consideration, sifting, analysis, inquest, hearing, questioning, inquisition.

inveterate adjective CONFIRMED, habitual, inured, hardened, chronic, die-hard, deep-dyed, dyed-in-the-wool, long-standing, addicted, hard-core, incorrigible.

invidious adjective ❶ invidious comparisons: DISCRIMINATORY, unfair, prejudicial, slighting, offensive, objectionable, deleterious, detrimental. ❷ an invidious position: UNPLEASANT, awkward, unpopular, repugnant, hateful.
– OPPOSITES fair, pleasant.

invigorate verb REVITALIZE, energize, fortify, strengthen, put new strength/life/heart in, brace, refresh, rejuvenate, enliven, liven up, animate, exhilarate, perk up, stimulate, motivate, rouse, excite, wake up, galvanize, electrify; *informal* pep up.
– OPPOSITES tire.

invincible adjective ❶ UNCONQUERABLE, undefeatable, unbeatable, unassailable, invulnerable, indestructible, impregnable, indomitable, unyielding, unflinching, dauntless. ❷ INSUPERABLE, unsurmountable, overwhelming, overpowering.
– OPPOSITES vulnerable.

inviolable adjective INALIENABLE, untouchable, unalterable, sacrosanct, sacred, holy, hallowed.

invisible adjective UNSEEABLE, out of sight, undetectable, imperceptible, indiscernible, indistinguishable, unseen, unnoticed, unobserved, hidden, concealed, inconspicuous, unnoticeable.

invite verb ❶ they invited him to dinner: ASK, bid, summon, request someone's company/presence. ❷ invite applications: ASK FOR, request, call for, solicit, look for, seek, appeal for, petition, summon. ❸ invite disaster: CAUSE, bring on, bring upon oneself, induce, provoke.

inviting adjective ATTRACTIVE, appealing, pleasant, agreeable, delightful, engaging, tempting, enticing, alluring, irresistible, ravishing, seductive.
– OPPOSITES repellent.

invocation noun CALL, prayer, request, petition, appeal, supplication, entreaty, solicitation, imploring, importuning; *poetic/literary* beseeching.

invoke verb CALL FOR, call up, pray for, request, supplicate, entreat, solicit, beg, implore, importune, call on, petition, appeal to; *poetic/literary* beseech.

involuntary adjective ❶ an involuntary reaction: REFLEXIVE, reflex, automatic, mechanical, unconditioned, spontaneous, instinctive, instinctual, unconscious, unthinking, unintentional, uncontrolled. ❷ involuntary help: UNWILLING, against one's will/wishes, reluctant, grudging, forced, coerced, coercive, compelled, compulsory, obligatory.
– OPPOSITES deliberate, voluntary.

involve verb ❶ ENTAIL, imply, mean, denote, betoken, connote, require, necessitate, presuppose. ❷ involve everyone: INCLUDE, count in, cover, embrace, take in, number, incorporate, encompass, comprise, contain, comprehend.

❸ something that involves them: INTEREST, be of interest to, absorb, engage, engage/hold someone's attention, rivet, grip, occupy, preoccupy, engross.
– OPPOSITES preclude, exclude.

involved adjective COMPLICATED, difficult, intricate, complex, elaborate, confused, confusing, mixed up, jumbled, tangled, entangled, convoluted, knotty, tortuous, labyrinthine, Byzantine.

iota noun BIT, mite, speck, atom, jot, whit, particle, fraction, morsel, grain; *informal* smidgen.

ironic adjective ❶ SATIRICAL, mocking, derisive, scornful, sardonic, wry, double-edged, sarcastic. ❷ PARADOXICAL, incongruous.

irons plural noun FETTERS, chains, shackles, bonds, manacles.

irrational adjective ❶ irrational fears: ILLOGICAL, unreasonable, groundless, unsound, implausible, absurd, ridiculous, silly, foolish, senseless, nonsensical, ludicrous, preposterous, crazy. ❷ an irrational person: ILLOGICAL, muddled, muddle-headed, confused, demented, insane, crazy, unstable.
– OPPOSITES rational.

irrefutable adjective INCONTROVERTIBLE, incontestable, indisputable, undeniable, unquestionable, beyond question, indubitable, beyond doubt, conclusive, decisive, definite.

irregular adjective ❶ an irregular coastline: ASYMMETRIC, unsymmetrical, uneven, broken, jagged, ragged, serrated, crooked, curving, craggy. ❷ an irregular pulse: UNEVEN, unsteady, shaky, fitful, variable, erratic, spasmodic, wavering, fluctuating, aperiodic. ❸ an irregular attender: INCONSISTENT, erratic, sporadic, variable, inconstant, desultory, haphazard, intermittent, occasional. ❹ it was most irregular: OUT OF ORDER, against the rules, unofficial, unorthodox, unconventional, abnormal.

irrelevant adjective IMMATERIAL, unrelated, unconnected, inapposite, inapt, inapplicable, non-germane, inappropriate, extraneous, beside the point, not to the point, out of place; *informal* nothing to do with it, neither here nor there.

irreparable adjective BEYOND REPAIR, past mending, irreversible, irrevocable, irretrievable, irrecoverable, irremediable, incurable, ruinous.

irreplaceable adjective PRICELESS, invaluable, precious, unique, worth its weight in gold, rare.

irrepressible adjective ❶ irrepressible optimism: INEXTINGUISHABLE, unquenchable, uncontainable, uncontrollable, unstoppable, unreserved, unchecked, unbridled. ❷ irrepressible children: BUOYANT, effervescent, ebullient, vivacious, animated, spirited, lively.

irreproachable adjective BEYOND REPROACH, blameless, faultless, guiltless, sinless, innocent, unimpeachable, inculpable, impeccable, immaculate, unblemished, stainless, pure.
– OPPOSITES reprehensible.

irresistible adjective ❶ an irresistible impulse: OVERWHELMING, overpowering, compelling, irrepressible, forceful, potent, imperative, urgent. ❷ an irresistible woman: FASCINATING, alluring, enticing, seductive, captivating, enchanting, ravishing, tempting, tantalizing.

irresolute adjective UNCERTAIN, unsure, doubtful, dubious, undecided, indecisive, unresolved, undetermined, unsettled, vacillating, wavering, hesitant, hesitating, tentative, in two minds, oscillating.
– OPPOSITES resolute.

irresponsible adjective ❶ irresponsible people: UNDEPENDABLE, unreliable, untrustworthy, careless, reckless, rash, flighty, giddy, scatterbrained, erratic, hare-brained, feather-brained, immature. ❷ irresponsible actions: THOUGHTLESS, ill-considered, unwise, injudicious, careless, reckless, immature.
– OPPOSITES sensible.

irreverent adjective ❶ DISRESPECTFUL, impertinent, insolent, impudent, rude, cheeky, discourteous, impolite, uncivil. ❷ IMPIOUS, irreligious, heretical, sacrilegious, ungodly, blasphemous, profane.
– OPPOSITES respectful.

irrevocable adjective UNALTERABLE, unchangeable, irreversible, fixed, settled, fated, immutable, predetermined, predestined.

irrigation noun WATERING, wetting, spraying, sprinkling, moistening, soaking, flooding, inundating.

irritable adjective BAD-TEMPERED, ill-tempered, ill-humoured, irascible, cross, edgy, testy, touchy, crabbed, peevish, petulant, cantankerous, grumpy, grouchy, crusty, dyspeptic, choleric, splenetic; *informal* snappish, snappy.
– OPPOSITES good-humoured, cheerful.

irritate verb ❶ ANNOY, vex, provoke, irk, nettle, get on someone's nerves, exasperate, infuriate, anger, enrage, incense, make someone's hackles rise, ruffle, disturb, put out, bother, pester, try someone's patience; *Brit.* rub up the wrong way; *informal* aggravate, peeve, get someone's goat, get someone's back up, get up someone's nose, drive up the wall, drive bananas. ❷ it irritated her skin: CHAFE, fret, rub, pain, hurt, inflame, aggravate.

irritation noun ❶ IRRITABILITY, annoyance, impatience, vexation, exasperation, indignation, crossness, ill temper, anger, fury, rage, wrath, displeasure; *informal* aggravation; *poetic/literary* ire. ❷ SOURCE OF ANNOYANCE, annoyance, irritant, pest, nuisance, thorn in the flesh; *informal* pain in the neck, pain.

isolate verb SET APART, segregate, cut off, separate, detach, abstract, quarantine, keep in solitude, sequester, insulate.

isolated adjective ❶ feeling isolated: ALONE, solitary, lonely, separated, exiled, forsaken, forlorn. ❷ an isolated place: REMOTE, out of the way, off the beaten track, outlying, secluded, hidden, unfrequented, lonely, desolate, godforsaken. ❸ an isolated example: SINGLE, solitary, unique, random, unrelated, unusual, uncommon, exceptional, abnormal, atypical, untypical, anomalous, freak.

issue noun ❶ debate the issue: MATTER, matter in question, point at issue, question, subject, topic, affair, problem, bone of contention, controversy, argument. ❷ the issue is still in doubt: RESULT, outcome, decision, upshot, end, conclusion, consequence, termination, effect, denouement. ❸ the next issue of the magazine: EDITION, number, printing, print run, impression, copy, instalment, version. ❹ the issue of the new shares: ISSUING, issuance, publication, circulation, distribution, supplying, supply, dissemination, sending out, delivery.
▶ verb ❶ issue a statement: PUT OUT, give out, deal out, send out, distribute, circulate, release, disseminate, announce, proclaim, broadcast. ❷ smoke issuing from the chimney: EMIT, exude, discharge, emanate, gush, pour forth, seep, ooze. ❸ people issued from the building: EMERGE, come out, come forth, appear, leave.

itch verb ❶ TINGLE, prickle, tickle, be irritated, be itchy. ❷ itch for something: LONG, have a longing, yearn, hanker, pine, ache, burn, hunger, thirst, lust, desire greatly, crave.
▶ noun ❶ TINGLING, irritation, itchiness, prickling, tickling; *Medicine* formication, paraesthesia. ❷ an itch for something: GREAT DESIRE, longing, yearning, craving, hankering, ache, burning, hunger, thirst, lust; *informal* yen.

item noun ❶ ARTICLE, thing, piece of merchandise, goods. ❷ POINT, detail, matter, consideration, particular, feature, circumstance, aspect, element, ingredient.

Jj

jab noun POKE, prod, dig, nudge, elbow, thrust, stab, bump, tap, punch; *informal* sock, biff.

jabber verb CHATTER, gibber, prattle, babble, gabble, prate, blather, clack, rattle, ramble.

jacket noun CASING, case, encasement, sheath, sheathing, envelope, cover, covering, wrapping, wrapper, wrap.

jaded adjective TIRED, weary, fatigued, worn out, exhausted, spent; *informal* played out, bushed, done, done in; *Brit. informal* fagged out; *N. Amer. informal* pooped.
– OPPOSITES fresh.

jagged adjective SERRATED, toothed, notched, indented, nicked, pointed, snaggy, spiked, barbed, uneven, rough, ridged, ragged, craggy, broken, cleft.
– OPPOSITES smooth.

jam verb ❶ WEDGE, sandwich, insert, force, ram, thrust, push, stick, press, cram, stuff. ❷ CRAM, pack, crowd, squeeze, crush. ❸ BECOME STUCK, stick, stall, halt, stop.
▶ noun ❶ TRAFFIC JAM, hold-up, obstruction, congestion,

bottleneck, stoppage; *N. Amer.* gridlock. ❷ PREDICAMENT, plight, straits, trouble, quandary; *informal* fix, pickle, hole, spot, tight spot, scrape; *Brit. informal* spot of bother.

jamboree noun RALLY, party, get-together, celebration, festivity, festival, carnival, jubilee, revelry, merrymaking, spree; *informal* do, shindig, blowout, bash; *Brit. informal* beanfeast, rave-up.

jar verb ❶ GRATE, rasp, scratch, squeak, screech. ❷ **her manner jarred on him:** GRATE ON, irritate, disturb, upset, discompose, irk, annoy, nettle, vex. ❸ **his views jarred with hers:** CLASH, conflict, be in opposition, be at variance, be at odds.

jargon noun CANT, slang, argot, idiom, usage, vernacular, dialect, patois; *informal* lingo.

jaundiced adjective CYNICAL, pessimistic, sceptical, distrustful, suspicious, misanthropic, bitter, resentful, jealous, envious.

jaunt noun TRIP, outing, excursion, expedition, tour, holiday, break, airing, stroll, ramble.

jaunty adjective SPRIGHTLY, bouncy, buoyant, lively, breezy, perky, frisky, merry, blithe, carefree, joyful. *See also* HAPPY (1).

jazz

■ **jazz up** BRIGHTEN UP, liven up, enliven, put some spirit into, put some animation into, add some colour to, enhance.

jazzy adjective FLASHY, fancy, stylish, smart, gaudy; *informal* flash, snazzy.

jealous adjective ❶ ENVIOUS, begrudging, grudging, resentful, green with envy, green-eyed, covetous, desirous, emulous. ❷ **a jealous lover:** SUSPICIOUS, possessive, distrustful, mistrustful, doubting, insecure. ❸ **jealous of something:** PROTECTIVE, vigilant, watchful, heedful, mindful, careful, solicitous, on guard, wary.
– OPPOSITES trusting.

jeer verb MOCK, ridicule, deride, taunt, gibe, scorn, cry down, hector, barrack, boo, hiss, tease, scoff at, laugh at, sneer at; *informal* knock.
– OPPOSITES cheer.

jell verb ❶ SET, stiffen, solidify, harden, thicken, congeal, coagulate. ❷ **ideas beginning to jell:** TAKE SHAPE, take form, form, crystallize, come together.

jeopardy noun RISK, danger, endangerment, peril, hazard, precariousness, insecurity, vulnerability, threat, menace.
– OPPOSITES safety.

jerk verb ❶ PULL, yank, tug, wrench, tweak, pluck. ❷ JOLT, lurch, bump, jump, bounce, jounce.
▶ **noun** ❶ PULL, yank, tug, wrench, tweak. ❷ JOLT, lurch, bump, start, jar. ❸ *See* IDIOT.

jerky adjective ❶ SPASMODIC, fitful, convulsive, twitchy, shaking, shaky, tremulous, uncontrolled. ❷ JOLTING, lurching, bumpy, bouncy, jouncing, rough; *informal* jumpy.
– OPPOSITES smooth.

jester noun ❶ COMIC, comedian, humorist, wag, wit. ❷ FOOL, clown, buffoon, merry andrew, harlequin, pantaloon.

jet noun ❶ STREAM, gush, spurt, spout, spray, rush, fountain, spring. ❷ NOZZLE, spout, nose, sprinkler, sprinkler head, spray,

rose, atomizer.
▶ **verb** SHOOT, gush, spurt, spout, well, rush, spray, squirt, spew, stream, surge, flow, issue.

jetty **noun** PIER, wharf, quay, harbour, dock, breakwater, mole, groyne.

jewel **noun** GEM, gemstone, precious stone, stone, brilliant; *informal* sparkler, rock.

jib **verb** BALK AT, recoil from, shrink from, stop short of, refuse.

jibe **noun** TAUNT, sneer, jeer, mocking, sneering, scoffing, scorn, derision, ridicule, teasing, sarcasm; *informal* dig.

jiffy **noun** MOMENT, second, split second, minute, instant, flash, trice, twinkling of an eye; *informal* two shakes of a lamb's tail.

jilt **verb** REJECT, cast aside, discard, throw over, leave, forsake; *informal* ditch, dump, give the brush-off to, give the heave-ho, give the elbow.

jingle **verb** ❶ CLINK, chink, jangle, rattle, clank. ❷ TINKLE, ding, go ding-dong, go ting-a-ling, ring, chime.
▶ **noun** DITTY, chorus, refrain, short song, limerick, piece of doggerel, carol, melody, tune, catchy tune.

job **noun** ❶ WORK, piece of work, task, undertaking, chore, assignment, venture, enterprise, activity, business, affair.
❷ OCCUPATION, profession, trade, employment, vocation, calling, career, field of work, means of livelihood, métier, pursuit, position, post, situation, appointment. ❸ DUTY, task, chore, errand, responsibility, concern, role, charge, office, commission, capacity, contribution.

jobless **adjective** UNEMPLOYED, without employment, out of work, without work, workless, idle, inactive, unoccupied.
– OPPOSITES employed.

jocular **adjective** HUMOROUS, funny, witty, comic, comical, facetious, joking, jesting, playful, roguish, waggish, whimsical, droll, jocose, teasing, sportive, amusing, entertaining, diverting, hilarious, farcical, laughable.
– OPPOSITES serious.

jog **verb** ❶ GO JOGGING, run slowly, dogtrot, trot, canter, lope. ❷ **jog him in the ribs:** NUDGE, prod, poke, push, elbow, tap. ❸ **the sight jogged her memory:** STIMULATE, activate, stir, arouse, prompt.

join **verb** ❶ FASTEN, attach, tie, bind, couple, connect, unite, link, splice, yoke, knit, glue, cement, fuse, weld, solder. ❷ **we joined them:** JOIN FORCES WITH, team up with, band together with, cooperate with, collaborate with, affiliate with. ❸ **join the army:** ENLIST, sign up, enrol, become a member of, enlist in, sign up for, enrol in. ❹ **his land joins ours:** ADJOIN, conjoin, abut on, border, border on, touch, meet, verge on, reach to, extend to.
– OPPOSITES detach, leave.

joint **noun** JOIN, junction, juncture, intersection, nexus, knot, seam, coupling.
▶ **adjective** COMMON, shared, joined, mutual, combined, collective, cooperative, allied, united, concerted, consolidated.
– OPPOSITES separate.

jointly **adverb** TOGETHER, in combination, in conjunction, as one, mutually, in partnership, cooperatively, in cooperation, in league, in collusion; *informal* in cahoots.

joke noun ❶ JEST, witticism, quip, yarn, pun, sally; *informal* wisecrack, crack, gag, funny. ❷ PRACTICAL JOKE, prank, trick, hoax, jape; *informal* leg-pull, lark. ❸ LAUGHING STOCK, butt, figure of fun, target, fair game, Aunt Sally.
▶ verb ❶ TELL JOKES, crack jokes, jest, banter, quip, wisecrack. ❷ FOOL, fool around, tease, pull someone's leg; *informal* kid, have someone on.

jolly adjective MERRY, joyful, joyous, jovial, happy, glad, mirthful, gleeful, cheerful, cheery, carefree, buoyant, lively, bright, light-hearted, jocund, sprightly, elated, exuberant, exhilarated, jubilant, high-spirited, sportive, playful; *dated* gay; *poetic/literary* blithe.
– OPPOSITES miserable.

jolt verb ❶ BUMP AGAINST, knock against, bump into, bang into, collide with, jostle, push, shove, elbow, nudge, jar. ❷ BUMP, bounce, jounce, start, jerk, lurch, jar. ❸ **the accident jolted him:** UPSET, disturb, perturb, shake, shake up, shock, stun, disconcert, discompose, disquiet, startle, surprise, astonish, amaze, stagger.

jostle verb ❶ BUMP AGAINST, knock against, bump into, bang into, collide with, jolt, push, shove, elbow. ❷ PUSH, thrust, shove, press, squeeze, elbow, force.

jot noun IOTA, whit, bit, scrap, fraction, atom, grain, particle, morsel, mite, speck, trace, trifle, tinge; *informal* smidgen, tad.

journal noun ❶ DIARY, daybook, notebook, commonplace book, log, logbook, chronicle, record, register. ❷ PERIODICAL, magazine, trade magazine, review, publication. ❸ NEWSPAPER, paper, daily newspaper, daily, weekly newspaper, weekly, gazette.

journalist noun REPORTER, newspaperman/woman, newsman/woman, news hound, pressman/woman, feature writer, columnist, correspondent, contributor, commentator, reviewer, editor, subeditor; *informal* stringer, sub.

journey noun TRIP, expedition, excursion, travels, tour, trek, voyage, cruise, safari, peregrination, roaming, roving, globetrotting, odyssey, pilgrimage, outing, jaunt.
▶ verb *see* TRAVEL (1).

jovial adjective JOLLY, jocular, jocose, jocund, happy, cheerful, cheery, glad, in good spirits, merry, mirthful, buoyant, animated, convivial, sociable, cordial; *dated* gay; *poetic/literary* blithe.
– OPPOSITES miserable.

joy noun ❶ DELIGHT, pleasure, gladness, enjoyment, gratification, happiness, rapture, glee, bliss, ecstasy, elation, rejoicing, exultation, jubilation, euphoria, ravishment, transport, felicity. ❷ SOURCE OF JOY, treasure, prize, gem, jewel, pride and joy, delight. ❸ **we had no joy:** SUCCESS, satisfaction, good fortune, luck, achievement.
– OPPOSITES misery.

joyful adjective ❶ OVERJOYED, elated, beside oneself, thrilled, delighted, pleased, gratified, happy, glad, gleeful, jubilant, ecstatic, exultant, euphoric, enraptured; *informal* over the moon, in seventh heaven, on cloud nine, tickled pink; *poetic/literary* blithe. ❷ **the joyful news:** GLAD, happy, good, pleasing, cheering, gratifying,

heart-warming. ❸ a joyful occasion: JOYOUS, happy, cheerful, merry, festive, celebratory; *dated* gay.
– OPPOSITES unhappy.

joyless adjective GLOOMY, dreary, drab, dismal, bleak, depressing, cheerless, grim, desolate, comfortless.

judge verb ❶ judge the contest: ADJUDICATE, adjudge, umpire, referee, arbitrate, mediate. ❷ judge his conduct: ASSESS, appraise, evaluate, weigh up, size up, gauge, examine, review, criticize, diagnose. ❸ judge the distance: ESTIMATE, assess, reckon, guess, surmise; *informal* guesstimate. ❹ judge him to be: CONSIDER, believe, think, form the opinion, deduce, gather, conclude.
▶ noun ❶ MAGISTRATE, sheriff, His/Her/Your Honour; *Brit.* m'lud; *Brit. informal* beak. ❷ APPRAISER, assessor, evaluator, critic, expert. ❸ ADJUDICATOR, umpire, referee, arbiter, arbitrator, mediator.

judgement noun ❶ he has no judgement: DISCERNMENT, acumen, shrewdness, common sense, good sense, sense, perception, perspicacity, percipience, penetration, discrimination, wisdom, judiciousness, prudence, sagacity, understanding, intelligence, powers of reasoning. ❷ he gave his judgement: VERDICT, decision, adjudication, ruling, finding, opinion, conclusion, decree, sentence. ❸ in her judgement: OPINION, view, belief, conviction, estimation, evaluation, assessment, appraisal.

judicial adjective ❶ JUDICIARY, juridical, judicatory, legal. ❷ JUDGELIKE, impartial, unbiased, critical, analytical, discriminating, discerning, perceptive.

judicious adjective WISE, prudent, politic, sagacious, shrewd, astute, sensible, common-sense, sound, well advised, well considered, well judged, considered, thoughtful, expedient, practical, discerning, discriminating, informed, intelligent, clever, enlightened, logical, rational, discreet, careful, cautious, circumspect, diplomatic; *informal* smart.
– OPPOSITES injudicious, foolish.

jug noun PITCHER, carafe, decanter, jar, urn, crock, vessel, receptacle, container.

juggle verb CHANGE AROUND, alter, tamper with, falsify, fake, manipulate, manoeuvre, rig, massage; *informal* fix, doctor, cook.

juice noun EXTRACT, sap, secretion, liquid, liquor, fluid, serum.

juicy adjective ❶ SUCCULENT, moist, lush, sappy, watery, wet, flowing. ❷ a juicy tale: RACY, risqué, spicy, sensational, thrilling, fascinating, colourful, exciting, vivid.
– OPPOSITES dry, dull.

jumble verb DISORGANIZE, muddle, confuse, disarrange, disorder, dishevel, tangle, shuffle, mix, mix up, mingle, put in disarray, make a shambles of, throw into chaos.
▶ noun CLUTTER, muddle, confusion, litter, mess, hodgepodge, hotchpotch, mishmash, confused heap, miscellany, motley collection, mixture, medley, gallimaufry, farrago.

jump verb ❶ SPRING, leap, bound, hop, bounce, skip, caper, gambol, frolic, frisk, cavort. ❷ jump over the rope: LEAP OVER, vault, pole-vault, hurdle, clear, go over,

sail over. ❸ START, flinch, jerk, recoil, twitch, quiver, shake, wince; *informal* jump out of one's skin. ❹ **they jumped him:** SET UPON, mug, pounce on, fall on, swoop down on, attack, assault.
▶ **noun** ❶ SPRING, leap, vault, bound, hop, bounce, skip. ❷ HURDLE, fence, rail, hedge, obstacle, barrier, gate. ❸ GAP, break, hiatus, interruption, space, lacuna, breach, interval. ❹ START, flinch, jerk, twitch, quiver, shake, wince.

jumpy **adjective** NERVOUS, nervy, edgy, on edge, agitated, fidgety, anxious, uneasy, restive, tense, alarmed, apprehensive, panicky; *informal* jittery.
– OPPOSITES calm.

junction **noun** ❶ JOIN, joint, juncture, link, bond, connection, seam, joining, coupling, linking, welding, union. ❷ CROSSROADS, crossing, intersection, interchange.

juncture **noun** POINT, point in time, time, stage, period, critical point, crucial moment, moment of truth, turning point, crisis, crux, extremity.

junior **adjective** YOUNGER, subordinate, lesser, lower, minor, secondary, inferior.
– OPPOSITES senior, older.

junk **noun** RUBBISH, refuse, litter, scrap, waste, garbage, trash, debris, leavings, leftovers, remnants, cast-offs, rejects, odds and ends, bric-a-brac, oddments.
▶ **verb** THROW OUT, throw away, discard, get rid of, dispose of, scrap; *informal* dump.

just **adjective** ❶ **a just judge:** FAIR, fair-minded, equitable, even-handed, impartial, unbiased, objective, neutral, disinterested, unprejudiced, open-minded. ❷ **just criticism:** VALID, sound, well founded, well grounded, justified, justifiable, warrantable, defensible, reasonable.
– OPPOSITES unjust, undeserved.

justice **noun** ❶ JUSTNESS, fairness, fair play, fair-mindedness, equitableness, equity, even-handedness, impartiality, lack of bias, objectivity, neutrality, disinterestedness, lack of prejudice, open-mindedness. ❷ **the justice of his criticism:** VALIDITY, justification, soundness, reasonableness. ❸ **demand justice:** AMENDS, recompense, redress, compensation, reparation, requital, retribution, penalty, punishment.
– OPPOSITES injustice.

justifiable **adjective** VALID, sound, well founded, lawful, legitimate, legal, tenable, right, defensible, supportable, sustainable, warrantable, reasonable, within reason, sensible, acceptable, plausible, vindicable.

justify **verb** ❶ **justify his behaviour:** GIVE GROUNDS FOR, give reasons for, show just cause for, explain, give an explanation for, rationalize, defend, stand up for, uphold. ❷ **justified our worries:** WARRANT, substantiate, bear out, show to be reasonable, prove to be right, confirm.

jut **verb** STICK OUT, project, protrude, poke out, bulge out, overhang, beetle.

juvenile **adjective** ❶ YOUNG, junior, minor. ❷ **a juvenile attitude:** CHILDISH, puerile, infantile, immature, inexperienced, callow, green, unsophisticated, naive; *informal* wet behind the ears.

Kk

kaleidoscopic adjective ❶ MANY-COLOURED, variegated, motley, rainbow-like, many-splendoured, psychedelic. ❷ a kaleidoscopic scene: CHANGEABLE, ever-changing, variable, varying, mutable, protean, ever-moving, fluid, mobile, unstable, unsteady, labile.

keen adjective ❶ EAGER, enthusiastic, willing, avid, earnest, intent, diligent, assiduous, conscientious, zealous, fervent, fervid, impatient. ❷ keen on something: FOND OF, devoted to, eager for, hungry for, thirsty for. ❸ keen to learn: EAGER TO, longing to, yearning to, impatient to; *informal* raring to, itching to. ❹ a keen edge: SHARP, sharp-edged, sharpened, fine-edged, razor-sharp. ❺ a keen sense of smell: SHARP, acute, discerning, perceptive, sensitive, discriminating. ❻ a keen mind: SHARP, astute, quick-witted, sharp-witted, shrewd, perceptive, penetrating, perspicacious, clever, bright, intelligent, brilliant, wise, canny, sagacious; *informal* brainy, smart; *formal* sapient. ❼ her keen wit: ACERBIC, acid, biting, caustic, tart, pointed, mordant, trenchant, incisive, razor-like, razor-sharp, finely honed, cutting, stinging, scathing, sardonic, satirical.
– OPPOSITES apathetic, blunt.

keep verb ❶ keep going: CARRY ON, continue, maintain, persist, persevere. ❷ he kept the ring she gave him: HOLD ON TO, keep hold of, retain; *informal* hang on to. ❸ he keeps all his old newspapers: SAVE UP, accumulate, store, hoard, amass, pile up, collect, garner. ❹ keeping the estate: LOOK AFTER, keep in good order, tend, mind, maintain, keep up, manage, superintend. ❺ keep a wife and children: PROVIDE FOR, support, maintain, sustain, subsidize, feed, nurture. ❻ keep a promise: KEEP TO, abide by, comply with, fulfil, carry out, keep faith with, stand by, honour, obey, observe; *formal* effectuate. ❼ keep the Sabbath: OBSERVE, hold, celebrate, commemorate, respect, ritualize, solemnize, ceremonialize. ❽ what kept you? KEEP BACK, hold back, hold up, delay, detain, retard, hinder, obstruct, impede, hamper, constrain, check, block.
■ **keep at** ❶ PERSIST, persevere, be persistent, be pertinacious, carry on, keep going, continue, work away, see it through; *informal* stick at it, stay the distance, hang on in there. ❷ KEEP ON AT, keep after, go on at, chivvy, badger, harp on at, nag, harass. **keep back** WITHHOLD, keep secret, keep hidden, hide, conceal, suppress.

keeper noun ❶ JAILER, warder, warden, guard, custodian, sentry; *informal* screw. ❷ CURATOR, conservator, attendant, caretaker, steward, superintendent, overseer, administrator.

keepsake noun MEMENTO, souvenir, remembrance,

reminder, token of remembrance, relic, favour.

kernel noun ❶ SEED, nut, grain, germ. ❷ NUB, nucleus, core, centre, heart, marrow, pith, substance, essence, essential part, gist, quintessence; *informal* nitty-gritty, nuts and bolts.

key noun ❶ the key to the problem: ANSWER, solution, explanation, guide, clue, cue, pointer, interpretation, explication, clarification, exposition. ❷ a musical key: TONE, pitch, timbre, tonality.

kick verb ❶ BOOT, punt. ❷ the gun kicked: RECOIL, spring back. ❸ kick the habit: GIVE UP, stop, abandon, leave off, desist from; *informal* quit.

kill verb ❶ TAKE SOMEONE'S LIFE, murder, do away with, do to death, slaughter, butcher, massacre, assassinate, liquidate, wipe out, destroy, erase, eradicate, exterminate, dispatch, put to death, execute; *informal* bump off, do in, knock off, top; *poetic/literary* slay. ❷ kill his hopes: DESTROY, put an end to, ruin, extinguish, scotch, quell. ❸ the walk will kill you: EXHAUST, overtire, tire out, fatigue, wear out, debilitate, enervate, prostrate, tax, overtax, strain; *Brit. informal* fag out. ❹ my feet were killing me: HURT, cause pain, cause discomfort, be uncomfortable, be painful.

killer noun MURDERER, slaughterer, butcher, assassin, liquidator, destroyer, exterminator, executioner, gunman; *informal* hit man; *poetic/literary* slayer.

killing noun ❶ MURDER, manslaughter, homicide, slaughter, butchery, massacre, bloodshed, carnage, liquidation, destruction, extermination, execution. ❷ FINANCIAL SUCCESS, bonanza, fortune, windfall, gain, profit, booty, coup; *informal* bomb, clean-up.

killjoy noun SPOILSPORT, dampener, damper; *informal* wet blanket, party-pooper.

kilter noun CONDITION, state, shape, fettle, trim, fitness, repair, order, working order.

kin noun RELATIVES, relations, family, connections, folks, people, kindred, kith and kin, kinsfolk, kinsmen, kinswomen.

kind[1] noun ❶ SORT, type, variety, brand, class, category, genus, species. ❷ NATURE, character, manner, aspect, disposition, humour, style, stamp, mould.

kind[2] adjective KIND-HEARTED, kindly, generous, charitable, giving, benevolent, magnanimous, big-hearted, warm-hearted, altruistic, philanthropic, humanitarian, humane, tender-hearted, soft-hearted, gentle, mild, lenient, merciful, clement, pitying, forbearing, patient, tolerant, sympathetic, compassionate, understanding, considerate, helpful, thoughtful, good, nice, pleasant, benign, friendly, genial, congenial, amiable, amicable, cordial, courteous, gracious, good-natured, warm, affectionate, loving, indulgent, obliging, accommodating, neighbourly; *Brit. informal* decent; *poetic/literary* bounteous.
– OPPOSITES unkind, nasty.

kindle verb ❶ kindle a fire: LIGHT, set alight, set on fire, set fire to, ignite, start, torch. ❷ kindle interest: STIMULATE, rouse, arouse,

excite, stir, awaken, inspire, inflame, incite, induce, provoke, actuate, activate, touch off.
– OPPOSITES extinguish.

kindred adjective ❶ RELATED, connected, of the same blood, of the same family, consanguineous, cognate. ❷ **kindred spirits:** LIKE, similar, resembling, corresponding, matching, congenial, allied.

king noun ❶ MONARCH, sovereign, ruler, crowned head, majesty, royal personage, emperor, overlord, prince. ❷ LEADING LIGHT, luminary, star, superstar, kingpin; *informal* mogul; *N. Amer. informal* big wheel.

kink noun ❶ TWIST, bend, coil, corkscrew, curl, twirl, knot, tangle, entanglement. ❷ FLAW, defect, imperfection, hitch, snag, difficulty, complication. ❸ QUIRK, whim, whimsy, caprice, vagary, eccentricity, foible, idiosyncrasy, crotchet, fetish, deviation.

kinky adjective ❶ QUIRKY, peculiar, odd, strange, queer, bizarre, eccentric, idiosyncratic, weird, outlandish, unconventional, unorthodox, whimsical, capricious, fanciful. ❷ PERVERTED, warped, deviant, unnatural, abnormal, depraved, degenerate, lascivious, licentious, lewd, sadistic, masochistic.

kit noun ❶ EQUIPMENT, apparatus, set of tools, tools, implements, instruments, utensils, tackle, supplies, paraphernalia, accoutrements, effects, trappings, appurtenances; *informal* gear, stuff. ❷ **football kit:** OUTFIT, clothing, dress, uniform, colours; *informal* rig-out, gear, strip.
■ **kit out** EQUIP, supply, provide, fit out, fix up, furnish, outfit, deck out, rig out, arm, accoutre.

kittenish adjective PLAYFUL, frisky, coquettish, coy; *poetic/literary* frolicsome.

knack noun TALENT, aptitude, gift, flair, bent, forte, ability, capability, capacity, expertise, expertness, skill, genius, facility, propensity, dexterity, ingenuity, proficiency, competence, handiness.

knead verb WORK, manipulate, press, squeeze, massage, rub, form, shape.

kneel verb GET DOWN ON ONE'S KNEES, fall to one's knees, genuflect, bow, bow down, stoop, make obeisance, kowtow.

knife noun BLADE, cutting tool.
▶ verb STAB, pierce, run through, impale, bayonet, transfix, cut, slash, lacerate, wound. *See also* WOUND verb.

knit verb ❶ LOOP, weave, interweave, crochet. ❷ **knit the community together:** LINK, bind, unite, draw together, ally.

knob noun ❶ DOORKNOB, handle, door handle, switch, on/off switch. ❷ BUMP, bulge, swelling, lump, knot, node, nodule, pustule, growth, tumour, protuberance, tumescence.

knock verb ❶ TAP, rap, bang, pound, hammer. ❷ STRIKE, hit, slap, smack, box, punch, cuff, buffet, thump, thwack, batter, pummel. ❸ KNOCK INTO, bang into, bump into, collide with, run into, crash into, crash against, smash into, dash against, jolt. ❹ CRITICIZE, find fault with, take apart, take to pieces, pick holes in, run down, carp at, cavil at, deprecate, belittle, disparage, censure, condemn.

knoll noun HILLOCK, hill, hummock, elevation, mound, hump, knob, barrow.

knot noun LOOP, twist, bend, intertwinement, interlacement, ligature.
▶ verb TIE, loop, bind, secure, tether, lash, leash.

know verb ❶ BE AWARE OF, notice, perceive, realize, be conscious of, be cognizant of, sense, recognize; *informal* latch on to. ❷ HAVE KNOWLEDGE OF, understand, comprehend, apprehend, be conversant with, be familiar with, be acquainted with. ❸ have known tragedy: BE FAMILIAR WITH, be acquainted with, experience, undergo, go through. ❹ HAVE MET, be acquainted with, have dealings with, associate with, be friends with, socialize with, fraternize with, be intimate with, be close to, be on good terms with.

knowing adjective ❶ a knowing look: ASTUTE, shrewd, perceptive, meaningful, well informed, significant, eloquent, expressive. ❷ a knowing girl: AWARE, astute, shrewd, perceptive, sophisticated, worldly, worldly-wise. ❸ a knowing infringement: CONSCIOUS, intentional, intended, deliberate, wilful, purposeful, calculated, on purpose, by design.

knowledge noun ❶ LEARNING, erudition, scholarship, letters, education, enlightenment, wisdom. ❷ his knowledge of the subject: UNDERSTANDING, grasp, comprehension, apprehension, cognition, adeptness, skill, expertise, proficiency; *informal* know-how. ❸ knowledge of the area: ACQUAINTANCESHIP, familiarity, conversance.

knowledgeable adjective ❶ WELL INFORMED, informed, educated, learned, erudite, scholarly, well read, cultured, cultivated, enlightened. ❷ HAVING A KNOWLEDGE OF, acquainted with, familiar with, experienced in, expert in, conversant with, having an understanding of.
– OPPOSITES ill-informed.

known adjective RECOGNIZED, acknowledged, admitted, declared, proclaimed, avowed, confessed, published, revealed.

Ll

label noun ❶ IDENTIFICATION TAG, tag, ticket, tab, sticker, marker, docket. ❷ EPITHET, name, nickname, title, sobriquet, designation, description, characterization; *formal* denomination.
▶ verb ❶ ATTACH LABELS TO, tag, tab, ticket, stamp, mark, put stickers on, docket. ❷ DESCRIBE, designate, identify, classify, class, categorize, brand, call, name, term, dub.

laborious adjective ❶ HARD, heavy, difficult, arduous, strenuous, fatiguing, tiring, wearying, wearisome, tedious. ❷ PAINSTAKING, careful,

meticulous, diligent, assiduous, industrious, hard-working, scrupulous, persevering, pertinacious, zealous. ❸ LABOURED, strained, forced.
– OPPOSITES easy, natural.

labour noun ❶ WORK, employment, job, toil, exertion, effort, industry, industriousness, hard work, hard labour, drudgery, slog, donkey work, sweat of one's brow; *poetic/literary* travail. ❷ TASK, job, chore, undertaking, commission, assignment, charge, venture. ❸ EMPLOYEES, workers, workmen, workforce, working people, hands, labourers. ❹ CHILDBIRTH, birth, parturition, delivery, contractions, labour pains; *poetic/literary* travail; *dated* confinement.
▶ verb WORK HARD, work away, toil, slave away, drudge, grub away, plod on/away, grind/sweat away, struggle, exert oneself, work like a slave, work one's fingers to the bone, work like a Trojan; *poetic/literary* travail.

laboured adjective ❶ laboured breathing: DIFFICULT, strained, forced, heavy, awkward. ❷ a laboured style: CONTRIVED, affected, studied, stiff, strained, stilted, forced, unnatural, artificial, overdone, overworked, heavy, ponderous, ornate, elaborate, over-elaborate, intricate, convoluted, complex, laborious.

labyrinth noun MAZE, warren, network, convolution, entanglement.

labyrinthine adjective ❶ MAZE-LIKE, meandering, winding, wandering, twisting, circuitous, tangled. ❷ labyrinthine plots: INTRICATE, complicated, complex, involved, tortuous, convoluted, tangled, entangled, confusing, puzzling, perplexing, mystifying, bewildering.

lacerate verb CUT, tear, gash, slash, cut open, rip, rend, mangle, mutilate, hurt, wound, injure, maim.

lack noun ABSENCE, want, need, deprivation, deficiency, privation, dearth, insufficiency, shortage, scarcity, scarceness, paucity.
– OPPOSITES plenty.
▶ verb BE LACKING, be without, have need of, need, stand in need of, require, want, be short of, be deficient in, miss.

laconic adjective BRIEF, concise, terse, succinct, short, elliptical, crisp, pithy, to the point, incisive, abrupt, blunt, curt.
– OPPOSITES verbose.

laden adjective LOADED, burdened, heavily laden, weighed down, weighted, encumbered, hampered, oppressed, taxed.

lady noun ❶ WOMAN, female. ❷ NOBLEWOMAN, gentlewoman, aristocrat.

ladylike adjective GENTEEL, refined, well bred, cultivated, polished, decorous, proper, correct, respectable, well mannered, courteous, polite, civil, gracious.
– OPPOSITES coarse.

lag verb FALL BEHIND, fall back, trail, not keep pace, bring up the rear, loiter, linger, dally, straggle, dawdle, hang back, delay, move slowly, drag one's feet.

laid-back adjective RELAXED, at ease, easy, leisurely, unhurried, casual, easy-going, free and easy, informal, nonchalant,

unexcitable, imperturbable, unflappable.
– OPPOSITES tense.

lair noun ❶ TUNNEL, dugout, hollow, cave, haunt. ❷ RETREAT, hideaway, refuge, sanctuary, sanctum, sanctum sanctorum.

lake noun POND, tarn, pool, reservoir, lagoon; *Scottish* loch; *N. Amer.* bayou.

lame adjective ❶ LIMPING, hobbling, halting, crippled, game, disabled, incapacitated, defective; *Brit. informal* gammy. ❷ **a lame reply**: WEAK, feeble, thin, flimsy, unconvincing, unsatisfactory, inadequate, insufficient, deficient, defective, ineffectual.

lament verb ❶ MOURN, grieve, sorrow, wail, moan, groan, weep, cry, sob, complain, keen, ululate, howl, beat one's breast. ❷ COMPLAIN ABOUT, bemoan, bewail, deplore.

lamentable adjective ❶ DEPLORABLE, regrettable, tragic, terrible, wretched, woeful, sorrowful, distressing, grievous. ❷ **a lamentable salary**: MISERABLE, pitiful, poor, meagre, low, unsatisfactory, inadequate; *informal* measly.

lamp noun LANTERN, table lamp, standard lamp, night light, light bulb, headlight, headlamp, sidelight, fog light, fog lamp.

lampoon verb SATIRIZE, send up, parody, caricature, ridicule, mock, make fun of, burlesque, take off, do a take-off of.

land noun ❶ DRY LAND, ground, solid ground, earth, terra firma. ❷ SOIL, earth, loam, dirt. ❸ GROUND, fields, open space, expanse, stretch, tract. ❹ PROPERTY, ground, acres, estate, realty, real estate. ❺ COUNTRY, nation, fatherland, motherland, state, realm, province, territory, district, region, area, domain.
▶ **verb** ❶ TOUCH DOWN, alight, make a landing, come in to land. ❷ MAKE A LANDING, bring down, put down, take down. ❸ BERTH, dock, reach the shore, come ashore, disembark, debark. ❹ **land a blow**: DEAL, deliver, deposit, give, catch; *informal* fetch.

landlady, landlord noun ❶ INNKEEPER, hotel keeper, hotelier, host, mine host; *Brit.* publican, pub-owner. ❷ OWNER, proprietor, lessor, householder, freeholder.

landscape noun COUNTRYSIDE, scene, scenery, outlook, view, aspect, prospect, vista, panorama, perspective.

landslide noun ❶ AVALANCHE, landslip, rockfall. ❷ **win by a landslide**: DECISIVE VICTORY, runaway victory, overwhelming majority.

language noun ❶ SPEECH, speaking, talking, words, vocabulary, utterances, verbal expression, verbalization, vocalization, communication, conversation, discourse, interchange. ❷ TONGUE, speech, parlance, mother tongue, native tongue; *informal* lingo.

languid adjective LANGUISHING, listless, languorous, lackadaisical, spiritless, vigourless, lacking energy, lethargic, torpid, idle, inactive, inert, indolent, lazy, sluggish, slow-moving, unenthusiastic, apathetic, indifferent.
– OPPOSITES energetic, vigorous.

languish verb ❶ DROOP, flag, wilt,

wither, fade, fail, weaken, decline, go into a decline, go downhill, waste away. ❷ WASTE AWAY, rot, decay, wither away, be abandoned, be neglected, be forgotten, be disregarded.
– OPPOSITES thrive.

languor noun LISTLESSNESS, lethargy, torpor, idleness, inactivity, inertia, indolence, laziness, sluggishness, sleepiness, drowsiness, somnolence, dreaminess, relaxation.
– OPPOSITES vigour.

lank adjective LIFELESS, lustreless, limp, straggling, straight, long.

lanky adjective TALL, spindly, gangling, gangly, lean, thin, angular, scraggy, bony, gaunt, raw-boned, gawky, rangy; *informal* weedy.
– OPPOSITES sturdy.

lap noun ❶ CIRCUIT, circle, loop, orbit, round, compass, ambit. ❷ the last lap: ROUND, tour, section, stage.

lapse noun ❶ SLIP, error, mistake, blunder, failing, fault, failure, omission, oversight, negligence, dereliction; *informal* slip-up. ❷ INTERVAL, gap, pause, intermission, interlude, lull, hiatus, break, passage. ❸ a lapse in standards: DECLINE, downturn, fall, falling, falling away, slipping, drop, deterioration, worsening, degeneration, backsliding.
▶ verb ❶ standards have lapsed: DECLINE, fall, fall off, drop, go downhill, deteriorate, worsen, degenerate, go to pot. ❷ the season ticket has lapsed: BECOME VOID, become invalid, expire, run out, terminate, become obsolete. ❸ lapse into silence: SLIDE, slip, drift, sink, subside, submerge.

larder noun PANTRY, storage room, storeroom, store, still room, cooler, scullery.

large adjective ❶ BIG, great, of considerable size, sizeable, substantial, goodly, tall, high, huge, immense, enormous, colossal, massive, mammoth, vast, prodigious, gigantic, giant, monumental, stupendous, gargantuan, man-size, king-size, giant-size, outsize, considerable; *informal* jumbo, whopping. ❷ a large man/woman: BIG, burly, heavy, bulky, thickset, powerfully built, heavy-set, chunky, strapping, hefty, ample, fat, obese, corpulent; *informal* hulking. ❸ a large supply: ABUNDANT, copious, plentiful, ample, liberal, generous. ❹ the large view: WIDE, wide-ranging, large-scale, broad, extensive, far-reaching, sweeping, comprehensive, exhaustive.
– OPPOSITES small.
■ **at large** AT LIBERTY, free, unconfined, unrestrained, roaming, on the loose, on the run, fugitive. **by and large** ON THE WHOLE, generally, in general, all things considered, taking everything into consideration, for the most part, in the main, as a rule.

largely adverb TO A LARGE EXTENT, to a great degree, chiefly, for the most part, mostly, mainly, in the main, principally, in great measure.

lascivious adjective LEWD, lecherous, lustful, licentious, promiscuous, libidinous, prurient, salacious, lubricious, concupiscent, debauched, depraved, degenerate, dissolute, dissipated.

lash verb WHIP, horsewhip, scourge, birch, switch, flog, flail, flagellate, thrash, beat, strike, batter, hammer; *informal* wallop, whack.

last[1] adjective ❶ **his last words:** FINAL, closing, concluding, ending, finishing, terminating, ultimate, terminal. ❷ **the last runner:** HINDMOST, rearmost, at the end, at the back, final, aftermost. ❸ **the last thing she wants:** LEAST LIKELY, most unlikely, least suitable, least wanted, least favourite. ❹ **last Thursday:** LATEST, most recent.

last[2] verb ❶ CONTINUE, go on, carry on, remain, persist, keep on. ❷ SURVIVE, exist, live, subsist, hold on, hold out. ❸ LAST LONG, wear well, stand up to wear, keep, endure.

late adjective ❶ BEHIND SCHEDULE, behind, not on time, tardy, overdue, delayed, dilatory, slow. ❷ **her late husband:** DECEASED, dead, departed, defunct, non-extant. ❸ **the late government:** FORMER, previous, preceding, past, prior.
– OPPOSITES punctual.

latent adjective DORMANT, quiescent, inactive, passive, hidden, unrevealed, concealed, unapparent, indiscernible, imperceptible, invisible, covert, undeveloped, unrealized, potential, possible.
– OPPOSITES evident.

lateral adjective SIDEWISE, sideways, sidelong, sideward, edgewise, edgeways, indirect, oblique, slanting.

latitude noun ❶ PARALLEL. ❷ SCOPE, freedom of action, freedom, liberty, free play, carte blanche, leeway, elbow room, licence, indulgence.
– OPPOSITES longitude, restriction.

latter adjective ❶ LAST-MENTIONED, second-mentioned, second of the two, second. ❷ LATER, hindmost, closing, end, concluding, final.
– OPPOSITES former.

laudable adjective PRAISEWORTHY, commendable, admirable, worthy of admiration, meritorious, deserving, creditable, worthy, estimable, of note, noteworthy, exemplary, excellent.
– OPPOSITES shameful.

laugh verb CHUCKLE, chortle, guffaw, giggle, titter, snigger, tee-hee, burst out laughing, roar/hoot with laughter, shake/be convulsed with laughter, split one's sides, be rolling in the aisles, be doubled up; *informal* be in stitches, die laughing, be creased up, fall about, crack up, break up.
■ **laugh at** MOCK, ridicule, deride, scoff at, jeer at, sneer at, make fun of, poke fun at, make a fool of, lampoon, satirize, taunt, tease; *informal* send up, take the mickey out of.

laughing stock noun FIGURE OF FUN, dupe, butt, fool, everybody's fool, stooge, fair game, everybody's target, victim, Aunt Sally; *informal* fall guy.

laughter noun LAUGHING, chuckling, chortling, guffawing, giggling, tittering, sniggering, amusement, entertainment, humour, mirth, merriment, gaiety, hilarity, glee, light-heartedness; *poetic/literary* blitheness.

launch verb ❶ **launch a rocket:** FIRE, discharge, propel, project, send forth, throw, cast, hurl, let fly, blast off. ❷ launch a search: SET IN MOTION, get going, begin, start, commence, embark upon, initiate, instigate, institute, inaugurate, establish, set up, organize, introduce, usher in.

lavatory noun TOILET, WC, water closet, public convenience, ladies, gents, cloakroom, powder room, privy, urinal, latrine; *N. Amer.* bathroom, washroom, rest room; *Nautical* head; *informal* little girls' room, little boys' room; *Brit. informal* loo, bog, khazi, lav; *N. Amer. informal* can, john.

lavish adjective ❶ a lavish supply: COPIOUS, abundant, superabundant, plentiful, profuse, prolific, unlimited. ❷ EXTRAVAGANT, excessive, immoderate, wasteful, squandering, profligate, prodigal, thriftless, improvident, intemperate, unrestrained. ❸ a lavish hostess: GENEROUS, liberal, bountiful, open-handed, unstinting, free, munificent, extravagant. ❹ a lavish display: LUXURIANT, lush, gorgeous, sumptuous, costly, opulent, pretentious, showy.
– OPPOSITES meagre.
▶ verb HEAP, shower, pour, deluge, give freely, give generously, bestow freely, waste, squander, dissipate.

law noun ❶ RULE, regulation, statute, enactment, act, decree, edict, command, order, ordinance, commandment, directive, pronouncement, covenant. ❷ RULE, principle, precept, standard, criterion, formula, tenet, doctrine, canon. ❸ a law of nature: GENERALIZATION, general truth, axiom, maxim, truism. ❹ go to law: LITIGATION, legal action, legal proceedings, lawsuit.

law-abiding adjective LAWFUL, righteous, honest, honourable, upright, upstanding, good, virtuous, orderly, peaceable, peaceful, dutiful, duteous, obedient, compliant, complying.
– OPPOSITES lawless.

lawful adjective ❶ lawful actions: LEGAL, legitimate, licit, just, valid, permissible, allowable, rightful, proper, constitutional, legalized, sanctioned, authorized, warranted, approved, recognized. ❷ a lawful person: *see* LAW-ABIDING.
– OPPOSITES illegal.

lawless adjective ❶ a lawless country: WITHOUT LAW AND ORDER, anarchic, disorderly, ungoverned, unruly, insurrectionary, insurgent, revolutionary, rebellious, insubordinate, riotous, mutinous, seditious, terrorist. ❷ lawless actions: UNLAWFUL, illegal, law-breaking, illicit, illegitimate, criminal, felonious, miscreant, transgressing, violating.
– OPPOSITES orderly, legal.

lawsuit noun SUIT, case, legal action, action, legal proceedings, proceedings, litigation, trial.

lawyer noun SOLICITOR, legal practitioner, legal adviser, barrister, advocate, counsel, Queen's Counsel, QC; *informal* brief; *N. Amer.* attorney.

lax adjective SLACK, slipshod, negligent, neglectful, remiss, careless, heedless, unmindful, inattentive, casual, easy-going, lenient, permissive, indulgent, overindulgent, complaisant, over-tolerant.

laxative noun PURGATIVE, aperient, cathartic, senna, ipecacuanha, castor oil.

lay verb ❶ SET, deposit, plant, settle, position. ❷ **lay the carpet:** POSITION, set out, arrange, dispose. ❸ **lay the blame:** ATTRIBUTE, assign, ascribe, allocate, allot, impute. ❹ **lay the burden:** IMPOSE, inflict, encumber, saddle, tax, charge, burden, apply.
■ **lay aside** PUT ASIDE, put to one side, keep, save, store. **lay bare** REVEAL, make known, disclose, divulge, show, expose, exhibit, uncover, unveil, unmask. **lay down** ❶ SURRENDER, relinquish, give up, yield, cede, turn over. ❷ SET DOWN, stipulate, prescribe, order, command, ordain, postulate, demand, proclaim, assert, maintain. **lay hold of** GET HOLD OF, get one's hands on, catch, seize, grab, snatch, clutch, grip, grasp, lay hands on. **lay in** STOCK UP WITH/ON, stockpile, store, accumulate, amass, heap up, hoard, collect. **lay into** SET ABOUT, set upon, assail, attack, hit out at, strike out at, let fly at. **lay off** ❶ LET GO, make redundant, dismiss, discharge, pay off; *informal* sack, fire. ❷ STOP, cease, desist from, refrain from, give up, discontinue, leave off, finish; *informal* give over.

layabout noun GOOD-FOR-NOTHING, ne'er-do-well, do-nothing, idler, loafer, lounger, shirker, wastrel, sluggard, laggard; *informal* waster; *Brit. informal* skiver.

layman noun AMATEUR, non-professional, dilettante.

lay-off noun REDUNDANCY, dismissal, discharge; *informal* sacking, firing.

laze verb IDLE, do nothing, loaf, lounge, lounge about, loll around, waste time, fritter away time.

laziness noun IDLENESS, indolence, slothfulness, sloth, inactivity, inertia, lethargy, languor, remissness, laxity.

lazy adjective IDLE, indolent, slothful, work-shy, inactive, inert, sluggish, lethargic, languorous, listless, torpid, slow-moving, remiss, negligent, lax.
– OPPOSITES industrious.

lead verb ❶ GUIDE, show someone the way, conduct, lead the way, usher, escort, steer, pilot. ❷ **led him to believe:** CAUSE, induce, prompt, move, incline, dispose, predispose, persuade, sway, influence, prevail upon, bring round. ❸ **lead to disaster:** CAUSE, result in, bring on, call forth, provoke, contribute to. ❹ **lead the procession:** BE AT THE HEAD OF, be at the front of, head. ❺ **lead the country/discussion:** COMMAND, direct, govern, rule, manage, be in charge of, regulate, preside over, head, supervise, superintend, oversee; *informal* head up. ❻ **he was leading:** BE IN THE LEAD, be in front, be out in front, be ahead, be first, come first, precede. ❼ **lead a happy life:** HAVE, live, pass, spend, experience, undergo.
▶ noun ❶ LEADING POSITION/PLACE, first place, advance position, van, vanguard. ❷ **a lead of half a lap:** MARGIN, gap, interval. ❸ **a lead to others:** EXAMPLE, model, pattern, standard of excellence. ❹ **the lead in the play:** LEADING ROLE, star/starring role, star part, title role, principal part. ❺ LEASH, tether, rein, cord, rope, chain.
■ **lead off** BEGIN, start, start off, commence, open; *informal* kick off. **lead on** DECEIVE, mislead, delude,

hoodwink, dupe, trick, beguile, tempt, entice, lure, tantalize, inveigle, seduce; *informal* string along. **lead up to** PREPARE THE WAY FOR, pave the way for, open the way for, do the groundwork for, work round/up to, make overtures about, make advances about, hint at, approach the subject of, introduce the subject of.

leader noun ❶ RULER, head, chief, commander, director, governor, principal, captain, manager, superintendent, supervisor, overseer, foreman, kingpin; *informal* boss, number one, skipper. ❷ a leader of fashion: PACESETTER, pacemaker, trendsetter, front runner, innovator, pioneer, trailblazer, pathfinder, ground-breaker, originator.
– OPPOSITES follower, supporter.

leading adjective ❶ the leading role: CHIEF, main, most important, principal, foremost, supreme, paramount, dominant, superior; *informal* number-one. ❷ a leading writer: CHIEF, most important, foremost, greatest, best, outstanding, pre-eminent, supreme, principal, top-rank, first-rate.
– OPPOSITES subordinate, minor.

leaflet noun PAMPHLET, booklet, brochure, handbill, flyer, bill, circular; *Brit. informal* advert.

league noun ALLIANCE, confederation, confederacy, federation, union, association, coalition, combine, consortium, affiliation, guild, corporation, conglomerate, cooperative, partnership, fellowship, syndicate, band, group.

leak noun ❶ DRIP, leaking, leakage, escape, seeping, seepage, oozing, percolation, discharge. ❷ OPENING, crack, crevice, chink, fissure, puncture, cut, gash, slit, rent, break, rift. ❸ DISCLOSURE, divulgence, revelation, uncovering.
▶ verb ❶ ESCAPE, drip out, seep out/through, ooze out, exude, discharge, issue, gush out. ❷ DISCLOSE, divulge, reveal, make known, make public, impart, pass on, relate, give away, let slip; *informal* let the cat out of the bag, spill the beans about, take the lid off.

lean verb ❶ BE SUPPORTED, be propped up, recline, repose. ❷ INCLINE, bend, slant, tilt, be at an angle, slope, bank, list, heel. ❸ he leans towards Labour: INCLINE TOWARDS, tend towards, have a tendency towards, have a propensity for, have a proclivity for, have a preference for, be attracted to, have a liking for, gravitate towards, have an affinity with. ❹ she leans on her husband: DEPEND ON, be dependent on, rely on, count on, pin one's faith on, have faith in, trust, have every confidence in.

leaning noun TENDENCY, inclination, bent, proclivity, propensity, penchant, predisposition, predilection, proneness, partiality, preference, bias, attraction, liking, fondness, taste.

leap verb ❶ JUMP, bound, bounce, hop, skip, romp, caper, spring, frolic, frisk, cavort, gambol, dance. ❷ JUMP, jump over, vault over, vault, spring over, bound over, hurdle, clear, cross over, sail over. ❸ leap to help: JUMP, hurry, hasten, rush, hurtle. ❹ prices have leapt: INCREASE RAPIDLY, soar, rocket, skyrocket, shoot up, escalate, mount.

learn verb ❶ **learn French:** ACQUIRE A KNOWLEDGE OF, gain an understanding of, acquire skill in, become competent in, grasp, master, take in, absorb, assimilate, pick up. ❷ **learn the poem:** LEARN BY HEART, get by heart, memorize, commit to memory, become word-perfect in, get off pat. ❸ **we learned that he had gone:** DISCOVER, find out, detect, become aware of, gather, hear, be informed, have it brought to one's attention, understand, ascertain, discern, perceive, get word of, get wind of.

learned adjective ERUDITE, scholarly, well educated, knowledgeable, well read, widely read, well versed, well informed, lettered, cultured, intellectual, academic, literary, bookish.
– OPPOSITES ignorant.

learner noun BEGINNER, trainee, apprentice, pupil, student, novice, tyro, neophyte, initiate; *N. Amer. informal* greenhorn.
– OPPOSITES veteran.

lease verb ❶ **lease a house:** RENT, hire, charter. ❷ **lease their house to him:** RENT, rent out, let, let out, hire, hire out, sublet.

leash noun ❶ LEAD, rein, tether, rope, cord, chain. ❷ REIN, curb, control, check, restraint, hold.

leathery adjective ❶ **leathery skin:** WRINKLED, wizened, weather-beaten, rough, rugged, coriaceous. ❷ **leathery meat:** TOUGH, hard, hardened.

leave[1] verb ❶ **leave hurriedly:** DEPART, go away, go, withdraw, retire, take oneself off, exit, take one's leave, make off, pull out, quit, be gone, decamp, disappear, say one's farewells/goodbyes; *informal* push off, shove off, cut, split, vamoose; *Brit. informal* do a bunk. ❷ **leave for France:** SET OFF, set sail. ❸ **leave his wife:** ABANDON, desert, forsake, discard, turn one's back on, leave in the lurch. ❹ **has left his job:** GIVE UP, abandon, move from; *informal* quit. ❺ **left his gloves at the hotel:** LEAVE BEHIND, forget, mislay. ❻ **leave the job to them:** ASSIGN, allot, consign, hand over, give over, refer, commit, entrust. ❼ **he left him his money:** BEQUEATH, will, endow, hand down, transfer, convey. ❽ **it left feelings of resentment:** LEAVE BEHIND, cause, produce, generate, result in.

■ **leave off** STOP, cease, finish, halt, end, desist from, break off, give up, discontinue, refrain from; *informal* give over, knock off. **leave out** MISS OUT, omit, fail to include, overlook.

leave[2] noun ❶ PERMISSION, consent, authorization, sanction, warrant, dispensation, concession, indulgence. ❷ HOLIDAY, vacation, break, time off, furlough, sabbatical, leave of absence; *informal* hols, vac. ❸ **they took their leave:** LEAVING, leave-taking, departure, parting, withdrawal, exit, farewell, goodbye, adieu.

lecherous adjective LUSTFUL, promiscuous, carnal, sensual, licentious, lascivious, lewd, salacious, libertine, libidinous, lubricious, concupiscent, debauched, dissolute, wanton, intemperate, dissipated, degenerate, depraved; *informal* horny, raunchy.
– OPPOSITES chaste.

lecture noun ❶ TALK, speech, address, discourse, disquisition, lesson, sermon, homily. ❷ SCOLDING, reprimand, rebuke, reproof, reproach, remonstration, upbraiding, berating, tirade, diatribe; *informal* dressing-down, telling-off, talking-to.
▶ verb ❶ TEACH, tutor in, instruct in, give instruction in, give lessons in. ❷ SCOLD, reprimand, rebuke, reprove, reproach, remonstrate with, upbraid, berate; *formal* castigate.

lecturer noun TEACHER, college teacher, tutor, reader, instructor, academic, academician.

ledge noun SHELF, sill, mantel, mantelpiece, mantelshelf, projection, protrusion, overhang, ridge, step.

leer verb OGLE, look lasciviously at, look suggestively at, eye, wink at, watch, stare, goggle, sneer, smirk grin; *informal* give someone the glad eye, give someone the once-over.

leery adjective WARY, chary, cautious, careful, guarded, on one's guard, suspicious, distrustful, mistrusting.

left adjective ❶ LEFT-HAND, sinistral; *Nautical* port; *Heraldry* sinister. ❷ LEFT-WING, leftist, socialist, radical, progressive, liberal, communist, communistic.
– OPPOSITES right.

leg noun ❶ LOWER LIMB, limb, member, shank; *informal* stump, peg, pin. ❷ **table legs**: SUPPORT, upright, prop, brace, underpinning. ❸ **the last leg**: PART, portion, segment, section, bit, stretch, stage, lap.

legal adjective ❶ LAWFUL, legitimate, licit, legalized, valid, right, proper, sound, permissible, permitted, allowable, allowed, above board, admissible, acceptable, authorized, sanctioned, warranted, licensed; *informal* legit. ❷ **legal processes**: JUDICIAL, juridical, forensic.
– OPPOSITES illegal.

legalize verb MAKE LEGAL, decriminalize, legitimize, legitimatize, legitimate, validate, ratify, permit, allow, admit, accept, authorize, sanction, warrant, license.

legend noun MYTH, saga, epic, folk tale, folk story, traditional story, tale, story, narrative, fable, romance.

legendary adjective ❶ MYTHICAL, heroic, traditional, fabled, fictitious, fictional, storybook, romantic, fanciful, fantastical, fabulous. ❷ CELEBRATED, acclaimed, illustrious, famous, famed, renowned, well known, popular, immortal.

legitimate adjective ❶ LEGAL, lawful, licit, within the law, going by the rules; *informal* legit. ❷ **the legitimate heir**: LAWFUL, rightful, genuine, authentic, real, true, proper, correct, authorized, sanctioned, warranted, acknowledged, recognized, approved. ❸ **a legitimate reason**: VALID, sound, admissible, acceptable, well founded, justifiable, reasonable, plausible, credible, believable, reliable, logical, rational.
– OPPOSITES illegitimate.

legitimize verb LEGALIZE, pronounce lawful, declare legal, legitimate, decriminalize, validate, permit, warrant, authorize, sanction, license, give the stamp of approval to.

leisure noun FREE TIME, spare time, idle hours, inactivity, time off, relaxation, recreation, freedom, holiday, vacation, breathing space, breathing spell, respite; *informal* time to kill.

leisurely adjective UNHURRIED, relaxed, easy, easy-going, gentle, comfortable, restful, slow, lazy, lingering; *informal* laid-back.
–OPPOSITES hurried.

lend verb ❶ LOAN, give someone the loan of, let someone have the use of, advance. ❷ IMPART, add, give, bestow, confer, provide, supply, furnish.
–OPPOSITES borrow.

length noun ❶ DISTANCE, extent, linear measure, span, reach. ❷ PERIOD, stretch, duration, term, span. ❸ PIECE, portion, section, measure, segment, swatch.

lengthen verb ❶ MAKE LONGER, elongate, let down. ❷ GROW LONGER, get longer, draw out, stretch. ❸ MAKE LONGER, prolong, increase, extend, expand, protract, stretch out, draw out.
–OPPOSITES shorten.

lengthy adjective LONG, long-lasting, prolonged, extended, protracted, long-drawn-out.
–OPPOSITES short.

lenient adjective MERCIFUL, clement, sparing, moderate, compassionate, humane, forbearing, tolerant, liberal, magnanimous, indulgent, kind, gentle, easy-going, mild.
–OPPOSITES severe.

less adjective SMALLER, slighter, not so much, not so great.
▶ **pronoun** A SMALLER AMOUNT, not so much.
▶ **adverb** TO A LESSER DEGREE, to a smaller extent, not so much.
▶ **preposition** MINUS, subtracting, excepting, without.

lessen verb ❶ GROW LESS, abate, decrease, diminish, subside, moderate, slacken, die down, let up, ease off, tail off, ebb, wane. ❷ RELIEVE, soothe, allay, assuage, alleviate, palliate, ease, dull, deaden, blunt, take the edge off.
–OPPOSITES increase.

lesson noun ❶ CLASS, period of instruction, exercise, schoolwork, homework, assignment, task. ❷ **a lesson to others:** EXAMPLE, warning, deterrent, message, moral, precept.

let verb ❶ ALLOW, permit, give permission to, give leave to, authorize, sanction, grant, license, assent to, consent to, agree to; *informal* give the thumbs up to, give the go-ahead to, give the green light to. ❷ LET OUT, rent, rent out, lease, hire, sublet.
■ **let down** FAIL, disappoint, disillusion, forsake, abandon, desert, leave, betray, leave in the lurch. **let in on** INCLUDE, count in, admit, allow to share in, let participate in, take in. **let off** ❶ EXPLODE, detonate. ❷ ACQUIT, release, discharge, reprieve, absolve, exonerate, pardon, forgive, exempt, spare. **let on** MAKE KNOWN, tell, disclose, divulge, let out, let slip, give away, leak. **let up** LESSEN, abate, decrease, diminish, subside, moderate, slacken, die down, ease off, tail off, ebb, wane.

let-down noun DISAPPOINTMENT, disillusionment, fiasco, anticlimax; *informal* washout.

lethal adjective FATAL, deadly, mortal, death-dealing, murderous, poisonous, toxic, dangerous, virulent, noxious,

destructive, disastrous, calamitous, ruinous.
– OPPOSITES harmless.

lethargic adjective SLUGGISH, inactive, slow, slothful, torpid, listless, languid, apathetic, passive, weary, enervated, fatigued, sleepy, indolent, dull, comatose.
– OPPOSITES energetic.

lethargy noun SLUGGISHNESS, inertia, inactivity, slowness, sloth, idleness, torpor, torpidity, lifelessness, dullness, listlessness, languor, languidness, apathy, passivity, weariness, lassitude, fatigue, sleepiness, drowsiness, somnolence, narcosis.
– OPPOSITES energy.

letter noun ❶ CHARACTER, sign, symbol. ❷ MESSAGE, note, line, missive, epistle, dispatch, love letter, billet-doux, fan letter, letter of thanks, thank-you letter, bread-and-butter letter, reply, acknowledgement.

lettered adjective LEARNED, erudite, academic, well educated, educated, well read, widely read, cultured, cultivated, scholarly, literary, highbrow.
– OPPOSITES ill-educated.

level adjective ❶ FLAT, smooth, even, uniform, plane, flush, horizontal. ❷ EVEN, uniform, regular, consistent, constant, stable, steady, unchanging, unvarying, unfluctuating. ❸ EQUAL, on a level, close together, neck and neck, level-pegging, side by side, on a par, with nothing to choose between them.
– OPPOSITES uneven, unsteady, unequal.
▶ **noun** ❶ HEIGHT, highness, altitude, elevation. ❷ LEVEL OF ACHIEVEMENT, position, rank, standing, status, station, degree, grade, stage, standard. ❸ LAYER, stratum, bed.
▶ **verb** ❶ LEVEL OUT, make level, even off, even out, make flat, flatten, smooth, smooth out, plane. ❷ **level the buildings:** RAZE, raze to the ground, pull down, knock down, tear down, demolish, flatten, bulldoze, lay waste, destroy.

level-headed adjective SENSIBLE, prudent, circumspect, shrewd, wise, reasonable, rational, sane, composed, calm, cool, collected, balanced, self-possessed, unruffled, even-tempered, imperturbable.
– OPPOSITES excitable.

liable adjective ❶ RESPONSIBLE, accountable, answerable, chargeable, blameworthy, at fault, censurable. ❷ EXPOSED, open, subject, susceptible, vulnerable, in danger of, at risk of. ❸ APT, likely, inclined, tending, disposed, predisposed, prone.

liar noun FIBBER, perjurer, falsifier, false witness, fabricator, deceiver, spinner of yarns.

libel noun DEFAMATION, denigration, vilification, disparagement, aspersions, calumny, slander, false report, traducement, obloquy, abuse, slur, smear; *formal* derogation, calumniation.
▶ **verb** DEFAME, vilify, blacken someone's name, denigrate, disparage, cast aspersions on, slander, traduce, abuse, revile, malign, slur, smear, fling mud at; *formal* derogate, calumniate.

libellous adjective DEFAMATORY, denigratory, vilifying, disparaging, derogatory, slanderous, false, misrepresentative, traducing, abusive, reviling, malicious, scurrilous, muckraking.

liberal adjective ❶ a liberal supply: ABUNDANT, copious, ample, plentiful, lavish, profuse, munificent, bountiful, rich, handsome, generous. ❷ liberal in his hospitality: GENEROUS, magnanimous, open-handed, unsparing, unstinting, lavish, munificent, bountiful, big-hearted, kind, philanthropic, charitable, altruistic, unselfish; *poetic/literary* bounteous. ❸ liberal ideas: UNPREJUDICED, unbiased, unbigoted, impartial, disinterested, broad-minded, enlightened, catholic, indulgent, permissive. ❹ a liberal interpretation: LOOSE, flexible, free, general, inexact, imprecise. ❺ liberal in her politics: ADVANCED, forward-looking, progressive, reformist, radical, latitudinarian. ❻ a liberal education: WIDE-RANGING, broad-based, general, humanistic.
– OPPOSITES conservative.

liberate verb SET FREE, free, release, let out, let go, discharge, set loose, unshackle, unfetter, unchain, deliver, rescue, emancipate, unyoke; *historical* manumit.

liberty noun ❶ FREEDOM, independence, autonomy, sovereignty, self-government, self-rule. ❷ FREEDOM, liberation, release, discharge, deliverance, emancipation; *historical* manumission.
■ **at liberty** FREE, loose, on the loose, at large, unconfined.

libidinous adjective LUSTFUL, lecherous, lascivious, lewd, carnal, sensual, salacious, prurient, concupiscent, lubricious, dissolute, debauched, degenerate, decadent, wanton, immoral, unchaste, impure, intemperate; *informal* horny; *Brit. informal* randy.

licence noun ❶ PERMIT, certificate, credentials, document, documentation, pass. ❷ PERMISSION, leave, liberty, freedom, consent, authority, authorization, sanction, approval, warranty.

license verb ❶ GRANT A LICENCE TO, authorize, warrant, accredit, charter, franchise. ❷ GIVE PERMISSION TO, permit, allow, grant leave to, entitle, give the freedom to, sanction, give one's approval to, empower.
– OPPOSITES ban.

lid noun COVER, top, cap, cork, stopper, plug.

lie[1] noun UNTRUTH, falsehood, fib, white lie, fabrication, made-up story, trumped-up story, invention, piece of fiction, falsification, falsity, fairy story, cock and bull story, dissimulation, departure from the truth; *informal* terminological inexactitude, tall tale, whopper.
▶ verb TELL A LIE, perjure oneself, fib, fabricate, invent/make up a story, falsify, dissemble, dissimulate, prevaricate, depart from the truth, be economical with the truth, bear false witness.

lie[2] verb ❶ RECLINE, be recumbent, be prostrate, be supine, be prone, be stretched out, sprawl, rest, repose, relax, lounge, loll. ❷ BE, be situated, be located, be placed, be positioned, be found.
■ **lie in** CONSIST, be inherent, inhere, be present, exist, reside. **lie low** HIDE, go into hiding, hide

out, conceal oneself, keep out of sight, keep a low profile, take cover, go to earth, go to ground, go underground; *informal* hole up.

life noun ❶ EXISTENCE, being, animation, aliveness, viability. ❷ **life on Mars**: LIVING THINGS, living beings, living creatures, human/animal/plant life, fauna, flora. ❸ PERSON, human being, individual, mortal, soul. ❹ **all her life**: LIFETIME, days, duration of life, course of life, lifespan, time on earth, existence, career; *informal* one's born days.

lifeless adjective ❶ DEAD, deceased, gone, cold, defunct. ❷ **lifeless countryside**: BARREN, sterile, bare, desolate, stark, arid, unproductive, uncultivated, empty, uninhabited, unoccupied. ❸ **a lifeless play**: SPIRITLESS, lacking vitality, lacklustre, apathetic, uninspired, colourless, dull, flat, stiff, wooden, tedious, uninspiring.
– OPPOSITES alive, lively.

lifelike adjective TRUE-TO-LIFE, realistic, photographic, faithful, authentic, exact, vivid, graphic, natural.
– OPPOSITES unrealistic.

lift verb ❶ PICK UP, uplift, hoist, heave up, raise, raise up, upraise, heft. ❷ RAISE HIGH, hold up, bear aloft. ❸ **lift their game**: IMPROVE, boost, enhance, make better, ameliorate, upgrade. ❹ **lift the ban**: RAISE, remove, withdraw, revoke, cancel, annul, void, countermand, relax, end, stop, terminate. ❺ **they lifted her purse**: STEAL, thieve, rob, pilfer, purloin, pocket, take, appropriate; *informal* filch, swipe; *Brit. informal* pinch, nick.

light[1] noun ❶ ILLUMINATION, luminescence, luminosity, shining, gleaming, brightness, brilliance, blaze, glare, incandescence, effulgence, refulgence, lambency, radiance, lustre. ❷ DAYLIGHT, daylight hours, daytime, day, hours of sunlight. ❸ **a different light**: ASPECT, angle, slant, approach, viewpoint, point of view.
▶ **verb** ❶ SET BURNING, set fire to, set a match to, ignite, kindle. ❷ ILLUMINATE, brighten, lighten, irradiate, flood with light, floodlight; *poetic/literary* illumine.
▶ **adjective** ❶ FULL OF LIGHT, bright, well lit, well illuminated, sunny. ❷ LIGHT-COLOURED, light-toned, pale, pastel, whitish, faded, bleached.

light[2] adjective ❶ SLIGHT, thin, slender, skinny, underweight, small, tiny. ❷ LIGHTWEIGHT, thin, flimsy, insubstantial, delicate, floaty, gossamer. ❸ **a light tap on the shoulder**: GENTLE, slight, delicate, soft, weak, faint, indistinct. ❹ **light tasks**: MODERATE, easy, simple, undemanding, untaxing, effortless, facile; *informal* cushy. ❺ **light reading**: LIGHT-HEARTED, entertaining, diverting, recreational, amusing, humorous, funny, frivolous, superficial, trivial, trifling.
– OPPOSITES heavy.

lighten[1] verb **lighten the load**: MAKE LIGHTER, lessen, reduce, ease, alleviate, mitigate, allay, relieve, assuage, ameliorate.
– OPPOSITES increase.

lighten[2] verb ❶ **the sky lightened**: BECOME LIGHTER, grow brighter, brighten. ❷ MAKE LIGHTER, make brighter, brighten, light up, illuminate, shed light on, cast

light on, irradiate.
– OPPOSITES darken.

lightly adverb ❶ snow falling lightly: SLIGHTLY, thinly, softly, gently. ❷ salt the food lightly: SPARINGLY, sparsely, slightly. ❸ dismiss the subject lightly: AIRILY, carelessly, heedlessly, uncaringly, indifferently, thoughtlessly, flippantly, frivolously, slightingly.

like[1] verb ❶ they like each other: BE FOND OF, have a liking for, be attracted to, be keen on, love, adore, have a soft spot for. ❷ he likes swimming: ENJOY, be keen on, find/take pleasure in, be partial to, love, adore, find agreeable, delight in, relish, revel in; *informal* get a kick from. ❸ we would like you to go: WISH, want, desire, prefer, had sooner, had rather.
– OPPOSITES dislike.

like[2] adjective SIMILAR, comparable, corresponding, resembling, analogous, parallel, equivalent, of a kind, identical, matching, akin.
– OPPOSITES dissimilar.
▶ preposition ❶ IN THE SAME WAY AS, in the manner of, in a similar way to, after the fashion of, along the lines of. ❷ TYPICAL OF, characteristic of, in character with.
▶ noun we'll not see his like again: EQUAL, match, counterpart, fellow, twin, mate, parallel, peer, compeer.

likeable adjective PLEASANT, nice, friendly, agreeable, amiable, genial, charming, engaging, pleasing, appealing, winning, attractive, winsome, lovable, adorable.
– OPPOSITES unpleasant.

likelihood noun LIKELINESS, probability, good chance, chance, prospect, good prospect, possibility.

likely adjective ❶ PROBABLE, possible, to be expected, on the cards, odds-on. ❷ APT, inclined, tending, liable, prone. ❸ a likely place: SUITABLE, appropriate, fit, fitting, acceptable, proper, right, qualified, relevant, reasonable. ❹ the most likely young people: PROMISING, talented, gifted; *informal* up-and-coming.
– OPPOSITES unlikely.

liken verb COMPARE, equate, analogize, draw an analogy between, draw a parallel between, parallel, correlate, link, associate.

likeness noun ❶ RESEMBLANCE, similarity, sameness, similitude, correspondence, analogy. ❷ GUISE, semblance, appearance, outward form, form, shape, character. ❸ PICTURE, drawing, sketch, painting, portrait, photograph, study, representation, image, bust, statue, statuette, sculpture.

liking noun FONDNESS, love, affection, desire, preference, partiality, penchant, bias, weakness, weak spot, soft spot, appreciation, taste, predilection, fancy, inclination, bent, leaning, affinity, proclivity, propensity, proneness, tendency.
– OPPOSITES dislike, aversion.

limb noun ❶ ARM, leg, wing, member, extremity, appendage. ❷ BRANCH, bough.

limber
■ **limber up** WARM UP, loosen up, stretch, exercise, get ready.

limelight noun FOCUS OF ATTENTION, public attention, public notice, public eye, public recognition, publicity, fame, renown, celebrity, stardom, notability, eminence, prominence, spotlight.

limit noun ❶ BOUNDARY, border, bound, frontier, edge, perimeter, confines, periphery. ❷ MAXIMUM, ceiling, limitation, restriction, curb, check, restraint.
▶ verb ❶ PLACE A LIMIT ON, restrict, curb, check, keep within bounds, hold in check, restrain, confine, control, ration, reduce. ❷ RESTRICT, curb, restrain, constrain, hinder, impede, hamper, check, trammel.

limitation noun ❶ RESTRICTION, curb, restraint, constraint, qualification, control, check, hindrance, impediment, obstacle, obstruction, bar, barrier, block, deterrent. ❷ INABILITY, incapability, incapacity, defect, frailty, weakness.

limited adjective ❶ **limited accommodation**: RESTRICTED, scanty, sparse, cramped, basic, minimal, inadequate. ❷ **limited experience**: RESTRICTED, little, narrow, scanty, basic, minimal, inadequate, insufficient.
– OPPOSITES ample, boundless.

limitless adjective ❶ **a limitless expanse**: INFINITE, endless, never-ending, interminable, immense, vast, extensive, measureless. ❷ **limitless enthusiasm**: UNLIMITED, boundless, unbounded, illimitable, infinite, endless, unceasing, interminable, inexhaustible, constant, perpetual.

limp adjective ❶ FLOPPY, drooping, droopy, soft, flaccid, flabby, loose, slack. ❷ TIRED, fatigued, weary, exhausted, worn out, lethargic, enervated, feeble, frail, puny, debilitated. ❸ WEAK, characterless, ineffectual, insipid, wishy-washy, vapid; *informal* wet.
– OPPOSITES stiff.

line noun ❶ RULE, bar, score, underline, underscore, stroke, slash. ❷ BAND, stripe, strip, belt, seam. ❸ FURROW, wrinkle, crease, crow's foot, groove, scar. ❹ OUTLINE, contour, configuration, shape, figure, delineation, silhouette, profile. ❺ BOUNDARY, boundary line, limit, border, borderline, frontier, edge, margin, perimeter, periphery. ❻ ROW, queue, procession, column, file, string, chain, array; *Brit. informal* crocodile. ❼ **a line of flight**: COURSE, route, track, channel, path, way, road, lane, trajectory. ❽ LINE OF WORK, line of business, business, field, area, trade, occupation, employment, profession, work, job, calling, career, pursuit, activity, province, speciality. ❾ **a noble line**: LINEAGE, descent, ancestry, parentage, family, extraction, heritage, stock, strain, race, breed. ❿ ROPE, string, cord, cable, wire, thread, twine, strand, filament.
▶ verb BORDER, edge, fringe, bound, skirt, hem, rim, verge.
■ **line up** ❶ FORM A LINE, get into rows/columns, file, form a queue, queue up, group together, fall in. ❷ GET TOGETHER, organize, prepare, assemble, lay on, get, obtain, procure, secure, produce, come up with.

linger verb ❶ STAY, remain, wait around, hang around, delay, dawdle, loiter, dally, take one's time; *informal* dilly-dally; *archaic* tarry. ❷ **the infection lingered**: PERSIST, continue, remain, stay, hang around, be protracted, endure.

link noun ❶ CHAIN RING, loop, connection, connective, coupling, joint, knot. ❷ COMPONENT, constituent, element, part, piece, member, division. ❸ a link between smoking and cancer: CONNECTION, relationship, relatedness, association, tie-up. ❹ strong family links: BOND, tie, attachment, connection, relationship, association, affiliation, mutual interest.
▶ verb ❶ CONNECT, fasten together, attach, bind, unite, couple, yoke. ❷ JOIN, connect, associate, relate, bracket.
– OPPOSITES detach, separate.

lionize verb MAKE MUCH OF, treat as a celebrity, glorify, exalt, acclaim, sing someone's praises, praise, extol, eulogize, fête, pay tribute to, put on a pedestal, hero-worship, worship, idolize, adulate, aggrandize; *formal* laud.
– OPPOSITES vilify.

lip noun EDGE, rim, brim, margin, border, verge, brink.

liquid noun FLUID, liquor, solution, juice, sap.

liquidate verb ❶ liquidate assets: CONVERT TO CASH, cash, cash in, sell off, sell up, realize. ❷ liquidate an enemy: KILL, murder, put to death, do away with, assassinate, put an end to, eliminate, dispatch, finish off, destroy, obliterate; *informal* do in, bump off, rub out, wipe out.

liquidize verb BLEND, crush, purée, pulverize, process.

list[1] noun CATALOGUE, inventory, record, register, roll, file, index, directory, listing, enumeration, table, tabulation, schedule, syllabus, calendar, programme, series.
▶ verb NOTE DOWN, write down, record, register, set down, enter, itemize, enumerate, catalogue, file, tabulate, schedule, chronicle, classify, alphabetize.

list[2] verb LEAN, lean over, tilt, tip, heel, heel over, careen, cant, incline, slant, slope.

listen verb PAY ATTENTION TO, be attentive to, hear, attend, hark, give ear to, lend an ear to, hang on someone's words, keep one's ears open, prick up one's ears; *informal* be all ears, pin back one's ears.

listless adjective LANGUID, lethargic, languishing, enervated, lackadaisical, spiritless, lifeless, inactive, inert, indolent, apathetic, passive, dull, heavy, sluggish, slothful, limp, languorous, torpid, supine, indifferent, uninterested, impassive.
– OPPOSITES energetic.

literal adjective WORD-FOR-WORD, verbatim, line-for-line, exact, precise, faithful, close, strict, undeviating, true, accurate.

literary adjective ❶ a literary man: WELL READ, widely read, educated, well educated, scholarly, learned, intellectual, cultured, erudite, bookish, studious, lettered. ❷ a literary word: FORMAL, poetic.

literate adjective ❶ scarcely literate: ABLE TO READ AND WRITE, educated, schooled. ❷ literate people: EDUCATED, well educated, well read, scholarly, learned, intellectual, erudite, cultured, cultivated, knowledgeable, well informed. ❸ literate prose: WELL WRITTEN, stylish, polished, articulate, lucid, eloquent.

literature noun ❶ WRITTEN WORKS, writings, printed works, published works, letters.

❷ literature about the course: PRINTED MATTER, brochure, leaflet, pamphlet, circular, information, data, facts; *informal* bumf.

lithe adjective AGILE, flexible, supple, limber, loose-limbed, pliant, pliable, lissom.

litigation noun LAWSUIT, legal case, case, legal dispute, legal contest, legal action, legal proceedings, suit, suit at law.

litter noun ❶ RUBBISH, debris, refuse, junk, odds and ends, fragments, detritus, flotsam; *N. Amer.* trash. ❷ a litter of pups: BROOD, young, offspring, progeny, family. ❸ an invalid on a litter: STRETCHER, portable bed/couch, palanquin.
▶ verb MAKE UNTIDY, mess up, make a mess of, clutter up, throw into disorder, disarrange; *informal* make a shambles of.

little adjective ❶ a little man: SMALL, short, slight, petite, tiny, wee, miniature, mini, diminutive, minute, infinitesimal, microscopic, minuscule, dwarf, midget, pygmy, bantam; *informal* teeny, teeny-weeny, pint-sized. ❷ when he was little: SMALL, young, junior. ❸ little difficulties: UNIMPORTANT, insignificant, minor, trivial, trifling, petty, paltry, inconsequential, negligible, nugatory. ❹ little advantage: HARDLY ANY, small, scant, meagre, skimpy, sparse, insufficient, exiguous; *informal* piddling. ❺ nasty little minds: MEAN, narrow, narrow-minded, small-minded, base, cheap, shallow, petty, illiberal, provincial, parochial, insular.
– OPPOSITES large.
▶ adverb little known: HARDLY, barely, scarcely, not much, only slightly, only just.

liturgy noun RITUAL, worship, service, ceremony, rite, observance, celebration, office, sacrament.

live adjective ❶ ALIVE, living, having life, breathing, animate, vital, existing, existent; *informal* in the land of the living. ❷ a real live tiger: ACTUAL, in the flesh, not imaginary, true to life, genuine, authentic. ❸ a live show: NOT PRERECORDED, unedited, with an audience. ❹ live coals: GLOWING, aglow, burning, alight, flaming, aflame, blazing, hot, smouldering. ❺ live electric wires: CHARGED, connected, active, switched on. ❻ a live issue: CURRENT, topical, active, prevalent, important, of interest, lively, vital, pressing, burning, pertinent, controversial, debatable, unsettled.
– OPPOSITES dead.

livelihood noun LIVING, subsistence, means of support, income, keep, maintenance, sustenance, upkeep, work, employment, occupation, trade, profession, career.

lively adjective ❶ FULL OF LIFE, active, animated, energetic, alive, vigorous, alert, spirited, high-spirited, vivacious, enthusiastic, keen, cheerful, buoyant, sparkling, bouncy, perky, sprightly, spry, frisky, agile, nimble; *informal* chirpy, chipper, peppy. ❷ a lively pace: BRISK, quick, rapid, swift, speedy, vigorous. ❸ a lively discussion: ANIMATED, spirited, stimulating, heated, enthusiastic, forceful. ❹ a lively scene: BUSY, crowded, bustling, hectic, swarming, teeming, astir, buzzing,

thronging. ❺ **things got lively:** EVENTFUL, exciting, busy, dangerous; *informal* hairy.
– OPPOSITES apathetic.

liven
■ **liven up** ENLIVEN, put some life into, brighten up, cheer up, perk up, put some spark into, add some zest to, give a boost to, animate, vitalize, vivify; *informal* pep up; *Brit. informal* hot up.

living adjective ❶ ALIVE, live, having life, breathing, animate, vital, existing, existent; *informal* in the land of the living. ❷ **living languages:** CURRENT, in use, extant, existing, contemporary, operating, active, continuing, surviving, persisting.
▶ noun LIVELIHOOD, subsistence, means of support, income, keep, maintenance, sustenance, upkeep, job, work, employment, occupation.

load noun ❶ CARGO, freight, charge, burden, lading, contents, consignment, shipment, lorryload, shipload, containerload, busload. ❷ BURDEN, onus, weight, responsibility, duty, charge, obligation, tax, strain, trouble, worry, encumbrance, affliction, oppression, handicap, trial, tribulation, cross, millstone, albatross, incubus.
▶ verb ❶ FILL, fill up, lade, freight, charge, pack, pile, heap, stack, stuff, cram. ❷ BURDEN, weigh down, weight, saddle, charge, tax, strain, encumber, hamper, handicap, overburden, overwhelm, oppress, trouble, worry. ❸ **load a gun:** PRIME, charge, fill. ❹ **load a dice:** WEIGHT, add weight to, bias, rig.

loaf verb LAZE, lounge, do nothing, idle, lie around, hang about, waste time, fritter away time, take things easy, twiddle one's thumbs, sit on one's hands.

loan noun ADVANCE, credit, mortgage.
▶ verb LEND, advance, give credit, give on loan, let out.

loath adjective RELUCTANT, unwilling, disinclined, not in the mood, against, averse, opposed, resisting.
– OPPOSITES eager.

loathe verb HATE, detest, abhor, despise, abominate, have an aversion to, not be able to bear, dislike, shrink from, recoil from, feel repugnance towards, be unable to stomach, execrate.
– OPPOSITES like, love.

loathing noun HATRED, hate, detestation, abhorrence, aversion, abomination, repugnance, disgust, revulsion, odium, antipathy, dislike, ill will, enmity, execration.

loathsome adjective HATEFUL, detestable, abhorrent, odious, repugnant, disgusting, repulsive, revolting, nauseating, abominable, vile, nasty, obnoxious, horrible, offensive, disagreeable, despicable, contemptible, reprehensible, execrable; *informal* yucky.

local noun ❶ LOCAL PERSON, native, inhabitant, resident, parishioner. ❷ **drinking in his local:** BAR, inn, tavern; *Brit.* PUB, public house; *informal* watering hole; *Brit. informal* boozer.

locale noun PLACE, site, spot, position, location, venue, area, neighbourhood, locality, setting, scene.

locality noun ❶ VICINITY, surrounding area, area,

neighbourhood, district, region, environs, locale. ❷ LOCATION, position, place, whereabouts, bearings; *technical* locus.

localize verb CONFINE, restrict, contain, limit, circumscribe, delimit.

locate verb ❶ FIND, find out, discover, identify, pinpoint, detect, uncover, track down, run to earth, unearth, hit upon, come across, reveal, pin down. ❷ SITUATE, site, position, place, put, build, establish, station, set, fix, settle.

location noun POSITION, place, situation, whereabouts, bearings, site, spot, point, scene, setting, venue, locale; *technical* locus.

lock verb ❶ BOLT, fasten, bar, secure, make secure, padlock. ❷ the wheels locked: JAM, become immovable, become rigid.
– OPPOSITES unlock.
▶ noun BOLT, catch, fastener, clasp, bar, hasp.
■ **lock up** *see* IMPRISON.

locker noun CUPBOARD, compartment, cabinet, cubicle, storeroom, storage room.

lodge verb ❶ BOARD, have lodgings, put up, reside, dwell, sojourn, stop; *informal* have digs. ❷ lodge money: DEPOSIT, put in, bank. ❸ REGISTER, submit, put forward, place, file, lay, put on record, record. ❹ the bullet lodged in his brain: BECOME FIXED, become embedded, become implanted, stick, become caught, come to rest.

lofty adjective ❶ TOWERING, soaring, tall, high, elevated, sky-high, sky-scraping. ❷ lofty contempt: ARROGANT, haughty, proud, self-important, conceited, overweening, disdainful, supercilious, condescending, patronizing, lordly, snobbish, scornful, contemptuous, insulting, cavalier; *informal* high and mighty, stuck up, snooty, toffee-nosed, uppity. ❸ lofty ideals: NOBLE, exalted, grand, sublime, imposing, esoteric.
– OPPOSITES low, modest, base.

log noun ❶ BLOCK, piece, chunk, billet, stump, trunk, branch, bole. ❷ a ship's log: LOGBOOK, record, register, journal, diary, daybook, chart, account, tally.

logic noun ❶ LINE OF REASONING, reasoning, argument, argumentation. ❷ REASON, sound judgement, judgement, wisdom, sense, good sense, common sense, rationale, relevance, coherence.

logical adjective ❶ a logical argument: REASONED, well reasoned, rational, sound, cogent, coherent, clear, consistent, relevant. ❷ the logical outcome: MOST LIKELY, likeliest, plausible, obvious. ❸ a logical person: REASONING, thinking, straight-thinking, rational, consistent.
– OPPOSITES illogical.

loiter verb HANG AROUND/ABOUT, linger, wait, skulk, loaf, lounge, idle, waste time, dawdle, take one's time, go at a snail's pace, dally, stroll, saunter, delay, loll.

lone adjective SINGLE, solitary, sole, unaccompanied.

lonely adjective ❶ feeling lonely: FRIENDLESS, companionless, lonesome, forlorn, forsaken, abandoned, rejected, isolated, outcast, sad, unhappy, despondent. ❷ a lonely landscape: DESOLATE, barren, isolated, out of the way, remote, secluded, off the

beaten track, deserted, uninhabited, unfrequented, unpopulated, godforsaken.
– OPPOSITES popular, crowded.

long[1] adjective ❶ LENGTHY, extended, extensive, stretched out, spread out. ❷ **a long speech**: LENGTHY, prolonged, protracted, extended, long-drawn-out, spun out, dragged out, interminable, long-winded, verbose, prolix, tedious.
– OPPOSITES short.

long[2]
■ **long for** WISH FOR, desire, want, yearn for, crave, hunger for, thirst for, covet, lust after, hope for, dream of, pine for, eat one's heart out over, have a fancy for, hanker for/after; *informal* itch for, have a yen for.

longing noun WISH, desire, wanting, yearning, craving, hunger, thirst, covetousness, lust, hope, dream, aspiration, pining, fancy, urge, hankering; *informal* itch, yen.

look verb ❶ SEE, take a look, glance, fix one's gaze, focus, observe, view, regard, eye, take in, watch, examine, study, inspect, scan, scrutinize, survey, check, contemplate, consider, pay attention to, run the eyes over, peep, peek, glimpse, gaze, stare, gape, ogle; *informal* take a gander, have a squint, gawp, rubberneck; *Brit. informal* take a butcher's, take a dekko, take a shufti; *N. Amer. informal* eyeball. ❷ **she looks ill**: SEEM, seem to be, appear, appear to be, give every appearance/ indication of being, look to be, strike someone as being. ❸ **the house looks on to the sea**: FACE, overlook, front, front on, give on to.
▶ noun ❶ SIGHT, glance, observation, view, examination, study, inspection, scan, survey, peep, peek, glimpse, gaze, stare, gape, ogle; *informal* eyeful, gander, look-see, once-over, squint; *Brit. informal* butcher's, dekko, shufti. ❷ EXPRESSION, face, countenance, features, mien.
■ **look after** TAKE CARE OF, care for, attend to, tend, mind, keep an eye on, watch, sit with, nurse, take charge of, supervise, protect, guard. **look down on** REGARD WITH CONTEMPT, scorn, disdain, hold in disdain, sneer at, spurn, disparage, despise; *informal* look down one's nose at, turn up one's nose at. **look for** SEARCH FOR, hunt for, seek, look around for, cast about for, forage for.

lookalike noun DOUBLE, twin, exact likeness, image, living image, exact match, clone, duplicate, Doppelgänger; *informal* spitting image, spit, dead ringer.

loom verb ❶ APPEAR, emerge, become visible, take shape, materialize, reveal itself. ❷ BE IMMINENT, impend, be close, be ominously close, threaten, menace.

loop noun COIL, hoop, noose, circle, ring, oval, spiral, curl, twirl, whorl, twist, convolution.
▶ verb FORM A HOOP WITH, make a circle with, bend into spirals/ whorls.

loophole noun LET-OUT CLAUSE, means of avoidance, means of escape, escape clause, escape route, ambiguity, omission.

loose adjective ❶ AT LARGE, at liberty, free, on the loose, unconfined, untied, unchained, untethered, unsecured, unshackled, unfastened,

unrestricted, unbound, freed, let go, liberated, released, set loose. ❷ WOBBLY, not secure, insecure, rickety, unsteady, movable. ❸ **loose hair**: UNTIED, unpinned, hanging free, flowing, floppy. ❹ **loose clothes**: LOOSE-FITTING, easy-fitting, generously cut, slack, baggy, saggy, sloppy. ❺ **a loose translation**: INEXACT, imprecise, vague, indefinite, ill-defined, broad, general, non-specific. ❻ **loose women/morals**: IMMORAL, disreputable, dissolute, corrupt, fast, promiscuous, debauched, dissipated, degenerate, wanton, whorish, unchaste, licentious, lascivious, lustful, libertine, abandoned, profligate, reprobate. ❼ **be/hang loose**: RELAXED, informal, uninhibited, unreserved, frank, open, unceremonious, unconstrained.
■ **let loose** SET FREE, unloose, turn loose, set loose, untie, unchain, untether, unfasten, detach, unleash, let go, release, free, liberate.

loosen verb ❶ **loosen a nut**: SLACKEN, slack, unstick, work loose, work free. ❷ **loosen control**: LOOSE, relax, slacken, weaken, lessen, moderate.
– OPPOSITES tighten.
■ **loosen up** RELAX, ease up/off; *informal* let up, hang loose, lighten up.

loot noun BOOTY, spoils, plunder, haul, stolen goods, pillage, prize; *informal* swag, the goods, hot goods, boodle.
▶ verb PLUNDER, pillage, rob, burgle, steal from, ransack, sack, maraud, ravage, despoil.

lop verb CUT OFF, chop, chop off, hack off, prune, sever, clip, dock, crop, remove, detach.

loquacious adjective TALKATIVE, garrulous, voluble, long-winded, wordy, verbose, effusive, chatty, gossipy; *informal* big-mouthed, gabby, gassy.
– OPPOSITES taciturn.

lose verb ❶ MISLAY, misplace, fail to keep/retain, fail to keep sight of, drop, forget. ❷ **losing a lot of blood**: BE DEPRIVED OF, suffer the loss of. ❸ **lose the police**: ESCAPE FROM, evade, elude, dodge, give the slip to, shake off, throw off, throw off the scent, duck, get rid of. ❹ SUFFER DEFEAT, be defeated, be the loser, be worsted, get/have the worst of it, be beaten, be conquered, be vanquished, be trounced, come off second-best, fail, come to grief, meet one's Waterloo; *informal* come a cropper.

loser noun RUNNER-UP, also-ran, the defeated, the vanquished, failure, born loser; *informal* flop, dud, non-starter, no-hoper, washout.
– OPPOSITES winner, success.

loss noun ❶ MISLAYING, misplacement, dropping, forgetting. ❷ **the loss of prestige**: LOSING, deprivation, privation, forfeiture, bereavement, disappearance, waste, squandering, dissipation. ❸ **losses in battle**: CASUALTY, fatality, dead, death toll, number killed. ❹ **firms making a loss**: DEFICIT, debit, debt, lack of profit, deficiency, losing, depletion.

lost adjective ❶ MISSING, strayed, gone missing/astray, mislaid, misplaced, vanished, disappeared, forgotten. ❷ STRAY, astray, off course, off-track, disorientated, having lost one's bearings, adrift, going round in circles, at sea. ❸ **lost opportunities**: MISSED, passed, forfeited, neglected, wasted, squandered, dissipated, gone by the board; *informal* down the drain.

lotion noun CREAM, salve, ointment, moisturizer, balm, emollient, lubricant, unguent, liniment, embrocation, pomade, hand lotion, body lotion.

lottery noun DRAW, raffle, sweepstake, game of chance, gamble, drawing of lots, bingo, tombola.

loud adjective ❶ BLARING, booming, noisy, deafening, resounding, reverberant, sonorous, stentorian, roaring, thunderous, tumultuous, clamorous, head-splitting, ear-splitting, ear-piercing, piercing, strident, harsh, raucous. ❷ **loud young women**: BRASH, brazen, bold, loud-mouthed, vociferous, raucous, aggressive, pushy, coarse, crude, rough, crass, vulgar, brassy. ❸ **loud colours**: GARISH, gaudy, flashy, bold, flamboyant, lurid, glaring, showy, obtrusive, vulgar, tawdry, tasteless, meretricious; *informal* flash, kitsch, camp, tacky; *Brit. informal* naff.
– OPPOSITES quiet.

lounge verb LAZE, lie, lie around, recline, relax, take it easy, sprawl, slump, loll, repose, loaf, idle, loiter, hang about, linger, skulk, waste time; *informal* hang out.
▶ **noun** SITTING ROOM, drawing room, living room, parlour.

lousy adjective ❶ **a lousy player**: VERY BAD, poor, incompetent, inadequate, unsatisfactory, inferior, careless, second-rate, terrible, miserable; *informal* rotten, no-good, poxy; *Brit. informal* duff. ❷ **a lousy trick**: DIRTY, low, mean, base, despicable, contemptible, hateful, detestable, loathsome, vile, wicked, vicious.

lout noun BOOR, oaf, dolt, churl, bumpkin, yahoo, barbarian; *informal* slob, clodhopper; *Brit. informal* yob, yobbo; *N. Amer. informal* lummox.

lovable adjective ADORABLE, dear, sweet, cute, charming, lovely, likeable, attractive, delightful, captivating, enchanting, engaging, bewitching, pleasing, appealing, winsome, winning, endearing, warm-hearted, cuddly.
– OPPOSITES hateful, loathsome.

love verb ❶ BE IN LOVE WITH, be fond of, feel affection for, be attracted to, be attached to, care fore, hold dear, adore, think the world of, dote on, worship, idolize, treasure, prize, cherish, be devoted to, desire, want, be infatuated with, lust after, long for, yearn for, adulate; *informal* have a crush on, lech after, have the hots for, be soft on; *Brit. informal* fancy. ❷ **she loves chocolate**: LIKE, have a liking for, have a weakness for, be partial to, have a soft spot for, be addicted to, enjoy, find enjoyment in, relish, savour, appreciate, take pleasure in, delight in; *informal* get a kick out of, have a thing about.
– OPPOSITES hate.
▶ **noun** ❶ AFFECTION, fondness, care, concern, attachment, regard, warmth, intimacy, devotion, adoration, passion, ardour, desire, lust, yearning, infatuation, adulation. ❷ LIKING FOR, weakness for, partiality for, enjoyment of, appreciation of, delight in, relish, passion for. ❸ BELOVED, loved one, true love, love of one's life, dear, dearest, dear one, darling, sweetheart,

sweet, sweet one, angel, lover, inamorato/inamorata.

love affair noun AFFAIR, romance, relationship, liaison, amour, intrigue, affair of the heart, affaire de cœur.

lovelorn adjective LOVESICK, unrequited in love, crossed in love, spurned, jilted, ill-starred, miserable, unhappy, pining, moping.

lovely adjective ❶ a lovely girl: BEAUTIFUL, pretty, attractive, good-looking, glamorous, handsome, sweet, fair, charming, adorable, enchanting, engaging, bewitching, winsome, seductive, ravishing; *archaic* comely. ❷ a lovely surprise: DELIGHTFUL, pleasant, nice, agreeable, pleasing, marvellous, wonderful; *informal* fabulous, terrific.
– OPPOSITES ugly, horrible.

lover noun ❶ BOYFRIEND, girlfriend, mistress, lady-love, other man, other woman, beau, loved one, beloved, sweetheart, inamorata, inamorato; *informal* bit on the side, bit of fluff, toy boy, fancy man, fancy woman; *archaic* paramour. ❷ ADMIRER, devotee, fan, enthusiast, aficionado; *informal* buff, freak.

loving adjective AFFECTIONATE, fond, devoted, caring, adoring, doting, solicitous, demonstrative, tender, warm, warm-hearted, friendly, kind, sympathetic, charitable, cordial, amiable, amorous, ardent, passionate.

low adjective ❶ SHORT, small, little, squat, stubby, stunted, truncated, dwarfish, knee-high. ❷ supplies are low: SPARSE, meagre, scarce, scanty, scant, few, little, deficient, inadequate, paltry, measly, trifling, reduced, depleted, diminished. ❸ a low hum: SOFT, quiet, muted, subdued, muffled, hushed, quietened, whispered, murmured, gentle, dulcet, indistinct, inaudible. ❹ feeling low: DEPRESSED, dejected, despondent, disheartened, downhearted, downcast, gloomy, glum, unhappy, sad, miserable, blue, morose, moody, heavy-hearted, forlorn; *informal* fed up, down in the mouth, down in the dumps; *Brit. informal* brassed off, cheesed off. ❺ low intelligence: LOW-GRADE, inferior, substandard, below par, second-rate, deficient, defective, wanting, lacking, inadequate, mediocre, unacceptable, worthless. ❻ a low opinion: UNFAVOURABLE, poor, bad, adverse, hostile, negative. ❼ low creatures: MEAN, nasty, foul, vile, despicable, contemptible, base, villainous, hateful, loathsome, reprehensible, depraved, debased, wretched, miserable, sorry. ❽ low comedy: VULGAR, crude, coarse, obscene, indecent, gross, ribald, smutty, bawdy, pornographic, rude, rough, unrefined, indelicate, improper, offensive; *informal* blue.

low-down noun INFORMATION, data, facts, facts and figures, intelligence, inside information; *informal* info, gen, dope.

lower[1] adjective ❶ of lower status: LESSER, lower-level, lower-grade, subordinate, junior, inferior, minor, secondary. ❷ lower prices/wages: CHEAPER, reduced, decreased, lessened, cut, slashed, curtailed, pruned.
– OPPOSITES higher.

lower[2] verb ❶ LET DOWN, take down, haul down, drop, let fall, let sink. ❷ lower one's voice: SOFTEN,

quieten, hush, tone down, muffle, turn down, mute. ❸ DEGRADE, debase, demean, downgrade, discredit, devalue, dishonour, disgrace, belittle, humble, humiliate, disparage. ❹ **lower prices:** REDUCE, bring down, decrease, lessen, cut, slash, curtail, prune. ❺ **the winds lowered:** ABATE, die down, subside, let up, moderate, slacken, dwindle, lessen, ebb, fade away, wane, taper off, lull.
– OPPOSITES raise.

lowly adjective ❶ **lowly people:** LOW, humble, low-born, low-ranking, plebeian, peasant, poor, common, ordinary, inferior, subordinate. ❷ **lowly ambitions:** LOW, simple, plain, ordinary, commonplace, run-of-the-mill, modest, unambitious, unpretentious, unaspiring.
– OPPOSITES aristocratic, exalted.

loyal adjective FAITHFUL, true, true-hearted, tried and true, trusted, trustworthy, trusty, true-blue, steadfast, staunch, dependable, reliable, devoted, dutiful, patriotic, constant, unchanging, unwavering, unswerving, firm, stable.
– OPPOSITES disloyal, treacherous.

loyalty noun FAITHFULNESS, fidelity, allegiance, trueness, true-heartedness, trustiness, trustworthiness, steadfastness, staunchness, dependability, reliability, devotion, duty, patriotism, constancy, stability; *historical* fealty.
– OPPOSITES disloyalty, treachery.

lucid adjective ❶ **a lucid description:** CLEAR, clear-cut, crystal-clear, comprehensible, intelligible, understandable, plain, simple, direct, straightforward, graphic, explicit. ❷ **he seemed lucid:** SANE, rational, in one's right mind, in possession of one's faculties, of sound mind, compos mentis, sensible, clear-headed.
– OPPOSITES confusing.

luck noun ❶ FATE, fortune, destiny, chance, fortuity, accident, hazard, serendipity. ❷ GOOD LUCK, good fortune, success, prosperity, advantage, advantageousness, felicity; *informal* lucky break.

lucky adjective ❶ **lucky people:** FORTUNATE, blessed with good luck, favoured, born under a lucky star, charmed, successful, prosperous, happy, advantaged. ❷ **a lucky guess:** FORTUNATE, fortuitous, providential, advantageous, timely, opportune, expedient, auspicious, propitious.
– OPPOSITES unlucky.

lucrative adjective PROFITABLE, profit-making, moneymaking, paying, high-income, well paid, high-paying, gainful, remunerative, productive, fat, fruitful, rewarding, worthwhile.
– OPPOSITES unprofitable.

ludicrous adjective ABSURD, ridiculous, laughable, risible, derisible, comic, comical, farcical, silly, crazy, zany, nonsensical, odd, outlandish, eccentric, incongruous, preposterous.
– OPPOSITES sensible.

lull verb SOOTHE, quiet, hush, silence, calm, still, quell, assuage, allay, ease, alleviate, pacify.
▶ **noun** RESPITE, interval, break, hiatus, let-up, calm, calmness, stillness, quiet, quietness, tranquillity, silence, hush.

lumber verb CLUMP, stump, plod, trudge, stamp, shuffle, shamble, stumble, waddle, lump along.

lumbering adjective AWKWARD, clumsy, heavy-footed, blundering, bumbling, inept, maladroit, ungainly, like a bull in a china shop, ungraceful, lumpish, ponderous; *informal* clodhopping.
– OPPOSITES graceful, agile.

luminous adjective ILLUMINATED, shining, bright, brilliant, radiant, dazzling, glowing, effulgent, luminescent, phosphorescent, vivid, resplendent.

lump noun ❶ CHUNK, wedge, hunk, piece, mass, cake, nugget, ball, dab, pat, clod, gobbet, wad, clump, cluster, mound; *Brit. informal* gob. ❷ BUMP, swelling, bruise, bulge, protuberance, growth, carbuncle, tumour, tumescence, node.

lunacy noun INSANITY, madness, mental illness/derangement, dementia, dementedness, loss of reason, unsoundness of mind, mania, frenzy, psychosis; *informal* craziness.
– OPPOSITES sanity.

lunatic noun MANIAC, madman, madwoman, imbecile, idiot, psychopath; *informal* loony, nut, nutcase, head case, headbanger, psycho; *Brit. informal* nutter; *N. Amer. informal* screwball.

lunge verb ❶ SPRING, jump, leap, bound, dash, charge, pounce, dive. ❷ STAB, jab, poke, thrust at, pitch into, lash out at, take a swing at, aim a blow at; *informal* take a swipe at.

lurch verb STAGGER, sway, reel, weave, stumble, totter.

lure verb ENTICE, cajole, attract, induce, inveigle, decoy, draw, lead, allure, tempt, seduce, beguile, ensnare.

lurid adjective ❶ lurid colours: BRILLIANT, glaring, flaming, dazzling, glowing, intense, vivid, showy, gaudy. ❷ lurid descriptions: SENSATIONAL, melodramatic, exaggerated, extravagant, graphic, explicit, unrestrained, shocking, startling.
– OPPOSITES muted, restrained.

lurk verb SKULK, lie in wait, lie low, hide, conceal oneself, take cover, crouch, sneak, slink, prowl, steal, tiptoe.

luscious adjective JUICY, sweet, succulent, mouth-watering, tasty, appetizing, delectable, palatable, toothsome, nectar-like; *informal* scrumptious, yummy.

lush adjective ❶ lush vegetation: LUXURIANT, abundant, profuse, exuberant, dense, thick, riotous, overgrown, prolific, rank, flourishing, verdant, green. ❷ lush rooms: LUXURIOUS, sumptuous, grand, palatial, opulent, lavish, elaborate, extravagant; *informal* plush, ritzy.

lustful adjective LECHEROUS, lascivious, lewd, libidinous, licentious, salacious, prurient, concupiscent, wanton, unchaste, hot-blooded, passionate, sensual, sexy; *informal* horny; *Brit. informal* randy.
– OPPOSITES chaste.

lustrous adjective SHINY, shining, glossy, gleaming, glowing, bright, burnished, polished, dazzling, sparkling, glistening, twinkling, shimmering, luminous.
– OPPOSITES dull.

lusty adjective ❶ lusty young men: HEALTHY, strong, vigorous, robust, hale and hearty, hearty, energetic, lively, blooming, rugged, sturdy, tough, stalwart, brawny, hefty, husky, burly, solidly built, powerful, virile, red-blooded. ❷ a lusty cry: LOUD, vigorous, hearty, powerful, forceful.

luxuriant adjective ❶ luxuriant vegetation: LUSH, abundant, profuse, exuberant, dense, thick, riotous, overgrown, prolific, teeming, verdant. ❷ ORNATE, elaborate, fancy, adorned, decorated, embellished, embroidered, extravagant, flamboyant, ostentatious, showy, baroque, rococo.

luxurious adjective OPULENT, affluent, sumptuous, expensive, rich, costly, de luxe, lush, grand, splendid, magnificent, lavish, well appointed, comfortable, extravagant, ornate, fancy; *informal* plush, ritzy, swanky; *Brit. informal* posh.
– OPPOSITES spartan.

luxury noun ❶ live in luxury: LUXURIOUSNESS, opulence, affluence, sumptuousness, grandeur, splendour, magnificence, lavishness, lap of luxury, bed of roses. ❷ life's luxuries: EXTRA, non-essential, frill, extravagance, indulgence, treat, refinement.
– OPPOSITES simplicity, necessity.

lying noun UNTRUTHFULNESS, fabrication, fibbing, perjury, falseness, falsity, dishonesty, mendacity, storytelling, dissimulation, dissembling, prevarication, deceit, guile; *informal* crookedness.
▶ adjective UNTRUTHFUL, fabricating, false, dishonest, mendacious, dissimulating, dissembling, prevaricating, deceitful, guileful, double-dealing, two-faced; *informal* crooked.
– OPPOSITES truthful.

lyrical adjective RHAPSODIC, effusive, rapturous, ecstatic, euphoric, carried away, emotional, impassioned.
– OPPOSITES unenthusiastic.

Mm

macabre adjective GRUESOME, grisly, grim, gory, morbid, ghastly, hideous, horrific, horrible, horrifying, horrendous, frightening, frightful, fearsome, shocking, dreadful.

Machiavellian adjective DEVIOUS, cunning, crafty, artful, wily, sly, scheming, designing, conniving, opportunistic, insidious, treacherous, perfidious, two-faced, double-dealing, unscrupulous, deceitful, dishonest.
– OPPOSITES straightforward.

machine noun APPLIANCE, apparatus, instrument, tool, device, contraption, gadget, mechanism, engine, motor, vehicle, car, bicycle, motor cycle, aeroplane.

machismo noun MASCULINITY, manliness, virility, toughness, chauvinism, male chauvinism, sexism.

mad adjective ❶ INSANE, deranged, crazy, demented, of unsound mind, crazed, lunatic, non compos mentis, unbalanced, unhinged, unstable, distracted, manic, frenzied, raving, distraught, frantic, hysterical, delirious, psychotic; *informal* not quite right, mad as a hatter, mad as a March hare, foaming at the mouth, off one's head, out of one's mind, off one's nut, nuts, nutty, off one's rocker, round the bend, raving mad, batty, bonkers, crackpot, cuckoo, loopy, loony, bananas, loco, dippy, screwy, with a screw loose, off the wall, not all there, not right upstairs; *Brit. informal* barmy, crackers, round the twist, not the full shilling, off one's trolley. ❷ *See* ANGRY. ❸ a mad idea: INSANE, foolish, stupid, lunatic, foolhardy, idiotic, crackbrained, irrational, unreasonable, illogical, senseless, nonsensical, absurd, impractical, silly, inane, asinine, ludicrous, wild, unwise, imprudent, preposterous. ❹ mad about jazz: *see* ENTHUSIASTIC.
– OPPOSITES sane, sensible.

madden verb ANGER, infuriate, enrage, incense, exasperate, irritate, inflame, annoy, provoke, upset, agitate, vex, irk, pique, gall, make someone's hackles rise, make someone's blood boil; *informal* make someone see red, get someone's back up.

madman noun MANIAC, lunatic, psychopath; *informal* loony, nut, nutcase, head case, headbanger, psycho; *Brit. informal* nutter; *N. Amer. informal* screwball.

madness noun INSANITY, craziness, dementia, mental illness, derangement, dementedness, instability of mind, unsoundness of mind, lunacy, distraction, mania, frenzy, psychosis.
– OPPOSITES sanity, calm.

magazine noun PERIODICAL, journal, publication, supplement, colour supplement; *informal* glossy.

magic noun ❶ SORCERY, witchcraft, wizardry, enchantment, spell-working, necromancy, the supernatural, occultism, the occult, black magic, black art, voodoo, hoodoo, thaumaturgy. ❷ SLEIGHT OF HAND, legerdemain, conjuring, illusion, prestidigitation, deception, trickery, juggling.
▶ adjective ❶ MAGICAL, enchanting, entrancing, spellbinding, fascinating, captivating, charming, glamorous, magnetic, irresistible, hypnotic. ❷ MARVELLOUS, wonderful, excellent; *informal* terrific, fab; *Brit. informal* brilliant, brill.

magician noun SORCERER, sorceress, witch, wizard, warlock, enchanter, enchantress, spell-worker, spell-caster, necromancer, thaumaturge.

magnanimity noun GENEROSITY, charitableness, charity, benevolence, beneficence, open-handedness, big-heartedness, kindness, munificence, bountifulness, largesse, altruism, philanthropy, unselfishness, selflessness, self-sacrifice, mercy, leniency.
– OPPOSITES meanness, selfishness.

magnanimous adjective GENEROUS, charitable, benevolent, beneficent, open-handed, big-hearted, great-hearted, kind, kindly, munificent, bountiful, liberal, altruistic, philanthropic, noble, unselfish, selfless, self-sacrificing, ungrudging, unstinting, forgiving, merciful, lenient, indulgent.
– OPPOSITES mean.

magnificent adjective ❶ SPLENDID, resplendent, grand, grandiose, impressive, imposing, striking, glorious, superb, majestic, august, noble, stately, exalted, awe-inspiring, royal, regal, kingly, princely, sumptuous, opulent, luxurious, lavish, rich, brilliant, radiant, elegant, gorgeous; *informal* ritzy; *Brit. informal* posh. ❷ EXCELLENT, masterly, skilful, virtuoso, splendid, impressive, fine, marvellous, wonderful.
– OPPOSITES ordinary, poor.

magnify verb ❶ AUGMENT, enlarge, expand, amplify, intensify, heighten, deepen, broaden, widen, dilate, boost, enhance. ❷ magnifying their troubles: EXAGGERATE, overstate, overdo, overemphasize, overplay, dramatize, colour, embroider, embellish, enhance, inflate, make a mountain out of a molehill.
– OPPOSITES minimize.

magnitude noun SIZE, extent, measure, proportions, dimensions, volume, weight, quantity, mass, bulk, amplitude, capacity.

mail noun POST, letters, packages, parcels, correspondence.

main adjective HEAD, chief, principal, leading, foremost, most important, central, prime, premier, primary, supreme, predominant, pre-eminent, paramount, cardinal, crucial, vital, critical, pivotal, urgent.
– OPPOSITES minor.

mainly adverb FOR THE MOST PART, mostly, in the main, on the whole, largely, by and large, to a large extent, to a great degree, predominantly, chiefly, principally, substantially, overall, in general, generally, usually, commonly, as a rule.

maintain verb ❶ maintain efficiency: CONTINUE, keep going, keep up, keep alive, keep in existence, carry on, preserve, conserve, prolong, perpetuate, sustain. ❷ maintain the roads: KEEP IN GOOD CONDITION, keep in repair, keep up, conserve, preserve, keep intact, care for, take good care of, look after. ❸ maintain his children: SUPPORT, provide for, keep, finance, feed, nurture, nourish, sustain. ❹ maintain that he is right: INSIST ON, hold to, declare, assert, state, announce, affirm, avow, profess, claim, allege, contend; *formal* aver.

maintenance noun ❶ UPKEEP, repairs, preservation, conservation, care. ❷ pay maintenance: ALIMONY, support, allowance, keep, upkeep, subsistence.

majestic adjective REGAL, royal, kingly, queenly, princely, imperial, noble, lordly, august, exalted, awesome, elevated, lofty, stately, dignified, distinguished, magnificent, grand, splendid, resplendent, glorious, impressive, imposing, marvellous, superb, proud.

major adjective ❶ major poets: GREATEST, best, most important,

leading, foremost, chief, main, outstanding, first-rate, notable, eminent, pre-eminent, supreme. ❷ **a major issue**: IMPORTANT, significant, crucial, vital, great, weighty, paramount, utmost, prime. ❸ **major surgery**: SERIOUS, radical, complicated.
– OPPOSITES minor.

majority noun ❶ LARGER PART/NUMBER, greater part/number, most, more than half, bulk, mass, main body, preponderance, lion's share. ❷ LEGAL AGE, coming-of-age, seniority, adulthood, manhood, womanhood, maturity, age of consent.
– OPPOSITES minority.

make verb ❶ BUILD, construct, assemble, put together, put up, erect, manufacture, produce, fabricate, create, form, fashion, model, mould, shape, forge. ❷ **make them pay**: FORCE TO, compel to, coerce into, press into, drive into, pressure into, pressurize into, oblige to, require to, prevail upon to, dragoon into, impel to, constrain to, urge to; *informal* railroad into, put the heat on, put the screws on, use strong-arm tactics on. ❸ **make a noise/scene**: CAUSE, create, give rise to, produce, bring about, generate, engender, occasion, effect. ❹ **make him president**: CREATE, appoint, designate, name, nominate, select, elect, vote in, install, invest, ordain, assign. ❺ **make a will**: COMPOSE, put together, frame, formulate, prepare, write, direct. ❻ **make money/a profit**: GAIN, acquire, obtain, get, realize, secure, win, earn, net, gross, clear, bring in, take home, pocket. ❼ **make tea**: PREPARE, get ready, put together, concoct, cook; *informal* whip up. ❽ **that makes £100**: COME TO, add up to, total, amount to. ❾ **what do you make it?** ESTIMATE, calculate, compute, gauge, reckon. ❿ **make a decision**: COME TO, settle on, determine on, conclude, establish, seal. ⓫ **make a speech**: GIVE, deliver, utter, give voice to, enunciate, recite, pronounce. ⓬ **make a great leader**: BE, act as, serve as, constitute, perform the function of, play the part of, represent, embody. ⓭ **make the first eleven**: ACHIEVE, attain, get into, gain access to, gain a place in. ⓮ **make the bus**: CATCH, arrive in time for, arrive at, reach, get to.
▶ noun BRAND, label, sort, type, variety, style, mark, marque.
■ **make away with** MAKE OFF WITH, run away with, abscond with, steal, purloin, kidnap, abduct; *informal* swipe, nab; *Brit. informal* nick. **make believe** PRETEND, fantasize, indulge in fantasy, daydream, dream, imagine, romance, play-act, act, enact. **make do** GET ALONG, scrape by, manage, cope, survive, muddle through, make the best of a bad job. **make off** RUN AWAY/OFF, leave, take off, beat a hasty retreat, flee, bolt, fly, make a/one's getaway.

make-believe noun PRETENCE, fantasy, daydreaming, dreaming, fabrication, play-acting, charade, masquerade.
▶ adjective PRETENDED, feigned, made up, fantasy, dream, imagined, imaginary, unreal, fictitious, mock, sham, pretend.

maker noun MANUFACTURER, builder, constructor, producer, creator, fabricator, author, architect, framer.

makeshift adjective STOPGAP, make-do, provisional, temporary, rough and ready, substitute, improvised, standby, jerry-built, thrown together.

maladroit adjective AWKWARD, clumsy, inept, bungling, bumbling, incompetent, unskilful, unhandy, ungainly, inelegant, graceless, gauche, all fingers and thumbs; *informal* butterfingered, ham-fisted, cack-handed.
– OPPOSITES skilful.

malediction noun CURSE, imprecation, execration, anathema, voodoo, damning, damnation.

malice noun MALEVOLENCE, maliciousness, malignity, malignancy, evil intentions, ill will, ill feeling, animosity, animus, hostility, enmity, bad blood, hatred, hate, spite, spitefulness, vindictiveness, rancour, bitterness, grudge, venom, spleen, defamation; *informal* bitchiness, cattiness.
– OPPOSITES benevolence.

malicious adjective MALEVOLENT, malign, malignant, evil, evil-intentioned, ill-natured, hostile, spiteful, baleful, vindictive, rancorous, bitter, venomous, pernicious, hurtful, destructive, defamatory; *informal* bitchy, catty.
– OPPOSITES friendly.

malign verb SLANDER, libel, defame, smear, blacken someone's name/character, vilify, speak ill of, spread lies about, cast aspersions on, misrepresent, traduce, denigrate; *formal* calumniate.
– OPPOSITES praise.

malnutrition noun UNDERNOURISHMENT, lack of food, starvation, famine, anorexia.

maltreat verb TREAT BADLY, ill-treat, ill-use, mistreat, misuse, abuse, handle/treat roughly, bully, injure, harm, hurt, molest.

maltreatment noun ILL-TREATMENT, ill use, mistreatment, abuse, rough handling, mishandling, manhandling, bullying, injury, harm.

manage verb ❶ **manage the organization:** BE IN CHARGE OF, run, be head of, head, direct, control, preside over, lead, govern, rule, command, superintend, supervise, oversee, administer, organize, conduct, handle, guide, be at the helm of; *informal* head up. ❷ **manage to survive:** SUCCEED IN, contrive, engineer, bring about/off, achieve, accomplish, effect. ❸ **will he manage?** COPE, deal with the situation, get along/on, carry on, survive, make do. ❹ **can you manage the dog?** COPE WITH, deal with, handle, control, master, influence.

manageable adjective ❶ **manageable tasks:** EASY, doable, practicable, possible, feasible, viable. ❷ **manageable people:** CONTROLLABLE, governable, tractable, pliant, compliant, docile, accommodating, amenable, yielding, submissive.
– OPPOSITES unmanageable.

management noun ❶ MANAGERS, employers, owners, proprietors, directors, board of directors, board, directorate, executives, administration; *informal* bosses, top brass. ❷ RUNNING, charge, care, direction, leadership, control, governing, ruling, command, superintendence, supervision, administration.

mandatory adjective OBLIGATORY, compulsory, binding, required, requisite, essential, imperative, necessary.
– OPPOSITES voluntary.

mangle verb MUTILATE, hack, cut about, lacerate, maul, tear at, rend, butcher, disfigure, deform.

mangy adjective ❶ SCABBY, scaly, diseased. ❷ SHABBY, moth-eaten, worn, shoddy, dirty, mean, squalid, filthy, seedy; *Brit. informal* grotty.

manhandle verb ❶ HANDLE ROUGHLY, push, pull, shove, maul, mistreat, ill-treat, abuse, injure, damage, beat, batter; *informal* knock about, rough up. ❷ HEAVE, haul, push, shove, pull, tug, manoeuvre; *informal* hump.

mania noun ❶ FRENZY, violence, wildness, hysteria, raving, derangement, dementia. ❷ OBSESSION, compulsion, fixation, fetish, fascination, preoccupation, passion, enthusiasm, urge.

maniac noun *see* MADMAN.

manifest adjective OBVIOUS, clear, plain, apparent, patent, noticeable, perceptible, visible, transparent, conspicuous, unmistakable, distinct, blatant, glaring.
– OPPOSITES secret.
▶ verb *see* SHOW verb (1, 3).

manifestation noun ❶ DISPLAY, show, exhibition, demonstration, presentation, exposition, illustration, exemplification, indication, declaration, expression, profession. ❷ EVIDENCE, proof, testimony, substantiation, sign, indication, mark, symbol, token, symptom.

manifold adjective MULTIFARIOUS, multiple, numerous, many, several, multitudinous, various.

manipulate verb ❶ HANDLE, wield, ply, work. ❷ manipulate someone: INFLUENCE, control, use to one's advantage, exploit, manoeuvre, direct, guide, pull the strings. ❸ manipulate the figures: JUGGLE, massage, falsify, doctor, tamper with, fiddle with, tinker with.

manipulator noun the manipulator of the tools: HANDLER, wielder, operator.

mankind noun MAN, homo sapiens, the human race, the human species, humankind, human beings, humans, people.

manly adjective MASCULINE, all-male, macho, virile, strong, robust, vigorous, muscular, powerful, well built, strapping, sturdy, rugged, tough.
– OPPOSITES effeminate.

manner noun ❶ WAY, means, method, system, approach, technique, procedure, process, methodology, routine, practice, fashion, mode, style, habit, custom. ❷ AIR, appearance, demeanour, aspect, mien, bearing, deportment, cast, behaviour, conduct. ❸ KIND, sort, type, variety, form, nature, breed, brand, stamp, class, category.

mannered adjective AFFECTED, put on, unnatural, artificial, pseudo, stilted, theatrical, posed, stagy, pretentious.
– OPPOSITES natural.

mannerism noun HABIT, characteristic, trait, idiosyncrasy, quirk, foible, peculiarity.

manoeuvre noun ❶ MOVEMENT, move, measure. ❷ TRICK, stratagem, tactic, machination, manipulation, artifice, subterfuge, device, dodge, ploy, ruse, scheme, plan, plot, intrigue; *informal* wangle.
▶ verb ❶ MOVE, work, negotiate, steer, guide, direct, manipulate. ❷ SCHEME, intrigue, plot, use trickery/artifice, machinate; *informal* pull strings.

mantle noun COVERING, cover, blanket, curtain, canopy, cloud, veil, cloak, shroud, screen.
▶ verb COVER, blanket, curtain, envelop, veil, cloak, wrap, shroud, cloud, conceal, hide.

manufacture verb MAKE, produce, mass-produce, build, construct, assemble, put together, create, fabricate, turn out, process, form, fashion, model, mould, shape, forge.

manufacturer noun MAKER, producer, builder, constructor, creator, fabricator, factory owner, industrialist, captain of industry.

many adjective A LOT OF, lots of, numerous, innumerable, a large/great number of, countless, scores of, myriad, great quantities of, multitudinous, multiple, copious, abundant.
– OPPOSITES few.

mar verb SPOIL, detract from, impair, damage, ruin, wreck, disfigure, blemish, scar, deface, harm, hurt, injure, deform, mutilate, maim, mangle.
– OPPOSITES enhance.

marauder noun RAIDER, plunderer, pillager, looter, ravager, robber, pirate, freebooter.

march noun WALK, step, pace, stride, tramp, hike, demonstration, parade, procession; *informal* demo.

margin noun ❶ EDGE, side, verge, border, perimeter, boundary, limits, periphery, brim. ❷ LEEWAY, latitude, scope, room, room for manoeuvre, space, allowance, extra, surplus.

marginal adjective SLIGHT, small, tiny, minute, low, minor, insignificant, minimal, negligible.

maritime adjective NAVAL, marine, nautical, seafaring, seagoing.

mark noun ❶ STAIN, blemish, blot, smear, trace, spot, speck, dot, blotch, smudge, bruise, scratch, scar, dent, pit, pock, chip, notch, nick, line, score, cut, incision, gash; *informal* splotch. ❷ MARKER, guide, pointer, landmark, direction post, signpost, milestone, waymark. ❸ **mark of respect:** SIGN, symbol, indication, symptom, feature, token, badge, emblem, evidence, proof, clue, hint.
▶ verb ❶ **mark the table:** STAIN, smear, smudge, scratch, scar, dent, chip, notch, score, cut, gash. ❷ **mark your property:** PUT ONE'S NAME ON, initial, label, tag, stamp, brand, earmark. ❸ **mark essays:** CORRECT, assess, evaluate, appraise, grade. ❹ **mark his birthday:** CELEBRATE, commemorate, honour, observe, recognize, acknowledge, solemnize.

marked adjective PRONOUNCED, decided, striking, clear, glaring, blatant, unmistakable, remarkable, prominent, signal, conspicuous, noticeable.
– OPPOSITES inconspicuous.

maroon verb ABANDON, forsake,

leave behind, desert, strand, leave stranded, leave isolated.

marriage noun ❶ their marriage lasted ten years: MARRIED STATE, matrimony, holy matrimony, wedlock, conjugal bond, union, match. ❷ invited to their marriage: MARRIAGE CEREMONY, wedding, wedding ceremony, nuptials. ❸ the marriage of their skills: ALLIANCE, union, merger, unification, amalgamation, combination, affiliation, association, connection, coupling; *informal* hook-up.

marrow noun CORE, kernel, nucleus, pith, heart, centre, soul, spirit, essence, quintessence, gist, substance, meat, stuff; *informal* nitty-gritty, nuts and bolts.

marry verb BE MARRIED, wed, be wed, become man and wife, become espoused; *informal* tie the knot, walk down the aisle, take the plunge, get spliced, get hitched, get yoked.

marsh noun MARSHLAND, bog, peat bog, swamp, swampland, morass, mire, quagmire, quag, slough, fen, fenland; *N. Amer.* bayou.

marshal verb GATHER TOGETHER, assemble, collect, muster, draw up, line up, align, set/put in order, arrange, deploy, dispose.

martial adjective MILITANT, warlike, combative, belligerent, bellicose, aggressive, pugnacious.

marvel noun WONDER, amazing thing, prodigy, sensation, spectacle, phenomenon, miracle. ■ **marvel at** BE AMAZED BY, be filled with amazement at, be awed by, be full of wonder at, wonder at.

marvellous adjective ❶ AMAZING, astounding, astonishing, awesome, breathtaking, sensational, remarkable, spectacular, stupendous, phenomenal, prodigious, miraculous, extraordinary; *poetic/literary* wondrous. ❷ a marvellous singer: EXCELLENT, splendid, wonderful, magnificent, superb, glorious, great; *informal* super, fantastic, terrific, fabulous, awesome, ace, mean, bad, wicked; *Brit. informal* smashing.

masculine adjective MALE, manly, manlike, virile, all-male, robust, vigorous, muscular, strapping, rugged, macho.
– OPPOSITES feminine.

mash verb CRUSH, pulp, purée, smash, squash, pound, beat.
▶ noun PULP, mush, paste, purée, slush, pap.

mask noun DISGUISE, guise, concealment, cover, cover-up, cloak, camouflage, veil, screen, front, false front, facade, blind, semblance, false colours, pretence.
▶ verb DISGUISE, hide, conceal, cover up, obscure, cloak, camouflage, veil, screen.

mass noun ❶ CONCENTRATION, conglomeration, aggregation, assemblage, collection. ❷ MAJORITY, greater part, major part, most, bulk, main body, preponderance.
▶ adjective WHOLESALE, universal, widespread, general, large-scale, extensive, pandemic, popular.
▶ verb AMASS, accumulate, assemble, gather, collect, draw together, join together.

massacre verb *see* KILL (1).

massage verb RUB, knead, pummel, manipulate.

master noun LORD, overlord, ruler, overseer, superintendent, director, manager, controller,

governor, commander, captain, chief, head, headman, principal, owner, employer; *informal* boss, top dog, big cheese.
▶ **verb** ❶ CONQUER, vanquish, defeat, overcome, overpower, subdue, subjugate, govern, quell, quash, suppress, control, curb, check, bridle, tame. ❷ LEARN, become proficient in, grasp; *informal* get the hang of, get clued up about.

masterful **adjective** AUTHORITATIVE, powerful, controlling, domineering, dictatorial, overbearing, overweening, imperious, peremptory, high-handed, arrogant, haughty.
– OPPOSITES weak.

mastermind **verb** DIRECT, manage, plan, organize, arrange, engineer, conceive, devise, forge, originate, initiate, think up, come up with; *informal* be the brains behind.

masterpiece **noun** MAGNUM OPUS, masterwork, chef-d'œuvre, work of art, creation, pièce de resistance.

match **verb** ❶ COMPLEMENT, blend with, harmonize with, go with, tone with, coordinate with, team with, tally with, correspond to, accord with. ❷ BE EQUAL TO, be a match for, measure up to, rival, vie with, compete with, compare with. ❸ PAIR UP, mate, couple, unite, join, combine, link, ally; *informal* hitch up, yoke.

matching **adjective** CORRESPONDING, equivalent, parallel, analogous, complementary, the same, paired, twin, coupled, double, duplicate, identical, like.
– OPPOSITES different.

mate **noun** ❶ FRIEND, companion, comrade, crony; *informal* pal, chum; *N. Amer. informal* buddy. ❷ ASSISTANT, helper, apprentice, subordinate.
▶ **verb** BREED, copulate, couple.

material **noun** ❶ MATTER, substance, stuff, medium, constituent elements. ❷ FABRIC, cloth, stuff, textile. ❸ DATA, information, facts, facts and figures, evidence, details.
▶ **adjective** CORPOREAL, physical, bodily, fleshly, tangible, substantial, concrete.

materialize **verb** ❶ COME INTO BEING, happen, occur, come about, take place; *poetic/literary* come to pass. ❷ APPEAR, turn up, become visible, come into view, come into sight, show oneself/itself, come to light, emerge.

matrimonial **adjective** MARITAL, conjugal, connubial, nuptial, spousal.

matter **noun** ❶ MATERIAL, substance, stuff. ❷ **no laughing matter**: AFFAIR, business, proceeding, situation, circumstance, event, happening, occurrence, incident, occasion, experience. ❸ **important matters**: SUBJECT, topic, issue, question, point, case.
▶ **verb** BE OF IMPORTANCE, be of consequence, make a difference, signify, be relevant, carry weight, count.

mature **adjective** ❶ ADULT, grown up, grown, fully grown, full-grown, of age. ❷ RIPE, ripened, mellow, ready, seasoned.
– OPPOSITES immature.
▶ **verb** GROW UP, develop fully, become adult, reach adulthood, come of age.

maudlin adjective MAWKISH, sentimental, tearful, lachrymose; *informal* weepy; *Brit. informal* soppy.

maverick noun NONCONFORMIST, rebel, dissenter, dissident, individualist, bohemian, eccentric.
– OPPOSITES conformist.

maxim noun APHORISM, proverb, adage, saw, saying, axiom, precept, epigram, gnome.

maximum noun MOST, utmost, uttermost, upper limit, ceiling, top, summit, peak, apogee, acme.
▶ adjective HIGHEST, greatest, biggest, largest, topmost, most, utmost, supreme.
– OPPOSITES minimum.

mayhem noun HAVOC, disorder, confusion, chaos, bedlam.

meadow noun FIELD, grassland, pasture, paddock, lea.

meagre adjective PALTRY, sparse, scant, scanty, spare, inadequate, insufficient, insubstantial, skimpy, miserly, niggardly, pathetic; *informal* stingy.
– OPPOSITES abundant.

mean[1] verb ❶ INDICATE, signify, express, convey, denote, designate, stand for, represent, symbolize, portend, connote, imply, purport, suggest, allude to, intimate, hint at, insinuate, drive at. ❷ he meant to do it: INTEND, have in mind, have in view, contemplate, set out, aim, aspire, desire, want, wish. ❸ this means war: INVOLVE, entail, lead to, result in, give rise to, bring about, cause.

mean[2] adjective ❶ MISERLY, niggardly, parsimonious, close-fisted, penny-pinching, grasping, greedy, avaricious, ungenerous, illiberal, close, near; *informal* stingy, tight, tight-fisted, mingy. ❷ a mean old woman: NASTY, disagreeable, unpleasant, unfriendly, offensive, obnoxious, cross, ill-natured, bad-tempered, irritable, churlish, surly, cantankerous, crotchety, crabbed. ❸ of mean birth: LOW, lowly, low-born, humble, modest, common, ordinary, base, proletarian, plebeian, obscure.
– OPPOSITES generous, kind, noble.

meander verb WIND, zigzag, snake, curve, turn, bend.

meaning noun ❶ the meaning of a word: DEFINITION, explanation, interpretation, elucidation, explication. ❷ life has no meaning: SIGNIFICANCE, point, value, worth, consequence, account.

meaningful adjective ❶ a meaningful relationship: SIGNIFICANT, important, serious, sincere, in earnest. ❷ a meaningful glance: SIGNIFICANT, pointed, suggestive, eloquent, expressive, pregnant.
– OPPOSITES meaningless.

meaningless adjective ❶ SENSELESS, unintelligible, incomprehensible, incoherent. ❷ a meaningless act: SENSELESS, pointless, purposeless, motiveless, irrational. ❸ meaningless lives: EMPTY, futile, pointless, aimless, valueless, worthless, trivial, insignificant.
– OPPOSITES meaningful.

means plural noun WAY, method, expedient, process, mode, manner, agency, medium, instrument, channel, avenue, course.

meanwhile adverb ❶ IN THE MEANTIME, for the time being, for now, for the moment, in the interim, in the interval. ❷ AT THE

SAME TIME, simultaneously, concurrently, coincidentally.

measure noun ❶ SIZE, dimension, proportions, magnitude, amplitude, mass, bulk, volume, capacity, quantity, weight. ❷ RULE, ruler, tape measure, gauge, meter, scale, level, yardstick. ❸ SHARE, portion, division, allotment, part, piece, quota, lot, ration, percentage; *informal* rake-off. ❹ **take measures:** ACTION, act, course, course of action, deed, proceeding, procedure, step, means, expedient.

▶ **verb** CALCULATE, compute, estimate, quantify, weigh, size, evaluate, rate, assess, appraise, gauge, measure out, determine, judge, survey.

■ **measure up** COME UP TO STANDARD, fulfil expectations, fit/fill the bill, pass muster, be adequate, be suitable; *informal* come up to scratch, make the grade, cut the mustard, be up to snuff.

measured adjective **measured words:** CAREFULLY CHOSEN, selected with care, well thought out, studied, calculated, planned, considered, deliberate, reasoned.

mechanical adjective ❶ AUTOMATED, automatic, machine-driven, motor-driven, power-driven. ❷ AUTOMATIC, unthinking, unconscious, unfeeling, unemotional, cold, involuntary, instinctive, routine, habitual.

– OPPOSITES manual.

mechanism noun ❶ MACHINE, apparatus, appliance, tool, device, instrument, contraption, contrivance. ❷ PROCESS, procedure, system, operation, method, means, medium, agency, channel.

meddle verb INTERFERE, butt in, intrude, intervene, interlope, pry, nose; *informal* stick one's nose in, horn in, snoop.

mediate verb ARBITRATE, negotiate, conciliate, intervene, intercede, interpose, moderate, umpire, referee, act as peacemaker, reconcile, restore harmony, make peace, bring to terms, step in.

mediator noun ARBITRATOR, arbiter, negotiator, go-between, middleman, intermediary, honest broker, peacemaker, intervenor, interceder, moderator, umpire, referee, judge, conciliator, reconciler.

medicinal adjective MEDICAL, therapeutic, curative, healing, remedial, restorative, health-giving, analeptic.

medicine noun ❶ MEDICATION, medicament, drug, remedy, cure; *archaic* physic. ❷ MEDICAL SCIENCE, practice of medicine, healing art.

mediocre adjective ❶ **her work is mediocre:** INDIFFERENT, average, middle-of-the-road, middling, ordinary, commonplace, pedestrian, run-of-the-mill, tolerable, passable, adequate, uninspired, undistinguished, unexceptional; *informal* so-so, fair-to-middling, nothing to write home about, no great shakes. ❷ **mediocre goods/actors:** INFERIOR, second-rate, second-dass, low-grade, poor, shabby, minor.

– OPPOSITES exceptional.

meditate verb CONTEMPLATE, think about/over, muse on/about, ponder on/over, consider, concentrate on, reflect on, deliberate about/on, ruminate about/on/over, brood over, mull over, be in a brown study over.

meditation noun CONTEMPLATION, thought, musing, pondering, consideration, reflection, deliberation, rumination.

medium noun ❶ MEDIAN, mid-point, middle, centre point, average, norm, standard, middle course, compromise, happy medium, golden mean. ❷ MEANS, agency, channel, avenue, vehicle, organ, instrument.
▶ adjective MIDDLE, mean, medial, median, midway, midpoint, intermediate.

meek adjective DOCILE, modest, humble, unassuming, unpretentious, submissive, yielding, unresisting, patient, long-suffering, forbearing, resigned, gentle, peaceful, compliant, acquiescent, deferential, weak, timid, frightened, spineless, spiritless; *informal* weak-kneed.
– OPPOSITES assertive.

meet verb ❶ ENCOUNTER, come face to face with, make contact with, run into, run across, come across, come upon, chance upon, happen upon, light upon; *informal* bump into. ❷ **where the land and sea meet**: COME TOGETHER, abut, adjoin, join, link up, unite, connect, touch, converge, intersect. ❸ **the committee met**: GATHER, assemble, come together, foregather, congregate, convene, muster, rally; *formal* convoke. ❹ **meet the proposal with hostility**: DEAL WITH, handle, treat, cope with, approach, answer. ❺ **meet the demands of the job**: SATISFY, fulfil, measure up to, come up to, comply with. ❻ **meet one's responsibilities**: CARRY OUT, perform, execute, discharge, take care of. ❼ **meet the cost**: PAY, settle, honour, square. ❽ **meet death bravely**: FACE, encounter, undergo, experience, go through, bear, suffer, endure.
– OPPOSITES avoid.

meeting noun ❶ ENCOUNTER, contact, assignation, rendezvous; *poetic/literary* tryst. ❷ GATHERING, assembly, conference, congregation, convention, convocation, conclave; *informal* get-together. ❸ ABUTMENT, junction, conjunction, union, convergence, confluence, concourse, intersection. ❹ MEET, race meeting, athletics meeting, sports meeting.

melancholy adjective DESPONDENT, dejected, depressed, down, downhearted, downcast, disconsolate, glum, gloomy, sunk in gloom, miserable, dismal, dispirited, low, in low spirits, in the doldrums, blue, mournful, lugubrious, woeful, woebegone, doleful, sorrowful, unhappy, heavy-hearted, low-spirited, sombre, pessimistic; *informal* down in the dumps, down in the mouth.
– OPPOSITES cheerful.

mellifluous adjective SWEET, sweet-sounding/toned, dulcet, honeyed, mellow, soft, soothing, smooth, silvery, euphonious, musical.

mellow adjective ❶ MATURE, well matured, soft, juicy, tender, luscious, sweet. ❷ **a mellow old man**: GENTLE, easy-going, pleasant, kindly, kind-hearted, amicable, amiable, good-natured, affable, gracious. ❸ **a mellow mood**: GENIAL, jovial, jolly, cheerful, happy, merry.

melodious adjective MELODIC, musical, tuneful, harmonious, lyrical, dulcet, sweet, sweet-sounding, sweet-toned, silvery, silvery-toned, euphonious.
– OPPOSITES discordant.

melodramatic adjective THEATRICAL, stagy, overdramatic, histrionic, over-sensational, extravagant, overdone, overemotional; *informal* actressy, camp, hammy.

melody noun TUNE, air, strain, music, refrain, theme, song.

melt verb DISSOLVE, deliquesce, thaw, unfreeze, defrost, soften, fuse.

member noun ❶ ADHERENT, associate, fellow. ❷ ORGAN, limb, appendage, extremity.

memorable adjective UNFORGETTABLE, not to be forgotten, momentous, significant, historic, notable, noteworthy, important, consequential, remarkable, outstanding, extraordinary, striking, impressive, distinctive, distinguished.
– OPPOSITES forgettable.

memorial noun MONUMENT, statue, plaque, shrine, tombstone.

memorize verb COMMIT TO MEMORY, remember, learn by heart, get by heart, learn off, learn, learn by rote.

memory noun ❶ REMEMBRANCE, recollection, powers of recall, recall, powers of retention, retention. ❷ **a statue in memory of him:** REMEMBRANCE, commemoration, honour, tribute.

menace noun THREAT, danger, hazard, jeopardy.
▶ **verb** THREATEN, intimidate, frighten, scare, alarm, terrify, bully, browbeat, cow, terrorize.

mend verb ❶ REPAIR, fix, put back together, patch up, restore, rehabilitate, renew, renovate, make whole, make well, cure, heal. ❷ GET BETTER, recover, recuperate, improve, be well, be cured. ❸ **mend matters:** PUT RIGHT, set straight, rectify, put in order, correct, amend, emend, improve.

menial adjective LOWLY, humble, low-grade, low-status, unskilled, routine, humdrum, boring, dull.
– OPPOSITES elevated.
▶ **noun** SERVANT, domestic, drudge, underling, lackey, flunkey; *Brit. informal* dogsbody, skivvy.

menstruation noun PERIOD, menses, menstrual cycle, monthly flow; *informal* the curse, monthlies, the usual.

mentality noun ❶ CAST OF MIND, frame of mind, turn of mind, way of thinking, mind, psychology, mental attitude, outlook, character, disposition, make-up. ❷ INTELLECT, intellectual capabilities, intelligence, IQ, brainpower, brains, mind, comprehension, understanding; *informal* grey matter.

mention verb ❶ REFER TO, allude to, touch on, speak briefly of, hint at. ❷ SAY, state, name, cite, quote, call attention to, adduce. ❸ TELL, speak about/of, utter, communicate, let someone know, disclose, divulge, breathe a word of, reveal, intimate, whisper; *informal* let on about.
▶ **noun** REFERENCE, allusion, observation, remark, statement, announcement, indication.

mentor noun ADVISER, counsellor, guide, guru, spiritual leader, confidant, teacher, tutor, coach, instructor.

mercenary adjective MONEY-ORIENTED, grasping, greedy, acquisitive, avaricious, covetous, bribable, venal; *informal* money-grubbing.

merchandise noun GOODS, wares, stock, commodities, produce, vendibles.

merchant noun TRADER, dealer, trafficker, wholesaler, broker, seller, salesman/woman/person, vendor, retailer, shopkeeper, distributor.

merciful adjective LENIENT, clement, compassionate, pitying, forgiving, forbearing, sparing, humane, mild, soft-hearted, tender-hearted, kind, sympathetic, liberal, tolerant, generous, beneficent, benignant.
– OPPOSITES merciless, cruel.

merciless adjective UNMERCIFUL, ruthless, relentless, inexorable, harsh, pitiless, unforgiving, unsparing, unpitying, implacable, barbarous, inhumane, inhuman, hard-hearted, heartless, callous, cruel, unsympathetic, unfeeling, illiberal, intolerant, rigid, severe, stern.
– OPPOSITES merciful, compassionate.

mercy noun LENIENCY, clemency, compassion, pity, charity, forgiveness, forbearance, quarter, humanity, humaneness, mildness, soft-heartedness, tender-heartedness, kindness, sympathy, liberality, tolerance, generosity, beneficence, benignancy.
– OPPOSITES severity, cruelty.

mere adjective NOTHING MORE THAN, no better than, no more important than, just a, only a, pure and simple.

merge verb ❶ JOIN TOGETHER, join forces, amalgamate, unite, combine, incorporate, coalesce, team up. ❷ BLEND, fuse, mingle, mix, intermix, homogenize.
– OPPOSITES separate.

merit noun ❶ EXCELLENCE, goodness, quality, worth, worthiness, value. ❷ **the merits of the scheme**: GOOD POINT, strong point, advantage, asset, plus.
▶ **verb** DESERVE, be deserving of, earn, be worthy of, be worth, be entitled to, have a right to, have a claim to, warrant, rate, incur.

meritorious adjective PRAISEWORTHY, laudable, commendable, admirable, estimable, creditable, excellent, exemplary, good, worthy, deserving.
– OPPOSITES discreditable.

merriment noun CHEERFULNESS, gaiety, high-spiritedness, high spirits, buoyancy, carefreeness, levity, sportiveness, joy, joyfulness, joyousness, jolliness, jollity, rejoicing, conviviality, festivity, merrymaking, revelry, mirth, glee, gleefulness, laughter, hilarity, amusement, fun.
– OPPOSITES misery.

merry adjective CHEERFUL, cheery, in good spirits, high-spirited, light-hearted, buoyant, carefree, sportive, joyful, joyous, rejoicing, jolly, jocund, convivial, festive, mirthful, gleeful, happy, glad, laughing; *dated* gay; *poetic/literary* frolicsome.
– OPPOSITES miserable.

mesh noun ❶ NETTING, net, tracery, web, lattice, latticework, lacework, trellis, reticulation,

plexus. ❷ TANGLE, entanglement, web, snare, trap.
▶ verb ❶ *gears meshing:* BE ENGAGED, connect, interlock. ❷ *our ideas do not mesh:* HARMONIZE, fit together, go together, coordinate, match, be on the same wavelength, dovetail.

mesmerize verb ❶ HYPNOTIZE, put into a trance, put under. ❷ HOLD SPELLBOUND, spellbind, entrance, enthral, bewitch, captivate, enchant, fascinate, grip, magnetize, hypnotize.

mess noun ❶ DISORDER, untidiness, disarray, dirtiness, filthiness, clutter, shambles, litter, jumble, muddle, chaos, confusion, disorganization, turmoil. ❷ PLIGHT, predicament, tight spot, tight corner, difficulty, trouble, quandary, dilemma, muddle, mix-up, confusion, imbroglio; *informal* jam, fix, pickle, stew, hole. ❸ MUDDLE, bungle; *informal* botch, screw-up; *Brit. informal* cock-up.
■ **mess up** ❶ DIRTY, befoul, litter, pollute, clutter up, disarrange, throw into disorder, dishevel; *poetic/literary* besmirch. ❷ BUNGLE, muff, make a mess of, mar, spoil, ruin; *informal* botch, make a hash of, muck up, foul up, screw up; *Brit. informal* cock up, make a muck of.

message noun ❶ COMMUNICATION, piece of information, news, word, tidings, note, memorandum, letter, missive, bulletin, communiqué, dispatch, memo. ❷ MEANING, import, idea, point, purport, intimation, theme, moral.

messenger noun MESSAGE-BEARER, courier, errand boy/girl, runner, envoy, emissary, agent, go-between, herald, harbinger.

messy adjective UNTIDY, disordered, dirty, filthy, grubby, slovenly, cluttered, littered, muddled, in a muddle, chaotic, confused, disorganized, sloppy, in disarray, disarranged, dishevelled, unkempt; *Brit. informal* shambolic.
– OPPOSITES orderly.

metamorphosis noun TRANSFORMATION, transfiguration, change, alteration, conversion, changeover, mutation, transmutation, sea change; *informal* transmogrification.

method noun ❶ PROCEDURE, technique, system, practice, modus operandi, process, approach, way, course of action, scheme, plan, rule, arrangement, form, style, manner, mode. ❷ *method in his madness:* ORDER, orderliness, sense of order, organization, arrangement, structure, form, planning, plan, design, purpose, pattern, regularity.

methodical adjective ORDERLY, well ordered, organized, systematic, structured, logical, well regulated, planned, efficient, businesslike.
– OPPOSITES disorganized.

meticulous adjective CONSCIENTIOUS, careful, scrupulous, punctilious, painstaking, demanding, exacting, thorough, perfectionist, fastidious, particular.
– OPPOSITES careless, slapdash.

microscopic adjective INFINITESIMAL, minuscule, tiny, minute.
– OPPOSITES massive.

middle adjective MID, mean,

medium, medial, median, midway, halfway, central, equidistant, intermediate, intermediary.
▶ **noun** MEAN, median, mid-point, halfway point, centre, dead centre.

middling **adjective** AVERAGE, medium, ordinary, fair, moderate; adequate, passable, tolerable, mediocre, indifferent, run-of-the-mill, unexceptional, unremarkable; *informal* fair-to-middling, so-so.

might **noun** FORCE, power, strength, mightiness, powerfulness, forcefulness, potency, toughness, robustness, sturdiness, muscularity.

mighty **adjective** ❶ FORCEFUL, powerful, strong, potent, tough, robust, sturdy, muscular, strapping, vigorous, energetic. ❷ HUGE, massive, vast, enormous, colossal, giant, gigantic, monumental, mountainous, towering.
– OPPOSITES puny, tiny.

migrant **adjective** MIGRATORY, wandering, drifting, nomadic, itinerant, peripatetic, vagrant.

mild **adjective** ❶ **a mild disposition:** TENDER, gentle, soft, soft-hearted, tender-hearted, sensitive, sympathetic, warm, compassionate, humane, forgiving, conciliatory, forbearing, placid, meek, docile, calm, tranquil, serene, peaceful, peaceable, good-natured, amiable, affable, genial, easy, easy-going, mellow. ❷ **mild winds:** GENTLE, soft, moderate, warm, balmy. ❸ **mild food:** BLAND, insipid, tasteless.
– OPPOSITES cruel, harsh, spicy.

milieu **noun** ENVIRONMENT, surroundings, background, setting, scene, location, sphere, element.

militant **adjective** AGGRESSIVE, combative, pugnacious, fighting, warring, combating, contending, embattled, in arms, belligerent, bellicose.
– OPPOSITES peaceful.
▶ **noun** ACTIVIST, extremist, partisan.

military **adjective** ARMY, service, soldierly, soldier-like, armed, martial.
▶ **noun** ARMY, armed forces, services, militia, soldiery, navy, air force, marines.

militate
■ **militate against** OPERATE AGAINST, go against, count against, tell against, weigh against, be detrimental to, be disadvantageous to, be to the disfavour of, be counter to the interests of, conflict with the interests of.

milk **verb** ❶ DRAW, draw off, express, siphon, tap, drain, extract. ❷ EXPLOIT, take advantage of, impose on, bleed, suck dry.

milky **adjective** WHITE, milk-white, whitish, creamy, pearly, nacreous, ivory, alabaster, off-white, clouded, cloudy.

mill **noun** FACTORY, plant, foundry, works, workshop, shop, industrial centre.
▶ **verb** GRIND, pulverize, pound, crush, powder, crunch, granulate; *technical* comminute, triturate.
■ **mill about/around** MOVE AROUND, wander around, amble, meander, crowd, swarm, throng.

mimic **verb** ❶ IMPERSONATE, give an impersonation of, imitate, copy, ape, caricature, parody;

informal take off. ❷ RESEMBLE, look like, have/take on the appearance of, echo, mirror, simulate.
▶ **noun** MIMICKER, impersonator, impressionist, imitator, parodist, copyist, parrot, ape.

mince **verb** ❶ CHOP/CUT INTO TINY PIECES, grind, crumble, hash. ❷ **she minced along:** WALK AFFECTEDLY, take tiny/baby steps, strike a pose, attitudinize, pose, posture, put on airs, be affected.

mind **noun** ❶ BRAIN, head, seat of intellect, psyche, ego, subconscious. ❷ BRAINPOWER, powers of thought, intellect, intellectual capabilities, mentality, intelligence, powers of reasoning, brain, brains, wits, understanding, comprehension, sense, ratiocination; *informal* grey matter. ❸ **bring it to mind:** MEMORY, recollection, remembrance. ❹ **of the same mind:** OPINION, way of thinking, thoughts, outlook, view, viewpoint, point of view, belief, judgement, attitude, feeling, sentiment. ❺ **one of the great minds:** GENIUS, intellect, intellectual, thinker; *informal* brain, egghead.
▶ **verb** ❶ BE OFFENDED BY, take offence at, object to, care about, be bothered by, be upset by, be affronted by, resent, dislike, disapprove of, look askance at. ❷ **mind the rules:** TAKE HEED OF, heed, pay heed to, pay attention to, attend to, concentrate on, listen to, note, mark, observe, respect, obey, follow, comply with, adhere to. ❸ **mind the baby:** LOOK AFTER, take care of, attend to, tend, have charge of, keep an eye on, watch.
■ **never mind** DO NOT BOTHER ABOUT, pay no attention to, do not worry about, disregard, forget, do not take into consideration, do not give a second thought to.

mindful **adjective** PAYING ATTENTION TO, heedful of, watchful of, careful of, wary of, chary of, cognizant of, aware of, conscious of, alert to, alive to, sensible of.
– OPPOSITES heedless.

mindless **adjective** STUPID, foolish, senseless, witless, empty-headed, unintelligent, dull, slow-witted, obtuse; *informal* birdbrained, dumb, dopey, moronic.
– OPPOSITES intelligent.

mine **noun** ❶ COLLIERY, pit, quarry, lode, vein, deposit, coal mine. ❷ SOURCE, reservoir, repository, store, storehouse, wealth.
▶ **verb** EXCAVATE, quarry for, dig for, dig up, extract, unearth.

mingle **verb** ❶ MIX, blend, combine, compound, homogenize, merge, unite, join, amalgamate, fuse. ❷ CIRCULATE, socialize, hobnob, fraternize, meet people.
– OPPOSITES separate.

miniature **adjective** SMALL-SCALE, scaled down, mini, midget, baby, toy, pocket, dwarf; *informal* pint-sized.
– OPPOSITES giant.

minimal **adjective** MINIMUM, least, smallest, slightest, nominal, token.
– OPPOSITES maximum.

minimize **verb** ❶ KEEP AT/TO A MINIMUM, reduce, decrease, curtail, cut back on, prune, slash. ❷ **minimize his achievement:** BELITTLE, make light of, decry, discount, play down, deprecate, depreciate, underestimate, underrate.

– OPPOSITES maximize, exaggerate.

minimum noun LOWEST LEVEL, bottom level, bottom, depth, nadir, least, lowest, slightest.
▶ adjective MINIMAL, lowest, smallest, littlest, least, least possible, slightest.
– OPPOSITES maximum.

minion noun LACKEY, flunkey, henchman, creature, toady, underling, hireling, servant, dependant, hanger-on, parasite.

minor adjective LESSER, insignificant, unimportant, inconsequential, inferior, trivial, negligible, trifling, lightweight, subordinate.
– OPPOSITES major.

minstrel noun MUSICIAN, singer, bard, troubadour; *historical* jongleur.

mint noun FORTUNE, small fortune, vast sum, king's ransom; *informal* pile, stack, heap, packet, bundle.
▶ adjective BRAND NEW, as new, unused, perfect, unblemished, undamaged, fresh.
▶ verb STAMP, punch, die, cast, strike, coin, make, manufacture, produce.

minute adjective TINY, minuscule, microscopic, miniature, diminutive, Lilliputian, little, small.
– OPPOSITES gigantic, huge.

minutely adverb IN DETAIL, exhaustively, meticulously, punctiliously, painstakingly, closely.

miracle noun WONDER, marvel, prodigy, phenomenon.

miraculous adjective SUPERNATURAL, fantastic, magical, inexplicable, unaccountable, preternatural, superhuman, thaumaturgic, phenomenal, prodigious, wonderful, remarkable; *poetic/literary* wondrous.

mire noun MARSH, bog, swamp, morass, quagmire, quag, slough, fen, fenland; *N. Amer.* bayou.
▶ verb SINK, sink down, bog down, stick in the mud.

mirror verb REFLECT, imitate, emulate, simulate, copy, follow, mimic, echo, ape, parrot, impersonate.

mirth noun GAIETY, merriment, high spirits, cheerfulness, cheeriness, hilarity, glee, laughter, jocularity.

misapprehension noun MISUNDERSTANDING, misinterpretation, misconstruction, misreading, misjudgement, misconception, the wrong idea, a false impression, delusion.

misappropriate verb EMBEZZLE, steal, thieve, swindle, pocket, help oneself to; *Brit. informal* nick, pinch; *formal* peculate.

misbehave verb BEHAVE BADLY, be bad, be naughty, be disobedient, get up to mischief, misconduct oneself, be guilty of misconduct, be bad-mannered, show bad/poor manners, be rude, fool around; *informal* carry on, act up.

misbehaviour noun MISCONDUCT, bad behaviour, disorderly conduct, badness, naughtiness, mischief, mischievousness, delinquency, misdeed, misdemeanour, bad/poor manners, rudeness; *informal* carrying on, acting up, shenanigans.

miscalculate verb CALCULATE

WRONGLY, make a mistake, go wrong, err, blunder, be wide of the mark; *informal* slip up, make a boo-boo; *Brit. informal* boob.

miscarriage noun ❶ FAILURE, foundering, ruination, non-fulfilment, misfiring. ❷ a miscarriage of justice: FAILURE, breakdown, mismanagement, perversion, thwarting, frustration. ❸ SPONTANEOUS ABORTION, termination.

miscarry verb ❶ HAVE A MISCARRIAGE, abort, lose the baby. ❷ GO WRONG, go awry, go amiss, be unsuccessful, fail, misfire, founder, come to nothing, come to grief, meet with disaster, fall through, be ruined, fall flat.
– OPPOSITES succeed.

miscellaneous adjective VARIED, assorted, mixed, diverse, sundry, variegated, diversified, motley, multifarious, jumbled, confused, indiscriminate, heterogeneous.

miscellany noun ASSORTMENT, mixture, mixed bag, variety, collection, medley, pot-pourri, conglomeration, jumble, confusion, mix, mishmash, hotchpotch, hodgepodge, pastiche, patchwork, farrago, gallimaufry.

mischief noun ❶ MISCHIEVOUSNESS, naughtiness, badness, bad behaviour, misbehaviour, misconduct, pranks, wrongdoing, delinquency; *informal* monkey business, shenanigans. ❷ do mischief: HARM, hurt, injury, damage, disruption, trouble.

mischievous adjective ❶ NAUGHTY, bad, badly behaved, misbehaving, disobedient, troublesome, vexatious, playful, rascally, roguish, delinquent; *poetic/literary* frolicsome. ❷ a mischievous smile: PLAYFUL, teasing, impish, roguish, waggish, arch.
– OPPOSITES well behaved.

misconception noun *see* MISAPPREHENSION.

miserable adjective ❶ feeling miserable: UNHAPPY, sorrowful, dejected, depressed, downcast, downhearted, down, despondent, disconsolate, desolate, wretched, glum, gloomy, dismal, blue, melancholy, low-spirited, mournful, woeful, woebegone, sad, doleful, forlorn, crestfallen; *informal* down in the mouth, down in the dumps. ❷ a miserable hovel: WRETCHED, mean, poor, shabby, squalid, filthy, foul, sordid, seedy, dilapidated. ❸ miserable wretches: POVERTY-STRICKEN, needy, penniless, impoverished, beggarly, destitute, indigent, down at heel, out at elbow. ❹ miserable salaries: MEAGRE, paltry, scanty, low, poor, niggardly, pathetic. ❺ miserable conditions: UNPLEASANT, disagreeable, displeasing, uncomfortable, wet, rainy, stormy.
– OPPOSITES happy.

miserly adjective MEAN, niggardly, parsimonious, close-fisted, penny-pinching, cheese-paring, penurious, grasping, greedy, avaricious, ungenerous, illiberal, close, near; *informal* stingy, mingy, tight, tight-fisted, money-grabbing; *N. Amer. informal* cheap.
– OPPOSITES generous.

misery noun ❶ DISTRESS,

wretchedness, hardship, suffering, affliction, anguish, torment, torture, agony, pain, discomfort, deprivation, poverty, grief, sorrow, heartbreak, despair, depression, dejection, desolation, gloom, melancholy, woe, sadness, unhappiness. ❷ endure untold miseries: TROUBLE, misfortune, adversity, affliction, ordeal, pain, sorrow, burden, load, blow, trial, tribulation, woe, torment, catastrophe, calamity, disaster.
– OPPOSITES happiness.

misfortune noun ❶ BAD LUCK, ill luck, ill fortune, poor/hard luck, accident, misadventure, mischance. ❷ TROUBLE, setback, reverse, adversity, misadventure, mishap, blow, failure, accident, disaster, tragedy, affliction, sorrow, misery, woe, trial, tribulation, catastrophe, calamity.

misgiving noun QUALM, doubt, reservation, suspicion, apprehension, unease, uncertainty.

misguided adjective MISTAKEN, deluded, erroneous, fallacious, wrong, unwarranted, uncalled for, misplaced, ill-advised, unwise, injudicious, imprudent, foolish.

mishap noun ACCIDENT, trouble, setback, reverse, adversity, misadventure, misfortune, stroke of bad luck, blow, disaster, trial, tribulation, catastrophe, calamity.

mislay verb LOSE, misplace, lose track of, miss, be unable to find.
– OPPOSITES find.

mislead verb MISINFORM, misdirect, delude, take in, deceive, fool, hoodwink, lead astray, throw off the scent, send on a wild-goose chase; *informal* lead up the garden path, take for a ride, pull the wool over someone's eyes.

misleading adjective *see* DECEPTIVE.

miss verb ❶ FAIL TO ATTEND, be too late for, absent oneself from, skip, be absent from, play truant from, take French leave from. ❷ miss an opportunity: FAIL TO SEIZE/GRASP, let slip, let go, pass up, overlook, disregard. ❸ they missed their father: REGRET THE ABSENCE/LOSS OF, feel the loss of, feel nostalgic for, long to see, long for, pine for, yearn for, ache for.

misshapen adjective DEFORMED, malformed, ill-proportioned, misproportioned, twisted, distorted, contorted, warped, curved, crooked, wry, bent, hunchbacked.

missing adjective LOST, mislaid, misplaced, nowhere to be found, absent, not present, gone, gone astray, unaccounted for.
– OPPOSITES present.

mission noun ❶ ASSIGNMENT, commission, task, job, errand, sortie, operation, work, chore, undertaking, duty, charge, trust. ❷ her mission in life: VOCATION, calling, pursuit, goal, aim, quest. ❸ a trade mission: DELEGATION, deputation, commission, legation.

missive noun COMMUNICATION, message, letter, memo, note, memorandum, bulletin, communiqué, report, dispatch.

mistake noun ERROR, fault, inaccuracy, slip, blunder, miscalculation, misunderstanding, oversight, gaffe, faux pas, solecism, misapprehension, misreading; *informal* slip-up, boo-boo, howler;

Brit. informal boob; *Brit. informal, dated* bloomer.
▶ **verb** **mistake his meaning:** GET WRONG, misunderstand, misapprehend, misinterpret, misconstrue, misread.
■ **be mistaken** BE WRONG, be in error, be at fault, be under a misapprehension, be misinformed, be misguided, be wide of the mark, be barking up the wrong tree, get the wrong end of the stick. **mistake for** TAKE FOR, mix up with, confuse with, misinterpret as.

mistakenly **adverb** BY MISTAKE, wrongly, in error, erroneously, incorrectly, falsely, fallaciously, misguidedly.
– OPPOSITES correctly.

mistreat **verb** MALTREAT, treat badly, ill-treat, ill-use, misuse, abuse, mishandle, harm, hurt, molest; *informal* beat up, rough up.

mistress **noun** LOVER, girlfriend, partner, lady-love, kept woman, inamorata; *archaic* paramour, concubine.

mistrust **verb** FEEL MISTRUSTFUL OF, distrust, feel distrustful of, have doubts about, be suspicious of, suspect, have reservations about, have misgivings about, be wary of, have no confidence in, question, doubt, lack faith in.
– OPPOSITES trust.

misty **adjective** HAZY, foggy, cloudy, blurred, fuzzy, dim, indistinct, vague, obscure, nebulous.
– OPPOSITES clear.

misunderstand **verb** MISAPPREHEND, misinterpret, misconstrue, misread, get the wrong idea, receive a false impression; *informal* get the wrong end of the stick, be barking up the wrong tree.

misunderstanding **noun** ❶ MISAPPREHENSION, mistake, error, mix-up, misinterpretation, misconstruction, misreading, misconception, misbelief, the wrong idea, a false impression; *informal* the wrong end of the stick. ❷ DISAGREEMENT, difference of opinion, falling-out, clash of views, dispute, quarrel, argument, squabble, conflict; *informal* spat, scrap, tiff.

misuse **verb** ❶ PUT TO WRONG USE, misapply, misemploy, abuse, squander, waste, dissipate. ❷ **misuse the children:** MALTREAT, mistreat, treat badly, ill-treat, ill-use, abuse, mishandle, manhandle, harm, hurt, bully, molest, beat up, rough up.
▶ **noun** ❶ WRONG USE, misapplication, misemployment, abuse, squandering, waste, dissipation. ❷ **misuse of the verb:** MISUSAGE, malapropism, barbarism, catachresis. ❸ **misuse of the children:** MALTREATMENT, mistreatment, ill-treatment, ill use, abuse, rough handling, mishandling, manhandling, bullying, injury, harm, molesting.

mitigate **verb** ALLEVIATE, reduce, diminish, lessen, weaken, attenuate, allay, assuage, palliate, appease, soothe, relieve, ease, soften, temper, mollify, lighten, still, quieten, quiet, tone down, moderate, modify, extenuate, calm, lull, pacify, placate, tranquillize.
– OPPOSITES aggravate.

mix **verb** ❶ BLEND, combine, mingle, compound, homogenize, alloy, merge, unite, join, amalgamate, fuse, coalesce,

interweave. ❷ SOCIALIZE, mingle, associate with others, meet people.
– OPPOSITES separate.
▶ noun MIXTURE, blend, combination, compound, alloy, merger, union, amalgamation, fusion.
■ **mix up** ❶ CONFUSE, get confused, muddle, muddle up, get muddled up, mistake, scramble. ❷ INVOLVE, implicate, entangle, embroil, draw into, incriminate.

mixed adjective ❶ ASSORTED, varied, miscellaneous, diverse, diversified, motley, heterogeneous. ❷ HYBRID, cross-bred, interbred, mongrel. ❸ **mixed reactions:** AMBIVALENT, equivocal, unsure, uncertain.
– OPPOSITES homogeneous.

mixed up adjective MALADJUSTED, ill-adjusted, disturbed, confused, muddled; *informal* screwed up, untogether.

mixture noun ❶ COMPOUND, blend, mix, brew, combination, concoction, alloy. ❷ ASSORTMENT, variety, melange, collection, medley, pot-pourri, conglomeration, jumble, mix, mishmash, hotchpotch, pastiche, farrago, mixed bag. ❸ CROSS, cross-breed, mongrel, hybrid.

moan noun GROAN, lament, lamentation, wail, whimper, whine.
▶ verb ❶ GROAN, wail, whimper, whine. ❷ COMPLAIN, whine, carp; *informal* grouse, gripe, grouch, whinge, beef.

mob noun CROWD, horde, multitude, rabble, mass, body, throng, host, gang, gathering, assemblage.
▶ verb CROWD AROUND, swarm around, surround, besiege, jostle.

mobile adjective ❶ ABLE TO MOVE, moving, walking, motile, ambulatory. ❷ TRANSPORTABLE, portable, travelling, peripatetic, locomotive. ❸ **a mobile face:** EXPRESSIVE, animated, ever-changing, changeable.
– OPPOSITES immobile.

mobilize verb ❶ MUSTER, rally, marshal, assemble, call to arms, organize, make ready, prepare, ready. ❷ **mobilize for action:** GET READY, prepare, ready oneself.

mock verb RIDICULE, jeer at, sneer at, deride, scorn, make fun of, poke fun at, laugh at, tease, taunt, twit, chaff, gibe at, insult; *informal* rag, kid, rib, take the mickey out of.
▶ adjective IMITATION, artificial, simulated, synthetic, ersatz, so-called, fake, sham, false, spurious, bogus, counterfeit, forged, pseudo, pretended.

mockery noun ❶ RIDICULE, jeering, derision, contempt, scorn, disdain, gibe, insult; *informal* ribbing. ❷ PARODY, travesty, caricature, lampoon, burlesque.

mocking adjective SNEERING, derisive, derisory, contemptuous, scornful, disdainful, sardonic, insulting, satirical.

model noun ❶ REPLICA, representation, mock-up, copy, dummy, imitation, facsimile, image. ❷ PROTOTYPE, archetype, type, mould, original, pattern, design, paradigm, sample, example, exemplar. ❸ STYLE, design, mode, form, mark, version, type, variety, kind, sort. ❹ **a model of tact:** IDEAL, paragon, perfect example, perfect specimen, exemplar, epitome, nonpareil, acme.

moderate adjective ❶ moderate

views: MIDDLE-OF-THE-ROAD, non-radical. ❷ **moderate demands:** REASONABLE, within reason, within due limits, fair, just. ❸ **moderate behaviour:** NOT GIVEN TO EXCESSES, restrained, controlled, temperate, sober, steady. ❹ **moderate success:** AVERAGE, middling, ordinary, fair, fairish, modest, tolerable, passable, adequate.
– OPPOSITES immoderate.
▶ **verb** ❶ ABATE, let up, die down, calm down, lessen, decrease, diminish, slacken. ❷ LESSEN, decrease, diminish, mitigate, alleviate, allay, assuage, ease, palliate.

moderately adverb QUITE, rather, somewhat, fairly, reasonably, to a certain degree, to some extent, within reason, within limits.

modern adjective ❶ **modern times:** CONTEMPORARY, present-day, present, current, twentieth-century, existing, existent. ❷ **very modern ideas:** UP TO DATE, up to the minute, fashionable, in fashion, in, in style, in vogue, voguish, modish, the latest, new, newfangled, fresh, advanced, progressive; *informal* trendy, with it.
– OPPOSITES old-fashioned.

modernize verb MAKE MODERN, update, bring up to date, renovate, remodel, remake, redo, refresh, revamp, rejuvenate; *informal* do over.

modest adjective ❶ SELF-EFFACING, humble, unpretentious, unassuming, free from vanity. ❷ SHY, bashful, self-conscious, diffident, reserved, retiring, reticent, quiet, coy, embarrassed, blushing, timid, fearful, meek. ❸ **modest demands:** MODERATE, fair, tolerable, passable, adequate, satisfactory, acceptable, unexceptional, small, limited.
– OPPOSITES conceited, grand.

modesty noun ❶ LACK OF VANITY, humility, self-effacement, lack of pretension, unpretentiousness. ❷ SHYNESS, bashfulness, self-consciousness, reserve, reticence, timidity, meekness.

modicum noun LITTLE, little bit, particle, iota, jot, atom, whit, speck, scrap, crumb, fragment, shred, mite, dash, drop.

modify verb ALTER, change, adjust, adapt, revise, recast, reform, reshape, refashion, rework, remould, redo, revamp, reorganize, refine, transform.

moist adjective WET, damp, clammy, humid, dank, rainy, drizzly, dewy, soggy, succulent, juicy, soft, spongy.

moisture noun WATER, liquid, wetness, wet, dampness, damp, humidity, dankness, rain, dew, drizzle, perspiration, sweat.

molest verb PESTER, annoy, plague, torment, harass, badger, harry, persecute, bother, worry, trouble, provoke; *informal* bug, needle, hassle.

mollify verb CALM DOWN, pacify, placate, appease, soothe, quiet.
– OPPOSITES enrage.

moment noun ❶ MINUTE, short time, second, instant; *informal* tick, jiffy. ❷ MINUTE, instant, point, point in time, time, juncture, stage.

momentary adjective BRIEF, short, short-lived, fleeting, passing, transient, transitory, ephemeral, evanescent, temporary, impermanent.
– OPPOSITES lengthy.

momentous adjective CRUCIAL, critical, vital, decisive, pivotal, serious, grave, important, significant, consequential, fateful, historic; *informal* earth-shattering.
– OPPOSITES insignificant.

momentum noun IMPETUS, impulse, propulsion, thrust, push, driving power, drive, power, energy, force.

money noun CASH, hard cash, ready money, finance, capital, funds, banknotes, currency, coin, coinage, silver, copper, legal tender, specie; *informal* wherewithal, dough, bread, loot, the necessary, the needful, shekels, tin, gelt, moolah, filthy lucre; *Brit. informal* dosh, brass, lolly, spondulicks, the ready, readies; *N. Amer. informal* mazuma.

moneyed adjective WELL-TO-DO, well off, affluent, rich, wealthy, prosperous; *informal* in the money, rolling in it, loaded, well heeled.
– OPPOSITES poor.

monitor noun DETECTOR, scanner, recorder, security camera, observer, watchdog, overseer, supervisor, invigilator.
▶ verb OBSERVE, scan, record, survey, follow, keep an eye on, keep track of, check, oversee, supervise, invigilate.

monopolize verb ❶ CORNER, control, take over, have sole rights in. ❷ monopolize the conversation: DOMINATE, take over, not let anyone else take part in.
– OPPOSITES share.

monotonous adjective UNVARYING, lacking/without variety, unchanging, repetitious, all the same, uniform, routine, humdrum, run-of-the-mill, commonplace, mechanical, uninteresting, unexciting, prosaic, wearisome, dull, boring, tedious, tiresome.
– OPPOSITES varied, interesting.

monster noun ❶ FIEND, beast, brute, barbarian, savage, villain, ogre, devil, demon. ❷ MONSTROSITY, malformation, abortion, freak, freak of nature, mutant.

monstrous adjective ❶ MALFORMED, unnatural, abnormal, grotesque, gruesome, repellent, freakish, mutant. ❷ a monstrous thing to do: OUTRAGEOUS, shocking, disgraceful, scandalous, atrocious, heinous, evil, abominable, terrible, horrible, dreadful, hideous, foul, vile, nasty, ghastly, odious, loathsome, intolerable, contemptible, despicable, vicious, cruel, savage.
– OPPOSITES lovely.

monument noun ❶ MEMORIAL, statue, shrine, reliquary, sepulchre, mausoleum, cairn, obelisk, dolmen, cromlech, megalith. ❷ MEMORIAL, commemoration, remembrance, reminder, testament, witness, token.

monumental adjective ❶ a monumental error: GREAT, huge, enormous, immense, vast, exceptional, extraordinary, tremendous, stupendous, prodigious, staggering. ❷ a monumental work of art: MASSIVE, impressive, striking, remarkable, magnificent, awe-inspiring, marvellous, majestic, stupendous, prodigious.

mood noun HUMOUR, temper, disposition, frame of mind, state of mind, spirit, tenor, vein.

moody adjective TEMPERAMENTAL,

changeable, unpredictable, volatile, mercurial, unstable, unsteady, erratic, fitful, impulsive, capricious.

moon verb LANGUISH, idle, mope, daydream, be in a reverie, be in a brown study.

moot adjective DEBATABLE, open to question, open, doubtful, disputable, arguable, contestable, controversial, unresolved, undecided.

moral noun LESSON, teaching, message, meaning, significance, point.

morale noun CONFIDENCE, heart, spirit, hope, hopefulness, optimism, determination, zeal.

morality noun MORALS, moral code, moral standards, ethics, principles of right and wrong, standards/principles of behaviour.

morass noun CONFUSION, muddle, tangle, entanglement, mix-up, jumble, clutter.

morbid adjective GRUESOME, grisly, macabre, hideous, dreadful, horrible, unwholesome.
– OPPOSITES wholesome.

more adverb TO A GREATER EXTENT, further, longer, some more.
▶ pronoun ADDITIONAL AMOUNT/NUMBER, greater quantity/part, addition, supplement, extra, increase, increment.
– OPPOSITES less.

moreover adverb BESIDES, furthermore, further, what is more, in addition, also, as well, into the bargain, to boot.

moron noun FOOL, idiot, dolt, dunce, ass, ignoramus, imbecile, simpleton; *informal* chump, booby, nincompoop, ninny, dunderhead, blockhead, fathead, halfwit, cretin, dummy, numbskull, dimwit; *Brit. informal* twerp, clot, twit, nitwit; *N. Amer. informal* schmuck.

morsel noun BITE, nibble, bit, crumb, grain, particle, fragment, piece, scrap, segment, soupçon, taste.

mortal adjective ❶ mortal beings: TEMPORAL, transient, ephemeral, passing, impermanent, perishable, human, earthly, worldly, corporeal, fleshly.
❷ mortal enemies: DEADLY, sworn, irreconcilable, bitter, implacable, unrelenting, remorseless.
– OPPOSITES immortal.

mortify verb HUMILIATE, humble, bring low, disgrace, shame, abash, chasten, degrade, abase, deflate, crush, discomfit, embarrass.

mostly adverb FOR THE MOST PART, on the whole, in the main, largely, mainly, chiefly, predominantly.

mother verb mother the orphans: LOOK AFTER, care for, tend, raise, rear, foster, cherish, fuss over, indulge.

motherly adjective MATERNAL, protective, comforting, caring, loving, affectionate, fond, warm, tender.

motion noun MOBILITY, locomotion, movement, moving, travel, travelling, progress, passing, passage, flow, action, activity.

motionless adjective UNMOVING, stock-still, at a standstill, stationary, immobile, immovable, static, at rest, frozen, inert, lifeless.
– OPPOSITES mobile.

motivate verb MOVE, cause, lead, persuade, prompt, actuate, drive, impel, spur, induce, provoke, incite, inspire.

motive noun MOTIVATION, reason, rationale, grounds, cause, basis, occasion, incentive, inducement, incitement, influence, stimulus, spur, goad; *informal* what makes one tick.

motley adjective ASSORTED, varied, miscellaneous, mixed, diverse, diversified, variegated.

mottled adjective BLOTCHED, blotchy, speckled, spotted, streaked, marbled, flecked, freckled, dappled, stippled; *informal* splotchy.

motto noun MAXIM, aphorism, adage, saying, saw, axiom, truism, precept, epigram, proverb.

mould verb SHAPE, form, fashion, model, create, design, carve, sculpt, chisel, forge.

mouldy adjective MILDEWED, blighted, musty, fusty, decaying, rotting, rotten, bad, spoiled.

mound noun HILLOCK, knoll, rise, hummock, tump, embankment, bank, dune.

mount verb ❶ ASCEND, go up, climb up, clamber up, make one's way up, scale. ❷ **prices/fear mounting:** INCREASE, grow, escalate, intensify. ❸ **mount an exhibition:** STAGE, put on, install, prepare, organize, arrange, set in motion, get up.
– OPPOSITES descend.

mountain noun PEAK, mount, height, elevation, eminence, pinnacle, fell, alp; *Scottish* ben.

mountainous adjective HILLY, high, highland, steep, lofty, towering, soaring, alpine, rocky.

mourn verb GRIEVE, sorrow, keen, lament, bewail, bemoan.

mournful adjective SAD, sorrowful, doleful, gloomy, sombre, melancholy, lugubrious, funereal, dejected, depressed, downcast, miserable, woeful, unhappy.
– OPPOSITES cheerful.

mouth noun ❶ LIPS, jaws, maw, muzzle; *informal* trap, chops, kisser; *Brit. informal* gob. ❷ OPENING, entrance, entry, inlet, door, doorway, gateway, hatch, aperture, orifice.

mouthful noun BITE, swallow, nibble, sip, sup, taste, drop, bit, piece, morsel, sample.

mouthpiece noun SPOKESMAN, spokeswoman, spokesperson, negotiator, intermediary, mediator, agent, representative.

move verb ❶ GO, walk, march, proceed, progress, advance. ❷ CARRY, transport, transfer, transpose, change over, shift, switch. ❸ **they must move soon:** TAKE ACTION, act, do something, get moving. ❹ MOVE HOUSE, relocate, move away, leave, go away. ❺ **moved by the performance:** AFFECT, touch, impress, upset, disturb, disquiet, agitate, make an impression on, have an impact on. ❻ **moved to tears:** PROVOKE, incite, actuate, rouse, excite, urge, incline, stimulate, motivate, influence, persuade, lead, prompt, cause, impel, induce. ❼ **move that he be sacked:** PROPOSE, put forward, advocate, recommend, urge, suggest.
▶ noun ❶ MOVEMENT, motion, moving, action, activity, gesture, gesticulation. ❷ **plan our next move:** ACTION, act, deed, measure, step, tack, manoeuvre, tactic, stratagem, ploy, ruse, trick. ❸ **it's your move:** TURN, go.
■ **get a move on** HURRY UP, make haste, speed up, move faster, get

moving; *informal* get cracking, make it snappy, step on it, shake a leg.

movement noun ❶ MOVING, carrying, transportation, transferral, shifting. ❷ MOVE, motion, action, activity, gesture, gesticulation. ❸ the clock's movement: MECHANISM, machinery, works, workings, action. ❹ a peace movement: CAMPAIGN, crusade, drive, group, party, organization, coalition, front.

moving adjective ❶ a moving story: AFFECTING, touching, emotive, emotional, poignant, stirring, arousing, upsetting, disturbing. ❷ moving parts: MOVABLE, mobile, motile, unfixed. ❸ the moving force: DRIVING, dynamic, impelling, motivating, stimulating, inspirational.

mow verb CUT, trim, crop, clip, scythe, shear.

muck noun ❶ DIRT, grime, filth, mud, slime, sludge, scum, mire; *informal* gunk; *Brit. informal* gunge. ❷ DUNG, manure, ordure, excrement, guano, droppings, faeces.

■ **muck up** BUNGLE, muff, make a mess of, mess up, mar, spoil, ruin, foul up; *informal* botch, screw up.

muddle verb ❶ CONFUSE, get confused, mix up, jumble, scramble, throw into disorder, get into a tangle, make a mess of, mess up. ❷ CONFUSE, disorientate, bewilder, befuddle, daze, perplex, puzzle, baffle, nonplus, confound.

muddy verb ❶ DIRTY, begrime, soil. ❷ muddy the issue: MAKE UNCLEAR, cloud, confuse, mix up, jumble, scramble, get into a tangle.

muffle verb ❶ WRAP UP, cover up, swathe, swaddle, envelop, cloak. ❷ muffle the sound: DEADEN, dull, dampen, stifle, smother, suppress, soften, quieten, mute.

mug verb ASSAULT, attack, beat up, knock down, rob; *informal* rough up, do over.

muggy adjective CLOSE, stuffy, sultry, oppressive, airless, humid, clammy, sticky.
– OPPOSITES fresh.

multiple adjective SEVERAL, many, numerous, various, collective, manifold.
– OPPOSITES single.

multiply verb ❶ BREED, reproduce. ❷ INCREASE, grow, accumulate, augment, proliferate, spread.

multitude noun CROWD, assembly, throng, host, horde, mass, mob, legion, army.

munch verb CHEW, champ, chomp, masticate, crunch, eat.

mundane adjective COMMON, ordinary, everyday, workaday, usual, prosaic, pedestrian, routine, customary, regular, normal, typical, commonplace, banal, hackneyed, trite, stale, platitudinous.
– OPPOSITES extraordinary.

municipal adjective CIVIC, civil, city, metropolitan, urban, town, borough.

murder noun KILLING, manslaughter, homicide, slaughter, assassination, butchery, carnage, massacre; *poetic/literary* slaying.
▶ verb *see* KILL (1).

murderer noun KILLER, slaughterer, cut-throat, assassin, butcher; *poetic/literary* slayer.

murderous adjective FATAL,

lethal, deadly, mortal, homicidal, savage, barbarous, brutal, bloodthirsty.

murky adjective DARK, dim, gloomy, dirty, muddy, dingy, dull, cloudy, turbid, opaque.
– OPPOSITES clear.

murmur noun ❶ WHISPER, undertone, mutter, mumble. ❷ BABBLE, burble, whisper, purl, rustle, buzzing, drone.
▶ verb ❶ WHISPER, speak in an undertone, speak sotto voce, mutter, mumble. ❷ BABBLE, burble, whisper, purl, rustle, buzz, drone.

muscular adjective BRAWNY, strapping, powerfully built, solidly built, hefty, sturdy, rugged, burly; *informal* beefy.
– OPPOSITES weak, puny.

muse verb THINK, meditate, ruminate, contemplate, reflect, deliberate, day dream, be in a reverie.

mushroom verb SPRING UP, shoot up, sprout, burgeon, boom, thrive, flourish, prosper.

musical adjective TUNEFUL, melodic, melodious, harmonious, mellifluous, dulcet, euphonious.

muster verb ASSEMBLE, bring together, call/gather together, call up, summon, rally, mobilize, round up, marshal, collect; *formal* convoke.

musty adjective MOULDY, mildewed, fusty, decaying, stale, stuffy, airless, damp, dank.

mutable adjective CHANGEABLE, variable, alterable, convertible, adaptable, modifiable.
– OPPOSITES invariable.

mutation noun CHANGE, variation, alteration, modification, transformation, metamorphosis, evolution, transmutation, transfiguration.

mute adjective SILENT, speechless, wordless, unspeaking, taciturn, uncommunicative; *informal* mum.
▶ verb *see* MUFFLE (2).

muted adjective SOFT, softened, subdued, subtle, discreet, toned down, quiet, understated.

mutinous adjective REBELLIOUS, insurgent, insurrectionary, revolutionary, subversive, seditious, traitorous, insubordinate, disobedient, riotous, unruly, restive, contumacious, refractory; *Brit. informal* bolshie.

mutiny noun REBELLION, revolt, insurrection, insurgence, insurgency, uprising, rising, revolution, disobedience, defiance, insubordination.

mysterious adjective ENIGMATIC, impenetrable, inscrutable, incomprehensible, inexplicable, unexplainable, unfathomable, unaccountable, dark, obscure, arcane, abstruse, cryptic, unknown, recondite, secret, preternatural, supernatural, uncanny, mystical, peculiar, strange, weird, curious, bizarre, undisclosed, mystifying, baffling, puzzling, perplexing, bewildering.

mystery noun ENIGMA, puzzle, secret, riddle, conundrum, question, question mark, closed book, unexplored ground, terra incognita.

mystic, mystical adjective SPIRITUAL, paranormal, transcendental, other-worldly, supernatural, preternatural, occult, metaphysical.

mystify verb CONFUSE, bewilder, confound, perplex, baffle, nonplus, puzzle, elude, escape; *informal* stump, beat, bamboozle.

myth noun ❶ LEGEND, saga, tale, story, fable, folk tale, allegory, parable, fairy story/tale. ❷ FANTASY, delusion, invention, fabrication, untruth, lie.

mythical adjective ❶ LEGENDARY, mythological, fabled, chimerical, fabulous, fantastical, fairy-tale, storybook, fictitious, allegorical. ❷ IMAGINED, imaginary, pretend, make-believe, unreal, fictitious, invented, fabricated, made up, untrue.
– OPPOSITES real.

Nn

nadir noun THE LOWEST POINT, rock bottom, the depths, all-time low, as low as one can get; *informal* the pits.
– OPPOSITES zenith.

nag verb SCOLD, carp, pick on, keep on at, harp on at, henpeck, bully, upbraid, berate, chivvy, criticize, find fault with, complain to, grumble to.
▶ **noun** SHREW, scold, harpy, termagant, carper, caviller, complainer, grumbler.

naive adjective INNOCENT, artless, childlike, simple, ingenuous, guileless, trusting, unsophisticated, unworldly, jejune, natural, unaffected, unpretentious, frank, open, candid.
– OPPOSITES worldly.

naked adjective STARK NAKED, nude, in the nude, bare, stripped, unclothed, undressed, uncovered, undraped, disrobed, au naturel; *informal* in the buff; *Brit. informal* starkers; *N. Amer. informal* buck naked.
– OPPOSITES clothed.

name noun DESIGNATION, title, label, tag, cognomen, sobriquet, epithet, first name, given name, surname, family name, maiden name, nickname, pet name, stage name, pseudonym, alias; *informal* moniker, handle; *formal* denomination, appellation.
▶ **verb** CHRISTEN, baptize, call, entitle, label, style, term, title, dub, denominate.

nameless adjective UNNAMED, untitled, unlabelled, untagged, anonymous, unidentified, undesignated, unspecified.

nap noun CATNAP, doze, light sleep, rest, lie-down; *informal* snooze, forty winks, shut-eye; *Brit. informal* kip.

narrate verb TELL, relate, recount, recite, unfold, chronicle, describe, detail, portray, sketch out, rehearse, repeat.

narrator noun REPORTER, describer, chronicler, annalist, storyteller, raconteur.

narrow adjective ❶ SLENDER, thin, slim, slight, spare, attenuated, tapering. ❷ a narrow range: LIMITED, restricted, select, exclusive.
– OPPOSITES wide.

narrow-minded adjective

INTOLERANT, illiberal, reactionary, close-minded, unreasonable, prejudiced, bigoted, biased, discriminatory, jaundiced, parochial, provincial, insular, small-minded, petty-minded, petty, mean-spirited, prudish, strait-laced.
– OPPOSITES broad-minded.

nasty adjective UNPLEASANT, disagreeable, distasteful, horrible, vile, foul, hateful, loathsome, revolting, disgusting, odious, obnoxious, repellent, repugnant, ugly, offensive, objectionable, squalid, dirty, filthy, impure, polluted, tainted, unpalatable, unsavoury, unappetizing, evil-smelling, foul-smelling, stinking, rank, fetid, malodorous; *poetic/literary* mephitic, noisome.
– OPPOSITES pleasant.

nation noun COUNTRY, land, state, kingdom, empire, realm, republic, commonwealth, people, race, tribe, society.

national adjective NATIONWIDE, countrywide, state, coast-to-coast, widespread, comprehensive, general.
▶ noun CITIZEN, subject, native.

native adjective ❶ INBORN, inherent, innate, intrinsic, instinctive, intuitive, natural, congenital, hereditary.
❷ INDIGENOUS, home-grown, domestic, local.

natural adjective ❶ natural produce: ORGANIC, pure, unrefined, unmixed, whole, plain, real, chemical-free, additive-free. ❷ her natural instincts: NATIVE, inborn, inherent, innate, intrinsic, instinctive, intuitive, congenital, hereditary, inherited, ingrained.
❸ natural charm: GENUINE, real, authentic, simple, unaffected, unpretentious, spontaneous, artless, ingenuous, candid, open, frank, relaxed, unstudied.
– OPPOSITES unnatural.

nature noun ❶ NATURAL FORCES, creation, the environment, the earth, mother earth, landscape, scenery. ❷ of this nature: KIND, sort, type, variety, description, category, class, classification.
❸ a pleasant nature: TEMPERAMENT, temper, personality, disposition, humour, mood, outlook.

naughty adjective MISCHIEVOUS, badly behaved, misbehaving, disobedient, defiant, unruly, roguish, wayward, delinquent, undisciplined, unmanageable, ungovernable, fractious, refractory, perverse, errant.
– OPPOSITES well behaved.

nausea noun SICKNESS, vomiting, retching, gagging, biliousness, queasiness, faintness.

nauseous adjective ❶ SICK, queasy, unwell, indisposed; *Brit.* off colour; *informal* green about the gills. ❷ DISGUSTING, revolting, repulsive, repellent, repugnant, offensive, loathsome, abhorrent, odious.

nautical adjective MARITIME, naval, marine, seagoing, seafaring.

navigable adjective NEGOTIABLE, passable, traversable, clear, unobstructed.

near adjective ❶ CLOSE, nearby, alongside, at close range/quarters, accessible, within reach, close/near at hand, at hand, neighbouring, adjacent, adjoining, bordering, contiguous, proximate. ❷ the time is near: APPROACHING, coming, imminent,

forthcoming, in the offing, impending, looming.
– OPPOSITES distant.

nearly adverb ALMOST, virtually, next to, close to, well-nigh, about, just about, practically, roughly, approximately, not quite.

neat adjective ❶ a neat house: TIDY, orderly, well ordered, in good order, spick and span. ❷ a neat person: TIDY, spruce, trim, smart, dapper, well groomed, well turned out. ❸ neat footwork: ADROIT, skilful, expert, practised, dexterous, deft, accurate, precise, nimble, agile.
– OPPOSITES untidy.

necessary adjective NEEDED, needful, essential, required, requisite, vital, indispensable, imperative, mandatory, obligatory, compulsory, de rigueur.
– OPPOSITES unnecessary.

need verb REQUIRE, necessitate, demand, call for, have occasion for, want, lack, be without.
▶ noun REQUIREMENT, want, wish, demand, prerequisite, requisite, essential, desideratum.

needless adjective UNNECESSARY, uncalled for, gratuitous, undesired, unwanted, pointless, useless, dispensable, expendable, inessential.
– OPPOSITES necessary.

negative adjective PESSIMISTIC, defeatist, gloomy, gloom-laden, cynical, jaundiced, critical, fault-finding, complaining, unhelpful, uncooperative.
– OPPOSITES positive.

neglect verb ❶ FAIL TO LOOK AFTER, fail to provide for, abandon, forsake, leave alone. ❷ LET SLIDE, skimp on, shirk, be remiss about, be lax about, not attend to, leave undone, procrastinate about.
▶ noun NEGLIGENCE, neglectfulness, remissness, carelessness, heedlessness, slackness, laxity, laxness, dereliction.
– OPPOSITES care, attention.

negligent adjective NEGLECTFUL, remiss, lax, careless, inattentive, heedless, thoughtless, unmindful, uncaring, forgetful, indifferent, offhand, cursory, slack, sloppy, slapdash, slipshod, procrastinating, dilatory.
– OPPOSITES attentive.

negligible adjective TRIVIAL, trifling, insignificant, of no account, paltry, petty, tiny, minute, small, minor, inconsequential, inappreciable, imperceptible.
– OPPOSITES significant.

negotiate verb BARGAIN, drive a bargain, hold talks, confer, debate, discuss, discuss terms, discuss a settlement, consult together, parley, haggle.

neighbourhood noun DISTRICT, area, region, locality, part, quarter, precinct, community; *informal* neck of the woods, stamping ground.

neighbouring adjective ADJACENT, adjoining, bordering, abutting, contiguous, nearby, near, very near, close/near at hand, not far away, in the vicinity.

nemesis noun DOWNFALL, undoing, ruin, destruction, Waterloo.

nervous adjective ON EDGE, edgy, tense, strained, anxious, nervy, agitated, worried, fretful, uneasy, disquieted, on tenterhooks, fidgety, ruffled, flustered, apprehensive, perturbed, fearful,

frightened, scared, with one's heart in one's mouth, quaking, trembling, shaking, shaky; *informal* jittery, twitchy, jumpy, in a state, uptight, wired.
– OPPOSITES calm.

nestle verb SNUGGLE, curl up, huddle together, cuddle up, nuzzle.

net noun NETTING, fishnet, mesh, latticework, lattice, openwork, webbing, tracery.
► **verb** CATCH, trap, snare, ensnare, entangle, enmesh, bag.

nettle verb IRRITATE, provoke, ruffle, annoy, incense, exasperate, irk, vex, pique, bother, pester, harass, torment, plague.

neurotic adjective UNSTABLE, maladjusted, obsessive, phobic, fixated, compulsive, oversensitive, hysterical, irrational.
– OPPOSITES stable.

neuter adjective ASEXUAL, sexless, unsexed.
► **verb** CASTRATE, geld, emasculate, spay, dress; *informal* fix, doctor.

neutral adjective IMPARTIAL, unbiased, unprejudiced, open-minded, non-partisan, without favouritism, even-handed, disinterested, non-aligned, dispassionate, objective, detached, uninvolved, uncommitted.

neutralize verb COUNTERACT, cancel, nullify, negate, annul, undo, invalidate, frustrate, be an antidote to.

new adjective MODERN, recent, advanced, state-of-the-art, present-day, contemporary, current, latest, up to date, up to the minute, new-fashioned, modish, brand new, newly arrived, modernist, ultra-modern, avant-garde, futuristic, newfangled.
– OPPOSITES old.

newcomer noun ARRIVAL, incomer, immigrant, settler, stranger, outsider, foreigner, alien, intruder, interloper; *informal* johnny-come-lately.

news plural noun INFORMATION, facts, data, report, story, news item, news flash, account, statement, announcement, press release, communiqué, message, bulletin, dispatch, disclosure, revelation, word, talk, the latest; *informal* gen, info.

newspaper noun PAPER, gazette, journal, tabloid, broadsheet, weekly, scandal sheet; *informal* rag.

next adjective ❶ FOLLOWING, succeeding, successive, subsequent, later, ensuing. ❷ NEIGHBOURING, adjacent, adjoining, bordering, contiguous.
– OPPOSITES previous.

nice adjective ❶ a nice time: GOOD, pleasant, enjoyable, pleasurable, agreeable, delightful, marvellous. ❷ a nice distinction: FINE, ultra-fine, subtle, minute, precise, exact, accurate, strict, close. ❸ a nice day: FINE, dry, sunny, warm, pleasant, agreeable.
– OPPOSITES unpleasant, rough, nasty.

nicety noun FINER POINT, subtlety, nuance, detail.

niggardly adjective MEAN, miserly, parsimonious, penny-pinching, cheese-paring; *informal* tight-fisted, stingy.
– OPPOSITES generous.

nimble adjective AGILE, lithe, sprightly, spry, graceful, skilful, deft.
– OPPOSITES clumsy.

nippy adjective ICY, chilly, bitter, raw, piercing, stinging.
– OPPOSITES warm.

no adverb ABSOLUTELY NOT, under no circumstances, by no means, never; *informal* not on your life, no way, nope.

noble adjective ❶ ARISTOCRATIC, patrician, blue-blooded, titled, landed. ❷ **noble acts:** NOBLE-MINDED, magnanimous, generous, self-sacrificing, honourable, virtuous, brave. ❸ **noble ideas:** LOFTY, grand, exalted, elevated. ❹ **noble appearance:** IMPRESSIVE, magnificent, striking, awesome, stately, grand, dignified.
– OPPOSITES common, dishonourable.

nod verb INCLINE, bob, bow, dip, duck.

noise noun SOUND, din, hubbub, clamour, racket, row, uproar, tumult, commotion, rumpus, pandemonium.
– OPPOSITES silence.

noisy adjective ❶ **noisy neighbours:** ROWDY, clamorous, boisterous, obstreperous, turbulent; *informal* rackety. ❷ **noisy music:** LOUD, blaring, blasting, deafening, ear-splitting.
– OPPOSITES quiet.

nomad noun ITINERANT, traveller, migrant, wanderer, transient, vagabond, vagrant, tramp.

nominal adjective ❶ IN NAME ONLY, titular, formal, theoretical, self-styled, purported, supposed. ❷ **a nominal sum:** TOKEN, symbolic, minimal, trivial, insignificant.

nominate verb NAME, propose, put forward, submit, present, recommend; *informal* put up.

nonchalant adjective SELF-POSSESSED, imperturbable, calm, cool, collected, cool as a cucumber, unconcerned, indifferent, blasé, casual, offhand, carefree, insouciant, easy-going, careless; *informal* laid-back.
– OPPOSITES anxious.

nonplus verb TAKE ABACK, stun, dumbfound, confound, astound, astonish, amaze, surprise, disconcert, stump, confuse, bewilder, embarrass, fluster; *informal* faze, flummox, floor.

nonsense noun RUBBISH, balderdash, drivel, gibberish, blather, trash, claptrap; *informal* twaddle, waffle, tripe, bilge, bull, tosh, bosh, gobbledegook, mumbo-jumbo, poppycock, stuff and nonsense; *Brit. informal* flannel; *informal, dated* bunkum, tommyrot.
– OPPOSITES sense.

nonsensical adjective MEANINGLESS, incomprehensible, unintelligible, senseless, foolish, absurd, silly, inane, stupid, ridiculous, ludicrous, preposterous, hare-brained, irrational, idiotic, insane; *informal* crazy, crackpot, nutty, wacky.
– OPPOSITES sensible.

non-stop adjective INCESSANT, unceasing, ceaseless, constant, continuous, continual, unbroken, unfaltering, steady, unremitting, relentless, persistent, endless, never-ending, unending, interminable.

nook noun CORNER, cranny, recess, alcove, niche, opening, cavity, crevice, gap.

normal adjective ❶ USUAL, standard, average, common, ordinary, natural, general, commonplace, conventional,

typical, regular, routine, run-of-the-mill, everyday, accustomed, habitual, prevailing, popular, accepted, acknowledged. ❷ he isn't normal: WELL ADJUSTED, well balanced, rational, compos mentis, sane.
– OPPOSITES abnormal.

normally adverb USUALLY, ordinarily, as a rule, as a general rule, generally, in general, mostly, commonly, habitually.

nose noun PROBOSCIS, bill, beak, snout, muzzle; *informal* snoot, hooter; *Brit. informal* conk; *N. Amer. informal* schnozz.
■ **nose around** PRY, search, peer, prowl; *informal* snoop. **nose out** SMELL OUT, sniff out, search for, detect, run to earth/ground.

nosy adjective INQUISITIVE, curious, interfering, meddlesome, intrusive; *informal* snooping, snoopy.

notable adjective ❶ a notable achievement: NOTEWORTHY, remarkable, outstanding, important, significant, momentous, memorable, unforgettable, pronounced, marked, striking, impressive, uncommon, unusual, particular, special, extraordinary. ❷ notable people: NOTED, of note, distinguished, eminent, pre-eminent, well known, prominent, illustrious, great, famous, famed, renowned, celebrated, acclaimed.
– OPPOSITES insignificant.

note noun ❶ RECORD, account, entry, item, notation, comment, jotting, inscription. ❷ LETTER, message, memorandum, memo, epistle, missive, communication. ❸ FOOTNOTE, annotation, commentary, gloss, marginalia, explanation, explication, exposition, exegesis. ❹ people of note: DISTINCTION, eminence, pre-eminence, illustriousness, greatness, prestige, fame, renown. ❺ a note of amusement: TONE, intonation, inflection, sound, indication, hint, element.
▶ verb ❶ WRITE DOWN, jot down, mark down, enter, mark, record, register. ❷ TAKE NOTE OF, take notice of, see, observe, perceive, behold, detect, take in.

noted adjective NOTABLE, distinguished, eminent, pre-eminent, well known, prominent, illustrious, great, famous, famed, renowned, celebrated, acclaimed.
– OPPOSITES unknown.

notice noun ❶ ATTENTION, attentiveness, heed, note, observation, cognizance, regard, consideration, watchfulness, vigilance. ❷ BULLETIN, poster, handbill, bill, circular, leaflet, pamphlet, advertisement.
▶ verb SEE, note, take note of, observe, perceive, discern, detect, behold, spot, distinguish, make out, take heed of, heed, pay attention to, take notice of, mark, regard.
– OPPOSITES overlook.

noticeable adjective OBSERVABLE, visible, discernible, perceptible, detectable, distinguishable, distinct, evident, obvious, apparent, manifest, patent, plain, clear, conspicuous, unmistakable, pronounced, striking, blatant.
– OPPOSITES imperceptible.

notify verb INFORM, tell, advise, acquaint, apprise, warn, alert, caution.

notion noun IDEA, belief, opinion, thought, impression, view, conviction, concept, assumption, presumption, hypothesis, theory, postulation, apprehension, understanding.

notorious adjective INFAMOUS, ill-famed, disreputable, dishonourable, of ill repute, well known, prominent, scandalous, opprobrious, legendary.

nourishing adjective NUTRITIOUS, nutritive, wholesome, healthy, health-giving, healthful, beneficial, good for one.
– OPPOSITES unhealthy.

nourishment noun FOOD, nutriment, nutrition, sustenance, subsistence, provisions; *informal* grub, chow; *Brit. informal* scoff; *dated* victuals.

novel adjective NEW, fresh, different, original, unusual, rare, unique, imaginative, unconventional, innovative, ground-breaking, trailblazing, modern, advanced.

novice noun BEGINNER, newcomer, apprentice, trainee, learner, probationer, student, pupil, recruit, tyro, initiate, neophyte; *informal* rookie; *N. Amer. informal* greenhorn.

now adverb AT PRESENT, at the present time, at this time, at the moment, for the time being, currently.

noxious adjective UNWHOLESOME, unhealthy, poisonous, toxic, harmful, injurious, malignant, detrimental, deleterious.
– OPPOSITES innocuous.

nuance noun SHADE, shading, gradation, subtlety, nicety, refinement, degree.

nucleus noun CORE, kernel, centre, heart, nub.

nude adjective *see* NAKED.

nudge verb POKE, jab, prod, dig, jog, elbow, touch, push, shove.

nuisance noun PEST, bother, plague, irritant, annoyance, trouble, burden, problem, difficulty, worry; *informal* drag.
– OPPOSITES blessing.

numb adjective WITHOUT FEELING, deadened, benumbed, insensible, insensate, dull, anaesthetized, dazed, stunned, stupefied, paralysed, immobilized, frozen.
– OPPOSITES sensitive.
▶ verb DEADEN, dull, anaesthetize, benumb, daze, stun, stupefy, paralyse, immobilize, freeze.

number noun ❶ FIGURE, digit, numeral, cipher, character, symbol, unit, integer. ❷ TOTAL, aggregate, score, tally, count, sum.
▶ verb COUNT, add up, enumerate, total, calculate, compute, reckon, tell, estimate, assess.

numerous adjective MANY, a lot, lots, innumerable, myriad, multitudinous, several, quite a few, various, diverse.
– OPPOSITES few.

nurse verb ❶ TAKE CARE OF, care for, look after, tend, attend to, minister to. ❷ SUCKLE, breast-feed, feed, wet-nurse.

nurture verb FEED, nourish, provide for, care for, take care of, tend, attend to, bring up, rear.

nutritious adjective *see* NOURISHING.

nuzzle verb NOSE, nudge, prod, push.

Oo

oaf noun LOUT, blunderer, bungler, boor, churl, bumpkin, yokel, brute, galoot; *informal* clodhopper; *N. Amer. informal* lummox.

oath noun ❶ VOW, promise, pledge, avowal, affirmation, attestation, bond, word of honour, word. ❷ CURSE, swear word, expletive, blasphemy, profanity, imprecation, malediction, obscenity, epithet, four-letter word, dirty word.

obedient adjective COMPLIANT, acquiescent, biddable, dutiful, deferential, respectful, tractable, amenable, malleable, governable, well trained, submissive, docile, meek, subservient, obsequious, servile.
– OPPOSITES disobedient.

obese adjective *see* FAT (1).

obey verb ❶ obey rules: ABIDE BY, comply with, adhere to, observe, conform to, respect, acquiesce in, consent to, agree to, follow. ❷ obey orders: PERFORM, carry out, execute, put into effect, fulfil, act upon.
– OPPOSITES disobey.

object noun ❶ THING, article, body, entity, item, device, gadget; *informal* thingamajig, thingamabob, thingummy, whatchamacallit, whatsit. ❷ OBJECTIVE, aim, goal, target, end, ambition, purpose, design, intent, intention, idea, point.
▶ verb PROTEST, demur, beg to differ, remonstrate, expostulate, take exception, argue against, oppose, be in opposition to, complain about.

objection noun PROTEST, protestation, complaint, demurral, opposition, remonstration, remonstrance, expostulation, dissatisfaction, disapproval, grievance, scruple, qualm; *informal* niggle.
– OPPOSITES approval.

objectionable adjective OFFENSIVE, obnoxious, unpleasant, disagreeable, unacceptable, nasty, disgusting, repulsive, repellent, abhorrent, repugnant, revolting, loathsome, hateful, detestable, reprehensible, deplorable, insufferable, intolerable, despicable, contemptible, odious, vile, obscene, foul, horrible, horrid, noxious.
– OPPOSITES agreeable.

objective adjective UNBIASED, unprejudiced, impartial, neutral, uninvolved, non-partisan, disinterested, detached, dispassionate, even-handed, equitable, fair, just, open-minded.
– OPPOSITES subjective.
▶ noun OBJECT, aim, goal, target, end, ambition, aspiration, intent, intention, purpose, design, plan, scheme, plot.

obligate verb OBLIGE, compel, require, necessitate, impel, force, constrain, press, pressure, pressurize.

obligatory adjective COMPULSORY, mandatory, enforced, necessary, essential, required, requisite,

imperative, de rigueur, unavoidable, unescapable.
– OPPOSITES voluntary.

oblige verb ❶ *See* OBLIGATE. ❷ DO SOMEONE A FAVOUR, do someone a kindness, do someone a service, help, accommodate, meet someone's wants/needs, put oneself out for, indulge, assist.

obliging adjective *see* HELPFUL (2).

oblique adjective ❶ SLANTING, slanted, sloping, sloped, inclined, at an angle, angled, tilted, listing, diagonal. ❷ an oblique compliment: INDIRECT, implied, roundabout, circuitous, circumlocutory, ambiguous, evasive, backhanded.
– OPPOSITES direct.

obliterate verb ERASE, eradicate, efface, blot out, rub out, wipe out, expunge, delete, destroy, annihilate, eliminate, extirpate, decimate, liquidate, demolish.

oblivious adjective HEEDLESS OF, unmindful of, unaware of, unconscious of, insensible of, ignorant of, blind to, unobservant of, deaf to, inattentive to, neglectful of, forgetful of, absent-minded, careless of, unconcerned with, abstracted, preoccupied, absorbed, far away.
– OPPOSITES conscious.

obscene adjective INDECENT, pornographic, off colour, risqué, lewd, salacious, smutty, lecherous, lascivious, licentious, prurient, lubricious, ribald, scatological, scabrous, bawdy, suggestive, vulgar, dirty, filthy, foul, coarse, gross, vile, nasty, offensive, immoral, impure, immodest, shameless, unchaste, improper, unwholesome, erotic, carnal, sexy; *informal* raunchy, blue.
– OPPOSITES decent.

obscenity noun ❶ INDECENCY, lewdness, salaciousness, lasciviousness, licentiousness, prurience, lubricity, ribaldry, scabrousness, bawdiness, suggestiveness, vulgarity, dirtiness. ❷ CURSE, oath, swear word, expletive, imprecation, blasphemy, epithet, profanity, four-letter word, dirty word.

obscure adjective ❶ obscure references: UNCLEAR, indeterminate, opaque, abstruse, recondite, unexplained, concealed, hidden, arcane, enigmatic, deep, cryptic, mysterious, puzzling, perplexing, confusing, involved, unfathomable, incomprehensible, impenetrable, vague, indefinite, hazy, uncertain, doubtful, dubious, ambiguous, equivocal. ❷ obscure shapes: INDISTINCT, vague, shadowy, hazy, blurred, fuzzy, cloudy. ❸ obscure writers: LITTLE KNOWN, unknown, unheard of, undistinguished, insignificant, inconspicuous, minor, unimportant, unrecognized, unsung.
– OPPOSITES clear, famous.

obsequious adjective SERVILE, subservient, submissive, slavish, menial, abject, fawning, grovelling, cringing, toadying, truckling, sycophantic, ingratiating, unctuous, oily, Uriah Heepish; *informal* bootlicking.

observant adjective ALERT, sharp-eyed, sharp, eagle-eyed, attentive, vigilant, wide awake, watchful, heedful, on the lookout, on guard, mindful, intent, aware,

conscious; *informal* not missing a thing/trick, on the ball.
– OPPOSITES inattentive.

observation noun ❶ SCRUTINY, scrutinization, watch, monitoring, surveillance, inspection, attention, consideration, study, review, examination. ❷ REMARK, comment, statement, utterance, pronouncement, declaration.

observe verb ❶ SEE, catch sight of, notice, note, perceive, discern, detect, espy, behold, watch, view, spot, witness; *informal* get a load of. ❷ **observe regulations**: KEEP, obey, adhere to, abide by, heed, follow, comply with, conform to, acquiesce in, consent to, accept, respect, defer to. ❸ **observe one's duty**: CARRY OUT, perform, execute, discharge, fulfil. ❹ **observe the holiday**: CELEBRATE, keep, recognize, commemorate, mark, remember, solemnize.

observer noun WATCHER, looker-on, onlooker, witness, eyewitness, spectator, bystander, beholder, viewer, spotter.

obsess verb PREOCCUPY, haunt, have a hold on, possess, consume, engross, have a grip on, grip, dominate, rule, control, be on someone's mind, prey on, plague, torment, hound, bedevil.

obsession noun PREOCCUPATION, fixation, consuming passion, mania, enthusiasm, infatuation, compulsion, phobia, complex, fetish, craze; *informal* bee in one's bonnet, hang-up.

obsessive adjective EXCESSIVE, overdone, consuming, compulsive, besetting, gripping, haunting.

obsolete adjective OUTWORN, discarded, discontinued, extinct, bygone, outmoded, antiquated, out of date, superannuated, old-fashioned, behind the times, old, dated, antique, archaic, ancient, antediluvian, time-worn, past its prime.
– OPPOSITES current.

obstacle noun BAR, barrier, obstruction, impediment, hindrance, hurdle, barricade, blockade, stumbling block, blockage, curb, check, snag, difficulty, catch, drawback.
– OPPOSITES advantage, aid.

obstinate adjective STUBBORN, mulish, pig-headed, wilful, self-willed, strong-minded, perverse, refractory, recalcitrant, contumacious, unmanageable, firm, steadfast, unyielding, inflexible, unbending, immovable, intransigent, intractable, uncompromising, persistent, tenacious, dogged, single-minded.
– OPPOSITES amenable, tractable.

obstreperous adjective UNRULY, disorderly, turbulent, rowdy, boisterous, rough, riotous, out of control, out of hand, wild, undisciplined, unrestrained, unmanageable; *Brit. informal* bolshie, stroppy.
– OPPOSITES orderly.

obstruct verb BLOCK, barricade, bar, cut off, shut off, choke, clog, hold up, bring to a standstill, stop, halt, hinder, impede, hamper, interfere with, frustrate, thwart, baulk, inhibit, curb, hamstring, encumber.
– OPPOSITES clear, facilitate.

obtain verb ❶ GET, get hold of, acquire, come by, procure, secure, gain, earn, achieve, attain, get one's hands on, seize, grab, pick up. ❷ BE IN FORCE, be effective, exist, stand, prevail, hold, be the case, reign, rule, hold sway.

obtrusive adjective NOTICEABLE, conspicuous, obvious, unmistakable, blatant, flagrant, bold, audacious, intrusive.
– OPPOSITES unobtrusive.

obtuse adjective *see* STUPID (1).

obvious adjective CLEAR, plain, visible, noticeable, perceptible, discernible, detectable, recognizable, evident, apparent, manifest, palpable, patent, conspicuous, unconcealed, overt, pronounced, transparent, prominent, unmistakable, indisputable, undeniable; *informal* sticking out like a sore thumb, sticking out a mile.
– OPPOSITES imperceptible, inconspicuous.

occasion noun ❶ TIME, juncture, point, situation, instance, case, circumstance. ❷ EVENT, incident, occurrence, happening, episode, affair, experience.
▶ verb CAUSE, give rise to, bring about, result in, lead to, prompt, provoke, produce, create, generate, engender.

occasional adjective INFREQUENT, intermittent, irregular, sporadic, odd, rare, casual, incidental.
– OPPOSITES regular, habitual.

occasionally adverb NOW AND THEN, now and again, from time to time, sometimes, at times, every so often, once in a while, on occasion, periodically, at intervals, irregularly, sporadically, infrequently, intermittently, off and on.

occupation noun ❶ JOB, profession, business, employment, employ, career, calling, vocation, trade, craft, line, field, province, area. ❷ OCCUPANCY, tenancy, tenure, residence, inhabitancy, habitation, possession, holding. ❸ INVASION, seizure, takeover, conquest, capture, overthrow, subjugation, subjection.

occupy verb ❶ LIVE IN, inhabit, reside in, dwell in, tenant, have one's residence/abode in, make one's home in. ❷ **occupy space/her time:** FILL, fill up, take up, use up, utilize, cover. ❸ **occupied their country:** INVADE, overrun, seize, take over.

occur verb ❶ HAPPEN, take place, come about, materialize, transpire, arise, crop up, turn up, eventuate; *poetic/literary* come to pass, befall. ❷ BE FOUND, be met with, be present, exist, obtain, appear, present itself, show itself, manifest itself.

occurrence noun ❶ HAPPENING, event, incident, circumstance, affair, episode, proceedings, adventure. ❷ EXISTENCE, appearance, manifestation, materialization.

odd adjective ❶ STRANGE, eccentric, queer, peculiar, idiosyncratic, unconventional, outlandish, weird, bizarre, freakish; *informal* offbeat, wacky, freaky. ❷ **does the odd piece of work:** OCCASIONAL, casual, temporary, part-time, seasonal, periodic, irregular, miscellaneous. ❸ **at odd moments:** OCCASIONAL, random, irregular, periodic, haphazard, chance, fortuitous. ❹ **odd socks:** UNMATCHED, unpaired, left over, spare, remaining, surplus, superfluous, lone, single, solitary, sole.
– OPPOSITES ordinary.

odious adjective ABHORRENT, offensive, repugnant, disgusting, repulsive, repellent, revolting, foul, vile, unpleasant, disagreeable, loathsome, detestable, hateful, despicable, contemptible.
– OPPOSITES delightful.

odour noun AROMA, smell, scent, perfume, fragrance, bouquet, essence, stench, stink; *Brit. informal* niff, pong; *poetic/literary* redolence.

offence noun ❶ CRIME, illegal act, wrongdoing, wrong, misdemeanour, misdeed, peccadillo, sin, transgression, shortcoming, fault, lapse; *Law* malfeasance. ❷ **cause offence**: ANNOYANCE, anger, indignation, exasperation, wrath, displeasure, disapproval, dislike, animosity, resentment; *poetic/literary* ire.

offend verb ❶ GIVE OFFENCE TO, affront, upset, displease, annoy, anger, incense, exasperate, vex, pique, put out, gall, irritate, provoke, ruffle, disgruntle, rankle with, outrage, insult, slight, humiliate; *informal* put someone's back up. ❷ COMMIT A CRIME, break the law, do wrong, sin, go astray, fall from grace, err, transgress.

offender noun WRONGDOER, culprit, criminal, lawbreaker, miscreant, delinquent, sinner, transgressor, malefactor.

offensive adjective ❶ HURTFUL, wounding, abusive, affronting, displeasing, annoying, exasperating, vexing, galling, irritating, provocative, objectionable, outrageous, insulting, rude, discourteous, uncivil, impolite. ❷ DISAGREEABLE, unpleasant, nasty, foul, vile, objectionable, odious, abominable, detestable, loathsome, repugnant, disgusting, obnoxious, repulsive, repellent.
– OPPOSITES complimentary.

offer verb ❶ PUT FORWARD, propose, advance, submit, propound, suggest, recommend. ❷ VOLUNTEER ONE'S SERVICES, volunteer, offer one's service, offer assistance/help, make oneself available.

offering noun CONTRIBUTION, donation, subscription, gift, present, handout.

offhand adjective CASUAL, unceremonious, cavalier, careless, indifferent, perfunctory, cursory, abrupt, brusque, discourteous, uncivil, impolite, rude.

office noun ❶ PLACE OF BUSINESS, base, workplace. ❷ POST, position, role, place, situation, station, function, responsibility, obligation, charge, tenure.

official adjective AUTHORIZED, accredited, approved, validated, authenticated, certified, endorsed, sanctioned, licensed, recognized, accepted, legitimate, legal, lawful, bona fide, proper, ex cathedra; *informal* kosher.
– OPPOSITES unofficial.

officiate verb TAKE CHARGE, be in charge, preside, oversee, superintend, conduct, run, take the chair.

officious adjective OVERZEALOUS, interfering, intrusive, meddlesome, importunate, forward, obtrusive, self-important, opinionated, dictatorial, domineering, pushy; *informal* nosy.
– OPPOSITES self-effacing.

offset verb COUNTERBALANCE,

counteract, countervail, balance, balance out, cancel out, neutralize, compensate for, make up for, make good.

offshoot noun BRANCH, subsidiary, adjunct, appendage.

offspring noun CHILDREN, family, progeny, young, descendants, heirs, successors, spawn; *informal* kids; *Law* issue.

often adverb FREQUENTLY, a lot, many a time, repeatedly, again and again, time and again, time after time, over and over, over and over again, {day in, day out}; *poetic/literary* oft, oft-times.
– OPPOSITES seldom, never.

oily adjective ❶ GREASY, fatty, buttery. ❷ **oily remarks**: SMOOTH, smooth-talking, flattering, fulsome, glib, unctuous, subservient, servile, oleaginous.

ointment noun CREAM, lotion, emollient, salve, balm, liniment, embrocation, unguent, gel.

old adjective ❶ **old men**: OLDER, elderly, aged, advanced in years, long in the tooth, mature, grey-haired, grizzled, hoary, past one's prime, ancient, decrepit, senile, venerable, senior; *Biology* senescent; *informal* getting on, past it, over the hill. ❷ **old buildings**: DILAPIDATED, run down, tumbledown, ramshackle, decaying, crumbling, disintegrating. ❸ **old ideas**: OUT OF DATE, outdated, old-fashioned, outmoded, passé, archaic, obsolete, extinct, antiquated, antediluvian, superannuated; *informal* old hat. ❹ **the old days**: BYGONE, past, early, earlier, primeval, primordial, prehistoric. ❺ **old habits**: AGE-OLD, long-standing, long-lived, long-established, time-honoured, enduring, lasting. ❻ **an old girlfriend**: EX-, former, previous, one-time, sometime, erstwhile; *formal* quondam.
– OPPOSITES young.

old age noun OLDNESS, elderliness, age, declining years, advanced years, winter/autumn of one's life, senility, dotage; *Biology* senescence.

old-fashioned adjective OUT OF FASHION, outmoded, unfashionable, out of style, out of date, outdated, dated, out, dead, old-time, behind the times, past, bygone, passé, archaic, obsolescent, obsolete, ancient, antiquated, superannuated, antediluvian, old-fangled; *informal* old hat, not with it.
– OPPOSITES up to date, fashionable.

omen noun PORTENT, sign, token, foretoken, harbinger, premonition, forewarning, warning, prediction, forecast, prophecy, augury.

ominous adjective THREATENING, menacing, minatory, black, dark, gloomy, heavy, sinister, bad, unpromising, unpropitious, pessimistic, inauspicious, unfavourable, unlucky.
– OPPOSITES auspicious.

omission noun ❶ EXCLUSION, exception, deletion, erasure, elimination, expunction. ❷ NEGLECT, negligence, dereliction, forgetfulness, oversight, disregard, default, failure.

omit verb ❶ LEAVE OUT, exclude, except, miss out, miss, fail to mention, pass over, drop; *informal* give something a miss. ❷ **omit to**

do it: FORGET TO, neglect to, fail to, leave undone, overlook, skip.

omnipotent adjective ALL-POWERFUL, almighty, supreme, pre-eminent, invincible.

onerous adjective ARDUOUS, strenuous, difficult, hard, burdensome, crushing, back-breaking, taxing, demanding, exacting, wearing, wearisome, fatiguing.
– OPPOSITES easy.

ongoing adjective IN PROGRESS, current, progressing, advancing, successful, developing, evolving, growing, extant.

onset noun START, beginning, commencement, inception, outbreak; *informal* kick-off.
– OPPOSITES end.

onslaught noun ASSAULT, attack, charge, storming, sortie, sally, raid, foray, push, thrust, drive, blitz.

onus noun BURDEN, weight, load, responsibility, liability, obligation, duty, charge, encumbrance.

open adjective ❶ open doors: NOT SHUT, not closed, unlocked, unbolted, unlatched, unbarred, unfastened, unsecured, ajar, wide open, agape, gaping, yawning. ❷ open boxes: UNCOVERED, topless, unsealed. ❸ open spaces: EXPOSED, unsheltered, wide, wide open, extensive, broad, spacious, sweeping, airy, uncrowded, uncluttered, undeveloped. ❹ open about her dislike: FRANK, candid, honest, forthright, direct, blunt, plain-spoken, downright. ❺ the shop is open: OPEN TO THE PUBLIC, open for business, admitting customers/visitors. ❻ open hostility: OBVIOUS, clear, noticeable, visible, apparent, evident, manifest, overt, conspicuous, patent, unconcealed, unhidden, undisguised, blatant, flagrant. ❼ open to abuse: WIDE OPEN TO, allowing of, permitting, vulnerable to, exposed to, susceptible to, liable to, at the mercy of, an easy target for. ❽ an open mind: UNBIASED, unprejudiced, non-partisan, impartial, objective, disinterested, dispassionate, detached.
▶ verb ❶ open the door: THROW OPEN, unlock, unbolt, unlatch, unbar, unfasten. ❷ open the parcel: UNWRAP, undo, untie, unseal. ❸ open his heart: LAY BARE, bare, uncover, expose, exhibit, disclose, divulge, pour out.
– OPPOSITES close.

opening noun ❶ GAP, aperture, space, hole, orifice, vent, slot, breach, crack, split, fissure, cleft, crevice, chink, interstice, rent, rupture. ❷ VACANCY, position, job, opportunity, chance; *informal* break, lucky break.

operate verb ❶ WORK, function, go, run, perform, act. ❷ WORK, run, use, utilize, employ, handle, manage, be in charge of. ❸ PERFORM AN OPERATION, perform surgery; *informal* put under the knife.

operational adjective OPERATIVE, workable, in operation, working, in working order, functioning, functional, going, in use, usable, in action, ready for action.

operative adjective ❶ IN OPERATION, in force, effective, valid. ❷ OPERATIONAL, workable, working, functioning, functional, usable.
– OPPOSITES inoperative.

▶ noun WORKER, workman, machinist, operator, mechanic, factory hand/employee.

opinion noun POINT OF VIEW, view, viewpoint, belief, thought, thinking, way of thinking, standpoint, theory, judgement, estimation, feeling, sentiment, impression, notion, assumption, conception, conviction, persuasion, creed, dogma.

opponent noun OPPOSITION, rival, adversary, opposer, contestant, competitor, enemy, foe, antagonist, contender, dissenter, disputant.
– OPPOSITES ally.

opportune adjective ADVANTAGEOUS, favourable, auspicious, propitious, good, lucky, happy, timely, well timed, fortunate, providential, felicitous, convenient, expedient, suitable, apt, fitting, relevant, pertinent.
– OPPOSITES unfavourable.

opportunity noun CHANCE, good time, golden opportunity, favourable time/occasion/ moment, right set of circumstances, appropriate time; *informal* break.

oppose verb BE HOSTILE TO, take a stand against, stand up to, take issue with, take on, contradict, counter, argue against, counter-attack, confront, resist, withstand, defy, fight, put up a fight against, combat, fly in the face of.
– OPPOSITES support.

opposite adjective ❶ FACING, face to face with; *informal* eyeball to eyeball with. ❷ **opposite opinions:** OPPOSING, differing, different, unlike, contrary, reverse, contradictory, conflicting, clashing, discordant, dissident, at variance, incompatible, irreconcilable, antipathetic, poles apart.

opposition noun ❶ HOSTILITY, dislike, disapproval, resistance, defiance. ❷ OPPONENT, opposing side, other side/team, rival, adversary, competition, antagonist, enemy, foe.

oppress verb SUBJUGATE, enslave, suppress, crush, subdue, quash, quell, bring someone to their knees, tyrannize, repress, abuse, maltreat, persecute, rule with a rod of iron, trample on, trample underfoot, ride roughshod over.

oppressed adjective ENSLAVED, crushed, subdued, repressed, persecuted, abused, maltreated, misused, browbeaten, downtrodden, disadvantaged, underprivileged.

oppression noun SUBJUGATION, subduing, tyranny, suppression, persecution, abuse, maltreatment, cruelty, brutality, injustice, ruthlessness, harshness.

oppressive adjective ❶ TYRANNICAL, despotic, Draconian, iron-fisted, high-handed, repressive, domineering, harsh, crushing, cruel, brutal, ruthless, merciless, pitiless, unjust. ❷ **oppressive weather:** MUGGY, close, airless, stuffy, stifling, suffocating, sultry, torrid.
– OPPOSITES lenient.

oppressor noun TYRANT, despot, autocrat, persecutor, bully, iron hand, slave-driver, hard taskmaster, scourge, dictator.

optimistic adjective POSITIVE, sanguine, hopeful, confident,

bullish, cheerful, buoyant; *informal* upbeat.
– OPPOSITES pessimistic.

optimum adjective ❶ MOST FAVOURABLE, best, most advantageous, most appropriate, ideal, perfect. ❷ PEAK, top, best, perfect, ideal, flawless, superlative, optimal.

option noun CHOICE, freedom of choice, alternative, other possibility, preference.

optional adjective NON-COMPULSORY, not required, voluntary, discretionary, at one's discretion, elective.
– OPPOSITES compulsory.

opulent adjective ❶ AFFLUENT, wealthy, rich, well off, well-to-do, moneyed, prosperous; *informal* well heeled, roiling in it. ❷ LUXURIOUS, sumptuous, lavishly appointed; *informal* plush, plushy, ritzy.
– OPPOSITES spartan, poor.

orbit noun ❶ REVOLUTION, circle, circuit, cycle, rotation. ❷ SPHERE, sphere of influence, range, reach, scope, ambit, sweep, domain.

ordeal noun TRIAL, test, tribulation, suffering, affliction, distress, agony, anguish, torture, torment, calamity, trouble, nightmare.

order noun ❶ ORDERLINESS, neatness, tidiness, trimness, harmony. ❷ METHOD, organization, system, plan, uniformity, regularity, symmetry, pattern. ❸ in working order: CONDITION, state, shape, situation. ❹ in alphabetical order: ARRANGEMENT, grouping, system, organization, form, structure, disposition, classification, categorization, codification, series, sequence, progression, succession, layout, set-up. ❺ give orders: COMMAND, direction, directive, instruction, decree, edict, injunction, law, rule, regulation, ordinance, stipulation, dictate. ❻ place an order: REQUEST, call, requirement, requisition, demand, booking, reservation, commission. ❼ the lower orders: RANK, class, caste, grade, level, degree, position, station. ❽ a religious order: BROTHERHOOD, sisterhood, community. ❾ a point of order: PROCEDURE, correct procedure, standard procedure, ruling.
▶ verb ❶ GIVE THE ORDER TO, command, instruct, direct, bid, enjoin. ❷ PUT IN/PLACE AN ORDER FOR, request, call for, requisition, book, reserve, contract for, apply for, send away for.

orderly adjective ❶ an orderly room: IN ORDER, neat, tidy, trim, shipshape, shipshape and Bristol fashion, in apple-pie order. ❷ an orderly person: ORGANIZED, well organized, methodical, systematic, efficient, businesslike. ❸ an orderly class: WELL BEHAVED, disciplined, quiet, peaceful, controlled, restrained.
– OPPOSITES disorderly.

ordinary adjective ❶ the ordinary way: USUAL, normal, standard, typical, stock, common, customary, habitual, accustomed, everyday, quotidian, regular, routine, established, settled, fixed, prevailing, humdrum; *poetic/literary* wonted. ❷ ordinary lives: RUN-OF-THE-MILL, common, conventional, standard, typical, average, commonplace, workaday, humdrum, unremarkable, unexceptional, undistinguished, unmemorable,

pedestrian, prosaic, unpretentious, modest, plain, simple.
– OPPOSITES unusual.

organic adjective ❶ LIVING, live, animate, biological. ❷ FUNDAMENTAL, basic, structural, integral, inherent, innate, intrinsic, vital, essential, indispensable.

organization noun ❶ ARRANGEMENT, regulation, coordination, systematization, categorization, administration, running, management. ❷ COMPANY, firm, concern, operation, corporation, institution, group, consortium, conglomerate, combine, syndicate, federation, confederation, association, body.

organize verb ❶ ARRANGE, dispose, regulate, marshal, put in order, put straight, coordinate, systematize, methodize, standardize, collocate, group, sort, sort out, classify, categorize, catalogue, codify, tabulate. ❷ BE RESPONSIBLE FOR, be in charge of, take care of, administrate, run, manage, lick/knock into shape, see to.
– OPPOSITES inefficient.

orientate verb ❶ FIND ONE'S BEARINGS, get the lie of the land, establish one's location. ❷ ADAPT, adjust, accommodate, familiarize, acclimatize, find one's feet. ❸ DIRECT, guide, lead, point someone in the direction of, turn.

orifice noun OPENING, hole, vent, aperture, gap, space, breach, break, rent, slot, slit, cleft, cranny, fissure, crevice, rift, crack, chink.

origin noun ❶ SOURCE, basis, base, derivation, root, roots, provenance, etymology, genesis, spring, wellspring, fountain, fountainhead, aetiology. ❷ **his origins**: DESCENT, ancestry, pedigree, lineage, heritage, parentage, extraction, beginnings.

original adjective ❶ **original inhabitants**: ABORIGINAL, indigenous, early, earliest, first, primary, primordial, primal, primeval, primitive, autochthonous. ❷ **original work**: INNOVATIVE, innovatory, inventive, new, novel, fresh, creative, imaginative, individual, ingenious, unusual, unconventional, unorthodox, unprecedented, ground-breaking.
– OPPOSITES unoriginal, derivative.

originate verb ❶ ARISE, stem, spring, result, derive, start, begin, commence. ❷ GIVE BIRTH TO, set in motion, set up, invent, dream up, conceive, discover, initiate, create, formulate, inaugurate, pioneer, introduce, establish, found, evolve, develop, generate.

ornament noun ❶ KNICK-KNACK, trinket, bauble, gewgaw, accessory, decoration, frill, whatnot, doodah. ❷ DECORATION, adornment, embellishment, trimming, garnish, garnishing.

ornamental adjective DECORATIVE, attractive, showy, embellishing, ornamenting.

ornate adjective ELABORATE, over-elaborate, decorated, embellished, adorned, ornamented, fancy, fussy, busy, ostentatious, showy, baroque, rococo; *informal* flash.
– OPPOSITES plain.

orthodox adjective ❶ **orthodox**

beliefs: DOCTRINAL, of the faith, of the true faith, sound, conservative, correct, faithful, true, devoted, strict, devout. ❷ orthodox behaviour: CONVENTIONAL, accepted, approved, correct, proper, conformist, established, traditional, usual, regular.
– OPPOSITES unconventional.

ostensible adjective APPARENT, seeming, professed, outward, alleged, claimed, purported, pretended, feigned, supposed.
– OPPOSITES genuinely.

ostentation noun SHOWINESS, show, conspicuousness, obtrusiveness, loudness, extravagance, flamboyance, gaudiness, flashiness, pretentiousness, affectation, exhibitionism; *informal* swank.

ostentatious adjective SHOWY, conspicuous, obtrusive, loud, extravagant, flamboyant, gaudy, flashy, pretentious, affected, overdone; *informal* flash, swanky.
– OPPOSITES unobtrusive.

ostracize verb COLD-SHOULDER, give someone the cold shoulder, send to Coventry, exclude, shut out, shun, spurn, avoid, boycott, repudiate, cast out, reject, blackball, blacklist.
– OPPOSITES welcome.

other adjective ❶ DIFFERENT, unlike, variant, dissimilar, distinct, separate, alternative. ❷ MORE, additional, further, extra.

outbreak noun ERUPTION, flare-up, upsurge, outburst, start, rash.

outburst noun BURST, explosion, eruption, outbreak, flare-up, attack, fit, spasm, paroxysm.

outclass verb SURPASS, be better than, outshine, eclipse, overshadow, outstrip, outdo, trounce, beat, defeat.

outcome noun RESULT, upshot, issue, product, conclusion, after-effect, aftermath, wake; *informal* pay-off.

outdated adjective OUT OF DATE, out of fashion, old-fashioned, unfashionable, outmoded, dated, passé, behind the times, antiquated, archaic.
– OPPOSITES modern.

outdo verb SURPASS, top, exceed, excel, get the better of, outstrip, outshine, eclipse, overshadow, outclass, overcome, beat, defeat.

outer adjective ❶ OUTSIDE, outermost, outward, exterior, external, surface, superficial. ❷ OUTLYING, distant, remote, faraway, peripheral, fringe, perimeter.
– OPPOSITES inner.

outgoing adjective ❶ EXTROVERT, demonstrative, affectionate, warm, friendly, genial, cordial, affable, sociable, communicative, open, expansive, talkative, gregarious, approachable. ❷ RETIRING, departing, leaving, withdrawing, ex-, former.
– OPPOSITES reserved, incoming.

outgoings plural noun COSTS, expenses, expenditure, outlay, overheads.

outlandish adjective STRANGE, unfamiliar, unknown, unheard of, odd, unusual, extraordinary, peculiar, queer, curious, singular, eccentric, quaint, bizarre, grotesque, preposterous, weird; *informal* freaky, wacky, far out, off-the-wall.
– OPPOSITES ordinary.

outline noun ❶ THUMBNAIL SKETCH, rough idea, quick rundown, abbreviated version, summary, synopsis, main points, bones, bare bones. ❷ CONTOUR, silhouette, profile, lineaments, delineation, configuration, perimeter, circumference.

outlook noun ❶ an outlook on life: VIEW, point of view, viewpoint, perspective, attitude, frame of mind, standpoint, slant, angle, interpretation, opinion. ❷ the house has a pleasant outlook: VIEW, vista, prospect, panorama, aspect.

outlying adjective OUTER, outermost, out of the way, remote, distant, far-flung, peripheral, isolated, inaccessible, off the beaten track.

output noun PRODUCTION, product, productivity, yield, harvest, crop.

outrage noun ❶ ATROCITY, crime, horror, enormity, brutality. ❷ OFFENCE, affront, insult, injury, abuse, scandal, desecration, violation. ❸ ANGER, fury, rage, indignation, wrath, annoyance, shock, resentment, horror.

outrageous adjective ❶ outrageous behaviour: INTOLERABLE, insufferable, insupportable, unendurable, unbearable, impossible, exasperating, offensive, provocative, maddening, distressing. ❷ outrageous acts: ATROCIOUS, heinous, abominable, wicked, vile, foul, monstrous, horrible, horrid, dreadful, terrible, horrendous, hideous, ghastly, unspeakable, gruesome.

outside adjective ❶ OUTER, outermost, outward, exterior, external. ❷ OUTDOOR, out of doors. ❸ an outside chance: UNLIKELY, improbable, slight, slender, slim, small, faint, negligible, marginal, remote, distant, vague.
– OPPOSITES inside.

outsider noun ALIEN, stranger, foreigner, outlander, immigrant, incomer, newcomer, parvenu, arriviste, interloper, intruder, gatecrasher, outcast, misfit.

outskirts plural noun VICINITY, neighbourhood, environs, outlying districts, fringes, margin, periphery, borders, boundary, suburbs.

outspoken adjective CANDID, frank, forthright, direct, straightforward, plain-spoken, explicit, blunt.
– OPPOSITES diplomatic.

outstanding adjective ❶ EXCELLENT, remarkable, exceptional, superlative, pre-eminent, eminent, well known, notable, noteworthy, distinguished, important, famous, famed, renowned, celebrated, great. ❷ outstanding debts: UNPAID, unsettled, owing, due.
– OPPOSITES unexceptional.

outwardly adverb ❶ EXTERNALLY, on the outside. ❷ ON THE SURFACE, superficially, on the face of it, to all appearances, as far as one can see, to all intents and purposes, apparently, evidently.

outwit verb GET THE BETTER OF, be cleverer than, outsmart, outmanoeuvre, steal a march on, trick, dupe, make a fool of; *informal* put one over on, pull a fast one on.

overall adjective COMPREHENSIVE, universal, all-embracing, inclusive, all-inclusive, general, sweeping, complete, blanket, umbrella, global.

▶ adverb ON THE WHOLE, in general, generally speaking.

overawe verb INTIMIDATE, daunt, disconcert, abash, dismay, frighten, alarm, scare, terrify, terrorize.

overcome verb CONQUER, defeat, vanquish, beat, prevail over, get the better of, triumph over, best, worst, trounce, rout, master, overpower, overwhelm, overthrow, subdue, subjugate, quell, quash, crush; *informal* thrash, lick, clobber, whip.
▶ adjective OVERWHELMED, emotional, moved, affected, speechless, at a loss for words; *informal* bowled over.

overdue adjective ❶ LATE, behind schedule, delayed, belated, tardy, unpunctual. ❷ UNPAID, owed, owing, outstanding, unsettled, in arrears.

overflow verb FLOW OVER, run over, spill over, brim over, well over, pour forth, stream forth, discharge, surge, debouch.

overhang verb STAND OUT, stick out, extend, project, protrude, jut, jut out, beetle, bulge out.

overhead adverb ABOVE, up above, high up, up in the sky, on high, aloft.

overlook verb ❶ FAIL TO NOTICE, miss, leave, neglect; *informal* slip up on. ❷ LEAVE UNDONE, ignore, disregard, omit, neglect, forget. ❸ LOOK OVER, look on to, front on to, have/afford a view of, command a view of.

overpowering adjective OVERWHELMING, burdensome, weighty, unbearable, unendurable, intolerable, shattering; *informal* mind-blowing.

overriding adjective MOST IMPORTANT, predominant, principal, primary, paramount, chief, main, major, foremost, central.

oversight noun ❶ CARELESSNESS, inattention, neglect, inadvertence, laxity, dereliction, omission. ❷ MISTAKE, error, blunder, gaffe, fault, omission, slip, lapse.

overt adjective OBVIOUS, noticeable, undisguised, unconcealed, apparent, plain, manifest, patent, open, public, blatant, conspicuous.
–OPPOSITES covert.

overtake verb PASS, get past, go past, go by, overhaul, leave behind, outstrip, go faster than.

overthrow verb *see* OVERCOME.

overtone noun IMPLICATION, innuendo, hint, suggestion, insinuation, association, connotation, undercurrent, nuance.

overwhelm verb ❶ OVERCOME, move, make emotional, daze, dumbfound, shake, take aback, leave speechless, stagger. ❷ overwhelmed with mail: INUNDATE, flood, deluge, engulf, submerge, swamp, bury, overload, overburden, snow under.

overwhelming adjective ❶ an overwhelming desire: UNCONTROLLABLE, irrepressible, irresistible, overpowering. ❷ the overwhelming majority: VAST, massive, great, large.

owe verb BE IN DEBT, be indebted, be under an obligation, be obligated, be beholden.

own verb POSSESS, have in one's possession, have, keep, retain, maintain, hold, enjoy.
■ **own up** *see* CONFESS.

Pp

pace noun ❶ STEP, stride. ❷ GAIT, walk, tread. ❸ SPEED, swiftness, fastness, quickness, rapidity, velocity.

pacify verb CALM DOWN, placate, conciliate, propitiate, appease, mollify, soothe, tranquillize, quieten.
– OPPOSITES enrage.

pack noun ❶ PACKET, container, package, carton. ❷ *a pack of thieves*: GANG, crowd, mob, group, band, company, troop, set; *informal* crew, bunch.
▶ verb ❶ FILL, store, stow, load, bundle, stuff, cram. ❷ *people packing the stadium*: FILL, crowd, throng, mob, cram, jam, press into, squeeze into.
■ **pack up** FINISH, leave off, halt, stop, cease, call it a day; *informal* jack it in.

packed adjective FULL, filled to capacity, crowded, thronged, mobbed, crammed, jammed, brimful, chock-full, chock-a-block, jam-packed.

pact noun AGREEMENT, treaty, deal, contract, settlement, bargain, compact, covenant, bond, concordat, entente.

pad noun ❶ PADDING, wadding, stuffing, buffer. ❷ CUSHION, pillow, bolster. ❸ NOTEPAD, writing pad, notebook; *Brit.* jotter; *informal* memo pad.
▶ verb PACK, stuff, line, cushion, protect.

paddle verb ROW, pull, oar, scull, pole, punt.

paddock noun FIELD, meadow, enclosure, yard, pen, pound, corral.

pagan noun UNBELIEVER, heathen, infidel, idolater, pantheist, polytheist.
▶ adjective HEATHEN, infidel, idolatrous, pantheistic, polytheistic.

pageant noun DISPLAY, spectacle, extravaganza, show, parade, scene, tableau.

pageantry noun SPECTACLE, magnificence, pomp, splendour, grandeur, glamour, theatricality, show, showiness; *informal* pizzazz.

pain noun ❶ SORENESS, hurt, ache, aching, agony, throb, throbbing, smarting, twinge, pang, spasm, cramp, discomfort, irritation, tenderness. ❷ SUFFERING, hurt, sorrow, grief, heartache, sadness, unhappiness, distress, misery, wretchedness, anguish, affliction, woe.

pained adjective HURT, aggrieved, reproachful, offended, insulted, upset, unhappy, distressed; *informal* miffed.

painful adjective ❶ SORE, hurting, aching, throbbing, smarting, tender, inflamed, agonizing, excruciating. ❷ DISAGREEABLE, unpleasant, nasty, distressing, disquieting, disturbing, miserable, wretched, agonizing, harrowing.

painless adjective ❶ PAIN-FREE, without pain. ❷ EASY, simple, trouble-free, effortless, plain

sailing; *informal* as easy as pie, as easy as falling off a log, child's play, a cinch.
– OPPOSITES painful, difficult.

painstaking adjective CAREFUL, thorough, assiduous, conscientious, meticulous, punctilious, sedulous, scrupulous.
– OPPOSITES careless.

painting noun PICTURE, illustration, portrayal, depiction, delineation, representation, likeness.

pair noun COUPLE, duo, brace, two, twosome, matched set, matching set.
■ **pair off** ARRANGE/GROUP IN PAIRS, pair up, put together, get together, join up, link up, team up.

palatable adjective ❶ TASTY, appetizing, pleasant-tasting, flavoursome, delicious, mouth-watering, savoury; *informal* scrumptious, yummy. ❷ AGREEABLE, pleasant, pleasing, pleasurable, nice, attractive, acceptable, satisfactory.
– OPPOSITES unpalatable.

palatial adjective LUXURIOUS, imposing, splendid, grand, magnificent, stately, majestic, opulent, sumptuous, plush.
– OPPOSITES humble.

pale adjective ❶ pale with fear: WHITE, white-faced, colourless, anaemic, wan, drained, pallid, pasty, peaky, ashen, waxen, as white as a sheet/ghost, deathly pale. ❷ pale shades: LIGHT, pastel, muted, low-key, restrained, faded, bleached, washed out, etoliated. ❸ pale light: DIM, faint, weak, feeble, thin.
– OPPOSITES dark.
▶ verb GROW/BECOME PALE, go/turn white, blanch, lose colour.

palliate verb RELIEVE, ease, soothe, alleviate, mitigate, assuage, abate, allay, dull, take the edge off, blunt.

pallid adjective *see* PALE adjective (1).

palpable adjective TANGIBLE, feelable, touchable, solid, concrete.
– OPPOSITES intangible.

paltry adjective ❶ a paltry sum: SMALL, meagre, trifling, minor, insignificant, trivial, derisory; *informal* piddling. ❷ a paltry excuse: WORTHLESS, despicable, contemptible, miserable, wretched, sorry, puny.
– OPPOSITES considerable.

pamper verb SPOIL, cosset, indulge, overindulge, humour, coddle, mollycoddle.

pamphlet noun LEAFLET, booklet, brochure, circular.

panache noun STYLE, verve, flamboyance, zest, dash, flourish, brio, elan; *informal* pizzazz.

pandemic adjective WIDESPREAD, universal, global, extensive, prevalent, wholesale, rife, rampant.

pander verb GRATIFY, indulge, humour, give in to, please, satisfy, cater for.

panegyric noun EULOGY, paean, encomium, extolment, accolade, testimonial, tribute; *formal* laudation.

panic noun ALARM, fright, fear, terror, horror, agitation, hysteria.
– OPPOSITES calm.
▶ verb BE ALARMED, take fright, be terrified/horrified, be agitated, be hysterical, lose one's nerve, overreact.

panic-stricken adjective PANICKY, alarmed, frightened, scared, terrified, terror-stricken, petrified, horror-stricken, horrified, aghast, agitated, hysterical, dismayed; *informal* in a tizzy.

panoply noun ARRAY, trappings, display, show, splendour.

panoramic adjective WIDE, extensive, sweeping, bird's-eye, comprehensive.

pant verb PUFF, huff and puff, blow, gasp, wheeze.

paper noun ❶ NEWSPAPER, magazine, journal, gazette, broadsheet, tabloid; *informal* rag. ❷ an academic paper: ESSAY, article, work, dissertation, treatise, thesis, monograph, study, report.
■ **paper over** HIDE, conceal, draw a veil over, disguise, camouflage, cover up, gloss over, whitewash.

parade noun PROCESSION, progression, cavalcade, spectacle, pageant, array.
▶ verb ❶ MARCH, go in columns, file by. ❷ parade their wealth: DISPLAY, show off, exhibit, show, demonstrate, make a show of, flaunt.

paradox noun CONTRADICTION, inconsistency, incongruity, anomaly, enigma, puzzle, absurdity, oxymoron.

paradoxical adjective SELF-CONTRADICTORY, inconsistent, incongruous, anomalous, enigmatic, puzzling, absurd.

parallel adjective ❶ SIDE BY SIDE, equidistant, collateral. ❷ SIMILAR, like, resembling, analogous, comparable, equivalent, corresponding, matching.
▶ noun COUNTERPART, equivalent, analogue, match, duplicate, equal.
▶ verb BE SIMILAR TO, be like, resemble, be analogous to, correspond to, compare with, be comparable/equivalent to.

paralyse verb IMMOBILIZE, numb, deaden, dull, incapacitate, debilitate, disable, cripple.

paralysis noun IMMOBILITY, powerlessness, lack of feeling, numbness, palsy, incapacity, debilitation; *Medicine* paresis.

paralytic adjective ❶ IMMOBILE, immobilized, powerless, numb, dead, incapacitated, debilitated, disabled, crippled. ❷ *See* DRUNK.

parameter noun LIMIT, limitation, limiting factor, restriction, specification, guidelines, framework.

parched adjective DRIED UP/OUT, dry, baked, burned, scorched, seared, desiccated, dehydrated, withered, shrivelled.

pardon noun ❶ FORGIVENESS, forbearance, indulgence, clemency, lenience, leniency, mercy. ❷ FREE PARDON, reprieve, release, acquittal, absolution, amnesty, exoneration, exculpation.
▶ verb ❶ EXCUSE, condone, let off. ❷ REPRIEVE, release, acquit, absolve, exonerate, exculpate.

pardonable adjective FORGIVABLE, excusable, allowable, condonable, understandable, minor, slight, venial.
– OPPOSITES inexcusable.

parentage noun FAMILY, birth, origins, extraction, ancestry, lineage, descent, heritage, pedigree.

pariah noun OUTCAST, leper,

persona non grata, untouchable, undesirable.

parliament noun LEGISLATIVE ASSEMBLY, congress, senate, chamber, house, convocation, diet.

parody noun LAMPOON, spoof, send-up, satire, pastiche, caricature, mimicry, take-off, burlesque.
▶ verb LAMPOON, satirize, caricature, mimic, take off, send up, burlesque.

parry verb WARD OFF, fend off, stave off, turn aside, avert, deflect, block, rebuff, repel, repulse, hold at bay.

part noun ❶ PORTION, division, section, segment, bit, piece, fragment, scrap, slice, fraction, chunk. ❷ SECTION, area, region, sector, quarter, territory, neighbourhood. ❸ his part in the project: FUNCTION, role, job, task, work, responsibility, capacity, participation. ❹ play the part: ROLE, character. ❺ a man of many parts: TALENT, gift, ability, capability, capacity, skill, attribute.
▶ verb ❶ DIVIDE, separate, split, break up, sever, disjoin. ❷ LEAVE, go away, say goodbye, say one's goodbyes, separate; *informal* split, push off, hit the road.

partial adjective ❶ PART, in part, limited, incomplete, imperfect, fragmentary. ❷ BIASED, prejudiced, partisan, one-sided, discriminatory, preferential, unjust, unfair.
– OPPOSITES complete, impartial.
■ **be partial to** *see* LIKE[1] (2).

participate verb TAKE PART IN, join in, engage in, play a part in, contribute to, be involved in, share in, have a hand in.

participation noun PART, contribution, association, involvement, partaking.

particle noun ❶ BIT, piece, speck, spot, atom, molecule. ❷ IOTA, jot, whit, grain, bit, scrap, shred, morsel, atom, hint, touch, trace, suggestion.

particular adjective ❶ this particular case: SPECIFIC, individual, single, distinct, precise. ❷ particular care: SPECIAL, especial, singular, peculiar, exceptional, unusual, uncommon, notable, noteworthy, remarkable. ❸ particular about something: FASTIDIOUS, discriminating, selective, fussy, painstaking, meticulous, punctilious, demanding, critical, finicky; *informal* pernickety, choosy, picky.
– OPPOSITES general, careless.

particularly adverb ❶ particularly good: ESPECIALLY, specially, singularly, peculiarly, distinctly, markedly, exceptionally, unusually, uncommonly. ❷ ask for him particularly: IN PARTICULAR, specifically, explicitly, expressly, specially, especially.

partisan noun ❶ GUERRILLA, resistance fighter, underground fighter. ❷ SUPPORTER, adherent, devotee, backer, follower, disciple.
▶ adjective *see* PARTIAL (2).

partition verb DIVIDE, divide up, subdivide, separate, separate off, screen off, wall off, fence off.

partly adverb IN PART, partially, not wholly, not fully, half, somewhat, to some extent/degree, in some measure, fractionally, slightly.
– OPPOSITES completely.

partnership noun ❶ ASSOCIATION, cooperation, collaboration, alliance, union, fellowship, companionship. ❷ COLLABORATION, collusion, connivance, conspiracy.

party noun ❶ GATHERING, function, reception, celebration, festivity, at-home, soirée, bacchanal; *informal* do, bash, shindig; *Brit. informal* rave-up. ❷ POLITICAL PARTY, alliance, association, grouping, faction, camp, set, caucus.

pass verb ❶ GO, move, proceed, progress, drive, run, travel, roll, flow, course. ❷ GO PAST, move past, go/get ahead of, go by, overtake, outstrip. ❸ HAND OVER, reach, let someone have, give, transfer. ❹ **the hours passed slowly**: GO BY, proceed, progress, advance, elapse. ❺ **pass the time**: SPEND, occupy, fill, take up, use, employ, while away. ❻ **pass exams**: GAIN A PASS IN, get through, be successful in, succeed in, pass muster in. ❼ **pass the motion**: VOTE FOR, accept, approve, adopt, authorize, ratify.

▶ noun PERMIT, warrant, authorization, licence, passport, visa, safe conduct, exeat.

■ **pass for** BE TAKEN FOR, be accepted as, be mistaken for. **pass out** FAINT, collapse, black out, keel over, swoon.

passable adjective ❶ ADEQUATE, all right, tolerable, fair, acceptable, satisfactory, mediocre, middling, ordinary, average, run-of-the-mill, not too bad, unexceptional, indifferent. ❷ OPEN, clear, crossable, traversable, navigable, unblocked, unobstructed.

passage noun ❶ PASSING, progress, advance, process, flow, course. ❷ JOURNEY, voyage, transit, trek, crossing, trip, tour. ❸ PASSAGEWAY, corridor, hall, hallway, entrance hall, entrance, vestibule, lobby. ❹ EXTRACT, excerpt, quotation, citation, section, verse.

passer-by noun BYSTANDER, onlooker, witness, spectator.

passion noun ❶ INTENSITY, fervour, ardour, zeal, vehemence, fire, emotion, feeling, zest, eagerness, excitement, animation. ❷ FASCINATION, keen interest, obsession, fixation, craze, mania.

passionate adjective ❶ **a passionate performance**: IMPASSIONED, intense, fervent, fervid, ardent, zealous, vehement, fiery, emotional, heartfelt, animated. ❷ **a passionate lover**: ARDENT, aroused, desirous, hot, sexy, amorous, sensual, erotic, lustful.

– OPPOSITES apathetic, frigid.

passive adjective ❶ INACTIVE, unassertive, uninvolved, unresisting, yielding, submissive, compliant, pliant, acquiescent, quiescent, resigned, obedient, tractable, malleable. ❷ IMPASSIVE, emotionless, unmoved, unresponsive, undemonstrative, dispassionate, detached, distant, remote, aloof, indifferent.

– OPPOSITES active.

past adjective ❶ **times past**: GONE BY, gone, bygone, elapsed, over, ended, former, long ago. ❷ **past achievements**: FORMER, previous, prior, erstwhile, one-time, sometime.

– OPPOSITES present.

pastel adjective PALE, soft,

delicate, muted, subdued, faint, low-key.
– OPPOSITES vivid.

pastime noun HOBBY, leisure activity, sport, game, recreation, diversion, amusement, entertainment, distraction, relaxation.

pastoral adjective RURAL, country, rustic, simple, idyllic, innocent, Arcadian, agricultural, bucolic, georgic.

pasture noun PASTURAGE, grazing, grassland, grass, field, meadow.

patch noun ❶ COVER, covering, pad, shield. ❷ **patch of ground**: PLOT, area, piece, tract, parcel.
▶ verb COVER, mend, repair, fix, sew up, stitch.

patchwork noun HOTCHPOTCH, hodgepodge, mishmash, jumble, medley, miscellany, pot-pourri, mosaic, blend, mixture.

patent adjective OBVIOUS, clear, plain, evident, apparent, manifest, transparent, conspicuous, blatant, unmistakable.

path noun ❶ PATHWAY, footpath, footway, track, trail, towpath, walk. ❷ COURSE, route, circuit, track, orbit, trajectory.

pathetic adjective ❶ PITIFUL, piteous, moving, touching, poignant, affecting, heartbreaking, heart-rending, sad, wretched, mournful, woeful. ❷ PITIFUL, lamentable, deplorable, miserable, wretched, feeble, woeful, poor, contemptible, inadequate, unsatisfactory, worthless.

pathological adjective COMPULSIVE, obsessive, irrational, unreasonable, illogical.

patience noun ❶ CALMNESS, composure, even-temperedness, equanimity, serenity, tranquillity, restraint, imperturbability, tolerance, indulgence, forbearance, endurance, resignation, stoicism, fortitude. ❷ PERSEVERANCE, persistence, endurance, tenacity, assiduity, diligence, staying power, indefatigability, doggedness, singleness of purpose.
– OPPOSITES impatience.

patient adjective UNCOMPLAINING, serene, calm, composed, even-tempered, tranquil, restrained, imperturbable, tolerant, accommodating, long-suffering, forbearing, indulgent, resigned, stoical, unflappable; *informal* cool.
– OPPOSITES impatient.

patriotic adjective NATIONALIST, nationalistic, chauvinistic, flag-waving, jingoistic.

patrol verb MAKE THE ROUNDS OF, range, police, keep watch on, guard, keep guard on, monitor.
▶ noun ❶ PATROLLING, round, policing, watch, guard, monitoring. ❷ SENTRY, guard, watchman, watch, nightwatchman, policeman/policewoman.

patron noun ❶ SPONSOR, backer, benefactor/benefactress, promoter, friend; *informal* angel. ❷ CUSTOMER, client, shopper, regular, frequenter.

patronize verb ❶ LOOK DOWN ON, talk down to, condescend to, treat condescendingly, treat scornfully/contemptuously, be snobbish to. ❷ BE A CUSTOMER OF, be a client of, frequent, shop at, buy from, do business with, deal with, trade with.

patronizing adjective

CONDESCENDING, supercilious, superior, haughty, lofty, lordly, snobbish; *informal* snooty, toffee-nosed.

pattern noun ❶ DESIGN, decoration, motif, ornamentation, device, figure. ❷ DESIGN, guide, blueprint, model, plan, template, instructions.

paucity noun SCARCITY, sparseness, dearth, shortage, insufficiency, deficiency, lack, want, meagreness.
– OPPOSITES abundance.

pause verb STOP, halt, cease, discontinue, take a break, desist, rest, hold back, delay, hesitate, waver; *informal* take a breather.
▶ noun BREAK, halt, stoppage, cessation, interruption, lull, respite, stay, discontinuation, gap, interlude, intermission, interval, rest, delay, hesitation.

pave verb CONCRETE, asphalt, flag, tile, tar, macadamize, floor.

pay verb ❶ SETTLE UP WITH, remunerate, reimburse, recompense. ❷ PAY OUT, spend, expend, lay out, part with, disburse, hand over, remit, render; *informal* shell out, fork out, cough up. ❸ the business doesn't pay: MAKE MONEY, be profitable, make a profit, be remunerative, make a return. ❹ it would pay you to listen: REPAY, be advantageous to, be of advantage to, be of benefit to, be beneficial to, be profitable to, be worthwhile to.
▶ noun PAYMENT, salary, wages, earnings, fee, remuneration, recompense, reimbursement, reward, stipend, emoluments.

payment noun ❶ SETTLEMENT, discharge, clearance, squaring, liquidation. ❷ *See* PAY noun. ❸ monthly payments: INSTALMENT, premium, amount, remittance.

peace noun ❶ PEACEFULNESS, tranquillity, serenity, calm, calmness, composure, placidity, rest, repose, contentment. ❷ PEACEFULNESS, peaceableness, accord, harmony, amity, amicableness, goodwill, friendship, cordiality; *formal* concord. ❸ the Peace of Versailles: TREATY, truce, agreement, armistice, cessation of hostilities, non-aggression, ceasefire.
– OPPOSITES anxiety, war.

peaceable adjective PEACE-LOVING, non-violent, easy-going, placid, gentle, mild, good-natured, even-tempered, amiable, amicable, pacific, pacifist, dovelike, dovish.
– OPPOSITES aggressive.

peaceful adjective TRANQUIL, restful, quiet, calm, still, serene, composed, placid, reposeful, undisturbed, untroubled, unworried, anxiety-free.
– OPPOSITES noisy, agitated.

peacemaker noun CONCILIATOR, mediator, arbitrator, pacifier, appeaser, peace-monger.

peak noun ❶ TOP, summit, crest, pinnacle, mountain, hill, height, alp. ❷ HEIGHT, high point, climax, culmination, zenith, acme, meridian, apogee, prime, heyday.
– OPPOSITES nadir.

peaky adjective PALE, wan, drained, drawn, pallid, pasty, white, anaemic, whey-faced, ill-looking, sickly-looking.

peccadillo noun MISDEMEANOUR, minor offence, petty offence, indiscretion, lapse, misdeed, error, infraction; *informal* slip-up.

peculiar adjective ❶ STRANGE,

odd, queer, funny, curious, unusual, abnormal, eccentric, unconventional, bizarre, weird, quaint, outlandish, out of the way, grotesque, freakish, offbeat, droll, comical; *informal* far out, way-out. ❷ CHARACTERISTIC, distinctive, distinct, individual, distinguishing, special, unique, idiosyncratic.
– OPPOSITES ordinary.

peculiarity noun ❶ STRANGENESS, oddness, queerness, abnormality, eccentricity, unconventionality, bizarreness, weirdness, outlandishness, grotesqueness, freakishness. ❷ CHARACTERISTIC, feature, quality, property, trait, attribute, mark, stamp, hallmark.

pedantic adjective PRECISE, exact, scrupulous, over-scrupulous, punctilious, meticulous, overnice, perfectionist, formalist, dogmatic, literalist, literalistic, quibbling, hair-splitting, casuistic, casuistical, pettifogging; *informal* nit-picking.

pedestal noun BASE, support, stand, foundation, pillar, column, plinth.

pedestrian noun WALKER, person on foot, hiker, footslogger.
▶ adjective ❶ PEDESTRIANIZED, for pedestrians. ❷ PLODDING, unimaginative, uninspired, unexciting, dull, flat, prosaic, turgid, stodgy, mundane, humdrum, banal, run-of-the-mill, commonplace, ordinary, mediocre.
– OPPOSITES inspired.

peek verb PEEP, glance, sneak a look, cast a brief look, look hurriedly, look; *informal* take a gander, have a look-see.

peephole noun APERTURE, opening, spyhole, judas, slit, crack, chink, crevice, fissure.

peer[1] verb LOOK CLOSELY, try to see, narrow one's eyes, screw up one's eyes, squint.

peer[2] noun ❶ NOBLE, nobleman, aristocrat, lord, patrician. ❷ COMPEER, fellow, equal, match, like, co-equal.

peerless adjective INCOMPARABLE, beyond compare, matchless, unmatched, unrivalled, unsurpassed, unequalled, without equal, unparalleled, superlative, second to none, nonpareil.

peeve verb IRRITATE, annoy, anger, vex, provoke, upset, exasperate, irk, pique, nettle, get on someone's nerves; *Brit.* rub up the wrong way; *informal* aggravate, miff.

penalize verb PUNISH, discipline, fine, correct; *formal* castigate.
– OPPOSITES reward.

penalty noun PENANCE, fine, forfeit, sentence, mulct.

penance noun ATONEMENT, reparation, amends, mortification.

penchant noun LIKING, fondness, preference, taste, partiality, inclination, bent, proclivity, predilection.

pending adjective IMMINENT, impending, on the way, coming, approaching, forthcoming, near, nearing, close, close at hand, in the offing.

penetrate verb ❶ PIERCE, bore, perforate, stab, prick, gore, spike. ❷ PERMEATE, pervade, fill, imbue, suffuse, seep through, saturate.

penitent adjective REPENTANT, contrite, regretful, remorseful,

sorry, apologetic, rueful, ashamed, abject, sorrowful.
– OPPOSITES unrepentant.

penniless adjective IMPECUNIOUS, penurious, impoverished, indigent, poor, poverty-stricken, destitute, bankrupt, hard up; *informal* broke; *Brit. informal* skint.
– OPPOSITES wealthy.

pensive adjective THOUGHTFUL, reflective, lost in thought, contemplative, meditative, cogitative, ruminative, absorbed, preoccupied.

penury noun POVERTY, impoverishment, indigence, need, want, neediness, destitution, privation, beggary.
– OPPOSITES affluence.

people noun ❶ PERSONS, individuals, human beings, humans, mortals, living souls, {men, women, and children}. ❷ RACE, tribe, clan, nation, country, population, populace. ❸ THE GENERAL PUBLIC, the public, the masses, the rank and file, commonalty, the mob, the multitude, the hoi polloi.

perceive verb ❶ SEE, catch sight of, spot, observe, glimpse, notice, make out, discern, behold, espy, detect, witness, remark. ❷ DISCERN, appreciate, recognize, be aware of, be conscious of, know, grasp, understand, comprehend, apprehend, see, sense.

perceptible adjective PERCEIVABLE, discernible, noticeable, detectable, distinguishable, appreciable, visible, observable, distinct, palpable, tangible.
– OPPOSITES imperceptible.

perception noun ❶ DISCERNMENT, appreciation, recognition, awareness, consciousness, knowledge, grasp, understanding, comprehension, apprehension, notion, conception, idea, sense. ❷ PERSPICACITY, discernment, perceptiveness, understanding, discrimination, insight, intuition, feeling, sensitivity.

perceptive adjective PENETRATING, astute, shrewd, discerning, perspicacious, percipient, understanding, discriminating, intuitive, responsive, sensitive.
– OPPOSITES obtuse.

perch noun POLE, rod, branch, roost, rest.
▶ verb SIT, rest, roost, settle, alight, land.

peremptory adjective IMPERIOUS, high-handed, overbearing, dogmatic, autocratic, dictatorial, domineering, arbitrary, tyrannical, despotic, arrogant.

perfect adjective ❶ FLAWLESS, faultless, unmarred, ideal, impeccable, consummate, immaculate, exemplary, superb, superlative, supreme, excellent, complete, full, whole, entire. ❷ **a perfect copy**: EXACT, precise, accurate, faithful, strict; *Brit. informal* spot on. ❸ **a perfect fool**: ABSOLUTE, complete, out-and-out, thorough, thoroughgoing, downright, utter, sheer, consummate, unmitigated, unqualified.
▶ verb MAKE PERFECT, render faultless/flawless, polish, refine, complete, consummate, put the finishing touches to.

perfection noun ❶ PERFECTING, polishing, refinement, completion, consummation.

❷ FLAWLESSNESS, faultlessness, impeccability, immaculateness, exemplariness, superbness.

perfidious adjective TREACHEROUS, traitorous, treasonous, false, untrue, disloyal, faithless, unfaithful, deceitful.
– OPPOSITES faithful.

perform verb ❶ DO, carry out, execute, discharge, conduct, effect, bring about, bring off, accomplish, achieve, fulfil, complete. ❷ ACT, play, appear. ❸ FUNCTION, work, operate, run, go.

performance noun ❶ EXECUTION, discharge, accomplishment, achievement, fulfilment. ❷ SHOW, production, entertainment, act, presentation; *informal* gig.

performer noun ACTOR/ACTRESS, player, entertainer, artist, artiste, Thespian, musician, singer, dancer.

perfume noun ❶ SCENT, fragrance, aroma, smell, bouquet; *poetic/literary* redolence. ❷ SCENT, fragrance, eau de Cologne, cologne.

perfunctory adjective CURSORY, superficial, desultory, mechanical, automatic, routine, sketchy, brief, hasty, hurried, rapid, fleeting, quick, fast, offhand, casual, indifferent, careless, inattentive, negligent.
– OPPOSITES careful, thorough.

perhaps adverb MAYBE, possibly, it is possible that, conceivably, feasibly, for all one knows; *poetic/literary* peradventure.

peril noun DANGER, jeopardy, risk, hazard, menace, threat.
– OPPOSITES safety.

perilous adjective DANGEROUS, risky, precarious, hazardous, chancy, threatening, unsafe.
– OPPOSITES safe.

perimeter noun BOUNDARY, border, frontier, limits, outer limits, confines, edge, margin, fringe, periphery.

period noun SPACE, spell, interval, term, stretch, span, age, era, epoch, aeon.

periodic adjective PERIODICAL, recurrent, recurring, repeated, cyclical, cyclic, regular, intermittent, occasional, infrequent, sporadic.

peripheral adjective ❶ OUTER, on the edge/outskirts, surrounding, neighbouring. ❷ **peripheral matters:** MINOR, lesser, secondary, subsidiary, ancillary, unimportant, superficial, irrelevant.
– OPPOSITES central.

perish verb ❶ DIE, lose one's life, be killed, lay down one's life, meet one's death, breathe one's last, draw one's last breath; *informal* bite the dust, kick the bucket. ❷ GO BAD, go off, go sour, rot, decay, decompose.

perk

■ **perk up** CHEER UP, brighten up, take heart; *informal* buck up, pep up.

permanent adjective LASTING, long-lasting, stable, fixed, established, everlasting, perpetual, eternal, enduring, perennial, abiding, constant, persistent, unending, endless, never-ending, immutable, unchangeable, unalterable, invariable.
– OPPOSITES impermanent.

permeate verb SPREAD THROUGH, pass through, pervade, saturate, fill, diffuse through, extend throughout, imbue, penetrate, infiltrate, percolate through.

permissible adjective PERMITTED, allowable, admissible, acceptable, tolerated, authorized, sanctioned, legal, lawful, legitimate, licit, within bounds; *informal* legit.
– OPPOSITES forbidden.

permission noun AUTHORIZATION, sanction, leave, licence, dispensation, empowerment, allowance, consent, assent, acquiescence, agreement, approval, approbation, tolerance, sufferance; *informal* green light, go-ahead, thumbs up.

permissive adjective LIBERAL, tolerant, broad-minded, open-minded, easy-going, indulgent, lenient, overindulgent, lax, unprescriptive.
– OPPOSITES intolerant, strict.

permit verb GIVE PERMISSION, allow, let, authorize, give leave, sanction, grant, license, consent to, assent to, acquiesce in, agree to, approve of, tolerate, countenance, suffer; *informal* give the green light to, give the go-ahead to, give the thumbs up to; *formal* brook.
– OPPOSITES forbid.
▶ noun LICENCE, authorization, warrant, sanction, pass, passport.

perpetual adjective
❶ EVERLASTING, eternal, never-ending, unending, endless, undying, perennial, permanent, lasting, abiding, persisting, enduring, constant, unfailing, unchanging, unvarying, invariable; *poetic/literary* perdurable. ❷ perpetual noise: INCESSANT, unceasing, ceaseless, unending, endless, non-stop, continuous, uninterrupted, unbroken, unremitting. ❸ perpetual complaints: INTERMINABLE, persistent, frequent, continual, recurrent, repeated; *informal* eternal.

perpetuate verb KEEP ALIVE, keep going, keep up, preserve, conserve, sustain, maintain, continue.

perplex verb PUZZLE, baffle, mystify, stump, bewilder, confound, confuse, nonplus, disconcert, dismay, dumbfound; *informal* bamboozle.

perquisite noun BENEFIT, advantage, bonus, dividend, extra, plus; *informal* perk, freebie.

persecute verb OPPRESS, tyrannize, abuse, mistreat, maltreat, ill-treat, molest, afflict, torment, torture, victimize, martyr.

persevere verb PERSIST, go on, keep on, keep at, keep going, continue, carry on, struggle, work, hammer away, be tenacious, be persistent, be pertinacious, be resolute, be purposeful, be obstinate, be insistent, be intransigent, be patient, be diligent; *informal* plug away.
– OPPOSITES give up.

persist verb *see* PERSEVERE.

persistent adjective ❶ persistent people: PERSEVERING, tenacious, pertinacious, determined, resolute, purposeful, obstinate, stubborn, insistent, intransigent, obdurate, intractable, patient, diligent. ❷ persistent rain: CONSTANT, continual, continuous, continuing, interminable, incessant, unceasing, endless, unremitting, unrelenting, relentless.
– OPPOSITES irresolute, intermittent.

person noun INDIVIDUAL, human being, human, creature, living soul, soul, mortal.

persona noun CHARACTER, personality, role, part, public face.

personable adjective PLEASANT, agreeable, amiable, affable, likeable, charming, nice, attractive, presentable, good-looking.
– OPPOSITES disagreeable.

personal adjective ❶ personal reasons: INDIVIDUAL, private, confidential, secret, one's own business. ❷ a personal style: PERSONALIZED, individual, idiosyncratic, characteristic, unique, peculiar. ❸ a personal letter: PRIVATE, confidential, intimate. ❹ personal attention: IN PERSON, individual, special. ❺ personal remarks: INSULTING, slighting, derogatory, disparaging, pejorative, offensive.
– OPPOSITES public, general.

personality noun ❶ NATURE, disposition, character, temperament, temper, make-up, psyche. ❷ FORCE OF PERSONALITY, character, charisma, magnetism, powers of attraction, charm. ❸ CELEBRITY, VIP, household name, dignitary, notable, personage, luminary, worthy.

personally adverb FOR MY PART, for myself, from my own point of view, as far as I am concerned.

personification noun EMBODIMENT, incarnation, epitome, quintessence, essence, symbol, representation, image.

personnel noun STAFF, employees, workers, workforce, labour force, manpower, human resources, liveware.

perspective noun ❶ OUTLOOK, view, viewpoint, point of view, standpoint, stance, angle, slant, attitude. ❷ VIEW, vista, bird's-eye view, prospect, scene, outlook, panorama, aspect, sweep.

persuade verb PREVAIL UPON, induce, convince, win over, talk into, bring round, influence, sway, prompt, coerce, inveigle, cajole, wheedle; *informal* sweet-talk, soft-soap.
– OPPOSITES discourage.

persuasive adjective EFFECTIVE, effectual, convincing, cogent, plausible, compelling, forceful, eloquent, weighty, influential, telling.
– OPPOSITES ineffective.

pertain verb BE CONNECTED, relate, be relevant, have relevance, concern, apply to, be pertinent to, have reference to, have a bearing upon.

pertinent adjective RELEVANT, appropriate, suitable, fitting, fit, apt, apposite, to the point, applicable, material, germane, to the purpose, apropos.
– OPPOSITES irrelevant.

perturb verb DISTURB, make anxious, worry, alarm, trouble, upset, disquiet, discompose, disconcert, vex, bother, agitate, unsettle, fluster, ruffle, harass.
– OPPOSITES reassure.

pervade verb SPREAD THROUGH, permeate, fill, pass through, suffuse, diffuse through, imbue, infuse, penetrate, infiltrate, percolate.

pervasive adjective PERVADING, permeating, prevalent, extensive, ubiquitous, omnipresent, rife, widespread, universal, suffusive.

perverse adjective CONTRARY, wayward, troublesome, difficult, awkward, unreasonable, disobedient, unmanageable, uncontrollable, rebellious, wilful, headstrong, capricious, stubborn, obstinate, obdurate, pertinacious, mulish, pig-headed, wrong-headed, querulous, fractious, intractable, refractory, intransigent, contumacious; *Brit. informal* bolshie, stroppy.

perversion noun ❶ a perversion of the truth: DISTORTION, misuse, misrepresentation, falsification, misinterpretation, misconstruction. ❷ sexual perversion: DEVIATION, aberration, abnormality, irregularity, unnaturalness, corruption, debauchery, depravity, vice; *informal* kinkiness.

pervert verb ❶ MISAPPLY, misuse, distort, garble, warp, twist, misinterpret, misconstrue. ❷ LEAD ASTRAY, corrupt, warp, deprave, debauch, debase, degrade.
▶ noun DEVIANT, deviate, degenerate, debauchee; *informal* perv.

perverted adjective DEPRAVED, debauched, debased, corrupt, deviant, abnormal, aberrant, warped, distorted, twisted, sick, unhealthy, immoral, evil, vile; *informal* kinky.

pessimist noun PROPHET OF DOOM, cynic, defeatist, fatalist, alarmist, doubter, doubting Thomas; *informal* doom merchant, gloom merchant.
– OPPOSITES optimist.

pessimistic adjective GLOOMY, gloom-ridden, cynical, defeatist, fatalistic, hopeless, distrustful, alarmist, doubting, suspicious, bleak, resigned, depressed, dejected, despairing.
– OPPOSITES optimistic.

pest noun NUISANCE, bother, irritant, thorn in the flesh, problem, trouble, worry, inconvenience, trial, tribulation, the bane of one's life; *informal* pain, pain in the neck.

pester verb BADGER, hound, irritate, annoy, bother, irk, nag, harass, chivvy, torment, plague, bedevil, harry; *informal* bug, hassle.

pet noun FAVOURITE, darling, idol, apple of one's eye; *Brit. informal* blue-eyed boy/girl; *N. Amer. informal* fair-haired boy/girl.
▶ verb STROKE, caress, fondle, pat.

peter
■ **peter out** FADE, wane, ebb, diminish, taper off, come to nothing, die out, fail, fall through, come to a halt, come to an end.

petition noun APPEAL, request, entreaty, supplication, plea, prayer, application, suit.
▶ verb APPEAL TO, request, ask, apply to, entreat, beg, plead with, make a plea to; *poetic/literary* beseech.

petrify verb ❶ TERRIFY, frighten, horrify, fill with fear, panic, alarm, scare someone out of their wits, paralyse, stun, stupefy, transfix. ❷ TURN TO STONE, fossilize, calcify, ossify.

petulant adjective QUERULOUS, complaining, peevish, fretful, impatient, cross, irritable, moody, crabbed, crabby, crotchety, touchy, bad-tempered, irascible, sulky; *informal* snappish; *Brit. informal* ratty.

phantom noun GHOST, apparition, spectre, shade, spirit, revenant, wraith, shadow; *informal* spook; *poetic/literary* phantasm.

phenomenal adjective EXTRAORDINARY, remarkable,

exceptional, singular, uncommon, unheard of, unique, unparalleled, unprecedented, amazing, astonishing, astounding, unusual, marvellous, prodigious, sensational, miraculous; *informal* mind-blowing.

phenomenon noun ❶ FACT, experience, occurrence, happening, event, incident, episode. ❷ MARVEL, prodigy, rarity, wonder, sensation, miracle, nonpareil.

philanderer noun WOMANIZER, ladies' man, flirt, Lothario, Casanova, Don Juan, trifler; *informal* ladykiller, stud.

philanthropic adjective BENEVOLENT, beneficent, benignant, charitable, almsgiving, generous, kind, munificent, bountiful, liberal, open-handed, giving, helping; *poetic/literary* bounteous.
– OPPOSITES selfish.

philistine adjective UNCULTURED, uncultivated, uneducated, unenlightened, unread, ignorant, boorish, barbaric.

philosophical adjective ❶ a philosophical mood: THOUGHTFUL, reflective, pensive, meditative, contemplative. ❷ remain philosophical: CALM, composed, cool, collected, self-possessed, serene, tranquil, stoical, impassive, phlegmatic, unperturbed, imperturbable, dispassionate, unruffled, patient, resigned, rational, logical, realistic, practical.

philosophy noun ❶ THOUGHT, thinking, reasoning, logic, wisdom. ❷ BELIEFS, convictions, ideology, ideas, doctrine, tenets, values, principles, attitude, view, viewpoint, outlook.

phlegmatic adjective CALM, cool, composed, collected, serene, tranquil, placid, impassive, imperturbable, dispassionate, philosophical.
– OPPOSITES excitable.

phobia noun AVERSION, fear, dread, horror, terror, dislike, hatred, loathing, detestation, distaste, antipathy, revulsion, repulsion; *informal* thing, hang-up.

phone verb TELEPHONE, call, give someone a call; *Brit.* ring, ring up; *informal* buzz, get on the blower to.

phoney adjective BOGUS, sham, counterfeit, imitation, spurious, mock, ersatz, fake, forged, feigned, simulated, make-believe, false, fraudulent.
– OPPOSITES genuine.

photograph noun PHOTO, snap, snapshot, picture, likeness, shot, print, slide, transparency.

photographic adjective ❶ PICTORIAL, in photographs. ❷ DETAILED, graphic, exact, accurate, precise.

phrase noun EXPRESSION, idiom, remark, saying, utterance, witticism, tag.
▶ verb PUT INTO WORDS, put, word, express, formulate, couch, frame.

phraseology noun PHRASING, wording, words, choice of words, language, vocabulary, terminology.

physical adjective MATERIAL, substantial, solid, concrete, tangible, palpable, visible, real, bodily, non-mental, corporeal, corporal.
– OPPOSITES mental, spiritual.

physician noun DOCTOR, medical practitioner, general practitioner,

GP, specialist, consultant; *informal* doc, medic, medico; *Brit. informal* quack.

physique noun BODY, build, shape, frame, form, figure.

pick verb ❶ CHOOSE, select, opt for, plump for, single out, hand-pick, decide upon, settle upon, fix upon, prefer, favour, elect. ❷ HARVEST, gather, collect, take in, pluck, pull, cull.
▶ noun ❶ CHOICE, selection, option, preference. ❷ the pick of the bunch: BEST, choicest, prime, cream, flower, prize.
■ **pick on** PUNISH REPEATEDLY, blame regularly, constantly find fault with, criticize, badger. **pick up** IMPROVE, get better, recover, rally, perk up, be on the mend, make headway, make progress, take a turn for the better.

picture noun ❶ PAINTING, drawing, sketch, oil painting, watercolour, print, canvas, delineation, portrait, portrayal, illustration, likeness, representation, similitude, semblance. ❷ *See* PHOTOGRAPH.
▶ verb ❶ SEE IN ONE'S MIND/MIND'S EYE, imagine, call to mind, visualize, see, evoke. ❷ PAINT, draw, sketch, depict, delineate, portray, illustrate, reproduce, represent.

picturesque adjective ❶ BEAUTIFUL, pretty, lovely, attractive, scenic, charming, quaint, pleasing, delightful. ❷ a picturesque description: VIVID, graphic, colourful, impressive, striking.
– OPPOSITES ugly.

pie noun PASTRY, tart, tartlet, pasty, quiche.

piebald adjective PIED, skewbald, dappled, brindled, spotted, mottled, speckled, flecked, variegated; *N. Amer.* pinto.

piece noun ❶ PART, bit, section, segment, unit. ❷ torn to pieces: BIT, fragment, smithereens, shard, shred. ❸ a piece of cheese: BIT, section, slice, chunk, lump, hunk, wedge. ❹ a piece of cloth: LENGTH, bit, remnant, scrap, snippet. ❺ a piece of his fortune: SHARE, slice, portion, allotment, allocation, quota, percentage, fraction, quantity.
■ **piece together** PUT TOGETHER, assemble, join up, fit together, unite.

piecemeal adverb PIECE BY PIECE, bit by bit, gradually, in stages, in steps, little by little, by degrees, in fits and starts.

pier noun ❶ JETTY, quay, wharf, dock, landing, landing place, promenade. ❷ SUPPORT, upright, pillar, post, column, pile, piling, buttress.

pierce verb PENETRATE, puncture, perforate, prick, stab, spike, enter, pass through, transfix, bore, drill.

piercing adjective ❶ a piercing glance: PENETRATING, sharp, keen, searching, alert, shrewd, perceptive, probing. ❷ a piercing shriek: PENETRATING, shrill, ear-splitting, high-pitched, loud. ❸ a piercing pain: PENETRATING, sharp, stabbing, shooting, intense, severe, fierce, excruciating, agonizing, exquisite.

piety noun PIOUSNESS, religiousness, holiness, godliness, devoutness, devotion, veneration, reverence, religious duty, spirituality, sanctity, religious zeal.
– OPPOSITES impiety.

pig noun HOG, boar, sow, porker, grunter, swine, piglet.

pile noun ❶ HEAP, bundle, stack, mound, mass, accumulation, collection, assemblage, store, stockpile, hoard, load, mountain. ❷ GREAT DEAL, a lot, lots, quantity, abundance, mountain; *informal* heap, ocean, stacks, oodles, scuds.
▶ verb ❶ HEAP, stack. ❷ ACCUMULATE, amass, collect, gather, stockpile, hoard, store up, assemble, lay by/in. ❸ FORM PILES, form heaps, heap up, amass, accumulate.

pile-up noun CRASH, collision, smash, smash-up, accident, road accident.

pill noun TABLET, capsule, pellet, lozenge, bolus.

pillage verb PLUNDER, rob, raid, loot, maraud, sack, ransack, ravage, lay waste, despoil.
▶ noun PLUNDER, robbery, raiding, looting, marauding, sacking, ransacking, ravaging, rapine, despoiling, laying waste, spoliation, depredation.

pillory verb STIGMATIZE, cast a slur on, denounce, hold up to shame, hold up to ridicule, ridicule, heap scorn on; *informal* show up.

pilot noun ❶ AIRMAN/AIRWOMAN, aviator, flier, captain, commander, co-pilot. ❷ NAVIGATOR, guide, steersman, helmsman.
▶ verb FLY, drive, operate, navigate, guide, steer, control, handle, manoeuvre.

pimple noun SPOT, pustule, boil, swelling, papule; *informal* zit.

pin verb ❶ ATTACH, fasten, affix, fix, stick, tack, nail. ❷ PINION, hold, press, restrain, constrain, hold fast, immobilize, pin down.

pinch verb ❶ NIP, tweak, squeeze, compress. ❷ *See* STEAL (1, 2). ❸ *See* ARREST.

pinched adjective DRAWN, haggard, worn, peaky, pale.
– OPPOSITES healthy.

pinnacle noun PEAK, height, culmination, high point, acme, zenith, climax, crowning point, summit, apex, vertex, apogee.
– OPPOSITES nadir.

pinpoint verb IDENTIFY, discover, distinguish, locate, spot, home in on, put one's finger on.

pioneer noun ❶ SETTLER, colonist, colonizer, explorer. ❷ DEVELOPER, innovator, ground-breaker, trailblazer, founder, founding father, architect.
▶ verb DEVELOP, introduce, launch, instigate, initiate, institute, originate, create, open up, blaze a trail, break new ground.

pious adjective ❶ RELIGIOUS, holy, godly, spiritual, devout, devoted, dedicated, reverent, God-fearing, righteous, faithful. ❷ SANCTIMONIOUS, hypocritical, self-righteous, unctuous, pietistic, holier-than-thou, goody-goody.
– OPPOSITES impious.

pipe noun TUBE, cylinder, conduit, main, duct, channel, pipeline, drainpipe.
▶ verb CONVEY, duct, channeL transmit, bring in, siphon.
■ **pipe down** BE QUIET, quieten down, be silent, hush, hold one's tongue; *informal* shut up, belt up.

piquant adjective ❶ SPICY, flavoursome, peppery, tangy, pungent, sharp, tart, zesty, biting, stinging. ❷ **a piquant piece of gossip:** STIMULATING, intriguing,

interesting, fascinating, alluring, racy, salty, provocative.
– OPPOSITES insipid.

pirate noun FREEBOOTER, marauder, raider; *historical* privateer; *archaic* buccaneer, corsair.

pit noun ABYSS, chasm, crater, hole, cavity, excavation, quarry, coal mine, mine, diggings, working.

pitch verb ❶ THROW, cast, fling, hurl, toss, lob, launch; *informal* chuck, heave, bung. ❷ **pitch a tent:** PUT UP, set up, erect, raise. ❸ **pitch forwards into the lake:** FALL HEADLONG, fall, tumble, topple, plunge, dive.
▶ noun ❶ FIELD, ground, park, stadium, arena, playing field. ❷ LEVEL, point, degree, height, extent, intensity.
■ **pitch in** HELP, assist, lend a hand, join in, participate, play a part, do one's bit, cooperate, collaborate.

piteous adjective PITIFUL, pitiable, pathetic, distressing, affecting, moving, sad, heart-rending, heartbreaking, poignant, emotional, emotive.

pitfall noun TRAP, snare, catch, stumbling block, hazard, peril, danger, difficulty.

pitiful adjective ❶ *See* PITEOUS. ❷ **a pitiful excuse:** CONTEMPTIBLE, despicable, poor, sorry, miserable, inadequate, worthless, base, shabby, pathetic.

pitiless adjective MERCILESS, ruthless, relentless, cruel, severe, harsh, heartless, callous, brutal, inhuman, inhumane, cold-hearted, hard-hearted, unfeeling, uncaring, unsympathetic.
– OPPOSITES merciful.

pity noun ❶ COMMISERATION, condolence, sympathy, compassion, fellow feeling, understanding, forbearance, distress, sadness, emotion, mercy, clemency, kindness. ❷ **it's a pity:** SHAME, crying shame, misfortune, sad thing, sin.
– OPPOSITES indifference.
▶ verb FEEL SORRY FOR, commiserate with, feel sympathy for, sympathize with, feel for.

pivot noun AXIS, fulcrum, axle, swivel, spindle, central shaft.

placate verb CALM, pacify, soothe, appease, conciliate, propitiate, mollify.

place noun ❶ LOCATION, spot, scene, setting, position, site, situation, venue, area, region, whereabouts; *technical* locus. ❷ POSITION, status, grade, rank, station, standing, footing, role, niche.
▶ verb ❶ PUT, position, set/lay down, deposit, rest, settle, station, situate. ❷ ORDER, rank, grade, group, arrange, sort, class, classify, categorize, bracket.

placid adjective ❶ STILL, calm, peaceful, at peace, pacific, tranquil, motionless, smooth, unruffled, undisturbed. ❷ CALM, cool, composed, self-possessed, serene, tranquil, equable, even-tempered, peaceable, easy-going, unmoved, undisturbed, unperturbed, imperturbable, unexcited, unexcitable, unruffled, unemotional.
– OPPOSITES excitable, bustling.

plagiarize verb COPY, pirate, poach, borrow, reproduce, appropriate; *informal* rip off, crib.

plague noun ❶ CONTAGION,

disease, pestilence, sickness, epidemic, pandemic. ❷ a plague of locusts: MULTITUDE, host, swarm, influx, infestation.
▶ **verb** AFFLICT, cause suffering to, torture, torment, bedevil, trouble.

plain adjective ❶ CLEAR, crystal-clear, obvious, evident, apparent, manifest, transparent, patent, unmistakable. ❷ a plain statement of facts: CLEAR, clear-cut, simple, straightforward, uncomplicated, comprehensible, intelligible, understandable, lucid, unambiguous. ❸ a plain lifestyle: SIMPLE, austere, stark, severe, basic, ordinary, unsophisticated, spartan. ❹ a plain child: UNATTRACTIVE, ugly, unprepossessing, unlovely, homely.
– OPPOSITES obscure, fancy, attractive.
▶ **adverb** just plain stupid: DOWNRIGHT, utterly, completely, totally, thoroughly, positively, incontrovertibly, unquestionably, simply.

plaintive adjective MOURNFUL, doleful, melancholy, sad, sorrowful, unhappy, disconsolate.

plan noun ❶ PLAN OF ACTION, scheme, system, procedure, method, programme, schedule, project, way, means, strategy, tactics, formula. ❷ SCALE DRAWING, blueprint, layout, sketch, diagram, chart, map, illustration, representation, delineation.
▶ **verb** ❶ plan a picnic: ARRANGE, organize, line up, schedule, programme. ❷ planning to emigrate: MAKE PLANS, intend, aim, propose, mean, purpose, contemplate, envisage, foresee.

plane adjective FLAT, level, horizontal, even, flush, smooth, regular, uniform.

plant noun ❶ FLOWER, vegetable, herb, shrub, weed. ❷ MACHINERY, equipment, apparatus; *informal* gear. ❸ FACTORY, works, foundry, mill, workshop, shop, yard.
▶ **verb** ❶ IMPLANT, set out, sow, scatter. ❷ PLACE, position, set, situate.

plaster verb COVER THICKLY, spread, coat, smear, overlay, bedaub.
■ **plaster down** FLATTEN, smooth down, sleek down.

plastic adjective ❶ MOULDABLE, malleable, workable, ductile, pliant, pliable, supple, flexible, soft. ❷ FALSE, artificial, synthetic, spurious, sham, bogus; *informal* phoney.

plate noun ❶ DISH, platter, dinner plate, side plate. ❷ PLAQUE, tablet, sign; *Brit.* brass. ❸ ILLUSTRATION, picture, photograph, print, lithograph. ❹ SHEET, panel, slab.

platform noun ❶ DAIS, rostrum, podium, stage, stand. ❷ a socialist platform: PROGRAMME, policy, manifesto, plan, objectives, principles, tenets.

platitude noun TRUISM, hackneyed expression, commonplace, stock expression, trite phrase, banality, bromide, inanity.

platter noun SERVING PLATE, salver, plate, dish, tray.

plausible adjective BELIEVABLE, credible, convincing, persuasive, likely, probable, conceivable, imaginable, tenable, cogent, reasonable.
– OPPOSITES implausible.

play verb ❶ AMUSE ONESELF, entertain oneself, enjoy oneself,

have fun, play games, frolic, frisk, gambol, romp, cavort. ❷ play Hamlet: PLAY THE PART OF, act, act the part of, perform, portray, represent, execute. ❸ play a trick on: PERFORM, carry out, execute, do, accomplish. ❹ play football: TAKE PART IN, participate in, engage in, be involved in. ❺ play them at football: COMPETE AGAINST, contend against, oppose, take on, challenge, vie with, rival.
▶ noun ❶ AMUSEMENT, entertainment, recreation, diversion, leisure, enjoyment, fun, merrymaking, revelry. ❷ play in the line: MOVEMENT, freedom of movement, free motion, slack, give.
■ **play at** PRETEND TO BE, give the appearance of, assume/affect the role of; *informal* make like. **play ball** COOPERATE, collaborate, play along, show willing, be willing. **play down** MAKE LIGHT OF, make little of, gloss over, minimize, diminish, set little store by, underrate, underestimate, undervalue, think little of; *informal* soft-pedal.

player noun ❶ COMPETITOR, contestant, participant, team member, sportsman/sportswoman. ❷ ACTOR/ACTRESS, performer, entertainer, artist, artiste, trouper, Thespian. ❸ PERFORMER, musician, instrumentalist, artist, artiste, virtuoso.

playful adjective ❶ FUN-LOVING, full of fun, high-spirited, frisky, skittish, coltish, sportive, mischievous, impish, puckish; *poetic/literary* frolicsome. ❷ a playful remark: IN FUN, joking, jesting, humorous, facetious, waggish, tongue-in-cheek, arch, roguish.
– OPPOSITES serious.

plea noun ❶ APPEAL, entreaty, supplication, petition, prayer, request, solicitation, suit, invocation. ❷ EXCUSE, pretext, claim, vindication.

plead verb ❶ APPEAL TO, beg, entreat, implore, petition, supplicate, importune, pray to, solicit, request, ask earnestly; *poetic/literary* beseech. ❷ plead insanity: PUT FORWARD, state, assert, argue, claim, allege.

pleasant adjective ❶ a pleasant experience: PLEASING, pleasurable, agreeable, enjoyable, entertaining, amusing, delightful, satisfying, gratifying, nice, good, fine. ❷ a pleasant person/manner: AGREEABLE, friendly, amiable, affable, genial, likeable, nice, good-humoured, charming, engaging, winning, delightful.
– OPPOSITES unpleasant.

please verb ❶ try to please her: GIVE PLEASURE TO, be agreeable to, make pleased/happy/glad etc., gladden, delight, cheer up, charm, divert, entertain, amuse. ❷ do as one pleases: WANT, wish, see fit, will, like, desire, be inclined, prefer.
– OPPOSITES displease.

pleased adjective HAPPY, glad, cheerful, delighted, thrilled, elated, contented, satisfied, gratified, fulfilled; *informal* over the moon; *Brit. informal* chuffed.

pleasure noun HAPPINESS, gladness, delight, joy, enjoyment, entertainment, amusement, diversion, satisfaction, gratification, fulfilment, contentment.

plebeian adjective LOWER-CLASS, low-class, low, low-born, working-class, proletarian,

common, peasant, mean, ignoble.
– OPPOSITES noble.

pledge noun ❶ PROMISE, word, word of honour, vow, assurance, undertaking, oath, covenant, warrant. ❷ SECURITY, surety, guarantee, collateral.
▶ verb ❶ PROMISE, give one's word, vow, give an undertaking, undertake, take an oath, swear, vouch, engage, contract.
❷ MORTGAGE, put up as collateral, guarantee, plight, pawn.

plentiful adjective ABUNDANT, copious, ample, profuse, lavish, liberal, generous, large, huge, bumper, infinite.
– OPPOSITES scanty.

plenty noun PLENTIFULNESS, affluence, prosperity, wealth, opulence, luxury, abundance, copiousness, fruitfulness, profusion; *poetic/literary* plenteousness.
■ **plenty of** ENOUGH, sufficient, a good deal of, a great deal of, masses of; *informal* lots of, heaps of, stacks of, piles of.

plethora noun OVER-ABUNDANCE, superabundance, excess, superfluity, surplus, surfeit, glut.
– OPPOSITES dearth.

pliable adjective ❶ FLEXIBLE, bendable, bendy, pliant, elastic, supple, stretchable, ductile, plastic. ❷ **a pliable person:** MALLEABLE, compliant, docile, biddable, tractable, manageable, governable, controllable, amenable.
– OPPOSITES rigid, obdurate.

plot noun ❶ PIECE OF GROUND, parcel, patch; *Brit.* allotment; *N. Amer.* lot. ❷ CONSPIRACY, intrigue, stratagem. ❸ **the plot of the film:** ACTION, theme, subject, story line, story, scenario, thread.
▶ verb ❶ MAP OUT, draw, draw a diagram of, draw the layout of, make a blueprint/chart of, sketch out, outline. ❷ TAKE PART IN A PLOT, scheme, conspire, participate in a conspiracy, intrigue, form an intrigue.

plough verb TILL, work, cultivate, break up, turn up.
■ **plough into** CAREER INTO, crash into, smash into, hurtle into, drive into.

ploy noun DODGE, ruse, scheme, trick, stratagem, manoeuvre, move.

plucky adjective COURAGEOUS, brave, valiant, valorous, heroic, intrepid, fearless, mettlesome, gritty, determined, bold, daring, spirited, audacious; *informal* gutsy, spunky.
– OPPOSITES cowardly.

plum adjective PRIZE, first-class, choice, best, excellent.

plummet verb FALL, fall headlong, plunge, hurtle, nosedive, dive, drop.

plump adjective CHUBBY, well rounded, of ample proportions, rotund, buxom, stout, fat, obese, corpulent, fleshy, portly, tubby, dumpy, roly-poly, well covered; *Brit. informal* podgy.
– OPPOSITES slim, skinny.

plunder verb ROB, pillage, loot, raid, ransack, strip, fleece, lay waste, despoil, maraud, sack, rape.
▶ noun LOOT, booty, spoils, prize, pillage, ill-gotten gains; *informal* swag.

plunge verb ❶ **plunge the dagger:** THRUST, stick, jab, push, drive.
❷ **plunge into the sea:** DIVE, nosedive, jump, plummet, drop, fall, descend.

plush adjective LUXURIOUS, luxury, sumptuous, lavish, gorgeous, opulent, rich, costly; *informal* ritzy, classy.
– OPPOSITES plain.

pocket noun POUCH, compartment, receptacle.
▶ adjective SMALL, little, miniature, compact, concise, abridged, potted.
▶ verb MISAPPROPRIATE, steal, thieve, purloin; *informal* lift, filch, swipe, snaffle; *Brit. informal* pinch, nick.

poet noun VERSIFIER, rhymester, sonneteer, balladeer, lyricist, bard, minstrel.

poetic adjective IMAGINATIVE, creative, figurative, symbolic, flowery.

poignant adjective MOVING, affecting, touching, tender, emotional, sentimental, heartfelt, sad, sorrowful, tearful, evocative.

point noun ❶ TIP, top, extremity, prong, spike, tine. ❷ PROMONTORY, headland, head, foreland, cape, bluff. ❸ PLACE, position, location, situation, site, spot, area, locality. ❹ TIME, juncture, stage, period, moment, instant. ❺ get to the point: MAIN POINT, central point, essential point, focal point, salient point, keynote, heart of the matter, essence, nub, core, pith, marrow, meat, crux. ❻ the point of the story: MEANING, significance, signification, import, essence, gist, substance, drift, thrust, burden, theme, tenor, vein. ❼ the point of the exercise: AIM, purpose, object, objective, goal, intention, reason for, use, utility. ❽ one of his strong points: CHARACTERISTIC, trait, attribute, quality, feature, property, predisposition, streak, peculiarity, idiosyncrasy.
▶ verb DIRECT, aim, level, train.
■ **point out** CALL ATTENTION TO, draw attention to, indicate, show, specify, designate, identify, mention, allude to.

pointed adjective ❶ SHARP, sharp-edged, edged; *formal* cuspidate, acicular. ❷ a pointed remark: CUTTING, trenchant, biting, incisive, penetrating, forceful, telling, significant.

pointless adjective FUTILE, useless, in vain, unavailing, to no purpose, valueless, unproductive, senseless, absurd, foolish, nonsensical, stupid, silly.
– OPPOSITES useful.

poise noun COMPOSURE, equanimity, self-possession, aplomb, self-assurance, calmness, coolness, serenity, dignity, imperturbability, suaveness, urbanity; *informal* cool.
▶ verb BALANCE, steady, position, support.

poised adjective ❶ a poised young woman: COMPOSED, serene, self-possessed, self-assured, calm, cool, imperturbable, unruffled, unflappable. ❷ poised to attack: READY, prepared, all set, standing by, waiting.
– OPPOSITES flustered.

poison noun ❶ VENOM, toxin. ❷ BLIGHT, contagion, cancer, canker, malignancy, corruption, pollution.
▶ verb ❶ CONTAMINATE, pollute, blight, spoil. ❷ CORRUPT, warp, pervert, deprave, defile, debauch.

poisonous adjective VENOMOUS, deadly, fatal, lethal, noxious.
– OPPOSITES non-toxic.

poke verb JAB, prod, dig, elbow, nudge, push, thrust, shove, stick.

poky adjective CONFINED, cramped, narrow, cell-like, small, little, tiny.
– OPPOSITES spacious.

polar adjective ARCTIC, Antarctic, frozen, freezing, icy, glacial.

polarity noun DIFFERENCE, separation, opposition, contrariety, antithesis, antagonism, conflict.

pole noun POST, upright, pillar, stanchion, standard, support, prop, rod, shaft, mast.

police noun POLICE FORCE, police officers; *Brit.* constabulary; *informal* the cops, the fuzz, the law, the boys in blue; *Brit. informal* the (Old) Bill, the rozzers, the force, the pigs, the filth.
▶ verb GUARD, keep guard over, keep watch on, protect, keep in order, control, keep under control, regulate.

police officer noun POLICEMAN, POLICEWOMAN; *Brit.* constable, PC, WPC; *N. Amer.* patrolman, trooper; *informal* cop; *Brit. informal* bobby, copper, rozzer.

policy noun PLAN, scheme, programme, schedule, code, system, approach, procedure, guideline, theory.

polish verb ❶ WAX, buff, rub up, burnish, shine. ❷ PERFECT, refine, improve, brush up, touch up, finish off.

polished adjective ❶ WAXED, buffed, burnished, shining, shiny, glossy, gleaming, lustrous, glassy, slippery. ❷ a polished manner: REFINED, cultivated, civilized, well bred, polite, well mannered, genteel, courtly, urbane, suave, sophisticated. ❸ a polished performance: EXPERT, accomplished, masterly, skilful, proficient, adept, impeccable, flawless, faultless, perfect, consummate, outstanding, remarkable.
– OPPOSITES dull, gauche, inexpert.

polite adjective ❶ WELL MANNERED, mannerly, courteous, civil, respectful, deferential, well behaved, well bred, genteel, polished, tactful, diplomatic. ❷ polite society: WELL BRED, civilized, cultured, refined, polished, genteel, urbane, sophisticated, elegant, courtly.
– OPPOSITES rude.

politic adjective WISE, prudent, sensible, advisable, judicious, well judged, sagacious, expedient, shrewd, astute, discreet, tactful, diplomatic.
– OPPOSITES unwise.

political adjective
❶ GOVERNMENTAL, ministerial, public, civic, administrative, bureaucratic. ❷ political reasons: FACTIONAL, partisan, bipartisan, power, status.

poll noun ❶ VOTE, ballot, canvass, headcount. ❷ RETURNS, count, tally.
▶ verb ❶ poll more votes: REGISTER, record, return, get, gain. ❷ poll one hundred people: BALLOT, canvass, question, interview, survey, sample.

pollute verb CONTAMINATE, adulterate, infect, taint, poison, befoul, foul.
– OPPOSITES purify.

pomp noun CEREMONY, ritual, display, pageantry, show, spectacle, splendour, grandeur, magnificence, majesty.

pompous adjective SELF-IMPORTANT, presumptuous, imperious, overbearing,

grandiose, affected, pretentious, arrogant, vain, haughty, proud, conceited, egotistic, supercilious, condescending, patronizing; *informal* uppity, uppish.
– OPPOSITES humble.

ponder verb THINK ABOUT, give thought to, consider, reflect on, mull over, contemplate, meditate on, deliberate about/on, dwell on, brood on/over, ruminate about/on/over, puzzle over, cogitate about/on, weigh up, review.

pontificate verb HOLD FORTH, expound, declaim, preach, lay down the law, sound off, dogmatize, sermonize; *informal* preachify.

poor adjective ❶ PENNILESS, hard up, badly off, poverty-stricken, needy, deprived, in need, needful, in want, indigent, impoverished, impecunious, destitute, penurious, beggared, in straitened circumstances, in the red, on one's beam-ends; *informal* broke, flat broke, on one's uppers; *Brit. informal* skint, stony broke. ❷ a poor diet/performance: INADEQUATE, deficient, insufficient, unsatisfactory, below standard, below par, inferior, imperfect, bad, low-grade. ❸ a poor crop: SPARSE, scanty, meagre, scarce, skimpy, paltry, miserable, exiguous. ❹ you poor thing: WRETCHED, pitiable, pitiful, unfortunate, unlucky, luckless, unhappy, hapless, ill-fated, ill-starred. ❺ a poor specimen of a man: MISERABLE, sad, sorry, spiritless, mean, low, base, despicable, contemptible, abject, pathetic.
– OPPOSITES rich.

populace noun THE GENERAL PUBLIC, the public, the people, the population, the common people, the masses.

popular adjective ❶ WELL LIKED, liked, favoured, in favour, favourite, well received, approved, admired, accepted. ❷ popular concern: PUBLIC, general, civic. ❸ popular beliefs: CURRENT, prevalent, prevailing, accepted, recognized, widespread, universal, general, common, customary, usual, standard, stock, conventional.
– OPPOSITES unpopular.

popularity noun ❶ FAVOUR, approval, approbation, admiration, acceptance. ❷ DEMAND, fashionableness, vogue.

populate verb ❶ INHABIT, dwell in, occupy, people. ❷ SETTLE, colonize, people.

population noun INHABITANTS, residents, community, people, citizenry, populace, society.

populous adjective DENSELY POPULATED, heavily populated, thickly populated, overpopulated, crowded.
– OPPOSITES deserted.

pore noun OPENING, orifice, hole, outlet.

pornographic adjective OBSCENE, indecent, erotic, dirty, smutty, filthy, salacious, lewd, prurient; *informal* porno, blue.

porous adjective ABSORBENT, permeable, penetrable, pervious, spongy, sponge-like.
– OPPOSITES impermeable.

port noun HARBOUR, harbourage, haven, anchorage, dock, mooring, marina.

portable adjective TRANSPORTABLE, movable, conveyable, easily carried, lightweight, compact, handy, manageable.

portend verb BE A SIGN OF, be a warning of, point to, be an omen of, herald, bode, augur, presage, forebode, foreshadow, foretell.

portion noun ❶ HELPING, serving, piece, quantity. ❷ SHARE, division, quota, part, bit, allocation, allotment, piece; *informal* cut; *Brit. informal* whack.

portly adjective STOUT, plump, fat, corpulent, obese, tubby, stocky.
– OPPOSITES slim.

portrait noun PORTRAYAL, representation, likeness, image, study, depiction.

portray verb ❶ PAINT, draw a picture of, draw, sketch, depict, represent, delineate. ❷ DESCRIBE, depict, characterize, put into words.

pose verb ❶ SIT, model, take up a position. ❷ ARRANGE, position, lay out, set out, dispose, place, put, locate, situate. ❸ STRIKE AN ATTITUDE, posture, put on an act, play-act, attitudinize, put on airs, show off. ❹ **pose problems:** PRESENT, set, create, cause, give rise to.
▶ noun ❶ POSTURE, stance, position, attitude. ❷ ACT, pretence, facade, front, masquerade, attitudinizing, affectation, airs.

poser[1] noun VEXED QUESTION, enigma, dilemma, puzzle, mystery, conundrum.

poser[2] noun ❶ MODEL, sitter, subject. ❷ *See* POSEUR.

poseur noun POSER, attitudinizer, posturer, play-actor, impostor, exhibitionist, show-off; *informal* phoney.

posh adjective ❶ **a posh hotel:** LUXURIOUS, luxury, sumptuous, opulent, lavish, rich, fancy; *informal* plushy, ritzy, swanky. ❷ **a posh accent:** UPPER-CLASS, aristocratic, upmarket, fancy; *informal* upper-crust.

position noun ❶ SITUATION, location, site, place, spot, area, locality, locale, scene, setting. ❷ **an upright position:** POSTURE, stance, attitude, pose, bearing. ❸ **his financial position:** SITUATION, state, condition, circumstance, predicament, plight, pass. ❹ **his position on the matter:** POINT OF VIEW, viewpoint, opinion, way of thinking, outlook, attitude, stand, standpoint, stance. ❺ **apply for a position:** POST, job, situation, appointment, role, office, place, capacity, duty. ❻ **his position in the class:** PLACE, level, grade, grading, rank, status, standing.
▶ verb PLACE, locate, situate, put, arrange, set, settle, dispose, array.

positive adjective ❶ **a positive attitude:** CONFIDENT, optimistic, assured, assertive, firm, forceful, determined, resolute, emphatic, dogmatic. ❷ **positive developments:** GOOD, favourable, effective, promising, encouraging, heartening. ❸ **positive proposals:** CONSTRUCTIVE, productive, helpful, practical, useful, beneficial.
– OPPOSITES negative.

possess verb ❶ OWN, be the owner of, have, be the possessor of, count among one's possessions, have to one's name, hold, be blessed with, enjoy, be endowed with, be gifted with. ❷ **possessed by the devil:** INFLUENCE, control, dominate, have mastery over, bewitch, enchant, put under a spell, obsess.

possessions plural noun BELONGINGS, things, property,

assets, luggage, baggage, personal effects, goods and chattels, accoutrements, paraphernalia, appendages, impedimenta.

possessive adjective ❶ ACQUISITIVE, greedy, grasping, covetous, selfish. ❷ OVERPROTECTIVE, clinging, controlling, dominating, jealous.

possibility noun FEASIBILITY, practicability, attainability, likelihood, potentiality, conceivability, probability.

possible adjective ❶ it's not possible: FEASIBLE, able to be done, practicable, doable, attainable, achievable, realizable, within reach; *informal* on. ❷ possible outcomes: LIKELY, potential, conceivable, imaginable, probable, credible, tenable.
– OPPOSITES impossible.

possibly adverb ❶ PERHAPS, maybe, for all one knows, very likely. ❷ CONCEIVABLY, by any means, by any chance, at all.

post noun STAKE, upright, pole, shaft, prop, support, column, stanchion, standard, stock, picket, pillar, palisade, baluster, newel.
▶ verb ❶ PUT UP, stick, stick up, pin, pin up, tack, tack up, attach, affix, hang, display. ❷ ANNOUNCE, make known, advertise, publish, publicize, circulate, broadcast.

poster noun PLACARD, bill, notice, public notice, sticker, advertisement, announcement, bulletin; *Brit. informal* advert.

postpone verb DEFER, put off, put back, delay, hold over, adjourn, shelve, table, pigeonhole; *informal* put on ice, put on the back burner.
– OPPOSITES advance.

postscript noun PS, subscript, afterthought, afterword, addendum, appendix, codicil, supplement.

postulate verb ASSUME, presuppose, suppose, presume, take for granted, posit, hypothesize, theorize.

posture noun ❶ POSITION, pose, attitude, carriage, bearing, stance. ❷ ATTITUDE, position, point of view, viewpoint, opinion, outlook, stand, standpoint, stance, angle, slant.
▶ verb POSE, strike an attitude, put on an act, act, play-act, attitudinize, show off.

potent adjective ❶ POWERFUL, forceful, strong, vigorous, mighty, influential, authoritative, commanding, dominant, energetic, dynamic; *poetic/literary* puissant. ❷ a potent argument: POWERFUL, forceful, strong, effective, cogent, compelling, convincing, persuasive, eloquent, impressive, telling.
– OPPOSITES impotent.

potential adjective ❶ a potential star: BUDDING, embryonic, developing, promising, prospective, likely, possible, probable. ❷ a potential accident: LIKELY, possible, probable.
▶ noun PROMISE, possibilities, capability, capacity, ability, aptitude.

potion noun DRINK, beverage, brew, concoction, mixture, draught, elixir, philtre.

potter verb DAWDLE, loiter, dally, dilly-dally; *informal* mess about/around.

pouch noun BAG, purse, wallet, container.

pounce verb SWOOP ON, spring on, lunge at, leap at, jump at/on, ambush, take by surprise, take unawares, attack suddenly.

pound[1] verb ❶ CRUSH, beat, pulverize, powder, smash, mash, grind; *technical* comminute, triturate. ❷ heart pounding: BEAT, pulsate, pulse, throb, thump, pump, palpitate.

pound[2] noun COMPOUND, enclosure, pen, yard.

pour verb ❶ GUSH, rush, stream, flow, course, spout, jet, spurt. ❷ pour the milk: LET FLOW, decant, splash, spill.

poverty noun ❶ PENNILESSNESS, neediness, need, want, hardship, deprivation, indigence, impoverishment, impecuniousness, destitution, penury, privation, beggary. ❷ poverty of imagination: DEFICIENCY, dearth, shortage, scarcity, paucity, insufficiency, lack, want, meagreness.
– OPPOSITES wealth.

powder verb ❶ DUST, sprinkle, scatter, strew. ❷ *See* POUND[1] (1).

powdery adjective POWDER-LIKE, fine, dusty, chalky, floury, friable, granulated, ground, crushed, pulverized.

power noun ❶ the power to do it: ABILITY, capability, capacity, potential, potentiality. ❷ lose the power of speech: ABILITY, capability, faculty, competence. ❸ the power behind the blow: POWERFULNESS, strength, force, might, weight. ❹ in his power: CONTROL, authority, mastery, domination, dominance, rule, command, ascendancy, supremacy, dominion, sway.

powerful adjective ❶ STRONG, sturdy, strapping, stout, robust, vigorous, tough. ❷ INFLUENTIAL, dominant, authoritative, commanding, forceful, strong, vigorous, potent. ❸ a powerful argument: FORCEFUL, strong, effective, cogent, compelling, convincing, persuasive, eloquent, impressive.
– OPPOSITES weak.

powerless adjective WEAK, feeble, impotent, helpless, unfit, ineffectual, inadequate, paralysed, disabled, incapacitated, debilitated.
– OPPOSITES powerful, strong.

practicable adjective FEASIBLE, possible, viable, workable, doable, achievable, attainable, accomplishable.
– OPPOSITES theoretical.

practical adjective ❶ practical knowledge: APPLIED, empirical, pragmatic, workaday, hands-on. ❷ practical clothing: FUNCTIONAL, useful, utilitarian, sensible. ❸ she's very practical: BUSINESSLIKE, sensible, down-to-earth, pragmatic, realistic, hard-headed; *informal* hard-nosed.
– OPPOSITES impractical.

practically adverb ALMOST, nearly, virtually, all but, in effect; *informal* pretty nearly/well.

practice noun ❶ put into practice: ACTION, operation, application, effect, exercise, use. ❷ TRAINING, preparation, study, exercise, drill, workout, rehearsal. ❸ standard practice: PROCEDURE, method, system, usage, tradition, convention.

practise verb ❶ practise self-control: CARRY OUT, perform, do, execute, follow, pursue, observe. ❷ practise her tennis: WORK AT, go through, run through, go over, rehearse, polish, refine.

❸ practise law: WORK AT, have a career in, pursue a career in, engage in.

praise verb ❶ EXPRESS ADMIRATION FOR, applaud, acclaim, express approval of, cheer, compliment, congratulate, pay tribute to, extol, sing the praises of, eulogize, cry up, throw bouquets at; *formal* laud. ❷ praise God: WORSHIP, glorify, honour, exalt, adore, pay tribute to, give thanks to; *formal* laud.
– OPPOSITES condemn.
▶ noun ❶ APPROBATION, applause, acclaim, approval, acclamation, compliments, congratulations, commendation, tributes, accolades, plaudits, eulogy, panegyric, encomium, extolment; *formal* laudation. ❷ WORSHIP, glory, honour, devotion, exaltation, adoration.

praiseworthy adjective COMMENDABLE, laudable, admirable, estimable, creditable, deserving, meritorious, worthy, excellent, exemplary, sterling, fine.

prance verb ❶ LEAP, spring, jump, skip, cavort, caper, frisk, gambol. ❷ PARADE, cavort, strut, swagger; *informal* swank.

prank noun TRICK, practical joke, joke, hoax, caper, stunt; *informal* lark.

pray verb ❶ OFFER PRAYERS TO, say prayers to. ❷ pray for mercy: APPEAL FOR, beg for, petition for, solicit, plead for.

prayer noun DEVOTION, communion, litany, collect.

preach verb GIVE/DELIVER A SERMON, sermonize, spread the gospel, evangelize.
■ **preach at** LECTURE, moralize at, admonish, harangue, sermonize.

preacher noun MINISTER, parson, clergyman, churchman, cleric, missionary, revivalist, evangelist, televangelist.

precarious adjective RISKY, hazardous, insecure, unstable, shaky, tricky, perilous, dangerous, touch-and-go; *informal* dicey, hairy.
– OPPOSITES safe.

precaution noun ❶ take a few precautions against burglary: PREVENTIVE MEASURE, preventative measure, safety measure, safeguard, provision. ❷ a situation which demands precaution: FORESIGHT, foresightedness, forethought, far-sightedness, anticipation, prudence, circumspection, caution, care, attentiveness, chariness, wariness.

precede verb ❶ GO BEFORE, come before, go/come ahead of, lead, usher in. ❷ LEAD TO, lead up to, antedate, antecede, usher in, herald, pave the way for.
– OPPOSITES follow.

precedence noun RANK, seniority, superiority, pre-eminence, eminence, supremacy, primacy, ascendancy.

precedent noun is there a precedent for such a severe punishment? PREVIOUS CASE, prior case, previous instance, prior instance, pattern, model, example, exemplar, paradigm, criterion, yardstick, standard.

precious adjective ❶ VALUABLE, costly, expensive, dear, priceless, rare, choice. ❷ VALUED, cherished, prized, treasured, favourite, dear, beloved, adored, revered, venerated.

precipitate verb HASTEN, accelerate, expedite, speed up, push forward, bring on, trigger. ▶ adjective HURRIED, rapid, swift, speedy, headlong, abrupt, sudden, unexpected, breakneck, precipitous.

precipitous adjective ❶ STEEP, sheer, perpendicular, abrupt, high. ❷ *See* PRECIPITATE adjective.

precise adjective ❶ EXACT, literal, actual, close, faithful, strict, express, minute, accurate, correct. ❷ that precise moment: EXACT, very, actual, particular, specific, distinct.
– OPPOSITES imprecise.

preclude verb PREVENT, prohibit, make impossible, rule out, eliminate, debar, interdict, block, bar, hinder, impede.

precocious adjective ADVANCED, ahead, far ahead, gifted, brilliant, quick, smart.
– OPPOSITES backward.

preconception noun PRECONCEIVED IDEA, assumption, presupposition, presumption, prejudgement, prejudice, bias.

predatory adjective ❶ HUNTING, predacious, rapacious, raptorial. ❷ EXPLOITATIVE, greedy, acquisitive, rapacious, vulturine.

predecessor noun PRECURSOR, forerunner, antecedent, ancestor, forefather, forebear, progenitor.
– OPPOSITES successor.

predestine verb FATE, predetermine, destine, foreordain, predestinate.

predicament noun DIFFICULT SITUATION, plight, tight corner, mess, emergency, crisis, dilemma, quandary, trouble; *informal* jam, hole, fix, pickle, scrape, tight spot.

predict verb FORECAST, foretell, prophesy, foresee, divine, prognosticate, forewarn, forebode, portend, presage, augur.

predictable adjective FORESEEABLE, expected, anticipated, probable, likely, certain, sure; *informal* on the cards.

predilection noun LIKING, fondness, preference, love, partiality, taste, weakness, penchant, fancy, inclination, leaning.
– OPPOSITES dislike.

predominate verb BE DOMINANT, be in control, rule, hold ascendancy, hold sway, have the upper hand, carry most weight.

pre-eminent adjective OUTSTANDING, leading, foremost, chief, excellent, distinguished, prominent, eminent, important, superior, unrivalled, unsurpassed.
– OPPOSITES undistinguished.

preface noun INTRODUCTION, foreword, preamble, prologue, prelude, front matter, proem, exordium, prolegomenon; *informal* prelims, intro.
▶ verb PRECEDE, prefix, introduce, begin, open, launch.

prefer verb LIKE BETTER, favour, fancy, be more partial to, incline towards, choose, select, pick, opt for, go for, plump for, single out.

preferable adjective BETTER, superior, more desirable, more suitable.

preference noun ❶ CHOICE, first choice, first option, liking, fancy, desire, wish, inclination, partiality, predilection, leaning, bias, bent. ❷ PREFERENTIAL TREATMENT, favour, precedence, priority, advantage.

preferential adjective SPECIAL, better, advantageous, favoured, privileged, partial, partisan.

pregnant adjective ❶ HAVING A BABY/CHILD, expectant, expecting, in the family way, with child, enceinte; *informal* preggers, with a bun in the oven; *Brit. informal* in the club; *technical* gravid. ❷ **a pregnant pause:** MEANINGFUL, significant, eloquent, expressive, suggestive, pointed, telling.

prejudice noun BIAS, discrimination, partisanship, partiality, preference, one-sidedness, chauvinism, bigotry, narrow-mindedness, intolerance, unfairness, unjustness, racism, sexism, ageism, heterosexism.
▶ verb BE PREJUDICIAL TO, be disadvantageous to, damage, injure, harm, hurt, mar, spoil, impair, undermine.

prejudiced adjective BIASED, discriminatory, partisan, partial, one-sided, jaundiced, chauvinistic, bigoted, intolerant, narrow-minded, unfair, unjust, racist, sexist, ageist.
– OPPOSITES impartial.

prejudicial adjective DETRIMENTAL, deleterious, unfavourable, damaging, injurious, harmful, hurtful, inimical.
– OPPOSITES beneficial.

preliminary adjective INTRODUCTORY, prefatory, prior, precursory, opening, initial, beginning, preparatory, initiatory.
– OPPOSITES final.

prelude noun ❶ PRECURSOR, forerunner, curtain-raiser, harbinger, herald, preliminary, introduction, start, beginning. ❷ INTRODUCTION, preface, prologue, preamble, proem, exordium, prolegomenon; *informal* intro.

premature adjective TOO SOON, too early, early, untimely, overhasty, precipitate, impulsive, impetuous, rash.
– OPPOSITES overdue.

premeditated adjective PLANNED, pre-planned, pre-arranged, intentional, intended, deliberate, calculated, wilful.
– OPPOSITES spontaneous.

premier noun HEAD OF GOVERNMENT, president, prime minister, PM.
▶ adjective LEADING, foremost, chief, principal, head, top, first, highest, main.

premonition noun FOREBODING, presentiment, intuition, feeling, hunch, suspicion, sneaking suspicion, misgiving, apprehension, fear, feeling in one's bones, funny feeling.

preoccupied adjective LOST IN THOUGHT, deep in thought, in a brown study, absorbed, engrossed, pensive, absent-minded, distracted, abstracted, distrait, oblivious, faraway, rapt.

preparation noun ❶ ARRANGEMENT, provision, preparatory measure, necessary step, groundwork, spadework. ❷ COACHING, training, grooming, priming. ❸ MIXTURE, compound, concoction, composition, tincture.

prepare verb ❶ GET READY, make ready, arrange, develop, put together, assemble, draw up, produce, construct, compose, concoct, fashion, work up. ❷ **prepare for the test:** REVISE, study, cram, do homework; *Brit. informal* swot. ❸ **prepare him for the test:** COACH, train, groom, prime.

preposterous adjective ABSURD, ridiculous, foolish, ludicrous, farcical, asinine, senseless, unreasonable, crazy, insane, outrageous, unbelievable, incredible, unthinkable.
– OPPOSITES sensible.

prerequisite adjective NECESSARY, needed, required, called for, essential, requisite, vital, indispensable, imperative, obligatory, mandatory.
– OPPOSITES unnecessary.
▶ noun REQUIREMENT, necessity, essential, requisite, precondition, condition, sine qua non; *informal* must.

prescribe verb ❶ ADVISE, recommend, commend, suggest. ❷ LAY DOWN, require, stipulate, specify, decree, order, command, ordain, enjoin.

presence noun ❶ EXISTENCE, being. ❷ COMPANY, proximity, neighbourhood, vicinity, closeness, nearness. ❸ a woman of presence: MAGNETISM, aura, charisma, personality, attraction, poise.
– OPPOSITES absence.

present[1] adjective ❶ EXISTING, existent, extant. ❷ PRESENT-DAY, existing, current, contemporary. ❸ IN ATTENDANCE, near, nearby, available, at hand, ready.
– OPPOSITES absent.
▶ noun TODAY, now, here and now, the present moment, the time being.

present[2] verb ❶ GIVE, hand over, confer, bestow, donate, award, grant, accord. ❷ INTRODUCE, make known, announce. ❸ present a performance: PUT ON, produce, perform, stage, mount.

present[3] noun GIFT, donation, offering, contribution, gratuity, handout, presentation, award, bounty, benefaction; *informal* freebie; *Brit. informal* pressie.

presentable adjective WELL GROOMED, smartly dressed, tidily dressed, tidy, spruce, of smart appearance, fit to be seen.

presentiment noun FOREBODING, premonition, intuition, feeling, hunch, apprehension.

preserve verb ❶ preserve wood: CONSERVE, protect, safeguard, care for. ❷ preserve from danger: KEEP, protect, defend, guard, safeguard, secure, shelter, shield. ❸ preserve for posterity: CONSERVE, save, keep, safeguard, maintain, perpetuate. ❹ preserve the old traditions: CONSERVE, keep up, keep alive, keep going, maintain, continue with, uphold, prolong, perpetuate.
– OPPOSITES neglect.

preside verb BE IN CHARGE OF, control, direct, run, conduct, supervise, govern, rule.

press verb ❶ press the button: DEPRESS, push down, force down, bear down on. ❷ press grapes: CRUSH, squeeze, compress, mash, reduce. ❸ press trousers: IRON, smooth out, flatten. ❹ press the soil down: FLATTEN, make flat, smooth out. ❺ pressing him to leave: URGE, entreat, exhort, implore, put pressure on, pressurize, force, compel, coerce.
▶ noun NEWSPAPERS, the media; *Brit.* Fleet Street.

pressing adjective *see* URGENT (1).

pressure noun ❶ FORCE, weight, heaviness, compression. ❷ FORCE, compulsion, coercion, constraint, duress. ❸ the pressure of work: STRAIN, stress, tension, burden,

load, weight, trouble; *informal* hassle.
▶ **verb** PUT PRESSURE ON, pressurize, press, force, compel, coerce, constrain, bulldoze, dragoon.

prestige **noun** STATUS, kudos, standing, stature, importance, reputation, fame, renown, esteem, influence, authority, supremacy, eminence, superiority, predominance.

prestigious **adjective** IMPORTANT, prominent, impressive, high-ranking, reputable, respected, esteemed, eminent, distinguished, of high standing, well known, celebrated, illustrious, renowned, famous.

presume **verb** ❶ ASSUME, take for granted, take it, take as read, suppose, presuppose, believe, think, imagine, judge, guess, surmise, conjecture, hypothesize, infer, deduce. ❷ HAVE THE TEMERITY, have the audacity, be so bold as, have the effrontery, go so far as, dare, venture.

presumptuous **adjective** OVERCONFIDENT, cocksure, arrogant, egotistical, conceited, bold, audacious, forward, pushy, insolent, impudent, bumptious; *informal* too big for one's boots.

pretence **noun** ❶ FALSE SHOW, show, semblance, appearance, false front, guise, facade, masquerade, mask, veneer, cover, charade. ❷ PRETEXT, false excuse, guise, sham, ruse, wile, trickery, lie, falsehood. ❸ PRETENTIOUSNESS, display, ostentation, affectation, showiness, flaunting, posturing.

pretend **verb** ❶ PUT ON AN ACT, act, play-act, put it on, dissemble, sham, feign, fake, dissimulate, make believe, put on a false front, posture, go through the motions. ❷ CLAIM, make believe, purport, affect, profess, make out, fabricate.

pretender **noun** CLAIMANT, claimer, aspirant.

pretentious **adjective** AFFECTED, ostentatious, showy, pompous, artificial, mannered, high-flown, high-sounding, flowery, grandiose, elaborate, extravagant, flamboyant, grandiloquent, bombastic, orotund; *informal* highfalutin.
– OPPOSITES plain, simple.

preternatural **adjective** EXTRAORDINARY, exceptional, unusual, uncommon, singular, abnormal, supernatural, paranormal.

pretty **adjective** LOVELY, attractive, good-looking, nice-looking, personable, prepossessing, appealing, charming, delightful, nice, engaging, pleasing, winning, winsome, as pretty as a picture; *Scottish & N. English* bonny; *N. Amer. informal* cute; *archaic* fair, comely.
– OPPOSITES ugly.
▶ **adverb** QUITE, rather, fairly, somewhat, moderately, reasonably; *informal* kind of.

prevail **verb** WIN, triumph, be victorious, carry the day, conquer, overcome, gain mastery.

prevalent **adjective** ❶ PREVAILING, current, frequent, usual, common, general, widespread, pervasive, universal, set, established, accepted, popular, fashionable, in fashion, in style, in vogue. ❷ WIDESPREAD, extensive, frequent, usual, endemic, universal, ubiquitous, rampant, rife.
– OPPOSITES uncommon.

prevaricate verb BE EVASIVE, shilly-shally, dodge the issue, hedge, beat about the bush, equivocate, quibble; *Brit.* hum and haw.

prevent verb PUT A STOP TO, halt, arrest, avert, nip in the bud, fend off, turn aside, stave off, ward off, block, check, hinder, impede, hamper, obstruct, baulk, foil, thwart, frustrate, forestall, inhibit, hold back, restrain, prohibit, bar, deter.
– OPPOSITES encourage.

preventative, preventive adjective PRECAUTIONARY, protective, deterrent, prophylactic.

previous adjective ❶ FORMER, ex-, past, sometime, one-time, erstwhile; *formal* quondam. ❷ PRECEDING, foregoing, earlier, prior, above, precursory, antecedent, anterior.
– OPPOSITES following.

previously adverb FORMERLY, earlier on, before, until now, hitherto, heretofore, once, at one time, in the past, in years gone by.

price noun ❶ COST, asking price, charge, fee, payment, rate, amount, figure, value, valuation, bill. ❷ RESULT, cost, penalty, sacrifice, forfeit, forfeiture, punishment.
▶ verb FIX/SET THE PRICE OF, cost, value, rate, evaluate, assess, estimate, appraise, assay.

priceless adjective ❶ INVALUABLE, precious, rare, incomparable, expensive, costly, rich, dear, irreplaceable, treasured, prized. ❷ *See* HILARIOUS.
– OPPOSITES worthless.

prick verb PIERCE, puncture, perforate, stab, nick, gash, slit, bore, spike.

prickle noun ❶ THORN, needle, barb, spike, spine, spur. ❷ TINGLE, tingling, sting, stinging, smarting, itching.
▶ verb TINGLE, sting, smart, itch.

pride noun ❶ SELF-ESTEEM, self-respect, ego, amour propre, self-worth, self-image, feelings, sensibilities. ❷ CONCEIT, vanity, arrogance, haughtiness, self-importance, self-love, egotism, presumption, hauteur, superciliousness, disdain; *informal* big-headedness. ❸ SATISFACTION, gratification, pleasure, joy, delight.
– OPPOSITES humility.
▶ verb BE PROUD OF, take pride in, take satisfaction in, congratulate oneself on, revel in, glory in, exult in, boast about, brag about, crow about.

priest noun CLERGYMAN, cleric, man/woman of the cloth, man/woman of God, father, padre.

priggish adjective PRUDISH, puritanical, prim, strait-laced, stuffy, starchy, self-righteous, sanctimonious, narrow-minded, censorious; *informal* holier-than-thou, goody-goody.
– OPPOSITES broad-minded.

prim adjective PROPER, demure, formal, precise, stuffy, starchy, strait-laced, prudish, prissy, old-maidish, priggish, puritanical.

primarily adverb BASICALLY, essentially, in essence, fundamentally, in the first place, first and foremost, chiefly, mainly, in the main, principally, mostly, for the most part, on the whole, predominantly, predominately.

primary adjective ❶ PRIME, chief, main, principal, leading, predominant, most important,

paramount, basic, fundamental, elemental, rudimentary, essential. ❷ EARLIEST, original, initial, beginning, first, opening.
– OPPOSITES secondary.

prime adjective ❶ *See* PRIMARY (1). ❷ TOP-QUALITY, highest, top, best, first-class, high-grade, grade A, superior, choice, select.
– OPPOSITES inferior.
▶ noun BEST PART, peak, pinnacle, best days, height, zenith, acme, culmination, apex, heyday, full flowering.

primitive adjective ❶ ANCIENT, earliest, primeval, primordial, primal, pristine. ❷ CRUDE, simple, rudimentary, undeveloped, unrefined, rough, unsophisticated, rude. ❸ UNCIVILIZED, barbarian, barbaric, savage, wild.
– OPPOSITES advanced.

principal adjective ❶ **principal members:** CHIEF, leading, pre-eminent, foremost, most important, most influential, dominant, controlling, ruling, in charge. ❷ **principal issues:** CHIEF, main, major, most important, leading, key, primary, prime, paramount.
– OPPOSITES subsidiary.
▶ noun ❶ HEAD TEACHER, headmaster, headmistress, head, rector, master, dean. ❷ LEADING PLAYER/PERFORMER, leading man/lady, lead, star.

principle noun ❶ THEORY, basis, fundamental, essence, assumption, rule, law, canon, tenet, code, maxim, axiom, dictum, postulate. ❷ **a woman of principle:** MORALS, ethics, integrity, uprightness, righteousness, probity, rectitude, honour, conscience, scruples.

print verb ❶ SET IN PRINT, send to press, publish, issue, run off, put to bed. ❷ IMPRINT, stamp, mark.
▶ noun ❶ TYPE, letters, lettering, typeface, newsprint. ❷ COPY, reproduction, replica.

prior adjective EARLIER, previous, anterior.
– OPPOSITES subsequent.
■ **prior to** BEFORE, until, up to, earlier than, preceding.

priority noun ❶ FIRST/PRIME CONCERN, most important thing. ❷ PRECEDENCE, preference, urgency.

prison noun JAIL, lock-up, penal institution, place of detention, place of confinement, dungeon; *N. Amer.* penitentiary, correctional facility; *informal* clink, cooler, slammer, stir, jug; *Brit. informal* nick; *N. Amer. informal* can, pen; *Brit. informal, dated* chokey.

prisoner noun CONVICT, captive, detainee, internee hostage; *informal* con, lag, lifer, jailbird.

pristine adjective UNMARKED, unblemished, unspoilt, spotless, immaculate, clean, in mint/perfect condition.
– OPPOSITES dirty, spoilt.

private adjective ❶ **private talks:** CONFIDENTIAL, secret, unofficial, off-the-record, in camera, closet, privileged; *informal* hush-hush. ❷ **her private thoughts:** PERSONAL, intimate, secret. ❸ **a private place:** SECLUDED, secret, remote, out of the way, quiet. ❹ **a private person:** RESERVED, retiring, self-contained, uncommunicative, diffident, secretive.
– OPPOSITES public, open, extrovert.

privation noun DEPRIVATION, want, need, neediness,

disadvantage, poverty, hardship, distress, indigence, destitution.

privileged adjective ❶ a privileged background: ADVANTAGED, socially advantaged, favoured, elite, indulgent, spoilt. ❷ privileged information: CONFIDENTIAL, private, off-the-record, secret, top secret; *informal* hush-hush.
– OPPOSITES disadvantaged, public.

prize noun TROPHY, medal, award, accolade, reward, premium, honour, laurels, palm, bays.
▶ adjective PRIZEWINNING, award-winning, winning, champion.
▶ verb VALUE, treasure, cherish, hold dear, esteem, hold in high regard.

probable adjective LIKELY, most likely, odds-on, expected, anticipated, predictable, foreseeable, on the cards, credible, quite possible, possible.
– OPPOSITES improbable.

probably adverb IN ALL PROBABILITY, in all likelihood, as likely as not, it is to be expected that, perhaps.

probe noun INVESTIGATION, scrutiny, inquest, exploration, examination, study.
▶ verb ❶ FEEL, feel around, prod, poke, explore. ❷ INVESTIGATE, scrutinize, inquire into, examine, study, research, analyse.

problem noun ❶ DIFFICULTY, complication, trouble, mess, predicament, plight, dilemma, quandary; *informal* pickle, can of worms. ❷ PUZZLE, poser, enigma, riddle, conundrum; *informal* teaser, brain-teaser.

problematic adjective ❶ PROBLEMATICAL, difficult, troublesome, complicated, puzzling, knotty, thorny, ticklish, tricky; *Brit. informal* dodgy. ❷ DOUBTFUL, uncertain, unsettled, questionable, open to question, debatable, arguable.
– OPPOSITES straightforward.

procedure noun ❶ COURSE OF ACTION, plan of action, policy, system, method, methodology, modus operandi, technique, means, practice, operation, strategy. ❷ STEP, process, measure, move, operation, transaction.

proceed verb ❶ MAKE ONE'S WAY, go, advance, carry on, move on, press on, progress. ❷ ARISE, originate, spring, stem, come, derive, result, follow, ensue, emanate, issue, flow.

proceedings plural noun ❶ ACTIVITIES, events, action, process, affairs, doings, happenings. ❷ CASE, lawsuit, litigation, trial. ❸ MINUTES, report, account, record, transactions.

proceeds plural noun TAKINGS, profits, returns, receipts, income, earnings.

process noun ❶ METHOD, system, technique, means, practice, way, procedure. ❷ DEVELOPMENT, evolution, changes, stages, steps.

procession noun ❶ PARADE, march, column, file, train, cortège, cavalcade, motorcade. ❷ STREAM, steady stream, succession, series, sequence, run.

proclaim verb ❶ ANNOUNCE, declare, make known, give out, notify, circulate, advertise, publish, broadcast, promulgate. ❷ proclaim him king: PRONOUNCE, announce, declare to be.

proclivity noun TENDENCY, inclination, leaning, propensity, bent, bias, penchant, predisposition, weakness.

procrastinate verb DELAY, postpone action, defer action, be dilatory, use delaying tactics, stall, temporize, play for time, play a waiting game, dally, dilly-daily, drag one's feet/heels.

procure verb OBTAIN, acquire, get, pick up, find, come by, get hold of, secure, lay/get one's hands on, gain.

prod verb ❶ POKE, jab, dig, nudge, elbow, butt, push, shove, thrust. ❷ *See* URGE verb (1).

prodigious adjective IMPRESSIVE, striking, startling, extraordinary, remarkable, exceptional, amazing, staggering, stupendous, phenomenal, miraculous.
– OPPOSITES small, unexceptional.

prodigy noun CHILD GENIUS, wonder child, wunderkind, gifted child, wonder, marvel, phenomenon, sensation.

produce verb ❶ MAKE, manufacture, create, construct, build, fabricate, put together, assemble, turn out, compose, originate, prepare, develop, fashion. ❷ PRESENT, offer, set forth, proffer, advance, show, exhibit, demonstrate, disclose, reveal. ❸ YIELD, bear, give, bring forth, supply, provide, furnish. ❹ GIVE BIRTH TO, bring forth, bear, breed, give life to, bring into the world, procreate. ❺ MOUNT, stage, put on, present.
▶ noun YIELD, crops, harvest, output.

product noun ❶ COMMODITY, artefact, goods, wares, merchandise. ❷ RESULT, outcome, effect, consequence, upshot, fruit, spin-off, legacy.

productive adjective ❶ productive soil: FERTILE, fruitful, fecund, rich, high-yielding. ❷ a productive worker: PROLIFIC, energetic, vigorous, efficient, effective, valuable.
– OPPOSITES sterile, unproductive.

profess verb DECLARE, announce, proclaim, assert, state, utter, affirm, avow; *formal* aver.

profession noun ❶ CAREER, job, calling, business, vocation, occupation, line of work, métier, position, situation. ❷ DECLARATION, announcement, proclamation, assertion, statement, affirmation, avowal; *formal* averment.

professional adjective ❶ a very professional worker: SKILLED, skilful, proficient, expert, adept, competent, efficient, experienced. ❷ a professional piece of work: SKILFUL, expert, adept, masterly, excellent, fine, polished, finished. ❸ a professional tennis player: NON-AMATEUR, paid.
– OPPOSITES amateurish, amateur.

proffer verb OFFER, tender, present, extend, give, submit, volunteer, suggest.
– OPPOSITES withdraw.

profile noun ❶ OUTLINE, silhouette, contour, lines, shape, form, figure. ❷ SHORT BIOGRAPHY, sketch, thumbnail sketch, portrait, vignette.

profit noun ❶ TAKINGS, proceeds, gain, yield, return, receipts, income, earnings, winnings.

❷ GAIN, benefit, advantage, good, value, use, avail.
– OPPOSITES loss.
▶ **verb** BENEFIT, be of benefit to, be of advantage to, be of use/value to, serve, help, be helpful to, assist, aid, stand in good stead.

profitable adjective
❶ MONEY-MAKING, commercial, gainful, remunerative, paying, lucrative. ❷ BENEFICIAL, advantageous, rewarding, helpful, productive, useful, worthwhile, valuable.
– OPPOSITES unprofitable.

profligate adjective
❶ EXTRAVAGANT, spendthrift, improvident, immoderate, reckless, wasteful. ❷ DISSOLUTE, dissipated, debauched, abandoned, corrupt, degenerate, depraved, immoral, promiscuous, loose, wanton, licentious, lascivious, lecherous.
– OPPOSITES frugal, moral.

profound adjective ❶ a profound thinker: DEEP, weighty, serious, learned, discerning, penetrating, thoughtful, philosophical, erudite, wise, sagacious. ❷ a profound love: DEEP, intense, keen, great, extreme, sincere, heartfelt. ❸ profound changes: FAR-REACHING, radical, extensive, exhaustive, thoroughgoing.
– OPPOSITES shallow, superficial.

profuse adjective ❶ profuse apologies: LAVISH, liberal, unstinting, generous, fulsome, extravagant, inordinate, immoderate, excessive. ❷ profuse vegetation: ABUNDANT, copious, ample, plentiful, bountiful, luxuriant.
– OPPOSITES meagre.

programme noun ❶ AGENDA, calendar, schedule, syllabus, list of events, order of the day. ❷ PRODUCTION, presentation, show, performance, broadcast. ❸ SYLLABUS, prospectus, schedule, list, curriculum, literature.

progress noun ❶ FORWARD MOVEMENT, headway, advance, going, passage, advancement, progression. ❷ PROGRESSION, improvement, betterment, upgrading, development, growth.
▶ **verb** ❶ GO FORWARD, move forward/on, make one's way, advance, go on, continue, proceed, push forward, forge ahead. ❷ MAKE PROGRESS, get better, improve, recover, recuperate.
– OPPOSITES regress.

progressive adjective
❶ progressive improvement: INCREASING, growing, intensifying, accelerating, escalating.
❷ progressive ideas: MODERN, advanced, radical, reforming, innovative, revolutionary, forward-looking, enlightened, avant-garde; *informal* go-ahead.
– OPPOSITES conservative.

prohibit verb ❶ FORBID, ban, bar, disallow, proscribe, veto, interdict, outlaw. ❷ PREVENT, stop, rule out, preclude, make impossible, hinder, impede, hamper, obstruct, restrict, constrain.
– OPPOSITES allow.

prohibitive adjective EXORBITANT, steep, extortionate, excessive, preposterous, high-priced, high-cost, sky-high.

project noun SCHEME, plan, programme, enterprise, undertaking, venture, activity, operation, campaign.
▶ **verb** ❶ PLAN, propose, map out, devise, design, outline. ❷ LAUNCH,

discharge, propel, hurl, throw, cast, fling, shoot. ❸ JUT OUT, protrude, extend, stick out, stand out, hang over, obtrude.

proliferate verb INCREASE, multiply, extend, expand, burgeon, accelerate, escalate, rocket, snowball, mushroom.
– OPPOSITES decrease.

prolix adjective OVERLONG, lengthy, long-winded, prolonged, protracted, verbose, wordy, pleonastic, discursive, digressive, rambling, wandering, circuitous.

prolong verb LENGTHEN, make longer, elongate, extend, stretch out, draw out, drag out, protract, spin out.

prominent adjective ❶ prominent cheekbones: PROTRUDING, protuberant, jutting, projecting, standing out, bulging. ❷ a prominent feature: CONSPICUOUS, noticeable, obvious, unmistakable, obtrusive, eye-catching, striking. ❸ a prominent person: EMINENT, important, pre-eminent, distinguished, notable, noted, illustrious, celebrated, well known, famous, renowned, leading.
– OPPOSITES inconspicuous.

promiscuous adjective DISSOLUTE, dissipated, fast, licentious, loose, profligate, abandoned, immoral, debauched, wanton, of easy virtue, unchaste.
– OPPOSITES chaste.

promise verb ❶ GIVE ONE'S WORD, give an undertaking, give one's assurance, swear, vow, pledge, contract. ❷ AUGUR, indicate, denote, signify, be a sign of, show signs of, suggest, betoken, presage.
▶ noun ❶ WORD, undertaking, assurance, guarantee, commitment, vow, oath, pledge, bond, contract, covenant. ❷ a musician of promise: POTENTIAL, flair, talent, ability, aptitude, capability, capacity.

promising adjective ENCOURAGING, hopeful, favourable, auspicious, propitious, optimistic, bright.
– OPPOSITES unfavourable, hopeless.

promontory noun HEADLAND, point, cape, foreland, bluff, cliff, precipice, overhang, height, projection, prominence.

promote verb ❶ ELEVATE, advance, move up, upgrade, prefer, aggrandize. ❷ promote the cause of peace: ADVANCE, further, assist, aid, help, contribute to, foster, boost. ❸ promoting their products: ADVERTISE, publicize, push, puff, beat the drum for; *informal* plug, give a plug to, hype.
– OPPOSITES demote, obstruct.

promotion noun ❶ UPGRADING, elevation, advancement, preferment, aggrandizement. ❷ ADVANCEMENT, furtherance, furthering, assistance, aid, help, contribution to, fostering, boosting. ❸ ADVERTISING, publicity, hard sell, puff, puffing; *informal* plug, hype, hyping.

prompt adjective ❶ a prompt reply: IMMEDIATE, instant, instantaneous, swift, rapid, speedy, quick, fast, expeditious, early, punctual, in good time, timely. ❷ prompt to help: SWIFT, rapid, speedy, quick, fast, ready, willing, eager.
– OPPOSITES slow.
▶ verb ❶ CAUSE, make, encourage, move, induce, urge, incite, impel, spur on, motivate, stimulate,

inspire, provoke. ❷ REMIND, jog someone's memory, refresh someone's memory, cue, help out.

promulgate verb MAKE KNOWN, make public, publicize, announce, spread, communicate, disseminate, circulate, broadcast.

pronounce verb ❶ ENUNCIATE, articulate, say, utter, sound, voice, vocalize. ❷ ANNOUNCE, declare, proclaim, assert, affirm, rule, decree.

pronounced adjective ❶ MARKED, noticeable, obvious, evident, conspicuous, striking, distinct, unmistakable. ❷ have pronounced views: DECIDED, definite, clear, strong, positive, distinct.
– OPPOSITES slight.

pronunciation noun ENUNCIATION, articulation, saying, uttering, utterance, sounding, voicing, vocalization.

proof noun EVIDENCE, demonstration, substantiation, corroboration, confirmation, attestation, testimony, certification, verification, authentication, validation.
▶ adjective IMPERVIOUS, impenetrable, resistant, repellent.

prop noun SUPPORT, upright, brace, buttress, stay, bolster, stanchion, truss, column, post, rod, pole, shaft.
▶ verb LEAN, rest, set, lay, stand, balance, steady.
■ **prop up** HOLD UP, shore up, bolster up, buttress, support, brace, underpin, reinforce, strengthen.

propaganda noun PUBLICITY MATERIAL, publicity, promotion, advertising, advertisement, information, agitprop.

propagate verb ❶ GROW, breed, multiply, reproduce. ❷ SPREAD, communicate, circulate, disseminate, transmit, distribute, broadcast, publish, publicize, proclaim, promulgate.

propel verb MOVE, set in motion, push forward, drive, thrust forward, force, impel.

propensity noun *see* PROCLIVITY.

proper adjective ❶ the proper equipment: RIGHT, suitable, fitting, appropriate, apt. ❷ the proper way to do it: RIGHT, correct, precise, accepted, established, orthodox, conventional, formal. ❸ their proper place: RIGHT, correct, own, individual, particular, respective, special, specific. ❹ a very proper upbringing: SEEMLY, decorous, respectable, decent, refined, genteel, formal, conventional, orthodox, strict, punctilious, sedate.
– OPPOSITES improper.

property noun ❶ POSSESSIONS, belongings, things, goods, effects, chattels, assets, resources. ❷ REAL ESTATE, buildings, land. ❸ healing properties: QUALITY, attribute, characteristic, feature, power, peculiarity, idiosyncrasy, quirk.

prophecy noun PREDICTION, forecast, prognostication, divination, augury.

prophesy verb PREDICT, foretell, forecast, foresee, forewarn of, presage, prognosticate, divine, augur.

prophet noun SEER, soothsayer, diviner, clairvoyant, prophesier, oracle, augur, sibyl, Cassandra.

prophylactic adjective PREVENTIVE, preventative, precautionary, protective, disease-preventing.

propitious adjective AUSPICIOUS, favourable, promising, optimistic, bright, advantageous, fortunate, lucky, happy, rosy, beneficial, opportune, suitable, timely.
– OPPOSITES inauspicious.

proponent noun ADVOCATE, supporter, upholder, adherent, backer, promoter, endorser, champion, sponsor, espouser.

proportion noun ❶ RATIO, distribution, relative amount/number, relationship. ❷ PORTION, part, segment, share, quota, division, percentage, fraction, measure; *informal* cut. ❸ the proportions of the room: BALANCE, symmetry, harmony, correspondence, congruity, agreement.

proportional adjective PROPORTIONATE, corresponding, commensurate, equivalent, comparable.
– OPPOSITES disproportionate.

proposal noun SCHEME, plan, project, programme, motion, bid, proposition, presentation, suggestion, recommendation, tender, terms.

propose verb ❶ PUT FORWARD, advance, offer, proffer, present, submit, tender, propound, suggest, recommend, advocate. ❷ INTEND, mean, plan, have in mind, aim, purpose. ❸ NOMINATE, name, put forward, put up, suggest, recommend.

proprieties plural noun ETIQUETTE, social niceties, protocol, civilities, formalities, rules of conduct, accepted behaviour, good manners, good form, the done thing, punctilio.

proprietor noun OWNER, possessor, title-holder, deed-holder, landowner, landlord/landlady.

prosaic adjective UNIMAGINATIVE, ordinary, uninspired, commonplace, dull, tedious, boring, dry, humdrum, mundane, pedestrian, lifeless, spiritless, stale, bland, vapid, banal, hackneyed, trite, insipid, monotonous, flat.
– OPPOSITES imaginative.

prosecute verb ❶ CHARGE, prefer charges against, bring an action against, try, bring to trial, put on trial, sue, bring a suit against, interdict, arraign. ❷ CARRY ON, conduct, direct, engage in, work at, proceed with, continue with.

prospect noun ❶ LIKELIHOOD, likeliness, hope, expectation, anticipation, chance, chances, odds, probability, possibility. ❷ VIEW, vista, outlook, perspective, panorama, scene, spectacle.
▶ verb EXPLORE, search, inspect, survey, examine, check out.

prospective adjective FUTURE, to-be, soon-to-be, intended, expected, would-be, potential, possible, likely, hoped for, looked for, awaited, anticipated.

prospects plural noun POTENTIAL, promise, possibilities, expectations, scope.

prosper verb DO WELL, get on well, thrive, flourish, be successful, succeed, get ahead, progress, advance, get on in the world, make headway, make good, become rich, be in clover.
– OPPOSITES fail.

prosperity noun AFFLUENCE, wealth, riches, prosperousness, success, good fortune, ease,

plenty, the good life, luxury.
– OPPOSITES hardship.

prosperous adjective WELL OFF, well-to-do, affluent, wealthy, rich, successful, moneyed, opulent, in clover; *informal* well heeled, in the money, on Easy Street.
– OPPOSITES poor.

prostitute noun CALL GIRL, whore; *informal* tart, pro, working girl, member of the oldest profession; *Brit. informal* tom; *N. Amer. informal* hooker, hustler; *dated* loose woman, woman of ill repute, streetwalker, woman of the streets, fallen woman; *archaic* courtesan, strumpet, harlot, trollop, wench.

prostrate adjective PRONE, lying down, flat, stretched out, horizontal, procumbent.
▶ verb KNOCK FLAT, flatten, knock down, floor, level.

protean adjective EVER-CHANGING, variable, changeable, mutable, kaleidoscopic, mercurial, volatile, labile, versatile.
– OPPOSITES constant.

protect verb ❶ KEEP SAFE, save, safeguard, shield, preserve, defend, shelter, secure. ❷ GUARD, mount/stand guard on, defend, secure, watch over, look after, take care of.
– OPPOSITES endanger.

protection noun ❶ SAFE KEEPING, safety, care, charge, keeping, preservation, defence, security. ❷ SAFEGUARD, shield, barrier, buffer, screen, cover.

protective adjective ❶ PROTECTING, safeguarding, shielding, covering. ❷ CAREFUL, watchful, vigilant, paternal/maternal, fatherly/motherly, overprotective, possessive, clinging.

protector noun DEFENDER, champion, bodyguard, guardian, guardian angel.

protest verb ❶ OBJECT TO, raise objections to, oppose, take issue about/on/over, make/take a stand against, put up a fight against, take exception to, complain about, demur at, remonstrate about, make a fuss about, demonstrate against; *informal* kick up a fuss about, beef about, bitch about. ❷ **protest their innocence**: DECLARE, announce, profess, proclaim, assert, affirm, argue, attest, maintain, insist on, avow; *formal* aver.
▶ noun OBJECTION, opposition, exception, complaint, disapproval, disagreement, dissent, demurral, remonstration, fuss, outcry, demonstration, protestation.

protocol noun ETIQUETTE, rules of conduct, code of behaviour, conventions, formalities, customs, propriety, proprieties, decorum, manners, courtesies, civilities, good form, politesse.

protract verb PROLONG, extend, stretch out, draw out, lengthen, make longer, drag out, spin out, keep going, continue.
– OPPOSITES curtail, shorten.

protuberant adjective BULGING, swelling, swollen, jutting, jutting out, protruding, protrusive, prominent, bulbous, gibbous.
– OPPOSITES sunken.

proud adjective ❶ **proud parents**: PLEASED, glad, happy, satisfied, gratified, content, appreciative. ❷ ARROGANT, conceited, vain, self-important, egotistical, boastful, haughty, disdainful, scornful, supercilious, snobbish, imperious, overbearing,

overweening, high-handed; *informal* high and mighty, stuck up, snooty, toffee-nosed. ❸ a proud day: GRATIFYING, satisfying, happy, memorable, notable, red-letter, glorious, marvellous.
– OPPOSITES ashamed, humble.

prove verb ESTABLISH, determine, demonstrate, show beyond doubt, substantiate, corroborate, verify, validate, authenticate, confirm.
– OPPOSITES disprove.

proverb noun SAYING, adage, maxim, saw, axiom, aphorism, dictum, apophthegm.

proverbial adjective LEGENDARY, notorious, infamous, famous, famed, renowned, well known, acknowledged, accepted, traditional, time-honoured.

provide verb ❶ SUPPLY, furnish, equip, accommodate, provision, outfit. ❷ provide scope: GIVE, bring, afford, present, offer, accord, yield, impart, lend.
■ **provide for** SUPPORT, maintain, keep, sustain, take care of, care for, look after.

provided conjunction PROVIDING THAT, on condition that, if, as long as, given, with the provision/proviso that, contingent upon, on the assumption that.

provident adjective FAR-SIGHTED, prudent, judicious, shrewd, cautious, careful, thrifty, canny, economical, frugal.

provincial adjective ❶ LOCAL, small-town, rural, country. ❷ UNSOPHISTICATED, parochial, limited, small-minded, insular, inward-looking, illiberal, narrow, narrow-minded, inflexible, bigoted, prejudiced, intolerant.
– OPPOSITES metropolitan, sophisticated.

provisional adjective PROVISORY, temporary, interim, stopgap, transitional, to be confirmed, conditional, tentative, contingent, pro tem.
– OPPOSITES permanent.

provisions plural noun SUPPLIES, stores, groceries, food and drink, foodstuffs, staples, rations, provender, eatables, edibles, comestibles; *poetic/literary* viands; *dated* victuals.

proviso noun CONDITION, stipulation, provision, clause, rider, qualification, restriction, reservation, limitation.

provocative adjective ❶ PROVOKING, annoying, irritating, exasperating, infuriating, maddening, vexing, galling, affronting, insulting, inflaming, goading; *informal* aggravating. ❷ a provocative dress: SEDUCTIVE, sexy, tempting, suggestive, arousing, exciting, alluring, erotic, titillating.

provoke verb ❶ ANNOY, anger, incense, enrage, irritate, exasperate, infuriate, madden, pique, nettle, vex, harass, irk, gall, affront, insult; *informal* make someone's blood boil, aggravate. ❷ INCITE, rouse, stir, move, stimulate, motivate, excite, inflame, prompt, induce, spur, goad, prod, egg on.
– OPPOSITES allay, pacify.

prowess noun SKILL, skilfulness, expertise, facility, ability, capability, talent, genius, adroitness, adeptness, aptitude, competence, proficiency; *informal* know-how.

prowl verb ROAM, range, move stealthily, slink, skulk, steal, sneak, stalk.

proxy noun REPRESENTATIVE,

deputy, substitute, agent, delegate, surrogate.

prudent adjective ❶ a prudent decision: WISE, well judged, judicious, sagacious, sage, shrewd, sensible, circumspect, far-sighted, politic. ❷ a prudent person: CAUTIOUS, careful, discreet, wary, vigilant, heedful, thrifty, economical, canny, sparing, frugal, provident.
– OPPOSITES imprudent.

prudish adjective PRIGGISH, prim, strait-laced, prissy, puritan, puritanical, stuffy, starchy, Victorian, Grundyish, old-maid, old-maidish, schoolmarmish; *informal* goody-goody.
– OPPOSITES permissive.

prune verb CUT, lop, chop, clip, snip, remove.

pry verb BE INQUISITIVE, interfere, meddle, intrude, be nosy, be a busybody; *informal* stick/poke one's nose in, stick one's oar in, snoop; *Austral./NZ informal* stickybeak.

pseudonym noun ASSUMED NAME, alias, false name, nom de plume, pen-name, stage name, professional name, sobriquet, nickname, nom de guerre.

psych
■ **psych out** UNSETTLE, upset, agitate, disturb, make nervous, put off, put off balance, put someone off their stroke, intimidate, frighten. **psych oneself up** STEEL ONESELF, prepare, get ready, gird one's loins, get in the mood, get in the right frame of mind.

psychological adjective MENTAL, of the mind, cerebral, psychic, psychical.

pub noun BAR, tavern, inn; *Brit.* public house; *Brit. informal* local, boozer.

puberty noun PUBESCENCE, adolescence, young adulthood, teenage years, teens.

public adjective ❶ public awareness: POPULAR, general, common, universal, widespread. ❷ make his views public: KNOWN, widely known, acknowledged, overt, in circulation, published, publicized, plain, obvious. ❸ public figures: PROMINENT, well known, important, eminent, respected, influential, prestigious, famous.
– OPPOSITES private.
▶ noun PEOPLE, population, country, nation, community, citizens, populace, the masses, the multitude, the mob, the hoi polloi.

publication noun ❶ PUBLISHING, production, issuing, issuance. ❷ BOOK, newspaper, magazine, periodical, journal, daily, weekly, monthly, quarterly, booklet, brochure, leaflet, pamphlet, handbill.

publicize verb ❶ MAKE PUBLIC, make known, announce, publish, broadcast, distribute, disseminate, promulgate. ❷ GIVE PUBLICITY TO, promote, advertise, puff, puff up, push, beat the drum for; *informal* hype, plug.
– OPPOSITES conceal.

publish verb ❶ PRODUCE, issue, print, bring out. ❷ *See* PUBLICIZE (1).

pucker verb SCREW UP, wrinkle, crease, furrow, knit, crinkle, corrugate.

puerile adjective CHILDISH, immature, infantile, juvenile, adolescent, foolish, silly, inane, asinine.
– OPPOSITES mature.

puff noun GUST, blast, whiff, breath, flurry, draught.

▶ **verb** ❶ PANT, blow, gasp, gulp. ❷ SWELL, distend, inflate, dilate, bloat. ❸ *See* PUBLICIZE (2).

pugnacious **adjective** BELLIGERENT, bellicose, combative, aggressive, antagonistic, argumentative, disputatious, hostile, threatening, irascible, ill-tempered, bad-tempered.
– OPPOSITES peaceable.

pull **verb** ❶ HAUL, drag, draw, trail, tow, tug. ❷ **pull a muscle:** STRAIN, sprain, wrench, stretch, tear, dislocate, damage.
– OPPOSITES push.
■ **pull back** WITHDRAW, retreat, draw back, fall back. **pull down** KNOCK DOWN, demolish, raze, level, destroy, bulldoze. **pull off** ACCOMPLISH, execute, succeed in. **pull oneself together** REGAIN ONE'S COMPOSURE/CALM, get a grip on oneself; *informal* snap out of it. **pull out** WITHDRAW, retreat from, leave, abandon, give up, quit. **pull someone's leg** TEASE, make fun of, poke fun at.

pulp **noun** PURÉE, mush, mash, pap, triturate.
▶ **verb** CRUSH, squash, mash, purée, pulverize, triturate.

pulsate **verb** BEAT, throb, vibrate, pulse, palpitate, pound, thud, thump, drum.

pulse **noun** BEAT, rhythm, throb, throbbing, vibration, pulsation, pounding, thud, thumping, thump, drumming.
▶ **verb** *see* PULSATE.

pump **verb** ❶ DRIVE, force, push, send. ❷ QUESTION, quiz, interrogate, cross-examine; *informal* grill.

punch **verb** STRIKE, hit, knock, thump, thwack, box, jab, cuff, slug, smash, slam, batter, pound, pummel; *informal* sock, biff, bash, bop, wallop, whack, clout.

punctilious **adjective** CAREFUL, scrupulous, meticulous, conscientious, exact, precise, particular, strict, nice, finicky, fussy.
– OPPOSITES careless.

punctual **adjective** ON TIME, on the dot, prompt, in good time, when expected, timely, well timed.
– OPPOSITES late.

puncture **noun** HOLE, perforation, flat, prick, rupture, cut, nick, slit, leak.
▶ **verb** MAKE A HOLE IN, hole, perforate, pierce, bore, prick, penetrate, rupture, cut, nick, slit.

pungent **adjective** ❶ **a pungent smell:** SHARP, acrid, acid, sour, biting, stinging, burning. ❷ **a pungent taste:** SHARP, acid, sour, biting, bitter, tart, tangy, spicy, highly flavoured, aromatic, piquant, peppery, hot, fiery. ❸ **pungent remarks:** CAUSTIC, acid, biting, cutting, sharp, incisive, scathing, pointed, acrimonious, trenchant, mordant, stringent.
– OPPOSITES bland, mild.

punish **verb** ❶ DISCIPLINE, teach someone a lesson, penalize, chastise, smack, slap, beat, cane, whip, flog, lash, scourge; *formal* castigate. ❷ MALTREAT, mistreat, abuse, manhandle, damage, harm.

punishing **adjective** ARDUOUS, demanding, taxing, strenuous, hard, exhausting, fatiguing, wearing, tiring, gruelling, uphill, back-breaking.

punitive **adjective** ❶ PENAL, DISCIPLINARY, corrective, correctional. ❷ **punitive taxation:** HARSH, severe, stiff, cruel, savage.

puny **adjective** WEAK, weakly, frail,

feeble, undersized, underdeveloped, stunted, small, slight, little.
– OPPOSITES strong.

pupil noun SCHOOLBOY/GIRL, schoolchild, scholar, student.

puppet noun ❶ MARIONETTE, string puppet, glove puppet, finger puppet. ❷ TOOL, instrument, cat's-paw, pawn, creature, dupe, mouthpiece; *Brit. informal* poodle.

purchase verb *see* BUY.
▶ noun ❶ ACQUISITION, order, investment; *informal* buy. ❷ GRIP, hold, foothold, footing, toehold, support, grasp, leverage.

pure adjective ❶ **pure gold**: UNALLOYED, unmixed, unadulterated, uncontaminated, flawless, perfect, genuine, real, true. ❷ **pure air**: CLEAN, clear, fresh, unpolluted, untainted, unadulterated, uncontaminated, uninfected, wholesome, natural. ❸ VIRGINAL, chaste, maidenly, virtuous, undefiled, unsullied. ❹ **a pure character**: STAINLESS, spotless, unsullied, unblemished, impeccable, immaculate, blameless, sinless. ❺ **pure madness**: SHEER, utter, absolute, downright, out-and-out, complete, total, perfect, unmitigated, unqualified.
– OPPOSITES adulterated, polluted, immoral.

purely adverb ENTIRELY, completely, totally, wholly, solely, only, simply, just, merely.

purge verb ❶ CLEANSE, clear, purify, make pure. ❷ **purge dissidents**: REMOVE, clear out, expel, eject, dismiss, oust, depose, eradicate, root out, weed out.

purify verb MAKE PURE, clean, cleanse, decontaminate, filter, refine, disinfect, sterilize, sanitize, fumigate.
– OPPOSITES contaminate.

puritanical adjective PRUDISH, prim, priggish, prissy, puritan, ascetic, austere, strait-laced, narrow-minded, rigid, stiff.
– OPPOSITES broad-minded.

purpose noun ❶ REASON, point, basis, motivation, cause, justification. ❷ AIM, intention, object, objective, goal, end, target, ambition, aspiration, desire, wish, hope. ❸ **he lacks purpose**: DETERMINATION, resolution, resolve, firmness, steadfastness, single-mindedness, persistence, perseverance, tenacity, doggedness.
▶ verb *see* INTEND (1).

purposeful adjective DETERMINED, resolute, resolved, firm, steadfast, single-minded, persistent, tenacious, dogged, unfaltering, unwavering.
– OPPOSITES aimless.

purposely adverb ON PURPOSE, intentionally, deliberately, by design, wilfully, wittingly, knowingly, consciously.

pursue verb ❶ GO AFTER, run after, follow, chase, hunt, stalk, track, trail, shadow; *informal* tail. ❷ FOLLOW, go on with, proceed with, keep/carry on with, continue with, continue, persist in. ❸ **pursue a career**: FOLLOW, engage in, work at, practise, prosecute, apply oneself to.

purvey verb PROVIDE, supply, furnish, sell, retail, deal in.

push verb ❶ SHOVE, thrust, propel, drive, ram, jolt, butt, jostle. ❷ **push the bell**: PRESS, depress, exert pressure on. ❸ **push him into it**: PRESS, urge, egg on, spur on,

prod, goad, incite, impel, dragoon, force, coerce, constrain, browbeat, strong-arm.
❹ PROMOTE, advertise, publicize, puff, puff up, boost, beat the drum for; *informal* plug, hype.
■ **push around** BULLY, ride roughshod over, browbeat, tyrannize, intimidate, domineer.

pushy **adjective** ASSERTIVE, self-assertive, aggressive, forceful, forward, bold, brash, bumptious, presumptuous, cocksure, loud, obnoxious.
– OPPOSITES submissive.

put **verb** ❶ PLACE, lay, set down, deposit, position, rest, stand, locate, situate, settle, install.
❷ **put the blame:** PLACE, attribute to, impute to, impose, fix, assign to, allocate to, lay, pin. ❸ **put it to the committee:** SET BEFORE, lay before, present, bring forward, forward, submit, tender, offer, proffer, put forward, set forth, advance.
■ **put about** SPREAD, bandy about, circulate, disseminate, make public, make known, give out, publicize, broadcast, propagate, announce, bruit. **put away** IMPRISON, confine, lock up, shut away/up. **put down** ❶ PUT TO SLEEP, put out of its misery, destroy, do away with, kill.
❷ SNUB, disparage, deprecate, belittle, denigrate, deflate, slight, humiliate, crush, mortify. **put it on** PRETEND, play-act, make believe, exaggerate. **put out** ❶ INCONVENIENCE, trouble, bother, impose upon, discommode, incommode. ❷ EXTINGUISH, quench, douse, stamp out.

putative **adjective** SUPPOSED, assumed, presumed, presumptive, alleged, reputed.

put-down **noun** SNUB, rebuff, slight, disparagement, sneer, humiliation.

puzzle **verb** PERPLEX, baffle, stump, beat, mystify, confuse, bewilder, nonplus, stagger, dumbfound, daze, confound; *informal* flummox.

puzzling **adjective** DIFFICULT, hard, unclear, perplexing, knotty, baffling, enigmatic, abstruse, mystifying, bewildering, unfathomable, inexplicable, incomprehensible, beyond one, above one's head.
– OPPOSITES clear.

Qq

quagmire **noun** ❶ BOG, marsh, quag, swamp, morass, mire, slough, fen. ❷ DIFFICULTY, quandary, dilemma, predicament, plight, tight corner, muddle.

quail **verb** FLINCH, shrink, recoil, shy away, pull back, draw back, cower, cringe, shudder, shiver, tremble, shake, quake, blench, blanch.

quake **verb** SHAKE, tremble, quiver, shiver, shudder, rock, vibrate, pulsate, throb.

qualification **noun** ❶ CERTIFICATION, training, competence, competency, accomplishment, eligibility, acceptability, suitableness, preparedness, fitness, proficiency, skilfulness, adeptness, capability, aptitude, skill, ability, attribute, endowment. ❷ MODIFICATION, limitation, restriction, reservation, stipulation, allowance, adaptation, adjustment, condition, proviso, provision, caveat.

qualified adjective ❶ TRAINED, certificated, equipped, prepared, competent, accomplished, proficient, skilled, skilful, adept, practised, experienced, expert, capable, able. ❷ **qualified approval:** MODIFIED, limited, conditional, restricted, bounded, contingent, confined, circumscribed, reserved, guarded, equivocal.

qualify verb ❶ CERTIFY, license, empower, authorize, allow, permit, sanction, warrant, fit, equip. ❷ **not qualify as poetry:** COUNT, be considered, be designated, be eligible, meet the requirements of. ❸ **qualify her statement:** MODIFY, limit, make conditional, restrict.

quality noun ❶ DEGREE OF EXCELLENCE, standard, grade, level, sort, type, kind, variety. ❷ FEATURE, trait, attribute, characteristic, aspect, property, peculiarity.

qualm noun DOUBT, misgiving, scruple, hesitation, hesitancy, reluctance, anxiety, apprehension, disquiet, uneasiness, concern.

quantity noun NUMBER, amount, total, aggregate, sum, quota, weight, capacity, mass, volume, bulk, extent, length, area.

quarrel noun ARGUMENT, fight, disagreement, difference of opinion, dispute, disputation, squabble, altercation, wrangle, misunderstanding, feud, vendetta; *informal* row, spat, scrap, tiff.
▶ verb ARGUE, have a fight, fight, dispute, squabble, bicker, spar, wrangle, have a misunderstanding, fall out; *informal* row, have a row.
– OPPOSITES agree.

quarrelsome adjective ARGUMENTATIVE, belligerent, disputatious, contentious, pugnacious, combative, ready for a fight, bellicose, litigious, hot-tempered, irascible, choleric, irritable.
– OPPOSITES peaceable.

quarry noun PREY, victim, prize.

quarter noun ❶ DISTRICT, area, region, part, side, neighbourhood, locality, zone. ❷ **receive no quarter:** MERCY, leniency, clemency, compassion, pity.
▶ verb PUT UP, house, board, billet, accommodate, lodge, install.

quarters plural noun ACCOMMODATION, billet, residence, habitation, lodgings, rooms, barracks; *informal* digs, pad; *formal* dwelling, abode, domicile.

quash verb ❶ **quash the sentence:** ANNUL, declare null and void, nullify, invalidate, void, cancel, overrule, override, overthrow, reject, set aside, reverse, revoke, rescind, repeal. ❷ **quash the rebellion:** CRUSH, put down, squash, quell, subdue, suppress, repress, quench, extinguish, stamp out, put a stop to, end, terminate, defeat, destroy.
– OPPOSITES validate.

quaver verb QUIVER, vibrate, tremble, shake, waver.

queasy adjective SICK, nauseated, ill, indisposed, dizzy, sick to one's stomach.

queer adjective ❶ ODD, strange, unusual, extraordinary, funny, curious, peculiar, weird, outlandish, singular, eccentric, unconventional, unorthodox, atypical, abnormal, irregular, anomalous, deviant, offbeat; *informal* off-the-wall. ❷ STRANGE, peculiar, suspicious, suspect, irregular, questionable, dubious, doubtful; *informal* fishy, shady.

quell verb ❶ quell their fears: ALLAY, lull, quiet, silence, calm, soothe, appease, assuage, abate, deaden, dull, pacify. ❷ *See* QUASH (2).

quench verb ❶ SATISFY, slake, sate, satiate. ❷ EXTINGUISH, put out, snuff out, blow out, douse.

quest noun ❶ SEARCH, seeking, pursuit, chase, hunt. ❷ ADVENTURE, expedition, journey, voyage, exploration, crusade.

question noun ❶ QUERY, enquiry, interrogation. ❷ the question of safety: ISSUE, problem, matter, point, subject, topic, theme, bone of contention.
– OPPOSITES answer.
▶ verb ❶ ASK QUESTIONS OF, interrogate, cross-examine, quiz, interview, sound out, examine; *informal* grill, pump. ❷ question his motives: CALL INTO QUESTION, query, raise doubts about, throw doubt on, have suspicions about, challenge.

questionable adjective OPEN TO QUESTION/DOUBT, doubtful, dubious, uncertain, debatable, in dispute, arguable, controversial, controvertible.
– OPPOSITES indisputable.

queue noun LINE, row, column, file, chain, string, train, succession, sequence, series, concatenation.

quibble noun CRITICISM, complaint, protest, objection, niggle, cavil, nicety.
▶ verb CAVIL, carp, pettifog, split hairs, chop logic; *informal* nit-pick.

quick adjective ❶ FAST, rapid, speedy, swift, fleet, express. ❷ a quick response: PROMPT, without delay, immediate, instantaneous, expeditious. ❸ a quick look: BRIEF, brisk, fleeting, momentary, hasty, hurried, cursory, perfunctory. ❹ she's very quick: QUICK-WITTED, sharp-witted, alert, intelligent.
– OPPOSITES slow, long.

quicken verb ❶ BECOME/GROW FASTER, speed up, accelerate, hurry, hasten. ❷ quicken his interest: *see* AROUSE.

quiet adjective ❶ the house was quiet: SILENT, hushed, noiseless, soundless, peaceful. ❷ a quiet voice: SOFT, low, inaudible. ❸ a quiet person: CALM, serene, composed, placid, tranquil, gentle, mild, temperate, unexcitable, phlegmatic, reserved, uncommunicative, taciturn, silent. ❹ a quiet village: PEACEFUL, sleepy, undisturbed, unfrequented, secluded, isolated, out of the way, off the beaten track. ❺ business is quiet: INACTIVE, not busy, sluggish.
– OPPOSITES noisy.

quieten verb ❶ SILENCE, hush, shush, quiet; *informal* shut up. ❷ quieten their fears: ALLAY, soothe, calm, appease, lull, pacify, mollify, palliate.

quintessence noun ESSENCE, core, heart, soul, spirit; *Philosophy* quiddity.

quit verb ❶ **quit smoking:** GIVE UP, stop, cease, leave off, abandon, abstain from, desist from. ❷ **quit his job:** LEAVE, depart from, vacate, walk out on.

quite adverb ❶ **he has quite recovered:** COMPLETELY, fully, entirely, totally, wholly, absolutely, in all respects. ❷ **he is quite talented:** FAIRLY, relatively, moderately, reasonably, to some extent/degree, rather, somewhat.

quiver verb TREMBLE, shiver, vibrate, quaver, quake, shudder, pulsate, convulse, palpitate.

quizzical adjective QUESTIONING, puzzled, perplexed, baffled, mystified, mocking, teasing.

quota noun SHARE, allowance, allocation, portion, ration, part, slice, measure, proportion; *informal* cut; *Brit. informal* whack.

quotation noun ❶ CITATION, reference, quote, allusion, excerpt, extract, selection, passage, line. ❷ ESTIMATE, estimated price, quote, cost, charge, figure.

quote verb ❶ REPEAT, iterate, recite, reproduce. ❷ CITE, give, name, instance, mention, refer to, make reference to, allude to. ❸ ESTIMATE FOR, price, set a price for.

Rr

rabble noun MOB, horde, swarm, crowd, throng.

race[1] noun ❶ CONTEST, competition, chase, pursuit, relay. ❷ CHANNEL, waterway, watercourse, sluice, spillway.
▶ verb ❶ RUN AGAINST, compete against, be pitted against. ❷ RUN, sprint, dash, dart, bolt, speed, hare, fly, tear, zoom, accelerate, career.

race[2] noun ETHNIC GROUP, people, bloodline, stock, line, lineage, breed, strain.

racial adjective RACE-RELATED, ethnic, ethnological.

racism noun RACIALISM, racial discrimination, racial prejudice/bigotry, chauvinism, xenophobia.

racist noun RACIALIST, bigot.
▶ adjective RACIALIST, discriminatory, prejudiced, bigoted, intolerant, illiberal.

rack noun FRAME, framework, stand, form, trestle, structure, holder, shelf.

racket noun NOISE, din, row, commotion, disturbance, uproar, hubbub, hullabaloo, clamour, pandemonium, tumult.

radiant adjective ❶ SHINING, bright, illuminated, brilliant, luminous, luminescent, lustrous. ❷ JOYFUL, happy, elated, ecstatic, delighted, pleased. *See also* HAPPY (1).
– OPPOSITES dark, gloomy.

radiate verb SEND OUT/FORTH, give off/out, emit, emanate, scatter, disperse, diffuse, spread, shed.

radical adjective ❶ FUNDAMENTAL, basic, rudimentary, elementary, elemental, constitutional. ❷ radical change: THOROUGH, complete, total, entire, absolute, utter, comprehensive, exhaustive, sweeping, far-reaching, profound, drastic. ❸ radical views: EXTREMIST, extreme, immoderate, revolutionary, rebel, rebellious, militant.
– OPPOSITES superficial, moderate.

raffle noun LOTTERY, draw, sweepstake, sweep, tombola.

rage noun FURY, anger, wrath, high dudgeon, frenzy, madness; *poetic/literary* ire.
▶ verb BE FURIOUS, be infuriated, be angry, seethe, be beside oneself, lose one's temper, boil over, rant, rave, storm, fume, fulminate; *informal* blow one's top, flip one's lid, freak out.

ragged adjective ❶ TATTERED, threadbare, frayed, the worse for wear, torn, rent, in holes, worn to shreds, falling to pieces. ❷ a ragged coastline: JAGGED, uneven, irregular, notched, serrated, saw-toothed, craggy.
– OPPOSITES smart.

raid noun SURPRISE ATTACK, assault, onslaught, invasion, incursion, thrust, sortie, sally.
▶ verb ❶ ATTACK, assault, invade, assail, storm, rush, set upon, descend upon, swoop upon. ❷ PLUNDER, pillage, loot, rifle, forage, ransack, steal from.

rail
■ **rail against** INVEIGH AGAINST, rage against, protest strongly, complain bitterly, criticize severely, censure, condemn, lambaste.

rain noun RAINFALL, precipitation, raindrops, drizzle, shower, rainstorm, cloudburst, torrent, downpour, deluge.
▶ verb POUR, pour/come down, precipitate; *informal* rain cats and dogs, come down in buckets.

rainy adjective WET, showery, drizzly, damp.

raise verb ❶ LIFT, lift up, raise aloft, elevate, uplift, upthrust, hoist, heave up. ❷ raise the cost: INCREASE, put up, escalate, inflate; *informal* step up, hike, jack up. ❸ raise the temperature: INCREASE, heighten, augment, amplify, intensify; *informal* step up. ❹ raise a statue: CONSTRUCT, build, erect, put up. ❺ raise an army: GET/GATHER TOGETHER, collect, assemble, muster, levy, accumulate, amass. ❻ raise objections: PUT FORWARD, introduce, advance, bring up, suggest, present, moot, broach. ❼ raise doubts: CAUSE, engender, create, kindle, arouse, awaken, excite, summon up, provoke, activate, evoke, incite. ❽ raise children: BRING UP, rear, nurture, educate.
– OPPOSITES lower.

rally verb ❶ COME/GET TOGETHER, assemble, group, band together, convene, unite. ❷ CALL/BRING TOGETHER, assemble, summon, round up, muster, marshall, mobilize. ❸ RECOVER, recuperate, revive, get better/well, improve, perk up.
▶ noun MEETING, gathering, assembly, convention, convocation.

ram verb ❶ FORCE, cram, stuff, compress, jam, squeeze, thrust, tamp. ❷ STRIKE, hit, run into, crash into, collide with, bump, slam.

ramble verb ❶ WALK, hike,

wander, stroll, amble, roam, range, rove, traipse. ❷ DIGRESS, wander, gabble; *informal* rattle on; *Brit. informal* rabbit on, witter on.

rambling adjective ❶ DIGRESSIVE, wandering, roundabout, circuitous, periphrastic, disconnected, disjointed, maundering, long-winded, verbose, wordy, prolix.
❷ SPRAWLING, spreading, unsystematic, straggling.
– OPPOSITES concise.

ramification noun CONSEQUENCE, aftermath, outcome, result, upshot, issue, sequel, complication, implication.

ramp noun SLOPE, incline, gradient, acclivity, rise.

rampage verb RUN RIOT, run amok, charge, tear, storm, go berserk.
▶ noun UPROAR, furore, mayhem, turmoil.

rampant adjective OUT OF CONTROL/HAND, unrestrained, unchecked, unbridled, widespread, pandemic, epidemic.
– OPPOSITES controlled.

rancorous adjective RESENTFUL, malicious, spiteful, hateful, malevolent, malignant, antipathetic, hostile, acrimonious, venomous, vindictive.

random adjective HAPHAZARD, chance, accidental, fortuitous, serendipitous, adventitious, arbitrary, hit-or-miss, indiscriminate, sporadic, stray, spot, casual, unsystematic, unmethodical, disorganized, unplanned.
– OPPOSITES systematic.

range noun ❶ SCOPE, compass, limits, bounds, confines, radius, span, scale, gamut, reach, sweep, extent, area, field, orbit, province, domain, latitude. ❷ ASSORTMENT, variety, kind, sort, type, class, rank, order, genus, species.
▶ verb ❶ EXTEND, stretch, reach, cover, go, run, pass, fluctuate between, vary between. ❷ ROAM, rove, ramble, traverse, travel over, wander, meander, amble, stroll, stray, drift.

rank[1] noun ❶ GRADE, level, echelon, stratum, class, status, position, station. ❷ NOBILITY, aristocracy, eminence, distinction. ❸ **break rank**: ARRAY, alignment, order, arrangement, organization.
▶ verb ❶ CLASSIFY, class, categorize, grade. ❷ HAVE A RANK, be graded, be placed, be positioned.

rank[2] adjective ❶ **rank vegetation**: *see* LUSH (1). ❷ **a rank smell**: *see* FOUL adjective (2).

rankle verb FESTER, annoy, anger, irk, vex, irritate, rile, chafe, gall, embitter; *informal* get someone's goat.

ransack verb ❶ *See* PLUNDER verb. ❷ *See* SEARCH verb (1).

rapacious adjective GRASPING, acquisitive, greedy, avaricious, covetous, insatiable, predatory, usurious.
– OPPOSITES generous.

rapid adjective QUICK, fast, swift, speedy, fleet, hurried, hasty, expeditious, express, brisk, lively, prompt, precipitate.
– OPPOSITES slow.

rapport noun AFFINITY, bond, empathy, sympathy, understanding.

rapture noun JOY, ecstasy, elation, exaltation, exhilaration, bliss, euphoria, rhapsody, enchantment, delight.

rare adjective ❶ **a rare specimen**:

UNUSUAL, uncommon, out of the ordinary, exceptional, atypical, singular, remarkable, unique. ❷ **a rare appearance:** INFREQUENT, few and far between, scarce, sparse, sporadic, scattered.
– OPPOSITES common.

rascal noun ❶ IMP, scamp, scallywag, mischief-maker, little devil. ❷ SCOUNDREL, rogue, ne'er-do-well, good-for-nothing, wastrel, reprobate; *dated* cad; *informal* creep, rat; *informal, dated* rotter; *archaic* blackguard.

rash adjective ❶ **a rash woman:** RECKLESS, impetuous, hasty, impulsive, bold, madcap, audacious, brash, daredevil, foolhardy, harum-scarum, devil-may-care, headstrong, hot-headed, incautious, careless, heedless, thoughtless, imprudent. ❷ **a rash act:** RECKLESS, impetuous, hasty, impulsive, incautious, careless, unthinking, foolish, imprudent, injudicious, hare-brained, unwary.
– OPPOSITES prudent.

rate noun ❶ PERCENTAGE, ratio, proportion, scale, degree, standard. ❷ PACE, stride, gait, motion, speed, tempo, velocity, measure.
▶ verb ❶ JUDGE, assess, appraise, evaluate, value, measure, weigh up, grade, rank, adjudge. ❷ REGARD AS, consider, deem, reckon, account.

rather adverb ❶ **would rather:** SOONER, preferably, more readily. ❷ **he is rather silly:** QUITE, fairly, a bit, a little, slightly, somewhat; *informal* sort of, kind of, pretty.

ratify verb CONFIRM, endorse, sign, sanction, warrant, approve, authorize, validate.
– OPPOSITES revoke.

ratio noun PROPORTION, comparative size/extent, correlation, correspondence, percentage, fraction, quotient.

ration noun ALLOWANCE, quota, allotment, portion, share, measure, part, lot, amount, helping, proportion, percentage.
▶ verb LIMIT, restrict, control, conserve, budget.

rational adjective SENSIBLE, reasonable, logical, sound, intelligent, wise, judicious, sagacious, prudent, circumspect, politic, astute, shrewd, perceptive, well advised, well grounded.
– OPPOSITES irrational.

rationalize verb ❶ EXPLAIN AWAY, account for, make excuses, make plausible, try to vindicate/justify. ❷ **rationalize the workforce:** STREAMLINE, trim, make cuts in, cut back on, retrench on.

rattle verb ❶ BANG, knock, rap, clatter, clang, clank, jangle, clink. ❷ DISCONCERT, disturb, fluster, upset, shake, perturb, faze, discompose, discomfit.
■ **rattle off** REEL OFF, list, recite, run through. **rattle on** GO ON, chatter, babble, gabble, prate.

raucous adjective STRIDENT, piercing, ear-splitting, shrill, screeching, harsh, sharp, grating, rasping, discordant, dissonant, jarring.
– OPPOSITES soft, quiet.

ravage verb DEVASTATE, lay waste, ruin, wreak havoc on, destroy, level, raze, demolish.

rave verb ❶ RANT AND RAVE, rage, storm, fulminate, explode in anger; *informal* fly off the handle, flip one's lid. ❷ RHAPSODIZE OVER, enthuse about, praise to the skies, gush over.

ravenous adjective STARVING, starved, famished, ravening, wolfish, voracious, insatiable, insatiate.

ravishing adjective BEAUTIFUL, lovely, stunning, gorgeous, dazzling, radiant, enchanting, bewitching, charming.
– OPPOSITES hideous.

raw adjective ❶ UNCOOKED, fresh. ❷ UNREFINED, crude, green, coarse, unprocessed, unprepared, untreated. ❸ INEXPERIENCED, untrained, unskilled, untutored, new, callow, immature, green; *informal* wet behind the ears. ❹ a raw day: COLD, chilly, freezing, bitter, biting, nippy, piercing, penetrating.
– OPPOSITES cooked, processed.

ray noun BEAM, shaft, streak, stream, gleam, glint, flash, glimmer.

raze verb TEAR/PULL DOWN, knock down, level, bulldoze, flatten, demolish, ruin, wreck.

reach verb ❶ STRETCH, extend, hold out, thrust out, stick out. ❷ reach her destination: GET AS FAR AS, get to, arrive at, come to. ❸ try to reach him: CONTACT, get in touch with, get hold of, get through to, communicate with.
▶ noun SCOPE, range, compass, latitude, ambit, orbit, sphere, area.

react verb ❶ HAVE A REACTION/RESPONSE TO, respond. ❷ BEHAVE, act, conduct oneself, proceed, operate, function, cope.

reactionary adjective ULTRA-CONSERVATIVE, conservative, obscurantist, diehard, rightist, right-wing; *Brit.* Colonel Blimp.
– OPPOSITES progressive.

read verb ❶ PERUSE, study, scan, pore over, scrutinize; *informal* wade through, dip into. ❷ INTERPRET, construe, decipher, deduce, understand, comprehend. ❸ REGISTER, record, display, show, indicate.

readable adjective ❶ LEGIBLE, easy to read, decipherable, clear, intelligible, understandable, comprehensible. ❷ ENJOYABLE, entertaining, interesting, gripping, enthralling, stimulating.
– OPPOSITES unreadable.

readily adverb ❶ WILLINGLY, gladly, happily, cheerfully, eagerly. ❷ EASILY, without difficulty, effortlessly.
– OPPOSITES reluctantly.

ready adjective ❶ dinner is ready: PREPARED, completed, finished, organized. ❷ ready to go: PREPARED, equipped, organized, all set, in a fit state; *informal* fit. ❸ a ready source of income: WITHIN REACH, available, on hand, present, near, near at hand, accessible, handy, convenient, on call, at one's fingertips; *informal* on tap. ❹ ready to collapse: ABOUT TO, on the verge/brink of, in danger of, liable to, likely to. ❺ ready for anything: PREPARED, eager, enthusiastic, anxious, keen; *informal* psyched up, geared up.

real adjective ❶ real fears: ACTUAL, existent, factual, non-fictitious. ❷ real leather: AUTHENTIC, genuine, bona fide. ❸ real feelings: SINCERE, heartfelt, earnest, fervent, unfeigned, unaffected, honest, truthful.
– OPPOSITES imaginary, false.

realistic adjective ❶ be realistic: PRACTICAL, pragmatic, rational, down-to-earth, matter-of-fact, sensible, no-nonsense,

commonsensical, level-headed, hard-headed, businesslike, hard-boiled, sober, unromantic, unsentimental, with both feet on the ground. ❷ a realistic model: LIFELIKE, true-to-life, true, faithful, close, representational, graphic, naturalistic, authentic, genuine.
– OPPOSITES unrealistic.

reality noun ❶ REAL WORLD, actuality, physical existence, corporeality, substantiality, materiality. ❷ harsh realities: FACT, actuality, truth.
– OPPOSITES fantasy.

realize verb ❶ UNDERSTAND CLEARLY, grasp, take in, know, comprehend, apprehend, appreciate, recognize, perceive, discern, conceive; *informal* latch on; *Brit. informal* twig. ❷ realize one's hopes: FULFIL, achieve, accomplish, bring about, bring off, bring to fruition, consummate, effect, perform, execute, actualize, reify; *formal* effectuate. ❸ realize a profit: MAKE, clear, acquire, gain, bring in, obtain, earn.

realm noun KINGDOM, country, land, state, province, empire, domain, monarchy, principality.

reap verb ❶ CUT, crop, harvest, gather in, bring in, take in. ❷ reap the benefits: REALIZE, receive, obtain, get, acquire, secure, procure.

rear[1] verb ❶ rear children: BRING UP, raise, care for, nurture, parent, educate, train, instruct. ❷ rear one's head: RAISE, lift up, hold up, elevate, upraise.

rear[2] noun BACK, back part, hind part, back end, tail, tail end.
– OPPOSITES front.

reason noun ❶ GROUNDS, cause, basis, motive, motivation, impetus. ❷ EXPLANATION, justification, argument, case, defence, vindication, apologia, rationalization, excuse, apology. ❸ REASONING, intellect, intelligence, intellectuality, mind, judgement, logic, rationality, thought, understanding, apprehension, comprehension, ratiocination. ❹ he has lost his reason: SANITY, mind, soundness of mind, senses.
▶ verb ❶ THINK, think straight, use one's mind, use one's brain/head, analyse, cogitate, cerebrate, intellectualize, ratiocinate; *informal* put on one's thinking cap. ❷ try reasoning with him: USE LOGIC ON, argue with, debate with, dispute with, try to persuade, plead with.

reasonable adjective ❶ a reasonable idea: LOGICAL, practical, rational, sensible, intelligent, wise, sound, judicious, advisable, well thought out, tenable, plausible. ❷ a reasonable man: OPEN TO REASON, fair, just, equitable, impartial, dispassionate, unbiased, disinterested. ❸ reasonable prices: MODERATE, low, modest, cheap, within one's means. ❹ reasonable work: TOLERABLE, passable, acceptable, average; *informal* OK.
– OPPOSITES unreasonable.

reasoned adjective LOGICAL, rational, well thought out, clear, systematic, methodical, organized, well expressed, well presented.

reassure verb PUT ONE'S MIND AT REST, put at ease, restore/give confidence to, encourage, hearten, buoy up, cheer up.

rebel noun REVOLUTIONARY,

revolutionist, insurrectionist, insurgent, mutineer.
▶ verb MUTINY, riot, revolt, rise up, rise up in arms, take to the streets.
– OPPOSITES conform.

rebellion noun ❶ REVOLT, revolution, insurrection, uprising, rising, mutiny. ❷ DEFIANCE, disobedience, resistance, dissent, nonconformity, heresy, apostasy, schism, recusancy.

rebellious adjective ❶ DEFIANT, disobedient, unruly, ungovernable, unmanageable, turbulent, disorderly, intractable, recalcitrant, incorrigible; *formal* contumacious. ❷ REVOLUTIONARY, insurrectionary, insurgent, mutinous.
– OPPOSITES obedient.

rebound verb ❶ BOUNCE BACK, recoil, ricochet, boomerang. ❷ the plan rebounded on her: MISFIRE, backfire, come back on, redound on.

rebuff noun REJECTION, repudiation, discouragement, snub, slight; *informal* brush-off, slap in the face.
▶ verb REJECT, refuse, turn down, turn away, spurn, brush off, repudiate, snub, slight.

rebuke verb REPRIMAND, tell off, scold, chide, admonish, reproach, reprove, remonstrate with, lecture, reprehend, berate, upbraid, take to task; *informal* bawl out; *Brit. informal* tick off, tear off a strip, carpet; *formal* castigate.
– OPPOSITES praise.

recalcitrant adjective INTRACTABLE, refractory, unmanageable, ungovernable, disobedient, insubordinate, defiant, contrary, wayward.
– OPPOSITES compliant.

recall verb ❶ SUMMON BACK, call back, bring back. ❷ *See* REMEMBER (1).

receive verb ❶ BE IN RECEIPT OF, accept delivery of, accept, take into one's possession. ❷ receive bad treatment: UNDERGO, experience, meet with, encounter, be subjected to, bear, suffer. ❸ receive **guests**: WELCOME, greet, entertain, be at home to.
– OPPOSITES give, send.

recent adjective ❶ NEW, fresh, novel, latest, late, modern, contemporary, latter-day, current, up to date. ❷ OCCURRING/APPEARING RECENTLY, not long past.

recently adverb LATELY, of late, latterly, in recent times, not along ago.

receptacle noun CONTAINER, holder, repository.

receptive adjective OPEN, open to suggestions, flexible, willing, perceptive, sensitive, alert, bright, quick, keen.
– OPPOSITES unresponsive.

recess noun ❶ ALCOVE, niche, nook, corner, cavity, bay, oriel. ❷ BREAK, respite, rest, interval, intermission, holiday, time off, vacation.

recession noun DOWNTURN, depression, slump.
– OPPOSITES boom.

recipe noun DIRECTIONS, instructions, guide, method, system, procedure.

reciprocal adjective MUTUAL, shared, common, exchanged, give and take, complementary, corresponding, correlative.

reciprocate verb RETURN, requite, repay, give back.

recital noun ❶ PERFORMANCE,

concert, show. ❷ ACCOUNT, report, telling, relation, description, detailing, rendering, record, chronicle.

recite verb SAY, repeat, read aloud, deliver, declaim, speak, render.

reckless adjective RASH, careless, thoughtless, incautious, heedless, unheeding, regardless, daredevil, devil-may-care, madcap, harum-scarum, wild, precipitate, headlong, hasty, irresponsible, hare-brained, foolhardy, imprudent, unwise, indiscreet, mindless, negligent.
– OPPOSITES cautious.

reckon verb ❶ BE OF THE OPINION, think, believe, suppose, assume. ❷ COUNT, calculate, add up, compute, total, tally, put a figure on, give a figure to.

reclaim verb HAVE RETURNED, get back, take back, regain, retrieve, recover.

recline verb LIE DOWN, be recumbent, rest, repose, loll, lounge, sprawl, stretch out.

recluse noun HERMIT, anchorite, eremite, solitary, lone wolf, loner.

recognize verb ❶ KNOW, know again, identify, place, spot, recall, recollect, remember, call to mind. ❷ REALIZE, see, be aware of, be conscious of, perceive, discern, appreciate, understand, apprehend, acknowledge, accept, admit, concede, allow, grant, confess, own. ❸ *recognize his claim*: ACKNOWLEDGE, accept, admit, concede, allow, grant, endorse, sanction, approve, validate, ratify, uphold.

recoil verb DRAW BACK, jump back, pull back, shrink, shy away, flinch, start, wince, cower, quail.

recollect verb REMEMBER, recall, call to mind, think of, summon up, place; *informal* put one's finger on.
– OPPOSITES forget.

recommend verb ADVOCATE, commend, put in a good word for, speak favourably of, endorse, approve, vouch for, suggest, offer, put forward, propose, advance.

recommendation noun COMMENDATION, endorsement, suggestion, tip, hint, proposal, good word, favourable mention, praise; *informal* plug.

reconcile verb REUNITE, bring together, restore harmony between, make peace between, bring to terms, pacify, appease, placate, propitiate, mollify.
– OPPOSITES estrange, quarrel.

recondite adjective OBSCURE, esoteric, abstruse, abstract, cryptic, incomprehensible, inscrutable, arcane, deep, profound, difficult, complex.
– OPPOSITES straightforward.

reconnaissance noun SURVEY, exploration, scouting, probe, inspection, observation; *informal* recce.

reconnoitre verb SURVEY, see how the land lies, spy out, take stockof, explore, scout, investigate, scrutinize, scan, inspect, observe; *informal* recce, check out.

reconsider verb RETHINK, review, re-examine, re-evaluate, reassess, think again, think twice, have second thoughts, change one's mind.

reconstruct verb REBUILD, remake, reassemble, refashion, recreate, remodel, revamp, renovate, recondition.

record noun ❶ DOCUMENT, register, log, logbook, file, official report/account, chronicle, documentation, minutes, notes, annals, archives. ❷ DISC, album, single, recording, release; *informal* platter.
▶ verb ❶ PUT ON RECORD, set down, write down, put in writing, take down, put down, enter, make a note of, document. ❷ REGISTER, read, indicate, show, display.

recount verb DESCRIBE, detail, enumerate, list, specify, itemize, cite, particularize, catalogue.

recover verb ❶ GET BACK, win back, regain, recoup, retrieve, reclaim, repossess, redeem, recuperate, recapture. ❷ GET BETTER, get well, recuperate, convalesce, heal, get back on one's feet, feel oneself again, improve, mend, pick up, perk up, rally, revive, pull through, bounce back.
–OPPOSITES deteriorate.

recovery noun ❶ RECOUPING, regaining, retrieval, reclamation, repossession, recapture. ❷ RECUPERATION, convalescence, healing, rallying, revival.

recreation noun ❶ RELAXATION, leisure, refreshment, amusement, entertainment, distraction, diversion. ❷ ACTIVITY, pastime, hobby, diversion, distraction.

recrimination noun COUNTER-ACCUSATION, countercharge, counter-attack, retaliation, reprisal.

recruit verb ENLIST, enrol, sign up, draft, conscript, levy, engage, obtain, acquire, procure, take on, round up, muster.
▶ noun ❶ DRAFTEE, conscript. ❷ NEWCOMER, initiate, beginner, learner, trainee, apprentice.

rectify verb PUT/SET RIGHT, right, correct, amend, emend, remedy, repair, fix, make good.

rectitude noun RIGHTEOUSNESS, virtue, honour, integrity, principle, probity, uprightness, good character, decency, honesty.

recuperate verb *see* RECOVER.

recur verb REOCCUR, happen/occur again, come back, return, reappear, be repeated, happen repeatedly.

recurrent adjective RECURRING, repeated, repetitive, reiterative, periodic, cyclical, regular, habitual, continual, frequent, intermittent, chronic.

recycle verb REUSE, reprocess, salvage, save.

red adjective ❶ SCARLET, vermilion, cherry, ruby, cardinal, carmine, claret, wine, coral, salmon-pink, cochineal, rose, reddish. ❷ FLUSHED, blushing, rosy, florid, ruddy, rubicund, roseate.

redden verb GO RED, blush, flush, colour, colour up, crimson.

redeem verb ❶ EXCHANGE, cash in, convert, turn in, trade in. ❷ SAVE, deliver from sin, turn from sin, convert, purge/absolve of sin.

redolent adjective ❶ EVOCATIVE, suggestive, reminiscent. ❷ SWEET-SMELLING, fragrant, scented, perfumed, aromatic.

reduce verb ❶ MAKE SMALLER, lessen, lower, decrease, diminish, cut, curtail, contract, shorten, abbreviate, moderate, dilute, alleviate, abate. ❷ **reduced to tears/begging:** BRING TO, bring to the point of, force to, drive to. ❸ **reduced in rank:** DEMOTE, downgrade, lower, lower in rank/status, humble. ❹ **reduced the**

stock: LOWER/CUT IN PRICE, lower, make cheaper, cheapen, cut, mark down, slash, discount, put on sale.
– OPPOSITES increase.

reduction noun ❶ LESSENING, lowering, decrease, diminution, cut, contraction, abbreviation, moderation, dilution, alleviation, abatement. ❷ DISCOUNT, deduction, cut, concession, allowance. ❸ DEMOTION, downgrading, lowering, humbling.

redundant adjective SURPLUS TO REQUIREMENTS, not required, unnecessary, inessential, unwanted, surplus, supernumerary.

reel verb ❶ STAGGER, lurch, sway, stumble, totter, wobble, falter, waver, pitch, roll. ❷ FEEL GIDDY/DIZZY, feel confused, be shaken, be in shock, be upset.

refer verb ❶ refer to his notes: CONSULT, turn to, look at, look up, have recourse to. ❷ refer it to a higher court: PASS, hand on, send on, transfer, remit, direct. ❸ he referred to her: MENTION, make mention of, make reference to, allude to, touch on, speak of, cite, hint at; *formal* advert to. ❹ figures refer to last year: APPLY TO, be relevant to, have relevance to, concern, relate to, belong to.

referee noun UMPIRE, judge, adjudicator, arbitrator, arbiter, mediator; *informal* ref.

reference noun ❶ MENTION, allusion, citation, hint. ❷ with reference to: REGARD, respect, relation, bearing, relevance, pertinence. ❸ a list of references: SOURCE, citation, authority, bibliography. ❹ he gave her a reference: TESTIMONIAL, recommendation, good word, credentials.

refine verb PURIFY, rarefy, clarify, clear, cleanse, strain, sift, filter, distil, process.

refined adjective ❶ PURIFIED, pure, rarefied, clarified, clear, filtered, distilled, processed. ❷ CULTIVATED, cultured, polished, civilized, civil, gracious, stylish, elegant, sophisticated, urbane, courtly, well mannered, well bred, gentlemanly, ladylike, genteel.
– OPPOSITES crude.

refinement noun ❶ PURIFICATION, processing, distillation, filtration. ❷ CULTIVATION, culture, taste, discrimination, polish, finish, civility, grace, graciousness, style, elegance, finesse, sophistication, urbanity, courtliness, good breeding, politeness, good manners, gentility. ❸ SUBTLETY, nicety, nuance, fine point.

reflect verb ❶ THROW BACK, cast back, send back, give back, scatter, diffuse. ❷ MIRROR, echo. ❸ THINK, consider, mull over, contemplate, deliberate, ponder, meditate, muse, ruminate, cogitate, brood.

reflection noun ❶ IMAGE, mirror image, echo. ❷ THOUGHT, thinking, consideration, contemplation, deliberation, meditation, rumination, cogitation. ❸ THOUGHT, opinion, view, idea, impression, comment, findings.

reflex adjective AUTOMATIC, involuntary, spontaneous, knee-jerk.
– OPPOSITES conscious.

reform verb ❶ IMPROVE, make better, ameliorate, amend, mend, rectify, correct, rehabilitate, change, make over, revamp, renovate. ❷ MEND ONE'S WAYS, change for the better, turn over a new leaf, improve; *informal* go straight.

refrain verb DESIST, abstain, hold back, forbear, forgo, do without, avoid, eschew, cease, stop, give up, leave off, renounce; *informal* quit.

refresh verb ❶ felt refreshed: FRESHEN, invigorate, revitalize, revive, brace, fortify, enliven, perk up, stimulate, energize, exhilarate, rejuvenate, regenerate, breathe new life into, inspirit. ❷ refresh someone's memory: STIMULATE, prompt, prod, jog, activate, rouse, arouse.
– OPPOSITES weary.

refreshing adjective FRESHENING, invigorating, revitalizing, reviving, bracing, stimulating, exhilarating, energizing.

refuge noun ❶ seek refuge: SHELTER, safety, security, protection, asylum, sanctuary. ❷ a refuge from the world: PLACE OF SAFETY, shelter, haven, retreat, bolt-hole, sanctuary, harbour.

refund verb GIVE BACK, return, repay, pay back, reimburse, make good, restore, replace.
▶ noun REPAYMENT, reimbursement.

refuse[1] verb ❶ TURN DOWN, decline, say no to, reject, spurn, rebuff, repudiate; *informal* pass up, knock back. ❷ DECLINE, be unwilling, baulk at, demur at, avoid, resist, protest at.
– OPPOSITES accept.

refuse[2] noun RUBBISH, waste, debris, litter, dross, dregs, leavings, sweepings; *N. Amer.* garbage, trash; *informal* junk.

refute verb PROVE WRONG, disprove, negate, invalidate, discredit.

regain verb GET BACK, win back, recover, recoup, retrieve, reclaim, repossess, redeem, recuperate, take back, retake, recapture.

regal adjective ROYAL, majestic, noble, proud, kingly, queenly, princely, fit for a king/queen/prince/princess.

regard verb ❶ WATCH, look at, gaze at, keep an eye on, stare at, observe, view, study, scrutinize, eye, mark, behold. ❷ regard the prospect: LOOK UPON, view, consider, contemplate, think of, weigh up, mull over, reflect on, deliberate on.
▶ noun ❶ LOOK, gaze, stare, observation, scrutiny. ❷ HEED, attention, notice, consideration, thought, mind. ❸ RESPECT, esteem, admiration, approval, approbation, favour.

regarding preposition WITH/IN REGARD TO, as regards, as to, with reference to, on the subject/matter of, apropos, concerning, about, respecting.

regardless
■ **regardless of** WITHOUT REGARD TO, disregarding, unmindful of, heedless of, without consideration of, indifferent to, negligent of.

regards plural noun BEST/GOOD WISHES, greetings, salutations, respects, compliments.

regenerate verb RENEW, breathe new life into, restore, invigorate, refresh, revitalize, revive, revivify, rejuvenate.

regiment verb ORGANIZE, order, control, discipline, keep a tight rein on, bring into line, rule with a rod of iron.

region noun AREA, province, territory, division, section, sector, zone, tract, part, quarter, locality.

register noun LIST, listing, roll, roster, index, directory, catalogue. ▶ verb ❶ RECORD, put on record, enter, set down, chronicle, write down, take down, note, minute, list, catalogue. ❷ READ, record, indicate, show, display. ❸ register surprise: SHOW, express, display, exhibit, evince, betray, reveal, manifest, demonstrate, reflect. ❹ it did not register: MAKE AN IMPRESSION, get through, sink in, penetrate, have an effect.

regress verb REVERT, relapse, lapse, backslide, fall away, go backwards, degenerate, retrogress, retrograde.
– OPPOSITES progress.

regret verb ❶ FEEL SORRY/CONTRITE ABOUT, feel remorse about, wish undone, repent, rue. ❷ LAMENT, bemoan, be upset/disappointed about, mourn, grieve over, weep over, fret about, pine over, deplore.
– OPPOSITES welcome.
▶ noun ❶ SORROW, remorse, contrition, repentance, pangs of conscience, compunction, ruefulness, self-reproach, penitence. ❷ DISAPPOINTMENT, lamentation, grief, mourning, pining.
– OPPOSITES satisfaction.

regretful adjective SORRY, apologetic, remorseful, contrite, repentant, conscience-stricken, rueful, penitent.
– OPPOSITES unrepentant.

regrettable adjective DEPLORABLE, reprehensible, disgraceful, blameworthy, unfortunate, unwelcome, ill-advised.

regular adjective ❶ his regular route: USUAL, normal, customary, habitual, routine, typical, everyday, daily, unvarying, common, average, commonplace. ❷ regular breathing: RHYTHMIC, steady, even, uniform, constant, unchanging. ❸ regular intervals: EVEN, uniform, consistent, orderly, systematic, fixed. ❹ the regular channels: OFFICIAL, established, conventional, formal, proper, orthodox, approved, sanctioned, standard, usual, traditional. ❺ he's a regular charmer: REAL, thorough, absolute, utter, complete.
– OPPOSITES occasional, erratic.

regulate verb ❶ CONTROL, direct, guide, govern, rule, manage, order, organize, conduct, run, supervise, oversee, superintend, monitor. ❷ ADJUST, balance, set, synchronize, modulate.

regulation noun ❶ CONTROL, direction, guidance, government, rule, management, administration, organization, supervision. ❷ RULE, ruling, order, directive, act, law, decree, statute, edict, ordinance.

rehearsal noun PRACTICE, preparation, trial performance, run-through, going-over.

rehearse verb PRACTISE, try out, run through, go over.

reign verb ❶ BE KING/QUEEN, sit on the throne, occupy the throne, wear the crown, wield the sceptre. ❷ BE IN POWER, govern, rule, be in charge/control, administer, hold sway.
▶ noun ❶ MONARCHY, sovereignty. ❷ POWER, government, rule, command, control, administration, charge.

rein
■ **rein in** CHECK, curb, restrain, constrain, hold back, restrict, control, bridle.

reinforce verb ❶ STRENGTHEN, fortify, bolster up, shore up, buttress, prop up, brace, support, back up, uphold, stress, underline, emphasize. ❷ **reinforce the troops:** AUGMENT, increase, add to, supplement.

reiterate verb REPEAT, say again, go over again, belabour, dwell on, harp on, hammer away at.

reject verb ❶ **reject an offer:** REFUSE, turn down, decline, say no to, spurn, rebuff, repudiate, veto, deny; *informal* pass up, knock back, give the thumbs down to. ❷ **reject someone:** CAST OUT, cast aside, discard, jettison, renounce, abandon, forsake, scrap, exclude, eliminate.
– OPPOSITES accept.
▶ **noun** ❶ SUBSTANDARD ARTICLE, discard, second. ❷ FAILURE, outcast, derelict; *informal* drop-out.

rejoice verb BE JOYFUL, be happy, be pleased, be glad, be delighted, be elated, be overjoyed, be jubilant, be euphoric, exult.
– OPPOSITES mourn.

rejoinder noun ANSWER, response, reply, riposte, retort; *informal* comeback.

relapse verb LAPSE, regress, retrogress, revert, backslide, fall away, go backwards, slip back, degenerate.
– OPPOSITES improve.
▶ **noun** LAPSE, regression, retrogression, reversion, backsliding, recidivism.

relate verb ❶ **relate the story:** RECOUNT, tell, narrate, describe, report, impart, communicate, recite, rehearse, present, detail, delineate, chronicle, set forth. ❷ **relate cause and effect:** CONNECT, associate, link, correlate, ally, couple, join. ❸ **relate to this matter:** APPLY TO, be relevant to, have relevance to, concern, refer to, have reference to, pertain to, bear on.

related adjective ❶ CONNECTED, interconnected, associated, linked, correlated, allied, affiliated, accompanying, concomitant, akin. ❷ **related through marriage:** CONNECTED, akin, kindred, agnate, cognate, consanguineous.
– OPPOSITES unrelated.

relation noun ❶ CONNECTION, association, link, tie-in, correlation, alliance, bond, relationship, interdependence. ❷ RELATIVE, family member, kinsman, kinswoman, connection, kin.

relationship noun ❶ *See* RELATION (1). ❷ FRIENDSHIP, love affair, affair, liaison.

relative adjective ❶ COMPARATIVE, comparable, respective, correlative, parallel, corresponding. ❷ PROPORTIONATE, in proportion/ratio, based.
▶ **noun** *see* RELATION (2).

relax verb ❶ **relax one's grip:** LOOSEN, slacken, weaken, lessen, let up, reduce, diminish. ❷ **muscles relaxed:** BECOME LESS TENSE/STIFF/RIGID, loosen, slacken. ❸ **relax the rules:** MODERATE, make less strict/formal, soften, ease. ❹ **learn to relax:** LOOSEN UP, ease up/off; *informal* unwind, take it easy, let it all hang out, hang loose.
– OPPOSITES tense, tighten.

relaxation noun ❶ LOOSENING, slackening, weakening, letting up. ❷ LESSENING, reduction, easing off, abatement. ❸ LEISURE, recreation, enjoyment, amusement, entertainment, pleasure, rest, refreshment.

relay verb PASS ON, hand on, communicate, send, transmit, broadcast, spread, circulate.

release verb ❶ SET FREE, free, let go, set/turn loose, let out, liberate, untie, undo, unloose, unbind, unchain, unfetter, unshackle, extricate, deliver, emancipate; *historical* manumit. ❷ release the news: MAKE PUBLIC, make known, issue, break, announce, reveal, divulge, unveil, present, disclose, publish, broadcast, put out, circulate, disseminate, distribute, spread.
– OPPOSITES imprison, suppress.

relent verb SOFTEN, become merciful/lenient, show mercy/pity, give quarter, capitulate, yield, give way, give in, unbend, come round, forbear, change one's mind.

relentless adjective ❶ a relentless tyrant: UNRELENTING, ruthless, merciless, pitiless, remorseless, unforgiving, implacable, inexorable, cruel, grim, harsh, hard, cold-hearted, fierce, strict, obdurate, unyielding, inflexible, unbending. ❷ relentless ambition: UNRELENTING, unremitting, persistent, unswerving, persevering, unflagging, unfaltering, unstoppable, incessant, unceasing.
– OPPOSITES lenient.

relevant adjective APPLICABLE, pertinent, apposite, material, appurtenant, to the point/purpose, germane, admissible, appropriate, apt, fitting.
– OPPOSITES irrelevant.

reliable adjective ❶ a reliable person: DEPENDABLE, trustworthy, trusty, true, faithful, devoted, steady, steadfast, constant, unfailing, certain, sure. ❷ reliable evidence: DEPENDABLE, trustworthy, well founded, well grounded, authentic, genuine, credible, sound.
– OPPOSITES unreliable.

relic noun ❶ ANCIENT/HISTORICAL OBJECT, artefact, antique, heirloom. ❷ VESTIGE, trace, survivor, remnant.

relief noun ❶ ALLEVIATION, mitigation, assuagement, palliation, ease, appeasement, abatement. ❷ AID, help, assistance, succour. ❸ RESPITE, remission, interruption, break, variation, diversion; *informal* let-up.
– OPPOSITES intensification.

relieve verb ❶ ALLEVIATE, mitigate, assuage, allay, soothe, soften, palliate, appease, ease, dull, abate, reduce, lessen, diminish. ❷ BRING AID TO, aid, help, assist, rescue, save, succour. ❸ BRING RESPITE TO, interrupt, break up, vary, lighten.
– OPPOSITES aggravate.

religious adjective ❶ religious festivals: CHURCH, holy, divine, theological, doctrinal, spiritual, sectarian. ❷ religious people: CHURCHGOING, God-fearing, godly, pious, devout. ❸ religious attention: SCRUPULOUS, conscientious, meticulous, zealous, strict, rigid, rigorous.
– OPPOSITES irreligious.

relinquish verb GIVE UP, renounce, resign, abdicate, surrender, sign away.
- OPPOSITES retain.

relish noun ENJOYMENT, delight, pleasure, satisfaction, gratification, appreciation, liking, zest, gusto.
▶ verb ENJOY, delight in, like, love, adore, appreciate, revel in, luxuriate in.
- OPPOSITES dislike.

reluctant adjective UNWILLING, disinclined, hesitant, unenthusiastic, grudging, loath, averse, slow, chary.
- OPPOSITES eager.

rely
■ **rely on** DEPEND ON, count on, bank on, trust, lean on, be confident/sure of, swear by.

remain verb ❶ BE LEFT, be left over, stay behind, survive, last, abide, endure, prevail. ❷ remain at home: STAY, wait, linger; *informal* stay put; *archaic* tarry. ❸ remain calm: STAY, continue, persist in being.

remainder noun REMNANT, residue, leavings, dregs, residuum, balance, surplus, excess, superfluity.

remains plural noun ❶ remains of a meal: REMNANTS, leftovers, leavings, scraps, residue, debris, detritus. ❷ Roman remains: RELICS, reliquiae, fragments, shards. ❸ CORPSE, dead body, body, carcass; *Medicine* cadaver; *informal* stiff.

remark verb ❶ MENTION, say, state, declare, pronounce, assert, observe. ❷ NOTE, notice, observe, mark, perceive, discern.
▶ noun COMMENT, statement, utterance, declaration, pronouncement, observation, reference, opinion.

remarkable adjective OUT OF THE ORDINARY, extraordinary, unusual, uncommon, conspicuous, singular, notable, noteworthy, memorable, signal, rare, exceptional, outstanding, striking, impressive, considerable, pre-eminent, significant, important, momentous, phenomenal, wonderful.
- OPPOSITES ordinary, commonplace.

remedy noun ❶ CURE, treatment, medicine, medication, medicament, therapy, antidote, restorative, nostrum, panacea. ❷ a remedy for the problem: CORRECTIVE, solution, redress, panacea.
▶ verb ❶ CURE, heal, treat, counteract, control. ❷ RECTIFY, solve, set to rights, put right, redress, fix, sort out.

remember verb ❶ RECALL, call to mind, recollect, think of, keep/bear in mind, not forget. ❷ REMINISCE ABOUT, look/think back on, hark back to, summon up.
- OPPOSITES forget.

remind verb CAUSE TO REMEMBER, jog/refresh someone's memory, prompt.

reminiscent adjective EVOCATIVE, suggestive, redolent.

remiss adjective NEGLIGENT, neglectful, lax, slack, slipshod, sloppy, careless, forgetful, inattentive, heedless, thoughtless, unthinking, culpable, delinquent.
- OPPOSITES careful, diligent.

remission noun ❶ CANCELLATION, revocation, repeal, rescinding.

❷ remission of pain: EASING, moderation, abatement, lessening, decrease, dwindling, wane, waning, ebb, ebbing, subsidence.

remit verb ❶ CANCEL, revoke, repeal, rescind, stop, halt. ❷ EASE, moderate, abate, lessen, decrease, dwindle, wane, ebb, subside. ❸ remit payment: SEND, dispatch, forward, transmit, post, mail.

remnant noun ❶ REMAINDER, residue, balance, remains, vestiges. ❷ PIECE, fragment, scrap.

remonstrate
■ **remonstrate with** TAKE ISSUE WITH, argue with, dispute with, protest to, complain to, expostulate with.

remorse noun REGRET, sorrow, contrition, penitence, repentance, guilty conscience, guilt, shame, self-reproach, ruefulness, pangs of conscience, compunction.

remorseful adjective SORRY, regretful, contrite, apologetic, penitent, repentant, guilt-ridden, conscience-stricken, ashamed, chastened, rueful.
– OPPOSITES unrepentant.

remorseless adjective *see* RELENTLESS.

remote adjective ❶ DISTANT, far, far-off, faraway, out of the way, outlying, inaccessible, off the beaten track, isolated, secluded, lonely, godforsaken. ❷ a remote possibility: UNLIKELY, improbable, implausible, negligible, insignificant, doubtful, dubious, slight, slender, slim, small, poor. ❸ she is rather remote: ALOOF, distant, detached, withdrawn, reserved, uncommunicative, unapproachable, stand-offish, cool, haughty, uninvolved, indifferent, unconcerned.
– OPPOSITES near, likely, friendly.

removal noun ❶ removal from office: DISMISSAL, eviction, ejection, expulsion, ousting, dislodgement, deposition. ❷ removal of privileges: TAKING AWAY, withdrawal, deprivation, abolition. ❸ removal of errors: DELETION, elimination, erasure, effacing, obliteration.

remove verb ❶ TAKE AWAY, carry away, move, shift, convey, transfer, transport. ❷ remove from office: DISMISS, get rid of, eject, expel, cast out, oust, throw out, dislodge, relegate, unseat, depose, displace; *informal* sack, fire. ❸ remove their coats: TAKE OFF, pull off, strip off; *Brit. informal* peel off. ❹ remove their privileges: TAKE AWAY, withdraw, do away with, abolish. ❺ remove the errors: DELETE, eliminate, erase, rub out, cross out, strike out, blue-pencil, efface, obliterate. ❻ remove the weeds: TAKE OUT, pull out, uproot, eradicate, extirpate, destroy, exterminate, annihilate. ❼ remove a branch: CUT OFF, amputate, lop off, chop off, excise.

remunerative adjective PROFITABLE, moneymaking, paying, lucrative, gainful, financially rewarding, rich.

render verb ❶ MAKE, cause to be/become, leave. ❷ services rendered: GIVE, contribute, make available, provide, supply, furnish. ❸ render an account: PRESENT, send in, submit, tender. ❹ render the role: ACT, perform, play, execute, interpret.

rendezvous noun APPOINTMENT,

date, engagement, meeting, assignation.

renegade noun DEFECTOR, deserter, turncoat, traitor, apostate, revolutionary, rebel, mutineer.

renege verb GO BACK ON ONE'S WORD, break one's promise, default, back out, welsh, pull out; *informal* cop out.
– OPPOSITES honour.

renounce verb ❶ **renounce his claim:** GIVE UP, relinquish, resign, abdicate, surrender, sign away, waive, forego. ❷ **renounce his son:** REPUDIATE, disown, cast off, discard, reject, disinherit, wash one's hands of, spurn, shun. ❸ **renounce drink:** GIVE UP, abstain from, desist from, swear off, eschew.
– OPPOSITES embrace.

renovate verb MODERNIZE, recondition, refurbish, rehabilitate, overhaul, restore, revamp, remodel, repair, redecorate, refit; *informal* do up, fix up.

renown noun FAME, repute, acclaim, celebrity, distinction, illustriousness, eminence, pre-eminence, prominence, mark, note, consequence, prestige.

renowned adjective FAMOUS, famed, well known, of repute, acclaimed, celebrated, distinguished, illustrious, eminent, pre-eminent, prominent, noted, notable, of note, of consequence, prestigious.
– OPPOSITES obscure.

rent[1] noun RENTAL, payment, hire fee.
▶ verb ❶ LEASE, hire, charter. ❷ LET, lease, hire, hire/let out, farm out.

rent[2] noun TEAR, rip, split, gash, slash, hole, perforation, break, crack, fracture, crevice, fissure, cleft.

repair[1] verb ❶ MEND, fix, put right, restore, adjust, regulate, overhaul. ❷ MEND, darn, sew, patch. ❸ **repair the omission:** PUT RIGHT, make good, rectify, correct, redress, compensate for.

repair[2]
■ **repair to** GO TO, withdraw to, head for, take off for, leave for, depart for.

repay verb ❶ PAY BACK, refund, reimburse, recompense, remunerate, square accounts with, settle up with. ❷ GET BACK AT, hit back, retaliate against, get even with, settle the score with; *informal* get one's own back on.

repeal verb REVOKE, rescind, abrogate, annul, nullify, make void, void, invalidate, quash, set aside, cancel, countermand, retract, overrule, override, reverse.

repeat verb ❶ SAY AGAIN, restate, retell, reiterate, recapitulate, recap, echo, parrot, quote. ❷ DO AGAIN, redo, duplicate, replicate.

repeated adjective RECURRENT, frequent, continual, incessant, constant, endless.

repel verb ❶ REPULSE, drive back, push back, thrust back, force back, beat back, ward off, fend off, keep at bay, keep at arm's length. ❷ REVOLT, disgust, sicken, nauseate, make someone sick, turn someone's stomach, be repugnant to, make someone's flesh creep; *informal* give someone the creeps.
– OPPOSITES welcome, attract.

repellent adjective REPULSIVE, revolting, disgusting, sickening,

nauseating, distasteful, repugnant, abhorrent, offensive, obnoxious, loathsome, off-putting, hateful, vile, nasty, odious, abominable, horrible, horrid, foul, heinous, obscene.
– OPPOSITES attractive.

repent verb BE SORRY, be contrite, be conscience-stricken, reproach oneself, be ashamed, regret, rue, be penitent.

repentant adjective PENITENT, sorrowful, apologetic, regretful, contrite, remorseful, conscience-stricken, rueful, ashamed, guilt-ridden.
– OPPOSITES unashamed.

repercussion noun EFFECT, result, consequence, reverberation, backlash.

repetitive adjective RECURRENT, unchanging, unvaried, monotonous, tedious, boring, mechanical, automatic; *Brit. informal* samey.

replace verb ❶ PUT BACK, return, restore. ❷ TAKE THE PLACE OF, succeed, supersede, follow after, come after, supplant, substitute for, stand in for, act for, fill in for, cover for.

replacement noun SUCCESSOR, substitute, stand-in, fill-in, locum, understudy, proxy, surrogate.

replenish verb REFILL, top up, fill up, recharge, reload.

replete adjective FULL, full up, satiated, sated, glutted, gorged, stuffed, well fed.

replica noun COPY, carbon copy, duplicate, facsimile, model, reproduction, imitation.

reply verb ❶ ANSWER, respond to, acknowledge, write back. ❷ ANSWER, respond, rejoin, retort, return, riposte, come back, counter.
▶ noun ANSWER, response, acknowledgement, rejoinder, retort, return, riposte; *informal* comeback.

report noun ❶ ACCOUNT, statement, record, exposition. ❷ ARTICLE, piece, story, write-up, communiqué, dispatch, bulletin. ❸ EXPLOSION, bang, boom, crack, crash.
▶ verb ❶ ANNOUNCE, pass on, communicate, relay, relate, tell, recount, give an account of, set forth, document, narrate, describe, delineate, detail, divulge, disclose, circulate. ❷ TELL ON, inform on, accuse, make a charge/complaint against; *informal* squeal on, rat on; *Brit. informal* grass on. ❸ PRESENT ONESELF, be present, appear, arrive, come, turn up, clock in; *Brit.* clock on; *informal* show up.

reporter noun JOURNALIST, newsman, newswoman, pressman, correspondent, writer, broadcaster, announcer, presenter; *informal* newshound, hack.

repose noun REST, relaxation, leisure, ease, inactivity, respite, sleep, slumber.

reprehensible adjective BLAMEWORTHY, culpable, erring, errant, wrong, bad, shameful, disgraceful, discreditable, dishonourable, objectionable, unpardonable, indefensible, unjustifiable, inexcusable.
– OPPOSITES praiseworthy.

represent verb ❶ STAND FOR, symbolize, personify, epitomize, typify, embody, incorporate, exemplify. ❷ DEPICT, portray, delineate, illustrate, picture, denote, paint, draw, sketch, exhibit, show, display, evoke. ❸ ACT FOR, appear for, speak for, be the representative of.

representation noun DEPICTION, portrayal, portrait, delineation, illustration, picture, painting, drawing, sketch, image, model.

representative adjective ❶ TYPICAL, archetypal, exemplary, characteristic, indicative, illustrative. ❷ a representative body: ELECTED, elective, chosen, delegated.
– OPPOSITES unrepresentative.
▶ noun ❶ SPOKESMAN, spokeswoman, spokesperson, agent, deputy, proxy. ❷ MEMBER OF PARLIAMENT, MP, Member, deputy, councillor.

repress verb ❶ SUBJUGATE, conquer, vanquish, overpower, overcome, crush, master, dominate, domineer, bully, intimidate, oppress. ❷ repress his desire: HOLD/KEEP BACK, hold in, bite back, restrain, suppress, keep in check, check, inhibit, bottle up, silence, muffle, stifle, smother.

repressed adjective ❶ SUBJUGATED, oppressed, tyrannized. ❷ a repressed laugh: RESTRAINED, suppressed, muffled, smothered. ❸ a repressed person: INHIBITED, withdrawn, restrained.

repression noun ❶ OPPRESSION, dictatorship, authoritarianism, tyranny, despotism, domination, coercion, suppression, subjugation. ❷ HOLDING BACK, biting back, restraint, suppression, smothering.

repressive adjective TYRANNICAL, despotic, dictatorial, authoritarian, oppressive, coercive, suppressive, harsh, severe, strict, cruel.

reprieve verb POSTPONE/DELAY PUNISHMENT OF, grant a stay of execution to, let off, pardon, let off the hook.

reprimand verb REBUKE, scold, chide, reproach, reprove, lecture, admonish, berate, upbraid, correct, take to task, haul over the coals; *informal* tell off, give someone a dressing-down, bawl out; *Brit. informal* tick off; *formal* castigate.
– OPPOSITES praise
▶ noun REBUKE, scolding, chiding, reproach, reproof, admonition, berating, upbraiding, tongue-lashing; *informal* talking-to, telling-off, dressing-down, bawling-out; *Brit. informal* ticking-off, wigging; *formal* castigation.
– OPPOSITES commendation.

reprisal noun RETALIATION, revenge, vengeance, retribution, redress, requital, recrimination, an eye for an eye; *informal* tit for tat.

reproach verb & noun *see* REPRIMAND.

reproachful adjective DISAPPROVING, disappointed, critical, censorious, admonitory, condemnatory, disparaging, reproving; *formal* castigatory.
– OPPOSITES approving.

reproduce verb ❶ COPY, duplicate, replicate, photocopy, recreate, redo, remake, imitate, follow, emulate, echo, mirror, parallel, match, mimic, ape. ❷ BREED, procreate, bear young, produce offspring, give birth, multiply, propagate, proliferate, spawn.

reproduction noun ❶ COPY, duplicate, replica, facsimile, imitation, print. ❷ BREEDING, procreation, propagation, proliferation.

reprove verb *see* REPRIMAND verb.

repudiate verb DISOWN, reject, cast off, cut off, abandon, forsake, desert, discard, renounce, disavow, abjure, turn one's back on, have nothing to do with, wash one's hands of.
– OPPOSITES embrace.

repugnant adjective ABHORRENT, revolting, repulsive, repellent, disgusting, sickening, nauseating, disagreeable, distasteful, offensive, objectionable, obnoxious, loathsome, off-putting, hateful, despicable, reprehensible, contemptible, abominable, horrible, horrid, foul, nasty, vile, ugly, odious, heinous.
– OPPOSITES agreeable.

repulsive adjective *see* REPUGNANT.

reputable adjective RESPECTABLE, respected, well thought of, esteemed, estimable, of good repute, worthy, creditable, reliable, dependable, conscientious, trustworthy, above board, legitimate, upright, virtuous, good, excellent.
– OPPOSITES disreputable.

reputation noun REPUTE, standing, name, character, position, status, station.

request noun ENTREATY, appeal, petition, plea, application, demand, solicitation, call, suit.
▶ verb ASK FOR, solicit, seek, apply for, put in for, call for, beg for, plead for, pray for, petition, implore, sue for, supplicate for, requisition, demand, desire; *poetic/literary* beseech.

require verb ❶ NEED, have need of, lack, be short of, want, wish, desire, crave, miss. ❷ CALL FOR, demand, necessitate, involve, take.

required adjective COMPULSORY, obligatory, mandatory, prescribed, recommended, requisite, set, essential, necessary, vital.
– OPPOSITES optional.

requirement noun NEED, want, lack, must, necessity, demand, prerequisite, requisite, precondition, specification, qualification, sine qua non, stipulation.

requisite adjective *see* REQUIRED.

requisition noun ❶ APPLICATION, order, claim, request, call, demand. ❷ COMMANDEERING, appropriation, possession, occupation, seizure, confiscation.
▶ verb ❶ APPLY FOR, order, put in a claim for, request, call for, demand. ❷ COMMANDEER, appropriate, take over, take possession of, occupy, seize, confiscate.

rescind verb REPEAL, revoke, reverse, abrogate, retract, countermand, overturn, annul, nullify, invalidate, cancel, set aside.
– OPPOSITES enforce.

rescue verb SAVE, come to someone's aid, free, set free, release, liberate, emancipate, get out, extricate, redeem, salvage, relieve.
▶ noun DELIVERANCE, freeing, release, liberation, emancipation, extrication, redemption, salvage, relief.

research noun EXPERIMENT, assessment, study, tests,

investigation, experimentation, fact-finding, testing, exploration. ▶ **verb** DO TESTS ON, investigate, inquire into, look into, probe, explore, analyse, study, examine.

resemblance **noun** LIKENESS, similarity, semblance, sameness, uniformity, correspondence, comparability, affinity, closeness, nearness, agreement, congruity, concurrence, conformity.

resemble **verb** BE LIKE, look like, bear a resemblance to, be similar to, remind one of, take after, echo, mirror, parallel, favour.

resent **verb** TAKE OFFENCE/UMBRAGE AT, take exception to, take amiss, be annoyed/angry at, begrudge, feel bitter about, dislike.
– OPPOSITES welcome.

resentful **adjective** AGGRIEVED, offended, indignant, irritated, displeased, annoyed, angry, irate, incensed, piqued, in high dudgeon, grudging, bitter, embittered, wounded; *informal* in a huff.

resentment **noun** OFFENCE, indignation, irritation, displeasure, annoyance, anger, pique, grudgingness, bitterness, animosity, hostility, hard feelings; *poetic/literary* ire.

reservation **noun** ❶ BOOKING, engagement, appointment. ❷ CONDITION, stipulation, qualification, proviso, provision, qualm, scruple, hesitancy, doubt.

reserve **verb** ❶ PUT/SET/LAY ASIDE, put away, keep back, keep, withhold, conserve, save, retain, store, hoard, stockpile; *informal* hang on to. ❷ BOOK, engage, arrange for, charter, hire.
▶ **noun** ❶ STORE, stock, supply, reservoir, pool, cache, fund, stockpile, accumulation, backlog, hoard. ❷ ALOOFNESS, detachment, distance, remoteness, formality, coolness, coldness, frigidity, reticence, unapproachability, uncommunicativeness, shyness, diffidence, taciturnity. ❸ **a nature reserve**: PRESERVE, reservation, sanctuary, park.

reserved **adjective** ALOOF, detached, remote, formal, unemotional, undemonstrative, cool, cold, frigid, reticent, unapproachable, uncommunicative, unsociable, unfriendly, unresponsive, unforthcoming, shy, retiring, diffident, secret, secretive, taciturn, silent.
– OPPOSITES outgoing.

reside
■ **reside in** LIVE IN, dwell in, stay in, inhabit, occupy.

residence **noun** HOUSE, home, habitation, quarters, lodgings; *formal* dwelling, domicile.

resident **noun** INHABITANT, occupant, householder, denizen; *Brit.* occupier.

residue **noun** REMAINDER, remnant, residuum, rest, surplus, extra, excess, remains, leftovers, dregs, lees.

resign **verb** ❶ GIVE NOTICE, hand in one's notice, leave; *informal* quit. ❷ RENOUNCE, relinquish, give up, abdicate, surrender, cede.

resilient **adjective** ❶ ELASTIC, springy, rubbery, whippy, flexible, pliant, supple, pliable, plastic. ❷ TOUGH, strong, hardy, quick to recover, difficult to keep down, irrepressible.

resist **verb** ❶ WITHSTAND, be proof against, repel. ❷ STOP, halt, prevent, check stem, curb, obstruct, hinder, impede, block, thwart, frustrate, inhibit, restrain.

resistant adjective PROOF AGAINST, impervious to, unaffected by, immune to.

resolute adjective DETERMINED, resolved, decided, firm, fixed, set, intent, steadfast, constant, earnest, staunch, bold, courageous, serious, purposeful, deliberate, inflexible, unyielding, unwavering, unfaltering, unhesitating, unswerving, unflinching, obstinate, obdurate, strong-willed, dogged, persevering, persistent, tenacious, relentless, unshakeable, dedicated.
– OPPOSITES irresolute.

resolution noun ❶ RESOLVE, determination, firmness, intentness, steadfastness, constancy, staunchness, boldness, courage, seriousness, purposefulness, obstinacy, obduracy, will power, doggedness, perseverance, persistence, tenacity, staying power, dedication. ❷ **pass a resolution:** MOTION, declaration, decree, verdict, judgement. ❸ **the resolution of the problem:** SOLVING, solution, answer, sorting out, working out, unravelling, disentanglement, cracking.

resolve verb ❶ DECIDE, make up one's mind, determine, settle on, undertake. ❷ SOLVE, answer, sort out, work out, clear up, fathom, unravel, disentangle, crack.
▶ noun *see* RESOLUTION (1).

resort verb FALL BACK ON, turn to, have recourse to, look to, make use of, use, avail oneself of, bring into play/service, exercise.
▶ noun ❶ HOLIDAY/TOURIST CENTRE, centre, spot, retreat. ❷ RECOURSE, source of help, expedient, alternative, choice, possibility, hope.

resound verb REVERBERATE, resonate, echo, ring.

resource noun ❶ ASSET, reserve, reservoir, store, stock, supply, pool, fund, stockpile. ❷ RESOURCEFULNESS, initiative, ingenuity, inventiveness, quick-wittedness, cleverness, native wit, talent, ability, capability.

respect noun ❶ ESTEEM, high regard, regard, high opinion, admiration, approval, appreciation, veneration, reverence, deference, honour, praise, homage. ❷ **in all respects:** ASPECT, facet, feature, way, sense, characteristic, particular, point, detail.
– OPPOSITES contempt.
▶ verb ESTEEM, have a high opinion of, think highly of, admire, approve of, appreciate, venerate, revere, honour, praise.
– OPPOSITES despise.

respectable adjective ❶ REPUTABLE, of good repute, upright, honest, honourable, trustworthy, above board, worthy, decent, good, virtuous, admirable, well bred, proper, decorous. ❷ **a respectable salary:** REASONABLE, fairly good, fair, considerable, ample, sizable, substantial; *informal* not to be sneezed at.
– OPPOSITES disreputable, paltry.

respective adjective INDIVIDUAL, separate, personal, own, particular, specific.

respects plural noun REGARDS, best wishes, greetings, compliments, remembrances.

respite noun REST, break,

interval, intermission, recess, lull, pause, hiatus, halt, relief, relaxation; *informal* breather, let-up.

respond verb ❶ ANSWER, reply to, say in response to, acknowledge. ❷ SAY IN RESPONSE, answer, reply, rejoin, retort, return, riposte, come back, counter.

response noun ANSWER, reply, acknowledgement, rejoinder, retort, return, riposte; *informal* comeback.
– OPPOSITES question.

responsibility noun ❶ DUTY, charge, onus, task, role, liability, accountability, answerability. ❷ BLAME, fault, guilt, culpability.

responsible adjective ❶ IN CHARGE/CONTROL OF, at the helm of, accountable for, liable for. ❷ ACCOUNTABLE, answerable, to blame, blameworthy, at fault, guilty, culpable. ❸ **a responsible child**: SENSIBLE, level-headed, rational, reasonable, sound, stable, reliable, dependable, trustworthy, competent, conscientious, hard-working, industrious.
– OPPOSITES irresponsible.

responsive adjective QUICK TO REACT, reactive, receptive, forthcoming, sensitive, perceptive, sympathetic, susceptible, impressionable, open, alive, awake, aware, sharp.

rest noun ❶ REPOSE, relaxation, leisure, ease, inactivity, respite, time off, breathing space, sleep, slumber. ❷ BREAK, interval, interlude, intermission, lull, pause, time off. ❸ STAND, base, holder, support, prop, shelf.
▶ verb ❶ TAKE A REST, relax, sit down, lie down, go to bed, sleep, take a nap, nap, catnap, doze, slumber; *informal* take it easy. ❷ BE SUPPORTED BY, be propped up by, lie on, be laid on, recline on, stand on, sit on. ❸ DEPEND, rely, hang, hinge, be based, be founded.

restful adjective QUIET, calm, tranquil, relaxed, peaceful, placid, still, languid, undisturbed, unhurried, sleepy.
– OPPOSITES hectic.

restless adjective ❶ **a restless night**: SLEEPLESS, wakeful, tossing and turning, fitful. ❷ **the crowd was restless**: UNEASY, ill at ease, on edge, agitated. ❸ **restless people**: UNSETTLED, roaming, roving, wandering, itinerant, travelling, nomadic, peripatetic.

restore verb ❶ RENOVATE, repair, fix, mend, set to rights, recondition, rehabilitate, refurbish, rebuild, reconstruct, remodel, revamp, redecorate, touch up; *informal* do up, fix up. ❷ RETURN, give back, hand back, send back. ❸ RE-ESTABLISH, reinstitute, reinstate, reinstall, reimpose.

restrain verb ❶ **restrain the crowd**: CONTROL, keep under control, hold in check, curb, keep within bounds, subdue. ❷ **restrain one's anger**: CONTROL, check, suppress, repress, contain, smother, stifle, bottle up, rein in; *informal* keep the lid on.

restraint noun ❶ CONSTRAINT, check, curb, block, hindrance, impediment, deterrent, inhibition. ❷ **behave with restraint**: SELF-RESTRAINT, self-control, self-discipline, moderation, temperateness, prudence, judiciousness.

restrict verb ❶ HINDER, impede, hamper, retard, handicap, cramp.

❷ LIMIT, set/impose limits on, keep under control, regulate, control, moderate.

restriction noun CONSTRAINT, limitation, control, check, curb, regulation, condition, provision, proviso, stipulation, qualification, demarcation.

result noun ❶ OUTCOME, consequence, issue, upshot, sequel, effect, repercussion, end, conclusion, termination, aftermath, product, byproduct, fruits. ❷ ANSWER, solution.
–OPPOSITES cause.
▶ verb FOLLOW, ensue, issue, develop, stem, evolve, emerge, emanate, occur, happen, come about, eventuate.
■ **result in** END IN, culminate in, finish in, terminate in.

resume verb CARRY ON, continue, recommence, begin again, reopen, reinstitute.

resurrect verb RAISE FROM THE DEAD, restore to life, bring back to life, revive, breathe new life into, give new life to.

retain verb ❶ KEEP, keep possession/hold of, hold on to, hang on to, preserve, maintain. ❷ retain a gardener: HIRE, employ, engage, commission.

retaliate verb TAKE/EXACT/WREAK REVENGE, avenge oneself, exact retribution, give as good as one gets, get one's own back, get back at, make reprisals, get even with, even the scores, settle a score.

retard verb SLOW DOWN, slow up, hold back, set back, hold up, delay, hinder, hamper, obstruct, impede, decelerate, put a brake on, check, arrest, interfere with, interrupt, thwart, frustrate.
–OPPOSITES expedite.

reticent adjective *see* RESERVED.

retire verb ❶ GIVE UP WORK, stop working, be pensioned off; *informal* be put out to grass. ❷ the jury retired: WITHDRAW, go out, depart, exit, leave, absent oneself. ❸ GO TO BED, go to sleep, turn in, call it a day; *informal* hit the sack.

retiring adjective SHY, diffident, bashful, self-effacing, shrinking, unassuming, reserved, reticent, timid, timorous, nervous, modest, demure.
–OPPOSITES brash.

retract verb ❶ DRAW IN, pull in, pull back. ❷ retract her statement: TAKE BACK, withdraw, revoke, repeal, rescind, annul, cancel, abrogate, disavow, abjure, renounce, recant, disclaim, backtrack on, renege on.

retreat verb ❶ WITHDRAW, pull back, fall back, back off, give way/ground, decamp, depart, leave, flee, take flight, turn tail, beat a retreat, beat a hasty retreat. ❷ GO BACK, recede, ebb.
▶ noun ❶ WITHDRAWAL, pulling back, departure, flight, evacuation. ❷ REFUGE, haven, shelter, sanctuary, sanctum sanctorum, hideaway, resort, asylum.

retribution noun REPRISAL, retaliation, revenge, vengeance, punishment, justice, nemesis, reckoning, requital, an eye for an eye, tit for tat.

retrieve verb GET BACK, recover, regain, win back, recoup, redeem, reclaim, repossess, recapture, salvage, rescue.

retrograde adjective RETROGRESSIVE, backwards, deteriorating, declining, on the wane.

retrospect
■ **in retrospect** ON REFLECTION, on looking/thinking back, with hindsight.

return verb ❶ GO BACK, come back, reappear, reoccur, come again, come round again. ❷ GIVE BACK, send back, take back, carry back, put back, replace, restore, reinstate, reinstall. ❸ RECIPROCATE, repay, requite, send/give in response to. ❹ return a profit: YIELD, bring in, earn, make, net.
– OPPOSITES depart.
▶ noun ❶ HOMECOMING, reappearance, reoccurrence. ❷ REPLACEMENT, restoration, reinstatement, reinstallation. ❸ PROFIT, yield, gain, income, revenue, interest.
– OPPOSITES departure.

reveal verb ❶ SHOW, display, exhibit, expose to view. ❷ BRING TO LIGHT, uncover, expose to view, lay bare, unearth, unveil, unmask. ❸ DISCLOSE, divulge, tell, let out, let on, let slip, give away, give out, leak, betray, make known/public, broadcast, publicize, publish, proclaim.
– OPPOSITES conceal, hide.

revel verb CELEBRATE, make merry, have a party, party, carouse, roister.
■ **revel in** DELIGHT IN, take pleasure in, bask in, rejoice in, relish, savour, gloat over, luxuriate in, wallow in.

revelation noun DISCLOSURE, divulgence, telling, leak, betrayal, broadcasting, publicizing, communication, publishing, proclamation.

revelry noun CELEBRATIONS, festivities, jollification, merrymaking, carousal.

revenge noun VENGEANCE, retaliation, retribution, reprisal, redress.
▶ verb TAKE REVENGE FOR, avenge, retaliate, exact retribution for, take reprisals for, requite.

revenue noun INCOME, return, yield, interest, profits, returns, receipts, proceeds, takings, rewards.
– OPPOSITES expenditure.

reverberate verb RESOUND, echo, ring, vibrate.

revere verb LOOK UP TO, think highly of, admire, respect, esteem, defer to, honour, venerate, exalt, put on a pedestal, idolize.
– OPPOSITES despise.

reverence noun ESTEEM, admiration, respect, deference, honour, veneration, worship, homage, adoration, devotion, awe, exaltation.
– OPPOSITES scorn.

reverent adjective REVERENTIAL, admiring, respectful, deferential, adoring, loving, devoted, awed, submissive, humble, meek.

reversal noun ❶ a policy reversal: TURNAROUND, turnabout, about-face, volte-face, U-turn, change of heart; *Brit.* about-turn. ❷ reversal of roles: CHANGE, exchange, trading, trade-off, swapping. ❸ reversal of the verdict: OVERTURN, overthrow, revocation, repeal, rescinding, annulment, invalidation.

reverse verb ❶ TURN ROUND, put back to front, turn upside down, upend, invert. ❷ MOVE/DIRECT BACKWARDS, back. ❸ reverse roles: CHANGE, exchange, trade, swap. ❹ reverse the verdict: SET ASIDE, overturn, overthrow, revoke,

repeal, rescind, annul, nullify, declare null and void, void, invalidate, quash.
▶ adjective REVERSED, backwards, inverted, transposed, turned round.
▶ noun ❶ OPPOSITE, contrary, converse, antithesis. ❷ OTHER SIDE, back, rear, underside, flip side. ❸ REVERSAL, upset, setback, failure, misfortune, mishap, blow, disappointment.

review noun ❶ STUDY, analysis, survey, examination, scrutiny, assessment, appraisal. ❷ CRITICISM, critique, notice, assessment, evaluation, rating.
▶ verb ❶ ANALYSE, examine, study, survey, scrutinize, assess, appraise. ❷ CRITICIZE, evaluate, assess, appraise, judge, weigh up, discuss.

revise verb ❶ AMEND, emend, correct, alter, change, edit, rewrite, redraft, rework, update, revamp. ❷ GO OVER, reread, run through, study; *informal* bone up on; *Brit. informal* swot up on.

revival noun RESUSCITATION, resurrection, rebirth, renaissance, comeback, restoration, reintroduction.

revive verb ❶ BRING ROUND, resuscitate, give artificial respiration to, save, restore to health; *informal* give the kiss of life to. ❷ REFRESH, restore, cheer up, comfort, enliven, revitalize.

revoke verb REPEAL, rescind, abrogate, countermand, annul, nullify, declare null and void, void, invalidate, quash.
– OPPOSITES enact.

revolt verb ❶ RISE UP, take to the streets, take up arms, rebel, mutiny. ❷ REPEL, disgust, sicken, nauseate, turn someone's stomach, be repugnant to, make someone's flesh creep, put off, offend, shock.

revolting adjective *see* REPELLENT.

revolution noun ❶ REBELLION, revolt, insurrection, uprising, rising, insurgence, coup, putsch. ❷ DRASTIC CHANGE, metamorphosis, sea change, upheaval, upset, transformation. ❸ ROTATION, single turn, whirl, round, spin, wheel.

revolutionary adjective ❶ REBELLIOUS, insurrectionary, mutinous, seditious, subversive, extremist. ❷ **revolutionary changes:** PROGRESSIVE, radical, innovative, new, novel, avant-garde, experimental, different, drastic.
▶ noun REBEL, insurgent, insurrectionist.

revolve verb GO ROUND, turn round, rotate, spin, circle, orbit, gyrate, whirl.

revulsion noun REPULSION, disgust, nausea, distaste, aversion, repugnance, abhorrence, loathing.
– OPPOSITES delight.

reward noun RECOMPENSE, payment, remuneration, bonus, bounty, present, gift, tip, gratuity, prize.
– OPPOSITES punishment.
▶ verb RECOMPENSE, pay, remunerate, give a present to, tip.

rewarding adjective SATISFYING, fulfilling, enriching, edifying, beneficial, profitable, advantageous, productive, valuable.

rhetoric noun BOMBAST, grandiloquence, magniloquence, hyperbole, pomposity, verbosity, prolixity, turgidity.

rhetorical adjective POMPOUS, high-flown, flamboyant, showy, flowery, florid, oratorical, declamatory, bombastic, grandiloquent, magniloquent, hyperbolical, verbose, long-winded, prolix, turgid, periphrastic.

rhythm noun BEAT, cadence, tempo, pulse, metre, pattern.

ribald adjective BAWDY, risqué, smutty, vulgar, coarse, earthy, off colour, rude, naughty, racy, suggestive, indecent, indelicate. *See also* OBSCENE.

rich adjective ❶ WEALTHY, affluent, well off, well-to-do, prosperous, moneyed, propertied; *informal* well heeled, filthy rich, loaded, made of money, rolling in it/money, flush, worth a packet/bundle, on Easy Street. ❷ OPULENT, expensive, costly, precious, valuable, priceless, beyond price, lavish, luxurious, lush, sumptuous, palatial, splendid, superb, resplendent, elegant, fine, exquisite, magnificent, grand, gorgeous. ❸ **rich in oil**: WELL PROVIDED, well supplied, well stocked, abounding, overflowing, replete, rife. ❹ **a rich soil**: FERTILE, productive, fecund, fruitful, lush. ❺ **a rich sauce**: CREAMY, fatty, heavy. ❻ **that's rich**: PREPOSTEROUS, outrageous, ridiculous, laughable, risible.
– OPPOSITES poor.

riches plural noun WEALTH, affluence, prosperity, money, capital, property, treasure, assets, resources.

richly adverb ❶ EXPENSIVELY, lavishly, luxuriously, sumptuously, palatially, splendidly, superbly, magnificently. ❷ **richly deserved**: FULLY, in full measure, well, thoroughly, completely, amply, utterly.
– OPPOSITES meanly.

rid verb DO AWAY WITH, remove, get rid of, dispense with, eliminate, dump, dispose of, unload, expel, eject, weed out, clear, cleanse, purge, purify.

riddle noun PUZZLE, poser, conundrum, brain-teaser, problem, enigma, mystery.

ride verb ❶ SIT ON, mount, be mounted on, bestride, manage, control. ❷ TRAVEL, go, move, progress.
▶ noun TRIP, outing, journey, jaunt; *informal* spin.

ridicule noun DERISION, mockery, laughter, scorn, jeering, gibing, teasing, taunting, chaff, banter, badinage, raillery, satire, sarcasm, irony; *informal* kidding, ribbing, ragging.
– OPPOSITES respect.
▶ verb DERIDE, mock, laugh at, scoff at, scorn, jeer at, gibe at, make fun of, poke fun at, make a fool of, tease, taunt, chaff; *informal* kid, rib, rag, take the mickey out of, send up.

ridiculous adjective ❶ ABSURD, comical, funny, laughable, hilarious, humorous, droll, farcical, facetious, ludicrous, risible, derisory. ❷ **a ridiculous thing to do**: POINTLESS, senseless, foolish, inane, fatuous, nonsensical, mindless. ❸ **it's ridiculous**: UNBELIEVABLE, incredible, outrageous, preposterous, shocking, monstrous.
– OPPOSITES sensible.

rife adjective WIDESPREAD, common, prevalent, predominant, general, extensive, ubiquitous, universal, global, rampant.

rifle
■ **rifle through** RANSACK, rummage through, go through, rake through, search.

rift noun ❶ SPLIT, break, breach, fissure, cleft, crevice, gap, crack, cranny, slit. ❷ DISAGREEMENT, fight, falling-out, breach, division, estrangement, schism, split, alienation, quarrel, altercation, conflict, feud; *informal* row.

rig[1]
■ **rig out** CLOTHE, dress, attire, accoutre, array, deck, bedeck, drape. **rig up** PUT TOGETHER, erect, assemble, throw together, cobble together.

rig[2] verb **rig the results:** FALSIFY, fake, tamper with, doctor, engineer, manipulate.

right adjective ❶ JUST, fair, equitable, impartial, good, upright, righteous, virtuous, proper, moral, ethical, honourable, honest, principled, lawful, legal. ❷ **the right way:** CORRECT, accurate, unerring, exact, precise, valid; *informal* on the mark; *informal* spot on, bang on. ❸ **the right owner:** RIGHTFUL, true, genuine, authentic, lawful, legal, legitimate; *informal* legit. ❹ **right for the job:** SUITABLE, appropriate, fit, proper, desirable, ideal. ❺ **the right moment:** OPPORTUNE, favourable, convenient, suitable, appropriate, propitious. ❻ **my right side:** RIGHT-HAND, dextral; *Nautical* starboard; *Heraldry* dexter. ❼ CONSERVATIVE, right-wing, Tory, reactionary.
– OPPOSITES wrong, left.
▶ **noun** ❶ LAWFULNESS, legality, goodness, righteousness, virtue, virtuousness, integrity, rectitude, propriety, justice, justness, fairness, equity, equitableness. ❷ **you had the right to do it:** PREROGATIVE, privilege, authority, power, licence, permission, entitlement.
▶ **verb** PUT TO RIGHTS, sort out, straighten out, rectify, fix, put in order, repair.

righteous adjective GOOD, virtuous, upright, moral, ethical, law-abiding, honest, honourable, pure, noble, God-fearing.
– OPPOSITES sinful.

rigid adjective ❶ STIFF, hard, taut, inflexible, unbendable, unbending, unyielding, inelastic, non-pliant. ❷ **rigid principles:** STRICT, severe, stern, stringent, rigorous, austere, spartan, harsh, inflexible, intransigent, uncompromising.
– OPPOSITES flexible.

rigorous adjective ❶ **a rigorous search:** METICULOUS, painstaking, thorough, laborious, scrupulous, conscientious, nice, exact, precise, accurate. ❷ **rigorous weather:** HARSH, severe, bad, bleak, extreme, inclement.
– OPPOSITES slapdash, mild.

rim noun BRIM, edge, lip, circumference, border, verge, margin, brink.

rind noun OUTER LAYER, peel, skin, husk, crust.

ring[1] noun ❶ BAND, circle, loop, circuit, halo, disc, round. ❷ ARENA, enclosure, area. ❸ **a spy ring:** GANG, syndicate, cartel, association, league.
▶ **verb** CIRCLE, encircle, circumscribe, encompass, loop, gird, enclose, surround, hem in, fence in, seal off.

ring[2] noun ❶ RINGING, tolling, peal,

pealing, knell, chime, clang, tinkle. ❷ CALL, telephone call, phone call; *informal* phone, buzz.
▶ **verb** ❶ TOLL, peal, sound, chime, ding, ding-dong, clang, tinkle. ❷ CALL, telephone, phone; *informal* buzz.

rinse **verb** WASH, wash out, clean, sluice, flush, drench.

riot **noun** STREET FIGHT, commotion, disturbance, uproar, tumult, melee, scuffle, fracas, fray, brawl, free-for-all, uprising, insurrection.
▶ **verb** RUN RIOT, rampage, go on the rampage, run wild/amok, go berserk, fight, brawl, take to the streets.

riotous **adjective** ❶ **riotous assembly**: DISORDERLY, uncontrollable, ungovernable, unmanageable, rowdy, wild, violent, brawling, lawless, anarchic, rebellious, mutinous. ❷ **a riotous party**: LOUD, noisy, boisterous, uproarious, rollicking, orgiastic. ❸ **a riotous show**: HILARIOUS, funny, uproarious, side-splitting.
– OPPOSITES peaceable.

ripe **adjective** ❶ MATURE, developed, full grown, ready to eat, ready, mellow, seasoned, tempered. ❷ **plans are ripe**: READY, all ready/set, developed, prepared, arranged, complete, finished. ❸ **ripe for development**: READY, fit, suitable, right.
– OPPOSITES immature.

ripen **verb** MATURE, come to maturity, develop, mellow.

riposte **noun** RETORT, rejoinder, reply, response, sally; *informal* comeback.

rise **verb** ❶ ARISE, come/go up, move up, ascend, climb up. ❷ RISE UP, tower, soar, loom, rear up. ❸ **costs rising**: GO UP, get higher, increase, soar, rocket, escalate. ❹ STAND UP, get to one's feet, get up, jump up. ❺ ARISE, get up, get out of bed, wake up, surface.
– OPPOSITES fall.
▶ **noun** ❶ INCLINE, elevation, slope, acclivity, rising ground, hillock, hill. ❷ **rise in costs**: INCREASE, escalation, upsurge, upswing.

risk **noun** ❶ CHANCE, possibility. ❷ DANGER, peril, jeopardy. ❸ CHANCE, hazard, uncertainty, speculation, venture.
– OPPOSITES impossibility, safety.
▶ **verb** ❶ PUT AT RISK, endanger, imperil, jeopardize. ❷ TAKE THE RISK OF, chance, venture. ❸ BET, gamble, hazard, chance, venture.

risky **adjective** DANGEROUS, hazardous, perilous, unsafe, precarious, touch-and-go, tricky, uncertain; *informal* chancy, dicey; *Brit. informal* dodgy.

rite **noun** RITUAL, ceremony, ceremonial, observance, service, sacrament, celebration, performance, act, practice, tradition, convention, formality, procedure, usage.

rival **noun** OPPONENT, opposition, adversary, antagonist, contestant, competitor, challenger, contender.
– OPPOSITES ally.
▶ **verb** COMPETE WITH, vie with, match, equal, emulate, measure up to, compare with, parallel.
▶ **adjective** OPPOSING, competing, in competition, contending, in conflict, conflicting.

rivalry **noun** OPPOSITION, competition, competitiveness, vying, contention, conflict.

road **noun** STREET, thoroughfare, highway.

roam verb WANDER, rove, ramble, meander, drift, range, travel, walk, tramp, traverse, trek, peregrinate.

roar verb BELLOW, yell, bawl, shout, howl, thunder, shriek, scream, cry, bay.

rob verb STEAL FROM, burgle, burglarize, hold up, break into, mug, defraud, swindle, cheat, mulct; *informal* rip off, diddle, bilk, do out of.

robber noun BURGLAR, thief, mugger, pilferer, housebreaker, looter, raider, bandit, brigand, pirate, highwayman.

robbery noun THEFT, burglary, stealing, housebreaking, larceny, pilfering, embezzlement, misappropriation, swindling, fraud, mugging, hold-up, break-in, raid; *informal* filching.

robe noun ❶ VESTMENT, habit, costume, gown. ❷ DRESSING GOWN, housecoat, wrapper, peignoir.

robot noun AUTOMATON, android, machine.

robust adjective ❶ HEALTHY, strong, vigorous, hale and hearty, energetic, muscular, powerful, tough, rugged, sturdy, stalwart, strapping, brawny, burly. ❷ **a robust attitude:** SENSIBLE, common-sense, no-nonsense, down-to-earth, practical, realistic, pragmatic, hard-headed.
– OPPOSITES weak.

rock[1] verb ❶ MOVE TO AND FRO, swing, sway, roll, lurch, pitch. ❷ STUN, shock, stagger, astound, astonish, dumbfound, shake, take aback.

rock[2] noun ❶ BOULDER, stone. ❷ FOUNDATION, cornerstone, support, prop, mainstay.

rocky[1] adjective ROCK-STREWN, stony, pebbly, rough.

rocky[2] adjective UNSTEADY, unstable, shaky, tottering, teetering, wobbly.
– OPPOSITES steady, stable.

rod noun BAR, stick, pole, baton, staff.

rogue noun VILLAIN, scoundrel, rascal, reprobate, swindler, fraudster, cheat, deceiver, confidence trickster, charlatan, mountebank, sharper, wretch, ne'er-do-well, wastrel, good-for-nothing, crook; *informal, dated* rotter, bounder; *dated* cad; *archaic* blackguard.

role noun ❶ PART, character, representation, portrayal. ❷ CAPACITY, function, position, place, situation, job, post, task.

roll verb ❶ GO ROUND, turn, turn round, rotate, revolve, spin, whirl, wheel. ❷ FURL, coil, fold. ❸ **the bus rolled along:** PASS, go, flow, travel. ❹ FLATTEN, level, smooth, even, press down, crush. ❺ TOSS, rock, pitch, lurch, sway, reel.
▶ noun ❶ TURN, rotation, revolution, spin, whirl. ❷ SPOOL, reel, bobbin, cylinder. ❸ REGISTER, list, file, index, roster, directory, catalogue.

romance noun ❶ FANTASY, fancy, whimsy, fabrication, glamour, mystery, legend, fairy tale, idyll. ❷ LOVE AFFAIR, affair, liaison, attachment, intrigue, courtship, amour.

romantic adjective ❶ **romantic words:** LOVING, amorous, passionate, fond, tender, sentimental, sloppy; *informal* mushy; *Brit. informal* soppy. ❷ **a romantic view:** UNREALISTIC, idealistic, visionary, utopian,

starry-eyed, optimistic, hopeful. ❸ a romantic figure: FASCINATING, mysterious, glamorous, exotic, exciting.
–OPPOSITES unsentimental.
▶ noun DREAMER, visionary, idealist, utopian.
–OPPOSITES realist.

room noun ❶ SPACE, area, territory, expanse, extent, volume, elbow room. ❷ room for improvement: SCOPE, capacity, margin, leeway, latitude, occasion, opportunity.
▶ verb HAVE ROOMS, lodge, board, stay, dwell, reside.

roomy adjective SPACIOUS, commodious, capacious, voluminous, ample, generous, sizeable, large, broad, wide, extensive.
–OPPOSITES cramped.

root noun ❶ ROOTSTOCK, tuber, tap root; *Botany* rhizome, radicle. ❷ SOURCE, origin, starting point, basis, foundation, beginnings, seat, cause, reason, rationale, occasion; *formal* radix.
▶ verb TAKE ROOT, grow roots, become established, set.
■ **root out** ERADICATE, get rid of, extirpate, weed out, remove, do away with, eliminate, abolish, destroy.

rope noun CORD, cable, line, strand, hawser.
■ **rope in** ENLIST, engage, inveigle, persuade, talk into, involve.

roster noun LIST, listing, rota, roll, register, schedule, agenda, calendar, directory, index, table.

rot verb ❶ DECOMPOSE, decay, crumble, disintegrate, corrode, perish. ❷ GO BAD, spoil, go sour, putrefy, fester; *informal* go off.
▶ noun ❶ DECOMPOSITION, decay, disintegration, corrosion, putrefaction, mould, blight. ❷ RUBBISH, nonsense, claptrap, drivel; *informal* bosh, twaddle, poppycock, guff, tosh; *Brit. informal* codswallop; *informal, dated* bunkum, bunk.

rotary adjective ROTATING, rotational, revolving, turning, gyrating, gyratory, spinning, whirling.

rotate verb ❶ GO ROUND, move round, turn, revolve, spin, whirl, swivel, reel, wheel, gyrate. ❷ ALTERNATE, take turns, take in turn.

rotten adjective ❶ BAD, off, mouldy, mouldering, spoiled, tainted, sour, rancid, rank, decaying, decomposed, putrid, putrescent, festering, fetid, stinking. ❷ NASTY, foul, mean, bad, dirty, filthy, contemptible, despicable.
–OPPOSITES fresh, kind.

rough adjective ❶ rough surfaces: UNEVEN, irregular, bumpy, broken, stony, rugged, craggy, lumpy, nodulous. ❷ a rough coat: SHAGGY, hairy, bushy, fuzzy, bristly. ❸ rough play: BOISTEROUS, rowdy, disorderly, wild, violent, savage. ❹ rough seas: TURBULENT, tumultuous, choppy. ❺ rough weather: STORMY, squally, wild, tempestuous, wintry. ❻ a rough character: COARSE, crude, uncouth, vulgar, unrefined, loutish, boorish, churlish, brutish, ill-mannered, unmannerly, impolite, discourteous, uncivil. ❼ rough treatment: : HARSH, severe, hard, tough, difficult, unpleasant, disagreeable, nasty, cruel. ❽ a rough sketch: ROUGH AND READY, hasty, quick, cursory, crude, incomplete, rudimentary, basic.

❾ a rough guess: APPROXIMATE, inexact, imprecise, vague, hazy. ❿ feeling rough: ILL, sick, unwell, unhealthy, below par; *Brit.* off colour.
– OPPOSITES smooth, exact.

round adjective ❶ CIRCULAR, ring-shaped, cycloid, discoid, disk-like, cylindrical, spherical, spheroid, ball-shaped, globe-like, convex, curved. ❷ WELL ROUNDED, ample, rotund, chubby, buxom, roly-poly, tubby, portly, stout, corpulent, fat, obese; *Brit. informal* podgy.
▶ noun ❶ SUCCESSION, sequence, series, cycle. ❷ CIRCUIT, course, beat, routine, schedule. ❸ STAGE, level, division, lap, heat.
▶ verb GO ROUND, travel round, sail round, circumnavigate.
■ **round off** *see* COMPLETE verb (2).

roundabout adjective INDIRECT, circuitous, meandering, winding, tortuous, discursive, oblique, circumlocutory, periphrastic.
– OPPOSITES direct.

rouse verb ❶ WAKE, wake up, rise, call, get up. ❷ STIR UP, excite, incite, egg on, induce, impel, inflame, agitate, whip up, galvanize, stimulate.
– OPPOSITES calm, pacify.

rout verb DEFEAT, trounce, worst, conquer, subjugate, overthrow, crush, beat; *informal* lick, thrash, give someone a pasting.
– OPPOSITES victory.

route noun COURSE, way, itinerary, road, path.

routine noun ❶ PATTERN, procedure, practice, custom, habit, programme, schedule, formula, method, system, order. ❷ ACT, performance, piece; *informal* spiel.
▶ adjective USUAL, normal, everyday, workaday, common, ordinary, typical, customary, habitual, scheduled, conventional, standard.
– OPPOSITES unusual.

row[1] noun LINE, column, queue, procession, chain, string; *Brit. informal* crocodile.

row[2] noun ❶ ARGUMENT, dispute, disagreement, falling-out, controversy, quarrel, squabble, fight, conflict, altercation, wrangle; *informal* set-to, tiff. ❷ NOISE, din, clamour, commotion, rumpus, uproar, tumult, hubbub, pandemonium.

rowdy adjective UNRULY, disorderly, noisy, boisterous, loud, obstreperous, wild, rough, unrestrained, lawless.
– OPPOSITES quiet.

royal adjective KINGLY, queenly, kinglike, queenlike, princely, regal, monarchical, sovereign.

rub verb ❶ MASSAGE, knead, stroke, caress, fondle. ❷ SCRUB, scour, wipe, clean.
■ **rub out** ERASE, wipe off, efface, obliterate, expunge, remove.

rubbish noun ❶ WASTE, refuse, litter, lumber, junk, debris, detritus, dross, rubble, sweepings, leavings, dregs, offscourings; *N. Amer.* garbage, trash. ❷ *See* NONSENSE.

ruddy adjective RED, reddish, pink, rosy, rosy-cheeked, rubicund, flushed, blushing, glowing, fresh, healthy.
– OPPOSITES pale.

rude adjective ❶ ILL-MANNERED, bad-mannered, mannerless, impolite, discourteous, impertinent, insolent, impudent, cheeky, uncivil, disrespectful,

churlish, curt, brusque, blunt, offhand, short, offensive. ❷ rude jokes: VULGAR, coarse, indelicate, smutty, dirty, naughty, risqué, ribald, bawdy, licentious; *informal* blue. ❸ rude tools: PRIMITIVE, crude, rudimentary, rough, rough-hewn, simple.
– OPPOSITES polite.

rudimentary adjective ❶ ELEMENTARY, basic, fundamental, introductory, early, primitive, crude, rough, simple. ❷ a rudimentary organ: UNDEVELOPED, immature, incomplete, vestigial.

rudiments plural noun BASICS, fundamentals, beginnings, elements, essentials, foundation; *informal* nuts and bolts.

rueful adjective REGRETFUL, apologetic, sorry, remorseful, contrite, repentant, penitent, woebegone, woeful, plaintive.

ruffle verb ❶ RUMPLE, dishevel, tousle, disarrange, discompose, disorder, derange, tangle, mess up; *informal* muss up. ❷ FLUSTER, agitate, harass, upset, disturb, discompose, perturb, unsettle, disconcert, worry, alarm, trouble, confuse, rattle, shake up.
– OPPOSITES smooth, soothe.

rugged adjective ❶ rugged terrain: ROUGH, uneven, irregular, bumpy, rocky, stony, broken up, jagged, craggy. ❷ rugged features: WRINKLED, furrowed, lined, gnarled, weather-beaten, leathery. ❸ a rugged man: TOUGH, hardy, robust, sturdy, strong, vigorous, stalwart, hale and hearty, muscular, brawny.
– OPPOSITES smooth, flimsy.

ruin noun ❶ DESTRUCTION, devastation, wreckage, demolition, disintegration, decay, disrepair. ❷ RUINATION, loss, failure, bankruptcy, insolvency, penury, impoverishment, indigence, destitution, calamity, disaster.
▶ verb ❶ DESTROY, devastate, lay waste, raze, demolish, damage, spoil, wreak havoc on.
❷ BANKRUPT, make insolvent, impoverish, pauperize.
– OPPOSITES save.

ruined adjective IN RUINS, ruinous, dilapidated, decaying, in disrepair, derelict, ramshackle, decrepit.

ruinous adjective ❶ DISASTROUS, devastating, calamitous, catastrophic, cataclysmic, dire, injurious, damaging, crippling. ❷ *see* RUINED.

rule noun ❶ RULING, law, regulation, statute, ordinance, tenet, order, decree, commandment, directive.
❷ PRINCIPLE, precept, standard, axiom, maxim. ❸ GOVERNMENT, administration, jurisdiction, reign, authority, control, direction, mastery, leadership, command.
▶ verb ❶ PRESIDE OVER, govern, control, dominate, direct, administer, manage, regulate.
❷ ORDER, decree, direct, pronounce, make a judgement, judge, adjudge, adjudicate, lay down, decide, determine, resolve, settle, establish.
■ **rule out** *see* EXCLUDE (2).

ruling noun JUDGEMENT, adjudication, finding, verdict, resolution, decree, pronouncement.

rumour noun REPORT, story, whisper, word, news, tidings, gossip, hearsay, talk.
▶ verb it is rumoured that they are wealthy: SAY, report.

run verb ❶ RACE, rush, hasten, hurry, dash, sprint, bolt, dart, gallop, career along, tear along, charge along, speed along, jog along; *informal* scoot, hare, step on it, hotfoot it. ❷ **trains are running:** MOVE, go, get along, travel. ❸ **the river runs by:** GLIDE, course, roll, slide. ❹ **the lease runs for a year:** OPERATE, be in operation, be valid, be current, continue. ❺ **the road runs along the coast:** GO, continue, proceed, extend, stretch. ❻ **water running:** FLOW, issue, stream, pour, gush, cascade, spurt, jet, trickle, leak. ❼ **run for president:** STAND FOR, stand for election as, stand as candidate for, be a contender for, put oneself forward for. ❽ **run a business:** OWN, operate, conduct, carry on, direct, manage, administer, be in charge of, control, head, lead, look after, organize, coordinate, supervise, superintend, oversee.
▶ **noun** ❶ JOG, sprint, dash, gallop, canter, headlong rush, scamper. ❷ DRIVE, ride, trip, outing, excursion, jaunt, short journey; *informal* spin. ❸ SPELL, stretch, streak, chain, string, round, cycle, sequence, series, succession.
■ **run after** *see* PURSUE (1). **run into** *see* MEET (1).

runner noun ❶ RACER, sprinter, hurdler, harrier, jogger, athlete. ❷ BRANCH, shoot, offshoot, tendril.

run-of-the-mill adjective ORDINARY, average, common, middling, mediocre, commonplace, everyday, undistinguished, unexceptional, passable, tolerable.
– OPPOSITES exceptional.

rupture noun BREAK, fracture, crack, split, burst, rent, tear, rift, fissure.
▶ **verb** ❶ BREAK, fracture, crack, split, breach, burst, rend, tear, puncture. ❷ SEVER, cut off, break off, disrupt, breach.

rural adjective PASTORAL, rustic, agricultural, agrarian, Arcadian.
– OPPOSITES urban.

rush verb HURRY, hasten, run, race, dash, sprint, bolt, dart, gallop, career, tear, charge, speed, scurry, scamper; *informal* step on it, get a move on, hotfoot it.
– OPPOSITES dawdle.
▶ **noun** ❶ ONSLAUGHT, attack, assault, charge. ❷ SURGE, flow, gush, stream, flood. ❸ HURRY, haste, speed, swiftness, rapidity, dispatch.

rushed adjective HURRIED, hasty, speedy, quick, fast, swift, rapid, expeditious, prompt.

rustle verb ❶ SWISH, whisper, whoosh. ❷ **rustle cattle:** STEAL, purloin, plunder, abduct, kidnap; *informal* filch.

rusty adjective ❶ RUSTED, corroded, oxidized. ❷ WEAK, below par, unpractised, out of practice, neglected, not what it was.

rut noun ❶ FURROW, groove, track, crack, hollow, hole, pothole. ❷ HUMDRUM EXISTENCE, routine job, boring routine, treadmill, dead end.

ruthless adjective MERCILESS, pitiless, relentless, unrelenting, remorseless, unforgiving, unsparing, inexorable, implacable, heartless, unfeeling, hard, harsh, severe, grim, cruel, vicious, brutal, barbarous, callous, savage, fierce, ferocious.
– OPPOSITES compassionate.

Ss

sabotage noun DAMAGE, destruction, vandalism, disruption, ruining, wrecking.
▶ verb DAMAGE, destroy, wreck, ruin, impair, incapacitate, cripple, vandalize, disrupt; *Brit.* throw a spanner in the works of; *informal* foul up.

saccharine adjective CLOYING, mawkish, maudlin, sentimental; *informal* mushy; *Brit. informal* soppy.

sack noun ❶ BAG, pack. ❷ DISMISSAL, discharge, redundancy; *informal* the boot, the chop, the axe; *Brit. informal* the push.
▶ verb ❶ DISCHARGE, dismiss, declare redundant; *informal* kick out, give someone their marching orders, boot out, give someone the sack/boot/chop/axe, give someone the old heave-ho; *Brit. informal* give someone the push, give someone their cards. ❷ *See* PLUNDER verb.

sacred adjective ❶ HOLY, blessed, blest, hallowed, consecrated, sanctified. ❷ RELIGIOUS, spiritual, devotional, church, churchly, ecclesiastical.
– OPPOSITES profane.

sacrifice noun ❶ GIVING UP, renunciation, abandonment, surrender, relinquishment, yielding, ceding, forfeiture. ❷ OFFERING, gifts, oblation.
▶ verb ❶ GIVE UP, forgo, renounce, abandon, surrender, relinquish, yield, cede, forfeit. ❷ OFFER UP, offer, immolate.

sacrilege noun DESECRATION, profanity, blasphemy, impiety, irreverence, irreligion, godlessness, disrespect.
– OPPOSITES piety.

sacrilegious adjective PROFANE, blasphemous, impious, irreverent, irreligious, godless, disrespectful.

sad adjective ❶ UNHAPPY, miserable, sorrowful, gloomy, melancholy, blue, mournful, woebegone, wretched, dejected, downcast, despondent, in low spirits, low-spirited, low, downhearted, depressed, doleful, glum, cheerless, dispirited, disconsolate, heartbroken, broken-hearted, sick at heart, grief-stricken, grieving; *informal* down, down in the dumps, down in the mouth, in the pits. ❷ sad events: UNHAPPY, unfortunate, sorrowful, miserable, sorry, depressing, upsetting, distressing, dispiriting, heartbreaking, heart-rending, pitiful, pitiable, grievous, tragic, disastrous, calamitous. ❸ in a sad state: SORRY, wretched, deplorable, lamentable, regrettable, unfortunate, pitiful, pitiable, pathetic, shameful, disgraceful.
– OPPOSITES happy.

sadden verb CAST DOWN, deject, depress, dishearten, dispirit, dampen someone's spirits, cast a gloom upon, desolate, upset, distress, grieve, break someone's heart, make someone's heart bleed.
– OPPOSITES cheer.

sadness noun UNHAPPINESS, misery, sorrow, gloom, melancholy, wretchedness, dejection, despondency, low spirits, depression, dolefulness, glumness, cheerlessness, disconsolateness, broken-heartedness, heartache, grief.
– OPPOSITES happiness.

safe adjective ❶ SAFE AND SOUND, secure, protected, sheltered, guarded, defended, free from harm/danger, out of harm's way. ❷ UNHARMED, all right, alive and well, well, unhurt, uninjured, unscathed, undamaged, out of danger; *informal* OK, out of the woods. ❸ **a safe place**: SECURE, sound, risk-free, riskless, impregnable, unassailable. ❹ **a safe person**: RELIABLE, dependable, responsible, trustworthy, tried and true, reputable, upright, honest, honourable. ❺ **a safe driver**: CAUTIOUS, circumspect, prudent, unadventurous, conservative, timid, unenterprising. ❻ **the drugs are safe for children**: HARMLESS, innocuous, non-toxic, non-poisonous, wholesome.
– OPPOSITES dangerous.
▶ **noun** STRONGBOX, safety-deposit box, safe-deposit box, cash box, repository, depository, locker, vault, crypt.

safeguard noun PROTECTION, defence, preventive, precaution, security, surety.
▶ **verb** PROTECT, look after, defend, guard, preserve, secure.
– OPPOSITES endanger.

safe keeping noun PROTECTION, care, charge, keeping, surveillance, custody, guardianship, trusteeship, wardship.

safety noun ❶ SAFENESS, security, secureness, soundness, impregnability. ❷ RELIABILITY, dependability, responsibility, trustworthiness. ❸ SHELTER, sanctuary, refuge.

sag verb SINK, subside, slump, curve down.

saga noun EPIC, chronicle, legend, history, romance.

sail verb ❶ CRUISE, ride the waves, go by water, go on a sea voyage, voyage. ❷ **we sail tonight**: SET SAIL, embark, put to sea, leave port/ dock, raise sail, put off, shove off. ❸ STEER, captain, pilot, navigate.

sailor noun SEAMAN, seafarer, mariner, salt, sea dog, boatman, yachtsman/woman; *Brit. informal* matelot; *informal, dated* tar, Jack Tar.

saintly adjective SAINTLIKE, sainted, holy, godly, pious, God-fearing, religious, devout, blessed, virtuous, righteous, good, innocent, sinless, blameless, pure, angelic.
– OPPOSITES ungodly.

sake noun WELL-BEING, welfare, behalf, benefit, advantage, interest, gain, profit, consideration, regard, concern, account, respect.

salary noun PAY, wages, earnings, remuneration, fee, emolument, stipend, honorarium.

sale noun SELLING, marketing, trade, traffic, vending, bargaining.
■ **on sale** FOR SALE, in stock, on the market, purchasable, available, obtainable.

salient adjective IMPORTANT, main, prominent, conspicuous, striking, noticeable, obvious, remarkable, pronounced, signal, arresting.
– OPPOSITES unimportant.

sallow adjective YELLOWISH,

jaundiced-looking, pallid, wan, pale, waxen, anaemic, colourless, pasty, pasty-faced, unhealthy-looking, sickly-looking.

sally noun SORTIE, foray, thrust, offensive, drive, attack, raid, assault.

salty adjective ❶ SALTED, saline, briny, brackish. ❷ SPICY, piquant, pungent, biting, zestful, tangy, lively, vigorous.

salubrious adjective HEALTHY, health-giving, beneficial, good for one's health, wholesome, salutary, refreshing, invigorating, bracing.
– OPPOSITES unhealthy.

salute noun ❶ GREETING, salutation, address, welcome. ❷ TRIBUTE, testimonial, honour, homage, recognition, acknowledgement.
▶ verb ❶ GREET, address, hail, acknowledge, pay one's respects to. ❷ PAY TRIBUTE TO, pay homage to, honour, recognize, acknowledge; *informal* take one's hat off to.

salvage noun ❶ RESCUE, saving, recovery, reclamation, salvation. ❷ WASTE MATERIAL, scrap, remains.
▶ verb RESCUE, save, recover, retrieve, reclaim, get back.

salvation noun REDEMPTION, deliverance, saving, rescue.
– OPPOSITES damnation, destruction.

same adjective ❶ the same person: IDENTICAL, the very same, selfsame, one and the same, the very. ❷ the same mannerisms: IDENTICAL, alike, duplicate, twin, indistinguishable, interchangeable, corresponding, equivalent. ❸ the same old food: UNCHANGING, unchanged, unvarying, unvaried, invariable, constant, consistent, uniform.
– OPPOSITES different.

sameness noun LACK OF VARIETY, repetition, monotony, similarity, uniformity, tedium, tediousness, routine, predictability.

sample noun ❶ SPECIMEN, example, instance, illustration, exemplification, representative type, model, pattern. ❷ CROSS-SECTION, sampling, test.
▶ verb TRY, try out, test, examine, inspect, taste.

sanctify verb CONSECRATE, make holy/sacred, bless, hallow, set apart, dedicate.

sanctimonious adjective SELF-RIGHTEOUS, holier-than-thou, pietistic, unctuous, smug, mealy-mouthed, hypocritical, Pharisaic, Tartuffian; *informal* goody-goody.

sanction noun ❶ AUTHORIZATION, warrant, accreditation, licence, endorsement, permission, consent, approval, backing, support, seal/stamp of approval, approbation, acceptance; *informal* thumbs up, go-ahead, the green light, OK. ❷ PENALTY, punishment, penalization, penance, sentence.
▶ verb AUTHORIZE, warrant, accredit, license, endorse, permit, allow, consent to, back, support, approve, accept; *informal* give the thumbs up to, give the green light to, OK.
– OPPOSITES reject.

sanctity noun ❶ SACREDNESS, holiness, inviolability. ❷ HOLINESS, godliness, saintliness, spirituality, religiosity, piety, devoutness, devotion, righteousness, goodness, virtue, purity.

sanctuary noun ❶ REFUGE,

haven, shelter, retreat, hideout, hiding place. ❷ HOLY PLACE, church, temple, shrine, altar, sanctum. ❸ PRESERVE, reserve, wildlife reserve, reservation. ❹ SAFETY, safe keeping, protection, shelter, security, immunity.

sane adjective ❶ OF SOUND MIND, in one's right mind, compos mentis, rational, lucid, in possession of one's faculties; *informal* all there. ❷ a sane decision: SENSIBLE, reasonable, balanced, judicious, responsible, prudent, wise, advisable.
– OPPOSITES insane.

sangfroid noun COMPOSURE, coolness, calmness, presence of mind, poise, equanimity, equilibrium, aplomb, nerve, imperturbability, unflappability.

sanguine adjective OPTIMISTIC, confident, assured, hopeful, buoyant, cheerful, spirited.
– OPPOSITES gloomy.

sanitary adjective HYGIENIC, clean, germ-free, antiseptic, aseptic, sterile, unpolluted, salubrious, healthy.

sanity noun ❶ SANENESS, soundness of mind, mental health, reason, rationality, lucidity. ❷ SENSE, sensibleness, common sense, good sense, reasonableness, rationality, soundness, judiciousness, prudence, wisdom, advisability.

sap noun ❶ FLUID, moisture, vital fluids, vital juices. ❷ VIGOUR, energy, vitality, vivacity, enthusiasm, spirit; *informal* pep, zip, oomph.
▶ verb DRAIN, enervate, exhaust, weaken, enfeeble, debilitate, devitalize. *See also* EXHAUST (1).

sarcasm noun DERISION, scorn, mockery, ridicule, irony, satire, trenchancy, acerbity, asperity, mordancy, bitterness, spitefulness.

sarcastic adjective DERISIVE, derisory, scornful, mocking, sneering, jeering, scoffing, taunting, ironic, sardonic, satirical, caustic, trenchant, acerbic, acrimonious, mordant, bitter, spiteful; *Brit. informal* sarky.

sardonic adjective DRY, wry, derisory, cynical, ironic, sarcastic, caustic, trenchant, acerbic, mordant, bitter.

satanic adjective DIABOLICAL, fiendish, devilish, demonic, demoniac, demoniacal, hellish, infernal, accursed, wicked, evil, sinful, iniquitous, malevolent, vile, foul.

satellite noun ❶ SPACECRAFT, space capsule, space station. ❷ PROTECTORATE, dependency, colony, dominion.

satire noun ❶ TAKE-OFF, spoof, send-up, burlesque, parody, travesty, caricature, lampoon, pasquinade. ❷ MOCKERY, ridicule, irony, sarcasm.

satirical adjective MOCKING, ridiculing, taunting, ironic, sarcastic, sardonic, caustic, biting, cutting.

satirize verb MOCK, ridicule, hold up to ridicule, take off, send up, deride, make fun of, poke fun at, parody, lampoon, burlesque, travesty, criticize, censure.

satisfaction noun FULFILMENT, gratification, pleasure, enjoyment, delight, happiness, pride, comfort, content, contentment, smugness.
– OPPOSITES dissatisfaction.

satisfactory adjective ADEQUATE, all right, acceptable, fine, good enough, sufficient, competent, up to standard, up to the mark, up to par, up to scratch, passable, average; *informal* OK, okay.
– OPPOSITES unsatisfactory.

satisfy verb ❶ **satisfy their thirst:** SATIATE, sate, slake, quench. ❷ **satisfy their desires:** FULFIL, gratify, appease, assuage, meet, indulge, content. ❸ **satisfy the police:** CONVINCE, persuade, assure, reassure, remove/dispel doubts, put someone's mind at rest.
– OPPOSITES frustrate.

saturate verb WET THROUGH, wet, soak, drench, souse, steep, douse, permeate, imbue, pervade, suffuse.

sauce noun ❶ RELISH, dressing, condiment, flavouring. ❷ *See* INSOLENCE.

saucy adjective IMPUDENT, cheeky, impertinent, insolent, rude, disrespectful, audacious, presumptuous, bold, brash; *informal* fresh.
– OPPOSITES demure, polite.

saunter verb STROLL, amble, wander, meander, walk, promenade; *informal* mosey.

savage adjective ❶ **a savage blow:** VICIOUS, ferocious, fierce, brutal, cruel, bloody, murderous, bloodthirsty, inhuman, harsh, grim, terrible, merciless, ruthless, pitiless, sadistic, barbarous, fell. ❷ **a savage animal:** FIERCE, ferocious, wild, untamed, undomesticated, feral. ❸ **a savage person:** FIERCE, ferocious, wild, rough, rugged, uncivilized, barbarous, barbaric. ❹ **savage tribes:** PRIMITIVE, uncivilized, uncultivated, wild.
– OPPOSITES mild, tame.
▶ noun BARBARIAN, wild man/woman, native, primitive, heathen.
▶ verb MAUL, lacerate, mangle, tear to pieces, attack.

save verb ❶ RESCUE, free, set free, liberate, deliver, snatch, bail out, salvage, redeem. ❷ PROTECT, safeguard, guard, keep, keep safe, shield, screen, preserve, conserve. ❸ **save a lot of trouble:** PREVENT, obviate, forestall, spare, make unnecessary, rule out. ❹ **save some money:** PUT ASIDE, set aside, put by, put away, lay by, keep, reserve, conserve, salt away, stockpile, store, hoard.

savings plural noun CAPITAL, assets, resources, reserves, funds, nest egg.

saviour noun RESCUER, liberator, deliverer, emancipator, champion, knight in shining armour, Good Samaritan, friend in need.

savour noun TASTE, flavour, tang, relish, smack, smell, aroma, fragrance.
▶ verb TASTE, enjoy, appreciate, delight in, take pleasure in, relish, revel in.

savoury adjective ❶ APPETIZING, mouth-watering, fragrant, flavoursome, palatable, tasty, delicious, delectable, luscious, toothsome; *informal* scrumptious. ❷ SALTY, piquant, tangy.
– OPPOSITES unpalatable, sweet.

saw noun SAYING, proverb, maxim, aphorism, axiom, adage, epigram, dictum, gnome, apothegm, platitude, cliché.

say verb ❶ MENTION, voice, pronounce, put into words, give utterance to, give voice to, vocalize. ❷ STATE, remark, announce, affirm, assert, maintain, declare, allege, profess, avow, opine; *informal* come out with; *formal* aver. ❸ ESTIMATE, judge, guess, hazard a guess, predict, speculate, conjecture, surmise, imagine, assume, suppose, presume. ❹ PROPOSE, advance, bring forward, offer, introduce, adduce, plead.

saying noun *see* SAW.

scaffold noun ❶ SCAFFOLDING, frame, framework, gantry. ❷ GALLOWS, gibbet.

scale[1] noun ❶ PLATE, flake; *technical* lamella, lamina, squama. ❷ COATING, coat, crust, encrustation, limescale; *Brit.* fur.

scale[2] noun ❶ PROGRESSION, succession, sequence, series, ranking, register, ladder, hierarchy; *informal* pecking order. ❷ EXTENT, scope, range, degree, reach.
▶ verb CLIMB, ascend, go up, clamber, mount, clamber up.
■ **scale down** REDUCE, cut down, cut back on, decrease, lessen, lower.

scaly adjective ❶ scaly creatures: *technical* squamous, squamate, lamellate. ❷ scaly patches on the skin: FLAKY, scurfy, rough, scabrous.

scamp noun RASCAL, rogue, imp, devil, monkey, scallywag, mischief-maker, troublemaker, prankster, tyke.

scan verb ❶ STUDY, examine, scrutinize, survey, inspect, take stock of, search, scour, sweep. ❷ SKIM, look over, glance over, run one's eye over, read through, leaf through, thumb through.

scandal noun ❶ DISGRACE, shame, dishonour, disrepute, discredit, odium, opprobrium, censure, obloquy. ❷ SLANDER, libel, calumny, defamation, aspersion, gossip, malicious rumours, dirt, muckraking, smear campaign.

scandalize verb SHOCK, appal, outrage, horrify, affront, disgust, offend, insult, cause raised eyebrows.

scandalous adjective
❶ scandalous behaviour: DISGRACEFUL, shameful, dishonourable, outrageous, shocking, monstrous, disreputable, improper, unseemly, discreditable, infamous, opprobrious.
❷ scandalous rumours: SLANDEROUS, libellous, defamatory, scurrilous, malicious, gossiping.

scant adjective LITTLE, minimal, limited, insufficient, inadequate, deficient.
– OPPOSITES abundant.

scanty adjective MEAGRE, scant, sparse, small, paltry, slender, negligible, skimpy, thin, poor, insufficient, inadequate, deficient, limited, restricted, exiguous.
– OPPOSITES ample, copious.

scapegoat noun WHIPPING BOY, dupe, victim; *informal* fall guy.

scar noun ❶ MARK, blemish, blotch, discoloration, cicatrix, disfigurement, defacement. ❷ DAMAGE, trauma, shock, injury, suffering, upset.
▶ verb ❶ MARK, blemish, blotch, discolour, disfigure, deface. ❷ DAMAGE, traumatize, shock, injure, upset.

scarce adjective ❶ IN SHORT SUPPLY, short, meagre, scant,

scanty, sparse, paltry, not enough, too little, insufficient, deficient, inadequate, lacking, at a premium, exiguous. ❷ RARE, infrequent, few and far between, seldom seen/found, sparse, uncommon, unusual.
– OPPOSITES plentiful, abundant.

scarcely adverb HARDLY, barely, only just.

scarcity noun ❶ DEARTH, shortage, undersupply, paucity, meagreness, sparseness, insufficiency, deficiency, inadequacy, lack, exiguity. ❷ RARITY, rareness, infrequency, sparseness, uncommonness.

scare verb FRIGHTEN, alarm, startle, make fearful, make nervous, terrify, terrorize, petrify, horrify, appal, shock, intimidate, daunt, awe, cow, panic, put the fear of God into, scare stiff, make someone's blood run cold, make someone's flesh creep, make someone's hair stand on end; *informal* scare the pants off; *Brit. informal* put the wind up.
▶ noun FRIGHT, alarm, start, fearfulness, nervousness, terror, horror, shock, panic.

scathing adjective VIRULENT, savage, fierce, ferocious, brutal, stinging, biting, mordant, trenchant, caustic, vitriolic, withering, scornful, harsh, severe, stern.
– OPPOSITES mild.

scatter verb ❶ DISSEMINATE, diffuse, spread, sow, sprinkle, strew, broadcast, fling, toss, throw. ❷ the crowd scattered: BREAK UP, disperse, disband, separate, dissolve.
– OPPOSITES gather, assemble.

scatterbrained adjective FORGETFUL, dreamy, irresponsible, wool-gathering, with one's head in the clouds, feather-brained, hare-brained, erratic, giddy.

scavenge verb SEARCH, look for, hunt, forage for, rummage for.

scenario noun PLOT, outline, synopsis, summary, precis, rundown, storyline, structure, scheme, plan, sequence of events.

scene noun ❶ PLACE, location, site, position, spot, setting, locale, whereabouts, arena, stage. ❷ EVENT, incident, happening, situation, episode, affair, moment, proceeding. ❸ FUSS, exhibition, outburst, commotion, to-do, row, upset, tantrum, furore, brouhaha.

scenery noun ❶ VIEW, outlook, landscape, vista, panorama, prospect. ❷ SET, stage set, setting, background, backdrop.

scenic adjective PICTURESQUE, pretty, beautiful, pleasing.

scent noun ❶ AROMA, perfume, fragrance, smell, bouquet, odour; *poetic/literary* redolence. ❷ TRACK, trail, spoor.

sceptic noun QUESTIONER, doubter, agnostic, unbeliever, doubting Thomas, disbeliever, dissenter, scoffer, cynic.

sceptical adjective DOUBTING, doubtful, dubious, questioning, distrustful, mistrustful, suspicious, hesitant, disbelieving, misbelieving, incredulous, unconvinced, scoffing, cynical.
– OPPOSITES certain, convinced.

scepticism noun DOUBT, doubtfulness, dubiety, agnosticism, distrust, mistrust, suspicion, hesitancy, disbelief, misbelief, incredulity, cynicism.

schedule noun PLAN, scheme, timetable, programme, diary, calendar, itinerary, agenda.
▶ verb ARRANGE, timetable, organize, plan, programme, book.

scheme noun ❶ PLAN, programme, project, course of action, system, procedure, strategy, design, tactics, contrivance. ❷ ARRANGEMENT, system, organization, disposition, schema. ❸ PLOT, ruse, ploy, stratagem, manoeuvre, machinations, intrigue, conspiracy; *informal* game, racket.
▶ verb PLOT, conspire, intrigue, manoeuvre, plan, lay plans.

scheming adjective CALCULATING, designing, conniving, wily, crafty, cunning, sly, artful, slippery, underhand, duplicitous, devious, Machiavellian; *informal* tricky.
– OPPOSITES ingenuous, honest.

schism noun DIVISION, breach, split, rift, break, rupture, separation, severance, detachment, discord, disagreement.

scholar noun MAN/WOMAN OF LETTERS, learned person, academic, highbrow, intellectual, pundit, savant; *informal* bookworm, egghead.

scholarly adjective LEARNED, erudite, academic, well read, intellectual, highbrow, scholastic, literary, studious, bookish, lettered.
– OPPOSITES ignorant.

scholarship noun ❶ LEARNING, knowledge, education, erudition, letters. ❷ GRANT, fellowship, endowment; *Brit.* bursary.

school noun ❶ EDUCATIONAL INSTITUTION, academy. ❷ SCHOOL OF THOUGHT, outlook, persuasion, opinion, point of view, belief, faith, creed.
▶ verb EDUCATE, teach, instruct, train, coach, drill, discipline, direct, guide, prepare, prime, verse.

scientific adjective SYSTEMATIC, methodical, orderly, regulated, controlled, exact, precise, mathematical.

scintillate verb ❶ SPARKLE, twinkle, flash, gleam, glitter, glint, glisten, coruscate. ❷ BE SPARKLING, be vivacious, be lively, be witty.

scintillating adjective SPARKLING, dazzling, vivacious, effervescent, lively, animated, ebullient, bright, brilliant, witty, exciting, stimulating, invigorating.
– OPPOSITES dull, boring.

scion noun DESCENDANT, heir, offspring, child; *Law* issue.

scoff verb JEER AT, mock at, sneer at, gibe at, taunt, laugh at, ridicule, poke fun at, make a fool of, make sport of, rag, revile, deride, belittle, scorn, knock; *informal* pooh-pooh.

scold verb *see* REPRIMAND verb.

scoop noun ❶ LADLE, spoon, dipper. ❷ EXCLUSIVE STORY, revelation, exposé.
■ **scoop out** HOLLOW OUT, gouge out, dig, excavate. **scoop up** GATHER UP, pick up, lift.

scope noun ❶ EXTENT, range, sphere, area, field, realm, compass, orbit, reach, span, sweep, confine, limit. ❷ OPPORTUNITY, freedom, latitude, capacity.

scorch verb BURN, singe, char, sear, discolour, blacken.

score noun ❶ NUMBER OF POINTS/

GOALS, total, result, outcome. ❷ NOTCH, mark scratch, scrape, groove, cut, nick, chip, gouge.
▶ verb ❶ *score a point:* WIN, gain, achieve, chalk up, notch up. ❷ *yet to score:* WIN A POINT/GOAL, gain a point. ❸ MAKE A NOTCH IN, mark, scratch, scrape, groove, cut, nick, chip, gouge.

scores plural noun CROWDS, throngs, multitudes, droves, swarms, armies, legions.

scorn noun CONTEMPT, contemptuousness, disdain, haughtiness, disparagement, derision, mockery, contumely.
– OPPOSITES praise.
▶ verb ❶ BE CONTEMPTUOUS, hold in contempt, look down on, disdain, disparage, slight, deride, mock, scoff at, sneer at. ❷ REBUFF, spurn, shun, refuse, reject, turn down.

scornful adjective CONTEMPTUOUS, disdainful, haughty, supercilious, disparaging, slighting, scathing, derisive, mocking, scoffing, sneering, contumelious.
– OPPOSITES respectful.

scoundrel noun VILLAIN, rogue, rascal, miscreant, reprobate, scapegrace, good-for-nothing, n'er-do-well, wastrel; *dated* cad; *informal, dated* rotter, bounder.

scour[1] verb *scour the bath:* SCRUB, rub, clean, cleanse, abrade, wash, wipe, polish, buff, burnish.

scour[2] verb *scour the countryside:* SEARCH, comb, go over, look all over, ransack, hunt through, rake through, rummage through, leave no stone unturned.

scourge noun ❶ BANE, curse, affliction, plague, trial, torment, torture, suffering, burden, cross to bear, thorn in one's flesh/side, nuisance, pest, punishment, penalty. ❷ WHIP, horsewhip, bullwhip, switch, lash, cat-o'-nine-tails, flail, strap, birch.
▶ verb WHIP, horsewhip, flog, lash, birch, cane, thrash, beat, leather; *informal* belt, wallop, tan someone's hide.

scout noun LOOKOUT, outrider, spy.
▶ verb RECONNOITRE, make a reconnaissance of, spy out, survey, inspect, investigate, examine, scan.

scowl verb FROWN, glower, glare, lower, look daggers.
– OPPOSITES smile.
▶ noun FROWN, glower, glare, black look, dirty look.

scraggy adjective *See* SCRAWNY.

scramble verb ❶ CLAMBER, climb, crawl. ❷ HURRY, hasten, rush, race, scurry. ❸ MIX UP, jumble, tangle, throw into confusion, disorganize.
▶ noun ❶ CLAMBER, climb, trek. ❷ HURRY, rush, race, scurry.

scrap[1] noun ❶ *a scrap of cloth:* FRAGMENT, piece, bit, snippet, remnant, tatter. ❷ *a scrap of food:* PIECE, bit, morsel, particle, sliver, crumb, bite, mouthful. ❸ WASTE, junk, rubbish, scrap metal.
▶ verb THROW AWAY, get rid of, discard, toss out, abandon, jettison, dispense with, shed; *informal* ditch, junk.
– OPPOSITES keep, preserve.

scrap[2] noun FIGHT, quarrel, argument, squabble, wrangle, fracas, brawl, scuffle, disagreement, clash; *informal* set-to, punch-up, dust-up, tiff; *Brit. informal* barney.
▶ verb FIGHT, quarrel, bicker, argue, squabble, wrangle, brawl, disagree.

scrape verb ❶ SCOUR, rub, scrub,

file, sandpaper, remove, erase. ❷ GRATE, rasp, grind, scratch. ❸ GRAZE, scratch, abrade, skin, cut, lacerate, bark.
▶ **noun** ❶ GRAZE, scratch, abrasion, cut, laceration, wound. ❷ TROUBLE, difficulty, straits, distress, mess, muddle, predicament, plight, tight spot, tight corner, fix.

scraps **plural noun** LEFTOVERS, leavings, scrapings, remains, residue, bits and pieces, odds and ends.

scratch **verb** ❶ SCRAPE, abrade, graze, skin, cut, lacerate, bark. ❷ *scratch an itchy part:* RUB, scrape, tear at.
▶ **noun** ❶ GRAZE, scrape, abrasion, cut, laceration, wound. ❷ *a scratch on the paintwork:* SCRAPE, mark, line, defacement.
■ **scratch about/around** SEARCH, hunt, cast about, rummage around, forage about, poke about.

scrawny **adjective** SKINNY, scraggy, thin, thin as a rake, gaunt, bony, angular, raw-boned.
– OPPOSITES plump.

scream **verb** SHRIEK, howl, shout, cry out, call out, yell, screech, wail, squawk, bawl; *informal* holler.
▶ **noun** SHRIEK, howl, shout, yell, cry, screech, wail, squawk.

screen **noun** ❶ SHIELD, protection, shelter, guard, safeguard, buffer. ❷ COVER, cloak, veil, mask, camouflage, disguise, facade, front, blind. ❸ SIEVE, riddle, strainer, colander, filter.
▶ **verb** ❶ PARTITION OFF, divide off, conceal, hide. ❷ SHELTER, shield, protect, guard, safeguard. ❸ VET, check, test, examine, investigate, scan.

scribble **verb** DASH OFF, jot down, scrawl.

scribe **noun** AMANUENSIS, copyist, transcriber, secretary, recorder.

scrimp **verb** SKIMP, economize, be frugal, be thrifty, husband one's resources, tighten one's belt, draw in one's horns.

script **noun** ❶ HANDWRITING, writing, hand, pen, calligraphy. ❷ TEXT, book, libretto, score, lines, words, manuscript.

scrounge **verb** BEG, borrow; *informal* sponge, cadge, bum; *N. Amer. informal* mooch.

scrounger **noun** BEGGAR, borrower, parasite; *informal* sponger, cadger, freeloader.

scrub **verb** RUB, scour, clean, cleanse, wash, wipe.

scruffy **adjective** UNTIDY, unkempt, dishevelled, ungroomed, ill-groomed, shabby, down at heel, ragged, tattered, slovenly, messy, slatternly, sluttish.
– OPPOSITES smart.

scruple **verb** HAVE QUALMS ABOUT, hesitate to, think twice about, balk at, demur about, be reluctant to, recoil from, shrink from, waver about, vacillate about.

scruples **plural noun** QUALMS, compunction, hesitation, second thoughts, doubt, misgivings, uneasiness, reluctance, restraint, wavering, vacillation.

scrupulous **adjective** ❶ METICULOUS, careful, painstaking, thorough, rigorous, strict, conscientious, punctilious, exact, precise, fastidious. ❷ HONEST, honourable, upright, righteous, right-minded, moral, ethical.
– OPPOSITES careless, unscrupulous.

scrutinize verb EXAMINE, study, inspect, survey, scan, look over, investigate, go over, peruse, probe, inquire into, sift, analyse, dissect.

scrutiny noun EXAMINATION, study, inspection, perusal, investigation, exploration, probe, inquiry, analysis, dissection.

sculpture noun STATUE, statuette, bust, figure, figurine.
▶ **verb** SCULPT, chisel, model, fashion, shape, cast, carve, cut, hew.

scum noun ❶ FILM, crust, algae, filth, dirt. ❷ LOWEST OF THE LOW, dregs of society, riff-raff, rabble.

scupper verb ❶ SINK, submerge. ❷ scupper their plans: RUIN, defeat, demolish, wreck, smash.

scurrilous adjective ABUSIVE, insulting, offensive, disparaging, defamatory, slanderous, gross, foul, scandalous.

scurry verb HURRY, hasten, make haste, rush, race, dash, run, sprint, scuttle, scamper, scramble.

seal noun ❶ EMBLEM, symbol, insignia, badge, crest, token, mark, monogram. ❷ SEALANT, sealer, adhesive.
▶ **verb** ❶ FASTEN, secure, shut, close up. ❷ MAKE AIRTIGHT, make watertight, close, shut, cork, stopper. ❸ seal the bargain: SECURE, clinch, settle, decide, complete.
■ **seal off** CLOSE OFF, shut off, cordon off, fence off.

seam noun ❶ JOINT, join, junction. ❷ LAYER, stratum, vein, lode.

sear verb BURN, singe, scorch, char, dry up, wither, discolour, brown.

search verb ❶ search the building: GO THROUGH, look through, hunt through, rummage through, forage through, rifle through, scour, ransack, comb, go through with a fine-tooth comb, sift through, turn upside down, turn inside out, leave no stone unturned in. ❷ search for clues: LOOK FOR, seek, hunt for, look high and low for, cast around for, ferret about for, scout out. ❸ search the prisoner: EXAMINE, inspect, check; *informal* frisk.
▶ **noun** ❶ HUNT, rummage, forage, ransacking. ❷ EXPLORATION, quest, probe.

season noun PERIOD, time, time of year, spell, term.
▶ **verb** ❶ FLAVOUR, add flavouring to, spice, add spices to; *informal* pep up, add zing to. ❷ MATURE, age, mellow, prime, prepare.

seasonable adjective OPPORTUNE, timely, well timed, appropriate, suitable, apt.

seasoned adjective EXPERIENCED, practised, well versed, established, long-serving, veteran, hardened, battle-scarred.
– OPPOSITES inexperienced.

seat noun ❶ CHAIR, bench, settle, stool, stall. ❷ the seat of government: HEADQUARTERS, location, site, base, centre, hub, heart. ❸ BUTTOCKS, rump, hindquarters; *Brit.* bottom; *informal* behind, backside; *Brit. informal* bum; *N. Amer. informal* butt, tail, fanny; *humorous* posterior.
▶ **verb** ❶ PLACE, position, put, situate, deposit. ❷ the hall seats 500: HOLD, take, have room for, accommodate.

secede verb WITHDRAW FROM, break away from, break with, sever relations with, split with, resign from, pull out of, drop out of, turn one's back on, repudiate, reject, renounce; *informal* quit.
– OPPOSITES join.

secluded adjective SHELTERED, concealed, hidden, private, solitary, lonely, sequestered, retired, out of the way, remote, isolated, off the beaten track, tucked away, cut-off.
– OPPOSITES accessible.

seclusion noun PRIVACY, solitude, retreat, retirement, withdrawal, sequestration, isolation, concealment, hiding, secrecy.

second[1] adjective ❶ SECONDARY, lower, subordinate, lesser, lower-grade, inferior. ❷ ADDITIONAL, extra, further.
▶ noun ASSISTANT, attendant, helper, supporter, backer, right-hand man/woman.
▶ verb ❶ ASSIST, help, aid, support. ❷ SUPPORT, give one's support to, back, approve, give one's approval to, endorse, promote.

second[2] noun MOMENT, instant, trice, twinkling, twinkling of an eye; *informal* sec, jiffy, tick, two shakes of a lamb's tail, two shakes.

secondary adjective ❶ LESSER, subordinate, minor, ancillary, subsidiary, non-essential, unimportant. ❷ **secondary infections**: NON-PRIMARY, derived, derivative, indirect, resulting, resultant. ❸ **a secondary line of action**: SECOND, back-up, reserve, relief, auxiliary, extra, alternative, subsidiary.
– OPPOSITES primary.

second-hand adjective USED, worn, nearly new, handed down, hand-me-down; *Brit. informal* reach-me-down.
– OPPOSITES new.
▶ adverb AT SECOND HAND, indirectly.
– OPPOSITES directly.

second-rate adjective SECOND-CLASS, low-class, inferior, lesser, substandard, poor-quality, low-quality, low-grade, shoddy, rubbishy, tawdry.
– OPPOSITES first-rate, excellent.

secret adjective ❶ **keep it secret**: CONFIDENTIAL, private, unrevealed, undisclosed, under wraps, unpublished, untold, unknown; *informal* hush-hush. ❷ **a secret drawer**: HIDDEN, concealed, camouflaged, disguised. ❸ **a secret love affair**: HIDDEN, clandestine, furtive, conspiratorial, undercover, surreptitious, stealthy, cloak-and-dagger, covert.
– OPPOSITES open, obvious.

secrete[1] verb DISCHARGE, emit, excrete, exude, ooze, leak, give off, send out.
– OPPOSITES absorb.

secrete[2] verb HIDE, conceal, cover up, stow away, sequester, cache; *informal* stash away.
– OPPOSITES reveal.

secretion noun DISCHARGE, emission, excretion, exudate, oozing, leakage.

secretive adjective SECRET, reticent, uncommunicative, unforthcoming, reserved, taciturn, silent, quiet, tight-lipped, close-mouthed, close, playing one's cards close to one's chest; *informal* cagey.
– OPPOSITES open.

secretly adverb IN SECRET, confidentially, privately, behind closed doors, in camera, sub rosa.

sectarian adjective BIGOTED, prejudiced, doctrinaire, partisan, narrow-minded, insular, hidebound, extreme, fanatic, fanatical.
– OPPOSITES tolerant.

section noun ❶ PART, segment, division, component, piece, portion, bit, slice, fraction, fragment. ❷ PART, division, department, branch.

sector noun ❶ PART, division, area, branch, department, category, field. ❷ ZONE, quarter, district, area, region.

secular adjective LAY, non-religious, non-spiritual, non-church, laical, temporal, worldly, earthly.
– OPPOSITES religious.

secure adjective ❶ SAFE, free from danger, out of harm's way, invulnerable, unharmed, undamaged, protected, sheltered, shielded. ❷ FASTENED, closed, shut, locked, sealed. ❸ STABLE, fixed, steady, strong, sturdy, solid. ❹ UNWORRIED, at ease, comfortable, confident, assured.
– OPPOSITES insecure.
▶ verb ❶ MAKE SAFE, make sound, fortify, strengthen, protect. ❷ FASTEN, close, shut, lock, bolt, chain, seal. ❸ ACQUIRE, obtain, gain, get, get hold of, procure, get possession of, come by; *informal* get one's hands on, land.

sedate[1] verb GIVE A SEDATIVE TO, put under sedation, tranquillize.

sedate[2] adjective ❶ CALM, tranquil, placid, dignified, formal, decorous, proper, demure, sober, earnest, staid, stiff. ❷ a sedate pace: SLOW, slow-moving, leisurely, measured, deliberate, dignified.
– OPPOSITES exciting, fast.

sedative noun TRANQUILLIZER, calmative, depressant, sleeping pill, narcotic, opiate; *informal* downer.
▶ adjective CALMING, tranquillizing, soothing, relaxing, assuaging, lenitive, soporific, narcotic.

sedentary adjective SITTING, seated, desk-bound, desk, inactive.
– OPPOSITES active.

sediment noun DREGS, lees, grounds, deposit, residue, precipitate, settlings.

seditious adjective REBELLIOUS, insurrectionist, insurgent, mutinous, subversive, dissident, disloyal, treasonous.

seduce verb ❶ PERSUADE TO HAVE SEX; *informal* have one's (wicked) way with, take advantage of; *dated* debauch. ❷ ATTRACT, lure, tempt, entice, beguile, ensnare.

seductive adjective ❶ ATTRACTIVE, alluring, tempting, provocative, exciting, arousing, sexy. ❷ ATTRACTIVE, appealing, inviting, alluring, tempting, enticing, beguiling.

see verb ❶ MAKE OUT, catch sight of, glimpse, spot, notice, observe, view, perceive, discern, espy, descry, distinguish, identify, recognize. ❷ I saw the programme: WATCH, look at, view. ❸ see what they mean: UNDERSTAND, grasp, get, comprehend, follow, take in, know, realize, get the drift of, make out, fathom. ❹ see what he wants: FIND OUT, discover, learn, ascertain, determine, ask, enquire, make enquiries, investigate. ❺ see trouble ahead: FORESEE, predict, forecast, anticipate, envisage, picture, visualize. ❻ see an old friend: MEET, encounter, run into, stumble upon, chance upon. ❼ see the doctor: VISIT, pay a visit to, consult, confer with. ❽ GO OUT

WITH, take out, keep company with, court; *informal* go steady with, date.

■ **see about** SEE TO, deal with, attend to, cope with, look after, take care of. **see through** NOT BE TAKEN IN BY, be wise to, get the measure of, penetrate; *informal* have someone's number.

seed noun ❶ OVULE, pip, kernel, stone, germ. ❷ SOURCE, origin, root, cause, reason.

seek verb ❶ SEARCH FOR, look for, be on the lookout for, be after, hunt for, be in quest of, be in pursuit of. ❷ ASK FOR, request, solicit, entreat, beg for.

seem verb APPEAR, appear to be, have the appearance of being, give the impression of being, look, look like, look to be, have the look of.

seemly adjective DECOROUS, proper, decent, becoming, fitting, suitable, appropriate, apt, apposite, meet, comme il faut, in good taste.
– OPPOSITES unbecoming.

seep verb OOZE, leak, exude, drip, drain, percolate.

see-saw verb FLUCTUATE, go from one extreme to the other, swing, oscillate.

seethe verb ❶ BOIL, bubble, fizz, foam, froth, ferment, churn. ❷ BE FURIOUS, be livid, be incensed, storm, fume.

segment noun SECTION, part, division, component, piece, portion, slice, wedge.

segregate verb SEPARATE, set apart, isolate, cut off, sequester, ostracize, discriminate against.
– OPPOSITES amalgamate.

segregation noun SEPARATION, setting apart, isolation, dissociation, sequestration, discrimination, apartheid, partition.

seize verb ❶ GRAB, grab hold of, take hold of, grasp, take a grip of, grip, clutch at. ❷ CONFISCATE, impound, commandeer, appropriate, sequester, sequestrate. ❸ SNATCH, abduct, take captive, kidnap, hijack.

seizure noun ❶ CONFISCATION, commandeering, appropriation, sequestration. ❷ SNATCHING, abduction, kidnapping, hijacking.

seldom adverb RARELY, hardly ever, scarcely ever, infrequently, only occasionally; *informal* once in a blue moon.
– OPPOSITES frequently.

select verb CHOOSE, pick, hand-pick, single out, opt for, decide on, settle on, prefer, favour.
▶ adjective ❶ CHOICE, hand-picked, prime, first-rate, first-class, finest, best, high-quality, top-quality. ❷ EXCLUSIVE, elite, limited, privileged, cliquish; *Brit. informal* posh.
– OPPOSITES inferior.

selection noun ❶ CHOICE, pick, option. ❷ VARIETY, assortment, anthology, miscellany, collection, range.

selective adjective PARTICULAR, discriminating, discriminatory, discerning, fussy, careful, cautious; *informal* choosy, picky.

self-assurance noun SELF-CONFIDENCE, confidence, assertiveness, positiveness.
– OPPOSITES diffidence.

self-centred adjective EGOCENTRIC, egotistical, self-absorbed, self-seeking, wrapped up in oneself, selfish, narcissistic.

self-confidence noun SELF-ASSURANCE, confidence, self-reliance, self-dependence, self-possession, poise, aplomb, composure, sangfroid.

self-conscious adjective AWKWARD, shy, diffident, bashful, blushing, timorous, nervous, timid, retiring, shrinking, ill at ease, embarrassed, uncomfortable.
– OPPOSITES confident.

self-control noun SELF-RESTRAINT, restraint, self-discipline, will power, strength of will.

self-denial noun SELF-DISCIPLINE, asceticism, abnegation, abstemiousness, temperance, abstinence, self-sacrifice, selflessness, unselfishness, altruism.
– OPPOSITES self-indulgence.

self-esteem noun SELF-RESPECT, self-regard, pride in oneself/one's abilities, faith in oneself, amour propre.

self-important adjective POMPOUS, vain, conceited, arrogant, swollen-headed, egotistical, presumptuous, overbearing, overweening, haughty, swaggering, strutting.
– OPPOSITES humble.

self-indulgence noun SELF-GRATIFICATION, lack of self-restraint, intemperance, immoderation, excess, pleasure-seeking, sensualism, dissipation.

selfish adjective SELF-SEEKING, self-centred, egocentric, egotistic, egoistic, self-interested, self-regarding, self-absorbed; *informal* looking out for number one.
– OPPOSITES unselfish, selfless.

selfless adjective UNSELFISH, altruistic, generous, self-sacrificing, self-denying, magnanimous, liberal, ungrudging.
– OPPOSITES selfish.

self-respect noun SELF-ESTEEM, self-regard, pride in oneself, pride in one's abilities, belief in one's worth, faith in oneself, amour propre.

self-righteous adjective SANCTIMONIOUS, holier-than-thou, pietistic, too good to be true, Pharisaic, unctuous, mealy-mouthed; *informal* goody-goody.
– OPPOSITES humble.

self-sacrifice noun SELF-DENIAL, selflessness, unselfishness, altruism.

self-seeking adjective SELF-INTERESTED, opportunistic, ambitious, mercenary, out for what one can get, fortune-hunting, gold-digging; *informal* on the make, looking out for number one.
– OPPOSITES altruistic.

self-willed adjective WILFUL, contrary, perverse, uncooperative, wayward, recalcitrant, refractory, intractable, stubborn, pig-headed, mulish, intransigent, difficult, disobedient; *informal* cussed.

sell verb ❶ PUT UP FOR SALE, put on sale, dispose of, vend, auction off, trade, barter, trade in, deal in, traffic in, stock, market, handle, peddle, hawk. ❷ BOUGHT, be purchased, go, move, be in demand. ❸ selling for £5: RETAIL, go for, be, be found for. ❹ sell the idea: GET ACCEPTANCE FOR, win

approval for, get support for, get across, promote.
– OPPOSITES buy.

seller noun VENDOR, retailer, salesman/woman/person, shopkeeper, trader, merchant, dealer, agent, representative, rep.

semblance noun APPEARANCE, show, air, guise, pretence, facade, front, veneer, mask, cloak, disguise, camouflage, pretext.

send verb ❶ DISPATCH, forward, mail, post, remit. ❷ THROW, fling, hurl, cast, let fly, propel, project. ❸ **send someone mad:** DRIVE, make, cause someone to be/become.
– OPPOSITES receive.
■ **send for** CALL FOR, summon, request, order.

senile adjective DODDERING, decrepit, failing, in one's dotage, in one's second childhood; *informal* past it.

senior adjective ❶ HIGH-RANKING, higher-ranking, superior. ❷ OLDER, elder.
– OPPOSITES junior.

sensation noun ❶ FEELING, sense, awareness, consciousness, perception, impression. ❷ STIR, excitement, agitation, commotion, furore, scandal.

sensational adjective ❶ **a sensational story:** SPECTACULAR, stirring, exciting, startling, staggering, dramatic, amazing, shocking, scandalous, lurid. ❷ **looking sensational:** MARVELLOUS, superb, excellent, exceptional, remarkable; *informal* fabulous, fab, out of this world.

sense noun ❶ FEELING, sensation, faculty, sensibility. ❷ APPRECIATION, awareness, understanding, comprehension. ❸ COMMON SENSE, practicality, wisdom, sagacity, sharpness, discernment, perception, wit, intelligence, cleverness, understanding, reason, logic, brains, nous. ❹ **a word with several senses:** MEANING, definition, import, signification, significance, implication, nuance, drift, gist, purport, denotation.
▶ verb FEEL, get the impression of, be aware of, be conscious of, observe, notice, perceive, discern, grasp, pick up, suspect, divine, intuit.

senseless adjective ❶ **a senseless act:** NONSENSICAL, stupid, foolish, silly, inane, idiotic, mindless, unintelligent, unwise, irrational, illogical, meaningless, pointless, absurd, ludicrous, fatuous, asinine, moronic, imbecilic. ❷ **knocked senseless by:** UNCONSCIOUS, insensible, out cold, out, stunned, numb, numbed, insensate.
– OPPOSITES wise.

sensible adjective PRACTICAL, realistic, down-to-earth, wise, prudent, judicious, sagacious, shrewd, discerning, perceptive, intelligent, clever, reasonable, rational, logical.
– OPPOSITES foolish.
■ **sensible of** AWARE OF, conscious of, mindful of, sensitive to, alive to, cognizant of, acquainted with.

sensitive adjective ❶ **sensitive skin:** DELICATE, fine, soft, fragile. ❷ **a sensitive person:** RESPONSIVE, receptive, perceptive, discerning, discriminatory, sympathetic, understanding, empathetic. ❸ **a sensitive issue:** DELICATE, difficult, problematic, ticklish.
– OPPOSITES resilient, impervious, uncontroversial.

■ **sensitive to** RESPONSIVE TO, easily affected by, susceptible to, reactive to, sentient of.

sensual adjective ❶ PHYSICAL, carnal, bodily, fleshly, animal, voluptuous, epicurean, sybaritic. ❷ VOLUPTUOUS, sexual, sexy, erotic.
– OPPOSITES spiritual.

sensuous adjective PLEASING, pleasurable, gratifying, aesthetic.

sentence noun ❶ JUDGEMENT, verdict, ruling, decision, decree. ❷ PRISON SENTENCE, jail sentence, prison term; *informal* time; *Brit. informal* porridge.
▶ verb IMPOSE A SENTENCE ON, pass judgement on, penalize, punish, condemn, doom.

sententious adjective MORALISTIC, moralizing, judgemental, sanctimonious, canting, pompous.

sentiment noun ❶ EMOTION, emotionalism, finer feelings, tender feelings, tenderness, softness. ❷ FEELINGS, attitude, belief, opinion, view, point of view.

sentimental adjective ❶ EMOTIONAL, romantic, mawkish, maudlin; *informal* mushy, slushy, schmaltzy, corny; *Brit. informal* soppy. ❷ EMOTIONAL, nostalgic, affectionate, loving, tender, warm.

sentiments plural noun FEELING, attitude, belief, thoughts, way of thinking, opinion, view, point of view, idea, judgement.

sentry noun GUARD, lookout, watch, watchman, sentinel.

separate adjective ❶ have separate residences: INDIVIDUAL, distinct, different, particular, autonomous, independent. ❷ problems are quite separate: UNCONNECTED, distinct, different, disconnected, unrelated, detached, divorced, divided, discrete.
▶ verb ❶ DISCONNECT, detach, sever, uncouple, divide, sunder. ❷ DIVIDE, come between, stand between, keep apart, partition. ❸ PART, part company, go their/your/our separate ways, go different ways, diverge, split, divide. ❹ BREAK UP, split up, part, become estranged, divorce.
– OPPOSITES join, unite.

separately adverb ❶ live separately: APART, individually, independently, autonomously. ❷ they left separately: INDIVIDUALLY, one by one, one at a time, singly, severally, independently.

septic adjective INFECTED, festering, poisoned, putrefying, putrefactive, putrid.

sepulchre noun TOMB, vault, burial place, grave.

sequel noun FOLLOW-UP, development, result, consequence, outcome, issue, upshot.

sequence noun CHAIN, course, cycle, series, progression, succession, set, arrangement, order, pattern.

serendipity noun CHANCE, luck, good fortune, fortuity, fortuitousness, accident, coincidence.

serene adjective CALM, composed, tranquil, peaceful, placid, still, quiet, unperturbed, imperturbable, undisturbed, unruffled, unworried, unexcited, unexcitable, unflappable.
– OPPOSITES excitable.

series noun SUCCESSION,

progression, sequence, chain, course, string, train, run, cycle, set, row, arrangement, order.

serious adjective ❶ SOLEMN, earnest, unsmiling, thoughtful, preoccupied, pensive, grave, sombre, sober, long-faced, dour, stern, grim, poker-faced. ❷ **serious problems**: IMPORTANT, significant, consequential, of consequence, momentous, weighty, far-reaching, urgent, pressing, crucial, vital, life-and-death. ❸ **serious injuries**: ACUTE, grave, bad, critical, grievous, dangerous, perilous. ❹ **serious about doing it**: EARNEST, in earnest, sincere, honest, genuine, firm, resolute, resolved, determined, fervent.
– OPPOSITES cheerful, minor, trivial.

sermon noun HOMILY, address, oration, lecture, preaching, teaching.

servant noun DOMESTIC, help, domestic help, maid, handyman, menial, drudge, scullion, retainer, attendant, lackey; *Brit. informal* char; *Brit. dated* charwoman.

serve verb ❶ **serve on the committee**: HAVE/HOLD A PLACE ON, be on, perform duties, carry out duties. ❷ **sofas serving as beds**: ACT AS, do duty as, function as, do the work of, be suitable for. ❸ **serve three years**: SPEND, go through, carry out, fulfil, complete. ❹ **serve food**: DISH UP, give out, distribute, set out, present, provide. ❺ **serve a customer**: ATTEND TO, look after, take care of, assist.

service noun ❶ **do someone a service**: GOOD TURN, assistance, help, advantage, benefit. ❷ **his conditions of service**: WORK, employment, labour, duty, business. ❸ **a wedding service**: CEREMONY, ritual, rite, sacrament. ❹ **the car is due for a service**: SERVICING, overhaul, check, maintenance, repair.
▶ verb CHECK, go over, overhaul, maintain, repair.

serviceable adjective ❶ FUNCTIONAL, utilitarian, practical, useful, durable, hard-wearing, tough, strong. ❷ USABLE, of use, functioning, operative, repairable.
– OPPOSITES impractical, unusable.

servile adjective ❶ **servile tasks**: MENIAL, low, lowly, humble, mean, base. ❷ **servile employees**: SUBSERVIENT, obsequious, sycophantic, fawning, toadying, grovelling, submissive; *informal* bootlicking.
– OPPOSITES assertive.

serving noun HELPING, portion, plateful.

servitude noun SLAVERY, enslavement, subjugation, subjection, domination, bondage; *historical* serfdom, vassalage, thraldom.
– OPPOSITES liberty.

session noun ❶ PERIOD, time, spell, stretch. ❷ MEETING, sitting, assembly, conference, discussion.

set[1] verb ❶ PUT, place, lay, lay down, deposit, position, rest, locate, lodge, situate, station; *informal* stick, park, plonk. ❷ FIX, embed, insert, lodge, mount, arrange, install. ❸ **set pen to paper**: PUT, apply, lay, place, bring into contact with, touch. ❹ **set one's watch**: ADJUST, regulate, synchronize, coordinate, harmonize, calibrate, rectify, set right. ❺ **set the table:** LAY, make ready, prepare, arrange. ❻ **set her hair:** FIX, style, arrange, curl, wave. ❼ **set things in motion:** PUT, cause to be, start, actuate, instigate. ❽ **concrete won't set:** SOLIDIFY, stiffen, thicken, jell, harden, cake, congeal, coagulate. ❾ **set a record:** ESTABLISH, fix, create, bring into being/existence, institute. ❿ **set a date:** FIX, fix on, agree on, appoint, decide on, name, specify, stipulate, determine, designate, select, choose, arrange, schedule.

set[2] noun ❶ COLLECTION, group, assemblage, series, batch, array, assortment, selection. ❷ **the set of his shoulders:** BEARING, carriage, cast, posture, position. ❸ STAGE SET, setting, scenery, backdrop.

set[3] adjective ❶ **set texts:** FIXED, prescribed, scheduled, specified, determined, arranged, appointed, established, decided, agreed. ❷ **all set for the journey:** READY, prepared, equipped, primed; *informal* fit.
– OPPOSITES variable, unprepared.

setback noun REVERSAL, reverse, upset, check, hitch, hold-up, hindrance, impediment, obstruction, disappointment, misfortune, blow.
– OPPOSITES breakthrough.

setting noun ❶ ENVIRONMENT, surroundings, milieu, background, location, place, site. ❷ STAGE SETTING, set, scene, stage, scenery, backdrop. ❸ MOUNTING, frame.

settle verb ❶ **settle in America:** MAKE ONE'S HOME, set up home, take up residence, put down roots, establish oneself, go to live, move to, emigrate to. ❷ **an area settled by Scots:** ESTABLISH/FOUND A COLONY, colonize, occupy, people, inhabit, populate. ❸ **they won't settle:** CALM DOWN, quieten down, be quiet, be still, relax. ❹ **a bird settling on a branch:** LIGHT, land, come down, descend, repose, rest. ❺ **settle a dispute:** RESOLVE, clear up, patch up, reconcile, conclude, bring to an end. ❻ **settle one's affairs:** PUT IN ORDER, order, arrange, set to rights, straighten out, organize, regulate, adjust, clear up.
– OPPOSITES agitate, rise.
■ **settle for** COMPROMISE ON, accept, agree to, accede to, acquiesce in. **settle on** DECIDE ON, agree on, determine, confirm, arrange, fix, choose, appoint, select.

settlement noun ❶ COMMUNITY, colony, village, hamlet, encampment, outpost. ❷ RESOLUTION, reconciliation, conclusion, agreement, contract, pact, compact. ❸ PAYMENT, discharge, defrayal, liquidation.

settler noun COLONIST, colonizer, pioneer, immigrant.

sever verb ❶ CUT OFF, chop off, lop off, hack off, break off, tear off. ❷ DIVIDE, split, cleave, dissect, halve. ❸ **sever relations:** BREAK OFF, discontinue, suspend, dissolve, end, terminate, stop, cease, conclude.
– OPPOSITES join, maintain.

several adjective ❶ SOME, a number of, a few. ❷ SEPARATE, different, diverse, disparate, divergent, respective, individual, own, particular, specific, various, sundry.

severe adjective ❶ **severe criticism/punishment:** HARSH, hard, stringent, rigorous, unsparing, relentless, merciless, ruthless,

painful, sharp, caustic, biting, cutting, scathing, serious, extreme. ❷ **a severe shortage**: EXTREME, very bad, serious, grave, acute, critical, dire, dangerous, perilous. ❸ **severe storms**: FIERCE, strong, violent, intense, powerful, forceful. ❹ **a severe test**: DEMANDING, taxing, exacting, tough, difficult, hard, fierce, arduous, punishing, onerous, burdensome. ❺ **a severe expression**: STERN, grim, cold, chilly, austere, forbidding, dour, disapproving, unsmiling, sombre, grave, sober, serious. ❻ **a severe style**: AUSTERE, stark, spartan, ascetic, plain, simple, modest, bare, unadorned, unembellished, restrained, functional, classic.
– OPPOSITES mild, friendly, ornate.

sew verb STITCH, seam, embroider, mend, darn.

sex noun ❶ SEXUALITY, sexual attraction, sexual chemistry, sexual desire, desire, sex drive, sexual appetite, libido. ❷ FACTS OF LIFE, sexual reproduction, reproduction; *informal* the birds and the bees. ❸ INTIMACY, coitus, coition, coupling, copulation, carnal knowledge, making love, mating, fornication. ❹ GENDER.

sexuality noun ❶ SEX, gender, sexual characteristics. ❷ SEXUAL DESIRE, sexual appetite, sexiness, carnality, physicalness, eroticism, lust, sensuality, voluptuousness. ❸ SEXUAL ORIENTATION, sexual preferences.

sexy adjective ❶ **sexy films**: EROTIC, titillating, suggestive, arousing, exciting, stimulating. ❷ **sexy clothes**: AROUSING, provocative, seductive, sensuous, slinky. ❸ **sexy women/men**: ATTRACTIVE, alluring, seductive, shapely. ❹ **a sexy new project**: EXCITING, stimulating, stirring, interesting, intriguing, fashionable; *informal* trendy.

shabby adjective ❶ **shabby furniture**: DILAPIDATED, broken-down, run down, tumbledown, ramshackle, in disrepair, scruffy, dingy, seedy, squalid, tatty; *informal* tacky. ❷ **shabby clothes**: WORN, worn out, threadbare, ragged, frayed, tattered, faded, scruffy, tatty, the worse for wear. ❸ **shabby treatment**: CONTEMPTIBLE, despicable, rotten, dishonourable, disreputable, mean, base, low, dirty, odious, shameful, ignoble, unworthy, cheap, shoddy.
– OPPOSITES smart.

shackle verb CHAIN, fetter, put in irons, manacle, tie up, bind, tether, hobble, handcuff.

shade noun ❶ SHADINESS, shadow, shadowiness, shadows, shelter, cover. ❷ COLOUR, hue, tone, tint, tinge. ❸ NUANCE, degree, gradation, difference, variety. ❹ GHOST, spectre, phantom, apparition, spirit.
– OPPOSITES light.
▶ verb ❶ SHUT OUT THE LIGHT FROM, block off light to, cast a shadow over, screen, darken, dim. ❷ COVER, obscure, mute, hide, conceal, veil, curtain.

shadow noun ❶ *See* SHADE noun (1). ❷ SILHOUETTE, outline, shape. ❸ CONSTANT COMPANION, close friend, bosom friend, intimate, alter ego; *informal* sidekick. ❹ **a shadow of a smile**: A TRACE, a hint, a suggestion, a suspicion, a ghost.

shadowy adjective ❶ SHADY, shaded, dim, dark, gloomy, murky, crepuscular, tenebrous.

❷ INDISTINCT, indeterminate, indefinite, unclear, vague, nebulous, ill-defined.
– OPPOSITES bright, distinct.

shady adjective ❶ *See* SHADOWY (1). ❷ DISREPUTABLE, suspicious, suspect, questionable, dishonest, dishonourable, untrustworthy, devious, shifty, slippery, underhand, unscrupulous; *informal* crooked, tricky, fishy.
– OPPOSITES honest.

shaft noun ❶ POLE, stick, rod, staff, shank, stem, handle, upright. ❷ RAY, beam, gleam, streak, pencil. ❸ PASSAGE, duct, tunnel, well, flue.

shaggy adjective HAIRY, hirsute, long-haired, rough, coarse, matted, tangled, unkempt, untidy.
– OPPOSITES sleek.

shake verb ❶ ROCK, bump, jolt, bounce, roll, sway, judder, swing, jar, oscillate, wobble, rattle, vibrate, jerk, joggle, jounce. ❷ SHIVER, tremble, quiver, quake, shudder. ❸ **shake the can:** JIGGLE, joggle, jolt, jerk, rattle, agitate, jounce. ❹ **shaken by the news:** AGITATE, upset, distress, shock, alarm, disturb, perturb, fluster, unsettle, discompose, disquiet, disconcert, unnerve, ruffle; *informal* rattle.

shaky adjective ❶ TREMBLING, tremulous, quivering, quivery, unsteady, wobbly, weak, tottering, teetering, doddering, staggering. ❷ **feeling a bit shaky:** INFIRM, unsound, unwell, ill, below par, indisposed; *informal* under the weather. ❸ **shaky reasoning:** QUESTIONABLE, dubious, tenuous, flimsy, weak, unsound, unreliable.
– OPPOSITES steady, sound.

shallow adjective ❶ **a shallow person:** FRIVOLOUS, foolish, unintelligent, unthinking, trivial, insincere, superficial. ❷ **shallow ideas:** SUPERFICIAL, unsubstantial, trifling, trivial, petty, empty, meaningless.
– OPPOSITES serious, deep.

sham verb FAKE, pretend, feign, counterfeit, put on, simulate, affect, imitate.
▶ **noun** ❶ COUNTERFEIT, fake, forgery, copy, imitation, hoax, pretence, simulation. ❷ IMPOSTOR, fake, fraud, pretender, masquerader, dissembler, charlatan; *informal* phoney.
▶ **adjective** PRETEND, feigned, artificial, synthetic, ersatz, fake, pseudo, contrived, simulated, affected, put on, artificial, insincere, false, bogus, spurious; *informal* phoney.
– OPPOSITES genuine.

shamble verb SHUFFLE, hobble, limp, falter, totter, dodder.

shambles plural noun CHAOS, muddle, mess, confusion, disorder, disarray, disorganization, anarchy; *informal* disaster area.

shame noun ❶ HUMILIATION, ignominy, mortification, loss of face, remorse, guilt, compunction, embarrassment, discomfort, discomposure. ❷ DISGRACE, dishonour, scandal, discredit, degradation, ignominy, disrepute, infamy, odium, opprobrium. ❸ **what a shame!** PITY, misfortune, bad luck, ill luck, source of regret.
– OPPOSITES pride, honour.

shamefaced adjective ❶ ASHAMED, embarrassed, guilty, conscience-stricken, remorseful, contrite, penitent, regretful, humiliated, mortified, shamed.

❷ SHY, bashful, timid, timorous, shrinking, coy, sheepish.
– OPPOSITES unrepentant.

shameful adjective ❶ *shameful behaviour*: DISGRACEFUL, base, mean, low, vile, outrageous, shocking, dishonourable, unbecoming, unworthy, discreditable, deplorable, despicable, contemptible, reprehensible, scandalous, atrocious, heinous. ❷ *shameful secrets*: SHAMING, humiliating, mortifying, embarrassing; *informal* blush-making.
– OPPOSITES admirable.

shameless adjective ❶ UNASHAMED, without shame, unabashed, uncontrite, impenitent. ❷ BRAZEN, impudent, bold, brash, forward, audacious, immodest, unseemly, improper, unbecoming, indecorous, wanton, abandoned, indecent.
– OPPOSITES modest.

shape noun ❶ FORM, figure, configuration, formation, conformation, contour, outline, silhouette, profile, outward form, external appearance. ❷ FORM, guise, appearance, likeness, look, semblance, image, aspect. ❸ *in poor shape*: CONDITION, state, health, trim, fettle.
▶ verb FORM, fashion, make, mould, model, cast, frame, block, carve, sculpt.

shapeless adjective ❶ AMORPHOUS, formless, unformed, unshaped, unfashioned, undeveloped, embryonic. ❷ *shapeless clothes*: FORMLESS, badly cut, sack-like, ill-proportioned, inelegant.

shapely adjective WELL FORMED, well proportioned, elegant, curvaceous, curvy.

share noun ALLOWANCE, ration, allocation, division, quota, allotment, portion, part, lot, measure, helping, serving; *informal* cut, rake-off, piece of the cake, piece of the action; *Brit. informal* whack.
▶ verb ❶ *share a job/costs*: DIVIDE, split, have in common, go halves in; *informal* go fifty-fifty in, go Dutch. ❷ DIVIDE, distribute, apportion, parcel out, deal out, dole out, give out.

sharp adjective ❶ EDGED, razor-edged, keen, cutting, serrated, knife-like, pointed, needle-like, barbed, spiky. ❷ *a sharp drop*: STEEP, sheer, abrupt, precipitous, vertical. ❸ *a sharp stop*: SUDDEN, abrupt, rapid, unexpected. ❹ *a sharp pain*: INTENSE, acute, keen, piercing, cutting, extreme, severe, stabbing, shooting, stinging. ❺ *a sharp taste*: PUNGENT, biting, bitter, acid, sour, tart, vinegary. ❻ *sharp words*: HARSH, curt, brusque, bitter, hard, cutting, scathing, caustic, biting, barbed, acrimonious, trenchant, venomous, malicious, vitriolic, hurtful, unkind, cruel. ❼ *a sharp pupil*: INTELLIGENT, bright, clever, quick. ❽ *a sharp intelligence*: KEEN, acute, quick, ready, knowing, shrewd, discerning, perceptive, penetrating; *informal* smart. ❾ *a sharp pace*: BRISK, rapid, quick, fast, swift, vigorous, spirited, animated. ❿ *a sharp dresser*: SMART, stylish, fashionable, chic, elegant; *informal* dressy, snappy, natty.
– OPPOSITES blunt.

sharpen verb PUT AN EDGE ON, edge, whet, hone, strop, grind.

shatter verb ❶ SMASH, break,

break into pieces, splinter, fracture, pulverize, crush, crack; *informal* bust. ❷ **shatter someone's dreams:** DESTROY, demolish, wreck, ruin, dash, blight, wipe out, devastate; *informal* torpedo.

shave **verb** ❶ CUT OFF, trim, snip off, crop. ❷ PARE, plane, shear. ❸ BRUSH, graze, touch, scrape, rub.

sheath **noun** ❶ CASE, casing, cover, covering, envelope, wrapper. ❷ CONDOM, contraceptive; *Brit. informal* rubber johnny; *N. Amer. informal* rubber.

shed[1] **noun** HUT, outhouse, lean-to, shack.

shed[2] **verb** ❶ LET FALL, let drop, cast off, slough off. ❷ **shed clothes:** TAKE OFF, remove, strip off, doff. ❸ **shed light:** SEND FORTH, radiate, disperse, scatter.

sheen **noun** SHINE, lustre, gleam, sparkle, gloss, burnish, polish, patina.

sheepish **adjective** EMBARRASSED, ashamed, shamefaced, abashed, uncomfortable, shy, bashful, diffident, foolish, silly.

sheer **adjective** ❶ **sheer madness:** UTTER, complete, thoroughgoing, total, absolute, veritable, downright, out-and-out, unqualified, unconditional, unmitigated, unalloyed, unadulterated. ❷ **a sheer drop:** STEEP, abrupt, sharp, precipitous, vertical. ❸ **sheer silk:** DIAPHANOUS, transparent, see-through, translucent, fine, thin.
– OPPOSITES gradual, thick.

sheet **noun** ❶ BEDSHEET, bedlinen. ❷ PIECE, pane, panel, plate, slab. ❸ PIECE OF PAPER, leaf, page, folio. ❹ **sheets of water:** EXPANSE, stretch, span, reach, sweep, covering, blanket, carpet.

shell **noun** ❶ CARAPACE, case, casing, husk, pod, integument. ❷ BULLET, grenade, shot, shrapnel. ❸ FRAMEWORK, frame, structure, chassis, hull, skeleton.
▶ **verb** BOMB, bombard, blitz, strafe, fire on.
■ **shell out** PAY OUT, spend, lay out, disburse; *informal* fork out.

shelter **noun** ❶ PROTECTION, shield, cover, screen, safety, security, defence. ❷ REFUGE, sanctuary, retreat, haven, harbour.
– OPPOSITES exposure.
▶ **verb** ❶ PROTECT, shield, screen, safeguard, provide refuge/sanctuary from, guard, harbour, conceal, hide. ❷ TAKE SHELTER, take refuge, seek protection, seek refuge/sanctuary.
– OPPOSITES expose.

sheltered **adjective** ❶ SHADY, shaded, protected, screened, shielded, secluded. ❷ **a sheltered life:** QUIET, withdrawn, retired, isolated, protected, cloistered, reclusive.

shepherd **verb** ESCORT, conduct, usher, convoy, guide, marshal, steer.

shift **verb** MOVE, carry, transfer, switch, reposition, rearrange.
▶ **noun** ❶ MOVE, movement, transference, switch, repositioning. ❷ **an eight-hour shift:** STINT, spell/period of work.

shiftless **adjective** LAZY, idle, indolent, slothful, inefficient, unambitious, unenterprising, worthless, good-for-nothing.

shifty **adjective** EVASIVE, slippery, devious, duplicitous, deceitful, underhand, untrustworthy, double-dealing, dishonest, wily, crafty, artful, sly, scheming, contriving.
– OPPOSITES honest.

shimmer verb GLISTEN, glint, flicker, twinkle, sparkle, gleam, glow, scintillate, dance.

shine verb ❶ GLEAM, glow, glint, sparkle, twinkle, flicker, glitter, glisten, shimmer, flash, dazzle, beam, radiate, illuminate, luminesce, incandesce. ❷ POLISH, burnish, buff, wax, gloss. ❸ **shine at tennis:** EXCEL, be expert, be brilliant, be very good, be outstanding.
▶ **noun** ❶ LIGHT, brightness, gleam, glow, glint, sparkle, twinkle, flicker, glitter, glisten, shimmer, flash, dazzle, glare, beam, radiance, illumination, luminescence, luminosity, lambency, effulgence. ❷ POLISH, burnish, gleam, gloss, lustre, sheen, patina.

shiny adjective SHINING, polished, burnished, gleaming, glossy, satiny, lustrous.
– OPPOSITES dull.

shirk verb AVOID, evade, dodge, sidestep, shrink from, shun, get out of, play truant from; *informal* funk; *Brit. informal* skive off.

shirker noun SLACKER, truant, absentee, malingerer, layabout, loafer, idler; *Brit. informal* skiver.

shiver verb TREMBLE, quiver, shake, shudder, quaver, quake, vibrate.
▶ **noun** TREMBLE, quiver, shake, quaver, shudder.

shock noun ❶ IMPACT, blow, collision, crash, dash, jolt, bump, jar, jerk. ❷ BLOW, upset, bombshell, bolt from the blue, disturbance, state of agitation/perturbation, source of distress, revelation; *informal* eye-opener.
▶ **verb** APPAL, horrify, scandalize, outrage, repel, revolt, disgust, nauseate, sicken, offend, traumatize, make someone's blood run cold, distress, upset, perturb, disturb, disquiet, unsettle, astound, dumbfound, stagger, amaze, astonish, stun.

shoddy adjective POOR-QUALITY, inferior, second-rate, tawdry, rubbishy, trashy, junky, gimcrack, cheapjack, jerry-built; *informal* tacky, tatty.
– OPPOSITES quality.

shoot verb ❶ **shoot a deer:** HIT, shoot down, bring down, pick off, bag, fell, kill; *informal* plug, zap; *poetic/literary* slay. ❷ **shoot arrows:** FIRE, discharge, launch, let fly, send forth. ❸ **he shot past:** RACE, dash, sprint, charge, dart, fly, hurtle, bolt, streak, flash, whisk, run, speed. ❹ **plants shooting:** BUD, burgeon, sprout, germinate, appear, spring up.
▶ **noun** BUD, offshoot, slip, scion, sucker, sprout, branch, twig, sprig, cutting, graft.

shop noun STORE, retail outlet, retailer, establishment, emporium, trading post.

shore[1] noun SEASHORE, seaside, beach, coast, seaboard, waterside, foreshore; *poetic/literary* strand.

shore[2]
■ **shore up** PROP UP, support, hold up, underpin, strengthen, brace, buttress.

short adjective ❶ **short people:** SMALL, little, slight, petite, tiny, squat, dwarfish, diminutive, dumpy, Lilliputian; *Scottish* wee; *informal* pint-sized, pocket-sized, knee-high to a grasshopper. ❷ **a short report:** BRIEF, concise, succinct, to the point, compact, terse, summary, crisp, pithy, epigrammatic, abridged, abbreviated, condensed,

summarized, contracted, curtailed, truncated. ❸ a short affair: BRIEF, momentary, temporary, short-lived, impermanent, short-term, cursory, fleeting, passing, transitory, transient, ephemeral, fugacious, evanescent. ❹ money is short: DEFICIENT, lacking, wanting, insufficient, inadequate, scarce, scanty, meagre, sparse, tight, low. ❺ he was short with her: CURT, sharp, abrupt, blunt, brusque, terse, gruff, surly, testy, tart, rude, discourteous, uncivil, impolite.
– OPPOSITES tall, long, plentiful.

shortage noun DEARTH, scarcity, lack, deficiency, insufficiency, paucity, deficit, inadequacy, shortfall, want, poverty.
– OPPOSITES abundance.

shortcoming noun DEFECT, fault, flaw, imperfection, failing, drawback, weakness, weak point, foible, frailty, infirmity.
– OPPOSITES strength.

shorten verb ABBREVIATE, condense, abridge, cut, cut down, contract, compress, reduce, lessen, decrease, diminish, curtail, duck, trim, pare down.
– OPPOSITES extend.

shortly adverb SOON, in a short while, in a little while, presently, before long, directly; *informal* before you can say Jack Robinson.

short-sighted adjective ❶ MYOPIC, near-sighted. ❷ a short-sighted attitude: IMPRUDENT, injudicious, unwise, ill-advised, thoughtless, unthinking, heedless, rash, incautious.

short-tempered adjective QUICK-TEMPERED, hot-tempered, irascible, touchy, testy, fiery, peppery, choleric; *Brit. informal* ratty.

shot noun ❶ CRACK, bang, report, blast, explosion, gunfire. ❷ PELLET, bullet, slug, projectile, ammunition. ❸ a shot of the house: PHOTOGRAPH, photo, snap, snapshot. ❹ have a shot at it: ATTEMPT, try, go, effort, endeavour, essay; *informal* stab, crack, bash, whack. ❺ a cheap shot: COMMENT, remark, statement, utterance.

shout verb CRY OUT, call out, yell, roar, howl, bellow, scream, bawl, call at the top of one's voice, raise one's voice; *informal* holler.
– OPPOSITES whisper.

shove verb PUSH, thrust, drive, force, shoulder, elbow, jostle, jolt.

shovel noun SPADE, scoop.
▶ verb SCOOP UP, dig, excavate, spade.

show verb ❶ grey hairs showing: BE VISIBLE, be seen, be in view, appear, put in an appearance. ❷ show it to them: EXHIBIT, display, present, demonstrate, set forth, uncover, reveal. ❸ show his grief: INDICATE, express, manifest, reveal, make known, make plain, make obvious, evince, evidence, disclose, betray, divulge. ❹ show them what to do: DEMONSTRATE, point out, explain, expound, teach, instruct in, give instructions in, tutor in, indoctrinate in. ❺ show them to their seats: ESCORT, accompany, usher, conduct, attend, guide, lead, direct, steer. ❻ he didn't show: APPEAR, put in an appearance, make an appearance, turn up, come, arrive, be present.
– OPPOSITES conceal.
▶ noun ❶ DISPLAY, array, arrangement, exhibition, presentation, exposition, spectacle. ❷ EXHIBITION, demonstration, display,

exposition, presentation. ❸ PERFORMANCE, production; *informal* gig. ❹ **a show of courage**: APPEARANCE, outward appearance, air, guise, semblance, pretence, illusion, pose, affectation, profession.

showdown noun CONFRONTATION, conflict, clash, face-off, moment of truth, crisis, culmination, climax.

shower noun ❶ FALL, drizzle, flurry, sprinkling. ❷ ABUNDANCE, profusion, plethora, flood, deluge. ▶ verb ❶ **shower with gifts**: DELUGE, inundate, overwhelm. ❷ **they showered gifts on him**: LAVISH, pour, load, heap.

show-off noun EXHIBITIONIST, extrovert, bragger, braggart, boaster; *N. Amer. informal* blowhard.

showy adjective OSTENTATIOUS, flamboyant, elaborate, fancy, pretentious, overdone, glittering. – OPPOSITES restrained.

shred noun ❶ SCRAP, fragment, wisp, sliver, bit, piece, remnant, snippet, tatter. ❷ **a shred of evidence**: SCRAP, bit, iota, whit, particle, atom, modicum, trace, speck.
▶ verb CUT UP, tear up, rip up, grate.

shrewd adjective ASTUTE, sharp, clever, intelligent, alert, quick-witted, discerning, perspicacious, perceptive, discriminating, wise, sagacious, far-seeing, canny, cunning, artful, crafty, wily, calculating; *informal* smart.
– OPPOSITES stupid.

shriek verb SCREAM, screech, squeal, yell, howl, shout, cry out, call out, whoop, wail; *informal* holler.

shrill adjective HIGH-PITCHED, high, sharp, piercing, ear-piercing, penetrating, ear-splitting, screeching, shrieking.

shrine noun ❶ HOLY PLACE, temple, church. ❷ MEMORIAL, monument, cenotaph. ❸ RELIQUARY, burial chamber, tomb, sepulchre.

shrink verb GET/BECOME/GROW SMALLER, contract, diminish, lessen, reduce, dwindle, narrow, decline, fall off, drop off, shrivel. – OPPOSITES expand, increase.
■ **shrink from** DRAW BACK, pull back, back away, shy away, recoil, retreat, withdraw, flinch, cringe, wince.

shrivel verb DRY UP, wither, desiccate, dehydrate, wrinkle, pucker up.

shroud noun COVER, covering, pall, cloak, mantle, blanket, cloud, veil, screen.
▶ verb COVER, enshroud, swathe, envelop, cloak, blanket, cloud, veil, screen, conceal, hide.

shrug
■ **shrug off** DISREGARD, take no notice of, not trouble about, dismiss, gloss over, play down, make light of, minimize.

shuffle verb ❶ SHAMBLE, hobble, limp, drag one's feet. ❷ **shuffle papers**: MIX, intermix, shift about, rearrange, reorganize, jumble.

shun verb AVOID, evade, eschew, steer clear of, shy away from, recoil from, keep away from, keep one's distance from, cold-shoulder, give a wide berth to.
– OPPOSITES seek.

shut verb CLOSE, draw to, pull to, fasten, bar, lock, secure, seal.
– OPPOSITES open.
■ **shut in** *see* IMPRISON. **shut out** EXCLUDE, leave out, omit, keep out,

bar, debar, ostracize, blackball, banish, exile, outlaw. **shut up** KEEP QUIET, be quiet, keep silent, hold one's tongue; *informal* keep mum, pipe down, keep one's trap shut.

shy adjective BASHFUL, diffident, reserved, reticent, retiring, self-effacing, withdrawn, timid, timorous, fearful, nervous, hesitant, wary, suspicious, chary, unconfident, self-conscious, embarrassed, abashed, modest.
– OPPOSITES brash, confident.

sick adjective ❶ UNWELL, ill, ailing, indisposed, poorly, below par, out of sorts, laid up, on the sick list; *informal* under the weather. ❷ NAUSEATED, queasy, bilious; *informal* green about the gills. ❸ sick of that music: TIRED, weary, bored, jaded, surfeited, satiated, glutted; *informal* fed up, have had something up to here. ❹ sick humour: MORBID, macabre, ghoulish, gruesome, sadistic, perverted, cruel.
– OPPOSITES well.
■ **be sick** VOMIT, throw up; *informal* spew, puke.

sicken verb ❶ MAKE SICK, nauseate, turn someone's stomach, make someone's gorge rise, revolt, disgust, repel, shock, appal. ❷ TAKE/FALL ILL, become ill, become infected, contract, be stricken.
– OPPOSITES recover.

sickening adjective *see* REPELLENT.

sickly adjective ❶ UNHEALTHY, in poor health, ill, delicate, frail, weak, feeble, puny. ❷ SENTIMENTAL, cloying, mawkish, maudlin, slushy, mushy, syrupy; *informal* schmaltzy; *Brit. informal* soppy.
– OPPOSITES healthy.

sickness noun ❶ ILLNESS, disease, disorder, ailment, complaint, affliction, malady, infirmity, indisposition; *informal* bug. ❷ NAUSEA, queasiness, biliousness.

side noun ❶ the side of the lake: EDGE, border, verge, boundary, margin, rim, fringe, skirt, flank, brink, brim, periphery. ❷ the east side of the city: PART, quarter, section, sector, neighbourhood. ❸ both sides of the question: ASPECT, angle, facet, point of view, viewpoint, view, opinion, standpoint, position, slant. ❹ on his side: CAMP, faction, caucus, party, wing, splinter group, sect.
■ **side with** TAKE SOMEONE'S SIDE, be on someone's side, take someone's part, support, give one's support to, back, give one's backing to, join with, favour.

sidelong adjective SIDE, sideways, oblique, indirect, covert.
– OPPOSITES overt.

sidetrack verb DIVERT, deflect, distract, lead away from.

sideways adverb ❶ SIDE FIRST, edgeways, edgewise. ❷ look sideways: OBLIQUELY, indirectly, sidelong.

siesta noun NAP, sleep, rest, catnap, doze; *informal* forty winks, snooze.

sieve noun STRAINER, filter, colander, riddle, screen.

sift verb ❶ FILTER, strain, riddle, screen. ❷ EXAMINE, scrutinize, study, investigate, analyse, review.

sigh verb BREATHE OUT, exhale.
■ **sigh for** YEARN FOR, long for, weep for, mourn for.

sight noun ❶ EYESIGHT, vision, power of sight. ❷ RANGE OF VISION,

field of vision, view. ❸ VIEW, glimpse, look.
▶ verb CATCH SIGHT OF, see, behold, spot, make out, descry, espy, perceive, observe, discern.

sign noun ❶ **a sign of strength:** INDICATION, symptom, hint, suggestion, trace, mark, clue, manifestation, token, evidence, proof. ❷ SIGNPOST, notice, placard, board, marker. ❸ **make a sign:** GESTURE, signal, motion, movement, wave, gesticulation. ❹ **mathematical signs:** SYMBOL, mark, cipher, code, hieroglyph. ❺ **look for a sign:** OMEN, portent, warning, forewarning, augury, presage.
▶ verb ❶ WRITE, inscribe, autograph, initial. ❷ *See* SIGNAL[1] verb (1).

signal[1] verb ❶ SIGN, give a sign to, indicate, beckon, gesture, motion, gesticulate, nod. ❷ BE A SIGN OF, mark signify, designate.
▶ noun ❶ SIGN, indicator, cue. ❷ SIGN, indication, token, evidence, hint.

signal[2] adjective EXCEPTIONAL, conspicuous, notable, noteworthy, significant, memorable, outstanding, striking.

significance noun ❶ MEANING, sense, import, signification, purport, point, gist, essence, implications. ❷ IMPORTANCE, consequence, momentousness, magnitude, seriousness.

significant adjective ❶ **significant words:** MEANINGFUL, eloquent, expressive, pregnant, knowing. ❷ **significant progress:** IMPORTANT, of importance, of consequence, momentous, of moment, weighty, material, impressive, serious, vital, critical.
– OPPOSITES insignificant.

signify verb ❶ BE A SIGN OF, indicate, mean, denote, suggest, point to, portend. ❷ MEAN, denote, represent, symbolize, stand for. ❸ MATTER, be of importance, be of consequence, be important, be significant, be of significance, carry weight, count.

silence noun ❶ QUIET, quietness, hush, still, stillness, peace, peacefulness, tranquillity, noiselessness, soundlessness. ❷ SPEECHLESSNESS, wordlessness, dumbness, muteness, taciturnity, reticence, uncommunicativeness.
– OPPOSITES noise.
▶ verb ❶ QUIET, quieten, hush, still, calm, pacify, subdue, quell. ❷ MUFFLE, deaden, abate, extinguish.

silent adjective ❶ QUIET, hushed, still, peaceful, tranquil, noiseless, soundless. ❷ SPEECHLESS, unspeaking, wordless, voiceless, dumb, mute, taciturn, reticent, uncommunicative, mum, tight-lipped, tongue-tied; *informal* struck dumb. ❸ **silent criticism:** UNSPOKEN, wordless, unvoiced, unsaid, unexpressed, unpronounced, tacit, implicit, understood, implied.
– OPPOSITES noisy, loquacious.

silhouette noun OUTLINE, contour, profile, delineation, form, shape.

silky adjective SILKEN, smooth, sleek, velvety, diaphanous.

silly adjective ❶ **a silly person:** FOOLISH, stupid, unintelligent, idiotic, brainless, witless, unwise, imprudent, thoughtless, reckless, foolhardy, irresponsible, mad, erratic, unstable, scatterbrained, feather-brained, flighty, frivolous, giddy, fatuous, inane, immature, childish, shallow, naive; *informal*

crazy, dotty, scatty, loopy, screwy; *Brit. informal* daft. ❷ **silly behaviour:** FOOLISH, stupid, unintelligent, senseless, mindless, idiotic, unwise, imprudent, inadvisable, injudicious, misguided, unsound, impractical, pointless, meaningless, purposeless, inappropriate, illogical, irrational, unreasonable, thoughtless, reckless, foolhardy, irresponsible, erratic, hare-brained, absurd, ridiculous, ludicrous, laughable, risible, farcical, preposterous, fatuous, asinine; *informal* half-baked, crazy, screwy; *Brit. informal* daft.
– OPPOSITES sensible.

similar adjective LIKE, alike, resembling, close, much the same, comparable, corresponding, analogous, parallel, equivalent, kindred, approximate.
– OPPOSITES dissimilar, different.

similarity noun RESEMBLANCE, likeness, sameness, similitude, comparability, correspondence, analogy, parallel, parallelism, equivalence, approximation, closeness, affinity, kinship.
– OPPOSITES dissimilarity, difference.

similarly adverb LIKEWISE, in the same way, in like matter, correspondingly, by the same token.

simmer verb BOIL, cook, bubble, stew, poach, seethe.

simple adjective ❶ **a simple task:** EASY, uncomplicated, straightforward, uninvolved, effortless, manageable, elementary, facile; *informal* like falling off a log, a piece of cake, a cinch, easy-peasy, no sweat. ❷ **simple language:** CLEAR, plain, intelligible, comprehensible, understandable, lucid, direct, straightforward, uncomplicated, uninvolved. ❸ **simple clothes:** PLAIN, classic, clean-cut, unelaborate, unadorned, undecorated. ❹ SIMPLE-MINDED, feeble-minded, retarded, backward, slow-witted, slow, dull-witted.
– OPPOSITES difficult, complex, ornate.

simplify verb MAKE SIMPLE/SIMPLER, make easy/easier, make plainer, clarify, decipher, disentangle, explain, paraphrase, translate.
– OPPOSITES complicate.

simplistic adjective OVERSIMPLE, oversimplified, facile, shallow, superficial, naive.

simply adverb ❶ CLEARLY, plainly, intelligibly, lucidly, directly, straightforwardly. ❷ PLAINLY, unfussily, without clutter, austerely, starkly, spartanly, with restraint, naturally, casually.

simultaneous adjective CONCURRENT, contemporaneous, concomitant, coinciding, coincident, synchronous, coexistent, parallel.

sin noun WRONG, wrongdoing, act of evil/wickedness, crime, offence, misdeed, misdemeanour, transgression, error, lapse, fall from grace; *archaic* trespass.
– OPPOSITES virtue.
▶ **verb** COMMIT A SIN, do wrong, offend, commit an offence, transgress, misbehave, go astray, stray from the straight and narrow, go wrong, fall from grace.

sincere adjective ❶ **sincere affection:** GENUINE, real, true, honest, unfeigned, unaffected, bona fide, wholehearted,

heartfelt, serious, earnest, fervent. ❷ sincere people: HONEST, above board, trustworthy, frank, candid, straightforward, plain-dealing, no-nonsense, genuine, artless, guileless, ingenuous; *informal* upfront.
– OPPOSITES insincere.

sincerely adverb ❶ thank them sincerely: WITH ALL SINCERITY, wholeheartedly, with all one's heart, earnestly, fervently. ❷ mean it most sincerely: GENUINELY, really, truly, in truth, without pretence, honestly, in good faith.

sinecure noun EASY JOB, soft option; *informal* cinch, cushy number, money for old rope, money for jam, picnic, gravy train.

sinewy adjective MUSCULAR, brawny, burly, powerfully built, stalwart, strapping.
– OPPOSITES puny.

sinful adjective WRONG, evil, wicked, bad, iniquitous, criminal, immoral, corrupt, unrighteous, ungodly, irreligious, irreverent, profane, blasphemous, impious, sacrilegious.
– OPPOSITES virtuous.

sing verb CAROL, trill, warble, pipe, quaver, croon, chant, yodel.

singe verb SCORCH, burn, sear, char, blacken.

single adjective ❶ ONE, sole, lone, solitary, unique, isolated, by itself, exclusive. ❷ INDIVIDUAL, particular, separate, distinct. ❸ UNMARRIED, unwed, unwedded, wifeless/husbandless, spouseless, partnerless, unattached, free.
■ **single out** SEPARATE OUT, set apart, put to one side, pick, choose, select, fix on, decide on.

single-handed adverb BY ONESELF, alone, on one's own, solo, independently, unaided, unassisted, without help.

single-minded adjective UNSWERVING, unwavering, undeviating, set, fixed, devoted, dedicated, committed, determined, dogged, tireless, purposeful, obsessive, monomaniacal.

singular adjective ❶ EXTRAORDINARY, exceptional, rare, unusual, unique, remarkable, outstanding, notable, noteworthy, striking, conspicuous, distinctive. ❷ STRANGE, unusual, odd, peculiar, curious, queer, bizarre, weird, abnormal, atypical.
– OPPOSITES ordinary.

sinister adjective ❶ a sinister figure: EVIL-LOOKING, villainous, malevolent, menacing, threatening, frightening. ❷ sinister reasons: EVIL, wicked, bad, criminal, base, vile, vicious, cruel, malicious, malign. ❸ sinister signs: OMINOUS, inauspicious, portentous.
– OPPOSITES innocent.

sink verb ❶ GO UNDER, submerge, founder, capsize. ❷ FALL, drop, descend, go down, go lower, plunge, plummet, slump. ❸ sink a shaft: DIG, bore, drill, excavate. ❹ sink posts: DRIVE, place, put down, plant, position. ❺ sink hopes: DESTROY, ruin, demolish, devastate; *informal* put the kibosh on, put the skids under; *Brit. informal* scupper.
– OPPOSITES float, rise.

sinner noun WRONGDOER, evil-doer, criminal, offender, miscreant, transgressor, reprobate; *archaic* trespasser.

sinuous adjective WINDING, curving, twisting, undulating, serpentine.

sit verb ❶ SIT DOWN, take a seat, settle down, be seated; *informal* take the load/weight off one's feet. ❷ BE PLACED, be positioned, be situated, rest, perch. ❸ **the committee is sitting:** BE CONVENED, meet, assemble, be in session.

site noun LOCATION, situation, position, place, locality, setting, scene.
▶ verb *see* SITUATE.

situate verb PLACE, position, locate, site, put, install, station, establish, set up.

situation noun ❶ PLACE, position, location, site, setting, milieu, environment. ❷ CIRCUMSTANCES, affairs, state of affairs, condition, case, predicament, plight; *informal* kettle of fish, ball game. ❸ POST, position, place, job, employment.

size noun DIMENSIONS, measurements, proportions, bigness, largeness, magnitude, vastness, bulk, area, expanse, extent.
■ **size up** APPRAISE, assess, judge, evaluate, gauge, estimate, rate.

skeleton noun ❶ FRAMEWORK, frame, structure, shell, chassis, support. ❷ OUTLINE, sketch, bones, bare bones, draft, rough draft, plan, blueprint.

sketch noun ❶ DRAWING, outline, diagram, plan, representation, delineation. ❷ OUTLINE, summary, abstract, precis, skeleton, bones, bare bones, draft, plan. ❸ SKIT, act, scene.
▶ verb DRAW, rough out, outline, represent, delineate, depict.

sketchy adjective ❶ **sketchy plans:** PRELIMINARY, provisional, unfinished, unrefined, unpolished, rough, crude. ❷ **sketchy information:** LIGHT, superficial, cursory, perfunctory, meagre, scrappy, skimpy, bitty, insufficient, inadequate, imperfect, incomplete.
– OPPOSITES detailed.

skilful adjective SKILLED, able, good, accomplished, adept, competent, efficient, adroit, deft, dexterous, masterly, expert, first-rate, experienced, trained, practised, professional, talented, gifted, clever; *informal* smart.
– OPPOSITES incompetent.

skill noun SKILFULNESS, ability, accomplishment, adeptness, competence, efficiency, adroitness, deftness, dexterity, aptitude, expertise, expertness, art, finesse, experience, professionalism, talent, cleverness; *informal* smartness.
– OPPOSITES incompetence.

skilled adjective *see* SKILFUL.

skim verb GLIDE OVER, move lightly over, brush, graze.
■ **skim through** READ QUICKLY, glance at, scan, run one's eye over, flip through, leaf through, thumb through.

skimp verb BE SPARING, be economical, economize, be frugal, be mean, be parsimonious, be niggardly, scrimp, cut corners; *informal* be stingy.
– OPPOSITES lavish.

skin noun ❶ INTEGUMENT, epidermis, cuticle, corium, derma. ❷ COMPLEXION, colouring. ❸ HIDE, pelt, fleece, fell, integument, tegument. ❹ PEEL, rind, hull, husk. ❺ FILM, coating, coat, layer, crust.

skinflint noun MISER, niggard, penny-pincher, Scrooge.

skinny adjective THIN, thin as a rake, scraggy, scrawny, emaciated, skeletal; *informal* skin and bone. *See also* THIN adjective (1).

skip verb ❶ BOUND, jump, leap, spring, hop, bounce, dance, caper, prance, trip, cavort, gambol, frisk, bob. ❷ OMIT, leave out, miss out, pass over, bypass, skim over.

skirmish noun BATTLE, fight, clash, conflict, encounter, confrontation, engagement, tussle, scrimmage, fracas.

skirt verb ❶ GO ROUND, move round, walk round, circle, circumnavigate. ❷ EVADE, avoid, dodge, steer clear of, sidestep, circumvent, bypass.

skittish adjective PLAYFUL, lively, frisky, sportive; *poetic/literary* frolicsome.

sky noun ATMOSPHERE, air, airspace; *poetic/literary* the heavens, the firmament, the blue, the (wide) blue yonder, the welkin.

slab noun HUNK, piece, chunk, lump, slice, wedge, portion.

slack adjective ❶ LOOSE, baggy, bagging, easy, hanging, flapping. ❷ **business is slack**: SLOW, quiet, inactive, sluggish. ❸ **he's a bit slack**: LAX, negligent, remiss, neglectful, careless, inattentive, offhand, slapdash, slipshod, sloppy, disorderly, disorganized, tardy.
– OPPOSITES tight.
▶ verb IDLE, shirk be inactive, be lazy, be indolent, be neglectful.

slacker noun IDLER, shirker, loafer, dawdler, layabout, malingerer, good-for-nothing, clock-watcher.

slake verb SATISFY, quench, assuage, relieve, take the edge off, gratify, satiate.

slam verb BANG, thump, crash, smash, dash, hurt, fling, throw.

slander noun DEFAMATION, misrepresentation, calumny, libel, aspersions, vilification, verbal abuse, muckraking, smear campaigning, backbiting, obloquy, disparagement, denigration.
▶ verb DEFAME, blacken someone's name, libel, cast aspersions on, malign, vilify, verbally abuse, smear, slur, backbite, disparage, denigrate, decry, run down; *formal* calumniate.

slanderous adjective DEFAMATORY, libellous, damaging, abusive, muckraking, malicious, backbiting, disparaging, denigrating; *formal* calumnious.
– OPPOSITES complimentary.

slang noun ❶ COLLOQUIALISM, informal language, lingo. ❷ JARGON, cant, argot; *informal* gobbledegook, technospeak, mumbo-jumbo.

slant verb ❶ SLOPE, tilt, be askew, lean, dip, shelve, list. ❷ GIVE A SLANT TO, give a bias to, bias, angle, distort, twist.
▶ noun ❶ SLOPE, tilt, dip, leaning, inclination, shelving, listing. ❷ BIAS, leaning, one-sidedness, prejudice, angle, distortion, twist.

slanting adjective SLANTED, aslant, at an angle, sloping, oblique, tilting, tilted, askew, leaning, dipping, shelving, listing, diagonal.

slap verb SMACK, strike, hit, cuff; *informal* wallop, clout, whack, biff, belt, sock.

slapdash adjective *see* CARELESS (1, 2).

slaughter verb KILL, butcher, massacre, murder, put to death, do to death, put to the sword; *poetic/literary* slay. *See also* KILL (1).
▶ noun MASSACRE, murder, butchery, killing, bloodshed, carnage.

slave noun *historical* serf, vassal; *archaic* bondsman/woman.
▶ verb TOIL, drudge, slog, labour, grind, work one's fingers to the bone, work day and night, work like a Trojan.

slaver verb SLOBBER, drool, dribble, salivate.

slavery noun ENSLAVEMENT, bondage, servitude, subjugation; *historical* serfdom, vassalage, thraldom.
– OPPOSITES freedom.

slavish adjective ❶ SERVILE, subservient, obsequious, sycophantic, deferential, grovelling, fawning, cringing, menial, abject. ❷ IMITATIVE, unoriginal, uninspired, unimaginative.

slay verb KILL, murder, slaughter, put to death, do to death, assassinate, do away with; *informal* rub out.

sleek adjective SMOOTH, glossy, shiny, lustrous, silken, silky, satiny, burnished.

sleep verb BE ASLEEP, slumber, doze, nap, drowse; *informal* snooze, crash, have forty winks, be in the land of Nod.
– OPPOSITES wake up.
▶ noun SLUMBER, doze, nap, rest, siesta, drowse; *informal* snooze, forty winks, a bit of shut-eye.

sleepiness noun DROWSINESS, tiredness, somnolence, somnolency, languor, languidness, lethargy, sluggishness, inactivity, lassitude, torpor, torpidity.

sleepless adjective WITHOUT SLEEP, wakeful, insomniac, restless, disturbed.

sleepy adjective ❶ DROWSY, tired, somnolent, languorous, lethargic, sluggish, inactive, heavy, torpid, comatose. ❷ a **sleepy town**: INACTIVE, quiet, peaceful, slow-moving, slumberous.
– OPPOSITES alert.

slender adjective ❶ SLIM, thin, slight, lean, svelte, willowy, sylphlike. ❷ a **slender hope**: SMALL, slight, slim, faint, remote, feeble, flimsy, tenuous, fragile.
– OPPOSITES fat.

sleuth noun DETECTIVE, investigator, private investigator; *informal* private eye, dick; *N. Amer. informal* gumshoe.

slice noun PIECE, portion, segment, sliver, wedge, chunk, hunk; *Brit. informal* wodge.
▶ verb CUT UP/THROUGH, carve, chop, divide, cleave, sever.

slick adjective ❶ a **slick presentation**: SMOOTH, well organized, streamlined, efficient, polished. ❷ a **slick reply**: SMOOTH, glib, fluent, plausible, specious. ❸ a **slick operator**: SUAVE, urbane, sophisticated, polished, glib, smooth, efficient, professional, smart, sharp, shrewd.
■ **slick down/back** SMOOTH, flatten, plaster.

slide verb SLIP, skid, slither, skate, skim, glissade, glide.

slight adjective ❶ a **slight change**: SMALL, little, tiny, minute, inappreciable, imperceptible, subtle, modest. ❷ a **slight figure**:

SLIM, slender, small, spare, delicate, frail.
– OPPOSITES large.
▶ **verb** SNUB, insult, affront, rebuff, give the cold shoulder to, cold-shoulder, keep at arm's length, disregard, ignore, neglect, take no notice of, disdain, scorn.
▶ **noun** SNUB, insult, affront, rebuff, inattention, scorn, disdain; *informal* slap in the face.

slightly **adverb** A LITTLE, a bit, somewhat, rather, to some degree.
– OPPOSITES very.

slim **adjective** ❶ SLENDER, thin, slight, lean, narrow, svelte, willowy, sylphlike. ❷ **slim hopes:** SLIGHT, small, slender, faint, remote, feeble, flimsy, tenuous, fragile.
– OPPOSITES fat, strong.
▶ **verb** LOSE WEIGHT, shed weight, diet, go on a diet.

slime **noun** SLUDGE, muck, ooze, mud; *informal* goo, gunk.

slimy **adjective** ❶ SLUDGY, mucky, oozy, muddy, slippery, sticky, viscous, mucous. ❷ OILY, unctuous, obsequious, sycophantic, servile, grovelling.

sling **verb** TOSS, fling, throw, cast, hurl, pitch, shy, lob; *informal* chuck, heave.

slink **verb** SKULK, lurk, sneak, creep, steal, slip, slide.

slip **verb** ❶ SKID, slither, lose one's footing, lose one's balance. ❷ **slip from her hands:** FALL, slide, drop. ❸ **slip from the house:** STEAL, slide, creep, sneak, slink. ❹ **the pound slipped:** GO DOWN, decline, decrease, lessen, depreciate, sink, slump, plummet.
▶ **noun** ❶ SLIP-UP, mistake, error, blunder, miscalculation, oversight; *informal* boo-boo; *Brit. informal* boob; *Brit. informal, dated* bloomer. ❷ UNDERSKIRT, petticoat.
■ **let slip** *see* REVEAL (3). **slip up** MAKE A MISTAKE, blunder, make a blunder, miscalculate, err; *informal* make a boo-boo, screw up; *Brit. informal* boob; *Brit. informal, dated* make a bloomer.

slippery **adjective** ❶ GREASY, oily, slimy, icy, glassy, smooth, soapy; *informal* slippy, skiddy. ❷ SHIFTY, devious, deceitful, duplicitous, crafty, cunning, sneaky, treacherous, perfidious, two-faced, dishonest, false, unreliable, untrustworthy; *informal* tricky, foxy.

slipshod **adjective** CARELESS, slovenly, sloppy, slapdash, disorganized, unsystematic, unmethodical.
– OPPOSITES meticulous.

slit **verb** CUT, split open, slash, gash, rip, make an incision in, tear, rend, pierce.
▶ **noun** CUT, split, slash, gash, rip, incision, tear, rent, fissure, opening.

slither **verb** SLIDE, slip, skid.

sliver **noun** CHIP, flake, splinter, shred, fragment, scrap.

slobber **verb** SLAVER, drool, dribble, splutter.

slog
■ **slog away** WORK, labour, toil, slave, drudge, plough.

slogan **noun** MOTTO, logo, catchword, jingle, rallying cry, shibboleth.

slop **verb** SPILL, overflow, splash, slosh, splatter, spatter.

slope **verb** DROP AWAY, fall away, slant, incline, lean, tilt, dip.
▶ **noun** SLANT, inclination, angle, skew, tilt, dip, gradient.

sloping adjective SLANTING, oblique, leaning, inclined, angled, askew, tilting, dipping.
– OPPOSITES level.

sloppy adjective ❶ WATERY, wet, soggy, splashy, slushy, sludgy. ❷ CARELESS, slapdash, slipshod, disorganized, unmethodical, untidy, messy, slovenly. ❸ SENTIMENTAL, mawkish, maudlin, gushing, effusive, banal, trite; *informal* mushy, schmaltzy; *Brit. informal* soppy.
– OPPOSITES meticulous.

slot noun ❶ SLIT, crack, hole, opening, aperture, groove, notch. ❷ PLACE, position, niche, space, opening, time, period.

sloth noun LAZINESS, indolence, idleness, sluggishness, inertia, inactivity, lethargy, langour, slothfulness, torpor.

slothful adjective LAZY, indolent, idle, work-shy, sluggish, inert, inactive, lethargic, languorous, torpid.
– OPPOSITES industrious.

slovenly adjective SLATTERNLY, untidy, dirty, unclean, messy, unkempt, dishevelled, bedraggled, tousled, rumpled.
– OPPOSITES tidy.

slow adjective ❶ SLOW-MOVING, unhurried, leisurely, measured, deliberate, ponderous, creeping, dawdling, loitering, lagging, laggard, sluggish, snail-like, tortoise-like. ❷ BACKWARD, retarded, slow-witted, dull-witted, dull, unintelligent, stupid, thick, dense; *informal* dumb, dopey. ❸ a slow process: TIME-CONSUMING, protracted, drawn-out, prolonged, interminable.
– OPPOSITES quick, bright.
▶ verb ❶ REDUCE SPEED, decelerate, put the brakes on. ❷ HOLD BACK, keep back, delay, detain, restrain.

slowly adverb AT A SLOW PACE, without hurrying, unhurriedly, at a leisurely pace, steadily, ploddingly, taking one's time, in one's own good time, with heavy steps, at a snail's pace.

sluggish adjective INACTIVE, inert, heavy, lifeless, apathetic, listless, lethargic, languid, languorous, torpid, phlegmatic, indolent, lazy, slothful, drowsy, sleepy.
– OPPOSITES energetic.

slumber verb & noun *see* SLEEP.

slump noun PLUNGE, nosedive, collapse, fall, falling-off, drop, downturn, downswing, slide, decline, decrease, lowering, devaluation, depreciation, depression.
▶ verb ❶ COLLAPSE, sink, fall, subside. ❷ PLUMMET, plunge, nosedive, fall, drop, go down, slide, decline, decrease, devalue.
– OPPOSITES rise.

slur noun INSULT, slight, aspersion, imputation, affront, defamation, slander, libel, misrepresentation, smear, stain, stigma.

sly adjective ❶ a sly person: CUNNING, crafty, wily, artful, conniving, scheming, devious, underhand, shrewd, astute; *informal* tricky, foxy, smart. ❷ a sly smile: ROGUISH, impish, mischievous, playful, arch, knowing.

smack noun & verb SLAP, blow, hit, whack, thump, cuff, punch, spank, buffet, rap, bang; *informal* wallop, clout, belt, sock.

small adjective ❶ a small toy: LITTLE, tiny, petite, slight, minute, miniature, pocket-size, mini, minuscule, diminutive,

undersized, puny; *informal* pint-sized, teeny, teeny-weeny, teensy-weensy; *Scottish* wee. ❷ **a small change/mistake:** SLIGHT, minor, unimportant, trifling, trivial, insignificant, inconsequential, inappreciable. ❸ **small beginnings:** HUMBLE, modest, lowly, simple, unpretentious, poor, inferior. ❹ **a small mind/man:** NARROW, narrow-minded, mean, petty.
– OPPOSITES big, large.

small-minded **adjective** NARROW-MINDED, bigoted, prejudiced, intolerant, hidebound, rigid, ungenerous, illiberal.
– OPPOSITES broad-minded.

small-time **adjective** PETTY, minor, unimportant, insignificant, of no account, of no consequence, inconsequential.
– OPPOSITES major.

smart **adjective** ❶ **looking smart:** WELL DRESSED, well turned out, fashionably dressed, fashionable, stylish, modish, elegant, chic, neat, spruce, trim; *informal* natty, snappy, out of a bandbox. ❷ **smart children:** CLEVER, bright, intelligent, gifted, sharp, quick-witted, nimble-witted, shrewd, ingenious. ❸ **a smart pace:** BRISK, quick, fast, swift, lively, energetic, spirited, vigorous, jaunty; *informal* cracking, spanking.
– OPPOSITES scruffy.
▶ **verb** STING, nip, burn, bite, pain.

smash **verb** ❶ BREAK, shatter, crash, shiver, pulverize, splinter, crack. ❷ CRASH, collide, wreck. ❸ DESTROY, ruin, shatter, devastate.

smattering **noun** BIT, modicum, dash, rudiments, elements.

smear **verb** ❶ SPREAD, daub, slap, plaster. ❷ SMUDGE, streak, blur. ❸ SULLY, tarnish, blacken, taint, stain, slur, defame, defile, vilify, slander, libel; *formal* calumniate.
▶ **noun** ❶ DAUB, spot, patch; *informal* splotch. ❷ SMUDGE, streak. ❸ TAINT, stain, slur, blot.

smell **verb** ❶ SCENT, sniff, get a sniff of; *Brit. informal* get a whiff of. ❷ HAVE A BAD SMELL, stink, be stinking, reek, be malodorous; *informal* stink to high heaven; *Brit. informal* pong, whiff, hum.
▶ **noun** ❶ ODOUR, scent, aroma, perfume, fragrance, bouquet; *poetic/literary* redolence. ❷ STINK, stench, reek; *Brit. informal* pong, whiff, hum.

smelly **adjective** SMELLING, evil-smelling, foul-smelling, stinking, high, malodorous, fetid; *Brit. informal* ponging, humming, whiffy; *poetic/literary* noisome, mephitic.

smirk **verb** LEER, sneer, simper, grin.

smitten **adjective** TAKEN WITH, infatuated with, enamoured of, attracted by, charmed by, captivated by, enchanted by, beguiled by; *informal* bowled over by.

smog **noun** HAZE, fog, pollution.

smoke **verb** ❶ SMOULDER, reek. ❷ CURE, dry, preserve.

smoky **adjective** SMOKE-FILLED, hazy, foggy, smoggy, reeky, murky.

smooth **adjective** ❶ **smooth surfaces:** EVEN, level, flat, plane, flush, unwrinkled. ❷ **smooth hair:** GLOSSY, shiny, sleek, silky, satiny, velvety, burnished. ❸ **smooth waters:** CALM, still, tranquil, flat, glassy, mirror-like. ❹ **smooth**

progression: EASY, effortless, trouble-free, simple, plain sailing. ❺ smooth running: STEADY, regular, rhythmic, uninterrupted, flowing, fluid. ❻ smooth sounds: SOFT, soothing, mellow, dulcet, mellifluous, melodious, musical. ❼ smooth young men: SMOOTH-TONGUED, suave, urbane, sophisticated, courteous, gracious, glib, persuasive, slick, oily, ingratiating, unctuous; *informal* smarmy.
– OPPOSITES rough.
▶ verb ❶ LEVEL, even, flatten, plane, press down, steamroll. ❷ EASE, make easy/easier, facilitate, clear the way for, pave the way for, open the door for, expedite, assist, aid, help, help along.

smother verb ❶ SUFFOCATE, stifle, asphyxiate, choke. ❷ OVERWHELM, shower, inundate, envelop, surround, cocoon.

smoulder verb ❶ SMOKE, reek. ❷ SEETHE, fume, burn, boil, foam, rage.

smudge noun MARK, spot, smear, streak, stain, blotch, blot, blur, smut; *informal* splotch.

smug adjective SELF-SATISFIED, complacent, pleased with oneself, superior, proud of oneself, conceited.

snack noun LIGHT MEAL, bite, nibbles, titbit, bite to eat, little something.

snag noun ❶ CATCH, drawback, hitch, stumbling block, obstacle, disadvantage, inconvenience, problem, complication. ❷ RIP, tear, run, hole.
▶ verb CATCH, rip, tear.

snap verb ❶ BREAK, fracture, splinter, separate, come apart, crack. ❷ HAVE A NERVOUS BREAKDOWN, break down, collapse, lose one's mind, lose one's reason, go mad, go insane. ❸ snap one's fingers: CRACK, click, crackle. ❹ dogs snapping: BITE, gnash, nip. ❺ SPEAK SHARPLY/BRUSQUELY, bark, snarl, growl, lash out at; *informal* jump down someone's throat, fly off the handle at.

snappy adjective ❶ IRRITABLE, irascible, cross, touchy, testy, crabbed, crotchety, grumpy, grouchy, peppery. ❷ a snappy dresser: SMART, fashionable, stylish, chic, modish, dapper; *informal* natty, trendy.
– OPPOSITES peaceable, slovenly.

snare verb TRAP, ensnare, catch, get hold of, seize, capture.
▶ noun TRAP, gin, springe, net, noose.

snatch verb ❶ SEIZE, grab, take hold of, pluck. ❷ GRAB, steal, make off with, appropriate; *informal* nab, swipe. ❸ KIDNAP, abduct, grab, take as hostage.

sneak verb ❶ CREEP, skulk, lurk, prowl, steal, slip, slide, slink, sidle. ❷ TELL TALES ON, inform on, report; *informal* tell on, squeal on, peach on; *Brit. informal* grass on.

sneaking adjective SECRET, private, hidden, concealed, unexpressed, unvoiced, undisclosed, undivulged, unconfessed, unavowed.

sneer verb ❶ CURL ONE'S LIP, smirk, snicker, snigger. ❷ SCOFF AT, scorn, be contemptuous of, hold in contempt, disdain, mock, jeer at, gibe at, ridicule, deride, taunt, insult, slight.
▶ noun ❶ SMIRK, snicker. ❷ JEER, jibe, taunt, insult, slight.

sniff verb ❶ SNUFFLE, inhale,

breathe in. ❷ SMELL, catch the scent of, scent; *Brit. informal* get a whiff of.

snigger verb SNICKER, sneer, smirk, titter, giggle, chortle.

snip verb CUT, cut into, nick, slit, notch, incise, snick.
▶ noun ❶ CUT, nick, slit, notch, incision, snick. ❷ BARGAIN; *informal* good buy, cheap buy, giveaway, steal.

snippet noun BIT, piece, scrap, fragment, particle, shred, snatch.

snivel verb ❶ WEEP, cry, sob, whimper; *informal* blub, blubber. ❷ SNIFFLE, snuffle, run at the nose, have a runny/running nose.

snobbish adjective SNOBBY, arrogant, proud, condescending, haughty, disdainful, supercilious, patronizing; *informal* snooty, uppity, stuck up, hoity-toity, toffee-nosed.

snoop verb PRY, spy, interfere, meddle; *informal* poke one's nose in.
▶ noun busybody, interferer, meddler; *informal* snooper, nosy parker; *Austral./NZ informal* stickybeak.

snooze verb DOZE, nap, catnap, drowse, sleep, slumber; *informal* take forty winks; *Brit. informal* have a kip, kip.
▶ noun DOZE, nap, catnap, siesta, sleep, slumber; *informal* forty winks; *Brit. informal* kip.

snub verb IGNORE, disregard, take no notice of, shun, rebuff, repulse, spurn, slight, give the cold shoulder to, cold-shoulder, insult, affront; *informal* give the brush-off to, give the go-by, put down.

snug adjective ❶ COSY, comfortable, warm, homelike, homely, sheltered; *informal* comfy. ❷ CLOSE-FITTING, tight, skin-tight.
– OPPOSITES bleak, loose.

snuggle verb NESTLE, cuddle, curl up, nuzzle.

soak verb ❶ DRENCH, wet through, saturate, make sopping. ❷ STEEP, immerse, souse.

soaking adjective SOAKED, soaked to the skin, wet through, drenched, sodden, saturated, sopping wet, dripping wet, wringing wet, streaming wet.
– OPPOSITES parched.

soar verb ❶ FLY, take flight, take off, ascend, climb, rise. ❷ **cost has soared**: RISE, go up, increase, climb, rapidly, spiral.
– OPPOSITES plummet.

sob verb WEEP, cry, shed tears, blubber, snivel, howl, bawl; *Scottish* greet; *informal* boohoo.

sober adjective ❶ NOT DRUNK/INTOXICATED, abstemious, teetotal, abstinent, temperate; *informal* on the wagon, dry. ❷ SERIOUS, solemn, thoughtful, grave, earnest, calm, composed, sedate, staid, dignified, steady, level-headed, self-controlled, strict, puritanical. ❸ **a sober account**: DISPASSIONATE, objective, rational, logical, well considered, circumspect, lucid, clear. ❹ **sober clothes/colours**: DARK, sombre, quiet, restrained, drab, severe, austere.
– OPPOSITES drunk.

sociable adjective FRIENDLY, affable, cordial, social, neighbourly, companionable, gregarious, convivial, communicative, genial, outgoing, approachable, accessible.
– OPPOSITES unsociable, unfriendly.

social adjective ❶ social problems: COMMUNITY, civil, civic, public, societal. ❷ social clubs: ENTERTAINMENT, recreation, amusement. ❸ *See* SOCIABLE.
– OPPOSITES individual.

socialize verb BE SOCIABLE/SOCIAL, mix, mingle, keep company, fraternize, consort, hobnob, get together, get out and about.

society noun ❶ MANKIND, humanity, civilization, the public, the general public, the people, the population, the world at large, the community. ❷ COMMUNITY, group, culture, civilization. ❸ HIGH SOCIETY, polite society, aristocracy, gentry, nobility, upper classes, the elite, the smart set, beau monde, haut monde; *informal* the upper crust, the top drawer, toffs, nobs, swells. ❹ ASSOCIATION, club, group, band, circle, body, fraternity, brotherhood, sisterhood, league, union, alliance, federation.

sodden adjective *see* SOAKING.

soft adjective ❶ PLIABLE, pliant, supple, elastic, flexible, ductile, malleable, plastic, mushy, squashy, pulpy, doughy, spongy; *informal* gooey. ❷ SMOOTH, velvety, cushiony, fleecy, downy, leathery, furry, silky, silken, satin; *informal* like a baby's bottom. ❸ soft winds: GENTLE, light, mild, moderate, calm, balmy, delicate. ❹ soft lights: LOW, dim, shaded, subdued, muted, mellow. ❺ soft tones: HUSHED, whispered, murmured, stifled, inaudible, low, quiet, mellow, melodious, mellifluous. ❻ soft with the pupils: EASY-GOING, tolerant, forgiving, forbearing, lenient, indulgent, permissive, liberal, lax. ❼ soft in the head: FEEBLE-MINDED, simple, silly; *informal* nutty; *Brit. informal* daft.
– OPPOSITES firm, hard.

soften verb ❶ soften the blow: EASE, cushion, temper, mitigate, assuage. ❷ the winds softened: ABATE, moderate, lessen, diminish, calm down. ❸ soften their approach: MODERATE, temper, tone down.
■ **soften up** WORK ON, persuade, win over, disarm.

soggy adjective SOAKING, saturated, sodden, sopping wet, soft, boggy, swampy, miry, waterlogged, over-moist.

soil[1] noun EARTH, ground, clay, dirt, land.

soil[2] verb DIRTY, stain, muddy, spot, smear, splash, smudge, sully, taint, blot; *poetic/literary* besmirch.

sojourn noun STAY, visit, stop, stopover, holiday, vacation.

solace noun COMFORT, consolation, condolence, support.

soldier noun FIGHTER, serviceman, servicewoman, warrior, trooper; *informal* cannon fodder.
■ **soldier on** PERSEVERE, keep going; *informal* plug away, stick it out.

solecism noun MISTAKE, error, blunder; *informal* howler; *Brit. informal* boob.

solemn adjective ❶ a solemn occasion: SERIOUS, grave, important, formal, profound. ❷ a solemn procession: DIGNIFIED, ceremonious, stately, majestic, imposing, impressive, grand. ❸ a solemn child: SERIOUS, sombre, unsmiling, pensive, thoughtful, gloomy, glum, grim. ❹ a solemn promise: EARNEST, sincere, honest, genuine, committed, heartfelt.
– OPPOSITES frivolous.

solicit verb ❶ ASK FOR, request, apply for, seek, beg, plead for, crave. ❷ WORK AS A PROSTITUTE, engage in prostitution, make sexual advances; *informal* hustle.

solicitous adjective CONCERNED, caring, attentive, considerate, anxious, worried, nervous, uneasy, apprehensive.

solid adjective ❶ FIRM, hard, thick, dense, concrete, compact, compressed, condensed. ❷ SOUND, substantial, strong, sturdy, stout, durable, well built, well constructed, stable. ❸ solid arguments: SOUND, well founded, well grounded, concrete, valid, reasonable, logical, cogent, weighty, authoritative, convincing, plausible, reliable. ❹ solid citizens: SENSIBLE, level-headed, down-to-earth, decent, law-abiding, upright, upstanding, worthy. ❺ solid work: SOUND, worthy, staid, unexciting, unimaginative, uninspired. ❻ a solid company: FINANCIALLY SOUND, solvent, creditworthy, in good standing, in the black, secure. ❼ a solid line: CONTINUOUS, uninterrupted, unbroken, undivided.
– OPPOSITES liquid, flimsy, unreliable.

solidarity noun UNITY, union, unanimity, singleness of purpose, like-mindedness, team spirit, camaraderie, harmony, esprit de corps.

solidify verb HARDEN, go hard, set, jell, congeal, cake.
– OPPOSITES liquefy.

solitary adjective ❶ a solitary life: LONELY, lonesome, companionless, friendless, antisocial, unsocial, unsociable, withdrawn, reclusive, cloistered, introverted, hermitic. ❷ a solitary spot: REMOTE, out of the way, isolated, secluded, hidden, concealed, private, unfrequented, unvisited, desolate. ❸ a solitary tree: LONE, single, sole, alone, by oneself/itself.
– OPPOSITES sociable, accessible.
▶ noun LONER, lone wolf, recluse, hermit, eremite, anchorite, stylite, cenobite.

solitude noun LONELINESS, remoteness, isolation, seclusion, privacy, retirement, desolation.

solution noun ❶ ANSWER, result, key, resolution, solving, resolving, explanation, clarification, elucidation, unravelling, unfolding. ❷ SUSPENSION, emulsion, mixture, mix, blend, compound.

solve verb FIND THE SOLUTION TO, answer, find the answer to, resolve, work out, figure out, fathom, find the key to, decipher, clear up, get to the bottom of, unravel, disentangle, unfold; *informal* crack.

solvent adjective FINANCIALLY SOUND, debt-free, creditworthy, in the black, viable.
– OPPOSITES insolvent.

sombre adjective ❶ DARK, dark-coloured, dull, dull-coloured, drab, dingy. ❷ GLOOMY, depressed, sad, melancholy, dismal, doleful, mournful, joyless, cheerless, lugubrious, funereal, sepulchral.
– OPPOSITES bright, cheerful.

somehow adverb BY SOME MEANS, in some way, in one way or other, no matter how, come what may, by fair means or foul, by hook or by crook; *informal* come hell or high water.

sometimes adverb OCCASIONALLY, on occasion, on

occasions, now and then, now and again, from time to time, once in a while, every so often, off and on.

somnolent adjective SLEEPY, drowsy, half asleep, heavy-eyed, dozy, groggy, comatose; *informal* dopey.

sonorous adjective DEEP, rich, full, round, resonant, resounding, booming, ringing, reverberating, vibrating, pulsating.

soon adverb SHORTLY, in a short time, in a little while, before long, in a minute, in a moment, any minute, in the near future, in a twinkling, in the twinkling of an eye; *informal* before you can say Jack Robinson, pronto, in two shakes of a lamb's tail.

soothe verb EASE, assuage, alleviate, allay, moderate, mitigate, temper, palliate, soften, lessen, reduce.
– OPPOSITES aggravate.

soothsayer noun SEER, augur, prophet, diviner, sibyl.

sophisticated adjective ❶ WORLDLY-WISE, worldly, experienced, seasoned, suave, urbane, cultured, cultivated, polished, refined, elegant, stylish, cosmopolitan, blasé. ❷ ADVANCED, highly developed, ultra-modern, complex, complicated, elaborate, intricate.
– OPPOSITES unsophisticated, crude.

soporific adjective SLEEP-INDUCING, sedative, tranquillizing, narcotic, opiate, somniferous.
– OPPOSITES invigorating.

soppy adjective MAWKISH, maudlin, sentimental, overemotional, sloppy; *informal* slushy, mushy, schmaltzy, corny.

sorcerer noun MAGICIAN, wizard, enchanter, warlock, necromancer, magus, thaumaturgist.

sorcery noun MAGIC, witchcraft, witchery, wizardry, necromancy, black art, enchantment, thaumaturgy.

sordid adjective ❶ FILTHY, dirty, foul, unclean, grimy, sooty, soiled, stained, mucky, squalid, shabby, seedy, seamy, slummy, sleazy. ❷ VILE, foul, base, low, debased, degenerate, dishonourable, disreputable, despicable, ignominious, ignoble, abhorrent, abominable. ❸ MEAN, greedy, avaricious, covetous, grasping, mercenary, miserly, niggardly; *informal* stingy.
– OPPOSITES clean.

sore adjective ❶ PAINFUL, in pain, aching, hurting, tender, inflamed, raw, smarting, stinging, burning, irritated, bruised, wounded, injured. ❷ DISTRESSED, upset, resentful, aggrieved, offended, hurt, pained, annoyed, angry, irritated, irked, nettled; *informal* peeved.
▶ noun WOUND, scrape, abrasion, cut, laceration, graze, boil, abscess, swelling.

sorrow noun ❶ SADNESS, unhappiness, grief, misery, distress, heartache, heartbreak, anguish, suffering, pain, woe, affliction, wretchedness, dejection, heaviness of heart, desolation, depression, disconsolateness, mourning. ❷ TROUBLE, worry, woe, misfortune, affliction, trial, tribulation.
– OPPOSITES joy.
▶ verb BE SAD, feel sad, be miserable, suffer, be wretched, be dejected, be heavy of, heart, pine, weep.

sorrowful adjective UNHAPPY, heartbroken, wretched, woebegone, tearful, miserable, dejected, desolated, depressed, disconsolate, mournful, doleful, melancholy, lugubrious. *See also* SAD (1).
–OPPOSITES happy.

sorry adjective ❶ REGRETFUL, apologetic, repentant, penitent, remorseful, contrite, ashamed, conscience-stricken, guilt-ridden, in sackcloth and ashes, compunctious. ❷ SYMPATHETIC, pitying, full of pity, compassionate, moved, commiserative, empathetic. ❸ SAD, unhappy, distressed, grieved, regretful, sorrowful, miserable, wretched.
–OPPOSITES glad, unsympathetic, unrepentant.

sort noun ❶ KIND, type, variety, class, category, style, group, set, genre, genus, family, order, breed, make, brand, stamp. ❷ **a good sort:** PERSON, individual, soul; *informal* fellow, guy, character, customer; *Brit. informal* bloke, chap.
▶ **verb** CLASSIFY, class, categorize, catalogue, grade, rank, group, divide, arrange, order, put in order, organize, assort, systematize, methodize.
■ **sort out** CLEAR UP, put straight, put right, solve, find a solution to.

sortie noun SALLY, foray, charge, rush, onrush, raid, attack.

so-so adjective MEDIOCRE, average, indifferent, unexceptional, undistinguished, tolerable, passable; *informal* fair-to-middling, no great shakes, nothing to write home about.

soul noun ❶ SPIRIT, psyche, inner self, true being, vital force, animating principle. ❷ **the soul of discretion:** PERSONIFICATION, embodiment, incarnation, essence, epitome. ❸ **not a soul there:** PERSON, human being, individual, creature. ❹ **play it with soul:** FEELING, emotion, intensity, fervour, ardour, vitality, animation, vivacity, energy, inspiration.

sound[1] noun ❶ NOISE, utterance, cry. ❷ HEARING, distance, earshot, range.
–OPPOSITES silence.
▶ **verb** ❶ RESOUND, reverberate, resonate. ❷ **sound the alarm:** OPERATE, set off, ring. ❸ **sound the letter 't':** PRONOUNCE, utter, voice, enunciate, articulate, vocalize. ❹ **sounds like it:** APPEAR, seem, give/create the impression that, strike someone that, give every indication that.

sound[2] adjective ❶ HEALTHY, in good health, in good condition, physically fit, hale and hearty, undamaged, unimpaired, in good shape, in fine fettle. ❷ SOLID, substantial, sturdy, well constructed, intact, whole, undamaged, unimpaired. ❸ **sound policies/arguments:** SOLID, well founded, well grounded, valid, reasonable, logical, cogent, weighty, authoritative, convincing, plausible, reliable. ❹ SOLVENT, creditworthy, in good financial standing, in the black, solid, secure. ❺ **a sound thrashing:** THOROUGH, complete, without reserve, unqualified, out-and-out, drastic, severe.
–OPPOSITES unhealthy, flimsy, insolvent.

sound[3] verb PLUMB, fathom, probe.
■ **sound out** INVESTIGATE, conduct a survey of, research, explore,

look into, examine, probe, canvass.

sour adjective ❶ ACID, acidy, acid-like, acetic, acidulous, tart, bitter, sharp, vinegary, pungent. ❷ TURNED, curdled, fermented, rancid, bad. ❸ a sour old man: EMBITTERED, nasty, unpleasant, disagreeable, bad-tempered, ill-tempered, ill-natured, sharp-tongued, irritable, crotchety, cross, crabbed, testy, touchy, peevish, churlish, grumpy; *informal* grouchy, snappish.
– OPPOSITES sweet, fresh, amiable.

source noun ❶ ORIGIN, derivation, commencement, beginning, start, rise, cause, wellspring, fountainhead, provenance, author, originator; *poetic/literary* begetter. ❷ WELLSPRING, well head, headspring. ❸ REFERENCE, authority.

sovereign noun RULER, monarch, king, queen, emperor, empress, tsar, crowned head, potentate.
▶ adjective ❶ SUPREME, absolute, unlimited, chief, paramount, principal, dominant, predominant, ruling. ❷ a sovereign state: INDEPENDENT, self-ruling, self-governing, autonomous.

sow verb SCATTER, spread, broadcast, disperse, strew, bestrew, disseminate, distribute.

space noun ❶ ROOM, expanse, extent, capacity, area, volume, spaciousness, scope, elbow room, latitude, margin, leeway. ❷ INTERVAL, gap, opening, interstice, break. ❸ TIME, duration, period, span, stretch, interval. ❹ OUTER SPACE, the universe, the galaxy, the solar system, infinity.
▶ verb PLACE AT INTERVALS, arrange, line up, range, order, interspace, set apart.

spacious adjective ❶ a spacious house: ROOMY, commodious, capacious, sizable, large, big, ample. ❷ spacious grounds: EXTENSIVE, broad, wide, expansive, ample, large, vast.
– OPPOSITES small.

span noun ❶ LENGTH, extent, reach, stretch, spread, distance. ❷ TIME, duration, period, space, stretch, interval.
▶ verb EXTEND OVER, stretch across, cover, range over, bridge, cross, traverse, pass over, arch over, vault over.

spank verb SMACK, slap, put over one's knee; *informal* tan someone's hide, give someone a hiding, warm someone's bottom, wallop, belt.

spare adjective ❶ EXTRA, additional, reserve, supplementary, auxiliary, surplus, supernumerary. ❷ spare time: FREE, leisure, unoccupied. ❸ a spare body: LEAN, thin, slim, slender, skinny, skin and bone, wiry, lank.
▶ verb ❶ AFFORD, part with, give, provide, dispense with, do without, manage without, get along without. ❷ BE MERCIFUL TO, show mercy to, be lenient to, deal leniently with, pardon, leave unpunished; *informal* let off, go easy on.

sparing adjective ECONOMICAL, frugal, thrifty, careful, prudent, parsimonious, niggardly; *informal* stingy, tight-fisted.
– OPPOSITES extravagant.

spark noun FLICKER, flash, flare, glint.

▶ **verb** SET OFF, spark off, start off, trigger off, touch off, precipitate, provoke, stir up, incite.

sparkle **verb** ❶ TWINKLE, flicker, shimmer, flash, glitter, glint, shine, gleam, glow, coruscate. ❷ BE VIVACIOUS, be lively, be animated, be ebullient, be effervescent, be witty, be brilliant.
▶ **noun** ❶ TWINKLE, flicker, shimmer, flash, glitter, glint, shining, gleam, glow, coruscation. ❷ VIVACITY, liveliness, life, animation, energy, vitality, spirit, enthusiasm, dash, dan, panache; *informal* pizzazz, vim, zip, zing.

sparse **adjective** SCANTY, meagre, slight, light, sparing, inadequate; *informal* thin on the ground.
– OPPOSITES abundant.

spartan **adjective** AUSTERE, harsh, frugal, stringent, rigorous, strict, severe, bleak, grim, ascetic, abstemious, self-denying.
– OPPOSITES luxurious.

spasm **noun** ❶ CONTRACTION, convulsion, cramp, twitch. ❷ FIT, paroxysm, convulsion, attack, bout, seizure, outburst, access.

spasmodic **adjective** INTERMITTENT, fitful, irregular, sporadic, erratic, periodic, recurring, recurrent.
– OPPOSITES regular.

spate **noun** RUSH, flood, deluge, torrent, outpouring, outbreak, cluster.

spatter **verb** SPLASH, spray, shower, bespatter, daub.

speak **verb** ❶ **speak the truth**: UTTER, voice, express, say, pronounce, articulate, enunciate, state, discourse upon, tell. ❷ **she spoke to him**: ADDRESS, talk to, converse with, communicate with, have a discussion with, chat with, have a chat with, have a word with, accost; *informal* have a chinwag with, chew the fat/rag with, pass the time of day with.
■ **speak for** ❶ REPRESENT, act for, act on behalf of, intercede for. ❷ SUPPORT, uphold, defend, stand up for, advocate. **speak out** SPEAK BOLDLY, speak frankly, speak openly, speak one's mind, sound off, stand up and be counted.

speaker **noun** PUBLIC SPEAKER, lecturer, orator, declaimer, haranguer, demagogue; *informal* tub-thumper, spieler.

spearhead **noun** VANGUARD, van, forefront, driving force.
▶ **verb** LEAD, head, set in motion, initiate, launch, pioneer.

special **adjective** ❶ EXCEPTIONAL, remarkable, unusual, rare, out of the ordinary, extraordinary, singular, distinctive, notable, outstanding, unique. ❷ **special meaning**: SPECIFIC, particular, individual, distinctive, exact, precise, definite. ❸ **special care**: ESPECIAL, extra special, particular, exceptional, out of the ordinary. ❹ **a special occasion**: SIGNIFICANT, momentous, memorable, festive, gala, red-letter.
– OPPOSITES ordinary.

specialist **noun** EXPERT, authority, professional, consultant, master.

speciality **noun** ❶ SPECIALTY, area of specialization, field of study. ❷ DISTINCTIVE FEATURE, forte, métier, talent, gift, claim to fame.

species **noun** SORT, kind, type, variety, class, category, group, genus, breed, genre.

specific **adjective** ❶ **specific instructions**: WELL DEFINED, clear-cut, unambiguous,

unequivocal, exact, precise, explicit, express, detailed. ❷ **a specific purpose**: PARTICULAR, specified, fixed, set, determined, distinct, definite.
– OPPOSITES vague, general.

specify verb STATE, mention, name, stipulate, define, set out, itemize, designate, detail, list, spell out, enumerate, particularize, catalogue, be specific about.

specimen noun SAMPLE, representative, example, illustration, instance, type, exhibit.

specious adjective MISLEADING, deceptive, fallacious, unsound, casuistic, sophistic.

speck noun ❶ SPOT, fleck, dot, speckle, stain, mark, smudge, blemish. ❷ PARTICLE, bit, piece, atom, iota, grain, trace.

speckled adjective MOTTLED, flecked, spotted, dotted, dappled, brindled, stippled.

spectacle noun ❶ SIGHT, vision, scene, picture. ❷ DISPLAY, show, exhibition, pageant, parade, extravaganza.

spectacles noun GLASSES, eyeglasses; *informal* specs.

spectacular adjective IMPRESSIVE, magnificent, splendid, eye-catching, breathtaking, glorious, dazzling, sensational, stunning, dramatic, exceptional, remarkable, unusual, picturesque; *informal* out of this world.
– OPPOSITES unimpressive, dull.

spectator noun VIEWER, observer, onlooker, looker-on, watcher, beholder, witness, eyewitness, bystander; *informal* rubberneck.
– OPPOSITES participant.

spectre noun APPARITION, ghost, phantom, wraith, spirit, shade, vision, revenant, manes; *informal* spook.

speculate verb ❶ CONJECTURE, theorize, hypothesize, guess, take a guess, surmise, muse, reflect, mediate, deliberate, cogitate, consider, think. ❷ GAMBLE, take a risk on, venture on; *informal* have a flutter on.

speculative adjective ❶ CONJECTURAL, theoretical, hypothetical, suppositional, notional, academic, tentative, unproven, vague, indefinite. ❷ RISKY, hazardous, gambling; *informal* chancy, dicey.

speech noun ❶ COMMUNICATION, talk, conversation, discussion, dialogue, colloquy. ❷ DICTION, articulation, enunciation, pronunciation. ❸ TALK, lecture, address, discourse, oration, sermon, harangue, diatribe, tirade; *poetic/literary* philippic. ❹ LANGUAGE, tongue, idiom, dialect, parlance; *informal* lingo.

speechless adjective ❶ STRUCK DUMB, dumbstruck, dumbfounded, astounded, thunderstruck. ❷ SILENT, unspoken, unexpressed, unsaid, unvoiced, tacit.

speed noun RAPIDITY, swiftness, quickness, fastness, haste, hurry, hurriedness, expeditiousness, expedition, alacrity, promptness, fleetness, celerity, velocity.
▶ verb ❶ HURRY, hasten, make haste, rush, race, dash, sprint, scurry, tear, scamper, charge; *informal* scoot. ❷ DRIVE TOO FAST, break the speed limit, exceed the speed limit; *informal* put one's foot down, step on it. ❸ **speed their recovery**: EXPEDITE, hasten, accelerate, advance, further,

forward, facilitate, promote, boost, aid, assist.
– OPPOSITES slow, hinder.
■ **speed up** *see* ACCELERATE.

speedy adjective ❶ RAPID, swift, quick, fast, expeditious, fleet, high-speed. ❷ **a speedy reply:** RAPID, swift, quick, fast, prompt, immediate, express.
– OPPOSITES slow, leisurely.

spell[1] verb MEAN, signify, amount to, add up to, signal, denote, result in, cause, bespeak, portend, augur, presage.
■ **spell out** SPECIFY, set out, itemize, detail, enumerate, particularize, stipulate, make clear, make plain, elucidate, clarify.

spell[2] noun ❶ INCANTATION, conjuration, charm, abracadabra. ❷ TRANCE, entrancement, enthralment, bewitchment.

spell[3] noun ❶ PERIOD, interval, stretch, course, extent, span, patch. ❷ TURN, stint, term, stretch, shift.

spellbound adjective RIVETED, entranced, enthralled, enraptured, transported, rapt, bewitched, fascinated, captivated, mesmerized, hypnotized; *informal* hooked.

spend verb ❶ PAY OUT, lay out, expend, disburse, dish out; *informal* fork out, shell out, splash out, splurge. ❷ **spend hours:** OCCUPY, fill, take up, use up, pass, while away.

spendthrift noun SQUANDERER, prodigal, profligate, wastrel; *informal* big spender.
– OPPOSITES miser.

spent adjective USED UP, consumed, exhausted, finished, depleted, drained, emptied; *informal* played out, burnt out.

sphere noun ❶ GLOBE, ball, orb, globule. ❷ AREA, field, range, scope, extent, compass, jurisdiction. ❸ SOCIAL CLASS, station, rank, status, social circumstances, walk of life.

spherical adjective GLOBE-SHAPED, globular, globoid, round, orb-like, orbicular.

spice noun ❶ FLAVOURING, seasoning, herb, condiment, relish. ❷ EXCITEMENT, interest, colour, piquancy, zest, gusto, pep; *informal* zip, zing, zap.

spicy adjective ❶ SPICED, seasoned, well seasoned, sharp, tart, hot, peppery, piquant, pungent. ❷ **spicy stories:** LIVELY, spirited, suggestive, racy, off colour, improper, indecent, offensive; *informal* raunchy.
– OPPOSITES bland, boring.

spill verb ❶ POUR, pour out, flow, overflow, brim over, run over, slop over, well over. ❷ REVEAL, disclose, divulge, leak, make known; *informal* let out, blab.
▶ noun FALL, tumble; *informal* header, nosedive.

spin verb ❶ REVOLVE, rotate, turn, turn round, circle, whirl, gyrate. ❷ WHIRL, reel, swim, be giddy.
■ **spin out** *see* PROLONG.

spine noun ❶ SPINAL COLUMN, vertebrae, vertebral column, backbone, dorsum. ❷ NEEDLE, spike, barb, quill.

spineless adjective WEAK, feeble, spiritless, irresolute, indecisive, cowardly, timorous, timid, submissive, unmanly, lily-livered; *informal* chicken, yellow, yellow-bellied, gutless.
– OPPOSITES brave.

spiral adjective COILED, corkscrew, winding, twisting, whorled,

helical, cochlear, cochleate, voluted.
▶ **noun** COIL, twist, whorl, corkscrew, wreath, curlicue, helix, volute.
▶ **verb** COIL, wind, twist, swirl, wreathe.

spirit noun ❶ SOUL, psyche, inner self, ego. ❷ BREATH OF LIFE, vital spark, animating principle, life force. ❸ APPARITION, ghost, phantom, spectre, wraith, shade, revenant, manes; *informal* spook. ❹ **a person of spirit:** COURAGE, bravery, braveness, valour, mettle, pluck, grit, pluckiness, will power, motivation, backbone, determination, firmness of purpose, resoluteness; *informal* guts. ❺ **in the wrong spirit:** ATTITUDE, way, state of mind, mood, frame of mind, point of view, reaction, feeling, humour. ❻ **the spirit of the age:** PREVAILING TENDENCY, animating principle, dominating characteristic, ethos, essence, quintessence, embodiment, personification.
– OPPOSITES body, flesh.

spirited adjective ❶ COURAGEOUS, brave, valiant, valorous, heroic, mettlesome, plucky, gritty, determined, resolute. ❷ ANIMATED, lively, vivacious, enthusiastic, fervent, fiery, passionate, energetic.
– OPPOSITES timid, lifeless.

spiritless adjective ❶ WEAK, feeble, spineless, irresolute, indecisive, cowardly, timorous, timid, submissive; *informal* chicken, yellow, yellow-bellied, gutless. ❷ **a spiritless performance:** LACKLUSTRE, dull, colourless, passionless, bland, insipid, vapid, indifferent, prosaic.
– OPPOSITES lively.

spiritual adjective
❶ NON-MATERIAL, incorporeal, ethereal, intangible, other-worldly, unworldly. ❷ RELIGIOUS, sacred, divine, holy, non-secular, churchly, ecclesiastic, devotional, devout.
– OPPOSITES physical, secular.

spit verb EXPECTORATE, hawk.
▶ **noun** SPITTLE, saliva, sputum.

spite noun MALICE, maliciousness, ill will, malevolence, venom, malignance, hostility, resentment, resentfulness, snideness, rancour, envy, hate, hatred, vengeance, vengefulness, vindictiveness.
– OPPOSITES benevolence.
■ **in spite of** DESPITE, despite the fact, notwithstanding, regardless of.

spiteful adjective MALICIOUS, ill-natured, malevolent, venomous, poisonous, malignant, malign, hostile, resentful, snide, rancorous, grudging, envious, vengeful, vindictive, splenetic; *informal* bitchy, catty.
– OPPOSITES benevolent.

splash verb ❶ SPATTER, sprinkle, spray, shower, splatter, squirt, slosh, slop; *Brit. informal* splodge. ❷ PADDLE, wade, wallow, dabble. ❸ BLAZON, display, exhibit, plaster, publicize, broadcast, headline, flaunt, trumpet.

splendid adjective ❶ **splendid furnishings:** MAGNIFICENT, imposing, superb, grand, sumptuous, resplendent, opulent, luxurious, plush, de luxe, rich, costly, lavish, ornate, gorgeous, glorious, dazzling, brilliant, showy, elegant, handsome. ❷ **a splendid reputation:** DISTINGUISHED, impressive, glorious, illustrious, brilliant, notable, noted,

remarkable, outstanding, eminent, celebrated, renowned, noble, venerable. ❸ **a splendid meal:** EXCELLENT, fine, first-class, first-rate, marvellous, wonderful, great; *informal* fantastic, terrific, fabulous, fab.
– OPPOSITES inferior, undistinguished.

splendour noun ❶ MAGNIFICENCE, grandeur, sumptuousness, opulence, luxury, luxuriousness, richness, lavishness, gloriousness, elegance. ❷ ILLUSTRIOUSNESS, brilliance, notability, eminence, renown, venerableness. ❸ GLORIOUSNESS, brilliance, brightness, gleam, glow, lustre, radiance.

splice verb INTERWEAVE, braid, plait, intertwine, interlace, join, unite, connect, bind.

splinter noun SLIVER, fragment, shiver, shard, chip, shaving, shred, piece, bit.
▶ verb SHATTER, fracture, split, disintegrate, crumble.

split verb ❶ BREAK, chop, hew, lop, cleave, rend, rip, tear, slash, slit, splinter. ❷ DIVIDE, separate, set apart, disunite. ❸ **split the money:** SHARE, divide, halve, apportion, distribute, dole out, parcel out, allot, allocate; *Brit. informal* divvy. ❹ BREAK UP WITH/FROM, separate from, part from, part company with, reach the parting of the ways, dissociate oneself from.
– OPPOSITES mend, unite, pool, converge.
▶ noun ❶ BREAK, cut, rent, rip, tear, slash, slit, crack, fissure, breach. ❷ DIVISION, rift, schism, rupture, separation, break-up, alienation, estrangement.
– OPPOSITES marriage.

spoil verb ❶ DAMAGE, impair, mar, blemish, disfigure, deface, injure, harm, ruin, destroy, wreck. ❷ **spoil our plans:** UPSET, mess up, disorganize, ruin, destroy, wreck. ❸ **spoil her son:** PAMPER, overindulge, mollycoddle, cosset, coddle, baby, spoon-feed, feather-bed, wait on hand and foot, kill with kindness. ❹ **the food will spoil:** GO BAD, go off, turn, go sour, become rotten, rot, become tainted, decompose, decay.
– OPPOSITES improve, further.

spoilsport noun KILLJOY, damper, dog in the manger; *informal* wet blanket, party-pooper, misery.

spoken adjective ORAL, verbal, uttered, voiced, expressed, by word of mouth, unwritten.
– OPPOSITES non-verbal, written.

sponge verb CLEAN, wash, wipe, mop, rub, swab.
■ **sponge off/on** LIVE OFF, impose on, be a parasite on, beg from, borrow from; *informal* scrounge from, freeload on, cadge from, bum from; *N. Amer. informal* mooch from.

spongy adjective SOFT, cushiony, squashy, springy, resilient, elastic, porous, absorbent.

sponsor noun PATRON, backer, promoter, subsidizer, guarantor, supporter, angel.
▶ verb BE A PATRON OF, back, put up the money for, fund, finance, promote, subsidize, support, lend one's name to.

spontaneous adjective ❶ VOLUNTARY, unforced, unconstrained, unprompted. ❷ UNPLANNED, unpremeditated, unrehearsed, impromptu, extempore, spur-of-the-moment, extemporaneous; *informal*

off-the-cuff. ❸ **a spontaneous smile:** NATURAL, instinctive, involuntary, automatic, impulsive, impetuous.
– OPPOSITES conscious, voluntary.

spoon-feed verb PAMPER, mollycoddle, cosset, coddle, feather-bed, wait on hand and foot, kill with kindness, overindulge, spoil.

sporadic adjective IRREGULAR, intermittent, scattered, random, infrequent, occasional, on and off, isolated, spasmodic.
– OPPOSITES frequent, regular.

sport noun ❶ PHYSICAL ACTIVITY, physical exercise, physical recreation, athletics, game, pastime. ❷ AMUSEMENT, entertainment, diversion, play, fun, pleasure, enjoyment.
▶ verb ❶ PLAY, have fun, amuse oneself, entertain oneself, divert oneself, frolic, gambol, frisk, romp, cavort, caper, disport oneself. ❷ **sport a new tie:** WEAR, exhibit, display, have on show, show off.

sporting adjective SPORTSMANLIKE, fair, just, honourable, generous.

sportive adjective PLAYFUL, high-spirited, sprightly, jaunty, rollicking, frisky, skittish, mischievous, waggish, prankish; *poetic/literary* frolicsome; *archaic* gamesome.

spot noun ❶ MARK, dot, speck, fleck, smudge, stain, blotch, patch; *informal* splotch. ❷ PIMPLE, pustule, papule, boil, whitehead, blackhead, blemish. ❸ STAIN, taint, blemish, defect, flaw, brand, stigma. ❹ **a picnic spot:** AREA, place, site, location, scene, setting, situation. ❺ **a spot of lunch:** LITTLE, bit, morsel, smidgen, bite. ❻ **in a spot:** DIFFICULTY, mess, trouble, plight, predicament, quandary, tight corner; *informal* hot water, fix, jam.
▶ verb ❶ CATCH SIGHT OF, see, notice, observe, espy, discern, descry, detect, make out, pick out, recognize. ❷ MARK, stain, dirty, soil, spatter; *poetic/literary* besmirch.

spotless adjective ❶ CLEAN, snowy-white, whiter-than-white, spick and span, immaculate, shining, gleaming. ❷ **a spotless character:** PURE, flawless, faultless, blameless, unstained, unsullied, untainted, unblemished, unimpeachable, above reproach.
– OPPOSITES dirty, impure.

spotlight noun LIMELIGHT, public eye, glare of publicity, publicity, public attention, public interest.

spotted adjective DAPPLED, mottled, pied, piebald, speckled.

spotty adjective ❶ PIMPLY, acned. ❷ *See* SPOTTED. ❸ PATCHY, irregular, non-uniform.

spouse noun HUSBAND/WIFE, partner, mate, companion, consort, helpmate; *informal* better half, old man/woman/lady, missis.

spout verb ❶ SPURT, gush, spew, squirt, jet, spray, emit, erupt, disgorge, pour, stream, flow. ❷ DECLAIM, orate, hold forth, ramble, rant, harangue, speechify, sermonize; *informal* spiel.

sprawl verb ❶ STRETCH OUT, lounge, lie around, repose, recline, slump, flop, loll, slouch. ❷ SPREAD, stretch, spill over, ramble, straggle, trail.

spray[1] noun ❶ SHOWER, jet, mist, drizzle, spindrift, foam, froth. ❷ ATOMIZER, vaporizer, aerosol, sprinkler.

▶ **verb** ❶ SPRINKLE, shower, disperse, disseminate. ❷ JET, spout, gush.

spray[2] **noun** SPRIG, posy, bouquet, nosegay, corsage, wreath, garland.

spread verb ❶ STRETCH, extend, open out, unfurl, unroll. ❷ STRETCH OUT, extend, enlarge, grow bigger, widen, broaden, grow, develop, branch out. ❸ STRETCH OUT, unfold, be on display, be exhibited, be on show, uncover, be unveiled, be revealed. ❹ COVER, coat, layer, lay on, put on, apply, smear on; *informal* plaster on. ❺ **the disease is spreading:** MUSHROOM, extend, increase, advance, proliferate, escalate. ❻ **spread rumours:** DISSEMINATE, circulate, transmit, make public, make known, broadcast, publicize, propagate, promulgate, bruit.
▶ **noun** ❶ EXTENT, stretch, span, reach, compass, sweep. ❷ **the spread of the disease:** INCREASE, advance, expansion, mushrooming, proliferation, escalation, diffusion. ❸ BEDSPREAD, bedcover, cover, coverlet, counterpane, throw. ❹ **a birthday spread:** FEAST, banquet, repast; *informal* blowout.

spree noun OUTING, fling, revel, junket, orgy, debauch, bacchanal, bacchanalia; *informal* binge, bender, jag.

sprightly adjective SPRY, lively, energetic, active, agile, nimble, supple, animated, vivacious, spirited, brisk, vital, light-hearted, cheerful, merry, jolly, jaunty, perky, frisky, playful, sportive; *poetic/literary* frolicsome, blithe.
– OPPOSITES inactive, lethargic.

spring verb JUMP, leap, bound, vault, hop.
▶ **noun** ❶ JUMP, leap, bound, vault, hop. ❷ BOUNCE, bounciness, liveliness, light-heartedness, merriment.
■ **spring from** ORIGINATE, have its origins in, derive from, stem from, arise in, emanate from, proceed from, start from. **spring up** APPEAR, come into being, come into existence, shoot up, develop quickly, mushroom, burgeon.

springy adjective BOUNCY, elastic, resilient, flexible, stretchy, tensile.
– OPPOSITES rigid.

sprinkle verb SPRAY, shower, splash, trickle, spatter, scatter, strew, dust, powder.

sprinkling noun ❶ SCATTERING, dusting. ❷ FEW, handful, trickle.

sprint verb RUN, race, rush, dash, put on a turn/burst of speed; *informal* scoot, tear, hare, hotfoot it.

sprout verb BUD, germinate, put forth shoots, shoot up, spring up, grow, develop, appear, mushroom, proliferate.

spruce adjective NEAT, well groomed, well turned out, smart, trim, dapper, elegant, chic; *informal* natty.
– OPPOSITES dishevelled.

spur noun GOAD, prod, stimulus, stimulant, incentive, inducement, encouragement, impetus.
– OPPOSITES disincentive.
▶ **verb** PROD, goad, stimulate, give the incentive to, induce, encourage, motivate, prompt, urge, impel.
– OPPOSITES discourage.

spurious adjective COUNTERFEIT, fraudulent, fake, bogus, sham, mock, feigned, pretended, pseudo, make-believe, imitation,

contrived, fictitious, deceitful, specious; *informal* phoney.
– OPPOSITES authentic, genuine.

spurn verb REJECT, turn away, repulse, rebuff, repudiate, snub, slight, cold-shoulder, disdain, look down one's nose at, scorn, despise, condemn; *informal* kick in the teeth, give the go-by.
– OPPOSITES welcome, accept.

spurt verb GUSH, squirt, shoot, surge, well, jet, spring, pour, stream, flow, issue, emanate.
▶ **noun** ❶ GUSH, surge, jet, spray, outpouring. ❷ **a spurt of speed**: BURST, outburst, fit, surge, access.

spy noun ENEMY AGENT, foreign agent, secret agent, undercover agent, intelligence agent, double agent, fifth columnist; *informal* mole, spook.
▶ **verb** CATCH SIGHT OF, spot, see, notice, observe, glimpse, make out, discern, descry, espy.
■ **spy on** KEEP UNDER SURVEILLANCE, watch, keep a watch on, keep an eye on, observe, keep under observation, follow, shadow, trail.

squabble noun DISPUTE, argument, wrangle, brawl; *informal* row, scrap, set-to, dust-up, run-in, spat; *Brit. informal* barney.
▶ **verb** HAVE A DISPUTE, argue, bicker, have a difference of opinion, have words, wrangle, brawl; *informal* row, have a tiff.

squalid adjective ❶ DIRTY, filthy, dingy, grubby, grimy, mucky, foul, vile, low, wretched, mean, nasty, seedy, sordid, sleazy, slovenly, repulsive, disgusting, ramshackle, broken-down, tumbledown; *informal* grungy; *Brit. informal* grotty. ❷ SORDID, vile, nasty, repulsive, horrible, disgraceful, shameful, abominable, odious, filthy, indecent, depraved.
– OPPOSITES clean, decent.

squander verb WASTE, misspend, dissipate, fritter away, run through, lavish, splurge, be prodigal with, spend like water, pour down the drain; *informal* blow.
– OPPOSITES save.

square noun ❶ PIAZZA, plaza, market square, marketplace, quadrangle. ❷ FOGY, old fogy, conservative, traditionalist, conventionalist, die-hard, conformist; *informal* stick-in-the-mud, fuddy-duddy.
▶ **adjective** ❶ EQUAL, even, level-pegging, drawn. ❷ FAIR, just, equitable, honest, straight, upright, above board, ethical; *informal* on the level.
❸ OLD-FASHIONED, behind the times, conservative, traditionalist, conventional, conformist, bourgeois, strait-laced, stuffy, unadventurous; *informal* fuddy-duddy.

squash verb ❶ CRUSH, squeeze, flatten, compress, press, smash, pulp, mash, pulverize, macerate. ❷ **people squashed in the hall**: CROWD, crush, cram, pack tight, jam, squeeze, wedge. ❸ **squash someone**: HUMILIATE, mortify, deflate, put someone in their place, take down a peg or two, intimidate, put down. ❹ **squash the rebellion**: PUT DOWN, quash, quell, crush, suppress, scotch.

squashy adjective PULPY, mushy, spongy, squishy, oozy, pappy.
– OPPOSITES firm.

squat adjective DUMPY, stubby, chunky, thickset, stocky, short.

squeak noun & verb SQUEAL, peep, pipe, yelp, whimper.

squeamish adjective ❶ EASILY NAUSEATED, liable to be made to feel sick, easily put off, nervous, unable to stand the sight of. ❷ SCRUPULOUS, particular, punctilious, finicky, fussy, fastidious.

squeeze verb ❶ COMPRESS, crush, squash, mash, pulp. ❷ GRIP, clutch, pinch, press, compress. ❸ CROWD, crush, cram, pack tight, jam, squash, wedge. ❹ PRESSURE, pressurize, strong-arm, blackmail; *informal* put the squeeze on, lean on, bleed, put the screws on, put the bite on.

squirm verb WRIGGLE, wiggle, writhe, twist, turn, shift.

squirt verb SPURT, spout, jet, stream, spray, gush, surge, pour, flow, issue, spew out.

stab verb KNIFE, pierce, puncture, run through, stick, skewer, gash, slash, wound, injure.
▶ **noun** ❶ PUNCTURE, gash, slash, incision, wound, injury. ❷ PANG, twinge, ache, throb, spasm. ❸ **have a stab**: TRY, attempt, endeavour, essay, effort, venture; *informal* go, crack.

stability noun FIRMNESS, solidity, steadiness, secureness, strength, fastness, stoutness, sturdiness, sureness, durability, constancy, permanence, reliability, dependability.
– OPPOSITES instability.

stable adjective ❶ FIRM, solid, steady, secure, fixed, strong, fast, stout, sturdy, immovable. ❷ **a stable relationship**: SECURE, solid, strong, steady, firm, sure, steadfast, unwavering, unfaltering, unswerving, long-lasting, deep-rooted, well founded, well grounded, abiding, durable, enduring, lasting, constant, permanent. ❸ **a stable person**: WELL BALANCED, balanced, steady, reasonable, sensible, responsible, equable, self-controlled, sane.
– OPPOSITES unstable.

stack noun ❶ HEAP, pile, mass, accumulation, collection, hoard, store, stock, stockpile, mound, mountain. ❷ **stacks of money**: ABUNDANCE, amplitude, a great deal, a lot; *informal* lots, bags, loads, heaps, tons, oodles, scads.
▶ **verb** HEAP, pile, pile up, amass, accumulate, collect, hoard, store, stockpile.

staff noun ❶ STICK, cane, crook, rod, pole, baton, truncheon. ❷ MACE, sceptre. ❸ EMPLOYEES, workers, workforce, personnel.
▶ **verb** MAN, people, provide with staff.

stage noun ❶ POINT, period, step, juncture, time, division, level. ❷ LAP, leg, phase, step. ❸ PLATFORM, dais, rostrum, podium.
▶ **verb** PUT ON, produce, direct, perform, mount, present.

stagger verb ❶ REEL, sway, teeter, totter, wobble, lurch, pitch, roll. ❷ AMAZE, astound, dumbfound, astonish, shock, shake, confound, nonplus, take aback, take someone's breath away, stupefy, stun, strike dumb; *informal* flabbergast.

stagnant adjective ❶ **stagnant water**: STILL, motionless, standing, foul, stale, dirty, filthy, brackish. ❷ **a stagnant economy**: SLUGGISH, slow-moving, quiet, inactive, dull, static.
– OPPOSITES fresh, active.

stagnate verb DO NOTHING, be sluggish, lie dormant, be inert, vegetate, idle, be idle, laze, loaf, hang about, languish.

staid adjective SEDATE, quiet, serious, grave, solemn, sombre, sober, proper, decorous, formal, demure, stiff, starchy; *informal* stuffy.
– OPPOSITES frivolous.

stain verb ❶ SOIL, mark, discolour, dirty, spot, blotch, blemish, smudge, smear, begrime; *poetic/literary* besmirch. ❷ BLACKEN, tarnish, sully, blemish, damage, mar, injure, defame, denigrate, dishonour, besmirch, defile, taint, blot, slur. ❸ VARNISH, dye, paint, colour.
▶ noun ❶ MARK, spot, blotch, blemish, smudge, smear. ❷ BLEMISH, damage, injury, taint, blot, slur, stigma. ❸ VARNISH, dye, paint, colourant.

stake[1] noun POST, pole, stick, upright, rod, spike, pale.
▶ verb ❶ SUPPORT, prop up, hold up, brace, tether. ❷ **stake a claim**: ESTABLISH, declare, state, lay claim to.

stake[2] noun ❶ WAGER, bet, ante. ❷ FINANCIAL INTEREST, interest, share, investment, involvement, concern.
▶ verb **stake money**: WAGER, bet, put on, gamble, pledge, chance, venture, risk, hazard.

stale adjective ❶ **stale bread/cheese**: DRY, dried out, hard, hardened, mouldy, decayed. ❷ **stale air**: STUFFY, close, musty, fusty; *Brit.* fuggy. ❸ **stale jokes**: HACKNEYED, tired, worn out, threadbare, banal, trite, stock, stereotyped, run-of-the-mill, commonplace, unoriginal, unimaginative, uninspired, flat, insipid, vapid; *informal* old hat.
– OPPOSITES fresh.

stalemate noun DEADLOCK, impasse, standstill, stand-off.

stalk[1] noun STEM, branch, shoot, twig.

stalk[2] verb ❶ PURSUE, chase, follow, shadow, trail, track down, creep up on, hunt; *informal* tail. ❷ **she stalked out**: STRIDE, march, flounce, strut, prance.

stall noun BOOTH, stand, table, counter.
▶ verb ❶ PLAY FOR TIME, use delaying tactics, delay, drag one's feet, beat about the bush; *Brit.* hum and haw. ❷ **stall his creditors**: HOLD OFF, stave off, keep at bay, keep at arm's length, evade, avoid.

stalwart adjective BRAVE, courageous, valiant, valorous, intrepid, fearless, manly, heroic, indomitable, bold, daring, plucky, spirited, adventurous; *informal* gutsy. *See also* BRAVE.
– OPPOSITES timid.

stamina noun ENDURANCE, staying power, indefatigability, resilience, fortitude, strength, vigour, energy, staunchness, robustness; *informal* grit, guts.

stammer verb STUTTER, stumble, mumble, splutter, hesitate, falter, pause.

stamp verb ❶ TRAMPLE, step on, tread on, trample on, crush. ❷ IMPRINT, inscribe, engrave, emboss, mark, sign.
▶ noun MARK, hallmark, label, brand, tag, characteristics, quality.
■ **stamp out** QUASH, suppress, put down, quell, crush, extinguish, scotch, put an end to, eradicate, eliminate.

stampede noun CHARGE, rush, flight, scattering.
▶ verb CHARGE, rush, flee, take flight, dash, race, run.

stance noun STAND, standpoint, position, line, policy, attitude, angle, slant, viewpoint, point of view, opinion.

stand verb ❶ BE UPRIGHT, be erect, rise, rise/get to one's feet, get up. ❷ BE SITUATED, be located. ❸ REMAIN/BE IN FORCE, remain/be valid, remain/be effective, hold, hold good, obtain, prevail, be the case. ❹ **can't stand him**: PUT UP WITH, tolerate, bear, take, endure, abide, countenance, stomach, cope with, handle; *informal* wear; *formal* brook; *archaic* suffer.
▶ noun ❶ STANDSTILL, halt, stop, rest. ❷ *See* STANCE. ❸ PLATFORM, stage, staging, dais, rostrum.
■ **stand by/stand up for** *see* SUPPORT verb (5). **stand out** BE NOTICEABLE, be noticed, be conspicuous, be striking, attract attention, catch the eye; *informal* stick out a mile, stick out like a sore thumb.

standard noun ❶ YARDSTICK, benchmark, gauge, measure, criterion, guide, guideline, norm, touchstone, model, pattern, example, exemplar, paradigm, ideal, archetype, specification, requirement, rule, principle, law, canon. ❷ LEVEL, grade, quality, worth, merit. ❸ FLAG, banner, pennant, streamer, ensign, colours. ❹ SUPPORT, prop, pole, cane, upright.
▶ adjective ❶ USUAL, ordinary, average, normal, habitual, common, regular, stock, set, fixed, conventional. ❷ **the standard work**: DEFINITIVE, established, classic, recognized, approved, accepted, authoritative, official.
– OPPOSITES unusual.

standardize verb MAKE UNIFORM, regulate, systematize, normalize, homogenize, regiment, bring into line.

standing noun STATUS, rank, social position, station, footing, place, circumstances.

stand-off noun DEADLOCK, impasse, stalemate.

stand-offish adjective ALOOF, distant, cold, cool, reserved, withdrawn, remote, detached, unapproachable, unfriendly, unsociable, haughty, disdainful.
– OPPOSITES friendly, approachable.

standpoint noun POINT OF VIEW, viewpoint, opinion, perspective, angle, slant, frame of reference.

standstill noun HALT, stop, dead stop, stoppage, rest, pause, cessation, stand.

staple adjective CHIEF, primary, main, principal, basic, fundamental, essential, indispensable.

star noun ❶ HEAVENLY BODY, celestial body. ❷ **read his stars**: HOROSCOPE, forecast, augury. ❸ SUPERSTAR, name, lead, celebrity, dignitary, notable, somebody, VIP; *informal* bigwig, big shot, big cheese, big wheel.

stare verb GAZE, gape, goggle, look; *informal* gawp.

stark adjective ❶ SHARP, sharply defined, obvious, evident, clear, clear-cut. ❷ **a stark landscape**: DESOLATE, bare, barren, arid, vacant, empty, forsaken, bleak, dreary, depressing, grim, harsh; *poetic/literary* drear.
– OPPOSITES indistinct, ornate.

start verb ❶ BEGIN, commence, make a start, get going, go ahead, set things moving, buckle to/down, turn to, put one's shoulder

to the wheel, put one's hand to the plough; *informal* get moving, start the ball rolling, get down to it, get down to business, get one's finger out, get the show on the road, take the plunge, kick off, pitch in, get off one's backside. ❷ START OUT, set out, set off, depart, leave, make a start; *informal* hit the road, push off, get the show on the road. ❸ SET IN MOTION, set moving, turn on, activate. ❹ **the machine started up:** BEGIN WORKING, start functioning, start operating. ❺ **he started at the noise:** JUMP, leap up, jerk, twitch, recoil, shrink, flinch, blench, wince, shy.
– OPPOSITES finish.
▶ noun ❶ BEGINNING, commencement, opening, inception, inauguration, dawn, birth; *informal* kick-off. ❷ JUMP, leap, jerk, twitch, flinch, blench, wince, spasm, convulsion.
– OPPOSITES end.

startle verb MAKE SOMEONE JUMP, disturb, agitate, perturb, unsettle, scare, frighten, alarm, surprise, astonish, shock; *informal* give someone a turn.

startling adjective DISTURBING, unsettling, alarming, surprising, unexpected, unforeseen, astonishing, amazing, staggering, shocking, extraordinary, remarkable.
– OPPOSITES predictable, ordinary.

starvation noun EXTREME HUNGER, lack of food, fasting, famine, undernourishment, malnourishment.

starving adjective STARVED, famished, ravenous, very hungry, fasting; *informal* able to eat a horse.

state[1] noun ❶ CONDITION, shape, situation, circumstances, state of affairs, position, predicament, plight. ❷ ANXIETY, nerves, panic, fluster; *informal* flap, tizzy. ❸ COUNTRY, nation, land, realm, kingdom, republic.

state[2] verb EXPRESS, voice, utter, say, tell, declare, set out, lay down, affirm, assert, announce, make known, reveal, disclose, divulge, pronounce, articulate, proclaim; *formal* aver.

stately adjective CEREMONIAL, dignified, solemn, majestic, royal, regal, magnificent, grand, glorious, splendid, elegant, imposing, impressive, august, lofty, pompous.

statement noun DECLARATION, account, recitation, report, affirmation, assertion, announcement, revelation, disclosure, divulgence, pronouncement, articulation, proclamation, presentation, promulgation; *formal* averment.

static adjective UNMOVING, unvarying, undeviating, changeless, constant, stable, steady, stationary, motionless, at a standstill, frozen.
– OPPOSITES mobile, variable.

station noun ❶ STOP, stopping place, terminus, terminal, depot. ❷ DEPOT, base, office, headquarters, seat. ❸ **at his station:** POST, place, position, location, site. ❹ **station in life:** CLASS, level, rank, grade, standing, status, caste.

stationary adjective ❶ UNMOVING, motionless, at a standstill, parked. ❷ CHANGELESS, unchanging, constant, unvarying, invariable, undeviating.
– OPPOSITES moving.

statue noun STATUETTE, sculpture, effigy, figure, figurine, bust, head.

statuesque adjective DIGNIFIED, stately, majestic, splendid, imposing, impressive, regal.

stature noun ❶ HEIGHT, tallness, size. ❷ STATUS, importance, import, standing, eminence, prominence, note, renown.

status noun STANDING, rank, level, grade, degree, position, importance, reputation, consequence.

staunch adjective LOYAL, faithful, dependable, reliable, steady, constant, stable, firm, steadfast, unswerving, unwavering, unhesitating, unfaltering.
– OPPOSITES disloyal.

stay[1] verb ❶ REMAIN, wait, stay put, continue, linger, pause, rest, delay; *archaic* tarry. ❷ LODGE, take a room, put up, be accommodated, sojourn, visit, reside, take up residence, dwell, live. ❸ CHECK, curb, arrest, stop, delay, hold, prevent, hinder, impede, obstruct.
– OPPOSITES leave.
▶ noun ❶ VISIT, sojourn, stop, stopover, holiday, vacation. ❷ POSTPONEMENT, suspension, adjournment, deferment, delay.

stay[2] noun PROP, support, brace, bolster, buttress.

steadfast adjective ❶ *See* STAUNCH. ❷ **a steadfast refusal:** FIRM, determined, resolute, unchanging, unwavering, unfaltering, unswerving, unyielding, inflexible, uncompromising, relentless, implacable.
– OPPOSITES irresolute.

steady adjective ❶ FIRM, fixed, stable, secure, immovable. ❷ STILL, motionless, unmoving, sure. ❸ **a steady gaze:** STEADFAST, fixed, immovable, unwavering, unfaltering. ❹ **a steady pace:** UNIFORM, even, regular, rhythmic, consistent. ❺ **a steady young man:** WELL BALANCED, balanced, sensible, level-headed, rational, settled, down-to-earth, calm, equable, imperturbable, reliable, dependable, serious-minded, serious.
– OPPOSITES unstable, shaky, fluctuating.
▶ verb ❶ MAKE STEADY, hold steady, stabilize, secure, balance, support. ❷ CALM, calm down, settle, compose, tranquillize, control, get a grip on.

steal verb ❶ THIEVE, take, appropriate, misappropriate, pilfer, purloin, walk off with, embezzle, pocket, abstract, shoplift; *informal* filch, snitch, swipe, lift, rip off; *Brit. informal* pinch, nick; *formal* peculate. ❷ PLAGIARIZE, copy, pirate, appropriate; *informal* lift, crib. ❸ **steal away:** SLIP, slide, tiptoe, sneak, creep, slink, slither, flit, glide.

stealing noun THEFT, thieving, thievery, robbery, larceny, burglary, appropriation, misappropriation, pilfering, pilferage, purloining, embezzlement, shoplifting; *informal* filching, swiping; *Brit. informal* pinching, nicking; *formal* peculation.

stealthy adjective SECRET, furtive, surreptitious, sly, sneaky, clandestine, covert, underhand, undercover; *informal* shady.
– OPPOSITES above board, open.

steam noun VAPOUR, fume, smoke, exhalation.

steamy adjective ❶ HUMID, muggy,

sticky, moist, damp, sweltering, boiling. ❷ EROTIC, sexy, passionate, tempestuous, sensuous, lustful, wanton.

steep adjective ❶ SHEER, abrupt, precipitous, sudden, sharp, perpendicular, vertical, declivitous. ❷ **a steep rise**: SHARP, rapid, sudden, precipitate. ❸ *See* EXPENSIVE.
– OPPOSITES gentle, gradual.

steeple noun SPIRE, tower, campanile, turret, minaret.

steer verb ❶ GUIDE, navigate, drive, pilot, be at the wheel of. ❷ GUIDE, lead, direct, conduct, usher.

stench noun STINK, foul smell/odour, reek; *Brit. informal* pong, whiff.

step noun ❶ STRIDE, pace, footstep, footfall, tread, tramp. ❷ WALK, gait, bearing, carriage. ❸ RUNG, tread. ❹ COURSE OF ACTION, move, act, action, deed, measure, manoeuvre, procedure, expedient, effort. ❺ STAGE, level, grade, rank, degree.
▶ **verb** WALK, tread, stride, pace, move, advance, proceed; *informal* hoof it.
■ **step down** RESIGN, give up one's job, retire, abdicate. **step in** *see* INTERVENE (2). **step up** *see* INCREASE verb (2).

stereotype noun RECEIVED IDEA, standardized image, hackneyed conception, cliché.
▶ **verb** TYPECAST, pigeonhole, conventionalize, standardize, label, tag, categorize.

stereotyped adjective TYPECAST, conventional, conventionalized, standardized, hackneyed, clichéd, banal, trite, platitudinous.

sterile adjective ❶ INFERTILE, barren, infecund. ❷ INFERTILE, unproductive, unfruitful, unyielding, arid, dry, barren. ❸ STERILIZED, germ-free, antiseptic, disinfected, aseptic, uncontaminated, unpolluted, pure, clean.
– OPPOSITES fertile, productive.

sterilize verb ❶ DISINFECT, purify, fumigate. ❷ MAKE INFERTILE, make barren, castrate, vasectomize, geld, neuter, spay, emasculate.

stern adjective ❶ STRICT, harsh, hard, severe, rigorous, stringent, rigid, exacting, demanding, cruel, relentless, unsparing, inflexible, unyielding, authoritarian, tyrannical, despotic, Draconian. ❷ SEVERE, forbidding, frowning, unsmiling, sombre, sober, austere.
– OPPOSITES lax, genial.

stew verb SIMMER, boil, casserole, fricassee.
▶ **noun** CASSEROLE, ragout, fricassee.

stick[1] noun PIECE OF WOOD, branch, twig, switch.

stick[2] verb ❶ PUSH, insert, jab, poke. ❷ PIERCE, penetrate, puncture, prick, spear, stab, run through, transfix, impale. ❸ GLUE, paste, gum, tape, sellotape, fasten, attach, fix, pin, tack. ❹ BECOME BOGGED DOWN, become embedded, become lodged, be unable to move. ❺ **stick it over there**: PUT, set down, place, lay, deposit, position, plant; *informal* plonk. ❻ PUT UP WITH, tolerate, bear, stand, take, abide, endure, stomach.
■ **stick at** KEEP AT, persist with, persevere with, work at; *informal* put one's back into. **stick by** STAND BY, be loyal to, remain faithful to, support, back, defend.

sticky adjective ❶ ADHESIVE, adherent, gummy, gluey, tacky. ❷ GLUEY, glutinous, viscous; *informal* gooey. ❸ CLOSE, humid, muggy, clammy, sultry, sweltering, oppressive. ❹ **a sticky situation**: AWKWARD, difficult, tricky, ticklish, delicate, thorny.

stiff adjective ❶ RIGID, inflexible, unyielding, inelastic, firm, hard, hardened, brittle. ❷ **stiff muscles**: TIGHT, tense, taut, aching; *informal* creaky. ❸ **a stiff climb**: DIFFICULT, hard, arduous, tough, laborious, exacting, demanding, formidable, challenging, tiring, fatiguing, exhausting, Herculean. ❹ **stiff punishment**: SEVERE, harsh, hard, stringent, rigorous, drastic, strong, heavy, Draconian. ❺ **stiff resistance**: STRONG, vigorous, determined, resolute, dogged, tenacious, unflagging, stubborn, obdurate. ❻ FORMAL, ceremonial, ceremonious, dignified, proper, decorous, pompous.
– OPPOSITES soft.

stiffen verb ❶ BECOME STIFF, thicken, set, jell, solidify, harden, congeal, coagulate. ❷ **stiffen their resolve**: STRENGTHEN, fortify, brace, steel, reinforce.
– OPPOSITES liquefy, weaken.

stifle verb ❶ **stifle a yawn**: SMOTHER, check, restrain, keep back, hold back, hold in, withhold, choke back, muffle, suppress, curb. ❷ **stifle dissent**: SUPPRESS, quash, quell, put an end to, put down, stop, extinguish, stamp out, crush, subdue, repress. ❸ SUFFOCATE, smother, asphyxiate, choke.

stigma noun SHAME, disgrace, dishonour, slur, stain, taint.
– OPPOSITES honour.

still adjective ❶ MOTIONLESS, unmoving, without moving, immobile, unstirring, inert, lifeless, stock-still, stationary, static. ❷ QUIET, silent, hushed, soundless, sound-free, noiseless, undisturbed.
– OPPOSITES moving, noisy.
▶ **noun** QUIETNESS, quiet, silence, hush, soundlessness, noiselessness, calmness, calm, tranquillity, peace, peacefulness, serenity.
▶ **adverb** ❶ AT THIS TIME, yet, up to this time, even now, until now. ❷ NEVERTHELESS, however, in spite of that, notwithstanding, for all that.

stilted adjective STIFF, unnatural, wooden, forced, laboured, constrained, unrelaxed, awkward.
– OPPOSITES natural.

stimulant noun ❶ TONIC, restorative, reviver, energizer, excitant, analeptic; *informal* upper, pick-me-up, bracer. ❷ STIMULUS, incentive, impetus, fillip, spur.
– OPPOSITES sedative, deterrent.

stimulate verb ACT AS A STIMULUS/INCENTIVE TO, encourage, prompt, spur on, activate, stir up, excite, whip up, kindle, incite, instigate, foment, fan.
– OPPOSITES discourage.

stimulating adjective ❶ RESTORING, restorative, reviving, energizing, analeptic; *informal* pick-me-up. ❷ INTERESTING, exciting, stirring, thought-provoking, inspiring, exhilarating, intriguing, provoking, provocative.
– OPPOSITES sedative, boring.

stimulus noun STIMULANT, incentive, fillip, spur, push, drive, encouragement, inducement, incitement, goad, jog, jolt; *informal* shot in the arm.

sting noun IRRITATION, smarting, tingling, tingle, pain, hurt.
▶ verb ❶ SMART, tingle, burn, be irritated. ❷ HURT, wound, distress, grieve, vex, pain, anguish, torture, torment, harrow.

stingy adjective MEAN, miserly, parsimonious, niggardly, cheese-paring, penny-pinching; *informal* tight, tight-fisted; *N. Amer. informal* cheap.
– OPPOSITES generous.

stink verb SMELL BAD, give off a bad smell, reek; *informal* smell to high heaven.
▶ noun BAD SMELL, foul smell, stench, reek, malodour.

stint verb SKIMP ON, limit, restrict, hold back on, be sparing with, be economical with, be frugal with, be mean with, be parsimonious with, be niggardly with.

stipulate verb SPECIFY, set down, lay down, state clearly, demand, require, insist upon, make a condition of, make a point of.

stipulation noun SPECIFICATION, demand, requirement, condition, precondition, provision, proviso, prerequisite.

stir verb ❶ MIX, blend, beat, whip. ❷ MOVE, disturb, agitate, rustle. ❸ refuse to stir: MOVE, move an inch, budge, get up, leave, depart. ❹ GET UP, get out of bed, rise, rouse oneself, bestir oneself, move about, be up and about, be active; *informal* shake a leg, look lively. ❺ stir his imagination: STIMULATE, excite, rouse, awaken, waken, kindle, quicken, inspire. ❻ stir them to action: ROUSE, incite, provoke, inflame, goad, spur, egg on, urge, encourage, motivate, drive, impel.
▶ noun EXCITEMENT, commotion, disturbance, fuss, uproar, to-do, flurry, ferment, brouhaha.

stirring adjective EXCITING, dramatic, thrilling, gripping, riveting, spirited, stimulating, moving, lively, animated, heady, passionate, impassioned.
– OPPOSITES dull, unexciting.

stitch verb SEW, sew up, repair, mend, darn.
■ **stich up** BETRAY, cheat, trick, deceive, hoodwink, defraud, swindle; *poetic/literary* cozen.

stock noun ❶ STORE, supply, range, selection, assortment, variety, collection, quantity. ❷ SUPPLIES, goods, merchandise, wares, articles for sale, commodities. ❸ STORE, supply, stockpile, reserve, reservoir, accumulation, pile, heap, load, hoard, cache. ❹ FARM ANIMALS, livestock, cattle, beasts, herds, sheep, flocks. ❺ SHARES, investment, holding, money. ❻ DESCENT, line of descent, lineage, ancestry, extraction, family, parentage, relatives, pedigree, genealogy, strain, breed, background.
▶ adjective ❶ stock sizes: STANDARD, regular, average, readily available. ❷ stock responses: USUAL, routine, run-of-the-mill, commonplace, conventional, traditional, stereotyped, clichéd, hackneyed, overused, worn out, banal, trite.
– OPPOSITES unusual, original.
▶ verb ❶ SELL, trade in, deal in, market, handle, supply, keep. ❷ EQUIP, fit, outfit, kit out, furnish, accoutre, supply, provide.

stockpile verb COLLECT, gather, accumulate, amass, store, lay in, put away, put down, deposit;

informal squirrel away, salt away, stash.

stocky adjective HEAVY-SET, thickset, dumpy, stubby, stumpy, squat, chunky, solid, sturdy, mesomorphic.
– OPPOSITES slender.

stodgy adjective ❶ **stodgy food:** HEAVY, solid, substantial, filling, starchy, leaden, indigestible. ❷ **stodgy prose:** DULL, uninteresting, boring, tedious, dry, wearisome, heavy-going, unimaginative, uninspired, monotonous, laboured, wooden, turgid.
– OPPOSITES light, interesting.

stoical adjective IMPASSIVE, dispassionate, unimpassioned, unemotional, self-controlled, self-disciplined, forbearing, patient, long-suffering, resigned, philosophical, fatalistic, imperturbable, calm, cool, unexcitable, unflappable, phlegmatic.
– OPPOSITES excitable.

stolid adjective IMPASSIVE, unemotional, apathetic, uninterested, unimaginative, indifferent, dull, stupid, bovine, lumpish, wooden, doltish, thick, dense.
– OPPOSITES lively, imaginative.

stomach noun ABDOMEN, belly, paunch, pot belly; *informal* tummy, gut, pot, breadbasket.
▶ **verb** STAND, put up with, bear, take, tolerate, abide, endure, swallow, submit to; *archaic* suffer.

stone noun ❶ PEBBLE, rock, boulder. ❷ PRECIOUS STONE, jewel, gem, brilliant; *informal* rock. ❸ TOMBSTONE, gravestone, headstone, memorial stone, monument. ❹ KERNEL, pit, nut, seed, pip.

stony adjective ❶ **stony ground:** ROCKY, pebbly, gravelly, shingly, gritty, rough, hard. ❷ **a stony stare:** COLD, chilly, frosty, icy, frigid, hard, stern, severe, rigid, fixed, expressionless, blank, poker-faced, deadpan. ❸ **a stony attitude:** UNFEELING, uncaring, unsympathetic, insensitive, callous, heartless, unmoved, unemotional, dispassionate, unresponsive, stern, severe, harsh, hard, cruel, cold-hearted, merciless, pitiless.
– OPPOSITES sympathetic.

stooge noun ❶ UNDERLING, subordinate, assistant, deputy; *informal* sidekick; *Brit. informal* dogsbody. ❷ BUTT, foil.

stoop verb ❶ BEND DOWN, lean over, lean down, crouch down, duck, bow. ❷ CONDESCEND, deign, lower oneself, humble oneself, demean oneself. ❸ SINK TO, descend to, lower oneself to, demean oneself to, resort to.

stop verb ❶ **stop the fight:** BRING TO A STOP, halt, bring to a halt, end, bring to an end, put an end to, finish, bring to a close, terminate, bring to a standstill, wind up, discontinue, cut short, interrupt, nip in the bud. ❷ **stop laughing:** DISCONTINUE, cease from, refrain from, desist from, leave off, break off, forbear from, abandon; *informal* quit, knock off, pack in. ❸ **work stopped:** COME TO A STOP, come to a halt, end, come to an end, finish, come to a close, be over, cease, conclude, terminate, come to a standstill, pause. ❹ **stop him escaping:** PREVENT, hinder, obstruct, impede, block, check. ❺ **stop the leak:** PLUG, seal, block, bung, staunch, stem.
– OPPOSITES begin, start.

▶ noun ❶ HALT, end, finish, close, cessation, conclusion, termination, standstill, stoppage, discontinuation, discontinuance. ❷ STOPPING PLACE, station, halt, stage, terminus, terminal, depot. ❸ BREAK, stop-off, stopover, stay, sojourn, overnight, rest.

stopgap noun TEMPORARY SUBSTITUTE, substitution, fill-in, makeshift, improvisation, expedient, last resort.

store noun ❶ SUPPLY, stock, stockpile, reserve, accumulation, pile, heap, cache, deposit, reservoir. ❷ STOREROOM, storehouse, warehouse, repository, depository. ❸ SHOP, department store, supermarket, retail outlet, emporium.
▶ verb STOCK UP WITH, get in supplies of, stockpile, collect, gather, accumulate, amass, lay in, put away, put down, deposit, hoard; *informal* squirrel away, salt away, stash.

storm noun ❶ GALE, hurricane, cyclone, tempest, squall, cloudburst, downpour, torrent. ❷ **a storm of protest:** OUTCRY, outburst, commotion, furore, brouhaha, clamour, tumult, row; *informal* to-do, rumpus, dust-up.
▶ verb ATTACK, charge, rush, make a raid/foray/sortie on, take by storm.

stormy adjective BLUSTERY, blustering, windy, gusty, squally, rainy, wild, tempestuous, turbulent.
– OPPOSITES calm.

story noun ❶ TALE, fairy tale, fable, myth, legend, anecdote, novel, novella, romance, narrative, chronicle; *informal* yarn. ❷ NEWS ITEM, news report, article, feature, scoop.

stout adjective ❶ FAT, fattish, plump, portly, tubby, obese, corpulent, rotund, big, heavy, thickset, overweight, bulky, burly, brawny, fleshy. ❷ **a stout stick:** STRONG, heavy, solid, substantial, sturdy. ❸ **a stout defender:** STOUT-HEARTED, brave, courageous, valiant, valorous, gallant, fearless, unafraid, intrepid, bold, plucky, heroic, lion-hearted, daring, tough, doughty; *informal* gutsy, spunky. ❹ **stout resistance:** FIRM, determined, resolute, staunch, steadfast, unyielding, unbending, unfaltering, unswerving, unwavering.
– OPPOSITES cowardly.

stow verb PLACE, deposit, put, put away, pack, store, load, bundle, stuff.
– OPPOSITES unload.

straggle verb ❶ WANDER, ramble, stray, roam, meander, rove, range, spread out. ❷ TRAIL BEHIND, fall behind, lag, string out, linger, loiter. ❸ GROW UNTIDILY, be messy, be dishevelled, be unkempt.

straight adjective ❶ DIRECT, undeviating, unswerving, straight as an arrow. ❷ **three straight wins:** SUCCESSIVE, consecutive, in a row, running, uninterrupted, solid, non-stop. ❸ IN ORDER, orderly, neat, tidy, spruce, in place, organized, arranged, sorted out. ❹ **a straight answer:** DIRECT, honest, faithful, sincere, frank, candid, forthright, straightforward, plain-speaking, matter-of-fact, outspoken, straight from the shoulder, unequivocal, unambiguous, unqualified, unmodified.
– OPPOSITES crooked, evasive.

straighten verb MAKE STRAIGHT, adjust, arrange, put in order, make tidy, tidy up, neaten, put to rights.

■ **straighten out** PUT IN ORDER, put right, sort out, clear up, settle, resolve, regulate, rectify, disentangle, unsnarl.

straightforward adjective ❶ STRAIGHT, direct, honest, frank, candid, forthright, plain-speaking, unambiguous, straight from the shoulder. ❷ UNCOMPLICATED, easy, simple, elementary, effortless, undemanding, routine; *informal* easy as falling off a log, easy as pie.
– OPPOSITES complicated.

strain verb ❶ DRAW TIGHT, tighten, make taut, tauten, stretch, extend, elongate, distend. ❷ strain one's eyes: TAX, overtax, exert to the limit, overwork, push to the limit, fatigue, tire. ❸ strain to win: MAKE EVERY EFFORT, strive one's utmost, push/drive oneself to the limit, struggle, labour; *informal* pull out all the stops, go all out, give it one's all. ❹ strain the mixture: SIEVE, silt, screen, riddle, separate.
▶ noun ❶ TIGHTNESS, tautness, tension, distension. ❷ STRESS, pressure, tension, overwork, exhaustion, anxiety.

strained adjective ❶ a strained smile: FORCED, artificial, unnatural, false, constrained, laboured, wooden, stiff, self-conscious. ❷ a strained silence: AWKWARD, embarrassed, uneasy, uncomfortable, tense, unrelaxed. ❸ strained relations: UNDER STRAIN, tense, troubled, uneasy, hostile.
– OPPOSITES natural, relaxed.

strainer noun SIEVE, colander, filter, screen, riddle.

strand noun ❶ THREAD, fibre, filament, length. ❷ ELEMENT, component, theme.

stranded adjective ❶ LEFT HELPLESS, left penniless, in dire straits, in difficulties, left in the lurch, left high and dry, abandoned, forsaken. ❷ stranded ships: GROUNDED, beached, shipwrecked, wrecked, marooned.

strange adjective ❶ PECULIAR, odd, bizarre, unusual, atypical, abnormal, surprising, curious, weird, funny, unfamiliar. ❷ a strange land: UNKNOWN, unfamiliar. ❸ a strange phenomenon: INEXPLICABLE, anomalous, unexpected, extraordinary.
– OPPOSITES ordinary, familiar.

stranger noun NEW PERSON, new arrival, newcomer, incomer, foreigner.

■ **a stranger to** UNFAMILIAR WITH, unacquainted with, unaccustomed to, new to, fresh to, unused to, inexperienced in, unpractised in, unversed in, unconversant with.

strangle verb ❶ THROTTLE, choke, strangulate, garrotte. ❷ SUPPRESS, inhibit, repress, check, restrain, hold back, curb, stifle, gag.

strap noun BAND, belt, thong, cord, tie.
▶ verb ❶ FASTEN, secure, tie, bind, lash, truss, pinion. ❷ BIND, bandage. ❸ FLOG, lash, whip, scourge, beat; *informal* belt.

stratagem noun TRICK, ruse, plot, plan, scheme, manoeuvre, tactic, artifice, machination, wile, subterfuge, dodge, deception.

strategic adjective ❶ CALCULATED, planned, plotted, tactical, diplomatic, politic, cunning, wily. ❷ CRUCIAL, key, vital, critical, essential, important.

strategy noun POLICY, approach, programme, scheme, plan of action, master plan, schedule, blueprint, game plan.

stratum noun ❶ LAYER, tier, seam, vein, lode. ❷ CLASS, level, grade, status, station, gradation.

stray verb ❶ WANDER, roam, rove, go astray, ramble, meander, drift. ❷ DIGRESS, wander, deviate, get off the subject, get sidetracked, go off at a tangent, lose the thread.
▶ adjective ❶ STRAYED, gone astray, lost, homeless, wandering, vagrant, abandoned, unclaimed. ❷ a stray bullet: ODD, random, isolated, scattered, occasional, incidental, accidental, chance, freak.

streak noun ❶ LINE, band, strip, dash, bar, score, striation, vein, slash, smear. ❷ STRAIN, vein, element, trace, touch, dash. ❸ SMEAR, smudge, mark. ❹ a winning streak: SPELL, period, course, stretch, series.
▶ verb ❶ BAND, stripe, mark, slash, striate, fleck, daub, smear. ❷ SMEAR, smudge, mark. ❸ streaking past: RACE, rush, speed, dash, sprint, hurtle, scurry, fly, flee, flash, whistle, zoom, zip; *informal* tear, whizz, go hell for leather.

stream noun ❶ RIVER, brook, rivulet, rill, freshet; *N. English* beck; *Scottish & N. English* burn; *N. Amer. & Austral./NZ* creek. ❷ a stream of blood: FLOW, rush, gush, surge, jet, outpouring, current, cascade.
▶ verb ❶ FLOW, run, pour, course, spill, gush, surge, flood, cascade, well. ❷ EMIT, issue, shed, spill. ❸ streaming in the breeze: FLOW, float, swing, flap, flutter. ❹ they streamed out: SURGE, pour, crowd.

streamer noun FLAG, pennant, banner, standard, ensign.

streamlined adjective ❶ SMOOTH, sleek, elegant. ❷ EFFICIENT, smooth-running, well run, modernized, rationalized, slick.

street noun ROAD, thoroughfare, terrace, avenue, drive, row, crescent.

strength noun ❶ POWER, might, force, brawn, muscle, muscularity, sturdiness, robustness, vigour, toughness, stamina. ❷ FORTITUDE, courage, bravery, pluck, firmness, stamina, backbone; *informal* grit, guts. ❸ its main strength: ADVANTAGE, asset, strong point, forte.
– OPPOSITES weakness.

strengthen verb ❶ MAKE STRONG, make stronger, give strength to, nourish, build up. ❷ GROW STRONG, grow stronger, gain strength, intensify, heighten. ❸ REINFORCE, support, back up, bolster, authenticate, confirm, substantiate, corroborate.
– OPPOSITES weaken.

strenuous adjective ❶ a strenuous task: ARDUOUS, laborious, taxing, demanding, difficult, hard, tough, uphill, heavy, weighty, burdensome, exhausting, tiring, fatiguing. ❷ strenuous efforts: ENERGETIC, active, vigorous, forceful, strong, spirited, bold, determined, resolute, tenacious, earnest, keen, zealous.
– OPPOSITES easy, half-hearted.

stress noun ❶ STRAIN, pressure, tension, worry, anxiety. ❷ EMPHASIS, priority, importance, weight, significance, value, worth, merit. ❸ EMPHASIS, accent, accentuation.

▶ **verb** ❶ LAY STRESS ON, emphasize, place emphasis on, give emphasis to, accentuate, underline, underscore, point up, highlight, spotlight, press home, dwell on, harp on, belabour. ❷ LAY STRESS ON, emphasize, place the accent on, accentuate. ❸ SUBJECT TO STRESS/STRAIN/TENSION, tax, overtax, pressurize, overwork, overstretch, overburden, push to the limit, push too far.
– OPPOSITES play down.

stretch **verb** ❶ BE STRETCHY, be elastic, be tensile. ❷ EXTEND, elongate, lengthen, expand, draw out, pull out, get larger, get bigger, enlarge, pull out of shape. ❸ EXTEND, spread, unfold, cover, range. ❹ **the job will stretch her:** BE A CHALLENGE TO, challenge, extend, tax, push to the limit. ❺ **stretch the truth:** STRAIN, overstrain, exaggerate, overdraw, push too far.
– OPPOSITES contract.
▶ **noun** ❶ EXPANSE, area, tract, extent, spread, sweep. ❷ PERIOD, time, spell, term, space, run, stint.

strict **adjective** ❶ **a strict interpretation:** PRECISE, exact, close, faithful, true, accurate, scrupulous, meticulous, conscientious, punctilious. ❷ **a strict upbringing:** STRINGENT, rigorous, severe, harsh, hard, stern, authoritarian, rigid, narrow, austere, illiberal, inflexible, unyielding, uncompromising. ❸ **strict confidence:** ABSOLUTE, utter, complete, total, perfect.
– OPPOSITES flexible, easy-going.

stricture **noun** ❶ CRITICISM, censure, blame, condemnation; *informal* flak. ❷ RESTRICTION, limitation, control, constraint, restraint, curb, check.
– OPPOSITES praise, freedom.

stride **verb** STEP, pace, walk, stalk.

strident **adjective** HARSH, raucous, rough, grating, discordant, rasping, jarring, shrill, loud, screeching, unmelodious, unmusical.
– OPPOSITES soft.

strife **noun** CONFLICT, friction, discord, disagreement, dissension, dispute, argument, quarrelling, wrangling, bickering, controversy, contention, ill feeling, hostility, animosity.
– OPPOSITES harmony.

strike **verb** ❶ BANG, beat, hit, pound, batter. ❷ HIT, slap, smack, beat, batter, thrash, thump, thwack, punch, cuff, box, rap, buffet, smite, cane, lash, whip; *informal* wallop, belt, clout, whack, bash, clobber, bop, biff, sock, plug. ❸ RUN INTO, knock into, bang into, bump into, smash into, collide with, be in collision with, dash against. ❹ ATTACK, charge, make an assault on, assault, storm, set upon, fall upon. ❺ **strike a balance:** REACH, achieve, arrive at, find, attain, effect. ❻ **strike a pose:** ASSUME, adopt, take on, affect, feign. ❼ GO ON STRIKE, take industrial action, walk out; *Brit. informal* down tools.
▶ **noun** ❶ HIT, slap, smack, thump, thwack, punch, cuff, box, knock; *informal* wallop, clout, whack, bop, buffet, plug. ❷ INDUSTRIAL ACTION, walkout.
■ **strike out** DELETE, cross out, erase, rub out, obliterate.

striking **adjective** ❶ NOTICEABLE, obvious, conspicuous, evident, visible, distinct, prominent, clear-cut, unmistakable,

remarkable, extraordinary, incredible, amazing. ❷ IMPRESSIVE, imposing, grand, splendid, magnificent, superb, marvellous, wonderful, dazzling; *Brit. informal* smashing.
– OPPOSITES unremarkable.

string noun ❶ TWINE, cord, yarn, rope, cable, line. ❷ QUEUE, line, row, procession, file, column, stream, succession, sequence.
▶ verb ❶ HANG, suspend, sling. ❷ STRETCH, sling, run, fasten, tie, secure together.
■ **string along** MAKE USE OF, take advantage of, mislead, deceive, make a fool of, fool, lead up the garden path. **string out** DRAW OUT, stretch, protract, spin out.

stringent adjective STRICT, firm, rigid, rigorous, severe, harsh, tough, tight, exacting, demanding, inflexible, hard and fast, uncompromising.
– OPPOSITES easy.

stringy adjective ❶ LANK, straggly, straggling. ❷ TOUGH, fibrous, gristly, leathery.

strip[1] verb ❶ STRIP NAKED, undress, take one's clothes off, remove one's clothes, disrobe. ❷ PEEL, pare, skin, excoriate. ❸ **stripped of the medal**: TAKE AWAY, dispossess of, deprive of, confiscate. ❹ **strip a machine**: DISMANTLE, take to pieces, take to bits, take apart.

strip[2] noun PIECE, bit, band, belt, ribbon, stripe, bar, swathe, slip, fillet.

stripe noun STRIP, band, belt, bar.

striped adjective STRIPY, banded, barred, striated, variegated.

stripling noun YOUTH, adolescent, youngster, boy, lad, teenager, child, juvenile, minor, young man; *informal* kid, nipper, young 'un.

strive verb TRY, attempt, endeavour, make an effort, make every effort, exert oneself, do one's best, do all one can, do one's utmost, labour, toil, strain, struggle; *informal* go all out, give it one's best shot.

stroke noun ❶ BLOW, hit, slap, smack, thump, thwack, punch, cuff, box, knock, rap, buffet, smite. ❷ MOVEMENT, action, motion. ❸ THROMBOSIS, embolism, cerebral vascular accident, CVA, seizure, shock, apoplexy.
▶ verb CARESS, fondle, pat, touch, rub, massage, soothe.

stroll verb SAUNTER, amble, wander, meander, ramble, dawdle, promenade, go for a walk, take a walk, stretch one's legs, take the air; *informal* mosey along.

strong adjective ❶ POWERFUL, mighty, brawny, muscular, well built, strapping, sturdy, burly, robust, vigorous, tough, hardy, lusty, Herculean, strong as an ox/horse/lion. ❷ COURAGEOUS, brave, plucky, firm, resolute, strong-minded; *informal* gutsy. ❸ DETERMINED, forceful, high-powered, assertive, tough, formidable, aggressive, redoubtable. ❹ **strong doors**: SOLID, well built, heavy, tough, secure, well fortified, well defended, well protected, impregnable, impenetrable. ❺ **strong material**: HEAVY-DUTY, solid, sturdy, durable, hard-wearing, long-lasting, enduring. ❻ **a strong interest**: KEEN, eager, deep, acute, dedicated, passionate, fervent, zealous. ❼ **strong feelings**: FORCEFUL, intense, vehement, passionate, fervent. ❽ **a strong supporter**: KEEN, eager,

enthusiastic, dedicated, staunch, loyal, steadfast, passionate, fierce, fervent. **9** **a strong argument:** POWERFUL, cogent, potent, weighty, compelling, convincing, plausible, effective, efficacious, sound, valid, well founded. **10** **a strong resemblance:** MARKED, pronounced, distinct, definite, clear-cut, obvious, evident, unmistakable, notable, remarkable. **11** **strong colours:** DEEP, intense, vivid, graphic. **12** **strong light:** BRIGHT, brilliant, intense, radiant, gleaming, dazzling, glaring. **13** **strong coffee:** CONCENTRATED, undiluted, highly flavoured.
– OPPOSITES weak.

structure noun **1** BUILDING, edifice, construction, erection, pile, complex. **2** CONSTRUCTION, form, configuration, conformation, shape, constitution, composition, make-up, organization, system, arrangement, design, frame, framework.
► verb CONSTRUCT, build, put together, assemble, shape, design, organize, arrange, order.

struggle verb **1** STRIVE, try hard, endeavour, make every effort, exert oneself, do one's best, do all one can, do one's utmost, battle, labour, toil, strain; *informal* go all out. **2** FIGHT, grapple, wrestle, scuffle, brawl; *informal* scrap.
► noun **1** STRIVING, battle, endeavour, effort, exertion, labour, toiling, pains. **2** FIGHT, scuffle, brawl, tussle; *informal* scrap, set-to, dust-up.

strut verb SWAGGER, prance, parade, flounce; *N. Amer.* sashay.

stubborn adjective OBSTINATE, headstrong, wilful, strong-willed, pig-headed, mulish, dogged, persistent, adamant, inflexible, uncompromising, unbending, unyielding, unmalleable, obdurate, intractable, refractory, recalcitrant, contumacious.
– OPPOSITES malleable.

stuck adjective **1** IMMOVABLE, immobile, fast, fixed, rooted. **2** BAFFLED, beaten, stumped, at a loss, perplexed, nonplussed, at one's wits' ends; *informal* up against a brick wall.

stuck-up adjective CONCEITED, proud, arrogant, swollen-headed, haughty, condescending, disdainful, patronizing, snobbish; *informal* high and mighty, snooty, uppity, uppish, big-headed, toffee-nosed, hoity-toity.
– OPPOSITES unassuming.

student noun UNDERGRADUATE, pupil, schoolboy, schoolgirl, trainee, apprentice, probationer.

studied adjective DELIBERATE, wilful, conscious, calculated, purposeful, contrived, affected, forced, feigned, artificial.
– OPPOSITES natural.

studious adjective SCHOLARLY, academic, intellectual, bookish, book-loving, serious, earnest.

study verb **1** **study hard:** APPLY ONESELF, revise, burn the midnight oil; *informal* cram, mug up; *Brit. informal* swot. **2** **study history:** LEARN, read up on, read, work at; *informal* mug up on. **3** **study its effects:** INVESTIGATE, inquire into, research, look into, examine, analyse, review, survey, conduct a survey of, scrutinize.

stuff noun **1** MATERIAL, fabric, matter, substance. **2** THINGS, objects, articles, items, luggage, baggage, belongings, possessions, goods, paraphernalia. ❸ **know one's stuff**: FACTS, information, data, subject.

▶ **verb** ❶ FILL, pack, pad. ❷ PACK, load, cram, squeeze, crowd, stow, press, force, compress, jam, wedge.

stuffy **adjective** ❶ AIRLESS, close, muggy, stifling, suffocating, musty, stale; *Brit. informal* fuggy. ❷ DULL, boring, dreary, staid, sedate, stiff, formal, pompous, starchy, prim, priggish, strait-laced, conventional, conservative, stodgy; *informal* fuddy-duddy, square.

– OPPOSITES airy, exciting.

stumble **verb** ❶ TRIP, slip, blunder, lumber, lurch, stagger, reel. ❷ STAMMER, stutter, hesitate, falter; *informal* fluff one's lines.

■ **stumble upon** CHANCE UPON, happen upon, light upon, hit upon, come across, find, discover, encounter.

stump **noun** END, stub, remnant, remains.

▶ **verb** BAFFLE, be too much for, put at a loss, nonplus, mystify, foil, perplex, puzzle, confound, bewilder; *informal* flummox.

stun **verb** ❶ DAZE, stupefy, knock senseless, knock out, lay out, knock stupid. ❷ SHOCK, astound, dumbfound, stupefy, overwhelm, overcome, overpower, devastate, stagger, amaze, astonish, bewilder, confuse; *informal* flabbergast; *Brit. informal* knock for six.

stunning **adjective** SENSATIONAL, ravishing, dazzling, wonderful, marvellous, magnificent, glorious, exquisite, impressive, splendid, beautiful, lovely, gorgeous.

– OPPOSITES ordinary.

stupendous **adjective** AMAZING, fantastic, astounding, astonishing, extraordinary, remarkable, wonderful, prodigious, phenomenal, staggering, breathtaking; *informal* mind-boggling, mind-blowing.

– OPPOSITES ordinary.

stupid **adjective** ❶ **a stupid person**: UNINTELLIGENT, foolish, dense, brainless, mindless, obtuse, dull-witted, dull, slow-witted, slow, dunce-like, doltish, simple-minded, half-witted, gullible, naive, moronic, imbecilic, cretinous; *informal* thick, dim, dumb, dopey; *Brit. informal* dozy. ❷ **a stupid error**: FOOLISH, silly, unintelligent, idiotic, brainless, mindless, crackbrained, nonsensical, senseless, irresponsible, unthinking, ill-advised, ill-considered, inept, unwise, injudicious, indiscreet, shortsighted, inane, absurd, ludicrous, ridiculous, laughable, fatuous, asinine, pointless, meaningless, futile, fruitless, mad, insane, lunatic; *informal* cock-eyed. ❸ **knocked stupid**: DAZED, stupefied, unconscious.

– OPPOSITES intelligent, sensible.

stupidity **noun** ❶ LACK OF INTELLIGENCE, foolishness, denseness, brainlessness, mindlessness, dull-wittedness, dullness, slow-wittedness, slowness, doltishness; *informal* thickness, dimness, dumbness, dopiness, doziness. ❷ FOOLISHNESS, folly, silliness, idiocy, brainlessness, senselessness, irresponsibility, injudiciousness, ineptitude, inaneness, inanity, absurdity, ludicrousness, ridiculousness, fatuousness, fatuity, asininity, pointlessness, meaninglessness, futility, fruitlessness, madness, insanity, lunacy.

sturdy adjective ❶ WELL BUILT, well made, muscular, athletic, strong, strapping, brawny, powerfully built, powerful, solid, substantial, robust, vigorous, tough, hardy, stalwart, mighty, lusty. ❷ *sturdy resistance*: STRONG, vigorous, stalwart, firm, determined, resolute, tenacious, staunch, steadfast, unyielding, unwavering, uncompromising. ❸ *See* STRONG (4, 5).
– OPPOSITES weak.

stutter verb STAMMER, stumble, hesitate, falter, splutter.

style noun ❶ KIND, type, variety, sort, design, pattern, genre. ❷ TECHNIQUE, method, methodology, approach, manner, way, mode, system. ❸ STYLISHNESS, smartness, elegance, polish, suavity, urbanity, chic, flair, dash, panache, elan; *informal* pizzazz, ritziness. ❹ FASHION, trend, vogue, mode.

stylish adjective FASHIONABLE, smart, elegant, chic, modish, à la mode, voguish, modern, up to date; *informal* trendy, dressy, natty, classy, nifty, ritzy, snazzy, snappy, with it.
– OPPOSITES unfashionable.

subdue verb ❶ CONQUER, defeat, vanquish, get the better of, overpower, overcome, overwhelm, subjugate, master, gain the upper hand at, triumph over, crush, quash, quell, tame, humble, bring someone to their knees, hold in check. ❷ CONTROL, curb, restrain, check, hold back, inhibit, rein in, repress, suppress, stifle.
– OPPOSITES arouse.

subdued adjective ❶ DIM, muted, toned down, softened, soft, lowered, shaded, low-key, subtle, unobtrusive. ❷ LOW-SPIRITED, downcast, dejected, depressed, restrained, repressed, inactive, lifeless, dull, passive, unexcited, unresponsive; *informal* down in the mouth.
– OPPOSITES bright, lively.

subject noun ❶ TOPIC, theme, question, substance, gist, text, thesis. ❷ BRANCH OF KNOWLEDGE, course of study, course, discipline. ❸ CITIZEN, national.
▶ verb SUBMIT, put through, expose, lay open, treat.
■ **subject to** ❶ CONDITIONAL UPON, contingent upon, dependent on. ❷ SUSCEPTIBLE TO, liable to, prone to, in danger of, vulnerable to.

subjective adjective PERSONAL, personalized, individual, biased, prejudiced, bigoted.
– OPPOSITES objective.

subjugate verb GAIN MASTERY OVER, gain control of, bring someone to their knees, bring to heel, bring under the yoke, conquer, vanquish, defeat, crush, quell, quash, overpower, overcome, subdue, tame, break, humble, tyrannize, oppress, enslave.
– OPPOSITES liberate.

sublime adjective NOBLE, exalted, lofty, awe-inspiring, majestic, imposing, glorious, supreme, grand, great, superb, perfect, ideal, wonderful, marvellous.

submerge verb ❶ GO UNDER WATER, dive, sink, plummet. ❷ IMMERSE, dip, plunge, duck dunk. ❸ FLOOD, inundate, deluge, engulf, swamp, overflow.

submission noun ❶ SURRENDER,

yielding, capitulation, agreement, acceptance, consent, accession, compliance. ❷ PRESENTATION, tender, proposal, suggestion. ❸ ARGUMENT, assertion, contention, statement, claim; *formal* averment.
– OPPOSITES defiance.

submissive adjective YIELDING, compliant, malleable, acquiescent, accommodating, tractable, manageable, unassertive, passive, obedient, biddable, dutiful, docile, meek, patient, resigned, subdued, humble, self-effacing, deferential, obsequious, servile, self-abasing; *informal* bootlicking.
– OPPOSITES intractable.

submit verb ❶ GIVE IN, yield, give way, capitulate, agree, accept, consent, accede, acquiesce, comply, conform. ❷ **submit a plan:** PUT FORWARD, present, proffer, tender, advance, propose, suggest, table, introduce, move.
– OPPOSITES resist, withdraw.

subordinate adjective LOWER-RANKING, junior, lower, lesser, inferior, minor, secondary, subsidiary, ancillary, auxiliary.
– OPPOSITES senior.
▶ **noun** JUNIOR, assistant, second, deputy, aide, subaltern, underling, inferior, second fiddle.
– OPPOSITES superior.

subscribe
■ **subscribe to** ❶ PAY A SUBSCRIPTION TO, buy regularly, take regularly. ❷ MAKE A DONATION TO, donate to, give to, give money to, make a contribution to, contribute towards; *informal* chip into. ❸ AGREE WITH, accede to, consent to, accept, believe in, endorse, back, support.

subscription noun ❶ FEE, membership fee, dues, annual payment. ❷ DONATION, contribution, offering.

subsequent adjective FOLLOWING, ensuing, succeeding, later, future, next, consequent.
– OPPOSITES previous.

subservient adjective SERVILE, submissive, deferential, obsequious, sycophantic, grovelling, fawning, ingratiating, toadying, unctuous, truckling; *informal* bootlicking.
– OPPOSITES domineering.

subside verb ❶ ABATE, let up, moderate, quieten down, calm, slacken, die out, peter out, taper off, recede, lessen, diminish, dwindle. ❷ GO DOWN, get lower, sink, settle, fall back, recede.
– OPPOSITES strengthen, rise.

subsidize verb PAY A SUBSIDY TO, contribute to, give money to, back, support, invest in, sponsor, finance, fund, underwrite, foot the bill for; *informal* pick up the tab for.

subsidy noun GRANT, contribution, backing, support, investment, sponsorship, finance, funding, subvention.

subsist
■ **subsist on** LIVE ON, exist on, eke out an existence on, survive on.

substance noun ❶ MATTER, material, stuff, medium, mass, fabric. ❷ SOLIDITY, body, corporeality, reality, actuality, materiality, concreteness, tangibility. ❸ MEANINGFULNESS, significance, weight, power, soundness, validity. ❹ **a man of substance:** WEALTH, affluence, prosperity, money, capital, means, resources, assets.

substantial adjective ❶ REAL,

material, weighty, sizeable, considerable, meaningful, significant, important, notable, major, marked, valuable, useful, worthwhile. ❷ SOLID, sturdy, stout, strong, well built, durable. ❸ substantial agreement: ESSENTIAL, basic, fundamental.
– OPPOSITES insubstantial.

substitute noun REPLACEMENT, deputy, relief, proxy, reserve, surrogate, fill-in, stand-in, standby, locum, stopgap.
▶ verb ❶ USE AS A REPLACEMENT, replace with, use instead of, exchange, switch, swap. ❷ TAKE THE PLACE OF, replace, deputize for, act as deputy for, relieve, fill in for, act as stand-in for, cover for, take over from.

subterfuge noun TRICK, ruse, wile, ploy, stratagem, artifice, dodge, manoeuvre, pretext, expedient, intrigue, scheme, deception.

subtle adjective ❶ a subtle flavour: DELICATE, faint, understated, low-key, muted, toned down. ❷ a subtle distinction: FINE, fine-drawn, nice, slight, minute, tenuous, indistinct, indefinite.
– OPPOSITES crude.

subtract verb TAKE AWAY, take from, deduct, remove, debit; *informal* knock off.
– OPPOSITES add.

suburb noun OUTLYING DISTRICT, residential area, dormitory area, purlieus.

suburban adjective PROVINCIAL, unsophisticated, parochial, insular.
– OPPOSITES cosmopolitan.

subversive adjective UNDERMINING, discrediting, destructive, disruptive, trouble-making, inflammatory, seditious, revolutionary, insurrectionary, treasonous, treacherous.

subvert verb OVERTHROW, overturn, wreak havoc on, sabotage, ruin, destroy, demolish, wreck, upset, disrupt, undermine, weaken.

subway noun UNDERGROUND RAILWAY, underground, metro, tube.

succeed verb ❶ TRIUMPH, achieve success, be successful, do well, flourish, thrive; *informal* make it, make the grade, make a name for oneself. ❷ BE SUCCESSFUL, turn out well, work, work out, come off; *informal* pan out, do the trick. ❸ COME AFTER, follow, replace, take the place of, supplant, supersede.
– OPPOSITES fail, precede.

success noun ❶ ACCOMPLISHMENT, achievement, attainment, fulfilment, victory, triumph. ❷ PROSPERITY, affluence, wealth, fame, eminence. ❸ BEST-SELLER, winner, triumph; *informal* hit, smash hit, sensation.
– OPPOSITES failure.

successful adjective ❶ VICTORIOUS, triumphant. ❷ successful people: PROSPEROUS, affluent, wealthy, well-to-do, famous, eminent, at the top, top. ❸ a successful business: FLOURISHING, thriving, booming, profitable, profit-making, moneymaking, lucrative.
– OPPOSITES unsuccessful.

succession noun SEQUENCE, series, progression, course, cycle, chain, train, run, continuation.

successor noun HEIR, heir apparent, next-in-line, replacement, supplanter.
– OPPOSITES predecessor.

succinct adjective SHORT, brief, concise, compact, condensed, crisp, terse, tight, to the point, pithy, summary, short and sweet.
– OPPOSITES lengthy.

succour noun ASSISTANCE, aid, help, comfort, relief, support.

succulent adjective JUICY, moist, luscious, mouth-watering.
– OPPOSITES dry.

succumb verb GIVE IN, give way, yield, submit, surrender, capitulate, be overcome/overwhelmed, fall victim.
– OPPOSITES resist.

suck verb SUCK UP, draw up, absorb, soak up, blot up.
■ **suck up to** TOADY TO, fawn upon, be obsequious/servile/sycophantic to.

sudden adjective ❶ IMMEDIATE, instantaneous, abrupt, unexpected, unforeseen, unanticipated, unlooked for, without warning. ❷ RAPID, swift, speedy, fast, quick, meteoric.
– OPPOSITES gradual.

suddenly adverb ALL OF A SUDDEN, all at once, instantaneously, abruptly, unexpectedly, without warning; *informal* out of the blue.
– OPPOSITES gradually.

sue verb TAKE TO COURT, bring an action against, prefer/bring charges against, charge, prosecute, bring to trial, summons, indict; *informal* have the law on.
■ **sue for** PETITION FOR, appeal for, solicit, request, ask for, beg for, plead for.

suffer verb ❶ BE IN PAIN, feel pain, be racked with pain, hurt, ache. ❷ BE DISTRESSED, be in distress, be upset, be miserable, be wretched, be hurt, hurt. ❸ **suffer loss:** EXPERIENCE, undergo, sustain, encounter, meet with, endure.
■ **suffer from** BE AFFECTED BY, be afflicted by, be troubled with.

suffice verb BE ENOUGH, be sufficient, do, serve, fulfil/meet someone's needs; *informal* hit the spot.

sufficient adjective ENOUGH, adequate, plenty of, ample, plenty.
– OPPOSITES insufficient.

suffocate verb SMOTHER, stifle, asphyxiate.

suffuse verb SPREAD OVER, cover, bathe, permeate, pervade, imbue.

sugary adjective ❶ SUGARED, sweet. ❷ SYRUPY, sentimental, maudlin, mawkish, sloppy, slushy, mushy; *informal* schmaltzy.
– OPPOSITES sour.

suggest verb ❶ PROPOSE, put forward, move, submit, recommend, advocate; *informal* throw out. ❷ INDICATE, lead to believe, give the impression, give the idea, insinuate, hint, imply, intimate.

suggestion noun ❶ PROPOSAL, proposition, plan, motion, submission, recommendation. ❷ HINT, trace, touch, suspicion. ❸ INSINUATION, hint, implication, intimation.

suggestive adjective PROVOCATIVE, titillating, sexual, sexy, indecent, indelicate, improper, off colour, smutty, ribald, risqué, lewd, salacious; *informal* blue.

suit noun ❶ SET OF CLOTHES, outfit, costume, ensemble. ❷ LAWSUIT, court case, action, proceedings, prosecution.
▶ verb ❶ BECOME, look attractive on, go well with, look right on.

❷ BE SUITABLE FOR, be convenient for, be acceptable to, meet someone's requirements, satisfy someone's demands.

suitable adjective ❶ CONVENIENT, acceptable, satisfactory. ❷ SUITED TO, befitting, appropriate to, relevant to, pertinent to, apposite to, in keeping with, in character with, tailor-made for. ❸ a suitable candidate: RIGHT, appropriate, fitting, apt, well qualified, ideal.
– OPPOSITES unsuitable.

sulk verb MOPE, pout, be sullen, be in a bad mood, be put out, be out of sorts, be grumpy; *informal* be in a huff.

sulky adjective MOPING, pouting, moody, sullen, piqued, disgruntled, ill-humoured, out of humour, bad-tempered, grumpy, churlish, glowering.
– OPPOSITES cheerful.

sullen adjective MOROSE, unresponsive, uncommunicative, unsociable, resentful, sulky, sour, glum, gloomy, dismal, cheerless, surly, cross, angry, frowning, glowering, grumpy.
– OPPOSITES cheerful.

sultry adjective ❶ CLOSE, airless, stuffy, stifling, suffocating, oppressive, muggy, humid, sticky, hot, sweltering. ❷ SENSUAL, sexy, voluptuous, seductive, provocative, alluring, tempting, passionate, erotic.

sum noun ❶ SUM TOTAL, grand total, tally, aggregate, answer. ❷ ARITHMETICAL PROBLEM, problem, calculation, reckoning, tally.
■ **sum up** GIVE A SUMMARY OF, summarize, encapsulate, put in a nutshell.

summarize verb GIVE/MAKE A SUMMARY OF, sum up, give a synopsis of, precis, give a precis of, give a résumé of, give an abstract of, abridge, condense, epitomize, outline, sketch, give the main points of, give a rundown of, review.

summary noun SYNOPSIS, precis, abstract, abridgement, digest, epitome, outline, sketch, rundown, review, summing-up.
▶ adjective IMMEDIATE, instant, instantaneous, direct, prompt, rapid, sudden, abrupt, peremptory.

summerhouse noun PAVILION, gazebo, arbour, bower, pergola.

summit noun ❶ TOP, peak, crest, crown, apex, vertex, apogee. ❷ PEAK, height, pinnacle, culmination, climax, crowning point, zenith, acme.
– OPPOSITES base, nadir.

summon verb ❶ SEND FOR, call for, bid, request someone's presence. ❷ ORDER, call, convene, assemble, muster, rally; *formal* convoke.

sumptuous adjective LAVISH, luxurious, de luxe, opulent, magnificent.
– OPPOSITES plain.

sundry adjective SEVERAL, various, varied, miscellaneous, assorted, diverse.

sunken adjective ❶ AT A LOWER LEVEL, below ground level, lowered. ❷ HOLLOW, hollowed, concave, drawn, haggard.

sunless adjective OVERCAST, dark, grey, gloomy, murky, dim, bleak.
– OPPOSITES sunny.

sunlight noun SUN, sunshine, light, daylight, light of day.

sunny adjective ❶ SUNLIT, bright, clear, cloudless, unclouded, without a cloud in the sky.

2 a sunny nature: *see* CHEERFUL.
– OPPOSITES dull.

sunrise noun DAWN, crack of dawn, daybreak, cockcrow; *N. Amer.* sun-up.

sunset noun NIGHTFALL, close of day, twilight, dusk; *N. Amer.* sundown.

sunshine noun *see* SUNLIGHT.

superannuated adjective **1** PENSIONED OFF, retired, elderly. **2** OLD, old-fashioned, antiquated, obsolete, broken-down; *informal* clapped out.

superb adjective SUPERLATIVE, excellent, first-rate, first-class, outstanding, remarkable, dazzling, marvellous, magnificent, wonderful, splendid, exquisite; *informal* fantastic, fabulous; *Brit. informal* brilliant.
– OPPOSITES poor.

supercilious adjective ARROGANT, haughty, conceited, proud, vain, disdainful, scornful, condescending, superior, patronizing, imperious, overbearing, lofty, lordly, snobbish, snobby; *informal* hoity-toity, uppity, snooty, stuck up.

superficial adjective **1** superficial damage: SURFACE, exterior, external, outer, outside, peripheral, slight. **2** a superficial examination: CURSORY, perfunctory, hasty, hurried, casual, sketchy, desultory, slapdash. **3** a superficial person: SHALLOW, empty-headed, trivial, frivolous, silly, lightweight, insignificant.
– OPPOSITES thorough, deep.

superfluous adjective SPARE, surplus, extra, unneeded, unrequired, excess, in excess, unnecessary, needless, inessential, uncalled for, unwarranted, gratuitous.
– OPPOSITES necessary, essential.

superhuman adjective **1** HERCULEAN, phenomenal, prodigious, stupendous, heroic, extraordinary. **2** DIVINE, god-like, holy, supernatural, preternatural, paranormal, other-worldly.
– OPPOSITES mundane.

superintend verb BE IN CHARGE OF, be in control of, preside over, direct, administer, manage, run, look after, supervise, oversee.

superior adjective **1** a superior player: BETTER, greater, more expert, more skilful, more advanced. **2** a superior position: HIGHER, higher-ranking, higher up. **3** superior quality: BETTER, higher-grade, greater, surpassing. **4** HAUGHTY, disdainful, condescending, supercilious, patronizing, lofty, lordly, snobbish, snobby; *informal* high and mighty, hoity-toity, uppity, snooty, stuck up, toffee-nosed.
– OPPOSITES inferior.

superlative adjective BEST, greatest, supreme, consummate, first-rate, first-class, of the first water, of the first order, brilliant, excellent, magnificent, outstanding, unsurpassed, unparalleled, unrivalled, peerless, matchless, transcendent.
– OPPOSITES poor.

supernatural adjective OTHER-WORLDLY, unearthly, spectral, ghostly, phantom, magical, mystic, unreal, paranormal, supernormal, psychic, miraculous, extraordinary, uncanny.

supersede verb **1** TAKE THE

PLACE OF, replace, take over from, displace, succeed, supplant, usurp. ❷ DISCARD, cast aside, throw out, dispose of, abandon, jettison; *informal* chuck out.

supervise verb SUPERINTEND, be in charge of, direct, administer, manage, run, oversee, keep an eye on, watch, observe, inspect, be responsible for, guide.

supervision noun ADMINISTRATION, management, direction, control, charge, superintendence, observation, inspection, guidance.

supervisor noun OVERSEER, superintendent, inspector, controller, manager, director, administrator, chief, guide, adviser; *informal* boss.

supine adjective ❶ FLAT ON ONE'S BACK, prostrate, horizontal. ❷ WEAK, passive, feckless, spineless, idle, inactive, indolent, lazy, slothful, languid, apathetic, indifferent; *informal* laid-back.

supplant verb TAKE THE PLACE OF, take over from, replace, displace, supersede, oust, usurp, overthrow, remove, unseat.

supple adjective ❶ LITHE, loose-limbed, limber. ❷ PLIANT, pliable, flexible, bendable, stretchable, elastic.
– OPPOSITES stiff.

supplement noun ❶ ADDITION, supplementation, additive, extra, add-on. ❷ PULL-OUT, insert, special-feature section, magazine section.
▶ verb ADD TO, augment, increase, top up, complement.

supplementary adjective ❶ SUPPLEMENTAL, additional, extra, add-on, complementary. ❷ ADDED, appended, attached, extra.

suppliant noun SUPPLICANT, petitioner, pleader, applicant, suitor, beggar, appellant.

supplicant noun *see* SUPPLIANT.

supplication noun PLEA, entreaty, begging, petition, appeal, solicitation, request, prayer, invocation; *poetic/literary* beseeching.

supplies noun PROVISIONS, stores, rations, food, provender; *dated* victuals.

supply verb ❶ PROVIDE, give, furnish, contribute, donate, grant, come up with; *informal* fork out, shell out. ❷ SATISFY, meet, fulfil.
▶ noun ❶ SUPPLYING, providing, provision, furnishing. ❷ STOCK, store, reserve, reservoir, stockpile, heap, pile, mass, hoard, cache. *See also* STOCK noun (2).

support verb ❶ BEAR, carry, hold up, prop up, bolster up, brace, keep up, shore up, underpin, buttress. ❷ **support his family**: MAINTAIN, provide for, sustain, take care of, look after. ❸ GIVE MORAL SUPPORT TO, give strength to, comfort, help, sustain, encourage, buoy up, hearten, fortify; *informal* buck up. ❹ **support his argument**: BACK UP, substantiate, give force to, bear out, corroborate, confirm, verify, validate, authenticate, endorse, ratify. ❺ **support the candidate**: BACK, champion, give help to, help, assist, aid, be on someone's side, side with, vote for, stand behind, stand up for, take up the cudgels for; *informal* stick up for. ❻ **support conservation**: ADVOCATE, promote, further, champion, be on someone's side, espouse, be in favour of, recommend, defend.
– OPPOSITES neglect, contradict, oppose.

▶ noun ❶ BASE, foundations, pillar, post, prop, underprop, underpinning, substructure, brace, buttress, abutment, bolster, stay. ❷ KEEP, maintenance, sustenance, food and accommodation, subsistence; *archaic* aliment. ❸ in need of support: MORAL SUPPORT, friendship, strength, encouragement, buoying up, heartening, fortification; *informal* bucking up. ❹ support for charity: BACKING, contribution, donation, money, subsidy, funding, funds, finance, capital. ❺ a support to his mother: HELP, assistance, comfort, tower of strength, prop, backbone, mainstay.

supporter noun ❶ BACKER, contributor, donor, sponsor, patron, friend, well-wisher. ❷ BACKER, helper, adherent, follower, ally, voter, apologist. ❸ BACKER, adherent, advocate, promoter, champion, defender, apologist. ❹ FAN, follower.

supportive adjective HELPFUL, encouraging, caring, sympathetic, understanding, loyal, interested, positive, reassuring.
– OPPOSITES unsympathetic.

suppose verb ❶ ASSUME, take for granted, dare say, take as read, presume, expect, imagine, believe, think, fancy, suspect, guess, surmise, reckon, conjecture, theorize, opine. ❷ TAKE AS A HYPOTHESIS, hypothesize, postulate, posit. ❸ PRESUPPOSE, require, imply.

supposed adjective PRESUMED, assumed, believed, professed, so-called, alleged, putative, reputed.

supposition noun ASSUMPTION, presumption, suspicion, guess, surmise, conjecture, speculation, theory, hypothesis, postulation.

suppress verb ❶ suppress the rebellion: VANQUISH, put an end to, crush, quell, conquer, squash, stamp out, extinguish, put out, crack down on, clamp down on. ❷ suppress his anger: RESTRAIN, keep a rein on, hold back, control, keep under control, check, keep in check, curb, bottle up, choke back. ❸ suppress the truth: KEEP SECRET, conceal, hide, keep hidden, keep silent about, withhold, cover up, smother, stifle, muzzle.
– OPPOSITES incite, reveal.

supremacy noun ASCENDANCY, dominance, superiority, predominance, paramountcy, dominion, sway, authority, mastery, control, power, rule, sovereignty, lordship.

supreme adjective ❶ HIGHEST-RANKING, highest, leading, chief, foremost, principal. ❷ supreme effort: EXTREME, greatest, utmost, uttermost, maximum, extraordinary, remarkable. ❸ supreme sacrifice: FINAL, last, ultimate.
– OPPOSITES subordinate, minimal.

sure adjective ❶ sure that he is honest: CERTAIN, definite, positive, convinced, confident, decided, assured, free from doubt, unhesitating, unwavering, unfaltering. ❷ sure of success: ASSURED OF, certain of, confident of, with no doubts about. ❸ a sure success: ASSURED, certain, guaranteed, inevitable, irrevocable. ❹ a sure remedy: CERTAIN, unfailing, infallible, never-failing, reliable,

dependable, trustworthy, tested, tried and true, foolproof, effective, efficacious; *informal* sure-fire. ❺ *a sure friend*: TRUE, reliable, dependable, trusted, trustworthy, trusty, loyal, faithful, steadfast. ❻ *a sure hand*: FIRM, steady, stable, secure, confident, unhesitating, unfaltering, unwavering.
– OPPOSITES unsure, uncertain.

surface noun ❶ OUTSIDE, exterior, top. ❷ OUTWARD APPEARANCE, superficial appearance, facade.
▶ adjective SUPERFICIAL, external, exterior, outward.
▶ verb ❶ COME TO THE SURFACE, come up, come to the top. ❷ REAPPEAR, appear, come to light, come up, emerge, crop up. ❸ GET UP, get out of bed, rise, wake, awaken.

surfeit noun EXCESS, surplus, oversupply, superabundance, superfluity, glut, too much.
– OPPOSITES dearth, lack.

surge noun GUSH, rush, outpouring, stream, flow, sweep, efflux.
▶ verb ❶ GUSH, rush, stream, flow. ❷ RISE, swell, heave, billow, roll, eddy, swirl.

surly adjective BAD-TEMPERED, ill-natured, crabbed, grumpy, crotchety, grouchy, cantankerous, irascible, testy, crusty, gruff, abrupt, brusque, churlish, uncivil, morose, sullen, sulky.
– OPPOSITES good-natured, friendly.

surmise verb GUESS, conjecture, suspect, deduce, assume, presume, gather, feel, be of the opinion, think, believe, imagine.

surmount verb GET OVER, overcome, conquer, triumph over, prevail over, get the better of beat.
– OPPOSITES descend.

surname noun LAST NAME, family name, patronymic.

surpass verb BE GREATER THAN, be better than, beat, exceed, excel, transcend, outdo, outshine, outstrip, overshadow, eclipse.

surplus noun EXCESS, remainder, residue, surfeit.
– OPPOSITES dearth, shortage.
▶ adjective EXCESS, in excess, superfluous, leftover, unused, remaining, extra, spare.

surprise verb ❶ ASTONISH, amaze, nonplus, take aback, startle, astound, stun, stagger, leave open-mouthed, take someone's breath away; *informal* flabbergast, bowl over, blow someone's mind. ❷ *surprise the burglar*: TAKE BY SURPRISE, catch unawares, catch off guard, catch red-handed, catch in the act, burst in on, spring upon, catch someone with their trousers down; *Brit. informal* catch on the hop.
▶ noun ❶ ASTONISHMENT, amazement, incredulity, wonder. ❷ SHOCK, bolt from the blue, bombshell, revelation.

surprised adjective ASTONISHED, amazed, nonplussed, startled, astounded, stunned, staggered, open-mouthed, speechless, thunderstruck; *informal* flabbergasted.

surprising adjective ASTONISHING, amazing, startling, astounding, staggering, incredible, extraordinary, remarkable; *informal* mind-blowing.
– OPPOSITES predictable.

surrender verb ❶ GIVE IN, give oneself up, yield, submit,

capitulate, lay down one's arms, raise/show the white flag, throw in the towel/sponge. ❷ **surrender a right:** GIVE UP, relinquish, renounce, forgo, forsake, cede, abdicate, waive. ❸ **surrender the keys:** HAND OVER, give up, deliver up, part with, let go of, relinquish.
– OPPOSITES resist.
▶ **noun** ❶ YIELDING, capitulation, submission. ❷ RELINQUISHMENT, renunciation, forgoing, ceding, cession, abdication.

surreptitious adjective STEALTHY, clandestine, secret, sneaky, sly, cunning, furtive, underhand, undercover, covert.
– OPPOSITES open, blatant.

surround verb ENCIRCLE, enclose, go around, encompass, ring, gird, girdle, fence in, hem in, confine.

surrounding adjective NEIGHBOURING, nearby, adjacent, adjoining, bordering.

surroundings plural noun ENVIRONMENT, setting, location, neighbourhood, vicinity, milieu, element, background.

surveillance noun OBSERVATION, watch, scrutiny, reconnaissance, spying, espionage.

survey verb ❶ LOOK AT, look over, take a look at, observe, view, contemplate, regard, examine, inspect, scan, study, consider, review, examine, inspect, scrutinize, take stock of; *informal* size up. ❷ **survey a building:** MAKE A SURVEY OF, value, carry out a valuation of, estimate the value of, appraise, assess, prospect, triangulate.
▶ **noun** ❶ STUDY, consideration, review, overview, examination, inspection, scrutinization, scrutiny. ❷ VALUATION, appraisal. ❸ INVESTIGATION, inquiry, research, study, review, probe, questionnaire.

survive verb ❶ REMAIN ALIVE, live, hold out, pull through, cling to life. ❷ **old customs survive:** LIVE ON, continue, remain, last, persist, endure, be extant, exist, be. ❸ **he survived his brother:** OUTLIVE, outlast, live after, remain alive after.

susceptible adjective IMPRESSIONABLE, credulous, gullible, innocent, defenceless, vulnerable, easily led, responsive, sensitive, thin-skinned.
– OPPOSITES immune, resistant.
■ **susceptible to** OPEN TO, responsive to, receptive to, vulnerable to, defenceless against.

suspect verb ❶ FEEL, have a feeling, be inclined to think, fancy, surmise, guess, conjecture, have a suspicion that, speculate, have a hunch, suppose, believe, think, conclude. ❷ DOUBT, have doubts about, harbour suspicions about, have misgivings about, be sceptical about, distrust, mistrust.

suspend verb ❶ HANG, put up, swing, dangle, sling. ❷ **suspend proceedings:** ADJOURN, interrupt, cut short, bring to an end, cease, discontinue, break off, arrest, put off, postpone, delay, defer, shelve, pigeonhole, table; *informal* put on ice. ❸ **suspended from his job:** DEBAR, shut out, exclude, keep out, remove.

suspense noun UNCERTAINTY, doubt, doubtfulness, anticipation, expectation, expectancy, excitement, tension, anxiety, nervousness, apprehension, apprehensiveness.

suspicion noun ❶ DOUBT,

misgiving, qualm, wariness, chariness, scepticism, distrust, mistrust, funny feeling. ❷ FEELING, surmise, guess, conjecture, speculation, hunch, supposition, belief, notion, idea, conclusion; *informal* gut feeling. ❸ TRACE, touch, suggestion, hint, soupçon, tinge, shade.

suspicious adjective ❶ **suspicious looks:** DOUBTFUL, unsure, wary, chary, sceptical, distrustful, mistrustful, disbelieving. ❷ **a suspicious person:** GUILTY-LOOKING, dishonest-looking, strange-looking, queer-looking, funny-looking; *informal* shifty, shady. ❸ **suspicious circumstances:** QUESTIONABLE, doubtful, odd, strange, irregular, queer, funny; *informal* fishy, shady.
– OPPOSITES trusting, innocent.

sustain verb ❶ BEAR, support, carry, keep up, prop up, shore up. ❷ SUPPORT, be a source of strength to, be a tower of strength to, comfort, help, assist, encourage, buoy up, cheer up, hearten; *informal* buck up. ❸ KEEP ALIVE, keep going, maintain, preserve, feed, nourish.

sustained adjective CONTINUING, steady, continuous, constant, prolonged, perpetual, unremitting.
– OPPOSITES intermittent.

sustenance noun FOOD, nourishment, provisions, rations, comestibles, provender; *informal* grub, chow; *Brit. informal* scoff; *dated* victuals; *archaic* aliment.

swagger verb STRUT, parade, prance.

swallow verb ❶ GULP DOWN, eat, drink, consume, devour, ingest; *informal* swig, swill; *Brit. informal* scoff. ❷ PUT UP WITH, tolerate, endure, stand, bear, abide, stomach, brook; *archaic* suffer. ❸ **swallow their story:** BELIEVE, accept; *informal* fall for, buy. ❹ **swallow his pride:** REPRESS, restrain, hold back, control, rein in.

swamp noun MARSH, bog, quagmire, mire, morass, fen, quag.
▶ verb ❶ FLOOD, inundate, deluge, wash out, soak, drench, saturate. ❷ OVERWHELM, engulf, snow under, overload, overburden, weight down, besiege, beset.

swampy adjective MARSHY, boggy, wet, soggy, spongy, waterlogged, miry, fenny, quaggy.
– OPPOSITES dry.

swap verb EXCHANGE, interchange, trade, barter, switch.

swarm noun ❶ HIVE, flight. ❷ CROWD, multitude, horde, host, mob, throng, army, flock, herd, pack, drove.
▶ verb FLOCK, crowd, throng, stream, surge.

swarthy adjective DARK, dark-coloured, dark-skinned, dark-complexioned, dusky, tanned.
– OPPOSITES pale, fair.

swashbuckling adjective DASHING, daring, adventurous, bold, gallant, swaggering.
– OPPOSITES timid.

swathe verb WRAP, envelop, bind, swaddle, bandage, bundle up, cover, shroud, drape.

sway verb ❶ SWING, shake, bend, lean, incline. ❷ WAVER, hesitate, fluctuate, vacillate, oscillate. ❸ **swayed by the argument:** INFLUENCE, affect, persuade,

prevail on, bring round, win over, induce.
▶ **noun** ❶ JURISDICTION, rule, government, sovereignty, dominion, control, command, power, authority, ascendancy, domination, mastery. ❷ CONTROL, domination, power, authority, influence, guidance, direction.

swear **verb** ❶ PROMISE, pledge, vow, give one's word, take an oath, swear on the Bible. ❷ VOW, insist, declare, assert, maintain, contend; *formal* aver. ❸ CURSE, blaspheme, utter profanities, be foul-mouthed, use bad language, swear like a trooper; *informal* turn the air blue.

swearing **noun** CURSING, blaspheming, profanity, imprecation, bad language.

sweat **verb** PERSPIRE, exude perspiration, drip with sweat, break out in a sweat.

sweaty **adjective** SWEATING, perspiring, clammy, sticky, moist, damp.

sweep **verb** BRUSH, clean, clean up, clear up.
■ **sweep away/aside** CAST ASIDE, discard, disregard, ignore, take no notice of, dismiss.

sweet **adjective** ❶ SWEETENED, sugary, sugared, honeyed, syrupy, saccharine. ❷ SWEET-SMELLING, fragrant, aromatic, perfumed, scented, balmy. ❸ SWEET-SOUNDING, musical, tuneful, dulcet, mellifluous, soft, harmonious, euphonious, silvery, silver-toned. ❹ **a sweet nature:** GOOD-NATURED, amiable, pleasant, agreeable, friendly, kindly, charming, likeable, appealing, engaging, winning, winsome, taking. ❺ DEAR, dearest, darling, beloved, loved, cherished, precious, treasured.
– OPPOSITES sour, savoury, harsh, disagreeable.
▶ **noun** ❶ DESSERT, pudding; *Brit. informal* afters. ❷ BONBON, sweetmeat; *N. Amer.* candy; *informal* sweetie.
■ **sweet on** FOND OF, taken with, in love with, enamoured of, infatuated with, keen on; *informal* gone on, mad about.

sweeten **verb** ❶ MAKE SWEET, add sugar to, sugar. ❷ **sweeten someone:** SOFTEN, soften up, mellow, pacify, appease, mollify.

sweetheart **noun** GIRLFRIEND, boyfriend, lover, suitor, admirer, beau, inamorato, inamorata; *poetic/literary* swain; *archaic* paramour.

swell **verb** ❶ EXPAND, bulge, distend, become distended, inflate, become inflated, dilate, become bloated, blow up, puff up, balloon, intumesce. ❷ **numbers have swelled:** INCREASE, grow larger, rise, mount, escalate, accelerate, step up, snowball, mushroom. ❸ **the music swelled:** GROW LOUD, grow louder, intensify, heighten.
– OPPOSITES contract.
▶ **adjective** EXPENSIVE, luxurious, de luxe, fashionable, elegant, grand; *informal* plush, ritzy; *Brit. informal* posh.

swelling **noun** BUMP, lump, bulge, blister, inflammation, protuberance, tumescence.

sweltering **adjective** HOT, torrid, tropical, stifling, suffocating, humid, sultry, sticky, muggy, clammy, close; *informal* boiling, baking.
– OPPOSITES freezing.

swerve **verb** CHANGE DIRECTION, go

off course, veer, turn aside, skew, deviate, sheer, twist.

swift adjective ❶ FAST, rapid, quick, speedy, fleet-footed, fleet, swift as an arrow; *informal* nippy. ❷ a swift change of plan: RAPID, sudden, abrupt, hasty, hurried. ❸ a swift reply: RAPID, prompt, immediate, instantaneous.
– OPPOSITES slow.

swill verb GULP DOWN, drink, quaff, swallow, down, drain, guzzle; *informal* swig.
■ **swill out** SLUICE, wash down, wash out, clean out, flush out, rinse out.

swim verb GO SWIMMING, bathe, dive in; *informal* have a dip.
■ **be swimming in** BE SATURATED IN, be drenched in, be soaked in, be steeped in, be immersed in.

swimmingly adverb VERY WELL, smoothly, effortlessly, like clockwork, with no hitch, without difficulty, as planned; *informal* like a dream.

swindle verb DEFRAUD, cheat, trick, fleece, dupe, deceive, rook, exploit; *informal* do, con, diddle, rip off, take for a ride, pull a fast one on, bilk.
▶ noun FRAUD, trick, deception, exploitation, sharp practice; *informal* con trick, con, diddle, rip-off, fiddle.

swindler noun FRAUDSTER, cheat, trickster, rogue, mountebank, exploiter; *informal* con man, con artist, shark, bilker.

swing verb ❶ HANG, be suspended, dangle, be pendent. ❷ MOVE BACK AND FORTH, sway, oscillate, wag. ❸ CURVE, veer, turn, lean, incline, wind, twist. ❹ CHANGE, fluctuate, oscillate, waver, see-saw, yo-yo. ❺ manage to swing a raise: ACHIEVE, obtain, acquire, get, manoeuvre.
▶ noun ❶ SWAYING, oscillation, wagging. ❷ MOVE, change, variation, turnaround.

swirl verb WHIRL, eddy, circulate, revolve, spin, twist, churn, swish.

switch noun ❶ CHANGE, change of direction, shift, reversal, turnaround, U-turn; *Brit.* about-turn. ❷ EXCHANGE, trade, swap.
▶ verb ❶ CHANGE, shift, reverse. ❷ EXCHANGE, interchange, trade, barter, swap.

swollen adjective EXPANDED, bulging, distended, inflated, dilated, bloated, blown up, puffed up, puffy, tumescent.

swoop verb POUNCE, dive, descend, sweep down on, drop down on.
■ **swoop up** TAKE UP, lift up, pick up, scoop up, seize, snatch, grab.

sybaritic adjective LUXURIOUS, self-indulgent, pleasure-seeking, sensual, voluptuous, hedonistic, epicurean, debauched, dissolute.
– OPPOSITES ascetic.

sycophant noun TOADY, flatterer, truckler, Uriah Heep; *informal* bootlicker, yes-man.

sycophantic adjective SERVILE, subservient, obsequious, toadying, flattering, ingratiating, unctuous, truckling, Uriah Heepish; *informal* bootlicking.

symbol noun ❶ a symbol of peace: EMBLEM, token, sign, badge, representation, figure, image, type. ❷ SIGN, character, mark.

symbolic adjective ❶ EMBLEMATIC, representative, typical. ❷ REPRESENTATIVE, illustrative, emblematic, figurative, allegorical.

symbolize verb BE A SYMBOL OF, stand for, be a sign of, represent, personify, exemplify, typify, betoken, denote, epitomize, signify, mean.

symmetrical adjective BALANCED, well proportioned, proportional, in proportion, regular, even, harmonious, uniform, consistent, in agreement.
– OPPOSITES asymmetrical.

sympathetic adjective ❶ COMPASSIONATE, commiserating, commiserative, pitying, condoling, consoling, comforting, supportive, caring, concerned, solicitous, considerate, kindly, kind, kind-hearted, warm, warm-hearted, understanding, charitable, empathetic. ❷ a sympathetic character: PLEASANT, agreeable, likeable, congenial, friendly, sociable, companionable, neighbourly, easy to get along with; *informal* simpatico. ❸ sympathetic to their cause: IN SYMPATHY WITH, well disposed to, favourably disposed to, approving of, pro, on someone's side.
– OPPOSITES unsympathetic.

sympathize verb SHOW/FEEL SYMPATHY FOR, be sympathetic towards, show compassion for, be compassionate towards, commiserate with, pity, offer condolences to, console, comfort, be supportive of, show understanding to, empathize with.

sympathy noun COMPASSION, commiseration, pity, condolence, consolation, comfort, solace, support, caring, concern, solicitude, solicitousness, consideration, kindness, kind-heartedness, warmth, warm-heartedness, charity, charitableness, understanding, empathy.
– OPPOSITES indifference.

symptom noun SIGN, indication, signal, warning, mark, characteristic, feature, token, evidence, demonstration, display.

symptomatic adjective INDICATIVE OF, signalling, characteristic of, suggesting, suggestive of.

synthesis noun COMBINATION, combining, union, unification, merging, amalgamation, fusion, coalescence, integration.

synthetic adjective MANUFACTURED, man-made, fake, artificial, mock, ersatz.
– OPPOSITES real, natural.

syrupy adjective OVERSWEET, sugary, sweet, honeyed, saccharine, sticky; *informal* gooey.

system noun ❶ STRUCTURE, organization, order, arrangement, set-up. ❷ METHOD, methodology, technique, process, procedure, approach, practice, line, means, way, modus operandi. ❸ METHOD, systematization, methodicalness, orderliness, planning, logic, tightness, routine.

systematic adjective STRUCTURED, organized, methodical, orderly, well ordered, planned, systematized, logical, efficient, businesslike.
– OPPOSITES unsystematic, chaotic.

systematize verb ARRANGE, organize, categorize, rationalize, standardize, codify, classify, catalogue, tabulate.

Tt

table noun ❶ COUNTER, bar, buffet, bench, stand. ❷ **a table of contents:** LIST, catalogue, tabulation, inventory, digest, itemization, index. ❸ CHART, diagram, figure, graph, plan.
▶ verb SUBMIT, put forward, propose, suggest, move, enter.

tableau noun ❶ PICTURE, painting, representation, portrayal, illustration. ❷ SPECTACLE, scene, sight.

tablet noun ❶ SLAB, panel, stone. ❷ PILL, capsule, lozenge. ❸ BAR, cake.

taboo adjective FORBIDDEN, prohibited, banned, proscribed, vetoed, ruled out, outlawed, not permitted, not acceptable, frowned on, beyond the pale.
– OPPOSITES acceptable.
▶ noun PROHIBITION, proscription, veto, interdiction, interdict, ban.

tabulate verb CHART, systematize, systemize, arrange, order, dispose, organize, catalogue, list, classify.

tacit adjective IMPLICIT, understood, implied, taken for granted, unstated, undeclared, unspoken, silent, wordless.
– OPPOSITES explicit.

taciturn adjective UNFORTHCOMING, uncommunicative, reticent, untalkative, tight-lipped, close-mouthed, quiet, silent.
– OPPOSITES loquacious.

tack noun ❶ DRAWING PIN, nail, pin, staple, rivet. ❷ **a different tack:** COURSE/LINE OF ACTION, method, approach, process, way, policy.
▶ verb NAIL, pin, staple, fix, fasten, affix, put up/down.

tackle noun EQUIPMENT, apparatus, outfit, tools, implements, accoutrements, paraphernalia, things, trappings; *informal* gear, stuff.
▶ verb ❶ UNDERTAKE, attempt, apply/address oneself to, get to grips with, set/go about, get to work at, embark on, set one's hand to, take on, engage in. ❷ GRAPPLE WITH, seize, take hold of, confront, face up to; *Brit. informal* have a go at.

tacky[1] adjective STICKY, gluey, gummy; *informal* gooey.

tacky[2] adjective TAWDRY, tasteless, kitsch, vulgar, crude, garish, gaudy, flashy; *informal* flash.
– OPPOSITES tasteful.

tact noun DIPLOMACY, discretion, sensitivity, understanding, thoughtfulness, consideration, delicacy, subtlety, finesse, skill, perception, judgement, prudence, judiciousness.
– OPPOSITES tactlessness.

tactful adjective DIPLOMATIC, politic, discreet, sensitive, understanding, thoughtful, considerate, delicate, subtle, perceptive, prudent, judicious.
– OPPOSITES tactless.

tactic noun MANOEUVRE, expedient, device, stratagem, trick, scheme, plan, ploy, course/line of action, method, approach, tack, means.

tactical adjective STRATEGIC, politic, planned, shrewd, skilful, adroit, clever, cunning, artful; *informal* smart.

tactless adjective UNDIPLOMATIC, impolitic, indiscreet, insensitive, inconsiderate, indelicate, unsubtle, rough, crude, clumsy, awkward, inept, bungling, maladroit, gauche, undiscerning, imprudent, injudicious.
– OPPOSITES tactful.

tag noun ❶ LABEL, ticket, sticker, docket. ❷ QUOTATION, stock phrase, platitude, cliché, epithet.
▶ verb LABEL, put a ticket/sticker on, mark.
■ **tag along** GO WITH, accompany, follow, trail behind, dog.

tail noun BRUSH, scut, dock.
▶ verb FOLLOW, shadow, stalk, trail, track, dog, keep under surveillance.
■ **tail off** *see* DECLINE verb (2, 3).

tailor noun OUTFITTER, dressmaker, couturier, clothier, costumier.
▶ verb FIT, suit, fashion, style, mould, shape, adapt, adjust, modify, convert, alter, accommodate.

take verb ❶ GET/LAY HOLD OF, grasp, grip, clutch. ❷ GET, receive, obtain, gain, acquire, secure, procure, come by, win. ❸ take hostages: SEIZE, catch, capture, arrest, carry off, abduct. ❹ who took his money? REMOVE, appropriate, make off with, steal, pilfer, purloin, pocket; *informal* filch, swipe; *Brit. informal* pinch, nick. ❺ take a room: RESERVE, book, engage, rent, hire, lease. ❻ take the bus: USE, make use of, utilize. ❼ it takes an hour: USE UP, require, call for, need, necessitate. ❽ take it with you: CARRY, fetch, bring, bear, transport, convey, cart, ferry. ❾ take her home: ESCORT, accompany, conduct, guide, lead, usher, convoy. ❿ take him for a fool: REGARD AS, consider as, view as, look upon as. ⓫ take a course: ENTER UPON, undertake, begin, set about. ⓬ the bucket takes three litres: HOLD, contain, have the capacity for, have space/room for, accommodate. ⓭ couldn't take criticism: BEAR, tolerate, stand, put up with, stomach; *formal* brook.
– OPPOSITES give.
■ **take after** *see* RESEMBLE. **take off** *see* IMITATE (2).

takings plural noun PROCEEDS, returns, receipts, earnings, winnings, pickings, profit, gain, income, revenue.

tale noun STORY, narrative, anecdote, legend, fable, myth, parable, allegory, epic, saga; *informal* yarn.

talent noun GIFT, flair, aptitude, facility, knack, bent, ability, capacity, faculty, aptness, endowment, strong point, forte, genius.

talented adjective GIFTED, accomplished, able, capable, apt, deft, adept, proficient, brilliant, expert, artistic.
– OPPOSITES incapable, inept.

talk verb ❶ SPEAK, give voice/utterance, discourse, chat, chatter, gossip, prattle, prate, gibber, jabber, babble, rattle on, gabble; *informal* yak, gab; *Brit. informal* natter, rabbit. ❷ COMMUNICATE, converse, speak to each other, discuss things, confer, consult each other, have negotiations, parley; *informal* chew the fat/rag, jaw, rap.
▶ noun ❶ TALKING, speaking, chatter, chatting, gossiping,

prattling; *Brit. informal* nattering. ❷ LECTURE, speech, address, discourse, oration, sermon, disquisition. ❸ GOSSIP, rumour, hearsay, tittle-tattle.

talkative adjective LOQUACIOUS, garrulous, voluble, chatty, gossipy, conversational, long-winded, gushing, effusive; *informal* gabby, mouthy, big-mouthed.
– OPPOSITES taciturn.

tall adjective ❶ **a tall person**: BIG, colossal, gigantic, lanky, rangy, gangling. ❷ **a tall building**: HIGH, lofty, towering, soaring, sky-high.
– OPPOSITES short.

tally noun COUNT, record, total, reckoning, enumeration, register, roll, census, poll.
▶ verb AGREE, accord, concur, coincide, conform, correspond, match, fit, harmonize.
– OPPOSITES disagree.

tame adjective ❶ DOMESTICATED, gentle. ❷ UNEXCITING, uninteresting, uninspired, dull, bland, flat, insipid, vapid, prosaic, humdrum, boring, tedious, wearisome.
– OPPOSITES wild.
▶ verb ❶ DOMESTICATE, break, train. ❷ SUBDUE, discipline, curb, control, master, overcome, suppress, repress, humble.

tamper
■ **tamper with** MEDDLE WITH, interfere with, monkey around with, mess about with, tinker with, fiddle with.

tan verb BECOME SUNTANNED, suntan, take a suntan/tan, brown, go/turn brown, darken.

tangible adjective ❶ TOUCHABLE, palpable, tactile, visible. ❷ **tangible proof**: CONCRETE, real, actual, solid, substantial, hard, well documented, definite, clear.
– OPPOSITES abstract.

tangled adjective ❶ ENTANGLED, twisted, snarled, ravelled, knotted, knotty, matted, tousled, messy. ❷ CONFUSED, jumbled, mixed up, messy, chaotic, complicated, involved, convoluted, complex.
– OPPOSITES simple.

tank noun ❶ CONTAINER, receptacle, vat, cistern. ❷ ARMOURED CAR, combat vehicle.

tantalize verb TEASE, torment, torture, frustrate, disappoint, thwart, lead on, entice, titillate, allure, beguile.

tantamount
■ **tantamount to** EQUIVALENT TO, equal to, as good as, synonymous with.

tape noun ❶ BAND, strip, string, ribbon. ❷ TAPE RECORDING, cassette, videotape, video cassette, video, audio tape, audio cassette.
▶ verb ❶ BIND, tie, fasten, stick, seal. ❷ RECORD, tape-record, video-record, video.

taper verb NARROW, thin, become narrow/thinner, come to a point.
– OPPOSITES thicken.
■ **taper off** *see* DECLINE verb (2, 3).

target noun ❶ OBJECTIVE, goal, object, aim, end, intention. ❷ BUTT, victim, scapegoat.

tariff noun ❶ PRICE LIST/SCHEDULE, list of charges. ❷ TAX, duty, toll, excise, levy, impost.

tarnish verb ❶ DULL, dim, discolour, rust. ❷ SULLY, besmirch, blacken, stain, blemish, blot, taint, befoul, drag through the mud.
– OPPOSITES polish, enhance.

tart[1] noun PASTRY, flan, tartlet, quiche, pie.

tart[2]
■ **tart up** DRESS UP, make up, smarten up, renovate, refurbish, redecorate, modernize.

tart[3] adjective SHARP, sour, tangy, piquant, pungent, bitter, acid, acidulous, vinegary.
– OPPOSITES sweet.

task noun JOB, duty, chore, charge, assignment, commission, mission, engagement, occupation, undertaking, exercise, errand, quest.

taste noun ❶ FLAVOUR, savour, relish, tang. ❷ MORSEL, bite, mouthful, spoonful, sample, sip, drop, swallow, touch, soupçon. ❸ LIKING, love, fondness, fancy, desire, preference, penchant, predilection, inclination, partiality, leaning, bent, hankering, appetite, palate, thirst, hunger. ❹ DISCRIMINATION, discernment, judgement, refinement, polish, finesse, elegance, grace, stylishness.
▸ verb ❶ SAMPLE, test, try, nibble, sip. ❷ MAKE OUT, perceive, discern, distinguish, differentiate.

tasteful adjective IN GOOD TASTE, aesthetic, artistic, harmonious, pleasing, elegant, graceful, beautiful, pretty, charming, handsome, discriminating, refined, restrained.
– OPPOSITES tasteless.

tasteless adjective
❶ FLAVOURLESS, bland, insipid, watery, watered down, weak, thin, unappetizing, uninteresting, vapid. ❷ VULGAR, crude, tawdry, garish, gaudy, loud, flashy, showy, cheap, gross, meretricious.
– OPPOSITES tasteful.

tasty adjective FLAVOURSOME, full-flavoured, appetizing, palatable, toothsome, delectable, delicious, luscious, mouth-watering, piquant, pungent, spicy; *informal* scrumptious, yummy, finger-licking.
– OPPOSITES bland.

tattle verb GOSSIP, tittle-tattle, chatter, prattle, prate, babble, rattle on; *informal* gab; *Brit. informal* rabbit on.

taunt verb GIBE AT, jeer at, sneer at, insult, chaff, tease, torment, provoke, ridicule, deride, mock, poke fun at.

taut adjective TIGHT, stretched, rigid, flexed, tensed.
– OPPOSITES slack.

tautology noun REPETITION, repetitiveness, reiteration, redundancy, pleonasm, wordiness, long-windedness, verbosity, prolixity.

tawdry adjective SHOWY, gaudy, flashy, garish, loud, tasteless, cheap, cheapjack, shoddy, meretricious, Brummagem; *informal* flash, tatty, tacky, kitsch.
– OPPOSITES tasteful.

tax noun LEVY, charge, duty, toll, excise, tariff, impost, tribute.
▸ verb ❶ LEVY A TAX ON, impose a toll on, charge duty on. ❷ MAKE DEMANDS ON, weigh heavily on, weigh down, burden, load, encumber, overload, push, stretch, strain, try, wear out, exhaust, sap, drain, enervate, fatigue, tire, weary, weaken.

teach verb ❶ GIVE LESSONS TO, instruct, educate, school, tutor, coach, train, drill, ground, enlighten. ❷ GIVE LESSONS/INSTRUCTION IN, instil, inculcate.

teacher noun SCHOOLTEACHER, schoolmaster, schoolmistress, master, mistress, instructor, educator, tutor, coach, trainer, lecturer, professor, don, pedagogue, guide, mentor, guru.

team noun GROUP, band, bunch, company, gang, crew, troupe, squad, side, line-up.

tear[1] noun RIP, split, hole, rent, run, rupture.
▶ verb RIP, split, rend, sever, rive, sunder, rupture.

tear[2] noun TEARDROP, drop, droplet, globule, bead.

tearful adjective IN TEARS, crying, weeping, weepy, sobbing, blubbering, snivelling, whimpering, wailing; *informal* blubbing.
– OPPOSITES cheerful.

tease verb MOCK, ridicule, poke fun at, torment, provoke, badger, bait, goad, pest, bother, worry, vex, irritate, annoy, gibe; *informal* needle.

technical adjective ❶ PRACTICAL, mechanical, scientific, technological. ❷ SPECIALIST, specialized, scientific.

technique noun ❶ METHOD, system, procedure, style, manner, way, course of action, mode, fashion, means. ❷ EXECUTION, skill, skilfulness, proficiency, expertise, expertness, mastery, artistry, art, craftsmanship, craft, ability.

tedious adjective WEARISOME, wearying, tiresome, tiring, fatiguing, soporific, overlong, long-winded, prolix, dull, deadly dull, boring, uninteresting, dry, dreary, drab, unexciting, lifeless, uninspired, flat, banal, vapid, insipid, monotonous, unvaried, prosaic, humdrum, run-of-the-mill, routine.
– OPPOSITES interesting.

teem verb ABOUND, be abundant, be plentiful, be copious, swarm, crawl, bristle, seethe, brim.

teenage adjective ADOLESCENT, youthful, young, juvenile.

teenager noun YOUNG PERSON, adolescent, youth, minor, juvenile; *informal* teeny-bopper.

teetotaller noun ABSTAINER, non-drinker, Rechabite.

telephone noun PHONE, handset, receiver; *informal* blower.
▶ verb CALL, call up, phone; *Brit.* ring up, ring; *informal* get on the blower to, buzz.

telescope verb CONCERTINA, crush, squash, squeeze, compress, compact.
– OPPOSITES elongate.

television noun TV; *informal* small screen; *Brit. informal* telly, the box, goggle-box; *N. Amer. informal* the tube, idiot box.

tell verb ❶ MAKE KNOWN, impart, communicate, announce, proclaim, broadcast, divulge, reveal, disclose, declare, state, mention, utter, voice, say, speak. ❷ INFORM, let know, make aware, apprise, notify. ❸ INSTRUCT, order, give orders, command, direct, bid, charge, enjoin, dictate to, call upon, require. ❹ DISTINGUISH, differentiate, discriminate.

telling adjective MARKED, significant, substantial, considerable, important, striking, impressive, potent, powerful, forceful, effective, influential, decisive.
– OPPOSITES insignificant.

temper noun ❶ TEMPERAMENT, disposition, nature, humour,

mood, character, frame of mind, mind, attitude, stamp. ❷ BAD MOOD, ill humour, fury, rage, passion, fit of temper/pique, tantrum; *Brit. informal* paddy.
▶ verb ❶ **temper the metal:** TOUGHEN, anneal, harden, strengthen, fortify. ❷ **temper justice with mercy:** MODERATE, soften, tone down, modify, mitigate, alleviate, allay, palliate, mollify, assuage, lessen, weaken.

temperament noun DISPOSITION, nature, humour, mood, character, personality, make-up, constitution, complexion, temper, spirit, mettle, frame of mind, cast of mind, mind, attitude, outlook stamp, quality.

temperamental adjective ❶ CONSTITUTIONAL, inherent, innate, inborn, congenital, deep-rooted, ingrained. ❷ EXCITABLE, emotional, volatile, mercurial, oversensitive, capricious, erratic, touchy, moody, hot-headed, explosive, impatient, petulant.
– OPPOSITES calm.

temperance noun MODERATION, self-control, abstemiousness, continence, abstinence, self-denial.
– OPPOSITES alcoholism.

temperate adjective MODERATE, mild, gentle, clement, balmy, pleasant, agreeable.
– OPPOSITES extreme.

tempest noun STORM, gale, hurricane, squall, cyclone, tornado, typhoon.

tempestuous adjective STORMY, turbulent, boisterous, violent, wild, uncontrolled, unrestrained, passionate, impassioned, emotional, intense, fierce.
– OPPOSITES calm.

temple noun PLACE OF WORSHIP, holy place, shrine, sanctuary.

tempo noun BEAT, rhythm, cadence, throb, pulse.

temporal adjective SECULAR, non-spiritual, worldly, material, earthly, carnal.
– OPPOSITES spiritual.

temporary adjective ❶ SHORT-TERM, impermanent, interim, provisional, pro tem. ❷ BRIEF, fleeting, passing, momentary, short-lived, transient, transitory, ephemeral, fugitive, evanescent.
– OPPOSITES permanent.

tempt verb ENTICE, lure, attract, appeal to, seduce, tantalize, incite, persuade, induce, egg on, urge, goad, prompt, sway, influence, cajole, coax.
– OPPOSITES discourage, deter.

tempting adjective ALLURING, enticing, attractive, captivating, appealing, beguiling, fascinating, tantalizing, appetizing, mouth-watering.
– OPPOSITES off-putting.

tenable adjective JUSTIFIABLE, defensible, defendable, arguable, maintainable, supportable, plausible, credible, reasonable, rational, sound, viable.
– OPPOSITES untenable.

tenacious adjective PERSISTENT, pertinacious, determined, dogged, resolute, firm, steadfast, purposeful, unshakeable, unswerving, relentless, inexorable, unyielding, inflexible, stubborn, obstinate, intransigent, obdurate, strong-willed.

tend[1] verb HAVE/SHOW A TENDENCY

TO, incline towards, be apt/ disposed/liable to, be likely to.

tend[2] verb LOOK AFTER, take care of, care for, attend to, minister to, see to, cater to, nurse, wait on, watch over, watch.
– OPPOSITES neglect.

tendency noun INCLINATION, disposition, predisposition, proclivity, propensity, proneness, aptness, bent, leaning, penchant, susceptibility, liability.

tender adjective ❶ EASILY DAMAGED, breakable, fragile, frail, delicate, sensitive. ❷ COMPASSIONATE, soft-hearted, kind, kindly, sympathetic, warm, caring, humane, gentle, solicitous, generous, benevolent, sentimental. ❸ LOVING, affectionate, warm, emotional, amorous. ❹ SORE, painful, aching, smarting, throbbing, inflamed, irritated, red, raw, bruised.
– OPPOSITES tough, hard-hearted.

tense adjective ❶ TIGHT, taut, rigid, stretched, strained. ❷ STRAINED, under a strain, under pressure, nervous, keyed up, worked up, overwrought, distraught, anxious, uneasy, worried, apprehensive, agitated, jumpy, edgy, on edge, restless, fidgety; *informal* uptight, wound up, jittery.
– OPPOSITES relaxed.

tension noun ❶ TIGHTNESS, tautness, rigidity. ❷ STRAIN, stress, stressfulness, suspense, pressure, anxiety, unease, disquiet, worry, apprehensiveness, agitation, jumpiness, edginess, restlessness.

tentative adjective ❶ **a tentative proposal**: SPECULATIVE, conjectural, exploratory, trial, provisional, test, pilot, untried, unproven. ❷ **tentative steps**: HESITANT, hesitating, faltering, wavering, uncertain, unsure, doubtful, cautious, diffident, timid.
– OPPOSITES definite, confident.

tenuous adjective SLIGHT, flimsy, weak, insubstantial, shaky, sketchy, doubtful, dubious, nebulous, hazy, vague, unspecific, indefinite.
– OPPOSITES definite.

term noun ❶ WORD, expression, phrase, name, title, appellation, designation; *formal* denomination. ❷ PERIOD, time, spell, interval, stretch, span, duration.
▶ verb CALL, name, entitle, style, dub, label, tag, designate, denominate.

terminal adjective FATAL, deadly, mortal, lethal, killing, incurable.
▶ noun ❶ TERMINUS, last stop, depot. ❷ WORKSTATION, visual display unit, VDU.

terminate verb BRING TO A CLOSE/ END/CONCLUSION, close, end, conclude, finish, stop, wind up, discontinue.
– OPPOSITES commence.

terminology noun LANGUAGE, phraseology, vocabulary, nomenclature, jargon, terms, expressions, words; *informal* lingo.

terrible adjective ❶ **a terrible bore**: GREAT, extreme, incorrigible, outrageous, awful, dreadful, frightful, impossible. ❷ **he's a terrible player**: BAD, poor, incompetent, useless, talentless; *informal* rotten; *Brit. informal* duff. ❸ **terrible experiences**: DREADFUL, terrifying, frightening, frightful, horrifying, horrible, horrific, horrendous, terrific, harrowing, hideous, grim, unspeakable, appalling, awful, gruesome.

terrific adjective ❶ TREMENDOUS, great, very great, very big, huge, sizeable, considerable, intense, extreme, extraordinary, excessive. ❷ VERY GOOD, excellent, superb, remarkable, magnificent, wonderful, marvellous, great, sensational; *informal* super, fantastic, fabulous, fab, Al, ace, unreal, awesome.

terrify verb FRIGHTEN, scare stiff, scare, petrify, horrify, make someone's blood run cold, make someone's flesh creep, make someone's hair stand on end, alarm, panic, intimidate.

territory noun ❶ REGION, area, terrain, tract. ❷ AREA, province, field, sector, department.

terror noun FRIGHT, dread, alarm, panic, intimidation, dismay, consternation, shock, horror; *informal* heebie-jeebies.

terrorize verb STRIKE TERROR IN/INTO, terrify, scare stiff, petrify, horrify.

terse adjective ❶ CONCISE, succinct, compact, brief, short, to the point, crisp, pithy, elliptical, epigrammatic. ❷ ABRUPT, curt, brusque, laconic, short, clipped, blunt.
– OPPOSITES long-winded.

test noun EXAMINATION, check, assessment, evaluation, appraisal, investigation, inspection, analysis, scrutinization, scrutiny, study, probe, exploration.
▶ verb PUT TO THE TEST, examine, check, assess, evaluate, appraise, investigate, scrutinize, study, probe.

testify verb GIVE EVIDENCE, bear witness, attest, be a witness.

testimonial noun REFERENCE, character reference, recommendation, commendation, credential, endorsement.

testimony noun EVIDENCE, attestation, sworn statement, deposition, affidavit.

testy adjective TETCHY, touchy, irritable, irascible, petulant, crotchety, crabbed, querulous; *informal* snappish.

text noun ❶ TEXTBOOK, book. ❷ THEME, subject matter, subject, matter, topic, issue. ❸ PASSAGE, verse, paragraph.

texture noun FEEL, touch, appearance, surface, grain.

thank verb OFFER/EXTEND THANKS TO, express/show gratitude to, show appreciation to.

thankful adjective GRATEFUL, appreciative, pleased, indebted, obliged, under an obligation, beholden.
– OPPOSITES ungrateful.

thankless adjective UNAPPRECIATED, unrewarded, unrewarding, unacknowledged, vain, in vain, fruitless, useless.
– OPPOSITES rewarding.

thanks plural noun GRATITUDE, gratefulness, appreciation, acknowledgement, recognition.

thaw verb DEFROST, unfreeze, melt, soften, liquefy.
– OPPOSITES freeze.

theatre noun ❶ DRAMA, dramaturgy, the stage, show business; *informal* show biz. ❷ AUDITORIUM, hall, playhouse.

theatrical adjective ❶ DRAMATIC, stage, dramaturgical, thespian. ❷ DRAMATIC, melodramatic, histrionic, emotional, exaggerated, overdone, ostentatious, showy, affected, mannered, stilted; *informal* hammy.

theft noun STEALING, robbery, thieving, thievery, burglary, larceny, misappropriation, pilfering, purloining, shoplifting, embezzlement.

theme noun ❶ TOPIC, subject, subject matter, matter, thesis, text, argument. ❷ THEME SONG, melody, tune, air, leitmotif.

theoretical adjective HYPOTHETICAL, conjectural, suppositional, speculative, notional, postulatory, assumed, presumed.
– OPPOSITES proven.

theorize verb FORM/EVOLVE A THEORY, speculate, conjecture, suppose, hypothesize.

theory noun HYPOTHESIS, thesis, conjecture, supposition, speculation, guess, notion, postulation, assumption, presumption, opinion, view.

therapy noun ❶ TREATMENT, remedy, cure. ❷ PSYCHOTHERAPY, psychoanalysis.

therefore adverb AND SO, so, then, thus, accordingly, consequently, as a result, for that reason.

thesis noun ❶ THEORY, hypothesis, contention, argument, proposal, proposition, premise, postulation, idea. ❷ DISSERTATION, paper, treatise, disquisition, essay, composition, monograph.

thick adjective ❶ BROAD, wide, large, big, bulky, solid, substantial, fat; *informal* beefy. ❷ **thick with ants:** TEEMING, swarming, crawling, alive, abounding, overflowing, covered. ❸ **a thick forest:** DENSE, close-packed, concentrated, crowded, condensed. ❹ **thick mists:** DENSE, heavy, opaque, soupy, murky, impenetrable. ❺ **he's a bit thick:** *see* STUPID (1).
– OPPOSITES thin.

thicken verb SET, gel, solidify, congeal, clot, coagulate, cake.

thief noun ROBBER, burglar, housebreaker, larcenist, pilferer, shoplifter, pickpocket, embezzler, bandit, swindler, fraudster, mugger.

thieve verb STEAL, rob, pilfer, purloin, embezzle, swindle; *informal* swipe, filch, rip off; *Brit. informal* nick, knock off.

thin adjective ❶ SLIM, slender, lean, slight, svelte, light, skinny, spindly, scrawny, scraggy, bony, skeletal, wasted, emaciated, shrunken, anorexic, undernourished, underweight. ❷ **thin materials:** FINE, light, delicate, flimsy, diaphanous, gossamer, sheer, transparent, see-through, gauzy, filmy, translucent. ❸ **a thin audience:** SPARSE, scarce, scanty, meagre, paltry, scattered. ❹ **a thin story:** FLIMSY, insubstantial, weak, feeble, lame, poor, shallow, unconvincing, inadequate, insufficient.
– OPPOSITES fat.
▶ verb ❶ DILUTE, water down, weaken. ❷ REDUCE IN NUMBER, lessen, decrease, diminish.

thing noun ❶ OBJECT, article; *informal* whatchamacallit, what's-its-name, whatsit, thingummy, thingamabob, thingamajig. ❷ ACTION, act, deed, exploit, feat, undertaking, task, job, chore. ❸ EVENT, happening, occurrence, incident, episode. ❹ QUALITY, characteristic, attribute, property, trait, feature.

think verb ❶ BELIEVE, suppose, expect, imagine, surmise, conjecture, guess, fancy. ❷ CONSIDER, deem, hold, reckon, regard as, assume, presume, estimate. ❸ PONDER, meditate, deliberate, contemplate, muse, cogitate, ruminate, concentrate, brood, rack one's brains, be lost in thought, be in a brown study.

thinker noun PHILOSOPHER, scholar, sage, theorist, intellect; *informal* brain.

thirst noun ❶ THIRSTINESS, dryness, dehydration. ❷ a thirst for something: DESIRE, craving, longing, hankering, yearning, avidity, keenness, eagerness, hunger, lust, appetite, passion, covetousness; *informal* yen.
■ **thirst for/after** DESIRE, crave, long for, hanker after, yearn for, hunger after, lust after, covet.

thirsty adjective ❶ PARCHED, dehydrated, dry. ❷ THIRSTING, avid, keen, eager, hungry, greedy, covetous.

thong noun STRIP, belt, strap, cord, lash, rope, tie, tether.

thorny adjective ❶ PRICKLY, spiky, barbed, spiny, spined, spinose, bristly, sharp, pointed. ❷ a thorny issue: *see* DIFFICULT (2).

thorough adjective ❶ a thorough investigation: IN-DEPTH, exhaustive, complete, comprehensive, intensive, extensive, widespread, sweeping, all-embracing, all-inclusive, detailed. ❷ he is thorough: METICULOUS, scrupulous, assiduous, conscientious, painstaking, punctilious, methodical, careful. ❸ a thorough villain: THOROUGHGOING, out-and-out, utter, downright, sheer, absolute, unmitigated, unqualified, complete, total, perfect.
– OPPOSITES cursory, careless.

thought noun ❶ THINKING, reasoning, pondering, meditation, cogitation, rumination, musing, mulling, reflection, introspection, contemplation, consideration, cerebration. ❷ IDEA, notion, line of thinking, theory, opinion. ❸ JUDGEMENT, conclusion, appraisal, assessment, estimation, opinion, point of view, position, stance, stand, feeling, sentiment, belief, conviction.

thoughtful adjective ❶ PENSIVE, reflective, introspective, meditative, contemplative, ruminative, cogitative, absorbed, rapt/lost in thought, in a brown study. ❷ a thoughtful book: PROFOUND, deep, serious, pithy, meaty, weighty. ❸ thoughtful acts: CONSIDERATE, attentive, caring, solicitous, helpful, kind, kindly, compassionate, tender, charitable.
– OPPOSITES thoughtless.

thoughtless adjective ❶ TACTLESS, undiplomatic, indiscreet, insensitive, inconsiderate, careless, selfish, impolite, rude. ❷ UNTHINKING, heedless, careless, unmindful, absent-minded, injudicious, ill-advised, ill-considered, imprudent, unwise, foolish, silly, stupid, reckless, rash, precipitate, negligent, remiss.
– OPPOSITES thoughtful.

thrash verb BEAT, whip, horsewhip, flog, lash, birch, cane, flagellate, scourge, leather, spank, chastise, belt, wallop.

thread noun ❶ YARN, cotton, filament, fibre. ❷ STRAND, line, streak, strip, seam.

threadbare adjective WORN, frayed, tattered, ragged, holey, shabby.

threat noun ❶ THREATENING REMARK, warning, ultimatum. ❷ a threat to aircraft DANGER, peril, hazard, menace, risk. ❸ the threat of bad weather POSSIBILITY, chance, probability, likelihood, risk.

threaten verb ❶ MAKE THREATS, menace, intimidate, browbeat, bully, pressurize, lean on. ❷ BE IMMINENT, impend, hang over, loom, foreshadow.

threatening adjective ❶ MENACING, warning, intimidating, bullying, minatory. ❷ OMINOUS, inauspicious, foreboding.

threesome noun TRIO, triumvirate, triad, trinity, troika, triunity.

threshold noun ❶ DOORWAY, doorstep, entrance. ❷ BEGINNING, commencement, start, outset, inception, opening, dawn, brink, verge, debut; *informal* kick-off.

thrifty adjective ECONOMICAL, careful, frugal, sparing, scrimping, parsimonious, penny-pinching, miserly.
– OPPOSITES spendthrift.

thrill noun ❶ EXCITEMENT, sensation of joy, wave of pleasure, glow, tingle; *informal* buzz, charge, kick. ❷ a thrill of terror: THROB, tremble, tremor, quiver, flutter, shudder, vibration.
▶ **verb** EXCITE, stimulate, arouse, stir, electrify, move, give joy/pleasure to; *informal* give a buzz/charge/kick to.
– OPPOSITES bore.

thrilling adjective EXCITING, stirring, electrifying, rousing, moving, gripping, riveting.
– OPPOSITES boring.

thrive verb FLOURISH, prosper, do/go well, boom, burgeon, succeed, advance, get ahead, make progress.
– OPPOSITES decline.

throb verb BEAT, pulse, pulsate, palpitate, pound, thump.

throng noun CROWD, horde, mob, mass, host, multitude, swarm, flock, pack, herd, drove, press, assemblage, gathering, congregation.

throttle verb CHOKE, strangle, strangulate, garrotte.

throw verb ❶ HURL, toss, cast, sling, pitch, shy, lob, propel, launch, project, send; *informal* heave, chuck. ❷ throw a shadow: CAST, project, send. ❸ the question threw me: DISCONCERT, discomfit, disturb, confound, astonish, surprise, dumbfound, discountenance.

thrust verb PUSH, shove, ram, drive, press, prod, propel.

thrusting adjective FORCEFUL, pushing, forward, pushy, energetic, assertive, aggressive, insistent, ambitious.
– OPPOSITES meek.

thug noun RUFFIAN, rough, hoodlum, bully boy, hooligan, villain, gangster; *informal* heavy, bovver boy, tough.

thunder noun BOOM, booming, rumble, rumbling, outburst, roar, roaring.
▶ verb BOOM, rumble, roar, blast, resound, reverberate.

thunderous adjective BOOMING, rumbling, roaring, resounding, reverberating, deafening, ear-splitting, loud, noisy, tumultuous.

thunderstruck adjective AMAZED, astonished, dumbfounded, astounded, speechless, struck dumb.

thwart verb FRUSTRATE, foil, baulk, check, block, stop, prevent, defeat, impede, obstruct, hinder, hamper, stymie.
– OPPOSITES assist.

tic noun TWITCH, spasm, jerk.

ticket noun ❶ PASS, token, stub, coupon, card. ❷ LABEL, tag, tally.

tickle verb ❶ STROKE, pet, touch. ❷ AMUSE, entertain, divert, cheer, gladden.

tide noun TIDAL FLOW, tidewater, tide race, flow, ebb, current, stream.

tidings plural noun NEWS, notification, word, communication, information, intelligence, advice, reports.

tidy adjective ❶ NEAT, trim, orderly, in order, in good order, well ordered, spruce, shipshape, well kept, clean, spick and span. ❷ ORDERLY, organized, well organized, methodical, systematic, businesslike.
– OPPOSITES untidy.
▶ verb CLEAN, clean up, put to rights, put in order, straighten, make shipshape, spruce up, groom, smarten, neaten, brush down.

tie verb ❶ TIE UP, fasten, attach, fix, bind, secure, tether, moor, lash, join, connect, link, couple, rope, chain. ❷ DRAW, be equal, be even, be neck and neck.

tier noun ROW, rank, bank, line, layer, level, storey.

tight adjective ❶ FAST, secure, fixed, clenched, clinched. ❷ TAUT, rigid, stiff, tense, stretched, strained. ❸ CRAMPED, restricted, limited, constricted. ❹ **security was tight**: STRICT, rigorous, stringent, tough, rigid, uncompromising, exacting. ❺ **a tight race**: CLOSE, even, evenly matched, neck and neck.
– OPPOSITES loose, slack.

tighten verb ❶ TAUTEN, make tight/taut, stretch, make rigid, rigidify, stiffen, tense. ❷ **tighten security**: INCREASE, make stricter, make rigorous/stringent/rigid.
– OPPOSITES slacken.

till verb CULTIVATE, work, farm, plough, dig, turn over.

tilt verb LEAN, list, slope, slant, incline, tip, cant.

time noun ❶ AGE, era, epoch, period. ❷ WHILE, spell, stretch, span, period, term. ❸ OCCASION, point, juncture. ❹ MOMENT, point, instant, stage. ❺ RHYTHM, measure, tempo, beat, metre.
▶ verb ❶ CLOCK, measure, calculate, regulate, count. ❷ SCHEDULE, arrange, fix, set, timetable, programme.

timeless adjective AGELESS, enduring, lasting, permanent, abiding, unending, ceaseless, undying, deathless, eternal, everlasting, immortal, changeless.
– OPPOSITES ephemeral.

timely adjective OPPORTUNE, well timed, convenient, appropriate, seasonable, felicitous.
– OPPOSITES ill-timed.

timetable noun SCHEDULE, programme, calendar, list, agenda.
▶ verb SCHEDULE, fix, set, programme.

timid adjective ❶ FEARFUL, apprehensive, timorous, afraid, frightened, scared, faint-hearted, cowardly, pusillanimous; *informal* chicken, yellow, lily-livered. ❷ SHY, diffident, bashful, reticent, timorous, shrinking, retiring, coy, demure.
– OPPOSITES bold.

tingle verb PRICKLE, prick, tickle, itch, sting, quiver, tremble.
▶ noun TINGLING, prickling, pricking, tickle, itch, quiver, trembling, pins and needles.

tinker
■ **tinker with** FIDDLE WITH, play with, toy with, tamper with, fool around with, mess about with.

tint noun SHADE, colour, tone, tinge, cast, tincture.

tiny adjective MINUTE, diminutive, miniature, mini, minuscule, infinitesimal, microscopic, dwarfish, midget, pocket-sized, Lilliputian, wee, small, little, insignificant, trifling, negligible, inconsequential; *informal* teeny, teeny-weeny, itsy-bitsy, pint-sized.
– OPPOSITES huge.

tip[1] noun ❶ POINT, peak, top, summit, apex, crown. ❷ END, extremity, point.
▶ verb CAP, top, crown.

tip[2] noun RUBBISH DUMP, dump, refuse dump, rubbish heap, midden.
▶ verb ❶ TILT, lean, list, cant, slant, topple, overturn, fall over, turn topsy-turvy, capsize. ❷ POUR, empty, unload, dump.

tirade noun DIATRIBE, harangue, stream of abuse, verbal onslaught, lecture, upbraiding.

tire verb ❶ FATIGUE, wear out, weary, exhaust, drain, enervate, debilitate, jade; *informal* take it out of, whack; *Brit. informal* fag out, knacker; *N. Amer. informal* poop; *Austral./NZ informal* bush. ❷ GET/GROW/BECOME TIRED, get fatigued, flag, droop.

tired adjective FATIGUED, worn out, weary, wearied, exhausted, drained, enervated, debilitated, jaded; *informal* done, done in, all in, dead beat, dog-tired, whacked, dead on one's feet, ready to drop; *Brit. informal* fagged out, knackered; *N. Amer. informal* pooped; *Austral./NZ informal* bush.
– OPPOSITES energetic, fresh.

tireless adjective UNTIRING, unflagging, indefatigable, energetic, industrious, vigorous, determined, resolute, dogged.
– OPPOSITES lazy.

tiresome adjective ❶ WEARISOME, laborious, wearing, tedious, boring, monotonous, dull, uninteresting, unexciting, humdrum, routine. ❷ TROUBLESOME, irksome, vexatious, irritating, annoying, exasperating, trying.
– OPPOSITES interesting, pleasant.

tiring adjective WEARYING, wearing, fatiguing, exhausting, draining, enervating, arduous, laborious, strenuous, exacting, taxing.

titillate verb EXCITE, arouse, stimulate, provoke, thrill, interest, fascinate, tantalize, seduce; *informal* turn on.

title noun ❶ NAME, designation, appellation, epithet, sobriquet; *informal* moniker, handle; *formal* denomination. ❷ ENTITLEMENT, right, claim, ownership, proprietorship, possession, holding.

▶ verb ENTITLE, name, call, designate, label, tag, style, term.

titter noun SNICKER, snigger, giggle, laugh, chuckle, chortle.

titular adjective NOMINAL, so-called, self-styled, soi-disant, token, puppet, putative.

toast verb ❶ BROWN, crisp, warm up, heat, heat up. ❷ DRINK THE HEALTH OF, drink to, pledge, salute.

toddle verb TOTTER, teeter, wobble, falter, dodder.

together adverb WITH EACH OTHER, in conjunction, jointly, in cooperation, as one, in unison, side by side, hand in hand, hand in glove, shoulder to shoulder, cheek by jowl.
– OPPOSITES separately.

toilet noun LAVATORY, ladies' room, powder room, convenience, outhouse, urinal, latrine, privy; *N. Amer.* washroom, bathroom; *informal* loo, bog, WC; *N. Amer. informal* john, can.

token noun ❶ SYMBOL, sign, emblem, badge, representation, indication, mark, manifestation. ❷ MEMENTO, souvenir, keepsake, remembrance, reminder, memorial.
▶ adjective PERFUNCTORY, superficial, nominal, slight, hollow.

tolerable adjective ❶ ENDURABLE, bearable, sufferable, supportable, acceptable. ❷ FAIRLY GOOD, fair, all right, passable, adequate, satisfactory, average, mediocre, ordinary, run-of-the-mill, indifferent, unexceptional; *informal* not bad, OK.
– OPPOSITES intolerable.

tolerance noun ❶ TOLERATION, open-mindedness, lack of prejudice, broad-mindedness, liberalism, forbearance, patience, magnanimity, understanding, charity, lenience. ❷ ENDURANCE, sufferance, acceptance.

tolerant adjective OPEN-MINDED, unprejudiced, unbiased, broad-minded, liberal, catholic, forbearing, long-suffering, magnanimous, sympathetic, understanding, charitable, lenient, indulgent, permissive, free and easy, easy-going.
– OPPOSITES intolerant.

tolerate verb ❶ PERMIT, allow, sanction, accept, countenance; *formal* brook. ❷ ENDURE, bear, suffer, take, stand, put up with, abide, accept, stomach, submit to.

toll noun ❶ CHARGE, fee, payment, levy, tariff. ❷ **a heavy toll**: COST, damage, loss, inroads.

tomb noun GRAVE, burial place/chamber, sepulchre, vault, crypt, catacomb, mausoleum.

tone noun ❶ SOUND, sound quality, colour, pitch, timbre, tonality. ❷ TONE OF VOICE, expression, intonation, inflection, modulation, accentuation. ❸ MOOD, air, attitude, character, manner, spirit, temper, tenor, vein, drift.

tongue noun LANGUAGE, speech, parlance, dialect, idiom, patois, vernacular; *informal* lingo.

tonic noun RESTORATIVE, stimulant, analeptic; *informal* pick-me-up.

tool noun IMPLEMENT, instrument, utensil, device, apparatus, gadget, appliance, machine, contrivance, contraption, aid.

top noun ❶ HIGHEST POINT/PART, summit, peak, pinnacle, crest, crown, tip, apex, vertex, apogee. ❷ UPPER PART, upper surface, upper layer. ❸ CAP, lid, stopper, cork, cover.
– OPPOSITES bottom.

▶ adjective ❶ TOPMOST, uppermost, highest. ❷ FOREMOST, leading, principal, pre-eminent, greatest, finest. ❸ MAXIMUM, maximal, greatest, utmost.
– OPPOSITES lowest, minimum.
▶ verb ❶ CAP, cover, finish, garnish. ❷ HEAD, lead, be first in. ❸ SURPASS, exceed, go beyond, transcend, better, best, beat, excel, outstrip, outdo, outshine, eclipse.

topic noun SUBJECT, theme, issue, matter, question, argument, thesis.

topical adjective CURRENT, up to date, up to the minute, contemporary, popular.
– OPPOSITES out of date.

topple verb ❶ FALL OVER, tip over, keel over, overturn, overbalance, capsize. ❷ OVERTHROW, oust, unseat, overturn, bring down, bring low.

torment noun AGONY, suffering, torture, pain, excruciation, anguish, hell, misery, distress, affliction, wretchedness.
▶ verb CAUSE AGONY/SUFFERING/PAIN TO, afflict, harrow, plague, torture, distress, worry, trouble.

torn adjective ❶ RIPPED, split, slit, cut, lacerated, rent. ❷ DIVIDED, wavering, vacillating, irresolute, uncertain, unsure, undecided.

torrent noun FLOOD, deluge, inundation, spate, cascade, rush, stream, current, downpour, rainstorm.
– OPPOSITES trickle.

tortuous adjective TWISTING, winding, curving, curvy, sinuous, undulating, coiling, serpentine, snaking, snaky, zigzag, convoluted, meandering.
– OPPOSITES straight.

torture noun ❶ ABUSE, ill-treatment, punishment, torment. ❷ AGONY, suffering, pain, excruciation, anguish, misery, distress.
▶ verb ❶ INFLICT PAIN/SUFFERING ON, abuse, ill-treat, punish, torment; *informal* work over. ❷ TORMENT, afflict, harrow, plague, distress, worry, trouble.

toss verb ❶ THROW, hurl, cast, sling, pitch, shy, lob, propel, launch, project; *informal* heave, chuck. ❷ ROLL, sway, undulate, pitch, lurch, heave.

total noun SUM, sum total, aggregate, whole, entirety, totality.
▶ adjective ❶ the total amount: COMPLETE, entire, whole, full, comprehensive, combined, aggregate, composite, integral. ❷ a total idiot: COMPLETE, thorough, utter, absolute, downright, out-and-out, outright, unmitigated, unqualified.
▶ verb ❶ ADD UP TO, come to, amount to. ❷ ADD UP, count, reckon, tot up.

totalitarian adjective AUTOCRATIC, authoritarian, absolute, despotic, dictatorial, tyrannical, undemocratic, oppressive.
– OPPOSITES democratic.

totter verb TEETER, wobble, stagger, stumble, reel, sway, roll, lurch.

touch verb ❶ BE IN CONTACT, come into contact, come together, meet, converge, be contiguous, adjoin, abut. ❷ PRESS LIGHTLY, tap, brush, graze, feel, stroke, pat, fondle, caress. ❸ AFFECT, move, make an impression on, influence, upset, disturb, make sad, arouse sympathy; *informal* get

to. ❹ REACH, attain, arrive at, come to.
▶ **noun** ❶ FEEL, feeling, sense of touch, tactile sense, tactility. ❷ TEXTURE, feel, grain, finish, surface, coating. ❸ BIT, trace, dash, taste, spot, drop, pinch, speck, smack, suggestion, hint, soupçon, tinge, whiff, suspicion.

touching **adjective** MOVING, impressive, affecting, warming, heart-warming.

touchy **adjective** SENSITIVE, oversensitive, hypersensitive, thin-skinned, tetchy, testy, irascible, irritable, grouchy, grumpy, peevish, querulous, bad-tempered, captious, crabbed, cross, surly.

tough **adjective** ❶ STRONG, durable, resistant, resilient, sturdy, firm, solid, hard, rigid, stiff. ❷ CHEWY, leathery, gristly, stringy, fibrous, sinewy. ❸ HARDY, strong, fit, sturdy, rugged, stalwart, vigorous, strapping, robust, resilient. ❹ **a tough job**: DIFFICULT, hard, arduous, onerous, laborious, strenuous, exacting, taxing, stressful. ❺ **tough on crime**: FIRM, strict, stern, severe, harsh, hard-hitting, adamant, inflexible. ❻ **that's tough**: UNFORTUNATE, unlucky, hard, regrettable; *informal* too bad.
– OPPOSITES tender, easy, lax.

toughen **verb** STRENGTHEN, fortify, reinforce, harden.

tour **noun** TRIP, excursion, journey, expedition, jaunt, outing, peregrination.
▶ **verb** TRAVEL ROUND/THROUGH, explore, holiday in, go round, visit.

tourist **noun** VISITOR, sightseer, holidaymaker, tripper.

tournament **noun** COMPETITION, contest, series, meeting, event.

tout
■ **tout for** ASK FOR, solicit, seek, petition for, appeal for, beg for.

tow **verb** PULL, draw, drag, haul, tug, trail, lug.

towering **adjective** ❶ HIGH, tall, lofty, elevated, sky-high. ❷ **a towering intellect**: OUTSTANDING, extraordinary, pre-eminent, superior, great, incomparable, unrivalled, peerless.

toxic **adjective** POISONOUS, venomous, virulent, noxious.
– OPPOSITES harmless.

trace **noun** ❶ MARK, sign, vestige, indication, evidence, remains, remnant. ❷ BIT, hint, suggestion, suspicion, trifle, dash, tinge, jot, iota.
▶ **verb** FIND, discover, detect, unearth, uncover, track down, turn up, ferret out, hunt down; *informal* dig up.

track **noun** ❶ MARK, trace, impression, footprint, trail, spoor, scent. ❷ PATH, line, course, orbit, route, trajectory. ❸ PATH, trail, route, way.
▶ **verb** FOLLOW, pursue, trail, trace, tail, shadow, stalk, dog.

trade **noun** ❶ COMMERCE, buying and selling, dealing, trafficking, business, merchandising. ❷ LINE OF WORK, line, occupation, job, career, profession, craft, vocation, calling, work, employment.
▶ **verb** ❶ BUY AND SELL, deal, traffic, market, merchandise. ❷ SWAP, exchange, switch, barter.

trader **noun** MERCHANT, dealer, buyer, seller, marketer, merchandiser, broker, tradesman, tradeswoman.

tradition **noun** CUSTOM, belief,

practice, convention, ritual, observance, habit, institution, usage, praxis.

traditional adjective CUSTOMARY, accustomed, conventional, established, ritual, ritualistic, habitual, set, fixed, routine, usual, old, time-honoured, historic, folk; *poetic/literary* wonted.

traduce verb DEFAME, slander, speak ill of, misrepresent, malign, vilify, blacken someone's name, cast aspersions on; *formal* calumniate.

tragedy noun DISASTER, calamity, catastrophe, misfortune, misadventure, affliction, adversity.

tragic adjective ❶ DISASTROUS, calamitous, catastrophic, fatal, terrible, dreadful, appalling, dire, awful, miserable, wretched, unfortunate. ❷ SAD, unhappy, pathetic, moving, distressing, pitiful, piteous, melancholy, doleful, mournful, dismal, gloomy.
– OPPOSITES fortunate, happy.

trail noun ❶ TRACK, scent, spoor, traces, marks, signs, footprints. ❷ PATH, pathway, footpath, track, road, route.
▶ verb ❶ DRAG, sweep, dangle, hang down, droop. ❷ FOLLOW, pursue, track, trace, tail, shadow, stalk, dog. ❸ LOSE, be down, be behind.

train noun ❶ PROCESSION, line, file, column, convoy, caravan. ❷ RETINUE, entourage, following, staff, household, followers, attendants.
▶ verb ❶ INSTRUCT, teach, coach, tutor, give lessons to, school, educate, drill, prepare, ground, guide. ❷ EXERCISE, do exercises, work out, practise, prepare. ❸ AIM, point, focus, direct, level, line up.

trait noun CHARACTERISTIC, attribute, feature, quality, property, idiosyncrasy, peculiarity, quirk.

traitor noun BETRAYER, turncoat, double-crosser, double-dealer, renegade, defector, deserter, apostate, Judas, quisling, fifth columnist.

traitorous adjective TREACHEROUS, double-crossing, double-dealing, disloyal, faithless, unfaithful, perfidious, false-hearted, false, untrue, renegade, apostate.
– OPPOSITES loyal.

trample verb TRAMP ON, tread on, walk over, stamp on, squash, crush, flatten.

trance noun DAZE, stupor, hypnotic state, dream, reverie, brown study.

tranquil adjective PEACEFUL, restful, reposeful, calm, quiet, still, serene, placid, undisturbed.

tranquillizer noun SEDATIVE, opiate; *informal* downer.
– OPPOSITES stimulant.

transaction noun BUSINESS, deal, undertaking, affair, bargain, negotiation.

transcend verb GO BEYOND, exceed, overstep, rise above, surpass, excel, be superior to, outdo, outstrip.

transfer verb ❶ CONVEY, move, shift, remove, take, carry, transport. ❷ MAKE OVER, turn over, sign over, hand on, hand down, pass on, transmit, assign, delegate.

transform verb CHANGE, alter,

convert, metamorphose, revolutionize, transfigure, transmogrify, remodel, redo, reconstruct, rebuild, reorganize, rearrange, renew, translate, transmute.

transformation noun CHANGE, alteration, conversion, metamorphosis, sea change, revolution, transfiguration, transmogrification, remodelling, reconstruction, reorganization, renewal, transmutation.

transgress verb GO BEYOND, overstep, exceed, infringe, breach, break, contravene, violate, defy, disobey.

transient adjective TRANSITORY, short-lived, short-term, impermanent, temporary, brief, short, ephemeral, evanescent, momentary, fleeting, flying, passing.
– OPPOSITES permanent.

transit noun MOVEMENT, transport, transportation, conveyance, haulage, travel, journeying, passage.

transition noun CHANGE, transformation, conversion, metamorphosis, shift, switch, jump, leap, progression, gradation, development, evolution, transmutation.

translate verb RENDER, interpret, paraphrase, reword, convert, decipher, decode, explain, elucidate.

transmission noun ❶ SENDING, conveyance, transport, dispatch, remission. ❷ BROADCASTING, relaying, sending out. ❸ BROADCAST, programme.

transmit verb ❶ SEND, convey, transport, dispatch, forward, remit. ❷ TRANSFER, pass on, hand on, communicate, impart, disseminate, spread, carry, diffuse. ❸ BROADCAST, relay, send out, put on air.

transparent adjective ❶ CLEAR, see-through, translucent, pellucid, crystal-clear, crystalline, limpid, glassy, transpicuous. ❷ *See* OBVIOUS.
– OPPOSITES opaque.

transpire verb COME ABOUT, take place, happen, occur, turn up, arise, chance; *poetic/literary* befall.

transport verb CONVEY, take, transfer, move, shift, bring, fetch, carry, bear, haul, cart, run, ship.
► noun TRANSPORTATION, conveyance, transit, carriage, freight.

transpose verb INTERCHANGE, exchange, switch, swap, transfer, reverse, invert, rearrange, reorder.

transverse adjective CROSSWISE, crossways, cross, athwart.

trap noun SNARE, net, mesh, gin, ambush, pitfall, booby trap.
► verb ❶ SNARE, ensnare, enmesh, entrap, catch, corner. ❷ TRICK, dupe, deceive, lure, inveigle, beguile.

trappings plural noun ACCOUTREMENTS, appurtenances, appointments, trimmings, paraphernalia, fittings, equipment, apparatus, gear, adornment, ornamentation, decoration, finery, frippery, panoply.

trash noun ❶ RUBBISH, waste, refuse, litter, garbage. ❷ RIFF-RAFF, scum, rabble, vermin, good-for-nothings.

traumatic adjective PAINFUL, agonizing, shocking, scarring, disturbing, distressing, damaging, injurious, harmful.

travel verb JOURNEY, take a trip, tour, voyage, cross, traverse, cover, wander, ramble, roam, rove.
▶ noun TRAVELLING, journeying, touring.

traveller noun TRIPPER, tourer, tourist, explorer, passenger, voyager, holidaymaker, sightseer, globetrotter.

traverse verb CROSS, go across, travel over, journey over, make one's way across, pass over, wander, roam, range.

treacherous adjective ❶ *See* TRAITOROUS. ❷ **treacherous roads:** HAZARDOUS, dangerous, unsafe, flooded, icy, ice-covered, slippery.

tread verb WALK, step, go, pace, march, tramp.
■ **tread on** RIDE ROUGHSHOD OVER, oppress, repress, suppress, subdue, subjugate, quell, crush.

treason noun BETRAYAL, treachery, disloyalty, faithlessness, sedition, subversion, mutiny, rebellion, lese-majesty.

treasure noun RICHES, valuables, wealth, fortune, hoard, jewels, gems, coins, gold.
▶ verb VALUE, prize, set great store by, think highly of, hold dear.

treat noun SURPRISE, celebration, entertainment, amusement, diversion.
▶ verb ❶ ACT TOWARDS, behave towards, deal with, handle, cope with, contend with, manage, use. ❷ REGARD, consider, view, look upon, deal with. ❸ GIVE TREATMENT TO, medicate, doctor, nurse, care for, attend to, minister to, cure, heal. ❹ **treat with chemicals:** APPLY TO, put on, use on, ply with. ❺ **treat to dinner:** PAY FOR, buy for, pay/foot the bill for, stand, finance, entertain, take out.

treatise noun DISCOURSE, exposition, disquisition, dissertation, thesis, study, essay, paper, monograph, tract, pamphlet.

treatment noun ❶ ACTION, behaviour, conduct, handling, management, use, dealings. ❷ MEDICAL CARE, medication, medicament, therapy, doctoring, nursing, first aid, care, ministration.

treaty noun AGREEMENT, pact, deal, compact, covenant, bargain, pledge, contract, alliance, concordat, convention, entente.

trek verb TRAMP, hike, trudge, march, slog, footslog, plod, walk, ramble, roam, range, rove, travel, journey; *Brit. informal* yomp.
▶ noun EXPEDITION, trip, journey, trudge, tramp, hike, march, slog, walk, odyssey.

tremble verb SHAKE, quiver, shudder, judder, teeter, totter, wobble, rock, vibrate, oscillate.

tremendous adjective ❶ **tremendous size:** GREAT, huge, enormous, immense, massive, vast, colossal, prodigious, stupendous, gigantic, gargantuan, mammoth. ❷ **a tremendous player:** EXCELLENT, very good, great, marvellous, remarkable, extraordinary, exceptional, wonderful, incredible; *informal* super, fabulous, terrific, fantastic.

tremor noun TREMBLE, shake, shaking, shiver, quiver, twitch, judder, spasm, paroxysm.

trend noun ❶ TENDENCY, drift, course, direction, bearing, current, inclination, bias, leaning, bent. ❷ FASHION, vogue, style, mode, look, craze; *informal* fad.

trendy adjective *see* FASHIONABLE.

trespass verb INTRUDE, encroach, infringe, invade, obtrude.

trial noun ❶ COURT CASE, case, hearing, inquiry, tribunal, litigation. ❷ TEST, try-out, trial/test run, check, assay, experiment; *informal* dry run. ❸ NUISANCE, pest, bother, worry, vexation, annoyance, irritant, irritation, bane, affliction, curse, burden, cross to bear; *informal* pain in the neck, hassle.

tribe noun ETHNIC GROUP, family, dynasty, clan, sect.

tribute noun ACCOLADE, commendation, testimonial, paean, eulogy, panegyric, encomium, applause, praise, homage, honour, exaltation, extolment, glorification, congratulations, compliments, bouquets; *formal* laudation.

trick noun ❶ STRATAGEM, ploy, artifice, ruse, dodge, wile, device, manoeuvre, deceit, deception, subterfuge, swindle, fraud; *informal* con. ❷ KNACK, art, gift, talent, technique, ability, skill, expertise; *informal* know-how. ❸ HOAX, practical joke, joke, prank, jape, antic, caper, frolic, lark, gambol; *informal* leg-pull, gag, put-on. ❹ SLEIGHT OF HAND, legerdemain, prestidigitation.
▶ verb DECEIVE, delude, mislead, take in, cheat, hoodwink, fool, outwit, dupe, hoax, gull, defraud, swindle; *informal* con, pull a fast one on, put one over on; *poetic/literary* cozen.

trickery noun DECEIT, deception, cheating, subterfuge, guile, artifice, wiliness, craftiness, chicanery, dishonesty, fraud, swindling, imposture, double-dealing, duplicity; *informal* monkey/funny business, hanky-panky; *Brit. informal* jiggery-pokery.
– OPPOSITES honesty.

trickle verb DRIP, dribble, leak, ooze, seep, exude, percolate.
– OPPOSITES pour, gush.

tricky adjective ❶ a tricky situation: DIFFICULT, problematic, awkward, delicate, sensitive, ticklish, thorny, knotty, touchy, risky. ❷ a tricky character: CUNNING, crafty, wily, artful, devious, scheming, sly, slippery, subtle, deceitful, deceptive; *informal* foxy.
– OPPOSITES honest.

trim adjective NEAT, tidy, neat and tidy, smart, spruce, well groomed, well dressed, well turned out, dapper, elegant; *informal* natty.
– OPPOSITES untidy.
▶ verb CUT, clip, snip, shear, prune, pare, even up, neaten, tidy up.

trip noun ❶ EXCURSION, tour, expedition, voyage, jaunt, outing, run. ❷ HALLUCINATION, drug experience, vision.
▶ verb ❶ STUMBLE, lose one's footing/balance, stagger, slip, slide, misstep, fall, tumble. ❷ SKIP, dance, hop, prance, bound, spring, gambol, caper, frisk, cavort, waltz. ❸ HALLUCINATE; *informal* get stoned/high.

triple adjective THREE TIMES, three times as much as, threefold, treble.

triumph noun ❶ CONQUEST, victory, win, ascendancy, mastery, success; *informal* walkover. ❷ EXULTATION, jubilation,

jubilance, elation, rejoicing, joy, joyfulness, pride.
– OPPOSITES failure, despair.
▶ **verb** WIN, succeed, come first, be the victor, be victorious, gain a victory, carry the day, take the honours/prize/crown.

triumphant **adjective** ❶ WINNING, victorious, successful, undefeated, unbeaten. ❷ EXULTANT, jubilant, elated, rejoicing, joyful, joyous, proud, cock-a-hoop, gloating, boastful.
– OPPOSITES unsuccessful, despondent.

trivial **adjective** UNIMPORTANT, insignificant, inconsequential, flimsy, insubstantial, petty, minor, of no account/matter, negligible, paltry, trifling, foolish, worthless; *informal* piddling.
– OPPOSITES significant.

troops **plural noun** ARMED FORCES, army, military, services, soldiers, soldiery, fighting men/women.

trouble **noun** ❶ PROBLEMS, worry, bother, anxiety, disquiet, unease, irritation, vexation, inconvenience, annoyance, agitation, harassment, difficulty, distress. ❷ DIFFICULTY, misfortune, adversity, hardship, bad luck, distress, pain, suffering, affliction, torment, woe, grief, unhappiness, sadness, heartache. ❸ **don't go to any trouble**: BOTHER, inconvenience, disturbance, fuss, effort, exertion, work, labour, attention, care, thoughtfulness; *informal* hassle. ❹ **stomach trouble**: DISORDER, disease, illness, dysfunction. ❺ **trouble at the match**: DISTURBANCE, disorder, unrest, fighting, strife, conflict, tumult, commotion, turbulence, law-breaking.
▶ **verb** ❶ WORRY, bother, disturb, annoy, irritate, vex, irk, fret, pester, torment, plague, inconvenience, upset, perturb, agitate, discompose, harass, distress; *informal* hassle. ❷ TAKE THE TROUBLE/TIME, bother, make the effort, exert/disturb oneself, go out of one's way.

troublemaker **noun** MISCHIEF-MAKER, agitator, instigator, rabble-rouser, demagogue.

troublesome **adjective** WORRYING, worrisome, bothersome, tiresome, disturbing, annoying, irritating, irksome, upsetting, perturbing, harassing, distressing, difficult, problematic, demanding, taxing.

trounce **verb** DEFEAT, beat, rout, drub, crush, overwhelm; *informal* thrash, make mincemeat of, walk all over, wipe the floor with, hammer, clobber, slaughter, give someone a pasting.

truancy **noun** ABSENTEEISM, absence, French leave, shirking, malingering; *informal* bunking off; *Brit. informal* skiving.

truant **noun** ABSENTEE, dodger, malingerer, shirker, deserter; *Brit. informal* skiver.
▶ **verb** STAY AWAY FROM SCHOOL, play truant; *Brit. informal* skive (off), bunk off; *N. Amer. informal* play hookey, goof off.

truce **noun** CEASE-FIRE, armistice, suspension/cessation of hostilities, peace, respite, moratorium.

true **adjective** ❶ TRUTHFUL, accurate, correct, right, valid, factual, exact, precise, faithful, genuine, reliable, honest; *formal* veracious. ❷ REAL, genuine, authentic, actual, bona fide, valid,

legitimate; *informal* honest-to-goodness. ❸ **true to his friends**: LOYAL, faithful, trustworthy, trusty, reliable, dependable, staunch, firm, fast, steady, constant, unswerving, unwavering, devoted, sincere, dedicated, supportive, dutiful.
– OPPOSITES untrue, false.

trump verb SURPASS, outperform, outdo.
■ **trump up** INVENT, make up, fabricate, devise, concoct, hatch, contrive, fake; *informal* cook up.

trust noun ❶ FAITH, confidence, belief, conviction, credence, assurance, certainty, reliance, hope, expectation.
❷ RESPONSIBILITY, duty, obligation, commitment.
▶ verb ❶ PUT/PLACE ONE'S TRUST IN, have faith/confidence in, be convinced by, pin one's hopes on. ❷ HOPE, assume, presume, expect, believe, suppose.
– OPPOSITES distrust.

trustful adjective TRUSTING, unsuspicious, unguarded, unwary, unsuspecting, unquestioning, credulous, gullible, ingenuous, naive, innocent.
– OPPOSITES suspicious.

trustworthy adjective RELIABLE, dependable, stable, staunch, loyal, faithful, trusty, responsible, sensible, level-headed, honest, honourable, upright, ethical, righteous, principled, virtuous.
– OPPOSITES untrustworthy.

truth noun ❶ TRUTHFULNESS, accuracy, correctness, rightness, validity, fact, factualness, factuality, genuineness, veracity, verity, honesty. ❷ REALITY, actuality, factuality.
– OPPOSITES falsehood, fiction.

truthful adjective ❶ HONEST, trustworthy, candid, frank, open, forthright, straight; *formal* veracious. ❷ **a truthful account**: TRUE, accurate, correct, right, valid, factual, exact, faithful, precise, genuine, reliable, honest; *formal* veracious.
– OPPOSITES untruthful, inaccurate.

try verb ❶ ATTEMPT, aim, endeavour, make an effort, exert oneself, undertake, strive, assay, seek, struggle, do one's best; *informal* have a go/shot/crack/stab.
❷ TRY OUT, test, put to the test, experiment with, assay, investigate, examine, appraise, evaluate, assess, experience, sample; *informal* check out.

trying adjective TROUBLESOME, bothersome, tiresome, irksome, vexatious, annoying, irritating, exasperating.

tuck verb GATHER, push, ease, insert, stuff.
■ **tuck into** EAT HEARTILY, gobble up, wolf down; *informal* get stuck into.

tug verb PULL, jerk, yank, wrench, drag, draw.

tumble verb FALL OVER, fall down, fall headlong, topple, fall head over heels, fall end over end, lose one's footing/balance, stumble, stagger, trip up.
– OPPOSITES rise.

tumbledown adjective DILAPIDATED, ramshackle, crumbling, disintegrating, falling to pieces/bits, decrepit, ruined, in ruins, rickety, shaky, tottering, teetering.

tumour noun LUMP, growth, swelling, excrescence, protuberance, tumefaction, intumescence.

tumult noun DIN, uproar, commotion, racket, hubbub, hullabaloo, clamour, shouting, yelling, pandemonium, babel, bedlam, noise.
– OPPOSITES tranquillity.

tumultuous adjective LOUD, noisy, clamorous, ear-shattering, deafening, ear-piercing, blaring, uproarious, unrestrained, boisterous, rowdy, unruly, disorderly, fierce, obstreperous, wild, violent.

tune noun MELODY, air, song, theme, strain, motif.

tunnel noun UNDERGROUND/ SUBTERRANEAN PASSAGE, underpass, subway, burrow.
▶ verb DIG, excavate, burrow, mine, penetrate.

turbulent adjective ❶ turbulent seas: TEMPESTUOUS, stormy, raging, foaming, rough, choppy, agitated. ❷ turbulent crowds: ROWDY, unruly, boisterous, disorderly, restless, agitated, obstreperous, wild, violent, lawless, noisy. ❸ turbulent emotions: DISTURBED, agitated, unsettled, unstable, troubled, distraught, in turmoil.
– OPPOSITES peaceful.

turgid adjective ❶ SWOLLEN, enlarged, bloated, distended, tumescent. ❷ BOMBASTIC, high-flown, high-sounding, rhetorical, oratorical, grandiloquent, magniloquent, extravagant, pretentious, pompous, flowery, fulsome, orotund, fustian.
– OPPOSITES simple.

turmoil noun AGITATION, ferment, confusion, disorder, disarray, upheaval, chaos, pandemonium, bedlam, tumult.
– OPPOSITES peace.

turn verb ❶ GO ROUND, rotate, revolve, circle, roll, spin, wheel, whirl, twirl, gyrate, swivel, pivot. ❷ TURN ROUND, change direction/ course, go back, return, reverse direction, make a U-turn. ❸ TURN OVER, reverse, invert, flip over, turn topsy-turvy. ❹ CHANGE, alter, transform, metamorphose, mutate. ❺ he turned nasty: BECOME, come to be, get, go. ❻ GO/ TURN SOUR, sour, curdle, become rancid, go bad, go off.
▶ noun ❶ ROTATION, revolution, circle, spin, whirl, twirl, gyration, swivel. ❷ TURNING, bend, curve, corner, twist, winding. ❸ it's your turn: TIME, opportunity, chance, stint, spell, move, try, attempt; *informal* go, shot, crack.
■ **turn down** *see* REJECT verb (1). **turn in** HAND IN, give in, submit, tender, hand over, deliver, return, give back, surrender. **turn up** ❶ INCREASE, raise, amplify, make louder, intensify. ❷ ARRIVE, appear, put in an appearance, present oneself, be present; *informal* show, show up.

turnover noun ❶ (GROSS) REVENUE, income, volume of business, business, financial flow. ❷ turnover of staff: RATE OF REPLACEMENT, change, movement.

tutor verb TEACH, instruct, coach, educate, school, train, drill, direct, guide.

twig noun BRANCH, stick, offshoot, shoot, spray, stem.

twilight noun DUSK, late afternoon, early evening, gloaming; *poetic/literary* crepuscule.

twin noun DOUBLE, lookalike, image, duplicate, clone; *informal* spitting image, spit, dead spit, dead ringer.
▶ verb JOIN, link, couple, pair, yoke.

twinge **noun** STAB OF PAIN, spasm, pain, pang, ache, throb, tweak, tingle, cramp, stitch.

twist **verb** ❶ BEND, warp, misshape, deform, contort, distort, wrench, wrest. ❷ **twisted his ankle:** WRENCH, turn, sprain, rick. ❸ **the path twisted:** WIND, curve, bend, twine, zigzag, meander, snake, worm. ❹ **twist their words:** DISTORT, pervert, warp, garble, misrepresent, falsify, misquote, misreport, change, alter.
▶ **noun** ❶ BEND, warp, kink, deformity, contortion, distortion. ❷ WRENCH, turn, sprain, rick. ❸ **a twist in the tale:** DEVELOPMENT, turn, change, alteration, variation, slant.

twitch **verb** JERK, jump, quiver, shiver, quaver.
▶ **noun** SPASM, jerk, jump, quiver, tremor, shiver, quaver.

two-faced **adjective** HYPOCRITICAL, insincere, deceitful, duplicitous, false, untrustworthy.
– OPPOSITES sincere.

type **noun** ❶ KIND, sort, variety, form, class, classification, category, group, order, set, genre, strain, species, genus, ilk. ❷ PRINT, fount, face, character.

typical **adjective** ❶ REPRESENTATIVE, classic, standard, stock, orthodox, conventional, true to type, quintessential, archetypal. ❷ NORMAL, average, ordinary, regular, general, customary, habitual, routine. ❸ CHARACTERISTIC, in character, in keeping, to be expected.
– OPPOSITES atypical.

typify **verb** EXEMPLIFY, characterize, personify, epitomize, symbolize, embody.

tyrannical **adjective** DESPOTIC, autocratic, dictatorial, authoritarian, high-handed, imperious, oppressive, coercive, domineering, bullying, harsh, strict, severe, cruel, brutal, unjust.

tyrant **noun** DESPOT, autocrat, dictator, absolute ruler, authoritarian, oppressor, martinet, slave-driver, bully.

Uu

ubiquitous **adjective** EVERYWHERE, omnipresent, ever-present, all-over, pervasive, universal.
– OPPOSITES rare.

ugly **adjective** ❶ UNATTRACTIVE, plain, homely, ill-favoured, unprepossessing, hideous, unlovely, unsightly, grotesque, horrible, horrid, frightful, vile, shocking, distasteful, disgusting, revolting; *informal* not much to look at. ❷ **an ugly situation:** THREATENING, menacing, ominous, sinister, dangerous, nasty, unpleasant, disagreeable.
– OPPOSITES beautiful.

ulterior **adjective** HIDDEN, concealed, unrevealed,

undisclosed, secret, covert, unapparent.
– OPPOSITES overt.

ultimate adjective ❶ LAST, final, eventual, concluding, conclusive, terminal, end, furthest. ❷ BASIC, fundamental, primary, elemental, radical.

umpire noun ADJUDICATOR, arbitrator, arbiter, judge, moderator, referee; *informal* ref.

unable adjective NOT ABLE, incapable, powerless, impotent, not up/equal to, inadequate, ineffectual, incompetent.
– OPPOSITES able.

unacceptable adjective UNSATISFACTORY, inadmissible, unsuitable, insupportable, intolerable, objectionable, offensive, obnoxious, undesirable, disagreeable, distasteful, improper.
– OPPOSITES acceptable.

unaccompanied adjective ALONE, on one's own, by oneself, solo, lone, solitary, single.

unaccustomed adjective UNUSED, not used, new, unpractised, unfamiliar, inexperienced, unversed.

unanimity noun AGREEMENT, accord, unity, consensus, like-mindedness; *formal* concord.
– OPPOSITES disagreement.

unanimous adjective IN COMPLETE AGREEMENT/ACCORD, of one mind, like-minded, in harmony, at one, of a piece, with one voice, united, concordant.
– OPPOSITES divided.

unassailable adjective IMPREGNABLE, invulnerable, invincible, secure, well defended.
– OPPOSITES defenceless.

unassuming adjective *see* MODEST (1).

unattached adjective UNMARRIED, unwed, unwedded, uncommitted, free, available, single, on one's own, by oneself, unescorted.
– OPPOSITES married.

unauthorized adjective UNOFFICIAL, unsanctioned, uncertified, unaccredited, unlicensed, unwarranted, unapproved, disallowed, prohibited, forbidden, illegal.
– OPPOSITES official.

unavoidable adjective INESCAPABLE, inevitable, bound to happen, inexorable, ineluctable, certain, fated, predestined, necessary, compulsory, required, obligatory, mandatory.

unaware adjective UNKNOWING, unconscious, ignorant, heedless, unmindful, oblivious, uninformed, unenlightened; *informal* inf in the dark.
– OPPOSITES conscious.

unbelievable adjective BEYOND BELIEF, incredible, unconvincing, far-fetched, implausible, improbable, inconceivable, unthinkable, unimaginable, impossible, astonishing, astounding, staggering, preposterous.
– OPPOSITES credible.

unbend verb ❶ STRAIGHTEN, align, flatten. ❷ RELAX, become less formal, unwind, loosen up, let oneself go; *informal* let it all hang out, hang loose.

unbending adjective *see* INFLEXIBLE (3).

unbiased adjective IMPARTIAL, unprejudiced, non-partisan, neutral, objective, disinterested, dispassionate, detached, even-handed, open-minded, equitable, fair, fair-minded, just. – OPPOSITES prejudiced.

unbounded adjective BOUNDLESS, unlimited, limitless, illimitable, infinite, unrestrained, unconstrained, uncontrolled, unchecked, unbridled, vast, immense, immeasurable. – OPPOSITES limited.

unbreakable adjective *see* INDESTRUCTIBLE.

uncertain adjective ❶ UNKNOWN, undetermined, unsettled, in the balance, up in the air. ❷ UNSURE, doubtful, dubious, undecided, unresolved, indecisive, irresolute, hesitant, wavering, vacillating, equivocating, vague, hazy, unclear, ambivalent, in two minds. ❸ an uncertain voice: HESITANT, hesitating, tentative, halting, unsure, unconfident. – OPPOSITES predictable, sure, confident.

uncharted adjective UNMAPPED, unsurveyed, unexplored, unplumbed, unfamiliar, unknown, strange.

uncivilized adjective ❶ BARBARIAN, barbarous, barbaric, primitive, savage, wild. ❷ UNCOUTH, coarse, rough, boorish, vulgar, philistine, uneducated, uncultured, uncultivated, unsophisticated, unrefined, unpolished.

unclean adjective *see* DIRTY adjective (1).

uncomfortable adjective UNEASY, ill at ease, nervous, tense, edgy, self-conscious, awkward, embarrassed, discomfited, disturbed, troubled, worried, anxious, apprehensive. – OPPOSITES relaxed.

uncommon adjective *see* UNUSUAL.

uncompromising adjective INFLEXIBLE, unbending, unyielding, hard-line, tough, immovable, firm, determined, dogged, obstinate, obdurate, tenacious, relentless, implacable, inexorable, intransigent. – OPPOSITES flexible.

unconcerned adjective *see* INDIFFERENT (1).

unconditional adjective COMPLETE, total, entire, full, absolute, downright, utter, all-out, thoroughgoing, unequivocal, conclusive, definite, positive, indubitable.

unconscionable adjective ❶ AMORAL, immoral, unethical, unprincipled, unscrupulous, dishonourable, dishonest, corrupt. ❷ EXCESSIVE, unwarranted, uncalled for, unreasonable, inordinate, immoderate.

unconscious adjective ❶ SENSELESS, insensible, comatose, knocked out, stunned, dazed; *informal* out like a light, out cold, out. ❷ UNAWARE, heedless, ignorant, in ignorance, oblivious, insensible. ❸ an unconscious insult: UNINTENTIONAL, unintended, accidental, unthinking, unwitting, inadvertent, unpremeditated. – OPPOSITES aware.

unconventional adjective UNORTHODOX, irregular, unusual, uncommon, unwonted, rare, out of the ordinary, atypical, singular, individual, individualistic, different, original, idiosyncratic, nonconformist, bohemian, eccentric, odd. – OPPOSITES orthodox.

uncouth adjective ROUGH, coarse, uncivilized, uncultured, uncultivated, unrefined, unpolished, unsophisticated, crude, gross, loutish, boorish, oafish, rude, impolite, discourteous, unmannerly, bad-mannered, ill-bred, vulgar.
– OPPOSITES refined.

uncover verb ❶ EXPOSE, lay bare, bare, reveal, unwrap. ❷ *See* DISCOVER (1).

unctuous adjective SYCOPHANTIC, ingratiating, obsequious, fawning, servile.

undaunted adjective UNAFRAID, unflinching, indomitable, resolute, intrepid, bold, valiant, brave, courageous.
– OPPOSITES fearful.

undemonstrative adjective UNEMOTIONAL, impassive, restrained, self-contained, reserved, uncommunicative, unresponsive, stiff.

underestimate verb ❶ MISCALCULATE, misjudge, set too low. ❷ UNDERRATE, rate too low, undervalue, set little store by, not do justice to.

undergo verb GO THROUGH, experience, sustain, endure, bear, tolerate, stand, withstand, put up with, weather.

underground adjective ❶ SUBTERRANEAN, below ground, buried, sunken. ❷ SECRET, clandestine, surreptitious, covert, undercover, concealed, hidden.

underhand adjective DECEITFUL, devious, sneaky, furtive, surreptitious, covert, dishonest, dishonourable, unscrupulous, fraudulent.
– OPPOSITES honest.

undermine verb ❶ WEAKEN, impair, damage, injure, sap, threaten, subvert, sabotage. ❷ TUNNEL UNDER, dig under, burrow under, excavate.
– OPPOSITES support.

underprivileged adjective DISADVANTAGED, deprived, in need, needy, in want, destitute, poor, impoverished, impecunious.
– OPPOSITES wealthy.

understand verb ❶ COMPREHEND, apprehend, grasp, see, take in, perceive, discern, make out, glean, recognize, appreciate, get to know, follow, fathom; *informal* get the hang/drift of, catch on, latch on to, tumble to, figure out; *Brit. informal* twig. ❷ APPRECIATE, accept, commiserate with, feel compassionate towards, sympathize with, empathize with. ❸ GATHER, hear, be informed, learn, believe, think, conclude.
– OPPOSITES misunderstand.

understanding noun ❶ COMPREHENSION, apprehension, grasp, perception, discernment, appreciation, interpretation. ❷ INTELLIGENCE, intellect, mind, brainpower, brains, powers of reasoning; *informal* grey matter. ❸ BELIEF, perception, view, notion, idea, fancy, conclusion, feeling. ❹ COMPASSION, sympathy, empathy, insight. ❺ AGREEMENT, gentleman's agreement, arrangement, bargain, pact, compact, contract.
▶ **adjective** COMPASSIONATE, sympathetic, sensitive, considerate, kind, thoughtful, tolerant, patient, forbearing.

understate verb DOWNPLAY, play down, make light of, minimize; *informal* soft-pedal.
– OPPOSITES exaggerate.

undertake verb TAKE ON, set about, tackle, shoulder, assume, enter upon, begin, start, commence, embark on, venture upon, attempt, try.

undertone noun ❶ LOW TONE/VOICE, murmur, whisper. ❷ UNDERCURRENT, hint, suggestion, intimation, insinuation, trace, tinge, touch, atmosphere, aura, tenor, flavour.

undervalue verb *see* UNDERESTIMATE (2).

underwater adjective SUBMARINE, undersea, submerged, immersed.

underwear noun UNDERCLOTHES, undergarments, underclothing, lingerie; *informal* undies, unmentionables; *Brit. informal* smalls.

undesirable adjective UNWANTED, unwished for, unpleasant, disagreeable, nasty, unacceptable.

undisciplined adjective ❶ UNRULY, disorderly, disobedient, obstreperous, recalcitrant, refractory, uncontrolled, unrestrained, wild, wilful, wayward. ❷ UNSYSTEMATIC, unmethodical, disorganized, unorganized.

undisguised adjective OPEN, obvious, evident, patent, manifest, transparent, overt, unconcealed, unmistakable.

undistinguished adjective *see* ORDINARY (2).

undo verb ❶ UNFASTEN, unhook, unbutton, untie, unlace, loosen, disentangle, release, free, open, unlock. ❷ DESTROY, ruin, wreck, smash, shatter, annihilate, obliterate, overturn.

undoubted adjective UNDISPUTED, not in doubt, uncontested, unquestioned, not in question, certain, unquestionable, indubitable, incontrovertible, irrefutable.

undress verb TAKE OFF ONE'S CLOTHES, remove one's clothes, strip, disrobe; *Brit. informal* peel off.

undue adjective UNWARRANTED, unjustified, unreasonable, inappropriate, unsuitable, improper, ill-advised, excessive, immoderate.
– OPPOSITES appropriate.

undying adjective *see* ETERNAL.

uneasy adjective ILL AT EASE, troubled, worried, anxious, apprehensive, alarmed, disturbed, agitated, nervous, nervy, on edge, edgy, restive, restless, unsettled, discomposed, discomfited, perturbed, upset; *informal* jittery.
– OPPOSITES calm.

unemotional adjective UNDEMONSTRATIVE, passionless, cold, frigid, cool, reserved, restrained, unfeeling, unresponsive, unexcitable, unmoved, impassive, apathetic, indifferent, phlegmatic, detached.

unemployed adjective JOBLESS, out of work, out of a job, workless, redundant, laid off, idle; *Brit. informal* on the dole.

unequal adjective ❶ DIFFERENT, differing, dissimilar, unlike, unalike, disparate, varying, variable. ❷ UNEVEN, asymmetrical, unsymmetrical, unbalanced, lopsided, irregular, disproportionate. ❸ UNFAIR, unjust, inequitable, uneven, one-sided, ill-matched.
– OPPOSITES identical, fair.

unequivocal adjective UNAMBIGUOUS, clear, clear-cut, plain, explicit, unqualified, categorical, direct,

straightforward, blunt, point-blank, straight from the shoulder, positive, certain, decisive.
– OPPOSITES ambiguous.

unethical adjective *see* IMMORAL.

uneven adjective ❶ ROUGH, bumpy, lumpy. ❷ *his work is uneven:* VARIABLE, varying, changeable, irregular, erratic, patchy. ❸ UNEQUAL, asymmetrical, unsymmetrical, unbalanced, lopsided, irregular, disproportionate.
– OPPOSITES flat, regular, equal.

uneventful adjective UNEXCITING, uninteresting, monotonous, boring, dull, tedious, routine, ordinary, run-of-the-mill, pedestrian, commonplace, everyday, unexceptional, unremarkable.
– OPPOSITES exciting.

unexpected adjective UNFORESEEN, unanticipated, unpredicted, not bargained for, sudden, abrupt, surprising, startling, astonishing, out of the blue, chance, fortuitous.
– OPPOSITES predictable.

unfair adjective ❶ UNJUST, inequitable, partial, partisan, prejudiced, biased, one-sided. ❷ UNDESERVED, unmerited, uncalled for, unreasonable, unjustifiable, unwarrantable, out of proportion, disproportionate, excessive, extreme, immoderate.
– OPPOSITES just, justified.

unfaithful adjective ❶ DISLOYAL, false-hearted, faithless, perfidious, treacherous, traitorous. ❷ ADULTEROUS, fickle, untrue, inconstant; *informal* two-timing.
– OPPOSITES loyal.

unfamiliar adjective UNKNOWN, new, strange, alien, unaccustomed, uncommon.

unfashionable adjective OUT OF FASHION/DATE, old-fashioned, outmoded, outdated, dated, behind the times, passé, archaic, obsolete, antiquated.

unfasten verb *see* UNDO (1).

unfavourable adjective ❶ *an unfavourable review:* ADVERSE, critical, hostile, inimical, unfriendly, negative, discouraging, poor, bad. ❷ *unfavourable circumstances:* DISADVANTAGEOUS, adverse, unfortunate, unhappy, detrimental.
– OPPOSITES positive.

unfeeling adjective *see* CALLOUS.

unfit adjective ❶ UNSUITED, ill-suited, unsuitable, unqualified, ineligible, unequipped, unprepared, untrained, incapable, inadequate, incompetent, not up to, not equal to. ❷ OUT OF CONDITION, in poor condition/shape, flabby, unhealthy, debilitated, weak.
– OPPOSITES suitable.

unflattering adjective UNCOMPLIMENTARY, critical, blunt, candid, honest, straight from the shoulder.

unfold verb OPEN OUT, spread out, stretch out, flatten, straighten out, unfurl, unroll, unravel.

unforgivable adjective INEXCUSABLE, unpardonable, unjustifiable, indefensible, reprehensible, deplorable, despicable, contemptible, disgraceful, shameful.
– OPPOSITES venial.

unfortunate adjective UNLUCKY, out of luck, luckless, ill-starred,

star-crossed, hapless, wretched, miserable, unhappy, poor.
– OPPOSITES lucky.

unfriendly adjective UNCONGENIAL, unsociable, inhospitable, unneighbourly, unsympathetic, aloof, cold, cool, distant, disagreeable, unpleasant, surly, sour, hostile, inimical, antagonistic, aggressive, quarrelsome.
– OPPOSITES friendly.

ungainly adjective *see* AWKWARD.

ungodly adjective GODLESS, irreligious, blasphemous, profane, immoral, sinful, wicked, iniquitous.

ungrateful adjective UNTHANKFUL, unappreciative, impolite, uncivil, rude.
– OPPOSITES grateful.

unhappy adjective ❶ SAD, miserable, sorrowful, dejected, despondent, disconsolate, broken-hearted, down, downcast, dispirited, crestfallen, depressed, melancholy, blue, gloomy, glum, mournful, woebegone. ❷ an unhappy choice: UNFORTUNATE, regrettable, inappropriate, unsuitable, inapt, tactless, ill-advised, injudicious.
– OPPOSITES cheerful.

unhealthy adjective ❶ IN POOR HEALTH, unwell, ill, ailing, sick, sickly, poorly, indisposed, unsound, weak, feeble, frail, delicate, debilitated, infirm. ❷ an unhealthy diet: UNWHOLESOME, unnourishing, detrimental, injurious, damaging, deleterious, noxious.

unheard of adjective ❶ unheard-of behaviour UNPRECEDENTED, exceptional, extraordinary, undreamed of, unbelievable, inconceivable, unimaginable, unthinkable. ❷ an unheard-of game UNKNOWN, unfamiliar, new.
– OPPOSITES common, well known.

unhinged adjective UNBALANCED, deranged, demented, out of one's mind, crazed, mad, insane, crazy.
– OPPOSITES sane.

unhurried adjective LEISURELY, leisured, easy, slow, slow-moving, deliberate, sedate.
– OPPOSITES hasty.

unidentified adjective NAMELESS, unnamed, unknown, anonymous, incognito, obscure, unmarked, undesignated, unclassified.

uniform adjective ❶ CONSTANT, consistent, invariable, unvarying, unvaried, unchanging, undeviating, stable, regular, even, equal. ❷ SAME, alike, like, selfsame, identical, similar, equal.
– OPPOSITES variable.
▶ noun LIVERY, regalia, dress, regimentals.

unify verb UNITE, bring together, merge, fuse, amalgamate, coalesce, combine, blend, mix, bind, link up, consolidate.
– OPPOSITES separate.

unimaginable adjective UNTHINKABLE, inconceivable, incredible, unbelievable, unheard of, unthought of, implausible, improbable, unlikely, impossible, undreamed of, fantastic; *informal* mind-boggling, mind-blowing.

unimportant adjective OF LITTLE/NO IMPORTANCE, insignificant, of no consequence, inconsequential, of no account, immaterial, irrelevant, not worth mentioning, minor, slight, trivial, petty, paltry, insubstantial, inferior, worthless, nugatory; *informal* no great shakes; *N. Amer. informal* dinky.

uninhabited adjective VACANT, empty, unoccupied, unpopulated, unpeopled, unsettled, abandoned, deserted, forsaken, barren, desert, desolate.

uninhibited adjective UNSELFCONSCIOUS, spontaneous, free and easy, relaxed, informal, open, candid, outspoken, unrestrained, unrepressed, unconstrained, uncontrolled, uncurbed, unchecked, unbridled.
– OPPOSITES repressed.

unintelligible adjective *see* INCOMPREHENSIBLE.

unintentional adjective UNINTENDED, accidental, inadvertent, unplanned, unpremeditated, uncalculated, chance, fortuitous, unconscious, involuntary, unwitting, unthinking.
– OPPOSITES deliberate.

uninterested adjective INDIFFERENT, unconcerned, uninvolved, apathetic, unresponsive, impassive, dispassionate, aloof, detached, distant.

uninteresting adjective UNEXCITING, dull, boring, tiresome, wearisome, tedious, dreary, flat, monotonous, humdrum, commonplace, pedestrian, prosaic, hackneyed, stale.
– OPPOSITES interesting.

uninterrupted adjective UNBROKEN, undisturbed, continuous, continual, constant, steady, sustained, non-stop, unending, endless, incessant, interminable, unremitting.

union noun ❶ JOINING, junction, merger, fusion, amalgamation, blend, mixture, coalition, combining, combination, consolidation, confederation. ❷ ASSOCIATION, alliance, league, coalition, consortium, syndicate, guild, confederation, federation, confederacy. ❸ MARRIAGE, wedding, wedlock.
– OPPOSITES separation.

unique adjective ❶ ONLY, one and only, single, sole, lone, solitary, exclusive. ❷ UNEQUALLED, without equal, unparalleled, unmatched, matchless, peerless, unsurpassed, unexcelled, incomparable, inimitable, second to none.

unit noun ❶ ENTITY, whole. ❷ COMPONENT, part, section, element, constituent, subdivision, portion, segment, module, item, member.

unite verb ❶ JOIN, link, connect, combine, amalgamate, fuse, weld. ❷ COMBINE, mix, commix, blend, mingle, homogenize; *technical* admix. ❸ JOIN TOGETHER, join forces, combine, amalgamate, band/club together, cooperate, work/pull together, pool resources.
– OPPOSITES separate.

united adjective ❶ COMBINED, amalgamated, allied, cooperative, concerted, collective, pooled. ❷ IN AGREEMENT, agreed, in unison, of the same opinion/mind, of like mind, like-minded, at one, in accord, unanimous.

unity noun AGREEMENT, harmony, accord, concurrence, unanimity, consensus, concert, togetherness, solidarity; *formal* concord.
– OPPOSITES disunity.

universal adjective GENERAL, all-embracing, all-inclusive, comprehensive, across the board,

worldwide, global, widespread, common, predominant, preponderant, omnipresent, ubiquitous, catholic.
- OPPOSITES particular.

unjust adjective ❶ UNFAIR, inequitable, prejudiced, biased, partisan, partial, one-sided. ❷ UNDESERVED, unmerited, unwarranted, uncalled for, unreasonable, unjustifiable.
- OPPOSITES fair.

unjustifiable adjective INDEFENSIBLE, inexcusable, unforgivable, unpardonable, uncalled for, unreasonable, blameworthy, culpable, unwarrantable.
- OPPOSITES justifiable.

unkempt adjective UNTIDY, dishevelled, disordered, tousled, rumpled, windblown, scruffy, slovenly, sloppy.
- OPPOSITES neat.

unkind adjective MEAN, cruel, vicious, spiteful, malicious, malevolent, harsh, pitiless, ruthless, unsympathetic, unfeeling, hard-hearted, heartless, cold-hearted, unfriendly, unkindly, unamiable, uncharitable, unchristian, inhospitable, ungenerous, nasty.
- OPPOSITES kind.

unknown adjective ❶ UNREVEALED, undisclosed, undetermined, unsettled, unascertained, in the balance, up in the air. ❷ UNIDENTIFIED, unnamed, nameless, anonymous, incognito, unheard of, little known, obscure. ❸ unknown regions: UNFAMILIAR, unexplored, uncharted, untravelled, undiscovered.
- OPPOSITES familiar.

unlawful adjective *see* ILLEGAL.

unlikely adjective ❶ IMPROBABLE, doubtful, dubious, faint, slight, remote. ❷ an unlikely excuse: IMPLAUSIBLE, questionable, improbable, unconvincing, incredible, unbelievable, inconceivable.
- OPPOSITES probable, believable.

unlimited adjective ❶ UNRESTRICTED, unconstrained, uncontrolled, unrestrained, unchecked, unhindered, unhampered, unimpeded, unfettered, untrammelled. ❷ LIMITLESS, boundless, unbounded, immense, extensive, immeasurable, incalculable, untold, infinite.
- OPPOSITES restricted, finite.

unloved adjective UNWANTED, unpopular, forsaken, rejected, jilted, disliked, hated, detested, loathed.

unlucky adjective ❶ an unlucky man: LUCKLESS, out of luck, down on one's luck, unfortunate, hapless, ill-fated, ill-starred. ❷ an unlucky attempt: UNSUCCESSFUL, failed, ill-fated.
- OPPOSITES fortunate.

unmanly adjective EFFEMINATE, effete, womanish; *informal* sissy.
- OPPOSITES virile.

unmarried adjective SINGLE, unwed, unwedded, divorced, unattached, bachelor, celibate, husbandless, wifeless.

unmistakable adjective *see* OBVIOUS.

unmitigated adjective *see* ABSOLUTE.

unnatural adjective ❶ an unnatural colour: UNUSUAL, uncommon, extraordinary,

strange, queer, odd, bizarre, preternatural. ❷ INHUMAN, heartless, uncaring, unconcerned, unfeeling, soulless, cold, hard, hard-hearted, callous, cruel, brutal, merciless, pitiless, remorseless, evil, wicked. ❸ an unnatural laugh: AFFECTED, artificial, feigned, false, self-conscious, contrived, forced, laboured, studied, strained, insincere, theatrical, stagy, mannered.
– OPPOSITES natural.

unnecessary adjective NEEDLESS, unneeded, inessential, non-essential, uncalled for, unrequired, gratuitous, useless, dispensable, expendable, redundant, superfluous.
– OPPOSITES necessary, essential.

unobtrusive adjective *see* INCONSPICUOUS.

unofficial adjective ❶ INFORMAL, casual, unauthorized, unsanctioned, unaccredited. ❷ an unofficial rumour: UNCONFIRMED, unauthenticated, uncorroborated, unsubstantiated.

unorthodox adjective ❶ HETERODOX, uncanonical, heretical, nonconformist. ❷ *See* UNCONVENTIONAL.
– OPPOSITES conventional.

unpalatable adjective UNSAVOURY, unappetizing, uneatable, inedible, nasty, disgusting, repugnant, revolting, nauseating, sickening, distasteful, disagreeable, unpleasant.
– OPPOSITES tasty.

unparalleled adjective WITHOUT PARALLEL, unequalled, without equal, matchless, unmatched, peerless, unrivalled, unprecedented.

unpleasant adjective ❶ an unpleasant taste: DISAGREEABLE, unpalatable, unsavoury, unappetizing, disgusting, repugnant, revolting, nauseating, sickening. ❷ an unpleasant person: DISAGREEABLE, unlikeable, unlovable, unattractive, nasty, ill-natured, cross, bad-tempered. ❸ an unpleasant task: DISAGREEABLE, irksome, troublesome, annoying, irritating, vexatious.
– OPPOSITES agreeable, likable.

unpopular adjective DISLIKED, unliked, unloved, friendless, unwanted, unwelcome, avoided, ignored, rejected, shunned, out in the cold, cold-shouldered, unattractive, undesirable, out of favour.

unpredictable adjective ERRATIC, fickle, capricious, whimsical, mercurial, volatile, unstable, undependable, unreliable.

unpremeditated adjective UNPLANNED, unintentional, extempore, impromptu, ad lib, spontaneous, spur of the moment, on the spot, impulsive, hasty; *informal* off the cuff.
– OPPOSITES planned.

unpretentious adjective SIMPLE, plain, ordinary, humble, unostentatious, unassuming, modest, unaffected, natural, straightforward, honest.
– OPPOSITES pretentious.

unprincipled adjective IMMORAL, amoral, unethical, dishonourable, dishonest, deceitful, devious, unscrupulous, corrupt, bad, wicked, evil, villainous; *informal* crooked.
– OPPOSITES ethical.

unprofessional adjective AMATEUR, amateurish, unskilled, inexpert, untrained, unqualified, inexperienced, incompetent.
–OPPOSITES professional.

unpromising adjective UNFAVOURABLE, adverse, unpropitious, inauspicious, gloomy, black, discouraging, portentous, ominous.
–OPPOSITES auspicious.

unquestionable adjective BEYOND QUESTION/DOUBT, indubitable, undoubted, indisputable, undeniable, irrefutable, incontestable, incontrovertible, certain, sure, definite, positive, conclusive, self-evident, obvious.

unravel verb ❶ UNTANGLE, disentangle, unwind, straighten out, separate out, unknot, undo. ❷ SOLVE, resolve, work out, clear up, puzzle out, get to the bottom of, fathom; *informal* figure out.
–OPPOSITES entangle.

unreal adjective IMAGINARY, make-believe, fictitious, mythical, fanciful, fantastic, fabulous, hypothetical, non-existent, illusory, chimerical, phantasmagoric.

unrealistic adjective IMPRACTICAL, impracticable, unworkable, unreasonable, irrational, illogical, improbable, foolish, wild, absurd, quixotic; *informal* half-baked.
–OPPOSITES pragmatic.

unreasonable adjective ❶ **unreasonable demands:** EXCESSIVE, immoderate, undue, inordinate, outrageous, extravagant, preposterous. ❷ **unreasonable people:** IRRATIONAL, illogical, blinkered, obstinate, obdurate, wilful, headstrong, temperamental, capricious. ❸ **unreasonable behaviour:** UNACCEPTABLE, outrageous, ludicrous, absurd, irrational, illogical.

unreliable adjective ❶ UNDEPENDABLE, irresponsible, untrustworthy, erratic, fickle, inconstant. ❷ **unreliable evidence:** SUSPECT, questionable, open to question/doubt, doubtful, implausible, unconvincing, fallible, specious.

unrepentant adjective IMPENITENT, unremorseful, shameless, unregenerate, abandoned.

unrest noun DISSATISFACTION, discontent, unease, disquiet, dissent, discord, strife, protest, rebellion, agitation, turmoil, turbulence.

unrestricted adjective UNLIMITED, open, free, unhindered, unchecked, unbounded; *informal* free-for-all, with no holds barred.

unsavoury adjective UNPLEASANT, disagreeable, nasty, objectionable, offensive, obnoxious, repellent, repulsive, disreputable, degenerate, coarse, gross, vulgar, boorish, churlish, rude, uncouth.

unscrupulous adjective UNPRINCIPLED, unethical, amoral, immoral, conscienceless, shameless, corrupt, dishonest, dishonourable, deceitful, devious, exploitative, wrongdoing, bad, evil, wicked; *informal* crooked.
–OPPOSITES honest.

unselfish adjective ALTRUISTIC, self-sacrificing, selfless, kind, self-denying, open-handed, generous, liberal, unsparing,

ungrudging, unstinting, charitable, philanthropic.
– OPPOSITES selfish.

unshakeable adjective FIRM, steadfast, resolute, staunch, constant, unswerving, unwavering, unfaltering.

unsightly adjective *see* UGLY (1).

unskilled adjective UNTRAINED, unqualified, inexpert, inexperienced, amateurish, unprofessional.

unsophisticated adjective ❶ UNWORLDLY, naive, simple, innocent, inexperienced, childlike, artless, guileless, ingenuous, natural, unaffected, unpretentious, unrefined, unpolished, gauche, provincial. ❷ CRUDE, unrefined, basic, rudimentary, primitive.

unspeakable adjective INDESCRIBABLE, unmentionable, appalling, shocking, horrible, frightful, terrible, dreadful, deplorable, despicable, contemptible, repellent, loathsome, odious, monstrous.

unspoilt adjective PRESERVED, intact, perfect, unblemished, unimpaired, undamaged, untouched, unaffected, unchanged.

unstable adjective ❶ UNSTEADY, infirm, rickety, shaky, wobbly, tottery, insecure, precarious. ❷ UNBALANCED, unhinged, irrational, deranged, mentally ill, insane, mad.
– OPPOSITES stable.

unstudied adjective NATURAL, unaffected, unpretentious, without airs, artless, guileless, informal, casual, spontaneous, impromptu.
– OPPOSITES affected.

unsubstantiated adjective UNCONFIRMED, uncorroborated, unproven, questionable, open to question, disputable.

unsuccessful adjective ❶ WITHOUT SUCCESS, failed, vain, unavailing, futile, useless, worthless, abortive, nugatory, ineffective, ineffectual, inefficacious, fruitless, unproductive, unprofitable, baulked, frustrated. ❷ FAILED, losing, unprosperous, unlucky, luckless, out of luck, unfortunate, ill-starred, ill-fated.

unsuitable adjective INAPPROPRIATE, inapt, inapposite, unfitting, incompatible, incongruous, out of place/keeping, ineligible, unacceptable, unbecoming, unseemly, indecorous, improper.
– OPPOSITES appropriate.

unsure adjective *see* UNCERTAIN (2).

unsuspecting adjective UNSUSPICIOUS, unwary, off guard, trusting, gullible, credulous, ingenuous, naive, innocent.
– OPPOSITES wary.

unsympathetic adjective UNCARING, unfeeling, insensitive, unconcerned, indifferent, unkind, unpitying, pitiless, unresponsive, apathetic, unmoved, untouched, heartless, cold, hard-hearted, stony-hearted, hard, harsh, callous.
– OPPOSITES sympathetic.

untangle verb *see* UNRAVEL.

untenable adjective INDEFENSIBLE, insupportable, unsustainable, unsound, weak, flawed, defective, implausible, groundless, unfounded.

unthinkable adjective *see* INCONCEIVABLE.

unthinking adjective *see* THOUGHTLESS (2).

untidy adjective DISORDERED, disorderly, disarranged, disorganized, chaotic, confused, muddled, jumbled, topsy-turvy, at sixes and sevens; *informal* higgledy-piggledy, every which way; *Brit. informal* like a dog's breakfast.
– OPPOSITES orderly.

untie verb *see* UNDO (1).

untiring adjective *see* TIRELESS.

untroubled adjective UNWORRIED, unruffled, unbothered, unconcerned, calm, cool, collected, composed, serene.

untrue adjective *see* FALSE (1).

unusual adjective ❶ unusual behaviour: UNCOMMON, atypical, abnormal, rare, singular, odd, strange, curious, queer, bizarre, surprising, unexpected, different, unconventional, unwonted, unorthodox, irregular; *informal* weird. ❷ an unusual talent: EXTRAORDINARY, exceptional, singular, rare, remarkable, outstanding.
– OPPOSITES common.

unwarranted adjective UNJUSTIFIABLE, unjustified, indefensible, inexcusable, unforgivable, unpardonable, uncalled for, gratuitous.
– OPPOSITES justified.

unwelcome adjective ❶ unwelcome visitors: UNWANTED, undesired, uninvited, unpopular. ❷ unwelcome news: UNPLEASANT, disagreeable, unpalatable, displeasing, distasteful, undesirable.

unwell adjective *see* ILL adjective (1).

unwieldy adjective CUMBERSOME, unmanageable, awkward, clumsy, massive, hefty, bulky, ponderous; *informal* hulking.
– OPPOSITES manageable.

unwilling adjective RELUCTANT, disinclined, unenthusiastic, grudging, involuntary, averse, loth, opposed, not in the mood.
– OPPOSITES willing.

unwind verb ❶ *See* UNRAVEL (1). ❷ *See* RELAX (4).

unwitting adjective UNKNOWING, unconscious, unintentional, unintended, inadvertent.
– OPPOSITES deliberate.

unworthy adjective ❶ NOT WORTHY, not good enough for, undeserving, ineligible for, unqualified for. ❷ DISREPUTABLE, dishonourable, base, contemptible, reprehensible.
– OPPOSITES deserving.

upbraid verb SCOLD, rebuke, reproach, reprove, chide, reprimand, berate, remonstrate with, criticize, censure; *formal* castigate.

upgrade verb IMPROVE, better, ameliorate, enhance, rehabilitate, refurbish.

upheaval noun DISRUPTION, disturbance, disorder, confusion, turmoil, chaos.

uphill adjective ARDUOUS, difficult, laborious, strenuous, hard, tough, burdensome, onerous, taxing, punishing.

uphold verb SUPPORT, back up, back, stand by, champion, defend, maintain, sustain.

upkeep noun MAINTENANCE, running, preservation, conservation, repairs.

upper adjective ❶ HIGHER, further up, loftier. ❷ SUPERIOR, higher-ranking, elevated, greater.
– OPPOSITES lower.

upright adjective ❶ ERECT, on end, vertical, perpendicular, standing up, rampant. ❷ HONEST, honourable, upstanding, decent, respectable, worthy, reputable, good, virtuous, righteous, law-abiding, ethical, moral.
– OPPOSITES horizontal, dishonourable.

uproar noun TUMULT, turmoil, turbulence, disorder, confusion, commotion, mayhem, pandemonium, bedlam, din, noise, clamour, hubbub, racket.
– OPPOSITES calm.

upset verb ❶ OVERTURN, knock over, push over, upend, tip over, topple, capsize. ❷ DISTURB, discompose, unsettle, disconcert, dismay, disquiet, trouble, worry, bother, agitate, fluster, ruffle, frighten, alarm, anger, annoy, distress, hurt, grieve. ❸ THROW INTO DISORDER/CONFUSION, disorganize, disarrange, mess up, mix up.

upshot noun RESULT, outcome, conclusion, issue, end, end result, denouement, effect, repercussion, reaction; *informal* pay-off.
– OPPOSITES cause.

upstart noun PARVENU, parvenue, social climber, nouveau riche, arriviste.

up to date adjective MODERN, current, prevalent, prevailing, present-day, recent, up to the minute, fashionable, voguish.
– OPPOSITES out of date.

upward adjective RISING, climbing, mounting, ascending, on the rise.
– OPPOSITES downward.

urbane adjective SUAVE, debonair, sophisticated, smooth, worldly, cultivated, cultured, civilized, polished.
– OPPOSITES uncouth.

urge verb ❶ PUSH, drive, propel, impel, force, hasten, hurry, spur, incite, stir up, stimulate, prod, goad, egg on, encourage, prompt, entreat, exhort, implore, appeal, beg, plead; *poetic/literary* beseech. ❷ **urge caution:** ADVISE, counsel, advocate, recommend, suggest, support, endorse, back, champion.
– OPPOSITES discourage.
▶ **noun** DESIRE, need, compulsion, longing, yearning, wish, fancy, impulse.

urgent adjective ❶ IMPERATIVE, vital, crucial, critical, essential, exigent, top-priority, high-priority, important, necessary, pressing, serious, grave. ❷ **an urgent whisper:** IMPORTUNATE, insistent, clamorous, earnest, pleading, begging.

urinate verb PASS WATER, micturate; *informal* spend a penny, pee, have a tinkle/leak; *Brit. informal* wee, have a slash.

usable adjective FOR USE, to be used, utilizable, available, ready/fit for use, in working order, functional.

use verb ❶ MAKE USE OF, utilize, employ, work, operate, wield, ply, avail oneself of, put to use, put into service. ❷ CONSUME, get through, exhaust, deplete, expend, spend, waste, fritter away.
▶ **noun** ❶ USEFULNESS, good, advantage, benefit, service, help, gain, profit, avail. ❷ **no use for it:** NEED, necessity, call, demand, purpose.
■ **used to** ACCUSTOMED TO, familiar with, at home with, in the habit of, given to, prone to.

used adjective SECOND-HAND, nearly new, cast-off, hand-me-down.
– OPPOSITES new.

useful adjective ❶ OF USE, functional, utilitarian, of service, practical, convenient. ❷ a useful experience: BENEFICIAL, advantageous, of help, helpful, worthwhile, profitable, rewarding, productive, valuable.
– OPPOSITES useless.

useless adjective ❶ a useless attempt: VAIN, in vain, to no avail/purpose, unavailing, unsuccessful, futile, purposeless, fruitless, unprofitable, unproductive, abortive. ❷ a useless player: WORTHLESS, ineffective, ineffectual, incompetent, incapable, inadequate; *informal* no good.
– OPPOSITES useful.

usual adjective ❶ HABITUAL, customary, accustomed, normal, regular, routine, everyday, established, set, familiar; *poetic/literary* wonted. ❷ COMMON, typical, ordinary, average, run-of-the-mill, expected, standard, stock, regular.
– OPPOSITES unusual.

usually adverb GENERALLY, as a rule, normally, by and large, in the main, mainly, mostly, for the most part, on the whole.

usurp verb TAKE OVER, seize, expropriate, appropriate, commandeer, assume.

utilitarian adjective PRACTICAL, functional, useful, to the purpose.

utter verb VOICE, say, pronounce, express, put into words, enunciate, articulate, verbalize, vocalize.

utterance noun ❶ VOICE, expression, articulation, enunciation, verbalization, vocalization. ❷ REMARK, word, comment, statement, opinion.

utterly adverb ABSOLUTELY, completely, totally, entirely, thoroughly, positively, extremely, categorically, perfectly, consummately, to the core.

vacancy noun ❶ OPENING, position, post, job, opportunity, slot. ❷ BLANKNESS, lack of expression, lack of emotion/interest, vacuousness.

vacant adjective ❶ EMPTY, void, without contents. ❷ UNOCCUPIED, unfilled, free, empty, available, unengaged, uninhabited, untenanted, not in use, unused, abandoned, deserted; *informal* up for grabs. ❸ a vacant expression: BLANK, expressionless, inexpressive, deadpan, poker-faced, emotionless, uninterested, vacuous, inane.
– OPPOSITES occupied.

vacate verb LEAVE, quit, depart from, evacuate, abandon, desert.

vacillate verb SHILLY-SHALLY, waver, dither, hesitate, equivocate, beat about the bush; *Brit.* hum and haw.

vacuous adjective VACANT, blank,

expressionless, deadpan, inane, unintelligent, brainless, stupid.
– OPPOSITES intelligent.

vacuum noun EMPTINESS, void, empty space, nothingness, vacuity.

vagary noun CAPRICE, whim, whimsy, fancy, notion, quirk.

vagrant noun TRAMP, beggar, person of no fixed address, itinerant, nomad, wanderer, vagabond; *N. Amer.* hobo; *N. Amer. informal* bum.

vague adjective ❶ a vague shape: INDISTINCT, indeterminate, ill-defined, unclear, nebulous, amorphous, shadowy, hazy, fuzzy, blurry, bleary, out of focus. ❷ a vague description: IMPRECISE, inexact, inexplicit, non-specific, loose, generalized, ambiguous, equivocal, hazy, woolly. ❸ she is rather vague: ABSENT-MINDED, abstracted, dreamy, vacuous; *informal* with one's head in the clouds.
– OPPOSITES definite.

vaguely adverb ❶ vaguely familiar: IN A GENERAL WAY, in a way, somehow, slightly, obscurely. ❷ smiling vaguely: ABSENT-MINDEDLY, abstractedly, vacantly, vacuously.

vain adjective ❶ CONCEITED, self-loving, narcissistic, self-admiring, egotistical, proud, haughty, arrogant, boastful, swaggering, imperious, overweening, cocky, affected. ❷ vain efforts: UNSUCCESSFUL, futile, useless, unavailing, to no avail, ineffective, inefficacious, fruitless, unproductive, abortive, unprofitable, profitless.
– OPPOSITES modest, successful.

valiant adjective BRAVE, courageous, valorous, heroic, intrepid, fearless, undaunted, bold, daring, audacious, staunch, stalwart, indomitable, resolute, determined.
– OPPOSITES cowardly.

valid adjective SOUND, well founded, well grounded, substantial, reasonable, logical, justifiable, defensible, vindicable, authentic, bona fide, effective, cogent, powerful, convincing, credible, forceful, weighty.
– OPPOSITES invalid.

validate verb RATIFY, legalize, legitimize, authorize, sanction, warrant, license, approve, endorse, set one's seal to.
– OPPOSITES invalidate.

valley noun DALE, dell, hollow, vale, depression; *Brit.* dene, combe; *Scottish* glen, strath.

valuable adjective ❶ COSTLY, high-priced, expensive, priceless, precious. ❷ a valuable lesson: USEFUL, helpful, beneficial, advantageous, worthwhile, worthy, important.
– OPPOSITES worthless.

value noun ❶ COST, face value, price, market price, worth. ❷ WORTH, merit, usefulness, advantage, benefit, gain, profit, good, avail, importance, significance.
▶ verb ❶ SET A PRICE ON, price, evaluate, assess, appraise. ❷ RATE HIGHLY, appreciate, esteem, hold in high regard, think highly of, set store by, respect, admire, prize, cherish, treasure.

van noun LORRY, truck, pantechnicon, camper.

vanguard noun ADVANCE GUARD, forefront, front, front line, front rank, leading position, van.
– OPPOSITES rear.

vanish verb DISAPPEAR, be lost to sight/view, be/become invisible, evaporate, dissipate, disperse, fade, fade away, evanesce, melt away, recede from view, withdraw, depart, leave.
– OPPOSITES appear.

vanity noun CONCEIT, conceitedness, narcissism, egotism, pride, haughtiness, arrogance, boastfulness, braggadocio, pretension, affectation, ostentation, show, airs.
– OPPOSITES modesty.

vapid adjective INSIPID, flat, lifeless, colourless, bland, dull, mute, uninteresting.
– OPPOSITES lively.

variable adjective VARYING, variational, changeable, changing, mutable, protean, shifting, fluctuating, wavering, vacillating, inconstant, unsteady, unstable, fitful, capricious, fickle; *informal* blowing hot and cold.
– OPPOSITES constant.

variation noun ❶ CHANGE, alteration, modification, diversification. ❷ VARIABILITY, changeability, fluctuation, vacillation, vicissitude. ❸ DIFFERENCE, dissimilarity.

varied adjective DIVERSE, assorted, miscellaneous, mixed, motley, heterogeneous.

variety noun ❶ VARIATION, diversification, diversity, multifariousness, many-sidedness, change, difference. ❷ ASSORTMENT, miscellany, range, mixture, medley, motley, collection, multiplicity. ❸ STRAIN, breed, kind, type, sort, class, category, classification, brand, make.
– OPPOSITES uniformity.

various adjective ❶ VARYING, diverse, different, differing, dissimilar, disparate, assorted, mixed, miscellaneous, variegated, heterogeneous. ❷ NUMEROUS, many, several, varled, sundry; *poetic/literary* divers.

varnish verb LACQUER, japan, shellac, enamel, glaze, veneer.

vary verb ❶ DIFFER, be different, be unlike, be dissimilar. ❷ CHANGE, be transformed, alter, metamorphose, suffer a sea change, vacillate, fluctuate. ❸ BE AT VARIANCE, disagree, be in disagreement, differ, conflict, clash, be at odds, be in opposition, diverge.

vast adjective IMMENSE, huge, enormous, massive, bulky, tremendous, colossal, prodigious, gigantic, monumental, elephantine, Brobdingnagian, extensive, broad, wide, expansive, boundless, limitless, infinite; *informal* hulking.
– OPPOSITES tiny.

vault[1] noun CELLAR, basement, underground chamber, tomb.

vault[2] verb JUMP, leap, jump over, leap over, spring over, bound over.

veer verb CHANGE COURSE/DIRECTION, turn, swerve, swing, sidestep, sheer, tack, be deflected.

vegetate verb DO NOTHING, idle, be inactive, laze around, lounge around, loaf around, languish, stagnate, moulder; *informal* go to seed.

vehemence noun FORCE, passion, forcefulness, emphasis, vigour, intensity, violence, earnestness, keenness, enthusiasm, zeal.

vehement adjective PASSIONATE, ardent, impassioned, fervent,

fervid, strong, forceful, forcible, powerful, emphatic, vigorous, intense, earnest, keen, enthusiastic, zealous, spirited.
– OPPOSITES mild.

vehicle noun ❶ MEANS OF TRANSPORT, transportation, conveyance, car, bus, lorry. ❷ CHANNEL, medium, means, agency, instrument, mechanism, organ, apparatus.

veil verb HIDE, conceal, cover up, camouflage, disguise, mask, screen.

vein noun ❶ BLOOD VESSEL, artery, capillary. ❷ LODE, seam, stratum. ❸ STREAK, stripe, line, thread, marking.

venal adjective CORRUPT, corruptible, bribable, buyable, mercenary, greedy, avaricious, grasping, rapacious.
– OPPOSITES honest.

veneer noun ❶ FACING, covering, coat, finish. ❷ FACADE, false front, show, outward display, appearance, semblance, guise, mask, pretence, camouflage.

venerable adjective VENERATED, respected, revered, reverenced, worshipped, honoured, esteemed, hallowed.

veneration noun RESPECT, reverence, worship, adoration, honour, esteem.

vengeance noun REVENGE, retribution, requital, retaliation, reprisal, an eye for an eye, quid pro quo; *informal* tit for tat.

venial adjective PARDONABLE, forgivable, excusable, allowable, tolerable, slight, minor, unimportant, insignificant, trivial.
– OPPOSITES unforgivable.

venom noun ❶ POISON, toxin, toxicant. ❷ *See* SPITE.

venomous adjective ❶ POISONOUS, toxic, lethal, deadly, fatal, noxious. ❷ *See* SPITEFUL.

vent noun OPENING, outlet, aperture, hole, gap, duct, flue.
▶ verb GIVE VENT/EXPRESSION TO, express, air, utter, voice, verbalize, let out, come out with.

ventilate verb AIR, aerate, oxygenate, freshen, cool, purify.

venture noun ENTERPRISE, undertaking, project, speculation, fling, plunge, gamble.
▶ verb DARE, take the liberty, make so bold as, presume to.

veracious adjective TRUE, truthful, accurate, exact, precise, factual, literal, realistic.

verbal adjective ORAL, spoken, said, uttered, articulated.

verbatim adjective WORD FOR WORD, literal, exact, faithful, precise.

verbose adjective WORDY, loquacious, garrulous, long-winded, prolix, diffuse, pleonastic, circumlocutory, periphrastic, tautological.
– OPPOSITES succinct.

verbosity noun VERBOSENESS, wordiness, loquacity, garrulity, long-windedness, logorrhoea, verbiage, prolixity, diffuseness, circumlocution, periphrasis, tautology.

verdict noun DECISION, judgement, adjudication, finding, conclusion, ruling, opinion.

verge noun EDGE, border, margin, rim, limit, boundary, end, extremity.
■ **verge on** APPROACH, incline to/towards, tend towards, border on, come near.

verification noun CONFIRMATION, evidence, proof, substantiation, corroboration, attestation, validation, authentication, endorsement, accreditation, ratification.

verify verb CONFIRM, substantiate, prove, give credence to, corroborate, attest to, testify to, validate, authenticate, endorse, accredit, ratify.
– OPPOSITES refute.

vernacular noun EVERYDAY/SPOKEN LANGUAGE, colloquial/native speech, conversational language, common parlance, non-standard language, jargon, cant, patois; *informal* lingo, patter.

versatile adjective ❶ a versatile person: ADAPTABLE, flexible, all-round, multifaceted, resourceful, ingenious, clever. ❷ a versatile tool: ADAPTABLE, adjustable, multi-purpose, all-purpose, handy.

verse noun ❶ STANZA, canto, couplet. ❷ POEM, lyric, sonnet, ode, limerick, piece of doggerel, ditty, song, ballad.

version noun ❶ ACCOUNT, report, story, rendering, interpretation, construction, understanding, reading, impression, side. ❷ ADAPTATION, interpretation, translation. ❸ VARIANT, variation, form, copy, reproduction.

vertical adjective UPRIGHT, erect, on end, perpendicular.
– OPPOSITES horizontal.

vertigo noun DIZZINESS, giddiness, light-headedness, loss of balance/equilibrium; *informal* wooziness.

verve noun ENTHUSIASM, vigour, force, energy, vitality, vivacity, liveliness, animation, sparkle, spirit, life, dash, brio, fervour, gusto, passion, zeal, feeling, fire; *informal* zing, zip, vim, get-up-and-go, pizzazz.

very adverb EXTREMELY, exceedingly, to a great extent, exceptionally, uncommonly, unusually, decidedly, particularly, eminently, remarkably, really, truly, terribly; *informal* awfully; *Brit. informal* jolly.
– OPPOSITES slightly.

vessel noun ❶ SHIP, boat, yacht, craft; *poetic/literary* barque. ❷ CONTAINER, receptacle.

vest verb BESTOW, confer, endow, entrust, invest, lodge, place, put in the hands of.

vet verb CHECK, check out, investigate, examine, appraise, look over, review, scrutinize; *informal* give the once-over, size up.

veteran noun OLD HAND, old-timer, old stager, past master, master; *informal* pro, old warhorse.
– OPPOSITES novice.
▶ adjective LONG-SERVING, seasoned, old, adept, expert.

veto verb REJECT, turn down, prohibit, forbid, interdict, proscribe, disallow, outlaw, embargo, ban, bar, preclude, rule out; *informal* give the thumbs down to, put the kibosh on.
– OPPOSITES approve.
▶ noun REJECTION, prohibition, interdict, proscription, embargo, ban.

vex verb ANGER, annoy, irritate, incense, irk, enrage, infuriate, exasperate, pique, provoke, nettle, disturb, upset, perturb, discompose, put out, try someone's patience, try; *informal* peeve, miff, bug, hassle, aggravate, drive up the wall.

vexatious adjective *see* ANNOYING.

viable adjective WORKABLE, sound, feasible, practicable, applicable, usable.
– OPPOSITES impractical.

vibrant adjective ❶ LIVELY, energetic, spirited, vigorous, animated, sparkling, vivacious, dynamic, electrifying. ❷ **vibrant colours:** VIVID, bright, strong, striking.
– OPPOSITES lifeless, pale.

vibrate verb SHAKE, oscillate, tremble, quiver, throb, pulsate, resonate, resound, reverberate, ring, echo.

vibration noun SHAKING, oscillation, throb, pulsation, resonance, reverberation, quivering, quiver.

vicarious adjective INDIRECT, second-hand, surrogate, by proxy, at one remove.

vice noun ❶ SIN, sinfulness, wrong, wrongdoing, wickedness, badness, immorality, iniquity, evil, evil-doing, venality, corruption, depravity, degeneracy. ❷ TRANSGRESSION, offence, misdeed, error, failing, flaw, defect, imperfection, weakness, foible, shortcoming.
– OPPOSITES virtue.

vicinity noun SURROUNDING DISTRICT, neighbourhood, locality, area, district, environs, precincts, purlieus; *informal* neck of the woods.

vicious adjective ❶ FIERCE, ferocious, savage, dangerous, ill-natured, bad-tempered, hostile. ❷ MALICIOUS, malevolent, malignant, spiteful, vindictive, venomous, backbiting, rancorous, caustic, mean, cruel; *informal* bitchy, catty. ❸ VIOLENT, savage, brutal, fierce, ferocious, inhuman, barbarous, fiendish, sadistic.
– OPPOSITES gentle.

vicissitude noun CHANGE, alteration, transformation, inconstancy, instability, uncertainty, unpredictability, chanciness, fickleness, ups and downs.

victim noun ❶ INJURED PARTY, casualty, sufferer. ❷ OFFERING, sacrifice, scapegoat.

victimize verb PERSECUTE, pick on, discriminate against, punish unfairly; *informal* have it in for, have a down on.

victor noun WINNER, champion, prizewinner, conquering hero; *informal* champ, top dog, number one.
– OPPOSITES loser.

victorious adjective CONQUERING, vanquishing, triumphant, winning, champion, successful, prizewinning, top, first.

vie verb COMPETE, contend, contest, struggle, strive.

view noun ❶ **come into view:** SIGHT, field/range of vision, vision, eyeshot. ❷ **the view from the mountain:** OUTLOOK, prospect, scene, spectacle, vista, panorama, landscape, seascape. ❸ **his views on politics:** POINT OF VIEW, viewpoint, opinion, belief, judgement, way of thinking, thinking, thought, notion, idea, conviction, persuasion, attitude, feeling, sentiment, impression.
▶ verb ❶ LOOK AT, watch, observe, contemplate, regard, behold, scan, survey. ❷ SEE OVER, be shown over, survey, examine, scrutinize, take stock of.

viewpoint noun POINT OF VIEW, frame of reference, perspective, angle, slant, standpoint, position, stance, vantage point.

vigilant adjective WATCHFUL, on the lookout, observant, sharp-eyed, eagle-eyed, attentive, alert, on the alert, awake, wide awake, on one's guard, careful, cautious, wary, circumspect, heedful.
– OPPOSITES inattentive.

vigorous adjective ❶ ROBUST, healthy, in good health, hale and hearty, strong, sturdy, fit, in good condition/shape/kilter, tough. ❷ ENERGETIC, lively, active, spry, sprightly, vivacious, animated, dynamic, full of life, sparkling.
– OPPOSITES weak, feeble.

vigour noun ❶ ROBUSTNESS, healthiness, strength, sturdiness, fitness, toughness. ❷ ENERGY, activity, liveliness, spryness, sprightliness, vitality, vivacity, verve, animation, dynamism, sparkle, zest, dash, gusto, pep; *informal* zip, zing, oomph, vim.
– OPPOSITES lethargy.

vile adjective FOUL, nasty, unpleasant, disagreeable, horrid, horrible, offensive, obnoxious, odious, repulsive, repellent, revolting, repugnant, disgusting, distasteful, loathsome, hateful, nauseating, sickening, base, low, mean, wretched, dreadful, ugly, abominable, monstrous.
– OPPOSITES pleasant.

vilify verb DEFAME, run down, impugn, revile, berate, denigrate, disparage, drag through the mud, speak ill of, cast aspersions at, criticize, decry, denounce, fulminate against, malign, slander, libel, traduce; *informal* bad-mouth, do a hatchet job on; *formal* calumniate.
– OPPOSITES commend.

villain noun ROGUE, scoundrel, wretch, cad, reprobate, evil-doer, wrongdoer, hoodlum, hooligan, miscreant; *informal* baddy, crook, rat, louse; *archaic* blackguard.

vindicate verb ACQUIT, clear, absolve, free from blame, exonerate, exculpate.

vindictive adjective VENGEFUL, revengeful, avenging, unforgiving, grudge-bearing, resentful, implacable, unrelenting, spiteful, rancorous, venomous, malicious, malevolent, malignant.
– OPPOSITES forgiving.

vintage adjective CLASSIC, ageless, enduring, high-quality, quality, prime, choice, select, superior, best.

violate verb ❶ violate a treaty: BREAK, breach, infringe, contravene, infract, transgress, disobey, disregard, ignore. ❷ violate a grave: DESECRATE, profane, defile, blaspheme. ❸ violate their privacy: DISTURB, disrupt, intrude on, interfere with, encroach on, invade.
– OPPOSITES respect.

violence noun FORCE, brute force, roughness, ferocity, brutality, savagery; *informal* strong-arm tactics.

violent adjective ❶ BRUTAL, vicious, destructive, savage, fierce, wild, intemperate, bloodthirsty, homicidal, murderous, maniacal. ❷ a violent temper: STRONG, powerful, uncontrolled, unrestrained, unbridled, uncontrollable, ungovernable, wild, passionate. ❸ a violent dislike: STRONG, great, intense, extreme, vehement, inordinate, excessive.
– OPPOSITES gentle, weak.

virginal adjective PURE, chaste, virtuous, uncorrupted.

virile adjective POTENT, manly, strong, vigorous, robust, muscular, rugged, strapping, sturdy, red-blooded; *informal* macho.
– OPPOSITES effeminate.

virtue noun ❶ GOODNESS, righteousness, morality, uprightness, integrity, rectitude, honesty, honourableness, honour, incorruptibility, probity, decency, respectability, worthiness, worth, trustworthiness. ❷ GOOD QUALITY/POINT, merit, asset, credit, attribute, advantage, plus, benefit, strength.
– OPPOSITES vice.

virtuoso adjective SKILFUL, masterly, impressive, outstanding, dazzling, bravura.
– OPPOSITES incompetent.

virtuous adjective ❶ GOOD, righteous, moral, ethical, upright, upstanding, honest, honourable, incorruptible, decent, respectable, worthy, trustworthy. ❷ VIRGINAL, celibate, pure, chaste, innocent, modest.
– OPPOSITES evil.

virulent adjective ❶ POISONOUS, toxic, venomous, deadly, lethal, fatal, noxious, harmful. ❷ SEVERE, extreme, violent, rapidly spreading, highly infectious/contagious, harmful, lethal. ❸ HOSTILE, spiteful, venomous, vicious, vindictive, malicious, malevolent, malignant, bitter, rancorous, acrimonious, abusive, aggressive, violent.
– OPPOSITES harmless, amicable.

visible adjective ❶ IN VIEW, perceptible, perceivable, discernible, detectable, seeable. ❷ APPARENT, evident, noticeable, observable, detectable, recognizable, manifest, plain, clear, obvious, patent, palpable, unmistakable, unconcealed, undisguised, conspicuous, distinct, distinguishable.
– OPPOSITES invisible.

vision noun ❶ EYESIGHT, sight, power of seeing. ❷ REVELATION, dream, hallucination, chimera, optical illusion, mirage, illusion, delusion, figment of the imagination. ❸ FORESIGHT, far-sightedness, prescience, breadth of view, discernment.

visionary adjective ❶ IDEALISTIC, impractical, unrealistic, utopian, romantic, quixotic, dreamy, dreaming; *informal* starry-eyed. ❷ FAR-SIGHTED, discerning, wise. ❸ visionary schemes: IMPRACTICAL, unrealistic, unworkable, unfeasible, theoretical, hypothetical, idealistic, utopian.
▶ noun MYSTIC, seer, prophet, dreamer, daydreamer, idealist, romantic, romanticist, fantasist, theorist, utopian.

visit verb PAY A VISIT TO, go/come to see, pay a call on, call on, call/look in on, stop by; *informal* pop/drop in on.
▶ noun CALL, social call, stay, sojourn, stopover.

visitation noun AFFLICTION, scourge, plague, pestilence, blight, disaster, tragedy, calamity, catastrophe, cataclysm.

visual adjective ❶ SEEING, optical, ocular. ❷ TO BE SEEN, seeable, perceivable, discernible.

visualize verb CONJURE UP, envisage, picture, envision, imagine, conceive.

vital adjective ❶ ESSENTIAL,

necessary, needed, indispensable, key, important, significant, imperative, urgent, critical, crucial, life-and-death. ❷ a vital person: LIVELY, animated, spirited, vivacious, vibrant, zestful, dynamic, energetic, vigorous, forceful.
– OPPOSITES unimportant, apathetic.

vitality noun LIFE, liveliness, animation, spirit, spiritedness, vivacity, vibrancy, zest, zestfulness, dynamism, energy, vigour, forcefulness.

vitriolic adjective CAUSTIC, mordant, acrimonious, bitter, acerbic, astringent, acid, acidulous, acrid, trenchant, virulent, spiteful, venomous, malicious, scathing, withering, sarcastic, sardonic; *informal* bitchy.

vivacious adjective LIVELY, full of life, animated, effervescent, bubbly, ebullient, sparkling, scintillating, light-hearted, spirited, high-spirited, merry, jolly, vibrant, vivid, dynamic, vital; *dated* gay.
– OPPOSITES dull.

vivid adjective ❶ vivid colours: STRONG, intense, colourful, rich, glowing, bright, brilliant, clear. ❷ a vivid account: GRAPHIC, clear, lively, stirring, striking, powerful, highly coloured, dramatic, memorable, realistic, lifelike, true to life.
– OPPOSITES dull.

vocal adjective ❶ VOICED, vocalized, spoken, said, uttered, expressed, articulated, oral. ❷ VOCIFEROUS, outspoken, forthright, plain-spoken, clamorous, strident, loud, noisy.

vocation noun PROFESSION, calling, occupation, walk of life, career, life's work, métier, trade, craft, job, work, employment, business, line, speciality.

vogue noun FASHION, mode, style, trend, taste, fad, craze, rage, latest thing.

voice noun ❶ POWER OF SPEECH/ ARTICULATION. ❷ EXPRESSION, utterance, verbalization, vocalization, airing.
▸ verb PUT INTO WORDS, express, give utterance to, utter, articulate, enunciate, mention, talk of, communicate, declare, assert, divulge, air.

void adjective ❶ EMPTY, emptied, vacant, bare, clear, free, unfilled, unoccupied, uninhabited, untenanted, tenantless. ❷ NULL AND VOID, nullified, invalid, cancelled, inoperative, ineffective, non-viable, useless, worthless, nugatory.
– OPPOSITES full, valid.

volatile adjective ❶ MERCURIAL, changeable, variable, capricious, whimsical, fickle, flighty, giddy, inconstant, erratic, unstable. ❷ EXPLOSIVE, eruptive, charged, inflammatory, tense, strained.
– OPPOSITES stable.

voluble adjective TALKATIVE, loquacious, garrulous, chatty, gossipy, chattering, articulate, eloquent, forthcoming, fluent, glib.
– OPPOSITES taciturn.

volume noun ❶ BOOK, publication, tome. ❷ SPACE, bulk, capacity. ❸ LOUDNESS, sound, amplification.

voluminous adjective CAPACIOUS, roomy, commodious, ample, full, big, vast, billowing.
– OPPOSITES small.

voluntary adjective OF ONE'S OWN FREE WILL, volitional, of one's own accord, optional, discretionary, at one's discretion, elective, non-compulsory, non-mandatory.
–OPPOSITES compulsory.

volunteer verb OFFER ONE'S SERVICES, present oneself, step forward.

voluptuous adjective ❶ HEDONISTIC, sybaritic, epicurean, self-indulgent, sensual, carnal, licentious, lascivious. ❷ CURVY, shapely, full-figured, ample, buxom, seductive, curvaceous.
–OPPOSITES ascetic, scrawny.

vomit verb ❶ THROW UP; *Brit.* be sick; *informal* spew, puke. ❷ BRING UP, regurgitate, spew up, spit up.

voracious adjective ❶ GLUTTONOUS, greedy, ravenous, ravening, starving, hungry, insatiable. ❷ COMPULSIVE, enthusiastic, eager.

vortex noun WHIRLPOOL, maelstrom, eddy, swirl, whirlwind.

vote noun BALLOT, poll, election, referendum, plebiscite.
▶ verb CAST ONE'S VOTE, go to the polls, mark one's ballot paper.

vouch
■ **vouch for** ATTEST TO, bear witness to, give assurance of, answer for, be responsible for, guarantee, go/stand bail for.

voucher noun CHIT, slip, ticket, token, document.

vow verb SWEAR, state under oath, pledge, promise, undertake, give one's word of honour.

voyage noun JOURNEY, trip, expedition, crossing, cruise, passage.
▶ verb TRAVEL, journey, take a trip, sail, cruise.

vulgar adjective ❶ RUDE, indecent, indecorous, indelicate, crude, unseemly, offensive, distasteful, obnoxious, suggestive, off colour, ribald, bawdy, obscene, lewd, salacious, licentious, concupiscent, smutty, dirty, filthy, pornographic, scatological; *informal* raunchy, blue. ❷ TASTELESS, gross, crass, unrefined, tawdry, ostentatious, showy, flashy, gaudy.
–OPPOSITES tasteful.

vulnerable adjective EXPOSED, unprotected, unguarded, open to attack, assailable, defenceless, easily hurt/wounded/damaged, powerless, helpless, weak, sensitive, thin-skinned.
–OPPOSITES invulnerable.

Ww

wad noun ❶ LUMP, mass, chunk, hunk, bail, plug, block. ❷ **a wad of notes:** BUNDLE, roll.

wadding noun STUFFING, filling, packing, padding, lining.

waddle verb SWAY, wobble, totter, toddle, shuffle.

wade verb FORD, cross, traverse, paddle.
■ **wade in** SET TO, set to work,

pitch in, buckle down, go to it, put one's shoulder to the wheel; *informal* get cracking, get stuck in.

waffle **noun** MEANINGLESS TALK/WRITING, padding, equivocation, prattle, jabbering, verbiage, logorrhoea; *Brit. informal* wittering.
▶ **verb** RAMBLE, prattle, jabber, babble; *Brit. informal* rabbit, witter.

waft **verb** ❶ FLOAT, glide, drift, be carried/borne/conveyed.
❷ CARRY, bear, convey, transport, transmit.

wag[1] **verb** ❶ SWING, sway, vibrate, quiver, shake, rock, twitch. ❷ **wag one's finger**: WAGGLE, wiggle, wobble, wave.

wag[2] **noun** WIT, humorist, jester, joker, jokester, comic, comedian, comedienne, wisecracker, punner, punster.

wage **noun** PAY, salary, earnings, payment, fee, remuneration, stipend, emolument.
▶ **verb** CARRY ON, conduct, execute, engage in, pursue, undertake, devote oneself to, practise.

wager **noun** BET, gamble, stake, pledge, hazard; *Brit. informal* flutter.
▶ **verb** LAY A WAGER, bet, place/make/lay a bet, lay odds, put money on, speculate.

waggish **adjective** PLAYFUL, roguish, impish, mischievous, joking, jesting, jocular, jocose, facetious, witty, amusing, entertaining, droll, whimsical.

wail **noun** CRY OF GRIEF/PAIN, lament, lamentation, weeping, sob, moan, groan, whine, complaint, howl, yowl, ululation.
▶ **verb** CRY, lament, weep, sob, moan, groan, whine, howl, yowl, ululate.

wait **verb** ❶ **wait here**: STAY, remain, rest, linger, abide; *archaic* tarry. ❷ **wait until he comes**: BE PATIENT, hold back, stand by, bide one's time, hang fire, mark time; *informal* cool one's heels, sit tight, hold one's horses, sweat it out.
▶ **noun** INTERVAL, stay, delay, hold-up.
■ **wait on** ACT AS A WAITER/WAITRESS TO, serve, attend to.

waiter, waitress **noun** STEWARD, stewardess, server, attendant.

waive **verb** RELINQUISH, renounce, give up, abandon, surrender, yield, cede, set aside, forgo, disregard, ignore.

wake **verb** ❶ AWAKE, awaken, waken, wake up, waken up, rouse, stir, come to, get up, arise.
❷ ROUSE, stir up, activate, stimulate, spur, prod, galvanize, provoke.
– OPPOSITES sleep.
▶ **noun** VIGIL, death watch, watch.

wakeful **adjective** ❶ UNSLEEPING, restless, tossing and turning, insomniac. ❷ ALERT, on the alert, vigilant, on the lookout, on one's guard, on the qui vive, watchful, observant, attentive, heedful, wary.
– OPPOSITES asleep, inattentive.

walk **verb** ❶ GO BY FOOT, travel on foot, foot it; *informal* hoof it.
❷ STROLL, saunter, amble, plod, trudge, hike, tramp, trek, march, stride, step out. ❸ **walk her home**: ACCOMPANY, escort, convey.
▶ **noun** ❶ STROLL, saunter, amble, promenade, ramble, hike, tramp, march, constitutional, airing.
❷ MANNER OF WALKING, gait, pace, step, stride. ❸ ROAD, avenue, drive, promenade, path, pathway, footpath, track, lane, alley.
■ **walk off/away with** MAKE/RUN OFF WITH, carry off, snatch, steal,

pilfer, embezzle; *informal* filch.
walk out on DESERT, abandon, forsake, leave, leave in the lurch, run away from, throw over, jilt; *informal* chuck, dump.

walkover noun EASY VICTORY; *informal* piece of cake, child's play, doddle, pushover.

wall noun ❶ PARTITION, room divider. ❷ FORTIFICATION, rampart, barricade, parapet, bulwark, stockade, breastwork.

wallet noun PURSE, pouch; *N. Amer.* billfold, pocketbook; *Brit. dated* notecase.

wallow verb ❶ ROLL, tumble about, lie around, splash around. ❷ **wallow in self-pity**: LUXURIATE IN, bask in, take pleasure/satisfaction in, indulge oneself in, delight in, revel in, glory in, enjoy.

wan adjective PALE, pallid, ashen, white, white as a sheet/ghost, anaemic, colourless, bloodless, waxen, pasty, peaky, tired-looking, washed out, sickly.
– OPPOSITES ruddy.

wand noun BATON, stick, staff, twig, sprig, withe, withy.

wander verb ❶ RAMBLE, roam, meander, rove, range, prowl, saunter, stroll, amble, peregrinate, drift; *informal* traipse; *Brit. informal* mooch. ❷ STRAY, depart, diverge, veer, swerve, deviate. ❸ BE INCOHERENT, ramble, babble, talk nonsense, rave, be delirious.
▶ noun RAMBLE, saunter, stroll, amble.

wanderer noun RAMBLER, roamer, rover, drifter, traveller, itinerant, wayfarer, nomad, bird of passage, rolling stone, gypsy, vagabond, vagrant, tramp, derelict, beggar.

wane verb DECREASE, decline, diminish, dwindle, shrink, contract, taper off, subside, sink, ebb, dim, fade away, vanish, die out, draw to a close, evanesce, peter out, wind down, be on the way out, abate, fail, become weak, deteriorate, degenerate.
– OPPOSITES strengthen.

want verb ❶ WISH, wish for, desire, demand, call for, long for, hope for, yearn for, pine for, fancy, crave, hanker after, hunger for, thirst for, lust after, covet, need; *informal* have a yen for. ❷ NEED, be/stand in need of, require. ❸ LACK, be lacking, be without, be devoid of, be bereft of, be short of, be deficient in, have insufficient of.
▶ noun ❶ LACK, absence, dearth, deficiency, inadequacy, insufficiency, shortness, paucity, shortage, scarcity, scarceness, scantiness. ❷ WISH, desire, demand, longing, yearning, fancy, craving, hankering, hunger, thirst, lust, covetousness. ❸ NEED, neediness, privation, poverty, destitution, penury, indigence.

wanting adjective LACKING, deficient, inadequate, imperfect, not up to standard/par, not good enough, disappointing, not acceptable, not up to expectations, flawed, faulty, defective, unsound, substandard, inferior, second-rate.
– OPPOSITES sufficient.

wanton adjective ❶ **wanton women**: PROMISCUOUS, fast, immoral, loose, immodest, shameless, unchaste, unvirtuous, of easy virtue, impure, abandoned, lustful, lecherous, lascivious, libidinous, licentious, libertine, dissolute, dissipated, debauched, degenerate. ❷ **wanton**

destruction: WILFUL, malicious, malevolent, spiteful, wicked, evil, cruel, unmotivated, motiveless, arbitrary, groundless, unjustifiable, unjustified, needless, unnecessary, uncalled for, unprovoked, gratuitous, senseless, pointless, purposefulness.

war noun WARFARE, conflict, hostilities, strife, combat, fighting, struggle, armed conflict, battle, fight, confrontation, skirmish.
– OPPOSITES peace.

ward noun ❶ ROOM, compartment, cubicle. ❷ ADMINISTRATIVE DISTRICT, district, division, quarter, zone. ❸ CHARGE, dependant, protégé, pupil.
■ **ward off** FEND OFF, stave off, parry, avert, deflect, turn aside, drive back, repel, repulse, beat back, rout, put to flight, scatter, disperse.

warder noun PRISON OFFICER, guard, warden, jailer; *informal* screw.

warehouse noun STORE, storehouse, depot, depository, stockroom.

wares plural noun GOODS, products, commodities, lines, merchandise, produce, stuff, stock.

warily adverb CAREFULLY, with care, cautiously, gingerly, circumspectly, guardedly, on one's guard, on the alert, watchfully, vigilantly, suspiciously, distrustfully, mistrustfully, charily.
– OPPOSITES trustingly.

warlike adjective AGGRESSIVE, belligerent, bellicose, pugnacious, combative, militaristic, militant, martial.
– OPPOSITES peaceful, peaceable.

warm adjective ❶ warm water: HEATED, tepid, lukewarm. ❷ a warm day: SUNNY, balmy. ❸ a warm person: KINDLY, friendly, affable, amiable, genial, cordial, sympathetic, affectionate, loving, tender, caring, charitable, sincere, genuine. ❹ a warm greeting: HEARTY, cordial, genial, friendly, hospitable, enthusiastic, eager, sincere, heartfelt, ardent, vehement, passionate, intense, fervent, effusive.
– OPPOSITES cool, cold.
▶ verb WARM UP, make warm, heat, heat up, reheat.

warn verb ❶ INFORM, notify, give notice, give prior notice, tell, let know, acquaint, give fair warning, forewarn; *informal* tip off, put wise. ❷ warn them to be careful: ADVISE, exhort, urge, counsel, caution, forewarn, put on the alert, make aware. ❸ GIVE A WARNING TO, admonish, remonstrate with.

warning noun ❶ INFORMATION, notification, notice, word, forewarning; *informal* tip-off. ❷ CAUTION, advice, exhortation, counselling. ❸ ADMONITION, remonstrance. ❹ OMEN, premonition, foretoken, token, augury, signal, sign, threat.

warrant noun ❶ AUTHORIZATION, consent, sanction, permission, validation, licence, imprimatur, seal of approval. ❷ AUTHORIZATION, official document, written order, papers.
▶ verb JUSTIFY, vindicate, excuse, be a defence of, explain away, account for, be a reason for, offer grounds for, support.

wary adjective CAREFUL, cautious, circumspect, leery, chary, on one's guard, alert, wide awake, on

one's toes, on the alert/lookout, on the qui vive, attentive, heedful, watchful, vigilant, observant.
– OPPOSITES unwary.

wash verb ❶ WASH ONESELF, have a wash, bath, shower, have a bath/ shower. ❷ CLEAN, cleanse, sponge, scrub, launder, shampoo. ❸ SPLASH AGAINST, dash against, break against, beat against. ❹ **his story won't wash:** BE ACCEPTED, be plausible, be convincing, hold up, hold water, stand up, bear scrutiny.
▶ **noun** CLEAN, cleaning, cleansing, bath, shower.

waspish adjective PETULANT, peevish, querulous, touchy, testy, irritable, irascible, cross, cantankerous, splenetic, short-tempered, bad-tempered, crabbed, crotchety, grumpy; *informal* snappish.

waste verb SQUANDER, dissipate, fritter away, misspend, misuse, spend recklessly, throw away, go through, run through; *informal* blow.
– OPPOSITES conserve.
▶ **noun** ❶ SQUANDERING, dissipation, frittering away, misspending, misuse, prodigality, unthriftiness. ❷ RUBBISH, refuse, debris, dross, dregs, leavings, garbage, trash.
▶ **adjective** ❶ LEFTOVER, unused, superfluous, supernumerary, unwanted, worthless, useless. ❷ DESERT, barren, uncultivated, unproductive, arid, bare, desolate, solitary, lonely, empty, void, uninhabited, unpopulated, wild, bleak, cheerless.
■ **waste away** GROW WEAK, wither, atrophy, become emaciated.

wasteful adjective PRODIGAL, profligate, thriftless, spendthrift, extravagant, lavish.
– OPPOSITES thrifty.

watch verb ❶ LOOK AT, observe, view, eye, gaze at, stare at, gape at, peer at, contemplate, behold, inspect, scrutinize, survey, scan, examine. ❷ KEEP WATCH ON, keep an eye on, keep in sight, follow, spy on; *informal* keep tabs on. ❸ **watch the children:** MIND, take care of, look after, supervise, superintend, tend, guard, protect, keep an eye on.
▶ **noun** ❶ WRISTWATCH, pocket watch, timepiece, chronometer. ❷ GUARD, vigil.

watchful adjective OBSERVANT, alert, vigilant, attentive, heedful, sharp-eyed, eagle-eyed, wary, circumspect. *See also* WARY, ALERT adjective (1).

watchman noun SECURITY GUARD/ MAN, guard, custodian, caretaker.

water noun ❶ ADAM'S ALE, tap water, mineral water, bottled water. ❷ SEA, river, lake, loch, pool, reservoir.
▶ **verb** ❶ **water the garden:** SPRINKLE, moisten, dampen, wet, water down, douse, hose, spray, drench, saturate, flood. ❷ **eyes watering:** EXUDE WATER, moisten, leak.
■ **hold water** BE TENABLE, ring true, bear examination, work out.
water down ❶ ADD WATER TO, dilute, thin, weaken, adulterate. ❷ PLAY DOWN, downplay, tone down, soft-pedal, understate, underemphasize.

waterfall noun FALLS, cascade, cataract.

watertight adjective ❶ WATERPROOF, sound. ❷ **a watertight excuse:** SOUND, flawless,

incontrovertible, indisputable, foolproof, unassailable, impregnable.
– OPPOSITES leaky, flawed.

watery adjective ❶ AQUEOUS, liquid, liquefied, fluid, hydrous. ❷ WET, damp, moist, sodden, soggy, squelchy, saturated, waterlogged, marshy, boggy, swampy, miry. ❸ THIN, runny, weak, dilute, diluted, watered down, adulterated, tasteless, flavourless; *informal* wishy-washy.
– OPPOSITES dry, thick.

wave verb ❶ UNDULATE, ripple, stir, flutter, flap, sway, swing, shake, quiver, oscillate. ❷ **wave one's hand:** MOVE UP AND DOWN, move to and fro, wag, waggle, flutter. ❸ GESTURE, gesticulate, signal, sign, beckon, indicate.
▶ **noun** ❶ BREAKER, roller, comber, ripple, billow, white horse, white cap, swell, surf. ❷ **a wave of visitors:** STREAM, flow, rush, surge, flood. ❸ **the waves in her hair:** UNDULATION, curl, kink. ❹ **a crime wave:** SURGE, upsurge, groundswell, welling up, rush, outbreak, rash.
■ **wave aside** SET ASIDE, dismiss, reject, disregard, ignore.

waver verb ❶ BECOME UNSTEADY, falter, wobble, hesitate. ❷ BE IRRESOLUTE/INDECISIVE, hesitate, dither, equivocate, vacillate, shilly-shally, blow hot and cold, pussyfoot around, beat about the bush; *Brit.* hum and haw. ❸ WEAVE, reel, totter, teeter, stagger, wobble.

wavy adjective UNDULATING, curvy, curling, squiggly, rippled, curving, winding.
– OPPOSITES straight.

wax verb GET BIGGER, increase in size, enlarge, grow, develop, extend, widen, broaden, spread, mushroom.
– OPPOSITES wane.

way noun ❶ DIRECTION, route, course, road, roadway, street, thoroughfare, track, path, pathway, lane, avenue, drive. ❷ METHOD, means, course of action, process, procedure, technique, system, plan, scheme, manner, modus operandi. ❸ MANNER, style, fashion, mode. ❹ CONDUCT, behaviour, practice, manner, style, nature, personality, temperament, disposition, character, habit, custom, characteristic, trait, attribute, mannerism, peculiarity, idiosyncrasy. ❺ DISTANCE, length, stretch, journey.

wayfarer noun TRAVELLER, walker, hiker, rambler, wanderer, roamer, rover, nomad, gypsy, vagabond, vagrant.

waylay verb LIE IN WAIT FOR, ambush, hold up, attack, accost, intercept, pounce on, swoop down on.

wayward adjective WILFUL, self-willed, headstrong, stubborn, obstinate, obdurate, perverse, contrary, uncooperative, refractory, recalcitrant, contumacious, unruly, ungovernable, unmanageable, incorrigible, intractable, difficult, fractious, disobedient, insubordinate.
– OPPOSITES docile.

weak adjective ❶ FRAIL, fragile, delicate, feeble, infirm, shaky, debilitated, incapacitated, ailing, indisposed, decrepit, puny, faint, enervated, tired, fatigued, exhausted, spent, worn out. ❷ COWARDLY, pusillanimous, timorous, timid, spineless,

ineffectual, useless, inept, effete, powerless, impotent, namby-pamby, soft; *informal* yellow, weak-kneed. ❸ **weak eyesight**: DEFECTIVE, faulty, poor, inadequate, deficient, imperfect, substandard, lacking, wanting. ❹ **weak excuses**: UNSOUND, feeble, flimsy, lame, hollow, pathetic, unconvincing, untenable, implausible, unsatisfactory. ❺ **a weak signal**: FAINT, low, muffled, stifled, muted, scarcely audible. ❻ **weak coffee**: UNDER-STRENGTH, dilute, diluted, watery, thinned down, thin, adulterated, tasteless, flavourless, insipid; *informal* wishy-washy.
– OPPOSITES strong.

weaken verb ❶ ENFEEBLE, debilitate, incapacitate, sap someone's strength, enervate, tire, exhaust, wear out. ❷ LESSEN, reduce, decrease, diminish, moderate, temper, sap, emasculate. ❸ ABATE, lessen, decrease, dwindle, diminish, ease up, let up. ❹ RELENT, give in, acquiesce, yield, give way, accede, come round.
– OPPOSITES strengthen.

weakling noun COWARD, mouse, milksop, namby-pamby; *informal* wimp, sissy, drip, wet, doormat, chicken, yellow-belly.

weakness noun ❶ FRAILTY, fragility, delicateness, delicacy, feebleness, infirmity, debility, incapacity, indisposition, decrepitude, puniness, enervation, fatigue. ❷ COWARDLINESS, timidity, spinelessness, ineffectuality, ineptness, powerlessness, impotence. ❸ DEFECTIVENESS, faultiness, inadequacy, deficiency. ❹ UNSOUNDNESS, feebleness, flimsiness, lameness, untenability, implausibility. ❺ FAINTNESS, low intensity, mutedness. ❻ THINNESS, wateriness, tastelessness; *informal* wishy-washiness. ❼ WEAK POINT, failing, foible, fault, flaw, defect, shortcoming, imperfection, blemish, Achilles' heel, chink in one's armour.
– OPPOSITES strength.

wealth noun ❶ MONEY, cash, capital, treasure, fortune, finance, property, riches, assets, possessions, resources, goods, funds; *informal* wherewithal, dough, bread. ❷ **a wealth of opportunities**: MASS, abundance, profusion, copiousness, plenitude, amplitude, bounty, cornucopia.
– OPPOSITES poverty, scarcity.

wealthy adjective RICH, well off, well-to-do, moneyed, affluent, prosperous, of means, of substance; *informal* well heeled, rolling in it/money, in the money, made of money, filthy/stinking rich, loaded, flush, on easy street, quids in.
– OPPOSITES poor.

wear verb ❶ BE DRESSED IN, dress in, be clothed in, clothe oneself in, have on, put on, don, sport. ❷ HAVE, assume, present, show, display, exhibit. ❸ ERODE, corrode, abrade, wash away, rub away, rub down, grind away, wear down. ❹ BECOME WORN, wear thin, fray, become threadbare, go into holes.
■ **wear off** LOSE EFFECTIVENESS/EFFECT, lose intensity/strength, fade, peter out, dwindle, decrease, diminish, disappear, subside, ebb, wane. **wear out** FATIGUE, tire, weary, exhaust, drain, strain,

stress, weaken, enfeeble, prostrate, enervate; *Brit. informal* knacker; *N. Amer. informal* poop.

weariness noun FATIGUE, tiredness, exhaustion, enervation, lassitude, languor, listlessness, lethargy.

wearisome adjective FATIGUING, tiring, exhausting, draining, wearing, trying, irksome, boring, tedious, dull, uninteresting, monotonous, humdrum, routine. – OPPOSITES refreshing.

weary adjective ❶ FATIGUED, tired, exhausted, drained, worn, worn out, spent, careworn, wearied; *informal* dead tired/beat, dead on one's feet, dog-tired, all in, done in, whacked; *Brit. informal* fagged out, knackered; *N. Amer. informal* pooped; *Austral./NZ informal* bush. ❷ BORED, discontented, jaded, uninterested, listless, lethargic; *informal* browned off, fed up, sick and tired; *Brit. informal* cheesed off. – OPPOSITES fresh, keen.
▶ verb ❶ FATIGUE, tire, exhaust, drain, wear out; *informal* wear to a frazzle; *Brit. informal* knacker. ❷ BORE, irk, make discontented/jaded; *informal* make fed up. ❸ GROW WEARY, tire, get bored, have enough, grow discontented/jaded. – OPPOSITES refresh, interest.

weather verb ❶ DRY, season, expose, expose to the elements. ❷ **weather the recession**: COME/GET THROUGH, survive, withstand, live/pull through, bear up against, stand, endure, ride out, rise above, surmount, overcome, resist; *informal* stick out.

weave[1] verb ❶ INTERLACE, intertwine, interwork, twist together, entwine, braid, plait. ❷ MAKE UP, fabricate, put together, construct, invent, create, contrive.

weave[2] verb ZIGZAG, wind, criss-cross.

web noun LACEWORK, lattice, latticework, mesh, net, netting.

wed verb GET MARRIED, marry, become man and wife; *informal* get hitched/spliced, tie the knot. – OPPOSITES divorce, separate.

wedding noun WEDDING/MARRIAGE CEREMONY, marriage, nuptials.

wedge verb THRUST, stuff, pack, ram, force, cram, squeeze, jam.

weep verb CRY, shed tears, sob, blubber, snivel, whimper, whine, moan, lament, grieve, mourn, keen, wail; *informal* boohoo, blub.

weigh verb ❶ MEASURE/GAUGE THE WEIGHT OF, put on the scales. ❷ HAVE A WEIGHT OF; *informal* tip the scales at. ❸ BALANCE, compare with, evaluate.
■ **weigh up** CONSIDER, contemplate, think over, mull over, ponder, deliberate upon, meditate on, muse on, brood over, reflect on. **weigh with** CARRY WEIGHT WITH, have influence with, be influential to, count with, tell with, matter to, be important/significant to.

weight noun ❶ HEAVINESS, load, quantity, poundage, tonnage, avoirdupois. ❷ BURDEN, load, onus, millstone, albatross, oppression, trouble, worry, strain. ❸ IMPORTANCE, significance, consequence, value, substance, force, influence; *informal* clout.

weird adjective ❶ STRANGE, queer, uncanny, eerie, mysterious, mystifying, supernatural, preternatural, unnatural, unearthly, ghostly; *informal* spooky, creepy. ❷ ODD, eccentric, bizarre,

outlandish, freakish, grotesque; *informal* offbeat, far out, way-out, out on a limb.
–OPPOSITES normal, conventional.

welcome noun GREETING, salutation, reception, warm reception.
▶ verb ❶ BID WELCOME, greet, receive, embrace, receive with open arms, roll out the red carpet for, meet, usher in. ❷ BE PLEASED BY, take pleasure in, feel satisfaction at.
▶ adjective ❶ WANTED, appreciated, popular, desirable. ❷ GLADLY RECEIVED, pleasant, pleasing, agreeable, cheering, to one's liking, to one's taste.
–OPPOSITES unwelcome.

welfare noun ❶ WELL-BEING, health, good health, soundness, happiness, comfort, security, prosperity, success, fortune, good fortune. ❷ STATE AID/BENEFIT, public assistance, social security, income support.

well[1] adjective ❶ HEALTHY, in good health, fit, strong, robust, hale and hearty, able-bodied, up to par. ❷ SATISFACTORY, all right, fine, good, thriving, flourishing; *informal* OK, fine and dandy.

well[2] noun ❶ SPRING, fountain, waterhole, pool, borehole. ❷ SOURCE, wellspring, fount, reservoir, repository, mine.

well advised adjective SENSIBLE, wise, prudent, judicious, circumspect, far-sighted, sagacious.

well balanced adjective ❶ well-balanced people: WELL ADJUSTED, sensible, reasonable, rational, level-headed, sound, practical, discerning, logical, sane, in one's right mind. ❷ a well-balanced diet: BALANCED, well proportioned, well ordered.

well bred adjective WELL BROUGHT UP, mannerly, well mannered, courteous, polite, civil, ladylike, gentlemanly, gallant, chivalrous, cultivated, refined, polished, cultured, debonair, urbane.
–OPPOSITES rude.

well built adjective STRONGLY BUILT, strong, muscular, brawny, sturdy, robust, strapping, husky, burly, big; *informal* hulking, hefty, beefy.
–OPPOSITES puny.

well known adjective ❶ KNOWN, widely known, familiar, common, usual, everyday. ❷ FAMOUS, famed, renowned, celebrated, noted, notable, illustrious, eminent.
–OPPOSITES unknown.

well-nigh adverb VIRTUALLY, next to, practically, all but, just about, almost, nearly, more or less.

well off adjective WEALTHY, rich, well-to-do, moneyed, affluent, prosperous, of means, of substance; *informal* well heeled, rolling in it/money, in the money, made of money, filthy/stinking rich, loaded, flush, on easy street, quids in.
–OPPOSITES poor.

well spoken adjective ARTICULATE nicely spoken, educated, polite, refined; *Brit. informal* posh.

wet adjective ❶ DAMP, moist, moistened, wet through, soaked, drenched, saturated, sopping/dripping/wringing wet, sopping, dripping, soggy, waterlogged. ❷ a wet day: RAINY, raining, pouring, showery, drizzling, damp, humid, dank, misty. ❸ FEEBLE, weak,

inept, ineffective, ineffectual, effete, timid, timorous, cowardly, spineless, soft; *informal* namby-pamby, weedy.
▶ **noun** WETNESS, damp, dampness, moisture, moistness, condensation, humidity, water, liquid.
▶ **verb** DAMPEN, damp, moisten, sprinkle, spray, splash, water, irrigate, douse.
– OPPOSITES dry.

wharf **noun** PIER, quay, jetty, dock, landing stage.

wheel **verb** TURN, go round, circle, rotate, revolve, spin, swivel round, pivot, whirl/twirl round, make a U-turn.

wheeze **verb** GASP, puff, pant, cough, whistle, hiss, rasp.

whereabouts **noun** LOCATION, site, position, situation, place, vicinity.

whet **verb** SHARPEN, put an edge on, edge, hone, strop, file, grind, rasp.
– OPPOSITES blunt.

whim **noun** NOTION, fancy, idea, impulse, urge, caprice, vagary, craze, passion, inclination, bent.

whimper **verb** WHINE, cry, sniffle, snivel, moan, wail, groan.

whimsical **adjective** CAPRICIOUS, fanciful, fantastical, playful, mischievous, waggish, quaint, unusual, curious, droll, eccentric, peculiar, queer, bizarre, weird, freakish.

whine **verb** ❶ WHIMPER, cry, wail, groan; *informal* grizzle. ❷ *See* COMPLAIN (2).

whip **verb** ❶ LASH, flog, scourge, flagellate, birch, switch, strap, cane, thrash, beat, strike, leather; *informal* belt, tan, give someone a hiding. ❷ BEAT, whisk, mix.
▶ **noun** LASH, scourge, horsewhip, bullwhip, cat-o'-nine-tails, knout, crop, riding crop.

whirl **verb** TURN ROUND, circle, spin, rotate, revolve, wheel, twirl, swirl, gyrate, reel, pirouette, pivot.

whirlpool **noun** VORTEX, maelstrom, eddy, whirl.

whirlwind **noun** TORNADO, hurricane, typhoon.
▶ **adjective** SWIFT, rapid, quick, speedy, hasty, headlong.

whisk **verb** WHIP, beat, mix, stir.
▶ **noun** MIXER, beater.

whisper **verb** MURMUR, mutter, speak softly, speak in muted/hushed tones.
– OPPOSITES roar.
▶ **noun** ❶ MURMUR, mutter, low voice, hushed tone, undertone. ❷ RUMOUR, report, insinuation, suggestion, hint, gossip, word.

whit **noun** PARTICLE, bit, jot, iota, mite, little, trifle.

white **adjective** ❶ PALE, wan, pallid, ashen, anaemic, colourless, bloodless, waxen, pasty, peaky, whey-faced, grey. ❷ GREY, silver, hoary, snowy-white, grizzled.

white-collar **adjective** NON-MANUAL, office, clerical, professional, executive, salaried.

whiten **verb** MAKE WHITE, make pale, bleach, blanch, fade, wash out, etiolate.

whole **adjective** ❶ ENTIRE, complete, full, total, solid, integral, unabridged, unreduced, undivided, uncut. ❷ INTACT, sound, flawless, in one piece, unimpaired, undamaged, unharmed, unhurt, uninjured, unmutilated.
– OPPOSITES incomplete.

wholehearted adjective UNRESERVED, unqualified, unstinting, complete, committed, hearty, emphatic, real, sincere, genuine.
– OPPOSITES half-hearted.

wholesale adjective INDISCRIMINATE, mass, all-inclusive, total, comprehensive, extensive, wide-ranging, sweeping, broad.
– OPPOSITES partial.

wholesome adjective ❶ wholesome food: NUTRITIOUS, nourishing, health-giving, healthful, good, strengthening. ❷ wholesome literature: MORAL, ethical, uplifting, edifying, helpful, beneficial.

wholly adverb COMPLETELY, fully, entirely, totally, utterly, thoroughly, altogether, comprehensively, in every respect, perfectly, enthusiastically, with total commitment, unreservedly, heart and soul.

wicked adjective ❶ a wicked man: EVIL, sinful, bad, black-hearted, villainous, base, vile, vicious, dishonourable, unprincipled, unrighteous, criminal, lawless, perverted, immoral, amoral, unethical, corrupt, dissolute, abandoned, dissipated, degenerate, reprobate, debauched, depraved, unholy, impious, irreligious, ungodly, godless, devilish. ❷ wicked deeds: EVIL, sinful, iniquitous, wrong, bad, vile, foul, base, mean, gross, odious, obnoxious, nefarious, heinous, infamous, dreadful, dire, grim, horrible, hideous, gruesome, monstrous, atrocious, abominable, abhorrent, loathsome, hateful, detestable, reprehensible, dishonourable, disgraceful, shameful, ignominious, lawless, unlawful, illicit, illegal, villainous, dastardly, unholy, impious, impure, ungodly, godless, irreverent, irreligious, damnable, devilish, demonic, diabolic; *archaic* blackguardly.
– OPPOSITES good, righteous.

wide adjective ❶ BROAD, extensive, spacious. ❷ wide hips: BROAD, large, outspread, spread out, ample. ❸ wide knowledge: BROAD, extensive, large, large-scale, vast, far-ranging, immense, wide-ranging, expansive, sweeping, encyclopedic, comprehensive, general, all-embracing, catholic, compendious.
– OPPOSITES narrow.

wide-eyed adjective ❶ SURPRISED, amazed, astonished, astounded. ❷ NAIVE, impressionable, ingenuous, credulous, trusting, unsuspicious, innocent, simple, unsophisticated, inexperienced, green; *informal* wet behind the ears.

widen verb ❶ MAKE WIDER, broaden, expand, extend, enlarge, increase, augment, add to, supplement. ❷ OPEN WIDE, dilate.

widespread adjective UNIVERSAL, common, general, far-reaching, prevalent, rife, extensive, sweeping, pervasive, epidemic.
– OPPOSITES limited.

width noun ❶ WIDENESS, breadth, broadness, span, diameter. ❷ WIDENESS, breadth, scope, range, span, extensiveness, vastness, immensity, expansiveness, comprehensiveness.
– OPPOSITES length, narrowness.

wield verb ❶ BRANDISH, flourish, wave, swing, use, employ, handle, ply, manipulate. ❷ EXERCISE, exert, be possessed of, have, have at one's disposal, hold, maintain, command, control.

wild adjective ❶ wild horses: UNTAMED, undomesticated, unbroken, feral, savage, fierce, ferocious. ❷ wild flowers: UNCULTIVATED, natural, native, indigenous. ❸ wild peoples: UNCIVILIZED, primitive, ignorant, savage, barbaric, barbarous, brutish, ferocious, fierce. ❹ a wild night: STORMY, tempestuous, turbulent, blustery, howling, violent, raging, furious, rough. ❺ a wild life: UNDISCIPLINED, unrestrained, unconstrained, uncontrolled, out of control, unbridled, unchecked, chaotic, disorderly. ❻ a wild crowd: ROWDY, unruly, disorderly, turbulent, violent, lawless, riotous, out of control, unmanageable, ungovernable, unrestrained, excited, passionate, frantic. ❼ he went wild: CRAZY, beside oneself, berserk, frantic, frenzied, in a frenzy, hysterical, crazed, mad, distracted, distraught, irrational, deranged, demented, raving, maniacal, rabid. ❽ wild schemes: EXTRAVAGANT, fantastical, impracticable, foolish, ill-advised, ill-considered, imprudent, unwise, madcap, impulsive, reckless, rash, outrageous, preposterous.
– OPPOSITES tame, cultivated, calm, disciplined.

wilderness noun DESERT, wasteland, waste, the wilds, jungle, no-man's-land.

wiles plural noun TRICKS, ruses, ploys, schemes, dodges, manoeuvres, subterfuges, artifices, guile, artfulness, cunning, craftiness.

wilful adjective ❶ wilful neglect: DELIBERATE, intentional, intended, conscious, purposeful, premeditated, planned, calculated. ❷ wilful children: HEADSTRONG, strong-willed, obstinate, stubborn, mulish, pig-headed, obdurate, intransigent, adamant, dogged, determined, persistent, unyielding, uncompromising, intractable, refractory, recalcitrant, disobedient, contrary, perverse, wayward, self-willed.
– OPPOSITES accidental.

will noun ❶ VOLITION, choice, option, decision, discretion, prerogative. ❷ DESIRE, wish, preference, inclination, fancy, mind. ❸ WILL POWER, determination, resolution, resolve, firmness of purpose, purposefulness, doggedness, single-mindedness, commitment, moral fibre, pluck, mettle, grit, nerve. ❹ LAST WILL AND TESTAMENT, testament, last wishes.

willing adjective ❶ PREPARED, ready, game, disposed, content, happy, so-minded, consenting, agreeable, amenable, in the mood, compliant. ❷ willing help: COOPERATIVE, gladly given, cheerful, accommodating, obliging.
– OPPOSITES unwilling.

willingly adverb VOLUNTARILY, of one's own free will, of one's own accord, by choice, by volition, spontaneously, unforced.

wilt verb ❶ DROOP, wither, shrivel, lose freshness, sag. ❷ DIMINISH, dwindle, lessen, grow less, flag,

fade, melt away, ebb, wane, weaken, fail.
– OPPOSITES flourish.

wily adjective CRAFTY, cunning, artful, sharp, astute, shrewd, scheming, intriguing, shifty, sly, guileful, deceitful, deceptive, fraudulent, cheating, underhand; *informal* crooked, foxy; *Brit. informal* fly.
– OPPOSITES naive.

win verb ❶ **win first prize:** ACHIEVE, attain, earn, gain, receive, obtain, acquire, procure, get, secure, collect, pick up, come away with, net, bag. ❷ BE VICTORIOUS, be the victor, gain the victory, overcome, achieve mastery, carry the day, carry all before one, finish first, come out ahead, come out on top, win out, succeed, triumph, prevail.
– OPPOSITES lose.

wind[1] noun ❶ AIR CURRENT, breeze, gust, blast, gale, storm, hurricane; *poetic/literary* zephyr. ❷ BREATH, respiration; *informal* puff. ❸ FLATULENCE, gas; *formal* flatus.

wind[2] verb TWIST, twist and turn, curve, bend, loop, zigzag, snake, spiral, meander, ramble.
■ **wind down** UNWIND, relax, become less tense, ease up, calm down, cool off. **wind up** BRING TO AN END/CONCLUSION, end, conclude, terminate, finish; *informal* wrap up.

windfall noun PIECE/STROKE OF GOOD LUCK, unexpected gain, godsend, manna from heaven, bonanza, jackpot.

windy adjective ❶ BREEZY, blowy, blustery, blustering, gusty, gusting, boisterous, squally, stormy, wild, tempestuous, turbulent. ❷ LONG-WINDED, loquacious, wordy, verbose, rambling, meandering, prolix, diffuse, turgid. ❸ NERVOUS, scared, frightened, alarmed, fearful, timid, timorous, cowardly.
– OPPOSITES still.

wink verb ❶ BLINK, flutter, bat; *technical* nictate. ❷ FLASH, twinkle, sparkle, glitter, gleam.

winner noun CHAMPION, victor, vanquisher, conqueror, prizewinner.
– OPPOSITES loser.

winning adjective ❶ VICTORIOUS, successful, triumphant, vanquishing, conquering. ❷ **a winning smile:** CAPTIVATING, enchanting, bewitching, beguiling, disarming, taking, engaging, endearing, winsome, charming, attractive, fetching, alluring, sweet, lovely, delightful, darling, pleasing.

wintry adjective COLD, chilly, icy, frosty, freezing, frozen, snowy, arctic, glacial, biting, piercing, nippy.
– OPPOSITES warm.

wipe verb RUB, brush, dust, mop, sponge, swab, clean, dry.
■ **wipe out** *see* DESTROY.

wiry adjective ❶ LEAN, spare, sinewy, tough, strong. ❷ BRISTLY, prickly, thorny, stiff, rigid.

wisdom noun ❶ SAGENESS, sagacity, cleverness, intelligence, erudition, learning, education, knowledge, enlightenment, reason, discernment, perception, insight. ❷ SENSE, common sense, prudence, judiciousness, judgement, shrewdness, astuteness, circumspection, strategy, foresight, reasonableness, rationality, logic, soundness, saneness; *informal* smartness.
– OPPOSITES folly.

wise adjective ❶ SAGE, sagacious, clever, intelligent, erudite, learned, educated, well read, knowledgeable, informed, enlightened, philosophic, deep-thinking, discerning, perceptive, experienced; *formal* sapient. ❷ SENSIBLE, prudent, well advised, judicious, politic, shrewd, astute, reasonable, rational, logical, sound, sane; *informal* smart.
– OPPOSITES unwise.

wish verb WANT, desire, long for, hope for, yearn for, pine for, have a fancy for, fancy, crave, hunger for, thirst for, lust after, covet, sigh for, set one's heart on, hanker after, have a yen for.
▶ noun DESIRE, liking, fondness, longing, hope, yearning, want, fancy, aspiration, inclination, urge, whim, craving, hunger, thirst, lust, hankering, yen.

wishy-washy adjective ❶ WEAK, feeble, puny, ineffectual, effete, spineless, weak-kneed. ❷ PALLID, pale, wan, sickly. ❸ TASTELESS, flavourless, insipid, watery, weak, diluted.
– OPPOSITES strong, tasty.

wistful adjective YEARNING, longing, forlorn, disconsolate, melancholy, sad, mournful, dreamy, in a reverie, pensive, reflective, musing, contemplative, meditative.

wit noun ❶ WITTINESS, humour, jocularity, funniness, facetiousness, drollery, waggishness, repartee, badinage, banter, raillery. ❷ HUMORIST, wag, funny person, comic, jokester, banterer; *informal* card.

witch noun SORCERESS, enchantress, magician, necromancer, hex.

witchcraft noun WITCHERY, sorcery, black art/magic, magic, necromancy, wizardry, occultism, the occult, sortilege, thaumaturgy, wonder-working.

withdraw verb ❶ TAKE BACK, pull back, take away, extract, remove. ❷ **withdraw that remark**: TAKE BACK, retract, recall, unsay. ❸ **withdraw the bill**: REVOKE, annul, nullify, declare void, rescind, repeal, abrogate. ❹ **the troops withdrew**: PULL BACK, fall back, retire, retreat, disengage, back down, depart, go, leave; *informal* make oneself scarce.
– OPPOSITES insert, enter.

withdrawn adjective RETIRING, reserved, uncommunicative, unforthcoming, unsociable, taciturn, silent, quiet, introverted, detached, aloof, self-contained, distant, private, shrinking, timid, timorous, shy, bashful, diffident.
– OPPOSITES outgoing.

wither verb ❶ DRY UP/OUT, shrivel, go limp, wilt, die. ❷ DECLINE, fade, ebb, wane, disintegrate, die, perish.
– OPPOSITES thrive.

withhold verb ❶ HOLD BACK, keep back, restrain, hold/keep in check, check, curb, repress, suppress. ❷ REFUSE TO GIVE/GRANT/ALLOW, refuse, decline, keep back.

withstand verb HOLD OUT AGAINST, stand up to, stand firm against, resist, fight, combat, oppose, endure, stand, tolerate, bear, put up with, take, cope with, weather, brave.

witness noun EYEWITNESS, observer, spectator, onlooker, looker-on, viewer, watcher, beholder, bystander.
▶ verb SEE, observe, view, watch, look on at, behold, perceive, be present at, attend.

witticism noun WITTY REMARK, clever saying, flash of wit, bon mot, quip, sally, pleasantry, riposte, joke, jest, epigram; *informal* wisecrack, crack, one-liner.

witty adjective CLEVER, original, ingenious, sparkling, scintillating, humorous, amusing, jocular, funny, facetious, droll, waggish, comic.

wizard noun SORCERER, warlock, enchanter, witch, necromancer, magician, magus.

wizened adjective WITHERED, shrivelled, dried up, shrunken, wasted, wrinkled, lined, gnarled, worn.

wobble verb ❶ ROCK, sway, see-saw, teeter, shake, vibrate. ❷ TEETER, totter, stagger, waddle, waggle.

woe noun ❶ **a tale of woe:** MISERY, wretchedness, misfortune, disaster, grief, anguish, affliction, suffering, pain, agony, torment, sorrow, sadness, unhappiness, distress, heartache, heartbreak, despondency, desolation, dejection, depression, gloom, melancholy. ❷ **her woes:** TROUBLE, misfortune, adversity, trial, tribulation, ordeal, burden, affliction, suffering, disaster, calamity, catastrophe.
– OPPOSITES joy.

woebegone adjective MISERABLE, sad, unhappy, sorrowful, disconsolate, mournful, downcast, dejected, doleful, desolate, depressed, despairing, tearful.
– OPPOSITES cheerful.

woeful adjective ❶ SAD, saddening, unhappy, sorrowful, miserable, dismal, wretched, doleful, gloomy, tragic, pathetic, grievous, pitiful, plaintive, heart-rending, heartbreaking, distressing, anguished, agonizing, dreadful, terrible. ❷ **woeful work:** POOR, bad, inadequate, substandard, lamentable, deplorable, disgraceful, wretched, disappointing, feeble; *informal* rotten, lousy, shocking; *Brit. informal* duff.
– OPPOSITES cheerful, excellent.

woman noun ❶ FEMALE, lady, girl, member of the fair/gentle sex; *informal* chick; *Brit. informal* bird; *N. Amer. informal* dame, broad. ❷ GIRLFRIEND, lady-love, sweetheart, partner, lover, wife, spouse.

wonder noun ❶ WONDERMENT, awe, surprise, astonishment, amazement, bewilderment, stupefaction, fascination, admiration. ❷ **the wonders of the world:** MARVEL, phenomenon, miracle, prodigy, curiosity, rarity, nonpareil, sight, spectacle.
▶ **verb** ❶ THINK, speculate, conjecture, ponder, meditate, reflect, deliberate, muse, ask oneself, puzzle, be curious about, be inquisitive about. ❷ MARVEL, stand amazed, stand in awe, be dumbfounded, gape, stare, goggle, look agog; *informal* be flabbergasted, gawk, boggle.

wonderful adjective MARVELLOUS, awe-inspiring, awesome, remarkable, extraordinary, phenomenal, prodigious, miraculous, amazing, astonishing, astounding, surprising, incredible, unprecedented, unparalleled, unheard of; *poetic/literary* wondrous. *See also* EXCELLENT.
– OPPOSITES dreadful.

wonted adjective CUSTOMARY,

accustomed, habitual, usual, normal, routine, regular, common, frequent, familiar, conventional.

woo verb ❶ PAY COURT TO, seek someone's hand, pursue, chase after; *dated* court, set one's cap at. ❷ IMPORTUNE, press, urge, entreat, beg, implore, supplicate, solicit, coax, wheedle.

wood noun ❶ FOREST, woodland, copse, thicket, coppice, grove. ❷ TIMBER, firewood, kindling, fuel.

wooded adjective WOODY, forested, tree-covered, tree-clad, timbered, sylvan.

wooden adjective ❶ MADE OF WOOD, wood, woody, timber. ❷ **a wooden performance**: STIFF, stolid, stodgy, expressionless, graceless, inelegant, ungainly, gauche, awkward, clumsy, maladroit. ❸ **a wooden expression**: EXPRESSIONLESS, inexpressive, blank, deadpan, empty, vacant, vacuous, glassy, impassive, lifeless, spiritless, unanimated, emotionless, unemotional, unresponsive.

woolly adjective ❶ WOOLLEN, made of wool, wool. ❷ FLEECY, fluffy, shaggy, hairy, furry. ❸ **a woolly description**: VAGUE, hazy, indefinite, muddled, confused, disorganized.

word noun ❶ TERM, expression, name. ❷ **give one's word**: WORD OF HONOUR, promise, pledge, assurance, guarantee, undertaking, vow, oath. ❸ **have had word of it**: NEWS, intimation, notice, communication, information, intelligence, message, report, account.
▶ **verb** EXPRESS, phrase, couch, put, say, utter, state.

wordy adjective LONG-WINDED, verbose, loquacious, garrulous, voluble, prolix, protracted, discursive, diffuse, rambling, digressive, maundering, tautological, pleonastic.

work noun ❶ EFFORT, exertion, labour, toil, slog, sweat, drudgery, trouble, industry; *informal* grind, elbow grease; *poetic/literary* travail. ❷ JOB, task, chore, undertaking, duty, charge, assignment, commission, mission. ❸ EMPLOYMENT, occupation, business, job, profession, career, trade, vocation, calling, craft, line, field, métier, pursuit.
– OPPOSITES leisure.
▶ **verb** ❶ BE EMPLOYED, have a job, hold down a job, earn one's living, do business, follow/ply one's trade. ❷ EXERT ONESELF, put in effort, make efforts, labour, toil, slog, sweat, drudge, slave; *informal* grind, plug away, knock oneself out. ❸ **work the machine**: OPERATE, control, drive, manage, direct, use, handle, manipulate, manoeuvre, ply, wield. ❹ **the machine won't work**: GO, operate, function, perform, run. ❺ **the plan won't work**: SUCCEED, be successful, have success, go well, be effective, be effectual.
– OPPOSITES rest, fail.

workable adjective PRACTICABLE, practical, viable, doable, feasible, possible.
– OPPOSITES impracticable.

worker noun EMPLOYEE, hand, workman, working man/woman/person, blue-collar worker, white-collar worker, labourer, artisan, craftsman, craftswoman, wage-earner, proletarian.

working adjective ❶ IN WORK, employed, in a job, waged.

❷ FUNCTIONING, operating, going, running, in working order.
– OPPOSITES unemployed, broken.

workmanship noun CRAFTSMANSHIP, craft, artistry, art, handicraft, handiwork, expertise, skill, technique, work.

workshop noun ❶ FACTORY, plant, mill, garage. ❷ WORKROOM, studio, atelier, shop. ❸ SEMINAR, study/discussion group, class.

world noun ❶ EARTH, globe, sphere, planet. ❷ **the academic world:** SOCIETY, sector, section, group, division.

worldly adjective ❶ EARTHLY, secular, temporal, material, materialistic, human, carnal, fleshly, corporeal, physical. ❷ WORLDLY-WISE, experienced, knowing, sophisticated, cosmopolitan, urbane.
– OPPOSITES spiritual, naive.

worldwide adjective UNIVERSAL, global, international, pandemic, general, ubiquitous, extensive, widespread, far-reaching, wide-ranging.
– OPPOSITES local.

worn adjective ❶ WORN OUT, threadbare, tattered, in tatters, ragged, frayed, shabby, shiny. ❷ HAGGARD, drawn, strained, careworn; *informal* done in, dog-tired, dead on one's feet, fit to drop, played out; *Brit. informal* knackered; *N. Amer. informal* pooped; *Austral./NZ informal* bush.

worried adjective ANXIOUS, disturbed, perturbed, troubled, bothered, distressed, concerned, upset, distraught, uneasy, ill at ease, disquieted, fretful, agitated, nervous, edgy, on edge, tense, overwrought, worked up, distracted, apprehensive, fearful, afraid, frightened; *informal* uptight; *N. Amer. informal* antsy.
– OPPOSITES carefree.

worry verb ❶ BE WORRIED, be anxious, fret, brood. ❷ MAKE ANXIOUS, disturb, trouble, bother, distress, upset, concern, disquiet, discompose, fret, agitate, unsettle.
▶ noun ❶ ANXIETY, disturbance, perturbation, trouble, bother, distress, concern, care, uneasiness, unease, disquiet, disquietude, fretfulness, agitation, edginess, tenseness, apprehension, fearfulness. ❷ NUISANCE, pest, plague, trial, trouble, problem, irritation, irritant, vexation, thorn in one's flesh.

worsen verb ❶ MAKE WORSE, aggravate, exacerbate, damage, intensify, increase, heighten. ❷ GET/GROW/BECOME WORSE, take a turn for the worse, deteriorate, degenerate, retrogress, decline, sink, slip, slide, go downhill.
– OPPOSITES improve.

worship noun REVERENCE, veneration, homage, respect, honour, adoration, devotion, praise, prayer, glorification, exaltation, extolment; *formal* laudation.
▶ verb ❶ REVERE, venerate, pay homage to, honour, adore, praise, pray to, glorify, exalt, extol; *formal* laud. ❷ ADORE, be devoted to, cherish, treasure, admire, adulate, idolize, hero-worship, lionize; *informal* be wild about.

worth noun ❶ FINANCIAL VALUE, value, price, cost. ❷ VALUE, use, usefulness, advantage, benefit, service, gain, profit, avail, help, assistance, aid.

worthless adjective ❶ VALUELESS, of little/no financial value; *informal* rubbishy, trashy. ❷ USELESS, of no use, of no benefit, to no avail, futile, ineffective, ineffectual, pointless, nugatory. ❸ GOOD-FOR-NOTHING, useless, despicable, contemptible, base, low, vile, corrupt, depraved; *informal* no-good, no-account.
– OPPOSITES valuable, useful, worthwhile.

worthwhile adjective WORTH IT, worth the effort, valuable, of value, useful, of use, beneficial, advantageous, helpful, profitable, gainful, productive, constructive, justifiable.

worthy adjective VIRTUOUS, good, moral, upright, righteous, honest, decent, honourable, respectable, reputable, trustworthy, reliable, irreproachable, blameless, unimpeachable, admirable, praiseworthy, laudable, commendable, deserving, meritorious.
– OPPOSITES disreputable.
■ **worthy of** DESERVING, meriting.

wound noun INJURY, lesion, cut, graze, scratch, gash, laceration, tear, puncture, slash, sore.
▶ verb CUT, graze, scratch, gash, lacerate, tear, puncture, pierce, stab, slash, injure, hurt, damage, harm.

wraith noun GHOST, spectre, shade, phantom, apparition, spirit.

wrap verb ❶ ENVELOP, enfold, encase, enclose, cover, swathe, bundle up, swaddle. ❷ WRAP UP, parcel up, package, do up, tie up, gift-wrap.
▶ noun SHAWL, stole, cloak, cape, mantle.
■ **wrap up** FINISH, end, bring to an end/close, conclude, terminate, wind up.

wrath noun ANGER, rage, fury, annoyance, exasperation, high dudgeon, bad temper, ill humour, irritation, crossness, displeasure, irascibility; *poetic/literary* ire.
– OPPOSITES happiness.

wreathe verb ❶ COVER, envelop, festoon, garland, adorn, decorate. ❷ TWIST, wind, coil, twine, entwine, curl, spiral, wrap.

wreck noun ❶ SHIPWRECK, sunken ship/vessel, derelict. ❷ WRECKING, wreckage, destruction, devastation, ruination, ruin, demolition, smashing, shattering, disruption, disintegration, undoing.
▶ verb ❶ SMASH, demolish, ruin, damage; *informal* write off. ❷ DESTROY, devastate, ruin, demolish, smash, shatter, disrupt, undo, spoil, mar, play havoc with. ❸ SHIPWRECK, sink, capsize, run aground.

wreckage noun WRECK, debris, ruins, remains, remnants, fragments.

wrench verb TWIST, pull, tug, yank, wrest, jerk, tear, force.

wrest verb TWIST, wrench, pull, snatch, take away, remove.

wretch noun ❶ POOR CREATURE/SOUL/THING, miserable creature, unfortunate, poor devil. ❷ SCOUNDREL, villain, ruffian, rogue, rascal, reprobate, criminal, delinquent, miscreant; *informal* creep, jerk, louse, rat, swine, skunk; *informal, dated* rotter; *archaic* blackguard.

wretched adjective ❶ MISERABLE, unhappy, sad, broken-hearted,

sorrowful, sorry, distressed, disconsolate, downcast, down, downhearted, dejected, crestfallen, cheerless, depressed, melancholy, gloomy, doleful, forlorn, woebegone, abject. **❷** POOR, bad, substandard, low-quality, inferior, pathetic, worthless.
– OPPOSITES cheerful, excellent.

wriggle **verb** TWIST, squirm, writhe, jiggle, wiggle, snake, crawl, slink.

wring **verb** **❶** TWIST, squeeze. **❷** EXTRACT, force, coerce, exact, extort, wrest, wrench, screw.

wrinkle **noun** CREASE, fold, pucker, gather, furrow, ridge, line, corrugation, crinkle, crumple, rumple.
▶ **verb** CREASE, pucker, gather, furrow, line, corrugate, crumple, rumple.

write **verb** **❶** **write their names:** WRITE DOWN, put in writing, put in black and white, commit to paper, jot down, note, set down, take down, record, register, list, inscribe, scribble, scrawl. **❷** **write an essay:** COMPOSE, draft, create, pen, dash off.
■ **write off** **❶** FORGET ABOUT, disregard, give up for lost, cancel, annul, nullify, wipe out, cross out, score out. **❷** DAMAGE BEYOND REPAIR, wreck, smash, crash, destroy, demolish; *N. Amer. informal* total.

writer **noun** AUTHOR, wordsmith, penman, novelist, essayist, biographer, journalist, columnist, scriptwriter; *informal* scribbler, pen-pusher.

writhe **verb** TWIST ABOUT, twist and turn, roll about, squirm, wriggle, jerk, thrash, flail, toss, struggle.

writing **noun** **❶** HANDWRITING, hand, penmanship, script, print, calligraphy, scribble, scrawl. **❷** WORK, opus, book, volume, publication, composition.

wrong **adjective** **❶** **the wrong answer:** INCORRECT, inaccurate, in error, erroneous, wide of the mark, mistaken, inexact, imprecise, unsound, faulty, false; *informal* off beam, barking up the wrong tree, off target. **❷** **the wrong moment:** UNSUITABLE, inappropriate, inapt, inapposite, undesirable, infelicitous. **❸** **it's wrong to steal:** IMMORAL, bad, wicked, evil, unlawful, illegal, illicit, lawless, criminal, delinquent, felonious, dishonest, dishonourable, corrupt, unethical, sinful, iniquitous, blameworthy, culpable; *informal* crooked. **❹** **something wrong with the phone:** AMISS, awry, out of order, not right, faulty, defective.
– OPPOSITES right.
▶ **noun** **❶** BADNESS, immorality, sin, sinfulness, wickedness, evil, iniquity, unlawfulness, crime, dishonesty, dishonour, injustice, transgression, abuse; *informal* crookedness. **❷** MISDEED, offence, injury, crime, infringement, infraction, injustice, grievance, outrage, atrocity.
– OPPOSITES right.
▶ **verb** **❶** ABUSE, mistreat, maltreat, harm, hurt, do injury to. **❷** MISREPRESENT, malign, dishonour, impugn, vilify, defame, slander, libel, denigrate, insult; *informal* bad-mouth.

wrongdoer **noun** LAWBREAKER, criminal, delinquent, culprit, offender, felon, villain, miscreant, evil-doer, sinner, transgressor, malefactor; *informal* wrong 'un.

wrongful adjective UNFAIR, unjust, improper, unjustified, unwarranted, unlawful, illegal, illegitimate, illicit.

wry adjective ❶ TWISTED, distorted, contorted, crooked, lopsided, askew. ❷ IRONIC, sardonic, mocking, sarcastic, dry, droll, witty, humorous.

yank verb PULL, tug, jerk, wrench. ▶ noun PULL, jerk, wrench.

yardstick noun MEASURE, standard, gauge, scale, guide, guideline, touchstone, criterion, benchmark, model, pattern.

yarn noun ❶ THREAD, fibre, strand. ❷ STORY, tale, anecdote, fable, traveller's tale; *informal* tall tale/story, cock and bull story.

yawning adjective WIDE, wide open, gaping, cavernous.

yearly adjective ANNUAL, once a year, every year.

yearn verb LONG, pine, have a longing, crave, desire, want, wish for, hanker after, covet, fancy, hunger for, thirst for; *informal* have a yen for.

yell verb SHOUT, cry out, howl, scream, shriek, screech, squeal, roar, bawl, whoop; *informal* holler.

yen noun HANKERING, desire, want, wish, fancy, longing, craving, hunger, thirst, lust.

yes adverb ALL RIGHT, of course, by all means, sure, certainly, in the affirmative; *informal* yeah, yah, yep, uh-huh; *Brit. informal* righto.
– OPPOSITES no.

yield verb ❶ GIVE, return, bring in, fetch, earn, net, produce, supply, provide, generate, furnish. ❷ GIVE UP, surrender, relinquish, part with, deliver up, turn over, give over, remit, cede, renounce, resign, abdicate, forgo. ❸ ADMIT/CONCEDE DEFEAT, surrender, capitulate, submit, lay down one's arms, give in, give up the struggle, succumb, raise/show the white flag, throw in the towel/sponge, cave in.
– OPPOSITES withhold, resist.

yoke noun ❶ HARNESS, collar, coupling. ❷ OPPRESSION, tyranny, enslavement, slavery, servitude, bondage, thrall.

yokel noun RUSTIC, countryman, countrywoman, peasant, country bumpkin, provincial; *N. Amer. informal* hayseed, hillbilly.

young adjective ❶ YOUTHFUL, juvenile, junior, adolescent, in the springtime of life, in one's salad days. ❷ NEW, recent, undeveloped, fledgling, in the making.
– OPPOSITES old.

youngster noun YOUNG ADULT/PERSON, youth, juvenile, teenager, adolescent, lad, boy, young man/woman, girl; *Scottish & N. English* lass; *informal* kid, shaver, young 'un.

youth noun ❶ YOUNG DAYS, early years, teens, early life, adolescence, boyhood, girlhood. ❷ BOY, young man, lad, youngster, juvenile, teenager, adolescent; *informal* kid.

youthful adjective YOUNG, active, vigorous, spry, sprightly.
– OPPOSITES old.

Zz

zany adjective ECCENTRIC, peculiar, odd, ridiculous, absurd, comic, clownish, madcap, funny, amusing, weird; *informal* screwy, wacky; *Brit. informal* daft; *N. Amer. informal* kooky.
– OPPOSITES conventional.

zeal noun ❶ ARDOUR, fervour, fervency, passion, fire, devotion, vehemence, intensity, enthusiasm, eagerness, keenness, earnestness, vigour, energy, verve, gusto, zest, fanaticism; *informal* zing. ❷ ZEALOTRY, fanaticism, extremism.
– OPPOSITES apathy.

zealot noun ENTHUSIAST, fanatic, extremist, radical, militant, bigot.

zealous adjective ARDENT, fervent, fervid, passionate, impassioned, devoted, intense, enthusiastic, eager, keen, earnest, vigorous, energetic, zestful, fanatical.
– OPPOSITES apathetic.

zenith noun HIGHEST/HIGH POINT, crowning point, height, top, acme, peak, pinnacle, climax, prime, meridian, apex, apogee, vertex.
– OPPOSITES nadir.

zero noun ❶ NOUGHT, nothing, cipher. ❷ NOTHING, naught, nil; *informal* zilch, not a sausage.
■ **zero in on** FOCUS ON, centre on, concentrate on, home in on, pinpoint.

zest noun ❶ RELISH, gusto, enthusiasm, eagerness, zeal, vigour, liveliness, energy, enjoyment, joy, delectation, appetite; *informal* zing, oomph. ❷ PIQUANCY, spice, pungency, flavour, relish, tang, savour, interest.

zone noun AREA, sector, section, belt, district, region, province.

zoom verb FLY, buzz, rush, dash, pelt, race, tear, shoot, scurry, speed, hurry, hasten, whizz, hare, zip, zap.

Wordfinder lists

1. Food and drink

Alcoholic drinks

absinthe
advocaat
alcopop
ale
amaretto
anisette
applejack
aquavit
Armagnac
arrack/arak
barley wine
beer
bitter
Bloody Mary
bourbon
brandy
Buck's Fizz
Calvados
cava
champagne
chartreuse
cherry brandy
cider
cognac
crème de menthe
curaçao
daiquiri
gimlet
gin
ginger wine
grappa
Harvey Wallbanger
highball
kirsch
kümmel
kvass
lager
liqueur
Madeira
malmsey
malt (whisky)
maraschino
marc
margarita
Marsala
mead
mild
ouzo
pastis
perry
Pils
pina colada
pink gin
pombe
port
porter
poteen
pulque
punch
raki
rum
St Clements
sake
sambuca
sangria
schnapps
screwdriver
scrumpy
shandy
sherry
slivovitz
sloe gin
snowball
spritzer
stout
tej
tequila
tequila sunrise
Tom Collins
vermouth
vodka
whisky/whiskey
whisky mac
whisky sour
wine

Bread

bagel
baguette
bannock
bap
bara brith
barmbrack
barm cake
barracouta
bialy
billy-bread
bloomer
boxty
bridge roll
brioche
bun
challah
chapatti
ciabatta
cob
cottage loaf
damper
farl
farmhouse loaf
flatbread
focaccia
French stick
granary bread
hoagie
injera
johnnycake
kaiser
kulcha
malt loaf
matzo
milk loaf
muffin
nan
pan dulce
panettone
panino
pan-loaf
paratha
petit pain
pitta
pone
poppadom
pumpernickel
puri
roti
soda bread
sourdough
split tin
spoon bread
stotty

Fruit

apple
apricot
Asian pear
avocado
banana
bilberry
blackberry
blackcurrant
blood orange
blueberry

boysenberry
breadfruit
cantaloupe
Cape gooseberry
carambola
cherry
Chinese gooseberry
citron
clementine
cloudberry
coconut
crab apple
cranberry
currant
damson
date
dewberry
elderberry
fig
galia melon
gooseberry
gourd
granadilla
grape
grapefruit
greengage
guava
honeydew melon
huckleberry
jackfruit
jujube
kiwi fruit
kumquat
lemon
lime
lingonberry
loganberry
lychee
mandarin
mango
mangosteen
melon
minneola
mulberry
muscat
musk melon
navel orange
nectarine
Ogen melon
olive
orange
ortanique
papaya
passionfruit
pawpaw
peach
pear
persimmon
physalis
pineapple
plantain
plum
pomegranate
pomelo
prickly pear
pumpkin
quince
rambutan
raspberry
redcurrant
roseapple
satsuma
sharon fruit
sloe
starfruit
strawberry
tangerine
tayberry
tomato
Ugli fruit (*trademark*)
watermelon
white currant
whortleberry

Herbs *See also* Spices.

anise
basil
bay leaf
bergamot
borage
camomile
chervil
chicory
chives
comfrey
coriander
dill
dittany
fennel
hyssop
lavender
lemon balm
lemon grass
lovage
marjoram
mint
oregano
parsley
peppermint
rosemary
rue
saffron
sage
savory
sorrel
spearmint
sweet cicely
tarragon
thyme
vervain

Meat

bacon
baron of beef
beef
belly
best end
brisket
chateaubriand
chine
chop
chuck
collar
cutlet
entrecôte
escalope
fillet
flank
fricandeau
game
gammon
gigot
ham
hand
hock
knuckle
leg
loin
mince
mutton
neck
noisette
pork
porterhouse steak
rack
rib
rump
saddle
shank
shoulder
shin
side
silverside
sirloin
skirt
spare rib
steak
T-bone
tenderloin
topside
tournedos
veal
venison

Nuts

almond
areca nut
beechnut
betel nut
Brazil nut
cashew
chestnut
cobnut
coco-de-mer
coconut
cola nut
earthnut
filbert
groundnut
hazelnut
macadamia
monkey nut
palm nut
peanut
pecan
pine nut
piñon
pistachio
walnut
water chestnut

Pasta

agnolotti
angel hair
annellini
bucatini
cannelloni
cappelletti
conchiglie
ditalini
farfalle
farfalline
fettuccine
fusilli
gemelli
gramigna
lasagne
linguine
macaroni
manicotti
orecchiette
orzo
paglia e fieno
pappardelle
penne
ravioli
rigatoni
rotelle
rotini
spaghetti
spaghettini
stelline
tagliatelle
tagliolini
taglioni
tortellini
tortelloni
tortiglioni
trenette
vermicelli
ziti

Spices *See also* **Herbs.**

allspice
capers
caraway seeds
cardamom
cayenne pepper
chilli
cinnamon
cloves
coriander
cumin
fennel seeds
fenugreek
garlic
ginger
ginseng
juniper berries
mace
mustard
nutmeg
paprika
pepper
pimento
star anise
turmeric
vanilla

Vegetables

adzuki/aduki bean
alfalfa
artichoke
asparagus
aubergine
avocado pear
bamboo shoots
bean
beet
beetroot
black bean
black-eyed bean
borlotti bean
butter bean
breadfruit
broad bean
broccoli
Brussels sprout
butter bean
butternut squash
cabbage
calabrese
cannellini bean
capsicum
cardoon
carrot
cassava
cauliflower
celeriac
celery
chard
chayote
chervil
chickpea
chicory
Chinese artichoke
Chinese cabbage
Chinese leaves
choko
collard
corn on the cob
cos lettuce
courgette
cress
cucumber
curly kale
cush-cush
custard marrow
dishcloth gourd
eggplant
endive
fennel
flageolet
French bean
garden pea
garlic
gherkin
globe artichoke
gobo
gourd
gumbo

haricot bean
kale
kidney bean
kohlrabi
Jerusalem artichoke
jicama
leek
lentil
lettuce
lima bean
mangetout
manioc
marrow
marrow squash
mizuna
mung bean
mustard
okra
onion
orache
oyster plant
pak choi
parsnip
pattypan
pea
pea bean
pepper
petits pois
pimiento
pinto bean
plantain
potato
puha
pumpkin
radish
radicchio
runner bean
rutabaga
salsify
savoy cabbage
scallion
scorzonera
sea kale
shallot
snap bean
spinach
spinach beet
spring onion
squash
string bean
succory
sugar bean
sugar-snap peas
swede
sweetcorn
sweet potato
taro
tomato
turnip
turnip greens
vegetable spaghetti
water chestnut
watercress
waxpod
yam
yam bean
zucchini

2. Animals and birds

Birds

adjutant bird
albatross
auk
avocet
bald eagle
barnacle goose
barn owl
bateleur
bearded tit
bee-eater
Bewick's Swan
bird of paradise
bittern
blackbird
blackcap
black grouse
black kite
black swan
bluebird
bluethroat
blue tit
booby
bowerbird
brambling
brent goose
bronzewing
brown owl
budgerigar
bullfinch
bunting
burrowing owl
bustard
butcher-bird
buzzard
Canada goose
canary
capercaillie
caracara
cardinal
cassowary
chaffinch
chat
chickadee
chicken
chiffchaff
chough
coal tit
cockatiel
cockatoo
cock-of-the-rock
collared dove
condor
coot
cormorant
corncrake
crane
crested tit
crossbill
crow
cuckoo
curlew
currawong
dabchick
dipper
diver
diving duck
dodo
dotterel
dove
duck
dunnock
eagle
eagle owl
egret
eider duck
elephant bird
emperor penguin
emu
erne
fairy penguin
fairy tern
falcon
fantail
ferruginous duck
fieldfare
finch
firecrest
fish eagle
flamingo
flycatcher
frigate bird
fulmar
galah
gannet
gentoo penguin
goldcrest
golden eagle
golden oriole

golden pheasant
goldfinch
goose
goshawk
great auk
great crested grebe
great tit
grebe
greenfinch
green woodpecker
greylag goose
grey parrot
griffon vulture
grouse
guillemot
guineafowl
gull
gyrfalcon
harpy eagle
harrier
Harris' hawk
Hawaiian goose
hawfinch
hawk
hawk owl
hedge sparrow
hen
hen harrier
heron
herring gull
hobby
honey buzzard
honeyeater
honeyguide
hooded crow
hoopoe
hornbill
horned owl
house martin
house sparrow
hummingbird
ibis
jackdaw
jay
junglefowl
kea
kestrel
kingbird
kingfisher
king penguin
kite
kittiwake
kiwi
kookaburra
lammergeier
lanner
lapwing
lark
laughing jackass
lily-trotter
linnet
little owl
long-tailed tit
loon
lorikeet
lovebird
lyrebird
macaroni penguin
macaw
magpie
mallard
malleefowl
mandarin duck
marabou stork
marsh harrier
martin
meadowlark
meadow pipit
merlin
mistle thrush
moa
mockingbird
moorcock
moorfowl
moorhen
Mother Carey's chicken
Muscovy duck
mute swan
mynah bird
nightingale
nightjar
noddy
nuthatch
oriole
ortolan
osprey
ostrich
ouzel
owl
oystercatcher
parakeet
parrot
partridge
passenger pigeon
peacock
peafowl
peewit
pelican
penguin
peregrine falcon
petrel
phalarope
pheasant
pied wagtail
pigeon
pilot bird
pipit
plover
pochard
prairie chicken
pratincole
ptarmigan
puffin
quail
quetzal
rail
raven
razorbill
red kite
redpoll
redstart
redwing
reed-bird
reed bunting
reed warbler
rhea
rhinoceros bird
ringed plover
ring ouzel
roadrunner
robin
rockhopper
rook
roseate tern
ruddy duck
ruddy shelduck
ruff
sacred ibis
sandgrouse
sand martin
sandpiper
sandwich tern
screech owl
sea eagle
seagull
secretary bird
sedge warbler
shag
shearwater
shelduck
shoveler
shrike
siskin
skua
skylark
snakebird
snipe
snow bunting
snow goose
snowy owl
song thrush
sooty tern
sparrow
sparrowhawk
spoonbill
spotted flycatcher
starling
stilt
stonechat
stone curlew
stork
storm petrel
sunbird
sunbittern
sungrebe
swallow
swan
swift
tawny owl
teal
tern
thrush
tit
titlark
titmouse
toucan
treecreeper
tree pipit
tree sparrow
tufted duck
turkey
turkey vulture
turtle dove
umbrellabird
vulture
wagtail
wallcreeper
warbler
water rail
waxwing
weaver bird
wheatear
whimbrel
whippoorwill
whooping crane
wigeon

willow warbler
woodchat
woodcock
wood duck
woodgrouse
wood ibis
woodlark
woodpecker
wood pigeon
wren
yellowhammer
zebra finch

Butterflies

Adonis blue
alpine
angle wings
apollo
arctic
argus
azure
birdwing
blue
brimstone
brown
buckeye
cabbage white
Camberwell Beauty
chalkhill blue
checkerspot
cleopatra
clouded yellow
comma
copper
diana
dog face
dryad
Duke of Burgundy
dusky wing
elfin
emperor
festoon
fritillary
gatekeeper
grayling
hairstreak
julia
map butterfly
marbled white
mazarine blue
meadow brown
metalmark
milkweed
monarch
morpho
mourning cloak
nettle-tree butterfly
nymph
orange tip
owl butterfly
painted lady
peacock butterfly
pearly eye
plain tiger
purple emperor
red admiral
ringlet
satyr
Scotch argus
silver-studded blue
skipper
snout butterfly
speckled wood
sulphur
swallowtail
tortoiseshell
two-tailed pasha
wall brown
white admiral
wood nymph
zebra

Deer and antelopes

addax
blackbuck
blesbok
bongo
bontebok
brocket
caribou
chamois
chevrotain
chital
dik-dik
duiker
eland
elk
fallow deer
gazelle
gemsbok
gerenuk
gnu
goat-antelope
goral
hartebeest
impala
klipspringer
kudu
lechwe
marsh deer
moose
mountain goat
mouse deer
mule deer
muntjac
musk deer
musk ox
nilgai
nyala
okapi
oribi
oryx
Père David's deer
pronghorn antelope
puku
red deer
reedbuck
reindeer
rhebok
roan antelope
roe deer
royal stag
rusa
sable antelope
saiga
sika
sitatunga
springbok
steenbok
suni
swamp deer
topi
wapiti
waterbuck
water deer
white-tailed deer
wildebeest

Fish

albacore
alewife
amberjack
anchovy
angelfish
angel shark
anglerfish
arapaima
archerfish
argus fish
balloonfish
bandfish
barbel
barracouta
barracuda

barramundi
basking shark
bass
beluga
bib
bitterling
black durgon
blackfish
blenny
bloodfin
blowfish
bluefin
bluefish
bluegill
bluehead
blue shark
bonefish
bonito
bonnethead
bonnetmouth
bowfin
boxfish
bream
brill
brisling
brown trout
bullhead
bummalo
burbot
butterfish
butterfly fish
cabezon
callop
candiru
candlefish
capelin
cardinal fish
carp
carpet shark
catfish
cat shark
cavefish
charr
chimera
chinook salmon
chub
clownfish
coalfish
cod
coelacanth
coley
comber
combfish
conger eel
cornetfish
cowfish
cow shark
cutlassfish
dab
dace
damselfish
darter
devil ray
discus
dogfish
dorado
dory
Dover sole
dragonet
dragonfish
drumfish
eel
eelpout
electric eel
electric ray
espada
fighting fish
filefish
flatfish
flathead
flounder
fluke
flying fish
frogfish
gaper
garden eel
garfish
garpike
glassfish
globefish
goatfish
goby
goldfish
goosefish
gourami
grayling
great white shark
grey mullet
grouper
grunion
grunt
gudgeon
guitarfish
gulper eel
gunnel
guppy
gurnard
haddock
hagfish
hake
halfbeak
halibut
hammerhead shark
harlequin fish
hatchetfish
hawkfish
herring
hogfish
hoki
horse mackerel
houndfish
huss
icefish
jackfish
jackknife fish
jawfish
jewelfish
John Dory
kingfish
koi carp
lamprey
lancetfish
lanternfish
leatherjacket
lemon sole
ling
lionhead
lizardfish
loach
lumpsucker
lungfish
lyrefish
mackerel
mako
manta
marlin
medusa fish
megrim
midshipman
milkfish
minnow
mirror carp
monkfish
moonfish
Moorish idol
moray eel
morwong
mudfish
mudminnow
mudskipper
mullet
muskellunge
musselcracker
needlefish
neon tetra
Nile perch
nurse shark
oarfish
orfe
paddlefish
paradise fish
parrotfish
perch
pike
pikeperch
pilchard
pilotfish
pipefish
piranha
plaice
platy
pollack
pollan
pomfret
porbeagle
porcupine fish
porgy
pout
prowfish
puffer fish
rabbitfish
ragfish
rainbow trout
rascasse
ratfish
ray
razorfish
redfin
red mullet
red snapper
remora
requiem shark
ribbonfish
roach
rock bass
rockfish
rockling
rock snapper
ronquil
rouget
roughy
rudd
ruffe
sablefish
sailfish
saithe
salmon
salmon trout
sand dab
sand eel
sandfish

sand shark
sardine
sawfish
scabbardfish
scad
scat
scorpionfish
sea bass
sea bream
sea horse
sea perch
sea trout
sergeant fish
sergeant major
shad
shark
shark-sucker
shovelhead
shubunkin
sild
silverside
skate
skilfish
skipjack tuna
skipper
smelt
smooth hound
snaggle-tooth
snailfish
snakehead
snapper
snipe eel
snipefish
snook
soapfish
sockeye salmon
soldierfish
sole
spadefish
sparling
spearfish
sprat
square-tail
squawfish
squirrelfish
stargazer
stickleback
stingaree
stingray
stockfish
stonefish
striped bass
sturgeon
sucker
sunfish
surfperch
surgeonfish
sweetlips
swordfish
swordtail
tai
tailorfish
tarpon
tench
tetra
thornback
threadfin
thresher shark
tiger fish
tiger shark
tilapia
toadfish
tope
topminnow
torpedo ray
triggerfish
trout
trumpeter
trumpetfish
trunkfish
tubesnout
tuna
tunny
turbot
unicorn fish
vendace
walleye
warbonnet
weakfish
weatherfish
weever
whale shark
whitebait
white bass
whitefish
whiting
wobbegong
wolf fish
wormfish
wrasse
wreckfish
wrymouth
X-ray fish
yellowfin
yellowtail
zander
zebra fish

Insects

ant
ant-lion
aphid
army ant
assassin bug
bedbug
bee
beetle
blackfly
bloodworm
blowfly
bluebottle
bombardier beetle
bookworm
botfly
bristletail
bumblebee
butterfly
cabbage root fly
caddis fly
cardinal beetle
carpenter bee
carpet beetle
carrion beetle
carrot fly
chafer
chigger
cicada
click beetle
cockchafer
cockroach
Colorado beetle
crab louse
crane fly
cricket
cutworm
daddy-long-legs
damselfly
death-watch beetle
demoiselle
devil's coach-horse
dor beetle
dragonfly
drosophila
dung beetle
earwig
elm bark beetle
fire ant
firefly
flea
flour beetle
fly
froghopper
fruit fly
furniture beetle
gadfly
gall wasp
glow-worm
gnat
goliath beetle
grasshopper
greenbottle
greenfly
honeybee
hornet
horsefly
housefly
hoverfly
ichneumon
katydid
lacewing
lac insect
ladybird
leafcutter ant
leaf insect
leaf miner
leatherjacket
locust
longhorn beetle
louse
mantis
mason bee
mason wasp
May bug
mayfly
meal beetle
mealworm
mealy bug
midge
mining bee

mosquito
moth
paper wasp
phylloxera
pond skater
praying mantis
red ant
rhinoceros beetle
root fly
sawfly
scale insect
scarab
sexton beetle
shield bug
silverfish
Spanish fly
springtail
stag beetle
stick insect
stink bug
stonefly
termite
thrips
thunderbug
thunderfly
tsetse fly
tumblebug
warble fly
wasp
water boatman
weevil
whirligig
whitefly
wireworm
witchetty grub
woodworm
woolly bear

Marsupials

antechinus
bandicoot
bettong
brushtail
cuscus
dunnart
glider
kangaroo
koala
kowari
mulgara
numbat
opossum
pademelon
phalanger
possum
potoroo
quokka
quoll
rat-kangaroo
ringtail
Tasmanian devil
Tasmanian tiger/wolf
thylacine
wallaby
wallaroo
wombat
yapok

Monkeys and apes

baboon
Barbary ape
capuchin monkey
chimpanzee
colobus
douroucouli
gelada
gibbon
gorilla
green monkey
grivet
guenon
hamadryas
hanuman langur
howler monkey
langur
lar gibbon
leaf monkey
macaque
mandrill
marmoset
orang-utan
proboscis monkey
rhesus monkey
spider monkey
squirrel monkey
tamarin
vervet
woolly monkey

Moths

angle shades
atlas moth
bagworm
bogong
brimstone
brown-tail
buff-tip
burnet
burnished brass
cabbage moth
cecropia
cinnabar
clearwing
Clifden nonpareil
clothes moth
codling/codlin moth
common heath
corn borer
crescent
dagger
death's head hawkmoth
diamondback moth
drinker
dun-bar
eggar
emerald
emperor
ermine
festoon
flour moth
footman
forester
fox moth
garden carpet
garden tiger
ghost moth
goat moth
gypsy moth
hawkmoth
heath
hooktip
hornet moth
io moth
Kentish moth
kitten
lackey
lappet
leaf miner
leaf roller
leopard moth
lobster moth
luna moth
magpie moth
meal moth
merveille du jour
minor
moon moth
Mother Shipton
noctuid

oak eggar
old lady
owlet
peach blossom
peppered moth
pine beauty
pink bollworm
plume moth
processionary
prominent
pug
puss moth
pyralid
rivulet
rustic
sallow
saturniid
shark
silk moth
silver-line
silver Y
snout
sphingid
swallow-tailed moth
swift
tabby
tapestry moth
thorn
tiger moth
tortrix
triangle
turnip moth
tussock moth
tussore moth
umber
underwing
vapourer
wainscot
wax moth
white spot
winter moth
yellow-tail
yellow underwing
yucca moth

Reptiles *See also* **Snakes**.

alligator
basilisk
bearded dragon
blindworm
caiman
chameleon
crocodile
gecko
gharial
Gila monster
goanna
hawksbill
iguana
Komodo dragon
leatherback
lizard
loggerhead turtle
marine iguana
moloch
monitor lizard
skink
slow-worm
terrapin
tortoise
turtle
whiptail

Rodents

acouchi
agouti
beaver
capybara
cavy
chinchilla
chipmumk
coypu
degu
desert rat
dormouse
field mouse
gerbil
gopher
groundhog
guinea pig
hamster
harvest mouse
house mouse
jerboa
kangaroo rat
lemming
mara
marmot
meerkat
mole rat
mouse
muskrat
paca
pacarana
porcupine
prairie dog
rat
springhare
swamp rat
tuco-tuco
viscacha
vole
water rat
water vole
woodchuck
wood mouse
wood rat

Shellfish

abalone
angel wings
argonaut
auger
clam
cockle
cone shell
coquina
cowrie
drill
file shell
jewel box
limpet
murex
mussel
nautilus
ormer
oyster
pandora
paua
piddock
quahog
razor shell
scallop
snail
teredo
triton
wentletrap
whelk
winkle

Snakes

adder
anaconda
asp
black mamba
blind snake
boa constrictor
brown snake
bullmaster
carpet snake
coachwhip
cobra
colubrid
copperhead
coral snake
cornsnake
diamondback
diamond python
egg-eating snake
fer de lance
flying snake
Gaboon viper
garter snake
gopher snake
grass snake
green snake
horned snake
indigo snake
king cobra
krait
mamba
massasauga
milk snake
night adder
pine snake
pit viper
puff adder
python
rat snake
rattlesnake
reticulated python
rinkhals
rock python
sea snake
sidewinder
smooth snake
spitting cobra
taipan
tiger snake
tree snake
viper
water snake
whip snake
wolf snake

Spiders and other arachnids

baboon spider
bird-eating spider
black widow
button spider
camel spider
cardinal spider
cobweb spider
crab spider
diadem spider
funnel-web spider
harvestman
hunting spider
jumping spider
katipo
money spider
orb-web spider
raft spider
redback
sun spider
tarantula
trapdoor spider
violin spider
wolf spider
zebra spider

Whales and dolphins

Amazon dolphin
baleen whale
beaked whale
beluga
blue whale
bottlenose dolphin
bottlenose whale
bowhead whale
cachalot
dusky dolphin
finback whale
fin whale
grampus
Greenland right whale
grey whale
humpback whale
killer whale
minke whale
narwhal
orca
pilot whale
porpoise
right whale
Risso's dolphin
river dolphin
rorqual
sei whale
sperm whale
spinner dolphin
toothed whale
tucuxi
whalebone whale
white whale

Wild cats

bobcat
caracal
cheetah
civet
clouded leopard
cougar
jaguar
jaguarundi
leopard
lion
lynx
margay
mountain lion
ocelot
panther
puma
serval
snow leopard
tiger

Collective names for animals and birds

Many of these are fanciful or humorous terms which probably never had any real currency but were popularized by antiquarian writers, notably Joseph Strutt in *Sports and Pastimes of England* (1801).

a shrewdness of **apes**
a herd or pace of **asses**
a troop of **baboons**
a cete of **badgers**
a sloth of **bears**
a swarm, drift, hive, or erst of **bees**
a flock, flight, or pod of **birds**
a herd, gang, or obstinacy of **buffalo**
a bellowing of **bullfinches**
a drove of **bullocks**
a clowder or glaring of **cats**
an army of **caterpillars**
a herd or drove of **cattle**
a brood, clutch, or peep of **chickens**
a chattering of **choughs**
a rag or rake of **colts**
a covert of **coots**
a herd of **cranes**
a bask of **crocodiles**
a murder of **crows**
a litter of **cubs**
a herd of **curlew**
a herd or mob of **deer**
a pack or kennel of **dogs**
a school of **dolphins**
a trip of **dotterel**
a flight, dole, or piteousness of **doves**
a paddling of **ducks** (on water)
a safe of **ducks** (on land)
a fling of **dunlin**
a herd or parade of **elephants**
a herd or gang of **elk**
a busyness of **ferrets**
a charm of **finches**
a shoal or run of **fish**
a swarm or cloud of **flies**
a skulk of **foxes**
a gaggle of **geese** (on land)
a skein, team, or wedge of **geese** (in flight)
a herd of **giraffe**
a cloud of **gnats**
a flock, herd, or trip of **goats**
a band of **gorillas**
a pack or covey of **grouse**
a down, mute, or husk of **hares**
a cast of **hawks**
a siege of **herons**
a bloat of **hippopotami**
a drove, string, stud, or team of **horses**
a pack, cry, or kennel of **hounds**
a flight or swarm of **insects**
a fluther or smack of **jellyfish**
a mob or troop of **kangaroos**
a litter or kindle of **kittens**
a desert of **lapwings**
a bevy or exaltation of **larks**
a leap of **leopards**
a pride or sawt of **lions**
a tiding of **magpies**
a sord or suit of **mallard**
a stud of **mares**
a richesse of **martens**
a labour of **moles**
a troop of **monkeys**
a span or barren of **mules**
a watch of **nightingales**
a parliament or stare of **owls**
a yoke of **oxen**
a pandemonium of **parrots**

a covey of **partridges**
a muster of **peacocks**
a muster, parcel, or rookery of **penguins**
a bevy or head of **pheasants**
a kit of **pigeons** (in flight)
a litter or herd of **pigs**
a congregation, stand, or wing of **plovers**
a rush or flight of **pochards**
a pod, school, herd, or turmoil of **porpoises**
a covey of **ptarmigan**
a litter of **pups**
a bevy or drift of **quail**
a bury of **rabbits**
a string of **racehorses**
an unkindness of **ravens**
a crash of **rhinoceros**
a bevy of roe **deer**
a parliament, building, or rookery of **rooks**
a hill of **ruffs**
a pod, herd, or rookery of **seals**
a flock, herd, trip, or mob of **sheep**
a dopping of **sheldrake**
a wisp or walk of **snipe**
a host of **sparrows**
a murmuration of **starlings**
a flight of **swallows**
a game or herd of **swans** (on land)
a wedge of **swans** (in flight)
a drift, herd, or sounder of **swine**
a spring of **teal**
a knot of **toads**
a hover of **trout**
a rafter of **turkeys**
a bale or turn of **turtles**
a bunch or knob of **waterfowl**
a school, herd, pod, or gam of **whales**
a company or trip of **wigeon**
a sounder of **wild boar**
a dout or destruction of **wild cats**
a team of **wild ducks** (in flight)
a bunch, trip, plump, or knob of **wildfowl**
a pack or rout of **wolves**
a fall of **woodcock**
a descent of **woodpeckers**
a herd of **wrens**
a zeal of **zebras**

Countries

country	related adjective/noun	currency unit
Afghanistan	Afghan	afghani = 100 puls
Albania	Albanian	lek = 100 qindarka
Algeria	Algerian	dinar = 100 centimes
America (*see* United States of America)		
Andorra	Andorran	euro = 100 cents (formerly French franc, Spanish peseta)
Angola	Angolan	kwanza = 100 lwei
Antigua and Barbuda	Antiguan, Barbudan	dollar = 100 cents
Argentina	Argentinian	peso = 10,000 centavos
Armenia	Armenian	dram = 100 luma
Australia	Australian	dollar = 100 cents
Austria	Austrian	euro = 100 cents (formerly schilling = 100 groschen)
Azerbaijan	Azerbaijani	manat = 100 gopik
Bahamas	Bahamian	dollar = 100 cents
Bahrain	Bahraini	dinar = 1,000 fils
Bangladesh	Bangladeshi	taka = 100 poisha
Barbados	Barbadian	dollar = 100 cents
Belarus	Belorussian *or* Byelorussian	rouble
Belgium	Belgian	euro = 100 cents (formerly franc = 100 centimes)
Belize	Belizian	dollar = 100 cents
Benin	Beninese	African franc
Bhutan	Bhutanese	ngultrum = 100 chetrum
Bolivia	Bolivian	boliviano = 100 centavos
Bosnia–Herzegovina	Bosnian	dinar = 100 paras
Botswana	Botswanan / Tswana	pula = 100 thebe
Brazil	Brazilian	real = 100 centavos
Brunei	Bruneian	dollar = 100 sen
Bulgaria	Bulgarian	lev = 100 stotinki
Burkina Faso	Burkinese	African franc
Burma (officially called **Myanmar**)	Burmese	kyat = 100 pyas
Burundi	Burundian	franc = 100 centimes
Cambodia	Cambodian	riel = 100 sen
Cameroon	Cameroonian	African franc
Canada	Canadian	dollar = 100 cents
Cape Verde Islands	Cape Verdean	escudo = 100 centavos
Central African Republic	–	African franc
Chad	Chadian	African franc
Chile	Chilean	peso = 100 centavos

country	related adjective/noun	currency unit
China	Chinese	yuan = 10 jiao or 100 fen
Colombia	Colombian	peso = 100 centavos
Comoros	Comoran	African franc
Congo	Congolese	African franc
Congo, Democratic Republic of (Zaire)	Congolese	franc = 100 centimes
Costa Rica	Costa Rican	colón = 100 centimos
Croatia	Croat *or* Croatian	kuna = 100 lipa
Cuba	Cuban	peso = 100 centavos
Cyprus	Cypriot	pound = 100 cents
Czech Republic	Czech	koruna = 100 haleru
Denmark	Danish/Dane	krone = 100 øre
Djibouti	Djiboutian	franc = 100 centimes
Dominica	Dominican	dollar = 100 cents
Dominican Republic	Dominican	peso = 100 centavos
Ecuador	Ecuadorean	sucre = 100 centavos
Egypt	Egyptian	pound = 100 piastres or 1,000 milliemes
El Salvador	Salvadorean	colón = 100 centavos
Equatorial Guinea	Equatorial Guinean	African franc
Eritrea	Eritrean	nakfa = 100 cents
Estonia	Estonian	kroon = 100 sents
Ethiopia	Ethiopian	birr = 100 cents
Fiji	Fijian	dollar = 100 cents
Finland	Finnish / Finn	euro = 100 cents (formerly markka = 100 penniä)
France	French	euro = 100 cents (formerly franc = 100 centimes)
Gabon	Gabonese	African franc
Gambia, the	Gambian	dalasi = 100 butut
Georgia	Georgian	lari = 100 tetri
Germany	German	euro = 100 cents (formerly Deutschmark = 100 pfennigs)
Ghana	Ghanaian	cedi = 100 pesewas
Greece	Greek	euro = 100 cents (formerly drachma = 100 leptae)
Grenada	Grenadian	dollar = 100 cents
Guatemala	Guatemalan	quetzal = 100 centavos
Guinea	Guinean	franc = 100 centimes
Guinea-Bissau	–	peso = 100 centavos
Guyana	Guyanese	dollar = 100 cents
Haiti	Haitian	gourde = 100 centimes
Holland (*see* Netherlands)		
Honduras	Honduran	lempira = 100 centavos
Hungary	Hungarian	forint = 100 filler

country	related adjective/noun	currency unit
Iceland	Icelandic / Icelander	krona = 100 aurar
India	Indian	rupee = 100 paisa
Indonesia	Indonesian	rupiah = 100 sen
Iran	Iranian	rial = 100 dinars
Iraq	Iraqi	dinar = 1,000 fils
Ireland, Republic of	Irish	euro = 100 cents (formerly pound [punt] = 100 pence)
Israel	Israeli	shekel = 100 agora
Italy	Italian	euro = 100 cents (formerly lira = 100 centesemos)
Ivory Coast	Ivorian	African franc
Jamaica	Jamaican	dollar = 100 cents
Japan	Japanese	yen = 100 sen
Jordan	Jordanian	dinar = 1,000 fils
Kazakhstan	Kazakh	tenge = 100 teins
Kenya	Kenyan	shilling = 100 cents
Kiribati	–	dollar = 100 cents
Kuwait	Kuwaiti	dinar = 1,000 fils
Kyrgyzstan	Kyrgyz	som = 100 tiyin
Laos	Laotian	kip = 100 ats
Latvia	Latvian	lat = 100 santims
Lebanon	Lebanese	pound = 100 piastres
Lesotho	Lesothan / Mosotho, *pl.* Basotho	loti = 100 lisente
Liberia	Liberian	dollar = 100 cents
Libya	Libyan	dinar = 1,000 dirhams
Liechtenstein	– / Liechtensteiner	Swiss franc
Lithuania	Lithuanian	litas = 100 centas
Luxembourg	– / Luxembourger	euro = 100 cents (formerly franc = 100 centimes)
Macedonia	Macedonian	denar = 100 deni
Madagascar	Malagasay *or* Madagascan	franc = 100 centimes
Malawi	Malawian	kwacha = 100 tambala
Malaysia	Malaysian	ringgit = 100 sen
Maldives	Maldivian	rufiyaa = 100 laris
Mali	Malian	African franc
Malta	Maltese	lira = 100 cents
Marshall Islands	Marshallese	US dollar
Mauritania	Mauritanian	ouguiya = 5 khoums
Mauritius	Mauritian	rupee = 100 cents
Mexico	Mexican	peso = 100 centavos
Micronesia, Federated States of	Micronesian	US dollar
Moldova	Moldovan	leu = 100 bani

country	related adjective/noun	currency unit
Monaco	Monegasque *or* Monacan	euro = 100 cents (formerly franc = 100 centimes)
Mongolia	Mongolian	tugrik = 100 mongos
Montenegro (*see* Yugoslavia)		
Morocco	Moroccan	dirham = 100 centimes
Mozambique	Mozambican	metical = 100 centavos
Myanmar (*see* Burma)		
Namibia	Namibian	rand = 100 cents
Nauru	Nauruan	Australian dollar
Nepal	Nepalese	rupee = 100 paisa
Netherlands, the	Dutch	euro = 100 cents (formerly guilder = 100 cents)
New Zealand	– / New Zealander	dollar = 100 cents
Nicaragua	Nicaraguan	cordoba = 100 centavos
Niger	Nigerien	African franc
Nigeria	Nigerian	naira = 100 kobo
North Korea	North Korean	won = 100 jun
Norway	Norwegian	krone = 100 øre
Oman	Omani	rial = 1,000 baiza
Pakistan	Pakistani	rupee = 100 paisa
Panama	Panamanian	balboa = 100 centésimos
Papua New Guinea	Papua New Guinean *or* Guinean	kina = 100 toea
Paraguay	Paraguayan	guarani = 100 centimos
Peru	Peruvian	nuevo sol = 100 cents
Philippines	Filipino *or* Philippine	peso = 100 centavos
Poland	Polish / Pole	zloty = 100 groszy
Portugal	Portuguese	euro = 100 cents (formerly escudo = 100 centavos)
Qatar	Qatari	riyal = 100 dirhams
Romania	Romanian	leu = 100 bani
Russia	Russian	rouble = 100 copecks
Rwanda	Rwandan	franc = 100 centimes
St Kitts and Nevis	–	dollar = 100 cents
St Lucia	St Lucian	dollar = 100 cents
St Vincent and the Grenadines	Vincentian, Grenadian	dollar = 100 cents
Samoa	Samoan	tala = 100 sene
San Marino	–	euro = 100 cents (formerly Italian lira)
São Tomé and Principe	–	dobra = 100 centavos
Saudi Arabia	Saudi Arabian *or* Saudi	riyal = 20 qursh or 100 halalas
Senegal	Senegalese	African franc
Serbia (*see* Yugoslavia)		
Seychelles, the	Seychellois	rupee = 100 cents
Sierra Leone	Sierra Leonean	leone = 100 cents

country	related adjective/noun	currency unit
Singapore	Singaporean	dollar = 100 cents
Slovakia	Slovak	koruna = 100 haleru
Slovenia	Slovene *or* Slovenian	tolar = 100 stotins
Solomon Islands	– / Solomon Islander	dollar = 100 cents
Somalia	Somali *or* Somalian	shilling = 100 cents
South Africa	South African	rand = 100 cents
South Korea	South Korean	won = 100 jeon
Spain	Spanish / Spaniard	euro = 100 cents (formerly peseta = 100 centimos)
Sri Lanka	Sri Lankan	rupee = 100 cents
Sudan	Sudanese	dinar = 10 pounds
Suriname	Surinamese	guilder = 100 cents
Swaziland	Swazi	lilangeni = 100 cents
Sweden	Swedish / Swede	krona = 100 öre
Switzerland	Swiss	franc = 100 centimes
Syria	Syrian	pound = 100 piastres
Taiwan	Taiwanese	New Taiwan dollar = 100 cents
Tajikistan	Tajik *or* Tadjik	somoni = 100 dirams
Tanzania	Tanzanian	shilling = 100 cents
Thailand	Thai	baht = 100 satangs
Togo	Togolese	African franc
Tonga	Tongan	pa'anga = 100 seniti
Trinidad and Tobago	Trinidadian, Tobagonian	dollar = 100 cents
Tunisia	Tunisian	dinar = 1,000 milliemes
Turkey	Turkish / Turk	lira = 100 kurus
Turkmenistan	Turkmen *or* Turkoman	manat = 100 tenge
Tuvalu	Tuvaluan	dollar = 100 cents
Uganda	Ugandan	shilling = 100 cents
Ukraine	Ukrainian	hryvna = 100 kopiykas
United Arab Emirates	—	dirham = 100 fils
United Kingdom	British / Briton	pound = 100 pence
United States of America	American	dollar = 100 cents
Uruguay	Uruguayan	peso = 100 centésimos
Uzbekistan	Uzbek	som
Vanuatu	Vanuatuan	vatu = 100 centimes
Vatican City	—	euro = 100 cents (formerly Italian lira)
Venezuela	Venezuelan	bolivar = 100 centimos
Vietnam	Vietnamese	dong = 10 hao or 100 xu
Yemen	Yemeni	riyal = 100 fils
Yugoslavia (Montenegro, Serbia)	Yugoslav (Montenegrin, Serbian)	dinar = 100 paras
Zaire (*see* Congo, Democratic Republic of)		
Zambia	Zambian	kwacha = 100 ngwee
Zimbabwe	Zimbabwean	dollar = 100 cents

Games and puzzles wordbuilder

These words can be particularly useful to players of word games. Proper names are excluded, as are abbreviations that are not pronounced as they are spelt, such *Dr* and *Mr*, since they are not allowed in most games.

Two-letter words

aa: rough lava containing cinders
ab: an abdominal muscle
ad: an advertisement
ag: (*S. African*) expressing various emotions, e.g. irritation, grief, or pleasure
ah: expressing surprise, sympathy, pleasure, etc.
ai: the three-toed sloth
am: the present tense of *be*
an: a form of the indefinite article
as: used to refer to extent or amount
at: expressing location or time
aw: expressing mild protest, entreaty, etc.
ba: (in Egyptian mythology) the soul
be: exist
bi: bisexual
bo: a kind of fig tree
by: beside
da: your father
DJ: a disc jockey
do: perform (an action)
dy: a type of sediment
eh: seeking explanation or agreement
El: an elevated railway or section of railway
em: a measuring unit in printing
en: a measuring unit in printing
er: expressing doubt or hesitation
ex: a former spouse or partner
fa: a musical note
Ga: a member of a people living in Ghana
GI: a soldier in the US army
go: move or travel
ha: expressing surprise, triumph, etc.
he: a male person or animal previously mentioned
hi: used as a greeting
ho: expressing surprise, triumph, etc.
id: a part of the mind
if: introducing a conditional clause
in: within
io: a North American moth
is: the present tense of *be*
it: a thing previously mentioned
ja: (*S. African*) yes
jo: (*Scottish, archaic*) a sweetheart
Ju: a kind of Chinese pottery
ka: (in Egyptian mythology) the spirit
ki: a plant of the lily family
KO: a knockout in a boxing match
la: a musical note
li: a Chinese unit of distance
lo: (*archaic*) used to draw attention to something
ma: your mother
MD: (*Brit.*) a managing director
me: myself
mi: a musical note
mo: a moment
MP: a Member of Parliament
mu: the 12th letter of the Greek alphabet
my: belonging to me
no: not any
nu: the 13th letter of the Greek alphabet
ob: a type of gene
od: a power once thought to pervade the natural world
of: belonging to
og: (*Austral., archaic*) a shilling

oh: expressing surprise, anger, disappointment, etc.
oi: used to attract attention
OK: used to express assent, agreement, etc.
om: a mystic syllable which constitutes a sacred mantra
on: supported by or covering
op: an operation
or: used to link alternatives
os: a bone
ou: a Hawaiian bird
ow: expressing pain
ox: a cow or bull
oy: = oi
Oz: Australia
pa: your father
pi: the 16th letter of the Greek alphabet
po: a chamber pot
qi: (in Chinese philosophy) the life force
ra: (in Norway and Sweden) a moraine
re: a musical note
ri: a Japanese unit of length
se: a Chinese musical instrument
si: = te
so: therefore
ta: thank you
te: a musical note
ti: = te
TV: television
uh: expressing hesitation
um: expressing hesitation
up: towards a higher position
us: myself and others
Wa: a member of a people living on the borders of China and Burma
we: myself and others
Wu: a dialect of Chinese
xi: the 14th letter of the Greek alphabet
xu: a unit of money in Vietnam
ye: (*archaic*) the plural form of *thou*
Yi: a people living in parts of China
yo: used as a greeting
yu: an ancient Chinese wine container

Words containing *q* not followed by *u*

qadi: a Muslim judge
qanat: an irrigation tunnel
qasida: an Arabic or Persian poem
qawwal: a qawwali singer
qawwali: Muslim devotional music
qi: (in Chinese philosophy) the life force
qibla: the direction towards Mecca
qigong: a Chinese system of physical exercises
qin: a Chinese musical instrument
qintar: a unit of money in Albania
qiviut: wool from the musk ox
qwerty: the standard layout of typewriters and keyboards
tariqa: the Sufi method of spiritual learning

Words beginning with *x*

xanthan: a polysaccharide
xanthate: a chemical compound
xanthene: a chemical compound
xanthic: yellowish
xanthin: a yellow colouring matter
xanthine: a biochemical compound
xanthoma: a yellow patch on the skin
xebec: a sailing ship
xeme: a fork-tailed gull
xenia: gifts to a guest or guests
xenial: relating to hospitality
xenon: a gas
xeric: very dry
xeroma: abnormal dryness of a body part

xerox: to photocopy
Xhosa: a South African people or their language
xi: the 14th letter of the Greek alphabet
xiphoid: sword-shaped
Xmas: Christmas
xoanon: a wooden image of a god
xography: a photographic process
xu: a unit of money in Vietnam
xylan: a compound found in wood
xylary: of or relating to xylem
xylem: plant tissue
xylene: a liquid hydrocarbon
xylite: a volatile liquid
xylol: = xylene
xylose: a plant sugar
xyrid: a sedge-like herb
xyster: a surgical instrument
xyston: an ancient Greek spear
xystus: an ancient Greek portico

Supplement contents